Fifth Edition

Essentials *of* Psychology

Douglas A. Bernstein

Universtiy of South Florida

WADSWORTH
CENGAGE Learning

Australia • Brazil • Japan • Korea • Mexico • Singapore • Spain • United Kingdom • United States

Essentials of Psychology, Fifth Edition
Douglas A. Bernstein

Senior Publisher: Linda Schreiber

Executive Editor: Jon-David Hague

Senior Sponsoring Editor: Jane Potter

Consulting Editor: William S. Altman

Managing Development Editor: Jeremy Judson

Assistant Editor: Rebecca Rosenberg

Editorial Assistants: Alicia McLaughlin, Nic Albert

Media Editor: Mary Noel

Executive Marketing Manager: Kim Russell

Marketing Associate: Molly Felz

Marketing Assistant: Anna Andersen

Executive Marketing Communications Manager: Talia Wise

Content Production Manager: Charlene M. Carpentier

Creative Director: Rob Hugel

Senior Art Director: Vernon Boes

Print Buyer: Linda Hsu

Text Permissions Editor: Roberta Broyer

Photo Permissions Editor: Don Schlotman

Production Service: Dovetail Publishing Services

Text Designer: Terri Wright

Photo Researcher: Stephen Forsling

Cover Designer: Terri Wright

Cover Image: Photodisc/Getty Images; Fotosearch

Compositor: Pre-Press PMG

For product information and technology assistance, contact us at
Cengage Learning Customer & Sales Support, 1-800-354-9706
For permission to use material from this text or product, submit all requests online at **cengage.com/permissions**
Further permissions questions can be emailed to
permissionrequest@cengage.com

Library of Congress Control Number: 2009936331

Student Edition:
ISBN-13: 978-0-495-81077-3
ISBN-10: 0-495-81077-0

Loose-leaf Edition:
ISBN-13: 978-0-8400-3268-3
ISBN-10: 0-8400-3268-4

Wadsworth
20 Davis Drive
Belmont, CA 94002-3098
USA

Cengage Learning is a leading provider of customized learning solutions with office locations around the globe, including Singapore, the United Kingdom, Australia, Mexico, Brazil, and Japan. Locate your local office at:
international.cengage.com/region

Cengage Learning products are represented in Canada by Nelson Education, Ltd.

To learn more about Wadsworth, visit **www.cengage.com/Wadsworth**
Purchase any of our products at your local college store or at our preferred online store www.ichapters.com.

Printed in the United States of America
1 2 3 4 5 6 7 13 12 11 10 09

For Doris

BRIEF CONTENTS

Detailed Contents

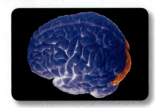

3 Sensation and Perception 83

4 Consciousness 137

5 Learning 171

6 Memory 209

7 Thought, Language, and Intelligence 247

8 Motivation and Emotion 297

9 Human Development 343

10 Health, Stress, and Coping 395

11 Personality 425

12 Psychological Disorders 461

13 Treatment of Psychological Disorders 509

14 Social Psychology 547

15 Industrial and Organizational Psychology 599

16 Neuropsychology 635

▶ ▶ ▶ Features

PREFACE

Psychology is a rich and varied science, covering the breadth and depth of human behavior—everything from fleeting reflexes to enduring memories, from falling asleep to falling in love. In my experience, most students enter the introductory course thinking that psychology concerns itself mainly with personality, psychological testing, mental disorders, psychotherapy, and other aspects of clinical psychology. Many of these students are surprised, then, when they find themselves reading about such topics as the structure of the brain, optical illusions, the effect of jet lag on athletic performance, AIDS and the immune system, and prenatal risk factors, to name just a few. Yet these are all topics under the umbrella that is psychology.

For all its diversity, psychology is also a remarkably integrated discipline whose subfields are linked through common interests and overarching research questions. As a psychologist and scholar, I wrote this book to portray the wide range of topics that make up the science of psychology. As a teacher, I focused on the essentials of the discipline—the core concepts of psychology that I hope will be especially accessible and interesting to students. I also tried to present these topics through an integrated, active pedagogical system designed to help students get the most out of the text.

In creating the fifth edition of *Essentials of Psychology,* I remained dedicated to presenting a textbook that not only is clear and enjoyable to read but that also provides features to support the learning process in all students, regardless of their academic background. Specifically, I set these goals:

- To focus on topics that represent the full range of psychology, from cell to society, without overwhelming the reader with details.

- To provide many active learning exercises that invite students to work with the text material in ways that can help them understand and remember it.

- To help students develop their ability to think critically and scientifically by examining the ways that psychologists have solved (or failed to solve) fascinating puzzles of behavior and mental processes.

- To explain the content of psychology with an emphasis on the doing of psychology, grounding all discussions in current and classic research studies. (I help students appreciate the importance of research by exploring one study in detail in a special feature in each chapter).

My discussion of research in psychology is also designed to remind students that although in some ways "people are people wherever you go," sociocultural factors—including gender, ethnicity, cultural background, and geography—often shape human behavior and mental processes. I repeatedly point out, therefore, that psychological research on the thinking styles, perceptual habits, psychological disorders, social pressures, and other phenomena seen in North America or Europe, for example, may or may not apply to other cultures, or even to subcultures within Western countries.

Rather than isolating discussion of sociocultural material in boxed features, I have woven it into every chapter so that students will encounter it repeatedly as they read. I introduce the importance of sociocultural factors in Chapter 1 and continue to reinforce it through coverage of such topics as the impact of culture and experience on perception (Chapter 3), classrooms across cultures (Chapter 5), ethnic differences in IQ (Chapter 7), social and cultural factors in sexuality (Chapter 8), gender differences in stress responses (Chapter 10), personality, culture, and human development (Chapter 11), gender and cultural differences in depression and suicide (Chapter 12), and cultural factors in aggression (Chapter 14), to cite just a few examples.

What's New in This Edition?

Feedback from faculty colleagues and students suggests that the changes made in the fourth edition of *Essentials* were well received. Accordingly, in creating the fifth edition, I have sought to update and upgrade all the book's best features rather than change them for the sake of change. I hope that the result of my effort is a book that offers even more of what faculty and students want and need.

Organization

Designed for presentation in a single semester, the book's fourteen-chapter organization has been retained, and the chapters appear in the same sequence as before. The sequence reflects the way I teach my introductory course, but I know that your preference for chapter sequencing may not match mine. Accordingly I have again ensured that each of the fourteen chapters appears as a freestanding unit so that you may assign the chapters in whatever order you wish. For example, many instructors prefer to teach the material on human development relatively late in the course, which is why it appears as Chapter 9. However, the chapter can be just as comfortably assigned earlier in the course. For the third edition, I added an optional fifteenth chapter, "Industrial and Organizational Psychology"; for the fourth edition, I added an optional sixteenth chapter, "Neuropsychology." Either chapter (or both) may be included in the textbook upon request. Note that end-of-book materials for these chapters, such as answer keys, references, credits, glossary, and index are printed in blue.

A Continued Emphasis on Learning by Doing

The added emphasis on active learning in the third edition was so popular with faculty and students that I have continued to emphasize it ever since. Three kinds of "Learn by Doing" features appear throughout the book.

- First, dozens of new or revised figure and photo captions help students understand and remember a psychological principle or phenomenon by suggesting ways they can demonstrate it for themselves. In the memory chapter, for example, a photo caption suggests that students show the photo to a friend and then ask questions about it to illustrate the operation of constructive memory. These captions are all identified with a Learn by Doing symbol.

- Second, I have placed Learn by Doing symbols in page margins at even more places where active learning opportunities occur in the narrative. At these points, I ask students to stop reading and try doing something to illustrate or highlight the psychological principle or phenomenon under discussion. For example, in the sensation and perception chapter, I ask the student to focus attention on various targets as a way of appreciating the difference between overt and covert attention shifts.

- Finally, I have carried the active learning theme through to the end of each chapter, where—as part of the built-in study guide I call Active Review—students will find sections called Put It in Writing and Personal Learning Activity. These sections invite students to (a) write about a specific chapter-related topic; and (b) collect, analyze, and discuss data on a chapter-related principle or phenomenon.

Active Review

The Put It in Writing and Personal Learning Activity sections are just two aspects of my effort to add educational value to the built-in Active Review study guide. The Active Review's other features include

- A Linkages diagram, which helps students understand and appreciate the ways the chapter they have just read relates to other subfields of psychology.

- Twenty-item multiple-choice self-tests. I have revised some of the questions, but (as in the fourth edition) they are focused on the applications as well as the definitions of principles, concepts, and phenomena.

- A Take Action to Learn More section, which—to highlight my emphasis on active learning—lists the courses students can take to further pursue chapter-related study and provides a newly expanded and annotated list of movies and books related to each chapter. I also refer students to the book companion Web site, where they will find chapter outlines, flashcards, Web links, tutorial quizzes, and more.

- A Review of Key Terms section, which invites students to write their own definitions of the most important terms presented in the chapter. These lists have been updated to include all the key terms discussed in the new edition.

Applying Psychology Photos

As in the fourth edition, I continue to emphasize the many ways psychological theory and research results are being applied to benefit human welfare. I further highlight the diversity of applied psychology by including a number of Applying Psychology photos that offer memorable examples. In the learning chapter, for example, a photo illustrates the use of classical conditioning principles in the humane control of predators that can threaten sheep ranchers' livelihoods. In the consciousness chapter, the Applying Psychology photo illustrates the value of stimulus control therapy for helping insomniacs get a better night's sleep.

Updated Content

As in the fourth edition, my goal in preparing this new edition of *Essentials* was to present the latest as well as the most established results of basic and applied research on topics that are both important to psychology and of high interest to students. Accordingly, I offer updated coverage of research on how drugs affect the brain (Chapter 2), the basis for optical illusions (Chapter 3), the effects of subliminal messages (Chapter 4), the importance of active learning in the classroom (Chapter 5), the accuracy of eyewitness testimony (Chapter 6), the origins of intelligence (Chapter 7), sources of sexual orientation (Chapter 8), the development of infants' minds (Chapter 9), the effects of stress on health (Chapter 10), what determines and shapes our personalities (Chapter 11), the causes of multiple personality disorder (Chapter 12), the effects of psychotherapy (Chapter 13), and the development of ethnic prejudice (Chapter 14).

In this new edition, students will also encounter the latest evidence on topics such as

- Epigenetics (Chapter 1)

- The value and limitations of fMRI in exploring behavior and mental processes; and the use of stem cells to repair damage to the central nervous system (Chapter 2)

- Individual differences in taste abilities, including how to determine if one is a "supertaster;" and the role of pheromones in human behavior (Chapter 3)

- The role of expectations on the effects of psychoactive drugs; and the effects of sleep deprivation on the solidification of traumatic memories (Chapter 4)

- The role of active learning processes in long term retention of information (Chapter 5)

- Factors that may make people more susceptible to reporting false memories (Chapter 6)

- The potential and limitations of artificial intelligence; the process of acquiring language; and the impact of stereotype threat on high-stakes tests of cognitive ability (Chapter 7)

- Factors that influence well-being; sexual activity among the elderly; the impact of previous pregnancies on the sexual orientation of later-born children; the effect of context on the interpretation of facial expressions (Chapter 8)

- The origins of infantile amnesia; uninvolved parenting; infants' theory of mind (Chapter 9)
- Social networks and happiness; and the "tend and befriend" response to stressors and its relationship to the traditional "fight-or-flight" syndrome (Chapter 10)
- Biological theories of personality; and honesty and humility as potential additions to the Five Factor Personality Model (Chapter 11)
- The origins of schizophrenia, depression, and anxiety; likely changes coming in DSM-V; the schizophrenia spectrum; and mirror neurons and autism (Chapter 12)
- The current status of psychologists' efforts to gain the right to prescribe psychoactive drugs; evidence based practice and empirically supported therapies; and deep brain stimulation (Chapter 13)
- Social neuroscience; Sternberg's duplex theory of love (Chapter 14)

Special Features

The fifth edition of *Essentials of Psychology* contains improved versions of a number of special features found in its predecessor. Designed to promote efficient learning and mastery of the material, these include, in each chapter, an integrated pedagogical system as well as sections on Thinking Critically, Focus on Research, and Linkages, along with an Active Review section.

An Integrated Pedagogical System

Our integrated pedagogical system is designed to help students get the most out of their reading. Based on the PQ4R study system (discussed in Chapter 6, "Memory"), learning aids in each chapter include the following elements.

Preview Section   To help students survey and question the material, each chapter opens with an outline and a brief preview statement. A question related to the key topic of each main section of the chapter appears at the beginning of each of those main sections, and these questions appear again in the Active Review, where they help to organize the chapter summary.

Margin Glossary   Key terms are defined in the margin of the page where they appear, reinforcing core concepts without interrupting the flow of reading. New to the fifth edition is a thorough revision of all key terms to match those in the American Psychological Association's *Thesaurus of Psychological Index Terms* (11th ed.) and in the *APA Dictionary of Psychology*. I believe that using key terms from these sources will help students do their own research by making it easier for them to use key-term searches in the field's most popular databases (PsycINFO & PsycARTICLES). Using these key terms will also improve students' abilities to transfer terms learned in introductory courses to their work in advanced courses. (For the fifth edition, I have revised many of the phonetic guides to make it even easier for students to correctly pronounce unfamiliar key terms as well as other terms whose pronunciation is not immediately obvious.) In the Active Review section at the end of each chapter, a definition exercise encourages students to restate these core concepts in their own words.

Instructional Captions   Captions for all figures, tables, photographs, and cartoons reiterate core concepts and help students learn to interpret visual information. And, as mentioned earlier, many of these captions prompt students to engage in various kinds of active learning experiences.

In Review Charts   In Review study charts summarize information in a convenient tabular format. I have placed two or three In Review charts strategically in each chapter to help students synthesize and assimilate large chunks of information—for example, on drug effects, key elements in personality theories, and stress responses and mediators. Fill-in-the-blank self-testing items at the bottom of each In Review chart further aid student learning and review of the chapter material. The answer key for these items can be found at the back of the book; answers printed in blue indicate those for the optional "Industrial and Organizational Psychology" and "Neuropsychology" chapters.

Active Review As mentioned earlier, the built-in Active Review study guide at the end of each chapter includes

- A Linkages diagram containing questions that illustrate three of the ways that material in each chapter is connected to other chapters in the book.

- A chapter summary organized around major topic headings and the related preview questions. The summary is presented in short, easy-to-read paragraphs that focus on the topics introduced by chapter subheadings.

- A Learn by Doing feature that is designed to promote active learning. Here, students will find Put It in Writing and Personal Learning Project sections that invite them to (a) write about a specific chapter-related topic; and (b) collect, analyze, and discuss some data on a chapter-related principle or phenomenon. For example, in the personality chapter, the Put It in Writing section suggests that students list a celebrity's personality traits and then summarize how various personality theories would account for the development of those traits. In the biology and behavior chapter, students are asked to write about how research on brain development might affect one's choice of an infant day care center. These Put It in Writing suggestions might be helpful as writing-across-the-curriculum assignments.

- Personal Learning Projects that suggest ways that students can do psychology as well as read about it. In the motivation and emotion chapter, for example, the Personal Learning Project section suggests a way that students can collect data on lie-detection skills. In the social psychology chapter, students are invited to test assumptions of evolutionary theories of mate selection by analyzing personals ads in a local newspaper. Each Personal Learning Project section ends by referring the student to additional projects listed in the study guide that accompanies the book.

- A Take Action to Learn More section, which (a) suggests courses students can take to pursue further chapter-related study; (b) presents an annotated list of movies and books related to each chapter; and (c) encourages students to visit the book's companion Web site, where they will find chapter outlines, flashcards, Web links, tutorial quizzes, and more.

- A Review of Key Terms, which invites students to write their own definitions of the most important terms presented in the chapter. These lists have been updated to include all the key terms discussed in the new edition, and (as already mentioned) all key terms now correspond to those used by the APA in its dictionary and thesaurus.

- A 20-item Multiple-Choice Self-Test designed to help students assess their understanding of the chapter's key points prior to taking quizzes and exams. As before, I provide an answer key at the back of the book that identifies and briefly explains each correct answer and refers students to the page on which the tested material was first discussed. Note that the answers printed in blue are for the optional "Industrial and Organizational Psychology" and "Neuropsychology" chapters.

Thinking Critically

A special Thinking Critically section in each chapter helps students hone their abilities in this vital skill. My approach centers on describing research on psychological phenomena in a way that reveals the logic of the scientific method, identifies possible flaws in design or interpretation, and leaves room for more questions and further research. In other words, as an author-teacher, I try to model critical thinking processes for my readers. The Thinking Critically sections are designed to make these processes more explicit and accessible by providing readers with a framework for analyzing evidence before drawing conclusions. The framework is built around five questions that the reader should find useful in analyzing not only psychological research studies but other forms of communication as well, including political speeches, advertising claims, and appeals for contributions. These five questions first appear in Chapter 1, where I introduce the importance of critical thinking, and they are repeated in every chapter's Thinking Critically section.

1. What am I being asked to believe or accept?
2. Is evidence available to support the claim?
3. Can that evidence be interpreted another way?
4. What evidence would help to evaluate the alternatives?
5. What conclusions are most reasonable?

Using this simple yet powerful framework, I explore issues such as subliminal persuasion, pornography and aggression, recovered memories, and the origins of sexual orientation, to name just a few. Page xii includes a complete list of the Thinking Critically features.

Focus on Research

Scientists in psychology have helped us better understand behavior and mental processes through their commitment to empirical research. They have posed vital questions about psychological phenomena and have designed research that can answer (or at least illuminate) those questions. In Chapter 1, I introduce readers to the methods of scientific research and to basic research designs in psychology. Every subsequent chapter features a Focus on Research section that highlights a particular research study to help students appreciate the value of research and the creativity with which psychologists have conducted it. Like the Thinking Critically sections, the Focus on Research features are organized around five questions designed to help readers organize their thinking about research questions and research results.

1. What was the researcher's question?
2. How did the researcher answer the question?
3. What did the researcher find?
4. What do the results mean?
5. What do I still need to know?

These Focus on Research sections help students see how psychologists have used experiments, surveys, observations, and other designs to explore phenomena such as learned helplessness, infant cognition, evolutionary theories of helping, and human sexual behavior. A full list of the Focus on Research features appears on page xii.

Linkages

In my experience, introductory psychology students are better able to appreciate the scope of our discipline when they look at it not as a laundry list of separate topics but as an interrelated set of subfields, each of which contributes to—and benefits from—the work being done in all the others. To help students see these relationships, I have built into the book an integrating tool called Linkages. There are three elements in the Linkages program.

- *Linkages diagrams*   The first element of the chapter's Active Review is a Linkages diagram, which presents a set of questions that illustrate three of the ways that material in the chapter is related to other chapters in the book. For example, the Linkages diagram in Chapter 2, "Biology and Behavior," contains questions that show how biological psychology is related to consciousness

("Does the brain shut down when I sleep?"), human development ("How do our brains change over a lifetime?"), and treatment of psychological disorders ("How do drugs help people who suffer from schizophrenia?"). These diagrams are designed to help students keep in mind how the content of each chapter fits into psychology as a whole. To introduce the concept of Linkages, the diagram in Chapter 1 appears within the body of the chapter.

- *Cross-references* The page numbers following each question in the Linkages diagrams direct the student to pages that carry further discussion of that question. There, the linking question is repeated in the margin alongside the discussion.

- *Linkages sections* One of the questions in each chapter's Linkages diagram reminds the student of the chapter's discussion of that question in a special section entitled, appropriately enough, Linkages (see page xii for a complete list of Linkages sections).

These three elements combine with the text narrative to highlight the network of relationships among psychology's subfields. This Linkages program is designed to help students see the "big picture" of psychology, no matter how many chapters their instructor assigns or in what sequence.

Teaching and Learning Support Package

Many useful instructional and pedagogical materials have been developed to support the *Essentials of Psychology* textbook and the introductory course. These are designed to enhance and maximize the teaching and learning experience. This fifth edition focuses on greater integration of the supplemental package components with the text itself. New features of several supplements reflect the text's emphasis on active learning and writing across the curriculum.

For the Instructor

Instructor's Resource Manual (ISBN: 0-495-90490-2) For each chapter of the textbook, the Instructor's Resource Manual includes learning objectives, a lecture outline, and numerous classroom "supplements," such as discussion, activity, and lecture suggestions and related handouts. The revised manual includes new Thinking Critically and Put It in Writing supplements similar to the exercises that appear in the textbook. The manual also includes a video guide and a pedagogical strategy section that covers active learning, critical thinking, using the Linkages feature, using the Research Focus supplements, and writing across the curriculum as well as suggestions on how to build a syllabus. For instructors switching from the fourth to the fifth edition of the text, the manual includes a detailed transition guide for each chapter, outlining the key changes between editions. Note that this revised Instructor's Resource Manual includes supporting material on the optional "Industrial and Organizational Psychology" and "Neuropsychology" chapters that was specially written for the fifth edition. As noted earlier, these chapters can be included in your text upon request—see your Cengage sales representative for details.

Test Bank (ISBN: 0-495-90387-6) The Test Bank, available in print or within ExamView,® a testing software program, includes 125 multiple-choice questions, five long essay questions, and five short answer questions per chapter. Over one-third of these are new, as are one-third of the essay questions. There is also a new section of short-answer questions for each chapter. Each multiple-choice question is keyed to pages in the student text and to the learning objectives that appear in the Instructor's Resource Manual and the Study Guide and that are also printed in the test bank. Each question is identified by whether it tests simple factual recall or deeper conceptual understanding.

Over 45 percent of the items have been class-tested with between 400 and 2,500 students. A statistical performance analysis is provided for those items. The computerized version allows instructors to edit questions, integrate their own questions, and generate paper or online exams. Both the print and computerized versions contain questions on the optional "Industrial and Organizational Psychology" and "Neuropsychology" chapters.

PowerLecture® with JoinIn™ and ExamView® (ISBN: 0-495-90491-0)   This one-stop lecture and class preparation tool contains ready-to-use PowerPoint slides (written by Tom Finn), enabling you to assemble, edit, publish, and present custom lectures for your course. PowerLecture lets you bring together text-specific lecture outlines and art from *Essentials* 5e along with videos or your own materials, culminating in a powerful, personalized media-enhanced presentation. PowerLecture also includes the JoinIn Student Response System that lets you pose book-specific questions and display students' answers seamlessly within the PowerPoint® slides of your own lecture in conjunction with the "clicker" hardware of your choice as well as the ExamView assessment and tutorial system, which guides you step by step through the process of creating tests.

WebTutor™
WebCT Printed Access Card (ISBN: 0-495-90930-0)
BlackBoard Printed Access Card (ISBN: 0-495-90928-9)
Save time managing your course, posting materials, incorporating multimedia, and tracking progress with this engaging, text-specific e-learning tool. Visit http://academic.cengage.com/webtutor.

ABC DVD: Introductory Psychology, Volumes 1-3
Volume 1 ISBN: 0-495-50306-1; Volume 2 ISBN: 0-495-59637-X;
Volume 3 ISBN: 0-495-60490-9
ABC Videos feature short, high-interest clips from current news events as well as historic raw footage going back 40 years. Perfect for discussion starters or to enrich your lectures and spark interest in the material in the text, these brief videos provide students with a new lens through which to view the past and present, one that will greatly enhance their knowledge and understanding of significant events and open up to them new dimensions in learning. Clips are drawn from such programs as *World News Tonight, Good Morning America, This Week, Primetime Live, 20/20,* and *Nightline* as well as from numerous ABC News specials and material from the Associated Press Television News and British Movietone News collections. VHS format is also available on request.

Wadsworth Psychology: Research in Action, Volumes 1 and 2
Volume 1 (ISBN: 0-495-60490-9); Volume 2 (ISBN: 0-495-59813-5)
Research in Action features the work of research psychologists to give students an opportunity to learn about cutting-edge research—not just who is doing it but also how it is done and how and where the results are being used. By taking students into the laboratories of both established and up-and-coming researchers and by showing research results being applied outside the laboratory, these videos offer insight into both the research process and the many ways that real people's lives are affected by research in the fields of psychology and neuroscience.

Wadsworth Guest Lecture Series (ISBN: 0-547-00401-X)   The Guest Lecture Series features many talented teachers sharing their teaching tips and best practices on a wide range of topics, including Rational Emotive Behavior Theory, Blogging as an Effective Tool, Demonstrations on Taste, Dramatizing Perspectives in Psychology, How to Teach Writing in Psychology, and many others.

Psych in Film (Intro) **(ISBN: 0-618-27530-4)**   The *Psych in Film®* DVD contains 35 clips from Universal Studios films illustrating key concepts in psychology. Clips from films such as *Schindler's List, Snow Falling on Cedars,* and many others are combined with commentary and discussion questions to help bring psychology alive for students and demonstrate its relevance to contemporary life and culture. Teaching tips are correlated to specific text chapters and concepts and are available on the instructor Web site.

***Revealing Psychology* (ISBN: 0-547-01453-8)**   The *Revealing Psychology* Video (available on DVD) is ideal for both classroom presentation and online study. The clips include a refreshed and innovative Candid Camera–like segment depicting people in socially challenging situations, with a focus on applications of concepts and experimental variations; classic experiments in real-world contexts with a new look and feel; and personal profiles with interviews of real people talking about their lives in ways that illustrate principles of social psychology.

For the Student

Book Companion Website   This outstanding site features chapter outlines, flashcards, Web links, tutorial quizzes, and more to help you succeed in your psychology course.

CengageNOW™ with CL eBook, Infotrac® College Edition, and Psychology Resource Center (Printed Access Card, ISBN: 0-538-49170-1)
CengageNOW Personalized Study is a diagnostic tool consisting of chapter-specific Pre-Tests, Study Plans, and Post-Tests that utilize text-specific resources to help you master the book's concepts and prepare for exams. You can work through learning modules featuring animations, discovery activities, videos, and eBook pages from the text.

***Study Guide*   The *Study Guide* augments the Active Review study materials built into every chapter of the textbook. Introductory sections in the guide provide tips on developing critical thinking skills, studying Linkages, reading a textbook, and (new to this edition) developing writing skills. For each chapter of the text—including the optional "Industrial and Organizational Psychology" and "Neuropsychology" chapters—the guide includes learning objectives, key term hints and examples, a Concepts and Exercises section that shows students how to apply their knowledge of psychology to everyday issues and concerns, a Critical Thinking exercise, and several Personal Learning Activities of the same type as those found in the text. In addition, each chapter concludes with two multiple-choice quizzes with wrong-answer rejoinders and a self-diagnostic quiz analysis to pinpoint weaknesses in topic and cognitive skill areas. A section of each chapter called What Should I Write About? provides advice on how to choose an appropriate term paper topic related to the chapter.

***Psychology in Context: Voices and Perspectives* (2nd ed.)**   The second edition of this exceptional reader, edited by David N. Sattler and Virginia Shabatay, may be shrink-wrapped with the text. It features engaging first-person narratives and essays by noted writers, with each article keyed to major psychological concepts.

***Psychology: Fields of Application*   This unique reader, edited by Astrid Stec and Douglas Bernstein, explores the most prominent areas of applied psychology. Each chapter features an expert's account of one area of application, including a brief history of the area's development, examples of research and how it has been applied, and the challenges facing the field.

***Success in College*   This guide is a skill-building booklet containing selected chapters from Walter Pauk's best-selling study skills text, *How to Study in College.* The booklet is based on the recently updated *How to Succeed in College* and offers time-tested advice on note-taking, time management, and test-taking.

***Writing with Style: APA Style Made Easy* (4th ed.)**   This accessible and invaluable workbook-style reference guide written by Lenore T. Szuchman will help students smoothly make the transition from writing for composition classes to writing for psychology classes.

Acknowledgments

Many people provided me with the help, criticism, and encouragement I needed to create *Essentials of Psychology* and to revise it into this fifth edition. I am of course indebted to my colleagues Louis Penner, Ed Roy, and Alison Clarke-Stewart, who, as co-authors of the Bernstein, Penner, Clarke-Stewart, and Roy textbook *Psychology* provided invaluable assistance in reviewing the revised *Essentials* manuscript as it developed. I also offer sincere thanks to Professor Paul Spector of the University of South Florida, who took the lead in helping to create the optional chapter on industrial and organizational psychology, and to Joel Shenker, M.D., Ph.D., who took the lead in helping to create the optional chapter on neuropsychology, each of which is available upon request for this edition. I am particularly grateful to William S. Altman of Broome Community College who worked closely with me on the revision of every chapter of this new edition. His extensive teaching experience, wisdom, and sense of humor were invaluable to me every step of the way. I also want to thank David Daniel of James Madison University for his ongoing support of *Essentials* and for his valuable suggestions for improving the teaching technology that accompanies it. I am indebted, too, to a number of other colleagues for their expert help and advice on the revision of various chapters that appeared in the fourth edition of *Essentials*. These colleagues include, for Chapter 3, Joel Shenker, M.D., Ph.D., and Larry Gotlob, University of Kentucky; for Chapter 5, Doug Williams, University of Winnipeg; for Chapter 6, Kathleen McDermott, Washington University; for Chapter 7, Paul Whitney, Washington State University, and Rose Mary Webb, Appalachian State University; for Chapter 8, Nancy Dess, Occidental College; for Chapter 10, Catherine Stoney, National Center for Complementary and Alternative Medicine; for Chapter 12, Geoff Kramer, Westshore Community College; for Chapter 13, Vicki Phares, University of South Florida; and for optional Chapter 15, Kim Schneider, Illinois State University.

Special thanks are also due to my dear friend and valued colleague, Sandra Goss Lucas, former Director of Introductory Psychology at the University of Illinois, who worked closely with me as I shaped and organized the new edition of *Essentials* and who helped me revise and improve the multiple-choice self-tests at the end of each chapter and create the Active Learning booklet that accompanies this new edition.

I also want to offer heartfelt thanks to my friends and colleagues who did such a wonderful job in creating revised versions of the ancillary materials for *Essentials*. Most of these people have worked with me for years, and many of them had been graduate student instructors in the University of Illinois introductory psychology program out of which this book emerged. They include Kelly Bouas Henry, Missouri Western State College; Sandra Goss Lucas, University of Illinois; Linda Lebie, Lakeland College; Chris Armstrong, University of Illinois; and David B. Strohmetz, Monmouth University.

I also extend my deep appreciation to the *Essentials'* Board of Consultants, eight dedicated instructors whose involvement in focus groups and surveys, comments on manuscript chapters, and answers to development queries shaped the first edition of this text.

CHARLES BLAIR-BROEKER, *Cedar Falls High School*

KEN LeSURE, *Cuyahoga Community College*

BARBARA LUSK, *Collin County Community College*

MALINDA JO MUZI, *Community College of Philadelphia*

MAGGIE SOKOLIK, *University of California, Berkeley*

NANCY SIMPSON, *Trident Technical College*

FRED WHITFORD, *Montana State University*

ROBERT WILDBLOOD, *Northern Virginia Community College*

I wish to thank several colleagues who helped me get the fifth edition off to a good start by reviewing and commenting on the strengths and weaknesses of the fourth edition.

JAMES BEAN, *Lock Haven University*

DORIS A. BITLER, *George Mason University*

J. PETER BURTON, *Santa Fe Community College*

BERNARDO J. CARDUCCI, *Indiana University Southeast*

DWAINE COCHRAN, *Stetson University*

MARCIE N. DESROCHERS, *College of Charleston*

KENNETH C. ELLIOT, *University of Maine at Augusta*

MATTHEW FANETTI, *Southwest Missouri State University*

LETICIA Y. FLORES, *Southwest Texas State University*

DIANE HERBERT, *Hofstra University*

JENNIFER M. LANCASTER, *St. Francis College*

DAVID S. MALCOLM, *Fordham University*

JOSEPH G. MARRONE, *Siena College*

BONNIE J. NICHOLS, *Missouri County Community College*

ARTHUR G. OLGUIN, *Santa Barbara City College*

SHEILA O'BRIEN QUINN, *Salve Regina University*

LES PARROTT, *Seattle Pacific University*

ELISABETH D. SHERWIN, *University of Arkansas at Little Rock*

JANE A. SMITH, *Concordia University*

MARY A. WATERSTREET, *St. Ambrose University*

I owe an enormous debt as well to the colleagues listed below for their thoughtful reviews of the manuscripts of the first, second, third, and fourth editions as they were being developed. Their advice and suggestions for improvement were responsible for many of the good qualities you will find in this book. If you have any criticisms, they probably involve areas these reviewers warned me about!

PATRICIA ABBOT, *D'Youville College*

GARY ALTMANN, *York University, U.K.*

ROBIN A. ANDERSON, *St. Ambrose University*

GRACE AUYANG, *University of Cincinnati*

ALAN BAXTER, *Technical Career Institutes, New York*

BETH BENOIT, *University of Massachusetts, Lowell, and Middlesex Community College*

JOSEPH J. BENZ, *University of Nebraska at Kearney*

WINFIELD BROWN, *Florence Darlington Technical College*

JAMES F. CALHOUN, *University of Georgia*

YIWEI CHEN, *Bowling Green State University*

SAUNDRA CICCARELLI, *Gulf Coast Community College*

SAMUEL CLAY, *Heartland Community College*

ANNE M. COOPER, *St. Petersburg Junior College*

NAT DEANDA, *Los Madanos College*

JOHN R. FOUST, *Parkland College*

LAURA FREBERG, *California Polytechnic State University, San Luis Obispo*

GRACE GALLIANO, *Kennesaw State University*

CHRISTOPHER GILBERT, *Bristol Community College*

CRAIG W. GRUBER, *Walt Whitman High School*

LYNN HALLER, *Morehead State University*

WEN HARRIS, *Lane Community College*

DEBRA HOLLISTER, *Valencia Community College*

GENE INDENBAUM, *SUNY Farmingdale*

JOHN S. KLEIN, *Castleton State College*

RONALD KLEINKNECHT, *Western Washington University*

JANET L. KOTTKE, *California State University, San Bernardino*

JOSEPH A. MAYO, *Gordon College*

DAVID MURPHY, *Waubonsee College*

SHEILA M. MURPHY, *Mount Wachusett Community College*

STEVE A. NIDA, *Franklin University*

CHRISTINE OFFUTT LINGENFELTER, *Lock Haven University*

RANDALL E. OSBORNE, *Indiana University East*

RALPH G. PIFER, *Sauk Valley Community College*

JAMES S. PREVITE, *Victor Valley College*

WAYNE J. ROBINSON, *Monroe Community College*

JOHN L. ROMANEK, *Jefferson Community College*

KENNETH M. ROSENBERG, *State University of New York, Oswego*

CYNTHIA J. SMITH, *Wheeling Jesuit University*

MITCHELL SPEAKS, *Keene State College*

HOLLY STRAUB, *University of South Dakota*

LINDA K. SWINDELL, *Anderson University*

PARSRAM S. THAKUR, *Community College of Rhode Island*

INGER THOMPSON, *Glendale Community College*

M. LISA VALENTINO, *Seminole Community College*

MICHAEL J. WENGER, *University of Notre Dame*

GORDON WHITMAN, *Sandhills Community College*

JEAN M. WYNN, *Manchester Community College*

C. VAN YOUNGMAN, *Art Institute of Philadelphia*

The process of creating *Essentials of Psychology* was greatly facilitated by the work of many dedicated people at Cengage Learning. From the sales representatives and sales managers who reinforced my colleagues' requests for the text to the marketing staff who worked to tell my colleagues what *Essentials* has to offer, it seems everyone at Cengage had a hand in shaping this book and now in revising it into its fifth edition. Several people in the editorial and production areas at Cengage deserve special mention, however, because they did an outstanding job in helping me develop and revise the *Essentials* manuscript and turn that manuscript into the beautiful book you are now holding. Managing Development Editor Jeremy Judson was involved in the shaping and development of the manuscript. The eagle-eyed copyediting of our copyeditor, Kate Babbitt, revealed and corrected all my little errors and some big ones, too. Thanks to both of you for all your help. And many thanks to Jonathan Peck for coordinating the myriad production tasks associated with this project and for keeping them, and me, on schedule. I also want to thank Stephen Forsling for his outstanding work in the creation of the art and photo program for *Essentials* 5e and Charlene Carpentier for her work as Production/Design Coordinator. Also my thanks go to Rebecca Rosenberg for her assistance in managing the print supplements. To Jane Potter, my friend and Senior Sponsoring Editor, I offer my sincere thanks. Without these people, and those who worked with them, the fifth edition of *Essentials of Psychology* would still be just an idea.

Finally, I want to thank my wife Doris for the loving support that sustains me in my work and in my life. *Je vous aime beaucoup, ma chérie.*

Doug Bernstein

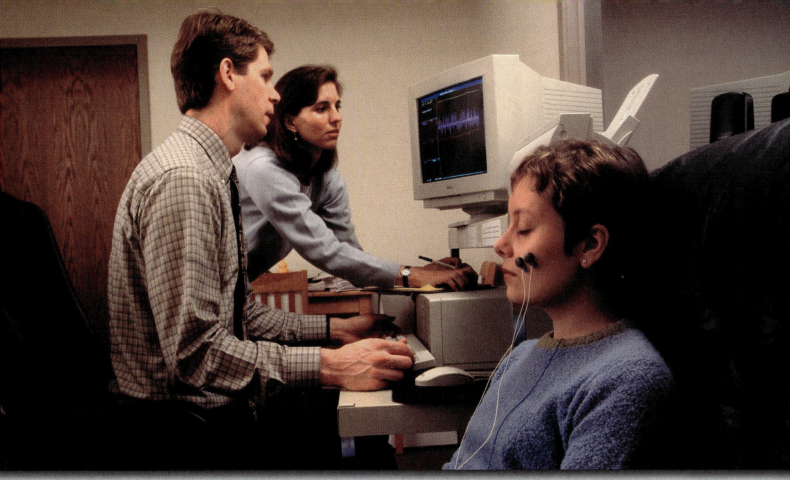

© Tom Stewart/Corbis

1 Introduction *to the* Science *of* Psychology

Preview

The following people all hold truly interesting jobs. What do you think they studied to qualify for those jobs? See if you can fill in the blank next to each job description with one of the fields of study listed in Table 1.1.

- **Kristen Beyer** works for the Federal Bureau of Investigation, where she develops questionnaires and conducts interviews aimed at identifying common features in the backgrounds of serial killers. _____

- **Jason Kring,** a professor at Embry-Riddle Aeronautical University, conducts research on how the gender composition of a team affects performance under the stress of spaceflight and military combat. _____

- **Anne Marie Apanovitch** is employed by a major drug company to study which of the company's marketing strategies are most effective in promoting sales. _____

- **Rebecca Snyder** studies the giant pandas at Zoo Atlanta in an effort to promote captive breeding and ultimately increase the wild population of this endangered species. _____

- **Michael Moon's** job at a software company is to find new ways to make Internet web sites easier for consumers to use. _____

- **Elizabeth Kolmstetter** works at the Transportation Security Administration, where, following the September 11, 2001, terrorist attacks, she took charge of a program to establish higher standards for hiring and training security screeners at U.S. airports. _____

- **Marissa Reddy,** co-director of the U.S. Secret Service's Safe Schools Initiative, tries to identify risk factors for violent behavior in high school students. _____

- **Sharon Lundgren,** founder of Lundgren Trial Consulting, Inc., helps prepare witnesses to testify in court and teaches attorneys how to present their evidence in the most convincing way. _____

- **Evan Byrne** works at the U.S. National Transportation Safety Board, where he investigates the role of memory lapses, disorientation, errors, and other human factors in causing airplane crashes. _____

- **Capt. Karen Orts,** chief of mental health services at a U.S. Air Force base, provides psychotherapy to military personnel suffering combat-related stress disorders and teaches leadership courses to commissioned and noncommissioned officers. _____

Because Captain Orts offers psychotherapy, you probably guessed that she is a psychologist, but what academic field did you associate with Rebecca Snyder, who studies giant pandas? It would have been perfectly reasonable to assume that she is a zoologist, but she, too, is a psychologist. So is Michael Moon, whose work on web site design might suggest that he was a computer science major. And although Sharon Lundgren spends her time working with witnesses and conducting mock trials, she is a psychologist, not a

TABLE 1.1 ■ WHAT'S MY LINE?

Try matching these educational backgrounds with the people described above by writing the correct field of study next to each person's job description.

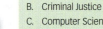

A. Engineering	F. Advertising
B. Criminal Justice	G. Biology
C. Computer Science	H. Education
D. Law	I. Zoology
E. Psychology	J. Business Administration

FIGURE 1.1 ■ HUSBAND AND FATHER-IN-LAW

This figure is called "Husband and Father-in-Law" (Botwinick, 1961) because you can see it as two different people, depending on how you mentally organize the features of the drawing. The elderly "father-in-law" faces to your right and is turned slightly toward you. He has a large nose, and the dark areas represent a coat pulled up to his chin. However, the tip of his nose can also be seen as the tip of a younger man's chin. The "husband" is in profile, also looking to your right, but away from you. The old man's mouth is the young man's neck band. Both men are wearing broad-brimmed hats. Can you see them? Cognitive psychologists point out that your ability to see two different figures in the same drawing—and to choose which one to see at any given moment—means that you actively manipulate incoming information rather than just passively receiving it.
Source: Botwinick (1961).

---

psychology   The science that seeks to understand behavior and mental processes and to apply that understanding in the service of human welfare.

positive psychology   A field of research that focuses on people's positive experiences and characteristics, such as happiness, optimism, and resilience.

cognitive psychologists   Psychologists whose research focus is analysis of the mental processes underlying judgment, decision making, problem solving, imagining, and other aspects of human thought or cognition.

---

lawyer. The fact is that *all* these people are psychologists! They may not all fit your image of what psychologists do, but as you will see in this chapter (and throughout this book), psychology is much broader and more diverse than you might have expected. We hope that reading this book will give you a fuller picture of psychology and that you will find our field as fascinating as we do.

This chapter begins our exploration of psychology with a brief look at some of its interrelated specialty areas, or *subfields*. We then tell the story of how psychology came to be and review several theories and approaches that guide psychologists in their work.

We also point out how the activities of psychologists in virtually every subfield are affected by human diversity, especially by age, gender, ethnicity, and other individual characteristics encountered in today's multicultural societies. Finally, we consider how critical thinking, scientific methods, and ethical standards guide psychologists as they conduct research and evaluate the evidence they collect. ■

The World of Psychology: An Overview

▶ *What is psychology, and how did it grow?*

Psychology is the science that seeks to understand behavior and mental processes and to apply that understanding in the service of human welfare. So although the ten people we have just described are engaged in many different kinds of work, they are all psychologists because they are all involved in studying, predicting, improving, or explaining some aspect of behavior and mental processes. But even this wide variety of jobs fails to capture the full scope of psychologists' interests. As a group, the world's half-million psychologists are interested in all the behaviors and mental processes that make you who you are and make other people who they are in every culture around the world. Many of these psychologists focus on what can go wrong in behavior and mental processes—on psychological disorders, problems in childhood development, stress-related illnesses, and the like—while others study what goes right. They explore the factors that lead people to be happy and satisfied with their lives, to achieve at a high level, to be creative, to help others, and to develop their full potential as human beings. This focus on the things that make life most worth living has become known as **positive psychology** (e.g., Peterson, 2006; Snyder & Lopez, 2007).

Subfields of Psychology

To appreciate how many things come under the umbrella of *behavior and mental processes,* think for a moment about how you would answer the question, Who are you? Would you describe your personality, the sharpness of your vision or hearing, your interests and goals, your job skills and accomplishments, your IQ, your cultural background, or your social skills? Perhaps you would describe a physical or psychological problem that bothers you. You could list these and dozens of other things about yourself, and every one of them would reflect some aspect of what psychologists mean by *behavior and mental processes.* When psychologists focus their work on particular aspects of behavior and mental processes, they enter one of psychology's many subfields. Let's take a quick look at the typical interests and activities of psychologists in these subfields now; we will focus on many of them in more detail in later chapters.

- **Cognitive psychologists** study basic mental processes such as sensation and perception (see Figure 1.1), learning and memory, judgment, decision making, and problem solving. Included in the wide range of fascinating topics they explore are such questions as whether people can forget (and then suddenly recover) traumatic memories, whether we can learn while asleep, and what role is played by intuition and other unconscious processes in guiding our thoughts and actions.

FIGURE 1.2   ■■   **WHERE WOULD YOU PUT A THIRD EYE?**

In a study of how thinking develops, children were asked to show where they would place a third eye if they could have one. Part A shows that nine-year-old children, who were still in an early stage of mental development, drew the extra eye between their existing eyes, "as a spare." Having developed more advanced thinking abilities, eleven-year-olds (Part B) drew the third eye in more creative places, such as the palm of their hand "so I can see around corners." *Source:* Shaffer (1973).

Drawing by a nine-year-old   Drawing by an eleven-year-old
(A)   (B)

- **Biological psychologists,** also called *physiological psychologists* or *neuroscientists,* study topics such as how genes and brain chemistry are related to the appearance of mental disorders, how brain cells communicate with each other in forming memories, whether certain patterns of brain activity can reveal that a person is lying, and how stress hormones weaken the body's immune system. Have you ever had the odd feeling that a new experience, such as entering an unfamiliar house, has actually happened to you before? Biological psychologists studying this experience of déjà vu (French for "already seen") suggest that it may be due to a temporary malfunction in the brain's ability to combine incoming information from the senses, creating the impression of two "copies" of a single event (Brown, 2004).

- **Personality psychologists** study individuality—the unique features of each person. Your personality traits, like your fingerprints, are different from those of all other people. Some personality psychologists use tests to describe how one individual compares with others in terms of openness to experience, emotionality, reliability, agreeableness, and sociability. Others study particular combinations of personality traits that may predict particular patterns of behavior. For instance, personality psychologists interested in positive psychology are identifying the characteristics of people who can remain optimistic even in the face of stress or tragedy and find happiness in life (Snyder & Lopez, 2006).

- **Developmental psychologists** study and describe changes in behavior and mental processes over the life span, trying to understand their causes and effects (see Figure 1.2). They explore areas such as the development of thought, friendship patterns, and parenting styles and whether everyone must face a midlife crisis. Some of their research has been used by judges and attorneys in deciding how old a child has to be in order to serve as a reliable witness in court or to responsibly choose which divorcing parent to live with.

- **Quantitative psychologists** develop and use statistical tools to analyze vast amounts of information generated by research results from all of psychology's subfields. Later in this chapter we show how quantitative psychologists use correlation coefficients and other statistical tools to evaluate psychological tests and to estimate the relative contributions of heredity and environment in determining our intelligence. To what extent are people born smart—or not so smart—and to what extent are their mental abilities affected by their environments? This is one of the hottest topics in psychology today, and quantitative psychologists are right in the middle of it.

biological psychologists   Psychologists who analyze the biological factors influencing behavior and mental processes.

personality psychologists   Psychologists who focus on people's unique characteristics.

developmental psychologists   Psychologists who seek to understand, describe, and explore how behavior and mental processes change over the course of a lifetime.

quantitative psychologists   Psychologists who develop statistical methods for evaluating and analyzing data from psychological research.

GOT A MATCH? ▶

Some commercial dating services apply social psychologists' research on interpersonal attraction in an effort to pair up people whose characteristics are most likely to be compatible.

applying psychology

- **Clinical, counseling, and community psychologists** study the causes of behavior disorders and offer services to help troubled people overcome these disorders. Generally, clinical psychologists have Ph.D. degrees in psychology; most provide therapy services, and many conduct research as well. A counseling psychologist might work as a mental health counselor, for example, and have either a Ph.D. or a master's degree in psychology. Community psychologists offer psychological services to the homeless and others who need help but tend not to seek it. By working for changes in schools and other social systems, they also try to prevent poverty and other stressful conditions that so often lead to disorder. All of these psychologists differ from *psychiatrists,* who are medical doctors who specialize in abnormal behavior (psychiatry).

- **Educational psychologists** conduct research and develop theories about teaching and learning. The results of their work are applied in programs designed to improve teacher training, refine school curricula, reduce dropout rates, and help students learn more efficiently. For example, they have supported the use of the "jigsaw" technique, a type of classroom activity in which children from various ethnic groups must work together to complete a task or solve a problem. These cooperative experiences appear to promote learning, generate mutual respect, and reduce intergroup prejudice (Aronson, 2004).

- **School psychologists** have traditionally specialized in intelligence testing, diagnosing learning disabilities and other academic problems, and setting up programs to improve students' achievement and satisfaction in school. Today, however, they are also involved in early detection of students' mental health problems and in crisis intervention following school violence (Benjamin & Baker, 2004; Elliot, Reynolds, & Kratochwill, 2006).

- **Social psychologists** study the ways that people influence one another. For example, they conduct research on social-influence strategies, such as the effectiveness of safe-sex advertising campaigns designed to halt the spread of AIDS. They also explore how peer pressure affects us, what determines whom we like (or even love), and why and how prejudice forms. They have found, for example, that although we may pride ourselves on not being prejudiced, we may actually hold unconscious beliefs about certain ethnic groups that negatively affect the way we relate to people from those groups (Vanman et al., 2004).

- **Industrial and organizational psychologists** study leadership, stress, competition, pay, and other factors that affect the efficiency, productivity, and satisfaction of workers and the organizations that employ them. They conduct research on topics such as increasing the motivation of current employees and helping companies select the best new workers. They also explore the ways in

clinical, counseling, and community psychologists Psychologists who seek to assess, understand, modify, and prevent behavior disorders.

educational psychologists Psychologists who study methods by which instructors teach and students learn and who apply their results to improving such methods.

school psychologists Psychologists who test IQ, diagnose students' academic problems, and set up programs to improve students' achievement.

social psychologists Psychologists who study how people influence one another's behavior and attitudes, especially in groups.

industrial and organizational psychologists Psychologists who examine factors that influence people's performance in the workplace.

FORENSIC PSYCHOLOGY ▶

Forensic psychologists may assist police and other agencies in profiling criminals, evaluating the mental competence of defendants, participating in jury selection, and performing many other tasks related to psychology and the law. Actor B. D. Wong's performance as forensic psychiatrist Dr. George Huang on *Law and Order: SVU* is so accurate that the Media Psychology division of the American Psychological Association gave the show its 2004 Golden Psi award for excellence in fictional portrayal of mental health professionals.

which businesses and industrial organizations work—or fail to work—and they make recommendations to help these organizations work better. Companies all over the world are applying research by industrial and organizational psychologists to foster *positive organizational behavior* through the development of employee training programs, effective goal-setting procedures, fair and reasonable evaluation methods, and systems for motivating and rewarding outstanding employee performance.

Our list of psychology's subfields is still not complete. For example, **health psychologists** study the effects of behavior on health and the impact of illness on behavior and emotion; **sport psychologists** search for the keys to maximum athletic performance; and **forensic psychologists** assist in jury selection, evaluate defendants' sanity and mental competence to stand trial, and deal with other matters involving psychology and the law. **Engineering psychologists,** also known as *human factors psychologists,* study the relationships of human beings to the computers, telephones, and other machines they use. Their research has been applied in the design of computer keyboards, Internet web sites, aircraft instrument panels, controls for hospital beds and nuclear power plants, and even on-screen programming and navigation systems for TV sets and mobile phones that make them more logical, easier to use, and less likely to cause errors. Finally, **environmental psychologists** study the effects of the environment on people's behavior and mental processes. The results of their research are applied by architects and interior designers as they plan or remodel residence halls, shopping malls, auditoriums, hospitals, prisons, offices, and other spaces to make them more comfortable and functional for the people who will occupy them. (See Table 1.2 for a summary of the typical activities and work settings of psychologists in the United States.)

Linkages Within Psychology and Beyond

We have listed psychology's subfields as though they were separate, but they often overlap, and so do the activities of the psychologists working in them. When developmental psychologists study the growth of children's thinking skills or friendships, for example, their research is linked to that of colleagues in cognitive or social psychology. Similarly, biological psychologists have one foot in clinical psychology when they look at how chemicals in the brain affect the risk of depression. And when social psychologists apply research on cooperation to promote group learning activities in the classroom, they are linking up with educational psychology. Even when psychologists work mainly in one subfield, they are still likely to draw on—and contribute to—the knowledge in other subfields.

So if you want to understand psychology as a whole, you have to understand the linkages among its subfields. To help you recognize these linkages, we highlight three

health psychologists Psychologists who study the effects of behavior on health and the impact of illness on behavior and emotion.

sport psychologists Psychologists whose research is aimed at maximizing athletic performance.

forensic psychologists Psychologists who are involved in many aspects of psychology and law.

engineering psychologists Psychologists who study and try to improve the relationships between human beings and the computers and other machines they use.

environmental psychologists Psychologists who study the relationship between people's physical environment and their behavior.

TABLE 1.2 ■ TYPICAL ACTIVITIES AND WORK SETTINGS FOR PSYCHOLOGISTS

The fact that psychologists can work in such a wide variety of settings and do so many interesting—and often well-paying—jobs helps account for the popularity of psychology as an undergraduate major (Snyder, Dillow, & Hoffman, 2008). Psychology courses also provide excellent background for students planning to enter medicine, law, business, and many other fields.

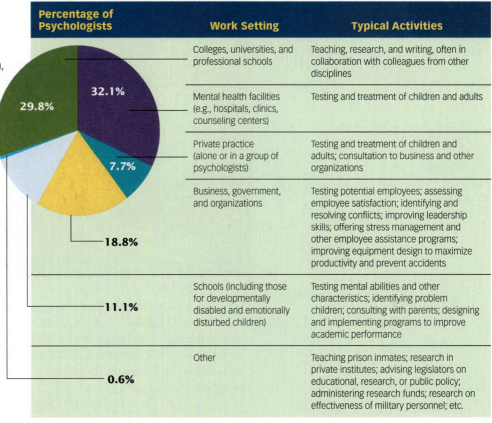

Percentage of Psychologists	Work Setting	Typical Activities
32.1%	Colleges, universities, and professional schools	Teaching, research, and writing, often in collaboration with colleagues from other disciplines
	Mental health facilities (e.g., hospitals, clinics, counseling centers)	Testing and treatment of children and adults
7.7%	Private practice (alone or in a group of psychologists)	Testing and treatment of children and adults; consultation to business and other organizations
18.8%	Business, government, and organizations	Testing potential employees; assessing employee satisfaction; identifying and resolving conflicts; improving leadership skills; offering stress management and other employee assistance programs; improving equipment design to maximize productivity and prevent accidents
11.1%	Schools (including those for developmentally disabled and emotionally disturbed children)	Testing mental abilities and other characteristics; identifying problem children; consulting with parents; designing and implementing programs to improve academic performance
0.6%	Other	Teaching prison inmates; research in private institutes; advising legislators on educational, research, or public policy; administering research funds; research on effectiveness of military personnel; etc.

29.8%

Source: Data from 2005 Doctorate Employment Survey (Wicherski & Kohout, 2007).

IMPROVING BAD DESIGNS ▶

Consultation by human factors psychologists, who apply cognitive research to the design of equipment, would surely have improved the layout of these self-service fuel pumps. The system will not operate until you press the red spot (see upper right) under the yellow "push to start" label, which is difficult to locate among all the other signs and stickers. Such user-unfriendly designs are all too common these days (e.g., Heller, 2008; Lee, 2006; Petroski, 2008a, 2008b; visit www.baddesigns.com for some amazing examples).

Photograph courtesy of www.baddesigns.com

PLANNING SPACES ▶

Environmental psychologists are often asked to consult on the design of offices. Here, the consultants suggested the use of aquariums filled with tropical fish to help reduce the stress that is created when many employees work in close quarters.

applying psychology

of them in a diagram, similar to the one in Figure 1.3, near the end of every chapter. Each chapter's Linkages diagram contains questions that illustrate three relationships between the topics discussed in that chapter and the topics of other chapters. The page numbers after each question indicate where discussions related to them appear (look for "Linkages" symbols on those pages). There are so many linkages throughout the book that we could not include them all in our diagrams, but we hope those diagrams will remind you to look for linkages that we didn't mention. This kind of detective work can actually help you to do better on exams and quizzes, because it is often easier to remember material in one chapter by relating it to linked material in other chapters.

Psychology itself is linked to other disciplines. Some of these connections occur because psychologists share interests with researchers in other fields. For example, cognitive psychologists are working with computer scientists to create artificial intelligence systems that can recognize voices, solve problems, and make decisions in ways that will equal or exceed human capabilities (Haynes, Cohen, & Ritter, 2009; Wang, 2007). Other links occur when research in one discipline is applied in another.

LINKING PSYCHOLOGY AND LAW ▶

Cognitive psychologists' research on the quirks of human memory has led to revised guidelines for police and prosecutors (U.S. Department of Justice, 1999). These guidelines warn that asking witnesses leading questions (e.g., "Do you remember seeing a gun?") can distort their memories, that false accusations are less likely if witnesses are told that the real criminal might not be in a lineup or in a group of photos, and that no one in a lineup should stand out from all the others (Doyle, 2005).

applying psychology

linkages

Is behavior influenced more by our genes or by our environment?
(ans. on p. 35)

Does psychotherapy work?
(ans. on p. 527)

Is it ethical to deceive people to learn about their social behavior? *(ans. on p. 577)*

Chapter 2
Biology and Behavior

Chapter 13
Treatment of Psychological Disorders

Chapter 14
Social Psychology

FIGURE 1.3 ■ LINKAGES

The questions listed in this diagram highlight just three of the many ways in which psychology's subfields are linked to one another. Three additional linking questions appear in the Linkages diagram included in every chapter to come. Each diagram lists the page number on which each question is answered. When you turn to that page, you will find a Linkages symbol in the margin where the answer is discussed. Sometimes the discussion is brief, but every chapter also contains a special Linkages feature that examines linked research in more detail. By staying alert to linkages among psychology's subfields, you will come away from this course not only with threads of knowledge about each subfield but also with an appreciation of the fabric of psychology as a whole.

For example, physicians and economists are using research by psychologists to better understand the thought processes that influence (good and bad) decisions about caring for patients and choosing investments (Basu, Chapman, & Galvani, 2008; Chapman & Coups, 2006; Leiser & Azar, 2008.; Leiser, Azar, & Hadar, 2008; Morgan et al., 2008). In fact, psychologist Daniel Kahneman recently won a Nobel Prize in economics for his work in this area. Other psychologists' research on memory has influenced how lineups are displayed to eyewitnesses attempting to identify criminals, how attorneys question eyewitnesses in court, and how judges instruct juries (Memon, Vrij, & Bull, 2004). And psychological studies of the effect of brain disorders on elderly patients' mental abilities are shaping doctors' recommendations about when those patients should stop driving cars (Baldock et al., 2007; Fiorentino, 2008; Rees et al., 2008).

This book is filled with examples of other ways that psychological theories and research have been applied to fields as diverse as health care, law, business, engineering, architecture, aviation, and sports.

A Brief History of Psychology

Psychology is a relatively new science, but its origins can be traced through centuries. Since at least the time of Socrates, Plato, and Aristotle in ancient Greece, philosophers have debated such psychological topics as where human knowledge comes from, the nature of mind and soul, the relationship of the mind to the body, and even the possibility of scientifically studying these matters.

Scientific psychology thus has its roots in philosophy, and especially in a philosophical view called **empiricism** (pronounced "im-PEER-eh-ciz-em"). In the 1600s, empiricists such as John Locke, George Berkeley, and David Hume challenged the claim—which had been made by philosophers as far back as Plato—that some of what we know is present at birth. Empiricists argued that our minds are more like a blank slate ("tabula rasa" in Latin) on which our experiences write a lifelong story. In other words, according to empiricism, knowledge comes to us only through our experiences and observations. For 130 years now, empiricism has guided psychologists in seeking

empiricism The view that knowledge comes from experience and observation.

WILHELM WUNDT (1832–1920) ▶

In an early experiment on the speed of mental processes, Wilhelm Wundt (third from left) first measured how quickly people could respond to a light by releasing a button they had been holding down. He then measured how much longer the response took when they held down one button with each hand and had to decide—based on the color of the light—which one to release. Wundt reasoned that the additional response time reflected how long it took to perceive the color and decide which hand to move. As noted in the chapter on thought, language, and intelligence, the logic behind this experiment remains a part of modern research on cognitive processes.

FIGURE 1.4   ■   A STIMULUS FOR INTROSPECTION

Look at this object and try to ignore what it is. Instead, try to describe only your conscious experience of it, such as redness, brightness, and roundness and how intense and clear these sensations and images are. If you can do this, you would have been an excellent research participant in Titchener's laboratory.

Learn BY Doing

knowledge about behavior and mental processes not through speculation but through observations governed by the rules of science.

Wundt and the Structuralism of Titchener   The birth date of modern scientific psychology is usually given as 1879. This is the year in which Wilhelm Wundt (pronounced "voont") established the first formal psychology research laboratory, at the University of Leipzig in Germany (Benjamin, 2000). Wundt was a physiologist, and like other physiologists of his day, he had been studying vision, hearing, and other sensory-perceptual systems. However, Wundt's ambitious goal was to use the methods of laboratory science to study **consciousness**—the mental experience that arises from these systems. In doing so, Wundt began psychology's transformation from the *philosophy* of mental processes to the science of mental processes.

Wundt wanted to describe the basic elements of consciousness, including how they are organized and how they relate to one another (Schultz & Schultz, 2002). In an attempt to study conscious experience, Wundt used *introspection,* which means "looking inward." Edward Titchener, an American who had been a student of Wundt, later used introspection in his own laboratory at Cornell University to study sensations, feelings, and images associated with conscious experience. To understand introspection, look at the object in Figure 1.4, but try to describe not what it is but only how intensely and clearly you experience its sensations and images (such as redness, brightness, and roundness). This was the difficult task that Wundt and Titchener set for carefully trained "introspectors" in their search for the building blocks of consciousness. Titchener called his approach *structuralism* because he was trying to define the structure of consciousness. Wundt and Titchener were not the only scientific researchers in psychology, and their work was not universally accepted. Other scientific psychologists in Europe were studying the limits of sensory abilities and the capability for learning and memory. They saw the structuralists' work as too simplistic.

Gestalt Psychology   Around 1912, another group of European psychologists, led by Max Wertheimer, Kurt Koffka, and Wolfgang Köhler, argued against the value of trying to break down human experience or consciousness into its component parts. They were called *Gestalt psychologists* because they pointed out that the whole (or *Gestalt,* in German) of conscious experience is not the same as the sum of its parts. Wertheimer noted, for example, that when two lights are placed near each other in a dark room and go on and off in just the right sequence, we experience not two lights but a single light "jumping" back and forth. This is called the *phi phenomenon,* and you have probably seen it in advertising signs that create the impression of a series of lights racing around

consciousness   The awareness of external stimuli and our own mental activity.

a display. Movies provide another example. Imagine how boring it would be to browse through the thousands of still images that are printed on a reel of film. Yet when those same images are projected onto a screen at just the right rate, they combine to create a rich emotional experience. In other words, said the Gestaltists, consciousness should be studied as a whole, not piece by piece.

Freud and Psychoanalysis   While Wundt was conducting scientific research on consciousness in Germany, Sigmund Freud, a physician, was in Vienna, Austria, exploring the unconscious. In the late 1880s, Freud began to question the assumption that biological factors were behind all behavior and mental processes, including illnesses. Using hypnosis and other methods, Freud suggested that the cause of some people's physical ailments was not physical. The real cause, he said, was deep-seated problems that the patients had pushed out of consciousness (Friedman & Schustack, 2003). He eventually came to believe that all behavior—from everyday slips of the tongue to severe forms of mental disorder—can be traced to *psychological processes,* especially to internal conflicts that he said take place without our being aware of them. He believed that many of these unconscious *psychodynamic* conflicts are created when our sexual and aggressive instincts clash with the rules set for us by society. For nearly fifty years, Freud revised and expanded his ideas into a body of work known as *psychoanalysis.* His theory included explanations of how personality and mental disorder develop as well as a set of treatment methods. Freud's ideas are by no means universally accepted, but he was a groundbreaker whose psychodynamic theories had a significant influence on psychology and many other fields.

William James and Functionalism   Psychology took root in North America not long after Wundt began his work in Germany. In the late 1870s, William James set up the first psychology laboratory in the United States, at Harvard University. His lab was used mainly to conduct demonstrations for his students (Schultz & Schultz, 2002), but in 1883, G. Stanley Hall at Johns Hopkins University established the first psychology research laboratory in the United States. The first Canadian psychology research laboratory was established in 1889 at the University of Toronto by James Mark Baldwin, Canada's first modern psychologist and a pioneer in research on child development.

William James rejected both Wundt's approach and Titchener's structuralism. Influenced by Darwin's theory of evolution, James wanted to understand how sensations, memories, and all the other mental events that make up our ever-flowing "stream of

WILLIAM JAMES'S LABORATORY ▶

William James (1842–1910) established this psychology demonstration laboratory at Harvard University in the late 1870s. Like the Gestalt psychologists, James saw the approach used by Wundt and Titchener as a scientific dead end; he said that trying to understand consciousness by studying its parts is like trying to understand a house by looking at individual bricks (James, 1884). He preferred instead to study the ways that consciousness functions to help people adapt to their environments.

consciousness" help us adapt to our changing environments (James, 1890, 1892). This idea was consistent with an approach to psychology called *functionalism,* which focused on the function of consciousness in guiding our ability to make decisions, solve problems, and the like. James's emphasis on the functions of mental processes encouraged other psychologists in North America to look at how those processes work to our advantage and how they differ from person to person. Some of these psychologists began to measure individual differences in learning, memory, and other aspects of intelligence and make recommendations for improving educational practices in the schools. A few even began to work with teachers on programs for children in need of special help (Kramer, Bernstein, & Phares, 2009).

John B. Watson and Behaviorism   Besides fueling James's interest in the functions of consciousness, Darwin's theory of evolution led other psychologists, especially in North America after 1900, to study animals as well as humans. If all species evolved in adaptive ways, perhaps their behavior and mental processes would follow the same, or similar, laws. Psychologists observed animal behavior in mazes and other experimental situations. From these observations, they drew conclusions about the animals' conscious experiences and about the general laws of learning, memory, problem solving, and other mental processes that might apply to people, too.

John B. Watson, a psychology professor at Johns Hopkins University, agreed that the behavior of animals and humans was the most important source of scientific information for psychology. In 1913, Watson wrote an article called "Psychology as the Behaviorist Views It." In this article, he argued that psychologists should ignore mental events and concern themselves only with *observable* behavior (Watson, 1913, 1919). His approach, known as *behaviorism,* did not address consciousness, as structuralism and functionalism did, let alone consider the unconscious, as the Freudian view did. Focusing on consciousness, said Watson, would prevent psychology from ever being a true science. Watson believed that learning is the most important cause of behavior. He was famous for claiming that if he had enough control over the environment, he could create learning experiences that would turn any infant into a doctor, a lawyer, or even a criminal.

American psychologist B. F. Skinner was another early champion of behaviorism. From the 1930s until his death in 1990, Skinner studied *operant conditioning,* a learning process through which rewards and punishments shape, maintain, and change behavior. Using what he called *functional analysis of behavior,* Skinner would explain, for example, how parents and teachers can unknowingly encourage children's tantrums by rewarding them with attention. He noted, too, that a virtual addiction to gambling can develop through the occasional and unpredictable rewards it brings. Skinner said that functional analysis not only reveals the learned foundations of behavior but also suggests what rewards and punishments should be changed in order to alter that behavior.

Watson's and Skinner's vision of psychology as the learning-based science of observable behavior found favor with many psychologists. Behaviorism dominated psychological research in North America from the 1920s through the 1960s. ("In Review: The Development of Psychology" summarizes behaviorism and the other schools of thought that have influenced psychologists over the years.)

Psychology Today   By end of the 1960s, however, more and more psychologists saw the behaviorists' lack of attention to mental processes as a serious limitation (e.g., Ericsson & Simon, 1994). As the computer age dawned, psychologists began to think about mental activity in a new way—as information processing. At the same time, progress in biotechnology began to offer psychologists new ways to study the biological bases of mental processes. Armed with ever-more-sophisticated research tools, many psychologists today are trying to do what Watson thought was impossible: to study mental processes and, as shown in Figure 1.5, even watch the brain perform them. Psychology has come full circle, once again accepting consciousness, in the form of cognitive processes, as a legitimate topic for research.

In Review

THE DEVELOPMENT OF PSYCHOLOGY

SCHOOL OF THOUGHT	FOUNDERS	GOALS	METHODS
Structuralism	Edward Titchener, trained by Wilhelm Wundt	To study conscious experience and its structure	Experiments; introspection
Gestalt psychology	Max Wertheimer	To describe organization of mental processes ("the whole is greater than the sum of its parts")	Observation of sensory/perceptual phenomena
Psychoanalysis	Sigmund Freud	To explain personality and behavior; to develop techniques for treating mental disorders	Study of individual cases
Functionalism	William James	To study how the mind works in allowing an organism to adapt to the environment	Naturalistic observation of animal and human behavior
Behaviorism	John B. Watson; B. F. Skinner	To study only observable behavior and explain behavior via learning principles	Observation of the relationship between environmental stimuli and overt responses

1. Darwin's theory of evolution had an especially strong influence on _____ ism and _____ ism.

2. Which school of psychological thought was founded by a European medical doctor? _____

3. In the history of psychology, _____ was the first school of thought to appear.

Improve Your Grade
Tutorial: Psychology Schools of Thought Timeline

FIGURE 1.5 ■ VISUALIZING BRAIN ACTIVITY

Magnetic resonance imaging (MRI) techniques allow biological psychologists to study the brain activity accompanying various mental processes (Cooper, 2007; deCharms, 2008; Harrison et al., 2008; Johnson et al., 2008). The study illustrated here found that while reading, males (left) and females (right) show different patterns of brain activity, as indicated by the brightly colored areas (Shaywitz et al., 1995).

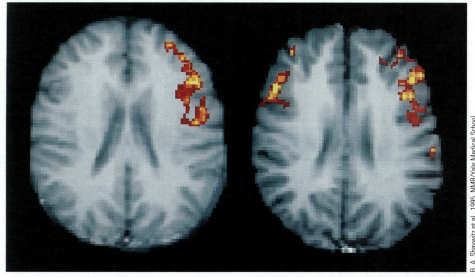

B. A. Shaywitz et al., 1995, NMR/Yale Medical School

Approaches to the Science of Psychology

 Why don't all psychologists explain behavior in the same way?

We have seen that the history of psychology is, in part, the history of the differing ways in which psychologists have thought about, or "approached," behavior and mental processes. Today, psychologists no longer refer to themselves as structuralists or functionalists but the psychodynamic and behavioral approaches remain, along with some newer ones known as the *biological, evolutionary, cognitive,* and *humanistic approaches.* Some psychologists adopt just one of these approaches, but most are eclectic. This means that they blend aspects of two or more approaches in an effort to more fully understand the behavior and mental processes in their subfield (e.g., Cacioppo et al., 2000). Some approaches to psychology are more influential than others these days, but we will review the main features of all of them so you can more easily understand why different psychologists may explain the same behavior or mental process in different ways.

The Biological Approach

As its name implies, the **biological approach** assumes that behavior and mental processes are largely shaped by biological processes. Psychologists who take this approach study the psychological effects of hormones and genes and the activity of the nervous system, especially the brain. When studying memory, for example, these researchers try to identify changes taking place in the brain as information is stored there. (Figure 6.14, in the chapter on memory, shows an example of these changes.) And when studying thinking, they might look for patterns of brain activity associated with, say, making quick decisions or reading a foreign language. Research discussed in nearly every chapter of this book reflects the enormous influence of the biological approach on psychology today.

The Evolutionary Approach

Biological processes are also highlighted in an approach to psychology that is based on Charles Darwin's 1859 book *On the Origin of Species.* Darwin argued that the forms of

THE BIOLOGY OF EMOTION ▶
Robert Levenson, a psychologist at the University of California at Berkeley, takes a biological approach to the study of social interactions. He measures heart rate, muscle tension, and other physical reactions as couples discuss problems in their relationships. He then looks for patterns of physiological activity in each partner (such as overreactions to criticism) that might be related to success or failure in resolving their problems.

biological approach   The view that behavior is the result of physical processes, especially those relating to the brain, to hormones, and to other chemicals.

Courtesy of Robert Levenson, Ph.D., Director, Institute of Personality and Social Research, University of California

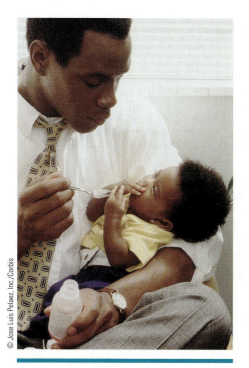

© Jose Luis Pelaez, Inc./Corbis

A FATHER'S LOVE ▲

Mothers are solely responsible for the care and protection of their young in almost all species of mammals. These species survive without male parenting, so why are some human fathers so active in child rearing? Do evolutionary forces make fathering more adaptive for humans? Is it a matter of learning to care? Is it a combination of both? Psychologists who take an evolutionary approach study these questions and others relating to the origins of human social behavior.

evolutionary approach   A view that emphasizes the inherited, adaptive aspects of behavior and mental processes.

psychodynamic approach   A view developed by Freud that emphasizes unconscious mental processes in explaining human thought, feelings, and behavior.

behavioral approach   A view based on the assumption that human behavior is determined mainly by what a person has learned in life, especially by rewards and punishments.

life we see today are the result of *evolution*—of changes in life forms that occur over many generations. He said that evolution occurs through *natural selection,* which promotes the survival of the fittest individuals. Those whose behavior and appearance allow them to withstand the elements, avoid predators, and mate are able to survive and produce offspring with similar characteristics. Those less able to adjust (or *adapt*) to changing conditions are less likely to survive and reproduce. Most evolutionists today see natural selection operating at the level of genes, but the process is the same. Genes that result in characteristics and behaviors that are adaptive and useful in a certain environment will enable the creatures that inherited them to survive and reproduce, thereby passing those genes on to the next generation. According to evolutionary theory, many (but not all) of the genes that animals and humans possess today are the result of natural selection.

The **evolutionary approach** to psychology assumes that the *behavior and mental processes* of animals and humans today are largely the result of evolution through natural selection. Evolutionary psychologists see aggression, for example, as a form of territory protection, and they see gender differences in mate selection preferences as reflecting different ways of helping genes survive in future generations (Griskevicius et al., 2009). The evolutionary approach has resulted in a growing body of research (Buller, 2005; Buss, 2004a, 2009); in later chapters, you will see how it is applied in relation to topics such as mental disorders, temperament, interpersonal attraction, and helping.

The Psychodynamic Approach

The **psychodynamic approach** to psychology offers a different slant on the role of inherited characteristics in shaping behavior and mental processes. Rooted in Freud's theory of psychoanalysis, this approach assumes that our behavior and mental processes reflect the constant (and mostly unconscious) psychodynamic conflicts that are said to rage within each of us. According to Freud, these conflicts occur when the impulse to instantly satisfy our instinctive needs—such as for food, sex, or aggression—are opposed by our learned need to follow society's rules about fairness and consideration for others. Psychologists taking the psychodynamic approach might see aggression as a triumph of raw impulses over self-control. At the same time, they consider anxiety, depression, and other psychological disorders as the outward evidence of inner conflict.

Freud's original theories are not as influential today as they once were (Mischel, 2004a), but in other chapters you will see that modern versions of the psychodynamic approach still appear in various theories of personality, psychological disorders, and psychotherapy.

The Behavioral Approach

The assumptions of the **behavioral approach** to psychology contrast sharply with those of the biological, evolutionary, and psychodynamic approaches. For one thing, the behavioral approach is rooted in the behaviorism of Watson and Skinner. As we mentioned earlier, behaviorism focused entirely on observable behavior in humans and animals and on how it is learned. Accordingly, psychologists who take a strict behavioral approach concentrate only on observable behavior. They want to know how life's rewards, punishments, and other learning experiences act on the "raw materials" provided by genes and evolution to shape behavior into what it is today. So whether they are trying to understand a person's aggressiveness, fear of spiders, parenting methods, or tendency to abuse drugs, behaviorists look mainly at that person's learning history. And because they believe that behavior problems develop through learning, behaviorists seek to eliminate those problems by helping people learn new and more adaptive responses.

Recall, though, that behaviorism was criticized precisely because it ignored everything but observable behavior. That criticism has had an impact on the many behaviorists who now apply their learning-based approach in an effort to understand

WHY IS HE SO AGGRESSIVE? ▶

Psychologists who take a cognitive behavioral approach suggest that there are several ways that children learn to be aggressive. Children might see others being rewarded for acting aggressively and then might be rewarded themselves for doing the same. Aggressiveness might also be made more likely if a child constantly hears that other people can be dangerous and that aggression is the only way to deal with threats, disagreements, and other conflict situations (Cooper, Gomez, & Buck, 2008; Wilkowski & Robinson, 2008).

cognitions (thoughts) as well as observable behavior. Those who take this *cognitive behavioral, or social-cognitive,* approach explore topics such as the ways that we learn our thoughts, attitudes, and beliefs and, in turn, how these learned cognitive patterns affect observable behavior.

The Cognitive Approach

The growth of the cognitive behavioral perspective reflects the influence of a more generally cognitive view of psychology. This **cognitive approach** focuses on how our behavior is affected by the ways we take in, mentally represent, process, and store information. Consider how the cognitive approach might guide the analysis of an incident of aggression: A person in line for movie tickets (1) *perceived* that someone had cut into the line, (2) *recalled* information stored in memory to judge that this act was inappropriate, (3) *decided* that the act was due to the other person's rudeness, (4) *labeled* the person as rude and inconsiderate, (5) *considered* several possible responses and their likely consequences, (6) *decided* that punching the other person was the best response, and then (7) *executed* that response. Psychologists who take a cognitive approach suggest that mental processes like these—some of which occur outside of awareness—can help us understand many kinds of individual and social behaviors, from decision making and problem solving to interpersonal attraction and intelligence. In the situation we just described, for example, the person's aggression would be seen as the result of poor problem solving because there were probably several better ways to deal with the problem of line cutting. The cognitive approach is especially important in the field of *cognitive science,* in which researchers from psychology, computer science, biology, engineering, linguistics, and philosophy study intelligent systems in humans and computers. Some of their progress in creating artificial intelligence in computers is described in the chapter on thought, language, and intelligence.

The Humanistic Approach

Mental processes play a different role in the humanistic approach to psychology (also known as the *phenomenological approach*). Psychologists who favor the **humanistic approach** see behavior as determined primarily by our capacity to choose how to think and act. They don't see these choices being guided by instincts, biological processes, or rewards and punishments but by each person's view of the world. So if you perceive the world as a friendly place, you are likely to be optimistic and secure. If you perceive

cognitive approach   A view that emphasizes research on how the brain takes in information, creates perceptions, forms and retrieves memories, processes information, and generates integrated patterns of action.

humanistic approach   A view of behavior as controlled by the decisions that people make about their lives based on their perceptions of the world.

it as full of hostile people, you will probably be defensive and anxious or perhaps unfriendly and aggressive. Like their cognitively oriented colleagues, then, psychologists taking a humanistic approach would agree that in the movie theater incident, the decision to punch the person who cut into line stemmed from a perception that aggression was justified. However, instead of trying to find general laws governing *all* people's thoughts and actions, humanistic psychologists try to understand how each individual's unique perceptions guide *that* person's thoughts and actions. In fact, many who prefer the humanistic approach claim that because no two people are exactly alike, the only way to understand behavior and mental processes is to focus on how they operate in each individual. Humanistic psychologists also believe that people are essentially good, that they are in control of themselves, and that they seek to grow toward their fullest potential.

The humanistic approach began to attract attention in North America in the 1940s, mainly through the writings of Carl Rogers and Abraham Maslow. As you will see in later chapters, their views have had a major influence on the way some psychologists think about the development of personality, how to do psychotherapy, and the reasons people are motivated to behave as they do. In fact, some of the roots of today's growing emphasis on positive psychology can be found in the writings of Maslow and Rogers (Peterson & Seligman, 2004; Strümpfer, 2005). Overall, however, the humanistic approach to psychology is less influential today than the biological, cognitive, behavioral, and evolutionary approaches. Many psychologists find humanistic concepts and predictions too vague to be expressed and tested scientifically. (All the approaches we have described are summarized in "In Review: Approaches to Psychology.")

MARY WHITON CALKINS (1863–1930) ▲

Mary Whiton Calkins studied psychology at Harvard University, where William James described her as "brilliant." Because she was a woman, though, Harvard would not grant her a doctoral degree unless she received it through Radcliffe, which was then an affiliated school for women. She refused that arrangement but went on to do research on memory, and in 1905 she became the first woman president of the American Psychological Association (APA). Margaret Washburn (1871–1939) encountered similar sex discrimination at Columbia University, so she transferred to Cornell University and became the first woman to earn a doctorate in psychology. In 1921, she became the second woman president of the APA.

In Review

APPROACHES TO PSYCHOLOGY

APPROACH	CHARACTERISTICS
Biological	Emphasizes activity of the nervous system, especially of the brain; the action of hormones and other chemicals; and genetics
Evolutionary	Emphasizes the ways that behavior and mental processes are adaptive for survival
Psychodynamic	Emphasizes internal conflicts, mostly unconscious, which usually pit sexual or aggressive instincts against environmental obstacles to their expression
Behavioral	Emphasizes learning, especially each person's experience with rewards and punishments
Cognitive	Emphasizes mechanisms through which people receive, store, retrieve, and otherwise process information
Humanistic	Emphasizes individual potential for growth and the role of unique perceptions in guiding behavior and mental processes

1. *Teaching people to be less afraid of heights reflects the _____ approach.*
2. *Charles Darwin was not a psychologist, but his work influenced the _____ approach to psychology.*
3. *Assuming that people inherit mental disorders suggests a _____ approach.*

Courtesy of Wilberforce University, Archives and Special Collections

GILBERT HAVEN JONES ▲
(1883–1966)
When Gilbert Haven Jones graduated from the University of Jena in Germany in 1909, he became one of the first African Americans to earn a doctorate in psychology. Many others were to follow, including J. Henry Alston, who was the first African American to publish research in a major U.S. psychology journal (Alston, 1920).

sociocultural factors   Social identity and other background factors, such as gender, ethnicity, social class, and culture.

culture   The accumulation of values, rules of behavior, forms of expression, religious beliefs, and occupational choices for a group of people who share a common language and environment.

Human Diversity and Psychology

▷ *How does your cultural background influence your behavior?*

Today, the diversity seen in psychologists' approaches to their work is matched by the diversity in their own backgrounds. This was not always the case. In the early twentieth century, most psychologists—like most members of other academic disciplines—were white, middle-class men (Walker, 1991). Even so, women and people of color played a part in psychology almost from the beginning (Schultz & Schultz, 2002). Throughout this book you will find the work of their modern counterparts, whose contributions to research, service, and teaching have all increased in tandem with their growing representation in psychology. In the United States, women now constitute about half of all psychologists holding doctoral degrees (National Science Foundation, 2004a). Women are also earning 72 percent of the new doctoral degrees awarded in psychology each year (Wicherski & Kohout, 2007). Moreover, 20 percent of new doctoral degrees in psychology are being earned by members of ethnic minority groups (Wicherski & Kohout, 2007). These numbers reflect continuing efforts by psychological organizations and governmental bodies, especially in the United States and Canada, to promote the recruitment, graduation, and employment of women and ethnic minorities in psychology (Maton et al., 2006).

The Impact of Sociocultural Diversity on Psychology

As diversity among psychologists has increased, so too has their interest in the diversity of the people they study and serve. This change is significant, because psychologists once assumed that all humans were essentially alike and that whatever principles emerged from research with one group would apply to people everywhere. They were partly right, because people around the world *are* alike in many ways. They tend to live in groups; have religious beliefs; and create rules, music, dances, and games. The principles of nerve cell activity or reactions to heat or a sour taste are the same in men and women everywhere, as is their recognition of a smile. This is not true of all characteristics, however. Research has shown that people's striving for achievement, their moral values, their styles of communicating, and many other aspects of behavior and mental processes are shaped by a variety of **sociocultural factors,** including gender, ethnicity, social class, and the culture in which they grow up (Miyamoto, Nisbett, & Masuda, 2006; Shiraev & Levy, 2004).

Culture has been defined as the sum total of the values, rules of behavior, forms of expression, religious beliefs, occupational choices, and the like among a group of people who share a common language and environment (Fiske et al., 1998). Culture is an organizing and stabilizing influence. It encourages or discourages particular behaviors and ways of thinking; it also allows people to understand others in that culture and know what to expect from them. It is a kind of group adaptation that is passed on by tradition and example (rather than by genes) from one generation to the next (Castro & Toro, 2004). Culture determines, for example, whether children's education will focus on skill in hunting or in reading, how close people stand when they talk to each other, and whether or not they form lines in public places.

Cultures can differ in many ways (Cohen, 2009). They may have strict or loose rules governing social behavior. They might place great value on achievement or on self-awareness. Some seek dominance over nature; others seek harmony with it. Time is of great importance in some cultures but not in others. Psychologists have tended to focus on the differences between cultures that can be described as individualist or collectivist (Triandis & Trafimow, 2001; see Table 1.3). In *individualist* cultures, such as those typical of North America and Western Europe, people tend to focus on and value personal rather than group goals and achievement. Competitiveness to distinguish oneself from others is common, but so is a sense of isolation. By contrast, in *collectivist* cultures, such as those found in Japan and other parts of Asia, people tend to think of themselves as part of family or work groups. Cooperative effort aimed at advancing the

TABLE 1.3 ■ SOME CHARACTERISTICS OF BEHAVIOR AND MENTAL PROCESSES TYPICAL OF INDIVIDUALIST VERSUS COLLECTIVIST CULTURES

Psychologists and anthropologists have noticed that cultures can create certain general tendencies in behavior and mental processes among the people living in them (Bhagat et al., 2002; Cohen, 2009). As shown here, individualist cultures tend to support the idea of placing one's personal goals before the goals of the extended family or work group, whereas collectivist cultures tend to encourage putting the goals of those groups ahead of personal goals. Remember, though, that these labels represent very rough categories. Cultures cannot be pigeonholed as being either entirely individualist or entirely collectivist, and not everyone raised in a particular culture always thinks or acts in exactly the same way.

Variable	Individualist	Collectivist
Personal identity	Separate from others	Connected to others
Major goals	Self-defined; be unique; realize your personal potential; compete with others	Defined by others; belong; occupy your proper place; meet your obligations to others; be like others
Criteria for self-esteem	Ability to express unique aspects of the self; ability to be self-assured	Ability to restrain the self and be part of a social unit; ability to be self-effacing
Sources of success and failure	Success comes from personal effort; failure, from external factors	Success is due to help from others; failure is due to personal faults
Major frame of reference	Personal attitudes, traits, and goals	Family, work group

welfare of those groups is highly valued. And although loneliness is rarely a problem, fear of rejection by the group is common. Many aspects of mainstream U.S. culture—from self-reliant movie heroes and bonuses for "top" employees to the invitation to "help yourself" at a buffet table—reflect its tendency toward an individualist orientation (see Table 1.4 on page 20).

We often associate cultures with particular countries, but in reality, most countries are *multicultural.* In other words, they host many cultural groups within their borders. For instance, the United States encompasses African Americans, Hispanic Americans, Asian Americans, and American Indians as well as European Americans whose families came from Italy, Germany, Britain, Greece, Poland, Sweden, Ireland, and many other places. In each of these groups, the individuals who identify with their cultural heritage tend to share behaviors, values, and beliefs based on their culture of origin. In other words, they form a *subculture.*

THE IMPACT OF CULTURE

Culture helps shape virtually every aspect of our behavior and mental processes, from how we dress to how we think to what we think is important. Because most people grow up immersed in a particular culture, they may not notice its influence on their thoughts and actions until—like these young women who emigrated from Africa to Denmark—they encounter people whose culture has shaped them in different ways (Luna, Ringberg, & Peracchio, 2008; Markus, 2008; Masuda et al., 2008; Nisbett & Masuda, 2007; Varnum et al., 2008).

© Francis Dean/The Image Works

TABLE 1.4   ■   CULTURAL VALUES AS SEEN IN ADVERTISING

The statements listed here appeared in advertisements in Korea and the United States. Those from Korea reflect collectivist values, whereas those from the United States emphasize a more individualist orientation (Han & Shavitt, 1994). See if you can tell which are which; then check the bottom of the next page for the answers. You might want to follow up on this exercise by identifying the cultural values appearing in the ads you see in newspapers and magazines and on billboards and television. By surfing the Internet or scanning international newspapers, you can compare the values conveyed by ads in your culture with those in ads from other cultures.

1.	"She's got a style all her own."
2.	"You, only better."
3.	"A more exhilarating way to provide for your family."
4.	"We have a way of bringing people closer together."
5.	"Celebrating a half-century of partnership."
6.	"How to protect the most personal part of the environment: Your skin."
7.	"Our family agrees with this selection of home furnishings."
8.	"A leader among leaders."
9.	"Make your way through the crowd."
10.	"Your business success: Harmonizing with (company name)."

Source: Brehm, Kassin, & Fein (1999).

Most of us don't realize how strongly our culture or subculture has shaped our thoughts and actions until we come in contact with people whose culture or subculture has shaped them differently. Consider hand gestures, for example. The "thumbs-up" sign means that "everything is OK" to people in North America and Europe, but it is considered a rude gesture in Australia, Nigeria, and Bangladesh. And though making eye contact during social introductions is usually seen as a sign of interest or sincerity in North America, it is likely to be considered rude in Japan (Axtell, 1998). Even some of the misunderstandings between people in the same culture can be traced to slight, culturally influenced differences in communication (Tannen, 2001). In the United States, for instance, women's efforts to connect with others by talking may be perceived by many men as "pointless" unless the discussion is geared to solving a particular problem. As a result, women often feel frustrated and misunderstood by men, who tend to offer well-meant but unwanted advice instead of conversation.

For decades, the impact of culture on behavior and mental processes was of concern mainly to a relatively small group of researchers working in *cross-cultural* psychology (Miller, 2002). As you will see in the chapters to come, however, psychologists in almost every subfield are now looking at how ethnicity, gender, age, and many other sociocultural factors can influence the behavior and mental processes of the people they serve and the people they study. In other words, psychology is striving to be the science of *all* behavior and mental processes, not just of those in the cultures in which it began.

Thinking Critically About Psychology (or Anything Else)

▶ *How can critical thinking save you money?*

In order to appreciate the effects of sociocultural factors on behavior and mental processes, psychologists had to think about their field in new ways. For one thing, they had to question the assumption that studying people of just one gender, age range, ethnic group, or culture can tell us about people in general. This kind of thinking can lead to new insights but it takes effort, and it sometimes upsets those who hold more traditional views. No wonder, then, that some people prefer to simply accept what they

TABLE 1.5 ■ SOME POPULAR MYTHS

Ask some friends and relatives what they think about the statements listed in the left-hand column of this table. Most people will probably agree with at least one of them, even though all of them are false. Perhaps you already knew that, but don't feel too smug. At one time or another, we all accept something we are told simply because the information seems to come from a reliable source or because "everyone knows" it is true.

Myth	Fact
Many children are injured each year in the United States when razor blades, needles, or poison are put in Halloween candy.	Reported cases are rare, most turn out to be hoaxes, and in the only documented case of a child dying from poisoned candy, the culprit was the child's own parent (Brunvald, 1989).
If your roommate commits suicide during the school term, you automatically get A's in all your classes for that term.	No college or university anywhere has ever had such a rule.
People have been known to burst into flames and die from fire erupting within their own bodies.	In rare cases, humans have been consumed by fires that caused little or no damage to the surrounding area. However, this phenomenon has not been duplicated in a laboratory, and each alleged case of "spontaneous human combustion" has been traced to an external source of ignition (Benecke, 1999; Nienhuys, 2001).
Most big-city police departments rely on the advice of psychics to help them solve murders, kidnappings, and missing persons cases.	Only about 35% of urban police departments ever seek psychics' advice, and that advice is virtually never more helpful than other means of investigation (Nickell, 1997; Wiseman, West, & Stemman, 1996).
Murders, suicides, animal bites, and episodes of mental disorder are more likely to occur when the moon is full.	Records of crimes, dog bites, and admissions to mental hospital do not support this common belief (Bickis, Kelly, & Byrnes, 1995; Chapman & Morrell, 2000; Rotton & Kelly, 1985).
You can't fool a lie detector.	Lie detectors can be helpful in solving crimes, but they are not perfect; their results can free a guilty person or send an innocent person to jail (see the chapter on motivation and emotion).
Viewers never see David Letterman walking to his desk after the opening monologue because his contract prohibits him from showing his backside on TV.	When questioned about this story on the air, Letterman denied it and, to prove his point, lifted his jacket and turned a full circle in front of the cameras and studio audience (Brunvald, 1989).
Psychics have special abilities to see into the future.	Even the most famous psychics are almost always wrong, as in these predictions for the year 2008: "a major supervolcano is poised to erupt, sending ash all over the earth"; "the era of global famine foreseen by Nostradamus will begin in 2008"; "terrorist attack on the Beijing Olympics"; "a terror attack right before the 2008 election which is the deciding factor in Rudi Giuliani becoming president"; "the 2007 WD5 asteroid will hit Mars, and the remains of an ancient civilization will be revealed"; and "the Earth will move slightly off its axis causing some havoc." No psychic's predictions for 2001 included the September 11 terrorist attacks on New York and Washington. When psychics do appear to be correct, it is usually because their forecasts are either vague ("US weather will be more severe than usual in the northeast and southwest") or easy to predict without special powers ("scandals will continue to plague the Bush White House") (Radford, 2008a, 2008b; 2008c; Sombrero, 2008).

are told, especially when it comes from a believable source (see Table 1.5). Some advertisers, politicians, and social activists hope for this kind of easy acceptance when they go after your money, your vote, or your loyalty. They want you to believe their promises or claims without careful thought on your part. In other words, they don't want you to think critically.

ANSWER KEY FOR TABLE 1.4: U.S. ads are numbers 1, 2, 6, 8, and 9.

Critical thinking is the process of assessing claims and making judgments on the basis of well-supported evidence (Wade, 1988). Let's consider some of the questions that arise from thinking critically about psychology (or anything else) and then review the scientific research methods that psychologists use to try to answer those questions.

Five Questions for Critical Thinking

Francine Shapiro, a clinical psychologist in northern California, had an odd experience while taking a walk one day in 1987. She had been thinking about some distressing events when she noticed that her emotional reaction to them was fading away. She realized that she had been moving her eyes from side to side, but had these eye movements caused the emotion-reducing effect? Perhaps, because when she made these same eye movements more deliberately, the effect was even stronger. Was this a fluke, or would the same thing happen to others? To find out, she tested the eye-movement effect in friends and colleagues and then with clients who had suffered childhood sexual abuse, military combat, rape, or other traumas. She asked the clients to recall these traumas while keeping their eyes focused on her finger as she moved it back and forth in front of their faces. They said that their emotional reactions to the memories, like Shapiro's, faded. They also reported that trauma-related problems such as nightmares, fears, and emotional flashbacks decreased dramatically, often after only one session (Shapiro, 1989a). These successful case studies led Shapiro to develop a new treatment called *eye movement desensitization and reprocessing,* or *EMDR* (Shapiro, 1991; Shapiro & Forrest, 2004). Today, Shapiro and 30,000 other therapists in 52 countries are using EMDR to treat an ever-widening range of anxiety-related problems in children and adults, including phobias and posttraumatic and other stress disorders, eating disorders, alcoholism, migraine headaches, marital conflicts and skin rashes (Beaulieu, 2003; Bloomgarden & Calogero, 2008; Cvetek, 2008; Edmond & Rubin, 2004; Gauvreau & Bouchard, 2008; Hase, Schallmayer, & Sack, 2008; Konuk et al., 2006; Lawson, 2004; Manfield & Shapiro, 2004; Marcus, 2008; Maxwell, 2003; Omaha, 2004; Russell, 2006; Russell et al., 2007; Silver et al., 2005; van der Kolk et al., 2007).

Would the phenomenal growth of EMDR be enough to convince you to spend your own money on it? If not, what would you want to know about EMDR before deciding? As a cautious person, you would probably ask some of the same questions that have occurred to many scientists in psychology: Are the effects of EMDR caused by the treatment itself or by the faith that clients might have in any new and impressive treatment? And are EMDR's effects faster, stronger, and longer lasting than those of other treatments?

Questioning what we are told is an important part of a more general critical thinking process that can help us make informed decisions, not only about psychotherapy options but also about many other things—such as which pain reliever or Internet service to choose, which college to attend, what apartment to rent, which candidate to vote for, and whether we believe that cell phones can cause cancer or that shark cartilage can cure it. One way of applying critical thinking to EMDR or any other topic is to ask the following five questions:

- What am I being asked to believe or accept?

In this case, you are asked to believe that EMDR reduces or eliminates anxiety-related problems.

- Is evidence available to support the claim?

Shapiro began her EMDR research on herself. When she found the same effects in others, coincidence became an unlikely explanation for the observed changes.

- Can that evidence be interpreted another way?

The dramatic effects that Shapiro's friends and clients experienced might have been due to their motivation to change or to their desire to please her, not to EMDR. And who

critical thinking The process of assessing claims and making judgments on the basis of well-supported evidence.

► Uncritically accepting claims for the value of astrologers' predictions, "get-rich-quick" investments, unproven therapies, or proposed government policies can be embarrassing, expensive, and sometimes dangerous. Critical thinkers carefully evaluate evidence for *and against* such claims before reaching a conclusion about them.

Doonesbury © 1993 G. B. Trudeau. Reprinted with permission of Universal Press Syndicate. All rights reserved.

knows? They might have eventually improved on their own without any treatment. In other words, even the most remarkable evidence cannot be accepted as confirming an assertion until all reasonable alternative explanations have been ruled out. Doing that leads to the next step in critical thinking: conducting scientific research.

• What evidence would help to evaluate the alternatives?

The ideal method for testing the value of EMDR would be to identify three groups of people who are identical in every way except for the anxiety treatment they receive. One group receives EMDR. The second group gets an equally motivating but useless treatment. The third group gets no treatment at all. If the EMDR group improves much more than the other two, then it is less likely that the changes following EMDR can be explained entirely by client motivation or the mere passage of time.

• What conclusions are most reasonable?

The evidence available so far has not yet ruled out alternative explanations for the effects of EMDR (e.g., Hertlein & Ricci, 2004). And although those effects are often greater than the effects of no treatment at all, they appear to be no stronger than those of several other kinds of treatment (Bisson, 2007; Cvetek, 2008; Hughes, 2006; Ironson et al., 2002; Lilienfeld & Arkowitz, 2008; Taylor, 2004; Taylor et al., 2003; Wanders, Serra, & de Jongh, 2008). Accordingly, the only reasonable conclusions to be drawn at this point are that (1) EMDR remains a controversial treatment, (2) it seems to have an impact on some clients, and (3) further research is needed in order to understand it.

Does that sound wishy-washy? Critical thinking sometimes does seem to be indecisive thinking, but the reason for that is that scientific conclusions must be guided by the evidence available. In the long run, though, critical thinking also opens the way to understanding. (To help you sharpen your critical thinking skills, we have included in every chapter to come a feature in which our five critical thinking questions are applied to a particularly interesting topic in psychology.) Let's now consider how psychologists translate critical thinking into scientific research.

Critical Thinking and Scientific Research

Scientific research often begins with questions based on curiosity, such as whether eye movements can reduce anxiety. Like many seemingly simple questions, this one is more complex than it first appears. Are we talking about horizontal, vertical, or diagonal eye movements? How long do they continue? How many treatment sessions should there be? Are we referring to mild or severe anxiety, and how will we measure improvement? In other words, scientists must ask specific questions in order to get meaningful answers.

Psychologists and other scientists clarify their questions about behavior and mental processes by phrasing them in terms of a **hypothesis**—a specific, testable statement or proposition about something they want to study. In the case of EMDR, the hypothesis might be as follows: EMDR treatment causes a significant reduction in anxiety.

hypothesis   In scientific research, a specific, testable proposition about a phenomenon.

TAKING YOUR LIFE IN YOUR HANDS? ▶

Does exposure to microwave radiation from cell phone antennas cause brain tumors? Do the dangers of hormone replacement therapy (HRT) outweigh its benefits for postmenopausal women? What about the value of herbal remedies, dietary supplements, and other "alternative" treatments for cancer, AIDS, and depression (Specter, 2004)? These questions generate intense speculation, strong opinions, and a lot of wishful thinking, but the answers ultimately depend on scientific research based on critical thinking. Even though there is no conclusive evidence that cell phones cause tumors (Christensen et al., 2005; Hepworth et al., 2006; Schoemaker et al., 2005), some scientists suggest there may be danger in long-term exposure (Hardell et al., 2007; Lonn et al., 2004; Manti et al., 2008; Sadetzki et al., 2008; Vijayalaxmi, 2008), and research continues. Evidence that HRT may be related to breast cancer and heart disease led to the cancellation of a large clinical trial in the United States (Kolata, 2003), and scientists are calling for new research on the safety of the testosterone replacement therapy that about 250,000 U.S. men receive each year (Groopman, 2002; Kolata, 2002).

operational definitions   Statements that define phenomena or variables by describing the exact research operations or methods used in measuring or manipulating them.

variables   Specific factors or characteristics that can take on different numerical values in research.

reliability   The degree to which test results or other research evidence occurs repeatedly.

validity   The degree to which evidence from a test or other research method measures what it is supposed to measure.

theory   An integrated set of propositions used to explain certain phenomena, including behavior and mental processes.

To make it easier to understand and objectively evaluate their hypotheses, scientists employ **operational definitions,** which are statements describing the exact operations or methods they will use in their research. In the hypothesis we just proposed, "EMDR treatment" might be operationally defined as a certain number of back-and-forth eye movements per second for a particular period of time. "Significant reduction in anxiety" might be operationally defined as a drop of at least ten points on a test that measures anxiety. The kind of treatment a client is given (say, EMDR versus no treatment) and the results of that treatment (how much anxiety reduction occurred) are examples of research **variables,** the specific factors or characteristics that are altered and measured in research.

In addition to collecting evidence, scientists must also check on how good it is. Usually, the quality of evidence is evaluated in terms of two characteristics: reliability and validity. **Reliability** is the consistency of the evidence that is obtained. **Validity** is the degree to which the evidence accurately represents the topic being studied. For example, if Shapiro had not been able to repeat (or *replicate*) the eye movement effects with others or if only a few clients had shown improvement, she would question the reliability of her evidence. If the clients' reports of improvement were not supported by, say, changes in their overt behavior or confirming statements by close relatives, she would doubt their validity.

The Role of Theories   After examining research evidence, scientists may begin to favor certain explanations as to why these results occurred. Sometimes they organize their explanations into a **theory,** which is a set of statements designed to explain certain phenomena. Shapiro's theory about EMDR suggests that eye movements activate parts of the brain in which information about trauma or other unpleasant experiences has been stored but never fully processed. EMDR, she says, promotes the "adaptive information processing" required for the elimination of anxiety-related emotional and behavioral problems (Shapiro & Forrest, 2004). Others (e.g. Lee, Taylor, & Drummond, 2006) suggest that EMDR may help troubled people think about stressful material in a more detached, less emotional way, perhaps as in a dream (Elofsson, von Schèele, Theorell, & Söndergaard, 2008). Because they are tentative explanations, theories must be subjected to scientific evaluation based on critical thinking about the evidence for and against them. For example, Shapiro's theory about EMDR has been criticized as vague, not well supported by evidence, and less plausible than other, simpler explanations (e.g., Carpenter, 2004; Gaudiano & Dalrymple, 2005; Herbert et al., 2000; Lohr et al.,

© Eric Bean/Getty Images

LITTLE REMINDERS ▲

If you asked this person what he needs to use various computer programs efficiently, he might not think to mention the notes on his monitor that list all his log-in names and passwords. Accordingly, researchers in human factors and in industrial and organizational psychology usually arrange to watch employees at work rather than just asking them what they do, how they do it, and how they interact with machines and fellow employees (Barriera-Viruet, Sobeih, Daraiseh, & Salem, 2006; Dempsey, McGorry, & Maynard, 2005).

observational methods Procedures for systematically watching behavior in order to summarize it for scientific analysis.

naturalistic observation The process of watching without interfering as a phenomenon occurs in the natural environment.

2003). Although a psychologist's theory may be based on research results, it usually also generates predictions that stimulate additional research. These predictions will be tested by many other psychologists and the theory will be revised or even abandoned if research does not support it.

The process of creating, evaluating, and revising psychological theories does not always lead to a single "winner." You will see in later chapters that there are several possible explanations for color vision, mental disorder, prejudice, and many other aspects of behavior and mental processes. As a result, we can't offer as many final conclusions about psychology as you might want. The conclusions we do offer are always based on what is known so far, and we always cite the need for additional research. We do that because research often raises at least as many questions as it answers. For example, a certain treatment might work well for mild depression in women, but would it work as well for men or for cases of severe depression? Answering those questions would require more research.

Keep this point in mind the next time you hear a talk-show guest giving simple solutions for complex problems such as obesity or anxiety or promoting easy formulas for a happy marriage and well-behaved children. These self-proclaimed experts—called "pop" (for *popular*) psychologists by the scientific community—tend to oversimplify issues, cite evidence for their views without concern for its reliability or validity, and ignore good evidence that contradicts their pet theories.

Psychological scientists must be more cautious, often delaying final judgments about behavior and mental processes until they have collected better evidence. In evaluating theories and deciding among conclusions, they are guided not only by the research methods described in the next section, but by the *law of parsimony* (also known as *simplicity*), sometimes referred to by nonscientists as KISS (Keep It Simple, Stupid). The principle of parsimony is based on experience in the long history of science. It suggests that when several alternative conclusions or several competing theories offer nearly equally convincing explanations of something, the correct explanation tends to be the simplest. Throughout this book you will see examples of how the parsimony principle has helped psychological scientists sift and refine explanatory theories in search of the ones that offer the simplest yet fullest understanding of behavior and mental processes.

You will also see that research in psychological science has created an enormous body of knowledge that is being put to good use in many ways. That knowledge forms the foundation for future research that will no doubt lead to even deeper understanding. Let's look now at the scientific methods that psychologists use in their research and at some of the pitfalls that lie in their path.

Research Methods in Psychology

▶ *How do psychologists learn about people?*

Like other scientists, psychologists try to achieve four main goals in their research: to *describe* a phenomenon, to *make predictions* about it, and to introduce enough *control* in their research to allow them to *explain* the phenomenon with some degree of confidence. Five research methods have proven especially useful for gathering the evidence needed to reach each of these goals. They include *observational methods, case studies, surveys, correlational studies,* and *experiments.*

Observational Methods: Watching Behavior

Sometimes, the best way to describe behavior is through **observational methods,** such as **naturalistic observation,** the process of watching without interfering as behavior occurs in the natural environment (Hoyle, Harris, & Judd, 2002). This method is especially valuable when more noticeable methods might alter the behavior you want to study. For example, if you ask people to keep track of how often they exercise, they

TRANSLATING OBSERVATIONS INTO EVIDENCE ▶

Observing people in natural settings can provide important clues to understanding social interaction and other aspects of behavior and mental processes (Floyd et al., 2008; Wakschlag et al., 2008). It is harder than it looks. Imagine you are studying these children at play, and make a list of the exact behaviors you would count as "aggressive," "shy," "fearful," "cooperative," and "competitive."

Learn BY Doing

might begin to exercise more than usual, and their records would give a false impression of their typical behavior. Much of what we know about, say, gender differences in how children play and communicate with one another has come from psychologists' observations in classrooms and playgrounds. Observations of adults, too, have provided valuable insights into friendships, couple communication patterns, and even responses to terrorism (e.g., Mehl & Pennebaker, 2003a, 2003b).

Observational methods can provide a lot of good information, but they are not without problems. For one thing, people tend to act differently when they know they are being observed (and research ethics usually require that they do know). To combat this problem, researchers typically observe people long enough for them to get used to the situation and begin behaving more naturally. Still, observations can be incomplete or misleading if the observers are not well trained or if they report what they expect to see rather than what actually occurs. Further, even the best observational methods do not allow researchers to draw conclusions about what is causing the behavior being observed.

Case Studies: Taking a Closer Look

Observations are often an important part of **case studies,** which are intensive examinations of behavior or mental processes in a particular individual, group, or situation. Case studies can also include tests, interviews, and the analysis of letters, school transcripts, or other written records. Case studies are especially useful when studying something that is new, complex, or relatively rare (Sacks, 2002). Francine Shapiro's EMDR treatment, for example, first attracted psychologists' attention through case studies of its remarkable effects on her clients (Shapiro, 1989b).

Case studies have played a special role in neuropsychology, which focuses on the relationships among brain activity, thinking, and behavior. Consider the case of Dr. P., a patient described by neurologist Oliver Sacks (1985). Dr. P. was a distinguished musician who began to show odd symptoms. He could not recognize familiar people or distinguish between people and things. For instance, while he and his wife were at the neurologist's office, Dr. P. mistook his foot for his shoe. When he rose to leave, he

case studies   Research involving the intensive examination of some phenomenon in a particular individual, group, or situation.

LEARNING FROM RARE CASES ▶

Dustin Hoffman's character in the movie *Rain Man* was based on the case of "Joseph," an autistic man who can, for example, mentally multiply or divide six-digit numbers. Other case studies have described autistic savants who can correctly identify the day of the week for any date in the past or the future or tell at a glance that, say, exactly 125 paper clips are scattered on the floor. By carefully studying such rare cases, cognitive psychologists are learning more about human mental capacities and how they might be maximized in everyone (Biever, 2009; Geddes, 2008).

tried to lift off his wife's head as if it were a hat and put it on his own head. He could not name common objects, but he could describe them. When handed a glove, for example, he said, "A continuous surface, infolded on itself. It appears to have . . . five outpouchings, if this is the word . . . a container of some sort." Only later, when he put it on his hand, did he exclaim, "My God, it's a glove!" (Sacks, 1985, p. 13). Using case studies such as this one, pioneers in neuropsychology have noted the symptoms suffered by people with particular kinds of brain damage or disease (Banich, 2004). Eventually, neuropsychologists were able to tie specific disorders to certain types of injuries, poisons, and other causes. In Dr. P.'s case, it was probably a large brain tumor that caused his symptoms.

Case studies do have limitations. They may not represent people in general, and they may contain only the evidence a particular researcher considered important (Loftus & Guyer, 2002). Nonetheless, when conducted and used with care, case studies can provide valuable raw material for further research and can serve as the testing ground for new treatments, training programs, and other applications of research.

Surveys: Looking at the Big Picture

In contrast to the individual close-ups provided by case studies, surveys offer wide-angle views of large groups. In **surveys,** researchers use interviews or questionnaires to ask people about their behavior, attitudes, beliefs, opinions, or intentions. Just as politicians and advertisers rely on opinion polls to test the popularity of policies or products, psychologists use surveys to gather descriptive data on just about any behavior or mental process, from parenting practices to sexual behavior. However, the validity of survey data depends partly on the way the survey questions are asked (Bhopal et al., 2004). In one survey study at a health clinic, patients were asked how frequently they experienced headaches, stomachaches, and other symptoms of illness (Schwarz & Scheuring, 1992). If the wording of the question suggested that most people frequently experience such symptoms, the patients said that they frequently experienced them too. But if the wording suggested that people rarely experience these symptoms, the patients said that they experienced the symptoms infrequently. A survey's validity also depends on who is surveyed. If the people surveyed do not represent the views of the population you are interested in, the survey results can be misleading (Gosling et al., 2004; Kraut et al., 2004). For example, if you were interested in Americans' views on

surveys Research that involves giving people questionnaires or interviews designed to describe their attitudes, beliefs, opinions, and intentions.

▶ **A Severely Flawed Survey** Using survey methods like this, you could probably get whatever results you want! Psychologists work hard to write questions and use methods that maximize the validity of their surveys' results.

© Scott Adams/Distributed by United Feature Syndicate, Inc.

how common ethnic prejudice is, you would come to the wrong conclusion if you surveyed only African Americans or only European Americans. To get a complete picture, you would have to survey people from all ethnic groups so that each group's opinions could be fairly represented.

Other limitations of the survey method are more difficult to avoid. For example, a poll conducted for the American Society for Microbiology (ASM) found that 92 percent of the U.S. adults surveyed said that they always wash their hands after using public toilet facilities. However, naturalistic observations of thousands of people in public restrooms across the United States revealed that the figure is closer to 77 percent (Harris Interactive, 2007). In other words, people may be unwilling to admit undesirable or embarrassing things about themselves or they may say what they believe they *should* say about an issue. And sometimes those who respond to a survey hold views that differ from those who do not respond (Visser, Krosnick, & Lavrakas, 2000). These factors all have the potential to distort survey results and the conclusions drawn from them (Hoyle, Harris, & Judd, 2002). Still, surveys provide an efficient way to gather large amounts of data about people's attitudes, beliefs, or other characteristics.

Correlational Studies: Looking for Relationships

Data collected using observational methods, case studies, and surveys provide valuable descriptions of behavior and mental processes, but they can do more than that. The data can also be examined for what they reveal about the relationships between research variables. For example, fear surveys show that most people have fears, but correlational

DESIGNING SURVEY RESEARCH ▶

How do various people feel about whether gay men and lesbians should have the right to legally marry? To appreciate the difficulties of survey research, try writing a question about this issue that you think is clear enough and unbiased enough to generate a valid portrait of people's views. Then ask some friends whether or not they agree that it would be a good survey question, and why.

Learn BY **Doing**

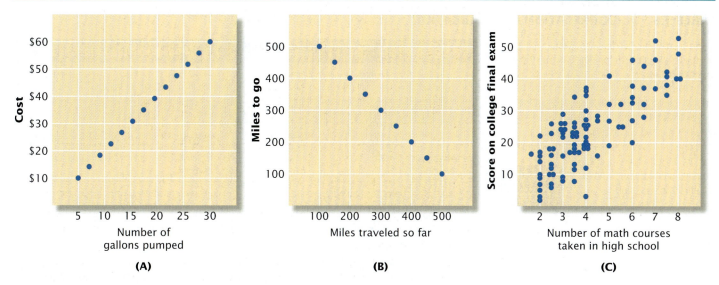

FIGURE 1.6 ■ THREE CORRELATIONS

The strength and direction of the correlation between variables can be seen in a graph called a scatterplot. Here are three examples. In Part A, we have plotted the cost of a gasoline purchase against the number of gallons pumped. The number of gallons is positively and perfectly correlated with their cost, so the scatterplot appears as a straight line and you can predict the value of either variable from a knowledge of the other. Part B shows a perfect negative correlation between the number of miles you have traveled toward a destination and the distance remaining. Again, one variable can be exactly predicted from the other. Part C illustrates a correlation of +.81 between the number of math courses students had taken in high school and their scores on a college math exam; each dot represents one student (Hays, 1981). As correlations decrease, they are represented by less and less organized scatterplots. A correlation of .00 would appear as a shapeless cloud.

correlational studies Research methods that examine relationships between variables in order to analyze trends, test predictions, evaluate theories, and suggest new hypotheses.

correlation The degree to which one variable is related to another.

analysis of those surveys also shows that fear is related to age. Specifically, as people get older, they tend to have fewer fears (e.g., Kleinknecht, 1991). **Correlational studies** examine relationships between variables in order to describe research data more fully, test predictions, evaluate theories, and suggest new hypotheses about why people think and act as they do.

Correlation refers to both the strength and the direction of the relationship between two variables. A *positive correlation* means that the two variables increase together or decrease together. A *negative correlation* means that the variables move in opposite directions. For example, James Schaefer observed 4,500 customers in 65 bars and found that the tempo of the jukebox music was negatively correlated with the rate at which the customers drank alcohol. The slower the tempo, the faster the drinking (Schaefer et al., 1988). Does this mean that Schaefer could have worn a blindfold and predicted exactly how fast people were drinking by timing the music? Could he have plugged his ears and determined the musical tempo just by watching people's sip rates? No and no, because the accuracy of predictions made about one variable from knowing the other depends on the *strength* of the correlation. Only a perfect correlation between two variables would allow you to predict the exact value of one from knowledge of the other. The weaker the correlation, the less one variable can tell you about the other.

Psychologists describe the strength and direction of correlations with a number called a *correlation coefficient,* which can range from a high of 1.00 to a low of .00 (see the "Statistics in Psychological Research" appendix). If the correlation between two variables is *positive*—if they both move in the same direction—the correlation coefficient will have a plus sign in front of it. If there is a minus sign, the correlation is *negative,* and the two variables will move in opposite directions. The larger the correlation coefficient, the stronger the relationship between the two variables. The strongest possible relationship is indicated by either +1.00 or −1.00 (see Figure 1.6 on page 30). A correlation of .00 indicates that there is virtually no relationship between variables.

Correlation coefficients can help to describe the results of correlational research and evaluate hypotheses, but psychological scientists must be extremely careful when interpreting what correlations mean. The mere fact that two variables are correlated does not guarantee that one is causing an effect on the other. And even if one variable actually does cause an effect on the other, a correlation coefficient can't tell us which variable is influencing which, or why (see Table 1.6). Consider the question of how aggression develops. Correlational studies of observational data indicate that children who are in day care for more than thirty hours a week are more aggressive than those who stay at home with a parent. Does separation from parents actually cause the heightened aggressiveness with which it is associated? It might, but psychologists must

TABLE 1.6 ■ CORRELATION AND CAUSATION

Look at the relationships described in the left-hand column, then ask yourself why the two variables in each case are correlated. Could one variable be causing an effect on the other? If so, which variable is the cause, and how might it exert its effect? Could the relationship between the two variables be caused by a third one? If so, what might that third variable be? We suggest some possible explanations in the right-hand column. Can you think of others?

Correlation	Possible Explanations
A survey found that the more sexual content U.S. teenagers reported watching on television, the more likely they were to begin having sex themselves during the following year (Collins et al., 2004).	It might have been some teens' greater interest in sex that led them to watch more sexually oriented shows and to become sexually active.
The number of drownings in the United States rises and falls during the year along with the amount of ice cream sold each month.	This relationship probably reflects a third variable—time of year—that affects both ice cream consumption and the likelihood of swimming and boating (Brenner et al., 2001).
In places where beer prices are increased, the number of new cases of sexually transmitted diseases falls among young people living in those places.	If price increases cause less beer consumption, people might stay sober enough to remember to use condoms during sexual encounters. The relationship could also reflect coincidence, because prices do not always affect alcohol use. More research is required to understand this correlation.
A study found that the more antibiotics a woman has taken and the longer she has taken them, the greater is her risk of breast cancer (Velicer et al., 2004).	Long-term antibiotic use might have impaired the women's immune systems, but the cancer risk might also have been increased by the diseases that were being treated with antibiotic drugs, not the drugs themselves. Obviously, much more research would be required before condemning the use of antibiotics.
The U.S. stock market rises during years when a team from the National Football Conference wins the Super Bowl and falls during years when an American Conference team wins.	The so-called "Super Bowl Effect" has occurred 31 times in 38 years; striking as this might seem, coincidence seems to be the most likely explanation.

be careful about jumping to that conclusion. The most obvious explanation for the relationship found in a correlational study may not always be the correct one. Perhaps the aggressiveness seen among some children in day care has something to do with the children themselves or with what happens to them in day care, not just with separation from their parents.

One way psychologists evaluate such alternative hypotheses is to conduct further correlational studies to look for trends that support or conflict with those hypotheses. Further analysis of day-care research, for example, shows that the aggressiveness seen in preschoolers who spend a lot of time in day care is the exception, not the rule. Most children don't show any behavior problems, no matter how much time they have spent in day care. This more general trend suggests that whatever effects separation has, it may be different for different children in different settings, causing some to express aggressiveness, others to display fear, and still others to find enjoyment. As described in the chapter on human development, psychologists are exploring this possibility by examining correlations between children's personality traits, qualities of different day-care programs, and reactions to day care (Belsky et al., 2007; NICHD Early Child Care Research Network, 2006a).

Throughout this book you will see many more examples of how correlational studies help shed light on a wide range of topics in psychology (Rutter, 2007).

Experiments: Exploring Cause and Effect

Still, to make the best choice among alternative explanations and to confirm cause-and-effect relationships between research variables, psychological scientists prefer to exert some control over those variables. This kind of controlled research usually takes the form of an experiment.

TABLE 1.7 ■ INDEPENDENT AND DEPENDENT VARIABLES

Fill in the names of the independent and dependent variables in each of these experiments (the answers are listed below the table). Remember that the independent variable is manipulated by the experimenter. The dependent variable is measured to determine the effect of the independent variable. How did you do on this task?

Learn BY Doing

1. Researchers measure the reading skills of children after they have taken either a special reading class or a standard reading class.	The independent variable is _____. The dependent variable is _____.
2. The memory of college students for German vocabulary words is tested after the students have had either a normal night's sleep or a night of no sleep.	The independent variable is _____. The dependent variable is _____.
3. Experiment title: "The effect of a daily walking program on elderly people's lung capacity."	The independent variable is _____. The dependent variable is _____.
4. People's ability to avoid "accidents" in a driving simulator is tested before, while, and after they talk on a cell phone.	The independent variable is _____. The dependent variable is _____.

experiment A situation in which the researcher manipulates one variable and observes the effect of that manipulation on another variable, while holding all other variables constant.

independent variable In an experiment, the variable manipulated by the researcher.

dependent variable In an experiment, the factor affected by the independent variable.

experimental group The group that receives the experimental treatment.

control group The group that receives no treatment or provides some other baseline against which to compare the performance or response of the experimental group.

In an **experiment,** the researcher makes a change in one variable and then observes the effect of that change on another variable while holding all the other variables constant. The variable that is changed, or manipulated, by the experimenter is called the **independent variable.** The variable that is measured following this manipulation is called the **dependent variable,** because it *depends* on the independent variable (see Table 1.7). So in an experiment on the effects of TV violence, for example, the independent variable might be the amount of violence that different groups of children are allowed to watch: a lot, a little, or none at all. The **experimental group** is the group that is exposed to an experience of interest to the experimenter (a lot of violent TV, for example). A group that receives no such exposure or a differing amount of exposure is called the **control group.** Control groups provide baselines against which to compare the performance of the experimental group. If everything about the groups is exactly the same except for exposure to some experience, then any differences between groups at the end of the experiment should be due to that experience.

Focus on RESEARCH

Studying EMDR

Let's consider how Francine Shapiro used the experimental method to explore whether her EMDR treatment was actually causing the improvements she observed in her clients. (Each chapter to follow contains a Focus on Research section like this one, which presents a different example of how researchers in psychology ask and answer questions about behavior and mental processes.)

▶ What was the researcher's question?

Like other scientists, Shapiro phrased her question about the value of EMDR in the form of a hypothesis, namely that *EMDR treatment causes a significant reduction in anxiety.* Does it?

▶ How did the researcher answer the question?

To find out, Shapiro operationally defined "EMDR treatment" as making a certain number of back-and-forth eye movements per second for a particular period of time. And she operationally

defined "significant reduction in anxiety" as a certain amount of reduction in clients' self-reported discomfort.

Shapiro then identified twenty-two people who were suffering the ill effects of traumas such as rape or military combat. These were her research participants. As shown in Figure 1.7, she assigned these participants to two groups. The experimental group received one 50-minute session of EMDR. The control group focused on their unpleasant memories for eight minutes but without moving their eyes back and forth (Shapiro, 1989b). The experimenter controlled whether EMDR treatment was given to each participant, so the presence or absence of treatment was the independent variable. The participants' anxiety level was the dependent variable. In Shapiro's experiment, having a control group allowed her to measure how much change in anxiety might be expected from exposure to bad memories without EMDR treatment.

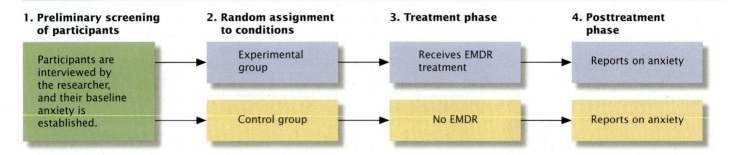

FIGURE 1.7   ■   A SIMPLE TWO-GROUP EXPERIMENT

Ideally, the only difference between the experimental and control group in experiments such as this one is whether the participants receive the treatment that the experimenter wants to evaluate. Under these ideal circumstances, at the end of the experiment any difference in the two groups' reported levels of anxiety (the dependent variable) should be attributable to whether or not they received treatment (the independent variable).

▶ **What did the researcher find?**

The results of Shapiro's experiment showed that participants receiving EMDR treatment experienced a complete and nearly immediate reduction in anxiety related to their traumatic memories. Those in the control group showed no such change.

▶ **What do the results mean?**

At this point, you might be ready to believe that the treatment caused the difference. Before coming to that conclusion, though, look again at the structure, or design, of the experiment. The treatment group's session lasted 50 minutes. The control group focused on their memories for only eight minutes. Would the people in the control group have improved if they, too, had spent 50 minutes focusing on their memories? We don't know, because the experiment did not compare methods of equal length.

▶ **What do we still need to know?**

Experiments have now been conducted that introduce enough control into the treatment situation to evaluate alternative explanations for the improvements seen in people treated with EMDR. Most of these studies cast doubt on whether the eye movements themselves are responsible (e.g., Davidson & Parker, 2001; Lazarus & Lazarus, 2002; Van Deusen, 2004), but we still don't know for sure what *is* producing the beneficial effects that so often

follow EMDR treatment (e.g., Cvetek, 2008). Considerable evidence suggests that EMDR may operate in much the same way as systematic desensitization therapy and other behavioral and cognitive behavioral treatments described in the chapter on treatment of psychological disorders. It may be that EMDR, like these other treatments, exposes people to unpleasant stimuli long enough for those stimuli to lose a lot of their emotional punch (Lilienfeld & Arkowitz, 2008; van der Does, 2006). As research on EMDR continues, it will be important for proponents and skeptics alike to avoid *confirmation bias,* the human tendency to look only for evidence that supports their own hypotheses. In fact, all scientists have a responsibility to combat confirmation bias by looking for evidence *for* and *against* even their most cherished hypotheses.

Shapiro's (1989b) experiment reminds us to be on the lookout for flaws in experimental design and control that might affect the conclusions we can draw from research results. In fact, we have to consider anything that could confuse, or *confound,* our interpretation of those results. Any factor that might have affected the dependent variable, along with or instead of the independent variable, may operate as a **confounding variable.** When confounding variables are present, we can't tell whether it was the independent variable or the confounding variable that produced the results. Let's consider three sources of confounding variables: random variables, participants' expectations, and experimenter bias.

Random Variables   In an ideal research world, everything about experimental and control groups would be the same except for their exposure to the independent variable (such as whether or not they received treatment). In the real world, however, there are always other differences between the groups that reflect random variables. **Random variables** are uncontrolled (and sometimes uncontrollable) factors, such as differences in the time of year when research takes place or differences in each

confounding variable   Any factor that affects the dependent variable along with, or instead of, the independent variable.

random variables   Uncontrolled or uncontrollable factors that affect the dependent variable along with, or instead of, the independent variable.

ANSWER KEY TO TABLE 1.7: The independent variable (IDV) in experiment 1 is the type of reading class; the dependent variable (DV) is reading skill. In experiment 2, the IDV is the quality of sleep; the DV is the score on a memory test. In experiment 3, the IDV is amount of exercise; the DV is lung capacity. In experiment 4, the IDV is using or not using a cell phone; the DV is performance on a simulated driving task.

participant's cultural background, personality, health, and sensitivity to stress. There are so many ways that participants might vary from each other that it is usually impossible to form groups that are matched on all of them. Instead, experimenters simply flip a coin or use some other random process to assign each research participant to experimental or control groups. These procedures, called **random assignment,** tend to spread the effects of uncontrolled variables randomly (and probably about evenly) across groups. This minimizes the chance that they will distort the results of the experiment (Shadish, Cook, & Campbell, 2002).

Participants' Expectations: The Placebo Effect Differences in what participants think about the experimental situation can act as another confounding variable. For example, if participants expect that a treatment will help them, they may try harder to improve than those in a control group who receive no treatment or a less impressive one. Improvement created by a participant's expectations is called the *placebo effect.* Although a **placebo** (pronounced "plah-SEE-boe") contains nothing known to be helpful, it still produces benefits because a person believes it will do so (Stewart-Williams & Podd, 2004; Wager et al., 2004).

How can researchers estimate the strength of placebo effects in an experiment? The most common strategy is to include in the experimental design a special control group that receives *only* a placebo. The researchers then compare results for the experimental group, the placebo group, and a group of participants receiving no treatment. In one stop-smoking study, for example, participants in a placebo group took sugar pills that the experimenter said would help them endure the stress of giving up cigarettes (Bernstein, 1970). These participants did as well at quitting as those in the experimental group, who had received extensive treatment. This result suggested that the experimental group's success may have been due largely to the participants' expectations, not to the treatment methods. Some early studies suggested the same conclusion about the effects of EMDR, because significant anxiety reduction was observed in clients who got a version of the treatment that did not involve eye movements or even focusing on traumatic memories (Cahill, Carrigan, & Frueh, 1999; Cusack & Spates, 1999; Rosen, 1999). More recent evidence suggests that EMDR can outperform placebo treatments, but the fact that its effects are not significantly better than those of other more established treatments has led many researchers to conclude that EMDR should not be a first-choice treatment for anxiety-related disorders (Bisson, 2007; Davidson & Parker, 2001; Goldstein et al., 2000; Lilienfeld & Arkowitz, 2008; Lohr et al., 2003; Taylor, 2004).

Experimenter Bias Another possible confounding variable is **experimenter bias,** the unintentional effect that researchers can exert on their own results. Robert Rosenthal (1966) was one of the first to demonstrate the power of experimenter bias. His participants were laboratory assistants who were asked to place rats in a maze. Rosenthal told some of the assistants that their rats were "maze-bright." He told the others that their rats were "maze-dull." In truth, both groups of rats were randomly drawn from the same population and had equal maze-learning capabilities. Still, the so-called maze-bright animals learned the maze significantly faster than the "maze-dull" ones. Why? Rosenthal concluded that the result had nothing to do with the rats and everything to do with the experimenters. He suggested that the assistants' expectations about their rats' supposedly superior (or inferior) capabilities caused them to slightly alter their training and handling techniques. These slight differences may have speeded (or slowed) the animals' learning. Similarly, when giving different kinds of anxiety treatments to different groups of people, experimenters who believe that one treatment will be the best might do a slightly better job with that treatment. When the results are in, this unintentional difference might make the favored treatment look better than the rest.

To prevent experimenter bias from confounding results, experimenters often use a **double-blind design.** In this design, the participants *and* those giving the treatments are unaware of ("blind" to) who is receiving a placebo and they do not know what results are to be expected of the various treatments. Only researchers who have no direct

EVER SINCE I STARTED WEARING THESE MAGNETS . . .
Placebo-controlled experiments are vital for establishing cause-effect relationships between treatments and outcomes with human participants. For example, many people swear that titanium bracelets and necklaces relieve the pain of sports injuries and even arthritis (Atkinson, 2006; Galdeira, 2006; Marchman, 2008; Siber, 2005). The web site of Phiten, the leading manufacturer and marketer of titanium accessories, presents many glowing testimonials and a scientific-sounding explanation of the technology behind titanium's alleged effects, but it offers no evidence from placebo-controlled experiments to support the company's claims (Boyles, 2008; Wagg, 2008).

random assignment A procedure through which random variables are evenly distributed in an experiment by placing participants in experimental and control groups on the basis of a coin flip or some other random process.

placebo A treatment that contains no active ingredient but produces an effect because the person receiving it believes it will.

experimenter bias A confounding variable that occurs when an experimenter unintentionally encourages participants to respond in a way that supports the hypothesis.

double-blind design A research design in which neither the experimenter nor the participants know who is in the experimental group and who is in the control group.

© Lee Christensen/Getty Images

SELECTING RESEARCH PARTICIPANTS ▶

Suppose that you want to study people's willingness to help each other. You have developed a way of measuring helpfulness, but now you need a sample of people to test. Take a minute to think about the steps necessary to select a truly random sample, then ask yourself how you might obtain a representative sample instead. Remember that although the names are similar, *random sampling* is not the same as *random assignment*. Random sampling helps ensure that the people studied are representative of some larger group. Random assignment is used in experiments to create equivalence among various groups.

Learn BY Doing

sampling   The process of selecting participants who are members of the population that the researcher wishes to study.

representative sample   A sample of research participants chosen from a larger population such that their age, gender, ethnicity, and other characteristics are typical of that larger population.

random sample   A group of research participants selected from a population each of whose members had an equal chance of being chosen.

biased sample   A group of research participants selected from a population each of whose members did not have an equal chance of being chosen.

contact with participants have this information, and they do not reveal it until the end of the experiment. Double-blind studies have not yet been conducted with EMDR, which is another reason for caution in drawing conclusions about this treatment.

In summary, experiments are vital tools for examining cause-and-effect relationships between independent and dependent variables, but they are also vulnerable to error. To maximize the value of their experiments, scientists try to eliminate as many confounding variables as possible. They then repeat their work to ensure consistent results and adjust their interpretation of those results to take into account the limitations or problems that remain.

Selecting Human Participants for Research

Visitors from another planet would be wildly mistaken if they tried to describe the typical earthling after meeting only Arnold Schwarzenegger, Paris Hilton, and a trained seal. Psychologists, too, can be led astray if the participants they encounter in their research are not typical of the people or animals about which they want to draw conclusions. Accordingly, one of the most vital steps in scientific research is the selection of participants, a process called **sampling.**

If they want to make accurate statements about the behavior and mental processes of any large group, psychologists must select a **representative sample** of participants whose characteristics mirror the rest of that group in terms of age, gender, ethnicity, cultural background, socioeconomic status, sexual orientation, disability, and the like. In theory, psychologists could draw representative samples—of people in general, of Canadians, of Florida college students, or of any other group—by choosing them at random from the entire population of interest. Doing this would require putting hundreds of thousands—perhaps millions—of names into a computer, running a program to randomly select participants, and then tracking them down to invite them to take part in the research. This method would result in a truly **random sample,** because every member of the population to be studied would have an equal chance of being chosen. (Any selection procedure that does not offer this equal chance is said to result in a **biased sample.**)

However, random sampling is usually too expensive and time-consuming to be practical, so psychologists may have to find their participants in populations that are more conveniently available. The populations from which these *convenience samples* are drawn depend to some extent on the size of the researcher's budget. They might include, for example, the students enrolled in a particular course, the students enrolled on

In Review

Methods of Psychological Research

METHOD	FEATURES	STRENGTHS	PITFALLS
Observational Methods (e.g., Naturalistic observation)	Observation of human or animal behavior in the environment in which it typically occurs	Provides descriptive data about behavior presumably uncontaminated by outside influences	Observer bias and participant self-consciousness can distort results.
Case studies	Intensive examination of the behavior and mental processes associated with a specific person or situation	Provide detailed descriptive analyses of new, complex, or rare phenomena	May not provide representative picture of phenomena.
Surveys	Standard sets of questions asked of a large number of participants	Gather large amounts of descriptive data relatively quickly and inexpensively	Sampling errors, poorly phrased questions, and response biases can distort results.
Correlational studies	Examine relationships between research variables	Can test predictions, evaluate theories, and suggest new hypotheses	Cannot confirm causal relationships between variables.
Experiments	Manipulation of an independent variable and measurement of its effects on a dependent variable	Can establish a cause-and-effect relationship between independent and dependent variables	Confounding variables may prevent valid conclusions.

1. The _____ method is most likely to use a double-blind design.
2. Research on a new treatment method is most likely to begin with _____.
3. Studying language by listening to people in public places is an example of _____ research.

online study center

Improve Your Grade
Tutorial: Research Methodologies

a local campus, the students who are willing to sign up for a study, or visitors to Internet web sites or chat rooms. Ideally, this selection process will yield a sample that fairly represents the population from which it was drawn. Scientific researchers are obliged to limit the conclusions they draw in light of the samples they draw (Kraut et al., 2004). Because of this obligation, psychologists often conduct additional studies to determine the extent to which their initial conclusions will apply to people who differ in important ways from their original sample (APA Office of Ethnic Minority Affairs, 2000; Case & Smith, 2000; Gray-Little & Hafdahl, 2000). For a recap of the strategies psychologists use in their research efforts, see "In Review: Methods of Psychological Research."

linkages

Is behavior influenced by our genes or by our environment? *(a link to Biology and Behavior)*

Linkages

Psychological Research and Behavioral Genetics

One of the most fascinating and difficult challenges in psychology is finding research methods that can help us understand the ways that genes and the environment—sometimes called *nature* and *nurture*—combine to influence behavior and mental processes (Moffitt, Caspi, & Rutter, 2005). Consider Mark and John, identical twins who were both adopted at birth because their parents were too poor to care for them. John grew up with a couple who made him feel secure and loved. Mark went from orphanage to foster home to hospital and, finally, back to his biological father's second wife. In other words, these genetically identical people encountered quite different environments. Yet, when they met for the first time at the age of twenty-four, they discovered similarities that went beyond physical appearance. They used the same aftershave, smoked the same brand of cigarettes, brushed with the same imported brand of toothpaste, and liked the same sports. They had joined the military within eight days of each other, and their IQ scores were nearly identical.

How did genetic influences operate in two different environments to result in such similarities? Exploring questions such as this has taken psychologists into the field of **behavioral genetics,** the study of how genes and environments work together to shape behavior and mental processes. They have already discovered that most behavioral tendencies can be influenced by many different genes but also by many environmental events and conditions, both before and after birth. Accordingly, research in behavioral genetics aims to explore the relative roles of genetic and environmental factors in creating differences among people in personality, mental ability, mental disorders, and other phenomena. It also seeks to identify specific genes that contribute to hereditary influences.

Some behavioral genetics research takes the form of experiments, mainly on the selective breeding of animals (Suomi, 2004). For example, Stephen Suomi (1999) identified monkeys whose genes predisposed them to react strongly or weakly to stress. He then mated strong reactors with other strong reactors and mated weak reactors with other weak reactors. Within a few generations, descendants of the strong-reactor pairs reacted much more strongly to stressors than did the descendants of the weak-reactor pairs. Selective-breeding studies must be interpreted with caution, though, because it is not specific behaviors that are inherited. What is inherited are differing sets of physical structures and capacities that make certain behaviors more or less likely. These behavioral tendencies are often very specific, and they can be altered by the environment (Grigorenko, 2002). For example, when Suomi (1999) placed young, highly stress-reactive monkeys with unrelated "foster mothers," he discovered that the foster mothers' own stress reactivity amplified or dampened the youngsters' genetically influenced behavioral tendencies. If stress-reactive monkeys were placed with stress-reactive foster mothers, they tended to be fearful of exploring their environments and had strong reactions to stressors. But if equally stress-reactive young monkeys had calm, supportive foster mothers, they appeared eager to explore their environments and were much less upset by stressors than their peers with stress-reactive foster mothers.

Research on behavioral genetics in humans must be interpreted with even greater care. Legal, moral, and ethical considerations obviously prohibit the selective breeding of people, so most research in human behavioral genetics depends on correlational studies, not controlled experiments. These usually take the form of family studies, twin studies, and adoption studies.

In *family studies,* researchers look at whether close relatives are more likely than distant ones to show similarities in behavior and mental processes. If increasing similarity is associated with closer family ties, the similarities might be inherited. For example, data from family studies suggest a genetic basis for schizophrenia, as Figure 1.8 shows. Remember, though, that a correlation between variables does not guarantee that one is causing the other. The appearance of similar disorders in close relatives might be due to environmental factors instead of, or in addition to, genetic ones. After all, close relatives tend to share environments as well as genes. So family studies alone cannot establish the role of genetic factors in mental disorders or other characteristics.

Twin studies explore the nature-nurture mix by comparing the similarities seen in identical twins with those of nonidentical twin pairs. Twins usually share the same environment and may also be treated very much the same by parents and others. If identical twins—whose genes are the same—are more alike on some characteristics than nonidentical twins (whose genes are no more similar than those of other siblings), those characteristics may have a significant genetic component.

Adoption studies take advantage of cases in which babies are adopted very early in life. The logic of these studies is that if adopted children's characteristics are more like

behavioral genetics   The study of how genes and environments combine to affect behavior and mental processes.

FIGURE 1.8 ■ FAMILY AND TWIN STUDIES OF SCHIZOPHRENIA

The risk of developing schizophrenia, a severe mental disorder, is highest for the siblings and children of patients with schizophrenia and lowest for those who are not genetically related to anyone with schizophrenia. Does this mean that schizophrenia is inherited? These results are consistent with that interpretation, but the question cannot be answered through family studies alone. Studies comparing identical and nonidentical twins suggest genetic influence, but even twin studies do not eliminate the role of environmental influences. Environmental factors, such as stressors that close relatives share, could also play an important role and may even contribute to genomic imprinting, as suggested by the epigenetic perspective discussed below (Crespi, 2008; Ivleva, Thaker, & Tamminga, 2008; Singh & O'Reilly, 2009; Tandon, Keshavan, & Nasrallah, 2008).

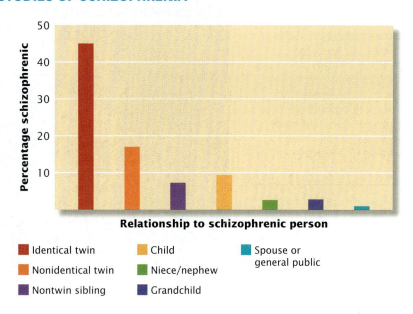

epigenetics The study of potentially inheritable changes in gene expression that are caused by environmental factors that do not alter a cell's DNA.

those of their biological parents than those of their adoptive parents, then genetics probably plays a clear role in those characteristics. In fact, the personalities of young adults who were adopted at birth do tend to be more like those of their biological parents than those of their adoptive parents. Adoption studies can be especially valuable when they focus on identical twins who, like Mark and John, were separated soon after birth. If identical twins show similar characteristics after years of living in very different environments, then the role of heredity in those characteristics is highlighted. Adoption studies of intelligence tend to support the role of genetics in variations in mental ability, but they show the impact of environmental influences, too.

Remember that family, twin, and adoption studies can tell us about the relative roles of heredity and environment in creating differences among individuals, but they cannot determine the degree to which a *particular* person's behavior or characteristics are due to heredity or environment. The two factors are too closely entwined in each of us to be separated that way. In the future, though, behavioral genetics research will be shaped by the results of the Human Genome Project, which has now unlocked the genetic code contained in the DNA that makes each human being unique (International Human Genome Sequencing Consortium, 2001; Venter et al., 2001). This achievement has allowed behavioral geneticists and other scientists to begin pinpointing some of the many genes that contribute to individual differences in disorders such as autism, learning disabilities, hyperactivity, and Alzheimer's disease, as well as to the differences in personality and mental abilities that we see all around us (Plomin et al., 2002; Saudino, Ronald, & Plomin, 2005). Finding the DNA differences responsible for certain personal attributes and behaviors will eventually make it possible to understand exactly how heredity interacts with the environment as development unfolds. Analysis of DNA—collected by rubbing a cotton swab inside an individual's cheek—may someday be used not only in behavioral genetics research but also in clinics, where it will help psychologists more precisely diagnose clients' problems and choose the most appropriate treatments (Plomin et al., 2002).

But DNA does not tell the whole story of behavioral genetics. Biological and psychological scientists have also begun to study the complex interactions between people's genetic inheritance (DNA) and the environments in which their genes operate (Champagne, 2009). This field of study, called **epigenetics**, describes the ways that events within cells can alter the *functions* of genes, even though the genetic code itself—the sequence of

TWINS AND BEHAVIORAL GENETICS ▶

Like other identical twins, each member of this pair has identical genes. Twin studies and adoption studies help reveal the interaction of genetic and environmental influences in human behavior and mental processes. Cases in which identical twins who have been separated at birth are found to have similar interests, personality traits, and mental abilities suggest that these characteristics are significantly influenced by genetic factors.

© George Shelley/Corbis

chemicals in the DNA—remains unchanged (Gräff & Mansuy, 2008; Keverne & Curley, 2008; Lickliter, 2007). The latest research suggests that the cellular environment can not only affect the expression of an individual's genetic characteristics but may also create structural changes in genes (called *imprinted genes*) that can be passed on to future generations (Keverne & Curley, 2008; Lamm & Jablonka, 2008; Lickliter, 2007). Epigenetic effects—which can be triggered by many environmental influences, including diseases and stress—have been linked to individual differences in learning, memory, and brain development (Gräff & Mansuy, 2008; Keverne & Curley, 2008; Lickliter, 2007), and they may also play a role in the appearance of cognitive disorders such as Alzheimer's disease, mental disorders such as schizophrenia and depression, illnesses such as cancer, and health problems such as obesity (Gräff & Mansuy, 2008; Keverne & Curley, 2008).

Statistical Analysis of Research Results

▶ *What does it mean when scientists announce that a research finding is "significant"?*

Observational methods, case studies, surveys, correlational studies, and experiments generate mountains of numbers—known as **data**—that represent research results and provide the basis for drawing conclusions about them (Keselman et al., 2004). These data might represent scores on intelligence tests, levels of stress hormones in blood samples, tiny differences in the time required to detect visual signals, ratings of people's personality traits, or whatever else a psychologist might be studying. Like other scientists, psychologists use descriptive and inferential *statistics* to summarize their data and interpret what they mean.

As the name implies, *descriptive statistics* are used to describe a set of data. For example, the performance of a group of students on a math test could be described statistically by the average score of the group. The difference between the performance of men and women could be described by the size of the difference between the average scores for each sex. And, as mentioned earlier, when psychologists want to describe the relationship between two variables, they use a descriptive statistic called the correlation coefficient.

data Numbers that represent research findings and provide the basis for conclusions.

Inferential statistics are mathematical procedures that help psychologists make inferences—that is, draw conclusions from their data and make assumptions about the meaning of results. Suppose, for example, that a group of trauma victims scored an average of ten points lower on an anxiety test after being treated with EMDR and that the scores of victims in a no-treatment control group dropped by an average of seven points. Does the three-point difference between these two groups reflect the impact of EMDR, or could it have been caused by random factors that made EMDR appear more powerful than it actually is? Inferential statistics allow researchers to estimate the likelihood that the difference between the average scores of the two groups reflects chance factors rather than the impact of the differing treatment they received. Other inferential statistics can help psychologists decide whether a correlation between two variables is large enough to suggest an important underlying relationship or is just a fluke.

When inferential statistics reveal that a correlation coefficient or the difference between groups is larger than what would be expected by chance alone, the results are said to be **statistically significant.** Statistical significance alone does not guarantee final "proof," but scientists do tend to pay more attention to correlations or other research findings that are statistically significant, especially when those results have been repeated, or *replicated,* in separate studies. When thinking critically about research, then, part of the process of evaluating evidence about hypotheses is to ask whether a researcher's results are statistically significant and repeatable. (For more details on descriptive and inferential statistics, see the "Statistics in Psychological Research" appendix).

Ethical Guidelines for Psychologists

▶ *Do psychologists deceive people when they do research?*

A few years ago, newspaper headlines claimed that hair dye causes cancer. Hairdressers were alarmed at first, then angry. The information given to the public was less than accurate. Rats—not humans—had been used in the research, and the animals developed cancer only after drinking the hair dye! Later research showed that using hair dye does not significantly increase people's cancer risk (Takkouche, Etminan, & Montes-Martinez, 2005).

Splashy headlines sell newspapers, but scientific psychologists have an ethical obligation not to manipulate, distort, or sensationalize their research results. The obligation to analyze and report research fairly and accurately is just one of the ethical standards that guide psychologists. Preserving the welfare and dignity of their research participants is another. So although researchers *could* measure anxiety by putting a loaded gun to people's heads or study marital conflicts by telling one partner that the other has been unfaithful, those methods could be harmful and are therefore unethical.

Whatever the research topic, psychologists' first priority is to investigate it in accordance with the highest ethical standards. They must find ways to protect their participants from harm while still gathering data that will have potential benefits for everyone. To measure anxiety, for example, a psychologist might ask people to enter a situation that is anxiety provoking but not traumatic (for example, approaching a feared animal or sitting in a dark room). And research on marital conflict usually involves observing couples as they discuss controversial issues in their relationship.

Psychologists take very seriously the obligation to minimize any immediate discomfort or risk for research participants as well as the need to protect those participants from long-term harm. They are careful to inform prospective participants about every aspect of the study that might influence their decision to participate, and they ensure that each person's involvement is voluntary. But what if the purpose of the study is to measure people's emotional reactions to being insulted? Participants might not react normally if they know ahead of time that an "insult" will be part of the experiment.

statistically significant Referring to a correlation, or a difference between two groups, that is larger than would be expected by chance.

© Michael Schwarz/The Image Works

CARING FOR RESEARCH ANIMALS ▲

Psychologists are careful to protect the welfare of animal participants in research. They do not wish to see animals suffer, and besides, undue stress on research animals can create reactions that can act as confounding variables. For example, in a study of how learning is affected by food rewards, the researcher could starve animals to make them hungry enough to want the rewards. But this would introduce discomfort, which would make it impossible to separate the effects of the reward from the effects of starvation.

When deception is necessary to create certain experimental conditions, ethical standards require the researcher to "debrief" participants as soon as the study is over by revealing all relevant information about the research and correcting any misconceptions it created.

Government regulations in the United States, Canada, and many other countries require that any research involving human participants must be approved by an Institutional Review Board (IRB) whose members have no connection with the research. If a proposed study is likely to create risks or discomfort for participants, IRB members weigh the potential benefits of the work in terms of knowledge and human welfare against any potential harm.

The obligation to protect participants' welfare also extends to animals, which are used in a small percentage of psychological research projects (American Psychological Association Committee on Animal Research and Ethics, 2006; Plous, 1996). Psychologists study animals partly because their behavior is interesting and partly because research with animals can provide information that would be impossible or unethical to collect from humans. For example, researchers can randomly assign animals to live alone and then look at how these conditions affect later social interactions. The same thing could not ethically be done with people, but animal studies offer clues about how social isolation might affect humans (see the chapter on motivation and emotion).

Contrary to the claims of some animal-rights activists, animals used in psychological research are not routinely subjected to extreme pain, starvation, or other inhumane conditions. Even in the small proportion of studies that require the use of electric shock, the discomfort created is mild, brief, and not harmful. High standards for the care and treatment of animal participants are outlined in the Animal Welfare Act, the National Institutes of Health's *Guide for the Care and Use of Laboratory Animals,* the National Institute of Mental Health's *Methods and Welfare Considerations in Behavioral Research with Animals,* the American Psychological Association's *Guidelines for Ethical Conduct in the Care and Use of Animals,* and other laws and regulations. In those relatively rare studies that require animals to undergo short-lived pain or other forms of moderate stress, legal and ethical standards require that funding agencies—as well as local committees charged with monitoring animal research—first determine that the discomfort is justified by the expected benefits to human welfare.

The responsibility for conducting research in the most humane fashion is one aspect of the *Ethical Principles of Psychologists and Code of Conduct* developed by the American Psychological Association (2002b). The main purpose of these standards is to protect and promote the welfare of society and those with whom psychologists work. For example, as teachers, psychologists should strive to give students complete, accurate, and up-to-date coverage of each topic, not a narrow and biased point of view. Further, psychologists should perform only those services and use only those techniques for which they are adequately trained. Psychologists should not reveal information obtained from clients or research participants except in the most unusual of circumstances (see the chapter on treatment of psychological disorders). Finally, they should avoid situations in which a conflict of interest might impair their judgment or harm someone else. They should not, for example, have sexual relations with their clients, students, or employees.

Despite these guidelines, doubt and controversy arise in some cases about whether a proposed experiment or a particular practice, such as deceiving participants, is ethical. The American Psychological Association has published a casebook to help psychologists resolve such issues (Nagy, 1999). The ethical principles themselves must continually be updated to deal with complex new questions—such as how to protect the confidentiality of e-mail communications—that psychologists face in their ever-expanding range of work (American Psychological Association, 2002b; Hays, 2006; Pipes, Holstein, & Aguirre, 2005).

SUMMARY ▶

The World of Psychology: An Overview

▶ *What is psychology, and how did it grow?*

Psychology is the science that seeks to understand behavior and mental processes. The broad concept of "behavior and mental processes" encompasses virtually all aspects of what it means to be a human being. Psychologists study a wide variety of topics, from the activity of individual nerve cells and the way we sense and perceive things to the way we think, make decisions, and experience emotion to the way people cooperate or compete with each other.

Because the subject matter of psychology is so diverse, most psychologists work in particular subfields within the discipline. For example, **cognitive psychologists** focus on basic psychological processes such as learning, memory, and perception. **Biological psychologists** explore the influence of brain chemistry and other physiological factors on behavior and mental processes. **Personality psychologists** focus on characteristics that set people apart from one another. **Developmental psychologists** specialize in trying to understand the development of behavior and mental processes over a lifetime. **Quantitative psychologists** develop methods for statistical analysis of data. **Clinical** and **counseling psychologists** provide direct service to troubled people and conduct research on abnormal behavior. **Community psychologists** work to prevent mental disorders and extend mental health services to those who need it. **Educational psychologists** conduct and apply research on teaching and learning, whereas **school psychologists** specialize in assessing and alleviating children's academic problems. **Social psychologists** examine questions regarding how people influence one another; **industrial and organizational psychologists** conduct research on topics such as increasing the motivation of employees and helping companies select the best new workers. **Health psychologists, sport psychologists, forensic psychologists, engineering psychologists,** and **environmental psychologists** work in some of psychology's many other subfields. Psychology's subfields often overlap, and psychologists often work in more than one subfield, sharing knowledge with colleagues in other subfields and contributing to knowledge in other disciplines.

Scientific psychology has its roots in philosophy, especially in a philosophical view called **empiricism**. The modern science of psychology began to emerge in the late nineteenth century as scientists in Germany and North America established laboratories to conduct research in psychology. In Germany, Wundt explored the building blocks of **consciousness;** Gestalt psychologists there later studied it as a whole. In Vienna, Freud explored the unconscious. At about the same time in the United States, James was applying Darwin's theory of evolution to the exploration of human behavior. In the early twentieth century, Watson argued that to be truly scientific, psychologists should focus only on observable behavior. He founded behaviorism, which dominated psychology for decades. Today, consciousness—in the form of cognitive processes—is being intensively studied once again.

Approaches to the Science Of Psychology

▶ *Why don't all psychologists explain behavior in the same way?*

Psychologists differ in their approaches to psychology—that is, in the assumptions, questions, and methods they believe will be most  helpful in their work. Psychologists who adopt a **biological approach** examine how physiological factors shape behavior and mental processes. Darwin's theory helped stimulate the **evolutionary approach,** which emphasizes the inherited, adaptive aspects of behavior and mental processes. The **psychodynamic approach** sees behavior and mental processes as a struggle to resolve conflicts between impulses and the demands made by society to control those impulses. Psychologists who take the **behavioral approach** consider behavior to be determined primarily by learning based on experiences with rewards and punishments. The **cognitive approach** assumes that behavior can be understood through analysis of the mental processes that underlie it. The **humanistic approach** views behavior as controlled by the decisions that people make about their lives based on their perceptions of the world.

Human Diversity and Psychology

▶ *How does your cultural background influence your behavior?*

Most of the prominent figures in psychology's history were white males, but women and people of color made important contributions from the start, and they  continue to do so. Psychologists are increasingly taking into account the influence of **culture** and other **sociocultural factors** such as gender and ethnicity in shaping human behavior and mental processes.

Thinking Critically About Psychology (or Anything Else)

▶ *How can critical thinking save you money?*

Critical thinking is the process of assessing claims and making judgments on the basis of well-supported evidence. This process  involves asking five questions: What am I being asked to believe or accept? Is evidence available to support the claim? Can that evidence be interpreted another way? What evidence would help to evaluate the alternatives? What conclusions are most reasonable?

Often, questions about psychological phenomena are phrased in terms of **hypotheses** about **variables** that are specified by **operational definitions.** Evidence for hypotheses must be evaluated for **reliability** and **validity.** After gathering research evidence, scientists may organize their findings into a **theory,** a set of statements designed to explain certain phenomena. Theories must be subjected to careful evaluation.

Research Methods in Psychology

▶ *How do psychologists learn about people?*

Research in psychology, as in other sciences, focuses on four main goals: description, prediction, control, and explanation.  Psychologists have found several research methods especially useful in gathering the evidence needed to reach each of these goals. **Observational methods,** such as **naturalistic observation** entail watching without interfering as behavior occurs in the natural environment. **Case studies** are intensive examinations of a particular individual, group, or situation. **Surveys** ask questions through interviews or questionnaires about behavior, attitudes, beliefs, opinions, and intentions. **Correlational studies** examine the **correlation** (the relationship) between variables in order to describe research data, test predictions, evaluate theories, and suggest hypotheses. In **experiments,** researchers manipulate an **independent variable** and observe the effect of that manipulation on a **dependent variable.** Participants who receive experimental treatment are called the **experimental group.** Participants in comparison conditions are called **control groups.** Experiments can reveal cause-and-effect relationships between variables, but only if researchers use **random assignment** and other strategies (such as **placebo** conditions and a **double-blind design**) to avoid being misled by **random variables, experimenter bias,** and other **confounding variables.**

Psychologists' research can be limited if their **sampling** procedures do not give them a **representative sample** of the population they want to study and about which they want to draw conclusions. Anything other than a truly **random sample** is said to be a **biased sample** of participants. In most cases, psychologists try to select a **representative sample** of the populations that are available to them.

Statistical Analysis of Research Results

▶ *What does it mean when scientists announce that a research finding is "significant"?*

Psychologists use descriptive and inferential statistical analyses to summarize and analyze **data,** which are the numbers that represent research

findings and provide the basis for conclusions. When a correlation coefficient, a difference between groups, or some other research finding is larger than would be expected by chance alone, it is said to be **statistically significant.**

Ethical Guidelines for Psychologists

▶ *Do psychologists deceive people when they do research?*

Ethical guidelines promote the protection of human and animal participants in psychological research and set the highest standards for behavior in all other aspects of psychologists' professional lives.

 Learn BY **Doing** ▶

Put It in Writing

Choose one or two recent newspaper, magazine, or Internet articles describing a research study in psychology and then, based on the article alone, try to answer the five critical thinking questions we described earlier (*What am I being asked to believe or accept? Is evidence available to support the claim? Can that evidence be interpreted another way? What evidence would help to evaluate the alternatives? and What conclusions are most reasonable?*). When you have finished, write a paragraph or two describing how well you think the popular media cover the results of scientific research in psychology and how that coverage could be improved.

Personal Learning Activity

Try designing an experiment on a hypothesis of your choice. First, state your hypothesis as specifically as possible, being sure to include operational definitions of the independent and dependent variables. Then tell how and where you will get your research participants, what the experimental and control groups will experience, and what all your research procedures will be. For example, if your hypothesis is that rock music played during studying improves students' memory for the material, then you should decide what you mean by "rock music" and "improved memory," what the experimental and control groups will hear while studying, what they will study, and how you will measure the students' memory for what they learned. *For additional projects, see the Personal Learning Activities in the corresponding chapter of the study guide that accompanies this book.*

Take Action to Learn More ▶

Now that you have finished reading this chapter, how about exploring some of the ideas and information that you found most interesting? Here are some courses, books, films, and Internet resources to get you started. Enjoy!

Courses

History and Systems of Psychology
Experimental Psychology

Movies

Me and Isaac Newton (scientific research methods)

Gorillas in the Mist; *Blow-Up*; *Kitchen Stories* (observational methods)
The Joy Luck Club; *Daughter from Danang* (cultural influences on behavior)
Mr. Baseball (collectivist versus individualist cultures)

Books

Ludy T. Benjamin and D. B. Baker, *From Seance to Science: A History of the Profession of Psychology in America* (Wadsworth, 2004). The development of clinical,

counseling, school, industrial, and organizational psychology.
Alan M. Goldstein (Ed.), *Forensic Psychology* (Wiley, 2006). Overview of the role of psychological science in the legal system.
Paul Bell, *Environmental Psychology* (Wadsworth, 2001). Applications of psychology to solving problems in natural and artificial environments, including college campuses.
Steve Jones, *Darwin's Ghost: The Origin of Species Updated* (Random House, 2000). Evolutionary theory explained with modern examples.

F. Barbara Orlans, Tom Beauchamp, Rebecca Dresser, and John Gluck (Eds.), *The Human Use of Animals: Case Studies in Ethical Choice* (Oxford University Press, 1998). Case studies related to animal research.

Peter Gay, *Freud: A Life for Our Time* (Norton, 1998). Comprehensive biography of the founder of psychoanalysis.

Roger Hock, *Forty Studies that Changed Psychology* (Prentice Hall, 1995). Reports of famous psychological studies.

Alice Wexler, *Mapping Fate* (University of California Press, 1996). The story of Nancy Wexler's discovery of the gene for Huntington's disease.

Joel Best, *Damned Lies and Statistics: Untangling Numbers from the Media, Politicians, and Activists* (University of California Press, 2001). Examples of why we need to think critically about statistics.

The Web

Essentials of Psychology Book Companion Website

www.cengage.com/psychology/bernstein

Visit the book companion website to access a wealth of resources, including chapter outlines, flashcards, web links, tutorial quizzes, and more!

CENGAGENOW™ Just what you need to know NOW! Spend time on what you need to master rather than on information you already have learned. Take a pre-test for this chapter, and CengageNOW will generate a personalized study plan based on your results. The study plan will identify the topics you need to review and direct you to online resources to help you master those topics. You can then take a post-test to help you determine the concepts you have mastered and what you will need to work on. Try it out! Go to www.cengage.com/login to sign in with an access code or to purchase access to this product.

Review of Key Terms ▶

Can you define each of the key terms in the chapter? Check your definitions against those on the pages shown in parentheses in the following list or in the Glossary at the end of the book.

behavioral approach (p. 15)
behavioral genetics (p. 36)
biased sample (p. 34)
biological approach (p. 14)
biological psychologists (p. 4)
case studies (p. 26)
clinical, counseling, and community psychologists (p. 5)
cognitive approach (p. 16)
cognitive psychologists (p. 3)
confounding variable (p. 32)
consciousness (p. 10)
control group (p. 31)
correlation (p. 29)
correlational studies (p. 29)
critical thinking (p. 22)
culture (p. 18)

data (p. 38)
dependent variable (p. 31)
developmental psychologists (p. 4)
double-blind design (p. 33)
educational psychologists (p. 4)
empiricism (p. 9)
engineering psychologists (p. 6)
environmental psychologists (p. 6)
epigenetics (p. 37)
evolutionary approach (p. 15)
experiment (p. 31)
experimental group (p. 31)
experimenter bias (p. 33)
forensic psychologists (p. 6)
health psychologists (p. 6)
humanistic approach (p. 16)
hypothesis (p. 23)
independent variable (p. 31)
industrial and organizational psychologists (p. 5)
naturalistic observation (p. 25)
observational methods (p. 25)

operational definitions (p. 24)
personality psychologists (p. 4)
placebo (p. 33)
positive psychology (p. 3)
psychodynamic approach (p. 15)
psychology (p. 3)
quantitative psychologists (p. 4)
random assignment (p. 33)
random sample (p. 34)
random variables (p. 32)
reliability (p. 24)
representative sample (p. 34)
sampling (p. 34)
school psychologists (p. 5)
social psychologists (p. 5)
sociocultural factors (p. 18)
sport psychologists (p. 6)
statistically significant (p. 39)
surveys (p. 27)
theory (p. 24)
validity (p. 24)
variables (p. 24)

MULTIPLE-CHOICE ▶ Self-Test

Select the best answer for each of the following questions. Then check your responses against the Answer Key at the end of the book.

1. The first research laboratory in psychology was established to study _____

   a. consciousness
   b. the unconscious
   c. perceptual processes
   d. the collective unconscious

2. Dr. Gauzz believes that low-income families who live in crowded conditions are more likely to need mental health services. Therefore, she works to eliminate overcrowded high-rises for low-income families. Dr. Gauzz is most likely a(n) _____ psychologist.

   a. developmental
   b. industrial-organizational
   c. community
   d. engineering

3. Dr. Hemmings believes that human behavior is influenced by genetic inheritance, unconscious motivations, and environmental influences. Dr. Hemmings uses a(n) _____ approach.
   a. evolutionary
   b. eclectic
   c. humanistic
   d. behavioral

4. Dr. Foreman studies what teachers actually do when they are teaching students to read. Dr. Foreman is most likely a(n) _____ psychologist.
   a. cognitive
   b. school
   c. educational
   d. community

5. Larry says that people act the way they have learned to act. He believes that if others stop rewarding a person's annoying behavior, that behavior will decrease. Larry most likely takes a(n) _____ approach to psychology.
   a. behavioral
   b. cognitive
   c. evolutionary
   d. humanistic

6. Marika just won a college scholarship because of her outstanding grades. If she is from a collectivist culture, she is most likely to say:
   a. "I've worked very hard for this honor and I appreciate the vote of confidence."
   b. "I had some tough times when I didn't think I would succeed, but this has made it all worthwhile."
   c. "I could not have won this award without the help of my teachers and family."
   d. "I am so happy that the committee recognized my hard work and perseverance and is rewarding it with this scholarship."

7. Dr. Rose, a cross-cultural psychologist, is most likely to find which behavior to be similar in all of the groups she studies?
   a. Striving for achievement
   b. Rules governing social behavior
   c. Styles of communication
   d. Recognition of a smile

8. You are watching an infomercial that claims that if you drink liquefied seaweed twice a day, you will lose ten pounds a month. As a wise consumer who knows the five critical thinking questions listed in this chapter, you would FIRST say to yourself:
   a. "I don't know whether the person making the claim about the weight-loss effects of seaweed is a doctor or not."
   b. "The only evidence they present in support of their claim is one woman's personal experience."
   c. "I'll bet you also have to exercise to lose the ten pounds."
   d. "They are asking me to believe that I can lose ten pounds a month by drinking seaweed."

9. Dr. Lucas is interested in the effect of color on people's moods. She has participants complete a mood survey in either a bright red room or a stark white one. A participant's score on the mood survey is her _____.
   a. descriptive statistic
   b. random variable
   c. independent variable
   d. operational definition of mood

10. Case studies are used to _____.
   a. avoid a placebo effect
   b. determine the effects of an independent variable
   c. collect descriptive data
   d. provide control in an experiment

11. Before using survey results to support a hypothesis, we must be sure about which of the following?
   a. The questions are properly worded.
   b. The sample used is representative of the population of interest.
   c. The responses are not strongly biased by efforts to appear socially acceptable.
   d. All of the above.

12. When Dr. Beren compares the performance of his experimental group and his control group, he finds the difference in their scores to be statistically significant. This means that _____.
   a. the difference is larger than would be expected by chance
   b. he used descriptive statistics
   c. his results were confounded by random variables
   d. he used a double-blind method

13. Dr. Daneli believes that memory is aided by an increase in a brain chemical called serotonin. To avoid the possibility that experimenter bias might confound the results of an experiment aimed at testing this hypothesis, she should use a(n) _____ design.
   a. operational   **c.** random
   b. naturalistic   **d.** double-blind

14. In Dr. Daneli's experiment, Group A receives serotonin before taking a memory test, whereas Group B takes the same test without receiving serotonin. In this experiment, performance on the memory test is the _____ variable.
   a. dependent
   b. independent
   c. control
   d. random

15. Angelica designed an experiment to test the effects of praise on the sharing behavior of children. Children in Group A will be praised after they share; children in Group B will only be observed. Group A is the _____ group.
   a. control
   b. experimental
   c. operational
   d. random

16. José wants to know whether growing up in an abusive family causes children to become physically violent. Which of the following research methods would create the greatest ethical problems in trying to scientifically study this question?

   a. case studies
   b. experiments
   c. observations
   d. surveys

17. Choose the strongest correlation coefficient.

   a. +.75   **c.** +.01
   b. -.99   **d.** -.01

18. A correlation coefficient can tell us all of the following except the _____ of a relationship between two variables.

   a. strength
   b. direction
   c. existence
   d. cause

19. Your psychology professor asks you to learn about the smoking habits of all students on your campus. The most practical yet scientific way to get participants for your study would be to find a _____.

   a. random sample of all students
   b. random sample of smokers
   c. representative sample of all students
   d. representative sample of all nonsmokers

20. Why do psychologists follow ethical guidelines?

   a. Psychologists would not want the cost of participating in an experiment to be too high in comparison with the information to be gained.
   b. The American Psychological Association has set standards for psychologists to follow when conducting research and treating clients.
   c. Stress and pain could act as confounding variables in an experiment.
   d. All of the above.

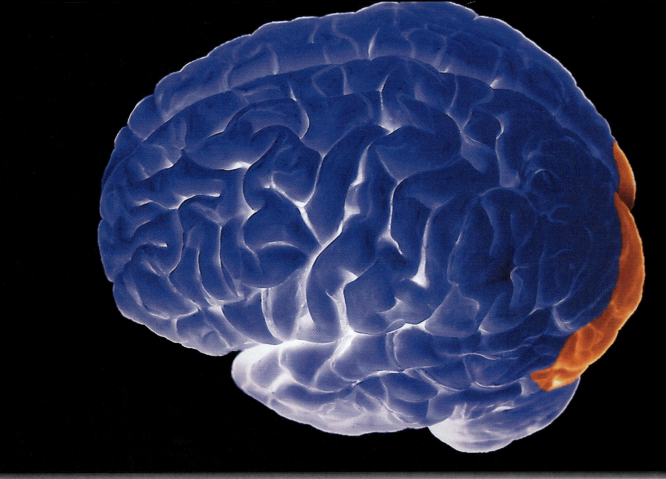

© ISM/Phototake

2 Biology *and* Behavior

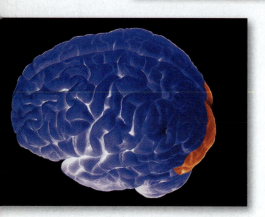

Before you read the next sentence, close your eyes and touch your nose. This task is easy, but it is not simple. To get the job done, your brain used specific nerves to tell your eyelids to close. It used other nerves to tell your hand to extend a finger and then sent a series of messages that moved your arm in just the right direction until it received a message that your finger and your nose were in contact. This example illustrates that everything you do—including how you feel and think—is based on some kind of biological activity in your body, especially in your brain. This chapter tells the story of that activity, beginning with a basic biological unit of the body, a specialized cell called the *neuron.* Collections of neurons form the systems that receive information from our senses, process that information, and biochemically translate it into behavior, thoughts, and emotions.

The fact is that biological factors are intimately related to *all* behavior and mental processes. The question of how they are related takes us into the realm of **biological psychology**—the study of cells, genes, and organs of the body and the physical and chemical changes involved in behavior and mental processes.

As we describe the biology of behavior and mental processes, we keep in mind the role of the environment in influencing those processes. You will see later, for example, that the experiences we have in the environment can change the chemistry and even the structure of our brains. Let's begin to consider in more detail the relationship between your body and your mind, between your brain and your behavior.

Understanding how we think, feel, act, and react requires some knowledge of the human body and how it works. Two primary systems—the nervous system and the endocrine system—direct the activities of the body. The nervous system receives information, sends messages from one part of the body to another, and begins actions. The endocrine (pronounced "END-oh-krin") system regulates internal activity of the body with glands that secrete chemicals, called *hormones,* into the bloodstream to control energy consumption, reactions to stress, sexual functioning, and the like. These are the basic pieces of the puzzle of the body. Putting the pieces together is the next step in understanding the biology of our complex behavior. ■

Cells of the Nervous System

▶ *What are neurons, and what do they do?*

We begin by considering the **nervous system,** a vast network of cells that tells you what is going on inside and outside your body and allows you to make appropriate responses. For example, if you are jabbed with a pin, your nervous system gets the message and immediately causes you to flinch. But the nervous system can do far more than detect information and make responses. When information about the world reaches the brain, that information is *processed*—it is combined with information about past experiences and current wants and needs—to allow you to make a decision about how to respond. We begin our exploration of the nervous system at the "bottom," with a description of its individual cells. Later we consider how these cells are organized to form the structures of the human nervous system.

biological psychology   The study of physical and chemical changes involved in behavior and mental processes.

nervous system   A network of billions of cells that detects what is going on inside or outside the body and guides appropriate responses.

FIGURE 2.1 ■ THREE FUNCTIONS OF THE NERVOUS SYSTEM

The nervous system's three main functions are to receive information (input), to integrate that information with past experiences (processing), and to guide actions (output). When the alarm clock goes off, this person's nervous system, like yours, gets the message, recognizes what it means, and takes action—by getting out of bed or perhaps hitting the snooze button.

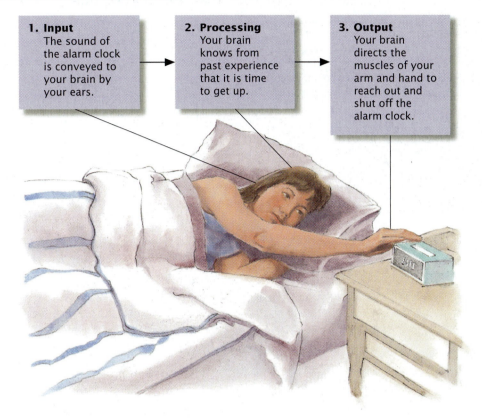

1. Input
The sound of the alarm clock is conveyed to your brain by your ears.

2. Processing
Your brain knows from past experience that it is time to get up.

3. Output
Your brain directs the muscles of your arm and hand to reach out and shut off the alarm clock.

Neurons

As Figure 2.1 shows, the nervous system is actually an information-processing system with three functions: input, processing, and output. These functions are possible partly because the nervous system is made up of cells that communicate with each other. Two major types of cells, neurons and glial cells, allow the nervous system to carry out its complex signaling tasks efficiently. The specialized cells that send and receive signals are called **neurons.**

Most of our discussion of brain cells concerns neurons, but glial cells are important, too. *Glial* means "glue," and scientists had long believed that glial cells did no more than hold neurons together. We now know, however, that **glial cells** also help neurons communicate by directing their growth, keeping their chemical environment stable, providing energy, and secreting chemicals to help repair damage (Rouach et al., 2008). Further, glial cells are capable of many of the functions of neurons, including releasing chemicals that influence neurons, responding to chemicals from neurons, and changing in response to experience (Barres, 2008). Without glial cells, neurons could not function, and malfunctions in glial cells may play a role in problems ranging from recurring pain to depression and other mental disorders (Miller, 2005a).

Every cell in the body has a skin, called an *outer membrane;* a cell body that (with the exception of red blood cells) contains a core called the *nucleus;* and tiny "engines," called *mitochondria* (pronounced "my-toh-CON-dree-uh"). Neurons are no different. A neuron's outer membrane acts like a screen, letting some substances pass in and out while blocking others. In the neuron's cell body, the nucleus (or center) carries genetic information that tells the cell what to do. And neurons' mitochondria turn oxygen and glucose into energy. This process is especially vital to brain cells, because although the brain accounts for only 2 percent of the body's weight, it uses more than 20 percent of the body's oxygen. All of this energy is required because brain cells transmit signals among themselves to an even greater extent than do cells in the rest of the body.

neurons Specialized cells of the nervous system that send and receive messages.

glial cells Nervous system cells that hold neurons together and help them communicate with each other.

FIGURE 2.2   ▬   THE NEURON

Part A shows fibers extending outward from the cell body of a neuron, which is a nervous system cell. These fibers are called *axons* and *dendrites.* Part B shows an enlarged drawing of the neuron's cell body. The cell body of a neuron includes an outer membrane, a nucleus, and mitochondria.

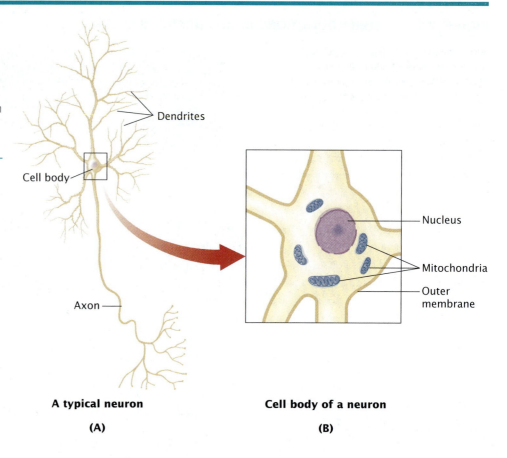

Dendrites

Cell body

Axon

Nucleus

Mitochondria

Outer membrane

A typical neuron

(A)

Cell body of a neuron

(B)

Neurons have special structural and chemical features that allow them to communicate with each other. Let's first examine their structure. Although neurons come in many shapes and sizes, they all have long, thin fibers that reach outward from the cell body like arms (see Part A in Figure 2.2). When these fibers get close to other neurons, communication between the cells can occur. The interweaving of these fibers with fibers from other neurons allows each neuron to be close to thousands or even hundreds of thousands of other neurons.

Fibers extending from the cell body are called axons and dendrites. As shown in Figure 2.2, each neuron generally has only one **axon,** whose function is to carry signals away from the cell body. An axon may have many branches along its stem, much like a tree. Axons can be short or long. In the brain, they may extend no more than a fraction of an inch, but the axon from your big toe to your spine is more than three feet long! **Dendrites** are the fibers that receive signals from the axons of other neurons and carry those signals to the cell body. As you can see in Figure 2.2, a neuron can have many dendrites, each of which usually has many branches. Remember that *axons* carry signals *away* from the cell body, and *dendrites detect* those signals.

Action Potentials

The communication signal between neurons begins with an electrochemical pulse called an **action potential,** which shoots down the axon. This is an "all-or-nothing" affair: The cell either fires its action potential at full strength or it does not fire at all. Once a cell has fired, a very short recovery time called the **refractory period** follows, during which the cell cannot fire again. Even so, neurons are able to fire as often as 1,000 times per second. The speed of an action potential ranges from about 5 to 260 miles per hour and depends on the thickness or diameter of the axon—larger ones are faster—and on the presence of myelin (pronounced "MY-a-lin"). *Myelin* is a fatty substance that wraps around some

axon   A fiber that carries signals away from the cell body.

dendrites   Fibers that receive signals from the axons of other neurons.

action potential   The electrochemical impulse or message that is sent down an axon and stimulates release of a neurotransmitter.

refractory period   A short recovery time after cell firing, during which the cell cannot fire again.

FIGURE 2.3 ▪ COMMUNICATION BETWEEN NEURONS

When stimulation of a neuron reaches a certain level, the neuron fires, sending an action potential shooting to the end of its axon and triggering the release of a neurotransmitter into the synapse. This process stimulates neighboring neurons and may cause them to fire their own action potentials.

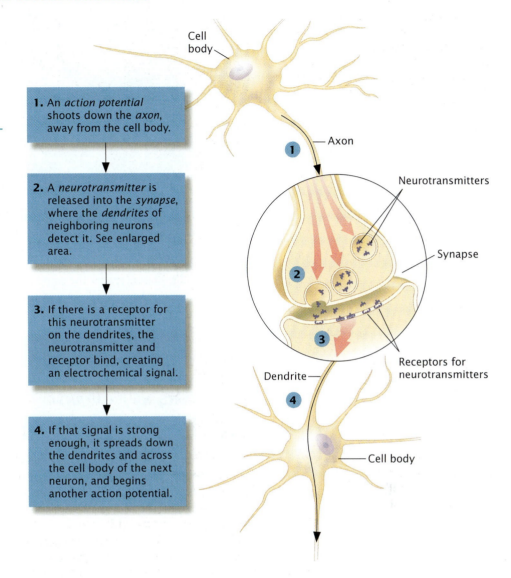

1. An *action potential* shoots down the *axon*, away from the cell body.

2. A *neurotransmitter* is released into the *synapse*, where the *dendrites* of neighboring neurons detect it. See enlarged area.

3. If there is a receptor for this neurotransmitter on the dendrites, the neurotransmitter and receptor bind, creating an electrochemical signal.

4. If that signal is strong enough, it spreads down the dendrites and across the cell body of the next neuron, and begins another action potential.

axons like a stocking and speeds up action potentials. When a neuron fires, dendrites in the next cell detect the message and send the signal to their cell body.

Synapses and Communication Between Neurons

How do the dendrites detect a signal from another neuron? As shown in Figure 2.3, it works a little like the game of tag you played as a child. In this neural communication tag game, however, one neuron "sends" a tag without actually touching the next neuron. When an action potential reaches the ends of an axon's branches, it stimulates the release of a chemical that is stored there in little "bags" called *vesicles* (pronounced "VESS-ick-els"). This chemical is called a **neurotransmitter** because it acts as a kind of messenger between neurons. Neurotransmitters flow across a tiny gap, less than a millionth of an inch wide, which separates the axon of one neuron and the dendrites of another. This is the *synaptic gap*, often referred to simply as the **synapse** (see Figure 2.4). When they reach the dendrite of the next cell, neurotransmitters chemically fit, or bind, to proteins called *receptors*. Like a key fitting into the right lock, a neurotransmitter snugly binds to its own receptors but not to receptors for other neurotransmitters. The receptors "recognize" only one type of neurotransmitter. In the dendrite, this binding

neurotransmitter A chemical that transfers messages across synapses.

synapse The tiny gap between the axon of one neuron and the dendrites of another.

FIGURE 2.4 ■ **A SYNAPSE**

This photograph taken with an electron microscope shows part of a synapse between neurons, magnified 50,000 times. The end of one neuron's axon is shaded green; the green ovals are mitochondria. The red spots are neurotransmitter-containing vesicles. The synapse itself appears as the narrow gap between the first cell's axon and the dendrite of the second cell, which is shaded blue.

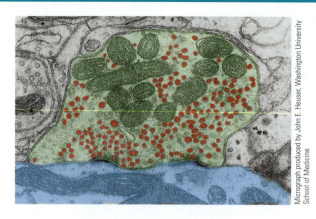

Micrograph produced by John E. Heuser, Washington University School of Medicine

creates an electrochemical signal that is called a *postsynaptic potential* because it occurs *after* the neurotransmitter has crossed the synapse. The postsynaptic potential, in turn, passes the message to the cell body for the signaling process to continue.

Generally, more than one message must go to a cell to make it fire. Signals from groups of cells often arrive at the same postsynaptic cell at about the same time. The messages from these many cells may conflict with one another. Some messages tell the

Improve Your Grade
Tutorial: Action Potential

In Review

NEURONS, NEUROTRANSMITTERS, AND RECEPTORS

PART	FUNCTION	TYPE OF SIGNAL CARRIED
Axon	Carries signals away from the cell body	The action potential, an all-or-nothing electrochemical signal that shoots down the axon to vesicles at the tip of the axon, releasing neurotransmitters
Dendrite	Detects and carries signals to the cell body	The postsynaptic potential, an electrochemical signal moving toward the cell body
Synapse	Provides an area for the transfer of signals between neurons, usually between axon and dendrite	Chemicals that cross the synapse and reach receptors on another cell
Neurotransmitter	A chemical released by one cell that binds to the receptors on another cell	A chemical message telling the next cell to fire or not to fire its own action potential
Receptor	Proteins on the cell membrane that receive chemical signals	Recognizes certain neurotransmitters, thus allowing it to begin a postsynaptic potential in the dendrite

?

1. For one neuron to communicate with another, a _____ has to cross the _____ between them.

2. The nervous system's main functions are to _____, _____, and _____ information.

3. The two main types of cells in the nervous system are _____ and _____.

FIGURE 2.5 ■ ORGANIZATION OF THE NERVOUS SYSTEM

The brain and spinal cord make up the bone-encased central nervous system (CNS), the body's central information processor, decision maker, and director of actions. The peripheral nervous system, which is not housed in bone, functions mainly to carry messages. The somatic subsystem of the peripheral nervous system transmits information to the CNS from the outside world and conveys instructions from the CNS to the muscles. The autonomic subsystem conveys messages from the CNS that alter the activity of organs and glands and it sends information about that activity back to the brain.

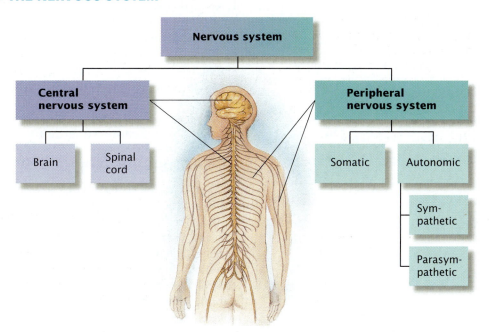

cell to fire, whereas others tell the cell not to fire. Whether it actually does fire depends on which kinds of signals are most numerous. So axons, neurotransmitters, synapses, and dendrites allow cells of the nervous system to communicate. If these components are damaged or disordered, however, serious problems can result. For example, spinal cord injuries may cut the neural communication lines that had once allowed victims to feel and move their bodies. And when the myelin surrounding some axons is destroyed by the brain disorder known as *multiple sclerosis (MS),* the result can be disruption of vision, speech, balance, and other important functions.

Organization of the Nervous System

Impressive as individual neurons are (see "In Review: Neurons, Neurotransmitters, and Receptors"), we can best understand their functions by looking at how they operate in groups called **neural networks.** The billions of neurons that make up the nervous system are organized into two main parts—the *central nervous system* and the *peripheral nervous system* (see Figure 2.5). We describe them in separate sections, but they work together closely to coordinate behavior and mental processes. The **central nervous system (CNS)** consists of the brain and spinal cord, which are encased in bone for protection. Like the chief executive officer in a company, the CNS receives information, processes it, and determines what actions should result. The **peripheral nervous system (PNS)** extends throughout the body and, like an e-mail or instant messaging service, relays information to and from the brain.

The Peripheral Nervous System: Keeping in Touch with the World

▶ *How do sights and sounds reach my brain?*

neural networks Neurons that operate together to perform complex functions.

central nervous system (CNS) The brain and spinal cord.

peripheral nervous system The part of the nervous system that sends messages to and from the central nervous system.

The peripheral nervous system sends sensory information from the eyes, ears, and other sense organs to the CNS. The PNS also carries messages from the brain and spinal cord to the muscles, glands, and other parts of the body. Unlike the CNS, it is not protected by bone. To accomplish its relay tasks, the peripheral nervous system has two subsystems—the somatic nervous system and the autonomic nervous system.

The Somatic Nervous System

Imagine that you are at the beach. It is hot, and the ocean smells salty. An attractive stranger approaches, catching your eye. The stranger smiles. You smile in return. The stranger continues walking away. In these few seconds, your nervous system has been busy. You feel the warmth of the sun and smell the ocean because your **somatic nervous system** takes in these pieces of sensory information and sends them to the central nervous system for processing. The CNS evaluates the warmth and the smells, sending messages through the somatic nervous system to the muscles that allow you to turn over, sit up, or put on more sunscreen. **Sensory neurons** bring information into the brain. **Motor neurons** carry information from the part of the brain that directs motion.

The Autonomic Nervous System

The **autonomic nervous system** carries messages back and forth between the CNS and the heart, lungs, and other organs and glands. For example, the autonomic nervous system takes that passing stranger's "attractive" rating from the CNS and translates it into an increase in heart rate, pupil dilation, and perhaps a little blushing. This system is called "autonomic" (pronounced "aw-toh-NOM-ic") because its activities, including digestion and sweating, for example, are generally autonomous, or independent of your control. With training and practice, some people can use a technique called *biofeedback* to bring some of their involuntary responses, such as heart rate, under conscious (CNS) control.

As shown in Figure 2.5, the autonomic system has two subsystems of its own—the *sympathetic nervous system* and the *parasympathetic nervous system*. These two subsystems work like a seesaw on a playground. Generally, the **sympathetic nervous system** readies your body for action in the face of stress. The **parasympathetic nervous system** calms you down once the crisis has passed. So the *sympathetic* nervous system *spends* energy, whereas the *parasympathetic* nervous system *preserves* energy.

The functions of the autonomic nervous system may not get star billing, but you would miss them if they were gone. Just as a race-car driver is nothing without a good pit crew, the somatic nervous system depends on the autonomic nervous system to get its job done. For example, when you want to move your muscles, you create a demand for energy. The autonomic nervous system fills the bill by increasing sugar fuels in the bloodstream. If you decide to stand up, you need increased blood pressure so that your blood does not flow out of your brain and settle in your legs. Again, the autonomic nervous system makes the adjustment. Disorders of the autonomic nervous system can make people sweat uncontrollably or faint whenever they stand up; they can also lead to other problems, such as an inability to have sex. We examine the autonomic nervous system in more detail in the chapter on motivation and emotion.

The Central Nervous System: Making Sense of the World

▶ *How is my brain "wired"?*

The amazing speed and efficiency of the central nervous system—the brain and spinal cord—have prompted many people to compare it to the central processor in a computer. But the CNS does not simply function as a high-powered computer. It certainly isn't laid out as neatly, either. The layout of the brain is more like the map of a college campus. There are clusters of offices for the administrators in one place, clusters of faculty offices in another place, and classrooms in yet another. Some of the sidewalks or hallways that connect these clusters are wide; others are narrow. There are many different but connected ways to get to the same place. Like a campus with its office clusters, the CNS has clusters of neuron cell bodies called **nuclei** (pronounced "NUKE-lee-eye"; *nuclei* is the plural of *nucleus*). The sidewalks and hallways of the CNS are axons that

somatic nervous system   The subsystem of the peripheral nervous system that transmits information from the senses to the central nervous system and carries signals from the CNS to the muscles that move the skeleton.

sensory neurons   The neurons that provide the brain with information about the environment.

motor neurons   The neurons that influence muscles and other organs to respond to the environment in some way.

autonomic nervous system   The subsystem of the peripheral nervous system that carries messages between the central nervous system and the heart, lungs, and other organs and glands in the body.

sympathetic nervous system   The subsystem of the autonomic nervous system that readies the body for vigorous activity.

parasympathetic nervous system   The subsystem of the autonomic nervous system that typically influences activity related to the protection, nourishment, and growth of the body.

nuclei   Clusters of nerve cell bodies in the central nervous system.

© ABC/Photofest

travel together in bundles called **fiber tracts,** or *pathways.* The axon (hallway) from any given cell (office) may merge with and leave many fiber tracts (sidewalks) and send branches out to other tracts. Let's consider a practical example of nervous system functioning to begin learning our way around the "campus" of the brain.

It is 6 A.M. and your alarm clock goes off, creating the simple case of information processing illustrated in Figure 2.1. Your ears receive sensory input in the form of sound from the alarm. The sound is converted into neural signals and sent to the brain. Your brain compares these signals with previous experiences stored in memory and correctly associates the sound with "alarm clock." Your muscle-guiding output is not yet at peak performance, though, because your brain activity has not yet reached the waking state. So you fumble to turn off the alarm, shuffle to the kitchen, and accidentally touch the coffeemaker's heating element. Things get more lively now. Heat energy activates sensory neurons in your fingers, generating action potentials that speed along fiber tracts going into the spinal cord. Your motor neurons are reflexively activated by the CNS, causing muscles in your arm to contract and quickly withdraw your hand.

The Spinal Cord

The **spinal cord** receives signals such as pain and touch from the senses and passes those signals to the brain. Neuron fibers within the cord also carry signals downward from the brain to the muscles. Some cells of the spinal cord can direct simple behaviors without instructions from the brain. These behaviors are called **reflexes,** because the response to the incoming signal is directly "reflected" back out, as shown in Figure 2.6. Spinal reflexes, such as the one that pulled your hand away from the heat, are very fast because they include few time-consuming synaptic links. Reflexes are called *involuntary* because they occur without instructions from the brain. As reflexes occur, though, action potentials are also sent along fiber tracts to the brain. So you officially "know" you have been burned a fraction of a second after your reflex got you out of trouble.

The spinal cord is an example of a *feedback system.* When touching something hot sets off a simple reflex, one set of arm muscles contracts, and an opposing set of

fiber tracts Bundles of axons that travel together.

spinal cord The part of the central nervous system that receives information from the senses, passes these signals to the brain, and sends messages from the brain to the body.

reflexes Simple, involuntary, unlearned behaviors directed by the spinal cord without instructions from the brain.

FIGURE 2.6 ■ A REFLEX PATHWAY

Sit on a chair, cross one leg over the other, and then use the handle of a butter knife or some other solid object to gently tap your top knee, just below the joint, until you get a knee-jerk reaction. Tapping your knee at just the right spot sets off an almost instantaneous sequence of events that begins with stimulation of sensory neurons that respond to stretch. When those neurons fire, their axons, which end within the spinal cord, cause spinal neurons to fire. This, in turn, stimulates the firing of motor neurons with axons ending in your thigh muscles. The result is a contraction of those muscles and a kicking of the lower leg and foot. Information about the knee tap and about what the leg has done also goes to your cerebral cortex, but the reflex is completed without waiting for guidance from the brain.

Learn BY **Doing**

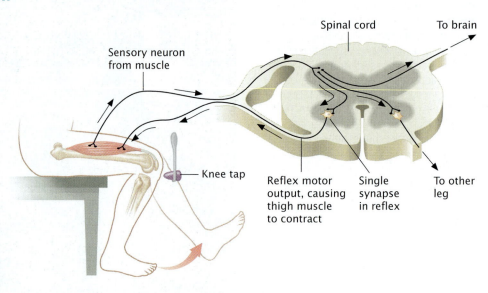

Sensory neuron from muscle

Spinal cord

To brain

Knee tap

Reflex motor output, causing thigh muscle to contract

Single synapse in reflex

To other leg

muscles relaxes. If this did not happen, the arm would go rigid. The muscles also have receptors that send information to the spinal cord to let it know how extended they are so that adjustments can be made for a smooth contracting motion. Information about the consequences of an action goes back to the source of the action for further adjustment. That is a feedback system.

The Brain

When pain messages from that hot burner reach your brain, you may become aware of more than just being burned. You might also realize that you have burned yourself twice before in the past week and get annoyed at your own carelessness. The brain is the most complex element in the central nervous system, and it is your brain's astonishing capacity for information processing that allows you to have these thoughts and feelings (Cacioppo & Decety, 2009). A variety of new brain-scanning techniques, combined with some older measures, are giving scientists ever better views of the workings of the human brain (Amaro & Barker, 2006; Miller, 2003; see Table 2.1).

Each technique can indirectly measure the activity of neurons firing, and each has different advantages and disadvantages. One of the earliest of these techniques, called the *electroencephalograph (EEG),* measures general electrical activity of the brain. Electrodes are pasted on the scalp to detect the electrical fields resulting from the activity of billions of neurons (Figure 4.3 in the consciousness chapter shows how EEG can be used to record brain activity during sleep). Although this tool can associate rapidly changing electrical activity with changes in the activity of the brain, it cannot tell us exactly where the active cells are.

A newer technique, called the *PET scan,* can locate brain cell activity by recording where radioactive substances become concentrated when injected into the bloodstream. *PET* stands for *positron emission tomography.* It records images from the brain that indicate the location of the radioactivity as the brain performs various tasks. For instance, PET studies have revealed that specific brain regions are activated when we look at fearful facial expressions or engage in certain kinds of thoughts or inhale cigarette smoke (Brody et al., 2006; Morris et al., 1998; Wharton et al., 2000). PET scans can tell us a lot about where changes in brain activity occur, but they can't reveal details of the brain's physical structure.

A detailed structural picture of the brain can be seen, however, using *magnetic resonance imaging,* or *MRI.* MRI exposes the brain to a magnetic field and measures

TABLE 2. 1 ■ TECHNIQUES FOR STUDYING HUMAN BRAIN FUNCTION AND STRUCTURE

Technique	What It Shows	Advantages (+) and Disadvantages (−)
EEG (electroencephalograph): Multiple electrodes are pasted to the outside of the head	Lines that chart the summated electrical fields resulting from the activity of billions of neurons	+ Detects very rapid changes in electrical activity, allowing analysis of stages of cognitive processing − Provides poor spatial resolution of the source of electrical activity; EEG is sometimes combined with magnetoencephalography (MEG), which localizes electrical activity by measuring magnetic fields associated with it.
PET (positron emission tomography) and SPECT (single-photon emission computed tomography): Positrons and photons are emissions from radioactive substances	An image of the amount and localization of any molecule that can be injected in radioactive form, such as neurotransmitters, drugs, or tracers for blood flow or glucose use (which indicates specific changes in neuronal activity)	+ Allows functional and biochemical studies + Provides visual image corresponding to anatomy − Requires exposure to low levels of radioactivity − Provides spatial resolution better than that of EEG but poorer than that of MRI − Cannot follow rapid changes (those faster than 30 seconds)
MRI (magnetic resonance imaging): Exposes the brain to a magnetic field and measures radio frequency waves	Traditional MRI provides high-resolution image of brain anatomy. Functional MRI (fMRI) provides images of changes in blood flow (which indicate specific changes in neural activity). A new variant, diffusion tensor imaging (DTI), shows water flow in neural fibers, thus revealing the "wiring diagram" of neural connections in the brain.	+ Requires no exposure to radioactivity + Provides high spatial resolution of anatomical details (smaller than 1 mm) + Provides high temporal resolution (less than one-tenth of a second)
TMS (transcranial magnetic stimulation): Temporarily disrupts electrical activity of a small region of brain by exposing it to an intense magnetic field.	Normal function of a particular brain region can be studied by observing changes after TMS is applied to a specific location.	+ Shows which brain regions are necessary for given tasks. − Long-term safety not well established.

the resulting radiofrequency waves to get amazingly clear pictures of the brain's anatomical details (see Figure 2.7). *Functional MRI,* or *fMRI,* combines the advantages of PET and MRI and is capable of detecting changes in blood flow and blood oxygen that reflect ongoing changes in the activity of neurons, providing a sort of "moving picture" of the brain (e.g., Shu et al., 2002). The newest techniques offer even deeper insight into brain activity, structure, and functioning. These techniques include a variant on fMRI called *diffusion tensor imaging (DTI),* which traces the activity of axon pathways, and a procedure called *transcranial magnetic stimulation (TMS)* which sets up magnetic fields outside the brain. These magnetic fields can either stimulate or disrupt neural activity (Lagopoulos & Malhi, 2008; López-Ibor, López-Ibor, & Pastrana, 2008). Some researchers have also begun combining fMRI and TMS in an effort to gain new insights into how the brain functions (Bestmann et al., 2008). For example, when one brain region is stimulated by TMS, and changes in activity are detected by fMRI in another region, that indicates that the two regions are functionally connected.

FIGURE 2.7 ■ COMBINING A PET SCAN AND MAGNETIC RESONANCE IMAGING

Researchers have superimposed images from PET scans and MRI to construct a three-dimensional view of the living brain. This figure shows the brain of a young epileptic girl. The picture of the outer surface of the brain is from the MRI; the pink area is from the PET scan and shows the source of epileptic activity. To the right of the figure are separate MRI and PET images taken at one plane, or "slice," through the brain (indicated by the line on the brain at the left).

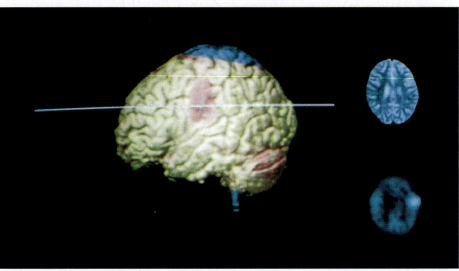

D. N. Levin, H. Xiaoping, K. K. Tan, S. Galhotra, C. A. Pelizzare, G. T. Y. Chen, R. N. Beck, C. T. Chen, M. D. Cooper, J. F. Mullan, J. Hekmatpanah, & J. P. Spire (1989). The Brain: Integrated three-dimensional display of MR and PET images. Radiology, 172: 783–789.

Thinking CRITICALLY

What Can fMRI Tell Us About Behavior and Mental Processes?

A picture may be worth a thousand words, but the pictures of brain activity offered by fMRI are generating millions of them. As of 2009, more than 8,000 scientific articles have reported the results of fMRI scans taken while people engaged in various kinds of thinking or experienced various emotions. Neuroscientists who use brain-imaging techniques can now be found in psychology departments around the world, and, as described in other chapters, their work is changing the research landscape in cognitive, social, and abnormal psychology. Excitement over fMRI is not confined to scientists, however. Popular and scientific magazines routinely carry fMRI pictures that appear to "show" people's thoughts and feelings as they happen, and readers see these articles as more believable than those offering the same data in less dramatic tables or graphs (McCabe & Castel, 2008).

▶ What am I being asked to believe or accept?

In the early 1800s, similar excitement surrounded *phrenology*, a technique that involved feeling bumps and depressions on the skull. It was claimed that these contours reflected the size of 27 structures on the brain's surface that determine personality traits, mental abilities, talents, and other characteristics. Although wildly popular with the public (Benjamin & Baker, 2004), phrenology did not survive the critical thinking of nineteenth-century scientists, and the technique has long been discredited. Today, some scientists wonder whether fMRI is a twenty-first-century version of phrenology, at least in the sense that their colleagues might be accepting its value too readily. These scientists point out that although fMRI images can indicate where brain activity occurs as people think and experience emotion, there is no guarantee that this activity is actually *causing* the associated thoughts and feelings (Aldridge, 2005). Questions are also being raised about the

assumption that particular thought processes or emotions occur in a particular brain structure or set of structures. It is easy to talk about "thinking" or "attention," but these psychological terms might not correspond to specific biological processes that can be isolated and located by *any* technology. In short, critics claim that the results of fMRI scans can be misleading and that they don't necessarily tell us much about how the mind works (Uttal, 2004). Perhaps it would be better to focus on *how* the brain produces thoughts and feelings instead of searching for their locations.

▶ Is evidence available to support the claim?

When the participant in an fMRI experiment thinks or feels something, you can actually see the colors in the brain scan change, much like the color changes you see on weather radar as a rainstorm intensifies or weakens. Looking at an fMRI scan, you get a clear impression that the brain areas that "light up" when a person experiences an emotion or performs a mental task are the ones involved in that emotion or task (see Figure 1.5 in the introduction to the science of psychology chapter).

These scans are not as precise as they seem, though, because fMRI doesn't directly measure brain cell activity. The colors seen in an fMRI scan reflect instead the flow of blood in the brain and the amount of oxygen the blood is carrying. Changes in blood flow and blood oxygen are *related* to changes in the firing rates of neurons, but the relationship is complex. For example, changes in an fMRI signal can depend on how much neural firing was taking place before a stimulus appeared (Maandag et al., 2007; Perthen et al., 2008). Further, when brain cells process information, their firing rates may either increase or decrease (Gonsalves et al., 2005). If the increases and decreases in a particular brain region happen to cancel each other out, an fMRI scan will miss the neuronal

EXPLORING BRAIN FUNCTIONS WITH FMRI ▶

As this participant performs a mental task, a functional magnetic resonance imaging scanner records blood flow and blood oxygen levels in her brain. The resulting computer analysis shows as "lit up" areas the parts of the brain that appear to be activated during the task, but critics doubt that fMRI scanning is as clear or accurate as its proponents suggest.

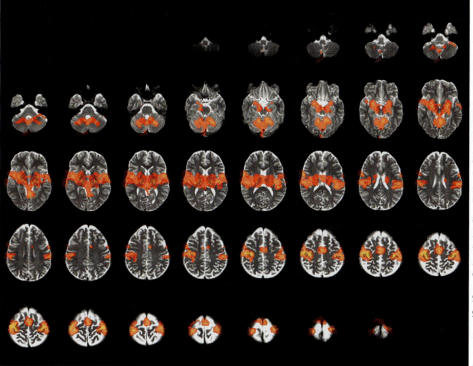

Image courtesy of Brad Sutton, Beckman Institute Biomedical Imaging Center, Univ. of Illinois at Urbana-Champaign

activity taking place in that region. In fact, compared with the direct measurement of brain cell activity that can be done in research with animals, fMRI technology is still quite crude. It takes coordinated changes in millions of neurons to produce a detectable change in the fMRI signal.

Critics also argue that the results of fMRI research can depend too much on how experimenters choose to interpret them. In a typical fMRI experiment, participants are shown some kind of display, such as pairs of photos, and asked to perform various tasks. One task might be to press a button if the photos are exactly the same. A second task might be to press the button if objects in the photos are arranged in the same way. In this second task, a participant should press the button if one photo shows, say, a short man standing to the left of a tall woman and the other photo shows a small dog standing to the left of a giraffe. Both versions of the task require the participant to compare two images, but only the second of them requires considering whether things that look different are actually similar in some way. The fMRI scans taken during these tasks might show certain brain areas "lighting up" only during the second task. If so, the researcher would suggest that those areas are involved in recognizing *analogies,* or the similarities between apparently different things (Wharton et al., 2000). The researcher would base this conclusion on a computer program that compares fMRI scans taken during two tasks, subtracts all the "lighted" areas that are the same in both scans, and keeps only those that are different. But what the computer classifies as "different" depends on a rule that is set by the experimenter. If the experimenter programs the computer to display only big differences between the scans, not many "lit up" areas will remain after the comparison process. But if even tiny differences are allowed to count as "different," many more "lighted" areas will remain after the subtraction

process. In our example, then, there could be large or small areas apparently associated with recognizing analogies, all depending on a rule set by the researcher.

These problems aside, critics wonder what it really means when fMRI research shows that certain brain areas appear activated during certain kinds of tasks or experiences. Their concern focuses on studies such as one from the new field of *neuroeconomics* that suggests that excessive activity in a particular brain area leads to bad investment decisions (Kuhnen & Knutson, 2005). Other studies have used fMRI to identify the neural activity associated with trust, religious belief, political liberalism or conservatism, and even the "neural basis of romantic love" (Amodio et al., 2007; Kapogiannis et al., 2009; Krueger et al., 2007). In this last study (Bartels & Zeki, 2000), investigators scanned people's brains as they looked at pictures of their romantic partners and compared these scans to those taken while the same people viewed nonromantic friends. According to the "difference" rule established by the experimenters, four brain areas were more active when viewing a romantic loved one than when viewing a friend. But does this result tell us anything about how or why these areas became active or what results this activity might have? In other words, do we know more about love? Critics of fMRI would say no.

▶ Can that evidence be interpreted another way?

Supporters of fMRI disagree with those critics. They believe that the colorful areas seen on fMRI scans can provide vital new information that will eventually allow scientists to answer important questions about behavior and mental processes. They point, for example, to fMRI research on brain mechanisms that help us to appreciate what other people are feeling—that is, to experience empathy—and to learn by watching others.

These *mirror neuron mechanisms* were discovered accidentally by scientists who had been using surgical techniques to directly record the activity of brain cells in monkeys' brains (Caggiano et al., 2009; Rizzolatti et al., 1996). They found that neurons in an area called F5 are activated not only when a monkey plans to reach for an object, such as a peanut, but also if the monkey sees *an experimenter* reach for a peanut! After fMRI scanning became available, researchers could begin looking for mirror mechanisms in the human brain. And in fact, some of the mirror systems they found in humans correspond to the F5 region in monkeys (Rizolatti & Arbib, 1998). One of them is called *Broca's area*, which, as described later, is an important component of our ability to speak. It makes sense that Broca's area contains a mirror mechanism, because language is a skill that we learn partly by imitation. The new fMRI findings suggest that Broca's area may also be important for many other skills that involve imitation. One study found that this area "lights up" when a guitar student learns chords by watching a professional guitarist (Buccino et al., 2004). Other fMRI research has found that mirror systems in other parts of the brain become active when a person sees someone experiencing emotion. For example, the brain area that is activated when you experience disgust (from the smell of rotten eggs, for example) is also activated if you see a video in which someone else reacts to a smell with disgust (Wicker et al., 2003).

So fMRI can be uniquely useful, say its defenders. Without it, research on mirror neurons in humans could not have taken place. And because of it, we have evidence that the experience of empathy comes about because seeing the actions and emotions of others activates the same brain regions that would be active if we were doing or feeling the same things ourselves. Some fMRI studies have also found that malfunctioning mirror mechanisms are associated with the impairments in language development, imitative skills, and empathy seen in children diagnosed with autistic disorder (Dapretto et al., 2006; Miller, 2005b; Oberman & Ramachandran, 2007; see the chapter on psychological disorders).

It may also be that fMRI can help answer centuries-old but still unanswered questions about the location of our consciousness and self-awareness. Studies using fMRI have suggested that these functions might be located in a region called the anterior insular cortex because this region appears to be involved in all kinds of subjective feelings and is activated by a wide range of experiences, including everything from pressure in the bowels to orgasm, from cigarette craving to maternal love and from decision making to sudden insight (Craig, 2009).

▶ What evidence would help to evaluate the alternatives?

As technology continues to be refined, the quality of fMRI scans will continue to improve, giving us ever better images of where brain activity is taking place. But the value of this scanning technology will depend on a better understanding of what it can and cannot tell us about how brain activity is related to behavior and mental processes. We also need more evidence about correlation and causation in fMRI research. For example, one study conducted fMRI scans on compulsive gamblers as they played a simple guessing game (Reuter et al., 2005). When they won the game, these people showed an unusually small amount of activity in a brain area that is normally activated by the experience of rewards, or pleasure. Noting the correlation between compulsive gambling and lower-than-normal activity in the reward area, the researchers suggested that an abnormality in the brain's reward mechanisms might be responsible for gambling addiction. But case studies also suggest that compulsive gambling appears in people taking a prescription drug that *increases* activity in reward areas—and that the gambling stops when the drug is discontinued (Cilia et al., 2008; Dodd et al., 2005; Ferrara & Stacy, 2008; Tippmann-Piekert et al., 2007).

As noted in the introduction to the science of psychology chapter, correlation does not guarantee causation. Is the brain activity reflected in fMRI scans causing the thoughts and feelings that take place during the scanning process? Possibly, but those thoughts and feelings might themselves be *caused by* activity elsewhere in the brain that affects the areas being scanned. The transcranial magnetic stimulation (TMS) procedures mentioned earlier might help identify causal versus correlational relationships in the brain. TMS is capable of temporarily disrupting neural activity in brain regions identified by fMRI as related to a particular kind of thought or feeling, so perhaps scientists can determine if those thoughts or feelings are temporarily disrupted when TMS occurs. Though TMS appears to be safe (López-Ibor, López-Ibor, & Pastrana, 2008), we don't yet know about its possible long-term negative side effects, so neuroscientists will have to proceed carefully in their use of this technique to explore basic questions about the mind and the brain.

Finding answers to questions like these will require continuing dialogue between those who dismiss fMRI and those who sing its praises. To make this interaction easier, a group of government agencies and private foundations has funded an fMRI Data Center (http://www.fmridc.org/f/fmridc). This facility stores information from fMRI experiments and makes it available to both critics and supporters of fMRI, who can review the research data, conduct their own analyses, and offer their own interpretations. Having access to an ever-growing database such as this will no doubt help scientists get the most out of fMRI technology and help them avoid either overstating or underestimating the meaning of fMRI research.

▶ What conclusions are most reasonable?

When the EEG was invented nearly 100 years ago, scientists had their first glimpse of brain cell activity, as reflected in the "brain waves" traced on a long sheet of paper rolling from the EEG machine (see Figure 4.3). To many of these scientists, EEG must have seemed like a golden gateway to an understanding of the brain and its relationship to behavior and mental processes. EEG has, in fact, helped to advance knowledge of the brain, but it certainly didn't solve all of its mysteries. When all is said and done, the same will probably be true of fMRI. It is an exciting new tool, and it offers previously undreamed-of images of the structure and functioning of the brain, but it is unlikely on its own to explain just how the brain creates our behavior and mental processes. It seems reasonable to conclude, then, that those who question the use of fMRI to study psychological processes are right in calling for a careful analysis of the value of this important high-tech tool.

FIGURE 2.8 ■ MAJOR STRUCTURES OF THE BRAIN

This side view of a section cut down the middle of the brain reveals the forebrain, midbrain, hindbrain, and spinal cord. Many of these subdivisions do not have clear-cut borders because they are all interconnected by fiber tracts. The brain's anatomy reflects its evolution over millions of years. Newer structures (such as the cerebral cortex, which is the outer surface of the forebrain) that handle higher mental functions were built on older ones (such as the medulla) that coordinate heart rate, breathing, and other, more basic functions

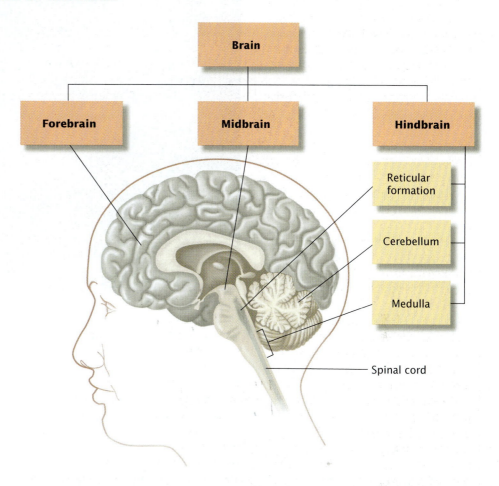

Although the meaning of fMRI data will remain a subject for debate, there is no doubt that brain-scanning techniques in general have opened new frontiers for biological psychology, neuroscience, and medicine. Let's now explore some of the structures highlighted by these techniques, starting with three major subdivisions of the brain: the hindbrain, the midbrain, and the forebrain.

The Hindbrain

Figure 2.8 shows the major structures of the brain. The **hindbrain** lies just inside the skull and is actually a continuation of the spinal cord. Signals coming from the spinal cord reach the hindbrain first. Many vital autonomic functions, such as heart rate, blood pressure, and breathing, are controlled by nuclei in the hindbrain, particularly in an area called the **medulla** (pronounced "meh-DUH-lah").

Weaving throughout the hindbrain and into the midbrain is a meshlike collection of cells called the **reticular formation** (*reticular* means "netlike"). This network is involved in arousal and attention. Cutting off fibers of the reticular system from the rest of the brain would put a person into a permanent coma. Some of the fibers that carry pain signals from the spinal cord connect in the reticular formation and immediately arouse the brain from sleep. Within seconds, the hindbrain causes your heart rate and blood pressure to increase. You are awake and aroused.

Axons from a small nucleus within the reticular formation, the locus coeruleus (pronounced "LOH-kus seh-ROO-lee-us"), branch extensively, making contact with as many as 100,000 other cells. Recent fMRI studies suggest that the **locus coeruleus** (which means "blue spot" in Latin) is involved in directing attention (Minzenberg et al., 2008). Abnormalities in the locus coeruleus have been linked to depression,

hindbrain   The portion of the brain that lies just inside the skull and is a continuation of the spinal cord.

medulla   The area of the hindbrain that controls vital autonomic functions such as heart rate, blood pressure, and breathing.

reticular formation   A collection of cells and fibers in the hindbrain and midbrain that are involved in arousal and attention.

locus coeruleus   A small nucleus in the reticular formation that is involved in directing attention.

A FIELD SOBRIETY TEST ▶

The cerebellum is involved in the balance and coordination required for walking. When the cerebellum's activity is impaired by alcohol, these skills are disrupted, which is why the police ask suspected drunk drivers to walk a straight line.

© Jonathan Kim/Jupiterimages

attention deficit hyperactivity disorder, sleep disorders, and posttraumatic stress disorder (Aston-Jones, 2005).

The **cerebellum** (pronounced "sair-a-BELL-um") is also part of the hindbrain. For a long time its primary function was thought to be control of finely coordinated movements, such as threading a needle. We now know that the cerebellum also allows the eyes to track a moving target accurately (Krauzlis & Lisberger, 1991) and that it may be the storehouse for well-rehearsed movements, such as those associated with dancing, playing a musical instrument, and athletics (McCormick & Thompson, 1984). The cerebellum might also be involved in the learning of these skills (Hazeltine & Ivry, 2002) as well as in more uniquely human tasks such as language and abstract thinking (Andreasen & Pierson, 2008; Bower & Parsons, 2003). Brain-imaging studies have led neuroscientists to believe that the cerebellum is involved in additional activities as well, including memory, emotion, language, impulse control, and other higher-order cognitive processes. For example, the cerebellum is important in timing (Manto, 2008), which plays a vital role in normal speech, integrating moment-to-moment feedback about vocal sounds with a sequence of precise movements of the lips and tongue (Leiner, Leiner, & Dow, 1993). When this process of integration and sequencing is disrupted, stuttering can result. Studies using fMRI have shown that the cerebellum is among the brain structures that show abnormal activity in young people who stutter (Watkins et al., 2008). Surgery that affects the cerebellum sometimes results in a syndrome called *cerebellar mutism*, in which patients become unable to speak for periods ranging from a few days to several years (Gelabert-Gonzalez & Fernandez-Villa, 2001). In short, the cerebellum seems to be involved in both physical and cognitive agility.

Reflexes and feedback systems are important in the hindbrain. For example, if blood pressure drops, heart action reflexively increases to make up for that decrease. If you stand up quickly, your blood pressure can drop so suddenly that you feel lightheaded until the hindbrain reflexively "catches up." You will faint if the hindbrain does not activate the autonomic nervous system to increase your blood pressure.

The Midbrain

A small region called the **midbrain** lies above the hindbrain. If you focus your eyes on another person and then move your head, midbrain circuits allow you to move your eyes smoothly in the direction opposite from your head movement so you never lose focus. When you swing a bat, swat a mosquito, or jump rope, part of the midbrain and its connections to the forebrain allow you to produce those movements smoothly. When

cerebellum The part of the hindbrain that controls finely coordinated movements.

midbrain A small region between the hindbrain and the forebrain that, among other things, helps produce smooth movements.

FIGURE 2.9 ■ MAJOR STRUCTURES OF THE FOREBRAIN

The structures of the forebrain are covered by an outer "bark" known as the cerebral cortex. This diagram shows some of the structures that lie within the forebrain. The amygdala, the hippocampus, and portions of the cerebral cortex are part of the limbic system.

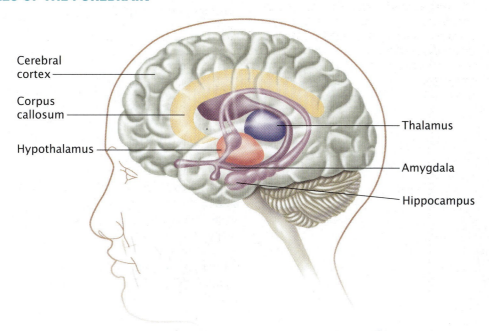

Cerebral cortex

Corpus callosum

Hypothalamus

Thalamus

Amygdala

Hippocampus

a car backfires, causing you to reflexively turn your head and look in the direction of the sound, it is again the midbrain at work. Together, the midbrain and parts of the hindbrain other than the cerebellum are called the *brainstem.*

The Forebrain

In humans, the **forebrain** controls the most complex aspects of behavior and mental life. It completely covers the rest of the brain. The outer surface of the forebrain is called the *cerebral cortex.* Figure 2.9 shows some structures of the forebrain.

Two structures deep within the forebrain, the *hypothalamus* and the *thalamus,* help operate basic drives, emotion, and sensation. The **thalamus** acts as a relay station for pain and sense-organ signals (except smell) from the body to the upper levels of the brain. The thalamus also processes and makes sense of these signals. The **hypothalamus** lies under the thalamus (*hypo* means "under") and helps regulate hunger, thirst, and sex drives. The hypothalamus is well connected to the autonomic nervous system and to other parts of the brain. Damage to parts of the hypothalamus upsets normal appetite, thirst, and sexual behavior.

Can you set an "internal alarm clock" to wake up in the morning at whatever time you want? If you can, it is with the help of a remarkable part of your hypothalamus called the *suprachiasmatic nuclei* that contains the brain's own clock. The suprachiasmatic (pronounced "soo-prak-eye-as-MAT-ik") nuclei operate on approximately a 24-hour cycle, controlling daily biological rhythms such as waking and sleeping as well as cycles of body temperature. Studies of the suprachiasmatic nuclei in animals suggest that having different night or morning energy times is biological and stable throughout a lifetime (Cofer et al., 1992). In humans, such differences may make some of us "morning people" and others "night people."

Other parts of the forebrain, especially the *amygdala* (pronounced "ah-MIG-duh-luh") and the *hippocampus,* help regulate memory and emotion. The **amygdala** links different kinds of sensory information in memory, such as the shape and feel of objects (Murray & Mishkin, 1985). If you close your eyes and pick up an object, your amygdala helps you recognize it. The amygdala also plays a role in fear and other emotions (LeDoux, 1995; Whalen, 1998), connecting emotion to sensation. People who suffer from posttraumatic stress disorder have unusual amygdala activity (Shin, Rauch, & Pitman, 2006). The amygdala may also influence our sensitivity to other people (Corden et al.,

forebrain   The part of the brain responsible for the most complex aspects of behavior and mental life.

thalamus   A forebrain structure that relays messages from most sense organs to higher brain areas.

hypothalamus   A forebrain structure that regulates hunger, thirst, and sex drives and has many connections to and from the autonomic nervous system and other parts of the brain.

amygdala   A forebrain structure that links information from various systems and plays a role in emotions.

2006). PET scans show a strong response of the amygdala when people view angry faces rather than neutral faces (Furmark et al., 2009). The amygdala, hippocampus, and some portions of the cerebral cortex are part of a group of brain structures called the *limbic system*, which is activated when emotions are being generated.

The **hippocampus** also helps you form new memories. In one case, a patient known as R. B. suffered a stroke (an interruption of blood flow to the brain) that damaged only his hippocampus. Although his intelligence remained above average and he could recall old memories, he was almost totally unable to build new ones (Squire, 1986). Damage to the hippocampus within a day of a mildly painful event seems to erase memories of the experience. However, if the damage occurs several days after the event, the memory remains. It seems that memories are not permanently stored in the hippocampus but instead are transferred from there to somewhere else in the brain.

It is not surprising, then, that certain aspects of memory are related to the size and level of activity in the hippocampus (Zimmerman et al., 2008). Studies using MRI have shown, for example, that having a relatively small hippocampus predicts the development of severe memory problems in the elderly (Devanand et al., 2007). Other studies suggest that some people's physical responses to stress includes a reduction in the number of neurons in the hippocampus (Caspi, Sugden, et al., 2003; Frodl et al., 2004). This effect was demonstrated in a study showing that compared to people who were more distant from the World Trade Center on 9/11, those who were exposed to the trauma at close range showed greater reductions in hippocampus volume, even three years after the event (Ganzel et al., 2008). The loss of neurons in this region may help explain the memory problems that appear in some people who have suffered depression or post-traumatic stress disorder (Bremner et al., 2003, 2004).

Disease, too, can affect the hippocampus and thus one's memory. On average, the hippocampus of a person with Alzheimer's disease has been found to be 40 percent smaller than that of a person without the disease. Alzheimer's disease is a major cause of senile dementia, which involves the decay of cognitive capabilities. About 10 percent of people over age 65 and 47 percent of people over 85 suffer from this disease (Kukull et al., 2002; U.S. Department of Health and Human Services, 2001a). The number of cases worldwide is expected to quadruple by 2050 (Ziegler-Graham et al., 2008). The financial cost of Alzheimer's disease is more than $148 billion a year in the United States alone (Alzheimer's Association, 2007), and the worldwide cost in human suffering is incalculable.

The Cerebral Cortex

On the surface of the forebrain is the **cerebral cortex.** The total area of the cerebral cortex is one to two square feet, but it fits into the skull because it is somewhat wrinkled and folded. (You can wad up a T-shirt and fit it into a small bowl in much the same way.) The cerebral cortex is much larger in humans than in most other animals (dolphins are an exception). It analyzes information from all the senses and controls voluntary movement, abstract thinking, and the other most complex aspects of our behavior and mental processes. The cerebral cortex looks somewhat round and has a long groove down the middle creating two halves, called *cerebral hemispheres.* The **corpus callosum,** a massive bundle of more than a million fibers, connects the two hemispheres.

The folds of the cerebral cortex give the surface of the human brain its wrinkled appearance, its ridges and valleys. The ridges are called *gyri* (pronounced "JI-rye"), and the valleys are known as *sulci* (pronounced "SUL-sigh") or *fissures.* As you can see in Figure 2.10, several deep sulci divide the cortex into four areas: the frontal (front), parietal (top), occipital (back), and temporal (side) lobes. The gyri and sulci provide landmarks for describing the structure of the cortex, but the *functions* of the cortex do not follow these boundaries. When divided according to function, the cortex includes areas of sensory cortex, motor cortex, and association cortex. ("In Review: Organization of the Brain" summarizes the major structures and functions of the brain.)

hippocampus A forebrain structure associated with the formation of new memories.

cerebral cortex The outer surface of the forebrain.

corpus callosum A bundle of fibers that connects the left and right cerebral hemispheres.

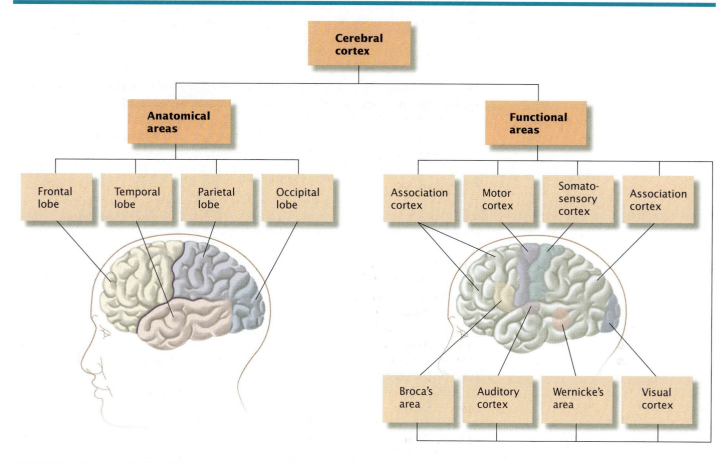

FIGURE 2.10 ■ THE CEREBRAL CORTEX (VIEWED FROM THE LEFT SIDE)

The brain's ridges (gyri) and valleys (sulci) are landmarks that divide the cortex into four lobes: the frontal, parietal, occipital, and temporal. These terms describe where the regions are (the lobes are named for the skull bones that cover them), but the cortex is also divided in terms of function. These functional areas include the motor cortex (which controls movement), sensory cortex (which receives information from various senses), and association cortex (which integrates information). Also labeled are Wernicke's area and Broca's area, two regions that are found only on the left side of the cortex and that are vital to the interpretation and production of speech (Heim, Eickhoff, & Amunts, 2008; Peña et al., 2003; Schnur et al., 2009; Sparing et al., 2008).

sensory cortex The part of the cerebral cortex located in the parietal, occipital, and temporal lobes that receives stimulus information from the skin, eyes, and ears, respectively.

motor cortex The part of the cerebral cortex that controls voluntary movement.

The Sensory and Motor Cortex

The **sensory cortex** lies in the parietal, occipital, and temporal lobes. Different regions of the sensory cortex receive information from different senses. Occipital lobe cells called the *visual cortex* receive visual information. Temporal lobe cells called the *auditory cortex* receive information from the ears. And information from the skin (such as sensations of touch, pain, and temperature) is received by cells in the parietal lobe. These skin-related areas are called the *somatosensory cortex* (*soma* is Greek for "body"). Information about skin sensations from neighboring parts of the body comes to neighboring parts of the somatosensory cortex. It is as if the outline of a tiny person, dangling upside down, determines the location of the information (see Figure 2.11). This pattern is called the *homunculus* (Latin for "little man"). The amount of sensory cortex that responds to particular sensory stimulation can be modified by experience (Schaefer, Heinze, & Rotte, 2008). For example, if a limb is lost, the part of the sensory cortex that had been stimulated by that limb will now be stimulated by other regions of skin. Similarly, practicing a musical instrument will increase the number of sensory neurons that respond to touch (Candia et al., 2005; Hyde et al., 2009); the same thing happens when blind people learn to read Braille with their fingertips (Amedi et al., 2005; Pascual-Leone & Torres, 1993).

In the frontal lobe, specific neurons of the **motor cortex** control voluntary movements in specific parts of the body (Indovina & Sanes, 2001). The arrangement of the motor cortex mirrors that of the somatosensory cortex; the parts of the motor cortex that control hand movement are near parts of the sensory cortex that receive sensory information from the hands.

In Review

ORGANIZATION OF THE BRAIN

MAJOR DIVISION	SOME MAJOR STRUCTURES	SOME MAJOR FUNCTIONS
Hindbrain	Medulla	Regulates breathing, heart rate, and blood pressure
	Reticular formation (also extends into midbrain)	Regulates arousal and attention
	Cerebellum	Controls finely coordinated movements and certain cognitive processes
Midbrain	Various nuclei	Relays sensory signals to forebrain; creates automatic responses to certain stimuli; initiates smooth movement
Forebrain	Thalamus	Interprets and relays sensory information
	Hypothalamus	Regulates hunger, thirst, and sex drives
	Amygdala	Connects sensations and emotions
	Hippocampus	Forms new memories
	Cerebral cortex	Analyzes sensory information; controls voluntary movements, abstract thinking, and other complex cognitive activity
	Corpus callosum	Transfers information between the two cerebral hemispheres

1. The oldest part of the brain is the _____.
2. Cells that operate as the body's twenty-four-hour "time clock" are found in the _____.
3. Memory problems seen in Alzheimer's disease are related to shrinkage of the _____.

Seems easy, doesn't it? You have a map of your body parts in your cerebral cortex, and you activate cells in the hand region of the cortex if you want to move your hand. In fact, the actual process is quite complex. Recall again your sleepy reach for the coffee-pot. To grasp its handle, your cortex must first translate the pot's location into a position relative to your body—to your left or right, for example. Next, the cortex must determine which muscles must be contracted to produce the desired movement toward that exact position. Groups of neurons work together to produce just the right combinations of direction and force in particular muscle groups. Making these determinations involves many interconnected areas of the cortex, and the specific neurons involved can change over time (Gallivan, Cavina-Pratesi, & Culham, 2009; Graziano, 2006). Computer models of neural networks are showing how these complex problem-solving processes might occur (Graziano, Taylor, & Moore, 2002; Krauzlis, 2002).

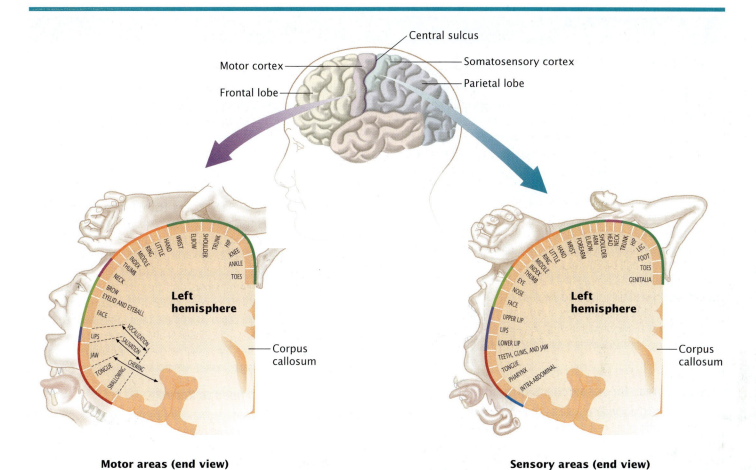

Motor areas (end view)

Sensory areas (end view)

FIGURE 2.11 ■ MOTOR AND SOMATOSENSORY CORTEX

The areas of the cortex that move parts of the body (motor cortex) and receive sensory input from body parts (somatosensory cortex) appear in both hemispheres of the brain. Here we show cross-sections of only those on the left side, looking from the back of the brain toward the front. Areas that control movement of neighboring parts of the body, such as the foot and leg, occupy neighboring parts of the motor cortex. Areas that receive input from neighboring body parts, such as the lips and tongue, are near one another in the sensory cortex. Notice that the size of these areas is uneven; the larger the area devoted to each body part, the larger that body part appears on the "homunculus."

Note: Did you notice the error in this classic drawing? (The figure shows the right side of the body, but the left hand and left side of the face.)

linkages

Where are the brain's language centers? *(a link to Thought, Language, and Intelligence)*

association cortex The parts of the cerebral cortex that integrate sensory and motor information and perform complex cognitive tasks.

Association Cortex

Parts of the cortex that do not directly receive specific sensory information or control specific movements are referred to as **association cortex.** The term *association* describes these areas well, because they receive input from more than one sense or input that combines sensory and motor information. For instance, these areas associate words with images. Association cortex appears in all lobes of the brain and forms a large part of the cerebral cortex in humans. For this reason, damage to association areas can create serious problems in a wide range of mental abilities.

Consider language. Language information comes from the auditory cortex for spoken language or from the visual cortex for written language. Areas of the motor cortex produce speech. Putting it all together in the complex activity known as language involves activity in association cortex. In the 1860s, a French surgeon named Paul Broca described the effects of damage to association cortex in the frontal lobe near motor areas that control face muscles. This part of the cortex is on the left side of the brain and is called *Broca's area* (see Figure 2.10). The hand and arm gestures that accompany speech are also controlled by neurons in this area (Gentilucci & Dalla Volta, 2008). Damage to Broca's area disrupts speech organization, a condition called *Broca's aphasia*. Victims have difficulty speaking, often making errors in grammar. Each word comes out slowly.

Other language problems result from damage to a portion of association cortex described in the 1870s by a Polish neurologist named Carl Wernicke (pronounced "VER-nick-ee"). Figure 2.10 shows that, like Broca's area, *Wernicke's area* is on the left side of the brain, but it is in the temporal lobe, near the area of the sensory cortex that receives information from the ears. Wernicke's area also receives input from the visual cortex and is involved in the interpretation of both speech and written words.

Focus on RESEARCH

The Case of the Disembodied Woman

Neurologist Oliver Sacks described the case of "Christina," a woman who had somehow lost the ability to feel the position of her own body (Sacks, 1985). This case study led to important insights about biological aspects of psychology that could not be studied through controlled experiments. It showed, for example, that the sense known as *kinesthesia* (pronounced "kin-es-THEE-see-uh") not only tells us where our body parts are but also plays an important role in our sense of self.

Christina was a healthy young woman who entered a hospital in preparation for some minor surgery. Before the surgery could be performed, however, she began to have difficulty holding onto objects. Then she had trouble moving. She would rise from bed and flop onto the floor like a rag doll. Christina seemed to have "lost" her body. She felt disembodied, like a ghost. On one occasion, for example, she became annoyed at a visitor for tapping her fingers on a tabletop. But it was Christina's fingers, not the visitor's, that were tapping. Her body was acting on its own, doing things she did not know about.

▶ What was the researcher's question?

Christina could not walk or use her hands and arms. Why was a seemingly normal healthy young woman falling and dropping things?

▶ How did the researcher answer the question?

A psychiatrist at the hospital thought that Christina was suffering from *conversion disorder,* a condition in which psychological problems cause physical disabilities (see the chapter on psychological disorders). Unconvinced, Sacks conducted a careful case study of Christina.

▶ What did the researcher find?

It turned out that the psychiatrist was wrong. Sacks's examinations and tests revealed that Christina had lost all sensory feedback about her joints and muscle tone and the position of her limbs. Christina had suffered a breakdown, or degeneration, of the sensory neurons that normally bring kinesthetic information to her brain. In other words, there was a biological reason that Christina could not walk or control her hands and arms.

▶ What do the results mean?

In his analysis of this case, Sacks noted that the sense we have of our bodies is provided partly through our experience of seeing but also partly through *proprioception* (sensing the self). Christina herself put it this way: "Proprioception is like the eyes of the body, the way the body sees itself. And if it goes, it's like the body's blind." With great effort and determination, Christina was eventually able to regain some of her ability to move about. If she looked intently at her arms and legs, she could coordinate their movement somewhat. She was able to leave the hospital and resume many of her normal activities, but Christina never recovered her sense of self. She still feels like a stranger in her own body.

▶ What do we still need to know?

Notice that Christina's case study did not confirm any hypotheses about kinesthesia in the way an experiment might. It did, however, focus attention on what it feels like to have lost this sense. It also highlighted a rare condition that, though almost unknown when Sacks reported it, has been observed more often in recent years, especially among people taking large doses of vitamin B6, also known as *pyridoxine*. These large doses—or even smaller doses taken over a long period of time—can damage sensory neurons (Dordain & Deffond, 1994). How and why vitamin B6 does such damage still needs to be determined. Are there other causes of this kinesthetic disorder? What treatments might best combat it? These questions remain to be answered by the research of psychologists and other scientists who continue to unravel the mysteries of behavior and mental processes.

Damage to Wernicke's area produces complicated symptoms. It can leave patients with the ability to speak but disrupts the ability to understand the meaning of words or to speak understandably.

Case studies illustrate the different effects of damage to each area (Lapointe, 1990). In response to the request "Tell me what you do with a cigarette," a person with Wernicke's aphasia replied, "This is a segment of a pegment. Soap a cigarette." This speech was fluent but without meaning. In response to the same request, a person with Broca's aphasia replied, "Uh.. uh.. cigarette [pause] smoke it." This speech was meaningful but halting and awkwardly phrased. Surprisingly, when a person with Broca's aphasia sings, the words come easily and correctly. Apparently, words set to music are handled by one part of the brain and spoken words by another (Jeffries, Fritz, & Braun, 2003). Some speech therapists take advantage of this fact through "melodic intonation" therapy, which helps Broca's aphasia patients to gain fluency by speaking in a singsong manner (Lapointe, 1990).

It appears that written language and spoken language require the use of different areas of association cortex. So does language involving specific parts of speech (Shapiro,

LANGUAGE AREAS OF THE BRAIN ▶

Have you ever tried to write notes while you were talking to someone? Like this teacher, you can probably write and talk at the same time because each of these language functions uses different areas of association cortex. However, stop reading for a moment and try writing one word with your left hand and a different word with your right hand. If you had trouble, it is partly because you asked the same language area of your brain to do two things at once.

Learn BY Doing

© Jose Luis Pelaez, Inc./Getty

Corpus callosum

Hemispheres

FIGURE 2.12 ■ THE BRAIN'S LEFT AND RIGHT HEMISPHERES

The brain's two hemispheres are joined by a core bundle of nerve fibers known as the corpus callosum. In this figure the hemispheres are separated so that the corpus callosum can be seen. The two cerebral hemispheres look nearly the same but perform somewhat different tasks. For one thing, the left hemisphere receives sensory input from and controls movement on the right side of the body. The right hemisphere senses and controls the left side of the body.

Moo, & Caramazza, 2006). For example, two women—H. W. and S. J. D—each had a stroke in 1985, causing damage to different language-related parts of their association cortex. Neither woman has difficulty speaking or writing nouns, but both have difficulty with verbs (Caramazza & Hillis, 1991). H. W. can write verbs but cannot speak them. S. J. D. can speak verbs but has difficulty writing them. Interestingly, H. W. has difficulty pronouncing *watch* when it is used as a verb in the sentence "I watch TV," but she speaks the same word easily when it appears as a noun in the sentence "My watch is slow."

Other association areas in the front of the brain, called the *prefrontal cortex*, are involved in the complex processes necessary for the conscious control of thoughts and actions and for understanding our world (Fincham & Anderson, 2006; Koechlin & Hyafil, 2007). For example, these areas of association cortex allow us to understand sarcasm or irony—that is, when someone says one thing but means the opposite. In one study, people with prefrontal cortex damage listened to sarcastic stories such as this: "Joe came to work, and instead of beginning to work, he sat down to rest. His boss noticed his behavior and said, 'Joe, don't work too hard.'" Normal people immediately realized that the boss was being sarcastic, but people with prefrontal brain damage did not (Shamay-Tsoory & Tomer, 2005).

The Divided Brain: Lateralization

A striking suggestion emerged from observations of people with damage to the language centers of the brain. Researchers noticed that damage to specific areas of the left hemisphere interfered with the ability to use or understand language. Damage to those same areas in the right hemisphere usually did not cause such problems. Could it be that the right and left hemispheres of the brain serve different functions?

This idea was not entirely new. It had long been understood that most sensory and motor pathways cross over from one hemisphere to the other as they enter or leave the brain. As a result, the left hemisphere receives information from and controls movements of the right side of the body. The right hemisphere receives input from and controls the left side of the body. Figure 2.12 shows the two hemispheres. The fact that language centers such as Broca's area and Wernicke's area almost always occur on the left side of the brain suggests that each hemisphere might be specialized to perform some functions almost independently of the other hemisphere (Stephan et al., 2003).

FIGURE 2.13 ■ APPARATUS FOR STUDYING SPLIT-BRAIN PATIENTS

When the person stares at the dot on the screen, images briefly presented on one side of the dot go to only one side of the brain. For example, a picture of a spoon presented on the left side of the screen goes to the right side of the brain. The right side of the brain can find the spoon and direct the left hand to touch it. However, the language areas on the left side of the brain did not see the spoon, so the person is unable to say what it is.

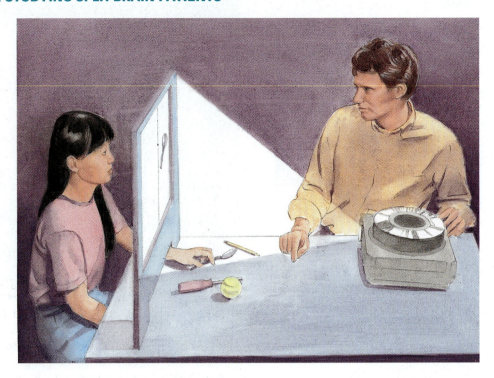

In the late 1800s there was great interest in the idea that the hemispheres might be specialized, but no techniques were available for testing it. Renewed interest grew out of studies during the 1960s by Roger Sperry, Michael Gazzaniga, and their colleagues.

Split-Brain Studies   Sperry studied *split-brain* patients—people who had undergone surgery in an attempt to control the severe seizures of epilepsy. Before the surgery, their seizures began in one hemisphere and then spread throughout the brain. As a last resort, surgeons isolated the two hemispheres from each other by cutting the corpus callosum, which had connected them.

After the surgery, researchers used a special device like the one shown in Figure 2.13 to present visual images to only one side of these patients' split brains. They found that cutting the tie between the hemispheres had dramatically changed the way these people thought about and dealt with the world. For example, when the image of a spoon was presented to the left, language-oriented, side of patient N. G.'s split brain, she could say what the spoon was. But when the spoon was presented to the right side of her brain, she could not describe the spoon in words. She still knew what the object was, because she could pick it out from a group of objects by feeling its shape with her left hand (controlled by the right hemisphere). When asked what she had just grasped, she replied, "A pencil." The right hemisphere recognized the object, but the patient could not say what it was because the left (language) half of her brain did not see or feel it (Sperry, 1968).

Although the right hemisphere has no control over spoken language in split-brain patients, it does have important abilities related to nonspoken language. For example, a split-brain patient's right hemisphere can guide the left hand in spelling out words with Scrabble tiles (Gazzaniga & LeDoux, 1978). Thanks to this finding, researchers concluded that split-brain patients have self-awareness and normal learning abilities in their right hemispheres. In addition, these patients' right hemispheres did better than their left hemispheres at tasks involving spatial relationships (especially drawing three-dimensional shapes) and recognizing human faces.

Having these two somewhat specialized hemispheres allows the normal brain to perform some tasks more efficiently, particularly difficult ones. But the differences between the hemispheres should not be exaggerated. Remember, the corpus callosum usually integrates the functions of the "two brains" (Rueckert et al., 1999). As a result, the hemispheres work closely together, each making up well for whatever lack of ability the other may have (Banich, 2004; Banich & Heller, 1998; Staudt et al., 2001).

Plasticity in the Central Nervous System

The central nervous system has a remarkable property called **neural plasticity** (also known as *neuroplasticity* or simply *plasticity*), which is the ability to strengthen neural connections at synapses as well as to establish new connections. Plasticity depends partly on neurons and partly on glial cells (Lee & Silva, 2009), and it provides the basis for the learning and memory processes described in other chapters. The connections between brain cells are not only highly changeable but can change in a fraction of a second (Bikbaev & Manahan-Vaughan, 2008; Stettler et al., 2006). Plasticity occurs throughout the central nervous system. Even the simplest reflex in the spinal cord can be modified by experience (Wolpaw & Chen, 2006). In the brain, plasticity is the basis of our ability to form new memories and learn new things. For example, more cells in the brain's motor cortex become involved in controlling hand movements in people who have learned to play a musical instrument. The process can be seen in brain-imaging studies; as nonmusicians get better at making rhythmic finger movements, the amount of motor cortex devoted to this task increases (Munte, Altenmuller, & Jancke, 2002). Even more amazing is that merely *imagining* practicing these movements causes changes in the motor cortex (Pascual-Leone, 2001). Athletes have long engaged in exercises in which they visualize skilled sports movements; brain-imaging research reveals that this "mental practice" can change the brain. However, the athlete must already be skilled at a task in order to visualize it properly. When practiced high jumpers visualize high jumping, fMRI reveals that their motor cortex is activated, but when novices visualize high jumping, their visual cortex is activated, as if they are seeing the movements from the outside rather than experiencing it from the inside (Olsson et al., 2008).

Repairing Brain Damage   There are limits to plasticity, though, especially when it comes to repairing damage in the brain and spinal cord. Unlike the skin or the liver, the adult central nervous system does not automatically replace damaged cells. As a result, most victims of severe stroke, Parkinson's disease, Alzheimer's disease, or spinal cord injury are permanently disabled in some way. Nevertheless, scientists are searching for ways to help a damaged central nervous system heal some of its own wounds.

One approach has been to transplant, or graft, tissue from the still-developing brain of a fetus into the brain of an adult animal. If the receiving animal does not reject it, the graft sends axons out into the brain and makes some functional connections. This treatment has reversed animals' learning difficulties, movement disorders, and other results of brain damage (Noble, 2000). The technique has also been used to treat a small number of people with Parkinson's disease—a disorder characterized by tremors, rigidity of the arms and legs, and poor balance (Lindvall & Hagell, 2001). The initial results have been encouraging (Mendez et al., 2005, 2008). Some patients showed improvement for several years, though improvement faded for others, and some patients suffered serious side effects (Freed et al., 2001). Brain tissue transplants in humans are controversial because they require the use of tissue from aborted fetuses. As an alternative, some scientists have tried transplanting neural tissue from another species, such as pigs, into humans (Drucker-Colin & Verdugo-Diaz, 2004). Russian physicians have even tried transplanting neural tissue from fruit flies into the brains of Parkinson's patients. The results were beneficial, and there were no immediate side effects (Saveliev et al., 1997), but the patients' bodies eventually rejected the fruit fly neurons (Korochkin, 2000).

The most promising source for new neurons now appears to be an individual's own tissues, because these cells would not be rejected. This is a revolutionary idea, because it was long believed that once humans reached adulthood, the cells of the

neural plasticity   A property of the central nervous system that has the ability to strengthen neural connections at synapses as well as to establish new connections.

central nervous system stopped dividing, leaving each of us with a fixed set of neurons (Rakic, 2002). Then came research showing that cell division *does* take place in the adult central nervous systems of humans, nonhuman primates, and other animals (Blakeslee, 2000; Eriksson et al., 1998; Gould et al., 1999; Steindler & Pincus, 2002). It turns out that the adult brain contains *neural stem cells,* a special kind of glial cells that are capable of dividing to form new tissue, including new neurons (Cheng, Tavazoie, & Doetsch, 2005; Sanai et al., 2004). The process of creating new neurons is called *neurogenesis.*

This discovery has created both excitement and controversy. There is excitement because stem cells raise hope that damaged tissue may someday be replaced by cells created from a person's own body, but there is controversy because stem cells are linked in many people's minds with the cloning of whole individuals. If brain cells can indeed be grown from cells found in bone marrow, the lining of the nose, or other sites, the benefits in treating brain disorders would be substantial (Murrell et al., 2005; Park et al., 2008; Yu et al., 2007). Patients suffering from spinal cord injuries as well as from Parkinson's disease and Alzheimer's disease might someday be cured by treatments that replace damaged or dying neurons with new ones grown from the patients' own stem cells (Chen, Magavi, & Macklis, 2004; Cowan et al., 2005; Horner & Gage, 2002; Mezey et al., 2003; Redmond et al., 2007; Takahashi & Yamanaka, 2006; Teng et al., 2002; Wernig et al., 2008; Zhao et al., 2003).

Generating new neurons is only half the battle, however. The new cells' axons and dendrites would have to reestablish all the synaptic connections that had been lost to damage or disease. Unfortunately, this process is hampered in the central nervous system by glial cells that actively suppress new connections between newly sprouted axons and other neurons (Olson, 1997). Several central nervous system proteins, including one aptly named *Nogo,* have the same suppressant effect.

Despite these challenges, scientists are reporting exciting results in their efforts to promote healing in damaged brains and spinal cords. They have found, for example, that blocking the action of Nogo in mice and rats with spinal cord injuries allows surviving neurons to make new axonal connections and repair the damage (Cummings et al., 2005; Kastin & Pan, 2005). Other research with animals has shown that both spontaneous recovery and the effectiveness of brain-tissue transplants can be greatly enhanced by naturally occurring proteins called *growth factors,* which promote the survival of neurons (Deshpande et al., 2006; Hoglinger et al., 2001). One of these proteins is called *nerve growth factor.* Another, called *glial cell line–derived neurotrophic factor,* or *GDNF,* actually causes neurons to produce the neurotransmitter needed to reverse the effects of Parkinson's disease (Kordower et al., 2000; Theofilopoulos et al., 2001). The best way to increase the amount of these growth factors in humans is still being studied. In one case, nerve growth factor was put directly into the brain of a patient with Alzheimer's disease (Seiger et al., 1993). The early results seemed encouraging, but the continuous infusion of the protein into the brain caused unacceptable side effects (Nabeshima & Yamada, 2000). Another way to deliver growth factors is through gene therapy, in which a gene for the desired growth factor is inserted into a patient's neurons (Bomze et al., 2001; Condic, 2001; Dass, Olanow, & Kordower, 2006; Tuszynski et al., 2002). Early results from the use of this high-tech treatment are encouraging (Tuszynski et al., 2005).

In the meantime, there are things that patients themselves can do to promote the neural plasticity needed to restore lost central nervous system functions. Special mental and physical exercise programs appear useful in restructuring communication in the brains of stroke victims and spinal cord injury patients, thus reversing some forms of paralysis and improving some sensory and cognitive abilities (Blakeslee, 2001; Liepert et al., 2000; Robertson & Murre, 1999; Taub, 2004). Christopher Reeve was an inspiring case in point. After his spinal cord injury, Reeve was told he would never again be able to move or feel his body. He refused to accept this gloomy prediction, and after years of devoted adherence to an exercise-oriented rehabilitation program, he regained some movement and in the years before his death was able to feel sensations from much of his body (Blakeslee, 2001).

© AP Photo

HE WAS A SUPER MAN   ▲

After a 1995 riding accident left actor/director Christopher Reeve paralyzed below his shoulders, he embarked on a long, intense rehabilitation regimen. He received electrical stimulation to maintain muscle tone and was strapped to a tilting table to maintain bone density. He was suspended in a harness over a treadmill while his legs were put through walking movements. In 1999, he began using a functional electrical stimulation bicycle, which sends computer-controlled electrical impulses to his legs, causing the muscles to contract and move the bike's pedals. By the end of 2002, he could move his fingers, right wrist, and upper legs. In a swimming pool, he could move his knees and upper arms. By the time of his death in 2004, he had also regained feeling in about 70 percent of his body. Research is continuing on other exercise programs to promote recovery from spinal cord injury (Dunlop, 2008; Raineteau, 2008).

linkages

How do our brains change over a lifetime? *(a link to Human Development)*

At birth

Six years old

Fourteen years old

FIGURE 2.14 ■ CHANGES IN NEURONS OF THE CEREBRAL CORTEX DURING DEVELOPMENT

During childhood, the brain overproduces neural connections, establishes the usefulness of certain connections, and then "prunes" the extra connections. Overproduction of synapses, especially in the frontal cortex, may be essential for infants to develop certain intellectual abilities. The changes that occur in the brain during adolescence are particularly important, as this is when many psychiatric disorders first appear (Paus, Keshavan, & Giedd, 2008). Adolescence is also a time of adjusting to and (sometimes) resisting negative peer influences. Research suggests that functional connectivity among brain regions in early adolescence is correlated with resisting such influences (Grosbras et al., 2007). *Source*: Conel (1939/1967).

Linkages

Human Development and the Changing Brain

Fortunately, most of the changes that take place in the brain are not the kind associated with damage and disease. How does the human brain change as we develop throughout our lives? Researchers are using PET and fMRI scans to begin to answer that question. For example, they have found that association areas of the cerebral cortex develop later than the sensory and motor cortexes do (Casey, Galvan, & Hare, 2005). There are also some interesting correlations between changes in neural activity and the behavior of newborns and infants. Among newborns, scans show that activity is relatively high in the thalamus but low in a portion of the forebrain related to smooth movement. This finding may be related to the way newborns move. They make random, sweeping movements of the arms and legs—much like patients with Huntington's disease, who have a hyperactive thalamus and a withering of the part of the forebrain that controls smooth movement (Chugani & Phelps, 1986). During the second and third months after birth, activity increases in many regions of the cortex. This change is correlated with the loss of certain reflexes, such as the grasping reflex. At eight or nine months of age, infants show increased frontal cortex activity, which correlates with the apparent beginnings of cognitive activity (Chugani & Phelps, 1986). The brain continues to mature even through adolescence, showing evidence of ever-more-efficient neural communication in its major fiber tracts (Gogtay et al., 2004; Paus et al., 1999; Thompson et al., 2000).

Most of these changes reflect plasticity—changes in axons and synapses—not the appearance of new cells. After birth, the number of dendrites and synapses increases. Although different areas of the cortex sprout at different rates, the number of synapses can increase tenfold in the first year after birth (Huttenlocher, 1990). In fact, by the time children are six or seven years old, their brains have more dendrites than those of adults, and they use twice as much energy. In early adolescence, the number of dendrites and neural connections actually drops, so the adult level is reached by about the age of fourteen. During childhood, the brain overproduces neural connections and then "prunes" the extra connections (Sowell et al., 2001). Figure 2.14 shows that as we grow, we develop more brainpower with less brain (Sowell et al., 2003).

As already mentioned, the brain's plasticity allows it to restructure itself to form new connections throughout life (Hua & Smith, 2004; Kozorovitskiy et al., 2005). Genes apparently determine the basic pattern of growth and the major lines of connections. However, the details of the connections depend on experience, including how stimulating and interesting the environment is. For example, researchers have compared the brains of rats raised individually with only a boring view of their cages to the brains of rats raised with toys and playmates. The cerebral cortex of the rats from the enriched environment had more and longer dendrites as well as more synapses than did the cortex of animals raised alone in bare cages (Klintsova & Greenough, 1999). Furthermore, the number of synapses increased when old animals who had been living in boring cages were moved to an enriched environment. Such changes in the brain following increased environmental stimulation may help explain why the maze-learning ability of genetically "maze-dull" rats raised in stimulating cages can equal that of genetically "maze-bright" animals.

Researchers have not yet determined whether an enriched environment stimulates the development of new connections or slows down normal pruning. Also not known is whether animals that are moved from a stimulating environment to a boring one will lose synaptic connections. If existing findings apply to humans, however, they have implications for how we raise children and treat the elderly. It is surely the case that within the limits set by genetics, interactions with the world mold the brain itself (Chang & Merzenich, 2003; Holtmaat et al., 2006).

The Chemistry of Behavior: Neurotransmitters

▶ *How do biochemicals affect my mood?*

We have already seen that neurons in the nervous system communicate with each other through chemical messengers called neurotransmitters. The neurotransmitters they use can differ from one set of nerve cells to another. A group of neurons that communicate using the same neurotransmitter is called a *neurotransmitter system*. Let's explore where neurotransmitters operate in the brain and how they affect behavior.

Three Classes of Neurotransmitters

The process of chemical neurotransmission was first demonstrated in frogs by Otto Loewi in 1921. Since then, about 100 neurotransmitters have been identified, but they fall into three main classes: *small molecules, peptides,* and *gases.* Let's consider some examples of each.

Small Molecules   The most important of the small-molecule chemicals that act as neurotransmitters are acetylcholine, norepinephrine, serotonin, dopamine, GABA, and glutamate. *Acetylcholine* (pronounced "uh-see-tull-KOE-leen") was the first to be identified as a neurotransmitter. Among the many neurons that communicate using acetylcholine are those active in controlling movement of the body, in making memories, and in slowing the heartbeat and activating the digestive system. No wonder, then, that disruption of acetylcholine systems can result in a wide variety of problems, including the loss of memory and (eventually) of all mental powers that is seen in Alzheimer's disease.

Systems of neurons that use *norepinephrine* (pronounced "nor-eppa-NEF-rin") affect arousal, wakefulness, learning, and mood. This neurotransmitter is involved when your nervous system prepares you to fight or to run away from a threat. Changes in norepinephrine systems have also been implicated in depression.

The neurotransmitter *serotonin* (pronounced "sair-oh-TOE-nin") is similar to norepinephrine in that it affects both sleep and mood. Serotonin may also be involved in the appearance of aggressive and impulsive behaviors. Unlike norepinephrine, though, the amount of serotonin in your brain can be affected by what you eat. For example, eating carbohydrates can increase serotonin, and the increase in serotonin normally reduces the desire for carbohydrates. Some researchers suspect that malfunctions in serotonin systems can result in the mood and appetite problems seen in some types of obesity, premenstrual tension, and depression, including disorders in which depressed mood, suicidal tendencies, and impulsivity appear together (Bach-Mizrachi et al., 2006; Oquendo & Mann, 2000). Antidepressant medications such as Prozac, Zoloft, and Paxil appear to relieve some of the symptoms of depression by acting on serotonin systems to maintain proper levels of this neurotransmitter.

Dopamine (pronounced "DOPE-uh-meen") is a neurotransmitter that is important for movement. Malfunctions of dopamine systems contribute to movement disorders such as Parkinson's disease and the shakiness experienced by people who have it. Parkinson's has been treated with some success using drugs that enable neurons to make more dopamine and by implanting dopamine-using neurons (Chase, 1998; Mendez et al., 2008). Permanently implanting an electrode that stimulates neurons in the brain's dopamine-influenced motor system offers an even more effective treatment but also carries a risk of surgical complications (Weaver et al., 2009). Other dopamine systems are involved in the experiencing of reward, or pleasure, which is vital in shaping and motivating behavior (Spanagel & Weiss, 1999). Animals will work very hard to receive a direct dose of dopamine to certain parts of the brain. These dopamine systems play a role in the rewarding properties of many drugs, including cocaine (Ciccocioppo, Sanna, & Weiss, 2001; Hyman, Malenka, & Nestler, 2006). Certain dopamine systems are also suspected to be partly responsible for the perceptual, emotional, and thought

PROMOTING RESEARCH ON PARKINSON'S DISEASE ▲

Actor Michael J. Fox suffers from Parkinson's disease, a condition related to malfunctioning of dopamine systems in the brain. He founded the Michael J. Fox Foundation for Parkinson's Research (http://www.michaeljfox.org/) to fund more research on treating, curing, and perhaps even preventing, Parkinson's disease.

© WireImage/Getty Images

disturbances associated with schizophrenia, a severe mental disorder (Marenco & Weinberger, 2000).

GABA stands for gamma-amino butyric acid. Unlike most neurotransmitters, which excite neurons to fire action potentials, GABA *reduces* the likelihood that neurons will fire. In fact, it is the main neurotransmitter for slowing, or inhibiting, the brain's activity. When you fall asleep, neurons that use GABA deserve part of the credit. Drugs that cause reduced neural activity often do so by amplifying the "braking" action of GABA. For example, alcohol's effect on GABA systems is partly responsible for the impairments in thinking, judgment, and motor skills that occur when people drink too much. Malfunctions of GABA systems contribute to severe anxiety and to *Huntington's disease,* an inherited disorder that causes its victims to suffer uncontrollable movement of the arms and legs along with a progressive loss of thinking abilities. Drugs that interfere with GABA's inhibitory effects produce intense repetitive electrical discharges, known as *seizures.* Researchers suspect that impaired GABA systems contribute to *epilepsy,* another brain disorder associated with seizures and convulsive movements. Repeated or sustained seizures can result in permanent brain damage. Drug treatments can reduce seizure frequency and severity, but completely effective drugs are not yet available.

Glutamate (pronounced "GLOO-tuh-mate") is used by more neurons than any other neurotransmitter, and it also helps glial cells provide energy for neurons (Rouach et al., 2008). Glutamate is particularly important because it helps the brain strengthen its synaptic connections, allowing messages to more easily cross the gap between neurons. This strengthening process is necessary for normal development and may be at the root of learning and memory (Newpher & Ehlers, 2008). Yet overactivity of glutamate synapses can cause neurons to die. This overactivity is the main cause of the brain damage that occurs when oxygen is cut off from neurons during a stroke. Glutamate can "excite neurons to death." Blocking glutamate receptors immediately after a brain trauma can prevent permanent brain damage (Colak et al., 2003). Glutamate may also contribute to the loss of brain cells that occurs in Alzheimer's disease (Cha et al., 2001).

Peptides Hundreds of chemicals called *peptides* have been found to act as neurotransmitters. The first of these, called *endorphins,* were discovered in the 1970s, when scientists were studying *opiates* such as morphine and heroin. Derived from poppy flowers, opiates can relieve pain, produce intense feelings of happiness, and, in high doses, bring on sleep. After marking morphine with a radioactive agent, researchers identified places where it became concentrated in the brain. They found that the opiates bound to receptors that had not been associated with any previously identified neurotransmitter. It is unlikely that the brain had developed opiate receptors just in case a person might want to use morphine or heroin, so researchers reasoned that the body must contain a substance that is similar to opiates. This hypothesis led to the search for a naturally occurring, or *endogenous,* morphine. (*Endogenous* is pronounced "en-DODGE-uh-niss"; *endorphin* is a contraction of the words *endogenous* and *morphine.*) As it turns out, there are many natural opiate-like compounds, and new ones are still being discovered. So the term *endorphin* refers to any neurotransmitter that can bind to the same receptors stimulated by opiates. Endorphins are used by neurons in several parts of the brain, including neuronal pathways that modify pain signals to the brain.

Gases Ideas about what substances can act as neurotransmitters were radically altered following the discovery that these chemicals include *nitric oxide* and *carbon monoxide*—two toxic gases that contribute to air pollution (Boehning & Snyder, 2003). When nitric oxide or carbon monoxide is released by a neuron, it spreads to nearby neurons, sending a signal that affects chemical reactions inside those neurons instead of binding to receptors on their surfaces. Nitric oxide is not stored in vesicles, as most other neurotransmitters are; it can be released from any part of the neuron. Nitric oxide appears to be one of the neurotransmitters responsible for such diverse functions as penile erection and the formation of memories—not at the same site, obviously.

CLASSES OF NEUROTRANSMITTERS

NEUROTRANSMITTER CLASS	NORMAL FUNCTION	DISORDER ASSOCIATED WITH MALFUNCTION
Small Molecules		
Acetylcholine	Memory, movement	Alzheimer's disease
Norepinephrine	Mood, sleep, learning	Depression
Serotonin	Mood, appetite, impulsivity	Depression
Dopamine	Movement, reward	Parkinson's disease, schizophrenia
GABA	Sleep, movement	Anxiety, Huntington's disease, epilepsy
Glutamate	Memory	Damage after stroke
Peptides		
Endorphins	Pain control	No established disorder
Gases		
Nitric oxide	Memory	No established disorder

1. *The main neurotransmitter for slowing, or inhibiting, brain activity is _____.*
2. *A group of neurons that use the same neurotransmitter is called a _____.*
3. *Which neurotransmitter's activity causes brain damage during a stroke?*

In summary, neurotransmitters acting throughout the body link our biochemistry with every aspect of our behavior and mental processes. In the chapter on sensation and perception, for example, we describe some of the neurotransmitters that help convey pain messages. In the consciousness chapter, we consider how neurotransmitters are affected by alcohol and illegal drugs. In the chapter on psychological disorders, we discuss the role that neurotransmitters play in schizophrenia and depression, and in the chapter on the treatment of psychological disorders, we explore ways that prescription drugs act on neurotransmitters to alleviate the symptoms of those disorders. ("In Review: Classes of Neurotransmitters" lists the most important of these neurotransmitters and the consequences of malfunctioning neurotransmitter systems.)

The Endocrine System: Coordinating the Internal World

▶ *How can my hormones help me in a crisis?*

endocrine system Cells that form organs called glands and that communicate with one another by secreting hormones.

glands Organs that secrete hormones into the bloodstream.

hormones Chemicals secreted by glands into the bloodstream, allowing stimulation of cells that are not directly connected.

Neurons are not the only cells that use chemicals to communicate with one another in ways that affect behavior and mental processes. Another kind of cell with this ability is found in the **endocrine system** (pronounced "EN-doh-krin"). Operating on orders from the brain, the endocrine system regulates growth, energy consumption, and sexual behavior, and it readies the body for action. The cells of the endocrine organs, or **glands,** communicate by secreting chemicals, much as neurons do. Figure 2.15 shows some major glands of the endocrine system. The chemicals that these glands secrete are called **hormones.**

FIGURE 2.15 ■ SOME MAJOR GLANDS OF THE ENDOCRINE SYSTEM

Each of the glands shown releases its hormones into the bloodstream. Even the hypothalamus, a part of the brain, regulates the nearby pituitary gland by secreting hormones.

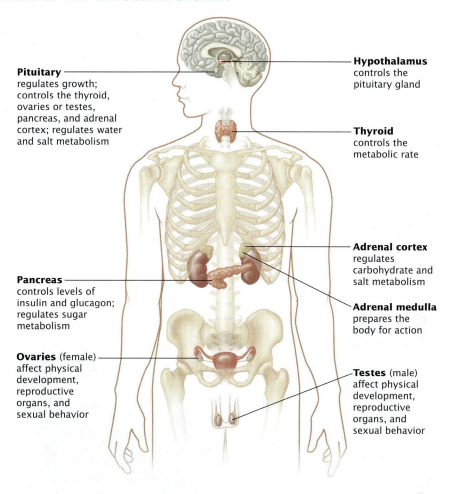

Pituitary regulates growth; controls the thyroid, ovaries or testes, pancreas, and adrenal cortex; regulates water and salt metabolism

Hypothalamus controls the pituitary gland

Thyroid controls the metabolic rate

Adrenal cortex regulates carbohydrate and salt metabolism

Pancreas controls levels of insulin and glucagon; regulates sugar metabolism

Adrenal medulla prepares the body for action

Ovaries (female) affect physical development, reproductive organs, and sexual behavior

Testes (male) affect physical development, reproductive organs, and sexual behavior

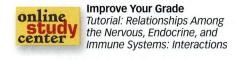

Improve Your Grade
Tutorial: Relationships Among the Nervous, Endocrine, and Immune Systems: Interactions

Hormones from endocrine organs are similar to neurotransmitters. In fact, many such chemicals, including norepinephrine and the endorphins, act both as hormones and as neurotransmitters. However, whereas neurons secrete neurotransmitters into synapses, endocrine organs release their chemicals into the bloodstream, which carries them throughout the body. In this way, endocrine glands can stimulate cells with which they have no direct connection. But not all cells receive the hormonal message. Hormones, like neurotransmitters, can influence only those cells with receptors capable of receiving them. Organs whose cells have receptors for a particular hormone are called *target organs*.

Each hormone acts on many target organs, producing coordinated effects throughout the body. For example, when a woman's ovaries secrete the sex hormone *estrogen*, it activates her reproductive system, causing the uterus to grow in preparation for nurturing an embryo. It enlarges the breasts to prepare them for nursing. It stimulates the brain to increase interest in sexual activity. And it stimulates the pituitary gland to release another hormone that causes a mature egg to be released by the ovary for fertilization. In males, sex organs called *testes* secrete *testosterone*, one of several sex hormones known as *androgens*. Androgens stimulate the maturation of sperm, increase a male's motivation for sexual activity, and increase his aggressiveness (Romeo, Richardson, & Sisk, 2002).

The brain, as a kind of "boss," has ultimate control over the secretion of hormones. The hypothalamus controls the pituitary gland, which in turn controls endocrine organs in the body. The brain is also a target organ for most hormones. In short, the endocrine system typically involves the brain, the pituitary gland, the endocrine organ, and the target organs (which include the brain). Each part in the system uses hormones to signal the next (Dubrovsky, 2005).

The secretion of each hormone is increased or decreased by other hormones. Consider stress-hormone systems, for example. When the brain interprets a situation as threatening, it stimulates the pituitary gland to release *adrenocorticotropic hormone (ACTH)*, which causes the adrenal glands to release the hormone *cortisol* into the bloodstream. Cortisol, in turn, acts on cells throughout the body, including the brain. One effect of cortisol is to activate the emotion-related limbic system, making it more likely that you will remember stressful or traumatic events. The combined effects of the adrenal hormones and the activation of the sympathetic nervous system result in the **fight-or-flight response.** The many components of this response prepare us for action in response to danger or other stress. The heart beats faster, the liver releases glucose into the bloodstream, fuels are mobilized from fat stores, and the body as a whole is placed in a state of high arousal. Without the endocrine system and the effects of its hormones on the brain, your life would not only be much less emotional but you also would be less able to escape or avoid threatening situations.

fight-or-flight response   Physical reactions triggered by the sympathetic nervous system that prepare the body to fight or to run from a threatening situation.

ACTIVE REVIEW   ▶ Chapter 2

Biology *and* Behavior

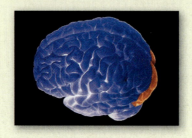

As noted in the introductory chapter, all of psychology's subfields are related to one another. Our discussion of developmental changes in the brain illustrates just one way that the topic of this chapter, biology and behavior, is linked to the subfield of developmental psychology, which is described in the chapter on human development. The Linkages diagram shows ties to two other subfields, and there are many more ties throughout the book. Looking for linkages among subfields will help you see how they all fit together and help you better appreciate the big picture that is psychology.

linkages

Does the brain shut down when we sleep? *(ans. on p. 145)*

Chapter 4
Consciousness

How do our brains change over a lifetime? *(ans. on p. 73)*

Chapter 9
Human Development

How do drugs help people who suffer from schizophrenia? *(ans. on p. 540)*

Chapter 13
Treatment of Psychological Disorders

SUMMARY ▶

Biological psychology focuses on the biological aspects of our being, which provide the physical basis for behavior and mental processes. Included among these aspects is the *nervous system,* which is composed of billions of cells that allow humans and other organisms to gain information about what is going on inside and outside the body and to respond appropriately.

Cells of the Nervous System

▶ *What are neurons, and what do they do?*

Much of our understanding of the biological aspects of psychology has stemmed from research on animal and human nervous systems at levels ranging from single cells to complex organizations of cells, including the brain. The fundamental units of the nervous system are cells called **neurons** and **glial cells.** Neurons are especially good at receiving signals from and transmitting signals to other neurons. Neurons have cell bodies and two types of fibers, called **axons** and **dendrites.** Axons usually carry signals away from the cell body, whereas dendrites usually carry signals to the cell body.

Neurons can transmit signals because of the structure of the axons and dendrites and the **synapses,** or gaps, between cells. A neuron can transmit, or fire, an **action potential** from one end of its axon to the other. The speed of the action potential is fastest in neurons covered in myelin. The very brief rest between firings is called the **refractory period.**

When an action potential reaches the end of an axon, the axon releases a chemical called a **neurotransmitter.** This chemical crosses the synapse and interacts with the postsynaptic cell at receptors that make the postsynaptic cell either more likely or less likely to fire its own action potential. Because the fibers of neurons have many branches, each neuron can interact with thousands of other neurons. Each neuron constantly integrates signals received at its many synapses; the result of this integration determines how often the neuron fires an action potential.

The cells of the nervous system are organized into two main parts: the **central nervous system (CNS)** and the **peripheral nervous system.**

The Peripheral Nervous System: Keeping in Touch with the World

▶ *How do sights and sounds reach my brain?*

The peripheral nervous system has two components. The first is the **somatic nervous system,** which transmits information from the senses to the CNS and carries signals from the CNS to muscles that move the skeleton. It performs these tasks through sensory systems that receive information from the environment and motor systems that influence the actions of muscles and other organs. The second component of the peripheral nervous system is the **autonomic nervous system,** whose subsystems, the **sympathetic nervous system** and the **parasympathetic nervous system,** carry messages back and forth between the CNS and the heart, lungs, and other organs and glands.

The Central Nervous System: Making Sense of the World

▶ *How is my brain "wired"?*

The CNS is laid out in interconnected groups of neuron cell bodies called **nuclei,** whose collections of axons travel together in **fiber tracts,** or pathways. The **spinal cord** receives information from the peripheral senses and sends it to the brain; it also relays messages from the brain to the rest of the body. In addition, cells of the spinal cord can direct simple behaviors called **reflexes** without instructions from the brain. The brain's major subdivisions are the **hindbrain,** the **midbrain,** and the **forebrain.** The hindbrain includes the **medulla** and the **cerebellum.** The **reticular formation** is found in both the hindbrain and the midbrain.

The forebrain is the largest and most highly developed part of the brain. Its structures include the **thalamus** and the **hypothalamus** as well as the **hippocampus** and the **amygdala,** which form part of the limbic system. The suprachiasmatic nuclei, a part of the hypothalamus, maintain a clock that determines biological rhythms. The outer surface of the cerebral hemispheres is called the **cerebral cortex;** it is responsible for many of the higher functions of the brain, including speech and reasoning. The functional areas of the cortex consist of the **sensory cortex,** the **motor cortex,** and the **association cortex.**

The right and left hemispheres of the cerebral cortex are specialized to some degree in their functions. In most people, the left hemisphere is more active in language and logical tasks and the right hemisphere in spatial tasks. The hemispheres are connected through the **corpus callosum,** allowing them to operate in a coordinated fashion.

The brain's *neural plasticity,* the ability to strengthen neural connections at its synapses as well as to establish new synapses, forms the basis for learning and memory. Scientists are studying ways to increase plasticity and stimulate neurogenesis—the formation of new neurons—following brain damage.

A child's growing and changing intellectual abilities are based on changing synaptic connections in the brain, not on an increase in the number of brain cells. The brain produces many more synaptic connections than it needs, pruning extra connections as experience strengthens useful connections. The ability to form new synapses continues even into old age.

The Chemistry of Behavior: Neurotransmitters

▶ *How do biochemicals affect my mood?*

Neurons that use the same neurotransmitter form a neurotransmitter system. There are three types of neurotransmitters: small molecules, peptides, and gases. Small molecules include acetylcholine, norepinephrine, serotonin, dopamine, GABA, and glutamate. Acetylcholine systems in the brain influence memory processes and movement. Norepinephrine is involved in arousal, mood, and learning. Serotonin is active in systems regulating mood and appetite. Dopamine systems are involved in movement and reward; Parkinson's disease and schizophrenia involve disturbances in dopamine systems. GABA is an inhibitory neurotransmitter involved in anxiety and epilepsy. Glutamate is the most common excitatory neurotransmitter; it is involved in learning and memory. In excess, though, it may cause neuronal death. Peptide neurotransmitters include the endorphins, which act like morphine by affecting pain pathways. Nitric oxide and carbon monoxide are two gases that can act as neurotransmitters.

The Endocrine System: Coordinating the Internal World

▶ *How can my hormones help me in a crisis?*

Like nervous system cells, the cells of the **endocrine system** communicate by releasing a chemical that signals other cells. However, the chemicals released by endocrine organs, or **glands,** are called **hormones** and are carried by the bloodstream to remote target organs. The brain is the main controller: Through the hypothalamus, it controls the pituitary gland, which in turn controls endocrine organs in the body. The brain is also a target organ for most endocrine secretions. The target organs often produce a coordinated response to hormonal stimulation. One example is the **fight-or-flight response,** which is set off by adrenal hormones that prepare for action in times of stress.

Put It in Writing

Suppose you are asked to help a young mother choose the infant care center that will be most likely to stimulate her one-year-old son's brain development. Write a page about what biological psychology research tells you about the role of environment on brain development. Does that research provide a useful guide for choosing the best day-care center? Why or why not?

Personal Learning Activity

To get a rough measure of the role played by your brain's left hemisphere in language, try the following test. First, see how long you can balance a yardstick on the tip of your right index finger, and then try the same task with your left hand. The difference in how long you can keep the stick balanced will probably be determined by whether you are right-handed or left-handed. Now try this balancing act eight more times, alternating hands on each trial so that you use your left index finger four times and your right index finger four times. Now here's where language might come in: On two of the four trials with each hand, count backward from 100 by 3s (100, 97, 94, 91, and so on) out loud while you try to keep the stick balanced. It has been suggested that this language task might interfere with your balancing skill, especially when you are using your right hand (Kemble, Filipi, & Gravlin, 1985; Kinsbourne & Cook, 1971). Why? If the left side of your brain is more involved with language, then counting backward while balancing with your right hand requires the left hemisphere to do two things at once. When counting while balancing with the left hand, the right hemisphere is handling the balancing and the left hemisphere is dealing with the language task. Is this what happened in your case? Try the same tests on your friends and summarize the results. *For additional projects, see the Personal Learning Activities in the corresponding chapter of the study guide that accompanies this book.*

Take Action to Learn More ▶

Now that you have finished reading this chapter, how about exploring some of the ideas and information that you found most interesting? Here are some courses, books, films, and Internet resources to get you started. Enjoy!

Courses

Biological Bases of Behavior
Physiological Psychology
Biological Psychology
Brain and Behavior
Introduction to Neuroscience
Anatomy and Physiology

Movies

Awakenings Neurotransmitters and mental functioning.
Brainstorm Trying to record thoughts and memories directly from the brain.
Iris; Complaints of a Dutiful Daughter Coping with a family member's Alzheimer's disease.

The Island of Doctor Moreau Nature and nurture issues—what makes us who we are?
Memento The role of the brain in anterograde amnesia.

Books

David Bainbridge, *Beyond the Zonules of Zinn: A Fantastic Journey Through Your Brain* (Harvard University Press, 2008). The title says it all.
William Calvin, *The Throwing Madonna: Essays on the Brain* (Bantam, 1991) Brain and behavior.
Steven Pinker, *How the Mind Works* (Norton, 1997) Brain and behavior.
V. S. Ramachandran, *Phantoms in the Brain: Probing the Mysteries of the Human Mind* (Quill, 1999) A doctor explores neurological disorders.
Bonnie Sherr Klein, *Slow Dance: A Story of Stroke, Love, and Disability* (PageMill Press, 1998) A personal account of recovery from a series of strokes.

Maryanne Wolf (2007). *Proust and the Squid: The Story and Science of the Reading Brain* (Harper, 2007) The story of all the systems in the brain that allow us to read.

The Web

Essentials of Psychology Book Companion Website

www.cengage.com/psychology/bernstein

Visit the book companion website to access a wealth of resources, including chapter outlines, flashcards, web links, tutorial quizzes, and more!

CENGAGENOW™ Just what you need to know NOW! Spend time on what you need to master rather than on information you already have learned. Take a pre-test for this chapter, and CengageNOW will generate a personalized study plan based on your results. The study plan will identify the topics you need to review and direct you to online resources to help you master those topics. You can then take a post-test to help you determine the concepts you have mastered and what you will need to work on. Try it out! Go to www.cengage.com/login to sign in with an access code or to purchase access to this product.

Review of Key Terms ▶

Can you define each of the key terms in the chapter? Check your definitions against those on the pages shown in parentheses in the following list or in the Glossary at the end of the book.

action potential (p. 50)
amygdala (p. 63)
association cortex (p. 67)
autonomic nervous system (p. 54)
axon (p. 50)
biological psychology (p. 48)
central nervous system (CNS) (p. 53)
cerebellum (p. 62)
cerebral cortex (p. 64)
corpus callosum (p. 64)
dendrites (p. 50)
endocrine system (p. 76)

fiber tracts (p. 55)
fight-or-flight response (p. 78)
forebrain (p. 63)
glands (p. 76)
glial cells (p. 49)
hindbrain (p. 61)
hippocampus (p. 64)
hormones (p. 76)
hypothalamus (p. 63)
locus coeruleus (p. 61)
medulla (p. 61)
midbrain (p. 62)
motor cortex (p. 65)
motor neurons (p. 54)
neural networks (p. 53)
nervous system (p. 48)
neural plasticity (p. 71)

neurons (p. 49)
neurotransmitter (p. 51)
nuclei (p. 54)
parasympathetic nervous system (p. 54)
peripheral nervous system (p. 53)
reflexes (p. 55)
refractory period (p. 50)
reticular formation (p. 61)
sensory cortex (p. 65)
sensory neurons (p. 54)
somatic nervous system (p. 54)
spinal cord (p. 55)
sympathetic nervous system (p. 54)
synapse (p. 51)
thalamus (p. 63)

MULTIPLE-CHOICE ▶ Self Test

Select the best answer for each of the following questions. Then check your responses against the Answer Key at the end of the book.

1. The nucleus of a cell _____, and the mitochondria _____.
   a. produces red blood cells; turn oxygen into glucose
   b. produces red blood cells; keep a stable chemical environment
   c. provides genetic information; turn oxygen into glucose
   d. provides genetic information; keep a stable chemical environment

2. A nurse has mixed up some test results on neurotransmitter function for several patients at the hospital where you work. To help her out, you tell her that the depressed patient's chart will show malfunctions in _____ systems and the Parkinson's patient's chart will show malfunctions in _____ systems.
   a. dopamine; norepinephrine
   b. dopamine; acetylcholine
   c. serotonin; dopamine
   d. acetylcholine; norepinephrine

3. Hannah had a stroke and oxygen was cut off from the neurons in her brain. This caused overactivity in _____ synapses, which led to brain damage.
   a. glutamate   c. acetylcholine
   b. dopamine   d. serotonin

4. Functional magnetic resonance imaging (fMRI) provides a way to _____.
   a. directly measure brain cell activity
   b. measure brain areas, showing changes in blood flow and oxygen levels
   c. locate the causes of particular mental processes
   d. locate where certain emotions take place in the brain

5. As you switch on your favorite TV medical show, a doctor charges through the emergency room doors and tells a worried spouse that her husband has a neurological problem. "The nerves that carry signals to his muscles are not functioning," the doctor says, "which means the _____ nervous system has been damaged."
   a. central   c. somatic
   b. autonomic   d. sympathetic

6. Kalli finishes a difficult final exam, then hurries home and flops down on her bed to relax. As Kalli relaxes, her _____ nervous system becomes less active, whereas her _____ nervous system becomes more active.
   a. central; somatic
   b. somatic; central
   c. parasympathetic; sympathetic
   d. sympathetic; parasympathetic

7. When Karena accidentally touched a hot stove, she instantly jerked her hand away. This automatic response was directed by neurons entering and leaving the _____, which is part of the _____ nervous system.
   a. spinal cord; central
   b. spinal cord; autonomic
   c. hypothalamus; central
   d. hypothalamus; autonomic

8. A neuron's action potential shoots down its axon with greater speed when the _____.
   a. axon is coated in myelin
   b. refractory period is longer
   c. neuron's diameter is smaller
   d. neuron is in the brain

9. Jessica has severe damage to her medulla. Most likely, Jessica _____.
   a. is dead
   b. will have memory problems
   c. will have difficulty with fine motor movements
   d. will not feel anything on the left side of her body

10. Damage in Lily's hindbrain caused her to lapse into a coma. The damage most likely occurred in the _____.
    a. cerebellum   c. hypothalamus
    b. hippocampus   d. reticular formation

11. Riley was an excellent pianist until he suffered brain damage. Now problems with fine motor skills make it impossible for him to play the piano. Riley most likely had damage to his _____.
    a. cerebellum
    b. hippocampus
    c. hypothalamus
    d. reticular formation

12. The hippocampus has been found to be significantly smaller in patients who are suffering from which of the following problems?
    a. Parkinson's disease
    b. Alzheimer's disease
    c. depression
    d. an eating disorder

13. A woman was rushed to an emergency room with severely burned hands. She had picked up an iron because she couldn't tell it was hot, and she still doesn't feel pain from her burns. The neurologist who examined her concluded that the woman's _____ system is malfunctioning.
    a. sensory   c. autonomic
    b. motor   d. parasympathetic

14. Reginald has suffered damage to his occipital lobe. This means that Reginald will have difficulty _____.
    a. feeling pain
    b. moving his body
    c. seeing
    d. regulating body temperature

15. Elnora wants to hit a nail with a hammer so she can hang a picture on the wall. This involves voluntary movements that are controlled by neurons in the _____ cortex, which is located in the _____ lobe.
    a. motor; frontal
    b. motor; parietal
    c. association; temporal
    d. sensory; occipital

16. Roberto, an actor, is recovering following a freak accident on the set of his latest movie. When asked about the accident, Roberto, once a confident and fluent speaker, can now only say, "Noise . . . acting . . . hurts." The part of Roberto's brain most likely involved in this type of speech problem is _____ area.
    a. Broca's
    b. Sperry's
    c. Wernicke's
    d. Sylva's

17. Joe experienced such severe seizures that doctors had to sever his corpus callosum. Following surgery, a psychologist presented the left hemisphere of Joe's brain with a picture of a car and asked Joe what he saw. Most likely, Joe could _____.
    a. correctly say "car"
    b. not identify the car in words
    c. only draw a car
    d. not understand the question

18. Edie is 80 and has suffered a paralyzing stroke. Her doctors are likely to tell her that _____.
    a. if she imagines moving her body, she can increase the number of neurons in her motor cortex
    b. the Nogo protein will help regenerate nerve cells
    c. neural stem cells will automatically repair the damage
    d. mental and physical exercise programs can help reverse some of the effects of the stroke

19. Ted is creating a study sheet to help him learn the differences between neurotransmitters and hormones. Which of the following statements on his list is *not* correct?
    a. Neurotransmitters travel through the bloodstream and hormones travel across synapses.
    b. Both hormones and neurotransmitters stimulate only those cells and organs that have receptors for them.
    c. Hormones and neurotransmitters regulate complex behaviors and mental processes.
    d. Hormones operate mainly in the endocrine system; neurotransmitters operate mainly in the nervous system.

20. When Mitch saw a woman in danger of drowning, he jumped into the water to save her. Mitch's endocrine system readied him for this exertion by releasing _____ and other stress hormones into his bloodstream.
    a. cortisol
    b. GABA
    c. glutamate
    d. BABA

© Inspirestock/Jupiterimages

3 Sensation *and* Perception

Preview

As you read and understand this sentence, you are performing a feat of immense proportions as the lines and squiggles of the letters become meaningful words. This is what sensation and perception are all about. You translate incoming stimulation, such as the light bouncing off this page, into neural activity called *sensations*. Then you interpret these sensations as meaningful experiences—in this case, as letters and words. These processes are so quick and automatic that you probably take them for granted. In this chapter, we draw your attention to these amazing processes. You will learn about how our sensory systems receive stimulation and how that stimulation is encoded into patterns of nerve activity that the brain can decode. The sensory systems include vision, hearing, taste, smell, and touch. You will also discover how the brain interprets, or perceives, this information from your senses. Principles for organizing the perceptual world allow you to recognize what you have seen, heard, tasted, smelled, or felt.

I t has been years since Fred Aryee lost his right arm below the elbow in a boating accident, yet he still "feels" sensations from his missing lower arm and hand. Once, his doctor asked Aryee to reach for a cup on the table in front of him with his right arm. When asked what he felt, Aryee said, "I feel my fingers clasping the cup" (Shreeve, 1993). People like Fred may also feel intense pain that seems to be coming from a lost limb (Glummarra et al., 2007; Ramachandran, 2008). Where do these "phantom limb" sensations and perceptions come from? Fred no longer has fingers to send messages to the brain, yet he experienced his "feeling" of the cup as real. Cases such as this one remind us that the "objective reality" we assume to be the same for everyone can actually differ from person to person (Bartoshuk, Fast, & Snyder, 2005). Just as someone can feel a hand that is not actually "there," every individual's senses actively shape information about the outside world to create a personal reality.

Psychologists distinguish between sensation (the stimulus message coming from the senses) and perception (the process of giving meaning to that message). So you do not actually sense a cat lying on the sofa. You sense shapes and colors, the visual sensations. You then use your knowledge of the world to interpret, or perceive, these sensations as a cat. However, it is impossible to draw a clear line between sensation and perception, because the process of interpreting sensations begins in the sense organs themselves. ■

Sensing and Perceiving the World

▶ *What is the difference between sensation and perception?*

To understand how sensory systems help us create reality, we need to have some basic information about the senses. A **sense** is a system that translates outside information into activity in the nervous system. For example, your eyes convert light into neural activity that tells the brain something about the source of the light or about the objects reflecting the light. Messages from the senses are called **sensations.** Sensations shape behaviors and mental processes by providing the vital link between the self and the world outside the brain.

sense   A system that translates data from outside the nervous system into neural activity.

sensations   Raw information from the senses.

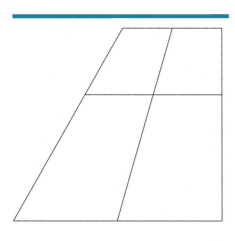

FIGURE 3.1 ■ WHAT DO YOU SEE?

Perception is the process of using information and your understanding of the world so that sensations become meaningful experiences. Perception is more than a passive process of absorbing and decoding incoming sensations. For example, look at Figure 3.1. It sends you only raw sensory information about a series of intersecting lines. But your perceptual system automatically interprets this image as a rectangle (or window frame) lying on its side. Perception is so quick and familiar that it is difficult to appreciate the processes that allow you to turn sensory signals into your personal experience of reality. By shaping this experience, your perceptions influence your thoughts, feelings, and actions. But before you can perceive something, you must be able to sense it.

Sensory Systems

▶ *How does information from my eyes and ears get to my brain?*

Your senses gather information about the world by detecting various forms of energy, such as sound, light, heat, and physical pressure. Your eyes detect light energy, your ears detect the energy of sound, and your skin detects the energy of heat and pressure. Humans depend mainly on vision, hearing, and the skin senses to gain information about the world. We depend less than other animals on smell and taste. To your brain, "the world" also includes the rest of your body, so specific sensory systems provide information about the location and position of your body parts.

All of these senses must detect information about stimuli (the plural of *stimulus*), encode it into neural activity, and then send this encoded information to the brain. Figure 3.2 illustrates these basic steps in sensation. At each step, sensory information is "processed" in some way. So the information that arrives at one point in the system is not exactly the same information that goes to the next step.

In some sensory systems, the first step in sensation involves **accessory structures,** which modify the incoming stimuli (Step 1 in Figure 3.2). For example, the lens of the eye is an accessory structure that changes incoming light by focusing it. The outer part of the ear is an accessory structure that collects sound.

The second step in sensation is **transduction,** which is the process of converting incoming energy into neural activity (Step 2 in Figure 3.2). Your cell phone receives electromagnetic energy and transduces it into sounds. In much the same way, your ears receive sound energy and transduce it into neural activity that you recognize as voices and music. Transduction takes place in structures called **neural receptors,** which are specialized cells that detect certain forms of energy. These receptors respond to incoming energy by firing an action potential and releasing neurotransmitters that send signals to neighboring cells. Sensory receptors respond best to *changes* in energy (Graziano et al., 2002). A constant level of stimulation usually produces **sensory adaptation,** or a decreasing responsiveness to the stimulus over time. This is the reason that the touch sensations you get from your glasses or wristwatch disappear shortly after you have put them on.

Sensory nerves carry information from receptors to the brain (Step 3 in Figure 3.2). For all the senses except smell, this information goes first to the thalamus, which does some initial processing before sending it on to the cerebral cortex (Step 4). The most complex processing occurs in the cortex (Step 5). (For a reminder of the location of these brain structures, see Figure 2.9.)

Encoding Sensations: Did You Feel That?

When receptors transduce, or convert energy, they must somehow *encode* the physical properties of the stimulus into patterns of neural activity. When organized by the brain, those neural patterns allow you to make sense of the stimulus. This processing lets you determine whether you are looking at a cat, a dog, or your next-door neighbor.

Each psychological dimension of a sensation, such as brightness or color, has a corresponding physical dimension that is encoded by the sensory receptors.

perception The process through which people take raw sensations from the environment and give them meaning, using knowledge, experience, and understanding of the world.

accessory structures Structures, such as the outer part of the ear, that modify a stimulus.

transduction The process of converting incoming physical energy into neural activity.

neural receptors Cells that are specialized to detect certain types of energy and convert it into neural activity.

sensory adaptation Decreasing responsiveness to an unchanging stimulus.

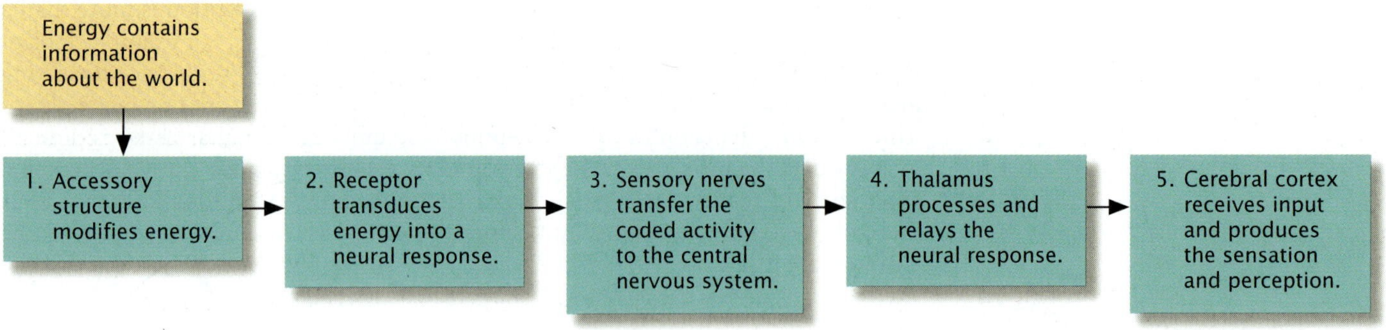

FIGURE 3.2 ■ **ELEMENTS OF A SENSORY SYSTEM**

Objects in the world generate energy that is focused by accessory structures and detected by sensory receptors, which convert the energy into neural signals. The signals are then relayed through parts of the brain, which processes them into perceptual experiences.

In other words, **encoding** translates the physical properties of a stimulus, such as the loudness of sound, into a pattern of neural activity that tells us what those physical properties are.

Absolute Thresholds: Is Something Out There?

How much stimulus energy does it take to trigger a conscious perceptual experience? Not much at all. Normal human vision can detect the light equivalent to a candle flame burning in the dark 30 miles away. The minimum detectable amount of light, sound, pressure, or other physical energy is called the *absolute threshold.* Table 3.1 lists absolute thresholds for human vision, hearing, taste, smell, and touch.

Psychologists discovered these thresholds by exploring *psychophysics,* the relationship between *physical* energy in the environment and your *psychological experience* of that energy. In a typical absolute threshold experiment, you would be seated in a darkened laboratory. After your eyes got used to the darkness, the researcher would show you brief flashes of light. These flashes would differ in brightness, or stimulus intensity. Each time, you'd be asked if you saw the light. Averaged over a large number of trials, your responses would probably form a curve like the one shown in Figure 3.3. As you can see, the absolute threshold is not an all-or-nothing affair. A stimulus at an intensity of three, which is below the absolute threshold in the figure, will still be detected 20 percent of the time it occurs. Because of such variability, psychophysicists redefined the **absolute threshold** as the smallest amount of energy that can be detected 50 percent of the time. Why does a supposedly "absolute" threshold vary? The two most important reasons have to do with "noise" and our response bias.

In psychophysics, the term internal **noise** is used to describe the random firing of cells in the nervous system that continues in varying amounts whether or not you are stimulated by physical energy. This ongoing neural activity is a little like "snow" on a television screen or static between radio stations. If the amount of internal noise happens to be high at a particular moment, your sensory systems might mistakenly interpret the noise as an external stimulus.

The second source of variation in absolute threshold is **response bias,** also known as the **response criterion,** which reflects a person's willingness to respond to a stimulus. A person's *motivation*—wants and needs—as well as *expectations* affect response bias. For example, if you were punished for reporting that a faint light appeared when it did not, then you might be motivated to raise your response criterion. That is, you would report the light only when you were quite sure you saw it. Similarly, expecting a faint stimulus to occur lowers the response criterion. Suppose, for example, that you worked at an airport security checkpoint, examining x-ray images of people's handbags, briefcases, and luggage. The signal to be detected in this situation is a weapon. If there has been a recent terrorist attack or if the threat level has just been elevated, your

encoding   Translation of the physical properties of a stimulus into a specific pattern of neural activity.

absolute threshold   The minimum amount of stimulus energy that can be detected 50 percent of the time.

noise   The spontaneous random firing of nerve cells that occurs because the nervous system is always active.

response bias (response criterion)   The internal rule a person uses to decide whether or not to report a stimulus.

TABLE 3.1 ■ SOME ABSOLUTE THRESHOLDS

Absolute thresholds can be amazingly low. Here are examples of the stimulus equivalents at the absolute threshold for the five primary senses. Set up the conditions for testing the absolute threshold for sound and see if you can detect this minimal amount of auditory stimulation. If you can't hear it, the signal detection theory we discuss in this section may help explain why.

Learn BY **Doing**

Human Sense	Absolute Threshold Is Equivalent to:
Vision	A candle flame seen at 30 miles on a clear night
Hearing	The tick of a watch under quiet conditions at 20 feet
Taste	One teaspoon of sugar in 2 gallons of water
Smell	One drop of perfume diffused into the entire volume of air in a 6-room apartment
Touch	The wing of a fly falling on your cheek from a distance of 1 centimeter

Source: Galanter (1962)

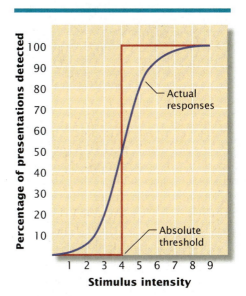

FIGURE 3.3 ■ THE ABSOLUTE THRESHOLD

The curved line shows the relationship between the physical intensity of a signal and the chance that it will be detected. If the absolute threshold were truly absolute, or exact, all signals at or above a particular intensity would always be detected and no signals below that intensity would ever be detected (as shown by the red line). But this response pattern almost never occurs, so the "absolute" threshold is defined as the intensity at which the signal is detected 50 percent of the time.

signal detection theory A mathematical model of what determines a person's report of a near-threshold stimulus.

sensitivity The ability to detect a stimulus.

Weber's law A law stating that the smallest detectable difference in stimulus energy (just-noticeable difference) is a constant fraction of the intensity of the stimulus.

airport will be on high alert. In that situation, your response criterion for saying that a questionable object on the x-ray image might be a weapon will be much lower than if terrorism were not so likely. You will be more likely to detect a weapon if there is one but you will also be more likely to mistake, say, a hairdryer for a gun.

Signal Detection Theory Once researchers understood that the detection of a stimulus depends on the combination of its physical energy, the effects of noise, and a person's response bias, they realized that measurement of absolute thresholds could never be more precise than the 50 percent rule mentioned earlier. So they abandoned the effort to pinpoint absolute thresholds and turned instead to signal detection theory.

Signal detection theory presents a mathematical model of how your personal sensitivity and response bias combine to determine your decision about whether or not a near-threshold stimulus occurred (Green & Swets, 1966). **Sensitivity** refers to your ability to discriminate a stimulus from its background. It is influenced by internal noise, the intensity of the stimulus, and the capacity of your sensory systems. As already mentioned, response bias is the internal rule that you use in deciding whether to report a signal. How likely is it that an airport security guard will spot a weapon in a passenger's x-rayed luggage? Signal detection theory provides a way to understand and predict such responses by guiding precise measurement of sensitivity to stimuli of any kind (MacMillan & Creelman, 2004; Swets, 1992, 1996).

Judging Differences Between Stimuli Sometimes our task is not to detect a faint stimulus but to notice small changes in a stimulus or to decide whether two stimuli are the same or different. Musicians who are tuning up for a concert must discern whether a particular note played on one instrument matches the same note played by another instrument. When you repaint part of a wall, you have to judge whether the color of the new paint matches the old color. And when you are cooking, you have to decide whether your soup tastes any spicier after you have added some pepper.

Your ability to judge differences between stimuli depends on the strength of the stimuli you are dealing with. The weaker those stimuli are, the easier it is to detect small differences between them. For example, if you are comparing the weight of two oranges, you will be able to detect a difference of as little as a fraction of an ounce. But if you are comparing two boxes weighing around 50 pounds each, you may not notice a difference unless it is a pound or more.

One of the oldest laws in psychology, named after German physiologist Ernst Weber (pronounced "VAY-ber"), describes the role of stimulus strength in our ability to detect differences. **Weber's law** states that the smallest detectable difference in stimulus energy is a constant fraction of the intensity of the stimulus. This smallest

DETECTING VITAL SIGNALS ▶

According to signal detection theory, the likelihood that security screeners will detect the outline of a bomb or other weapon in x-ray images of passengers' luggage depends partly on the sensitivity of their visual systems and partly on their criterion, their bias for responding to a questionable stimulus as a possible weapon. That bias, in turn, is affected by their expectations about how often weapons actually appear and by how motivated they are to look carefully for them. Airport security officials occasionally attempt to smuggle a simulated weapon through a checkpoint, not only to evaluate inspectors' performance but also to improve it by keeping their response criterion low enough to avoid missing real weapons (McCarley et al., 2004; Fleck & Mitroff, 2007; Wolfe et al., 2007).

FIGURE 3.4   ■   THE DIMENSIONS OF A WAVE

Wavelength is the distance from one peak of a wave to the next. *Frequency* is the number of complete waves, or cycles, that pass a given point in a given amount of time, such as one second. *Amplitude* is the height of a wave from baseline to peak.

just-noticeable difference (JND) The smallest detectable difference in stimulus energy. Also called difference threshold.

wavelength The distance between peaks in a wave of light or sound.

frequency The number of complete waves, or cycles, that pass a given point per unit of time.

amplitude The distance between the peak and the baseline of a wave.

detectable difference is called the *difference threshold,* or **just-noticeable difference (JND).** According to Weber's law, if an object weighs 25 pounds, the JND is only half a pound. So if you added a small container of yogurt to a grocery bag with three gallons of milk in it, you would not be able to tell the difference in weight. But candy snatchers beware: It takes a change of only two-thirds of an ounce to determine that someone has been into a two-pound box of chocolates! The size of the just-noticeable difference differs from one sense to the next. The human visual system, for example, is more sensitive than the human taste system; that is why we will notice smaller differences in the brightness of a light than in, say, the saltiness of a salad.

Sensory Energy   The sensory energies of light and sound vibrate as *waves* passing through space. These waves result from reflected light or from changes in air pressure caused when vocal cords and other objects move. The eye and ear detect the waves as light and sound. Waves of light and sound can be described in terms of wavelength, frequency, and amplitude, and it is these properties that determine what is sensed and perceived. **Wavelength** is the distance from one peak of the wave to the next. Wave **frequency** is the number of complete waves, or cycles, that pass a given point in a given amount of time. **Amplitude** is the height of the wave from baseline to peak (see Figure 3.4). Different wavelengths, frequencies, and amplitudes create different visual and sound experiences. Let's now consider how these physical properties of light and sound waves become sights and sounds.

Seeing

▶ *Why do some people need eyeglasses?*

Soaring eagles have the incredible ability to see a mouse move in the grass from a mile away. Cats have special "reflectors" at the back of their eyes that help them see even in very dim light. Nature has provided each species with a visual system uniquely adapted to its way of life. The human visual system is also adapted to do many things well. It combines great sensitivity with great sharpness, enabling us to see objects near and far, during the day and at night. Our night vision is not as good as that of some animals, but our color vision is excellent. Not a bad tradeoff; after all, being able to experience a sunset's splendor seems worth an occasional stumble in the dark.

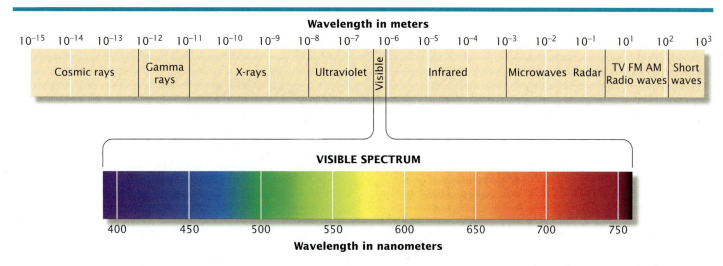

Wavelength in meters

| 10⁻¹⁵ | 10⁻¹⁴ | 10⁻¹³ | 10⁻¹² | 10⁻¹¹ | 10⁻¹⁰ | 10⁻⁹ | 10⁻⁸ | 10⁻⁷ | 10⁻⁶ | 10⁻⁵ | 10⁻⁴ | 10⁻³ | 10⁻² | 10⁻¹ | 10¹ | 10² | 10³ |

Cosmic rays | Gamma rays | X-rays | Ultraviolet | Visible | Infrared | Microwaves | Radar | TV FM AM Radio waves | Short waves

VISIBLE SPECTRUM

400   450   500   550   600   650   700   750

Wavelength in nanometers

FIGURE 3.5 ■ **THE SPECTRUM OF ELECTROMAGNETIC ENERGY**

The human eye is sensitive to only a narrow range of electromagnetic wavelengths. To detect energy outside this range, we rely on radios, cell phones, TV sets, radar detectors, infrared night-vision scopes, and other electronic instruments that can "see" this energy, just as the eye sees visible light.

Light

Light is a form of energy known as *electromagnetic radiation*. Most electromagnetic radiation, including x-rays, radio waves, television signals, and radar, is invisible to the human eye. In fact, as shown in Figure 3.5, the range, or spectrum, of *visible light* is just the tiny slice of electromagnetic radiation that vibrates at wavelengths from just under 400 nanometers to about 750 nanometers. (*A nanometer* is one-billionth of a meter.) It is correct to refer to light as either *light waves or light rays.*

Sensations of light depend on the intensity and wavelength of light waves. **Light intensity,** which refers to how much energy the light contains, determines the brightness of light, and what color you sense depends mainly on **light wavelength.** At a given intensity, different wavelengths produce sensations of different colors. For instance, 440-nanometer light appears violet blue, and 700-nanometer light appears orangish red.

Focusing Light

The eye transduces light energy into neural activity. First, accessory structures of the eye modify incoming light rays. The light rays enter the eye by passing through the curved, transparent, protective layer called the **cornea.** As shown in Figure 3.6,

FIGURE 3.6 ■ **MAJOR STRUCTURES OF THE EYE**

As shown in this top view of the eye, light rays bent by the combined actions of the cornea and the lens are focused on the retina, where the light energy is converted into neural activity. Nerve fibers from the retina combine to form the optic nerve, which leaves the back of the eye and continues to the brain.

light intensity A physical dimension of light waves that refers to how much energy the light contains and that determines our experience of its brightness.

light wavelength A physical dimension of light waves that refers to their length and that produces sensations of different colors.

cornea The curved, transparent, protective layer through which light rays enter the eye.

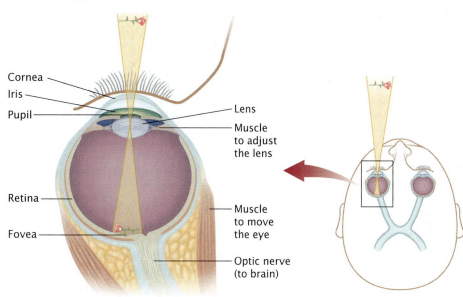

Cornea
Iris
Pupil
Lens
Muscle to adjust the lens
Retina
Fovea
Muscle to move the eye
Optic nerve (to brain)

FIGURE 3.7 ■ THE LENS AND THE RETINAL IMAGE

To see objects as they are, your brain must rearrange the upside-down and reversed images that the lens focuses on the retina. If light rays are out of focus when they reach the retina, glasses usually correct the problem. In some older people, vision is impaired by cataracts, a condition in which a "cloudy" lens severely reduces incoming light. Cataracts can be cleared up with laser surgery or by replacing the natural lens with an artificial one (Snellingen et al., 2002).

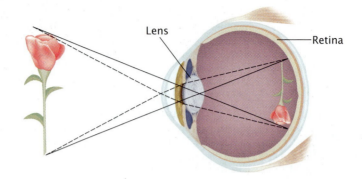

Lens — Retina

the light then passes through the **pupil,** the opening just behind the cornea. The **iris,** which gives the eye its color, adjusts the amount of light allowed into the eye by constricting to reduce the size of the pupil or dilating to enlarge it. Directly behind the pupil is the **lens.** Both the cornea and lens of the eye are curved so that they bend light rays. (A camera lens works the same way.) This bending process focuses light rays coming from various angles into a sharp image on the inner surface at the back of the eye. This surface is called the **retina.** Light rays from the top of an object are focused at the bottom of the image on the retinal surface. Light rays from the right side of the object end up on the left side of the retinal image (see Figure 3.7). The brain rearranges this upside-down and reversed image so that we can see the object as it is.

The muscles that hold the lens adjust its shape so that either near or far objects can be focused on the retina. To illustrate this for yourself, try reading the next sentence while holding the book as close to your face as possible. To maintain a focused image at close range, your muscles have to tighten your lenses, making them more curved. This ability to change the shape of the lens to bend light rays is called **ocular accommodation.** As the lens loses some of its flexibility over the years, accommodation becomes more difficult. Converging light rays may come into focus either before or after they reach the retina, causing images to be blurry. This is why most older people become "farsighted," seeing distant objects clearly but needing glasses for reading or close work. A more common problem in younger people is "nearsightedness," in which close objects are in focus but distant ones are blurry. This condition has a genetic component, but it can also be influenced by environmental factors such as reading habits (Quinn et al., 1999; Zadnik, 2001). These vision problems can usually be solved with glasses or contact lenses that assist in the light-bending process. Another option is Laser-Assisted In-Situ Keratomileusis (LASIK) surgery, which reshapes and stretches the cornea (Feit, 2003). LASIK increases the degree to which the cornea bends light rays, thus requiring the lens to do less accommodation and eliminating the need for glasses or contacts.

Converting Light into Images

The conversion of light energy into neural activity takes place in the retina, which contains neurons that are actually an extension of the brain. The word *retina* is Latin for "net," and the retina is in fact an intricate network of cells (Masland, 2001).

Rods and Cones   Specialized cells in the retina called **photoreceptors** convert light energy into neural activity. There are two main types of photoreceptors: rods and cones. **Rods** and **cones** are retinal cells that are named for their shapes and that contain chemicals that respond to light. When light strikes these chemicals, they break apart, creating a signal that can be transferred to the brain.

pupil   An opening in the eye just behind the cornea through which light passes.

iris   The part of the eye that gives it its color and adjusts the amount of light entering it.

lens   The part of the eye directly behind the pupil.

retina   The surface at the back of the eye onto which the lens focuses light rays.

ocular accommodation   The ability of the lens to change its shape and bend light rays so objects are in focus.

photoreceptors   Specialized cells in the retina that convert light energy into neural activity.

rods   Photoreceptors in the retina that allow sight even in dim light but that cannot distinguish colors.

cones   Photoreceptors in the retina that are less light sensitive than rods but that can distinguish colors.

RODS AND CONES ▶

This electron microscope view of rods (blue) and cones (aqua) shows what your light receptors look like. Rods are more light-sensitive, but they do not detect color. Cones can detect color, but they require more light in order to be activated. To experience the difference in how these cells work, try looking at an unfamiliar color photograph in a room where there is barely enough light to see. This dim light will activate your rods and allow you to make out images in the picture. But because there is not enough light to activate your cones, you will not be able to see colors in the photo.

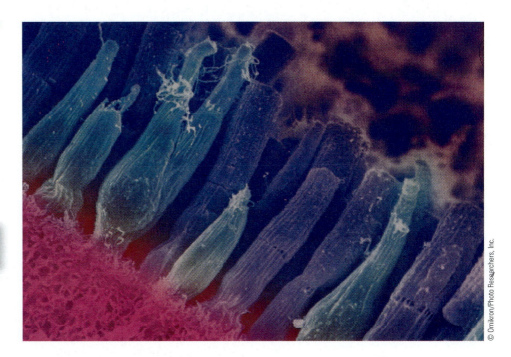

© Omikron/Photo Researchers, Inc.

The process of rebuilding these light-sensitive chemicals after they break down takes a little time. This explains why you cannot see when you first come from bright sunshine into a dark room (Mahroo & Lamb, 2004). In the dark, as your rods build up their light-sensitive chemicals, your ability to see gradually increases. The increasing ability to see in the dark over time is called **dark adaptation.** You become about 10,000 times more sensitive to light after about half an hour in a darkened room.

There are three kinds of light-sensitive chemicals in cones, and they provide the basis for color vision. Rods have only one kind of chemical, so they cannot discriminate colors. However, rods are more sensitive to light than cones. Rods allow you to see in dim light, as on a moonlit night, but they don't allow you to see colors. It's only at higher light intensities that the cones, with their ability to detect colors, become most active. As a result, you might put on what looked like a matched pair of socks in a darkened bedroom only to go outside and discover that one is dark blue and the other is dark green.

Cones are concentrated in the center of the retina in a circular region called the **fovea,** which is where the eye focuses incoming light. Differences in the density of cones in the fovea can lead to differences in various people's visual *acuity,* or ability to see details (Beirne, Zlatkova, & Anderson, 2005). There are no rods in the human fovea. With increasing distance from the fovea, though, the number of cones gradually decreases and the proportion of rods gradually increases. So if you are trying to detect a weak light, such as the light from a faint star, it is better to look slightly away from where you expect to see it. This focuses the weak light on the very light-sensitive rods outside the fovea. Because cones do not work well in low light, looking directly at the star will make it seem to disappear.

From the Retina to the Brain

If the eye simply transferred to the brain the images it focused on the retina, we would experience something like a slightly blurry TV picture. Instead, the eye first sharpens visual images. How? The key lies in the interactions among cells of the retina.

Light rays pass through several layers of retinal cells before striking the rods and cones. Signals generated by the rods and cones then go back toward the surface of the retina, making connections with *bipolar cells* and *ganglion cells,* which allow the eye to begin analyzing visual information even before that information leaves the retina. Ganglion cells in the retina have axons that form the **optic nerve,** which then goes to

dark adaptation   The increasing ability to see in the dark as time passes.

fovea   A region in the center of the retina.

optic nerve   A bundle of fibers that carries visual information to the brain.

FIGURE 3.8   ■   FIND YOUR BLIND SPOT

There is a blind spot where the optic nerve exits the eye. To "see" your blind spot, cover your left eye and stare at the cross inside the circle. Move the page closer and farther away, and at some point the dot to the right should disappear from view. However, the vertical lines around the dot will probably look continuous, because the brain tends to fill in visual information at the blind spot. We are normally unaware of this "hole" in our vision because the blind spot of one eye is in the normal visual field of the other eye.

Learn BY Doing

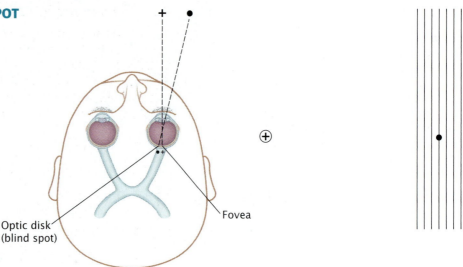

Optic disk (blind spot)

Fovea

the brain. Because there are no receptors for visual stimuli at the point where the optic nerve exits the eyeball, a **blind spot** is created, as Figure 3.8 demonstrates.

After leaving the retina, about half the optic nerve fibers cross over to the opposite side of the brain, creating a structure called the *optic chiasm. (Chiasm* means "cross" and is pronounced "KYE-az-um.") The fibers from the inside half of each eye (nearest to the nose) cross over. The fibers from the outside half of each eye do not. So no matter where you look, all the visual information about the right half of the visual world goes to the left hemisphere of your brain and all the visual information from the left half of the visual world goes to the right hemisphere (Roth, Lora, & Heilman, 2002).

The optic chiasm is part of the bottom surface of the brain. Beyond this chiasm, optic fibers extend into the brain itself. The axons from most of the retina's ganglion cells form synapses in the thalamus. Neurons there send the visual input to the primary visual cortex in the occipital lobe at the back of the brain. The primary visual cortex sends visual information to many association areas of the brain for processing (see Figure 2.10).

Certain cells in the brain's cerebral cortex are called **feature detectors** because they respond to specific characteristics of objects in the visual world (Hubel & Wiesel, 1979). For example, one type of feature detector specializes in responding to straight lines. Others respond to corners, to angles, or to some other feature. The combined responses of several types of feature-detecting cells allow us to sense the shapes of objects such as rectangles or triangles. Most people can also detect color. Let's explore how color vision works.

Seeing Color

Like beauty, color is in the eye of the beholder. Many animals see only shades of gray, even when they look at a rainbow, but for humans, color is an important feature of vision.

Wavelengths and Color Sensations   At a given intensity, each wavelength of light is sensed as a certain color. However, the eye rarely (if ever) encounters pure light of a single wavelength. Sunlight, for example, is a mixture of all wavelengths of light. When sunlight passes through a droplet of water, each different wavelength of light bends to a different degree, separating into a colorful rainbow. The spectrum of color found in the rainbow illustrates an important concept: The sensation produced by a *mixture* of different wavelengths of light is not the same as the sensations produced by separate wavelengths.

blind spot   The point at which the optic nerve exits the eyeball.

feature detectors   Cells in the cortex that respond to a specific feature of an object.

FIGURE 3.9 ■ THE COLOR CIRCLE

Arranging colors according to their psychological similarities creates a color circle that predicts the result of additive mixing of two colored lights. For example, mixing equal amounts of pure green and pure red light will produce yellow, the color that lies at the midpoint of the line connecting red and green. (Note: Nm stands for nanometers, the unit in which light wavelengths are measured.)

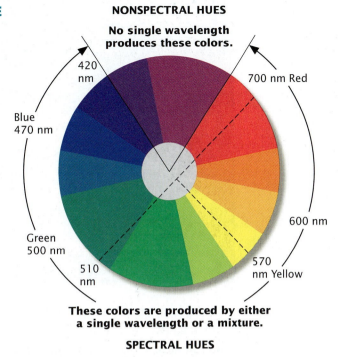

NONSPECTRAL HUES

No single wavelength produces these colors.

420 nm

700 nm Red

Blue 470 nm

600 nm

Green 500 nm

510 nm

570 nm Yellow

These colors are produced by either a single wavelength or a mixture.

SPECTRAL HUES

The sensation of a color results from features of the wavelength mixtures striking the eye. The three separate aspects of this sensation are hue, color saturation, and brightness. These labels refer to the *psychological* dimensions of what we experience when the light arrives, and they correspond roughly to the light's physical properties. **Hue,** the essential "color," is determined by the dominant wavelength in the mixture of the light. Black, white, and gray are not considered hues because they do not have a dominant wavelength. **Color saturation** is related to the purity of the color. A color is said to be more *saturated* (more pure) if just one wavelength is more intense (contains more energy) than other wavelengths. The yellow of a school bus and the red of a stop sign are saturated colors. When many other wavelengths are added in, the color is said to be *desaturated.* Pastels are colors that have been desaturated by the addition of whiteness. **Brightness** refers to the overall intensity of the wavelengths making up light.

The *color circle* shown in Figure 3.9 arranges hues according to their perceived similarities. Mix two different light wavelengths of equal intensity and the color you sense is midway between the two original colors on the color circle. This process is called *additive color mixing,* because the effects of the wavelengths are added together. Keep adding different colored lights and you eventually get white, which is the combination of all wavelengths. You are probably more familiar with a different form of color mixing, called *subtractive color mixing,* which occurs when, for example, paints are combined. Paint, like other physical objects, reflects certain wavelengths and absorbs others. Green paint is green because it absorbs all wavelengths except wavelengths perceived as green. (White objects appear white because they reflect all wavelengths.) So if you keep combining different colored paints, all of the wavelengths will eventually be subtracted, resulting in black.

Theories of Color Vision

Psychologists have long tried to explain how color vision works, but only two theories have stood the test of time: trichromatic (or "three-color") theory and opponent-process theory.

hue The essential color determined by the dominant wavelength of a light.

color saturation The purity of a color.

brightness The overall intensity of the wavelengths making up light.

THE SENSATION OF COLOR ▶

The vivid array of colored powders offered by this vendor in India allows him to create virtually any combination of hue (color), saturation (purity), and brightness that a customer might request.

The Trichromatic Theory of Color Vision   In the early 1800s, Thomas Young proved that mixing pure versions of blue, green, and red light in different ratios could produce any other color; Hermann von Helmholtz later confirmed these findings. The Young and von Helmholtz theory of color vision is called the **trichromatic theory.**

Support for trichromatic theory comes from research on cones in the retina. There are three types of cones, and each is most sensitive to particular wavelengths. *Short-wavelength* cones respond most to light in the blue range. *Medium-wavelength* cones are most sensitive to light in the green range. *Long-wavelength* cones respond best to light in the reddish-yellow range, but by tradition they are known as "red" cones. No single cone by itself can signal the color of a light; it is the *ratio* of the activities of the three types of cones that determines what color will be sensed. As you can see in Figure 3.10, the exact mixture of these three cone types can differ from person to person. The trichromatic theory was applied in the creation of color television screens, which contain microscopic elements of red, green, and blue. A television broadcast excites these elements to varying degrees, mixing their colors to produce many other colors. You see color mixtures, not patterns of red, green, and blue dots, because the dots are too small and close together to be seen individually.

trichromatic theory   A theory of color vision stating that information from three types of visual elements combines to produce the sensation of color.

opponent-process theory   A theory of color vision stating that the visual elements that are sensitive to color are grouped into red-green, blue-yellow, and black-white pairs.

FIGURE 3.10 ■ **INDIVIDUAL DIFFERENCES IN CONE TYPES**

These photographs show that people can differ widely from one another in the distribution of blue, green, and red cones in their retinas (Roorda & Williams, 1999). J. W., whose retina is shown in Part A, has an especially high population of red cones, whereas green cones predominate in A. N., whose retina is shown in Part B. Both have normal color vision, but J. W. will be somewhat more sensitive to long wavelengths of light, whereas A.N. will be somewhat more sensitive to light of medium wavelengths.

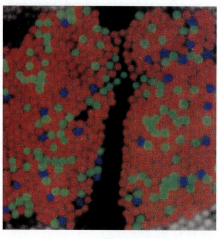

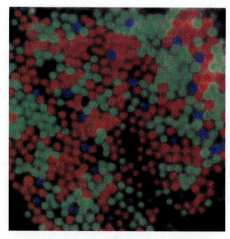

(A)

(B)

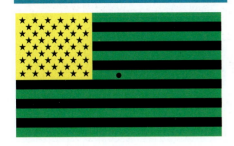

FIGURE 3.11 ■ AFTERIMAGES PRODUCED BY THE OPPONENT-PROCESS NATURE OF COLOR VISION

Stare at the black dot in the flag for at least thirty seconds and then focus on the dot in the white space below it. The afterimage you will see can be explained by the opponent process theory of color vision. What colors appeared in the afterimage you saw?

Learn BY Doing

The Opponent-Process Theory of Color Vision

Although it is essentially correct, the trichromatic theory cannot explain some aspects of color vision, such as afterimages. To see an afterimage, stare at the black dot in the flag in Figure 3.11 for thirty seconds and then look at the black dot in the white space below it. What was yellow in the original image will be blue in the afterimage. What was green before will appear red, and what was black will now appear white.

This type of observation led Ewald Hering to offer another theory of color vision, called the **opponent-process theory.** Hering suggested that color-sensitive visual elements in the eye are arranged into three kinds of pairs and that the members of each pair oppose, or inhibit, each other. Each element signals one color or the other (red or green, blue or yellow, black or white), but never both. This theory explains color afterimages. When one member of an opponent pair is no longer stimulated, the other is activated. So in Figure 3.11, if the original image you look at is green, the afterimage will be red.

Summing Up

Together, the trichromatic and opponent-process theories encompass most of what we now know about the complex process of color vision. We see color because our three types of cones have different sensitivities to different wavelengths. We sense different colors when the three cone types are stimulated in different ratios. Because there are three types of cones, any color can be produced by mixing three pure wavelengths of light. But there is more to it than that. The cones connect to ganglion cells containing pairs of opposing elements that respond to different colors and inhibit each other. This arrangement provides the basis for afterimages. Therefore, the trichromatic theory explains color vision as it relates to rods and cones, whereas the opponent-process theory explains color vision as it relates to the ganglion cells. Both theories are needed to account for the complexity of our visual sensations of color (Jacobs, 2008).

Color vision also depends on what happens in the brain—especially in the thalamus and visual cortex—where encoded color information from the retinas is assembled and processed (Gegenfurtner & Kiper, 2003). As a result, certain kinds of brain damage can weaken or destroy color vision, even though all the cones in the retina are working normally (Bouvier & Engel, 2006). ("In Review: Seeing" summarizes our discussion of vision.)

In Review

Seeing

ASPECT OF SENSORY SYSTEM	ELEMENTS	KEY CHARACTERISTICS
Energy	Visible light: electromagnetic radiation with a wavelength of about 400 nm to about 750 nm	The intensity, wavelength, and complexity of light waves determine the brightness, hue, and saturation of visual sensations.
Accessory structures of the eye	Cornea, pupil, iris, lens	Light rays are bent to focus on the retina.
Conversion of visual stimuli to neural activity	Photoreceptors (rods and cones) in the retina	Rods are more sensitive to light than cones, but cones discriminate among colors. Sensations of color depend first on the cones, which respond differently to different light wavelengths, and then on processing by ganglion cells.
Pathway to the brain	Optic nerve to optic chiasm to thalamus to primary visual cortex	Neurons in the brain respond to particular aspects of the visual stimulus, such as shape.

1. The ability to see in very dim light depends on photoreceptors called _____.
2. Color afterimages are best explained by the _____ theory of color vision.
3. Nearsightedness and farsightedness occur when images are not focused on the eye's _____.

FIGURE 3.12   ▬   ARE YOU COLORBLIND?

At the upper left is a photo as it appears to people whose cones have all three types of color-sensitive chemicals. The other photos simulate how colors appear to people who are missing chemicals for short wavelengths (lower left), long wavelengths (upper right), or medium wavelengths (lower right). If any of these photos look to you just like the one at the upper left, you may have a form of colorblindness.

Colorblindness

Cones normally contain three kinds of chemicals, each of which responds best to a particular wavelength of light. People who have cones containing only two of these three color-sensitive chemicals are described as *colorblind* (Carroll et al., 2004). They are not really blind to all color, but they discriminate fewer colors than do other people, as Figure 3.12 shows. Red-green colorblindness, for example, means that reds and greens appear to be the same brownish-gray color. Colorblindness is more common in men than in women.

Hearing

▶ *How would my voice sound on the moon?*

In 1969, when Neil Armstrong became the first person ever to set foot on the moon, millions of people back on earth heard his radio transmission: "That's one small step for a man, one giant leap for mankind." But if Armstrong had been foolish enough to take off his space helmet and shout, "Whoo-ee! I can moonwalk!" not even an astronaut three feet away could have heard him. Why? Because he would have been speaking into airless empty space. **Sound** is a repeating fluctuation—a rising and falling—in the pressure of a substance, such as air. Because the moon has almost no atmosphere and almost no air pressure, sound cannot exist there.

Sound

Vibrations of an object produce the fluctuations in pressure that make sound. When you speak, your vocal cords vibrate, causing fluctuations in air pressure that spread as sound waves. Figure 3.13 shows how these changes in air pressure can be represented as sound waveforms. The waveforms are drawn in only two dimensions, but remember that sound waves actually move through the air in all directions. This is the reason that when people talk to each other during a movie or a lecture, others all around them are distracted by the conversation.

Just as the amplitude and wavelength of light waves affect our experience of light, the characteristics of sound waves affect our experience of sound. The psychological

sound   A repetitive fluctuation in the pressure of a medium such as air.

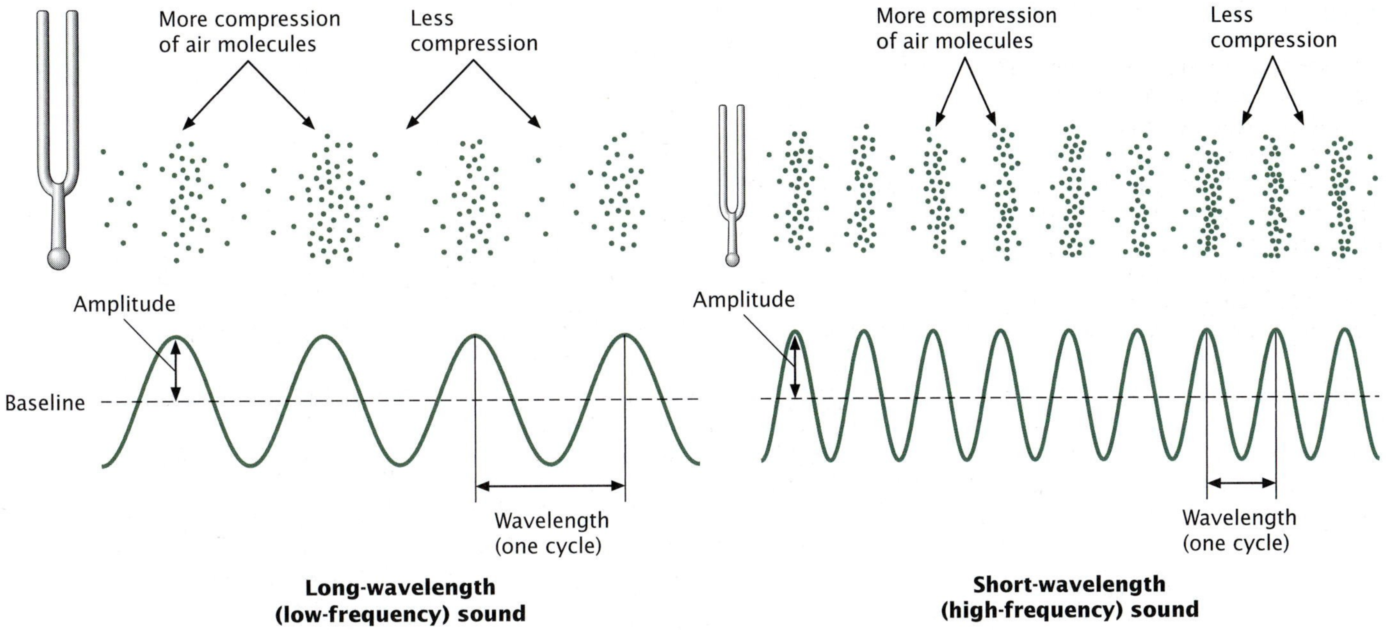

FIGURE 3.13 ■ SOUND WAVES AND WAVEFORMS

Sound is created when objects, such as a tuning fork, vibrate. The vibration creates alternating regions of greater and lesser compression of air molecules, which can be represented as a waveform. The point of greatest compression is the peak of the wave. The lowest point of the wave is where compression is least. In each particular substance, or *medium*, such as air, a sound's wavelength (the distance between peaks) is related to its frequency (the number of waves per second). The longer the wavelength, the lower the sound frequency. The shorter the wavelength, the higher the frequency.

TABLE 3.2 ■ INTENSITY OF SOUND SOURCES

Sound intensity varies across an extremely wide range. A barely audible sound is, by definition, 0 decibels; every increase of 20 decibels reflects a tenfold increase in the amplitude of sound waves. So the 40-decibel sounds of an office are actually 10 times as intense as a 20-decibel whisper; and traffic noise of 100 decibels is 10,000 times as intense as that whisper.

Source	Sound Level (decibels)
Spacecraft launch (from 45 meters)	180
Loudest rock band on record	160
Pain threshold (approximate)	140
Large jet motor (at 22 meters)	120
Loudest human shout on record	111
Heavy auto traffic	100
Conversation (at about 1 meter)	60
Quiet office	40
Soft whisper	20
Threshold of hearing	0

Source: Levine & Schefner (1981)

loudness A psychological dimension of sound determined by the amplitude of a sound wave.

experience we call **loudness** is determined by the amplitude, or height, of the sound wave. The greater the amplitude, the louder the sensation of sound. Loudness is described in units called *decibels* (abbreviated *dB*). By definition, 0 decibels is the minimum detectable sound for normal hearing. Table 3.2 gives examples of the intensity, or loudness, of some common sounds.

FIGURE 3.14 ■ STRUCTURES OF THE EAR

The outer ear (pinna and ear canal) channels sound waves into the middle ear, where the vibrations of the tympanic membrane are amplified by the delicate bones that stimulate the cochlea. In the cochlea in the inner ear, the vibrations are converted, or transduced, into changes in neural activity, which is sent along the acoustic nerve to the brain.

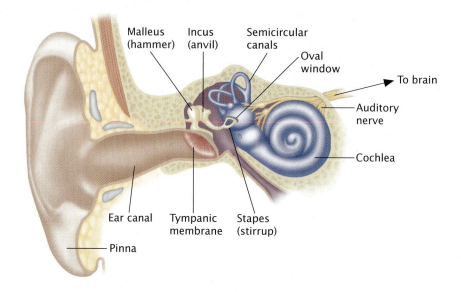

The psychological dimension of **pitch**—how high or low a tone sounds—depends on the frequency of the sound wave. Frequency is the number of complete waves or cycles that pass a given point in one second. It is described in units called *hertz,* abbreviated *Hz* (for Heinrich Hertz, a nineteenth-century physicist). One cycle per second is 1 hertz. High-frequency waves are sensed as sounds of high pitch. The highest note on a piano has a frequency of about 4,000 hertz, and the lowest note has a frequency of about 50 hertz. Humans can hear sounds ranging from about 20 to 20,000 hertz.

Most sounds are a mixture of many frequencies and amplitudes, and this mixture creates a sound's **timbre** (pronounced "TAM-ber"), the psychological dimension of sound quality. Complex wave patterns added to the *fundamental,* or lowest, frequency of sound determine its timbre. The extra waves allow you to tell the difference between, say, a note played on a flute and the same note played on a clarinet.

The Ear

The human ear converts sound energy into neural activity through a series of accessory structures and transduction mechanisms. The crumpled part of the ear on the side of the head, called the **pinna,** collects sound waves in the outer ear. (People trying to hear a faint sound may cup a hand to their ear because this action tilts the pinna forward and enlarges the area that is collecting sound. Try this for a moment, and you will notice a clear difference in the sounds you hear.) The pinna funnels sound down through the ear canal. At the end of the ear canal, the sound waves reach the **middle ear** (see Figure 3.14). There they strike the **tympanic membrane,** a tightly stretched structure also known as the **eardrum.** The sound waves set up vibrations in the tympanic membrane. The *hammer,* the *anvil,* and the *stirrup,* three tiny bones named for their shapes, amplify these vibrations and direct them onto a smaller membrane called the *oval window.*

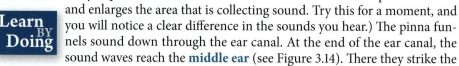

The Inner Ear   Sound vibrations passing through the oval window enter the inner ear, reaching the **cochlea** (pronounced "KOK-lee-ah"), where transduction occurs. The cochlea is rolled into a coiled spiral. (*Cochlea* comes from the Greek word for "snail.") A fluid-filled tube runs down its length. The **basilar membrane** forms the floor of this tube, as you can see in Figure 3.15. When a sound wave passes through the fluid in the tube, it makes the basilar membrane rise and fall (Ren, 2002). This movement,

pitch   How high or low a tone sounds; pitch depends on the frequency of a sound wave.

timbre   The quality of a sound that identifies it.

pinna   The crumpled part of the outer ear that collects sound waves.

middle ear   The part of the ear that contains the hammer, anvil, and stirrup, which transmit sound from the tympanic membrane to the oval window.

tympanic membrane (eardrum)   A tightly stretched membrane in the middle ear that generates vibrations that match the sound waves striking it.

cochlea   A fluid-filled spiral structure in the inner ear in which auditory transduction occurs.

basilar membrane   The floor of the fluid-filled duct that runs through the cochlea.

FIGURE 3.15 ■ THE COCHLEA

This drawing shows how the vibrations of the stirrup set up vibrations in the fluid inside the cochlea. The coils of the cochlea are unrolled in this illustration to show the path of the fluid waves along the basilar membrane. Movements of the basilar membrane stimulate hair cells, which transduce the vibrations into changes in neural firing patterns.

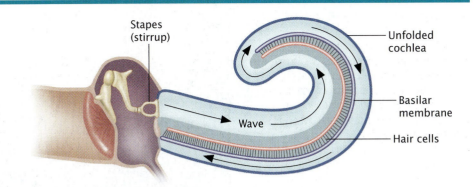

in turn, bends *hair cells* on the membrane. These hair cells make connections with fibers from the **acoustic nerve,** a bundle of axons that goes into the brain. Bending the hair cells stimulates the acoustic nerve, also known as the *auditory nerve,* which sends encoded signals to the brain about the amplitude and frequency of the sound waves (Griesinger, Richards, & Ashmore, 2005). These signals allow you to sense loudness, pitch, and timbre.

Deafness

The middle and inner ear are among the most delicate structures in the body, and damage to them can lead to deafness. One form of deafness is caused by problems with the bones of the middle ear. Over time they can fuse together, preventing accurate conduction of vibrations from one bone to the next. This condition, called *conduction deafness,* can be treated by surgery to break the bones apart or to replace the natural bones with plastic ones (Ayache et al., 2003). Hearing aids that amplify incoming sounds can also help.

Nerve deafness results when the acoustic nerve or, more commonly, the hair cells are damaged (Shepherd & McCreery, 2006). Hair-cell damage occurs gradually with age, but it can also be caused by very loud sounds, including amplified rock music (Goldstein, 2002). High-intensity sound can actually rip off the hair cells of the inner ear. Generally, any sound loud enough to produce ringing in the ears causes some damage. In humans, small amounts of damage gradually build up and can produce significant hearing loss by middle age—as many older rock musicians (and their fans) are finding out (Levine, 1999). Listening to music at high volume through the earphones of iPods and other devices can also cause hearing loss (Petrescu, 2008; Vogel et al., 2009).

Hair cells can be regenerated in chickens' ears (Cotanche, 1997), and a related kind of inner-ear hair cell has been regenerated in mammals (Malgrange et al., 1999). Scientists hope that human hair-cell regeneration might someday be accomplished by treating damaged areas with growth factors similar to those being used to repair damaged brain cells (Shepherd et al., 2005; see the chapter on biology and behavior). Inserting genes that might stimulate the regrowth of damaged hair cells (Izumikawa et al., 2005) and using stem cells to create new hair cells (Beisel et al., 2008) are two other promising approaches. If successful, these efforts could revolutionize the treatment of nerve deafness, which cannot be overcome by conventional hearing aids. In the meantime, scientists have developed an artificial cochlea that can be implanted in the human ear to stimulate the acoustic nerve (Wilson & Dorman, 2008).

Auditory Pathways to the Brain

Before sounds can be heard, the information encoded in the firing of the many axons that make up the acoustic nerve must be sent to the brain for further analysis. This transmission process begins when the acoustic nerve conveys the information to the thalamus. From there, the information is relayed to the *primary auditory cortex,* an area in the temporal lobe of the brain (see Figure 2.10). It is in the primary auditory cortex that information about sound is subjected to the most

acoustic nerve The bundle of axons that carries messages from the hair cells of the cochlea to the brain.

SHAPING THE BRAIN ▶

The brain region known as the primary auditory cortex is larger in trained musicians than in people whose jobs are less focused on fine gradations of sound. How much larger this area becomes is correlated with how long the musicians have studied their art. This finding reminds us that, as described in the chapter on biology and behavior, the brain can literally be shaped by experience and other environmental factors (Baumann, Meyer, & Jäncke, 2008; Lotze et al., 2003; Shahin et al., 2008).

intense and complex analysis (Ciocca, 2008). Cells in the auditory cortex have *preferred frequencies*. That is, individual cells there respond most vigorously to sounds of a particular frequency. Each neuron in the acoustic nerve also has a "favorite," or characteristic, frequency, though each also responds to some extent to a range of frequencies (Schnee et al., 2005). The auditory cortex examines the pattern of activity of many neurons to determine the frequency of a sound. This auditory analysis may be especially efficient in people who are deprived of visual experience because of blindness early in life (Stevens & Weaver, 2009).

Some parts of the auditory cortex are devoted to processing certain types of sounds. One part, for example, specializes in information from human speech (Belin, Zatorre, & Ahad, 2002); others are particularly responsive to sounds coming from animals, tools, or musical instruments (Lewis et al., 2005; Zatorre, 2003). This specialization in the auditory cortex can be seen in fMRI brain scans. Observing which brain areas become activated by which kind of sound has allowed researchers to detect whether a person is listening to words spoken by a familiar or unfamiliar voice and even to identify some details about what is being said (Formisano et al., 2008). The primary auditory cortex receives information from other senses as well. For example, it is activated when you watch someone say words (but not when the person makes other facial movements). This is the biological basis for the lip-reading that helps you hear what people say (Campbell & Capek, 2008).

Encoding Sounds

Most people can hear a wide range of sound intensities. The faintest sound that can be heard barely moves the ear's hair cells. Sounds more than a trillion times more intense can also be heard. Between these extremes, the auditory system encodes intensity in a rather simple way: The more intense the sound, the more rapid the firing of a given neuron. We are also very good at detecting differences between sound frequencies that allow us to hear differences in pitch (Shera, Guinan, & Oxenham, 2002). Information about frequency differences appears to be encoded in two ways: by their location on the basilar membrane and by the rate at which the auditory neurons fire.

place theory   A theory of hearing that states that hair cells at a particular place on the basilar membrane respond most to a particular frequency of sound.

volley theory   A theory of hearing that states that the firing rate of an acoustic nerve matches a sound wave's frequency. Also called frequency-matching theory.

As sound waves move down the basilar membrane, they reach a peak and then taper off, much like an ocean wave that crests and then dissolves. The waves produced by high-frequency sounds peak soon after they start down the basilar membrane. Waves produced by lower-frequency sounds peak farther down the basilar membrane. According to **place theory,** the greatest response by hair cells occurs at the peak of the wave. Because the location of the peak varies with the frequency of sound, it follows that hair cells at a particular place on the basilar membrane are most responsive to a particular frequency of sound. When cells with a particular characteristic frequency fire, we sense a sound of that frequency.

But place theory cannot explain the encoding of very low frequencies (such as deep bass notes) because none of the acoustic nerve fibers have very low preferred frequencies. However, humans can hear frequencies as low as twenty hertz, so they must be encoded somehow. The answer appears to be *frequency matching*, a process in which certain neurons in the acoustic nerve fire each time a sound wave passes. So a sound wave whose frequency is 25 cycles per second would cause those neurons to fire 25 times per second. Frequency-matching theory is sometimes called the **volley theory** of frequency encoding because the outputs of many cells can combine to create a *volley* of firing.

The nervous system apparently uses more than one way to encode the range of audible frequencies. The lowest frequencies are encoded by frequency matching. Low to moderate frequencies are encoded by frequency matching as well as by the place on the basilar membrane where the wave peaks. And high frequencies are encoded solely by the place on the basilar membrane where the wave peaks. ("In Review: Hearing" summarizes the encoding process and other aspects of the auditory system.)

In Review

Hearing

ASPECT OF SENSORY SYSTEM	ELEMENTS	KEY CHARACTERISTICS
Energy	Sound: pressure fluctuations of air produced by vibrations	Amplitude, frequency, and complexity of sound waves determine the loudness, pitch, and timbre of sounds.
Accessory structures of the ear	Pinna, tympanic membrane, hammer, anvil, stirrup, oval window, basilar membrane	Changes in pressure produced by the original wave are amplified.
Conversion of sound frequencies into neural activity	Hair cells in the inner ear	Frequencies are encoded by the location of the hair cells receiving the greatest stimulation (place theory) and by the combined firing rate of neurons (volley theory).
Pathway to the brain	Acoustic nerve to thalamus to primary auditory cortex	Auditory cortex examines patterns of information from the auditory nerve, allowing us to sense loudness, pitch, and timbre.

1. *Sound energy is converted to neural activity in an inner ear structure called the _____.*
2. *Hearing loss due to damage to hair cells or the auditory nerve is called _____.*
3. *How high or low a sound sounds is called _____ and is determined by the _____ of a sound wave.*

The Chemical Senses: Taste and Smell

▶ *Why can't I taste anything when I have a cold?*

Some animals cannot see and some cannot hear, but all animals have some form of chemical sense. Chemical senses arise from the interaction of chemicals and receptors. **Olfactory perception,** also known as *olfaction,* or our **sense of smell,** detects chemicals that are airborne, or volatile. **Taste perception,** also known as *gustatory perception*, detects chemicals in solution that come into contact with receptors inside the mouth. These systems are connected.

Smell, Taste, and Flavor

If you have a stuffy nose, everything tastes like cardboard. Why? Because smell and taste act as two components of a single system known as *flavor* (Rozin, 1982). Most of the properties that make food taste good are actually odors detected by the olfactory system, not chemicals detected by the taste system. The scent and taste pathways converge in the cerebral cortex (de Araujo et al., 2003), which is how smell and taste come to seem like one sensation.

Both tastes and odors prompt strong emotional responses. People have an inborn dislike of bitter flavors, but we have to learn to associate emotions with odors (Bartoshuk, 1991). Many animals easily learn taste aversions to particular foods when the taste is associated with nausea, but humans learn aversions to odors more readily than to tastes (Bartoshuk & Wolfe, 1990).

Variations in the state of our nutrition also affect our experience of taste and flavor and our motivation to eat particular foods. If we are deprived of food or don't get enough salt, sweet or salty things taste better. Nutrition has a less direct influence on protein and fat intake. Protein and fat molecules have no particular taste or smell, so preferring or avoiding foods that contain these nutrients is based on associations between scent cues from other volatile substances in food and on the nutritional results of eating the foods (Bartoshuk, 1991; Schiffman et al., 1999).

We experience warm foods as sweeter, but temperature does not alter our experience of saltiness (Cruz & Green, 2000). Warming releases aromas that rise from the mouth into the nose and create more flavor sensations. This is why some people find hot pizza delicious and cold pizza disgusting. Spicy "hot" foods actually stimulate pain fibers in the mouth because they contain a substance called *capsaicin* (pronounced "kap-SAY-uh-sin") that stimulates pain-sensing neurons that are also stimulated by heat.

Our Sense of Smell

Pinching your nose prevents you from smelling odors, and putting a dilator strip on the bridge of your nose opens your nasal passages and intensifies odors (Raudenbush & Meyer, 2002). These effects occur because the nose (and the mouth, to some extent) acts as an accessory structure that collects airborne odor molecules for encoding and analysis by the olfactory system (see Figure 3.16). As odor molecules pass into the moist lining of the upper part of the nose—called the *mucous membrane*—they bind to receptors on the dendrites of olfactory neurons, causing a biochemical change. This change, in turn, leads to changes in the firing rates of these neurons, whose axons combine to form the *olfactory nerve* (Dionne & Dubin, 1994). It takes only a single molecule of an odorous substance to cause a change in the activity of an olfactory neuron, but it takes about fifty such molecules before a human will detect the odor (Menini, Picco, & Firestein, 1995). The number of molecules needed to trigger an olfactory sensation can vary, however. For example, women are more sensitive to odors during certain phases of their menstrual cycles (Navarrete-Palacios et al., 2003).

olfactory perception (sense of smell) The sense that detects chemicals that are airborne. Also called olfaction.

taste perception The sense that detects chemicals in solution that come into contact with receptors inside the mouth. Also called gustatory sense.

FIGURE 3.16 ■ THE OLFACTORY SYSTEM: THE NOSE AND THE ROSE

Airborne odor molecules reach the olfactory area either through the nose or through an opening in the palate at the back of the mouth. This opening allows us to sample odors from our food as we eat. Nerve fibers pass directly from the olfactory area to the olfactory bulb in the brain, and from there signals pass to areas that are involved in emotion. This arrangement helps explain why odors often trigger strong emotional memories.

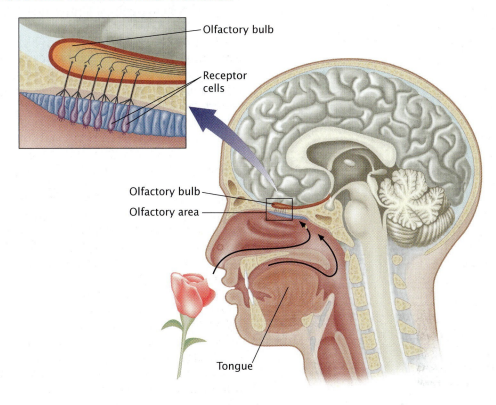

Olfactory bulb

Receptor cells

Olfactory bulb

Olfactory area

Tongue

There are about a thousand different receptors for odors, but there are even more possible odors in the world. Any particular odor is sensed as a particular *pattern* of responses by these odorant receptors, and humans can discriminate among tens of thousands of different odors (Kajiya et al., 2001; Zou & Buck, 2006). So a rose, a pizza, and your favorite cologne each have a different smell because they stimulate their own unique patterns of activity in your odorant receptors. Scientists are just beginning to understand exactly how this odor encoding system works (Ma, 2007). Their work has taken on special importance since the September 11, 2001, terrorist attacks in the United States. Researchers have intensified their efforts to develop an "electronic nose" capable of detecting odorants associated with guns and explosives (Thaler, Kennedy, & Hanson, 2001). Versions of these devices are already in use at some airports. An "electronic nose" has also been developed that can detect the presence of diseases that might not be evident to an examining doctor (Machado et al., 2005), and other artificial olfactory devices are being used to examine the condition and composition of food products and the air we breathe (Marin et al., 2007).

Unlike other senses, our sense of smell does not send its messages through the thalamus. Instead, axons from olfactory neurons in the nose extend through a bony plate and directly into the brain, reaching a structure called the **olfactory bulb**, where odor processing continues (Kay & Sherman, 2007). Connections from the olfactory bulb spread throughout the brain (Zou, Li, & Buck, 2005), but they are especially plentiful in the amygdala, a part of the brain involved in emotional experience and learning. In humans, the amygdala is especially active in response to disgusting odors (Zald & Pardo, 1997).

The unique anatomy of the olfactory system may help account for the intense relationship between smells and emotion (Stevenson & Boakes, 2003). Associations between particular odors and experiences—especially emotional experiences—are

olfactory bulb A brain structure that receives messages regarding smell.

not weakened much by time or later experiences (Lawless & Engen, 1977). So catching a whiff of the cologne once worn by a lost loved one can reactivate intense feelings of love or sadness associated with that person. Odors can also bring back accurate memories of experiences linked with them, especially positive experiences (Engen, Gilmore, & Mair, 1991; Mohr et al., 2001). These special features of the olfactory system may account for the fact that losing the sense of smell can be an early sign of disease in areas of the brain involved in memory and emotion (Albers, Tabert, & Devanand, 2006).

Species ranging from humans to worms have remarkably similar neural mechanisms for sensing smell. And all mammals, including humans, have brain systems for detecting the source of smells by comparing the strength of sensory inputs reaching the left and right nostrils (Porter et al., 2005). Different species vary considerably, however, in their sensitivity to odor and in the degree to which they depend on it for survival. Humans have about 9 million olfactory neurons, compared with about 225 million in dogs, a species that is far more dependent on smell to identify food, territory, and receptive mates. Dogs and many other species also have an accessory olfactory system that detects pheromones. **Pheromones** (pronounced "FAIR-oh-mohns") are chemicals that are released by one creature and when detected by another can shape the second animal's behavior or physiology (Zufall & Leinders-Zufall, 2007). For example, when a male snake detects a chemical on the skin of a female snake, it is stimulated to court the female.

The role of pheromones in humans is much less clear, but it appears that we do have some sort of pheromone-like system (Bhutta, 2007). A possible human gene for pheromone receptors has been found (Rodriguez et al., 2000), and pheromones have been shown to cause reproduction-related physiological changes in humans (Grammer, Fink, & Neave, 2005). Specifically, pheromonal signals secreted in women's perspiration can influence nearby women's menstrual cycles. As a result, women living together eventually tend to menstruate at about the same time (Stern & McClintock, 1998). Furthermore, odorants that cannot be consciously detected can nevertheless influence mood and stimulate activity in non-olfactory areas of the brain (Jacob & McClintock, 2000; Jacob et al., 2001; Savic et al., 2001).

Despite steamy ads for cologne and perfume, however, there is little or no evidence that humans give off or can detect pheromones that act as sexual attractants. In one study, for example, exotic dancers reported that their income from customer tips increased during the ovulation phase of their menstrual cycles (Miller, Tyber, & Jordan, 2007), but the difference was probably not due to pheromones. During ovulation females tend to speak in a more sexually attractive manner (Pipitone & Gallup, 2008), to be more interested in erotic stimuli (Mass et al., 2008), and to be more receptive to courtship (Gueguen, 2008; Rosen & López, 2009). So it could well be that differences in their behavior, and not pheromones, were responsible for their higher tip income during ovulation (Miller, Tyber, & Jordan, 2007).

If a certain scent does enhance a person's readiness for sex, it is probably because the person has learned to associate that scent with previous sexual experiences. There are many other examples of people using olfactory information in social situations. For instance, after just a few hours of contact with their newborn babies, mothers can usually identify their infant by smell (Porter, Cernich, & McLaughlin, 1983). And if infants are breastfed, they can discriminate their own mother's odor from that of other breastfeeding women and appear to be comforted by it (Porter, 1991). Recognizing this odor may help establish the mother-infant bond discussed in the chapter on human development.

pheromones Chemicals that are released by one creature and detected by another, shaping the second creature's behavior or physiology.

papillae Structures in the mouth on which taste buds are grouped.

Our Sense of Taste

Our receptors for taste are in the taste buds, which are grouped together in structures called **papillae** (pronounced "puh-PILL-ee"). Normally, there are about 10,000 taste buds in a person's mouth, mostly on the tongue but also on the roof of the mouth and on the back of the throat.

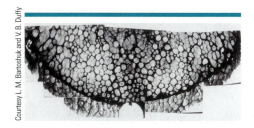

Courtesy L. M. Bartoshuk and V. B. Duffy

FIGURE 3.17 ■ **ARE YOU A SUPERTASTER?**

This photo shows papillae on the tongue of a "supertaster." If you don't mind a temporary stain on your mouth and teeth, you can look at your own papillae by painting the front of your tongue with a cotton swab soaked in blue food coloring. Distribute the dye by moving your tongue around and swallowing; then look into a magnifying mirror as you shine a flashlight on your tongue. The pink circles you see against the blue background are papillae, each of which has about six taste buds buried in its surface. Get several friends to do this test, and you will see that genes create wide individual differences in taste-bud density.

Learn BY **Doing**

In Review

Smell and Taste

ASPECT OF SENSORY SYSTEM	ELEMENTS	KEY CHARACTERISTICS
Energy	Smell: volatile chemicals Taste: chemicals in solution	The amount, intensity, and location of the chemicals determine taste and smell sensations.
Structures of taste and smell	Smell: chemical receptors in the mucous membrane of the nose Taste: taste buds grouped in papillae in the mouth	Odor and taste molecules stimulate chemical receptors.
Pathway to the brain	Olfactory bulb and taste buds	Axons from the nose and mouth bypass the thalamus and extend directly to the olfactory bulb.

?

1. The flavor of food arises from a combination of _____ and _____.
2. Emotion and memory are linked especially closely to our sense of _____.
3. Perfume ads suggest that humans are affected by _____ that increase sexual attraction.

The human taste system detects only a few basic sensations: sweet, sour, bitter, and salty. Each taste bud responds best to one or two of these categories (Zhang et al., 2003), but it responds weakly to others, too. Research has also revealed two additional taste sensations (Rolls, 1997). One, called *umami* (which means "delicious" in Japanese), enhances other tastes and is produced by certain proteins as well as by monosodium glutamate (MSG) (Kondoh & Torii, 2008). The other, called *astringent,* is the taste produced by tannins, which are found in tea, for example. About 25 percent of us are *supertasters*—individuals whose genes have given them an especially large number of papillae on their tongues (Bartoshuk, 2000; see Figure 3.17). Supertasters are more sensitive than other people to bitterness, as revealed in their reactions to foods such as broccoli, soy products, and grapefruit.

Scientists are learning more and more about how interactions between foods and taste receptors signal various tastes (Chandrashekar et al., 2006; Small et al., 2003; Stillman, 2002), and they are putting the information to good use. Understanding the chemistry of sweetness, for example, has led to new chemicals that fit into sweetness receptors and taste thousands of times sweeter than sugar. When used in products such as artificial sweeteners, they offer new ways to enjoy good-tasting but low-calorie sweets. ("In Review: Smell and Taste" summarizes our discussion of these senses.)

Sensing Your Body

⊙ *Which is the largest organ in my body?*

Some senses are not located in one place, such as in the eye or the ear. These are the *somatic senses*, also called *somatosensory systems,* and they are spread throughout the body. The **cutaneous senses** include the skin senses of touch, temperature,

cutaneous senses Senses including touch, temperature, pain, and kinesthetic perception that are spread throughout the body rather than located in a specific organ. Also called somatosensory systems.

and pain. Another body sense, called *kinesthesia,* or *kinesthetic perception,* tells the brain where the parts of the body are. Kinesthetic perception is closely related to our sense of balance. Although balance is not strictly a somatosensory system, we describe it here.

Touch and Temperature

People can function and prosper without vision, hearing, or smell. But a person without a sense of touch would have difficulty surviving. Without this sense, you could not even swallow food, because you could not tell where it was in your mouth and throat. You receive touch sensations through your skin, which is the body's largest organ. The skin covers nearly two square yards of surface area, weighs more than twenty pounds, and has hair virtually everywhere on it. The hairs on your skin do not sense anything directly. However, when the hairs are bent, they push against the skin beneath them. Neural receptors in and just below the skin send the "touch" message to the brain.

Encoding Touch Information　　The sense of touch encodes information about two aspects of an object contacting the skin: its weight and its location. The *intensity* of the stimulus—how heavy it is—is encoded both by the firing rate of individual neurons and by the number of neurons stimulated. A heavy object triggers a higher rate of firing and stimulates more neurons than a light object. The brain "knows" where the touch occurs based on the *location* of the nerves that sense the touch information.

Adapting to Touch Stimuli　　Continuous input from all your touch neurons would provide a lot of unnecessary information. Once you get dressed, you do not need to be constantly reminded that you are wearing clothes. Thanks in part to the process of sensory adaptation described earlier, you do not continue to feel your clothes against your skin.

Changes in touch (as when your belt or shoe suddenly feels loose) provide the most important sensory information. The touch sense emphasizes these changes and filters out the excess information. How? Typically, a touch neuron responds with a burst of firing when a stimulus is applied then quickly returns to its base-line firing rate, even though the stimulus may still be in contact with the skin. If the touch pressure increases, the neuron again responds by increasing its firing rate and then slowing down. A few neurons adapt more slowly, however, continuing to fire as long as pressure is applied. By attending to this input, you can sense a constant stimulus (try doing this by focusing on touch sensations from your clothes or shoes, or the surface you are sitting on).

Sensing Temperature   Some of the skin's sensory neurons respond to a change in temperature but not to simple contact. "Warm fibers" and "cold fibers" respond to specific temperature changes only. However, many fibers that respond to temperature also respond to touch, so these sensations sometimes interact. For example, if you touch an object made up of alternating warm and cool sections, you will have the sensation of intense heat (Thunberg, 1896, cited in Craig & Bushnell, 1994).

Pain

Touch can feel pleasurable, but if the intensity of touch stimulation increases too much, it can turn into a pain sensation. Pain tells you about the impact of the world on your body. It also has a distinctly negative emotional component that interrupts whatever you are doing (Eccleston & Crombez, 1999).

Pain as an Information Sense   The receptors for pain are free nerve endings that come from the spinal cord, enter the skin, and then simply end. Painful stimuli cause the release of chemicals that fit into these specialized receptors in pain neurons, causing them to fire. The axons of pain-sensing neurons release neurotransmitters not only near the spinal cord (thus sending pain information to the brain) but also near the skin (causing inflammation).

A LIFE WITH NO PAIN ▶

Ashlyn Blocker, shown here at age 5 being checked for injuries, was born with a rare genetic disorder that prevented the development of pain receptors. As a result, she feels no pain if she is cut or bruised, if she bites her tongue while eating, or even if she is burned by hot soup or a hot stove. She only knows she has been injured if she sees herself bruised or bleeding, so she will have to find ways to protect herself from danger without the vital information provided by the pain system. Ashlyn doesn't yet understand the seriousness of her condition, but her worried mother says "I would give anything for her to feel pain" (Associated Press, 2004).

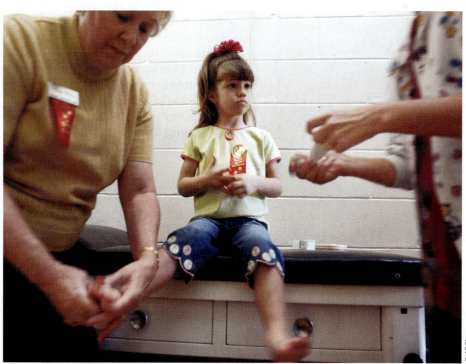

Two types of nerve fibers carry pain signals from the skin to the spinal cord. *A-delta* fibers carry sharp, pricking pain sensations; *C-fibers* carry dull, continuous aches and burning sensations. When you stub your toe, for example, that immediate wave of sharp, intense pain is signaled by A-delta fibers, whereas that slightly delayed wave of gnawing, dull pain is signaled by C-fibers. When pain impulses reach the spinal cord, they form synapses with neurons that relay the pain signals to the thalamus and other parts of the brain. Different pain neurons are activated by different types and degrees of painful stimulation (Ploner et al., 2002).

Emotional Aspects of Pain   There are specific pathways that carry the emotional component of a painful stimulus to areas of the hindbrain, the reticular formation, and the cortex via the thalamus (Johansen, Fields, & Manning, 2001). However, our overall emotional response to pain depends greatly on how we think about it (Spinhoven et al., 2005; Wager, 2005; Weich et al., 2008). In one study, some participants were told about the kind of painful stimulus they were to receive and when to expect it. Others were not informed. Those who knew what to expect objected less to the pain, even though the sensation was reported to be equally noticeable in both groups (Mayer & Price, 1982). People can lessen their emotional responses to pain by using pain-reducing strategies such as listening to music (McCaffrey & Locsin, 2006) or focusing on distracting thoughts (Patterson et al., 2006), especially if they expect these strategies to succeed (Bantick et al., 2002). Scientists are also developing special biofeedback systems that may someday allow patients to relieve chronic pain by reducing activity in the brain regions involved in pain perception (deCharms et al., 2005).

The Gate Control Theory of Pain   Pain is useful because it can protect you from harm. There are times, though, when enough is enough. Fortunately, the nervous system has several mechanisms for controlling the experience of pain. One theory about how these mechanisms work is called the **gate control theory of pain** (Melzack & Wall, 1965). This theory suggests that there is a "gate" in the spinal cord that either allows pain signals to reach the brain or stops them. Some details of the original theory were incorrect, but more recent work supports the idea that natural mechanisms can indeed block pain sensations at the level of the spinal cord (DeLeo, 2006).

For example, input from other skin senses can come into the spinal cord at the same time the pain gets there and take over the pathways that the pain impulses would have used. This may be why we can temporarily relieve pain by rubbing the skin around a wound or using electrical stimulation or creams that produce temperature sensations (Henderson, 2008; Slavin, 2008). It also helps explain why scratching relieves itching; itchy sensations involve activity in fibers located close to pain fibers (Andrew & Craig, 2001). Unfortunately, pain gates can sometimes be "left open." Chronic pain conditions can be caused by damage or inflammation in the peripheral nervous system that sensitizes incoming pain pathways, making them more likely to send pain signals to the brain (D'Mello & Dickenson, 2008).

The brain itself can close the gate to pain impulses by sending signals down the spinal cord. These messages from the brain block incoming pain signals at spinal cord synapses. The result is **analgesia** (pronounced "ann-nuhl-JEE-zhah"), a reduction in pain sensation in the presence of a normally painful stimulus. Aspirin and other *analgesic* drugs can dull pain sensations, but it may also be possible to help the brain close the pain gate without them. For example, research participants who received fifteen minutes of transcranial magnetic stimulation (see Table 2.1 in the chapter on biology and behavior) found it easier to withstand a painful heat stimulus (Borckardt et al., 2007), and patients suffering from pain caused by brain damage are being helped by other brain-stimulation techniques (Arle & Shils, 2008).

gate control theory of pain   A theory suggesting the presence of a "gate" in the spinal cord that either permits or blocks the passage of pain impulses to the brain.

analgesia   Reduction in the sensation of pain in the presence of a normally painful stimulus.

NATURAL ANALGESIA ▶

The stress of athletic exertion causes the release of endorphins, natural painkillers that have been associated with pleasant feelings known as "runner's high" (Benedetti, 2007; Lipscombe & Raingo, 2006).

Natural Analgesics   As described in the chapter on biology and behavior, natural opiates called *endorphins* play a role in the brain's ability to block pain signals. Endorphins are natural painkillers that act as neurotransmitters at many levels of the pain pathway. In the spinal cord, for example, they block the synapses of the fibers that carry pain signals. Endorphins may also relieve pain when the adrenal and pituitary glands secrete them into the bloodstream as hormones. The more endorphin receptors a person has inherited, the more pain tolerance that person has (Kest, Wilson, & Mogil, 1999; Uhl, Sora, & Wang, 1999).

Several conditions can cause the body to ease its own pain. For example, endorphins are released where inflammation occurs (Cabot, 2001). During the late stages of pregnancy, a spinal cord endorphin system develops to reduce the mother's labor pains (Dawson-Basoa & Gintzler, 1997). An endorphin system is also activated when people believe they are receiving a painkiller, even when they are not (Colloca & Benedetti, 2005; Zubieta et al., 2005); this may help explain the placebo effect, as described in the introduction to the science of psychology chapter (Stewart-Williams, 2004). Interestingly, the resulting pain inhibition is experienced in the part of the body where it was expected to occur, but not elsewhere (Benedetti, Arduino, & Amanzio, 1999). Physical or psychological stress can also activate natural analgesic systems. Stress-induced release of natural analgesics may account for the fact that injured soldiers and athletes sometimes continue to perform in the heat of battle or competition with no apparent pain (Colloca & Benedetti, 2005).

THINKING CRITICALLY

Does Acupuncture Relieve Pain?

Acupuncture, a widely used 3000-year-old Asian medical treatment, is said to relieve pain (Lin & Chen, 2008). The treatment is based on the idea that body energy, called *Qi*, flows along lines called *channels* that link the internal organs to places on the surface of the skin (Vincent & Richardson, 1986; see Figure 3.18). According to this theory, there are fourteen main channels and a person's health depends on the balance of energy flowing in them. Stimulating the channels by inserting fine needles into the skin and twirling them is said to restore a balanced flow of energy. The needles produce an aching and tingling sensation called *Teeh-ch'i* at the site of stimulation and they relieve pain in distant, seemingly unrelated parts of the body (Liu & Akira, 1994; Yan et al., 1992).

▶ What am I being asked to believe or accept?

Acupuncturists claim that twirling needles in the skin can relieve pain caused by everything from tooth extraction to cancer.

▶ Is evidence available to support the claim?

There is no scientific evidence for the existence of the energy channels proposed by acupuncturists (Wang, Kain, & White, 2008). However, there *is* evidence from positron emission tomography (PET) and magnetic resonance imaging (MRI) studies that stimulating acupuncture sites changes activity in brain regions related to pain regulation and to the targets of treatment (Lewith, White, & Pariente, 2005; Yan et al., 2005; Zhang et al., 2009). Numerous studies have also shown positive results in 50 to 80 percent of patients treated by acupuncture for various kinds of pain (Brinkhaus et al., 2006; Manheimer et al., 2005; Witt et al., 2005). One summary of eleven such studies found greater overall reductions in headache pain among patients who had been randomly assigned to receive acupuncture as compared to those randomly assigned to receive standard drug therapies (Linde et al., 2009). Adding acupuncture to a program of drugs and exercise was followed by a greater reduction in the pain of fibromyalgia, and the difference remained apparent three months after treatment (Targino et al., 2008). Another study found that acupuncture before surgery reduced postoperative pain and nausea, decreased the need for pain-relieving drugs, and reduced patients' stress responses (Kotani et al., 2001). Yet another found electrical-stimulation acupuncture to be more effective than either drugs or fake stimulation at reducing nausea following major breast surgery; the acupuncture group also reported the least postoperative pain (Gan et al., 2004).

Well-controlled studies of acupuncture are rare, however, and their results can be contradictory. Some studies of patients with back or neck pain, for example, have found acupuncture to be no better than placebo treatments or massage therapy (Assefi et al., 2005; Foster et al., 2007; Linde et al., 2009); others have found that acupuncture benefits only certain patients (Yuan et al., 2008).

Drugs that slow the breakdown of opiates also prolong the pain relief produced by acupuncture (He, 1987). The pain-reducing effects of acupuncture during electrical stimulation of a tooth can be reversed by naloxone, a substance that blocks the pain-killing effects of endorphins and other opiate drugs. These findings suggest that acupuncture does somehow activate the body's natural pain-killing system. Is this activation brought about only by a placebo effect? Probably not entirely, because acupuncture produces naloxone-reversible pain relief even in monkeys and rats, who obviously have no expectations about acupuncture (Ha et al., 1981; Kishioka et al., 1994).

▶ Can that evidence be interpreted another way?

Yes. Evidence about acupuncture might be interpreted as simply confirming that the body's pain-killing system can be stimulated by external means. Acupuncture may merely provide one activating method (Pariente et al., 2005). There may be other methods for doing so that are even more efficient (Petrovic et al., 2005; Ulett, 2003). We already know, for example, that successful placebo treatments for human pain appear to operate by activating the endorphin system.

▶ What evidence would help to evaluate the alternatives?

More placebo-controlled studies of acupuncture are needed, but it has been difficult to control for the placebo effect in acupuncture treatment, especially in double-blind fashion (e.g., Kaptchuk, 2001).

FIGURE 3.18 ■ LINKING INTERNAL ORGANS TO THE SKIN'S SURFACE

These diagrams illustrate the skin locations which are said by acupuncturists to be linked to the large intestine (LI4), the lung (Lu 5), the gallbladder (GB34), and the stomach (ST36).

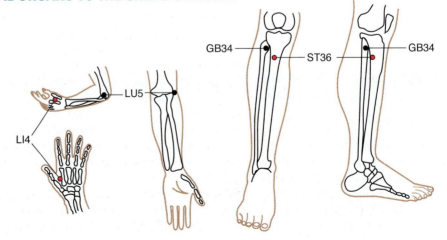

How could a study be set up so that therapists would not know whether the treatment they are giving is acupuncture or not? What placebo treatment could look and feel like having a needle inserted and twirled in the skin? Some researchers have created single-blind placebo acupuncture using "sham" techniques in which the needles do not actually break the skin or are inserted but not twirled or are inserted in locations that should not, according to acupuncturists, have any effect on pain. In one study of "sham" techniques, research participants were indeed unable to tell whether or not they were getting genuine acupuncture (Enblom et al., 2008). So far, only a few studies have used sophisticated "sham" methods (Madsen, Gøtzsche, Hróbjartsson, 2009), and some have found acupuncture to be no more effective than placebo methods (e.g. Haake et al., 2007; Linde et al., 2009). Future controlled experiments should eventually reveal the degree to which placebo effects play a role in the results of acupuncture treatment.

Researchers must also learn more about what factors govern whether acupuncture will activate the endorphin system. Other important unknowns include the types of pain for which acupuncture is most effective, the types of patients who respond best, and the precise procedures that are most effective. Knowing more about the general relationship between internal pain-killing systems and external methods for stimulating them would also be valuable.

▶ What conclusions are most reasonable?

Although acupuncture is by no means a cure-all, it appears that in some circumstances it may help to relieve pain and reduce nausea (British Medical Association, 2000; National Institutes of Health Consensus Conference, 1998). What we still don't know is exactly why this may be and through what mechanism any genuine effects might operate. So acupuncture remains a fascinating phenomenon, a treatment used on millions of people all over the world, and a continuing source of controversy. Some critics argue that further expenditures for acupuncture research are not warranted, but it seems likely that studies will continue. The quality of these studies' methodology and the nature of their results will determine whether acupuncture finds a more prominent place in Western medicine.

Sensing Body Position

Most sensory systems receive information from the outside world, such as the light reflected from a flower or the feeling of cool water. But as far as the brain is concerned, the rest of the body is "outside" too. You know about the position of your body and what each of its parts is doing only because sensory systems provide this information to your brain. Your sense of body movement and position is called **proprioception** (meaning "received from one's own," pronounced "pro-pree-oh-SEP-shun").

Kinesthetic Perception   In the biology and behavior chapter, we describe the case of Christina, a woman who did not recognize her own body. She had lost her **kinesthetic perception** (pronounced "kin-es-THEH-tic"), which tells us where the parts of the body are in relation to one another. To better appreciate kinesthetic perception, try this: Close your eyes; then hold your arms out in front of you and touch your two index fingers together. You probably did this easily because your kinesthetic sense told you where each finger was with respect to your body. You depend on kinesthetic information to guide all your movements, from walking to complex athletic actions such as running down a basketball court while dribbling a ball and avoiding an opposing player. These movement patterns become simple and fluid because with practice the brain uses kinesthetic information automatically. Normally, kinesthetic information comes primarily from **proprioceptors,** which are special receptors in the joints and muscles (Proske, 2006). These receptors send information to the brain about the stretching of muscles. When the position of the bones changes, receptors in the joints set off neural activity. This encoded information goes to the spinal cord and then to the thalamus, along with sensory information from the skin. Finally it goes to the cerebellum and to the somatosensory cortex, both of which help coordinate movements (see Figures 2.8, 2.9, and 2.10).

Balance   Have you ever been on a roller coaster? How did you feel when the ride ended? Your **sense of equilibrium,** sometimes called the **vestibular sense** (pronounced "ves-TIB-u-ler"), tells your brain about the position of your head (and, to some degree,

proprioception   The sensory processes that tell us about the location of our body parts and what each is doing.

kinesthetic perception   The proprioceptive sense that tells us where the parts of the body are with respect to one another.

proprioceptors   Neural receptors that provide information about movement and body position.

sense of equilibrium (vestibular sense)   The proprioceptive sense that provides information about the position of the head and its movements.

the rest of your body) in space and about its general movements. You have probably heard it referred to as the *sense of balance.* People usually become aware of the sense of equilibrium only when they overstimulate it and become dizzy or experience motion sickness.

The inner ear contains the organs for the vestibular sense. Each ear has two *vestibular sacs* that are filled with fluid and contain small crystals called *otoliths* ("ear stones") that rest on hair endings. Three arc-shaped tubes, called the *semicircular canals,* are also filled with fluid (see Figure 3.14). Tiny hairs extend into the fluid in the canals. When your head moves, the otoliths shift in the vestibular sacs and the fluid moves in the semicircular canals, stimulating hair endings. These responses to head movement activate neurons that travel along the acoustic nerve, signaling the brain about the amount and direction of head movement (Angelaki & Cullen, 2008).

Neural connections from the vestibular system to the cerebellum help coordinate bodily movements. Connections to the part of the autonomic nervous system that affects the digestive system help create the nausea that may follow overstimulation of the vestibular system—by a roller-coaster ride, for instance. Finally, connections to the eye muscles produce *vestibular-ocular reflexes,* which cause your eyes to move opposite to your head movements. These reflexes allow you to focus on one spot even when your head is moving. You can experience these reflexes by having a friend spin you around on a stool for a while. When you stop, try to fix your gaze on one point in the room. You'll be unable to do so, because the excitation of the vestibular system will cause your eyes to move repeatedly in the direction opposite from the way you were spinning. (See "In Review: Body Senses" for a summary of our discussion of touch, temperature, pain, and kinesthesia.)

Learn BY Doing

In Review

BODY SENSES

SENSE	ENERGY	CONVERSION OF PHYSICAL ENERGY TO NERVE ACTIVITY	PATHWAYS AND CHARACTERISTICS
Touch	Mechanical deformation of skin	Neural receptors in the skin (may be stimulated by hair on the skin)	Nerve endings respond to changes in weight (intensity) and location of touch.
Temperature	Heat	Sensory neurons in the skin	Changes in temperature are detected by warm-sensing and cool-sensing fibers. Temperature interacts with touch.
Pain	Increases with intensity of touch or temperature	Free nerve endings in or near the skin surface	Changes in intensity cause the release of chemicals detected by receptors in pain neurons. Some fibers convey sharp pain; others convey dull aches and burning sensations.
Kinesthetic perception	Mechanical energy of joint and muscle movement	Neural receptors in muscle fibers	Information from muscle fibers is sent to the spinal cord, thalamus, cerebellum, and cortex.
Sense of equilibrium	Mechanical energy of head movement	Neural receptors in the inner ear.	Information about fluid moving in the semicircular canals is sent to the brain along the acoustic nerve.

1. Gate control theory offers an explanation of why we sometimes do not feel _____.
2. Professional dancers look at the same spot as long as possible during repeated spins. They are trying to avoid the dizziness caused when the sense of _____ is overstimulated.
3. Without your sense of _____ you would not be able to swallow food without choking.

Perception

 *How do sensations become perceptions?*

So far, we have explored how sensory information reaches the brain. Let's now consider the processes of perception that allow the brain to make sense of that information. These perceptual processes can sometimes make the difference between life and death. For example, at a traffic circle in Scotland, fourteen fatal accidents occurred in one year, partly because drivers did not slow down as they approached the circle. After warning signs failed to solve the problem, Gordon Denton, a British psychologist, found a clever solution. He recommended that white lines be painted across the road leading to the circle, in a pattern something like this:

/ / / / / / //

Crossing these lines, which were spaced progressively more closely, gave drivers the impression that they were speeding up, so their automatic response was to slow down (Denton, 1980). During the fourteen months after Denton's idea was implemented, there were only two fatalities at the traffic circle! Similar kinds of striping patterns are now widely used throughout Britain and on approaches to some towns and intersections in the United States. Denton's solution depended partly on his knowledge of sensation but mostly on the principles of human perception.

Some perceptual tasks take attention and effort, as when a child struggles to recognize printed letters. But as experienced readers know, a lot of the perceptual work that transforms sensory information into meaningful experiences happens automatically without conscious awareness. To illustrate the workings of these complex processes, psychologists draw attention to *perceptual failures*—cases in which we perceive stimuli incorrectly. Just as drivers at the traffic circle incorrectly perceived themselves as speeding up, you will probably perceive the two lines in Figure 3.19 as differing in length, even though they are the same.

FIGURE 3.19 ■ MISPERCEIVING REALITY

Measure lines A-C and A-B. They are exactly the same length, but you probably perceived A-C as longer. Why? Partly because your visual system tries to interpret all stimuli as three-dimensional, even when they are not. A three-dimensional interpretation of this drawing would lead you to see the two lines as the edges of two parallel paths, one of which ends closer to you than the other. Your eyes tell you that the two paths start at about the same point (the castle entrance), so you assume that the closer line must be the longer of the two.
Source: Gardner (1988).

Learn BY **Doing**

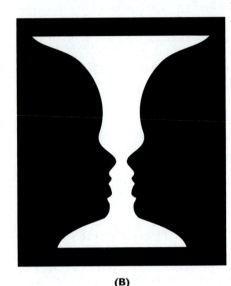

(A)

(B)

FIGURE 3.20 ■ **REVERSIBLE IMAGES**

These *reversible images* can be organized by your perceptual system in two ways. If you perceive Part A as the word "figure," the space around the letters becomes meaningless background. Now emphasize the word "ground," and what had stood out a moment ago now becomes background. In Part B, when you emphasize the white vase, the black profiles become background; if you organize the faces as the figure, what had been a vase now becomes background. We normally tend to see smaller, lower elements in a scene as figure and larger, higher elements as ground (Vecera, Vogel, & Woodman, 2002), but images like these don't allow us to use that rule of thumb.

Learn BY Doing

---

figure   The part of the visual field that has meaning.

ground   The contourless part of the visual field; the background.

figure ground discrimination   The ability to organize a visual scene so that it contains meaningful figures set against a less relevant ground.

Organizing the Perceptual World

▶ *What determines how I perceive my world?*

To further appreciate the wonder of the complicated perceptual work you do every day, imagine yourself driving on a busy road searching for Barney's Diner, an unfamiliar restaurant where you are to meet a friend. The roadside is crammed with signs of all shapes and colors, some flashing, some rotating. If you are ever to recognize the sign that says "Barney's Diner," you will have to impose some sort of organization on this overwhelming mixture of visual information. How do you do this? How do you know where one sign ends and another begins? And how do you know that an apparently tiny sign is not really tiny but just far away?

Principles of Perceptual Organization

Before you can recognize the Barney's Diner sign, your perceptual system must separate that sign from its background of lights, colors, letters, and other competing stimuli. Two basic principles—*figure ground perception* and *grouping*—guide this initial organization.

Figure and Ground   When you look at a complex scene or listen to a noisy environment, your perceptual apparatus automatically emphasizes certain features, objects, or sounds. These emphasized features become the **figure.** This part of the visual field has meaning, stands in front of the rest, and always seems to include contours or edges. These contours and edges separate the figure from the less relevant background, called the **ground** (Rubin, 1915). As you drive toward an intersection, a stop sign will become a figure that stands out clearly against the background of trees or buildings.

To experience your own **figure ground discrimination** ability, look at Figure 3.20. Notice that you can decide how to organize the stimuli in the drawings. You can repeatedly reverse figure and ground to see faces, then a vase, then faces again (3.20B) or to see the word *figure* or the word *ground* (3.20A). The fact that you can mentally manipulate these "reversible" images shows that your perceptual systems are not just recording devices that passively absorb incoming sensations; you play an active part in organizing what you perceive. We also usually organize sensory stimulation into only one perceptual category at a time. This is why it is difficult to see both a vase and two faces—or the words *figure* and *ground*—at the same time.

Grouping   Why is it that certain parts of the world become figure and others become ground, even when nothing in particular stands out in the pattern of light that falls on the retina? The answer is that certain properties of stimuli lead you to group them together more or less automatically.

In the early 1900s, several German psychologists described the principles behind this grouping of stimuli. They argued that people perceive sights and sounds as organized wholes. These wholes, they said, are different from the sum of the individual sensations, just as a house is something other than a pile of bricks and wood and glass. Because the German word meaning (roughly) "whole figure" is *Gestalt* (pronounced "ge-SHTALT"), these researchers became known as *Gestalt psychologists*. They proposed a number of principles that describe how the perceptual system "glues" raw sensations together in particular ways (Kimchi, 2003):

1. *Proximity.* The closer objects or events are to one another, the more likely they are to be perceived as belonging together, as Figure 3.21(A) illustrates.
2. *Similarity.* Similar elements are perceived to be part of a group, as in Figure 3.21(B). This is why students wearing the same school colors at a stadium will be perceived as belonging together even if they are not seated close together.
3. *Continuity.* Sensations that appear to create a continuous form are perceived as belonging together, as in Figure 3.21(C).

FIGURE 3.21 ■ GESTALT PRINCIPLES OF PERCEPTUAL GROUPING

We tend to perceive Part A as two groups of two circles plus one single circle rather than as, say, five circles. In Part B, we see two columns of Xs and two columns of Os, not four rows of XOXO. We see the X in Part C as being made out of two continuous lines, not a combination of the odd forms shown. In Part D, we fill gaps so as to perceive a hollow cube. In Part E, we tend to pair up dots in the same oval even though they are far apart. Part F shows that connected objects are grouped together.

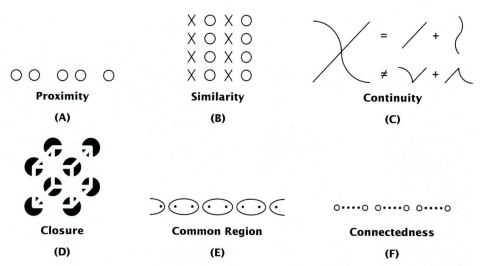

Proximity
(A)

Similarity
(B)

Continuity
(C)

Closure
(D)

Common Region
(E)

Connectedness
(F)

4. *Closure.* We tend to mentally fill in missing parts of incomplete objects, as in Figure 3.21(D). The gaps are easy to see, but the tendency to link disconnected parts can be so strong that you may perceive faint connections that are not actually there (Meng, Remus, & Tong, 2005).

5. *Texture.* When basic features of stimuli have the same texture (such as the angle of several elements), we tend to group those stimuli together. So we group standing trees together and perceive them as separate from their fallen neighbors.

6. *Simplicity.* We tend to group features of a stimulus in a way that provides the simplest interpretation of the world. You can see the simplicity principle in action in Figure 3.21(D), where it is simpler to see a single cube than an assortment of separate and unrelated arrows and Ys.

7. *Common fate.* Sets of objects that move in the same direction at the same speed are perceived together. So even though individual birds in a flock are separated from each other in space, they will be perceived as a group as they fly south. Choreographers and marching-band directors use this principle of common fate when they arrange for groups or subgroups of dancers or musicians to move in unison, causing the audience to perceive waves of motion or a single large moving object.

Stephen Palmer (1999) has identified three additional grouping principles:

1. *Synchrony.* Stimuli that occur at the same time are likely to be perceived as coming from the same source. For example, if you see a car up ahead stop violently at the same instant that you hear a crash, you will probably perceive these visual and auditory stimuli as part of the same event.

2. *Common region.* Stimuli located within some boundary tend to be grouped together. The boundary can be created by an enclosing perimeter, as in Figure 3.21(E), a region of color, or other factors.

3. *Connectedness.* Stimuli that are connected by other elements tend to be grouped together. In Figure 3.21(F), the circles connected by dotted lines seem to go together even though they are farther apart than some pairs of unconnected circles. Here, the principle of connectedness appears more important than the principle of proximity.

Perception of Depth and Distance

depth perception Perception of distance, allowing us to experience the world in three dimensions.

We are able to experience the world in three-dimensional depth even though the visual information we receive from it is projected onto two-dimensional retinas. This is possible because of **depth perception,** our ability to perceive distance. Depth perception,

FIGURE 3.22 ■ STIMULUS CUES FOR DEPTH PERCEPTION

See if you can identify the cues of relative size, interposition, linear perspective, height in the visual field, textural gradient, and shadows that combine to create a sense of three-dimensional depth in this photograph. Notice, too, that sidewalk artist Kurt Wenner has used some of these same cues to create a dramatic illusion of depth in his drawing. (You can see more of Wenner's amazing work at http://www.kurtwenner.com/street/.)

Learn BY **Doing**

in turn, is made possible by *stimulus cues* provided by the environment and also by the properties of our visual system (Anderson, 2004).

Stimulus Cues   To some extent, people perceive depth through the same cues that artists use to create the impression of depth and distance on a two-dimensional canvas. Figure 3.22 demonstrates several of these cues:

- One of the most important depth cues is *interposition*: Closer objects block the view of things farther away. This cue is illustrated in Figure 3.22 by the couple walking away from the camera. Because their bodies block out part of the buildings, we perceive them as being closer to us than the buildings are.

- You can see the principle of *relative size* operating in Figure 3.22 by measuring the images of that same couple and comparing it to the size of the man in the foreground. If two objects are assumed to be about the same size, the object producing a larger image on the retina is perceived as closer than the one producing a smaller image.

- Another cue comes from *height in the visual field*: On the ground, objects that are more distant are usually higher in the visual field than those that are nearby. Because the building in the center of Figure 3.22 is higher than the people in the restaurant, the building appears to be farther away from you. This is one reason why objects higher in the visual field are more likely to be interpreted as the background for objects that are lower in a scene (Vecera, Vogel, & Woodman, 2002).

- The tiny figures near the center of Figure 3.22 are seen as very far away because they are near a point where the buildings on each edge of the plaza, like all parallel lines that recede into the distance, appear to converge toward a single

FIGURE 3.23 ■ LIGHT, SHADOW, AND DEPTH PERCEPTION

The shadows cast by these protruding rivets and deep dents make it easy to see them in three dimensions. But if you turn the book upside down, the rivets now look like dents, and the dents look like bumps. This reversal in depth perception occurs partly because people normally assume that illumination comes from above and interpret the pattern of light and shadow accordingly (Adams, Graf, & Ernst, 2004; Cook et al., 2008). With the picture upside down, light coming from the top would produce the observed pattern of shadows only if the circles were dents, not rivets.

Learn BY Doing

point. This apparent *convergence* provides a cue called linear perspective. The closer together two converging lines are, the greater the perceived distance.

- Notice that the street in Figure 3.22 fades into a hazy background. Increased distance usually produces less clarity, and this *reduced clarity* is interpreted as a cue for greater distance. (Hazy, distant objects also tend to take on a bluish tone, which is why art students are taught to add a little blue when mixing paint for deep background features.)

- *Light and shadow* also contribute to the perception of three dimensions (Kingdom, 2003; Ramachandran, 1988). The buildings in Figure 3.22 are seen as three-dimensional, not flat, because of the shadows on some of their surfaces. Figure 3.23 shows a more dramatic example.

- An additional stimulus-based depth cue comes from continuous changes across the visual field, called *gradients*. For example, a textural gradient is a graduated change in the texture, or "grain," of the visual field, as you can see in the plaza and the street in Figure 3.22. Texture appears finer and less detailed as distance increases. As the texture of a surface changes across the retinal image, you perceive a change in distance.

Cues Based on Properties of the Visual System Some depth cues result from the way human eyes are built and positioned. Recall that to bring an image into focus on the retina, the lens of the eye changes shape, or *accommodates*. Information about the muscle activity involved is relayed to the brain, and this *accommodation cue* helps create the perception of distance.

Two other depth cues are produced by the relative location of our two eyes. The first is **eye convergence.** Each eye is located at a different place on the skull, so the eyes

must converge, or rotate inward, to project the same image on each retina. The closer the object, the more the eyes must converge. Eye muscles send information about this convergence to the brain, which processes it as a distance cue. You can experience this feedback from your eye muscles by holding up a finger at arm's length and then trying to keep it in focus as you move it toward your nose.

Second, because they are in slightly different locations, each eye sees the world from a slightly different angle. The difference between these different retinal images is called **retinal disparity,** also known as **binocular disparity.** The difference, or disparity,

eye convergence A depth cue that results when the eyes rotate to project the image of an object on each retina.

retinal disparity A depth cue based on the difference between the retinal images received by each eye.

© AP Photo

A CASE OF DEPTH ▲
MISPERCEPTION

The runner in this photo is actually farther away than the man on the pitcher's mound. But because he is lower, not higher, in the visual field—and because his leg can be seen as in front of, not behind, the pitcher's leg—the runner appears smaller than normal rather than farther away (Vecera, Vogel, & Woodman, 2002).

between images gets smaller for objects that are far away and larger for objects that are nearby. The brain not only combines the two images of an object but also takes into account how much they differ. This information helps generate the impression of a single object that has depth as well as height and width and is located at a particular distance. Three-dimensional movies and some virtual reality systems use these *binocular cues* to create the appearance of depth in a two-dimensional stimulus. They show each eye an image of a scene as viewed from a slightly different angle.

In short, many cues—some present in the environment and in retinal images, others arising from the structure of the visual system—combine to give us a powerful and accurate sense of depth and distance.

Perception of Motion

Sometimes the most important property of an object is its motion—how fast it is going and where it is heading. Many cues about motion come from *optical flow,* or the changes that take place in retinal images across the visual field. As in the case of depth perception, you automatically translate this two-dimensional information into a three-dimensional experience. One particularly meaningful pattern of optical flow is known as **looming,** the rapid expansion in the size of an image so that it fills the retina. When an image looms, there is an automatic tendency to perceive it as an approaching object. If the expansion is as fast to the right as to the left and as fast above as below, this information signals that the object is directly approaching the eyes. In other words: Duck!

We are lucky that movement of the retinal image is not the only factor contributing to motion perception. If it were, everything in sight would appear to move every time you moved your eyes and head (Ölveczky, Baccus, & Meister, 2003). This does not happen, because as noted earlier, the brain receives and processes information about the motion of the eyes and head (Wexler, 2005). If you look around you right now, tables, chairs, and other stationary objects will not appear to move because your brain determines that all the movement of images on your retinas is due to the movement of your eyes and head (Goltz et al., 2003). But now close one eye and wiggle your open eyeball by gently pushing your lower eyelid. Because your brain receives no signals that your eye is being moved by its own muscles, everything in the room will appear to move.

When your body is moving, as in a car, the flow of visual information across the retina combines with information from the vestibular and touch senses to give you the experience of being in motion. If the car accelerates, you feel pressure from the back of the seat and feel your head tilting backward. If visual flow is perceived without appropriate sensations from other parts of the body, particularly the vestibular senses, motion sickness may result. This explains why you might feel nauseous while in a motion simulator or playing certain video games, especially those with virtual reality technology. The images suggest that you are moving through space when there is no real motion.

Other illusions of motion are more enjoyable. The most important of these occurs when still images appear, one at a time, in rapid succession, as they do on films, videos, and DVDs. Because each image differs slightly from the preceding one, the brain sees the objects in each image at one location for only a fraction of a second before they disappear and immediately reappear in a slightly different location. The entertaining result is the **stroboscopic illusion** of motion; when objects disappear and then quickly reappear nearby, the brain assumes that they have moved smoothly from one location to another. The same illusion is at work when it appears that flashing lights on a theater or casino sign are moving around the sign.

Perceptual Constancy

Suppose that one sunny day you are watching someone walking toward you along a tree-lined path. The visual sensations produced by this person are actually very strange. For one thing, the size of the image on your retinas keeps getting larger as

looming A motion cue whereby rapid expansion in the size of an image fills the available space on the retina.

stroboscopic illusion An illusion of motion that is created when we see slightly different images or slightly displaced lights flashed in rapid succession.

RETINAL DISPARITY AND DISTANCE ▶

There is a smaller difference, or disparity, between each eye's view of an object when the object is far away than when it is close by. The amount of this retinal disparity helps us estimate the object's distance from us. To see for yourself how retinal disparity changes with distance, hold a pencil vertically about six inches in front of your nose; then close one eye and notice where the pencil is in relation to the background. Now open that eye, close the other one, and notice how much the pencil "shifts." These are the two different views your eyes have of the pencil. Repeat this procedure while holding the pencil at arm's length. Notice that there is now less disparity or "shift," because there is less difference in the angles from which your two eyes see the pencil.

© PictureNet/Corbis

the person gets closer. To see this for yourself, hold out a hand at arm's length and look at someone far away. The retinal image of that person will be so small that you can cover it with your hand. If you do the same thing when the person is three feet away, the retinal image will be too large to be covered by your hand, yet you will perceive the person as being closer now, not bigger. Similarly, as you watch the person pass from bright sunshine through the shadows of trees, your retinas receive images that shift back and forth from light to dark, but you perceive the person's coloring as staying the same.

These examples illustrate **perceptual constancy,** the perception that objects keep their size, shape, color, and other properties despite changes in their retinal image. Without this aspect of perception, you would experience the world as a place where solid objects continuously changed their properties.

Size Constancy Why does an object's perceived size stay more or less constant, regardless of changes in the size of its retinal image? One reason is that the brain perceives a change in the distance of an object and automatically adjusts the perception of size. Specifically, the *perceived size* of an object is equal to the size of the retinal image multiplied by the perceived distance (Holway & Boring, 1941). As an object moves closer, the size of its retinal image increases but the perceived distance decreases at the same rate. So the perceived size remains constant. If a balloon is inflated in front of your eyes, perceived distance remains constant and the perceived size (correctly) increases as the size of the retinal image increases.

Shape Constancy The principles behind shape constancy are closely related to those of size constancy. To see shape constancy at work, close this book (remember what page you are on) and tilt it toward and away from you several times. The book will continue to look rectangular, even though the shape of its retinal image changes dramatically as you move it. Your brain automatically combines information about retinal images and distance as movement occurs. In this case, the distance information has to do with the difference in distance between the near and far edges of the book.

Brightness Constancy Even with dramatic changes in the amount of light striking an object, our perception of the object's brightness remains relatively constant

perceptual constancy The perception that objects retain the same size, shape, color, and other properties despite changes in their retinal image.

A FAILURE OF SHAPE CONSTANCY ▶

When certain stimuli are viewed from an extreme angle, the brain's ability to maintain shape constancy can break down. Traffic engineers take this phenomenon into account in the design of road markings, as shown in these photos from a London airport. The arrow in the top photo appears to be about the same height as the lettering below it, but it isn't. The arrow had to be greatly elongated, as shown in the side view, so that approaching drivers would see its shape clearly. If the arrow had been painted to match the height of the accompanying letters, it would appear "squashed," and only half as tall as the lettering.

applying psychology

Phillip Kent/www.anamorphosis.com

(MacEvoy & Paradiso, 2001). To see this for yourself, place a piece of charcoal in sunlight and a piece of white paper in nearby shade. The charcoal will look very dark and the paper very bright, yet a light meter would tell you that much more light energy is reflected from the sun-bathed coal than from the shaded paper. The reason is partly that the charcoal is the darkest object relative to its sunlit background and the paper is the brightest object relative to its background of shade. As shown in Figure 3.24, the brightness of an object is perceived in relation to its background.

Learn BY **Doing**

FIGURE 3.24   ■   BRIGHTNESS CONTRAST

At first glance, the inner rectangle on the left probably looks lighter than the inner rectangle on the right. But carefully examine the inner rectangles alone (covering their surroundings) and you will see that both are of equal intensity. The brighter surround in the right-hand figure leads you to perceive its inner rectangle as relatively darker.

Learn BY **Doing**

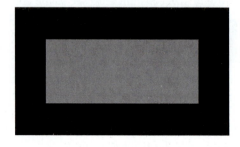

FIGURE 3.25 ■ THREE SIZE ILLUSIONS

These illusions are named for the scientists who described them. In Part A, a version of the Ponzo illusion, the upper monster looks bigger but is actually the same size as the lower one. In the Müller-Lyer illusion (Part B), both vertical lines are actually of equal length; in the Ebbinghaus illusion shown in Part C, both center circles are exactly the same size. To prove that you can't always believe your eyes, measure these drawings for yourself.

Learn BY Doing

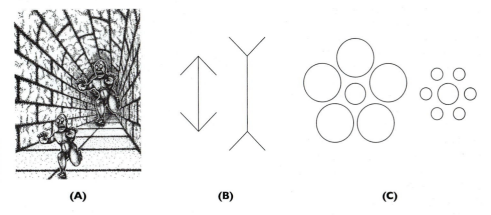

(A) (B) (C)

Size Illusions

Usually the visual perceptual system works automatically and perfectly to create correct impressions of depth, distance, and size. Sometimes, though, it can fail, resulting in *size illusions* such as the ones shown in Figure 3.25. Why does the monster that is placed higher in Figure 3.25(A) look larger than the lower one even though they are exactly the same size? The converging lines in the tunnel provide depth cues telling you that the higher monster is farther away. Because the retinal image of the "distant" monster is the same size as the "closer" one, your perceptual system calculates that the more distant monster must be bigger. This is the principle of size constancy at work: When two objects have retinal images of the same size, you perceive the one that seems farther away as larger. Now look at Figure 3.25(B). The two vertical lines are the same length, but the

In Review

PRINCIPLES OF PERCEPTUAL ORGANIZATION AND CONSTANCY

PRINCIPLE	DESCRIPTION	EXAMPLE
Figure ground discrimination	Certain objects or sounds automatically become identified as figure, whereas others become meaningless background.	You see a person standing against a building, not a building with a person-shaped hole in it.
Grouping	Properties of stimuli lead us to automatically group them together. These include proximity, similarity, continuity, closure, texture, simplicity, common fate, synchrony, common region, and connectedness.	People who are sitting together, or who are dressed similarly, are perceived as a group.
Depth perception	The world is perceived as three-dimensional, with help from stimulus cues (such as relative size, height in the visual field, interposition, linear perspective, reduced clarity, light and shadow, and gradients) and from visual system cues (such as accommodation, convergence, and binocular disparity).	A person who looks tiny and appears high in the visual field will be perceived as being of normal size, but at a great distance.
Perceptual constancy	Objects are perceived as constant in size, shape, color, and other properties despite changes in their retinal images.	A train coming toward you is perceived as getting closer, not larger; an advertising sign is perceived as rotating, not changing shape.

1. The movement we see in movies, videos, and DVDs is due to a perceptual illusion called _____.
2. People who have lost an eye also lose the depth cue called _____.
3. The grouping principle of _____ allows you to identify objects seen through a picket fence.

one on the right looks longer. Why? One possible reason is that the perceived length of an object is based on what frames it. When the frame is perceived as larger, as on the right side of Figure 3.25(B), the line segment within it is perceived as larger too (Rock, 1978). In Figure 3.25(C), the inner circle at the left looks smaller than the one at the right because, like the brightness of the center rectangles in Figure 3.24, the inner circles are judged in relation to what surrounds them. Because perception is based on many principles, illusions like these probably reflect the violation of more than one of them. (See "In Review: Principles of Perceptual Organization and Constancy.")

Recognizing the Perceptual World

 How do I recognize familiar people?

In discussing how people organize the perceptual world, we have set the stage for addressing one of the most vital questions that perception researchers must answer: How do we recognize what objects are? If you are driving in search of Barney's Diner, exactly what happens when your eyes finally locate the pattern of light that spells out its name?

To know that you have finally found what you have been looking for, your brain must analyze incoming patterns of information and compare them with information about the target that you have stored in memory. If the brain finds a match, recognition takes place. Once you recognize a stimulus as belonging to a particular category, your perception of the stimulus may never be the same again. Look at Figure 3.26. Do you see anything familiar? If not, turn to Figure 3.27; then look at Figure 3.26 again. You should now see it in an entirely new light. The difference between your "before" and "after" experiences is the difference between the sensory world before and after a perceptual match occurs and recognition takes place.

How does this matching process occur? Some aspects of recognition begin at the "top." That is, they are guided by knowledge, expectations, and other psychological factors. This phenomenon is called **top-down processing,** because it involves high-level, knowledge-based information. Other aspects of recognition begin at the "bottom,"

FIGURE 3.26 ■ CATEGORIZING PERCEPTIONS

What do you see here? For the identity of this figure, turn to Figure 3.27.

top-down processing Aspects of recognition guided by higher-level cognitive processes and by psychological factors such as expectations.

"Satan In the Smoke" © Mark D. Phillips/markdphillips.com

WHAT DOES IT LOOK LIKE TO YOU? ▲

Some people see the devil's face in this photo of smoke from the World Trade Center under attack on September 11, 2001. This perception results partly from top-down processes, such as knowledge about the evil of the attack, that make it easier to see something demonic. People who don't expect to see a face in the smoke—or whose cultural background doesn't include the "devil" concept—may not see one until that interpretation is suggested. To check that possibility, show this photo to people from various religions and cultures (cover the caption). Ask if they see anything in the smoke but don't immediately tell them what to look for. How many, and which ones, identified a demonic face before you mentioned it?

Learn BY Doing

bottom-up processing Aspects of recognition that depend first on information about stimuli that come up to the brain from the sensory systems.

schemas Mental representations of what we know and expect about the world.

relying on specific detailed information from the sensory receptors and assembling them into a whole. This phenomenon is called **bottom-up processing,** because it begins with basic information units that serve as a foundation for recognition.

Bottom-Up Processing

All along the path from the eye to the brain, certain cells respond to selected features of a stimulus. The stimulus is first analyzed into these *basic features,* which are then recombined to create the perceptual experience.

What are these features? As mentioned earlier, certain cells specialize in responding to lines, edges, corners, and stimuli that have specific orientations in space (Hubel & Wiesel, 1979). For example, some cells in the cerebral cortex fire only in response to a diagonal line, so they act as *feature detectors* for diagonal lines. The analysis by such feature detectors early in the sensation-perception sequence may contribute to recognition of letters or judgments of shape. Color and motion are other sensory features that appear to be analyzed separately in different parts of the brain before full perceptual recognition takes place (Beatty, 1995; Cowey, 1994; Treisman, 1999).

The brain also apparently analyzes patterns of light and darkness in the visual scene. Analyzing these patterns may help us perceive textural gradients, which in turn help us to judge depth and recognize the general shape of blurry images.

Top-Down Processing

Bottom-up feature analysis can explain why you recognize the letters in a sign for Barney's Diner. But why is it that you can recognize the sign more easily if it appears where you were told to expect it rather than a block earlier? And why can you recognize it even if a few letters are missing from the sign? Top-down processing seems to be at work in those cases. In top-down processing, people rely on their knowledge to make inferences (or "educated guesses") that help them recognize objects, words, or melodies, especially when sensory information is vague or ambiguous (DeWitt & Samuel, 1990; Rock, 1983). For example, once you knew that there was a dog in Figure 3.26, it became much easier for you to perceive one. Similarly, police officers find it easy to recognize familiar people on blurry security-camera videos, but it is much more difficult for them to recognize strangers (Burton et al., 1999).

Top-down processing illustrates that our experiences create **schemas,** mental representations of what we know and expect about the world. Schemas can bias our perception toward one recognition or another by creating a *perceptual set*—that is, a readiness to perceive a stimulus in a certain way. These expectations operate automatically, whether we are aware of them or not. For example, look again at Figure 3.21D. We see a hollow cube floating above the circles because once the closure principle has filled in the gaps, our experience tells us that the most likely interpretation of the resulting pattern of lines is a cube—even though it is not really there. A tragic example of a more conscious perceptual set occurred on the evening of November 13, 2007, when New York City police officers shot to death a highly agitated man after a 911 operator told them he had a gun. The man approached the officers holding a black object, and when he ignored their orders to stop, they fired. The object in his hand turned out to be a hairbrush, but it was dark, so they interpreted the object in accordance with their expectations.

Expectancy can be shaped by the *context* in which a stimulus occurs. For example, we know of a woman who saw a masked man in the darkened hallway of a house she was visiting. Her first perception was that the man who lived there was playing a joke; in fact, she had confronted a burglar. Context has biasing effects for sounds as well as sights. When shots are heard on a downtown street, they are often perceived as firecrackers or a car backfiring. The same sounds heard at a shooting range would immediately be interpreted as gunfire.

Motivation is another aspect of top-down processing that can affect perception. A hungry person, for example, might initially mistake a sign for Burger's Body Shop as indicating a place to eat. Similarly, perhaps you remember a time when an obviously

FIGURE 3.27   ■   ANOTHER VERSION OF FIGURE 3.26

Now that you can identify a dog in this figure, it should be much easier to recognize when you look back at the original version.

incompetent referee incorrectly called a penalty on your favorite sports team. You knew the call was wrong because you clearly saw the other team's player at fault. But suppose you had been cheering for that other team. The chances are good that you would have seen the referee's call as the right one.

Top-Down and Bottom-Up Processing Together

Top-down and Bottom-up processing usually work together to help us recognize the perceptual world. This interaction is beautifully illustrated by the process of reading. When the quality of the raw stimulus on the page is poor, as in Figure 3.28, top-down processes compensate to make continued reading possible. They allow you to fill in the gaps where words or letters are missing, thus giving you a general idea of the meaning of the text.

You can fill in the gaps because the world is *redundant;* it provides multiple clues about what is going on. So even if you lose or miss one stimulus in a pattern, other clues can help you recognize the pattern. There is so much redundancy in written language, for instance, that many of the words and letters you see are not needed. Fo- ex-mp-e, y-u c-n r-ad -hi- se-te-ce -it- ev-ry -hi-d l-tt-r m-ss-ng. Similarly, vision in three dimensions normally provides multiple cues to depth, making recognition of distance easy and clear. It is when many of these cues are eliminated that ambiguous stimuli create the sorts of depth illusions discussed earlier.

In hearing, too, top-down processing can compensate for ambiguous stimuli. In one experiment, participants heard strings of five words in meaningless order, such as "wet brought who socks some." There was so much background noise, however, that participants who heard this sequence could recognize only about 75 percent of the words (Miller, Heise, & Lichten, 1951). The words were then read to a second group of participants in a meaningful order (e.g., "who brought some wet socks"). The second group was able to recognize almost all of the words, even under the same noisy conditions. In fact, it took twice as much noise to reduce their performance to the level of the first group. Why? When the words were in meaningless order, only bottom-up processing was available. Recognizing one word was no help in identifying the next. Meaningful sentences, however, provided a more familiar context and allowed for some top-down processing. Hearing one word helped the listener make a reasonable guess

FIGURE 3.28 ■ INTERACTION OF TOP-DOWN AND BOTTOM-UP PROCESSING

Which obscured line do you find easier to read: the one on the top or the one on the bottom? Top-down processing should help you read the obscured text on the top line. However, in the bottom line, the words are not related, so top-down processing cannot operate.

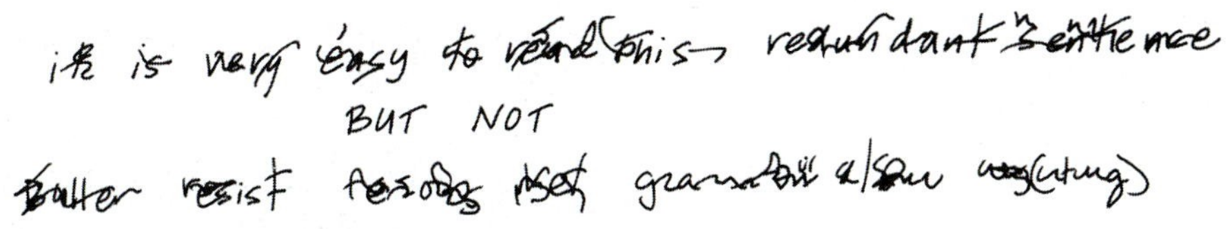

(based on knowledge and experience) about the others. (See "In Review: Mechanisms of Pattern Recognition" for a summary of bottom-up and top-down processing.)

Culture, Experience, and Perception

We have been talking as if all aspects of perception work or fail in the same way for everyone everywhere. The truth is, though, that virtually all perceptual abilities are shaped to some extent by the sensory experiences we have or have not had (Kitayama et al., 2003). For example, people are better at judging the size and distance of familiar objects than of unfamiliar ones. Size and shape constancy, too, depend partly on the knowledge and experience that tell us that most solid objects do not suddenly change their size or shape. The experience-based nature of perception can also be seen in brightness constancy: You perceive charcoal to be darker than a sheet of writing paper partly because no matter how much light the charcoal reflects, you *know* charcoal is black. Experience even teaches us when to ignore certain stimulus cues (Yang & Kubovy, 1999). To fully experience the depth portrayed in a painting, for example, you have to ignore ridges, scratches, dust, or other texture cues from the canvas that

In Review

MECHANISMS OF PATTERN RECOGNITION

MECHANISM	DESCRIPTION	EXAMPLE
Bottom-up processing	Raw sensations from the eye or the ear are analyzed into basic features, such as edges, color, or movement; these features are then recombined at higher brain centers, where they are compared with stored information about objects or sounds.	You recognize a dog as a dog because its features—four legs, barking, panting—match your perceptual category for "dog."
Top-down processing	Knowledge of the world and experience in perceiving allow people to make inferences about the identity of stimuli, even when the quality of raw sensory information is low.	On a dark night, a small, vaguely seen blob pulling on the end of a leash is recognized as a dog because the stimulus occurs at a location where we would expect a dog to be.

?

1. *Your ability to read a battered old sign that has some letters missing is a result of _____ processing.*

2. *When stimulus features match the stimuli we are looking for, _____ takes place.*

3. *Schemas can create a _____ that makes us more likely to perceive stimuli in a particular way.*

FIGURE 3.29   ■   CULTURE AND DEPTH CUES

People in various cultures were shown drawings like these and asked to judge which animal is closer to the hunter. Those in cultures that provide lots of experience with pictured depth cues choose the antelope, which is at the same distance from the viewer as the hunter. Those in cultures less familiar with such cues may choose the elephant, which, though closer on the page, is more distant when depth cues are considered. *Source*: Hudson (1960).

would remind you of its flatness. And the next time you are watching TV, notice the reflections of objects in the room that appear on the screen. You have learned to ignore these reflections, so it will take a little effort to perceive them and a lot of effort to focus on them for long.

What if you hadn't had a chance to learn or practice these perceptual skills? One way to explore this question is through case studies of people who have been blind for decades and then have had surgery that restored their sight. It turns out that these people can immediately recognize simple objects and perceive movement, but they usually have problems with other aspects of perception (Gregory, 2005). For example, M. M. had been blind from early childhood. When his vision was restored in his forties, he adjusted well overall, but he still has difficulty with depth perception and object recognition (Fine et al., 2003). Often, as people move toward or away from him, they appear to shrink or inflate. Identifying common objects can be difficult for him, and faces pose a particular challenge. To recognize individuals, he depends on features such as hair length or eyebrow shape. M. M. also has trouble distinguishing male faces from female ones and has great difficulty recognizing the meaning of facial expressions. He is unable to experience many of the perceptual illusions shown in this chapter, such as the closure illusion in Figure 3.21(D) or the size illusions in Figure 3.25. M. M.'s early blindness appears to have prevented his brain from fully developing the neural connections necessary for drawing accurate inferences about the visual world.

For the rest of us, too, the ability to experience perceptual illusions depends on our sensory history. People who grow up in significantly different sensory environments are likely to have noticeably different perceptual experiences. For example, the size illusion shown in Figure 3.25(A) is strongest in the "carpentered world," where seeing straight lines is an everyday experience (Leibowitz et al., 1969). Responses to illusions such as this one are not as strong for people from rural Africa and other places in which the visual environment contains more irregular and curved lines than straight ones (Coren & Girgus, 1978). Similarly, responses to depth cues in pictures and paintings differ in cultures that do and do not use such images to represent reality. People in the Me'n or the Nupa cultures of Africa, who have little experience with pictorial representation, have a more difficult time judging distances shown in pictures than do people in picture-oriented cultures (see Figure 3.29). These individuals also tend to have a harder time sorting pictures of three-dimensional objects into categories, even though they can easily sort the objects themselves (Derogowski, 1989). And residents of dense tropical rain forests, where most objects are seen over relatively short distances, may have some difficulty when asked to judge the distance of remote objects on an open plain (Turnbull, 1961). In other words, although the structure and principles of human perceptual systems tend to create generally similar views of the world for all of us, our perception of reality is also shaped by experience, including the experience of living in a particular culture (Chua, Boland, & Nisbett, 2005; Hedden et al., 2008).

linkages

How do infants perceive the world?
(a link to Human Development)

Linkages

Perception and Human Development

We have seen that perception is influenced by the knowledge and experience we gain over time, but what perceptual abilities do we start with? To learn about infants' perception, psychologists have studied two inborn patterns called *habituation* and *dishabituation*. Infants stop looking when they repeatedly see stimuli that they perceive to be the same. This is habituation. If they see a stimulus that is perceived to be new and different, they resume looking. This is dishabituation. Using the habituation/dishabituation technique, researchers have found that newborns can perceive differences in stimuli showing various amounts of black-and-white

FIGURE 3.30 ■ INFANTS' PERCEPTIONS OF HUMAN FACES

Newborns show significantly greater interest in the face-like pattern at the far left than in any of the other patterns. Evidently some aspects of face perception are innate. *Source*: Johnson et al. (1991).

contrast but that they cannot yet distinguish differences between colors (Burr, Morrone, & Fiorentini, 1996). Other studies using the same methods have shown that newborns can perceive differences in the angles of lines (Slater et al., 1991). Taken together, these studies suggest that we are born with the basic components of feature detection.

Are we also born with the ability to combine features into perceptions of whole objects? This is still a matter of debate. We know that at one month, infants concentrate their gaze on one part of an object, such as the corner of a triangle (Goldstein, 2002). By two months, though, their eyes systematically scan around the edges of the object. This change suggests that they are now perceiving the pattern, or shape, of the object, not just its component features. However, other researchers have found that newborns show dishabituation (that is, they pay attention) when a familiar set of features are combined in a new way. So even newborns appear to notice and keep track of the ways some stimulus features are put together (Slater et al., 1991).

Infants may also be innately tuned to perceive at least one important complex pattern of features: the human face. In one study of newborns, patterns such as those in Figure 3.30 were moved slowly past the infants' faces (Johnson et al., 1991). The infants moved their heads and eyes to follow these patterns. But they tracked the face-like pattern shown on the left side of Figure 3.30 significantly farther than any of the nonfaces. The differences in tracking in this study and others indicates that infants can tell faces from nonfaces and are more interested in faces, or at least in face-like patterns (Simion et al., 2003; Valenza et al., 1996). Why should this be? Investigators who take an evolutionary approach suggest that interest in human faces is adaptive because it helps newborns focus on their only source of food and care.

Other research on perceptual development suggests that our ability to accurately perceive depth and distance develops more slowly than our ability to recognize shapes (see Figure 3.31). For example, infants' ability to use binocular disparity and motion cues to judge depth appears to develop sometime after about three months of age (Yonas, Arterberry, & Granrud, 1987). They do not use textural gradients and linear perspective as cues to depth until they are five to seven months old (Arterberry, Craton, & Yonas, 1993; Bhatt & Bertin, 2001).

In summary, there is little doubt that many of the basic building blocks of perception are present within the first few days after birth. The basics include such organ-based cues to depth as accommodation and convergence. Maturation of the visual system adds to these basics as time goes by. Over the first few months after birth, the eye's fovea gradually develops the number of cone cells necessary for high visual acuity and perception of fine details (Goldstein, 2002). Visual experience is also necessary. Experience teaches the infant to recognize unified patterns and objects and to interpret depth and distance cues and use them to move safely through the world (Johnson, 2005; Quinn & Bhatt, 2005). Like so many aspects of human psychology, perception is the result of a blending of heredity and environment. From infancy onward, the perceptual system creates a personal reality.

FIGURE 3.31 ■ THE VISUAL CLIFF

The *visual cliff* is a glass-topped table that creates the impression of a sudden dropoff. A ten-month-old placed at what looks like the edge will calmly crawl across the shallow side to reach a parent but will hesitate and cry rather than crawl over the "cliff" (Gibson & Walk, 1960). Changes in heart rate show that infants too young to crawl also perceive the depth but are not frightened by it. Here is another example of the adaptive interaction of nature and nurture: Depth perception appears shortly after birth, but fear and avoidance of dangerous depth do not develop until an infant is old enough to crawl into trouble.

© Mark Richards/PhotoEdit

Attention

▶ *Can you run out of attention?*

Believe it or not, you still haven't found Barney's Diner! By now, you understand *how* you will recognize the right sign when you perceive it. But how can you be sure you *will* perceive it? The diner's sign will appear as one small piece of a sensory puzzle that also includes road signs, traffic lights, sirens, talk radio, and dozens of other stimuli. You can't perceive all of them at once. To find Barney's, you are going to have to be sure that the information you process includes the stimuli that will help you reach your goal. In short, you are going to have to pay attention.

Attention is the process of directing and focusing certain psychological resources to enhance perception, performance, and mental experience. We use attention to *direct* our sensory and perceptual systems toward certain stimuli, to *select* specific information for further processing, to *allocate* the mental energy required to do that processing, and to *regulate* the flow of resources necessary for performing a task or coordinating several tasks at once (Wickens & Carswell, 2006).

Psychologists have discovered three important characteristics of attention. First, it *improves mental processing*. You often need to concentrate attention on a task to do your best at it. Second, attention takes *effort*. Prolonged concentration of attention can leave you drained (McNay, McCarty, & Gold, 2001). When you are already tired, focusing attention on anything becomes more difficult. Third, attention is *limited*. When your attention is focused on reading this book, for instance, you will have less attention left over to listen to a conversation in the next room.

Directing Attention

To experience the process of attention, try "moving it around" a bit. When you finish reading this sentence, look at something behind you, then face forward and notice the next sound you hear, then visualize your best friend, then focus on how your tongue feels. You just used attention to direct your perceptual systems toward different aspects of your external and internal environments. When you looked behind you, shifting attention involved *overt orienting*—pointing sensory systems at a particular stimulus. But you were able to shift

Learn BY Doing

attention The process of directing and focusing certain psychological resources to enhance perception.

Courtesy Dr. Ronald Rensink

FIGURE 3.32 ■ CHANGE BLINDNESS

Can you see the difference between these photos? If not, or if it took you a while to see it, you may have been focusing your attention on the similarity of main features, resulting in blindness to one small, but obvious difference. (see below for the answer). Just as we are usually unaware of our visual blind spot (see Figure 3.8), we tend to be blind to inattentional blindness. We think we can see everything around us, but accidents are caused everyday because people sometimes fail to see what is right in front of their eyes (Galpin, Underwood, & Crundall, 2009).

Learn BY Doing

The difference between the photos in Figure 3.32 is that the top picture includes a clump of trees just to the left of the statue.

attention to an image of your friend's face without having to move a muscle. This is called *covert orienting.* (We have heard a rumor that students sometimes use covert orienting to shift their attention from their lecturer to thoughts that have nothing to do with the lecture.)

How do you control, or allocate, your attention? Research shows that control over attention can be voluntary or involuntary (Yantis, 1993). *Voluntary,* or goal-directed, control over attention occurs when you purposely focus so that you can perform a task. Voluntary control reflects top-down processing because attention is guided by knowledge-based factors such as intention, beliefs, expectations, and motivation. As people learn certain skills, they voluntarily direct their attention to information they once ignored. For example, the experienced driver notices events taking place farther down the road than the first-time driver does.

When some aspect of the environment—such as a loud noise—diverts your attention, control is said to be *involuntary,* or stimulus driven. Stimulus characteristics that tend to capture attention include abrupt changes in lighting or color (such as flashing signs), movement, and the appearance of unusual shapes (Folk, Remington, & Wright, 1994). Engineering psychologists' findings on which stimuli are most likely to attract—and distract—attention have been used in the design of everything from Internet web sites and billboard ads to operator warning devices for airliners, nuclear power plants, and other complex systems (Clay, 2000; Laughery, 1999). Other psychologists use the results of attention research to help design advertisements, logos, and product packaging that grab potential customers' attention.

As already mentioned, attending to some stimuli makes us less able to attend to others. In other words, attention is *selective.* It is like a spotlight that can illuminate only a part of the external or internal environment at any particular moment. So if you focus intently on your reading or on a computer game, you may fail to perceive even dramatic changes in other parts of your environment. This phenomenon has been called *inattentional blindness* (Mack, 2003; Mack & Rock, 1998). In one study, a researcher asked college students for directions to a campus building (Simons & Ambinder, 2005). During each conversation, two "workmen" carrying a large door passed between the researcher and the student. As the door hid the researcher from the student's view, one of the "workmen" took his place. This new person then resumed the conversation with the student as though nothing had happened. Amazingly, only half of the students noticed that they were suddenly talking to a new person! The rest had apparently been paying so much attention to the researcher's question or to the map he was showing that they did not notice what he looked like. Magicians take advantage of inattentional blindness when they use sudden movements or other attention-grabbing stimuli to draw our attention away from the actions that lie behind their tricks. To experience a type of inattentional blindness known as "change blindness," take a look at the photos in Figure 3.32.

Your search for Barney's Diner will be helped by your ability to overtly allocate attention to a certain part of the environment. It would be made even easier if Barney's had the only flashing sign on the road. As the most intense stimulus around you, it would attract your attention automatically. Psychologists describe this ability to search for targets rapidly and automatically as *parallel processing.* It is as if you can examine all nearby locations at once (in parallel) and rapidly detect the target no matter where it appears.

Dividing Attention

Often you can divide your attention efficiently enough to allow you to perform more than one activity at a time (Damos, 1992). You can drive a car, listen to the radio, sing along, and keep a beat by drumming on the steering wheel. However, your attention cannot be divided beyond a certain point without a loss in performance and mental-processing ability. For example, automobile drivers are much more likely to miss important signals, make errors in following directions, and react more slowly to potentially dangerous situations when talking on a mobile phone, even if it is a hands-free model (Strayer & Drews, 2007). The reason is that attention is a limited resource. If you try to spread it over too many targets, you "run out" of attention.

BLUE   GREEN
GREEN   ORANGE
PURPLE   ORANGE
GREEN   BLUE
RED   RED
GRAY   GRAY
RED   BLUE
BLUE   PURPLE

FIGURE 3.33 ■ **THE STROOP TASK**

Look at this list of words and as rapidly as possible call out the *color of the ink* in which each word is printed. How did you do?

Improve Your Grade
Tutorial: The Stroop Task

Still, it can sometimes be hard to keep your attention focused rather than divided. Look at the list of words in Figure 3.33 and as rapidly as possible call out the *color of the ink* in which each word is printed. This *Stroop task* (Stroop, 1935) is not easy, because your brain automatically processes the meanings of the familiar words in the list. These meanings then compete for attention with the responses you are supposed to give. To do well, you must focus on the ink color and not allow your attention to be divided between color and meaning. Children just learning to read have far less trouble with this task because they don't yet process the meanings of words as automatically as experienced readers do.

Although you can walk while talking or drive while listening to music, you would find it virtually impossible to read and talk at the same time. Why is it sometimes so easy and at other times so difficult to do two things at once? When one task is so automatic as to require little or no attention, it is usually easy to do something else at the same time (Schneider, 1985). Even when two tasks require attention, it may still be possible to perform them simultaneously if each taps into different kinds of attention (Wickens, 2002; Wickens et al., 1992). Some types of attention are devoted to perceiving incoming stimuli. Others handle making responses. This specialization of attention allows a skilled pianist to read musical notes and press keys simultaneously the first time through a piece. Apparently, the human brain can manage more than one type of attention and more than one spotlight of attention (Wickens, 1989). This notion of different types of attention also helps explain why an experienced driver can listen to the radio while steering safely. If two tasks require the same kind of attention, however, performance on both tasks will suffer (Just et al., 2001).

FOCUS ON RESEARCH

Attention and the Brain

What happens in the brain as people try to attend to more than one source of information at the same time?

What was the researchers' question?

If directing attention to more than one task causes extra mental work to be done, there should be evidence of that work in brain activity. One possibility is that information-processing activity in the brain should slow down. Does it? This was the question asked by one research team.

How did the researchers answer the question?

Allan J. Nash and Mercedes Fernandez (1996) examined the brain-processing speed of participants engaged in various tasks. Sixteen college students heard high and low tones and saw red and green light flashes. They were asked to respond as quickly as possible to the identified target stimulus. On some trials they were to ignore tones and respond only to one of the lights, and on other trials they were to respond to one light and keep a running count of one of the tones. In short, the participants either attended to one task (responding to a light) or split their attention between two tasks (responding to a light and counting tones). The speed of the participants' reactions to the flashing light was measured throughout the experiment.

What did the researchers find?

When attention had to be shared between information required for two tasks, reaction times were slower than they were in response to the single-attention task.

What do the results mean?

The finding that reaction times were slower on split-attention trials suggests that information processing in the brain was slower too. Further evidence for this conclusion has been provided by PET scans. They reveal increased blood flow to regions of the brain where mental processing is taking place (Corbetta et al., 1991; Just et al., 2001). When attention is focused on only one stimulus feature, increased blood flow appears only in the part of the brain where that feature is analyzed. But when attention is divided, the added supply of blood is shared between two locations.

What do we still need to know?

Still to be determined are the limits of attention, the means by which attention is shared, and the specific parts of the brain that are involved in attention, whether divided or undivided. So far, research using PET scans, surgery on laboratory animals, and case studies of humans with brain damage has shown that switching the spotlight of visual attention involves at least three different parts of the brain (e.g., Braver, Reynolds, & Donaldson, 2003; Posner & Raichle, 1994). Attention appears to be a linked set of resources that improve mental processing at several levels and locations in the brain. No single brain region has yet been identified as an "attention center" (Posner & Peterson, 1990; Sasaki et al., 2001).

ACTIVE REVIEW ▶ Chapter 3

Sensation *and* Perception

As noted in the introductory chapter, all of psychology's subfields are related to one another. Our discussion of the development of perception illustrates just one way that the topic of this chapter, sensation and perception, is linked to the subfield of developmental psychology, which is described in the

chapter on human development. The Linkages diagram shows ties to two other subfields, and there are many more ties throughout the book. Looking for linkages among subfields will help you see how they all fit together and help you better appreciate the big picture that is psychology.

linkages

How do infants perceive the world?
(ans. on p. 126)

Do people perceive hallucinations as real sensory events? (ans. on p. 490)

Do we sometimes perceive people the same way we perceive objects?
(ans. on p. 551)

Chapter 9
Human Development

Chapter 12
Psychological Disorders

Chapter 14
Social Psychology

SUMMARY ▶

Sensing and Perceiving the World

▶ *What is the difference between sensation and perception?*

A **sense** is a system that translates information from outside the nervous system into neural activity. Messages from the senses are called **sensations.** **Perception** is the process through which people actively use knowledge and understanding of the world to interpret sensations as meaningful experiences.

Sensory Systems

▶ *How does information from my eyes and ears get to my brain?*

The first step in sensation involves **accessory structures,** which collect and modify sensory stimuli. The second step is **transduction,** the

process of converting incoming energy into neural activity; it is accomplished by sensory **neural receptors,** neural cells specialized to detect energy of some type. **Sensory adaptation** takes place when receptors continue to receive stimulation that does not change. Except in the case of smell, neural activity is transferred through the thalamus, which relays it to the cerebral cortex.

Encoding is the translation of physical properties of a stimulus into a pattern of neural activity that specifically identifies those physical properties. It is the language the brain uses to describe sensations.

The minimum amount of light, sound, pressure, or other physical energy that can be detected 50 percent of the time is called the

absolute threshold. Internal noise is the spontaneous random firing of cells in the nervous system that occurs whether or not you are stimulated by physical energy. Your **response bias, or response criterion,** reflects your willingness to respond to a stimulus or ignore it. **Signal detection theory** addresses whether you will perceive a stimulus. **Sensitivity** refers to your ability to discriminate a stimulus from its background. **Weber's law** states that the smallest detectable difference in stimulus energy is a constant fraction of the intensity of the stimulus. This smallest detectable difference in a stimulus is called the difference threshold or **just-noticeable difference (JND). Wavelength** is the distance from one peak of a sound wave or light wave to the next. Wave **frequency** is the number of complete waves, or cycles, that pass a given point per unit of time. **Amplitude** is the height of the wave from baseline to peak.

Seeing

▶ *Why do some people need eyeglasses?*

Visible light is electromagnetic radiation with a wavelength of about 400 to about 750 nanometers. *Light intensity,* or the amount of energy in light, determines its brightness. Differing *light wavelengths* are sensed as different colors.

Accessory structures of the eye include the *cornea,* the *pupil,* the *iris,* and the *lens.* Through *ocular accommodation* and other means, these structures focus light rays on the *retina* (the net-like structure of cells at the back of the eye).

Photoreceptors in the retina—*rods* and *cones*—convert light into neural activity. Rods and cones differ in shape, sensitivity to light, ability to discriminate colors, and distribution across the retina. Photoreceptors, especially rods, contribute to *dark adaptation.* The *fovea,* the area of highest acuity, has only cones, which are color sensitive. Rods are more sensitive to light but do not discriminate colors; they are distributed in areas around the fovea. From the photoreceptors, neural activity is transferred to bipolar cells and then to ganglion cells. A *blind spot* is created at the point where axons of ganglion cells leave the eye as a bundle of fibers called the *optic nerve.* Half of these fibers cross over at the optic chiasm. *Feature detectors* are cells in the cerebral cortex that respond to specific characteristics of objects in the visual field. The color of an object depends on which of the wavelengths striking it are absorbed and which are reflected. The sensation of color has three psychological dimensions: *hue, color saturation,* and *brightness.*

According to the *trichromatic* (or Young and von Helmholtz) *theory,* color vision results from the fact that the eye includes three types of cones, each of which is most sensitive to short, medium, or long wavelengths. Information from the three types combines to produce the sensation of color. According to the *opponent-process* (or Hering) *theory,* there are red-green, blue-yellow, and black-white visual elements and the members of each pair inhibit each other so that only one member of a pair may produce a signal at a time. Opponent-process theory explains color afterimages.

Hearing

▶ *How would my voice sound on the moon?*

Sound is a repetitive fluctuation in the pressure of a medium such as air; it travels in waves. The frequency (which is related to wavelength) and

amplitude of sound waves produce the psychological experiences of *pitch* and *loudness,* respectively. *Timbre,* the quality of sound,

depends on complex wave patterns added to the basic frequency of sound.

The energy from sound waves is collected and transmitted to the *cochlea* through a series of accessory structures, including the *pinna,* and components of the *middle ear,* including the *tympanic membrane,* the hammer, the anvil, the stirrup, and the oval window. Transduction occurs when sound energy stimulates hair cells on the *basilar membrane* of the cochlea, which in turn stimulate the *acoustic nerve.* Auditory information is relayed through the thalamus to the primary auditory cortex.

The intensity of a sound stimulus is encoded by the firing of auditory neurons. *Place theory* describes the encoding of high frequencies. They are encoded by the place on the basilar membrane at which the sound wave peaks. Each neuron in the acoustic nerve is most sensitive to a specific frequency (its preferred frequency). According to *volley theory,* some frequencies may be matched by the firing rate of a group of neurons.

The Chemical Senses: Taste and Smell

▶ *Why can't I taste anything when I have a cold?*

The chemical senses include smell (olfaction) and taste (gustatory perception). Our *olfactory perception* (sense of smell) detects volatile chemicals that come into contact with olfactory receptors in the nose. Olfactory signals are sent through the olfactory nerve to the *olfactory bulb* in the brain without passing through the thalamus. *Pheromones* are odors from one creature that change the physiology or behavior of another. *Taste perception* detects chemicals that come into contact with taste receptors in *papillae* in the mouth, especially on the tongue. The basic taste sensations are sweet, sour, bitter, salty, umami, and astringent. The senses of smell and taste interact to produce flavor.

Sensing Your Body

▶ *Which is the largest organ in my body?*

The *cutaneous senses,* also called somatosensory systems, include the skin senses and are

related to *proprioception.* The skin senses detect touch, temperature, and pain. When they are mechanically stimulated, nerve

endings in the skin generate touch sensations. Some nerve endings are sensitive to temperature and some respond to both temperature and touch.

Pain provides information about intense stimuli. Sharp pain is carried by A-delta fibers; dull, chronic pain is carried by C-fibers. The emotional response to pain depends on how the painful stimulus is interpreted. According to the *gate control theory of pain,* pain signals can be blocked on their way to the brain, sometimes by messages sent from the brain down the spinal cord, resulting in *analgesia.* Endorphins act at several levels in pain systems to reduce sensations of pain.

Proprioception includes *kinesthetic perception,* which provides information about the position of body parts with respect to one another, and the *sense of equilibrium*, or *vestibular sense* (balance), which provides information about the position of the head in space. This information is provided by *proprioceptors*, which are sensory receptors for movement and body position.

Perception

▶ *How do sensations become perceptions?*

Perception is the knowledge-based interpretation of sensations. Much of this interpretation takes place automatically, but sometimes conscious effort is required to translate sensations into meaningful experience.

Organizing the Perceptual World

▶ *What determines how I perceive my world?*

Our perceptual systems automatically engage in *figure ground discrimination* to sense the difference between *figure* and *ground.*

They also automatically group stimuli into patterns on the basis of the Gestalt principles of proximity, similarity, continuity, closure, texture, simplicity, common fate, and three others known as synchrony, common region, and connectedness.

The perception of distance, or *depth perception,* depends partly on stimulus cues and partly on the physical structure of the visual system. Stimulus cues include relative size, height in the visual field, interposition, linear perspective, reduced clarity, light and shadow, and textural gradients. Cues based on the structure of the visual system include *eye convergence* (the fact that the eyes must move to focus on the same object), *retinal disparity* (the fact that the eyes are set slightly apart), and accommodation (changes in the shape of the lenses as objects are brought into focus).

The perception of motion results, in part, from the movement of stimuli across the retina. Expanding or *looming* stimulation is perceived as an approaching object. Movement of the retinal image is interpreted along with information about movement of the head, eyes, and other body parts so that one's own movement can be discriminated from the movement of external objects. The *stroboscopic illusion* is a movement illusion arising when a series of slightly different still images is seen in rapid succession.

Because of *perceptual constancy,* the brightness, size, and shape of objects are seen as constant despite changes in the sensations received from those objects. Size constancy and shape constancy depend on the relationship between the retinal image of the object and one's knowledge-based perception of how far away the object is. Brightness constancy depends on the perceived relationship between the brightness of an object and its background.

Size illusions are distortions of reality that result when principles of perception are applied inappropriately. Many of these illusions occur when we misread depth cues or when we are overly influenced by the contexts (surroundings) in which visual stimuli appear.

Recognizing the Perceptual World

▶ *How do I recognize familiar people?*

Both *bottom-up processing* and *top-down processing* contribute to our recognition of the world. Our ability to recognize objects is based on our capacity to match the pattern of sensations organized by the perceptual system and a pattern that is stored in memory. Bottom-up processing seems to be accomplished as the brain analyzes features, or combinations of features, such as form, color, motion, and depth. Top-down processing is influenced by our knowledge, expectations and motivation. *Schemas* based on our past experiences can create a perceptual set; that is, a readiness or predisposition to perceive stimuli in certain ways. Expectancies can also be created by the context in which a stimulus appears. Top-down and bottom-up processing commonly work together to create recognition. Top-down processing can fill in gaps in physical stimuli, in part because the environment provides redundant stimuli.

To the extent that the visual environments of people in different cultures differ, their perceptual experiences—and their responses to perceptual illusions—may differ as well.

The ability to perceive color, basic shape features, and possibly the human face is present at or near birth. Other abilities, such the ability to recognize forms, develop later. Depth is also perceived early, but its meaning is learned later. Perceptual abilities are modified by both experience and maturation.

Attention

▶ *Can you run out of attention?*

Attention is the process of focusing psychological resources to enhance perception, performance, and mental experience. We can shift attention overtly (by moving the eyes, for example) or covertly (without any movement of sensory systems). Attention is selective; it is like a spotlight that illuminates different parts of the external environment or specific mental processes. Control over attention can be voluntary and knowledge based or involuntary and driven by environmental stimuli. People can sometimes attend to two tasks at once, but there are limits to how much they can divide their attention.

Learn BY Doing ▶

Put It in Writing

Which of your five sensory systems—vision, hearing, touch, taste, or smell—do you think you could most easily do without? Which could you least easily do without? Write a page describing why you chose each of these sensory systems and listing what you would do to try to make up for the loss of each of these two systems.

Personal Learning Activity

Have you ever noticed how large the moon appears to be when it has just risen above the horizon? Some researchers suggest that the moon appears larger on the horizon than when it is overhead because the horizon moon—seen across a space filled with houses, trees, and terrain—appears to be farther away than when it is overhead (Kaufman & Kaufman, 2000). According to principles of size constancy discussed in this chapter, the greater perceived distance causes the horizon moon to be perceived as larger. This explanation has been questioned, though, because the horizon moon sometimes seems larger even when the observer cannot see the intervening terrain. The next time you see what appears to be a bigger-than-normal full moon just above the horizon, turn your back to it and then bend over and look at the moon, upside down, between your legs. Does the "moon illusion" remain, or is it destroyed when you look at the moon so that terrain appears above it rather than below it? What do you think causes the moon illusion? *For additional projects, see the Personal Learning Activities in the corresponding chapter of the study guide that accompanies this book.*

Take Action to Learn More ▶

Now that you have finished reading this chapter, how about exploring some of the ideas and information that you found most interesting? Here are some courses, books, films, and Internet resources to get you started. Enjoy!

Courses

Sensation and Perception
Speech and Hearing
Biological Psychology
Vision
Artificial Intelligence

Movies

The Miracle Worker. The story of Helen Keller, who was both deaf and blind.

Wait Until Dark. Thriller about a blind woman menaced by killers.

At First Sight. Changes and problems that occur when a man who was blind from birth can suddenly see.

The Matrix. A futuristic film that raises the question, what is reality?

Rashomon. A single event is perceived in vastly different ways by different people.

Daredevil; The Five Senses; Spiderman. Heightened sensory powers.

Sound and Fury. Controversy over cochlear implants.

Beethoven Lives Upstairs; Children of a Lesser God; Goya in Bordeaux. Deafness.

Life Is Beautiful. The power of perception to change one's view of life in a concentration camp.

Harold and Maude. Different perceptions of the meaning of life and death.

If You Could See What I Hear; Mr. Magoo; Ongezien; Scent of a Woman. Blindness.

Books

CHANDLER BURR, *The Emperor of Scent* (Random House, 2003). About the perfume industry and a scientist who is testing a new theory of smell.

RICHARD CYTOWIC, *The Man Who Tasted Shapes* (MIT Press, 2003). About synesthesia, a condition in which senses are mixed.

HENRY GRUNWALD, *Twilight: Losing Sight, Gaining Insight* (Knopf, 1999). Former editor-in-chief of *Time* writes about going blind.

MICHAEL POSNER AND MARCUS RAICHLE, *Images of Mind* (W. H. Freeman, 1997). Brain imaging.

RICHARD L. GREGORY AND J. HARRIS (Eds.), *The Artful Eye* (Oxford University Press, 1995). Visual perception.

RICHARD L. GREGORY AND ANDREW M. COLMAN (Eds.), *Sensation and Perception* (Longman, 1995). The senses and psychophysics.

OLIVER SACKS, *The Island of the Colorblind* (Knopf, 1997). About a Pacific island where colorblindness is common.

OLIVER SACKS, *The Man Who Mistook His Wife for a Hat* (Touchstone Books, 1998). Descriptions of patients with sensory and perceptual disorders.

OLIVER SACKS, *Seeing Voices: A Journey into the World of the Deaf* (Vintage, 2000). How deaf people experience the world.

ROGER SHEPARD, *Mind Sights* (W. H. Freeman, 1990). Visual illusions, ambiguous figures.

J. RICHARD BLOCK AND HAROLD YUKER, *Can You Believe Your Eyes?* (Gardner Press, 1989). More illusions and visual oddities.

The Web

***Essentials of Psychology* Book Companion Website**

www.cengage.com/psychology/bernstein

Visit the book companion website to access a wealth of resources, including chapter outlines, flashcards, web links, tutorial quizzes, and more!

CENGAGENOW™   Just what you need to know NOW! Spend time on what you need to master rather than on information you already have learned. Take a pre-test for this chapter, and CengageNOW will generate a personalized study plan based on your results. The study plan will identify the topics you need to review and direct you to online resources to help you master those topics. You can then take a post-test to help you determine the concepts you have mastered and what you will need to work on. Try it out! Go to www.cengage.com/login to sign in with an access code or to purchase access to this product.

Review of Key Terms ▶

Can you define each of the key terms in the chapter? Check your definitions against those on the pages shown in parentheses in the following list or in the Glossary at the end of the book.

absolute threshold (p. 86)
accessory structures (p. 85)
acoustic nerve (p. 99)
amplitude (p. 88)
analgesia (p. 108)
attention (p. 128)
basilar membrane (p. 98)
blind spot (p. 92)
bottom-up processing (p. 123)
brightness (p. 93)
cochlea (p. 98)

color saturation (p. 93)
cones (p. 90)
cornea (p. 89)
cutaneous senses (p. 105)
dark adaptation (p. 91)
depth perception (p. 115)
eardrum (p. 98)
encoding (p. 86)
eye convergence (p. 117)
feature detectors (p. 92)
figure (p. 114)
figure ground discrimination (p. 114)
fovea (p. 91)
frequency (p. 88)
gate control theory of pain (p. 108)
ground (p. 114)

hue (p. 93)
iris (p. 90)
just-noticeable difference (JND) (p. 88)
kinesthetic perception (p. 111)
lens (p. 90)
light intensity (p. 89)
light wavelength (p. 89)
looming (p. 118)
loudness (p. 97)
middle ear (p. 98)
neural receptors (p. 85)
noise (p. 86)
ocular accommodation (p. 90)
olfactory bulb (p. 103)
olfactory perception (sense of smell) (p. 102)
opponent-process theory (p. 95)

MULTIPLE-CHOICE ▶ Self Test

Select the best answer for each of the following questions. Then check your responses against the Answer Key at the end of the book.

1. Sandra reads English but not Chinese. So when she looks at a Chinese newspaper, the process is _____. When she reads an English newspaper, the process is _____.

   a. sensation; perception
   b. perception; sensation
   c. perception; transduction
   d. sensation; transduction

2. As Jeremy listens to music on his iPod, sound waves are converted by his auditory system into neural signals. This process is called _____.

   a. attention
   b. transduction
   c. adaptation
   d. accommodation

3. In an experiment, Dante raises his hand each time he hears a tone through a set of headphones. The tone gets quieter and quieter until he fails to hear it half the time. After repeating the same procedure many times, the researcher ends the experiment because she has found Dante's _____.

   a. absolute threshold
   b. difference threshold
   c. internal noise
   d. response criterion

4. Jane is told that she will be paid $100 for each needle she can find in a haystack. According to signal detection theory, this information should _____ Jane's _____.

   a. raise; response criterion
   b. lower; response criterion
   c. raise; sensitivity
   d. lower; sensitivity

5. Matt finishes his can of soda as he walks across campus with Brad and Andy, and now he wants to slip the empty can into one of their open backpacks. Brad's pack has several heavy textbooks in it; Andy's contains only a notebook. Weber's law suggests that to avoid detection, Matt should put the can in _____ pack because the change in weight will be _____ than a just-noticeable difference.

   a. Andy's; less
   b. Brad's; less
   c. Andy's; more
   d. Brad's; more

6. Bianca wants Bruce to see the distant star she wishes on every night. Because the star is so faint, to have him see it she should have him look _____.

   a. directly at the star
   b. slightly away from where the star is expected to be
   c. at the star's reflection in a mirror
   d. at the star when there is a full moon

7. A projection-screen TV aims green, red, and blue lights at a screen. Because the TV can show a full range of colors by combining the green, red, and blue lights in differing amounts, it best illustrates the _____ theory of color vision.

   a. convergence
   b. frequency-matching
   c. opponent-process
   d. trichromatic

8. When Sarah stubbed her toe, she immediately began to rub it. According to the gate control theory of pain, the rubbing _____.

   a. created sensations that "took over" the pain pathways
   b. released serotonin
   c. created an increase in pain tolerance
   d. shut down the brain's pain-sensing mechanisms

9. Mick has been a rock musician for fifty years. The constant loud noise from his band has caused hair-cell damage, literally ripping off hair cells from his inner ear. We would expect that Mick now has _____.

   a. extremely acute hearing
   b. conduction deafness
   c. nerve deafness
   d. normal hearing loss for someone his age

10. Jeremy developed a disease that destroyed his thalamus. The only sense that was unaffected was _____.

   a. vision
   b. hearing
   c. touch
   d. smell

11. Your blind spot is located _____.

   a. where the optic nerve leaves the eye
   b. where visual fibers cross at the optic chiasm
   c. in the center of the fovea
   d. where accommodation takes place

12. In cooking school, Natalie studied flavor. She learned that the flavor of food can be altered by _____.

a. changing its texture
b. changing its temperature
c. changing its color
d. both a and b

13. Andrea cannot yet read but Lorraine can. They are each shown a list of color names (e.g., blue, red, yellow) on which each word is printed in a color that doesn't match the word. They are asked to say the color of the ink each word is printed in, not the word itself. _____ will do better at this Stroop task because _____.

a. Andrea; she can use top-down processing
b. Lorraine; she is older
c. Andrea; she will not be distracted by word meanings
d. Lorraine; word meaning will help focus on the ink color

14. Ally has lost her sense of kinesthetic perception. She will most likely be unable to _____.

a. know that her hand is raised without looking at it
b. identify the flavor of her ice cream cone
c. feel the warmth of the sun on her face
d. feel pain

15. Shanelle likes the lights that appear to race around her Christmas tree as they flash on and off in sequence. This illusion is known as _____

a. the motion parallax
b. the stroboscopic illusion
c. dishabituation
d. texture gradient

16. Four swimmers practicing their synchronized swimming routine are perceived as a group because they are performing the same movements at the same speed. This is an example of _____.

a. synchrony
b. common fate
c. orientation
d. interposition

17. When you perceive an object as being closer to you because it blocks out part of the background, you are using the depth cue called _____.

a. linear perspective
b. interposition
c. reduced clarity
d. movement gradient

18. As Cliff walks out his front door, he sees a snowball coming straight at him. The retinal image of the snowball is increasing and he realizes that the snowball is approaching, not getting larger. This example illustrates _____.

a. induced motion
b. looming
c. the movement gradient
d. stroboscopic motion

19. Jeff and Larry were making chili. Jeff tasted the chili and thought it was perfectly seasoned. Then, while Jeff's back was turned, Larry added some more salt. When they sat down to eat Jeff immediately said the chili was too salty. Because he didn't know about the added salt, Jeff's perception must have been based on _____.

a. top-down processing
b. bottom-up processing
c. pattern recognition
d. selective attention

20. Although José appears to be listening as Rich talks about his new clothes, vacation plans, and exercise routine, José is thinking about the list of errands he has to run. José is _____.

a. covertly orienting
b. overtly orienting
c. using parallel distributed processing
d. using serial processing

© Trinette Reed/Getty Images

4 Consciousness

Preview

Have you ever "spaced out" while driving on a boring highway? Has your mind wandered far and wide during a dull lecture? These experiences contrast sharply with how it feels to focus your attention on playing a video game or to concentrate on a complicated recipe, but all of them represent differing versions of consciousness. In this chapter, we delve into both "normal" and altered states of consciousness. Most of the altered states—sleep, dreaming, hypnosis, meditation—differ psychologically and physiologically from normal waking consciousness. We examine how they differ and we look at the effects of psychoactive drugs, which, in addition to altering consciousness, have complex physiological effects.

© David Welling/Animals Animals

KEEPING AN EYE OUT ▲

Humans are not the only creatures capable of processing information while apparently unconscious. While ducks sleep, one hemisphere of their brains can process visual information from an eye that remains open. Birds positioned where they are most vulnerable to predators, such as at the end of a row, may spend twice as much time in this "alert" sleep than do birds in more protected positions (Rattenborg, Lima, & Amlaner, 1999).

consciousness The awareness of external stimuli and our own mental activity.

There is an old *Sesame Street* episode in which Ernie is trying to find out whether Bert is asleep or awake. In other words, Ernie is trying to determine Bert's state of consciousness. Ernie observes that Bert's eyes are closed, and he comments that Bert usually closes his eyes when he is asleep. Ernie also notes that when Bert is asleep, he does not respond to pokes, so naturally he delivers a few. At first, Bert does not respond, but after being poked a few times, he awakes, very annoyed, and yells at Ernie for waking him. Ernie then informs Bert that he just wanted to let him know it was time for his nap.

Doctors face a similar situation in dealing with the more than 30 million people each year who receive general anesthesia during surgery. All these patients certainly appear to go to sleep, but there is no reliable way of knowing whether they are actually unconscious (Alkire, Hudetz, & Tononi, 2008). It turns out that about two people in a thousand retain some degree of consciousness during the surgical procedure (Ekman et al., 2004; Sigalovsky, 2003). In rare cases, patients have conscious awareness of pain and remember the trauma. Although their surgical wounds heal, these people may be psychologically scarred by the experience and may even show symptoms of posttraumatic stress disorder (Schwender et al., 1995). To reduce the possibility of performing surgery on someone who appears unconscious but may not be, some physicans suggest that patients' brain activity should be monitored during every operation (Jameson & Sloan, 2006). Unfortunately, even this precaution does not entirely eliminate the problem (Avidan et al., 2008).

The fact that people can be conscious while "asleep" under the influence of powerful anesthetic drugs makes defining consciousness quite difficult (Edelman, 2003; Seth et al., 2006). In fact, after decades of discussion and research by philosophers, psychologists, and even physicists, some believe that consciousness is still not yet understood well enough to be precisely defined. Given the ethical and legal concerns raised by the need to ensure that patients are not subjected to pain during surgery, doctors tend to define consciousness as awareness that is demonstrated by any ability to recall an experience (Schwender et al., 1995). In psychology, the definition is somewhat broader: **Consciousness** is generally defined as your awareness of the outside world and of your mental processes, thoughts, feelings, and perceptions (Metzinger, 2000; Zeman, 2001). Let's see how this definition applies as we explore the scope of consciousness and various states of consciousness. ■

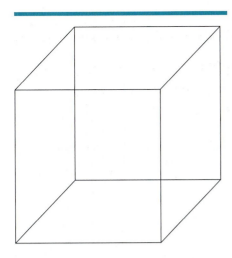

FIGURE 4.1 ■ THE NECKER CUBE

Each of the two squares in the Necker cube can be perceived as either the front or rear surface of the cube. Try to make the cube switch back and forth between these two orientations. Now try to hold only one orientation. You probably cannot maintain the whole cube in consciousness for longer than about three seconds before it "flips" from one orientation to the other.

Learn BY Doing

The Scope of Consciousness

▶ *Can unconscious thoughts affect your behavior?*

Mental activity changes constantly. The features of consciousness at any instant—what reaches your awareness, the decisions you are making, and so on—make up what is called your **consciousness state** at that moment (Tassi & Muzet, 2001). Possible *states of consciousness* include coma, deep sleep, hypnosis, meditation, daydreaming, and alert wakefulness. Consciousness can also be altered by drugs and other influences.

Consciousness States

Consciousness states can be viewed as different points along a scale or continuum of consciousness. For example, suppose you are aboard an airliner flying from New York to Los Angeles. The pilot calmly scans instrument displays while talking to an air traffic controller. In the seat next to you, a lawyer finishes her second cocktail while planning a courtroom strategy. Across the aisle, a young father gazes out the window, daydreaming, while his small daughter sleeps in his lap, dreaming dreams of her own. All these people are experiencing different states of consciousness. Some states are active and some are passive. The daydreaming father lets his mind wander, passively noticing images, memories, and other mental events that come to mind. Like the pilot, the lawyer actively directs her mental processes. In her case, though, as she evaluates various options and considers their likely outcomes, she is altering her state of consciousness by sipping alcohol.

Generally, people spend most of their time in a *waking* state of consciousness. Mental processing in this state varies with changes in attention or arousal (Taylor, 2002). While reading, for example, you may temporarily ignore sounds around you. Similarly, if you are upset or bored or talking on a mobile phone, you may tune out important cues from the environment, making it dangerous to perform complex activities such as driving a car.

Levels of Consciousness

The events and mental processes that you are aware of at any given moment are said to exist at the **conscious level.** For example, look at the Necker cube in Figure 4.1. If you are like most people, you can hold the cube in one orientation for only a few seconds before the other version "pops out" at you. The version that you experience at any moment is at your conscious level of awareness for that moment.

Some events, however, cannot be experienced consciously. For example, you are not directly aware of your brain regulating your blood pressure. Such mental processing occurs at the **nonconscious level,** totally removed from conscious awareness. Some people can learn to alter a nonconscious process through *biofeedback training*. In this training, you receive information about your biological processes and try to change them. Usually special equipment is required, but you can approximate a biofeedback session by having a friend take your pulse at one-minute intervals while you sit quietly.

First, establish a baseline pulse, then imagine a peaceful scene or think about lowering your pulse rate. Then ask your friend to softly say whether your pulse is higher or lower compared with the baseline. After four or five minutes of having this information "fed back" to you, you will probably be able to keep your pulse below the original baseline. Yet the pulse-regulating processes themselves remain out of consciousness.

Some mental events are not conscious but can become conscious or can influence conscious experience. These mental events make up the *cognitive unconscious* (Reber, 1992), which includes the preconscious and the subconscious. Mental events that are outside awareness but that can easily be brought into awareness are said to exist at the **preconscious level.** What did you have for dinner last night? The information you

---

consciousness state The characteristics of consciousness at any particular moment.

conscious level The level of consciousness at which mental activities accessible to awareness occur.

nonconscious level The level of consciousness at which reside processes that are totally inaccessible to conscious awareness.

preconscious level The level of consciousness at which reside mental events that are not currently conscious but can become conscious at will.

▶ Research shows that some surgery patients can hear, and later comply with, instructions or suggestions given while they were under anesthesia, even though they have no memory of what they were told (Bennett, Giannini, & Davis, 1985). People also have physiological responses to emotionally charged words even when they are not paying attention to them (Von Wright, Anderson, & Stenman, 1975). These and other similar studies provide evidence for the operation of subconscious mental processing (Deeprose & Andrade, 2006).

BLOOM COUNTY   **by Berke Breathed**

Permission granted by International Creative Management Inc. Copyright © 1996 by Burke Breathed. Cartoon first appeared in *The Washington Post*.

needed to answer this question was probably not already in your conscious awareness, but it was at the preconscious level. So when you read the question, you could answer it immediately. Similarly, when you play trivia games, you draw on your large storehouse of preconscious memories to come up with obscure facts.

Other mental activities can alter thoughts, feelings, and actions but are more difficult to bring into awareness. Sigmund Freud suggested that these **unconscious** activities, especially those involving unacceptable sexual and aggressive urges, are actively kept out of consciousness. Most psychologists do not accept Freud's view, but they still use the term *unconscious,* or **subconscious,** to describe mental activity that influences us in various ways but that occurs outside of awareness (Dijksterhuis & Nordgren, 2006).

Mental Processing Without Awareness

A fascinating demonstration of mental processing without awareness was provided by an experiment with patients who had surgery under general anesthesia. After their operations but while the patients were still unconscious from the anesthesia, a recording of fifteen word pairs was played over and over for them in the recovery room. After regaining consciousness, the patients could not say what words were on the recording or even whether a recording had been played at all. However, when given one word from each of the word pairs and asked to say the first word that came to mind, the patients were able to come up with the other member of the word pair from the recording (Cork, Kihlstrom, & Hameroff, 1992).

Even when conscious and alert, you can sometimes process and use information without being aware of it (Fu, Fu, & Dienes, 2008; Schmidt et al., 2007). In one study, participants watched a computer screen as an X flashed in one of four locations. The task was to indicate where the X appeared. The location of the X seemed to vary randomly but was actually determined by a set of complex rules. (One such rule was "If the X moves horizontally twice in succession, its next move will be vertical.") Participants' responses became progressively faster and more accurate. Then, unknown to the participants, the rules were abandoned and the X appeared in *truly* random locations. Participants' accuracy and speed deteriorated instantly. Apparently, the participants had learned the rules without being aware of them and had applied them to improve their performance. However, even when offered $100 to state the rules that had guided the location sequence, they could not do so, nor were they sure that any such rules existed (Lewicki, 1992).

Visual processing without awareness may even occur in certain cases of blindness. When blindness is caused by damage only to the brain's primary visual cortex, pathways from the eyes are still connected to other brain areas that process visual information. Some of these surviving connections may permit visual processing but without visual awareness—a condition known as *blindsight* (Binsted et al., 2007; Galpin, Underwood, & Chapman, 2008; Sahraie et al., 2006). So though patients say they see nothing, if forced to guess, they can still locate visual targets, identify the direction of moving images, reach for objects, name the color of lights, and even discriminate happy from fearful faces (Morris et al., 2001). The same blindsight phenomenon has been created in visually normal volunteers using magnetic brain stimulation to

unconscious The term used to describe a level of mental activity said by Freud to contain unacceptable sexual, aggressive, and other impulses of which an individual is unaware.

subconscious Another term that describes the mental level at which influential but normally inaccessible mental processes take place.

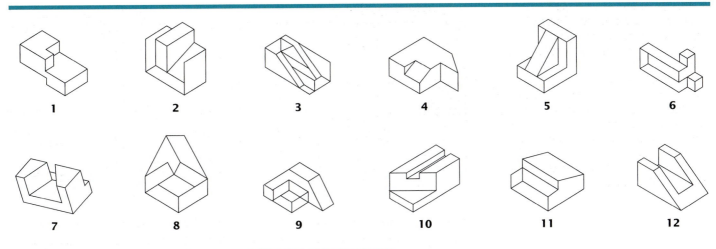

FIGURE 4.2 ■ **STIMULI USED IN A PRIMING EXPERIMENT**

Look at these figures and decide, as quickly as you can, whether each can actually exist. Priming studies show that this task would be easier for figures you have seen in the past, even if you don't recall seeing them. How did you do? The correct answers appear below. *Source*: Schacter et al. (1991).

Learn BY Doing

4.2: Figures 1, 4, 5, 7, 10, and 12 can exist in three-dimensional space.

Improve Your Grade
Tutorial: Priming

temporarily disable the primary visual cortex (Boyer, Harrison, & Ro, 2005; Christensen et al., 2008; Jolij & Lamme, 2005).

Research on *priming* also demonstrates mental processing without awareness. In a typical priming study, people tend to respond faster or more accurately to stimuli they have seen before. This is true even when they cannot consciously recall having seen those stimuli (Arndt et al., 1997; Bar & Biederman, 1998; Kouider & Dupoux, 2005). In one study, for example, people looked at figures like those in Figure 4.2. They had to decide which figures could actually exist in three-dimensional space and which could not. The participants were better at classifying pictures they had seen before, even when they could not remember having seen them (Schacter et al., 1991). Some priming effects are short lived, but others can last for years (Mitchell, 2006).

There is even evidence that some of the decisions and choices we make in everyday life may be guided to some extent by mental processes that occur without our awareness (Dijksterhuis et al., 2006; Galdi, Arcuri, & Gawronski, 2008; Ruiz-Padial & Vila, 2007). For example, your "lucky" choice of the fastest-moving supermarket checkout line might seem to have been based on nothing more than a hunch, a gut feeling, or intuition, but previous visits to that store might have given you useful information that you didn't know you had about the various clerks (Adolphs et al., 2005). In a laboratory study that supports this notion, people watched videotaped television commercials while the changing stock prices of fictional companies crawled across the bottom of the screen. Later, these people were asked to choose which of these companies they liked best. They couldn't recall anything they had seen about the companies' stock, so they had to make their choice on the basis of their gut reaction to the company names. Nevertheless, their choices were not random; they more often chose companies whose stock prices had been rising rather than those whose stock had been falling (Betch et al., 2003).

Thinking **CRITICALLY**

Can Subliminal Messages Change Your Behavior?

The research we have described suggests that we don't always have to be aware of information in order for it to affect us, but how strong can this influence be? In 1957, an adman named James Vicary claimed that a New Jersey theater flashed messages such as "buy popcorn" and "drink Coke" on a movie screen, too briefly to be noticed, while customers watched the movie *Picnic*. He said that these messages caused a 15 percent rise in sales of Coca-Cola and a 58 percent increase in popcorn sales. Can messages perceived at a *subliminal* level—that is, below conscious awareness—act as a form of "mind control"? Many people seem to think so. Each year, they spend millions of dollars on audiotapes, CDs, and videos whose subliminal messages are supposed to help people lose weight, raise self-esteem, quit smoking, make more money, or achieve other goals.

◗ *What am I being asked to believe or accept?*

Two types of claims have been made about subliminal stimuli. The more general one is that subliminal stimuli can influence our behavior. The second, more specific claim is that subliminal stimuli provide an effective means of changing people's buying habits, political opinions, self-confidence, and other complex attitudes and behaviors, with or without their awareness or consent.

◗ *Is evidence available to support the claim?*

Evidence that subliminal messages can affect conscious judgments comes in part from laboratory studies that present visual stimuli too briefly to be perceived consciously. In one such study, participants saw slides showing people performing ordinary acts such as washing dishes. Unknown to the participants, each slide was preceded by a subliminal exposure to a photo of "positive" stimuli (such as a child playing) or "negative" stimuli (such as a monster). Later, participants rated the people on the visible slides as more likable, polite, friendly, successful, and reputable when their images had been preceded by a positive subliminal photo (Krosnick et al., 1992). The subliminal photos not only affected participants' liking of the people they saw but also shaped beliefs about their personalities.

In another study, participants were exposed to subliminal presentations of slides showing snakes, spiders, flowers, and mushrooms. Even though the slides were impossible to perceive at a conscious level, participants who were afraid of snakes or spiders showed physiological arousal (and reported feeling fear) in response to slides of snakes and spiders (Öhman & Soares, 1994).

The results of studies such as these support the notion that subliminal information can have an impact on judgments and emotion, but they say little or nothing about the value of subliminal recordings for achieving self-help goals. In fact, no laboratory evidence exists to support the effectiveness of these recordings. Their promoters offer only the reports of satisfied customers.

◗ *Can that evidence be interpreted another way?*

Many claims for subliminal advertising—including the New Jersey movie theater case—have turned out to be publicity stunts using phony data (Haberstroh, 1995; Pratkanis, 1992). And testimonials from satisfied customers could be biased by what these people would like to believe about the subliminal recordings they bought. In one study designed to test this possibility, half the participants were told that they would be listening to recordings containing subliminal messages for improving memory. The rest were told that the subliminal messages would promote self-esteem. However, half the participants in the memory group actually got self-esteem messages, and half of the self-esteem group actually got memory messages. Regardless of which version they received, participants who thought they had heard memory enhancement messages reported improved memory; those who thought they had received self-esteem messages said their self-esteem had improved (Pratkanis, Eskenazi, & Greenwald, 1994). In other words, the effects of the recordings were determined by the listeners' expectations, not by the subliminal content of the recordings. These results suggest that customers' reports about the value of subliminal self-help recordings may reflect placebo effects based on optimistic expectations rather than the effects of subliminal messages.

◗ *What evidence would help to evaluate the alternatives?*

The effectiveness of self-help recordings and other subliminal products must be evaluated through further experiments, such as the one just mentioned, that carefully control for expectations. Those who support and sell subliminal-influence methods are responsible for conducting those experiments, but as long as customers are willing to buy subliminal products on the basis of testimonials alone, scientific evaluation efforts will probably come only from those interested in protecting consumers from fraud.

◗ *What conclusions are most reasonable?*

The available evidence suggests that subliminal perception occurs but that it has no potential for "mind control" (Greenwald, Klinger, & Schuh, 1995). Subliminal effects are usually small and short lived and they mainly affect simple judgments and general measures of overall arousal. As for subliminal messages aimed at long-term behavior change, most researchers agree that such messages have no special power to create needs, goals, skills, or actions (Pratkanis, 1992). In fact, advertisements, political speeches, and other messages that we *can* perceive consciously have far stronger persuasive effects.

Focus on RESEARCH

Subliminal Messages in Rock Music

Would the persuasive power of subliminal messages be increased if they were presented at normal speed but in reverse, so that we could not consciously understand them? According to numerous Internet web sites, this is exactly how satanic or drug-related messages have been hidden in the recorded music of rock bands such as Marilyn Manson, Nine Inch Nails, Judas Priest, Led Zeppelin, and the Rolling Stones. These alleged "backmasked" subliminal messages are said to have influenced listeners to commit suicide or murder. For this claim to be true, however, the subliminal backward message would have to be perceived at some level of consciousness.

◗ *What was the researchers' question?*

There is no good evidence that backward messages are actually present in most of the music cited. However, John R. Vokey and J. Don Read (1985) asked whether any backward messages that

SUBLIMINAL MESSAGES IN ROCK MUSIC? ▶

These picketers are protesting at the site of a Marilyn Manson concert. Some people claim that Manson's music, as well as that of rock stars ranging from Michael Jackson to Madonna, contains subliminal messages about drug use, violence, and Satanism, as well as about other, far more ordinary things (for an example of such claims, visit www.reversespeech.com/music_reversals.htm).

might exist could be perceived and understood while the music was playing forward. They also asked whether such a message, if perceived at all, would have any effect on the listener's behavior.

▶ *How did the researchers answer the question?*

First, Vokey and Read made tape recordings of a person reading portions of the 23rd Psalm and Lewis Carroll's poem "Jabberwocky." This poem includes many nonsense words, but it follows the rules of grammar (e.g., "'Twas brillig, and the slithy toves . . ."). These recordings were then played backward to college students, who were asked to judge whether what they heard would have been meaningful or nonsensical if played forward.

▶ *What did the researchers find?*

When the students heard the readings being played backward, they could not discriminate sense from nonsense. Nor could they tell the difference between declarative sentences and questions. They could not even identify the original material on which the recordings were based. In short, the participants could not understand the backward messages at a conscious level. Could they do so subconsciously? To find out, the researchers asked the participants to sort the backward statements they heard into one of five categories: nursery rhymes, Christian, satanic, pornographic, or advertising. They reasoned that if some sort of meaning could be subconsciously understood, the participants would be able to sort the statements nonrandomly. As it turned out, however, the participants did no better at this task than random chance would predict.

Perhaps backward messages might influence people's behavior even if the messages were not perceived consciously. To check

on this possibility, Vokey and Read (1985) conducted another study. This time, they presented a backward version of a message whose sentences contained homophones (words that sound alike but have two spellings and two different meanings, such as "feat" and "feet"). When heard in the normal forward direction, such messages affect people's spelling of ambiguous words that are read aloud to them at a later time. (For example, they tend to spell out f-e-a-t rather than f-e-e-t if they had previously heard the sentence "It was a great feat of strength.") This example of priming occurs even if people do not recall having heard the message. After hearing a *backward* version of the message, however, the participants in this study did not produce the expected spelling bias.

▶ *What do the results mean?*

Obviously, it wasn't possible for the participants to subconsciously understand meaning in the backward messages. Backward messages are evidently not consciously or unconsciously understood, nor do they influence behavior (Vokey, 2002).

▶ *What do we still need to know?*

Researchers would like to understand why the incorrect idea persists that backward messages can influence behavior. Beliefs and suspicions do not simply disappear in the face of contrary scientific evidence (Sagan, 1996; Vyse, 2000; Winer et al., 2002). Perhaps such evidence needs to be publicized more widely in order to lay the misconceptions to rest, but it seems likely that some people so deeply want to believe in the existence and power of backward messages in rock music that such beliefs will forever hold the status of folk myths in Western culture.

Altered States of Consciousness

altered state of consciousness
A condition that exists when changes in mental processes are extensive enough to produce noticeable differences in psychological and behavioral functioning.

When changes in mental processes are great enough for you or others to notice significant differences in how you function, you are said to have entered an **altered state of consciousness.** In an altered state, mental processing shows distinct changes unique to that state. Cognitive processes or perceptions of yourself or the world may change and normal inhibitions or self-control may weaken (Vaitl et al., 2005).

The phrase *altered states of consciousness* recognizes waking consciousness as the most common state, a baseline against which altered states are compared. However, this is not to say that waking consciousness is universally considered more normal, proper, or valued than other states. In fact, judgments about the status and meaning of certain states of consciousness vary considerably across cultures (Ward, 1994).

Consider, for instance, *hallucinations,* which are perceptual experiences (such as hearing voices) that occur without sensory stimulation from the outside world. In the United States, hallucinations are usually viewed as so undesirable that even normal people who develop visual hallucinations due to an eye disorder may be ashamed to seek the medical help they need to solve the problem (Menon et al., 2003). If mental patients hallucinate, they often feel stress and self-blame and may choose not to report their hallucinations. Those who do report them tend to be considered more disturbed and may receive more drastic treatments than patients who keep their hallucinations to themselves (Wilson et al., 1996). Among the Moche of Peru, however, hallucinations have a culturally approved place. When someone experiences illness or misfortune, a healer conducts an elaborate ritual to find causes and treatments. During the ceremony, the healer takes mescaline, a drug that causes hallucinations. These hallucinations are thought to give the healer spiritual insight into the patient's problems

ALTERED STATES AND CULTURAL VALUES ▶

Cultures differ in their definitions of which altered states of consciousness are approved and which are inappropriate. Here we see members of a Brazilian spirit possession cult in various stages of trance and, in Peru, a Moche curandero, or "curer," attempting to heal an ailing patient by using fumes from a potion—and a drug from the San Pedro cactus—to put himself in an altered state of consciousness.

© Jacques Jangoux/Photo Researchers, Inc.

© Nathan Benn/National Geographic Image Collection

(de Rios, 1989). In many other tribal cultures, too, purposeful hallucinations are respected, not rejected (Grob & Dobkin de Rios, 1992).

In other words, states of consciousness differ not only in their characteristics but also in their value to members of particular cultures. In the sections that follow, we describe some of the most interesting altered states of consciousness, beginning with the most common one: sleep.

linkages

Does the brain shut down when we sleep? *(a link to Biology and Behavior)*

online study center Improve Your Grade
Tutorial: EEG and Different Stages of Sleep

Sleeping and Dreaming

▶ *Does your brain go to sleep when you do?*

According to ancient myths, sleepers lose control of their minds and flirt with death as their souls wander freely. Early researchers thought sleep was a time of mental inactivity, but sleep is actually an active, complex state (Hobson, 2005).

Stages of Sleep

Sleep researchers study the brain's electrical activity during sleep by taping tiny discs to a person's scalp and connecting them to an *electroencephalograph,* or *EEG.* The resulting EEG recordings, often called *brain waves,* vary in height (amplitude) and speed (frequency) as behavior or mental processes change. The brain waves of an awake, alert person are irregular, small, and closely spaced; that is, high frequency and low amplitude. A relaxed person with closed eyes shows more rhythmic brain waves occurring at slower speeds, about eight to twelve cycles per second (cps). During a normal night's sleep, your brain waves show distinctive and systematic changes in amplitude and frequency as you pass through various stages of sleep (Durka et al., 2005).

Non-REM Sleep   Imagine that you are participating in a sleep study. You are hooked up to an EEG and various monitors and a video camera watches as you sleep through the night. If you were to view the results, here's what you'd see: At first, you are relaxed; your eyes are closed, but you are awake. At this point, your muscle tone and eye movements are normal and your EEG shows the slow brain waves associated with relaxation. Then, as you drift into sleep, your breathing deepens, your heartbeat slows, and your blood pressure falls. Over the next half-hour, you descend through four stages of sleep that are characterized by even slower brain waves with even higher amplitude (see Figure 4.3). The deepest of these, stages 3 and 4, are known as slow-wave sleep. When you reach stage 4, it is quite difficult to be awakened. If you were roused from this stage of deep sleep, you would be groggy and confused. Together, these four stages are called **NREM, or Non-REM, sleep** because they do not include the rapid eye movements (REM) described in the next section.

REM Sleep   After thirty to forty-five minutes in stage 4, you quickly return to stage 2 and then enter a special stage in which your eyes move rapidly under your closed eyelids. This is called **REM** (rapid eye movement) sleep, or paradoxical sleep. It is called paradoxical because its characteristics contain a paradox, or contradiction. In REM sleep, your EEG resembles that of an awake, alert person, and your physiological arousal—heart rate, breathing, and blood pressure—is also similar to when you are awake. However, your muscles are nearly paralyzed. Sudden, twitchy spasms appear, especially in your face and hands, but your brain actively suppresses other movements (Blumberg & Lucas, 1994). In other words, there are two distinctly different types of sleep, REM sleep and *non-REM,* or *NREM,* sleep (Lu et al., 2006).

A Night's Sleep   Most people pass through the cycle of sleep stages four to six times each night. Each cycle lasts about ninety minutes but the pattern of stages and length of the stages changes somewhat. Early in the night, most of the time is spent in

NREM (non-rapid eye movement) sleep   Sleep stages 1, 2, 3, and 4; they are accompanied by gradually slower and deeper breathing; a calm, regular heartbeat; reduced blood pressure; and slower brain waves. (Stages 3 and 4 are called slow-wave sleep.)

REM (rapid eye movement) sleep   The stage of sleep during which muscle tone decreases dramatically but the EEG resembles that of someone who is awake.

FIGURE 4.3   ■   EEG DURING SLEEP

EEG recordings of brain wave activity show four relatively distinct stages of sleep. Notice the regular patterns of brain waves that occur just before a person goes to sleep, followed by the slowing of brain waves as sleep becomes deeper (stages 1 through 4). In REM (rapid eye movement) sleep, the frequency of brain waves increases dramatically. In some ways the brain waves of REM sleep resemble patterns seen in people who are awake.
Source: Horne (1998).

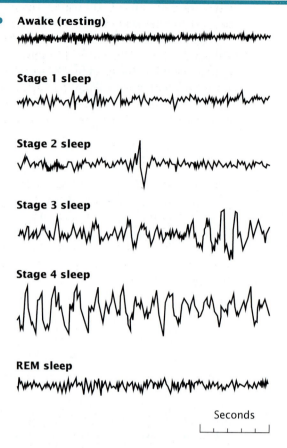

NREM with only a few minutes in REM (see Figure 4.4). As sleep continues, though, it is dominated by stage 2 and REM sleep, from which sleepers finally awaken.

Sleep patterns change with age. The average infant sleeps about sixteen hours a day. The average 70-year-old sleeps only about six hours (Roffwarg, Muzio, & Dement, 1966), and elderly people tend to wake more often during the night than younger people do (Floyd, 2002). The composition of sleep changes, too. REM accounts for half of total sleep in newborns but less than 25 percent in young adults. Individuals vary widely from these averages, though. Some people feel well rested after four hours of

FIGURE 4.4   ■   A NIGHT'S SLEEP

During a typical night, a sleeper goes through this sequence of EEG stages. Notice that sleep is deepest during the first part of the night and shallower later on, when REM sleep becomes more prominent.
Source: Cartwright (1978).

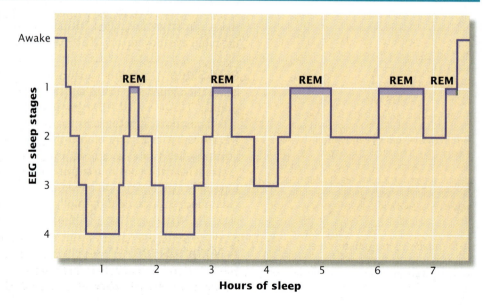

sleep, whereas others of similar age require ten hours to feel satisfied. To some extent, too, sleep patterns are a matter of choice or necessity. For example, North American college students get less sleep than other people their age (Hicks, Fernandez, & Pellegrini, 2001). This trend has grown over the last 30 years as students balance academic and job responsibilities with family obligations and a variety of social and recreational activities—including those late-night sessions playing computer games or surfing the Internet. You have probably noticed the results of sleep deprivation as your classmates (or you?) struggle to stay awake during lectures.

Sleep Disorders

Some time in life, most people experience sleep-related problems (Silber, 2001). These can range from occasional nights of tossing and turning to the more serious and long-term sleep disorders that affect as many as 70 million people in the United States alone (Institute of Medicine, 2006; Morin et al., 2009). The most common sleep disorder is **insomnia,** in which people feel fatigue during the day because they have trouble falling asleep or staying asleep. If you have difficulty getting to sleep or staying asleep that persists for longer than one month at a time, you may be suffering from insomnia. Besides being tiring, insomnia is associated with mental distress, impairment of functioning, and reduction in one's sense of well-being (Hamilton et al., 2007). Overall, insomniacs are three times more likely to show a mental disorder than individuals with no sleep complaints (Ohayon & Roth, 2003). Insomnia is especially associated with depressive and anxiety disorders (Harvey, 2008). It is unclear from such correlations, however, whether insomnia causes mental disorders, mental disorders cause insomnia, or some other factor causes both.

Sleeping pills can relieve insomnia. However, they may interact dangerously with alcohol, may disturb REM sleep, and may eventually lead to increased sleeplessness (Curry, Eisenstein, & Walsh, 2006; Poyares et al., 2004). In the long run, learning-based treatments may be more helpful (Perlis et al., 2001; Stepanski & Perlis, 2000; Yang, Spielman, & Glovinsky, 2006). These include the cognitive behavior therapy methods described in the chapter on treatment of psychological disorders and progressive relaxation training techniques mentioned in the chapter on health, stress, and coping. Both have been shown to promote better sleeping by reducing anxiety, tension, and other reactions to stress (Bernstein, Borkovec, & Hazlett-Stevens, 2000; Jacobs et al., 2004). Short daytime naps and moderate evening exercise can also help some people get to sleep more easily, sleep better, and experience better mood and performance the next day (Tanaka et al., 2001).

Narcolepsy is a disturbing daytime sleep disorder that is typically first seen in people who are between 15 and 25 years old (Dyken & Yamada, 2005; Zeman et al., 2004). People with narcolepsy abruptly enter REM sleep directly from the waking state, usually as they are laughing or experiencing some other emotional state. Because of the loss of muscle tone in REM, narcoleptics may experience *cataplexy,* meaning that they collapse and remain briefly immobile even after awakening. The most common cause of narcolepsy appears to be the absence or deficiency of a neurotransmitter called *orexin,* which is also known as *hypocretin* (Miyagawa et al., 2008; Wurtman, 2006). A combination of regular naps and stimulant drugs can be a helpful treatment (Rogers, Aldrich, & Lin, 2001; Schwartz, 2005).

People who suffer from **sleep apnea** briefly stop breathing hundreds of times each night, waking each time long enough to resume breathing. In the morning, victims do not recall the awakenings. However, they feel tired and tend to suffer headaches, reduced attention, and learning difficulties (Naëgelé et al., 1995). In one tragic case, two members of a train crew—both of whom had apnea—fell asleep on the job, resulting in a collision that killed two people (Pickler, 2002). Apnea has many causes, including genetic predisposition, obesity, problems with brain mechanisms that control breathing, and compression of the windpipe (Kadotani et al., 2001; Macey et al., 2002; Richards et al., 2002). Effective treatments include weight loss and use of a mask that provides a steady stream of air (Ayas, FitzGerald et al., 2006; Dixon, Schachter, & O'Brien, 2005; Gupta &

STIMULUS CONTROL THERAPY ▲

Insomnia can often be reduced through a combination of relaxation techniques and stimulus control therapy, in which the person goes to bed only when sleepy and gets out of bed if sleep does not come within fifteen to twenty minutes. The goal is to have the bed become a stimulus associated with sleeping, and perhaps sex, but not with reading, eating, watching television, worrying, or anything else that is incompatible with sleep (Edinger et al., 2001).

applying psychology

insomnia   A sleep disorder in which a person has trouble falling asleep or staying asleep at night.

narcolepsy   A daytime sleep disorder in which a person suddenly switches from an active waking state into REM sleep.

sleep apnea   A sleep disorder in which a person briefly but repeatedly stops breathing during the night.

SUDDEN INFANT DEATH SYNDROME (SIDS) ▲

In SIDS cases, seemingly healthy infants stop breathing while asleep in their cribs. All the causes of SIDS are not known, but health authorities now urge parents to ensure that infants sleep on their backs, as this baby demonstrates.

---

sudden infant death syndrome (SIDS)   A disorder in which a sleeping baby stops breathing, does not awaken, and dies.

sleepwalking   A phenomenon that starts primarily in non-REM sleep, especially in stage 4, and involves walking while asleep.

nightmares   Frightening dreams that take place during REM sleep.

sleep terror disorder (night terrors)   The occurrence of horrific dream images during stage 4 sleep, followed by a rapid awakening and a state of intense fear.

REM behavior disorder   A sleep disorder in which the decreased muscle tone normally seen in REM sleep does not appear, thus allowing dreams to be acted out.

Reiter, 2004; Lam et al., 2006). In some cases surgery may be required to widen the air passageway in the upper throat (Friedman et al., 2003; Patel et al., 2003).

In cases of **sudden infant death syndrome (SIDS),** sleeping infants stop breathing and die. SIDS is the most common cause of unexpected infant death in Western countries (Daley, 2004). In the United States, it strikes about two of every thousand infants, especially very low-birthweight babies, usually when they are two to four months old (Smith & White, 2006; Vernacchio et al., 2003). Some SIDS cases may be caused by exposure to cigarette smoke, problems with brain systems that regulate breathing, or genetic factors (Anderson, Johnson, & Batal, 2005; Audero et al., 2008; Creery & Mikrogianakis, 2004). Correlational evidence suggests that about half of apparent SIDS cases might actually be accidental suffocations that occur when infants sleep face down on a soft surface (Gilbert et al., 2005). In the United States, for example, SIDS may be particularly common when caregivers place babies in the face-down position (Corwin et al., 2003; Hauck et al., 2002; Shields et al., 2005). The danger of the face-down position is especially great for babies who do not usually sleep in that position, who are not breastfed, or who do not sleep with a pacifier in their mouths (Li et al., 2006; Vennemann et al., 2009a, 2009b). Since doctors began a "back to sleep" program, which advises parents to be sure their babies sleep face up, the number of infants dying from SIDS in the United States and United Kingdom has dropped by 50 percent (Blair et al., 2006; Daley, 2004; Moon, Calabrese, & Aird, 2008; Rasinski et al., 2003). Babies who sleep face up may also be less likely to inhale potentially toxic bacteria that grow in some foam mattresses (Jenkins & Sherbum, 2005; Weber et al., 2008).

Sleepwalking occurs in non-REM sleep, usually in childhood (Guilleminault et al., 2003; Pilon, Montplaisir, & Zadra, 2008; Masand, Popli, & Welburg, 1995). By morning, most sleepwalkers have forgotten their travels. Despite myths to the contrary, waking a sleepwalker is not harmful. Drugs help, but most children simply outgrow the problem. One adult sleepwalker was cured when his wife blew a whistle whenever he began a nighttime stroll (Meyer, 1975).

Nightmares are frightening REM dreams that occur in 4 to 8 percent of the general population but in a much higher percentage of people who suffer from posttraumatic stress disorder following military combat or rape (Kryger, Roth, & Dement, 2000; Zadra & Donderi, 2000). **Sleep terror disorder** (also known as **night terrors**) involves horrific dream images during stage 4 sleep. Sleepers often awaken from a night terror with a bloodcurdling scream and remain intensely afraid for up to 30 minutes. Yet they may not recall the episode in the morning. Sleep terror disorder is especially common in children, but adults can suffer milder versions, and it appears to be partly inherited (Nguyen et al., 2008). The condition is sometimes treatable with drugs.

In **REM behavior disorder,** the near-paralysis that normally accompanies REM sleep does not occur, so sleepers move as if acting out their dreams (Abad & Guilleminault, 2004; Oudiette et al., 2009). If the dreams are violent, the disorder can be dangerous to the dreamer or those nearby. One nine-year-old boy in New York City was seriously injured when he jumped from a third-floor window while dreaming that his parents were being murdered. In another case, a Minnesota man grabbed his wife's throat while dreaming about breaking a deer's neck (Brown, 2003). REM behavior disorder sometimes occurs in tandem with daytime narcolepsy (Schenck & Mahowald, 1992) and in one case was caused by a brain tumor (Zambelis, Paparrigopoulos, & Soldatos, 2002). REM behavior disorder is also common in patients with Parkinson's disease and is often the first sign of a degenerative brain condition (Gagnon, Postuma, & Montplaisir, 2006). Fortunately, prescription drugs are usually effective in treating REM behavior disorder (Gagnon et al., 2006; Takeuchi et al., 2001).

Why Do People Sleep?

People need a certain amount of uninterrupted sleep to function normally. In fact, most living creatures sleep. In trying to understand why people sleep, psychologists have studied what sleep does for us and how the brain shapes the characteristics of sleep (Siegel, 2005).

Sleep as a Circadian Rhythm   Humans and almost all animals display cycles of behavior and physiology that repeat about every 24 hours (Markov & Goldman, 2006). These patterns are called **circadian rhythms** (also known as **human biological rhythms**). (*Circadian,* pronounced "sir-KAY-dee-en," comes from the Latin *circa dies,* meaning "about a day.") Longer and shorter rhythms also occur, but they are less common.

Circadian rhythms are linked to signals such as the light of day and the dark of night (Ohta, Yamazaki, & McMahon, 2005). However, most of these rhythms continue even when no time signals are available. Volunteers living for months without external light and dark cues maintain daily rhythms in sleeping and waking, eating, urination, hormone release, and other physiological functions. Under such conditions, these cycles repeat about every 24 hours (Czeisler et al., 1999).

Disruption of the sleep-wake cycle can create problems. For example, air travel across several time zones often causes **jet lag,** a pattern of fatigue, irritability, inattention, and sleeping problems that can last for several days (Akerstedt, 2007; Reilly, Atkinson, et al., 2007; Reilly, Waterhouse, et al., 2007). The traveler's body feels ready to sleep at the wrong time for the new location. It tends to be easier to stay awake longer than usual than to go to sleep earlier than usual. That is the reason that the symptoms of jet lag are usually more intense after a long eastward trip (when time is lost) than after a long westward journey (when time is gained; Lemmer et al., 2002). Symptoms similar to those of jet lag also appear in workers who repeatedly change between day and night shifts and in people who try to go to sleep early on a Sunday night after a weekend of later-than-usual bedtimes (Czeisler et al., 2005; Di Milia, 2006). For these people, Monday morning "blues" may actually be symptoms of a disrupted sleep-wake cycle (Yang & Spielman, 2001).

The length of circadian sleep rhythms can vary from person to person such that some have a natural tendency to stay up later at night ("owls") or to wake up earlier in the morning ("larks"). But because our sleep-wake rhythms stay about the same even without external cues about light and dark, we must have an internal biological clock that keeps track of time. This clock is in the *suprachiasmatic nuclei* (*SCN*) of the hypothalamus (Kalsbeek et al., 2006), as shown in Figure 4.5. The SCN receives light information from a special set of photoreceptors in the eyes and then sends signals to

FIGURE 4.5 ■ SLEEP, DREAMING, AND THE BRAIN

This diagram shows the location of some of the brain structures thought to be involved in sleep and dreaming, as well as in other altered states discussed later in the chapter. For example, one area near the suprachiasmatic nuclei acts as a "master switch" to promote sleep (Saper, Chou, & Scammell, 2001). If it is damaged, sleep may be nearly impossible. Another nearby area promotes wakefulness; individuals with damage to this area sleep virtually all the time (Salin-Pascual et al., 2001).

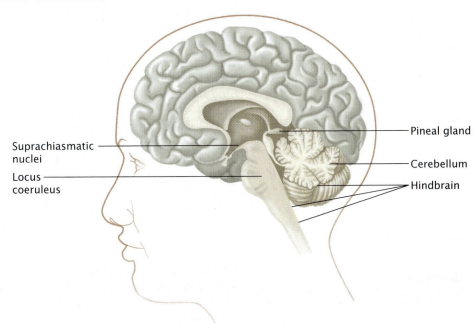

circadian rhythm (human biological rhythm)   A cycle, such as waking and sleeping, that repeats about once a day.

jet lag   Fatigue, irritability, inattention, and sleeping problems caused by air travel across several time zones.

hindbrain areas that initiate sleep or wakefulness (Albus et al., 2005; Lee et al., 2003; Saper, Scammell, & Lu, 2005). When animals with SCN damage receive transplanted SCN cells, their circadian rhythms become like those of the donor animal (Menaker & Vogelbaum, 1993). SCN neurons also regulate the release of the hormone *melatonin*. Melatonin, in turn, appears to be important in maintaining circadian rhythms (Beaumont et al., 2004; Cardinali et al., 2002). In fact, many of the symptoms associated with jet lag and other disruptions in sleep-wake cycles can be prevented or treated by taking melatonin (Lack & Wright, 2007; Revell & Eastman, 2005), although regular use, such as by commercial airline crewmembers, is not recommended (Simons & Valk, 2009). There is some evidence, too, that sildenafil (a drug normally prescribed for erectile dysfunction) can speed recovery from jet lag after eastbound (but not westbound) travel (Stephenson, 2007). It may also be possible to reduce jet lag through diet, exercise, and exposure to natural lighting conditions upon daytime arrival or to dim light upon nighttime arrival (Armstrong, 2006; Edwards, Reilly, & Waterhouse, 2009; Evans, Elliott, & Gorman, 2009).

The Functions of Sleep   Examining the effects of **sleep deprivation** may help explain why people sleep at all. People who go without sleep for as long as a week usually don't suffer serious long-term effects. However, extended sleeplessness does lead to fatigue, irritability, memory problems, and inattention (Drummond et al., 2000; Smith & Maben, 1993; Turner et al., 2007). Even short-term sleep deprivation—a common condition among busy adolescents and adults—can take its toll (Arnedt et al., 2005; Heuer et al., 2004; Stapleton, 2001; Steptoe, Peacey, & Wardle, 2006). For example, sleep deprivation can reduce the ability of the body's immune system to fight off colds (Cohen et al., 2009), and serious mistakes in patient care are more likely when medical interns work sleep-disrupting extended hospital shifts than when they work more normal hours (Ayas, Barger et al., 2006; Landrigan et al., 2004). Most fatal car crashes in the United States occur during the "fatigue hazard" hours of midnight to 6 A.M. (Coleman, 1992), and sleepiness resulting from long work shifts or other causes is a major factor in up to 25 percent of all auto accidents (Barger et al., 2005; Garbarino et al., 2001; Philip et al., 2001). The fact that "sleepy driving" can be as dangerous as drunk driving has led at least one U.S. state (New Jersey) to expand the definition of reckless driving to include "driving while fatigued" (i.e., having had no sleep in the previous 24 hours). Fatigue also plays a role in many injuries suffered by sleepy young children at play or in day care (Valent, Brusaferro, & Barbone, 2001). Learning, too, is more difficult after sleep deprivation (Yoo et al., 2007); but certain parts of the cerebral cortex actually increase their activity when a sleep-deprived person faces a learning task, so we are able to compensate for a while (Drummond et al., 2000).

Scientists are looking for drugs that can combat the effects of sleep deprivation, but there appears to be no substitute for sleep itself. Some researchers suggest that sleep helps restore the body and the brain for future activity and helps consolidate memories of newly learned facts (Gais et al., 2007; Korman et al., 2007; Orban et al., 2006; Rasch & Born, 2008; Walker & Stickgold, 2006). This restorative function is especially associated with non-REM sleep, which would help explain why most people get their non-REM sleep in the first part of the night (see Figure 4.4).

There is also an apparent need for REM sleep. For example, after total sleep deprivation, people don't need to make up every hour of lost sleep. Instead, they sleep about 50 percent more than usual, then wake up feeling rested. But their "recovery" night includes an unusually high percentage of REM sleep (Feinberg & Campbell, 1993). And if people are deprived *only* of REM sleep, they compensate even more directly. In one study, participants were awakened whenever their EEGs showed REM. When allowed to sleep normally the next night, they "rebounded," nearly doubling the percentage of time spent in REM (Dement, 1960). This research suggests that REM has its own special functions. What those functions might be is still unclear, but there are several interesting possibilities.

First, REM may improve the functioning of neurons that use norepinephrine (Siegel & Rogawski, 1988), a neurotransmitter released by cells in the *locus coeruleus*

sleep deprivation   A condition in which people do not get enough sleep; it may result in reduced cognitive abilities, inattention, and increased risk of accidents.

(pronounced "lo-kus seh-ROO-lee-us"; see Figure 4.5). During waking hours, it affects alertness and mood. But the brain's neurons lose their sensitivity to norepinephrine if it is released continuously for too long. Researchers suggest that because the locus coeruleus is almost completely inactive during REM sleep, REM helps restore sensitivity to norepinephrine and thus its ability to keep us alert (Steriade & McCarley, 1990). Animals deprived of REM sleep show unusually high norepinephrine levels and decreased daytime alertness (Brock et al., 1994).

REM sleep may also be a time for creating and strengthening connections between nerve cells in the brain (Graves, Pack, & Abel, 2001; Maquet, 2001; Peigneux et al., 2001). If so, it would explain why infants and children—whose brains are still developing—spend so much time in REM. Evidence favoring this possibility comes from animal research showing that REM sleep helps in the creation of neural connections following new learning experiences (Frank et al., 2001). There is also evidence that REM sleep deprivation slows the creation of these connections (Kim, Mahmoud, & Grover, 2005). So REM sleep may help to solidify and absorb the day's experiences and skills (Fenn, Nusbaum, & Margoliash, 2003; Fischer et al., 2002; Ishikawa et al., 2006; Sejnowski & Destexhe, 2000; Stickgold, James, & Hobson, 2000). Other studies have found that information, including emotional information, is remembered better and longer when followed immediately by sleep, especially REM sleep (Gais, Lucas, & Born, 2006; Gomez, Bootzin, & Nadel, 2006; Hu, Stylos-Allan, & Walker, 2006). In one study, people who were deprived of REM sleep showed poorer performance at a skill they had learned the day before when compared with people who were either deprived of non-REM sleep or had slept normally (Karni et al., 1994). Another study found that establishing memories of emotional information was particularly dependent on REM sleep (Wagner, Gais, & Born, 2001). Accordingly, some researchers have suggested that sleep deprivation in the aftermath of a traumatic event might reduce or even prevent the appearance of posttraumatic stress disorder (Wagner et al., 2006). Even 60- to 90-minute naps in which REM sleep appears can be enough to solidify the learning of visual information (Mednick, Nakayama, & Stickgold, 2003).

Dreams and Dreaming

We have seen that the brain is active in all sleep stages (for a summary of our discussion, see "In Review: Sleep and Sleep Disorders"). Some of this brain activity during sleep is experienced as the story-like sensations and perceptions known as **dreaming.** Dreams may be as short as a few seconds or last for many minutes. They may be organized or chaotic, realistic or fantastic, peaceful or exciting.

Some dreaming occurs during non-REM sleep, but most dreams—and the most bizarre and vivid dreams—occur during REM (Casagrande et al., 1996; Dement & Kleitman, 1957; Stickgold, Rittenhouse, & Hobson, 1994). Even when they seem to make no sense, dreams may contain a certain amount of logic. For example, people can tell the difference between written dream reports whose sentences had been randomly rearranged and those that had been left alone (Stickgold, Rittenhouse, & Hobson, 1994). And although dreams often involve one person transforming into another or one object turning into another object, it is rare that objects become people or vice versa (Cicogna et al., 2006).

Daytime activities may influence the content of dreams to some extent (Foulkes, 1985; Valli et al., 2006; Wegner, Wenzlaff, & Kozak, 2004). In one study, an unusually high number of animal characters appeared in the dreams reported by people who had just attended an animal rights conference (Lewis, 2008). In another, people with more health problems reported more dreams that included illness or injury (King & DiCicco, 2007), and several studies have found that dream images of violence, terrorism, and disaster became more common in the days and weeks following the September 11, 2001, terrorist attacks in the United States (Bulkeley & Kahan, 2008). It is also sometimes possible for people to intentionally direct their dream content. This is called **lucid dreaming,** because the sleeper is aware of dreaming while a dream is occurring (Stickgold, Malia, et al., 2000).

dreaming The production during sleep of story-like sequences of images, sensations, and perceptions that last from several seconds to many minutes; it occurs mainly during REM sleep.

lucid dreaming Being aware that a dream is a dream while it is occurring.

In Review

SLEEP AND SLEEP DISORDERS

TYPES OF SLEEP	CHARACTERISTICS	POSSIBLE FUNCTIONS
NREM (non–rapid eye movement) Stages 3 and 4 are also called slow-wave sleep	Includes the deepest stages of sleep, characterized by slowed heart rate and breathing, reduced blood pressure, and low-frequency, high-amplitude brain waves	Refreshing of body and brain; memory consolidation
REM (rapid eye movement) sleep	Characterized by eye movements, waking levels of heart rate, breathing, blood pressure, and brain waves, but near-paralysis in muscles	Restoring sensitivity to norepinephrine, thus improving waking alertness; creating and solidifying nerve cell connections; consolidating memories and new skills

SLEEP DISORDERS	CHARACTERISTICS	POSSIBLE CAUSES
Insomnia	Difficulty (lasting at least a month) in falling asleep or staying asleep	Worry, anxiety
Narcolepsy	Sudden switching from a waking state to REM sleep	Absence or deficiency in *orexin* (*hypocretin*)
Sleep apnea	Frequent episodes of interrupted breathing while asleep	Genetic predisposition, obesity, faulty breathing-related brain mechanisms, windpipe compression
Sudden infant death syndrome (SIDS)	Interruption of an infant's breathing, resulting in death	Genetic predisposition, faulty breathing-related brain mechanisms, exposure to cigarette smoke
Nightmares	Frightening dreams during REM sleep	Stressful or traumatic events or experiences
Sleep terror disorder (night terrors)	Frightening dream images during non-REM sleep	Stressful or traumatic events or experiences
REM behavior disorder	Lack of paralysis during REM sleep allows dreams to be enacted, sometimes with harmful consequences	Malfunction of brain mechanism normally creating REM paralysis

1. *Jet lag occurs because of a disruption in a traveler's _____.*
2. *The importance of non-REM sleep is suggested by its appearance _____ in the night.*
3. *The safest sleeping position for babies is _____.*

Research leaves little doubt that everyone dreams during every night of normal sleep. Even blind people dream, although their perceptual experiences are usually not visual. Whether you remember a dream depends on how you sleep and wake up. Recall is better if you awaken abruptly and lie quietly while writing or recording your recollections.

Why do we dream? Theories abound (Antrobus, 2001; Domhoff, 2001; Eiser, 2005). Some see dreaming as a process through which all species with complex brains analyze and consolidate information that is personally important or has survival value (Payne & Nadel, 2004; Porte & Hobson, 1996; Zadra, Desjardins, & Marcotte, 2006). This view is supported by the fact that dreaming appears to occur in most mammals, as indicated by the appearance of REM sleep. For example, after researchers disabled the neurons that cause REM sleep paralysis, sleeping cats ran around and attacked or seemed alarmed by unseen objects, presumably the images from dreams (Winson, 1990).

According to Freud (1900), dreams are a disguised form of *wish fulfillment,* a way to satisfy unconscious urges or resolve unconscious conflicts that are too upsetting to deal with consciously. For example, a person's sexual desires might appear in a dream as the rhythmic motions of a horseback ride. Conflicting feelings about a parent might appear as a dream about a fight. Seeing his patients' dreams as a "royal road to a knowledge of the unconscious," Freud interpreted their meaning as part of his psychoanalytic therapy methods (see the chapter on the treatment of psychological disorders).

In contrast, the *activation-synthesis theory* describes dreams as the meaningless by-products of REM sleep (Hobson, 1997). According to this theory, hindbrain arousal during REM sleep creates random messages that *activate* the brain, especially the cerebral cortex. Dreams result as the cortex connects, or *synthesizes,* these messages as best as it can, using stored memories and current feelings to organize this random brain activity into something more coherent. From this perspective, dreams represent the brain's attempt to make sense of meaningless stimulation during sleep, much as we might try to find meaningful shapes in cloud formations (Bernstein & Roberts, 1995; Rittenhouse, Stickgold, & Hobson, 1994; Tierney, 2009).

Even if dreams arise from random brain activity, their content may still have psychological significance. Some psychologists believe that dreams give people a chance to review and address some of the problems they face during waking hours (Cartwright, 1993). This view is supported by evidence suggesting that people's current concerns can affect both the content of their dreams and the way in which dreams are organized and recalled (Domhoff, 1996, 1999; Stevens, 1996). However, high-tech imaging research shows that while we are asleep, brain areas involved in emotion tend to be overactivated, whereas those areas controlling logical thought tend to be suppressed (Braun, Balkin, & Wesensten, 1998; Hobson et al., 1998). In fact, as we reach deeper sleep stages and then enter REM sleep, thinking subsides and hallucinations increase (Fosse, Stickgold, & Hobson, 2001). This is probably why dreams rarely provide realistic, logical solutions to our problems (Blagrove, 1996).

Hypnosis

▶ *Can you be hypnotized against your will?*

The word *hypnosis* comes from the Greek word *hypnos,* meaning "sleep." However, hypnotized people are not sleeping. Even those who say afterward that their bodies felt "asleep" also report that their minds were active and alert. **Hypnosis** has been defined as an altered state of consciousness that is brought on by special techniques and produces responsiveness to suggestions for changes in experience and behavior (Kirsch, 1994a). Most hypnotized people do not feel forced to follow the hypnotist's instructions. They simply see no reason to refuse (Hilgard, 1965). In fact, the more that people want to cooperate with the hypnotist, the more likely it is they will experience hypnosis (Lynn et al., 2002). People cannot be hypnotized against their will.

Experiencing Hypnosis

Hypnosis often begins with suggestions that the person feels relaxed and sleepy. The hypnotist may then gradually focus the person's attention on a particular and often monotonous set of stimuli, such as a swinging pendant. The hypnotist suggests that the individual should ignore everything else and imagine certain feelings.

There are special tests to measure **hypnotic susceptibility,** the degree to which people respond to hypnotic suggestions (Gfeller, 1994). Different tests can yield somewhat different results (Barnes, Lynn, & Pekala, 2009), but in general, they show that about 10 percent of adults are difficult or impossible to hypnotize (Hilgard, 1982). At the other extreme are people whose hypnotic experiences are so vivid that they can't tell the difference between images the hypnotist asked them to imagine and images projected on a screen (Bryant & Mallard, 2003). Hypnotically susceptible people typically

© David Parker/Photo Researchers, Inc.

INDUCING HYPNOSIS ▲

In the late 1700s, Austrian physician Franz Anton Mesmer used a forerunner of hypnosis to treat physical disorders. His procedure, known as mesmerism, included elaborate trance-induction rituals, but we now know that hypnosis can be induced far more easily, often simply by staring at an object, as this woman did.

hypnosis A phenomenon that is brought on by special techniques and is characterized by varying degrees of responsiveness to suggestions for changes in a person's behavior and experiences.

hypnotic susceptibility The degree to which a person responds to hypnotic suggestion.

FIGURE 4.6 ■ **HYPNOTIC AGE REGRESSION**

Here are the signatures of two adults before hypnotically induced age regression (top of each pair) and while age regressed (bottom of each pair). The lower signatures in each pair look less mature, but was the change due to hypnosis? To find out, ask a friend to sign a blank sheet of paper, first as usual, and then as if he or she were five years old. If the two signatures look significantly different, what does this say about the cause of certain age-regression effects? *Source:* Hilgard (1965).

Learn BY Doing

state theories of hypnosis Theories proposing that hypnosis creates an altered state of consciousness.

nonstate theories of hypnosis Theories, such as role theory, proposing that hypnosis does not create an altered state of consciousness.

differ from others in having a better ability to focus attention and ignore distractions (Crawford, Brown, & Moon, 1993; Iani et al., 2006). They also tend to have more active imaginations (Spanos, Burnley, & Cross, 1993), a tendency to fantasize (Lynn & Rhue, 1986), a capacity for processing information quickly and easily (Dixon, Brunet, & Laurence, 1990), a tendency to be suggestible (Kirsch & Braffman, 2001), and positive attitudes and expectations about hypnosis (Benham et al., 2006; Fassler, Lynn, & Knox, 2008; Gfeller, 1994).

The results of hypnosis can be fascinating. People told that their eyes are locked shut may struggle unsuccessfully to open them. They may appear deaf or blind or insensitive to pain. They may seem to forget their own names. Some appear to remember forgotten things. Others show *age regression,* apparently recalling or reenacting their childhoods (see Figure 4.6). These hypnotic effects can be extended for hours or days through *posthypnotic suggestions,* which are instructions about how to behave after hypnosis has ended (such as smiling whenever someone says "Paris"). Some individuals show *posthypnotic amnesia,* an inability to recall what happened while they were hypnotized, even after being told what happened (Barnier, 2002).

Ernest Hilgard (1965, 1992) described the main changes that people display during hypnosis. First, hypnotized people *tend not to begin actions on their own,* waiting instead for the hypnotist's instructions. One participant said, "I was trying to decide if my legs were crossed, but I couldn't tell, and didn't quite have the initiative to move to find out" (Hilgard, 1965). Second, hypnotized people tend to ignore all but the hypnotist's voice and whatever it points out: Their *attention is redistributed.* Third, hypnosis *enhances the ability to fantasize.* Participants more vividly imagine a scene or relive a memory. Fourth, hypnotized people *readily take on roles.* They more easily act as though they were people of a different age or sex than nonhypnotized people do. Fifth, hypnotized individuals show *reduced reality testing.* They tend not to question whether statements are true and they are more willing to accept distortions of reality. So a hypnotized person might shiver in a warm room if a hypnotist says it is snowing.

Explaining Hypnosis

Hypnotized people look and act different from nonhypnotized people (Hilgard, 1965). Do these differences indicate an altered state of consciousness?

Advocates of **state theories of hypnosis** say that they do. They point to the notable changes in brain activity that occur during hypnosis (Egner, Jamieson, & Gruzelier, 2005; Mohr, Binkofski et al., 2005; Raij et al., 2005) and to the dramatic effects that hypnosis can produce, including insensitivity to pain and the disappearance of warts (Noll, 1994). They also note that there are slight differences in the way hypnotized and nonhypnotized people carry out suggestions. In one study, hypnotized people and those pretending to be hypnotized were told to run their hands through their hair whenever they heard the word "experiment" (Orne, Sheehan, & Evans, 1968). The pretenders did so only when the hypnotist said the cue word. Hypnotized participants complied no matter who said it. Another study found that hypnotized people complied more often than pretenders with a posthypnotic suggestion to mail postcards to the experimenter (Barnier & McConkey, 1998).

However, there are also several **nonstate theories of hypnosis.** Supporters of role theory, for example, maintain that hypnosis is *not* a special state of consciousness. They point out that some of the changes in brain activity associated with hypnosis can also be created without hypnosis (Mohr, Binkofski et al., 2005). They suggest that hypnotized people are merely complying with the demands of the situation and acting in accordance with a special social role (Kirsch, 1994b). From this perspective, hypnosis provides a socially acceptable reason to follow someone's suggestions, much as a checkup at your doctor's office provides a socially acceptable reason to remove your clothing on request. Support for role theory comes from several sources. First, nonhypnotized people sometimes display behaviors that are usually associated with hypnosis. For example, contestants on television game shows and reality shows do lots of odd, silly, disgusting, or even dangerous things without first being hypnotized. Second, laboratory studies show that motivated but nonhypnotized volunteers can duplicate

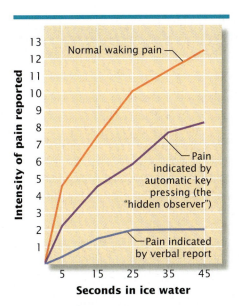

FIGURE 4.7 ■ **REPORTS OF PAIN IN HYPNOSIS**

This graph compares the intensity of pain reported by three groups of participants while one of their hands was immersed in ice water. The orange line represents nonhypnotized participants. The blue line represents hypnotized participants who were told they would feel no pain. The purple line shows the reports of hypnotized participants who were told they would feel no pain but were asked to press a key if "any part of them" felt pain. The key pressing by this "hidden observer" suggests that under hypnosis, the experience of pain was dissociated from conscious awareness (Hilgard, 1977).

many aspects of hypnotic behavior, from arm rigidity to age regression (Dasgupta et al., 1995; Orne & Evans, 1965). Other studies have found that people rendered blind or deaf by hypnosis can still see or hear, even though their actions and beliefs suggest that they cannot (Bryant & McConkey, 1989). Still others indicate that people's responses to hypnotic suggestions can vary from one occasion to the next, depending on situational factors (Fassler, Lynn, & Knox, 2008).

Hilgard's (1992) *dissociation theory* blends role and state theories. He suggested that hypnosis is not a single specific state but a general condition that temporarily reorganizes or breaks down our normal control over thoughts and actions. Hypnosis, he said, activates a process called *dissociation,* meaning a split in consciousness (Hilgard, 1979). Dissociation allows body movements normally under voluntary control to occur on their own and normally involuntary processes (such as overt reactions to pain) to be controlled voluntarily.

Hilgard argued that this relaxation of control is possible because of a social agreement between the hypnotized person and the hypnotist to share control. In other words, people usually decide for themselves how to act or what to attend to, perceive, or remember. During hypnosis, the hypnotist is given permission to control some of these experiences and actions. Compliance with a social role may tell part of the story, Hilgard said, but hypnosis also leads to significant changes in mental processes.

Support for Hilgard's theory comes from brain-imaging studies showing that the ability to dissociate certain mental processes is greater in people who are more hypnotically susceptible (Bob, 2008; Egner, Jamieson, & Gruzelier, 2005). Dissociation was also demonstrated behaviorally by asking hypnotized participants to immerse a hand in ice water (Hilgard, Morgan, & MacDonald, 1975). They were told that they would feel no pain but were asked to press a key with their other hand if "any part of them" felt pain. The results are shown in Figure 4.7. The participants' oral reports indicated almost no pain, but their key-pressing told a different story. Hilgard concluded that a "hidden observer" was reporting on pain that was reaching these people but that had been separated, or dissociated, from conscious awareness (Hilgard, 1977).

Much remains to be learned about the nature of hypnosis. However, traditional distinctions between state and role theories have become less important as researchers focus on larger questions, such as why people are susceptible to hypnosis and the biological, social, and cognitive factors that underlie hypnosis (e.g., Lynn & Kirsch, 2006; Raz, Fan, & Posner, 2005).

Applications of Hypnosis

Whatever hypnosis is, it has proven useful, especially in relation to pain (Patterson & Jensen, 2003). Magnetic resonance imaging (MRI) studies of hypnotized pain patients show altered activity in the anterior cingulate cortex, a brain region associated with the emotional component of pain (Faymonville et al., 2000; Mohr, Binkofski et al., 2005). Hypnosis seems to be the only anesthetic some people need to block the pain of dental work, childbirth, burns, and surgery (D. Patterson, 2004; Van Sickel, 1992). For others, hypnosis relieves chronic pain from arthritis, nerve damage, migraine headaches, and cancer (Stewart, 2005). Hypnotic suggestion can also help eliminate diarrhea (Tan, Hammond, & Joseph, 2005), reduce nausea and vomiting due to chemotherapy (Redd, 1984), limit surgical bleeding (Gerschman, Reade, & Burrows, 1980), and speed postoperative recovery (Astin, 2004).

Other applications of hypnosis are more controversial, especially the use of hypnosis to aid memory. For example, hypnotic age regression is sometimes used in an attempt to help people recover lost memories. However, the memories of past events reported by age-regressed individuals are not as accurate as those of nonhypnotized individuals (Lynn, Myers, & Malinoski, 1997). Similarly, it is doubtful that hypnosis can help witnesses recall the details of a crime. In fact, their positive expectations about the value of hypnosis may lead them to unintentionally distort or reconstruct memories of what they saw and heard (Garry & Loftus, 1994; Weekes et al., 1992; Wells & Olson, 2003). Being hypnotized may also make witnesses more confident about their reports, even if those reports are not accurate.

linkages

Does meditation relieve stress? *(a link to Health, Stress, and Coping)*

SURGERY UNDER HYPNOSIS ▲

Bernadine Coady, of Wimblington, England, has a condition that makes general anesthesia dangerous for her. In April 1999, she faced a foot operation that would have been extremely painful without anesthesia. She arranged for a hypnotherapist to help her through the procedure, but when he failed to show up, she was forced to rely on self-hypnosis as her only anesthetic. She said she imagined the pain as "waves lashing against a sea wall . . . [and] going away, like the tide." Coady's report that the operation was painless is believable because, in December 2000, she had the same operation on her other foot, again using only self-hypnosis for pain control (Morris, 2000).

applying psychology

psychoactive drugs   Chemical substances that act on the brain to create psychological effects.

psychopharmacology   The study of psychoactive drugs and their effects.

Linkages

Meditation, Health, and Stress

Meditation provides a set of techniques intended to create an altered state of consciousness characterized by inner peace and tranquility (Shapiro & Walsh, 1984; Walsh & Shapiro, 2006). Techniques to achieve a meditative state differ, depending on belief and philosophy (e.g., Eastern meditation, Sufism, yoga, or prayer). However, in the most common meditation methods, attention is focused on just one thing until the meditator stops thinking about anything else and experiences nothing but "pure awareness" (Benson, 1975). In this way, the individual becomes more fully aware of the present moment rather than being caught up in the past or the future.

To organize their attention, meditators may focus on the sound or tempo of their breathing or slowly repeat a soothing word or phrase, called a mantra. During a typical meditation session, breathing, heart rate, muscle tension, blood pressure, and oxygen consumption decrease, whereas blood flow in the brain to the thalamus and frontal lobes increases (Cahn & Polich, 2006; Newberg et al., 2001; Wallace & Benson, 1972). During most forms of meditation, EEG activity is similar to that seen in a relaxed, eyes-closed, waking state (see Figure 4.3). Meditation is also associated with increases in dopamine, a neurotransmitter that is involved in the experience of reward or pleasure, and fMRI scans show that during meditation, activity increases in brain areas involved in concentrated attention (Brefczynski-Lewis et al., 2007; Kjaer et al., 2002).

Some people claim that meditation improves their awareness and understanding of themselves and their environment. It has also been associated with better immune system functioning, reductions in high blood pressure, anxiety, and insomnia, longer survival among heart patients, and enhanced performance in everything from work to tennis (Beauchamp-Turner & Levinson, 1992; Bodian, 1999; Davidson et al., 2003; Paul-Labrador et al., 2006; Oman, Hedberg, & Thoreson, 2006; Schneider et al., 2005). More generally, meditators' scores on personality tests indicate increases in overall mental health, self-esteem, and social openness (Janowiak & Hackman, 1994; Sakairi, 1992; Tang et al., 2007). Exactly how meditation produces these benefits is unclear, though its activation of dopamine brain systems may tell an important part of the story. Whatever the mechanism, it is probably not unique to meditation. Many of the benefits associated with meditation have also been reported in association with other techniques, such as biofeedback, hypnosis, tai chi, or just relaxing (Bernstein et al., 2000; Beyerstein, 1999; Wang, Collet, & Lau, 2004).

Psychoactive Drugs

▶ *How do drugs affect the brain?*

The altered states we have discussed so far serve a biological need (sleep) or rely on the chemistry of the brain and body (hypnosis and meditation). Other altered states are brought on by outside agents, namely drugs. Every day, most people in the world use drugs that alter brain activity and consciousness (Levinthal, 2001). For example, 80 to 90 percent of people in North America use caffeine, the stimulant found in coffee and tea. A *drug* is a chemical that is not required for normal physiological functioning yet has an effect on the body. You may say that you "need" a cup of coffee in the morning, but you will still wake up without it; accordingly, the caffeine in coffee is defined as a drug. Drugs whose effects on the brain alter consciousness and other psychological processes are called **psychoactive drugs** (Julien, 2008). The study of psychoactive drugs is called **psychopharmacology.**

FIGURE 4.8 ■ AGONISTS AND ANTAGONISTS

In Part A, a molecule of neurotransmitter interacts with a receptor on a neuron's dendrites by fitting into and stimulating it. Part B shows a drug molecule acting as an agonist, affecting the receptor in the same way a neurotransmitter would. Part C depicts an antagonist drug molecule blocking a natural neurotransmitter from reaching and acting on the receptor.

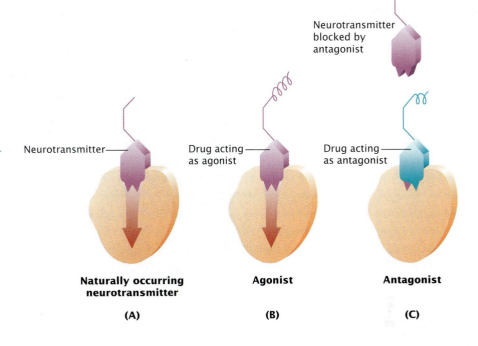

Neurotransmitter blocked by antagonist

Neurotransmitter —

Drug acting as agonist —

Drug acting as antagonist —

Naturally occurring neurotransmitter

(A)

Agonist

(B)

Antagonist

(C)

Psychopharmacology

Most psychoactive drugs affect the brain by altering the interactions between neurotransmitters and their receptors, as described in the chapter on biology and behavior. To create their effects, these drugs must cross the **blood-brain barrier,** a feature of blood vessels in the brain that prevents some substances from entering brain tissue (Neuwelt, 2004). Once past this barrier, a psychoactive drug's effects depend on several factors, such as which neurotransmitter systems the drug interacts with, how the drug affects those neurotransmitters and their receptors, and the psychological functions normally performed by the brain systems that use those neurotransmitters.

Drugs can affect neurotransmitters or their receptors through several mechanisms. Neurotransmitters fit into their own receptors, as Figure 4.8 shows. Some drugs, such as morphine, are similar enough to a particular neurotransmitter to fool its receptors. These drugs, called **agonists,** bind to receptors and imitate, or mimic, the effects of the normal neurotransmitter. Other drugs, called **antagonists,** are similar enough to a neurotransmitter to occupy its receptors but cannot mimic its effects. When they bind to receptors, they prevent the normal neurotransmitter from binding. Still other drugs work by increasing or decreasing the release of a specific neurotransmitter. Finally, some drugs work by speeding or slowing the *removal* of a neurotransmitter from synapses.

Predicting a psychoactive drug's effects on behavior is complicated. For one thing, most of these drugs interact with many neurotransmitter systems. Also, the nervous system may compensate for a given drug's effects. For instance, repeated exposure to a drug that blocks receptors for a certain neurotransmitter often leads to an increase in the number of receptors available to accept that neurotransmitter.

The Varying Effects of Drugs

Unfortunately, chemical properties that give drugs their medically desirable main effects, such as pain relief, often create undesirable side effects as well.

Drug Abuse One side effect may be the potential for abuse. **Drug abuse** (also referred to as *substance abuse*) is a pattern of use that causes serious social, legal, or interpersonal

blood-brain barrier A characteristic of blood vessels in the brain that prevents some substances from entering brain tissue.

agonists Drugs that bind to a receptor and mimic the effects of the neurotransmitter that normally fits that receptor.

antagonists Drugs that bind to a receptor and prevent the normal neurotransmitter from binding.

drug abuse (substance abuse) The use of psychoactive drugs in ways that deviate from cultural norms and cause serious problems for the user.

FIGURE 4.9   ■   CHANGING VIEWS OF DRUGS

The legal and social status of a drug can vary across cultures and over time (Weiss & Moore, 1990). For example, in the United States cocaine was once a respectable, commercially available drug; today it is illegal. And alcohol, which is legal in the United States and many other nations, is banned in countries such as Kuwait, Iran, and Saudi Arabia.

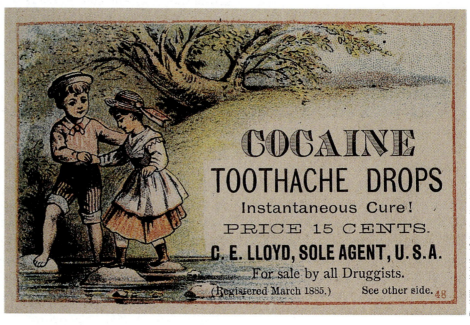

problems for the user (American Psychiatric Association, 2000). Of course, as a culture changes, which drugs cause a person social and legal problems may also change, as Figure 4.9 illustrates.

Substance abuse can lead to psychological or physical dependence. People displaying *psychological dependence* on a drug will continue to use it even though it has harmful effects. They need the drug for a sense of well-being and become preoccupied with getting the drug if it is no longer available. However, they can still function without the drug. Psychological dependence can occur with or without addiction, also known as *physical dependence.* **Addiction** is a physiological state in which there is not only a strong craving for the drug but also in which using the drug becomes necessary to prevent the unpleasant experience of **drug withdrawal** (sometimes called a *withdrawal syndrome*). Withdrawal symptoms vary depending on the drug, but they often include an intense desire for the drug and physical effects generally opposite to those of the drug itself. Eventually, drug users may develop **drug tolerance,** a condition in which increasingly larger drug doses are required to produce the same effect (Sokolowska, Siegel, & Kim, 2002). With the development of drug tolerance, many addicts need the drug just to prevent the negative effects of not taking it. However, most researchers believe that a craving for the positive effects of drugs is what keeps addicts coming back to them (Ciccocioppo, Martin-Fardon, & Weiss, 2004; Everitt & Robbins, 2005; George et al., 2001).

It may be tempting to think of "addicts" as being different from the rest of us, but we should never underestimate the ease with which drug dependence can develop in anyone, including ourselves. Physical dependence can develop gradually, without our awareness. In fact, scientists believe that the changes in the brain that underlie addiction may be similar to those that occur during learning (Koob & Kreek, 2007; Nestler, 2001). All addictive drugs stimulate the brain's "pleasure centers," regions that are sensitive to the neurotransmitter dopamine (Nestler, 2005). Neuron activity in these areas of the brain produces intensely pleasurable feelings in most people (Boyd, 2006; Cannon, 2005; Maldonado, Valverde, & Berrendero, 2006). It also helps generate the pleasant feelings associated with a good meal, a "runner's high," gambling, or sex (Grunberg, 1994; Harris & Aston-Jones, 1995; Reuter et al., 2005). It is no wonder, then, that addictive drugs have the capacity for creating tremendously rewarding effects in most people (Kelley & Berridge, 2002). In fact, the changes created in the brain

addiction   Development of a physical need for a psychoactive drug.

drug withdrawal   A set of symptoms associated with ending the use of an addictive substance.

drug tolerance   A condition in which increasingly larger drug doses are needed to produce a given effect.

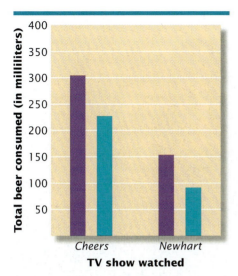

Alcohol-positive adjectives
Neutral adjectives

FIGURE 4.10 ■ EXPECTANCIES AND ALCOHOL CONSUMPTION

People may drink more when their expectancies about the positive effects of alcohol have been primed. In this study, some participants watched Cheers (a TV show in which people enjoy themselves while drinking alcohol) and were exposed to adjectives associated with positive expectancies about alcohol. They later drank more (nonalcoholic) beer than participants who watched a non-alcohol-related show and were not exposed to the alcohol-positive adjectives (Roehrich & Goldman, 1995).

CNS depressant drugs Psychoactive drugs that inhibit the functioning of the central nervous system.

by drug addiction can remain long after drug use ends (Diana, Spiqa, & Acquas, 2006), which is one reason that people who succeed in giving up addictive drugs may still be in danger of relapse months or even years later.

Expectations and Drug Effects Drug effects are not determined by biochemistry alone. The *expectations* we learn through experience with drugs and/or drug users also play a role (Bartholow & Heinz, 2006; Cumsille, Sayer, & Graham, 2000; Siegel, 2005; Stein, Goldman, & Del Boca, 2000). Several experiments have shown that research participants who consume nonalcoholic drinks that they *think* contain alcohol are likely to behave in line with their expectations about alcohol's effects. So they tend to feel drunk and to become more aggressive, more interested in violent and sexual material, and more easily sexually aroused (Darkes & Goldman, 1993; George & Marlatt, 1986; Lang et al., 1975; Lansky & Wilson, 1981). And because they know that alcohol impairs memory, these participants are more vulnerable to developing false memories about a crime they witnessed on videotape (Assefi & Garry, 2003).

Expectations about drug effects develop in part as people watch other people react to drugs (Sher et al., 1996), and these expectations can influence how much of a drug they themselves consume (see Figure 4.10). What they see can differ from one individual and culture to the next, so drug effects vary considerably throughout the world (MacAndrew & Edgerton, 1969). In the United States, for example, drinking alcohol is commonly associated with uninhibited behavior, including impulsiveness, anger, violence, and sexual promiscuity. These effects are not seen in all cultures, however. In Bolivia's Camba culture, people sometimes engage in extended bouts of drinking a brew that is 89 percent alcohol (178 proof). During these binges, the Camba repeatedly pass out, wake up, and start drinking again—all the while maintaining friendly social relations. Other studies have shown that learned expectations also contribute to the effects of heroin, cocaine, and marijuana (Robbins & Everitt, 1999; Schafer & Brown, 1991; Smith et al., 1992).

In short, the effects of psychoactive drugs are complex and variable. Here, we consider several major categories of psychoactive drugs that people use primarily to produce altered states of consciousness. They include depressant drugs, stimulating drugs, opiates, and hallucinogenic drugs.

CNS Depressant Drugs

Drugs such as alcohol and barbiturates are called **CNS depressant drugs** because they reduce or depress activity in the central nervous system (CNS), mainly in the brain. They do so partly by increasing the effects of the neurotransmitter GABA. As described in the chapter on biology and behavior, GABA reduces the activity of neurons in various brain circuits. So if a drug increases the amount of GABA available, activity in those circuits will be lower than usual, creating feelings of relaxation, drowsiness, and sometimes depression (Hanson & Venturelli, 1995).

Alcohol The most common CNS depressant drug by far is alcohol. In the United States, more than 100 million people drink it, and alcohol is equally popular worldwide (Leigh & Stacy, 2004). Alcohol affects several neurotransmitters, including glutamate, serotonin, and GABA, among others (Daglish & Nutt, 2003; Enoch, 2003; Vinod et al., 2006). The effect on GABA is especially significant. In fact, animal studies show that the intoxicating effects of alcohol can be blocked by drugs that prevent it from interacting with GABA receptors (Suzdak et al., 1986).

Alcohol also enhances the effect of endorphins, the body's natural painkillers. The fact that endorphins produce a sense of well-being may explain why people initially feel "high" when drinking alcohol. It may also explain why drugs that block endorphins are better than placebos at reducing alcohol cravings and relapse rates in recovering alcoholics (Garbutt et al., 2005). The pleasurable effects of alcohol are due in part to its interaction with the dopamine systems that are part of the brain's reward mechanisms (Thanos et al., 2001). Prolonged alcohol use can have lasting effects on the

DRINKING AND DRIVING DON'T MIX ▶

Though practice makes it seem easy, driving a car is a complex information processing task. As described in the chapter on thought, language, and intelligence, such tasks require constant vigilance, quick decisions, and skillful execution of responses. Alcohol can impair all these processes, as well as the ability to judge the degree of impairment—thus making drinking and driving a deadly combination that results in almost 13,000 deaths each year in the United States alone (National Highway Traffic Safety Administration, 2008).

brain's ability to regulate dopamine levels (Tiihonen et al., 1995). Dopamine agonists reduce alcohol cravings and the effects of alcohol withdrawal (Lawford et al., 1995).

Alcohol affects specific brain regions. It depresses activity in the locus coeruleus, an area that, as described in our discussion of sleep, normally helps activate the cerebral cortex. The resulting reduction in cortical activity, in turn, tends to cause cognitive changes and a loosening of control over normally inhibited behaviors (Casbon et al., 2003). Some drinkers begin talking loudly, acting silly, or telling others what they think of them. Emotional reactions range from giddy happiness to despair. Normally shy people may become impulsive or violent (Giancola & Corman, 2007). Alcohol also impairs the hippocampus, making it more difficult to process information and form new memories (Givens, 1995). The effects on the hippocampus may be permanent; brain-imaging studies have shown that the hippocampus is smaller in heavy drinkers than in nondrinkers (Beresford et al., 2006). Alcohol's suppression of the cerebellum causes poor motor coordination, including difficulty in walking (Rogers et al., 1986). Alcohol's ability to depress hindbrain mechanisms required for breathing and heartbeat can make overdoses fatal.

As mentioned earlier, some effects of alcohol—such as anger and aggressiveness—depend on both biochemical factors and learned expectations (Goldman, Darkes, & Del Boca, 1999; Kushner et al., 2000). But other effects—especially disruptions in motor coordination, speech, and thought—result from biochemical factors alone. These biological effects depend on the amount of alcohol the blood carries to the brain. It takes the liver about an hour to break down one ounce of alcohol (the amount in one typical drink), so alcohol has milder effects if consumed slowly. Faster drinking or drinking on an empty stomach speeds absorption of alcohol into the blood and heightens its effects. Even after allowing for differences in average male and female body weight, researchers have found metabolic differences that make male bodies able to tolerate somewhat greater amounts of alcohol. So a given quantity of alcohol may have a stronger effect on a woman than on a man. Overindulgence by either sex results in unpleasant physical hangover effects that cannot be prevented or relieved by aspirin, bananas, vitamins, coffee, eggs, exercise, fresh air, honey, pizza, herbal remedies, more alcohol, or any of the dozens of other "surefire" hangover cures you may have heard about (Pittler, Verster, & Ernst, 2005).

Genetics also seems to play a role in determining the biochemical effects of alcohol (Scholz, Franz, & Heberlein, 2005). Evidence suggests that some people have a genetic predisposition toward alcohol dependence (Agarwal, 1997; Enoch, 2003), though the genes involved have not yet been identified. Other groups (the Japanese, for example) may have inherited metabolic characteristics that enhance the adverse effects of alcohol, possibly inhibiting the development of alcohol abuse (Iwahashi et al., 1995).

Barbiturates   Sometimes called "downers" or sleeping pills, *barbiturates* are highly addictive. In small doses, their psychoactive effects include relaxation, mild pleasure, loss of muscle coordination, and lowered attention. Higher doses cause deep sleep, but continued use actually distorts sleep patterns (Kales & Kales, 1973). So long-term use of barbiturates as sleeping pills may be unwise. Overdoses can be fatal. Withdrawal symptoms are among the most severe for any drug and can include intense agitation, violent outbursts, seizures, hallucinations, and even sudden death.

GHB   *Gamma hydroxybutyrate (GHB)* is a naturally occurring substance similar to the neurotransmitter GABA (Drasbek, Christensen, & Jensen, 2006; Wong, Gibson, & Snead, 2004). In recent years, a laboratory-manufactured version of GHB (also known as "G") has become a popular "club drug" known for creating relaxation, feelings of elation, loss of inhibitions, and increased sex drive. Unfortunately, it can also cause nausea and vomiting, headaches, memory loss, dizziness, loss of muscle control or paralysis, breathing problems, loss of consciousness, and even death—especially when combined with alcohol or other drugs (Miotto et al., 2001; Stillwell, 2002). As with other CNS depressants, long-term use of GHB can lead to dependence. If dependent users abruptly stop taking the drug, they may experience a withdrawal syndrome that can include seizures, hallucinations, agitation, coma, or death (Tarabar & Nelson, 2004).

CNS Stimulating Drugs

Whereas depressants slow down central nervous system activity, **CNS stimulating drugs** speed it up. Amphetamines, cocaine, caffeine, and nicotine are all examples of CNS stimulating drugs.

Amphetamines   Often called "uppers" or "speed," *amphetamines* increase the release of norepinephrine and dopamine into synapses, affecting sleep, learning, and mood (Bonci et al., 2003; Kolb et al., 2003). Amphetamines also slow the removal of both substances at synapses, leaving more of them there, ready to work. The increased activity at these neurotransmitters' receptors results in alertness, arousal, and appetite suppression. These effects are amplified by the fact that amphetamines also reduce activity of the inhibitory neurotransmitter GABA (Centonze et al., 2002). Amphetamines' rewarding properties are probably associated with their effect on dopamine activity, because taking dopamine antagonists reduces amphetamine use (Holman, 1994).

People who abuse amphetamines usually begin taking these drugs in an effort to lose weight, stay awake, or "get high." Continued use leads to anxiety, insomnia, heart problems, brain damage, movement disorders, confusion, paranoia, nonstop talking, and psychological and physical dependence (Thompson et al., 2004; Volkow et al., 2001). In some cases, the symptoms of amphetamine abuse are almost identical to those of paranoid schizophrenia, a serious mental disorder linked to dopamine malfunction.

Cocaine   Like amphetamines, *cocaine* increases norepinephrine and dopamine activity and decreases GABA activity, so it produces many amphetamine-like effects (Kolb et al., 2003). Cocaine's particularly powerful and rapid effect on dopamine activity may underlie its remarkably addictive nature (Bonci et al., 2003; Ciccocioppo, Martin-Fardon, & Weiss, 2004; Ungless et al., 2001). In fact, most drugs with rapid onset and short duration are more addictive than others (Kato, Wakasa, & Yamagita, 1987), which helps explain why *crack*—a purified, fast-acting, highly potent, smokable form of cocaine—is especially addictive.

CNS stimulating drugs Psychoactive drugs that increase behavioral and mental activity.

DEADLY DRUG USE ▲

John Entwistle, bass player for The Who, died of a cocaine-related heart attack in 2002. He joined a long list of celebrities (including Chris Farley and Righteous Brother Bobby Hatfield) and an even longer list of ordinary people whose lives have been destroyed by the abuse of cocaine or other drugs.

Cocaine stimulates self-confidence, a sense of well-being, and optimism. Continued use, though, brings nausea, overactivity, insomnia, paranoia, a sudden depressive "crash," hallucinations, sexual dysfunction, and seizures. Overdoses, especially overdoses of crack cocaine, can be deadly. Even small doses can cause a fatal heart attack or stroke (Klausner & Lewandowski, 2002). Using cocaine during pregnancy harms the fetus (e.g., Hurt et al., 1995). However, many of the severe, long-term behavioral problems seen in "cocaine babies" may have as much to do with poverty and neglect after birth as with the mother's cocaine use beforehand. Early intervention can reduce the effects of both cocaine and the hostile environment that confronts most cocaine babies (Mayes et al., 2003; Singer et al., 2004).

Caffeine   *Caffeine* may be the world's most popular drug. It is found in chocolate, in many soft drinks, and in tea and coffee. A typical cup of coffee has 58–259 mg of caffeine, and even "decaffeinated" coffee may still contain up to 15.8 mg (McCusker, Goldberger, & Cone, 2003; McCusker et al., 2006). Caffeine reduces drowsiness and can enhance cognitive performance, including problem solving and vigilance (Beaumont et al., 2001; Ritchie et al., 2007). It also increases the capacity for physical work and raises urine production (Warburton, 1995). At high doses it causes anxiety and tremors. People can develop tolerance to caffeine, and it can be physically addictive (Strain et al., 1994). Withdrawal symptoms—including headache, fatigue, anxiety, shakiness, and craving—appear on the first day of abstinence and last about a week (Silverman et al., 1992). Caffeine may make it harder for women to become pregnant, and heavy use may increase the risk of miscarriage, stillbirth, or of having a low-birthweight baby (Balat et al., 2003; Bech et al., 2005; CARE Study Group, 2008; Rasch, 2003; Weng, Odouli, & Li, 2008; Wisborg et al., 2003). Moderate daily caffeine use may also cause slight increases in blood pressure (James, 2004), but otherwise it appears to have few, if any, negative effects (Kleemola et al., 2000; Lopez-Garcia et al., 2008; Winkelmayer et al., 2005).

Nicotine   A powerful autonomic nervous system stimulant, *nicotine* is the main psychoactive ingredient in tobacco. It enhances the action of acetylcholine and increases the availability of glutamate, the brain's primary excitatory neurotransmitter. It also activates the brain's dopamine-related pleasure systems (Balfour, 2002; McGehee et al., 1995). Nicotine has many psychoactive effects, including elevated mood and improved memory and attention (Domino, 2003; Ernst et al., 2001). Like heroin and cocaine, nicotine can be physically addictive (White, 1998). It doesn't create the "rush" characteristic of many drugs of abuse, but stopping nicotine use often creates a withdrawal syndrome that includes craving, irritability, anxiety, reduced heart rate, and lower activity in the brain's reward pathways (Epping-Jordan et al., 1998; Hughes, Higgins, & Bickel, 1994). The tendency to become physically dependent on nicotine appears to be at least partly inherited (Bierut et al., 2008; Li, 2006), so some smokers appear to develop only a psychological dependence on nicotine (Robinson & Pritchard, 1995). In either case, there is no doubt that smoking tobacco can be a difficult habit to break (Breteler et al., 2004). It is also clearly recognized as a major risk factor for cancer, heart disease, and respiratory disorders (U.S. Department of Health and Human Services, 2001).

MDMA   The stimulant "Ecstasy," or *MDMA* (short for 3,4-methylenedioxymethamphetamine), is a popular drug on college campuses in the United States (Strote, Lee, & Wechsler, 2002). MDMA increases the activity of dopamine-releasing neurons, so it leads to some of the same effects as those produced by cocaine and amphetamines. These include a sense of well-being, increased sex drive, and a feeling of greater closeness to others. Unfortunately, MDMA may also cause dry mouth, hyperactivity, jaw muscle spasms that may result in "lockjaw," elevated blood pressure, fever, dangerously abnormal heart rhythms, and visual hallucinations (Smith, Larive, & Romananelli, 2002). The hallucinations may appear because MDMA is a serotonin agonist and it also increases serotonin release. On the day after using MDMA—also known as "XTC," "clarity," "essence," "E," and "Adam"—people often report muscle aches, fatigue, depression, and poor concentration.

Even though it does not appear to be physically addictive, MDMA is a dangerous, potentially deadly drug, especially when taken by women (Liechti, Gamma, & Vollenweider, 2001; National Institute on Drug Abuse, 2000). It permanently damages the brain, killing serotonin-sensitive neurons as well as neurons that use dopamine. As you might expect, the danger of brain damage increases with higher doses and continued use. MDMA also impairs memory (Reneman et al., 2001; Rodgers, 2000; Zakzanis & Young, 2001), and users may develop the symptoms of panic disorder, which include intense anxiety and a sense of impending death (see the chapter on psychological disorders). Research on humans and nonhumans indicates that many of these impairments remain even after MDMA's use is discontinued (Kalechstein et al., 2007; Smith, Tivarus et al., 2006).

Opiates

The **opiates** (opium, morphine, heroin, and codeine) are unique in their capacity for inducing sleep and relieving pain (Julien, 2008). *Opium,* derived from the poppy plant, relieves pain and causes feelings of well-being and dreamy relaxation (Cowan et al., 2001). One of its most active ingredients, *morphine,* was first isolated in the early 1800s. It is used worldwide for pain relief. Percodan and Demerol are some common morphine-like drugs. *Heroin* is derived from morphine but is three times more powerful, causing intensely pleasurable reactions. Opiates have complex effects on consciousness. Drowsy, cloudy feelings occur because opiates depress activity in some areas of the cerebral cortex. They also create excitation in other parts, causing some users to experience euphoria, or elation. Opiates exert many of their effects by stimulating the receptors normally stimulated by endorphins, the body's own painkillers. This action "tricks" the brain into an exaggerated activation of its painkilling and mood-altering systems (Julien, 2008).

Opiates are highly addictive, partly because they stimulate a type of glutamate receptor in the brain's neurons that causes physical changes in these neurons. It may be, then, that opiates alter neurons so that they come to require the drug to function properly (Bajo et al., 2006; Martin et al., 2004). Beyond the hazard of addiction itself, heroin addicts risk death through overdoses, contaminated drugs, or AIDS contracted through sharing needles (Hser et al., 2001).

Hallucinogenic Drugs

Hallucinogenic drugs, also called *psychedelic drugs,* create a loss of contact with reality and alter other aspects of emotion, perception, and thought. They can cause distortions in body image (the user may feel gigantic or tiny), loss of identity (confusion about who one actually is), dreamlike fantasies, and hallucinations. Because these effects resemble many severe forms of mental disorder, hallucinogenic drugs are also called *psychotomimetics* ("mimicking psychosis").

LSD   One of the most powerful hallucinogenic drugs is *lysergic acid diethylamide,* or *LSD.* It was first synthesized from a rye fungus by Swiss chemist Albert Hofmann. In 1938, after Hofmann accidentally ingested a tiny amount of the substance, he discovered the drug's strange effects in the world's first LSD "trip" (Julien, 2008). LSD hallucinations can be quite bizarre. Time may seem distorted, sounds may cause visual sensations, and users may feel as if they have left their bodies. These experiences probably result from LSD's action as a serotonin agonist, because serotonin antagonists greatly reduce LSD's hallucinatory effects (Leonard, 1992).

The effects of LSD on a particular person are unpredictable. Unpleasant hallucinations and delusions can occur during a person's first—or two hundredth—LSD experience. Although LSD is not addictive, tolerance to its effects does develop. Some users suffer lasting side effects, including severe short-term memory loss, paranoia, violent

opiates   Psychoactive drugs that produce both sleep-inducing and pain-relieving effects.

hallucinogenic drugs   Psychoactive drugs that alter consciousness by producing a temporary loss of contact with reality and changes in emotion, perception, and thought.

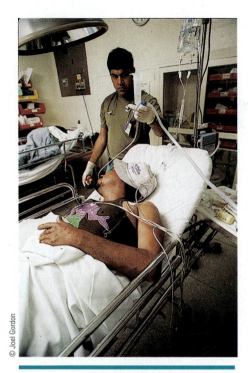

ANOTHER DRUG DANGER ▲

Oxycodone, a morphine-like drug prescribed by doctors under the label OxyContin, has become popular among recreational substance abusers. It was designed as a timed-release painkiller, but when people crush OxyContin tablets and then inject or inhale the drug, they get a much stronger and potentially lethal dose, especially when they are also using other drugs such as alcohol or cocaine (Cone et al., 2004). Deaths from OxyContin abuse have been on the rise in the United States in recent years (U.S. Drug Enforcement Administration, 2002).

outbursts, nightmares, and panic attacks (Gold, 1994). Sometimes "flashbacks" can occur, in which a person suddenly returns to an LSD-like state of consciousness weeks or even years after using the drug.

Ketamine   *Ketamine* is an anesthetic used by veterinarians to ease pain in animals (Hirota, 2006; Robakis & Hirsch, 2006), but because it also has hallucinogenic effects, it is being stolen and sold as a recreational drug known as "Special K." Its effects include dissociative feelings that create what some users describe as an "out-of-body" or "near-death" experience. Ketamine use can also lead to lasting memory problems (Curran & Monaghan, 2001; Smith, Larive, & Romananelli, 2002), possibly because it damages memory-related brain structures such as the hippocampus (Jevtovic-Todorovic et al., 2001).

Marijuana   A mixture of crushed leaves, flowers, and stems from the hemp plant (*Cannabis sativa*) makes up *marijuana*. The active ingredient is *tetrahydrocannabinol*, or *THC*. When inhaled, THC is absorbed in minutes by many organs, including the brain, and it continues to affect consciousness for a few hours (O'Leary et al., 2002). THC tends to collect in fatty deposits of the brain and reproductive organs, where it can remain for weeks. Low doses of marijuana may initially create restlessness and hilarity, followed by a dreamy, carefree relaxation, an expanded sense of space and time, more vivid sensations, food cravings, and subtle changes in thinking (Kelly et al., 1990).

There is an ongoing debate about the dangers and potential benefits of marijuana. Its dangers are suggested by the fact that a mild withdrawal syndrome has been reported in rats; in humans, withdrawal from marijuana may be accompanied by increases in anxiety, depression, irritability, restlessness, and aggressiveness (Budney et al., 2001, 2003; Haney et al., 1999; Kouri, Pope, & Lukas, 1999; Rodriguez de Fonseca et al., 1997; Smith, 2002). Further, marijuana interacts with the same dopamine and opiate receptors that heroin acts on (Tanda, Pontieri, & Di Chiara, 1997), leading some researchers to speculate that marijuana might be a "gateway" to the use of more addictive drugs (Lynskey et al., 2003; Spano et al., 2007). Other researchers have cautioned that the interpretation of these results is not clear cut, because even though the rewarding effects of sex and chocolate occur by activating these same neurotransmitter receptors, those pleasures are not generally viewed as gateways to drug addiction!

Regardless of whether marijuana is addicting or leads to the use of opiates, it can create a number of problems. It disrupts memory formation, making it difficult to carry out mental or physical tasks and, despite users' impressions, it actually reduces creativity (Bourassa & Vaugeois, 2001; Pope & Yurgelun-Todd, 1996). And because marijuana disrupts muscle coordination, driving while under its influence can be dangerous. In fact, motor impairment continues well after the subjective effects of the drug have worn off. Marijuana easily reaches a developing fetus and therefore should not be used by pregnant women (Fried, Watkinson, & Gray, 1992; Spano et al., 2007). Finally, long-term use can lead to psychological dependence (Stephens, Roffman, & Simpson, 1994) as well as to impairments in reasoning and memory that last for months or years after marijuana use stops (Bolla et al., 2002; Solowij et al., 2002). Research has also shown that adults who frequently used marijuana scored lower than nonusers with equal IQs on a twelfth-grade academic achievement test (Block & Ghoneim, 1993). Heavy use by teenagers has been associated with smaller than normal volume in brain areas involved in emotion and memory as well as with the later appearance of anxiety, depression, and other even more serious symptoms of mental disorder (Moore et al., 2007; Patton et al., 2002; Yücel et al., 2008; Zammit et al., 2002).

Marijuana may have considerable value in some domains, however. Doctors have successfully used it in the treatment of asthma, glaucoma, epilepsy, chronic pain, and nausea from cancer chemotherapy; it may even help in treating some types of cancer (Abrams et al., 2007; Gorter et al., 2005; Parolaro et al., 2002; Rog et al., 2005; Tramer et al., 2001). But critics say medical legalization of marijuana is premature until more

© Joel Gordon

In Review

MAJOR CLASSES OF PSYCHOACTIVE DRUGS

DRUG	TRADE/STREET NAME	MAIN EFFECTS	POTENTIAL FOR PHYSICAL/ PSYCHOLOGICAL DEPENDENCE
CNS Depressant Drugs			
Alcohol	"booze"	Relaxation, anxiety reduction, sleep	High/high
Barbiturates	Seconal, Tuinal, Nembutal ("downers")	Relaxation, anxiety reduction, sleep	High/high
GHB	G, Jib, Scoop, GH Buddy	Relaxation, euphoria	High/high
CNS Stimulating Drugs			
Amphetamines	Benzedrine, Dexedrine, Methadrine ("speed," "uppers," "ice")	Alertness, euphoria	Moderate/high
Cocaine	"coke," "crack"	Alertness, euphoria	Moderate to high/high
Caffeine		Alertness	Moderate/moderate
Nicotine	"smokes," "coffin nails"	Alertness	High (?)/high
MDMA	"Ecstasy," "clarity"	Hallucinations	Low/(?)
Opiates			
Opium		Euphoria	High/high
Morphine	Percodan, Demerol	Euphoria, pain control	High/high
Heroin	"junk," "smack"	Euphoria, pain control	High/high
Hallucinogenic Drugs			
LSD/ketamine	"acid"/"Special K"	Altered perceptions, hallucinations	Low/low
Marijuana (cannabis)	"pot," "dope," "reefer"	Euphoria, relaxation	Low/moderate

1. Physical dependence on a drug is a condition more commonly known as _____.
2. Drugs that act as antagonists _____ the interaction of neurotransmitters and receptors.
3. Drug effects are determined partly by what we learn to _____ the effects to be.

controlled research is available to establish its medicinal value. They point out, too, that even though patients tend to prefer marijuana-based drugs, other medications may be equally effective and less dangerous (e.g., Campbell et al., 2001; Fox et al., 2004; Hall & Degenhardt, 2003).

Nevertheless, in Canada, it is legal to grow and use marijuana for medicinal purposes, and the same is true in thirteen U.S. states, despite federal laws to the contrary and the threat of federal intervention to enforce those laws. The American Medical Association has rejected the idea of medical uses for marijuana, but scientists are intent on objectively studying its potential value in the treatment of certain diseases as well as its possible dangers. Their work is being encouraged by the National Institute of Medicine (Joy, Watson, & Benson, 1999), and drug companies are working on new cannabis-based medicines (Altman, 2000; Tuller, 2004). The United Nations, too, has recommended that governments worldwide sponsor additional work on the medical uses of marijuana (Wren, 1999). ("In Review: Major Classes of Psychoactive Drugs" summarizes our discussion of these substances.)

Consciousness

As noted in the introductory chapter, all of psychology's subfields are related to one another. Our discussion of meditation, health, and stress illustrates just one way that the topic of this chapter, consciousness, is linked to the subfield of health psychology, which is described in the chapter on health, stress, and coping. The Linkages diagram shows ties to two other subfields, and there are many more ties throughout the book. Looking for linkages among subfields will help you see how they all fit together and help you better appreciate the big picture that is psychology.

linkages

Do forgotten memories remain in consciousness? *(ans. on p. 234)*

Chapter 6
Memory

Does meditation relieve stress? *(ans. on p. 156)*

Chapter 10
Health, Stress, and Coping

Can subconscious processes alter our reaction to people? *(ans. on p. 560)*

Chapter 14
Social Psychology

SUMMARY   ▶

Consciousness can be defined as awareness of the outside world and of one's own thoughts, feelings, perceptions, and other mental processes.

The Scope of Consciousness

▶ *Can unconscious thoughts affect your behavior?*

A person's *con-sciousness state* is constantly chang-ing. When the changes are partic-ularly noticeable, they are called *altered states of consciousness*. Examples of al-tered states include sleep, hypnosis, meditation, and some drug-induced conditions. Cultures dif-fer in the value they place on particular states of consciousness.

Differing levels of consciousness are de-scribed as variations in awareness of your own mental functions. The *preconscious level* includes mental activities that are outside awareness but that can easily be brought to the *conscious level*. *Subconscious* and *unconscious* mental activity is said to involve thoughts, memories, and processes that are more difficult to bring to awareness. Men-tal processes that cannot be brought into aware-ness are said to occur at the *nonconscious level*.

Awareness is not always required for men-tal operations. For example, research on priming shows that people's responses to stimuli speed up and improve as stimuli are repeated, even when there is no conscious memory of which stimuli are old and which are new. And some decisions that seem intuitive may be guided by informa-tion that is outside of awareness.

Sleeping and Dreaming

▶ *Does your brain go to sleep when you do?*

Sleep is an active and complex state. Different stages of sleep are defined on the basis of changes in brain activity (as mea-sured by an electroencephalograph, or EEG) and physiological arousal. Sleep normally begins with stage 1 sleep and progresses gradually to stage 4 sleep. The two deepest stages of this **NREM (non rapid eye movement)** sleep are also called slow-wave sleep. After passing back to stage 2, people enter **REM (rapid eye movement) sleep,** or para-doxical sleep. The sleeper passes through these stages several times each night, gradually spending more time in stage 2 and REM sleep later in the night.

Sleep disorders can disrupt the natural rhythm of sleep. Among the most common is **insomnia,** a condition in which one has trouble falling asleep or staying asleep. **Narcolepsy** produces sudden daytime sleeping episodes. In cases of **sleep apnea,** people briefly but repeatedly stop breathing during sleep. **Sudden infant death syndrome (SIDS)** may be due to brain abnormalities or accidental suffocation. **Sleepwalking** happens most frequently during childhood. **Nightmares** and **sleep terror disorder (night terrors)** involve different kinds of frightening dreams. **REM behavior disorder** is potentially dangerous because it allows people to act out REM dreams. The cycle of waking and sleeping is a natural **circadian rhythm** or **human biological rhythm,** controlled by the suprachiasmatic nuclei of the brain. **Jet lag** can be one result of disrupting the normal sleep-wake cycle.

The purpose of sleep is still unclear. Non-REM sleep may aid bodily rest and repair. REM sleep may help maintain activity in brain areas that provide daytime alertness or it may allow the brain to "check circuits," eliminate useless information, and solidify learning from the previous day. **Sleep deprivation** leads to fatigue, irritability, and inattention and is a major factor in poor decision-making, learning and memory difficulties, and traffic accidents.

Most dreaming occurs during REM sleep. **Dreaming** is the production of story-like sequences of images, sensations, and perceptions that occur during sleep. Evidence from research on **lucid dreaming** suggests that people may be able to control their own dreams. Some claim that dreams are the meaningless by-products of brain activity, but our recall of dreams may still have psychological significance.

Hypnosis

▶ *Can you be hypnotized against your will?*

Hypnosis is a well-known but still poorly understood phenomenon. Tests of *hypnotic susceptibility* suggest that some people  cannot be hypnotized and that others are hypnotized easily. Hypnotized people tend to focus attention on the hypnotist and passively follow instructions. They become better at fantasizing and role taking. They may exhibit apparent age regression, experience posthypnotic amnesia, and obey posthypnotic suggestions.

State theories of hypnosis see hypnosis as a special state of consciousness. **Nonstate theories of hypnosis** such as **role theory** suggest that hypnosis creates a special social role that frees people to act in unusual ways. *Dissociation theory* combines aspects of role and state theories, suggesting that hypnotized individuals enter into a social contract with the hypnotist to allow normally integrated mental processes to become dissociated and to share control over these processes.

Hypnosis is useful in the control of pain and the reduction of nausea associated with cancer chemotherapy. Meditation is a set of techniques designed to create an altered state of consciousness characterized by inner peace and increased awareness. The consistent practice of meditation has been associated with reductions in stress-related problems such as anxiety and high blood pressure.

Psychoactive Drugs

▶ *How do drugs affect the brain?*

Psychoactive drugs affect the brain, changing consciousness and other psychological processes. **Psychopharmacology** is the field  that studies drug effects and their mechanisms. Psychoactive drugs exert their effects primarily by influencing specific neurotransmitter systems and hence certain brain activities. To reach brain tissue, drugs must cross the **blood-brain barrier.** Drugs that mimic the receptor effects of a neurotransmitter are called agonists; drugs that block the receptor effects of a neurotransmitter are called antagonists. Some drugs alter the release or removal of specific neurotransmitters, thus affecting the amount of neurotransmitter available for receptor effects.

Adverse effects such as **drug abuse** often accompany the use of psychoactive drugs. Psychological dependence, **addiction** (physical dependence), **drug tolerance,** and symptoms of **drug withdrawal** (withdrawal syndrome) may result. Drugs that produce dependence share the property of directly stimulating certain dopamine-sensitive areas of the brain known as pleasure centers. The consequences of using a psychoactive drug depend both on how the drug affects neurotransmitters and on the user's expectations.

Alcohol and barbiturates are examples of **CNS depressant drugs.** They reduce activity in the central nervous system, often by enhancing the action of inhibitory neurotransmitters. They have considerable potential for producing both psychological and physical dependence.

CNS stimulating drugs, such as amphetamines and cocaine, increase behavioral and mental activity mainly by increasing the action of dopamine and norepinephrine. These drugs can produce both psychological and physical dependence. Caffeine, one of the world's most popular stimulants, may also create dependence. Nicotine is a potent stimulant. And MDMA, which has both stimulant and hallucinogenic properties, is one of several psychoactive drugs that can permanently damage brain tissue.

Opiates such as opium, morphine, and heroin are highly addictive drugs that induce sleep and relieve pain.

LSD and marijuana are examples of **hallucinogenic drugs,** or psychedelic drugs. They alter consciousness by producing a temporary loss of contact with reality and changes in emotion, perception, and thought.

Learn BY **Doing** ▶

Put It in Writing

Watch a prime-time television program and make notes on the role played in the story by alcohol, nicotine, cocaine, or other psychoactive drugs. Now think about what you saw and write a one-page paper describing the messages the show sent to viewers about drugs. Did it directly or indirectly approve or disapprove of drug use? Did it lead viewers to expect particular effects from particular drugs? Conclude by considering what effects these drug-related messages might have on viewers, especially young children.

Personal Learning Activity

For the next two weeks, keep a notepad or voice recorder by your bed and write down or record your dreams as soon as you awaken. During this same period, use a diary or calendar to jot down significant events, problems, and emotional reactions in your waking life. Then compare the two sets of information. Do you see any correlation? For example, did any of your life events appear in your dreams? Did any dreams contain wished-for solutions to the problems or challenges you were facing at the time? What do you think your own data might say about the meaning of dreams in general? *For additional projects, see the Personal Learning Activities in the corresponding chapter of the study guide that accompanies this book.*

Take Action to Learn More

Now that you have finished reading this chapter, how about exploring some of the ideas and information that you found most interesting? Here are some courses, books, films, and Internet resources to get you started. Enjoy!

Courses

History of Psychology
Neuropsychology
Cognitive Psychology
Psychopharmacology
Computational Neuroscience
Sleep

Movies

Dune. Altered consciousness states.
An American Werewolf in London; Nightmare. Nightmares.
Boyz n the Hood; Wasted. The role of drugs and alcohol in adolescent development.
Days of Wine and Roses; Ironweed; The Lost Weekend; Leaving Las Vegas; When a Man Loves a Woman. Alcoholism.
Deadly Dreams; Joseph and the Amazing Technicolor Dreamcoat. Portrayal of dreams as glimpses of the future.
All That Jazz; Basketball Diaries; Bird; Love and Diane; Ray; Rush; Trainspotting; 21 Grams. Drug addiction.
Brainscan; Dead Again; Hypnosis; Mesmer; Stir of Echoes. Myths and misconceptions about hypnosis.
Sacred Sleep: The Power of Dreams. Various cultures view the meaning of dreams.

Books

SUSAN CHEEVER, *Note Found in a Bottle: My Life as a Drinker* (Washington Square Press, 2000). Memoir of an alcoholic.

BARNABY CONRAD, *Time Is All We Have* (Cameron, 1992). A month at the Betty Ford Treatment Center.
NICHOLAS HUMPHREY, *A History of the Mind: Evolution and the Birth of Consciousness* (Copernicus, 1999). Description of how consciousness has arisen from brain activity.
ERNEST KEEN, *Chemicals for the Mind: Pharmacology and Human Consciousness* (Praeger, 2000). Theories of consciousness and drugs' effects on it.
CAROLINE KNAPP, *Drinking: A Love Story* (Delta, 1997). A woman explores the roots of her alcohol addiction.
ROBERT M. JULIEN, *A Primer of Drug Action: A Concise, Nontechnical Guide to the Actions, Uses, and Side Effects of Psychoactive Drugs* (11th ed.; Worth, 2008). The title says it all.
DANIEL GOLEMAN, *The Meditative Mind: Varieties of Meditative Experience* (J. P. Tarcher, 1996). Meditation and its effects.
STEVEN J. LYNN AND IRVING KIRSCH, *Essentials of Clinical Hypnosis: An Evidence-Based Approach.* (American Psychological Association, 2005). Summary of hypnotic techniques, evidence for the clinical use of hypnosis, and theories of hypnosis.
STEVEN J. LYNN, IRVING KIRSH, AND JUDITH RHUE, *Casebook of Clinical Hypnosis* (American Psychological Association, 2006). Case studies in the use of hypnotic techniques in clinical treatment.
JOSEPH BARBER, ED., *Hypnosis and Suggestion in the Treatment of Pain* (Norton, 1996). Case studies in pain management using hypnosis.
STANLEY COREN, *Sleep Thieves: An Eye-Opening Exploration into the Science and Mysteries of Sleep* (Free Press, 1996). An introduction to sleep research.
EDWARD F. PACE-SCHOTT, MARK SOLMS, MARK BLAGROVE, AND STEVAN HARNAD, EDS., *Sleep and Dreaming: Scientific Advances and Reconsiderations* (Cambridge University Press, 2003). A comprehensive set of research articles on sleep and dreaming.

The Web

***Essentials of Psychology* Book Companion Website**

www.cengage.com/psychology/bernstein

Visit the book companion website to access a wealth of resources, including chapter outlines, flashcards, web links, tutorial quizzes, and more!

CENGAGENOW™ Just what you need to know NOW! Spend time on what you need to master rather than on information you already have learned. Take a pre-test for this chapter, and CengageNOW will generate a personalized study plan based on your results. The study plan will identify the topics you need to review and direct you to online resources to help you master those topics. You can then take a post-test to help you determine the concepts you have mastered and what you will need to work on. Try it out! Go to www.cengage.com/loginto sign in with an access code or to purchase access to this product.

Review of Key Terms ▶

Can you define each of the key terms in the chapter? Check your definitions against those on the pages shown in parentheses in the following list or in the Glossary at the end of the book.

addiction (p. 158)
agonists (p. 157)
altered state of consciousness (p. 143)
antagonists (p. 157)

blood-brain barrier (p. 157)
circadian rhythm (p. 149)
CNS depressant drugs (p. 159)
CNS stimulating drugs (p. 161)
consciousness (p. 138)
consciousness state (p. 139)
dreaming (p. 151)
drug abuse (substance abuse) (p. 157)
drug tolerance (p. 158)

drug withdrawal (p. 158)
hallucinogenic drugs (p. 163)
human biological rhythm (see circadian rhythm) (p. 149)
hypnosis (p. 153)
hypnotic susceptibility (p. 153)
insomnia (p. 147)
jet lag (p. 149)
lucid dreaming (p. 151)

narcolepsy (p. 147)
nightmares (p. 148)
night terrors (see sleep terror disorder)
    (p. 148)
nonconcious level (p. 139)
nonstate theories of hypnosis (p. 154)
NREM (nonrapid eye movement) sleep (p. 145)

opiates (p. 163)
preconcious level (p. 139)
psychoactive drugs (p. 156)
psychopharmacology (p. 156)
REM behavior disorder (p. 148)
REM (rapid eye movement) sleep (p. 145)
sleep apnea (p. 147)

sleep deprivation (p. 150)
sleep terror disorder (p. 148)
sleepwalking (p. 148)
state theories of hypnosis (p. 154)
subconscious (p. 140)
sudden infant death syndrome (SIDS) (p. 148)
unconscious (p. 140)

MULTIPLE-CHOICE ▶ Self Test

Select the best answer for each of the following questions. Then check your responses against the Answer Key at the end of the book.

1. Tyrrell is undergoing biofeedback training to help him regulate his blood pressure, a bodily function typically regulated at which level of consciousness?
   a. Nonconscious   c. Subconscious
   b. Preconscious   d. Unconscious

2. Dr. Eplort is staying in a cave for several months with no external light cues and no way to keep time. He goes to sleep when he feels sleepy and gets up when he is awake. Dr. Eplort will most likely sleep _____.
   a. fewer hours than he did before
   b. more hours than he did before
   c. about the same as he did before
   d. on a varying and unpredictable schedule

3. Zandra knew nothing about art, and during her first semester on campus she had not noticed the framed Rembrandt prints in the hallway of her classroom building. But when she took an art appreciation class the next semester, she found that the paintings she liked best were those same Rembrandt images. Her preference was most likely affected by _____.
   a. the prosopagnosia effect
   b. supraliminal perception
   c. priming
   d. visual masking

4. Edie has purchased a tape that contains subliminal messages designed to help her lose weight. According to the Thinking Critically section in this chapter, Edie's success in losing weight most likely depends on _____.
   a. the content of the subliminal messages
   b. her expectation that the subliminal messages will help
   c. how relaxed the subliminal messages make her feel
   d. the number of times the subliminal messages occur

5. Mitch noticed that after his friends smoked marijuana, they soon began giggling, acting silly, and singing "We're Off to See the Wizard." After he smoked marijuana himself for the first time, he found himself doing the very same things. Mitch's specific responses to marijuana were most likely due to _____.
   a. an altered state of consciousness
   b. reversion to a preconscious state
   c. priming
   d. learned expectations

6. The telephone rang several hours after Leroy fell asleep. It takes Leroy a while to locate the phone, and he is so groggy when he answers that in the morning, he can't remember who called or what was said. When the phone rang, Leroy was most likely in _____ sleep.
   a. stage 1   c. stage 4
   b. stage 2   d. REM

7. Alan's wife is concerned because he often gets out of bed during the night and acts out his dreams. One night he boxed with an invisible opponent, and last night he was fighting a phantom bull. Alan most likely would be diagnosed as having _____.
   a. sleep apnea   c. REM behavior disorder
   b. narcolepsy   d. sleep terror disorder

8. The "back to sleep" program, which advises parents to have their babies sleep face up, has greatly reduced the incidence of _____ in the United States.
   a. SIDS
   b. sleep terror disorder
   c. REM behavior disorder
   d. insomnia

9. Dr. Franklin was flying from Los Angeles to Paris, where he was to give a speech shortly after arrival. To minimize the effects of jet lag, his physician would most likely recommend that Dr. Franklin should _____.
   a. be sure to sleep eight hours a night for at least a week before his trip
   b. take melatonin
   c. stay awake for 24 hours before departure, then sleep throughout the flight
   d. reverse his sleep-wake cycle for a week before departure

10. Sleep research suggests that REM sleep may be important for all of the following *except* _____.
    a. improving the functioning of neurons that use norepinephrine
    b. developing, checking, and expanding the brain's nerve connections
    c. restoring the body's and brain's energy stores for the next day's activity
    d. establishing memories of emotional information

11. According to the activation-synthesis theory, dreams _____.
    a. help our brains analyze and consolidate information
    b. satisfy unconscious urges and resolve unconscious conflicts
    c. are hallucinations
    d. are meaningless, random byproducts of REM sleep

12. Lavonne, a hypnotist, wanted to present a dramatic demonstration of hypnosis. Which of the following people should she select as her hypnotic subject?
    a. Alex, who is easily distracted.
    b. Bobbi, who doesn't believe in hypnosis.
    c. Carl, who is good at focusing his attention.
    d. Dellena, whose imagination is limited.

13. Hypnosis has been especially effective in _____.
    a. connecting with past lives
    b. improving memory
    c. pain control
    d. lowering cholesterol

14. Norman has been meditating for over a year. By now, according to your textbook, we would expect Norman to _____.
    a. be less anxious
    b. need less sleep to feel refreshed
    c. have a better memory
    d. daydream more

15. Candice was given morphine to ease the pain of back surgery. Her doctor explained that morphine occupies the same receptors and has the same effect as endorphins, the body's natural painkillers. In other words, morphine is an endorphin _____.
    a. agonist   c. reuptake blocker
    b. antagonist   d. placebo

16. Vincent has been using heroin for some time, and now he finds that he needs larger amounts of the drug to achieve the same effect he used to get from smaller doses. Vincent is experiencing painkillers _____.
    a. drug tolerance
    b. learned expectations
    c. withdrawal
    d. synaptic potential

17. Which of the following is true about alcohol?
    a. A given amount of alcohol will affect a man more than a woman.
    b. Alcohol's effects are the same whether it is consumed slowly or quickly.
    c. There are no genetic predispositions toward alcohol abuse.
    d. Dopamine agonists reduce alcohol cravings.

18. A young man experiencing hallucinations is brought to a hospital emergency room. Which of the following drugs could his doctor rule out as a likely cause of the hallucinations?
    a. MDMA
    b. Cocaine
    c. Caffeine
    d. LSD

19. Abel took a drug to reduce the pain in his broken arm. The drug Abel took to reduce his pain would be classified as a(n) _____.
    a. depressant
    b. opiate
    c. hallucinogen
    d. stimulant

20. Yeh is doing research for a term paper about legalizing the use of marijuana in the United States. If her research is accurate, she is likely to learn all of the following *except* which one?
    a. Marijuana has been used successfully in treating asthma, glaucoma, chronic pain, and nausea from chemotherapy.
    b. Marijuana increases memory function and creativity.
    c. It is legal to grow and use marijuana for medicinal purposes in Canada.
    d. Doctors have found that marijuana may help treat some types of cancer.

© David R. Frazier/The Image Works

5 Learning

Preview

Live and learn. This simple phrase captures the idea that learning is a lifelong process that affects our behavior every day. Understanding how learning takes place is an important part of understanding ourselves. Sometimes learning involves one event signaling another, as when we learn to associate wailing sirens with ambulances. Other times learning depends on what happens after we do something—whether we receive praise or punishment, for example. But learning is more than these kinds of associations. What we think and how we feel about life's signals and consequences also have an impact on what we learn to do and not to do. Blend in practice and feedback about our behavior, mix well, and you have all the ingredients of the learning process.

Like most newborn babies, Jeffrey cried until he was fed. He awakened at 3 A.M. nearly every morning, hungry and crying for food. And as she had done every day since he was born, his mother would put on her slippers and walk down the tiled hallway to his bedroom. After a quick change of his diaper came the feeding. By the time he was four months old, Jeffrey would cry for about a minute and then quietly wait a few more minutes for his mother to arrive for his feeding. One particular morning, as his mother was halfway down the hall, she stopped in her tracks as she felt a sneeze coming. She pinched her nostrils together and the urge to sneeze passed. However, she noticed that Jeffrey had begun to cry again. This was unusual. She began to walk again and he quieted. Her scientific curiosity aroused, she walked a few steps, then stopped, then started, then stopped. She discovered that Jeffrey stopped crying when he heard her footsteps but resumed crying when the sound of footsteps stopped.

Jeffrey had learned a lot in the four months since his birth. He could anticipate events and predict outcomes based on the meaning of certain sounds. Like the rest of us, he showed an ability to learn about relationships in the environment and adjust to them. This adjustment to changes in the environment is called *adaptation*. Along with adaptation come expectations and predictions about what is and what is not likely to occur in our world.

The entire process of development, from birth to death, involves adapting to increasingly complex, ever-changing environments using continuously updated knowledge and skills gained through experience. This ability to adapt is especially impressive in humans, but it appears to varying degrees in every species. Charles Darwin highlighted the importance of adaptation in his theory of evolution, noting that individuals who do not adapt may not survive to reproduce. Many forms of adaptation fo!low the principles of learning.

Learning is a relatively permanent change in behavior or knowledge due to experience. We are born with some behaviors and knowledge, we acquire others automatically as we grow (through maturation), and we learn still others. Some of our sayings, such as "Once burned, twice shy" and "Fool me once, shame on you; fool me twice, shame on me," reflect this vital learning process. In fact, learning plays a central role in most aspects of human behavior. If you want to know who you are and how you became the person you are today, examining what and how you have learned is a good place to start.

This chapter describes what psychologists now know about the fundamental principles of learning. These include a form of learning called *operant conditioning* in which rewards and punishments affect the frequency of observable behavior. There is

learning   The modification of preexisting behavior and understanding.

also *classical conditioning*, a form of learning in which specific signals come to trigger behavior. In addition, cognitive processes underlie some of the most complex forms of learning, such as the ability to learn from watching others. Some learning takes place consciously, as when you study for an exam, but as mentioned later, you can also learn things without being aware that you are doing so (Watanabe, Náñez, & Sasaki, 2001). Let's begin by considering classical conditioning. ■

Classical Conditioning: Learning Signals and Associations

▶ *How did Russian dogs teach psychologists about learning?*

Improve Your Grade
Tutorial: Classical Conditioning—Pavlov's Study

At the first notes of the national anthem, an athlete's heart may start to pound because those sounds signal that the game is about to begin. A flashing red light on the instrument panel might raise your heart rate, too, because it means that something is wrong with your car. People are not born with these reactions. They have learned them by observing relationships, or *associations,* between events in the world. The experimental study of this kind of learning was begun, almost by accident, by Ivan Petrovich Pavlov.

Pavlov's Discovery

Pavlov is one of the best-known figures in psychology, but he was not a psychologist. He was a Russian physiologist who won the Nobel Prize in 1904 for his research on the digestive system of dogs. In the course of this research, Pavlov noticed a strange phenomenon. His dogs sometimes salivated, or drooled, when no food was present. For instance, they salivated when they saw the assistant who normally brought their food, even if he was empty-handed.

Pavlov devised a simple experiment to determine why salivation occurred without an obvious physical cause, such as food. First he performed an operation to divert a dog's saliva into a container so that the amount of salivation could be measured. Next he placed the dog in an apparatus similar to the one shown in Figure 5.1. The experiment had three phases.

FIGURE 5.1 ■ APPARATUS FOR MEASURING CONDITIONED RESPONSES

In this more elaborate version of Pavlov's original apparatus, the amount of saliva flowing from a dog's mouth is measured precisely and then recorded on a slowly revolving drum of paper.

Pen recording on cylinder

In the first phase, Pavlov and his associates confirmed that when meat powder was placed in the dog's mouth, the dog automatically salivated (Anrep, 1920). They also confirmed that the dog did not automatically salivate in response to a musical tone. The researchers had now established the two basic components of Pavlov's experiment: (1) a quick automatic response called a *reflex*; and (2) a neutral stimulus that does not trigger that reflex.

In the second phase of Pavlov's experiment, the tone was sounded and then meat powder was placed in the dog's mouth. The dog salivated. This pairing of the tone and the meat powder was repeated several times. So the tone always preceded the arrival of the meat powder, but had the dog learned that relationship? It had. In the third phase of the experiment, the tone was sounded but no meat powder was presented. Even so, the dog still salivated. The tone alone was now enough to trigger salivation. You may have seen a similar process if you regularly open pet food with an electric can opener. The sound of the opener probably brings your pet running (and salivating) because that sound means that food is on its way.

Pavlov's experiment demonstrated what we now call **classical conditioning.** In this procedure, a neutral stimulus is repeatedly paired with a stimulus that already triggers an automatic reflexive response. As a result of this pairing, the previously neutral stimulus itself comes to trigger a response that is similar to that reflex. Figure 5.2 shows the basic elements of classical conditioning. The stimulus that naturally elicits a response without conditioning, such as the meat powder in Pavlov's experiment, is called the **unconditioned stimulus (UCS).** The automatic, unlearned, reflexive response to this stimulus is called the **unconditioned response (UCR).** After being paired with the unconditioned stimulus (meat powder), the previously neutral stimulus becomes the **conditioned stimulus (CS)** and the response it comes to trigger is a learned or **conditioned response (CR).**

Conditioned Responses over Time: Extinction and Spontaneous Recovery

If you have ever been bitten by a barking dog, you might have learned to feel distress whenever you hear a dog's bark. The more bad experiences you have had with dogs, the stronger will be your learned distress in response to barking sounds. In the language of classical conditioning, continued pairings of a conditioned stimulus (CS/bark) with an

classical conditioning A procedure in which a neutral stimulus is paired with a stimulus that triggers a reflexive response until the neutral stimulus alone comes to trigger a similar response.

unconditioned stimulus (UCS) A stimulus that triggers a response without conditioning.

unconditioned response (UCR) The automatic, unlearned, reflexive reaction to a stimulus.

conditioned stimulus (CS) An originally neutral stimulus that now triggers a conditioned response.

conditioned response (CR) The response triggered by the conditioned stimulus.

FIGURE 5.2 ■ CLASSICAL CONDITIONING

Before classical conditioning has occurred, meat powder on a dog's tongue produces salivation but the sound of a tone—a neutral stimulus—brings only orienting responses such as turning toward the sound. During the process of conditioning, the tone is repeatedly paired with the meat powder. After classical conditioning has taken place, the sound of the tone alone acts as a conditioned stimulus, producing salivation.

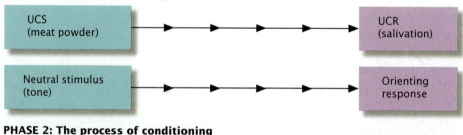

PHASE 1: Before conditioning has occurred

UCS (meat powder) → UCR (salivation)

Neutral stimulus (tone) → Orienting response

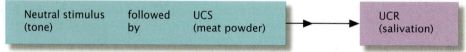

PHASE 2: The process of conditioning

Neutral stimulus (tone) followed by UCS (meat powder) → UCR (salivation)

PHASE 3: After conditioning has occurred

CS (tone) → CR (salivation)

FIGURE 5.3 ■ CHANGES OVER TIME IN THE STRENGTH OF A CONDITIONED RESPONSE

As the conditioned stimulus (CS) and the unconditioned stimulus (UCS) are repeatedly paired during initial conditioning, the strength of the conditioned response (CR) increases. If the CS is then repeatedly presented without the UCS, the CR weakens—and eventually disappears—through a process called extinction. If the CS is presented again later on, a weaker version of the CR will reappear (Rescorla, 2004). This phenomenon, called spontaneous recovery, is only temporary, though. Unless the UCS is again paired with the CS, the recovered CR soon disappears.

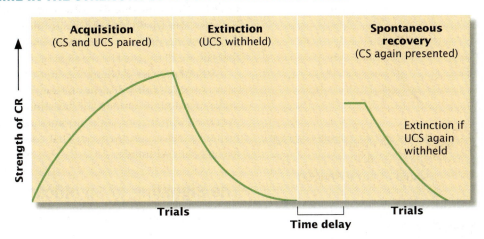

unconditioned stimulus (UCS/bite) strengthen the conditioned response (CR/distress). The curve on the left side of Figure 5.3 shows an example: Repeated associations of a tone (CS) with meat powder (UCS) caused Pavlov's dogs to increase their salivation (CR) to the tone alone.

What if the tone (CS) is repeatedly sounded but the meat powder (UCS) is no longer given? As you might expect, if the unconditioned stimulus is not paired with the conditioned stimulus at least now and then, the conditioned response will gradually disappear. This loss of the conditioned response is known as **extinction** (see the center section of Figure 5.3). The term is not entirely accurate, though. *Extinction* suggests that like the dinosaurs, the conditioned response has been wiped out, never to return. In fact, though, if the CS (tone) and the UCS (meat powder) are again paired after the conditioned response has been extinguished, that conditioned response will return to its original strength after as few as one or two trials. This quick relearning of a conditioned response after extinction is called **reconditioning.** Reconditioning takes much less time than the original conditioning, so it appears that extinction does not entirely erase the association between the conditioned stimulus and the conditioned response (Bouton, 1993, 2002; Myers & Davis, 2007).

The right side of Figure 5.3 provides more evidence for this conclusion. After a conditioned response has been extinguished it will temporarily reappear if the conditioned stimulus occurs again. This is called **spontaneous recovery,** the temporary reappearance of a conditioned response after extinction (and without further CS-UCS pairings). In general, the longer the time between extinction and the reappearance of the CS, the stronger the recovered conditioned response (Devenport, 1998; Rescorla, 2005). Unless the UCS is again paired with the CS, extinction will reoccur and will further suppress the conditioned response (Leung & Westbrook, 2008). Still, even after many years, spontaneous recovery can create a ripple of emotion—a conditioned response—when we hear a song or catch a scent associated with a long-lost lover or a departed relative.

Stimulus Generalization and Discrimination

Once a conditioned stimulus is able to trigger a conditioned response, stimuli similar to the conditioned stimulus will also trigger some version of that response. This phenomenon, called **stimulus generalization,** is illustrated by the fact that a person who was bitten by one particular dog may now show some fear of all dogs. Usually, the greater the similarity between a new stimulus and the original conditioned stimulus, the stronger the conditioned response will be. If the person was bitten by a small, curly-haired dog, fear responses would be strongest to other small dogs with similar types of hair. Figure 5.4 shows an example involving sounds.

extinction   The gradual disappearance of a conditioned response.

reconditioning   The relearning of a conditioned response following extinction.

spontaneous recovery   The temporary reappearance of a conditioned response after extinction.

stimulus generalization   A process in which a conditioned response is triggered by stimuli similar to the original conditioned stimulus.

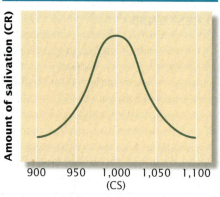

Sound of buzzer (hertz)

FIGURE 5.4 ■ **STIMULUS GENERALIZATION**

The strength of a conditioned response (CR) is greatest when the original conditioned stimulus (CS) occurs. However, some version of the CR is also triggered by stimuli that closely resemble the CS. Here, the CS is the sound of a buzzer at a frequency of 1,000 hertz (Hz), and the CR is salivation. Notice that the CR generalizes well to stimuli at 990 or 1,010 Hz but that it gets weaker and weaker as the buzzer sounds less and less similar to the CS.

Stimulus generalization has some obvious advantages. For example, it is important for survival that if you get sick after drinking sour-smelling milk, you now avoid dairy products that have a similar odor. Generalization would be a problem if it had no limits, however. You would probably be justifiably frightened if you found a lion in your living room, but imagine how disruptive it would be if your fear response generalized so widely that you were panicked by the sight of lions on TV or even by the word "lion" in a book.

Stimulus generalization does not run wild because it is usually balanced by a process called **stimulus discrimination.** Through stimulus discrimination, we learn to make distinctions among similar stimuli. Many parents find that the sound of their own baby whimpering soon becomes a conditioned stimulus, triggering a conditioned response that wakes them up. That conditioned response may not occur if a visiting friend's baby whimpers.

The Signaling of Significant Events

Early research suggested that classical conditioning involves nothing more than automatic associations that allow one stimulus (the conditioned stimulus, or CS) to substitute for another (the unconditioned stimulus, or UCS) in triggering a reflex. That view has turned out to be too simplistic. For example, a rat's unconditioned, reflexive response to a mild shock (UCS) will be flinching and jumping. But the animal's conditioned response to the sound of a tone (CS) that always precedes shock will not be to flinch and jump but to freeze—much as it would if threatened by a predator (Domjan, 2005). In other words, classical conditioning involves more than the appearance of robot-like, reflexive responses. Many psychologists now believe that classical conditioning provides a means through which people, and some other animals, develop expectations and other *mental representations* of the relationships between events in their environment (Shanks, 1995). These representations aid in adaptation and survival. When two events repeatedly take place together, we can predict that one will occur based on what we know about the other. Baby Jeffrey predicted his feeding from hearing his mother's footsteps. You have learned that a clear blue sky means dry weather, that too little sleep makes you irritable, that you can reach someone on the telephone by pressing certain buttons, and that yelling orders motivates some people and angers others.

What determines whether conditioned responses are learned? In general, these responses develop when one event *signals* the appearance of another. Other important factors are the timing, predictability, and intensity of the unconditioned stimulus as well as the amount of attention that is devoted to the conditioned stimulus and how prepared an organism is to associate paired events.

Timing   If your instructor always dismisses class at 9:59 and a bell rings at 10:00, the bell cannot prepare you for the dismissal. It comes too late to be a useful signal. For the same reason, classical conditioning works best when the conditioned stimulus comes before the unconditioned stimulus. This arrangement makes sense for adaptation and survival. Usually, the presence of food, predators, or other significant stimuli is most reliably signaled by smells, sounds, or other events that come just before their appearance (Einhorn & Hogarth, 1982). So it is logical that the brain should be "wired" to form associations most easily between things that occur at about the same time. How close together do they have to be? There is no single "best" interval for every situation. Classical conditioning can occur when the interval between the CS and the UCS is less than a second or more than a minute. It all depends on the particular CS, UCS, and UCR that are involved (Longo, Klempay, & Bitterman, 1964; Ross & Ross, 1971). However, classical conditioning will always be weaker if the interval between the CS and the UCS is longer than what is ideal for the stimuli and responses in a given situation.

Predictability   It is not enough for the CS merely to come before the UCS. Suppose your dogs, Moxie and Fang, have very different personalities. When Moxie growls, she sometimes bites, but sometimes she doesn't. Fang growls only before biting. Your conditioned fear response to Moxie's growl will probably occur slowly, because her growl does not reliably signal the danger of a bite. However, you are likely to quickly develop

stimulus discrimination   A process through which people learn to differentiate among similar stimuli and respond appropriately to each one.

a classically conditioned fear response to Fang's growl. It always means that you are in danger of being bitten. Classical conditioning proceeds most rapidly when the CS *always* signals the UCS and only the UCS. Even if both dogs provide the same number of pairings of the CS (growl) and the UCS (bite), it is only with Fang that the CS *reliably* predicts the UCS (Rescorla, 1968).

Intensity A conditioned response will be learned more rapidly if the UCS is strong than if it is weak. For example, a CS that acts as a predictive signal will be more rapidly associated with a strong shock (UCS) than with a weak one. As with the importance of timing, the effect of signal strength on classical conditioning makes adaptive sense. It is more important to be prepared for major events than for those that have little impact.

Attention In Pavlov's laboratory, just one conditioned stimulus, a tone, was linked to an unconditioned stimulus (meat powder). In the natural environment, a wide variety of stimuli might be present just before a UCS occurs. Suppose you are at the beach. You're eating a hot dog, reading a magazine, listening to your favorite CD, digging your toes in the warm sand, and enjoying the smell of suntan lotion when you are stung by a bee. Which of these stimuli is most likely to become a conditioned stimulus that might later trigger discomfort? It depends partly on where you were focusing your attention at the moment you were stung. The stimulus you most closely attended to—the one you most fully perceived—is most likely to become a CS. In general, loud tones, bright lights, and other intense stimuli tend to get extra attention, so they are the ones most rapidly associated with an unconditioned stimulus.

Biopreparedness Certain kinds of signals or events are especially likely to become associated with other signals or events (Logue, 1985). So which beach stimulus becomes a conditioned stimulus for fear will depend not only on attention but also on whether the stimulus is a sight, a sound, or a taste and what kind of unconditioned stimulus follows it. The apparently natural tendency for certain events to become linked suggests that organisms are "biologically prepared" to develop certain conditioned associations (Öhman & Soares, 1993, 1998).

The most dramatic example of this *biopreparedness* phenomenon is seen in conditioned taste aversions. In one study, rats were either shocked or made nauseous in the presence of a light, a buzzer, and flavored water. The rats formed only certain conditioned associations. Animals that had been shocked developed a conditioned fear response to the light and the buzzer but not to the flavored water. Those that had been made nauseous developed a conditioned avoidance of the flavored water, but they showed no particular response to the light or buzzer (Garcia & Koelling, 1966). These results reflect an adaptive process. Nausea is more likely to be caused by something we eat or drink than by a noise or a light. So nausea is more likely to become a conditioned response to an internal stimulus, such as a flavor, than to an external stimulus. In contrast, the sudden pain of a shock is more likely to have been caused by an external stimulus, so it makes evolutionary sense that the organism should be "tuned" to associate shock or sudden pain with a sight or sound.

Conditioned taste aversion shows that for certain kinds of stimuli, classical conditioning can occur even when there is a long delay between the CS (taste) and the UCS (sickness). Poisons do not usually produce their effects for many minutes or hours, but people who have experienced food poisoning may never again eat the type of food that made them ill. Organisms that are biologically prepared to link taste signals with illness, even a delayed illness, are more likely to survive than organisms not so prepared.

Other evidence for biopreparedness comes from research showing that people are much more likely to develop a conditioned fear of harmless dogs or nonpoisonous snakes than of electrical outlets, knives, or other more dangerous objects (Öhman & Mineka, 2001, 2003). And experiments with animals suggest that they tend to learn the type of associations that are most relevant to survival in their environment (Staddon & Ettinger, 1989). Birds of prey, which strongly depend on vision to find food, may develop taste aversions on the basis of appearance. Coyotes and rats depend more on their sense of smell, so they tend to develop aversions related to odor.

© Matt Bowman/FoodPix/Jupiterimages

TASTE AVERSIONS ▲

Humans can develop classically conditioned taste aversions, even to preferred foods. For example, Ilene Bernstein (1978) gave one group of cancer patients Mapletoff ice cream an hour before they received nausea-provoking chemotherapy. A second group ate this same kind of ice cream on a day they did not receive chemotherapy. A third group got no ice cream. Five months later, the patients were asked to taste several ice cream flavors. Those who had never tasted Mapletoff and those who had not eaten it in association with chemotherapy chose it as their favorite. Those who had eaten Mapletoff before receiving chemotherapy found it distasteful.

THE POWER OF HIGHER ORDER CONDITIONING ▶

Cancer patients may feel queasy when they enter a chemotherapy room because they have associated the room with nausea-producing treatment. Through higher order conditioning, almost anything associated with the room can also become a conditioned stimulus for nausea. One cancer patient who was flying out of town on a business trip became nauseated just by seeing her hospital from the air.

Higher Order Conditioning   Once we learn that a conditioned stimulus (CS) signals the arrival of an unconditioned stimulus (UCS), the CS may operate as if it actually were that UCS. For instance, suppose that a child endures a painful medical procedure (UCS) at the doctor's office and the pain becomes associated with the doctor's white coat. The white coat might then become a conditioned stimulus (CS) that can trigger a conditioned fear response. Once the white coat is able to set off a conditioned fear response, the coat may take on some properties of an unconditioned stimulus. So if the child later sees a white-coated pharmacist at the drugstore, that once-neutral store can become a conditioned stimulus for fear because it signals the appearance of a white coat, which in turn signals pain. When a conditioned stimulus (the white coat) acts like an unconditioned stimulus, creating conditioned stimuli (the drugstore) out of events associated with it, the process is called **higher order conditioning.**

This process serves as an adaptive "early warning system." It prepares us for threatening events (UCS) that are signaled not only by a CS but also by associated events that precede—and thus predict—that CS. But higher order conditioning can also cause problems. For example, the high blood pressure seen in medical patients who are known as white-coat hypertensives (Myers et al., 1996; Ugajin et al., 2005) does not reflect a physical disorder. It occurs simply because the sight of a doctor or nurse has become a conditioned stimulus for fear. Medical staff must be alert to such cases if they are to avoid giving blood pressure medication to patients who don't need it.

Some Applications of Classical Conditioning

The principles of classical conditioning are summarized in "In Review: Basic Processes of Classical Conditioning." These principles have proven useful in many areas, including in recent efforts to use insects to help detect explosive material. In one study, for example, after the taste of sugar water was associated with the smell of a chemical used in certain explosives, wasps quickly developed a conditioned response to the smell alone. When several of these trained insects were placed in a plastic tube and brought near the target chemical, they displayed an immediate attraction to it (Rains, Utley, & Lewis, 2006). Researchers hope that it may someday be possible to use these so-called Wasp Hounds and other similar devices to detect explosives or drugs concealed in airline passengers' luggage (Tomberlin, Rains, & Sanford, 2008). Classical conditioning principles have also been applied in overcoming fears and understanding certain aspects of drug addiction.

higher order conditioning   A process through which a conditioned stimulus comes to signal another conditioned stimulus that is already associated with an unconditioned stimulus.

Phobias   *Phobias* are intense, irrational fears of objects or situations—such as public speaking—that are not dangerous or that are less dangerous than the fear response

In Review

BASIC PROCESSES OF CLASSICAL CONDITIONING

PROCESS	DESCRIPTION	EXAMPLE
Acquisition	A neutral stimulus and an unconditioned stimulus (UCS) are paired. The neutral stimulus becomes a conditioned stimulus (CS), eliciting a conditioned response (CR).	A child learns to fear (conditioned response) the doctor's office (conditioned stimulus) by associating it with the reflexive emotional reaction (unconditioned response) to a painful injection (unconditioned stimulus).
Stimulus generalization	A conditioned response is elicited not only by the conditioned stimulus but also by stimuli similar to the conditioned stimulus.	A child fears most doctors' offices and places that smell like them.
Stimulus discrimination	Generalization is limited so that some stimuli similar to the conditioned stimulus do not elicit the conditioned response.	A child learns that his mother's doctor's office is not associated with the unconditioned stimulus.
Extinction	The conditioned stimulus is presented alone, without the unconditioned stimulus. Eventually the conditioned stimulus no longer elicits the conditioned response.	A child visits the doctor's office several times for a checkup but does not receive a shot. Fear may eventually cease.

1. *If your conditioned fear of spiders is triggered by the sight of other creatures that look somewhat like spiders, you are demonstrating stimulus _____.*
2. *Because of _____ , we are more likely to learn a fear of snakes than a fear of cars.*
3. *Feeling sad upon hearing a song associated with a long-lost relationship illustrates _____.*

would suggest. Classical conditioning often plays a role in the development of phobias (Bouton, Mineka, & Barlow, 2001). As mentioned earlier, a person frightened by a dog may learn a fear that is so intense and generalized that it leads the person to avoid all dogs and all situations in which dogs might be encountered. Classically conditioned fears can be extremely long lasting, especially when they are based on experiences with strong unconditioned stimuli. Combat veterans and victims of violent crime, terrorism, or other traumatic events may show intense fear responses to trauma-related stimuli for many years afterward.

Classical conditioning has also been used to treat phobias (see the chapter on treatment of psychological disorders). Joseph Wolpe (1958) was a pioneer in this effort. He showed that irrational fears could be relieved through *systematic desensitization,* a procedure that associates a new response, such as relaxation, with a feared stimulus. To treat a thunderstorm phobia, for instance, a therapist might first teach the client to relax deeply and then associate that relaxation with increasingly intense sights and sounds of thunderstorms presented on videotape (Öst, 1978). Because, as Wolpe (1958) noted, a person cannot be relaxed and afraid at the same time, the new conditioned response (relaxation) to thunderstorms replaces the old one (fear).

Drug Addiction   When people repeatedly use heroin or other addictive drugs, their responses to the drugs become weaker. This reduction in responsiveness to a repeated stimulus is called **habituation.** According to Richard Solomon's (1980) *opponent-process theory,* habituation is the result of two processes that balance each other, like a seesaw. The first process is a quick, automatic, involuntary response—essentially an unconditioned response (UCR) to the drug. The second—or

habituation   Reduced responsiveness to a repeated stimulus.

PREDATOR CONTROL THROUGH CONDITIONING ▶

In the western United States, some ranchers lace a sheep carcass with enough lithium chloride to make wolves and coyotes nauseous (Pfister et al., 2003). The predators associate nausea with the smell and taste of sheep and afterward stay away from the ranchers' flocks. A similar program in India has greatly reduced the human death toll from tiger attacks. Stuffed dummies are connected to a shock generator and placed in areas where tigers have killed people. When the animals approach the dummies, they receive a shock (UCS). After learning to associate shock with the human form (CS), the tigers tend to avoid people (CR).

applying psychology

opponent—process is a response that follows and counteracts the first. When a person is taking addictive drugs, this opponent response can be learned, or conditioned (McDonald & Siegel, 2004). So if the unconditioned response to a drug injection includes an increase in body temperature, the conditioned response will include an opponent process that reduces body temperature somewhat, creating the sensation of "chills." As the addict continues drug injections day after day, the learned opponent process ("chills") gets stronger and occurs sooner. As this CR strengthens, the rise in temperature caused by the drug gets smaller, resulting in habituation. In the same fashion, the intense pleasure first experienced as an unconditioned response to the drug begins to be weakened over time by an unpleasant opponent process (CR) that becomes faster and stronger. The addict begins to take larger drug doses in an effort to achieve the "high" once created by smaller doses. As described in the chapter on consciousness, people who display this pattern are said to have developed a *tolerance* for the drug.

The location where a drug is usually taken and the rituals that precede an injection (such as preparing the syringe) can become conditioned stimuli that trigger conditioned opponent-process responses even before the drug enters the bloodstream. These stimuli signal that the drug is coming, and the body begins to brace itself. But what if a person takes the drug in a new location or doesn't follow the usual ritual? According to opponent-process theory, in the absence of these conditioned environmental stimuli, the conditioned responses that normally dampen the user's unconditioned responses to the drug will not be as strong. As a result, the drug dose the addict took in the usual way yesterday might cause a potentially fatal overdose today (Melchior, 1990; Siegel et al., 1982; Siegel, 2005).

Instrumental and Operant Conditioning: Learning the Consequences of Behavior

▶ *How do reward and punishment work?*

Classical conditioning is an important form of learning, but it cannot explain most of what you learn on a daily basis. In classical conditioning, neutral and unconditioned stimuli are predictably paired. The result is an association of the two. This association is reflected in the fact that the conditioned stimulus now triggers the conditioned response. Notice that both stimuli occur before or along with the conditioned response. But you also learn many associations between responses and the stimuli that *follow* them, between behavior and its consequences. A child learns to say "please" to get a piece of candy. A headache sufferer learns to take a pill to escape the pain. A dog learns to "shake hands" to get a treat.

FIGURE 5.5 ▪ THORNDIKE'S PUZZLE BOX

This drawing illustrates the kind of puzzle box used in Thorndike's research. His cats learned to open the door and reach food by stepping on the pedal, but the learning occurred gradually. Some cats actually took longer to get out of the box on one trial than on a previous trial.

From the Puzzle Box to the Skinner Box

Edward L. Thorndike, an American psychologist, did much of the fundamental research on the consequences of behavior. While Pavlov was exploring classical conditioning, Thorndike was studying animals' intelligence, including their ability to solve problems. For example, he placed a hungry cat in a *puzzle box* like the one in Figure 5.5. The cat had to learn some response—such as stepping on a pedal—to unlock the door and get food. During the first few trials in the puzzle box, the cat explored and prodded until it finally hit the pedal. The animal eventually solved the puzzle, but very slowly. It did not appear to understand, or suddenly gain insight into, the problem (Thorndike, 1898). After many trials, though, the cat solved the puzzle quickly each time it was placed in the box. What was it learning? Thorndike argued that any response (such as pacing or meowing) that did not produce a satisfying effect (opening the door) gradually became weaker. And any response (pressing the pedal) that did have a satisfying effect gradually became stronger. The cat's learning, said Thorndike, is governed by the **law of effect.** According to this law, if a response made to a particular stimulus is followed by a satisfying effect (such as food or some other reward), that response is more likely to occur the next time the stimulus is present. In contrast, responses that produce discomfort are less likely to be performed again. Thorndike described this kind of learning as *instrumental conditioning* because responses are strengthened when they are instrumental in producing rewards (Thorndike, 1905).

About thirty years after Thorndike published his work, B. F. Skinner extended and formalized many of Thorndike's ideas. Skinner noted that during instrumental conditioning, an organism learns a response by *operating on* the environment. So he used the term **operant conditioning** to refer to the learning process in which behavior is changed by its consequences, specifically by rewards and punishments. To study operant conditioning, Skinner devised some new tools. One of these was a small chamber that, despite Skinner's objections, came to be known as the *Skinner box* (see Figure 5.6).

Basic Components of Operant Conditioning

The chamber Skinner designed allowed researchers to arrange relationships between a particular response and its consequences. If an animal pressed a lever in the chamber, for example, it might receive a food pellet. The researchers could then analyze how consequences affect behavior. It turned out that stimulus generalization, stimulus discrimination, extinction, spontaneous recovery, and other phenomena seen in classical conditioning also appear in operant conditioning. However, research in operant conditioning also focused on concepts known as operants, reinforcers, and discriminative conditioned stimuli.

Operants and Reinforcers Skinner coined the term *operant*, or *operant response,* to distinguish the responses in operant conditioning from those in classical

law of effect A law stating that if a response made in the presence of a particular stimulus is rewarded, the same response is more likely to occur when that stimulus is encountered again.

operant conditioning A process in which responses are learned on the basis of their rewarding or punishing consequences.

FIGURE 5.6 ■ B. F. SKINNER (1904–1990)

In the operant conditioning chamber shown here, the rat can press a bar to obtain food pellets from a tube. Operant and instrumental conditioning are similar in most respects, but they do differ in one way. Instrumental conditioning is measured by how long it takes for a response (such as a bar press) to occur. Operant conditioning is measured by the rate at which responses occur. In this chapter, the term operant conditioning refers to both.

© Nina Leen/Time & Life Pictures/Getty Images

conditioning. In classical conditioning, the conditioned response does not affect whether or when the stimulus occurs. Pavlov's dogs salivated when a tone sounded. The salivation had no effect on the tone or on whether food was presented. In contrast, an **operant** has some effect on the world. It is a response that operates on the environment. When a child says, "Momma, I'm hungry" and is then fed, the child has made an operant response that influences when food will appear.

A **reinforcer** is a stimulus that increases the probability that the operant behavior will occur again. There are two main types of reinforcers: positive and negative. **Positive reinforcers** strengthen a response if they are presented after that response occurs. The food given to a hungry pigeon after it pecks a key is a positive reinforcer for key pecking. For people, positive reinforcers can include food, smiles, money, and other desirable outcomes. Presentation of a positive reinforcer after a response is called *positive reinforcement*. **Negative reinforcers** are the *removal* of unpleasant stimuli, such as pain or noise. For example, the disappearance of a headache after you take a pain reliever acts as a negative reinforcer that makes you more likely to take that pain reliever in the future. When a response is strengthened by the removal of an unpleasant stimulus such as pain, the process is called *negative reinforcement*.

Notice that **reinforcement** always increases the likelihood of the behavior that precedes it, whether the reinforcer is adding something pleasant or removing something unpleasant. Figure 5.7 shows this relationship.

Escape and Avoidance Conditioning   The effects of negative reinforcement can be seen in both escape conditioning and avoidance conditioning. **Escape conditioning** occurs when we learn responses that stop an unpleasant stimulus. The left-hand panel of Figure 5.8 shows an example from an animal laboratory, but escape conditioning operates in humans, too. Not only do we learn to take pills to stop pain, but some parents learn to stop their child's annoying demands for a toy by agreeing to buy it. And television viewers learn to use the mute button to shut off obnoxious commercials.

When an animal or a person responds to a signal in a way that *avoids* an aversive stimulus before it arrives, **avoidance conditioning** has occurred (see the right-hand

operant   A response that has some effect on the world.

reinforcer   A stimulus event that increases the probability that the response immediately preceding it will occur again.

positive reinforcers   Stimuli that strengthen a response if they follow that response.

negative reinforcers   The removal of unpleasant stimuli.

reinforcement   The process through which a particular response is made more likely to recur.

escape conditioning   The process of learning responses that stop an aversive stimulus.

avoidance conditioning   The process of learning particular responses that avoid an aversive stimulus.

FIGURE 5.7 ■ POSITIVE AND NEGATIVE REINFORCEMENT

Remember that behavior is strengthened through positive reinforcement when something pleasant or desirable occurs following the behavior. Behavior is strengthened through negative reinforcement when the behavior results in the removal or termination of something unpleasant. To see how these principles apply in your own life, list two examples of situations in which your behavior was affected by positive reinforcement and two in which you were affected by negative reinforcement.

Learn BY Doing

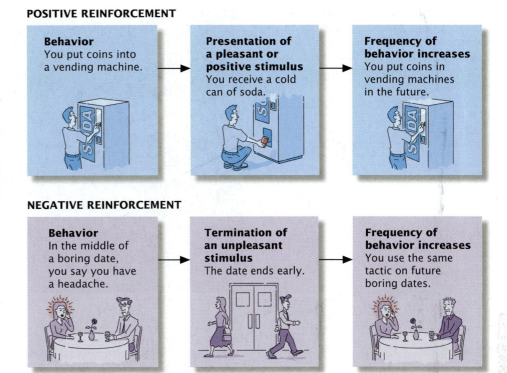

POSITIVE REINFORCEMENT

Behavior
You put coins into a vending machine.

→

Presentation of a pleasant or positive stimulus
You receive a cold can of soda.

→

Frequency of behavior increases
You put coins in vending machines in the future.

NEGATIVE REINFORCEMENT

Behavior
In the middle of a boring date, you say you have a headache.

→

Termination of an unpleasant stimulus
The date ends early.

→

Frequency of behavior increases
You use the same tactic on future boring dates.

sections of Figure 5.8). Avoidance conditioning is an important influence on everyday behavior. We go to work even when we would rather stay in bed, we stop at red lights even when we are in a hurry, and we apologize for our mistakes even before they are discovered. Each of these behaviors helps us avoid a negative consequence, such as lost pay, a traffic ticket, or a scolding.

Avoidance conditioning represents a marriage of classical and operant conditioning. If, as shown in Figure 5.8, a buzzer predicts shock (an unconditioned stimulus), the buzzer becomes a conditioned stimulus (CS). Through classical conditioning, the

Escape conditioning

Avoidance conditioning

FIGURE 5.8 ■ A SHUTTLE BOX

A shuttle box has two sections that are usually separated by a barrier; its floor is an electric grid. Shock can be administered through the grid to either section. The left-hand panel shows escape conditioning, in which an animal learns to get away from a mild shock by jumping over the barrier when the electricity is turned on. The next two panels show avoidance conditioning. Here, the animal has learned to avoid shock altogether by jumping over the barrier when it hears a warning buzzer just before shock occurs. *Source*: Adapted from Hintzman (1978).

FIGURE 5.9   ■   STIMULUS DISCRIMINATION

This rat could jump from a stand through any of three doors, but it was reinforced only if it jumped through the door that differed from the other two. The rat learned to do this quite well: On this occasion, it discriminated vertical from horizontal stripes.

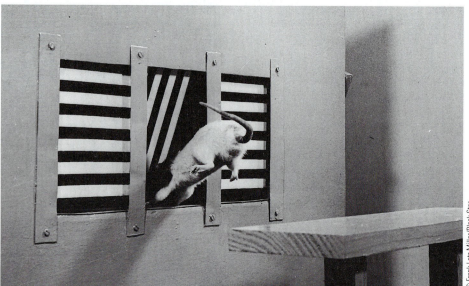

buzzer (now a CS) triggers a conditioned fear response (CR). Like the shock itself, conditioned fear is an unpleasant internal sensation. The animal then learns the instrumental response of jumping the barrier. The instrumental response (jumping) is reinforced because it reduces fear.

Once learned, avoidance is a difficult habit to break, because avoidance responses continue to be reinforced by fear reduction (Solomon, Kamin, & Wynne, 1953). So even if the shock is turned off in a shuttle box, animals may keep jumping when the buzzer sounds because they never discover that avoidance is no longer necessary. The same is often true of people. Those who avoid escalators out of fear never get a chance to find out that they are safe. Those with limited social skills may avoid potentially embarrassing social situations, but doing so also prevents them from learning how to be successful in those situations.

The study of avoidance conditioning has not only expanded our understanding of negative reinforcement but also has led some psychologists to consider more complex cognitive processes in operant learning. These psychologists suggest, for example, that in order for people to learn to avoid an unpleasant event (such as getting fired or paying a fine), they must have established an expectancy or other mental representation of that event. The role of such mental representations is emphasized in the cognitive theories of learning described later in this chapter.

Discriminative Conditioned Stimuli and Stimulus Control   The consequences of our behavior often depend on the situation we are in. Most people know that a flirtatious comment about someone's appearance may be welcomed on a date but not at the office. And even if you have been rewarded for telling jokes, you are not likely to do so during a funeral. In the language of operant conditioning, situations serve as **discriminative conditioned stimuli,** which are stimuli that signal whether reinforcement is available if a certain response is made. *Stimulus discrimination* occurs when an organism learns to make a particular response in the presence of one stimulus but not another (see Figure 5.9). The response is then said to be under *stimulus control*. Stimulus discrimination allows people or animals to learn what is appropriate (reinforced) and inappropriate (not reinforced) in particular situations.

Stimulus generalization also occurs in operant conditioning. That is, an animal or person will perform a response in the presence of a stimulus that is similar to (but not exactly like) a stimulus that has signaled reinforcement in the past. The more similar the new stimulus is to the old one, the more likely it is that the response will be

discriminative conditioned stimuli   Stimuli that signal whether reinforcement is available if a certain response is made.

© Frank Lotz Miller/Black Star

▶ Although the artist may not have intended it, this cartoon nicely illustrates one way in which discriminative stimuli can affect behavior.

"Oh, not bad. The light comes on, I press the bar, they write me a check. How about you?"

performed. Suppose you ate a wonderful meal at a restaurant called "Captain Jack's," which was decorated to look like the inside of a sailing ship. You might later be attracted to other restaurants with nautical names or with interiors that look something like the one where you had that great meal.

Stimulus generalization and stimulus discrimination complement each other. In one study, for example, pigeons received food for pecking a key, but only when they saw certain kinds of artwork (Watanabe, Sakamoto, & Wakita, 1995). As a result, these birds learned to *discriminate* the works of the impressionist painter Claude Monet from those of the cubist painter Pablo Picasso. Later, when the birds were shown new paintings by other impressionist and cubist artists, they were able to *generalize* from the original artists to other artists who painted in the same style, as if they had learned the conceptual categories of "impressionism" and "cubism." We humans learn to place people and objects into even more finely detailed categories, such as "honest," "dangerous," or "tax deductible." We discriminate one stimulus from another and then through generalization respond similarly to all those we perceive to be in a particular category. This ability to respond in a similar way to all members of a category can save us considerable time and effort, but it can also lead to the development of unwarranted prejudice against certain groups of people (see the chapter on social psychology).

Forming and Strengthening Operant Behavior

Your daily life is full of examples of operant conditioning. You go to movies, parties, classes, and jobs primarily because doing so brings reinforcement. What is the effect of the type or timing of your reinforcers? How do you learn new behaviors? How can you get rid of old ones?

Improve Your Grade
Tutorial: Shaping

Shaping   Let's say you want to train your dog, Sugar, to sit and "shake hands." You figure that positive reinforcement should work, so you decide to give Sugar a treat every time she sits and shakes hands. But there's a problem with this plan. Smart as Sugar is, she may never make the desired response on her own, so you might never be able to give the reinforcer. The way around this problem is to shape Sugar's behavior. **Shaping** is the process of reinforcing *successive approximations*—that is, responses that come successively closer to the desired behavior. For example, you might first give Sugar a treat whenever she sits down. Next, you might reinforce her only when she sits and partially lifts a paw. Finally, you might reinforce only complete paw lifting. Eventually, you would require Sugar to perform the entire sit-lift-shake sequence before giving the treat. Shaping is a powerful tool. Animal trainers have used it to teach chimpanzees to roller-skate, dolphins to jump through hoops, and pigeons to play Ping-Pong (Coren, 1999).

shaping   The reinforcement of responses that come successively closer to some desired response.

GETTING THE HANG OF IT ▲

Learning to eat with a spoon is, as you can see, a hit-and-miss process at first. However, this child will learn to hit the target more and more often as the food reward gradually shapes a more efficient (and far less messy) pattern of behavior.

primary reinforcers Events or stimuli that satisfy physiological needs basic to survival.

secondary reinforcers Rewards that people or animals learn to like.

Secondary Reinforcement   Operant conditioning often begins with the use of **primary reinforcers,** which are events or stimuli—such as food or water—that satisfy needs that are basic to survival. The effects of primary reinforcers are powerful and automatic. But constantly giving Sugar food as a reward can disrupt training, because she will stop to eat after every response. Also, once she gets full, food will no longer act as an effective reinforcer. To avoid these problems, animal trainers, parents, and teachers rely on the principle of secondary reinforcement.

Secondary reinforcers are previously neutral stimuli that take on reinforcing properties after being paired with stimuli that are already reinforcing. In other words, they are rewards that people or animals learn to like. If you say "Good girl!" just before feeding Sugar, those words will become reinforcing after a few pairings. "Good girl!" can then be used alone to reinforce Sugar's behavior. It helps if the words are again paired with food every now and then. Does this remind you of classical conditioning? It should, because the primary reinforcer (food) is an unconditioned stimulus. If the words "Good girl!" become a reliable signal for food, they will act as a conditioned stimulus (CS). For this reason, secondary reinforcers are sometimes called *conditioned reinforcers.*

The power of operant conditioning can be greatly increased by using secondary reinforcers. Consider the secondary reinforcer we call money. Some people will do almost anything for it despite the fact that it tastes terrible and won't quench your thirst. Its reinforcing power lies in its association with the many rewards it can buy. Smiles and other forms of social approval (such as the words "Good job!") are also important secondary reinforcers for human beings. However, what becomes a secondary reinforcer can vary widely from person to person and culture to culture. Tickets to a rock concert may be an effective secondary reinforcer for some people but not for others. A ceremony honoring outstanding job performance might be strongly reinforcing in an individualist culture, but the same experience might be embarrassing for a person in a collectivist culture, where group cooperation is given greater value than personal distinction (Miller, 2001). When carefully chosen, however, secondary reinforcers can build or maintain behavior, even when primary reinforcement is absent for long periods.

Delay and Size of Reinforcement   Much of our behavior is learned and maintained because it is regularly reinforced. But many of us overeat, smoke, drink too much, or procrastinate, even though we know these behaviors are bad for us. We may want to eliminate them, but they are hard to change. We seem to lack self-control. If behavior is controlled by its consequences, why do we do things that are ultimately self-defeating?

Part of the answer lies in the timing of reinforcers. For example, the good feelings (positive reinforcers) that follow excessive drinking are immediate. But because hangovers and other negative consequences are usually delayed, their effects on future drinking are weakened. In other words, operant conditioning is stronger when reinforcers appear soon after a response occurs (Rachlin, 2000). Under some conditions, delaying a positive reinforcer for even a few seconds can decrease the effectiveness of positive reinforcement. (An advantage of praise and other secondary reinforcers is that they can easily be delivered as soon as the desired response occurs.) The size of the reinforcer is also important. In general, conditioning is faster when the reinforcer is large than when it is small.

Reinforcement Schedules   When a *continuous reinforcement schedule* is in effect, a reinforcer is delivered every time a particular response occurs. This schedule can be helpful when teaching someone a new skill, but it can be impractical in the long run. Imagine how inefficient it would be, for example, if an employer had to deliver praise or pay following every little task employees performed all day long. In most cases, reinforcement is given only some of the time, on a *partial,* or *intermittent, reinforcement schedule*. Intermittent schedules are described in terms of when and how reinforcers are given. "When" refers to the number of responses that have to occur,

REINFORCEMENT SCHEDULES ON THE JOB ▲

Make a list of all the jobs you have ever held, along with the reinforcement schedule on which you received your pay for each. Which of the four types of schedules (fixed ratio, fixed interval, variable ratio, or variable interval) was most common, and which was most satisfying to you?

Learn BY Doing

or the amount of time that must pass, before a reinforcer will occur. "How" refers to whether the reinforcer will be delivered in a predictable or unpredictable way.

1. *Fixed-ratio (FR) schedules* provide reinforcement following a fixed number of responses. Rats might receive food after every tenth time they press the lever in a Skinner box (FR 10) or after every twentieth time (FR 20). Technicians working at computer help centers might be allowed to take a break after every fifth call they handle, or every tenth.

2. *Variable-ratio (VR) schedules* also call for reinforcement after a certain number of responses, but that number varies. As a result, it is impossible to predict which particular response will bring reinforcement. On a VR 30 schedule, for example, a rat will be reinforced after an *average* of thirty lever presses. This means that the reward sometimes comes after ten presses, sometimes after fifteen, and other times after fifty or more. Gambling offers humans a similar variable-ratio schedule. Casino slot machines pay off only after a frustratingly unpredictable number of button-pushes, averaging perhaps one in twenty.

3. *Fixed-interval (FI) schedules* provide reinforcement for the first response that occurs after some fixed time has passed since the last reward. On an FI 60 schedule, for instance, the first response after sixty seconds has passed will be rewarded, regardless of how many responses have been made during that interval. Some radio stations make use of fixed-interval schedules. Listeners who have won a call-in contest might have to wait at least ten days before they are eligible to win again.

4. *Variable-interval (VI) schedules* reinforce the first response after some period of time, but the amount of time varies unpredictably. So on a VI 60 schedule, the first response that occurs after an *average* of 60 seconds is reinforced, but the actual time between reinforcements might vary anywhere from 1 to 120 seconds or more. Police in Illinois and California have used a VI schedule to encourage seat belt use and careful driving. They stopped drivers at random times and awarded prizes to those who were buckled up and driving safely (Associated Press, 2007; Mortimer et al., 1988). Kindergarten teachers use VI schedules when they give rewards to children who are in their seats when a chime sounds at random intervals.

As shown in Figure 5.10, different **reinforcement schedules** produce different patterns of responding (Skinner, 1961). Both fixed-ratio and variable-ratio schedules produce especially high response rates overall. The reason, in both cases, is that the frequency of reward depends directly on the rate of responding. Under a fixed-interval schedule, it does not matter how many responses are made during the time between rewards. Because the timing of the reinforcement is so predictable, the rate of responding typically drops immediately after reinforcement and then increases as the time for another reward approaches. When teachers schedule quizzes on the same day each week, most students will study just before each quiz and then almost cease studying immediately afterward. By contrast, the possibility of unpredictable "pop" quizzes (on a variable-interval schedule) typically generates more consistent studying patterns (Kouyoumdjian, 2004).

Schedules and Extinction Ending the relationship between an operant response and its consequences weakens that response. In fact, failure to reinforce a response eventually extinguishes it. The response occurs less and less often and eventually may disappear. If you keep sending text messages to someone who never replies, you eventually stop trying. But extinction in operant conditioning does not erase learned relationships (Delamater, 2004). If a discriminative stimulus for reinforcement reappears some time after an operant response has been extinguished, that response may recur (spontaneously recover). And if it is reinforced again, the response will quickly return to its former level, as though extinction had never happened.

In general, behaviors learned under a partial reinforcement schedule are far more difficult to extinguish than those learned on a continuous reinforcement schedule. This phenomenon is called the **partial reinforcement effect.** Imagine, for example, that

reinforcement schedules In operant conditioning, rules that determine how and when certain responses will be reinforced. They are usually based on the number of responses made (ratio schedules) or the amount of time since the last reinforced response (interval schedules).

partial reinforcement effect A phenomenon in which behaviors learned under a partial reinforcement schedule are more difficult to extinguish than those learned on a continuous reinforcement schedule.

FIGURE 5.10 ■ RESULTS OF FOUR PARTIAL REINFORCEMENT SCHEDULES

These curves illustrate the patterns of behavior typically seen under different reinforcement schedules. The steeper the curve, the faster the response rate was. The thin diagonal lines crossing the curves show when reinforcement was given. In general, the rate of responding is higher under ratio schedules than under interval schedules. *Source*: Adapted from Skinner (1961).

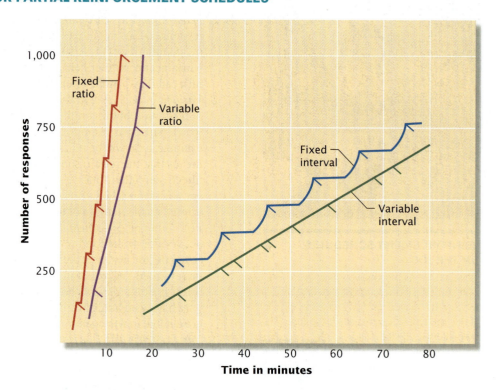

you are in a gambling casino, standing near a broken candy machine and a broken slot machine. You might deposit money in the broken candy machine once, but this behavior will probably stop (extinguish) very quickly. The candy machine should deliver its goodies on a continuous reinforcement schedule, so you can easily tell that it is not going to provide a reinforcer. But you know that slot machines give rewards on an unpredictable, intermittent schedule. So you might put in coin after coin, unsure of whether the machine is broken or is simply not paying off at the moment.

Partial reinforcement helps explain why superstitious behavior is so resistant to extinction (Vyse, 2000). Suppose you had been out for a run just before hearing that you passed an important exam. The run did nothing to cause this outcome. The reward followed it through sheer coincidence. Still, for some people, this kind of *accidental reinforcement* can strengthen the behavior that appeared to "cause" good news (Pronin et al., 2006). These people might decide that it is "lucky" to go running after taking an exam. Similarly, someone who wins the lottery or a sports bet while wearing a particular shirt may begin wearing the "lucky shirt" more often (Hendrick, 2003). Of course, if the person wears the shirt often enough, something good is bound to follow every now and then, thus further strengthening the superstitious behavior on a sparse partial schedule.

Why Reinforcers Work

What makes a reinforcer reinforcing? For primary reinforcers, at least, the reason could be that they satisfy basic physiological needs for survival. Yet artificial sweeteners, which have no nutritional value, can be as powerfully reinforcing as sugar, which is nutritious. And what about addictive drugs, which are also powerful reinforcers even though they threaten the health of those who use them?

Research by biological psychologists suggests that reinforcers may work by exerting particular effects on the brain. In a classic study on this point, James Olds and Peter Milner (1954) discovered that mild electrical stimulation of certain areas of the brain's hypothalamus can be a powerful reinforcer. Hungry rats will ignore food if they can press a lever that stimulates these "pleasure centers" (Olds, 1973). It has since been discovered that activation of brain systems that use the chemical dopamine is

SUPERSTITION AND PARTIAL REINFORCEMENT ▶

Partial reinforcement helps sustain superstitious athletic rituals—such as a fixed sequence of actions prior to hitting a golf ball or shooting a free throw in basketball. If the ritual has preceded success often enough, failure to execute it may upset the player and disrupt performance. Oakland Athletics' infielder Nomar Garciaparra tugs, loosens, and retightens each batting glove after every pitch. Those who watch sports have their superstitious rituals, too. One Pittsburgh Steelers football fan we know insists on wearing the same outfit while watching every game and eats a particular brand of lime-flavored corn chips to be sure his team will score.

associated with the pleasure of many stimuli, including food, music, sex, the uncertainty of gambling, and some addictive drugs such as cocaine (Berns et al., 2001; Blood & Zatorre, 2001; Ciccocioppo, Sanna, & Weiss, 2001; Reuter et al., 2005; Tobler, Fiorillo, & Schultz, 2005). Current research suggests that complex and widespread patterns of brain activity are involved in our response to reinforcers, allowing us to enjoy them, to learn to want them, and to learn how to get them (Montague, Hyman, & Cohen, 2004; Pessiglione et al., 2006; Robinson et al., 2005).

Punishment

Positive and negative reinforcement increase the frequency of a response, either by presenting something pleasurable or by removing something that is unpleasant. In contrast, **punishment** *reduces* the frequency of an operant behavior by presenting an unpleasant stimulus or removing a pleasant one. Shouting "No!" and swatting your cat when it begins chewing on your plants is an example of the kind of punishment that presents an aversive stimulus following a response. Taking away a child's TV privileges because of rude behavior is a second kind of punishment—sometimes called *penalty*—that removes a positive stimulus (see Figure 5.11).

Punishment is often confused with negative reinforcement, but the two are quite different. Just remember that reinforcement of any type always *strengthens* behavior, whereas punishment always *weakens* behavior. If shock is *turned off* when a rat presses a lever, this is negative reinforcement. It increases the probability that the rat will press the lever when shock occurs again. But if shock is *turned on* when the rat presses the lever, this is punishment. The rat will be less likely to press the lever again.

Although punishment can change behavior, it has some drawbacks (Gershoff & Bitensky, 2007). First, it does not "erase" an undesirable behavior. It merely suppresses the behavior temporarily. In fact, people often repeat punished acts when they think they can do so without getting caught. Second, punishment can produce unwanted side effects. If you punish a child for swearing, the child may associate the punisher with the punishment and end up fearing you. Third, punishment is often ineffective unless it is given immediately after the undesirable behavior and each time that behavior occurs. If a child gets into the cookie jar and enjoys a few cookies before being discovered

punishment The presentation of an aversive stimulus or the removal of a pleasant one following some behavior.

FIGURE 5.11   ■   TWO KINDS OF PUNISHMENT

In one form of punishment, a behavior is followed by an aversive, or unpleasant, stimulus. In a second form of punishment, sometimes called penalty, a pleasant stimulus is removed following a behavior. In either case, punishment decreases the chances that the behavior will occur in the future. Now you decide: When a toddler reaches toward an electric outlet and her father says "NO!" and gently taps her hand, is that punishment or negative reinforcement? If you said punishment, you are right, because it will reduce the likelihood of her touching outlets in the future.

PUNISHMENT 1

| **Behavior** You touch a hot iron. | **Presentation of an unpleasant stimulus** Your hand is burned. | **Frequency of behavior decreases** You no longer touch hot irons. |

PUNISHMENT 2 (Penalty)

| **Behavior** You're careless with your ice cream cone. | **Removal of a pleasant stimulus** The ice cream falls on the ground. | **Frequency of behavior decreases** You're not as careless with the next cone. |

and punished, the effect of the punishment will be greatly reduced. Fourth, physical punishment can become aggression, even abuse, if given in anger. And because children tend to imitate what they see, frequent punishment may lead them to behave aggressively themselves (Eriksen & Jensen, 2006; Lansford & Dodge, 2008). Finally, punishment lets people know they have done something wrong, but it doesn't specify what they should do instead. An "F" on a term paper means that the assignment was poorly done, but the grade alone tells the student nothing about how to improve.

When used properly, however, punishment can be a valuable tool (Baumrind, Larzelere, & Cowan, 2002). As shown in Figure 5.12, for example, it can help children

FIGURE 5.12   ■   LIFE-SAVING PUNISHMENT

This child suffered from chronic ruminative disorder, a condition in which he vomited everything he ate. At left, the boy was approximately one year old and had been vomiting for four months. At right is the same child thirteen days after punishment with electric shock had eliminated the vomiting response; his weight had increased 26 percent. He was physically and psychologically healthy when tested six months, one year, and two years later (Lang & Melamed, 1969). *Source:* Lang & Melamed (1969).

applying psychology

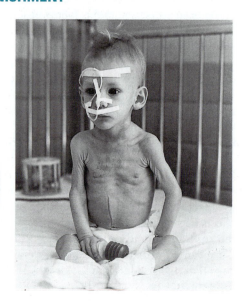
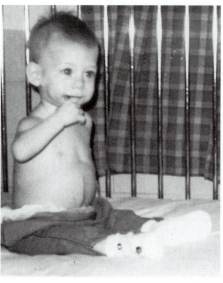

© Lang and Melamed, 1969

LEARNING CULTURAL VALUES ▲

The use of alcohol varies considerably from culture to culture, in part because some cultures reward it more than others. In Japan, for example, drinking alcohol after work is considered appropriate and is even encouraged. In some Islamic cultures, any use of alcohol is actively discouraged and may even be illegal.

who suffer from certain developmental disorders or who purposely injure themselves (Flavell et al., 1982). Punishment is especially effective when a few guidelines are followed. First, to prevent the development of a general fear of the punisher, specify why punishment is being given. Second, emphasize that the behavior, not the person, is being punished. Third, without being abusive, make sure the punishment is immediate and noticeable enough to eliminate the undesirable response. A half-hearted "Quit it" may actually reinforce a child's misbehavior, because almost any attention is rewarding to some children. And once a child gets used to mild punishment, the parent may resort to punishment that is far more severe than would have been necessary if stern, but moderate, punishment had been used in the first place. (You may have witnessed this *escalation effect* in grocery stores or restaurants where children ignore their parents' initially weak efforts to stop their misbehavior.) Fourth, identify and positively reinforce more appropriate responses.

When these guidelines are not followed, the beneficial effects of punishment may be wiped out or may be only temporary. As prison systems demonstrate, punishment alone does not usually lead to rehabilitation. Following their release, about two-thirds of U.S. prison inmates are rearrested for felonies or serious misdemeanors within three years, and about 50 percent will go back to prison (Cassel & Bernstein, 2007; U.S. Department of Justice, 2002).

Some Applications of Operant Conditioning

Although the principles of operant conditioning were originally worked out with animals in the laboratory, they are valuable for understanding human behavior in an endless variety of everyday situations. ("In Review: Reinforcement and Punishment" summarizes some key concepts of operant conditioning.) Effective use of reinforcements and punishments by parents, teachers, and peers is vital to helping children learn what is and is not appropriate behavior at the dinner table, in the classroom, or at a birthday party. People learn how to be "civilized" in their culture partly through experiencing positive and negative responses from others. And differing patterns of rewards and punishments for boys and girls underlie the development of behavior that fits culturally approved *gender roles,* a topic explored in more detail in the chapter on human development.

The scientific study of operant conditioning has led to numerous treatment programs for altering problematic behavior. Behavior modification programs that combine the use of rewards and extinction (or carefully administered punishment) have helped countless mental patients, mentally retarded or brain-damaged individuals, autistic children, and hard-to-manage preschoolers develop the behaviors they need to live happier and more productive lives (e.g., Alberto, Troutman, & Feagin, 2002; Pear & Martin, 2002). These programs include establishing goal behaviors, choosing reinforcers and punishers, and developing a systematic plan for applying them to achieve desired changes. Many self-help books also incorporate the principles of positive

In Review

REINFORCEMENT AND PUNISHMENT

CONCEPT	DESCRIPTION	EXAMPLE OR COMMENT
Positive reinforcement	Increasing the frequency of a behavior by following it with the presentation of a positive reinforcer— a pleasant, positive stimulus or experience	You say "Good job!" after someone works hard to perform a task.
Negative reinforcement	Increasing the frequency of a behavior by following it with the removal of an unpleasant stimulus or experience	You learn to use the mute button on the TV remote control to remove the sound of an obnoxious commercial.
Escape conditioning	Learning to make a response that removes an unpleasant stimulus	A little boy learns that crying will cut short the time that he must stay in his room.
Avoidance conditioning	Learning to make a response that avoids an unpleasant stimulus	You slow your car to the speed limit when you spot a police car, thus avoiding being stopped and reducing the fear of a fine; very resistant to extinction.
Punishment	Decreasing the frequency of a behavior by either presenting an unpleasant stimulus (punishment 1) or removing a pleasant one (punishment 2, or penalty)	You swat the dog after it steals food from the table or you take a favorite toy away from a child who misbehaves. A number of cautions should be kept in mind before using punishment.

1. *Taking an aspirin can relieve headache pain, so people learn to do so through the process of _____ reinforcement.*

2. *The "walk" sign that tells people it is safe to cross the street is an example of a _____ stimulus.*

3. *Response rates tend to be higher under _____ schedules of reinforcement than under _____ schedules.*

online study center

Improve Your Grade
Tutorial: Reinforcement and Punishment

reinforcement, recommending self-reward following each small victory in people's efforts to lose weight, stop smoking, avoid procrastination, or reach other goals (e.g., Grant & Kim, 2002; Rachlin, 2000).

When people cannot do anything to alter the consequences of a behavior, discriminative conditioned stimuli may hold the key to changing that behavior. For example, people often find it easier to quit smoking if they temporarily avoid bars and other places where there are powerful discriminative conditioned stimuli for smoking. Stimulus control can also help alleviate insomnia. Insomniacs tend to use their beds for activities such as watching television, writing letters, reading magazines, worrying, and so on. Soon the bedroom becomes a discriminative stimulus for so many activities that relaxation and sleep become less and less likely. *Stimulus control therapy* encourages insomniacs to use their beds only for sleeping (and perhaps sex), making it more likely that they will sleep better when in bed (Edinger et al., 2001).

linkages

How are learned associations stored in memory? *(a link to memory)*

Linkages

Networks of Learning

Associations between conditioned stimuli and reflexes or between responses and their consequences play an important role in learning, but how are they actually stored in the brain? No one yet knows for sure, but associative network models provide a good way of thinking about the process. As suggested in the chapter on memory, the associations we form among stimuli and events are represented in complex

FIGURE 5.13   ■   AN ASSOCIATIVE NETWORK

Here is an example of a network of associations to the word "dog." Network theorists suggest that the connections shown here represent patterns of connections among nerve cells in the brain.

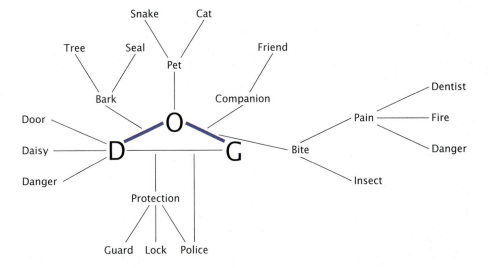

networks of connections among brain cells, or neurons. Consider the word "dog." As shown in Figure 5.13, each person's experience builds many associations to this word, and the strength of each association will reflect the frequency with which "dog" has been mentally linked to the other objects, events, and ideas in that person's life.

Using what they know about the laws of learning and the way neurons communicate and alter their connections, psychologists have developed computer models of how these associations are established (Messinger et al., 2001). An important feature of these *parallel distributed processing* models is the idea of distributed memory or distributed knowledge. These models suggest, for example, that your knowledge of "dog" does not lie in a single spot, or node, in your brain. Instead, that knowledge is distributed throughout the network of associations that connect the letters D, O, and G, along with other dog-related experiences. In addition, as shown in Figure 5.13, each of the interconnected nodes that make up your knowledge of "dog" is connected to many other nodes as well. So the letter D will be connected to "daisy," "danger," and many other concepts.

Neural network models of learning focus on how these connections develop through experience (Hanson & Burr, 1990). For example, suppose you are learning a new word in a foreign language. Each time you read the word and associate it with its English equivalent, you strengthen the neural connections between the sight of the letters forming that word and all of the nodes activated when its English equivalent is brought to mind. Neural network, or *connectionist,* models of learning predict how much the strength of each linkage grows (in terms of the likelihood of neural communication between the two connected nodes) each time the two words are experienced together.

The details of various theories about how these connections grow are very complex, but a theme common to many of them is that the weaker the connection between two items, the greater the increase in connection strength when they are experienced together. So in a classical conditioning experiment, the connections between the nodes that characterize the conditioned stimulus and those that characterize the unconditioned stimulus will show the greatest increase in strength during the first few learning trials. Notice that this prediction nicely matches the typical learning curve shown in Figure 5.3 (Rescorla & Wagner, 1972).

Neural network models have yet to fully explain the learning of complex tasks, and they cannot easily account for how people adapt when the "rules of the game" are suddenly changed and old habits must be unlearned and replaced. Nevertheless, further research on neural network models is likely to produce a better understanding of what we mean by *associations* (Anthony & Bartlett, 1999; Boden, 2006; Goldblum, 2001; Houghton, 2005).

Cognitive Processes in Learning

▶ *Can people learn to be helpless?*

In the first half of the twentieth century, psychologists in North America tended to look at learning through the lens of behaviorism. That is, they saw classical and operant conditioning as the automatic, unthinking formation or modification of associations between observable stimuli and observable responses. They gave little consideration to the role of mental activity that might accompany the learning process.

As mentioned earlier, though, this strictly behavioral view of classical and operant conditioning is now challenged by the cognitive approach, which has become increasingly influential in recent decades. Cognitive psychologists see a common thread in these apparently different forms of learning (Blaisdell, Sawa, & Leising, 2006). They see classical and operant conditioning as helping animals and people detect and understand what causes what (Young, 1995). They argue that both types of conditioning result not only from automatic associations but also from more complex mental processes—including how information is represented, stored, and used. These processes, they say, underlie our ability to adapt to and understand the world around us (Dickinson, 2001; Kirsch et al., 2004).

Cognitive psychologists have found, for example, that a classically conditioned fear response is more likely to develop if an unconditioned stimulus comes as a surprise than if it is expected (Kamin, 1969). Even the brain's reaction to a given stimulus can differ depending on whether that stimulus was expected or unexpected (Waelti, Dickinson, & Schultz, 2001). As discussed in the chapter on thought, language, and intelligence, cognitive theorists also emphasize the idea that the learned behavior of humans and perhaps other mammals, too, is affected by their ability to calculate the likely consequences of differing courses of action (Lohrenz et al., 2007; Tanaka, Balleine, & O'Doherty, 2008).

In other words, according to the cognitive view, learning is affected not only by the nature of the stimuli we experience but also by our expectations about them. Further, just as our perceptions depend on the meaning we attach to sensations (see the chapter on sensation and perception), learning can depend on the meaning we attach to events. So being praised by a boss we respect may be more reinforcing than getting the same good evaluation from a boss we hate.

The importance of cognitive processes has also been demonstrated in research on learned helplessness, latent learning, cognitive maps, insight, and observational learning.

Learned Helplessness

online study center

Improve Your Grade
Tutorial: Learned Helplessness

learned helplessness A process in which a person or animal stops trying to exert control after experience suggests that no control is possible.

Babies learn that crying attracts attention. Children learn how to make the TV louder. Adults learn what actions lead to success or failure in the workplace. On the basis of this learning people come to expect that certain actions on their part will cause certain consequences. But sometimes events are beyond our control. What happens when our actions have no effect on events, and especially when our escape or avoidance behaviors fail? If these circumstances last long enough, one result may be **learned helplessness,** a tendency to give up on efforts to control the environment (Overmier, 2002; Seligman, 1975).

Learned helplessness was first demonstrated in animals. As described earlier, dogs in a shuttle box will learn to jump over a partition to escape a shock (see Figure 5.8). But if the dogs first receive shocks that they cannot escape, they later do not even try to escape when the shock is turned on in the shuttle box (Overmier & Seligman, 1967). It is as if the animals had learned that "shock happens, and there is nothing I can do about it." Do people learn the same lesson?

Focus on RESEARCH

The "I Can't Do It" Attitude

What lessons do abused and neglected children learn about their ability to get what they need from the environment? Do they learn that even their best efforts result in failure? Do they give up even trying? Why would a student with above average ability tell a counselor, "I can't do math"? How do people develop an "I can't do it" attitude?

▶ What was the researcher's question?

Can lack of control over the environment lead to helplessness in humans? Donald Hiroto (1974) conducted an experiment to test the hypothesis that people develop learned helplessness either after experiencing lack of control or after simply being told that their control is limited.

▶ How did the researcher answer the question?

Hiroto (1974) randomly assigned research participants to one of three groups. One group heard a series of thirty bursts of loud, obnoxious noise and, like dogs receiving inescapable shock, had no way to stop it. A second group could control the noise by pressing a button to turn it off. The third group heard no noise at all. After this preliminary phase, all three groups were exposed to eighteen additional bursts of noise, each preceded by a red warning light. During this second phase, all participants could prevent the noise if they pushed a lever quickly enough. However, they didn't know whether to push the lever left or right on any given trial. Before these new trials began, the experimenter told half the participants in each group that avoiding or escaping the noise depended on their skill. The other half were told that their success would be a matter of chance.

▶ What did the researcher find?

The people who had previously experienced lack of control now failed to control noise on about four times as many trials as did those who had earlier been in control (50 percent versus 13 percent). This finding was similar to that of the research with dogs and inescapable shock. When the dogs were later placed in a situation in which they could escape or avoid shock, they did not even try. Humans, too, seem to use prior experiences to guide later efforts to try, or not to try, to control their environment.

Expectation of control, whether accurate or not, also had an effect on behavior. In Hiroto's study, those participants who expected that skill could control the noise exerted control on significantly more trials than did those who expected chance to govern the result. This outcome occurred regardless of whether the participants had experienced control before.

▶ What do the results mean?

These results support Hiroto's hypothesis that people, like animals, tend to make less effort to control their environment when prior experience suggests that those efforts will be of no use. But unlike animals, humans need only be *told* that they have no control or are powerless in order for this same effect to occur.

Hiroto's (1974) results appear to reflect a general phenomenon. When prior experience leads people to *believe* that there is nothing they can do to change their lives or control their destiny, they may stop trying to improve their lot (Faulkner, 2001; LoLordo, 2001; Peterson, Maier, & Seligman, 1993). Instead, they may passively endure painful situations. Has this ever happened to you?

▶ What do we still need to know?

Further research is needed on when and how learned helplessness affects people's thoughts, feelings, and actions. For example, could learned helplessness explain why some battered women remain with abusive partners? We do know that learned helplessness experiences are associated with the development of a generally pessimistic way of thinking that can produce depression and other mental disorders (Peterson & Seligman, 1984). People with this *pessimistic explanatory style* see the good things that happen to them as temporary and due to chance and the bad things as permanent and due to internal factors such as lack of ability. This explanatory style has, in fact, been associated with poor grades, inadequate sales performance, health problems, and other negative outcomes (Bennett & Elliott, 2002; Seligman & Schulman, 1986; Taylor, 2002). The exact mechanisms responsible for this connection are still unknown, but understanding how pessimistic (or optimistic) explanatory styles can lead to negative (or positive) consequences remains an important focus of research (e.g., Brennan & Charnetski, 2000). Research is also focusing on how best to minimize learned helplessness and maximize learned optimism in areas such as education, parenting, and psychotherapy (e.g., Jackson, Sellers, & Peterson, 2002).

Latent Learning and Cognitive Maps

Decades ago, Edward Tolman studied cognitive processes in learning by watching rats try to find their way to food that was waiting for them at the end of a complex maze. At first, the rats took many wrong turns. Over time, though, they made fewer and fewer mistakes. The behavioral interpretation of this result was that the rats learned a long

FIGURE 5.14   ■   LATENT LEARNING

This graph shows the average number of wrong turns that Tolman's rats made on their way to the end of a maze (Tolman & Honzik, 1930). Notice that when rats in Group C did not receive food reinforcement, they continued to make many errors. The day after first finding food at the end of the maze, however, they took almost no wrong turns! The reinforcement, argued Tolman, affected only the rats' performance; they must have learned the maze earlier, without reinforcement.

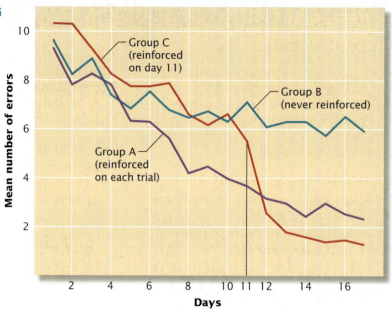

chain of turning responses that were reinforced by food. Tolman disagreed and offered evidence for a cognitive interpretation.

In one of Tolman's studies, three groups of rats were placed in the same maze once a day for several days (Tolman & Honzik, 1930). For Group A, food was placed at the end of the maze on each trial. As shown in Figure 5.14, these rats gradually improved their performance. Group B also ran the maze once a day, but there was never any food waiting for them. The animals in Group B continued to make many errors. Neither of these results is surprising.

The third group of rats, Group C, was the critical one. For the first ten days, they received no reinforcement for running the maze and continued to make many mistakes. On the eleventh day, food was placed at the end of the maze for the first time. What do you think happened? On the day after receiving reinforcement, these rats made almost no mistakes (again, see Figure 5.14). In fact, their performance was as good as that of the group that had been reinforced every day. The single reinforcement trial on day 11 produced a dramatic change in their performance the next day.

Tolman argued that these results support two conclusions. First, because the rats in Group C improved their performance the first time they ran the maze after being reinforced, the reinforcement on day 11 could not have significantly affected their *learning* of the maze. Rather, the reinforcement simply changed their subsequent *performance*. They must have learned the maze earlier as they wandered around making mistakes on their way to the end of the maze. These rats demonstrated **latent learning**—learning that is not evident when it first occurs. (Latent learning occurs in humans, too; for example, after years of experience in your neighborhood, you could probably tell a visitor that the corner drugstore is closed on Sundays, even if you had never tried to go there on a Sunday yourself.) Second, the rats' sudden improvement in performance after the first reinforcement trial could have occurred only if the rats had earlier developed a cognitive map of the maze. A **cognitive map** is a mental representation of some physical arrangement—in this case, a maze.

Tolman concluded that cognitive maps develop naturally through experience, even in the absence of any overt response or reinforcement. Research on learning in the natural environment has supported this view. We develop mental maps of shopping malls and city streets even when we receive no direct reward for doing so (Tversky & Kahneman, 1991). Having such a map allows you to tell that neighborhood visitor exactly how to get to the corner drugstore from where you are standing.

latent learning   Learning that is not demonstrated at the time it occurs.

cognitive map   A mental representation of the environment.

from The Mentality of Apes by W. Köhler, 1976. Courtesy of Routledge

FIGURE 5.15 ■ **INSIGHT**

Here are three impressive examples of problem solving by chimpanzees. At left, a chimp fixed a 15-foot pole in the ground, climbed to the top, and dropped down after grabbing a piece of fruit. In the center photo, the animal stacked two boxes from different areas of the compound, climbed to the top, and used a pole to knock down the fruit. The chimp at right stacked three boxes and climbed them to reach the fruit. *Source*: Köhler (1976).

Insight and Learning

Wolfgang Köhler was a psychologist whose work on the cognitive aspects of learning happened almost by accident. He was visiting Tenerife, an island in the Atlantic Ocean, when World War I broke out in 1914. As a German in territory controlled by Germany's enemy, Britain, Köhler was confined there until the war ended in 1918. He used this time to study problem solving in a colony of local chimpanzees (Köhler, 1924).

For example, Köhler would put a chimpanzee in a cage and place a piece of fruit where the chimp could see it but not reach it. He sometimes hung the fruit too high to be reached or placed it on the ground too far outside the animal's cage to be retrieved. Many of the chimps overcame these obstacles easily. If the fruit was out of reach beyond the cage, some chimps looked around, found a long stick, and used it to rake in the fruit. Surprised that the chimpanzees could solve these problems, Köhler tried more difficult tasks. Again, the chimps quickly got to the fruit, as Figure 5.15 illustrates.

Three aspects of Köhler's observations convinced him that animals' problem solving does not have to depend on trial and error and the gradual association of responses with consequences. First, once a chimpanzee solved one type of problem, it would immediately do the same thing in a similar situation. In other words, it acted as if it understood the problem. Second, Köhler's chimpanzees rarely tried a solution that did not work. Apparently, the solution was not discovered randomly but "thought out" ahead of time and then acted out successfully. Third, the chimps often reached a solution quite suddenly. When confronted with a piece of fruit hanging from a string, for instance, a chimp would jump for it several times. Then it would stop jumping, look up, and pace back and forth. Finally it would run over to a wooden crate, place it directly under the fruit, and climb on top of it to reach the fruit. Once, when there were no other objects in the cage, a chimp went over to Köhler, dragged him by the arm until he stood beneath the fruit, and then started climbing up his back!

Köhler believed that the only explanation for these results was that the chimpanzees had experienced **insight,** a sudden understanding of the problem as a

insight A sudden understanding of what is required to solve a problem.

LEARNING BY IMITATION ▶

Much of our behavior is learned by imitating others, especially those who serve as role models. To appreciate the impact of social learning in your life, list five examples of how your own actions, speech, appearance, or mannerisms have come to match those of a parent, a sibling, a friend, a teacher, or even a celebrity.

Learn BY **Doing**

© Paul Chesley/Getty Images

whole. Was he right? Possibly, but what Köhler saw as sudden insight might not have been so sudden. Other psychologists found that previous trial-and-error experience with objects, such as boxes and sticks, is necessary for "insight" in chimps (Birch, 1945). In fact, some psychologists argue that all known cases of "insight" by humans and nonhumans alike include a long history of experience with the objects that are used to solve the problem (Epstein et al., 1984; Kounios et al., 2006; Wynne, 2004). So although Köhler's work helped highlight the importance of cognitive processes in learning, questions remain about whether it demonstrated true insight in chimps.

Observational Learning: Learning by Imitation

People and animals learn a lot from personal experience, but they can also learn by observing what others do and what happens to them when they do it (e.g., Akins & Zentall, 1998; Mattar & Gribble, 2005). Learning by watching others—a process called **observational learning,** or **social learning**—is efficient and adaptive. We don't have to find out for ourselves that a door is locked or an iron is hot if we have just seen someone else try the door or suffer a burn.

Children are particularly influenced by the adults and peers who act as *models* for appropriate behavior. In a classic experiment, Albert Bandura showed nursery school children a film starring an adult and a large, inflatable, bottom-heavy Bobo doll (Bandura, 1965). The adult in the film punched the doll in the nose, kicked it, threw things at it, and hit its head with a hammer while saying things like "Sockeroo!" There were different endings to the film. Some children saw an ending in which the aggressive adult was called a "champion" by a second adult and rewarded with candy and soft drinks. Some saw the aggressor scolded and called a "bad person." Some saw a neutral ending in which there was neither reward nor punishment. After the film, each child was allowed to play alone with a Bobo doll. The way they played in this and similar studies led to some important conclusions about learning and the role of cognitive factors in it.

Bandura found that children who saw the adult rewarded for aggression showed the most aggressive acts in play (see Figure 5.16). They had received *vicarious conditioning,* a kind of observational learning through which a person is influenced by watching or hearing about the consequences of others' behavior. The children who

observational learning (social learning)
Learning by watching the behavior of others.

FIGURE 5.16 ■ OBSERVATIONAL LEARNING

Bandura found that after observing an aggressive model, many children imitate the model's acts precisely, especially if the model's aggression was rewarded.
Source: Bandura, Ross, & Ross (1963).

© Albert Bandura, Stanford University

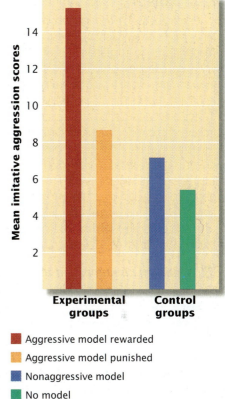

- ■ Aggressive model rewarded
- ■ Aggressive model punished
- ■ Nonaggressive model
- ■ No model

had seen the adult punished for aggressive acts showed less aggression, but they still learned something. When later offered rewards for imitating all the aggressive acts they had seen in the film, these children displayed just as many of these acts as the children who had watched the adult being rewarded. Observational learning can occur even when there are no vicarious consequences; many children in the neutral condition also imitated the model's aggression.

Like direct reward and punishment, observational learning is a powerful force in the *socialization* process through which children learn about which behaviors are—and are not—appropriate in their culture (Bandura, 1999). For example, children show long-term increases in their willingness to help and share after seeing a demonstration of helping by a friendly, impressive model (Schroeder et al., 1995). Fears, too, can be learned partly by the sight of fearfulness in others (Askew & Field, 2008).

Thinking CRITICALLY

Does Watching Violence on Television Make People More Violent?

If observational learning is important, then surely television—and televised violence—must teach children a great deal. It is estimated that the average child in the United States spends about three hours each day watching television (Annenberg Public Policy Center, 2000). Much of what children see is violent. In addition to the real-life violence portrayed on the news (Van der Molen, 2004),

prime-time entertainment programs in the United States present an average of five acts of simulated violence per hour. Some Saturday morning cartoons include more than twenty per hour (American Psychological Association, 1993; Gerbner, Morgan, & Signorielli, 1994). As a result, the average child will have witnessed at least 8,000 murders and more than 100,000 other acts of televised violence before finishing elementary school and twice that number by age 18 (Annenberg Public Policy Center, 1999; Kunkel et al., 1996; Parents Television Council, 2006).

Psychologists have long speculated that watching so much violence might be emotionally arousing, making viewers more likely to react violently to frustration (Huston & Wright, 1989). In fact, there is evidence that exposure to media violence can trigger or amplify viewers' aggressive thoughts and feelings, thus increasing the likelihood that they will act aggressively (Anderson & Dill, 2000; Bushman, 1998). Televised violence might also provide models that viewers imitate, particularly if the violence is carried out by the "good guys" (Huesmann et al., 2003). Finally, prolonged viewing of violent TV programs might desensitize viewers, making them less distressed when they see others suffer, less likely to help them, and less disturbed about inflicting pain on others (Aronson, 1999; Bushman & Anderson, 2009; Smith & Donnerstein, 1998). Concern over the influence of violence on television has led to the development of a violence-blocking V-Chip for new television sets in the United States.

▶ What am I being asked to believe or accept?

Many have argued that watching violence on television causes violent behavior in viewers (Anderson et al., 2003; Anderson & Bushman, 2002b; Bushman & Huesmann, 2000; Eron et al., 1972; Huesmann, 1998). In 1993, a National Academy of Sciences report concluded that "overall, the vast majority of studies, whatever their methodology, showed that exposure to television violence resulted in increased aggressive behavior, both contemporaneously and over time" (Reiss & Roth, 1993, p. 371). An American Psychological Association Commission on Violence and Youth reached the same conclusion (American Psychological Association, 1993).

▶ Is evidence available to support the claim?

Three types of evidence back up the claim that watching violent television programs increases violent behavior. First, there are anecdotes and case studies. Children have poked one another in the eye after watching the Three Stooges appear to do so on television. And adults have claimed that watching TV shows prompted them to commit murders or other violent acts matching those seen on the shows (Werner, 2003).

Second, many correlational studies have found a strong link between watching violent television programs and later acts of aggression and violence (Christakas & Zimmerman, 2007; Johnson, Cohen et al., 2002). One such study tracked people from the time they were six or seven (in 1977) until they reached their early twenties (in 1992). Those who watched more violent television as children were significantly more aggressive as adults (Huesmann et al., 1997, 2003) and more likely to engage in criminal activity (Huesmann, 1995). They were also more likely to use physical punishment on their own children, who themselves tended to be much more aggressive than average. These latter results were found not only in the United States but also in Israel, Australia, Poland, the Netherlands, and even Finland, where the number of violent TV shows is very small (Centerwall, 1990; Huesmann & Eron, 1986).

Finally, the results of numerous experiments support the view that TV violence increases aggression among viewers (American

Psychological Association, 1993; Paik & Comstock, 1994; Reiss & Roth, 1993). In one study, groups of boys watched either violent or nonviolent programs in a controlled setting and then played floor hockey (Josephson, 1987). Boys who had watched the violent shows were more likely than those who had watched nonviolent programs to behave aggressively on the hockey floor. This effect was greatest for boys who had the most aggressive tendencies to begin with. More extensive experiments in which children are exposed for long periods to carefully controlled types of television programs also suggest that exposure to large amounts of violent activity on television results in aggressive behavior (Eron et al., 1972).

▶ Can that evidence be interpreted another way?

To some, this evidence leaves no doubt that media violence causes increases in aggressive and violent behavior, especially in children (Anderson et al., 2003). Others suggest that the evidence is not conclusive and is open to some qualifications and alternative interpretations (e.g., Browne & Hamilton-Giachritsis, 2005; Freedman, 2002; Thakkar, Garrison, & Christakis, 2006).

Anecdotal reports and case studies are certainly open to different interpretations. If people face imprisonment or execution for their violent acts, how believable are their claims that their actions were triggered by television programs? How many other people might say that the same programs made them less likely to be violent? Anecdotes alone do not provide a good basis for drawing solid scientific conclusions.

What about the correlational evidence? A correlation between two variables does not necessarily mean that one caused the other. Both might be caused by a third factor. At least two possible "third factors" might account for the observed relationship between watching TV violence and acting aggressively.

First, certain people may prefer both to watch more violent TV programs and to behave aggressively toward others. In other words, personality may partly account for the observed correlations (e.g., Aluja-Fabregat & Torrubia-Beltri, 1998). Second, perhaps poverty, unemployment, or the effects of drugs and alcohol leave certain people more time to watch television and leave them with frustration or other stressors that trigger aggressive behavior.

As for the results of controlled experiments on the effects of televised violence, some researchers suggest that those effects may be short lived and may not apply beyond the experimental situation (Anderson, Lindsay, & Bushman, 1999; Browne & Hamilton-Giachritsis, 2005; Freedman, 2002). Who is to say, for example, whether an increase in aggressive acts during a hockey game has any later bearing on a child's tendency to commit an act of violence?

▶ What evidence would help to evaluate the alternatives?

By their nature, correlational studies of the role of TV violence in violent behavior can never be conclusive. As we've pointed out, a third, unidentified causal variable could always be responsible for the results. More important would be further evidence from controlled experiments in which equivalent groups of people were given different long-term "doses" of TV violence and its effects on their subsequent behavior were observed for many years. Such experiments could also explore the circumstances under which different people (for example, children versus adults) are affected by various forms of violence. However, conducting studies such as these would create an ethical dilemma. If watching violent television programs really does cause violent behavior, are psychologists justified in creating conditions that might lead some people to be more violent? If such violence occurred, would the researchers be partly responsible to the victims and to society? If some participants commit violent acts, should the researchers continue the experiment to establish a pattern or should they terminate the participation of those individuals? Difficulty in answering questions such as these is partly responsible for the use of short-term experiments and correlational designs in this research area, as well as for some of the remaining uncertainty about the effects of television violence.

▶ **What conclusions are most reasonable?**

The evidence collected so far makes it reasonable to conclude that watching TV violence is one cause of violent behavior, especially in some children and especially in boys (Anderson & Bushman, 2002a; Browne & Hamilton-Giachritsis, 2005; Bushman & Anderson, 2001; Huesmann et al., 1997; Robinson et al., 2001; Smith &

Donnerstein, 1998). Playing violent video games may be another (Anderson, 2004; Anderson & Bushman, 2001; Anderson et al., 2008). But a cause-and-effect relationship between watching TV violence and acting violently is not inevitable and may not always be long lasting (Browne & Hamilton-Giachritsis, 2005). Further, there are many circumstances in which the effect does not occur (Charleton, Gunter, & Coles, 1998; Freedman, 1992, 2002). Parents, peers, and other environmental influences as well as personality factors may dampen or amplify the effect of watching televised violence. Indeed, not every viewer interprets violence in the same way, and not every viewer is equally vulnerable (Ferguson, 2002; Feshbach & Tangney, 2008; Wood, Wong, & Chachere, 1991). The most vulnerable may be young boys, especially those who are most aggressive or violence-prone in the first place, a trait that could well have been acquired by observing the behavior of parents or peers (Huesmann et al., 1997).

Still, the fact that violence on television can have a causal impact on violent behavior is reason for serious concern. This issue continues to influence public debate about what should and should not be aired on television.

"I have HAD it with you two and your violent video games!"

▲ The violence that may affect children's aggressive behavior may not be limited to what they see on television and video games.

Using Research on Learning to Help People Learn

▶ *What should teachers learn about learning?*

The study of how people learn obviously has important implications for improved teaching in our schools (Bjork & Linn, 2006; Halpern & Hakel, 2003; Lambert, 1999; Li, 2005; Woolfolk-Hoy, 1999) and for helping people develop skills.

Classrooms Across Cultures

Many people have expressed concern that schools in the United States are not doing a very good job. The average performance of U.S. students on tests of reading, math, and other basic academic skills has tended to fall short of that of youngsters in other countries, especially Asian countries (Mullis et al., 2007; National Center for Education Statistics, 2000, 2002; Program for International Student Assessment, 2004, 2005). In one early comparison study, Harold Stevenson (1992) followed a sample of pupils in Taiwan, Japan, and the United States from the first grade, in 1980, to the eleventh grade, in 1991. In the first grade, the Asian students scored no higher than their U.S. peers on tests of mathematical aptitude and skills and they did not enjoy math more. However, by the fifth grade, the U.S. students had fallen far behind. Corresponding differences were seen in reading skills. More recent studies have found similar results (Mullis et al., 2004, 2007).

Some possible causes of these differences were found in the classroom itself. In a typical U.S. classroom, teachers talked to students as a group, then students worked at their desks independently. Reinforcement or other feedback about performance on their work was usually delayed until the next day or not provided at all. In contrast, the typical Japanese classroom placed greater emphasis on cooperative work among students (Kristof, 1997). Teachers provided more immediate feedback on a one-to-one basis. And there was an emphasis on creating teams of students with varying abilities, an arrangement in which faster learners help teach slower ones. However, before

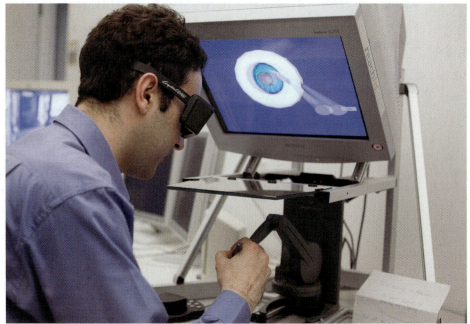

concluding that the differences in performance are the result of social factors alone, we must consider another important distinction: The Japanese children practiced more. They spent more days in school during the year and, on average, spent more hours doing homework.

Although the significance of these cultural differences in learning and teaching is not yet clear, the educational community in the United States is paying attention to them (e.g., Felder & Brent, 2001). Psychologists and educators are also considering how various principles of learning can be applied to improve education. For example, anecdotal and experimental evidence suggests that some of the most successful educational techniques are those that apply basic principles of operant conditioning, offering frequent testing, positive reinforcement for correct performance, and immediate corrective feedback following mistakes (Oppel, 2000; Roediger, McDaniel, & McDermott, 2006).

Further, research in cognitive psychology (e.g., Cepeda et al., 2008; Pashler, Rohrer, & Cepeda, 2006) suggests that students will retain more of what they learn if they study in several sessions distributed over time rather than in a single "cramming" session on the night before a test. To encourage this kind of *distributed practice*, researchers say, teachers should give enough exams and quizzes (some unannounced, perhaps) that students will be reading and studying more or less continuously. And because learning is aided by repeated opportunities to use new information, these exams and quizzes should cover material from throughout the term, not just the material from recent classes. These recommendations are not necessarily popular with students, but there is good evidence that they promote long-term retention of course material (e.g., Bjork, 2001; Bjork & Linn, 2006).

Active Learning

The importance of cognitive processes in learning is apparent in instructional methods that emphasize *active learning* (Bonwell & Eison, 1991). These methods take many forms, including, for example, small-group problem-solving tasks, discussion of "one-minute essays" written in class, use of student response devices ("clickers") or just "thumbs up" or "thumbs down" gestures to indicate agreement or disagreement

RECIPROCAL TEACHING ▲

Ann Brown and her colleagues (1992) demonstrated the success of reciprocal teaching, in which children take turns teaching each other. This technique, which is similar to the cooperative arrangements seen in Japanese education, has become increasingly popular in North American schools (Palincsar, 2003).

applying psychology

VIRTUAL SURGERY ▶

Using a virtual reality system, this medical student can actively learn and practice eye surgery skills before working with real patients. Computer-based human body simulators are also giving new doctors active learning experience in emergency room diagnosis and treatment; heart, lung, and abdominal surgery; and other medical skills (Aggarwal, Cheshire, & Darzi, 2008; Ganai et al., 2007; Groopman, 2005; Heinrichs et al., 2008; Kanno et al., 2008; Katsavelis et al., 2007; Prabhudesai et al., 2008; Seymour, 2008; Tsang et al., 2008).

with the instructor's lecture, and multiple-choice questions that give students feedback about their understanding of the previous fifteen minutes of a lecture (Goss Lucas & Bernstein, 2005; Heward, 1997). Students typically find classes that include active learning experiences to be interesting and enjoyable (Bruff, 2009; Moran, 2000; Murray, 2000). In addition, active learning methods help students go beyond memorizing isolated facts. These methods encourage students to think more deeply, to consider how new material relates to what they already know, and to apply it in new situations. This kind of thinking also makes the material easier to remember, which is why we have included so many opportunities for you to actively learn, rather than just passively read, the material in this book.

Studies of students in elementary schools, high schools, community colleges, and universities have found that compared with instructional techniques that are more passive, active learning approaches result in better test performance and greater class participation (e.g., Hake, 1998; Kellum, Carr, & Dozier, 2001; Meyers & Jones, 1993; Saville et al., 2006). In one study, a fifth-grade teacher spent some days calling only on students whose hands were raised. On other days, all students were required to answer every question by holding up a card with their response written on it. Scores on next-day quizzes and biweekly tests showed that students remembered more of the material covered on the active learning days than on the "passive" days (Gardner, Heward, & Grossi, 1994). In another study of two consecutive medical school classes taught by the same instructor, scores on the final exam were significantly higher when students learned mainly through small-group discussions and case studies than when they were taught mainly through lectures (Chu, 1994). Similarly, among adults being taught to use a new computer program, active learning with hands-on practice was more effective than passively watching a demonstration video (Kerr & Payne, 1994). Finally, high school and college students who passively listened to a physics lecture received significantly lower scores on a test of lecture content than did those who participated in a virtual reality lab that allowed them to interact with the physical forces covered in the lecture (Brelsford, 1993).

Results like these have fueled the development of other science education programs that place students in virtual laboratory environments in which they actively manipulate materials and test hypotheses (e.g., Horwitz & Christie, 2000). Despite the enthusiasm generated by active learning methods, rigorous experimental research is still needed to compare their short- and long-term effects with those of more traditional methods in teaching various kinds of course content (Moran, 2006).

Skill Learning

The complex action sequences, or *skills,* that people learn to perform in everyday life develop through learning processes that include feedback and, of course, lots of practice (Ackerman, 2007). In fact, *practice*—the repeated performance of a skill—is critical to mastery (Howe, Davidson, & Sloboda, 1998). For perceptual-motor skills such as playing pool or piano, both physical and mental practice are beneficial (Druckman & Bjork, 1994). To be most effective, practice should continue past the point of correct performance until the skill can be performed automatically, with little or no attention. Feedback about the correctness of the response is also necessary. As with any learning process, the feedback should come soon enough to be effective but not so quickly that it interferes with the learner's efforts to learn independently.

Large amounts of guidance may produce very good performance during practice, but too much guidance may hurt later performance (Kluger & DeNisi, 1998; Wickens, 1992). For instance, coaching students about correct responses in math may impair their ability later to retrieve the correct response from memory on their own. Independent practice at retrieving previously learned responses or information requires more effort, but it is critical for skill development (Ericsson & Charness, 1994). There is little or no evidence to support "sleep learning" or similar schemes designed to make learning effortless (Druckman & Bjork, 1994). In short, "no pain, no gain."

Learning

As noted in the introductory chapter, all of psychology's subfields are related to one another. Our discussion of associative network models illustrates just one way that the topic of this chapter, learning, is linked to the subfield of memory, which is described in the chapter by that name.

The Linkages diagram shows ties to two other subfields, and there are many more ties throughout the book. Looking for linkages among subfields will help you see how they all fit together and help you better appreciate the big picture that is psychology.

linkages

How are learned associations stored in memory? *(ans. on p. 192)*

Chapter 6
Memory

Who teaches boys to be men and girls to be women? *(ans. on p. 372)*

Chapter 9
Human Development

Are psychological disorders learned behaviors? *(ans. on p. 467)*

Chapter 12
Psychological Disorders

SUMMARY   ▶

Individuals adapt to changes in the environment through the process of *learning*, which is the modification, through experience, of preexisting behavior and understanding.

Classical Conditioning: Learning Signals and Associations

 How did Russian dogs teach psychologists about learning?

One form of learning is **classical conditioning.** It occurs when a previously neutral **conditioned stimulus,** or **CS** (such as a tone), is repeatedly paired with an **unconditioned stimulus,** or **UCS** (such as meat powder on a dog's tongue), which naturally brings about an **unconditioned response,** or **UCR** (such as salivation). Eventually the conditioned stimulus will elicit a response, known as the **conditioned response,** or **CR,** even when the unconditioned stimulus is not presented.

In general, the strength of a conditioned response grows as CS-UCS pairings continue. If the UCS is no longer paired with the CS, the conditioned response eventually disappears; this is **extinction.** After extinction, the conditioned response often reappears if the CS is presented after some time; this is **spontaneous recovery.** In addition, if the conditioned and unconditioned stimuli are paired once or twice after extinction, **reconditioning** occurs; that is, the conditioned response regains much of its original strength.

Because of **stimulus generalization,** conditioned responses occur to stimuli that are similar (but not identical to) conditioned stimuli. Generalization is limited by **stimulus discrimination,** which prompts conditioned responses to some stimuli but not to others.

Classical conditioning involves learning that the CS is an event that predicts the occurrence of another event, the UCS. Many psychologists see the conditioned response as a means through which animals and people develop mental representations of the relationships between events. Classical conditioning works best when the conditioned stimulus precedes the unconditioned stimulus by intervals ranging from less than a second to a minute or more, depending on the stimuli involved. Conditioning is also more likely when the CS reliably signals the UCS. In general, the speed of conditioning increases as the intensity of the UCS increases. Which particular stimulus is likely to become a CS linked to a subsequent UCS depends in part on which stimulus was being attended to when the UCS occurred; more intense stimuli are more likely to attract attention. *Higher order conditioning* occurs when one conditioned stimulus signals a conditioned stimulus that is already associated with an unconditioned stimulus. Some stimuli become associated more easily than others; taste aversions provide illustrations that organisms seem to be biologically prepared to learn certain associations.

Classical conditioning plays a role in the development and treatment of phobias. *Habituation* is reduced responsiveness to a repeated stimulus. According to Solomon's opponent-process theory, habituation is the result of two processes that balance each other. The first process is a relatively automatic, involuntary response—essentially a UCR. The second, or opponent, process is a learned or conditioned response that follows and counteracts the first. These conditioned responses may help explain the development of drug tolerance and some cases of drug overdoses.

Instrumental and Operant Conditioning: Learning the Consequences of Behavior

▶ *How do reward and punishment work?*

Learning occurs not only through associating stimuli but also through associating behavior with its consequences. Thorndike's *law of effect* holds that any response that produces  satisfaction becomes more likely to occur again and that any response that produces discomfort becomes less likely to recur. Thorndike referred to this type of learning as instrumental conditioning. Skinner called the process *operant conditioning.*

An *operant* is a response that has some effect on the world. A *reinforcer* increases the probability that the operant preceding it will occur again. There are two types of reinforcers: *positive reinforcers,* desirable stimuli that strengthen a response if they are presented after that response occurs, and *negative reinforcers,* which are the removal of an unpleasant stimulus following some response. Both kinds of reinforcers strengthen the behaviors that precede them. When behavior is strengthened by a positive reinforcer, the process is called positive *reinforcement.* When behavior is strengthened by a negative reinforcer, the process is called negative *reinforcement. Escape conditioning* results when a behavior stops an unpleasant stimulus. *Avoidance conditioning* results when behavior prevents an unpleasant stimulus from occurring; it reflects both classical and operant conditioning. Behaviors learned through avoidance conditioning are hard to extinguish. *Discriminative conditioned stimuli* signal whether reinforcement is available for a particular behavior.

Complex responses can be learned through *shaping,* which involves reinforcing successive approximations of the desired response. *Primary reinforcers* are innately rewarding; *secondary reinforcers* are rewards that people or animals learn to like because of their association with primary reinforcers. In general, operant conditioning proceeds more quickly when the delay in receiving reinforcement is short rather than long and when the reinforcer is large rather than small. Reinforcement may be delivered on a continuous reinforcement schedule or on one of four types of partial, or intermittent, *reinforcement schedules:* fixed-ratio (FR), variable-ratio (VR), fixed-interval (FI), and variable-interval (VI) schedules. Ratio schedules lead to a rapid rate of responding. Behavior learned through partial reinforcement is very resistant to extinction; this phenomenon is called the *partial reinforcement effect.* Partial reinforcement is involved in superstitious behavior, which results when some action is followed by but does not actually cause a reinforcer.

Research in neuroscience suggests that reinforcers act as rewards largely because of their ability to create activity in "pleasure centers" in the brain's hypothalamus as well as in other brain areas that use the chemical dopamine.

Punishment decreases the frequency of a behavior by following it either with an unpleasant stimulus or with the removal of a pleasant one. Punishment can be useful when performed properly, but it can have drawbacks. It only suppresses behavior; fear of punishment may generalize to the person doing the punishing; it is ineffective when delayed; it can be physically harmful and may teach aggressiveness; and it

teaches only what not to do, not what should be done to obtain reinforcement.

The principles of operant conditioning have been applied in many areas, from teaching social skills to treating sleep disorders.

Cognitive Processes in Learning

▶ *Can people learn to be helpless?*

Cognitive processes—how people represent, store, and use information— play an important role in learning. *Learned helpless-*  *ness* appears to result when people believe that their behavior has no effect on the world. Both animals and humans display *latent learning.* They also form *cognitive maps* of their environments, even in the absence of any reinforcement for doing so. Experiments on *insight* also suggest that cognitive processes play an important role in learning. The process of learning by watching others is called *observational learning,* or *social learning.* Some observational learning occurs through *vicarious conditioning,* in which a person is influenced by seeing or hearing about the consequences of others' behavior. Observational learning is more likely to occur when the observed model's behavior is seen to be rewarded. It is a powerful source of socialization.

Using Research on Learning to Help People Learn

▶ *What should teachers learn about learning?*

Research on how people learn has implications for improved teaching and for the development of a wide range of skills. The degree  to which learning principles such as immediate reinforcement are used in teaching varies considerably from culture to culture. The importance of cognitive processes in learning is seen in active learning methods designed to encourage people to think deeply about and apply new information instead of just memorizing isolated facts. Observational learning, practice, and corrective feedback play important roles in the learning of skills.

Put It in Writing

Imagine that you have just been hired as the new principal at a high school where students' attendance and test performance has been poor and the dropout rate has been high. At a meeting with your teachers, you explain that the principles of classical and operant conditioning could be used to improve the situation. Write a one-page paper describing how these principles could be used to increase students' class attendance, study skills, and test performance. Be sure to label all the concepts and principles you use (such as "conditioned stimulus," "positive reinforcement," "conditioned response," "discriminative conditioned stimulus," "shaping," and the like).

Personal Learning Activity

Select a pair of friends or relatives of about the same age and intelligence and try teaching each of them something that is new to them but that you know well—perhaps the words to a song, a popular dance, or how to operate a digital camera, tie a tie, hit a tennis ball, or use a skateboard. Teach one person simply by telling or showing what you want him or her to learn, but for the second person, work out a set of active learning methods. (Recall that active learning requires the learner to get involved in the learning process by doing something other than just listening to a lesson.) Keep a record of which student does better at this learning task and how long it takes each student to learn. Which method was more efficient? Which student enjoyed the learning process more? Did your results confirm or conflict with research on active learning in the classroom? *For additional projects, see the Personal Learning Activities in the corresponding chapter of the study guide that accompanies this book.*

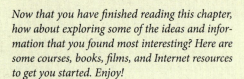

Take Action to Learn More ▶

Now that you have finished reading this chapter, how about exploring some of the ideas and information that you found most interesting? Here are some courses, books, films, and Internet resources to get you started. Enjoy!

Courses

Learning
Animal Behavior
Behavior Modification

Movies

The Deer Hunter; Quiet Rage; Schindler's List. Learned helplessness.
A Christmas Carol; The Miracle Worker. Shaping and reinforcement.
A Clockwork Orange; The Manchurian Candidate. Misconceptions about the power of classical conditioning.
Babe; Day of the Dolphin; Free Willy. Reinforcement and animal behavior.
The War. Observational learning, modeling.
Dangerous Minds; Dead Poets Society; Educating Rita; The History Boys; Mona Lisa Smile; Renaissance Man; To Sir, with Love. Learning principles in education.

Books

Kieran Egan, *The Educated Mind: How Cognitive Tools Shape Our Understanding* (University of Chicago Press, 1997). How children learn.
James Garbarino, *Lost Boys: Why Our Sons Turn Violent and How We Can Save Them* (Free Press, 1999). Development of violence examined from several perspectives, including learning theories.
Laurence Steinberg, *The Ten Basic Principles of Good Parenting* (Simon & Schuster, 2004). Learning-based parenting skills.
Martin Seligman, *What You Can Change and What You Can't: The Complete Guide to Successful Self-Improvement* (Fawcett Books, 1995). Using learning principles for self-improvement.
Martin Seligman, with Karen Reivich, Lisa Jaycox, and Jane Gillham, *The Optimistic Child* (Harper Perennial Library, 1996). The role of cognitive processes in learning and behavior.

The Web

Essentials of Psychology Book Companion Website

www.cengage.com/psychology/bernstein

Visit the book companion website to access a wealth of resources, including chapter outlines, flashcards, web links, tutorial quizzes, and more!

CENGAGENOW™ Just what you need to know NOW! Spend time on what you need to master rather than on information you already have learned. Take a pre-test for this chapter, and CengageNOW will generate a personalized study plan based on your results. The study plan will identify the topics you need to review and direct you to online resources to help you master those topics. You can then take a post-test to help you determine the concepts you have mastered and what you will need to work on. Try it out! Go to www.cengage.com/login to sign in with an access code or to purchase access to this product.

Review of Key Terms ▶

Can you define each of the key terms in the chapter? Check your definitions against those on the pages shown in parentheses in the following list or in the Glossary at the end of the book.

avoidance conditioning (p. 182)
classical conditioning (p. 174)

cognitive map (p. 196)
conditioned response (CR) (p. 174)
conditioned stimulus (CS) (p. 174)
discriminative conditioned stimuli (p. 184)
escape conditioning (p. 182)
extinction (p. 175)

habituation (p. 179)
higher order conditioning (p. 178)
insight (p. 197)
latent learning (p. 196)
law of effect (p. 181)
learned helplessness (p. 194)
learning (p. 172)

MULTIPLE-CHOICE ▶ Self Test

Select the best answer for each of the following questions. Then check your responses against the Answer Key at the end of the book.

1. Which saying best reflects learning?
   a. "A watched pot never boils."
   b. "A stitch in time saves nine."
   c. "Once burned, twice shy."
   d. "If you will it, it is no dream."

2. In a classical conditioning experiment, a puff of air was blown into Ralph's eye and he reflexively blinked. The experimenter then began flashing a green light just before presenting the puff of air. After many pairings of the green light and the puff of air, Ralph began to blink as soon as the green light appeared, whether or not the air puff followed. In this experiment, the green light is the
   a. unconditioned stimulus.   **c.** conditioned response.
   b. conditioned stimulus.   **d.** unconditioned response.

3. Suppose that the experimenter in the previous question continues presenting the green light but never again follows it with the puff of air. Ralph will soon _____ through the process of _____.
   a. blink faster; reconditioning
   b. stop blinking in response to the green light; extinction
   c. blink slower; stimulus control
   d. stop blinking; spontaneous recovery

4. Kim has gone out with both Alan and Brad this week. Even though she said she hates rock concerts, Alan took her to one, and she came home with a headache. Brad takes her to a movie she had been wanting to see. According to _____, Kim would be more likely to date Brad in the future.
   a. the law of effect
   b. the Premack principle
   c. classical conditioning theory
   d. all of the above

5. After being bitten by a dog at a young age, Najla became fearful of all dogs. Now, when Najla sees a dog, her heart races and she feels like running away. Najla has developed _____ through _____ conditioning.
   a. habituation; operant
   b. habituation; classical
   c. a phobia; operant
   d. a phobia; classical

6. The idea that knowledge is located in many areas throughout the brain rather than in one particular place is a basic assumption of _____.
   a. neural network theories
   b. classical conditioning
   c. observational learning
   d. stimulus generalization

7. Because of birth defects, Justin, a four-year-old, has had to have a number of surgical operations. As a result, just seeing a doctor or nurse in a surgical mask makes Justin fearful and tearful. At Halloween this year, Justin had the same reaction to children wearing masks. This is an example of _____.
   a. stimulus generalization
   b. stimulus discrimination
   c. vicarious learning
   d. observational learning

8. Laverne lost control and ate an entire coconut cream pie. Later that day she got the flu, complete with nausea and vomiting. After this experience, Laverne associated coconut cream pie with being sick, and now she can't even stand the smell of it. This is an example of _____, which supports the concept of _____.
   a. escape conditioning; spontaneous recovery
   b. discriminative conditioning; biopreparedness
   c. taste aversion; biopreparedness
   d. latent learning; spontaneous recovery

9. When baby Sally cries after being put to bed, her parents check to see that she is all right but otherwise ignore her. After several evenings of this treatment, Sally's bedtime crying stopped. This is an example of _____.
   a. extinction
   b. habituation
   c. higher order conditioning
   d. shaping

10. Manuel has learned that every time he cleans his room, his mother makes his favorite dessert. This is an example of _____.
   a. classical conditioning
   b. operant conditioning
   c. negative reinforcement
   d. extinction

11. Loretta gets a backache every day, but if she sits in a hot bath, the pain goes away. So she decides to take a hot bath every day. She has learned to do this through _____.

    a. positive reinforcement
    b. negative reinforcement
    c. stimulus discrimination
    d. shaping

12. Doug hates to hear children misbehaving in the grocery store, so he always shops late at night when children are not present. Doug's choice of shopping time is an example of _____.

    a. escape conditioning   b. avoidance conditioning
    c. shaping   d. secondary reinforcement

13. Ten minutes before a movie starts, the theater is filled with people who are talking and laughing. As soon as the lights go out, everyone becomes quiet. Sudden darkness serves as a _____ in this example of operant conditioning.

    a. positive reinforcer
    b. negative reinforcer
    c. punishment
    d. discriminative conditioned stimulus

14. Craig wanted to teach his dog, JoJo, to sit up and beg using operant conditioning principles. He started by giving JoJo a treat when she was simply standing. Then he gave her a treat only if she was sitting. Next, he gave her a treat only if she was sitting and had raised one paw, and so on. This is an example of _____.

    a. stimulus discrimination
    b. stimulus generalization
    c. negative reinforcement
    d. shaping

15. When Jamey has washed the dinner dishes on five evenings, his parents take him to the movies. Susan's dad occasionally gives her a dollar after she washes the dishes. Jamey is on a _____ reinforcement schedule, and Susan is on a _____ schedule.

    a. fixed interval; variable interval
    b. fixed ratio; variable ratio
    c. variable ratio; fixed interval
    d. variable interval; fixed ratio

16. Which of the following is a potential problem with using punishment to change behavior?

    a. It can produce unwanted side effects.
    b. Frequent punishment can teach children to behave aggressively.
    c. It signals that inappropriate behavior occurred but doesn't indicate what should be done instead.
    d. These are all potential problems with using punishment.

17. Whenever Javier asked his next-door neighbor to turn down her loud music, she ignored him. Later, when a new neighbor moved in next door and began playing loud music, Javier did not even bother to complain. His case demonstrates _____.

    a. latent learning
    b. learned helplessness
    c. observational learning
    d. trial and error

18. When Kenzi got a flat tire not far from campus, he walked down the street to a service station he drove by every day but had never visited. The fact that he immediately knew where it was illustrates _____.

    a. insight learning
    b. observational learning
    c. latent learning
    d. vicarious learning

19. After watching a number of people petting and playing with a dog, Najla decides that dogs aren't as scary as she'd thought. The next day, at her neighbors' house, she pets their dog. Najla's fear has been reduced through _____.

    a. classical conditioning
    b. operant conditioning
    c. spontaneous recovery
    d. observational learning

20. Whether the skill you want to learn involves a foreign language, the words of a speech, or a golf swing, the most important thing you can do is _____.

    a. delay feedback until you have almost reached perfection
    b. read all you can about the task you want to learn
    c. engage in all the practice you can
    d. work in a group

© Asia Images/Alamy

6 Memory

Have you ever forgotten where you parked your car? Have you ever had a name on the tip of your tongue but couldn't quite recall it? Researchers in the field of memory explore these common experiences. They have found that memory is a complex system. You use different kinds of memory for storing different types of information, such as personal experiences, specific skills, and abstract concepts. They have also found that once information is stored in memory, recalling it can sometimes be difficult. In this chapter, you will learn about some techniques that can help you to retrieve memories. What psychologists have learned about memory has been used to create study techniques that really work!

"'Il make him an offer he can't refuse." "I'll be back." "Trust no one." "Life is like a box of chocolates." "I see dead people." "Show me the money." "Is that your final answer?" Do you remember where you heard these words? They are memorable lines from *The Godfather, The Terminator, The X-Files, Forrest Gump, The Sixth Sense, Jerry Maguire*, and *Who Wants to Be a Millionaire*. Can you say who Private Ryan was and why he needed to be saved? And do you know which classic film character said "Play it again, Sam"? (If you don't, ask a friend who knows about old movies.) The most common answer to the latter question is Rick, the café owner played by Humphrey Bogart in *Casablanca*. Bogart never actually said this often-quoted line, though many people are sure they "remember" it.

Your memory stores vast amounts of useful and not-so-useful information from all of your experiences. This chapter will help you understand the nature of memory—how you form memories, how memory errors happen, and how you forget. ■

The Nature of Memory

▶ *How does information turn into memories?*

Memory is a funny thing. You might be able to remember the name of your first-grade teacher but not the name of someone you met five minutes ago. Mathematician John Griffith estimated that in an average lifetime, a person stores roughly five hundred times as much information as can be found in all the volumes of the *Encyclopaedia Britannica* (Hunt, 1982). Keep in mind, however, that although we retain a great deal of information, we also lose a great deal (Wixted, 2004). Consider Tatiana Cooley. She was the U.S. National Memory Champion for three years in a row, but she confesses that she is so absent-minded that she relies on Post-it Notes to remember everyday errands (Schacter, 2001). Obviously, our memory is made up of many different abilities, some of which may be better than others from person to person and from time to time.

Memory plays a critical role in your life. Without it, you wouldn't know how to shut off your alarm, take a shower, get dressed, recognize objects, or communicate. You would be unaware of your own likes and dislikes. You would have no idea of who you are. The impressive capacity of human memory depends on the operation of a complex mental system.

FIGURE 6.1 ▪ BASIC MEMORY PROCESSES

Remembering something requires, first, that the information be encoded—put in a form that can be placed in memory. It must then be stored and, finally, retrieved, or recovered. If any of these processes fails, forgetting will occur.

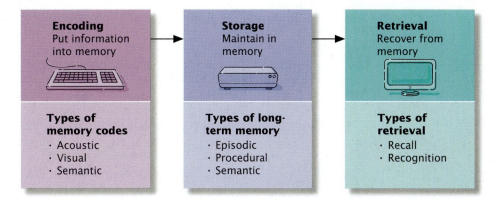

Encoding Put information into memory	Storage Maintain in memory	Retrieval Recover from memory
Types of memory codes · Acoustic · Visual · Semantic	**Types of long-term memory** · Episodic · Procedural · Semantic	**Types of retrieval** · Recall · Recognition

Basic Memory Processes

In February 2002, prison warden James Smith lost his set of master keys to the West-ville Correctional Facility. As a result, 2,559 inmates were kept under partial lockdown for eight days while the Indiana Department of Correction spent $53,000 to change locks in the affected areas. As it turned out, the warden had put the keys in his pocket when he went home, forgot he had done so, and reported the keys "missing" when they were not in their usual place in his office the next day (Associated Press, 2002). What went wrong? There are several possibilities. Memory depends on three basic processes: encoding, storage, and retrieval (see Figure 6.1). Our absent-minded warden might have had problems with any one of these processes.

First, information must be put into memory, a step that requires encoding. **Encoding** is a process that puts information to be remembered into a form that our memory system can accept and use. We use *memory codes* to translate information from the senses into mental representations of that information. Codes for **acoustic memory** (also known as **auditory memory**) represent information as sequences of sounds, such as a tune or a rhyme. Codes for **visual memory** represent information as pictures, such as the image of your best friend's face. Codes for **semantic memory** represent the general meaning of an experience. So if you see a billboard that reads "Huey's Going-Out-of-Business Sale," you might encode the sound of the words as if they had been spoken (acoustic encoding), the image of the letters as they were arranged on the sign (visual encoding), or the fact that you recently saw an ad for Huey's (semantic encoding). The type of encoding we use influences what we remember. Semantic encoding might allow you to remember the fact that an unfamiliar car was parked in your neighbors' driveway just before their house was robbed. If little or no other encoding took place, however, you might not be able to remember the make, model, or color of the car.

The second basic memory process is storage. **Storage** refers to the holding of information in your memory over time. When you recall a vacation you took in childhood or find that you can use a pogo stick many years after you last played with one, you are depending on the storage capacity of your memory.

The third memory process—**retrieval**—occurs when you find information stored in memory and bring it into consciousness. Retrieving stored information such as your address or telephone number is usually so fast and effortless that it seems automatic. The search-and-retrieval process becomes more noticeable, however, when you read a quiz question but cannot quite recall the answer. Retrieval involves both recall and recognition. To **recall** information, you have to retrieve it from memory without much help; this is what is required when you answer an essay test question or play *Jeopardy!* In **recognition,** retrieval is aided by clues, such as the response alternatives given on multiple-choice tests and the questions on *Who Wants to Be a Millionaire*. Accordingly, recognition tends to be easier than recall.

---

encoding The process of putting information into a form that the memory system can accept and use.

acoustic memory (auditory memory) Mental representations of stimuli as sounds.

visual memory Mental representations of stimuli as pictures.

semantic memory Memory for generalized knowledge about the world.

storage The process of maintaining information in the memory system over time.

retrieval The process of finding information stored in memory.

recall Retrieving information stored in memory.

recognition Awareness, based on retrieval cues, that particular information is in one's memory.

© Rick Gomez/Corbis

HOW DOES SHE DO THAT?   ▲

As she practices, this youngster is developing procedural memories of how to ride a bike that may be difficult to put into words. To appreciate the special nature of procedural memory, try writing a step-by-step description of exactly how you tie a shoe.

Learn BY **Doing**

---

episodic memory   Memory for events in one's own past.

semantic memory   Memory for generalized knowledge about the world.

procedural knowledge (procedural memory)   A type of memory containing information about how to do things.

explicit memory   Information retrieved through a conscious effort to remember something.

implicit memory   The unintentional recollection and influence of prior experiences.

Types of Memory

When was the last time you made a phone call? Who was the first president of the United States? How do you keep your balance on skates? Answering each of these questions involves different aspects of memory. To answer the first question, you must remember a particular event in your life. To answer the second one, you have to recall general knowledge that is unlikely to be tied to a specific event. And the answer to the third question is easier to demonstrate than to describe. So how many types of memory are there? No one is sure, but most research suggests that there are at least three. Each type of memory is named for the kind of information it handles: episodic, semantic, and procedural (Rajaram & Barber, 2008).

Any memory of a specific event that happened while you were present is an **episodic memory** (Tulving, 2005). It is a memory of an episode in your life. What you had for dinner yesterday, what you did last summer, or where you were last Friday night are episodic memories. **Semantic memory** contains generalized knowledge of the world—such as the fact that twelve items make a dozen—that does not involve memory of a specific event. So if you were asked "Are wrenches pets or tools?" you could answer using your semantic memory; you don't have to remember a specific episode in which you learned that wrenches are tools. As a general rule, people report episodic memories by saying, "I remember when . . ." whereas they report semantic memories by saying, "I know that . . ." (Tulving, 2000). Memory of how to do things, such as riding a bike, folding a map, or playing golf, is called **procedural memory,** or **procedural knowledge** (Cohen & Squire, 1980). Procedural knowledge often consists of a sequence of movements that are difficult or impossible to put into words. As a result, teachers of music, dance, cooking, woodworking, and other skills usually prefer to first show their students what to do rather than describe how to do it.

Many activities require all three types of memory. Consider the game of tennis. Knowing the official rules or the number of sets needed to win a match involves semantic memory. Remembering who served last requires episodic memory. And knowing how to hit the ball involves procedural memory.

Recalling these three kinds of memories can be either intentional or unintentional. When you deliberately try to remember something, such as where you went on your last vacation, the information you retrieve is an **explicit memory** (Masson & McLeod, 1992). In contrast, **implicit memory** involves the unintentional recollection and influence of prior experiences (McDermott, 2002). For example, if you were to read this chapter twice, implicit memories from your first reading would help you to read it more quickly the second time. For the same reason, you can solve a puzzle faster if you have solved it in the past. This improvement of performance—often called *priming*—is automatic, and it occurs without conscious effort. In fact, people are often unaware that their actions have been influenced by previous events (see the chapter on consciousness). Have you ever found yourself disliking someone you just met but you didn't know why? The person might have triggered an implicit memory of a similar-looking person who once treated you badly. In such cases, we are usually unaware of any connection between the two individuals (Lewicki, 1992). Because some influential events cannot be recalled even when people try to do so, implicit memory has been said to involve "retention without remembering" (Roediger, Guynn, & Jones, 1995).

Models of Memory

We remember some information far better than other information. Suppose your friends throw a surprise party for you. When you enter the room, you might barely notice the flash of a camera. Later, you cannot recall it at all. And you might forget in a few seconds the name of a person you met at the party. But if you live to be a hundred, you will never forget where the party took place or how surprised and pleased you were. Why do some things stay in memory forever, whereas others barely make an impression? Each of four ways of thinking about memory, called *models* of memory, provides a somewhat different explanation. Let's see what the levels-of-processing, transfer-appropriate processing, parallel distributed processing, and information-processing models have to say about memory.

Levels of Processing

The **levels-of-processing model of memory** suggests that memory depends on the extent to which you encode and process information when you first encounter it (Craik & Lockhart, 1972). Consider, for example, the task of remembering a phone number you just heard on the radio. If you were unable to write it down, you would probably repeat the number over and over to yourself until you could find a pen or get to your phone. This repetition process is called **maintenance rehearsal.** It can be an effective method for encoding information temporarily, but what if you need to remember something for hours, months, or years? In that case, you would be better off using **elaborative rehearsal,** a process in which you relate new material to information you already have stored in memory. For example, instead of trying to remember a new person's name by simply repeating it to yourself, you could try thinking about how the name is related to something you know well. So if you are introduced to a man named Jim Crews, you might think, "He is as tall as my Uncle Jim, who always wears a crew cut."

Study after study has shown that memory is improved when people use elaborative rehearsal rather than maintenance rehearsal (Jahnke & Nowaczyk, 1998). According to the levels-of-processing model of memory, the reason is that material is processed more "deeply" when elaborative rehearsal is used (Lockhart & Craik, 1990; Roediger & Gallo, 2001; Roediger, Gallo, & Geraci, 2002). The more you think about new information, organize it, and relate it to something you already know, the "deeper" the processing and the better your memory of the information becomes. Teachers use this idea when they ask students not only to define a new word but also to use it in a sentence. Figuring out how to use the new word takes deeper processing than merely defining it does. (The next time you come across an unfamiliar word in this book, don't just read its definition. Try to use the word in a sentence by coming up with an example of the concept that is related to your knowledge and experience.)

Learn BY Doing

Transfer-Appropriate Processing

Level of processing is not the only factor that affects memory (Baddeley, 1992). Another critical factor, suggested by the **transfer-appropriate processing model of memory,** is how the encoding process matches up with what is later retrieved. In one study, for example, half the students in a class were told that their next exam would contain multiple-choice questions. The rest of the students were told to expect essay questions. Only half the students actually got the type of exam they expected, however. These students did much better on the exam than those who took an unexpected type of exam. Apparently, in studying for the exam the two groups used encoding strategies that were most appropriate to the type of exam they expected. Those who tried to retrieve the information in a way that did not match their encoding method had a harder time (d'Ydewalle & Rosselle, 1978). Results such as these indicate that how well the encoding method transfers to the retrieval task is just as important as the depth of processing.

Parallel Distributed Processing

A third way of thinking about memory is based on **parallel distributed processing (PDP) models of memory** (Rumelhart & McClelland, 1986). These models suggest that new experiences do more than provide specific facts that are stored and later retrieved one at a time. Those facts are also combined with what you already know so that each new experience changes your overall understanding of the world and how it operates. For example, when you first arrived on campus, you learned lots of specific facts, such as where classes are held, what time the library closes, and where to get the best pizza. Over time, these and many other facts about student life form a network of information that creates a more general understanding of how the whole system works. The development of this network makes experienced students not only more knowledgeable than new

levels-of-processing model of memory A model that suggests that memory depends on the degree or depth to which we mentally process information.

maintenance rehearsal A memorization method that involves repeating information over and over to keep it in memory.

elaborative rehearsal A memorization method that relates new information to information already stored in memory.

transfer-appropriate processing model of memory A model that suggests that memory depends on how the encoding process matches up with what is later retrieved.

parallel distributed processing (PDP) models of memory Memory models in which new experiences are seen as changing one's overall knowledge base.

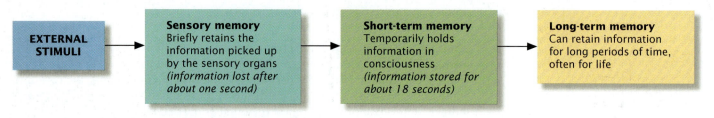

FIGURE 6.2   ■   THREE STAGES OF MEMORY

This traditional information-processing model describes the three stages in the memory system.

© Frank Siteman/Stock, Boston

SENSORY MEMORY AT WORK ▲

In a darkened room, ask a friend to hold a small flashlight and move it very slowly in a circle. You will see a moving point of light. If it appears to have a "tail," like a comet, that is your sensory memory of the light before it fades. Now ask your friend to move the light faster. You should now see a complete circle of light, because as the light moves, its impression on your sensory memory does not have time to fade before the circle is completed. A similar process allows us to see "sparkler circles."

Learn BY Doing

information-processing model of memory A model that suggests that information must pass through sensory memory, short-term memory, and long-term memory in order to become firmly embedded in memory.

students but also more sophisticated. It allows them to, say, allocate their study time in order to do well in their most important courses and to plan a schedule that doesn't conflict with work commitments and maybe even avoids early morning classes—and certain professors.

Using this network concept, PDP models of memory see each unit of knowledge as connected to every other unit. The connections between units become stronger as they are experienced together more frequently. In other words, your knowledge about the world is distributed across a network of associations that all operate at the same time, in parallel. This network allows you to quickly and efficiently draw inferences and generalizations about the world. For example, because of your network of associations, just seeing the word "chair" allows you to know immediately what a chair looks like, what it is used for, where it tends to be located, who might buy one, and the like. PDP models of memory explain this process very effectively.

Information Processing   The **information-processing model of memory** is probably the most influential and comprehensive memory model. It suggests that for information to be firmly implanted in memory, it must pass through three stages of mental processing: sensory memory, short-term memory, and long-term memory (Atkinson & Shiffrin, 1968; see Figure 6.2).

In *sensory memory*, information from the senses—sights or sounds, for example—is held very briefly before being lost. But if information in sensory memory is attended to, analyzed, and encoded as a meaningful pattern, we say that it has been *perceived* (see the chapter on sensation and perception). Information in sensory memory that has been perceived can now enter *short-term memory*. If nothing further is done with it, that information will disappear in less than twenty seconds. However, if the information in short-term memory is further processed, it may be encoded into *long-term memory*, where it may remain indefinitely.

The act of reading illustrates all three stages of memory processing. As you read any sentence in this book, light energy reflected from the page reaches your eyes, where it is converted to neural activity and registered in your sensory memory. If you pay attention to these visual stimuli, your perception of the patterns of light can be held in short-term memory. This stage of memory holds the early parts of the sentence so that they can be integrated and understood as you read the rest of the sentence. As you read, you are constantly recognizing words by matching your perceptions of them with the patterns and meanings you have stored in long-term memory. In other words, all three stages of memory are necessary for you to understand a sentence.

Today's versions of the information-processing model emphasize these constant interactions among sensory, short-term, and long-term memory. For example, sensory memory can be thought of as that part of your knowledge base (or long-term memory) that is momentarily activated by information sent to the brain via the sensory nerves. And short-term memory can be thought of as that part of your knowledge base that is the focus of attention at any given moment (Cowan, 2008; Massaro & Cowan, 1993). Like perception, memory is an active process, and what is already in long-term memory influences how new information is encoded (Cowan, 1988). To understand this interaction better, try the exercise in Figure 6.3.

FIGURE 6.3 ■ THE ROLE OF LONG TERM MEMORY IN UNDERSTANDING NEW INFORMATION

Read the paragraph shown here, then turn away and try to recall as much of it as you can. It probably didn't make make much sense, and it was probably difficult to remember. But if you read it again after checking the footnote on page 216, the meaning will not only be clearer but it will now be much easier to remember (try it again!). Why? Because knowing the title of the paragraph allows you to retrieve from long-term memory what you already know about the topic (Bransford & Johnson, 1972).

Learn BY Doing

Source: Howard (1983).

The procedure is actually quite simple. First, you arrange items into different groups. Of course, one pile may be sufficient, depending on how much there is to do. If you have to go somewhere else due to lack of facilities that is the next step; otherwise, you are pretty well set. It is important not to overdo things. That is, it is better to do too few things at once than too many. In the short run, this may not seem important, but complications can easily arise. A mistake can be expensive as well. At first, the whole procedure will seem complicated. Soon, however, it will become just another facet of life. It is difficult to foresee any end to the necessity for this task in the immediate future, but then, one never can tell. After the procedure is completed, one arranges the materials into different groups again. Then they can be put into their appropriate places. Eventually they will be used once more, and the whole cycle will then have to be repeated. However, that is part of life.

"In Review: Models of Memory" summarizes the four memory models we have discussed. Each of these models provides an explanation of why we remember some things and forget others, but which model offers the best explanation? The answer is that more than one model may be required to understand memory. Just as it is helpful for physicists to characterize light in terms of both waves and particles, psychologists find it useful to think of memory as both a sequential process, as suggested by the information-processing model, and as a parallel process, as suggested by parallel distributed processing models.

In Review

Models of Memory

MODEL	ASSUMPTIONS
Levels of processing	The more deeply material is processed, the better our memory of it.
Transfer-appropriate processing	Retrieval is improved when we try to recall material in a way that matches how the material was encoded.
Parallel distributed processing (PDP)	New experiences add to and alter our overall knowledge base; they are not separate, unconnected facts. Networks of associations allow us to draw inferences and make generalizations about the world.
Information-processing	Information is processed in three stages: sensory memory, short-term memory, and long-term memory.

?

1. The value of elaborative rehearsal over maintenance rehearsal has been cited as evidence for the _____ model of memory.

2. Deliberately trying to remember something means using your _____ memory.

3. Playing the piano uses _____ memory.

Storing New Memories

▶ *What am I most likely to remember?*

The storage of information is critical to memory because we can retrieve only information that has been stored. According to the information-processing model, sensory memory, short-term memory, and long-term memory each provide a different type of storage. Let's take a closer look at these three memory systems in order to better understand how they work—and sometimes fail.

Sensory Memory

To recognize incoming information, the brain must analyze and compare it with what is already stored in long-term memory. This process is very quick, but it still takes time. The major function of **sensory memory** is to hold information long enough for it to be processed further (Nairne, 2003). This "holding" function is the job of the **sensory registers,** which act as temporary storage bins. There is a separate register for each of the five senses. Each register can store a nearly complete representation of a sensory stimulus, but it can do so only briefly, often for less than one second (Eysenck & Keane, 2005).

Sensory memory helps us experience a constant flow of information, even if that flow is interrupted. To see this for yourself, move your head and eyes slowly from left to right. It may seem as though your eyes are moving smoothly, like a movie camera scanning a scene, but that's not what is happening. Your eyes fixate at one point for about one-fourth of a second and then rapidly jump to a new position. You perceive smooth motion because you hold the scene in your visual sensory register (also known as your **iconic memory**) until your eyes fixate again. Similarly, when you listen to someone speak, your auditory sensory register allows you to experience a smooth flow of information, even though there are actually short silences between or within words.

The fact that sensory memories fade quickly if they are not processed further is actually an adaptive characteristic of the memory system (Baddeley, 1998). You simply cannot deal with all of the sights, sounds, odors, tastes, and touch sensations that come to your sense organs at any given moment. Using **selective attention,** you focus your mental resources on only part of the stimuli around you, thus controlling what information is processed further in short-term memory.

Short-Term Memory and Working Memory

The sensory registers allow your memory system to develop a representation of a stimulus. However, they can't perform the more thorough analysis needed if the information is going to be used in some way. That function is accomplished by short-term memory and working memory.

Short-term memory (STM) is the part of your memory system that stores limited amounts of information for up to about eighteen seconds. When you check the building directory to see which floor your new dentist's office is on, and then keep that number in mind as you press the correct elevator button, you are using short-term memory. **Working memory** is the part of the memory system that allows us to mentally work with, or manipulate, the information being held in short-term memory. When you mentally calculate what time you have to leave home in order to have lunch on campus, return a library book, and still get to class on time, you are using working memory.

Short-term memory is actually a component of working memory, and together these memory systems allow us to do many kinds of mental work (Baddeley, 2003; Engle & Oransky, 1999). Suppose you are buying something for eighty-three cents. You go through your change and pick out two quarters, two dimes, two nickels, and three

ANSWER FOR FIGURE 6.3: The title of the paragraph is "Washing Clothes."

---

sensory memory   A type of memory that is very brief but lasts long enough to connect one impression to the next.

sensory registers   Memory systems that briefly hold incoming information.

iconic memory   The sensory register for visual information.

selective attention   The process of focusing mental resources on only part of the stimulus field.

short-term memory (STM)   A stage of memory in which information normally lasts less than twenty seconds; a component of working memory.

working memory   Memory that allows us to mentally work with, or manipulate, information being held in short-term memory.

```
9 2 5
8 6 4 2
3 7 6 5 4
6 2 7 4 1 8
0 4 0 1 4 7 3
1 9 2 2 3 5 3 0
4 8 6 8 5 4 3 3 2
2 5 3 1 9 7 1 7 6 8
8 5 1 2 9 6 1 9 4 5 0
9 1 8 5 4 6 9 4 2 9 3 7
```

FIGURE 6.4 ■ THE CAPACITY OF SHORT-TERM MEMORY

Here is a test of your immediate memory span (Howard, 1983). Ask someone to read to you the numbers in the top row at the rate of about one per second, then try to repeat them back in the same order. Then try the next row and the one after that, until you make a mistake. Your immediate memory span is the maximum number of items you can repeat back perfectly.

Learn BY **Doing**

immediate memory span The maximum number of items a person can recall perfectly after one presentation of the items.

chunking Organizing individual stimuli so that they will be perceived as larger units of meaningful information.

pennies. To do this you use both short-term memory and working memory to remember the price, retrieve the rules of addition from long-term memory, and keep a running count of how much change you have so far. Now try to recall how many windows there are on the front of the house or apartment where you grew up. In answering this question, you probably formed a mental image of the building. You used one kind of working-memory process to form that image and then you maintained the image in short-term memory while you "worked" on it by counting the windows. So working memory has at least two components: *maintenance* (holding information in short-term memory) and *manipulation* (working on that information).

 Learn BY **Doing**

Encoding in Short-Term Memory

The encoding of information in short-term memory is much more elaborate and varied than encoding in the sensory registers (Brandimonte, Hitch, & Bishop, 1992). Acoustic encoding (by sound) seems to dominate. This conclusion comes from research on the mistakes people make when encoding information in short-term memory. These mistakes tend to involve the substitution of similar sounds. For instance, Robert Conrad (1964) showed people strings of letters and asked them to repeat the letters immediately. Among their most common mistakes was the replacement of the correct letter with another that sounded like it. So if the correct letter was *C*, it was often replaced with a *D*, *P*, or *T*. The participants made these mistakes even though the letters were presented visually, without any sound. Studies in several cultures have also shown that items are more difficult to remember if they sound similar. For example, native English speakers do less well when they try to remember a string of letters like *ECVTGB* (which all have similar sounds) than when trying to remember one like *KRLDQS* (in which there are different sounds).

Encoding in short-term memory is not always acoustic, however. Information in short-term memory also can be encoded visually, semantically, and even kinesthetically (in terms of physical movements; Best, 1999). In one study, deaf people were shown a list of words and then asked to immediately write down as many as they could remember (Shand, 1982). When these participants made errors, they wrote words that are expressed through similar *hand movements* in American Sign Language rather than words that *sounded* similar to the correct words. Apparently, these individuals had encoded the words on the basis of the movements they would use when making the signs for them.

Storage Capacity of Short-Term Memory

How much information can you hold in short-term memory? The simple test presented in Figure 6.4 will help you determine your **immediate memory span,** which is the largest number of items you can recall perfectly after one presentation. If your memory span is like most people's, you can repeat six or seven items from the test in this figure. And you should come up with about the same result whether you use digits, letters, words, or virtually anything else (Pollack, 1953). George Miller (1956) noticed that many studies using a variety of tasks showed the same limit on the ability to process information. This "magic number," which is seven plus or minus two, appears to be the immediate memory span or capacity of short-term memory, at least in laboratory settings. In addition, the "magic number" refers not only to discrete elements, such as words or digits, but also to *chunks*, meaningful groupings of information that are produced by a process called **chunking.**

To see the difference between discrete elements and chunks, read the following letters to a friend, pausing at each dash: *FB-IAO-LM-TVQ-VCB-MW*. The chances are very good that your friend will not be able to repeat this string of letters perfectly. Why? There are fifteen letters, which exceeds most people's immediate memory span. Now, give your friend the test again, but group the letters like this: *FBI-AOL-MTV-QVC-BMW*. Your friend will probably repeat the string easily. Although the same fifteen letters are involved, they will be processed as only five meaningful chunks of information.

 Learn BY **Doing**

The Power of Chunking

Chunks of information can be quite complex. If you heard someone say, "The boy in the red shirt kicked his mother in the shin," you could

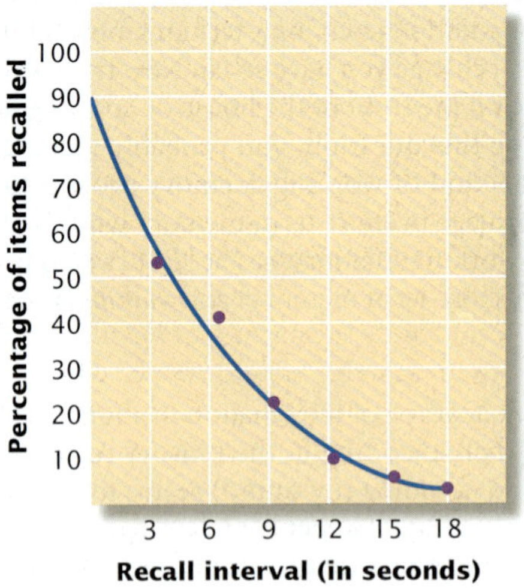

FIGURE 6.5 ■ **FORGETTING IN SHORT-TERM MEMORY**

This graph shows the percentage of items recalled after various intervals during which rehearsal was prevented. Notice that forgetting was virtually complete after a delay of eighteen seconds. *Source*: Data from Peterson & Peterson (1959).

probably repeat the sentence perfectly. Yet it contains twelve words and forty-three letters. How can you repeat the sentence so effortlessly? The answer is that you are able to build bigger and bigger chunks of information (Ericsson & Staszewski, 1989). In this case, you might represent "the boy in the red shirt" as one chunk of information rather than as six words or nineteen letters. Similarly, "kicked his mother" and "in the shin" represent separate chunks of information.

Learning to use bigger and bigger chunks of information can improve short-term memory. In fact, children's short-term memories improve partly because they gradually become able to hold as many as seven chunks in memory and also because they get better at grouping information into chunks (Servan-Schreiber & Anderson, 1990). Adults also can greatly increase the capacity of their short-term memory by using more efficient chunking. For example, after extensive training, one college student increased his immediate memory span from seven to eighty digits (Neisser, 2000a). So although the capacity of short-term memory is more or less constant (from five to nine chunks of meaningful information), the size of those chunks can vary tremendously.

Duration of Short-Term Memory   Why don't you remember every phone number you ever called or every conversation you ever had? The answer is that unless you do something to retain it, information in short-term memory is soon forgotten. This feature of short-term memory is adaptive because it gets rid of a lot of useless information; indeed, there are rare cases of people whose inability to forget interferes with their ability to concentrate (Parker, Cahill, & McGaugh, 2006). But it can also be inconvenient. You may have discovered this if you ever looked up a phone number, got distracted before you could call it, and then forgot the number.

How long does information remain in short-term memory if you don't keep rehearsing it? John Brown (1958) and Lloyd and Margaret Peterson (1959) devised the **Brown-Peterson distractor technique** to measure the duration of short-term memory when no rehearsal is allowed. In this procedure, participants are presented with a group of three letters, such as *GRB*. They then count backward by threes from some number until they get a signal. Counting serves as a distraction that prevents the participants from rehearsing the letters. At the signal, they stop counting and try to recall the letters. By varying the number of seconds spent counting backward, the experimenter can determine how much forgetting takes place over time. As you can see in Figure 6.5, information in short-term memory is forgotten rapidly: After only eighteen seconds, participants can remember almost nothing. Evidence from other such experiments also suggests that unrehearsed information can be held in short-term memory for no more than about eighteen seconds. However, if the information is rehearsed or processed further in some other way, it may be encoded into long-term memory.

Long-Term Memory

When people talk about memory, they are usually referring to long-term memory. **Long-term memory (LTM)** is the part of the memory system where encoding and storage capabilities can produce memories that last a lifetime.

Encoding in Long-Term Memory   Some information is encoded into long-term memory even if we make no conscious effort to memorize it (Ellis, 1991). However, putting information into long-term memory is often the result of more elaborate and more conscious processing that usually involves *semantic encoding*. As we mentioned earlier, semantic encoding often leaves out details in favor of the more general underlying meaning of the information.

In a classic study, Jacqueline Sachs (1967) demonstrated the dominance of semantic encoding in long-term memory. Her participants first listened to tape recordings of people speaking. She then showed them sets of similar sentences and asked them to say which contained the exact wording heard on the tape. Participants did well at this task when tested immediately, using mainly short-term memory. However, after twenty-seven seconds, they couldn't be sure which of two sentences they had heard.

Brown-Peterson distractor technique A method for determining how long unrehearsed information remains in short-term memory.

long-term memory (LTM) The stage of memory that researchers believe has an unlimited capacity to store new information.

For example, they could not remember whether they had heard "He sent a letter about it to Galileo, the great Italian scientist" or "A letter about it was sent to Galileo, the great Italian scientist." They didn't do as well after the delay because they had to recall information from long-term memory, where they had encoded the general meaning of what they had heard but not the exact wording.

Perhaps you are thinking, "So what?" After all, the two sentences mean the same thing. Unfortunately, when people encode the general meaning of information they hear or read, they can make mistakes about the details (Brewer, 1977). For example, after listening to a list of words such as *cold, white, ice, winter, frosty, blizzard, frozen, drift, flurries, parka, shovel, skis, sled,* and *flakes,* people often remember having heard the related word "snow" even though it was not presented (Gallo, 2006; Roediger & McDermott, 1995). This kind of false memory can be a problem when recalling exact words is important—such as in the courtroom, during business negotiations, and in discussions between students and teachers about previous agreements. Later in this chapter we show that such mistakes occur partly because people encode into long-term memory not only the general meaning of information but also what they think and assume about that information (McDermott & Chan, 2006).

Counterfeiters depend on the fact that people encode the general meaning of visual stimuli rather than specific details. For example, look at Figure 6.6 and find the correct drawing of a U.S. penny (Nickerson & Adams, 1979). Research shows that most people from the United States are unsuccessful at this task. People from other countries do poorly at recognizing their country's coins, too (Jones, 1990). This research has prompted the U.S. Department of the Treasury to begin using more distinctive drawings on the paper currency it distributes.

Storage Capacity of Long-Term Memory   The capacity of long-term memory is extremely large. In fact, many psychologists believe that it is literally unlimited (Matlin, 1998). There is no way to prove this, but we do know that people store vast quantities of information in long-term memory that can be remembered remarkably well after long periods of time. For example, people are amazingly accurate at recognizing the faces of their high school classmates after having not seen them for over twenty-five years (Bruck, Cavanagh, & Ceci, 1991). They also do surprisingly well on tests of a foreign language or algebra fifty years after having formally studied these subjects (Bahrick & Hall, 1991; Bahrick et al., 1994).

But long-term memories are also subject to distortion. In one study illustrating this point, students were asked to describe where they were and what they were doing at the moment they heard about the not-guilty verdict in the 1995 O. J. Simpson murder trial (Schmolck, Buffalo, & Squire, 2000). The students first reported their recollections three days after the verdict and then again after either fifteen or thirty-two months. Only half the recollections reported at fifteen months were accurate, and 11 percent contained major errors or distortions. Among those reporting after thirty-two months, 71 percent of their recollections were inaccurate, and just over 40 percent contained major errors or distortions. For example, three days after the verdict, a student said he heard about it while in a campus lounge with many other students around him. Thirty-two months later, this same person recalled hearing the news in the living room of his home with his father and sister. Amazingly, most of the students whose

---

FIGURE 6.6 ◼ **ENCODING INTO LONG-TERM MEMORY**

Which is the correct image of a U.S. penny? (See page 220 for answers.) *Source*: Nickerson & Adams (1979).

(A)

(B)

(C)

(D)

(E)

A REMARKABLE MEMORY ▶

Using only his long-term memory, Franco Magnani created amazingly accurate paintings of his hometown in Italy even though he had not seen it for more than 30 years (Sacks, 1992). People like Magnani display *eidetic imagery,* commonly called *photographic memory.* About 5 percent of school-age children have eidetic imagery, but it is extremely rare in adults (Haber, 1979). You can test yourself for eidetic imagery by drawing a detailed picture or map of a place that you know well but have not seen recently, then comparing your version with a photo or map of the same place. How did you do?

Learn BY Doing

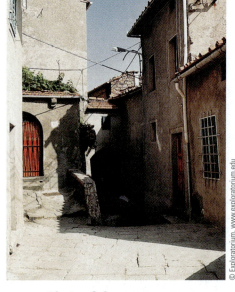

Magnani's painting   **Photo of the same scene**

memories had been greatly distorted over time were unaware of the distortion; they were very confident that their reports were accurate. Similar findings have been reported in relation to people's memories of the September 11, 2001, terrorist attacks on New York and Washington, D.C. Even when these memories changed as time went by, people remained confident in their accuracy (Talarico & Rubin, 2003). Later, we see that such overconfidence can also appear in courtroom testimony by eyewitnesses to crime.

Improve Your Grade
Tutorial: Memory: Primacy and Recency Effect

Distinguishing Between Short-Term and Long-Term Memory

Some psychologists argue that short-term memory and long-term memory have different features and obey different laws (Cowan, 1988; Talmi et al., 2005). ("In Review: Storing New Memories" summarizes the characteristics of these systems.) Evidence that information is transferred from short-term memory to a distinct storage system comes primarily from experiments on recall.

You can conduct your own recall experiment by reading aloud a list of words at a slow pace (about one word every two seconds). After reading the list just once, look away and write down as many of the words as you can, in any order. Here is a list you can use: *desk, chalk, pencil, chair, paperclip, book, eraser, folder, briefcase, essays, tree, soup, ocean, cabin, monster, bridge.* Did you notice anything about which words you remembered and which ones you forgot? If you are like most people, your recall depended partly on where each word appeared on the list—its serial position. As shown in the serial-position curve in Figure 6.7, memory researchers have found that recall tends to be very good for the first two or three words in a list. This result is called the **primacy effect.** The probability of recall decreases for words in the middle of the list and then rises dramatically for the last few words. The ease of recalling words near the end of the list is called the **recency effect.** The primacy effect may reflect the rehearsal that puts early words into long-term memory. The recency effect may occur because the last few words are still in short-term memory when you try to recall the list (Glanzer & Cunitz, 1966; Koppenaal & Glanzer, 1990).

Learn BY Doing

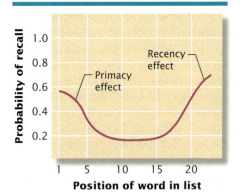

FIGURE 6.7 ■ A SERIAL-POSITION CURVE

This curve shows the probability of recalling items that appear at various serial positions in a list. Generally, the first several items and the last several items are most likely to be recalled.

ANSWER FOR FIGURE 6.6: Drawing A shows the correct penny image.

In Review

STORING NEW MEMORIES

STORAGE SYSTEM	FUNCTION	CAPACITY	DURATION
Sensory memory	Briefly holds representations of stimuli from each sense for further processing	Large: absorbs all sensory input from a particular stimulus	Less than one second
Short-term and working memory	Hold information in awareness and manipulate it to accomplish mental work	Five to nine distinct items or chunks of information	About 18 seconds
Long-term memory	Stores new information indefinitely	Unlimited	Unlimited

1. *If you looked up a phone number but forgot it before you could call it, the information was probably lost from _____ memory.*
2. *The capacity of short-term memory is about _____ to _____ items.*
3. *Encoding is usually _____ in short-term memory and _____ in long-term memory.*

Retrieving Memories

 How do I retrieve stored memories?

Most people have trouble remembering things at one time or another. Have you ever been unable to recall the name of a musical group or movie star, only to think of it the next day? Remembering requires not only the encoding and storing of information but also the ability to bring it into consciousness. In other words, you have to be able to *retrieve* it.

Retrieval Cues and Encoding Specificity

Retrieval cues are stimuli that help you retrieve information from long-term memory. As mentioned earlier, retrieval cues are what make recognition tasks (such as multiple-choice tests) easier than recall tasks (such as essay exams).

The effectiveness of retrieval cues depends on the extent to which they tap into information that was encoded at the time of learning (Tulving, 1983). This rule is known as the **encoding specificity principle.** Because long-term memories are often encoded in terms of their general meaning, cues that trigger the meaning of the stored information tend to work best. Imagine that you have learned a long list of sentences. One of them was either (1) "The man lifted the piano" or (2) "The man tuned the piano." Now suppose that on a later recall test, you were given the retrieval cue "something heavy." This cue would probably help you to remember the first sentence (because you probably encoded something about the weight of a piano as you read it) but not the second sentence (because it has nothing to do with weight). Similarly, the cue "makes nice sounds" would probably help you recall the second sentence but not the first (Barclay et al., 1974).

Context and State Dependence

Have you ever taken a test in a classroom other than the one where you learned the material for that test? If so, was your performance affected? Research has shown that people tend to recall more of what they have learned when they are in the place where they learned it (Smith, Glenberg, & Bjork, 1978). Why? Because if they have encoded features of the environment where the learning occurred, these features can later act as retrieval cues (Richardson-Klavehn & Bjork, 1988). In one experiment, people studied a series of photos while in the presence of a particular odor. Later, they reviewed a larger set of photos and tried to recognize the ones they had seen earlier. Half of the

primacy effect A characteristic of memory in which recall is particularly good for the first two or three items in a list.

recency effect A characteristic of memory in which recall is particularly good for the last few items in a list.

retrieval cues Stimuli that allow or help people to recall information.

encoding specificity principle A principle that states that the ability of a cue to aid retrieval depends on how well it taps into information that was originally encoded.

CONTEXT-DEPENDENT MEMORIES ▶

Many people attending a reunion at their old high school find that being in the building again provides context cues that help bring back memories of their school days. Visit your elementary school or high school and see if it helps you to remember things you'd forgotten. Be sure to look into specific rooms where you had classes or assemblies, and check out the restroom and your old locker, too.

Learn
BY
Doing

© Mary Kate Denny/PhotoEdit

people were exposed to the original odor while taking the recognition test. The rest were tested in the presence of another odor. Those who smelled the same odor during learning and testing did significantly better on the recognition task than those who were tested in the presence of a different odor. The matching odor served as a powerful retrieval cue (Cann & Ross, 1989).

Context-specific memories, also known as **context-specific learning,** refers to memories that are helped or hindered by similarities or differences in environmental context. This context-specificity effect is not always strong (Smith, Vela, & Williamson, 1988), but some students do find it helpful to study for a test in the classroom where the test will be given.

Sometimes we also encode information about how we were feeling during a learning experience, and this information, too, can act as a retrieval cue. When our internal state influences retrieval, we have a **state-dependent memory,** also known as **state-dependent learning.** For example, if people learn new material while under the influence of marijuana, they tend to recall it better if they are also tested under the influence of marijuana (Eich et al., 1975). Similar effects have been found with alcohol (Overton, 1984) and other psychoactive drugs (Eich, 1989), although memory is best when people aren't using any drugs during encoding or retrieval. Mood states, too, can affect memory (Eich & Macaulay, 2000). College students are more likely to remember pleasant events when they are feeling good at the time of recall (Bower, 1981; Eich & Macaulay, 2007). Negative events are more likely to be recalled when people are feeling sad or angry (Lewinsohn & Rosenbaum, 1987). These *mood congruency* effects are strongest when people try to recall personally meaningful episodes (Eich & Metcalfe, 1989). The more meaningful the experience, the more likely it is that the memory has been colored by their mood. (See "In Review: Factors Affecting Retrieval from Long-Term Memory.")

Retrieval from Semantic Memory

The retrieval situations we have discussed so far are relevant to episodic memory—our memory for events. But how do we retrieve information from semantic memory, where we store our general knowledge about the world? Researchers studying this question typically ask participants general knowledge questions, such as (1) Are fish minerals? (2) Is a beagle a dog? (3) Do birds fly? and (4) Does a car have legs? As you might imagine, most people answer such questions correctly. But by measuring how long it takes to answer them, psychologists gain important clues about how semantic memory is organized and how we retrieve information from it.

context-specific memory (context-specific learning) Memories that are helped or hindered by similarities or differences between the contexts in which they are learned and recalled.

state-dependent memory (state-dependent learning) Memory that is helped or hindered by similarities or differences in a person's internal state during learning versus recall.

In Review

Factors Affecting Retrieval from Long-Term Memory

PROCESS	EFFECT ON MEMORY
Encoding specificity	Retrieval cues are effective only to the extent that they tap into information that was originally encoded.
Context-specific memory	Retrieval is most successful when it occurs in the same environment where the information was originally learned.
State-dependent memory	Retrieval is most successful when people are in the same physiological or psychological state as when they originally learned the information.

1. Stimuli called _____ help you recall information stored in long-term memory.
2. If it is easier to remember something in the place where you learned it, you have _____ learning.
3. The tendency to remember the last few items in a list is called the _____ effect.

Semantic Networks

Semantic Networks   One view of semantic memory suggests that virtually everything we know about, including concepts such as "bird" or "animal," is represented in a dense network of associations (Churchland, 1989). Figure 6.8 presents just a tiny part of what our *semantic memory network* might look like. In general, semantic network theories suggest that information is retrieved from memory through the principle of **spreading activation** (Medin, Ross, & Markman, 2001). In other words, when you think about some concept, it becomes activated in the network and this activation begins to "spread" down all the paths that are related to it. So if you are asked if a robin is a bird, the concepts of both "robin" and "bird" will become activated and the spreading activation from each will intersect somewhere in these paths. When they do, you know what answer to give.

Some associations in the network are stronger than others, as illustrated by the thicker lines between some concepts in Figure 6.8. For instance, you probably have a stronger association between "bat" and "wings" than between "bat" and "mammal." Spreading activation travels faster along stronger paths than along weaker ones. As a result, you'd probably respond more quickly to "Can a bat fly?" than to "Is a bat a mammal?"

Because of the tight organization of semantic networks and the speed at which activation spreads through them, we can gain access to an enormous body of knowledge about the world quickly and effortlessly. We can retrieve not only facts we have learned from others but also knowledge that allows us to draw our own conclusions and inferences (Matlin, 1998). For example, imagine answering these two questions: (1) Is a robin a bird? and (2) Is a robin a living thing? You can probably answer the first question "directly," because you probably learned this fact at some point in your life. However, you may never have consciously thought about the second question, so answering it requires some inference. Figure 6.8 illustrates the path to that inference. Because you know that a robin is a bird, a bird is an animal, and animals are living things, you infer that a robin must be a living thing. As you might expect, however, it takes slightly longer to answer the second question than the first.

Retrieving Incomplete Knowledge

Retrieving Incomplete Knowledge   Figure 6.8 shows that concepts such as "bird" or "living thing" are represented in semantic memory as unique sets of features or attributes. As a result, there may be times when you can retrieve some features of a

spreading activation   In semantic network theories of memory, a principle that explains how information is retrieved.

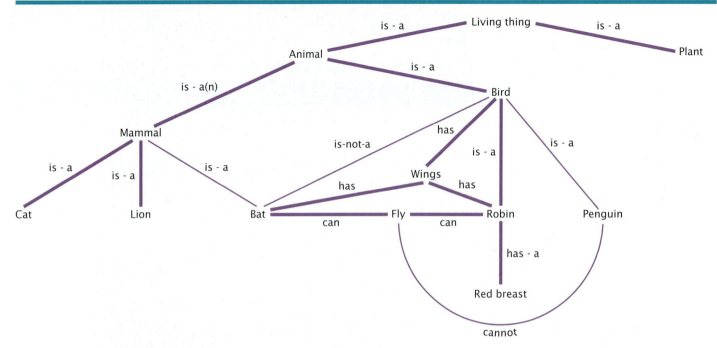

FIGURE 6.8 ■ SEMANTIC MEMORY NETWORKS

This drawing represents just a small part of a network of semantic associations. Semantic network theories of memory suggest that networks like these allow us to retrieve specific pieces of previously learned information, draw conclusions about how concepts are related, and make new inferences about the world.

concept from your semantic network but not enough of them to identify the concept. For example, you might know that there is an animal that has wings, can fly, and is not a bird and yet be unable to retrieve its name (Connor, Balota, & Neely, 1992). When this happens, you are retrieving *incomplete knowledge*. (The animal in question is a bat.)

You have probably experienced a particular example of incomplete knowledge called the *tip-of-the-tongue phenomenon*. In a typical experiment on this phenomenon, participants listen to dictionary definitions and are asked to name the word being defined (Brown & McNeill, 1966). If they can't recall the correct word, they are asked if they can recall any feature of it, such as its first letter or how many syllables it has. People are surprisingly good at this task, indicating that they are able to retrieve at least some knowledge of the word (Brennen et al., 1990). Most people experience the tip-of-the-tongue phenomenon about once a week; older people tend to experience it more often than younger people (Brown, 1991; Brown & Nix, 1996).

Constructing Memories

 How accurate are my memories?

Our memories are affected by what we experience but also by what we already know about the world (Schacter, Norman, & Koutstaal, 1998). We use that existing knowledge to organize the new information we encounter and we fill in gaps in that information as we encode and retrieve it (Sherman & Bessenoff, 1999). These processes are called *constructive memory*.

In one study of constructive memory, undergraduates were asked to wait for several minutes in the office of a graduate student (Brewer & Treyens, 1981). Later, they were asked to recall everything that was in the office. Most of the students mistakenly "remembered" seeing books, even though there were none. Apparently, the general knowledge that graduate students read many books influenced the participants' memory of what was in the room (Roediger, Meade, & Bergman, 2001). In another study, participants read one of two versions of a story about a man and woman at a ski lodge. One version ended with the man proposing marriage to the woman.

CONSTRUCTIVE MEMORY ▶

Here is a photo of the office used in the Brewer & Treyens (1981) study. Ask a friend to examine it for a minute or so (cover this caption). Then close the book and ask whether each of the following items appeared in the office: chair, wastebasket, bottle, typewriter, coffeepot, and book. If your friend reports having seen a wastebasket or a book, the experiment will have demonstrated constructive memory.

Learn BY **Doing**

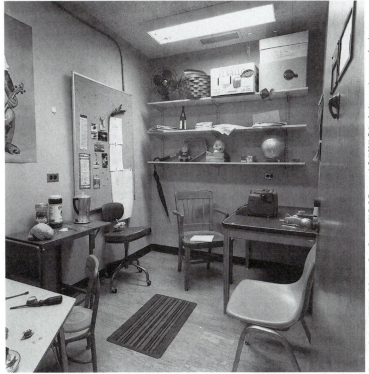

Courtesy Professor William F. Brewer. From Brewer, W. F., & Treyens, J. C. (1981). Role of schemata in memory for places. *Cognitive Psychology, 13, 207–230.*

The second version was identical until the end, when instead of proposing, the man sexually assaulted the woman. A few days after reading the story, all the participants were asked what they remembered from it. Those who had read the "proposal" version recalled nice things about the man, such as that he wanted the woman to meet his parents. Those who read the "assault" version recalled negative things, such as that the man liked to drink a lot. However, neither kind of information had actually been part of the original story. The participants had "recalled" memories of the man that they had constructed in accordance with their overall impression of him (Carli, 1999).

FOCUS ON RESEARCH

I Could Swear I Heard It!

By constructing our own versions of what we have seen and heard, we may remember an event differently from the way it actually happened. These errors, called *false memories,* can occur in relation to anything from the objects present in a room to the identity of an armed robber (Clancy et al., 2000). Later, we consider how false memories might color eyewitness testimony and reports of sexual abuse in childhood. For now, though, let's take a look at how researchers study false memories about less dramatic everyday experiences.

▶ What was the researchers' question?

How easy is it for people to form false memories? Henry Roediger and Kathleen McDermott (1995) addressed this question in an experiment to test for false memories as people recalled lists of words that had been read to them.

▶ How did the researchers answer the question?

On each of sixteen trials, college students heard a different list of words. Each list related to a particular theme. For example, the "cold" list contained fifteen words such as *sleet, slush, frost, white, snow,* and so on. Yet the list's theme word—in this case, *cold*—was not included. In half of these trials, the students were simply asked to recall as many words as possible from the list they had just heard. But in the other half, the students did math problems instead of trying to recall the words. Once all sixteen lists had been presented, the students were given a new list of words and asked to say which of them they recognized as having been on the lists they had heard earlier. Some of the words on this new list were theme words, such as *cold,* that had not been presented earlier. Would the students "remember" hearing these theme words on the list even though they hadn't? And if so, how confident would they be about their "memory" of these words?

been included on the lists created a "memory" that they *were* presented.

▶ *What did the researchers find?*

The students falsely, but confidently, recognized the theme words from twelve of the sixteen lists. In fact, theme words were falsely recognized as often as listed words were correctly recognized. As you might expect, the chance of accurately recognizing the listed words was greater when the students had been allowed to recall them shortly after hearing them. However, false memory of never-presented theme words occurred in both conditions.

▶ *What do the results mean?*

The results of this study suggest that the participants could not always distinguish words they had heard from those they had not heard. Why? The never-presented theme words "belonged" with the lists of presented words and apparently were "remembered" because they fit logically into the gaps in the students' memories. In short, the students' knowledge of words that *should* have

▶ *What do we still need to know?*

Studies such as this one make it clear that memory is constructive and that memory distortion and inaccuracy are commonplace (Schacter, Norman, & Koutstaal, 1998; Schmolck, Buffalo, & Squire, 2000). We still need to identify the processes behind such distortion. In addition, we are not yet sure why false memories can seem as real to us as our memories of actual events. Perhaps the more frequently we recall an event (as when students were allowed to rehearse some lists), the stronger is our belief that we have accurately recalled it. There is also evidence that merely thinking about certain objects or events or hearing sounds or seeing photos associated with them appears to make false memories of them more likely (Garry & Gerrie, 2005; Henkel, Franklin, & Johnson, 2000). Questions about how false memories are created lead to even deeper questions about the degree to which our imperfect memory processes might distort our experiences of reality. Is there an objective reality, or do we each experience our own version of reality?

© AP Photo

PDP MODELS AND CONSTRUCTIVE MEMORY

If you hear that "our basketball team won last night," your schema about basketball might prompt you to encode, and later retrieve, the fact that the players were men. Such spontaneous, though often incorrect, generalizations associated with PDP models of memory help explain the appearance of constructive memories.

Constructive Memory and PDP Models

Parallel distributed processing models of memory offer one way of explaining how semantic and episodic information become integrated in constructive memories. As mentioned earlier, PDP models suggest that newly learned facts alter our general knowledge of the world. In these network models, learned associations between specific facts come together. Let's say, for example, that your own network "knows" that your friend Joe is a male European American business major. It also "knows" that Claudia is a female African American student, but it has never learned her major. Now suppose that every other student you know is a business major. In this case, the connection between "students you know" and "business majors" would be so strong that you would conclude that Claudia is a business major, too. You would be so confident in this belief that it would take overwhelming evidence for you to change your mind (Rumelhart & McClelland, 1986). In other words, you would have constructed a memory about Claudia.

PDP networks also produce *spontaneous generalizations.* So if your friend tells you that she just bought a new car, you would know without asking that like all other cars you have experienced, it has four wheels. This is a spontaneous generalization from your knowledge base. Spontaneous generalizations are obviously helpful, but they can also create significant errors if the network is based on limited or biased experience with a class of objects or people.

If it occurs to you that ethnic prejudice can result from spontaneous generalization errors, you are right (Greenwald & Banaji, 1995). Researchers are actually encouraged by this aspect of PDP networks, though, because it accurately reflects human thought and memory. Virtually all of us make spontaneous generalizations about males, females, European Americans, African Americans, the young, the old, and many other categories (Rudman et al., 1999). Is prejudice, then, a process that we have no choice in or control over? Not necessarily. Relatively unprejudiced people tend to recognize that they are making generalizations and consciously try to ignore or suppress them (Amodio et al., 2004).

Schemas PDP models also help us understand constructive memory by explaining the operation of the schemas that guide it. As described in the chapters on social

FIGURE 6.9 ■ THE EFFECT OF SCHEMAS ON RECALL

In a classic experiment, people were shown figures like these, along with labels designed to activate certain schemas (Carmichael, Hogan, & Walter, 1932). For example, when showing the top figure, the experimenter said either "This resembles eyeglasses" or "This resembles a dumbbell." When the participants were later asked to draw these figures from memory, their drawings tended to resemble the items mentioned by the experimenter. In other words, their memory had been altered by the schema-activating labels.

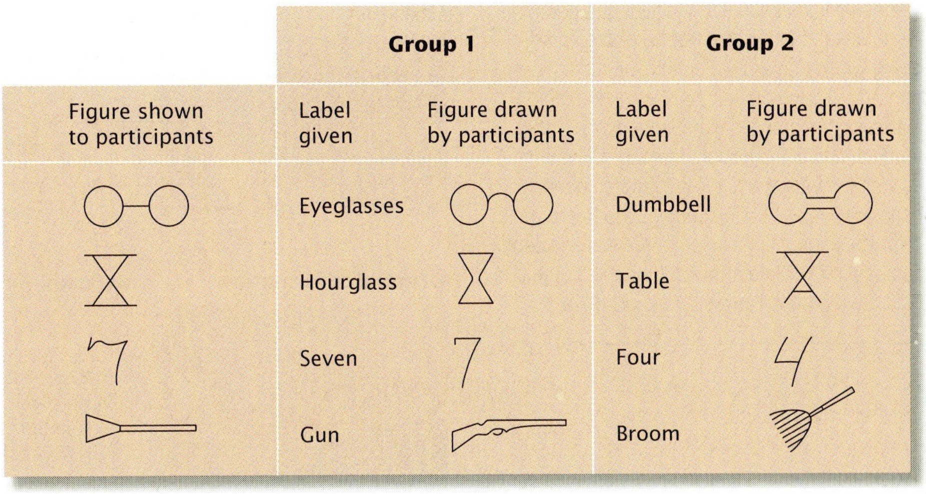

Figure shown to participants	Group 1		Group 2	
	Label given	Figure drawn by participants	Label given	Figure drawn by participants
○—○	Eyeglasses	○○	Dumbbell	○—○
⋈	Hourglass	⋈	Table	⋈
7	Seven	7	Four	4
⊐——	Gun	(gun drawing)	Broom	(broom drawing)

psychology and on thought, language, and intelligence, **schemas** are mental representations of categories of objects, places, events, and people. For example, most North Americans have a schema for *baseball game,* so simply hearing these words is likely to activate whole clusters of information in long-term memory, including the rules of the game and images of players, bats, balls, a green field, summer days, and perhaps hot dogs and stadiums. The generalized knowledge contained in schemas provides a basis for making inferences about new information during the encoding stage. So if you hear that a baseball player was injured, your schema about baseball might prompt you to encode the incident as game related, even though the cause was not mentioned. Later, you are likely to recall the injury as having occurred during a game (see Figure 6.9 for another example).

linkages

How accurate is eyewitness testimony? *(a link to Sensation and Perception)*

Linkages

Memory and Perception in the Courtroom

There are few situations in which accurate retrieval of memories is more important— and constructive memory is more dangerous—than when an eyewitness testifies in court about a crime. Let's consider the accuracy of eyewitness memory and how it can be distorted. To a jury, the most compelling evidence a lawyer can provide is that of an eyewitness, but eyewitnesses often make mistakes (Loftus & Ketcham, 1991; Wells, Memon, & Penrod, 2006; Wells, Olson, & Charman, 2002). In 1984, for example, North Carolina college student Jennifer Thompson confidently identified Ronald Cotton as the man who had raped her at knifepoint. Mainly on the basis of Thompson's testimony, Cotton was convicted of rape and sentenced to life in prison. He was released eleven years later, when DNA evidence revealed that he was innocent (and identified another man as the rapist). The eyewitness/victim's certainty had convinced a jury, but her memory had been faulty (O'Neill, 2000).

Like the rest of us, eyewitnesses can remember only what they perceive, and they can perceive only what they attend to (Backman & Nilsson, 1991). The task of the witnesses is to report as accurately as possible what they saw or heard. But no matter how hard they try to be accurate, there are limits to how valid their reports can be (Kassin, Rigby, & Castillo, 1991). For example, hearing new information about a crime (including in the form of a lawyer's question) can alter a witness's memory (Belli & Loftus, 1996; Wells & Quinlivan, 2009). Experiments show that when witnesses are asked "How fast were the

schemas Mental representations of categories of objects, places, events, and people.

FIGURE 6.10 ■ THE IMPACT OF QUESTIONS ON EYEWITNESS MEMORY

After seeing a filmed traffic accident, people were asked, "About how fast were the cars going when they (smashed into, hit, or contacted) each other?" As shown here, the witnesses' responses were influenced by the verb used in the question. "Smashed" was associated with the highest average speed estimates. A week later, people who heard the "smashed" question remembered the accident as being more violent than did people in the other two groups (Loftus & Palmer, 1974).

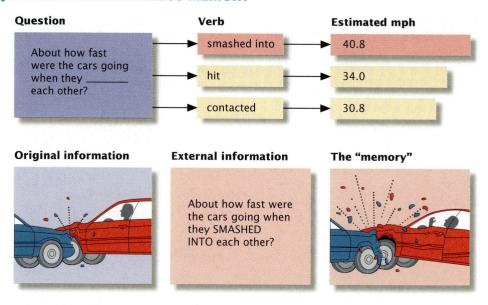

Question

About how fast were the cars going when they _____ each other?

Verb

smashed into → **Estimated mph** 40.8

hit → 34.0

contacted → 30.8

Original information

External information

About how fast were the cars going when they SMASHED INTO each other?

The "memory"

cars going when they *smashed into* each other?" they are likely to recall a higher speed than when asked "How fast were the cars going when they hit each other?" (Loftus & Palmer, 1974; see Figure 6.10). There is also evidence that an object mentioned during questioning about an incident is often mistakenly remembered as having been there during the incident (Roediger, Meade, & Bergman, 2001). So if a lawyer says that a screwdriver was lying on the ground when it was not, witnesses may recall with great certainty having seen it (Ryan & Geiselman, 1991). This *misinformation effect* can occur in several ways (Loftus & Hoffman, 1989). In some cases, hearing new information can make it harder to retrieve the original memory (Tversky & Tuchin, 1989). In others, the new information may be integrated into the old memory, making it impossible to distinguish from what was originally seen (Loftus, 1992). In still others, an eyewitness report might be influenced by the person's assumption that if a lawyer or police officer says an object was there or that something happened, it must be true (Chan, Thomas, & Bulevich, 2009).

Jurors' belief in a witness's testimony often depends as much (or even more) on how the witness presents evidence as on the content or relevance of that evidence (Leippe, Manion, & Romanczyk, 1992). For example, many jurors are particularly impressed by witnesses who give lots of details about what they saw. Extremely detailed testimony from prosecution witnesses is especially likely to lead to guilty verdicts, even when the details reported are irrelevant (Bell & Loftus, 1989). Apparently, when a witness reports details, such as the exact time of the crime or the color of the criminal's shoes, jurors assume that the witness had paid especially close attention or has a particularly good memory. This assumption seems reasonable, but there are limits on how much people can pay attention to, particularly when they are emotionally aroused and the crime happens quickly. Witnesses whose attention was drawn to details such as shoe color might not have had time to accurately perceive the criminal's facial features (Backman & Nilsson, 1991). So the fact that an eyewitness reports many details doesn't guarantee that all of them were remembered correctly.

Jurors also tend to believe witnesses who are confident about their testimony (Leippe, Manion, & Romanczyk, 1992). Unfortunately, research shows that witnesses' confidence is frequently much higher than the accuracy of their reports (Shaw, 1996; Wells, Olson, & Charman, 2002). In some cases, repeated exposure to misinformation and the repeated recall of that misinformation can lead witnesses to feel certain about their testimony even when—as in the Jennifer Thompson case—it may not be correct (Lamb, 1998; Mitchell & Zaragoza, 1996; Roediger, Jacoby, & McDermott, 1996).

The weaknesses inherent in eyewitness memory can be amplified by the use of police lineups and certain other criminal identification procedures (Haw & Fisher, 2004; Wells,

▶ This is exactly the sort of biased police lineup that *Eyewitness Evidence: A Guide for Law Enforcement* (U.S. Department of Justice, 1999) is designed to avoid. Based on research in memory and perception, this guide recommends that no suspect should stand out from all the others in a lineup, that witnesses should not assume that the real criminal is in the lineup, and that they should not be encouraged to "guess" when making an identification.

"Thank you, gentlemen—you may all leave except for No. 3."

Memon, & Penrod, 2006; Wells & Olson, 2003). In one study, for example, participants watched a videotaped crime and then tried to identify the criminal from a set of photographs (Wells & Bradfield, 1999). None of the photos showed the person who had committed the crime, but some participants nevertheless identified one of them as the criminal they saw on tape. When these mistaken participants were led to believe that they had correctly identified the criminal, they became even more confident in the accuracy of their false identification (Semmler, Brewer, & Wells, 2004; Wells, Olson, & Charman, 2003). These incorrect but confident witnesses became more likely than other participants to claim that it had been easy for them to identify the criminal from the photos because they had had a good view of him and had paid careful attention to him.

Since 1973, at least 130 people, including Ronald Cotton, have been released from U.S. prisons after DNA tests or other evidence revealed that they had been falsely convicted—mostly on the basis of faulty eyewitness testimony (Death Penalty Information Center, 2009). DNA evidence freed Charles Fain, who had been convicted of murder and spent almost 18 years on death row in Idaho (Bonner, 2001). Maryland officials approved $900,000 in compensation for Bernard Webster, who served 20 years in prison for rape before DNA revealed that he was innocent (Associated Press, 2003). Frank Lee Smith, too, would have been set free after the sole eyewitness at his murder trial retracted her testimony, but he had already died of cancer while awaiting execution in a Florida prison. Research on memory and perception helps explain how these miscarriages of justice can occur, and it is also guiding efforts to prevent such errors in the future. The U.S. Department of Justice has acknowledged the potential for errors in eyewitness evidence as well as the dangers of asking witnesses to identify suspects from lineups and photo arrays. The result is *Eyewitness Evidence: A Guide for Law Enforcement* (U.S. Department of Justice, 1999), the first-ever guide for police and prosecutors involved in obtaining eyewitness evidence. The guide warns these officials that asking leading questions about what witnesses saw can distort their memories. It also suggests that witnesses should examine photographs of possible suspects one at a time and points out that false identifications are less likely if witnesses viewing suspects in a lineup are told that the real perpetrator might not be included (Beresford & Blades, 2006; Wells & Olson, 2003; Wells et al., 2000).

Forgetting

● *What causes me to forget things?*

The frustrations of forgetting—where you left your keys, the answer to a test question, an anniversary—are apparent to most people nearly every day (Neisser, 2000b). Let's look more closely at the nature of forgetting and what causes it.

How Do We Forget?

Hermann Ebbinghaus, a German psychologist, began the systematic study of memory and forgetting in the late 1800s, using only his own memory as his laboratory. He read aloud a list of nonsense syllables (such as *POF*, *XEM*, and *QAL*) at a constant pace and then tried to recall the syllables.

Ebbinghaus devised a special **relearning method** to measure how much he forgot over time. He compared the number of repetitions (or trials) it took him to learn a list of items and the number of trials needed to relearn that same list later. Any reduction in the number of relearning trials represents the *savings* from one learning to the next. If it took Ebbinghaus ten trials to learn a list and another ten trials to relearn it, there would be no savings. Forgetting would have been complete. If it took him ten trials to learn the list and only five trials to relearn it, there would be a savings of 50 percent.

Ebbinghaus's research produced two lasting discoveries. One is the shape of the forgetting curve shown in Figure 6.11. Even when psychologists substitute words, sentences, and stories for nonsense syllables, the forgetting curve shows the same strong initial drop in memory, followed by a more moderate decrease over time (Slamecka & McElree, 1983; Wixted, 2004). Of course we remember sensible stories better than nonsense syllables, but the shape of the curve is the same no matter what type of material is involved (Davis & Moore, 1935). Even the forgetting of events from daily life tends to follow Ebbinghaus's forgetting curve (Thomson, 1982).

Ebbinghaus also discovered just how long-lasting "savings" in long-term memory can be. Psychologists now know from the method of savings that information about everything from algebra to bike riding is often retained for decades (Matlin, 1998). So although you may forget something you have learned if you do not use the information, it is very easy to relearn the material if the need arises, indicating that the forgetting was not complete (Hall & Bahrick, 1998).

IT'S ALL COMING BACK TO ME   ▲

This grandfather hasn't fed an infant for decades, but his memory of how to do it is not entirely gone. He showed some "savings"; it took him less time to relearn the skill than it took him to learn it initially.

relearning method   A method for measuring forgetting.

FIGURE 6.11   ■   EBBINGHAUS'S CURVE OF FORGETTING

List 30 words, selected at random from a dictionary, and spend a few minutes memorizing them. After an hour has passed, write down as many words as you can remember, but don't look at the original list again. Test yourself again eight hours later, a day later, and two days later. Now look at the original list and see how well you did on each recall test. Ebbinghaus found that most forgetting occurs during the first nine hours after learning, especially during the first hour. If this was not the case for you, why do you think your results were different?

Learn BY Doing

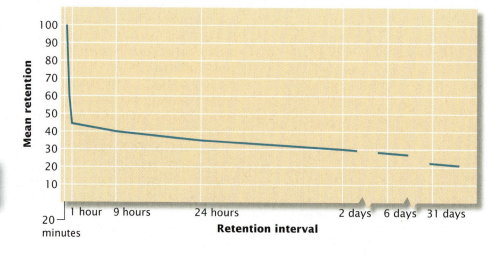

Why Do We Forget?

We have seen how forgetting occurs, but *why* does it happen? In principle, one of two processes can be responsible (Best, 1999). One process is described by **decay theory,** which suggests that information gradually disappears from memory. Decay occurs in memory in much the same way that the inscription on a ring or bracelet wears away and fades over time. Forgetting might also occur because of interference. Through **interference,** either the storage or the retrieval of information is impaired by the presence of other information. Interference might occur because one piece of information actually displaces other information, pushing it out of memory. It might also occur because one piece of information makes storing or recalling other information more difficult.

In the case of short-term memory, if an item is not rehearsed or thought about, memory of it decreases consistently over the course of about eighteen seconds. So decay appears to play the main role in forgetting information in short-term memory. But interference through displacement can also be operating. Like the top of a desk, short-term memory can hold only so much. Once it is full, adding additional items tends to make others "fall off" and become unavailable (Haberlandt, 1999). Displacement is one reason why the phone number you just looked up is likely to drop out of short-term memory if you read another number immediately afterward. Rehearsal prevents displacement by continually reentering the same information into short-term memory.

The cause of forgetting from long-term memory appears to be more directly tied to interference. Sometimes the interference is due to **retroactive inhibition,** in which learning new information interferes with our ability to recall older information (Wixted, 2005). Interference can also occur because of **proactive inhibition**, a process by which old information interferes with our ability to learn or remember new information. Retroactive inhibition would help explain why studying French vocabulary this term might make it more difficult to remember the Spanish words you learned last term. And because of proactive inhibition, the French words you are learning now might make it harder to learn German vocabulary next term. Figure 6.12 outlines the types

decay theory   The view that sees forgetting as the gradual disappearance of information from memory.

interference   The process through which storage or retrieval of information is impaired by the presence of other information.

retroactive inhibition   A cause of forgetting whereby new information placed in memory interferes with the ability to recall information already in memory.

proactive inhibition   A cause of forgetting whereby previously learned information interferes with the ability to remember new information.

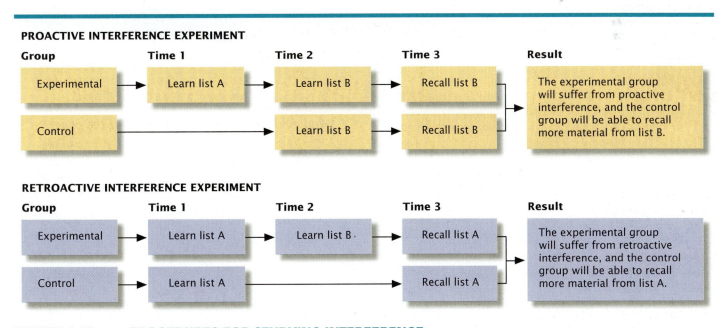

FIGURE 6.12 ■ PROCEDURES FOR STUDYING INTERFERENCE

To remember the difference between the two types of interference, keep in mind that the prefixes—pro and retro— indicate directions in time. Pro means "forward," and retro means "backward." In proactive inhibition, previously learned material "comes forward" to interfere with new learning; retroactive inhibition occurs when new information "goes back" to interfere with the recall of past learning.

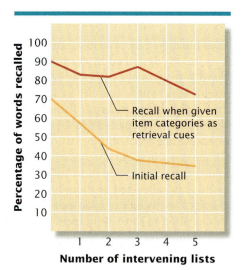

FIGURE 6.13 ■ RETRIEVAL FAILURES AND FORGETTING

Tulving and Psotka (1971) found that people's ability to recall a list of items was strongly affected by the number of other lists they learned before being tested on the first one. When retrieval cues were provided on a second test, however, retroactive inhibition from the intervening lists almost disappeared.
Source: Tulving & Psotka (1979).

of experiments used to study the influence of each form of interference in long-term memory.

Does interference push information out of memory or does it merely make it harder to retrieve the information? To find out, Endel Tulving and Joseph Psotka (1971) presented people with lists of words that represented a particular category. For example, there was a "buildings" list (e.g., *hut, cottage, cabin, hotel*) and a geographical features list (e.g., *cliff, river, hill, volcano*). Some people learned a list and then recalled as many of its words as possible. Other groups learned one list and then learned up to five additional lists before trying to recall the first one.

The results were dramatic. As the number of additional lists increased, the number of words that people could recall from the original list decreased. This finding reflected strong retroactive inhibition; the new lists were interfering with recall of the first one. Then the researchers gave a second test, but this time they provided a retrieval cue by telling the category of the words (such as "types of buildings") to be recalled. Now the number of additional lists had almost no effect on the number of words recalled from the original list, as Figure 6.13 shows. These results indicate that the words from the first list were still in long-term memory: They had not been pushed out, but the participants could not remember them without appropriate retrieval cues. In short, faulty retrieval caused the original forgetting. Putting more and more information in long-term memory may be like putting more and more CDs in a storage cabinet. Although none of the CDs disappears, it becomes increasingly difficult to find the one you are looking for.

Some theorists have suggested that all forgetting from long-term memory is due to retrieval failure (Ratcliff & McKoon, 1989). Does this mean that everything in long-term memory remains there for life, even if you cannot always (or ever) recall it? No one knows for sure yet, but as described in the next section, this question lies at the heart of some highly controversial court cases.

Thinking CRITICALLY

Can Traumatic Memories Be Repressed, Then Recovered?

In 1989, Eileen Franklin told California police that when she looked into her young daughter's eyes one day, she suddenly remembered seeing her father kill her childhood friend more than 20 years earlier. On the basis of her testimony about this memory, her father, George Franklin, Sr., was sent to prison for murder (Loftus & Ketcham, 1994).

▶ What am I being asked to believe or accept?

The prosecution in the Franklin case successfully argued that Eileen had recovered her long-buried memory of a murder. Similar arguments in other cases tried in the early 1990s also resulted in imprisonment as adult children claimed to have recovered childhood memories of physical or sexual abuse at the hands of their parents. The juries in these trials accepted the assertion that all memory of shocking events can be *repressed,* or pushed into an inaccessible corner of the mind where subconscious processes keep it out of awareness for decades yet potentially subject to accurate recall (Hyman, 2000). Jurors are not the only ones who believe in this **repressed memory** phenomenon. A few years ago a large American news organization reported that the United States had illegally used nerve gas during the war in Vietnam. This story

was based, in part, on a Vietnam veteran's account of recovered memories of having been subjected to a nerve gas attack.

▶ What evidence is available to support the claim?

Proponents of the recovered-memory argument point to several lines of evidence to support their claims. First, as discussed in the chapter on consciousness, a lot of mental activity occurs outside of awareness (Kihlstrom, 1999). Second, research on implicit memory shows that our behavior can be influenced by information that we are not aware of (Betch et al., 2003; Kouider & Dupoux, 2005; Schacter, Chiu, & Ochsner, 1993). Third, research on *motivated forgetting* suggests that people may sometimes be able to wilfully suppress information so that it is no longer accessible on a later memory test (Anderson & Green, 2001). Even suppressing one's emotional reactions to events can interfere with memories of those events (Richards & Gross, 2000). And people appear more likely to forget unpleasant rather than pleasant events (Erdelyi, 1985). In one study, a psychologist kept a detailed record of his daily life over a six-year period. When he later tried to recall these experiences, he remembered more than half of the positive events but only a third of the negative ones (Waagenaar, 1986). In another study,

38 percent of women who had been brought to a hospital when they were children because of sexual abuse did not report the incident when they were interviewed as adults (Williams, 1994). Fourth, retrieval cues can help people recall memories that had previously been inaccessible to conscious awareness (Andrews et al., 2000; Landsdale & Laming, 1995). For example, these cues have helped soldiers remember for the first time the circumstances under which they had been wounded many years before (Karon & Widener, 1997). Finally, there is the confidence with which people report recovered memories; they say they are just too vivid to be anything but real.

▶ Can that evidence be interpreted another way?

Those who are skeptical about repressed memories know that subconscious memory and retrieval processes exist (Kihlstrom, 1999). They also recognize that, sadly, child abuse and other traumas are all too common. But to these psychologists, the available evidence is not strong enough to support the conclusion that traumatic memories can be repressed and then accurately recalled. Any given "recovered" memory, they say, may actually be a distorted or constructed memory (Clancy et al., 2000; Hyman, 2000; Loftus, 1998). Our recall of past events is affected by what happened at the time, what we knew beforehand, and everything we have experienced since. The people in the study mentioned earlier who "remembered" nonexistent books in an office inadvertently used their prior knowledge of what is usually in graduate students' offices to construct a false memory of seeing books. Similarly, that Vietnam veteran's "recovered memory" of a nerve gas attack appears to have had no basis in fact; the news organization that published the story later retracted it.

As we saw in the Focus on Research section, false memories—distortions of actual events and the recall of events that didn't actually happen—can be just as vivid as real, accurate memories, and people can be just as confident about them (Brainerd & Reyna, 2005; Brainerd et al., 2003; Loftus, 2004; Nourkova, Bernstein, & Loftus, 2004; Roediger & McDermott, 2000). Most of us have experienced everyday versions of false memories. It is not unusual to "remember" turning off the coffeemaker or mailing the rent check, only to discover later that we didn't. Researchers have demonstrated that false memories can occur in relation to more emotional events, too. In one case study, a teenager named Chris was given descriptions of four incidents from his childhood and asked to write about each of them every day for five days (Loftus, 1997a). One of these incidents—being lost in a shopping mall at age five—never really happened. Yet Chris eventually "remembered" this event, and even added many details about the mall and the stranger whose hand he was supposedly found holding. He also rated this (false) memory as being more vivid than two of the other three (real) incidents he wrote about. Similar results occurred with about half of 77 child participants in other case studies (Porter, Yuille, & Lehman, 1999). The same pattern of results has appeared in formal experiments about planting emotion-laden false memories (Hyman & Pentland, 1996; Loftus & Pickrell, 1995). Researchers have been able to create vivid and striking (but completely false) memories of events that

people thought they experienced when they were one day old (DuBreuil, Garry, & Loftus, 1998). In other experiments, children who were repeatedly asked about a nonexistent trauma (getting a hand caught in a mousetrap) eventually developed a clear and unshakable false memory of experiencing it (Ceci et al., 1994). Some people will even begin to avoid a certain food after researchers create in them a false memory of having been ill after eating that food as a child (Bernstein & Loftus, 2009; Geraerts et al., 2008a).

In other words, people sometimes have a difficult time distinguishing between what has happened to them and what they have only imagined or have come to believe has happened (Garry & Polaschek, 2000; Henkel, 2004; Johnson & Raye, 1998; Mazzoni & Memon, 2003; Zaragoza et al., 2001). Some studies have found that people who are prone to fantasy, who easily mistake real and imagined stimuli, and who tend to have lapses in attention and memory are more likely than others to develop false memories and possibly more likely to report the recovery of repressed memories (McNally, 2003; McNally et al., 2000a, 2000b, 2005; Porter et al., 2000; Wilson & French, 2006). Two other studies have found that women who have suffered physical or sexual abuse are more likely to falsely remember words on a laboratory recall test (Bremner, Shobe, & Kihlstrom, 2000; Zoellner et al., 2000). This tendency appears strongest among abused women who show signs of posttraumatic stress disorder (Bremner, Shobe, & Kihlstrom, 2000). Another study found that the tendency to have false memories during a word recall task was greater in women who reported recovered memories of sexual abuse than in nonabused women or in those who had always remembered the abuse they suffered (Clancy et al., 2000).

Why would anyone "remember" a trauma that did not actually occur? Elizabeth Loftus (1997b) suggests that popular books such as *The Courage to Heal* (Bass & Davis, 1994), *Secret Survivors* (Blume, 1998), and *Surviving Babylon* (Garson, 2006) may lead people to believe that anyone who experiences guilt, depression, low self-esteem, overemotionality, or virtually any other psychological problem is harboring repressed memories of abuse. This message, says Loftus, is reinforced and elaborated by some therapists, particularly those who specialize in using guided imagination, hypnosis, and other methods to "help" clients recover repressed memories (Lindsay et al., 2004; McHugh, 2009; Pendergrast, 1996). In so doing, these therapists may influence their clients to construct false memories by encouraging them to imagine experiencing events that might never have actually occurred or that occurred only in a dream (Mazzoni & Loftus, 1996; Olio, 1994). As one client described her therapy, "I was rapidly losing the ability to differentiate between my imagination and my real memory" (Loftus & Ketcham, 1994, p. 25). To such therapists, a client's failure to recover memories of abuse or refusal to accept that they exist is evidence of denial of the truth (Loftus, 1997a; Tavris, 2003).

The possibility that recovered memories might actually be false memories has led to dismissed charges or not-guilty verdicts for defendants in some repressed memory cases. In other cases, previously convicted defendants have been released. (George Franklin's conviction was overturned, but only after he spent five

EXPLORING MEMORY PROCESSES ▶
Elizabeth Loftus (at the far right) is shown here with her students and Alan Alda, who hosted a documentary about her research. Loftus and other cognitive psychologists have demonstrated mechanisms through which false memories can be created. They have shown, for example, that false memories appear even in research participants who are told about them and asked to avoid them (McDermott & Roediger, 1998). Their work has helped focus scientific scrutiny on reports of recovered memories, especially those arising from contact with therapists who assume that most people have repressed memories of abuse.

linkages

Do forgotten memories remain in the subconscious? *(a link to Consciousness)*

Courtesy of Elizabeth Loftus

years in prison.) Concern over the potential damage resulting from false memories prompted the establishment in 1992 of the False Memory Syndrome Foundation, an organization of families affected by abuse accusations stemming from allegedly repressed memories. More than a hundred of these families (including George Franklin's) have filed lawsuits against hospitals and therapists. In 1994, California winery executive Gary Ramona received $500,000 in damages from two therapists who had "helped" his daughter recall his alleged sexual abuse of her. A more recent suit led to a $2 million judgment against a Minnesota therapist whose client discovered that her "recovered" memories of childhood were false; a similar case in Wisconsin brought a $5 million judgment against two therapists. And an Illinois case resulted in a $10.6 million settlement and the suspension of the license of the psychiatrist who had "found" his patient's lost memories (Loftus, 1998).

▶ What evidence would help to evaluate the alternatives?

Evaluating reports of recovered memories would be easier if we had more information about whether it is possible for people to repress memories of traumatic events. If it is possible, we also need to know how common it is and how accurate recovered memories might be. So far we know that some people apparently forget intense emotional experiences but that most people's memories of them are vivid and long lasting (Alexander et al., 2005; Goodman et al., 2003; Pope et al., 1998; Porter & Peace, 2007). Some memories are called *flashbulb memories* because they preserve particular experiences in great detail (Brown & Kulik, 1977; McGaugh, 2003). In fact, many people who live through trauma are *unable* to forget it, though they wish they could (Henig, 2004). In the sexual abuse study mentioned earlier, for example (Williams, 1994), 62 percent of the victims recalled as adults the trauma that had been

documented in their childhoods. A similar study of a different group of adults found that about 92 percent of them recalled the abuse that had been documented in their childhoods (Alexander et al., 2005; Goodman et al., 2003). The true recall figures might actually be even higher in such studies, because some people who remember abuse may not wish to talk about it. In any case, additional studies like these—studies that track the fate of memories in known abuse cases—would not only help estimate the prevalence of this kind of forgetting but also might offer clues as to the kinds of people and events most likely to be associated with it.

It would also be valuable to know more about the processes through which repression might occur. Is there a mechanism that specifically pushes traumatic memories out of awareness and then keeps them at a subconscious level for long periods? Despite some suggestive results (Anderson & Green, 2001; Anderson, Ochsner et al., 2004; DePrince & Freyd, 2004), cognitive psychologists have so far not found reliable evidence for such a mechanism (Bulevich et al., 2006; Geraerts et al., 2006; Loftus, 1997a; McNally, Clancy, & Schacter, 2001; McNally, 2003; McNally et al., 2000a; Pope et al., 1998).

▶ What conclusions are most reasonable?

An objective reading of the research evidence suggests that the recovery of traumatic memories is at least possible but that the implantation of false memories is also possible—and has been demonstrated repeatedly in controlled experiments. With this in mind, it is not easy to decide whether any particular case is an instance of recovered memory or false memory, especially when there is no objective corroborating evidence to guide the decision.

The intense conflict between those who uncritically accept claims of recovered memories and those who are more wary about the accuracy of such claims reflects a fundamental disagreement about evidence (Tavris, 2003). To many therapists who deal daily with victims of sexual abuse and other traumas, clients' reports constitute stronger proof of recovered memories than do the results of laboratory experiments. Client reports are viewed with considerably more skepticism by psychologists who engage in, or rely on, empirical research on the processes of memory and forgetting (Loftus, 2003, 2004; Pope, 1998). They would like to have additional sources of evidence, including from research on brain activity "signatures" that might someday distinguish true memories from false ones (e.g., Cabeza et al., 2001; Sederberg et al., 2007; Slotnick & Schacter, 2004).

So people's responses to claims of recovered memory may be determined by the relative weight that they assign to reports of personal experiences versus evidence from controlled experiments.

Still, the apparent ease with which false memories can be created should lead judges, juries, and the general public to exercise great caution before accepting unverified memories of traumatic events as the truth. At the same time, we should not automatically reject the claims of people who appear to have recovered memories (Geraerts et al., 2007; McNally & Geraerts, 2009). Perhaps the wisest course is to use all the scientific and circumstantial evidence available to carefully and critically examine claims of recovered memories while keeping in mind the possibility that constructive memory processes might have influenced those memories (Alison, Kebbell, & Lewis, 2006; Geraerts et al., 2007). This careful scientific approach is vital if we are to protect the rights of those who report recovered memories as well as those who face accusations arising from them (Geraerts et al., 2008b).

linkages

Where are memories stored? *(a link to Biology and Behavior)*

repressed memory A painful memory that is said to be kept out of consciousness by psychological processes.

Biological Bases of Memory

▶ *How does my brain change when I store a memory?*

Many psychologists who study memory focus on explicit and implicit mental processes (e.g. Schott et al., 2005). Others explore the physical, electrical, and chemical changes that take place in the brain when people encode, store, and retrieve information (Abraham, 2006; Jonides, Lacey, & Nee, 2005; Fields, 2005; Touzani, Puthanveettil, & Kandel, 2007).

The Biochemistry of Memory

As described in the chapter on biology and behavior, communication among brain cells takes place at the synapses between axons and dendrites using chemicals called *neurotransmitters* that are released at the synapses. The formation and storage of new memories are associated with at least two kinds of changes in synapses.

The first kind of change occurs when stimulation from the environment promotes the formation of *new* synapses. Scientists can now actually see this process occur. As shown in Figure 6.14, repeatedly sending signals across a particular synapse increases the number of special little branches, called *spines*, that appear on the receiving cell's dendrites (Hofer et al., 2009; Lang et al., 2004; Nägerl et al., 2008). The second kind of

FIGURE 6.14 ▬ BUILDING MEMORIES

These models are based on electron microscope images of synapses in the brain. The model on the left shows that before signals were repeatedly sent across the synapse, just one spine (shown in white) appears on this part of the dendrite. Afterward, as shown in the other model, there are two spines, which helps improve communication across the synapse. The creation and changing of many individual synapses in the brain appears to underlie the formation and storage of new memories. *Source*: Toni et al. (1999).

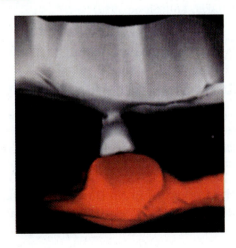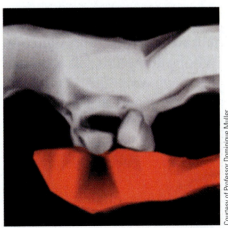

Courtesy of Professor Dominique Muller

FIGURE 6.15   ■   BRAIN STRUCTURES INVOLVED IN MEMORY

Combined neural activity in many parts of the brain allows us to encode, store, and retrieve memories. The complexity of the biological bases of these processes is underscored by research showing that different aspects of a memory—such as the sights and sounds of some event—are stored in different parts of the cerebral cortex.

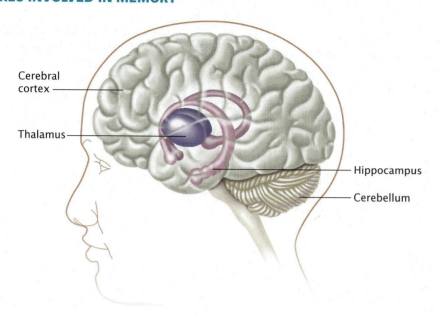

change occurs as new experiences change the operation of *existing* synapses. For example, when two neurons fire at the same time and together stimulate a third neuron, that other neuron will later be more responsive than before to stimulation by either neuron alone (Sejnowski, Chattarji, & Stanton, 1990). This process of "sensitizing" synapses is called *long-term potentiation* (Li et al., 2003; Mozzachiodi et al., 2008; Rioult-Pedotti, Friedman, & Donoghue, 2000). Other patterns of electrical stimulation can weaken synaptic connections, a process called *long-term depression* (Malenka, 1995). Changes in the sensitivity of synapses could account for the development of conditioned responses and other types of learning and for the operation of working memory (Olson et al., 2006; Mongillo, Barak, & Tsodyks, 2008; Whitlock et al., 2006).

In the hippocampus (see Figure 6.15), these changes appear to occur at synapses that use the neurotransmitter *glutamate* (Malenka & Nicoll, 1999). Other neurotransmitters, such as *acetylcholine,* also play important roles in memory formation (e.g., Furey, Pietrini, & Haxby, 2000; Li et al., 2003). The memory problems seen in Alzheimer's patients are related to a lack of neurons that use acetylcholine and send fibers to the hippocampus and the cortex (Muir, 1997). Drugs that interfere with the action of acetylcholine impair memory, and drugs that increase the amount of acetylcholine in synapses can improve memory somewhat in aging animals and humans (Pettit, Shao, & Yakel, 2001; Sirvio, 1999).

In summary, research has shown that the formation of memories is associated with changes in many individual synapses that, together, strengthen and improve the communication in networks of neurons.

Brain Structures and Memory

Are the biochemical processes involved in memory concentrated in certain brain regions, or are they distributed throughout the brain? The latest research suggests that memory involves both specialized regions where various types of memories are formed and widespread areas for storage (Takashima et al., 2006).

The Impact of Brain Damage   Studies of how brain injuries affect memory provide evidence about which parts of the brain are involved in various kinds of memory. For example, damage to the hippocampus, nearby parts of the cerebral cortex, and the thalamus often results in **anterograde amnesia,** a loss of memory for any event occurring after the injury. People who suffer this kind of damage are unable to form new memories.

The case of H. M. provides a striking example of anterograde amnesia (Milner, 1966). When H. M. was 27 years old, part of his hippocampus was removed in order to stop his severe epileptic seizures. After the operation, his long-term and short-term memory appeared normal, but something was wrong. Two years later, he still believed that he was 27. When his family moved into a new house, he couldn't remember the new address or how to get there. When his uncle died, he grieved in a normal way, but soon afterward he began to ask why his uncle had not visited him. He had to be repeatedly reminded of the death and, each time, H. M. began the mourning process all over again. The surgery had apparently destroyed the mechanism that transfers information from short-term to long-term memory. Until his death in 2008, H. M. lived in a nursing home, where his only long-term memories were from 50 years earlier, before the operation. He was still unable to recall events and facts he had experienced since then—not even the names of people he saw every day (Corkin, 2002; Hathaway, 2002; Squire, 2009).

Although patients with damage to the hippocampus cannot form new episodic memories, they may still be able to form implicit memories. For example, H. M.'s performance on a complicated puzzle improved steadily over several days of practice, just as it does with normal people, and eventually it became virtually perfect. But each time he tried the puzzle, he insisted that he had never seen it before (Cohen & Corkin, 1981). A musician with a similar kind of brain damage was able to use his implicit memory to continue leading choral groups (Vattano, 2000). So it appears that the hippocampus is crucial in the formation of new episodic memories but that implicit memory, procedural memory, and working memory are governed by other regions of the brain (Schott et al., 2005; Squire, 1992; Touzani, Puthanveettil, & Kandel, 2007).

Retrograde amnesia involves loss of memory for events prior to some brain injury. Often, a person with this type of amnesia can't remember anything that took place in the months or years before the injury. In 1994, head injuries from a car crash left 36-year-old Perlene Griffith-Barwell with retrograde amnesia so severe that she forgot virtually everything she had learned about everything and everyone she had known over the previous 20 years. She thought she was still 16 and did not recognize her husband, Malcolm, or her four children. She said, "The children were sweet, but they didn't seem like mine," and she "didn't feel anything" for Malcolm. Her memories of the previous 20 years never fully returned. She is divorced, but at last report, she was living with her children, working in a bank, and planning to remarry (Echo News, 2000; Weinstein, 1999).

A FAMOUS CASE OF RETROGRADE AMNESIA ▶

After Ralf Schumacher slammed his race car into a wall during the United States Grand Prix in June of 2004, he sustained a severe concussion that left him with no memory of the crash. Retrograde amnesia is relatively common following concussions, so if you ride a bike or a motorcycle, wear that helmet!

anterograde amnesia A loss of memory for events that occur after a brain injury.

retrograde amnesia A loss of memory for events that occurred prior to a brain injury.

© Paul Gilham/Getty Images

Unlike Perlene, most victims of retrograde amnesia gradually recover their memories (Riccio, Millin, & Gisquet-Verrier, 2003). The most distant events are recalled first, then the person gradually regains memory for events leading up to the injury. Recovery is seldom complete, however, and the person may never remember the last few seconds before the injury. One man received a severe blow to the head after being thrown from his motorcycle. Upon regaining consciousness, he claimed that he was 11 years old. Over the next three months, he slowly recalled more and more of his life. He remembered when he was 12, 13, and so on—right up until the time he was riding his motorcycle the day of the accident. But he was never able to remember what happened just before the accident (Baddeley, 1982). Those final events were probably encoded into short-term memory, but apparently they were never transferred into long-term memory (Dudai, 2004).

Other conditions that suppress neural activity in the brain can also disrupt the transfer of information from short-term to long-term memory. These conditions include anesthetic drugs, poisoning by carbon monoxide or other toxins, and strong electrical impulses such as those in the electroconvulsive therapy that is sometimes used to treat cases of severe depression (see the chapter on treatment of psychological disorders).

Multiple Storage Areas   Obviously, the hippocampus does not permanently store long-term memories (Bayley, Hopkins, & Squire, 2003; Rosenbaum et al., 2000). (If it did, H. M. would not have retained memories from the years before part of his hippocampus was removed.) The hippocampus and thalamus send nerve impulses to the cerebral cortex, and it is in and around the cortex that long-term semantic and episodic memories are probably stored—but not just in one place (Levy, Bayley, & Squire, 2004; Maviel et al., 2004; Miceli et al., 2001). As described in the chapter on biology and behavior, different regions of the cortex receive messages from different senses. Specific aspects of an experience are probably stored in or near these regions. For example, damage to the auditory association cortex disrupts memory for sounds (Colombo et al., 1990). A memory, however, involves more than one sensory system. Even in the simple case of a rat remembering a maze, the experience of the maze involves vision, smell, movements, and emotions, each of which may be stored in different regions of the brain (Gallagher & Chiba, 1996). So memories are both localized and distributed. Certain brain areas store specific aspects of each remembered event, but many brain systems are involved in experiencing a whole event (Brewer et al., 1998; Kensinger & Corkin, 2004). For example, the cerebellum (see Figure 6.15) is involved in the storage of procedural knowledge, such as dance steps and other movements.

What happens in the brain as we retrieve memories? Brain imaging studies show that the hippocampus and various regions of the cerebral cortex are active during memory retrieval (Cabeza et al., 2001; McDermott, Szpunar, & Christ, in press). There is also evidence to suggest that retrieving memories of certain experiences, such as a conversation or a tennis game, reactivates the sensory and motor regions of the brain that had been involved during the event itself (Nyberg et al., 2001). Research shows, too, that when animals recall a stored emotional (fear-related) memory, that memory may have to be stored again. During this biological restorage process, it may be distorted (Eisenberg et al., 2003; Lee, Everitt, & Thomas, 2004; Nader, Schafe, & Le Doux, 2000). Researchers are exploring the question of whether the same restorage and distortion processes occur humans (Dudai, 2004; Walker et al., 2003). Cognitive neuroscientists are also trying to determine whether different patterns of brain activity are associated with the storage and retrieval of accurate versus inaccurate memories (Gonsalves & Paller, 2000; Slotnick & Schacter, 2004; Urbach et al., 2005). Another new line of work concerns the ability to think about the future (Atance & O'Neill, 2001). Scientists have found, for example, that patients with amnesia due to damage to the medial temporal lobe are not only unable to recollect the past but they also cannot vividly envision future events, such as their next birthday party (Hassabis et al., 2007). It appears from neuroimaging studies that the same brain regions involved in remembering are important for envisioning, too (Addis et al., 2007; Szpunar, Watson, & McDermott, 2007; Szpunar, Chan, & McDermott, in press).

Improving Your Memory

● *How can I remember more information?*

Some questions remain about what memory is and how it works, but the results of memory research offer many valuable guidelines to help people improve their memories (Neisser, 2000a).

Mnemonic Strategies

One way to improve your memory is to use mnemonic strategies (pronounced "nee-MON-ik"). **Mnemonic strategies** are ways to put information into an organized framework in order to remember it more easily. To remember the names of the Great Lakes, for example, you could use the acronym HOMES (for Huron, Ontario, Michigan, Erie, and Superior). Verbal organization is the basis for many mnemonic strategies. You can link items by weaving them into a story, a sentence, or a rhyme. To help customers remember where they left their cars, some large parking lots have replaced traditional section designations such as "A1" or "G8" with the names of colors, months, or animals. Customers can then tie the location of their cars to information already in long-term memory—for example, "I parked in the month of my mother's birthday."

One simple but powerful mnemonic strategy is called the *method of loci* (pronounced "LOW-sigh"), or the "method of places." To use this method, first think about a set of familiar locations. Use your home, for example. You might imagine walking through the front door, around all four corners of the living room, and through each of the other rooms. Next, imagine that each item you want to remember is in one of these locations. Creating vivid or unusual images of how the items appear in each location seems to be particularly effective (Kline & Groninger, 1991). For example, tomatoes smashed against the front door or bananas hanging from the bedroom ceiling might be helpful in recalling these items on a grocery list. Whenever you want to remember a new list, you can create new images using the same locations in the same order.

Guidelines for More Effective Studying

The success of mnemonic strategies demonstrates again the importance of relating new information to knowledge already stored in memory. All mnemonic systems require that you have a well-learned body of knowledge (such as locations) that can be used to provide a framework, or context, for organizing incoming information (Hilton, 1986).

When you want to remember complex material, such as a textbook chapter, the same principle applies (Palmisano & Herrmann, 1991). You can improve your memory for text material by first creating an outline or other overall context for learning, rather than by just reading and rereading (Glover et al., 1990). Repetition may *seem* effective because it keeps material in short-term memory, but for retaining information over long periods, repetition alone tends to be ineffective, no matter how much time you spend on it (Bjork, 1999; Bjorklund & Green, 1992). In short, "work smarter, not harder."

In addition, spend your time wisely. **Distributed practice** is much more effective than **massed practice** for learning and retaining new information. If you are going to spend 10 hours studying for a test, you will be much better off studying for ten 1-hour blocks, separated by periods of sleep and other activity. "Cramming" for one 10-hour block will not be as successful (Rohrer & Pashier, 2007). By scheduling more study sessions, you will stay fresh and be able to think about the material from a new perspective during each session. This method will help you elaborate on the material, as in elaborative rehearsal, and thus remember it better.

Reading a Textbook   More specific advice for remembering textbook material comes from a study that examined how successful and unsuccessful college students approached their reading (Whimbey, 1976). Unsuccessful students tended to read the material straight through. They did not slow down when they reached a difficult section.

---

mnemonic strategies   Methods for organizing information in order to remember it.

distributed practice   Learning new information in many study sessions that are spaced across time.

massed practice   Trying to learn complex new information in a single long study period.

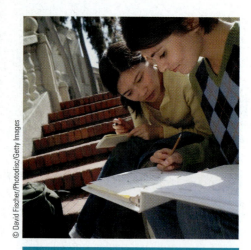

UNDERSTAND AND REMEMBER ▲

Research on memory suggests that students who simply read their textbooks won't remember as much as those who, like this woman, read for understanding using strategies such as the PQ4R method. Further, memory for the material is likely to be better if you read and study it over a number of weeks rather than in one marathon session on the night before a test.

applying psychology

They kept going even when they did not understand what they were reading. In contrast, successful college students monitored their understanding, reread difficult sections, and periodically stopped or reviewed what they had learned. (This book's In Review features are designed to help you do that.) In short, effective learners engage in a deep level of processing. They are active learners. They think of each new fact in relation to other material, and they develop a context in which many new facts can be organized effectively.

Research on memory suggests two specific guidelines for reading a textbook. First, make sure that you understand what you are reading before moving on (Herrmann & Searleman, 1992). Second, try the PQ4R *method* (Thomas & Robinson, 1972). PQ4R stands for six activities to engage in when you read a chapter: *preview, question, read, reflect, recite,* and *review*. These activities are designed to increase the depth to which you process the information you read and should be done as follows:

1. **Preview.** Begin by skimming the chapter. Look at the section headings and any boldfaced or italicized terms. Get a general idea of what material will be discussed, the way it is organized, and how its topics relate to one another and to what you already know. Some people find it useful to survey the entire chapter once and then survey each major section a little more carefully before reading it in detail.
2. **Question.** Before reading each section, ask yourself what content will be covered and what information you should be getting from it.
3. **Read.** Read the text, but think about the material as you read. Are the questions you raised earlier being answered? Do you see the connections between and among the topics?
4. **Reflect.** As you read, think of your own examples—and create visual images—of the concepts and phenomena you encounter. Ask yourself what the material means and consider how each section relates to other sections in the chapter and other chapters in the book (this book's Linkages features are designed to promote this kind of reflection).
5. **Recite.** At the end of each section, recite the major points. Resist the temptation to be passive and say, "Oh, I remember that." Be active. Put the ideas into your own words by reciting them aloud to yourself or by summarizing the material in a mini-lecture to a friend or study partner.
6. **Review.** When you reach the end of the chapter, review all of its material. You should now see connections not only within each section but also among sections. The objective is to see how the material is organized. Once you grasp that organization, the individual facts will be far easier to remember.

By following these procedures, you will learn and remember the material better. You will also save yourself considerable time.

Lecture Notes   Students and employees often have to learn and remember material from lectures or other presentations. Taking notes will help, but effective note taking is a learned skill that improves with practice (Pauk, 2005). Research on memory suggests some simple strategies for taking and using notes effectively.

Recognize first that in note taking, more is not necessarily better. Taking detailed notes on everything requires that you pay close attention to unimportant as well as important content, leaving little time for thinking about the material. Note takers who concentrate on expressing the major ideas in relatively few words remember more than those who try to catch every detail (Pauk & Fiore, 2000). In short, the best way to take notes is to think about what is being said. Draw connections with other material in the presentation. Then summarize the major points clearly and concisely (Kiewra, 1989).

Once you have a set of lecture notes, review them as soon as possible after the lecture so that you can fill in missing details. (Remember: Most forgetting from long-term memory occurs during the first hour after learning.) When the time comes for serious study, use your notes as if they were a chapter in a textbook. Write a detailed outline. Think about how various points are related. Once you have organized the material, the details will make more sense and will be much easier to remember. ("In Review: Improving Your Memory" summarizes tips for studying.)

In Review

IMPROVING YOUR MEMORY

GOAL	HELPFUL TECHNIQUES
Remembering lists of items	Use mnemonic strategies. Look for meaningful acronyms. Try the method of loci.
Remembering textbook material	Follow the PQ4R system. Allocate your time to allow for distributed practice. Read actively, not passively.
Taking lecture notes	Take notes, but record only the main points. Think about the overall organization of the material. Review your notes as soon after the lecture as possible in order to fill in missing points.
Studying for exams	Write a detailed outline of your lecture notes rather than passively reading them.

1. *Using mnemonic strategies and the PQ4R system to better remember course material are examples of the value of _____ rehearsal.*
2. *"Cramming" illustrates _____ practice that usually leads to _____ long-term retention than _____ practice.*
3. *To minimize forgetting, you should review lecture notes _____ after a lecture ends.*

ACTIVE REVIEW ▶ Chapter 6

Memory

As noted in the introductory chapter, all of psychology's subfields are related to one another. Our discussion of eyewitness testimony illustrates just one way that the topic of this chapter, memory, is linked to the subfield of sensation and perception, as discussed in the chapter by that name.

The Linkages diagram shows ties to two other subfields, and there are many more ties throughout the book. Looking for linkages among subfields will help you see how they all fit together and help you better appreciate the big picture that is psychology.

 linkages

Where are memories stored?
(ans. on p. 235)

Chapter 2
Biology and Behavior

How accurate is eyewitness testimony? *(ans. on p. 227)*

Chapter 3
Sensation and Perception

Why does memory improve during childhood? *(ans. on p. 357)*

Chapter 9
Human Development

SUMMARY ▶

The Nature of Memory

▶ *How does information turn into memories?*

Human memory depends on a complex mental system. There are three basic memory processes. *Encoding* transforms stimulus information  into some type of mental representation. Codes for *auditory* (or *acoustic*) *memory* represent information as sounds, codes for *visual memory* represent information as images, and codes for semantic memory represent information as general meanings. *Storage* maintains information in the memory system over time. *Retrieval* is the process of gaining access to previously stored information.

Most psychologists agree that there are at least three types of memory. *Episodic memory* refers to memory for specific events in a person's life. *Semantic memory* refers to generalized knowledge about the world. *Procedural memory,* or *procedural knowledge,* refers to information about how to do things. Research on memory focuses on *explicit memory,* the information we retrieve through a conscious effort to remember something, and *implicit memory,* the unintentional recollection and influence of prior experiences.

Four models of memory have guided most research. The *levels-of-processing model of memory* suggests that the most important determinant of memory is how extensively information is encoded or processed when it is first received. In general, *elaborative rehearsal* is more effective than *maintenance rehearsal* in learning new information, because it represents a deeper level of processing. According to the *transfer-appropriate processing model of memory,* the critical determinant of memory is not how deeply information is encoded but whether the processes used during retrieval match those used during encoding. *Parallel distributed processing (PDP) models of memory* suggest that new experiences not only provide specific information but also become part of (and alter) a whole network of associations. The *information-processing model of memory* suggests that for information to become firmly embedded in memory, it must pass through three stages of processing: sensory memory, short-term memory, and long-term memory.

Storing New Memories

▶ *What am I most likely to remember?*

Sensory memory maintains information about incoming stimuli in the *sensory registers,* such as in *iconic memory,* for a very brief time. *Selective attention,* which focuses mental resources on only part of the stimulus field, controls what information in the sensory registers is actually perceived and transferred to short-term memory.

Working memory is a system that allows us to store, organize, and manipulate information in order to think, solve problems, and make decisions. The storage, or maintenance, component of working memory is referred to as *short-term memory (STM).* Various memory codes can be used in short-term memory, but acoustic codes seem to be used in most verbal tasks. Studies of the *immediate memory span* indicate that the capacity of short-term memory is approximately seven meaningful groupings of information, created by *chunking.* Studies using the *Brown-Peterson distractor technique* show that information in short-term memory is usually forgotten in about eighteen seconds if it is not rehearsed.

Long-term memory (LTM) normally results from semantic encoding, which means that people tend to encode the general meaning of information, not the surface details, into long-term memory. The capacity of long-term memory to store new information is extremely large and perhaps unlimited. The appearance of a *primacy effect* and a *recency effect* suggests that short-term and long-term memory may be distinct systems.

Retrieving Memories

▶ *How do I retrieve stored memories?*

Retrieval cues help people remember things that they would otherwise not be able to recall.  The effectiveness of retrieval cues follows the *encoding specificity principle:* Cues help retrieval only if they match some feature of the information that was originally encoded. All else being equal, memory may be better when we attempt to retrieve information in the same environment in which it was learned; this is called *context-specific memory,* or *context-specific*

learning. When our internal state can affect retrieval, we have a *state-dependent memory,* or *state-dependent learning.* Researchers usually study retrieval from semantic memory by examining how long it takes people to answer general knowledge questions. It appears that ideas are represented as associations in a dense semantic memory network and that the retrieval of information occurs by a process of *spreading activation.* Each concept in the network is represented as a unique collection of features or attributes. The tip-of-the-tongue phenomenon illustrates the retrieval of incomplete knowledge.

Constructing Memories

▶ *How accurate are my memories?*

In the process of constructive memory, people use generalized knowledge, or *schemas,* to fill in gaps in the information they encode  and retrieve. PDP models provide one explanation of how people make spontaneous generalizations about the world.

Eyewitnesses can remember only what they perceive, and they can perceive only what they attend to. As a result, eyewitness testimony is often much less accurate than witnesses—and jurors—think it is.

Forgetting

▶ *What causes me to forget things?*

In his research on long-term memory and forgetting, Ebbinghaus devised a *relearning method* to measure the amount of time that is saved when previously learned material is learned again af-  ter a delay. He found that most forgetting from long-term memory occurs during the first hour after learning and that savings can be extremely long lasting. *Decay theory* and *interference* describe two mechanisms of forgetting. There is evidence of both decay and interference in short-term memory; it appears that most forgetting from long-term memory is due to interference caused by either *retroactive inhibition* or *proactive inhibition.* There is considerable controversy over the possibility of *repressed memory* of traumatic events, especially about whether recovered memories of such events are more likely to be true recollections or false, constructed ones.

Biological Bases of Memory

▶ *How does my brain change when I store a memory?*

Research has shown that memories can result from new synapses forming in the brain and improved communication at existing synapses. Studies of *anterograde amnesia, retrograde amnesia,* and other consequences of brain damage provide information about the brain structures involved

in memory. For example, the hippocampus and thalamus are known to play a role in the formation of memories. These structures

send nerve impulses to the cerebral cortex, and it is there that memories are probably stored. Memories appear to be both localized and distributed throughout the brain.

Improving your Memory

▶ *How can I remember more information?*

Mnemonic strategies are methods that can be used to remember things better. One of the simplest but most powerful mnemonic strate-

gies is the method of loci. It is useful because it provides a context for organizing material effectively. Another key memory strat-

egy is to space out your study sessions over time. This *distributed practice* is much more effective than *massed practice* ("cramming"), in which you try to learn a lot of information all at once. The key to remembering textbook material is to read actively rather than passively. One way to do this is to follow the PQ4R method: preview, question, read, reflect, recite, and review. Similarly, to take lecture notes or to study them effectively, organize the points in a meaningful outline and think about how each main point relates to the others.

Put It in Writing

Write a paragraph describing your views on the accuracy of eyewitness's memories of crimes. Be sure to mention what evidence leads you to think as you do about this topic. For example, indicate whether you tend to give more weight to the testimony of witnesses who seem very sure of their stories or to the results of scientific research on constructed and distorted memories. Be sure to say why you prefer one kind of evidence over another and whether you think the debate over the accuracy of eyewitness testimony will ever be resolved to everyone's satisfaction. If you wish, go on to write another paragraph describing your views on, and the evidence for and against, claims of recovered memories of childhood abuse.

Personal Learning Activity

When you study for your next quiz or exam, try using some of the memory tips contained in this chapter. Use one or more mnemonic devices to help you to remember lists of information, and try the PQ4R method with the next chapter you read. Did these memory-enhancing methods make it easier for you to study and to do well on your next quiz or exam? Why or why not? *For additional projects, see the Personal Learning Activities in the corresponding chapter of the study guide that accompanies this book.*

Take Action to Learn More ▶

Now that you have finished reading this chapter, how about exploring some of the ideas and information that you found most interesting? Here are some courses, books, films, and Internet resources to get you started. Enjoy!

Courses

Cognitive Psychology
Social Cognition
Experimental Psychology
Learning and Memory

Movies

The Bourne Identity; Hancock; The Majestic; Mulholland Drive. Amnesia.

Memento; The Lazarus Man; Anastasia; Blackout; Lapse of Memory; Regarding Henry. Memory loss.

Rashomon; Stagecoach. Constructive memory. *On Golden Pond.* Memory and aging.

Memory; Photographic Memory; Total Recall; Eternal Sunshine of the Spotless Mind; Overboard; 50 First Dates; Men in Black II. Futuristic, fantasy, and comedy films about constructing and losing memories; try spotting the errors in how memory processes are portrayed.

Books

Douglas J. Herrmann, Cathy McEvoy, and Christopher Hertzog (Eds.), *Basic and*

Applied Memory Research: Theory in Context (Lawrence Erlbaum Associates, 1996). Overview of memory research.

Steven Pinker, *How the Mind Works* (Norton, 1997). Biology of memory and thought.

William H. Calvin, *The Cerebral Code: Thinking a Thought in the Mosaics of the Mind* (MIT Press, 1996). Brain function and memory.

Akira Miyake and Priti Shah (Eds.), *Models of Working Memory* (Cambridge University Press, 1999). Theories of short-term memory.

Elizabeth Loftus and Katherine Ketcham, *The Myth of Repressed Memory* (St. Martin's Press, 1996). Research casting doubt on the validity of some recovered memories.

E. Sue Blume, *Secret Survivors: Uncovering Incest and Its Aftereffects in Women* (Ballantine, 1998). Presents the position of some therapists who believe in the validity of all reports of recovered memories.

Elizabeth Loftus, *Eyewitness Testimony* (Harvard University Press, 1996). Summarizes research on limitations of eyewitness testimony.

Lawrence Wright, *Remembering Satan: A Tragic Case of Recovered Memory* (Vintage, 1994). False memories led to convictions of sexual abuse for Paul Ingram.

Kathryn Lyon, *Witch Hunt* (Avon, 1998). Sexual abuse hysteria in Washington State in the 1990s led to dozens of false convictions.

Moira Johnson, *Spectral Evidence* (Westview, 1997). The Gary Ramona case that found a

therapist liable for inducing false memories of sexual abuse.

Susan Clancy, *Abducted: How People Come to Believe They Were Kidnapped by Aliens* (Harvard University Press, 2006). A fascinating summary of research on this topic.

Walter Pauk, *How to Study in College* (Houghton Mifflin, 2005). Effective study methods based on the results of memory research.

The Web

Essentials of Psychology Book Companion Website

www.cengage.com/psychology/bernstein

Visit the book companion website to access a wealth of resources, including chapter outlines, flashcards, web links, tutorial quizzes, and more!

CENGAGENOW™ Just what you need to know NOW! Spend time on what you need to master rather than on information you already have learned. Take a pre-test for this chapter, and CengageNOW will generate a personalized study plan based on your results. The study plan will identify the topics you need to review and direct you to online resources to help you master those topics. You can then take a post-test to help you determine the concepts you have mastered and what you will need to work on. Try it out! Go to www.cengage.com/login to sign in with an access code or to purchase access to this product.

Review of Key Terms ▶

Can you define each of the key terms in the chapter? Check your definitions against those on the pages shown in parentheses in the following list or in the Glossary at the end of the book.

auditory memory (acoustic memory) (p. 211)
anterograde amnesia (p. 237)
Brown-Peterson distractor technique (p. 218)
chunking (p. 217)
context-specific learning (p. 222)
context-specific memory (p. 222)
decay theory (p. 231)
distributed practice (p. 239)
elaborative rehearsal (p. 213)
encoding (p. 211)
encoding specificity principle (p. 221)
episodic memory (p. 212)
explicit memory (p. 212)

iconic memory (p. 216)
immediate memory span (p. 217)
implicit memory (p. 212)
information-processing model of memory (p. 214)
interference (p. 231)
levels-of-processing model of memory (p. 213)
long-term memory (LTM) (p. 218)
maintenance rehearsal (p. 213)
massed practice (p. 239)
mnemonic strategies (p. 239)
parallel distributed processing (PDP) models of memory (p. 213)
primacy effect (p. 221)
proactive inhibition (p. 231)
procedural knowledge (p. 212)
procedural memory (p. 212)
recall (p. 211)
recency effect (p. 221)
recognition (p. 211)

relearning method (p. 230)
repressed memory (p. 235)
retrieval (p. 211)
retrieval cues (p. 221)
retroactive inhibition (p. 231)
retrograde amnesia (p. 237)
schemas (p. 227)
selective attention (p. 216)
semantic memory (p. 211)
sensory memory (p. 216)
sensory registers (p. 216)
short-term memory (STM) (p. 216)
spreading activation (p. 223)
state-dependent learning (p. 222)
state-dependent memory (p. 222)
storage (p. 211)
transfer-appropriate processing model of memory (p. 213)
visual memory (p. 211)
working memory (p. 216)

MULTIPLE CHOICE ▶ Self Test

Select the best answer for each of the following questions. Then check your responses against the Answer Key at the end of the book.

1. Ludwig had an extraordinary memory for sound. Even when he lost his hearing in his later years, he was still able to create beautiful music. This demonstrates his well-developed _____ codes.

   a. acoustic   **c.** semantic

   b. visual   **d.** auditory

2. Henry is talking about his high school graduation ceremony. He remembers that his parents and grandparents were there and that afterward they gave him a laptop computer. Henry's memory of this event is both _____ and _____.

   a. semantic; explicit

   b. episodic; explicit

   c. semantic; implicit

   d. episodic; implicit

3. Riesa was uncomfortable when she was introduced to her roommate's cousin. She was not aware of it, but the cousin reminded her of a hated classmate in elementary school. This incident provides an example of the operation of _____ memory.
   a. procedural
   b. semantic
   c. implicit
   d. explicit

4. Raquel was still studying ten minutes before her test. As she entered the classroom, she kept repeating the last sentence she had read: "Henry VIII had six wives." She was using _____ to keep this information in mind.
   a. elaborative rehearsal
   b. maintenance rehearsal
   c. mnemonic strategies
   d. spreading activation

5. In a memory study, half the students in a class were told to expect multiple-choice questions on their upcoming exam and the other half was told to expect essay questions. Students did better if they got the type of exam they expected, which is consistent with the _____ model of memory.
   a. levels-of-processing
   b. transfer-appropriate processing
   c. parallel distributed processing
   d. information-processing

6. Reepal listens as her father describes a party the family is planning. She also smells popcorn from the kitchen, hears the radio playing, notices flashes of lightning outside, and feels too warm in her sweater. Yet Reepal is able to transfer the information about the party to her short-term memory, primarily because of _____.
   a. elaborative rehearsal
   b. implicit memory cues
   c. selective attention
   d. transfer-appropriate processing

7. Larry was thrilled when he met the girl of his dreams at the mall. She told him her phone number before she left, but if Larry doesn't use any rehearsal methods, he will remember the number for only about _____.
   a. one second.
   b. eighteen seconds.
   c. one minute.
   d. five minutes.

8. Remembering your bank account number (2171988) as your birthday (February 17, 1988) is an example of _____.
   a. chunking
   b. the Brown-Peterson distractor technique
   c. the PQ4R method
   d. the method of loci

9. Lisbeth's mother once told her to remember that "the nail that stands out will get pounded down." But when Lisbeth tried to tell a friend about this saying, she remembered it as "if you stand out too much you'll get in trouble." Her problem in recalling the exact words is probably due to the fact that encoding in long-term memory is usually _____.
   a. acoustic
   b. visual
   c. semantic
   d. state dependent

10. Raul went to a lecture on the structure of DNA but forgot his notebook and pen. He tried to remember as much of it as possible so that he could make some notes later. Research by Ebbinghaus suggests that Raul will forget most of the lecture within about _____ after it ends.
    a. eighteen seconds
    b. a minute
    c. an hour
    d. twenty-four hours

11. Nesta had made a list of twenty CDs that she wanted to check out of the library, but she forgot to bring it with her. Nesta is most likely to remember the CDs that were at the _____ of the list.
    a. beginning
    b. middle
    c. end
    d. beginning and end

12. Janetta has been studying for tomorrow's test while drinking strong caffeinated coffee. A friend tells Janetta that her test score can improve improved if she takes advantage of state-dependent memory by _____.
    a. drinking strong, caffeinated coffee just before the test.
    b. doing the rest of her studying where the test will be given.
    c. avoiding any kind of coffee just before the test.
    d. using mnemonic strategies to remember key terms.

13. Molly, a high school student, knows that she knows the name of her kindergarten teacher, but she can't quite remember it when asked. This experience is called _____.
    a. constructive memory block.
    b. sensory memory impairment.
    c. the tip-of-the-tongue phenomenon.
    d. the tip-of-the-nose phenomenon.

14. When asked if there was a fever thermometer in her doctor's office, Careen says she remembers seeing one, even though it wasn't actually there. This is an example of _____, which is influenced by _____.
    a. the tip-of-the-tongue phenomenon; schemas
    b. the tip-of-the-tongue phenomenon; selective attention
    c. constructive memory; schemas.
    d. constructive memory; selective attention.

15. Recent use of DNA evidence has had what effect on the U.S. legal system's view of eyewitness testimony?

    a. It has tended to back up eyewitness testimony.
    b. It has demonstrated that eyewitness testimony, though not always accurate, is much better than anyone thought it was.
    c. It has revealed that eyewitness testimony has put many people in prison for crimes they did not commit.
    d. It has had little effect.

16. Robin memorized the names of all of the U.S. presidents when she was 10. Two years later, she had forgotten most of them, so she was pleasantly surprised that she could learn them a second time much more quickly than the first. This faster relearning time is an example of what Ebbinghaus called _____.

    a. mnemonic strategies
    b. state dependence
    c. savings
    d. context dependence

17. Berean studied French during his first year at college and then started learning Spanish in his second year. Now he is having difficulty remembering his Spanish vocabulary because the French words keep popping into his mind. This is an example of _____.

    a. retrograde amnesia
    b. anterograde amnesia
    c. proactive inhibition
    d. retroactive inhibition

18. When her brother said he had gotten a job in a bookstore, Danielle immediately assumed it would be a large room with books along the walls, a magazine section, a children's section, and cash registers near the door. But he had been hired by an online store, so Danielle was wrong. Her mistaken assumptions occurred because of _____, which is/are predicted by the _____ model of memory.

    a. spontaneous generalizations; PDP
    b. spontaneous generalizations; information-processing
    c. constructive memory; depth of processing
    d. semantic memory; transfer-appropriate

19. Jerry, a factory worker, suffered a brain injury when a steel beam fell on his head. Jerry cannot remember anything that has happened since the accident. Jerry is experiencing _____ amnesia.

    a. retrograde   c. proactive
    b. anterograde   d. retroactive

20. Loretta wanted to remember a list of important memory researchers, so she pictured them all visiting her apartment. She imagined Elizabeth Loftus playing video games in the living room, Hermann Ebbinghaus napping in the bathtub, Henry Roediger and Kathleen McDermott dancing in the kitchen, and so on. Loretta is using the memory strategy called _____.

    a. the method of loci
    b. procedural memorization
    c. encoding cues
    d. context dependence

© artparadigm/Digital Vision/Getty Images

7 Thought, Language, *and* Intelligence

"Say what you mean, and mean what you say." This is good advice, but following it is not always easy, partly because our thoughts don't always come to us in clear, complete sentences. We have to construct those sentences—using the language we have learned—from the words, images, ideas, and other mental material in our minds. Often, the complexity of that material makes it difficult to accurately express what we are thinking. We all manage to do it, but with varying degrees of success. In this chapter, we explore what thoughts are, what language is, and how people translate one into the other. We also consider how thinking guides decision making and problem solving and how psychologists measure individual differences in these and other cognitive abilities that are commonly described as *intelligence*.

D r. Joyce Wallace, a New York City physician, was having trouble figuring out what was the matter with a 43-year-old patient, "Laura McBride." Laura reported pain in her stomach and abdomen, aching muscles, irritability, occasional dizzy spells, and fatigue (Rouéché, 1986). The doctor's first hypothesis was iron-deficiency anemia, a condition in which there is not enough oxygen-carrying hemoglobin in the blood. There was some evidence to support that hypothesis. A physical examination revealed that Laura's spleen was somewhat enlarged, and blood tests showed low hemoglobin and high production of red blood cells, suggesting that her body was attempting to compensate for the loss of hemoglobin. However, other tests revealed normal iron levels. Perhaps she was losing blood through internal bleeding, but other tests ruled that out. Had Laura been vomiting blood? She said no. Blood in the urine? No. Abnormally heavy menstrual flow? No.

As Dr. Wallace puzzled over the problem, Laura's condition worsened. She reported more intense pain, cramps, shortness of breath, and severe loss of energy. Her blood was becoming less and less capable of sustaining her, but if it was not being lost, what was happening to it? Finally, the doctor looked at a smear of Laura's blood on a microscope slide. What she saw indicated that a poison was destroying Laura's red blood cells. What could it be? Laura spent most of her time at home, and her teenage daughters, who lived with her, were perfectly healthy. Dr. Wallace asked herself, "What does Laura do that the girls do not?" She repairs and restores paintings. Paint. Lead! She might be suffering from lead poisoning! When the next blood test showed a lead level seven times higher than normal, Dr. Wallace knew she had found the answer at last.

To solve this medical mystery, Dr. Wallace relied on her intelligence, part of which can be seen in her ability to think, solve problems, and make judgments and decisions. She put these vital cognitive abilities to use in weighing the pros and cons of various hypotheses and in reaching decisions about what tests to order and how to interpret them. In consulting with the patient and other physicians, she relied on another remarkable human cognitive ability known as *language.* Let's take a look at what psychologists have discovered about these complex mental processes, how to measure them, and how to compare people in terms of intelligence. We begin by examining a general framework for understanding human thinking and then go on to look at some specific cognitive processes. ■

FIGURE 7.1 ■ **THE CIRCLE OF THOUGHT**

The circle of thought begins as our sensory systems receive information from the world. Our perceptual system describes and elaborates this information, which is represented in the brain in ways that allow us to make decisions, formulate plans, and guide our actions. As those actions change our world, we receive new information, which begins another journey around the circle of thought.

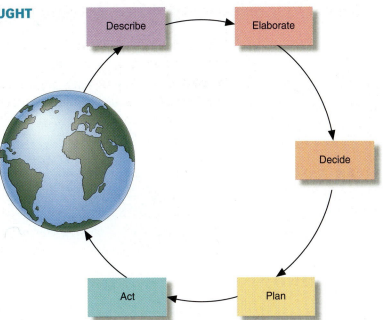

Basic Functions of Thought

● *What good is thinking, anyway?*

Understanding the mental processes that Dr. Wallace used to solve her problem begins by realizing that her thinking, like yours, involves five main operations or functions: describing, elaborating, deciding, planning, and guiding action. Figure 7.1 shows how these functions can be organized into a circle of thought.

The Circle of Thought

Consider how the circle of thought operated in Dr. Wallace's case. It began when she received the information about Laura's symptoms that enabled her to describe the problem. Next, Dr. Wallace elaborated on this information by using her knowledge, experience, and powers of reasoning to consider what disorders might cause such symptoms. Then she made a decision to investigate a possible cause, such as anemia. To pursue this decision, she formulated a plan—and then acted on that plan. But the circle of thought did not stop there. Information from the blood test provided new descriptive information, which Dr. Wallace elaborated further to reach another decision, create a new plan, and guide her next action. Each stage in the circle of thought was also influenced by her overall intention—in this case, to find and cure her patient's problem.

The processes making up the circle of thought usually occur so quickly and are so complex that slowing them down for careful analysis might seem impossible. Some psychologists approach this difficult task by studying thought processes as if they were part of a computer-like information-processing system. An **information-processing system** receives information, represents the information with symbols, and then manipulates those symbols (e.g. Anderson, Bothell et al., 2004). In an information-processing model, **thinking** is defined as the manipulation of mental representations. Figure 7.2 shows how an information-processing model might describe the sequence of mental events that make up one trip around the circle of thought.

information-processing system Mechanisms for receiving information, representing it with symbols, and manipulating it.

thinking The manipulation of mental representations.

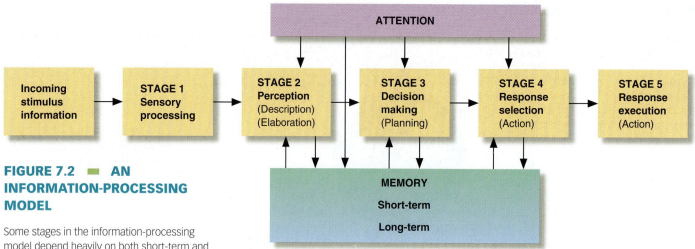

FIGURE 7.2 ■ **AN INFORMATION-PROCESSING MODEL**

Some stages in the information-processing model depend heavily on both short-term and long-term memory and require some attention, the limited supply of mental resources required for information processing to be carried out efficiently.

In the first stage, information about the world reaches your brain through the senses we discussed in the chapter on sensation and perception. This stage does not require attention. In the second stage, you must perceive and recognize the information—processes that do require attention. Also in this stage, you consciously elaborate information using the short-term and working-memory processes described in the memory chapter. These processes allow you to think about new information in relation to knowledge that is already stored in your long-term memory. Once the information has been elaborated in this way, you must decide what to do with it. This third stage—decision making—demands attention, too. Your decision might be to store the information or to take some action. If the decision is to act, it is at this stage that you plan what to do. In the fourth and fifth stages, the action is carried out. Your action usually affects the environment, providing new information that is "fed back" to the system for processing in the ongoing circle of thought.

"AUTOMATIC" THINKING ▶

The sensory, perceptual, decision-making, response-planning, and action components of the circle of thought can occur so rapidly that—as when playing a fast-paced video game—we may only be aware of the incoming information and our quick response to it. In such cases, our thinking processes become so well practiced that they are virtually automatic.

© AP Photo

Mental Representations: The Ingredients of Thought

▶ *What are thoughts made of?*

Just as measuring, stirring, and baking are only part of the story of cookie making, describing the processes of thinking tells only part of the story behind the circle of thought. Psychologists usually describe the ingredients of thought as information. But that is like saying that you make cookies with "stuff." What specific forms can information take in our minds? Cognitive psychologists have found that information can be mentally represented in many ways, including as concepts, propositions, schemas, scripts, mental models, images, and cognitive maps. Let's explore these ingredients of thought and how people manipulate them as they think.

Concepts

When you think about anything—dogs, happiness, sex, movies, pizza—you are manipulating a basic ingredient of thought called concepts. **Concepts** are categories of objects, events, or ideas with common properties. Some concepts, such as "round" and "red," are visual and concrete. Concepts such as "truth" and "justice" are more abstract and harder to define. To have a concept is to recognize the properties, or features, that tend to be shared by members of a category. For example, the concept of "bird" includes such properties as having feathers, laying eggs, and being able to fly. The concept of "scissors" includes such properties as having two blades, a connecting hinge, and a pair of finger holes. Concepts allow you to relate each object or event you encounter to a category that you already know. Using concepts, you can say, "No, that is not a dog," or "Yes, that is a car." Concepts also make it possible for you to think logically. If you have the concepts "whale" and "bird," you can decide whether a whale is a bird without having either creature in the room with you.

Types of Concepts   Some concepts—called *formal concepts*—clearly define objects or events by a set of rules and properties, so that every member of the concept has all of the concept's defining properties and nonmembers do not. For instance, the concept "square" can be defined as "a shape with four equal sides and four right-angle corners." Any object that does not have all of these features is simply not a square. Formal concepts are often used to study concept learning in the laboratory because the members of these concepts can be neatly defined (Trabasso & Bower, 1968).

In contrast, try to define the concepts "home" or "game." You might say that "home" is the place where you live and that a "game" is a competition between players. However, some people define "home" as the place where they were born, and almost everyone thinks of solitaire as a card game even though it involves only one player. These are just two examples of *natural concepts.* Unlike formal concepts, natural concepts don't have a fixed set of defining features. Instead, natural concepts have a set of typical or *characteristic* features, and members don't need to have all of them. For example, the ability to fly is a characteristic feature of the natural concept "bird," but an ostrich is still a bird even though it can't fly. It is a bird because it has enough other characteristic features of "bird" (such as feathers and wings). Having just one bird property is not enough, though. A snake lays eggs and a bat can fly, but neither animal is a bird. It is usually a combination of properties that defines a concept. In most situations outside the laboratory, people are thinking about natural rather than formal concepts. These natural concepts include object categories, such as "bird" or "house." They also include abstract idea categories, such as "honesty" or "justice," and goal-related categories, such as "things to pack for my vacation" (Barsalou, 1993).

The boundaries of a natural concept are fuzzy, so some members are better examples of it than others. A robin, a chicken, an ostrich, and a penguin are all birds. But

concepts   Categories of objects, events, or ideas that have common properties.

the robin is a better example of the bird concept than the others, because it is closer to what most people have learned to think of as a typical bird. A member of a natural concept that possesses all or most of its characteristic features is called a **prototype.** The robin is a *prototypical* bird. The more prototypical of a concept something is, the more quickly you can decide whether it is an example of the concept. This is the reason people can answer just a little more quickly when asked "Is a robin a bird?" than when asked "Is a penguin a bird?" Because prototypes are fundamental to the way we perceive and understand the world, understanding the nature of people's prototypes can have great practical value. For example, smokers—particularly young male smokers—are at greater risk for long-term cigarette use if their prototype for "smoker" includes traits such as "smart and independent" (Piko, Bak, & Gibbons, 2007). This is why health psychologists' anti-smoking programs often include efforts to create in smokers' minds a more negative prototype of the "typical smoker."

Propositions

We often combine concepts in units known as propositions. A **proposition** is a mental representation that expresses a relationship between concepts. Propositions can be true or false. Suppose you hear someone say that your friend Heather broke up with her boyfriend Jason. Your mental representation of this event will include a proposition that links your concepts of "Heather" and "Jason" in a particular way. This proposition could be diagrammed (using unscientific terms) as follows: Heather → dumped → Jason.

The arrows indicate that this statement is a proposition rather than a sentence. Propositions can be expressed as sentences, but they are actually general ideas that can be conveyed in any number of specific ways. In this case, the words "Jason was dumped by Heather" and "Heather is not willing to date Jason anymore" would all express the same proposition. If you later discovered that it was Jason who caused the breakup, the diagram of your proposition about the event would change to reflect this new information, shown here as reversed arrows: Heather ← dumped ← Jason.

Schemas, Scripts, and Mental Models

Sets of propositions are often so closely associated that they form more complex mental representations called *schemas*. As mentioned in the chapters on sensation and perception, memory, and human development, **schemas** are generalizations that we develop about categories of objects, places, events, and people. Our schemas help us

prototype   A member of a natural concept that possesses all or most of its characteristic features.

proposition   a mental representations that express a relationship between concepts.

schemas   Generalizations about categories of objects, places, events, and people.

YOU CAN'T JUDGE A BOOK BY ITS COVER ▶

Does this person look like a millionaire to you? Our schemas tell us what to expect about objects, places, events, and people, but those expectations can sometimes be wrong. This was dramatically illustrated in October 1999 when Gordon Elwood died. The Medford, Oregon, man, who dressed in rags and collected cans, left over $9 million to charity (McMahon, 2000).

© Jeff Greenberg/PhotoEdit

understand the world. If you borrow a friend's car, your "car" schema will give you a good idea of where to put the ignition key, where the accelerator and brake are, and how to raise and lower the windows. Schemas also generate expectations about objects, places, events, and people—telling us that stereo systems have speakers, that picnics occur in the summer, that rock concerts are loud, and so on.

Scripts   Schemas about familiar activities, such as going to a restaurant, are known as **scripts** (Anderson, 2000). Your "restaurant" script represents the sequence of events you can expect when you go out to eat. That script tells you what to do when you are in a restaurant and helps you understand stories involving restaurants (Whitney, 2001). Scripts also shape your interpretation of events. For example, on your first day of college, you no doubt assumed that the person standing at the front of the class was a teacher, not a security guard or a janitor.

If our scripts are violated, however, it is easy to misinterpret events. In one case, a heart attack victim in London lay for nine hours in the hallway of an apartment building after an ambulance crew smelled alcohol on his breath and assumed he was "sleeping it off." The crew's script for what happens in the poorer sections of big cities told them that someone slumped in a hallway is drunk, not sick. Because script-violating events are unexpected, our reactions to them tend to be slower and less effective than our reactions to expected events. Your "grocery shopping" script, for example, probably includes pushing a cart, putting items in it, going to the checkout stand, paying, and leaving. But suppose you are at the back of the store when a robber near the entrance fires a gun and shouts at the manager to open the safe. People sometimes ignore these script-violating events, interpreting gunshots as a car backfiring and shouted orders as "someone fooling around." Others simply freeze, unsure of what to do or not realizing that they could call the police on their cell phones.

Mental Models   The relationships among concepts can be organized not only as schemas and scripts but also as **mental models** (Johnson-Laird, 1983). For example, suppose someone tells you, "My living room has blue walls, a white ceiling, and an oval window across from the door." You will mentally represent this information as propositions about how the concepts "wall," "blue," "ceiling," "white," "door," "oval," and "window" are related. However, you will also combine these propositions to create in your mind a three-dimensional model of the room. As more information about the world becomes available, either from existing memories or from new information we receive, our mental models become more complete.

Accurate mental models are excellent guides for thinking about, and interacting with, many of the things we encounter every day (Ashcraft, 2006). If our mental models are incorrect, however, we are likely to make mistakes (see Figure 7.3). For example, college students make more effective Internet searches if their mental models of search engines recognize that computers require precise search terms. Students who think that human operators read and interpret the meaning of the search terms they enter are less likely to use precise terms and thus tend to get less useful results (Zang, 2008). Similarly, people who hold an incorrect mental model of how physical illness is cured might stop taking their antibiotic medication when their symptoms begin to disappear, well before the bacteria causing those symptoms have been eliminated (Medin, Ross, & Markman, 2001). Others overdose on medication because according to their faulty mental model, "if taking three pills a day is good, taking six would be even better."

Images and Cognitive Maps

Think about how your best friend would look in a clown suit. The mental picture you just got illustrates that thinking often involves the manipulation of **images**—mental representations of visual information. We can manipulate these images in a way that is similar to manipulating the objects themselves (Reed, 2000; see Figure 7.4). Our ability to think using images extends beyond the manipulation of stimuli such as those in Figure 7.4. We also create mental images that serve as mental models of descriptions

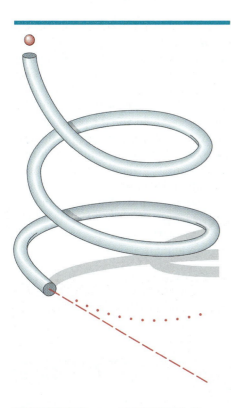

FIGURE 7.3 ■ APPLYING A MENTAL MODEL

Try to imagine the path that the ball will follow when it leaves the curved tube. In one study, most people drew the incorrect (curved) path indicated by the dotted line, rather than the correct (straight) path indicated by the dashed line (McCloskey, 1983). Their error was based on the construction of a faulty mental model of the behavior of physical objects.   **Learn BY Doing**

scripts   Mental representations of familiar sequences of activity.

mental models   Sets of propositions that represent people's understanding of how things look and work.

images   Mental representations of visual information.

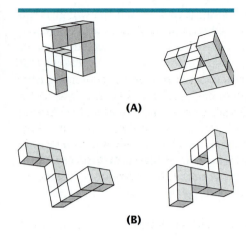

(A)

(B)

FIGURE 7.4 ■ MANIPULATING IMAGES

Are these pairs of objects the same or different? To decide, you will have to rotate one member of each pair. Because manipulating mental images, like manipulating actual objects, takes some time, the speed of your decision will depend on how far you have to mentally rotate one object to line it up with the other for comparison. (The top pair matches; the bottom pair does not.) Brain imaging studies have confirmed that manipulating mental images activates some of the same visual and spatial areas of the brain that are active during comparable tasks with real objects (Mazoyer et al., 2002). *Source*: Shepard & Metzler (1971).

Learn BY **Doing**

Improve Your Grade
Tutorial: Rotating Mental Objects

we hear or read (Mazoyer et al., 2002). For example, you probably created an image a minute ago when you read about that blue-walled room.

The same thing happens when someone gives you directions to a new pizza place in town. In this case, you scan your **cognitive map**—a mental model of familiar parts of your world—to find the location. In doing so, you use a mental process similar to the visual process of scanning a paper map (Anderson, 2000; Taylor & Tversky, 1992). Manipulating images on a different cognitive map would help you if a power failure left your home pitch dark. Even though you couldn't see a thing, you could still find a flashlight or candle because your cognitive map would show the floor plan, furniture placement, door locations, and other physical features of your home. You would not have this mental map in a hotel room or an unfamiliar house; there, you would have to walk slowly, arms outstretched, to avoid wrong turns and painful collisions. In the chapter on learning we describe how experience shapes cognitive maps that help animals navigate mazes and people navigate shopping malls. ("In Review: Ingredients of Thought" summarizes the ways we mentally represent information.)

In Review

INGREDIENTS OF THOUGHT

INGREDIENT	DESCRIPTION	EXAMPLES
Concepts	Categories of objects, events, or ideas with common properties; basic building blocks of thought	"Square" (a formal concept); "game" (a natural concept)
Propositions	Mental representations that express relationships between concepts; can be true or false	Assertions such as "The cow jumped over the moon."
Schemas	Sets of propositions that create generalizations and expectations about categories of objects, places, events, and people	A schema might suggest that all grandmothers are elderly, are gray haired, and bake a lot of cookies.
Scripts	Schemas about familiar activities and situations that guide behavior in those situations	You pay before eating in fast-food restaurants and after eating in fancier restaurants.
Mental models	A representation of how concepts relate to each other in the real world; can be correct or incorrect	Mistakenly assuming that airflow around an open car will send thrown objects upward, a driver tosses a lighted cigarette butt overhead, causing it to land in the back seat.
Images	Mental representations of visual information	Hearing a description of your blind date creates a mental picture of him or her.
Cognitive maps	Mental representations of familiar parts of the world	You can get to class by an alternate route even if your usual route is blocked by construction.

?
1. *Thinking is the manipulation of _____.*
2. *Arguments over what is "fair" occur because "fairness" is a _____ concept.*
3. *Your _____ of "hotel room" would lead you to expect yours to include a bathroom.*

cognitive map A mental model that represents familiar parts of the environment.

Thinking Strategies

▶ *Do people always think logically?*

We have seen that our thinking capacity is based largely on our ability to manipulate mental representations—the ingredients of thought—much as a baker manipulates the ingredients of cookies. The baker's food-processing system combines and transforms these ingredients into a delicious treat. Our information-processing system combines, transforms, and elaborates mental representations in ways that allow us to engage in reasoning, problem solving, and decision making. Let's begin our discussion of these thinking strategies by considering **reasoning:** the process through which we generate and evaluate arguments, as well as reach conclusions about them.

Formal Reasoning

Astronomers tell us that the temperature at the core of the sun is about 27 million degrees Fahrenheit. How do they know this? They can't put a temperature probe inside the sun, so their estimate is based on *inferences* from other things that they know about the sun and about physical objects in general. For example, telescopic observations allowed astronomers to calculate the energy coming from one small part of the sun. They then used what geometry told them about the surface area of spheres to estimate the sun's total energy output. Further calculations told them how hot a body would have to be to generate that much energy.

In other words, astronomers' estimates of the sun's core temperature are based on **formal reasoning** (also called *logical reasoning*)—the process of following a set of rigorous steps for reaching valid, or correct, conclusions. Some of these steps included applying specific mathematical formulas to existing data in order to generate new data. Such formulas are examples of **algorithms**—systematic methods that always reach a correct solution to a problem if a correct solution exists.

The astronomers also followed the rules of **logic,** a set of statements that provide a formula for drawing valid conclusions about the world. For example, each step in the astronomers' thinking took the form of if-then propositions: if we know how much energy comes from one part of the sun's surface and if we know how big the whole surface is, then we can calculate the total energy output. You use the same logical reasoning processes when you conclude, for example, that if your friend José is two years older than you are, then his twin brother, Juan, will be two years older, too. This kind of reasoning is called *deductive reasoning*, because it takes a general rule (e.g., twins are the same age) and applies it to deduce conclusions about specific cases (e.g., José and Juan).

Most of us try to use logical or deductive reasoning to reach valid conclusions and avoid invalid ones. However, even when our logic is perfect, we can make mistakes if we base our reasoning on false assumptions. Likewise, correct assumptions combined with faulty logic can lead to errors. Do you think the following example leads to a valid conclusion?

> Assumption 1: *All women want to be mothers.*
> Assumption 2: *Jill is a woman.*
> Conclusion: *Jill wants to be a mother.*

If you said that the first assumption is not necessarily correct, you're right. Now consider this example:

> Assumption 1: *All gun owners are people.*
> Assumption 2: *All criminals are people.*
> Conclusion: *All gun owners are criminals.*

Here, the assumptions are correct but the logic is faulty. According to the rules of logic, if "all As are B" and "all Cs are B," it does not follow that "all As are C." So it is

reasoning   The process by which people generate and evaluate arguments and reach conclusions about them.

formal reasoning   A set of rigorous procedures for reaching valid conclusions.

algorithms   Systematic procedures that cannot fail to produce a correct solution to a problem.

logic   A system of formulas for drawing valid conclusions.

PITFALLS IN LOGICAL REASONING   ▲

"Elderly people cannot be astronauts; this is an elderly man; therefore, he cannot be an astronaut." The logic is correct, but because the first statement is wrong, so is the conclusion. In 1962, John Glenn became the first American astronaut to orbit the earth. Here he is in 1998, at the age of 77, just before he returned to space as a full-fledged member of the crew of the space shuttle *Discovery*.

► Formal reasoning follows the rules of logic, but there are no foolproof rules for informal reasoning, as this fool demonstrates.

true that all gun owners are people and that all criminals are people, but it does not follow that all gun owners are criminals.

Psychologists have discovered that both kinds of pitfalls we just described can lead people to make errors in logical reasoning. This finding is one reason that misleading advertisements or speeches can still attract sales and votes (Cialdini, 2001).

Informal Reasoning

Using the rules of formal logic to deduce answers about specific cases is an important kind of reasoning, but it is not the only kind. A second kind, **informal reasoning,** comes into play when we are trying to assess the *believability* of a conclusion based on the evidence available to support it. Informal reasoning is also known as *inductive reasoning,* because its goal is to induce a general conclusion to appear on the basis of specific facts or examples. Psychologists use informal reasoning when they design experiments and other research methods whose results will provide evidence for (or against) their theories. Jurors use informal reasoning when weighing evidence for the guilt or innocence of a defendant. And air crash investigators use it in their efforts to discover and eliminate the causes of aviation accidents.

Formal reasoning is guided by algorithms, or formulas, but there are no foolproof methods for informal reasoning. For instance, how many white swans would you have to see before concluding that all swans are white? Fifty? A hundred? A million? Formal logic would require that you observe every swan in existence. A more practical approach is to base your conclusion on the number of observations that some mental rule of thumb leads you to believe is enough. In other words, you would take a mental shortcut to reach a conclusion that is probably, but not necessarily, correct (there are, in fact, black swans). Such mental shortcuts are called **heuristics** (pronounced "hyoor-IST-ix").

Heuristics can be helpful, but they can also bias our thinking and cause errors. Suppose your rule of thumb is to vote for all the candidates in a particular political party instead of researching the views of each individual. You might end up voting for someone with whom you strongly disagree on some issues. The extent to which heuristics are responsible for important errors in judgment and decision making is still being studied and debated by cognitive psychologists (e.g., Hilton, 2002; Medin & Bazerman, 1999). Nevertheless, Amos Tversky and Daniel Kahneman (1974; 1993) have described three potentially problematic heuristics that often affect people's judgments. These are the *anchoring heuristic* (also known as *anchoring bias*), the *representativeness heuristic,* and the *availability heuristic.*

The Anchoring Bias   People use the **anchoring bias** (also called the **anchoring heuristic**) when they estimate the probability of some event by adjusting their existing estimate rather than starting from scratch on the basis of new information (Rottenstreich & Tversky, 1997). This strategy sounds reasonable, but their existing estimate biases their final judgment. So even if new information suggests that their first estimate is way off, people may not adjust that estimate enough. It is as if they have dropped a "mental

Improve Your Grade
Improve Your Grade Tutorial: Common Heuristics

informal reasoning   The process of evaluating a conclusion based on the evidence available to support it.

heuristics   Mental shortcuts or rules of thumb.

anchoring bias (anchoring heuristic)   A shortcut in the thought process that involves adding new information to existing information to reach a judgment.

anchor" that keeps them from drifting too far from their original judgment. Suppose you think that the chance of being mugged in Los Angeles is 90 percent, but then you see evidence that the figure is closer to 1 percent. You might reduce your estimate, but only to 80 percent, so your new estimate is still quite inaccurate. The anchoring heuristic presents a challenge for defense attorneys in U.S. criminal courts because the prosecution presents its evidence first. Once this evidence has created the impression that a defendant is guilty, some jurors mentally anchor to that impression and may not be swayed much by defense evidence to the contrary (Hogarth & Einhorn, 1992). In a similar way, first impressions of people are not easily shifted by later evidence (see the chapter on social psychology).

The Representativeness Heuristic   People use the **representativeness heuristic** when they conclude that something belongs in a certain class based on how similar it is to other items in that class. For example, consider this personality sketch:

> *Tom W. is of high intelligence although lacking in true creativity. He has a need for order and clarity and for neat and tidy systems in which every detail finds its appropriate place. His writing is rather dull and mechanical, occasionally enlivened by somewhat corny puns and by flashes of imagination of the sci-fi type. He has a strong drive for competence. He seems to have little feeling and little sympathy for other people and does not enjoy interacting with others. Self-centered, he nonetheless has a deep moral sense.*

Do you think it is more likely that Tom is majoring in computer science or psychology? Research by Kahneman and Tversky (1973; Tversky & Kahneman, 1974) showed that most people would choose *computer science*. But this answer would probably be wrong. True, the description given is more similar to the prototypical computer science major than to the prototypical psychology major. However, there are many more psychology majors than computer science majors in the world. So there are probably more psychology majors than computer science majors who match this description. In fact, almost any personality sketch is more likely to describe a psychology major than a computer science major.

The representativeness heuristic affects many real-life judgments and decisions. For example, jury decisions depend partly on the degree to which a defendant's actions are representative of a particular crime category. So someone who abducts a child and asks for ransom is more likely to be convicted of kidnapping than someone who abducts an adult and demands no ransom (Smith, 1991). Both crimes constitute kidnapping, but the first is a more representative example.

The Availability Heuristic   People use the **availability heuristic** when they judge the likelihood of an event or the correctness of a hypothesis by how easy it is to think of that event or hypothesis (Tversky & Kahneman, 1974). In other words, they tend to choose the hypothesis or predict the event that is most mentally "available," much as they might select the box of cereal that happens to be at the front of the supermarket shelf. Although the availability heuristic tends to work well, it too can lead to biased judgments—especially when the mental availability of events doesn't match their actual frequency (Morewedge, Gilbert, & Wilson, 2005). For example, news reports about shark attacks and urban shootings lead many people to overestimate how often these memorable but relatively rare events actually occur (Ungemach, Chater, & Stewart, 2009). As a result, people may suffer undue anxiety over swimming in the ocean or being in certain cities (Bellaby, 2003). Similarly, many students stick with their first responses to multiple-choice test questions because it is especially easy to recall those galling occasions on which they changed a right answer to a wrong one. Research shows, though, that an answer that is changed in light of further reflection is more likely to be correct than incorrect (Kruger, Wirtz, & Miller, 2005).

The three heuristics we have presented represent only a few of the many mental shortcuts that people use more or less automatically in making judgments in daily life (Todd & Gigerenzer, 2007), and they describe only some of the biases and limitations

representativeness heuristic   A mental shortcut that involves judging whether something belongs in a given class on the basis of its similarity to other members of that class.

availability heuristic   A mental shortcut through which judgments are based on information that is most easily brought to mind.

that operate in human reasoning. Other biases and limitations are described in the following sections, as we consider two important goals of thinking: problem solving and decision making.

Problem Solving

 What's the best way to solve a problem?

Suppose that you're lost, you don't have a map or a navigation system, and there's nobody around to ask for directions. You have a *problem.* The circle of thought suggests that the most efficient approach to solving it would be to first diagnose the problem in the elaboration stage, then formulate a plan for solving it, then execute the plan, and finally evaluate the results to determine whether the problem remains. But people's problem-solving efforts are not always so systematic. This is one reason why medical tests are sometimes given unnecessarily, diseases are sometimes misdiagnosed, and auto parts are sometimes replaced when there is nothing wrong with them.

Strategies for Problem Solving

When you are trying to get from one place to another, the best path may not necessarily be a straight line. In fact, obstacles may require going in the opposite direction to get around them. So it is with problem solving. Sometimes the best strategy does not involve mental steps aimed straight at your goal. For example, when a problem is especially difficult, it can sometimes be helpful to allow it to "incubate" by setting it aside for a while. A solution that once seemed out of reach may suddenly appear after you have been thinking about other things. The benefits of *incubation* probably arise from forgetting incorrect ideas that may have been blocking the path to a correct solution (Anderson, 2000). Other effective problem-solving strategies are more direct.

One of these strategies is called *means-end analysis.* It involves continuously asking where you are in relation to your final goal and then deciding on the means by which you can get one step closer to that goal (Newell & Simon, 1972). In other words, rather than trying to solve the problem all at once, you identify a subgoal that will take you toward a solution (this process is also referred to as *decomposition*). After reaching that subgoal, you identify another one that will get you even closer to the solution, and you continue this step-by-step process until the problem is solved. Some students apply this approach to the problem of writing a major term paper. The task might seem overwhelming at first, but their first subgoal is simply to write an outline of what they think the paper should cover. When the outline is complete, they decide whether a paper based on it will satisfy the assignment. If it will, the next subgoal might be to search the library and the Internet for information about each section. If they decide

▶ Simply knowing about problem-solving strategies, such as decomposition, is not enough. As described in the chapter on motivation and emotion, people must believe that the effort required is worth the rewards it can bring.

CALVIN AND HOBBES © Watterson Reprinted with permission of UNIVERSAL PRESS SYNDICATE. All rights reserved.

anchor" that keeps them from drifting too far from their original judgment. Suppose you think that the chance of being mugged in Los Angeles is 90 percent, but then you see evidence that the figure is closer to 1 percent. You might reduce your estimate, but only to 80 percent, so your new estimate is still quite inaccurate. The anchoring heuristic presents a challenge for defense attorneys in U.S. criminal courts because the prosecution presents its evidence first. Once this evidence has created the impression that a defendant is guilty, some jurors mentally anchor to that impression and may not be swayed much by defense evidence to the contrary (Hogarth & Einhorn, 1992). In a similar way, first impressions of people are not easily shifted by later evidence (see the chapter on social psychology).

The Representativeness Heuristic   People use the **representativeness heuristic** when they conclude that something belongs in a certain class based on how similar it is to other items in that class. For example, consider this personality sketch:

> *Tom W. is of high intelligence although lacking in true creativity. He has a need for order and clarity and for neat and tidy systems in which every detail finds its appropriate place. His writing is rather dull and mechanical, occasionally enlivened by somewhat corny puns and by flashes of imagination of the sci-fi type. He has a strong drive for competence. He seems to have little feeling and little sympathy for other people and does not enjoy interacting with others. Self-centered, he nonetheless has a deep moral sense.*

Do you think it is more likely that Tom is majoring in computer science or psychology? Research by Kahneman and Tversky (1973; Tversky & Kahneman, 1974) showed that most people would choose *computer science*. But this answer would probably be wrong. True, the description given is more similar to the prototypical computer science major than to the prototypical psychology major. However, there are many more psychology majors than computer science majors in the world. So there are probably more psychology majors than computer science majors who match this description. In fact, almost any personality sketch is more likely to describe a psychology major than a computer science major.

The representativeness heuristic affects many real-life judgments and decisions. For example, jury decisions depend partly on the degree to which a defendant's actions are representative of a particular crime category. So someone who abducts a child and asks for ransom is more likely to be convicted of kidnapping than someone who abducts an adult and demands no ransom (Smith, 1991). Both crimes constitute kidnapping, but the first is a more representative example.

The Availability Heuristic   People use the **availability heuristic** when they judge the likelihood of an event or the correctness of a hypothesis by how easy it is to think of that event or hypothesis (Tversky & Kahneman, 1974). In other words, they tend to choose the hypothesis or predict the event that is most mentally "available," much as they might select the box of cereal that happens to be at the front of the supermarket shelf. Although the availability heuristic tends to work well, it too can lead to biased judgments—especially when the mental availability of events doesn't match their actual frequency (Morewedge, Gilbert, & Wilson, 2005). For example, news reports about shark attacks and urban shootings lead many people to overestimate how often these memorable but relatively rare events actually occur (Ungemach, Chater, & Stewart, 2009). As a result, people may suffer undue anxiety over swimming in the ocean or being in certain cities (Bellaby, 2003). Similarly, many students stick with their first responses to multiple-choice test questions because it is especially easy to recall those galling occasions on which they changed a right answer to a wrong one. Research shows, though, that an answer that is changed in light of further reflection is more likely to be correct than incorrect (Kruger, Wirtz, & Miller, 2005).

The three heuristics we have presented represent only a few of the many mental shortcuts that people use more or less automatically in making judgments in daily life (Todd & Gigerenzer, 2007), and they describe only some of the biases and limitations

representativeness heuristic   A mental shortcut that involves judging whether something belongs in a given class on the basis of its similarity to other members of that class.

availability heuristic   A mental shortcut through which judgments are based on information that is most easily brought to mind.

that operate in human reasoning. Other biases and limitations are described in the following sections, as we consider two important goals of thinking: problem solving and decision making.

Problem Solving

 What's the best way to solve a problem?

Suppose that you're lost, you don't have a map or a navigation system, and there's nobody around to ask for directions. You have a *problem*. The circle of thought suggests that the most efficient approach to solving it would be to first diagnose the problem in the elaboration stage, then formulate a plan for solving it, then execute the plan, and finally evaluate the results to determine whether the problem remains. But people's problem-solving efforts are not always so systematic. This is one reason why medical tests are sometimes given unnecessarily, diseases are sometimes misdiagnosed, and auto parts are sometimes replaced when there is nothing wrong with them.

Strategies for Problem Solving

When you are trying to get from one place to another, the best path may not necessarily be a straight line. In fact, obstacles may require going in the opposite direction to get around them. So it is with problem solving. Sometimes the best strategy does not involve mental steps aimed straight at your goal. For example, when a problem is especially difficult, it can sometimes be helpful to allow it to "incubate" by setting it aside for a while. A solution that once seemed out of reach may suddenly appear after you have been thinking about other things. The benefits of *incubation* probably arise from forgetting incorrect ideas that may have been blocking the path to a correct solution (Anderson, 2000). Other effective problem-solving strategies are more direct.

One of these strategies is called *means-end analysis*. It involves continuously asking where you are in relation to your final goal and then deciding on the means by which you can get one step closer to that goal (Newell & Simon, 1972). In other words, rather than trying to solve the problem all at once, you identify a subgoal that will take you toward a solution (this process is also referred to as *decomposition*). After reaching that subgoal, you identify another one that will get you even closer to the solution, and you continue this step-by-step process until the problem is solved. Some students apply this approach to the problem of writing a major term paper. The task might seem overwhelming at first, but their first subgoal is simply to write an outline of what they think the paper should cover. When the outline is complete, they decide whether a paper based on it will satisfy the assignment. If it will, the next subgoal might be to search the library and the Internet for information about each section. If they decide

▶ Simply knowing about problem-solving strategies, such as decomposition, is not enough. As described in the chapter on motivation and emotion, people must believe that the effort required is worth the rewards it can bring.

Calvin and Hobbes   by Bill Watterson

that this information is adequate, the next subgoal would be to write a rough draft of the introduction, and so on.

A second strategy in problem solving is to *work backward.* Many problems are like a tree. The trunk is the information you are given; the solution is a twig on one of the branches. If you work forward by taking the "givens" of the problem and trying to find the solution, it's easy to branch off in the wrong direction. Sometimes the more efficient approach is to start at the twig end and work backward. Consider the problem of planning a climb to the summit of Mount Everest. The best strategy is to figure out, first, what equipment and supplies are needed at the highest camp on the night before the attempt to reach the summit, then how many people are needed to stock that camp the day before, then how many people are needed to supply those who must stock the camp, and so on until a plan for the entire expedition is established. People often overlook the working-backward strategy because it runs counter to the way they have learned to think. It is hard to imagine that the first step in solving a problem could be to assume that you have already solved it. Sadly, it was partly because of failure to apply this strategy that six climbers died on Everest in 1996 (Krakauer, 1997).

A third problem-solving strategy is trying to find *analogies,* or similarities, between today's problem and others you have encountered before. A supervisor may discover that a seemingly hopeless problem between co-workers can be resolved by the same compromise that worked during a recent family squabble. Of course, to take advantage of analogies, you must first recognize the similarities between current and previous problems. Then you will be in a position to recall the solution that worked before. Unfortunately, most people are surprisingly poor at seeing the similarities between new and old problems (Anderson, 2000). They tend to concentrate on the surface features that make problems appear different.

© AP Photo

WORKING BACKWARD TO FORGE AHEAD ▲

Whether you are organizing a family vacation or preparing to sail alone in an around-the-world race, as Ellen MacArthur did, working backward from the final goal through all the steps necessary to reach that goal is a helpful approach to solving complex problems.

Focus on RESEARCH

Problem-Solving Strategies in the Real World

The value of using analogies in problem solving was beautifully illustrated in relation to the Hubble Space Telescope. In 1990, this telescope was placed in an earth orbit to take detailed photographs of distant galaxies, but because its main mirror was not focusing light properly, the pictures were blurry. When NASA engineer James Crocker happened to notice the way a hotel room showerhead pivoted, it gave him the idea for a system of movable mirrors to correct for the flaw in the Hubble's mirror. Shuttle astronauts installed these mirrors in 1993, and the problem was solved (Stein, 1993).

How do people use the other problem-solving strategies we have described to solve real-world problems? To explore this question, researchers have reconstructed problem-solving strategies associated with major inventions and scientific discoveries (Klahr & Simon, 1999; Weber, 1992).

▶ What was the researcher's question?

On December 17, 1903, Wilbur and Orville Wright successfully flew the first heavier-than-air flying machine. Gary Bradshaw (1993a, 1993b) was interested in identifying the problem-solving strategies that led to this momentous event. He found that 49 individuals or teams had worked on the problem of heavier-than-air flight, but only the Wright brothers were successful. In fact, it took them only four years to develop the airplane, whereas others worked for

decades without success. Bradshaw asked, How did the Wright brothers solve the problem of creating a heavier-than-air flying machine when so many others had failed?

▶ How did the researcher answer the question?

Bradshaw compared the written records left by all the individuals and teams who had worked on an airplane design. Using this *comparative case study* method, he was able to see patterns in the ways they approached the flying machine problem.

▶ What did the researcher find?

Bradshaw found several factors that might have contributed to the Wright brothers' success. First, as bachelors, they had a lot of spare time to work on their designs. Second, they owned a bicycle shop, so they were familiar with lightweight but sturdy structures. Third, they were brothers who had a good working relationship. And finally, as mechanics, they were good with their hands. Were any of these features directly responsible for their successful invention of the airplane?

Perhaps, but Bradshaw's use of the comparative case study method revealed that everyone else working on the problem of flight shared at least one of these features with the Wright brothers. For instance, an engineer named Octave Chanute was good with his hands and familiar with lightweight, sturdy structures.

And two other pairs of brothers had worked together to try to invent a flying machine.

However, Bradshaw found one feature that was unique to the Wright brothers' approach. Of all the inventors working on the problem, only the Wrights spent considerable time and energy testing aircraft components before field-testing complete machines. This feature was important because even the best designs of the day flew for only a few seconds—far too briefly to reveal what was working and what was not. As a result, inventors had to guess about what to fix and often ended up with an "improved" model that was worse than the previous one.

▶ What do the results mean?

Bradshaw's comparative case study method suggested that the problem-solving strategy of decomposition was the basis for the Wright brothers' success. By testing components, they were able to collect the information they needed to develop an efficient propeller, improve the shape of the wings for maximum lift, and refine other vital components of their aircraft.

▶ What do we still need to know?

Decomposition is a strategy often seen in the laboratory, and as demonstrated by the case of the Wright brothers, it is a potentially important aspect of major inventions and discoveries beyond the laboratory. But is decomposition, or means-end analysis, used in other real-world settings as well? To find out, researchers will need to conduct additional studies of the mental strategies people use as they attempt to solve problems ranging from how to install a new computer to how to efficiently search the Internet.

Obstacles to Problem Solving

The failure of the Wright brothers' competitors to use decomposition is just one example of the obstacles that face problem solvers every day. Difficulties frequently occur at the start, during the diagnosis stage, when a person forms and then tests hypotheses about a problem.

As a case in point, consider this true story: In September 1998, John Gatiss was in the kitchen of his rented house in Cheltenham, England, when he heard a faint "meowing" sound. Worried that a kitten had become trapped somewhere, he called for the fire brigade to rescue the animal. The sound seemed to be coming from the electric stove, so the rescuers dismantled it, disconnecting the power cord in the process. The sound stopped, but everyone assumed that wherever the kitten was, it was now too frightened to meow. The search was reluctantly abandoned and the stove was reconnected. Four days later, however, the meowing began anew. This time, Gatiss and his landlord called the Royal Society for the Prevention of Cruelty to Animals (RSPCA), whose inspectors heard the kitten in distress and asked the fire brigade to come back. They spent the next three days searching for the cat. First, they dismantled parts of the kitchen walls and ripped up the floorboards. Next, they called in plumbing and drainage specialists, who used cables tipped with fiber-optic cameras to search remote cavities where a kitten might hide. Rescuers then brought in a disaster search team, which tried to find the kitten with acoustic and ultrasonic equipment normally used to locate victims trapped under earthquake debris. Not a sound was heard. Increasingly concerned about how much longer the kitten could survive, the fire brigade tried to coax it from hiding with the finest-quality fish, but to no avail. Suddenly, there was a burst of "purring" that, to everyone's surprise (and the landlord's dismay), was traced by the ultrasonic equipment to the clock in the electric stove! Later, the landlord commented that everyone assumed Gatiss's original hypothesis was correct—that the "meowing" came from a cat trapped in the kitchen. "I just let them carry on. If there is an animal in there, you have to do what it takes. The funniest thing was that it seemed to reply when we called out to it" (*London Daily Telegraph*, 1998).

How could fifteen fire-rescue workers, three RSPCA inspectors, four drainage workers, and two acoustics experts waste eight days and cause nearly $2,000 in damage to a house in pursuit of a nonexistent kitten? The answer lies in the fact that they, like the rest of us, were prone to four main obstacles to efficient problem solving, described in the following sections.

Multiple Hypotheses   Often we begin to solve a problem with only a hazy notion of which hypotheses to test. Suppose you heard a strange sound in your kitchen.

FIGURE 7.5 ■ THE JAR PROBLEM

The task here is to come up with the number of quarts of water shown in the first column by using jars with the capacities shown in the next three columns. Each line represents a different problem and you have an unlimited supply of water for each one. Try to solve all seven problems without looking at the answers in the text.

Learn BY Doing

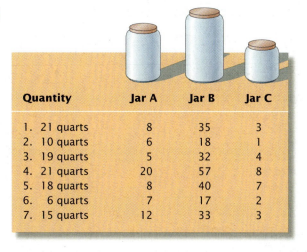

Quantity	Jar A	Jar B	Jar C
1. 21 quarts	8	35	3
2. 10 quarts	6	18	1
3. 19 quarts	5	32	4
4. 21 quarts	20	57	8
5. 18 quarts	8	40	7
6. 6 quarts	7	17	2
7. 15 quarts	12	33	3

FIGURE 7.6 ■ THE NINE-DOT PROBLEM

The problem is to draw no more than four straight lines that run through all nine dots on the page without lifting your pencil from the paper. Figure 7.8 shows two ways of going beyond mental sets to solve this problem.

Learn BY Doing

mental set The tendency for old patterns of problem solving to persist.

functional fixedness The tendency to think about familiar objects in familiar ways.

It could be caused by several different things, but which hypotheses should you test, and in what order?

People have a difficult time working with more than two or three hypotheses at a time (Mehle, 1982). The limited capacity of short-term memory may be part of the reason (Halford et al., 2005). As discussed in the memory chapter, a person can hold only about seven chunks of information in short-term memory. Because a single hypothesis, let alone two or three, might include more than seven chunks, it may be difficult or impossible to keep them all in mind at once. Further, the availability and representativeness heuristics may lead people to choose the hypothesis that comes most easily to mind and seems most likely to fit the circumstances (Tversky & Kahneman, 1974). That hypothesis may be wrong, though, meaning that the correct hypothesis is never considered. Mr. Gatiss diagnosed what he heard as distressed meowing because it sounded more like a kitten than a clock and because it was easier to imagine an animal trapped behind the stove than a suddenly faulty clock inside it.

Mental Sets Sometimes people are so blinded by one hypothesis or strategy that they stick with it even when better alternatives should be obvious. This is a clear case of the anchoring heuristic at work. Once Gatiss reported hearing a "trapped kitten,"

Learn BY Doing his description created an assumption that everyone else accepted and no one challenged. Figure 7.5 shows a problem-solving situation in which such errors often appear. The first problem in the figure is to come up with 21 quarts of liquid by using 3 jars that have capacities of 8, 35, and 3 quarts, respectively. Before you read any further, try to solve this problem and all the others listed in Figure 7.5.

How did you do? You probably figured out that the solution to the first problem is to fill Jar B to its capacity of 35 quarts, and then use its contents to fill Jar A to its capacity of 8 quarts, leaving 27 quarts in Jar B. Finally, you pour from Jar B to fill Jar C twice, leaving 21 quarts in Jar B [27 − (2 × 3) = 21]. You probably found that a similar solution worked for each problem. In fact, by the time you reached Problem 7, you might have developed a **mental set**, a tendency for old patterns of problem solving to persist (Luchins, 1942; Sweller & Gee, 1978). If so, your mental set probably caused you to use the same old formula (B − A − 2C) even though a simpler one (A + C) would have worked just as well. Figures 7.6 and 7.8 show another way in which mental sets can restrict our perception of the possible solutions to a problem.

Another restriction on problem solving may come from experience with objects. Once people become familiar with using an object for one purpose, they may be blinded to other ways of using it. Long experience may produce **functional fixedness,** a tendency to use familiar objects in familiar rather than creative ways (German &

FIGURE 7.7 ■ AN EXAMPLE OF FUNCTIONAL FIXEDNESS

Before reading further, look at this drawing and ask yourself how you would fasten together two strings that are hanging from the ceiling but are too far apart for you to grasp at the same time. Several tools are available, yet most people don't think of attaching, say, a hammer to one string and swinging it like a pendulum until it can be reached while holding the other string. This solution is not obvious because we tend to fixate on the hammer's function as a tool rather than as a weight. People are more likely to solve this problem if the tools are scattered around the room. If the hammer is in a toolbox, its function as a tool is emphasized, and functional fixedness becomes nearly impossible to break.

Learn BY **Doing**

FIGURE 7.8 ■ TWO CREATIVE SOLUTIONS TO THE NINE-DOT PROBLEM

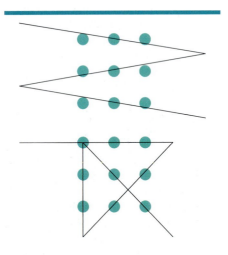

Many people find problems like this difficult because mental sets create artificial limits on the range of solutions. In this case, the mental sets involve the tendency to draw within the frame of the dots and to draw through the middle of each dot. As shown here, however, there are other possibilities.

confirmation bias   The tendency to pay more attention to evidence in support of one's hypothesis about a problem than to evidence that refutes that hypothesis.

Barrett, 2005). Figure 7.7 provides an example. An incubation strategy often helps to break mental sets.

Ignoring Negative Evidence   On September 26, 1983, Lt. Col. Stanislav Petrov was in command of a secret facility that analyzed information from Russian early-warning satellites. Suddenly alarms went off as computers found evidence that five U.S. missiles were being launched toward Russia. Tension between the two countries was high at the time, so based on the availability heuristic, Petrov hypothesized that a nuclear attack was under way. He was about to alert his superiors to launch a counterattack on the United States when it occurred to him that if this were a real nuclear attack, it would involve many more than five missiles. Fortunately for everyone, he realized that the "attack" was a false alarm (Hoffman, 1999). As this near-disaster shows, the absence of symptoms or events can sometimes provide important evidence for or against a hypothesis. Compared with evidence that is present, however, symptoms or events that do not occur are less likely to be noticed (Hunt & Rouse, 1981). People have a difficult time using the absence of evidence to help eliminate hypotheses from consideration (Hyman, 2002). In the "trapped kitten" case, when the "meowing" stopped for several days after the stove was unplugged and reconnected, rescuers assumed that the animal was frightened into silence. They ignored the possibility that their hypothesis was incorrect in the first place.

Confirmation Bias   Anyone who has had a series of medical tests knows that diagnosis is not a one-shot affair. Instead, physicians choose their first hypothesis on the basis of observed symptoms and then order tests or evaluate additional symptoms to confirm or eliminate that hypothesis (Trillin, 2001). This process can be distorted by a **confirmation bias:** Humans have a strong bias to confirm rather than reject the hypothesis they have chosen, even in the face of strong evidence against the hypothesis (Aronson, Wilson, & Akert, 2005; Groopman, 2007). In other words, people are quite willing to perceive and accept data that support their hypothesis, but they tend to ignore information that is inconsistent with it (Groopman, 2000). Confirmation bias may be seen as a form of the anchoring heuristic. Once you've "anchored" to your first hypothesis, you may be unwilling to abandon it. The would-be rescuers of John

Gatiss's "trapped kitten" were so intent on their efforts to pinpoint its location that they never stopped to question its existence. Similarly, as described in the chapter on social psychology, we tend to look for and pay extra attention to information that is consistent with our first impressions of other people. This tendency can create positive or negative bias in, say, a teacher's views of children's cognitive abilities or an interviewer's judgments of a job candidate's skills (Jussim & Eccles, 1992; Reich, 2004). (For a summary of problem solving and its pitfalls, see "In Review: Solving Problems.")

Problem Solving by Computer

Researchers have created artificial limbs, retinas, cochleas, and even hearts to help disabled people move, see, hear, and live more normally. They are developing artificial brains, too, in the form of computer systems that not only see, hear, and manipulate

In Review

Solving Problems

STEPS	PITFALLS	REMEDIES
Define the problem.	Inexperience: the tendency to see each problem as unique	Gain experience and practice in seeing the similarity between present problems and previous problems.
Form hypotheses about solutions.	Availability heuristic: the tendency to recall the hypothesis or solution that is most available to memory	Force yourself to write down and carefully consider many different hypotheses.
	Anchoring bias, or mental set: the tendency to anchor on the first solution or hypothesis and not adjust your beliefs in light of new evidence or failures of the current approach	Break the mental set, stop, and try a fresh approach.
Test hypotheses.	The tendency to ignore negative evidence	In evaluating a hypothesis, consider the things you should see (but don't) if the hypothesis is true.
	Confirmation bias: the tendency to seek only evidence that confirms your hypothesis	Look for disconfirming evidence that, if found, would show your hypothesis to be false.

1. People stranded without water could use their shoes to collect rain, but they may not do so because of an obstacle to problem solving called _____.

2. Because of the _____ heuristic, once sellers set a value on their house, they may refuse to take much less for it.

3. If you tackle a massive problem one small step at a time, you are using an approach called _____.

ARTIFICIAL INTELLIGENCE ▶

Chess master Garry Kasparov had his hands full when he was challenged by Deep Blue, a chess-playing computer that was programmed so well that it has won games against the world's best competitors, including Kasparov. Still, even the most sophisticated computers cannot perceive and think about the world in general anywhere near as well as humans can. Some observers believe that this situation will eventually change as progress in computer technology—and a deepening understanding of human cognitive processes—leads to dramatic breakthroughs in artificial intelligence.

objects but also reason and solve problems. These systems are the product of research in **artificial intelligence (AI),** a field that seeks to develop computers that imitate the processes of human perception and thought (O'Reilly, 2006).

Symbolic Reasoning and Computer Logic   An IBM computer known as Deep Blue has won chess games against the world's best chess masters. This result is not surprising, because chess is a clearly defined, logical game at which computers can perform effectively. However, it is precisely their reliance on logic and formulas that accounts for the shortcomings of today's artificial intelligence systems. For example, these systems are successful only in narrowly defined fields, not in general problem solving. This limitation stems from the fact that AI systems are based on logical symbolic manipulations that depend on if-then rules. Unfortunately, it is difficult to tell a computer how to recognize the "if" condition in the real world (Dreyfus & Dreyfus, 1988). Consider this simple if-then rule: "If it is a clock, then set it." Humans recognize all kinds of clocks because they have the natural concept of "clock," but computers are still not very good at forming natural concepts. Doing so requires putting into the same category many examples that have very different physical features, from your bedside digital alarm clock to London's Big Ben. The fact that computers cannot yet do this allows online businesses to protect themselves from potentially dangerous computer programs that pose as human customers. So when ordering something online, you may be shown a set of distorted, odd-looking letters and numbers and then be asked to type them. By doing so, you are proving that you are a human being, not a computer.

Neural Network Models   Recognizing the problems posed by the need to teach computers to form natural concepts, many researchers in AI have moved toward a connectionist, or neural network, approach. This approach uses computers to simulate the information processing taking place at many different but interconnected locations in the brain. Neural network models have helped researchers develop computers that are able to recognize voices, understand speech, read print, guide missiles, and perform many other complex tasks (Ashcraft, 2006). Some of these computer simulations are being used to improve speech recognition software and to test theories of how infants learn to recognize speech (e.g., Roy & Pentland, 2002; Sroka & Braida, 2005). Others have been used to improve on human decision making. One program, called PAP-NET, can outperform human technicians at detecting abnormal cells in smears collected during cervical examinations (Kok & Boon, 1996). Indeed, computerized expert systems can now perform as well as (and sometimes better than) humans at solving complex problems in medical diagnosis and business decision making (Khan et al., 2001; Workman, 2004).

artificial intelligence (AI)   The field that studies how to program computers to imitate the products of human perception, understanding, and thought.

Unfortunately, however, most computer models of neural networks still fall well short of the capacities of the human perceptual system. For example, computers are slow to learn how to classify visual patterns, which has led to disappointment in efforts to develop computerized face recognition systems capable of identifying terrorists and other criminals in public places (Feder, 2004). But even though neural networks are far from perfect "thinking machines," they are sure to play an important role in psychologists' efforts to build ever more intelligent systems and to better understand the principles of human problem solving (Gamez, 2008).

One approach to overcoming the limitations of both computers and humans is to have them work together in ways that create a better outcome than either could achieve alone. In medical diagnosis, for example, the human's role is to establish the presence and nature of a patient's symptoms. The computer then combines this information in a completely unbiased way to identify the most likely diagnosis (Swets, Dawes, & Monahan, 2000). This kind of human-machine teamwork can also help in the assessment of psychological problems (Kramer, Bernstein, & Phares, 2009).

Creative Thinking

One of the greatest challenges in the development of artificial intelligence will be to program computers in a way that allows their thinking and problem solving to be as creative as that of humans. Consider the case that opened this chapter. It was Dr. Wallace's knowledge of the chemicals in paint—which has no obvious connection to human body chemistry—that led her to figure out what was causing Laura McBride's illness. Computers are still not nearly as good as humans are at recognizing that information from one area can be used to solve a problem in a seemingly unrelated area.

The ability to blend knowledge from many different domains is only one aspect of the creative thinking that humans display every day. People demonstrate **creativity** by producing original but useful solutions to all sorts of challenges (Simonton, 1999, 2004; Sternberg & Grigorenko, 2004a). Executives and homemakers, scientists and artists—all may be creative to varying degrees. How do we know when people are thinking creatively? Psychologists have defined *creativity* as mental activity that can be inferred from performance on certain tests, as well as from the writings, computer programs, artwork, and other products resulting from the creative process (Sternberg & Dess, 2001). To measure creativity, some psychologists have generated tests of **divergent thinking**—the ability to think along many paths to generate multiple solutions to a problem (Diakidoy & Spanoudis, 2002). The Consequences Test is an example. It contains items such as "Imagine all of the things that might possibly happen if all national and local laws were suddenly abolished" (Guilford, 1959). Divergent-thinking tests are scored by counting the number of sensible responses that a person can give to each item and how many of these responses differ from those given by most people.

Only sensible responses to creativity tests are counted, because creativity involves divergent thinking that is appropriate for a given problem or situation. To be productive rather than just weird, a creative person must be firmly anchored in reality, understand society's needs, and learn from the experience and knowledge of others (Sternberg & Lubart, 1992). Theresa Amabile has identified three kinds of cognitive and personality characteristics necessary for creativity (Amabile, 1996; Amabile, Hennessey, & Grossman, 1986):

1. *Expertise* in the field of endeavor, which is directly tied to what a person has learned. For example, a painter or composer must know the paints, techniques, or instruments available.
2. A set of *creative skills,* including persistence at problem solving, capacity for divergent thinking, ability to break out of old problem-solving habits (mental sets), and willingness to take risks. Amabile believes that training can influence many of these skills, some of which are closely linked to the strategies for problem solving discussed earlier.
3. The *motivation* to pursue creative work for internal reasons, such as satisfaction, rather than for external reasons, such as prize money. In fact,

creativity The capacity to produce original solutions or novel compositions.

divergent thinking The ability to generate many different solutions to a problem.

Amabile and her colleagues found that external rewards can deter creativity. They asked groups of children and adults to produce creative projects such as paintings or stories. Some were simply asked to work on these projects. Others were told that the projects would be judged for creativity and excellence and that rewards would be given or winners announced. Experts, who had no idea which products were created by which group, judged those from the "reward" group to be significantly less creative. Similar effects have been found in other studies (Deci, Koestner, & Ryan, 1999, 2001).

Is creativity inherited? To some extent, perhaps it is (Lykken, 1998a), but evidence suggests that the social, economic, and political environment in which a person grows and lives also influences creative behavior (Amabile, 2001; Nakamura & Csikszentmihalyi, 2001). Do you have to be smart to be creative? Creativity does appear to require a certain degree of intelligence. For example, longitudinal studies have shown that individuals identified as particularly smart in adolescence were up to eight times more likely than other people to show creativity as adults by patenting inventions or producing scientific publications (Park, Lubinski, & Benbow, 2008; Wai, Lubinski, & Benbow, 2005). But you don't have to be a genius to be creative (Simonton, 1984, 2002; Sternberg, 2001). In fact, although correlations between scores on creativity tests and intelligence tests are almost always positive, they are relatively modest (Simonton, 1999). This finding is not surprising, because creativity involves divergent thinking about many solutions to a problem. As described later, high scores on most intelligence tests require **convergent thinking,** which uses logic and knowledge to narrow down the number of possible solutions to a problem. Research on creativity and its relationship to intelligence has intensified in recent years (Sternberg & Dess, 2001). One result of that research has been to see intelligence and creativity in the same person as contributing to the broader trait of *wisdom* (Baltes & Smith, 2008; Sternberg, 2001; Sternberg & O'Hara, 1999).

Decision Making

▶ *How can I become a better decision maker?*

Paper or plastic? Do I watch TV or study for the test? Should I get out of this relationship? Is it time to start thinking about a nursing home for Mom? Life is full of decisions. Some are quick and easy to make; others are painfully difficult and require considerable time, planning, and mental effort. Even carefully considered decisions can lead to undesirable outcomes, though, because the world is an uncertain place. Decisions made when the outcome is uncertain are called *risky decisions* or *decisions under uncertainty.* Chance aside, psychologists have discovered reasons why human decisions sometimes lead to unsatisfactory outcomes. Let's consider some of these reasons.

Evaluating Options

Suppose that you have to choose between (1) an academic major you love but that is unlikely to lead to steady employment or (2) a less exciting major that almost guarantees a high-paying job. The fact that each option has positive and negative features greatly complicates decision making. Deciding which car to buy, which college to attend, or even how to spend the evening are all examples of choices that require you to weigh several options. Such choices are often based on the positive or negative value, or **utility,** that you place on each feature of each option. Listing the pros and cons of each option is a helpful way of keeping them all in mind as you think about your decisions. You also have to estimate the probabilities and risks associated with the possible outcomes of each choice. For example, you must consider how likely it is that job opportunities in your chosen major will have faded by the time you graduate. In studying risky decision making, psychologists begin with the assumption that the best decision

convergent thinking   The ability to apply the rules of logic and what one knows about the world to narrow down the possible solutions to a problem.

utility   In decision making, any subjective measure of value.

► Analyzing your choices and the possible outcomes of each takes some time and effort, but the results are usually worth it. Like Dilbert's boss, many people prefer to make decisions more impulsively, and although their decisions sometimes turn out well, they often don't (Gladwell, 2005; Myers, 2004).

maximizes *expected value.* The **expected value** of a decision is the average benefit you could expect to receive if the decision were repeated on several occasions.

Biases and Flaws in Decision Making

Most people think of themselves as logical and rational, but in making decisions about everything from giving up smoking to investing in the stock market, they don't always act in ways that maximize expected value (Farmer, Patelli, & Zovko, 2005; Shiller, 2001). Why not?

Gains, Losses, and Probabilities   For one thing, our pain over losing a certain amount is usually greater than the pleasure we feel after gaining the same amount (Kermer et al., 2006). This phenomenon is called *loss aversion* (Dawes, 1998; Tversky & Kahneman, 1991). Because of loss aversion, you might go to more trouble to collect a $100 debt than to win a $100 prize. In addition, the value of a gain doesn't depend on the amount of the gain but on what you start with. Suppose you could have a $10 gift certificate from a restaurant but you would have to drive 10 miles to pick it up. This gain has the same monetary value as having an extra $10 added to your paycheck. However, most people tend to behave as if the difference between $0 and $10 is greater than the difference between, say, $300 and $310. So a person who won't drive across town after work to earn a $10 bonus on next week's paycheck might gladly make the same trip to pick up a $10 gift certificate. Understanding these biases and how they affect people's purchasing patterns and other economic decisions has proven so important that Daniel Kahneman received the 2002 Nobel Prize in economics for his research in this area.

People are also biased in how they think about probability. For example, we tend to overestimate the probability of rare events and to underestimate the probability of frequent ones (Kahneman & Tversky, 1984). This bias helps explain why people gamble in casinos and enter lotteries. The odds are against them and the decision to gamble has a negative expected value, but because people overestimate the probability of winning, they associate a positive expected value with gambling. In one study, not even a course that highlighted gambling's mathematical disadvantages could change university students' gambling behavior (Williams & Connolly, 2006). The tendency to overestimate rare events is amplified by the availability heuristic: vivid memories of rare gambling successes and the publicity given to lottery winners encourage people to recall gains rather than losses.

Sometimes our bias in estimating probability costs more than money. For example, many people underestimate the risk of infection by HIV/AIDS and continue to engage in unprotected sex (Specter, 2005). And after the September 11, 2001, terrorist attacks on the United States, the risks of flying seemed so high that many more people than usual decided to travel by car instead. Yet driving is more dangerous overall than flying, so the decision to drive might actually have increased these people's risk of death, especially if stress associated with the attacks made these drivers less careful (Su et al., 2008). With more cars on the road, there were 353 more traffic fatalities in the last three

expected value   The total benefit to be expected of a decision if it were repeated on several occasions.

A HIGHLY UNLIKELY OUTCOME ▶

Lottery agencies try to attract business by creating memorable images of big winners. They know that, like other decisions, people's ticket buying will be guided by the availability heuristic and the tendency to overestimate the probability of rare events. Did you ever notice that lottery ads and websites never show or talk about the millions of players who win nothing?

months of 2001 than there were during the same period in previous years (Gigerenzer, 2004). Similar bias in risk perception leads many people to buy a big, heavy sport utility vehicle that makes them feel safe, even though the chances of serious injury in an SUV are actually greater than in a minivan or family sedan (Gladwell, 2004). Their heightened sense of safety may even lead some SUV drivers to drive less carefully, which further increases their risk of injury (Bener et al., 2008; Thomas & Walton, 2007).

Another bias in estimating probability is called the *gambler's fallacy:* People believe that the probability of future events in a random process will change depending on past events. This belief is false. For example, if you flip a coin and it comes up heads ten times in a row, what is the likelihood of tails on the next flip? Although some people think otherwise, the chance that it will come up tails on the eleventh flip is still 50 percent, just as it was for the first ten flips. Yet many gamblers continue feeding a slot machine that has not paid off much for hours, because they believe it is "due."

Poor decision making can also stem from the human tendency to be unrealistically confident in the accuracy of our predictions. Baruch Fischoff and Donald MacGregor (1982) devised a clever way to study this bias. People were asked whether they believed a certain event would occur and then were asked to say how confident they were about their prediction. For example, they were asked whether a particular sports team would win an upcoming game. After the events were over, the accuracy of the people's forecasts was compared with their level of confidence. Sure enough, their confidence in their predictions was consistently greater than their accuracy. This overconfidence operates even when people make predictions concerning the accuracy of their own memories (Bjork, 1998).

How Biased Are We?   Almost everyone makes decisions that they later regret, but these outcomes may not be due entirely to biased thinking about gains, losses, and probabilities. Some decisions are not intended to maximize expected value but rather to satisfy other goals, such as minimizing expected loss, producing a quick and easy resolution, or preserving a moral principle (Arkes & Ayton, 1999; Galotti, 2007; McCaffery & Baron, 2006). Often decisions depend not just on how likely we are to gain or lose a particular amount of something but also on what that something is. A decision that could cost or save a human life may be made differently than one that could cost or gain a few dollars, even though the probabilities of each outcome are exactly the same in both cases.

Even the "goodness" or "badness" of decisions is often difficult to measure. Many decisions depend on personal values (utilities), which can vary from person to person and from culture to culture. People in individualist cultures, for example, may tend to assign high utilities to attributes that promote personal goals, whereas people in collectivist cultures might place greater value on attributes that bring group harmony and the approval of family and friends (Markus, Kitayama, & Heiman, 1996).

linkages

Do groups solve problems more effectively than individuals?
(a link to Social Psychology)

Linkages

Group Processes in Problem Solving and Decision Making

Problem solving and decision making often take place in groups. The factors that influence an individual's problem solving and decision making continue to operate when the individual is in a group, but group interactions also shape the outcome.

When groups are trying to make a decision, for example, they usually begin by considering the preferences or opinions stated by various members. Not all of these views have equal influence, though. Views that are shared by the greatest number of group members will have the greatest impact on the group's final decision (Tindale & Kameda, 2000). This means that extreme proposals or opinions will usually have less effect on group decisions than those that are more representative of the majority's views.

Nevertheless, group discussions sometimes result in decisions that are more extreme than the group members would make individually. This tendency toward extreme decisions is called *group polarization* (Baron, Branscombe, & Byrne, 2008). Two mechanisms appear to underlie group polarization. First, most arguments presented during the discussion favor the majority view and most criticisms are directed at the minority view. In fact, confirmation bias leads group members to seek additional information that supports the majority position (Schulz-Hardt et al., 2000). In this atmosphere, those who favor the majority view find it reasonable to adopt an even stronger version of it (Kassin, Fein, & Markus, 2008). Second, once some group members begin to agree that a particular decision is desirable, other members may try to associate themselves with it, perhaps by suggesting an even more extreme version (Kassin, Fein, & Markus, 2008).

Are people better at problem solving and decision making when they work in groups or on their own? This is one of the questions about human thinking that is studied by social psychologists. In a typical experiment, a group of people is asked to solve a problem like the one in Figure 7.6 or to decide the guilt or innocence of the defendant in a fictional court case. Each person is asked to work alone and then to join with the others to try to agree on a decision. These studies have found that when problems have solutions that can be easily demonstrated to everyone, groups will usually outperform individuals at solving them (Laughlin, 1999). When problems have less obvious solutions, groups may be somewhat better at solving them than their average member but usually no better than their most talented member (Hackman, 1998). And because of phenomena such as *social loafing* and *groupthink* (discussed in the social psychology chapter), people working in a group are often less productive than people working alone (Williams & Sommer, 1997).

Other research suggests that a critical element in successful group problem solving is the sharing of individual members' unique information and expertise (e.g., Stasser, Stewart, & Wittenbaum, 1995). For example, when asked to diagnose an illness, groups of physicians were much more accurate when they pooled their knowledge (Larson et al., 1998). However, *brainstorming,* a popular strategy that supposedly encourages group members to generate new and innovative solutions to a problem, may actually produce fewer ideas than are generated by individuals working alone (Baumeister & Bushman, 2008). This result may occur because comments from other group members may interfere with some members' ability to think clearly and creatively. Further, some participants in a brainstorming session may be reluctant to offer an idea, even a good one, for fear

▶ One disadvantage of brainstorming sessions is that running comments and bizarre ideas from some group members can interfere with the creative process in others (Nijstad, Stroebe, & Lodewijkx, 2003).

it will be rejected or ridiculed by the group (Kerr & Tindale, 2004). To prevent these problems, some brainstorming groups are specifically instructed to disagree with one another and to debate the quality of individual ideas. Following these procedures has been shown to elevate the level of performance by brainstorming groups significantly above what is typically found in such groups (Nemeth et al., 2004). Other researchers arrange for brainstorming groups to meet electronically using a special e-mail system that allows each member to offer suggestions without being identified or interrupted yet still gives everyone access to the ideas of all the other members. The levels of trust and the patterns of communication that develop in these groups appear comparable to those seen in face-to-face groups (Wilson, Straus, & McEvily, 2006), and because electronic brainstorming allows people to think more clearly and express themselves without fear, these groups may actually outperform those that meet in person (Nijstad, Stroebe, & Lodewijkx, 2003).

As they work to solve a problem, group members experience their own thoughts as concepts, propositions, images, or other mental representations. How does each member share these private events to help the group perform its task? The answer lies in the use of language.

Language

▶ *How do babies learn to talk?*

Many pet owners swear that their animals "talk" to them. Maybe Harry barks in a particular way when he wants to go outside or Cleo meows to be fed. But are Harry's barks and Cleo's meows really language? Probably not. These pets are communicating something to their owners, but the noises they make lack many of the components of human language (Rendall, Cheney, & Seyfarth, 2000; Slocombe & Zuberbühler, 2005). So although Harry may let out three high-pitched yelps when he wants to go outside, he may bark in exactly the same way when his owner asks him whether he agrees with the local leash laws. For this reason, we wouldn't call his barking "language." Humans, however, can use language to express everything from simple requests to abstract principles. They can create stories that pass on cultural information and traditions from one generation to the next. Our language abilities are usually well integrated with our memory, thinking, and other cognitive abilities. As a result, we can speak about our thoughts and memories and think about what people tell us. It is only when strokes or other forms of damage interfere with the brain's language areas that we are reminded that language is a very special kind of cognitive ability (Kohnert, 2004).

A **language** has two basic elements: symbols such as words and a set of rules called **grammar** for combining those symbols. With their knowledge of approximately 50,000 to 100,000 words (Miller, 1991), humans can create and understand an infinite number of sentences. Yet all of the sentences ever spoken are created from just a few

language Symbols (and a set of rules for combining them) that are used as a means of communicating.

grammar A set of rules for combining the symbols, such as words, used in a given language.

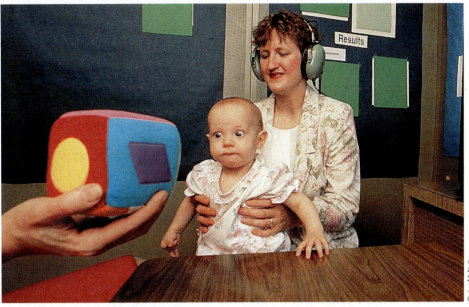

GETTING READY TO TALK ▶

Long before they say their first words, babies are getting ready to talk. Experiments in Patricia Kuhl's laboratory show that even six-month-olds tend to look longer at faces whose lip movements match the sounds of spoken words. This tendency reflects babies' abilities to focus on, recognize, and discriminate the sounds of speech, especially in their native language. These abilities are crucial to the development of language (Mayberry, Lock, & Kazmi, 2002).

dozen categories of sounds. The power of language comes from the way these rather unimpressive raw materials are organized according to certain rules.

Learning to Speak: Stages of Language Development

Children the world over develop language with impressive speed; the average six-year-old already has a vocabulary of about 13,000 words (Pinker, 1994). But acquiring language involves more than just learning vocabulary. We also have to learn how words are combined and how to produce and understand sentences. Psychologists who study the development of language have found that the process begins in the earliest days of a child's life and follows some predictable steps (Saffran, Senghas, & Trueswell, 2001).

The First Year   In their first year, infants become more and more attuned to the sounds that will be important in acquiring their native language. In fact, this early experience with language appears to be vital. Without it, as described later, language development can be impaired (Mayberry & Lock, 2003). The first year is also the time when babies begin to produce particular kinds of **infant vocalizations,** called **babblings,** patterns of meaningless sounds that first resemble speech. These alternating consonant and vowel sounds (such as "bababa," "dadada," and "mamimamima") appear at about four months of age, once the infant has developed the necessary coordination of the tongue and mouth. Though meaningless to the baby, babblings are a delight to parents. Infants everywhere begin with the same set of babbling sounds, but at about nine months of age, they begin to produce only the sounds that occur in the language they hear the most. At about the same time, their babbling becomes more complex and begins to sound like "sentences" in the babies' native language (Goldstein, King, & West, 2003). Infants who hear English, for example, begin to shorten some of their vocalizations to "da," "duh," and "ma." They use these sounds to convey joy, anger, interest, and other messages in specific contexts and with obvious purpose (Blake & de Boysson-Bardies, 1992).

By ten to twelve months of age, babies can understand several words—certainly more words than they can say (Fenson et al., 1994). Proper names and object words—such as *mama, daddy, cookie, doggy,* and *car*—are among the earliest words they understand. These are also the first words children are likely to say when they begin to talk at around twelve months of age (some talk a little earlier and some a little later). Infants acquire nouns for simple object categories (*dog, flower*) before they acquire

infant vocalizations   Early sounds, such as babblings, made by babies.

babblings   Repetitions of syllables; the first sounds infants make that resemble speech.

more general nouns (*animal, plant*) or more specific names (*collie, rose*) (Rosch et al., 1976).

Of course, these early words do not sound exactly like adult language. English-speaking babies usually reduce them to a shorter, easier form, like "duh" for *duck* or "mih" for *milk.* Children make themselves understood, however, by using gestures, voice tones, facial expressions, and endless repetitions. Once they have a word for an object, they may "overextend" it to cover more ground. So they might use *doggy* to refer to cats, bears, and horses; they might use *fly* for all insects and perhaps for other small things such as raisins and M&Ms (Clark, 1983, 1993). Children make these "errors" because their vocabularies are limited, not because they fail to notice the difference between dogs and cats or because they want to eat a fly (Fremgen & Fay, 1980; Rescorla, 1981). Being around people who don't understand these over-extensions encourages children to learn and use more precise words (Markman, 1994). During this period, children build up their vocabularies one word at a time. They also use their limited vocabulary one word at a time. They cannot yet put words together into sentences, but they are getting ready to do so. Their language skills will blossom during the years from two to four, and the richness of the vo-cabulary they eventually develop will be influenced by the richness of the language that they hear and the encouragement they receive for their earliest efforts to communicate using both words and gestures (Goldstein & Schwade, 2008; Rowe & Goldin-Meadow, 2009).

The Second Year   The **one-word stage** of speech lasts for about six months. Then, some time around eighteen months of age, children's vocabularies expand dramatically (Gleitman & Landau, 1994). They may learn several new words each day, and by the age of two, most youngsters can use 50 to well over 100 words. They also start using two-word combinations to form efficient little sentences. These two-word sentences are called telegraphic because, like telegrams or text messages, they are brief and to the point, leaving out anything that is not absolutely essential. So if she wants her mother to give her a book, a 20-month-old might first say, "Give book," then "Mommy give," and if that does not work, "Mommy book." The child also uses rising tones to indicate a question ("Go out?") and emphasizes certain words to indicate location ("Play *park*") or new information ("*Big* car").

Three-word sentences come next in the development of language. They are still telegraphic but they are more nearly complete: "Mommy give book." The child's sen-tences now begin to have the subject-verb-object form typical of adult sentences. Other words and word endings begin appearing, too. In English, these include the suffix *-ing,* the prepositions *in* and *on,* the plural *-s,* and irregular past tenses such as "It broke," and "I ate" (Brown, 1973; Dale, 1976). Children learn to use the suffix *-ed* for the past tense ("I walked"), but they often overapply this rule to irregular verbs that they had previously used correctly, saying, for example, "It breaked," "It broked," or "I eated" (Marcus, 1996). Children also expand their sentences with adjectives, although at first they make some mistakes. For example, they are likely to use both *less* and *more* to mean "more" (Smith & Sera, 1992).

The Third Year and Beyond   By age three or so, children begin to use auxiliary verbs ("Adam is going") and to ask questions using what, where, who, and why. They begin to put together clauses to form complex sentences ("Here's the ball I was looking for"). By age five, children have acquired most of the grammatical rules of their native language.

How Is Language Acquired?

Despite all that has been learned about the steps children follow in acquiring language, mystery and debate still surround the question of just how they do it. We know that children pick up the specific content of language from the speech they hear around

one-word stage   A stage of language development during which children tend to use one word at a time.

How do we learn to speak? *(a link to Human Development)*

them: English children learn English; French children learn French. But how do children come to follow the rules of grammar?

Conditioning, Imitation, and Rules

Perhaps children learn grammar because their parents reward them for using it. This idea sounds reasonable, but observational research suggests that positive reinforcement (which we describe in the learning chapter) is not the main character in the story of language acquisition. Parents are usually more concerned about what is said than about its grammatical form (Hirsch-Pasek, Treiman, & Schneiderman, 1984). So when the little boy with chocolate crumbs on his face says, "I not eat cookie," his mother is more likely to respond, "Yes, you did" than to ask the child to say, "I did not eat the cookie" and then praise him for his grammatical correctness.

Learning through imitation appears to be more influential. Children learn grammar most rapidly when adult models demonstrate the correct form in the course of conversation. For example:

Child:	*Mommy fix.*
Mother:	*Okay, Mommy will fix the truck.*
Child:	*It breaked.*
Mother:	*Yes, it broke.*

But if children learn grammar by imitation, why do children who at one time said "I went" later say "I goed"? Adults don't use this form of speech, so neither imitation nor reward can account for its sudden appearance. It appears more likely that children analyze for themselves the underlying patterns in the language they hear around them and then learn the rules governing those patterns (Bloom, 1995).

Biological Bases for Language Acquisition

The ease with which children the world over discover these patterns and develop language has led some to argue that language acquisition is at least partly innate, or automatic. Noam Chomsky (1965) believes that we are born with a built-in universal grammar, a mechanism that allows us to identify the basic dimensions of language (Baker, 2002; Chomsky, 1986; Nowak, Komarova, & Niyogi, 2001). According to Chomsky, a child's universal grammar might tell the child that word order is important to the meaning of a sentence. In English, for example, word order tells us who is doing what to whom (the sentences "Heather dumped Jason" and "Jason dumped Heather" contain the same words, but they have different meanings). In Chomsky's view, then, we don't entirely learn language—we develop it as genetic predispositions interact with experience (Senghas & Coppola, 2001). So a child's innate assumption that word order is important to grammar would change if the child heard language in which word order did not have much effect on the meaning of a sentence.

Other theorists disagree with Chomsky, arguing that the development of language reflects the development of more general cognitive skills, not just innate, language-specific mechanisms (e.g., Bates, 1993). Still, other evidence supports the existence of biological factors in language acquisition. For example, the unique properties of the human mouth and throat, the language-related brain regions described in the chapter on biology and behavior, and genetic research all suggest that humans are innately "prewired," or biologically programmed, for language (Buxhoeveden et al., 2001; Lai et al., 2001). In fact, researchers are even beginning to uncover genetic mechanisms behind some speech and language disorders (e.g., Fisher, 2005). In addition, there appears to be a period in childhood during which we can learn language more easily than at any other time (Ridley, 2000). The existence of this *critical period* is supported by evidence from cases in which unfortunate children spent their early years in isolation from human contact and the sound of adult language. Even after years of therapy and language training, these individuals are not able to combine ideas into sentences

LEARNING A SECOND LANGUAGE ▶

As these international students are discovering, people who learn a second language as adults do so more slowly, and with less proficiency, than younger people (Johnson & Newport, 1989; Patkowski, 1994) and virtually never learn to speak it without an accent (Lenneberg, 1967). Still, the window of opportunity for learning a second language remains open long after the end of the critical period in childhood during which first-language acquisition must occur (Hakuta, Bialystok, & Wiley, 2003).

© Michael Grecco/Stock, Boston

(Rymer, 1993). Such cases suggest that in order to acquire the complex features of language, we must be exposed to speech before a certain age.

Bilingualism   Does trying to learn two languages at once, even before the critical period for language learning is over, impair the learning of either? Research suggests just the opposite. Like some children in any situation, the early language of children from a bilingual environment may be confused or delayed, but they eventually show enhanced performance in each language (de Houwer, 1995). There is also some evidence that balanced bilinguals—those who have roughly equal mastery of two languages in childhood—are superior to other children in cognitive flexibility, concept formation, and creativity. It is as if each language offers a slightly different perspective on thinking and this dual perspective makes the brain more flexible (Hong et al., 2000).

ANIMAL LANGUAGE?   ▶

Several chimpanzees and gorillas have been taught to use American Sign Language (ASL), as demonstrated here by Nim Chimpsky (who was named after Noam Chomsky). Are nonhuman primates' accomplishments with ASL the same as human language abilities? Probably not (Fitch & Hauser, 2004; Povinelli & Bering, 2002; Rendall, Cheney, & Seyfarth, 2000; Zuberbühler, 2005). For example, apes, like humans, use many gestures in a flexible way to communicate, but they don't point at things, as humans do from a young age as they develop language and use it in joint communication (e.g. Tomasello, 2006). Still, research suggests that with the right tools and training, these animals can master language-like skills.

© Susan Kuklin/Photo Researchers, Inc.

Testing Intelligence

▶ *How is intelligence measured?*

People who are good at using and understanding language and skilled at thinking, problem solving, and decision making are likely to be seen as *intelligent*. But intelligence is not limited to these abilities alone. Over the years, psychologists studying people in various cultures around the world have proposed that the concept of "intelligence" is a broad umbrella that can also include attributes such as efficiently storing and retrieving memories; effectively focusing—or dividing—attention; rapidly processing information; quickly learning new things; profiting from experience; adapting well to changing environments; having a good sense of direction; appreciating patterns in nature; being good at music, dance, or athletics; showing eye-hand coordination; understanding oneself and others; and displaying polished social skills (Berry & Bennett, 1992; Eysenck, 1986; Gardner, 1999; Hunt, 1983; Meyer & Salovey, 1997; Sternberg, 1996; Sternberg, Lautrey, & Lubart, 2003).

So what exactly is intelligence? Psychologists have never been able to agree on a precise answer to this question, but the vast majority of them tend to agree that **intelligence** includes three main characteristics: (1) abstract thinking or reasoning abilities, (2) problem-solving abilities, and (3) the capacity to acquire knowledge (Gottfredson, 1997a; Snyderman & Rothman, 1987).

Standard tests of intelligence measure some of these characteristics, but they don't address all of them. Accordingly, some psychologists argue that these tools are not able to capture all that should be tested if we want to get a complete picture of someone's intelligence in its broadest sense. Others say that broadening the definition of intelligence too much will make it meaningless. Still others suggest dropping the term altogether in favor of the more descriptive and less emotionally charged concept of *cognitive ability*. To better understand the controversy, let's take a look at how standard intelligence tests were created, what they are designed to measure, and how well they do their job. Later, we will consider some alternative intelligence tests that have been proposed by those who find fault with traditional ones.

A Brief History of Intelligence Tests

The story of modern intelligence tests begins in 1904, when the French psychologist Alfred Binet (pronounced "bih-NAY") was appointed to a government committee whose job was to identify, study, and provide special educational programs for children who were not doing well in school. As part of his work, Binet developed a set of mental tasks that provided the model for today's intelligence tests. Binet assumed that reasoning, thinking, and problem solving all depend on intelligence, so he chose tasks that would highlight individual differences in children's ability to do these things (Binet & Simon, 1905). Children taking Binet's test were asked to unwrap a piece of candy, repeat numbers or sentences from memory, identify familiar objects, and the like (Rogers, 1995).

Binet also assumed that children's cognitive abilities increase with age. So after trying out test items on children of various ages, he categorized each item according to how old a child had to be to get the item right. For example, a "six-year-old item" was one that a large majority of six-year-olds could answer correctly but that five-year-olds could not. In other words, Binet's test contained a set of *age-graded* items (Binet & Simon, 1908). It measured a child's "mental level," later called *mental age*, by determining the age level of the most advanced items that the child could consistently answer correctly. Children whose mental age equaled their actual age, or *chronological age*, were considered to be of "regular" intelligence (Schultz & Schultz, 2000).

At about the time Binet published his test, Lewis Terman at Stanford University began to develop an English-language version that has come to be known as the **Stanford-Binet Intelligence Scale** (Terman, 1906, 1916). Table 7.1 gives examples of the kinds of items included on the test. Terman added items to measure the intelligence of adults and revised the scoring scale. He divided mental age by chronological age and multiplied the result by 100. He called this figure the **intelligence quotient,** or

intelligence The possession of knowledge, the ability to efficiently use that knowledge to reason about the world, and the ability to use that reasoning adaptively in different environments.

Stanford-Binet Intelligence Scale A test for determining a person's intelligence quotient, or IQ.

intelligence quotient (IQ) A number that was originally determined by dividing mental age by chronological age and multiplying the result by 100. It now reflects the degree to which a person's score on an intelligence test differs from the average score of others in his or her age group.

TABLE 7. 1 ▬ **THE STANFORD-BINET INTELLIGENCE SCALE**

Here are samples of the types of items included on Lewis Terman's original Stanford-Binet Intelligence Scale. As in Alfred Binet's test, an age level was assigned to each item.

Age	Task
2	Place geometric shapes into corresponding openings; identify body parts; stack blocks; identify common objects.
4	Name objects from memory; complete analogies (e.g., fire is hot; ice is _____); identify objects of similar shape; answer simple questions (e.g., "Why do we have schools?").
6	Define simple words: explain differences (e.g., between a fish and a horse); identify missing parts of a picture; count out objects.
8	Answer questions about a simple story; identify absurdities (e.g., in statements like "John had to walk with crutches because he hurt his arm"); explain similarities and differences among objects; tell how to handle certain situations (e.g., finding a stray puppy).
10	Define more difficult words; give explanations (e.g., about why people should be quiet in a library); list as many words as possible; repeat six-digit numbers.
12	Identify more difficult verbal and pictured absurdities; repeat five-digit numbers in reverse order; define abstract words (e.g., sorrow); fill in a missing word in a sentence.
14	Solve reasoning problems; identify relationships among points of the compass; find similarities in apparently opposite concepts (e.g., "high" and "low"); predict the number of holes that will appear when folded paper is cut and then opened.
Adult	Supply several missing words for incomplete sentences; repeat six-digit numbers in reverse order; create a sentence using several unrelated words (e.g., forest, businesslike, and dismayed); describe similarities between concepts (e.g., "teaching" and "business").

Improve Your Grade
Tutorial: Determining IQ— Stanford-Binet and IQ Tests

IQ. So a child whose mental age and chronological age were equal would have an IQ of 100, which is considered "average" intelligence. A ten-year-old who scored at the mental age of twelve would have an IQ of $12/10 \times 100 = 120$. From this method of scoring came the term *IQ test,* a name now widely used for any test designed to measure intelligence on an objective, standardized scale.

The method used to score the Stanford-Binet allowed testers to rank people based on their IQs. This goal was important to Terman and others who promoted the test in the United States. Terman believed that IQ tests could pinpoint who did and who did not have a suitable "amount" of intelligence. These beliefs were controversial and in some instances led to prejudice and discrimination as enthusiasm for testing outpaced understanding of what was being tested. For example, in 1917, as the United States moved closer to entering World War I, a team of psychologists was asked to develop group-administered tests that could identify the cognitive ability of army recruits. Scores on these tests were used to guide the assignment of each recruit to the most appropriate military job. Soldiers who could speak and read English were tested on mental tasks that required verbal skills, such as defining words, whereas the rest were asked to visualize objects and perform other nonverbal tasks. Unfortunately, the verbal tests contained items that were unfamiliar to many recruits. Further, tests were often given under stressful conditions in crowded rooms where instructions were not always audible or (for those who did not speak English) understandable. As a result, almost half of the soldiers tested appeared to have a mental age of thirteen or lower (Yerkes, 1921), leading testers to draw seriously incorrect conclusions about their lack of intelligence—especially in the cases of those who did not speak English (Brigham, 1923). Later, David Wechsler (1939, 1949) developed intelligence tests that were designed to correct some of the weaknesses of earlier ones.

Intelligence Tests Today

Today's editions of the Wechsler tests and the Stanford-Binet are among the most widely used of all individually administered intelligence tests. The Wechsler Adult Intelligence Scale (WAIS-III) includes fourteen subtests. Seven of them require verbal skills and make up the *verbal scale* of the test. These subtests include such items as remembering a series

of digits, solving arithmetic problems, defining vocabulary words, and understanding and answering general-knowledge questions. The other seven subtests have little or no verbal content and make up the *performance scale*. They include tasks that require understanding the relationships between objects and manipulation of various materials—tasks such as assembling blocks, solving mazes, arranging pictures to form a story, and completing unfinished pictures. Testers using the WAIS-III can compute a verbal IQ, a performance IQ, and an overall IQ, as well as "index" scores that reflect a person's mental processing speed, memory ability, perceptual skills, and understanding of verbal information. The latest edition of the Wechsler Intelligence Scale for Children (WISC-IV; Wechsler, 2003) yields four similar index scores and an overall IQ (see Figure 7.9).

The latest edition of the Stanford-Binet (SB5) also contains subtests (Roid, 2003). However, the SB5 subtests are designed to measure five different abilities: *fluid reasoning* (e.g., completing verbal analogies, such as "hot is to cold as _____ is to low"), *knowledge* (e.g., defining words, detecting errors in pictures), *quantitative reasoning* (e.g., solving math problems), *visual-spatial processing* (e.g., assembling a puzzle), and *working memory* (e.g., repeating a sentence). Each of these five abilities is measured by one verbal and one nonverbal subtest, so it is possible to calculate a score for each of the five abilities, a total score on all the verbal tests, a total score on all the nonverbal tests, and an overall score for all ten tests combined.

Calculating IQ

IQ is no longer calculated by dividing mental age by chronological age and multiplying by 100. If you take an intelligence test today, the points you earn for each correct subtest or age-level answer are added up. Your total score is then compared with the scores earned by other people. The average score obtained by people at each age level is given the IQ value of 100. Other scores are given IQ values that reflect how much each score differs from the average. So if you do better on the test than the average person in your age group, you will receive an IQ above 100. How far above depends on how much better than average you do. Similarly, a person scoring below the age-group average will have an IQ below 100. This procedure is based on a well-supported assumption about many characteristics: most

FIGURE 7.9 ■ PERFORMANCE ITEMS SIMILAR TO THOSE ON THE WECHSLER INTELLIGENCE SCALE FOR CHILDREN (WISC-IV)

The WISC-IV includes ten standard and five supplemental subtests, grouped into four clusters. The *perceptual reasoning* cluster includes tasks, such as those shown here, that involve assembling blocks, solving mazes, and reasoning about pictures. Tests in the *verbal comprehension* cluster require defining words, explaining the meaning of sentences, and identifying similarities between words. Tests in the *working memory* cluster ask children to recall a series of numbers, put a random sequence of numbers into logical order, and the like. The *processing speed* cluster tests children's ability to search for symbols on a page and to decode simple coded messages. *Source*: Simulated items similar to those in the Wechsler Intelligence Scales for Adults and Children. Copyright © 1949, 1955, 1974, 1981, 1991, and 1997 by Harcourt Assessment, Inc. Reproduced with permission. All rights reserved. "Wechsler" is a trademark of Harcourt Assessment, Inc. registered in the United States of America and/or other jurisdictions.

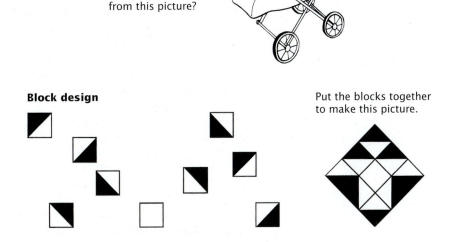

FIGURE 7.10 ■ THE DISTRIBUTION OF IQ IN THE POPULATION

When the IQs in the general population are plotted on a graph, a bell-shaped curve appears. The average IQ of any given age group is 100. Half of the scores are higher than 100 and half are below 100. Approximately 68 percent of the IQs of any age group fall between 84 and 116; about 16 percent fall below 84, and about 16 percent fall above 116.

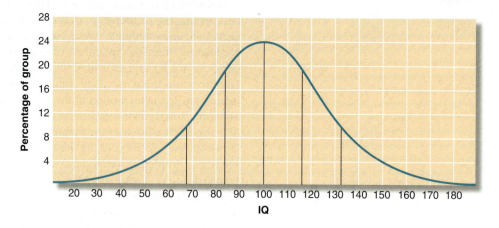

people's scores fall in the middle of the range of possible scores, creating a bell-shaped curve that approximates the normal distribution (see Figure 7.10). Half of those tested score below 100, the average for any given age group. The other half score above 100. In short, your IQ reflects your relative standing within a population of your age.

Evaluating Intelligence Tests

> ● *How good are IQ tests?*

We have said that no intelligence test can accurately measure all aspects of what various people think of as intelligence. So what does your IQ say about you? Can it predict your performance in school or on the job? Is it a fair summary of your cognitive abilities? To scientifically answer questions such as these, we have to measure the quality of the tests that yield IQs, using the same criteria that apply to tests of personality, language skills, driving, or anything else. Let's review these criteria and then see how they are used to evaluate IQ tests.

A **test** is a systematic procedure for observing behavior in a standard situation and describing it with the help of a numerical scale or system of categories (Cronbach, 1990). Tests are *standardized,* meaning that they present the same tasks, under similar conditions, to each person who takes them. Standardization helps ensure that test results will not be significantly affected by factors such as who gives and scores the test. Because the biases of those giving and scoring a test are minimized, a standardized test is said to be *objective.* Test scores can be used to calculate **norms,** which are descriptions of the frequency of particular scores. Norms tell us, for example, what percentage of high school students obtained each possible score on a college entrance exam. They also allow us to say whether a particular IQ or entrance-exam score is above or below the average score. Any test, including IQ tests, should fairly and accurately measure a person's performance. The two most important things to know about when determining the value of a test are its statistical reliability and validity.

Statistical Reliability If you stepped on a scale, checked your weight, stepped off, stepped back on, and found that your weight had increased by twenty pounds, you would know it was time to buy a new scale. A good scale, like a good test, must have **statistical reliability;** in other words, the results must be repeatable or stable. The test must measure the same thing in the same way every time it is used. Let's suppose you receive a very high score on a test of reasoning, but when you take the same test the next day, you get a very low score. Your reasoning ability probably didn't change much overnight, so the test is probably unreliable. The higher the reliability of a test, the less likely it is that its results will be affected by temperature, hunger, or other random and irrelevant changes in the environment or the test taker.

test A systematic observation of behavior in a standard situation, described by a numerical scale or category.

norms Descriptions of the frequency of particular scores on a test.

statistical reliability The degree to which test results or other research evidence occurs repeatedly.

▲ If only measuring intelligence were this easy!

Statistical Validity Most scales reliably measure your weight, giving you about the same reading day after day. But what if you use these readings as a measure of your height? This far-fetched example illustrates that a reliable scale reading can be incorrect, or invalid, if it is misinterpreted. The same is true of tests. Even the most reliable test might not provide a correct, or valid, measure of intelligence, of anxiety, of typing skill, or of anything else if those are not the things the test really measures. In other words, we can't say that a test itself is "valid" or "invalid." Instead, **statistical validity** refers to the degree to which test scores are interpreted appropriately and used properly (American Educational Research Association, American Psychological Association, & National Council on Measurement in Education, 1999; Messick, 1989). As in our scale example, a test can be valid for one purpose but invalid for another.

Researchers evaluate the statistical reliability of a test by obtaining two sets of scores on the same test from the same people. They then calculate a correlation coefficient between the two sets of scores (see the introductory chapter). When the correlation is high and positive (usually above +.80), the test is considered reliable. Evaluating a test's statistical validity usually means calculating a correlation coefficient between test scores and something else. What that "something else" is depends on what the test is designed to measure. Suppose, for example, you wanted to know if a creativity test is valid for identifying creative people. You could do so by computing the correlation between people's scores on the creativity test and experts' judgments about the quality of those same people's artistic creations. If the correlation is high, the test has high validity as a measure of creativity.

The Statistical Reliability and Validity of Intelligence Tests

The statistical *reliability* of intelligence tests is generally evaluated on the basis of their stability, or consistency. The statistical *validity* of intelligence tests is usually based on their accuracy in guiding statements and predictions about people's cognitive abilities.

Statistical Reliability IQs obtained before the age of seven are only moderately correlated with scores on intelligence tests given later (Fagan & Detterman, 1992; Fagan, Holland, & Wheeler, 2007; Rose & Feldman, 1995). There are two key reasons. First, the test items used with very young children are different from those used with older children. Second, cognitive abilities change rapidly in the early years (see the chapter on human development). During the school years, IQs tend to remain stable (Allen & Thorndike, 1995; Mayer & Sutton, 1996). So for teenagers and adults, the reliability of intelligence tests is high, as seen in correlation coefficients that are generally between + .85 and + .95.

Of course, a person's score may vary from one occasion to another if there are significant changes in the person's motivation, anxiety, health, or other factors. Overall, though, modern IQ tests usually provide exceptionally consistent results, especially compared with most other kinds of mental tests.

Statistical Validity If everyone agreed on exactly what intelligence is (having a good memory, for example), we could evaluate the statistical validity of IQ tests simply by correlating people's IQs with their performance on various tasks (in this case, memory tasks). IQ tests whose scores correlated most highly with scores on memory tests would be the most valid measures of intelligence. But because psychologists do not fully agree on a single definition of intelligence, they don't have a single standard against which to compare intelligence tests. Therefore, they cannot say whether these tests are valid measures of intelligence. Because intelligence is always displayed in the course of specific tasks and specific social situations, psychologists can only assess the validity of intelligence tests for specific purposes.

The results of their research suggest that intelligence test scores are most valid for assessing aspects of intelligence that are related to schoolwork, such as abstract reasoning and understanding verbal material. Their validity—as measured by correlating IQs with high school grades—is reasonably good, about +.50 (Brody & Erlichman, 1998). Scores on tests that focus more specifically on reasoning skills show even higher

statistical validity The degree to which test scores are interpreted appropriately and used properly.

correlations with school performance (Kuncel, Hezlett, & Ones, 2004; Lohman & Hagen, 2001). For example, the correlation between people's intelligence test scores and the level of education they achieve ranges from +.60 to +.80 (e.g., Colom & Flores-Mendoza, 2007; Lynn & Mikk, 2007).

There is also evidence that employees who score high on verbal and mathematical reasoning tests tend to perform better at work than those who earn lower scores (Borman, Hanson, & Hedge, 1997; Johnson & Neal, 1998; Pulakos et al., 2002), especially if their jobs require complex reasoning and judgment skills (Gottfredson, 1997b; Schmidt & Hunter, 2004). Later we describe a study that kept track of people for 70 years and found that those who had high IQs as children tended to be well above average in terms of academic and financial success in adulthood (Cronbach, 1996; Oden, 1968; Terman & Oden, 1947). IQs also appear to be highly correlated with performance on routine tasks such as reading medicine labels and using a telephone book (Gottfredson, 1997b, 2004).

So by the standard measures for judging psychological tests, scores on intelligence tests have good reliability and good validity for predicting success in school and in many life situations and occupations (Sackett, Borneman, & Connelly, 2008). However, IQ is not a perfect measure of how "smart" a person is. Because intelligence tests do not measure the full array of cognitive abilities, a particular test score tells only part of the story, and even that part may be distorted. Many factors other than cognitive ability, including reactions to the testing situation, can influence test performance. For example, children who are suspicious of strangers and adults who fear making mistakes may become anxious and fail even to try answering certain questions, thus artificially lowering their IQs (Fagan, 2000). Claude Steele and his colleagues have suggested that some people's test-related anxiety stems from a phenomenon known as *stereotype threat* (Steele & Aronson, 2000). According to Steele, concern over negative stereotypes about the cognitive abilities of the group to which they belong can impair the performance of some women and some members of ethnic minorities. As a result, the test scores they earn, in laboratory settings at least, underestimate those abilities (Blascovich et al., 2001; Cadinu et al., 2005; Murphy, Steele, & Gross, 2007; Schmader, Johns, & Forbes, 2008). However, research on the performance of females and minority group members on high-stakes tests such as the SAT has yielded mixed results. Some studies suggest that scores on these tests can be reduced by stereotype threat (Davis, Aronson, & Salinas, 2006; Lesko & Corpus, 2006), while others find no effects or only a weak effect (Cullen, Hardison, & Sackett, 2004; Cullen, Waters, & Sackett, 2006; Sackett, Hardison, & Cullen, 2004; Fischer & Massey, 2007; Stricker & Ward, 2004). So the extent to which stereotype threat impairs performance on cognitive abilities tests in real-world settings remains uncertain.

IQ as a Measure of Inherited Ability

Alfred Binet believed that intelligence could be improved with training and practice at mental tasks. Lewis Terman saw it as an inherited characteristic. Both were partly right. Years of research have led psychologists to conclude that intelligence is *developed ability.* This means that intelligence is influenced partly by genetics and partly by educational, cultural, and other environmental factors and experiences that shape the knowledge, reasoning, and other skills that intelligence tests measure (Atran, Medin, & Ross, 2005; Garlick, 2003; Plomin & Spinath, 2004).

To explore the influence of genetics on individual differences in IQs, psychologists have compared the correlations in scores between people who share varying degrees of similarity in genetic makeup and environment. For example, they have examined the IQs of identical twins (pairs with exactly the same genes) who were separated when very young and raised in different environments. They have also examined the scores of identical twins raised together. In other studies, they have compared individual children's IQs before and after environmental changes such as adoption. (Research designs used in these *behavioral genetics* studies are described in the introductory chapter.)

These studies find, first, that genetic factors are strongly related to IQ. In one study, when identical twins who were separated at birth and adopted by different families were tested many years later, the correlation between their scores was moderately high and positive, at least +.60 (Bouchard, 1999). If one twin earned a high score on an intelligence test, the other probably did, too; if one was low, the other was likely to be low as well. In another study, children who had been adopted soon after birth were tested after years of living in their adopted homes. Those whose biological parents were from higher socioeconomic groups (where higher IQs are more common) had higher IQs than those whose biological parents came from lower socioeconomic groups, regardless of the socioeconomic status of the adopted homes (Capron & Duyme, 1989, 1996). These findings are supported by data from the Colorado Adoption Project (Cardon & Fulker, 1993; Cardon et al., 1992), and they suggest that a genetic component of the children's cognitive abilities continued to exert an influence in the adoptive environment (McGue & Bouchard, 1998).

However, studies of IQ correlations also highlight the importance of the environment (Scarr, 1998). Consider any two people—twins, siblings who are not twins, or unrelated children—brought up together in a foster home. No matter what the degree of genetic similarity in these pairs, the correlation between their IQs is higher if they share the same home than if they are raised in different homes, as Figure 7.11 shows (Scarr & Carter-Saltzman, 1982).

The role of environmental influences is also seen in adoption studies (van IJzendoom & Juffer, 2005). Generally, when children from relatively impoverished backgrounds are adopted into homes offering a more enriching intellectual environment—including interesting materials and experiences and a supportive, responsive adult—they show modest increases in their IQs (Weinberg, Scarr, & Waldman, 1992). In one study, the IQs rose by twelve to fifteen points (Capron & Duyme, 1989). Programs designed to enhance young children's school readiness and academic ability have also been associated with improved scores on tests of intelligence (Neisser et al., 1996; Ripple et al., 1999). These early intervention programs may be partly responsible for the steady increase in average IQs seen throughout the world over the past six decades (Flynn, 1999; Neisser, 1998).

Some researchers have concluded that the influences of genetic and environmental factors on intelligence appear to be about equal. Others see a somewhat larger role for genetic factors (Herrnstein & Murray, 1994; Loehlin, 1989; Petrill et al., 1998; Plomin, 1994), and they are working to identify specific groups of genes that might be

FIGURE 7.11 ■ CORRELATIONS OF IQ

The correlation in IQ between pairs increases with increasing similarity in heredity or environment.
Source: Bouchard & McGue (1981).

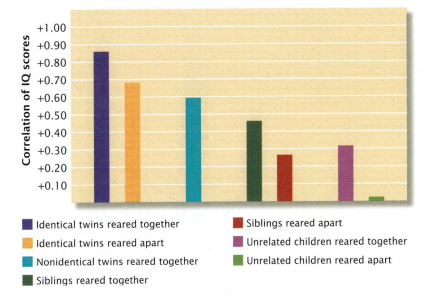

Identical twins reared together
Identical twins reared apart
Nonidentical twins reared together
Siblings reared together
Siblings reared apart
Unrelated children reared together
Unrelated children reared apart

associated with variations in cognitive abilities (Posthuma & de Geus, 2006). Still, it is important to understand that any estimates of the relative contributions of heredity and environment apply only to groups, not to individuals. It would be inaccurate to say that 50 percent of your IQ is inherited and 50 percent learned. It is more accurate to say that about half of the variability in the IQs of a group of people can be attributed to genetic influences. The other half can be attributed to other influences, including shared and nonshared environmental influences and measurement error. (As discussed in the appendix, *variability* is the degree to which scores spread out around an average score.)

Group Differences in IQ

Much of the controversy over the roles played by genes and the environment in intelligence has been sparked by efforts to explain differences in the average IQs of particular groups of people. For example, the average scores of Asian Americans are typically the highest among various ethnic groups, followed, in order, by European Americans, Hispanic Americans, and African Americans (e.g., Fagan, 2000; Herrnstein & Murray, 1994; Lynn, 2006; Taylor & Richards, 1991). Further, the average IQs of people from high-income areas in the United States and elsewhere are consistently higher than those of people from low-income communities with the same ethnic makeup (Jordan, Huttenlocher, & Levine, 1992; McLoyd, 1998; Rowe, Jacobson, & Van den Oord, 1999).

To understand these differences and where they come from, we must remember two things. First, group scores are just that; they do not describe individuals. So even though the average IQ of Asian Americans is higher than the average IQ of European Americans, there will still be many European Americans who score well above the Asian American average and large numbers of Asian Americans who score below the European American average (see Figure 7.12). Second, inherited characteristics are not necessarily fixed. As already mentioned, living in a favorable environment can improve a child's intellectual performance somewhat (Humphreys, 1984). There is also evidence that living in an impoverished environment can impair the development of cognitive skills (Turkheimer et al., 2003).

Socioeconomic Differences   We have already mentioned that there is a positive correlation between socioeconomic status (SES) and scores on IQ and other cognitive ability tests (e.g. Sackett et al., 2009). Why should this be? Four factors seem to account

---

FIGURE 7.12 ■   A REPRESENTATION OF ETHNIC GROUP DIFFERENCES IN IQ

The average IQ of Asian Americans is about four to six points higher than the average IQ of European Americans, who average twelve to fifteen points higher than African Americans and Hispanic Americans. Notice, however, that the variation *within* each of these groups is much greater than the variation *among* them.

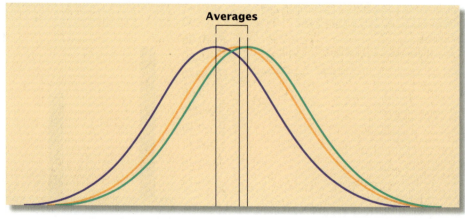

— African Americans and Hispanic Americans
— European Americans
— Asian Americans

How does motivation affect IQ?
(a link to Motivation and Emotion)

for it. First, parents' jobs and status depend on characteristics related to their own intelligence. And this intelligence is partly determined by a genetic component that, in turn, contributes to their children's cognitive ability level. Second, parents' income affects their children's environment in ways that can increase or decrease the children's IQs (Bacharach & Baumeister, 1998). Third, motivational differences may play a role. Parents in upper- and middle-income families tend to provide more financial and psychological support for their children's motivation to succeed and excel in academic endeavors (Erikson et al., 2005; Nelson-LeGall & Resnick, 1998). As a result, children from middle- and upper-income families may exert more effort in testing situations and therefore obtain higher scores (Bradley-Johnson, Graham, & Johnson, 1986; Zigler & Seitz, 1982). Fourth, because colleges, universities, and businesses usually select people with higher scores on various cognitive ability tests, those with higher IQs—who tend to do better on such tests—may have greater opportunities to earn more money (Sackett et al., 2001).

Ethnic Differences   Some have argued that the average differences in IQ among various ethnic groups in the United States and other developed countries are due at least partly to heredity (Rowe, 2005; Rushton & Jensen, 2005). However, the existence of hereditary differences among individuals *within* groups does not indicate whether differences *between* groups result from similar genetic causes. Notice again in Figure 7.12 that variation within ethnic groups is much greater than variation among the mean scores of those groups (Zuckerman, 1990).

We must also take into account the large differences among the environments in which the average African American, Hispanic American, Asian American, and European American child grows up. To take only the most blatant evidence, the latest U.S. Census Bureau figures show that 24.5 percent of African American families and 21.8 percent of Hispanic American families live below the poverty level, compared with 10.2 percent of Asian American families and 8.2 percent of European American families (U.S. Census Bureau, 2008). Compared with European Americans, African American children are more likely to have parents with less extensive educational backgrounds and to have less access to good nutrition, health care, and schools (Evans, 2004;

In Review

INFLUENCES ON IQ

SOURCE OF EFFECT	DESCRIPTION	EXAMPLES OF EVIDENCE FOR EFFECT
Genetics	Genes appear to play a significant role in IQ test performance.	The IQs of siblings who share no common environment are positively correlated. There is a greater correlation between scores of identical twins than between those of nonidentical twins.
Environment	Environmental conditions interact with genetic inheritance. Nutrition, medical care, sensory and intellectual stimulation, interpersonal relations, and influences on motivation are all significant features of the environment.	IQs have risen among children who are adopted into homes that offer a stimulating, enriching environment. Correlations between IQs of twins reared together are higher than for those reared apart.

1. Intelligence is influenced by both _____ and _____.
2. Children living in poverty tend to have _____ IQs than those in middle-income families.
3. IQs of children whose parents encourage learning tend to be _____ than those of children whose parents do not.

Wilson, 1997). All of these conditions are likely to pull down scores on intelligence tests (Brooks-Gunn, Klebanov, & Duncan, 1996). Cultural factors may also contribute to differences among the average scores of various ethnic groups. For example, those differing averages may partly reflect differences in the degree to which parents in each group tend to encourage their children's academic achievement (Steinberg, Dornbusch, & Brown, 1992).

In short, it appears that some important nongenetic factors serve to decrease the average scores of African American and Hispanic American children. Whatever heredity might contribute to children's performance, it may be possible for them to improve, given the removal of negative environmental conditions. ("In Review: Influences on IQ" summarizes our discussion of environmental and genetic factors affecting performance on intelligence tests.)

Thinking CRITICALLY

Are Intelligence Tests Unfairly Biased Against Certain Groups?

Summarizing a person's cognitive abilities with an IQ runs the risk of oversimplifying reality and making errors, but intelligence tests can also prevent errors. If boredom makes a child appear mentally slow, or even retarded, a properly conducted test is likely to reveal the child's potential. And, as Binet had hoped, intelligence tests have been enormously helpful in identifying children who need special educational attention. These tests can minimize the chances of assigning children to special classes that they don't need or to advanced work that they cannot yet handle.

Still, there is great concern over the fact that members of ethnic minorities and other environmentally disadvantaged groups have not had an equal chance to develop the knowledge and skills that are required to achieve high IQs.

▶ What am I being asked to believe or accept?

Some critics claim that, indeed, standard intelligence tests are not fair. They argue that a disproportionately large number of people in some ethnic minority groups score low on intelligence tests for reasons that are unrelated to cognitive ability, job potential, or other criteria that the tests are supposed to predict (Helms, 1992, 1997; Kwate, 2001; Neisser et al., 1996). They say that using intelligence tests to make decisions about people—such as assigning them to particular jobs or special classes—causes members of certain groups to be unfairly deprived of equal employment or educational opportunities.

▶ Is evidence available to support the claim?

Research reveals several possible sources of bias in intelligence test scores. First, noncognitive factors can influence a person's performance on IQ tests and may put certain groups at a disadvantage. We have seen, for example, that children from some ethnic and socioeconomic groups may be less motivated than other children to perform well on standardized tests. They may also be less comfortable in the testing situation and less likely to trust adult testers (Steele, 1997). So the differences in test scores

may partly reflect motivational or emotional differences among various groups, not intellectual ones.

Second, many intelligence test items are still drawn from the vocabulary and experiences of the dominant middle-class culture in the United States. As a result, these tests often measure achievement in acquiring knowledge valued by that culture. Not all cultures value the same things, however (Nisbett, 2003; Serpell, 1994; Sternberg & Grigorenko, 2004b). For example, a study of Cree Indians in northern Canada revealed that Cree words and phrases meaning "competent" included *good sense of direction*. At the "incompetent" end of the scale was the phrase *lives like a white person* (Berry & Bennett, 1992). A European American might not perform well on a Cree intelligence test based on these criteria. In fact, as illustrated in Figure 7.13, poor performance on a culture-specific test is probably due more to unfamiliarity with culture-based concepts than to lack of cognitive ability.

Third, some tests may reward those who interpret questions as expected by the test designer. Conventional intelligence tests have clearly defined "right" and "wrong" answers. Yet a person may interpret test questions in a manner that is "intelligent" or "correct" but that produces a "wrong" answer. For example, when one child was asked, "In what way are a pen and a pencil alike?" he replied, "They can both poke holes in paper." The fact that you don't give the answer that the test designer was looking for does not mean that you *can't*. When Liberian rice farmers were asked to sort objects, they tended to put a knife in the same group as vegetables. This was the clever way to do it, they said, because the knife is used to cut vegetables. When asked to sort the objects as a "stupid" person would, the farmers grouped the cutting tools together, the vegetables together, and so on, as most North Americans would (Segall et al., 1990).

▶ Can that evidence be interpreted another way?

The same evidence might be interpreted as showing that although traditional intelligence tests do not provide a pure measure of

FIGURE 7.13 ■ AN INTELLIGENCE TEST?

How did you do on this "intelligence test"? If, like most people, you are unfamiliar with the material being tested by these rather obscure questions, your score was probably low. Would it be fair to say, then, that you are not very intelligent?

Learn BY Doing

Take a minute to answer each of these questions, and check your answers against the key below.

1. What fictional detective was created by Leslie Charteris?
2. What dwarf planet travels around the sun every 248 years?
3. What vegetable yields the most pounds of produce per acre?
4. What was the infamous pseudonym of broadcaster Iva Toguri d'Aquino?
5. What kind of animal is Dr. Dolittle's Pushmi-Pullyu?

inherited cognitive ability, they do provide a fair test of whether a person is likely to succeed in school or in certain jobs. When some people have had more opportunity than others to develop their abilities, the difference will be reflected in higher IQs. From this point of view, intelligence tests are fair measures of the cognitive abilities people have developed while living in a society that, unfortunately, contains some unfair elements. In other words, the tests may be accurately detecting knowledge and skills that are not represented equally in all groups. That doesn't mean that the tests discriminate *unfairly* among those groups (Sackett, Borneman, & Connelly, 2008).

To some observers, concern over cultural bias in intelligence tests stems from a tendency to think of IQs as measures of innate ability. These psychologists suggest instead that intelligence tests are measuring ability that is developed and expressed in a cultural context—much as athletes develop the physical skills needed to play certain sports (Lohman, 2004). Eliminating language and other cultural elements from intelligence tests, they say, would eliminate a vital part of what the term *intelligence* means in any culture (Sternberg, 2004). This may be the reason that "culture-fair" tests do not predict academic achievement as well as conventional intelligence tests do (Aiken, 1994; Lohman, 2005). Perhaps familiarity with the culture reflected in intelligence tests is just as important for success at school or work in that culture as it is for success on the tests themselves. After all, the ranking among groups on measures of academic achievement is similar to the ranking for average IQs (Sue & Okazaki, 1990).

▶ What evidence would help to evaluate the alternatives?

If the problem of test bias is really a reflection of differences between various groups' opportunities to develop their cognitive skills, it will be important to learn more about how to reduce those differences. Making "unfair" cultures fairer by enhancing the skill development opportunities of traditionally disadvantaged groups should lead to smaller differences between groups on tests of cognitive ability (Martinez, 2000). It will also be important to find better

ways to encourage members of disadvantaged groups to take advantage of those opportunities (Sowell, 2005).

At the same time, alternative tests of cognitive ability must also be explored, particularly those that include assessment of problem-solving skills and other abilities not measured by most intelligence tests (e.g., Sternberg & Kaufman, 1998). If new tests show smaller between-group differences than traditional tests but have equal or better predictive validity, many of the issues discussed in this section will have been resolved. So far, efforts in this direction have not been successful.

▶ What conclusions are most reasonable?

The effort to reduce unfair cultural biases in tests is well founded, but "culture-fair" tests will be of little benefit if they fail to predict academic or occupational success as well as conventional tests do (Anastasi & Urbina, 1997; Sternberg, 1985). Whether one considers this situation good or bad, fair or unfair, it is important for people to have the information and skills that are valued by the culture in which they live and work. So using tests that are designed to predict success in such areas seems reasonable as long as the tests accurately measure a person's skills and access to culturally valued information.

In other words, there is probably no value-free or experience-free or culture-free way to measure the concept known as intelligence. The reason is that the concept is defined in terms of the behaviors that a culture values and that are developed through experience in that culture (Sternberg, 1985, 2004). This conclusion has led some researchers to worry less about how cultural influences might "contaminate" tests of cognitive abilities and to focus instead on how to help people develop the abilities that are required for success in school and society. As mentioned earlier, if more attention were focused on combating poverty, poor schools, inadequate nutrition, lack of health care, and other conditions that result in lower average IQs and reduced economic opportunities for certain groups of people, many of the reasons for concern about test bias might be eliminated.

Diversity in Intelligence

▶ *Is there more than one type of intelligence?*

Intelligence test scores can tell us some things—and predict some things—about people, but we have seen that they don't tell the whole story of intelligence. Let's see how diverse intelligence can be by looking at some nontraditional aspects of intelligence and at some people whose intellectual abilities are unusually high or low.

Practical and Creative Intelligence

According to Robert Sternberg (1988b, 1999), a complete theory of intelligence must deal with three different types of intelligence: analytic, creative, and practical. *Analytic intelligence,* the kind that is measured by traditional intelligence tests, would help you solve a physics problem; *creative intelligence* is what you would use to compose music; and you would draw on *practical intelligence* to figure out what to do if you were stranded on a lonely road during a blizzard. Sternberg's *triarchic theory* of intelligence deals with all three types of intelligence.

Sternberg recognizes the importance of analytic intelligence for success in academics and other areas, but he argues that universities and companies should not select people solely on the basis of tests of this kind of intelligence (Sternberg, 1996; Sternberg & Williams, 1997). Why? Because the tasks posed by tests of analytic intelligence are often of little interest to the people taking them and typically have little relationship to these people's daily experiences. In contrast, the practical problems people face every day are generally of personal interest and are related to more common life experiences (Sternberg et al., 1995). It is no wonder, then, that children who do poorly in school and on intelligence tests may also show high degrees of practical intelligence. Some Brazilian street children, for example, can do the math required for their street businesses despite having failed mathematics in school (Carraher, Carraher, & Schliemann, 1985).

Sternberg and his colleagues have developed new intelligence tests designed to assess analytic, practical, and creative intelligence (see Figure 7.14). They offer evidence that scores on these tests can predict success at some jobs at least as well as standard intelligence tests (Leonhardt, 2000; Sternberg & Kaufman, 1998; Sternberg et al., 1995; Sternberg and the Rainbow Project Coordinators, 2006), but other researchers have questioned this interpretation (Brody, 2003).

Multiple Intelligences

Many people with only average scores on intelligence tests have exceptional ability in specific areas. Even those with very low IQs have been known to show incredible ability in narrowly defined skills. One such child, whose IQ was only 50, could instantly and correctly state the day of the week for any date between 1880 and 1950 (Scheerer, Rothmann, & Goldstein, 1945). He could also play melodies on the piano by ear and sing Italian operatic pieces he had heard. He could spell—forward or backward—any word spoken to him and could memorize long speeches. However, he had no understanding of what he was doing.

Cases such as this are part of the evidence that led Howard Gardner to suggest that everyone possesses a number of intellectual potentials, or "intelligences," each of which involves a somewhat different set of aptitudes (Gardner, 1993, 2002). Biology, he says, provides raw capacities for *multiple intelligences*; cultures provide symbolic systems (such as language) that enable people to use their raw capacities. According to Gardner, the various intelligences normally interact but can function with some independence and individuals may develop certain intelligences further than others, often in response to the opportunities and demands found in their culture.

ANSWERS TO FIGURE 7.13: (1) Simon Templar (2) Pluto (3) Cabbage (4) Tokyo Rose (5) A two-headed llama

FIGURE 7.14 ■ TESTING FOR PRACTICAL AND CREATIVE INTELLIGENCE

Robert Sternberg argues that traditional IQ tests measure mainly analytic intelligence. Here are sample items from tests he developed that mesaure practical and creative intelligence as well. The answers are given at the bottom of the figure. How did you do?
Source: Sternberg (1996).

PRACTICAL

1. Think of a problem that you are currently experiencing in real life. Briefly describe the problem, including how long it has been present and who else is involved (if anyone). Then describe three different practical things you could do to try to solve the problem. *(Students are given up to 15 minutes and up to 2 pages.)*

2. Choose the answer that provides the **best** solution, given the specific situation and desired outcome.
   John's family moved to Iowa from Arizona during his junior year in high school. He enrolled as a new student in the local high school two months ago but still has not made friends and feels bored and lonely. One of his favorite activities is writing stories. What is likely to be the most effective solution to this problem?
   A. Volunteer to work on the school newspaper staff.
   B. Spend more time at home writing columns for the school newsletter.
   C. Try to convince his parents to move back to Arizona.
   D. Invite a friend from Arizona to visit during Christmas break.

3. Each question asks you to use information about everyday things. Read each question carefully and choose the best answer.

   Mike wants to buy two seats together and is told there are pairs of seats available only in Rows 8, 12, 49, and 95–100. Which of the following is not one of his choices for the total price of the two tickets?

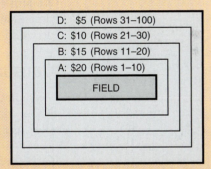

   A. $10.   **B.** $20.   **C.** $30.   **D.** $40.

CREATIVE

1. Suppose you are the student representative to a committee that has the power and the money to reform your school system. Describe your ideal school system, including buildings, teachers, curriculum, and any other aspects you feel are important. *(Students are given up to 15 minutes and up to 2 pages.)*

2. Each question has a "Pretend" statement. You must suppose that this statement is true. Decide which word goes with the third underlined word in the same way that the first two underlined words go together.
   Colors are audible.
   flavor is to tongue as shade is to
   A. ear.   **B.** light.   **C.** sound.   **D.** hue.

3. First, read how the operation is defined. Then, decide what is the correct answer to the question.
   *There is a new mathematical operation called **flix.**
   It is defined as follows:*
   A flix $B = A + B$, if $A > B$
   but A flix $B = A \times B$, if $A < B$
   and A flix $B = A / B$, if $A = B$
   How much is 4 flix 7?
   A. 28.   **B.** 11.   **C.** 3.   **D.** −11.

The specific intelligences that Gardner (1999) proposes are (1) *linguistic* intelligence (reflected in good vocabulary and reading comprehension); (2) *logical-mathematical* intelligence (as indicated by skill at arithmetic and certain kinds of reasoning); (3) *spatial* intelligence (seen in the ability to visualize the relationships among objects in the environment); (4) *musical* intelligence (as in abilities involving rhythm, tempo, and sound identification); (5) *body-kinesthetic* intelligence (reflected in skill at dancing, athletics, and eye-hand coordination); (6) *intrapersonal* intelligence (displayed by self-understanding); (7) *interpersonal* intelligence (seen in the ability to understand and interact with others); and (8) *naturalistic* intelligence (the ability to see patterns in nature). Other researchers have suggested that people also possess *emotional* intelligence, which involves the capacity to perceive, use, understand, and manage their emotions (Meyer & Salovey, 1997; Salovey & Grewal, 2005). Gardner says that standard IQ tests sample only the first three of these diverse intelligences, mainly because they are the forms of intelligence most valued in school. Gardner's view of intelligence is appealing, partly because it supports the flattering idea that almost everyone is especially intelligent in at least one way. However, his critics argue that including athletic or musical skill as part of intelligence dilutes the usefulness of the concept, especially as it is applied to performance in school and in many kinds of jobs. They also point out that Gardner's theory lacks the empirical evidence necessary to challenge other, more established theories of intelligences (Klein, 1997; Waterhouse, 2006a, 2006b). The ultimate value of the theory and of methods for assessing multiple intelligences will be determined by further research.

Unusual Intelligence

Psychologists' understanding of intelligence has been advanced by studying people whose cognitive abilities are unusual—especially the gifted and the mentally retarded (Robinson, Zigler, & Gallagher, 2000).

Giftedness   People who show remarkably high levels of accomplishment in particular areas are often referred to as gifted. Giftedness is typically measured by school achievement. A child's potential for high achievement is usually measured by intelligence tests, but researchers warn that it is risky to predict academic potential from a single measure, such as IQ (Hagen, 1980; Lohman & Hagen, 2001; Thorndike & Hagen, 1996).

For one thing, not all people with unusually high IQs become famous and successful in their chosen fields, although they are more likely than others to do so. One of the best-known studies of the intellectually gifted was conducted by Lewis Terman and his colleagues (Oden, 1968; Sears, 1977; Terman & Oden, 1947, 1959). This study began in 1921 with the identification of more than 1,500 boys and girls whose IQs were very high—most higher than 135 by age ten. Periodic interviews and tests over the next seventy years revealed that few, if any, became world-famous scientists, inventors, authors, artists, or composers. But only 11 failed to graduate from high school, and more than two-thirds graduated from college—this at a time when completing a college education was relatively rare, particularly for women. Ninety-seven went on to earn Ph.D.'s; 92, law degrees; and 57, medical degrees. In 1955 their median family income was well above the national average (Terman & Oden, 1959). In general, they were physically and mentally healthier than the general population and appeared to have led happier lives (Cronbach, 1996). More recent studies also show that people with higher IQs tend to live longer (Deary et al., 2004; Gottfredson, 2004; Hart et al., 2003), perhaps because they have the reasoning and problem-solving skills that lead them to take better care of themselves and avoid danger (Breslau, Lucia, & Alvarado, 2006; Deary & Der, 2005b; Gottfredson & Deary, 2004; see the Focus on Research section in the chapter on health, stress, and coping).

In other words, higher IQs tend to predict greater success in life (Lubinski et al., 2006; Simonton & Song, 2009; Wai, Lubinski, & Benbow, 2005; Whalley & Deary, 2001), but an extremely high IQ does not guarantee special distinction. Some research

ANSWERS TO FIGURE 7.14. Practical: (2) A, (3) B. Creative: (2) A, (3) A.

suggests that gifted children are not fundamentally different kinds of people. They just have more of the same basic cognitive abilities seen in all children (Dark & Benbow, 1993; Singh & O'Boyle, 2004). Other work suggests that gifted people may be different in other ways, too, such as having unusually intense motivation to master certain tasks or areas of intellectual endeavor (Lubinski et al., 2001; Winner, 2000).

Mental Retardation   People whose IQs are lower than about 70 and who fail to display the skills at daily living, communication, and other tasks that are expected of those their age have traditionally been described as mentally retarded (American Psychiatric Association, 1994). They are now often referred to as developmentally disabled, developmentally delayed, or mentally challenged. People within this very broad category differ greatly in their cognitive abilities and in their ability to function independently in daily life (see Table 7.2).

Some cases of mental retardation have a clearly identifiable cause. The best-known example is *Down syndrome,* which occurs when an abnormality during conception results in an extra copy of chromosome 21 (Hattori et al., 2000). Children with Down syndrome typically have IQs in the range of 40 to 55, though some may score higher than that. There are also several inherited causes of mental retardation. The most common of these is *fragile X syndrome,* a defect on chromosome 23 (known as the *X chromosome*). Retardation can also result from environmental causes, such as exposure to German measles (rubella), alcohol, or other toxins before birth; oxygen deprivation during birth; and head injuries, brain tumors, and infectious diseases (such as meningitis or encephalitis) in childhood (U.S. Surgeon General, 1999).

Cultural-familial mental retardation (also called psychosocial mental retardation) refers to the 30 to 40 percent of (usually mild) cases of mental retardation that have no obvious genetic or environmental cause (American Psychiatric Association, 1994). These cases appear to result from a complex and as yet unknown interaction between heredity and environment that researchers are continuing to explore (Croen, Grether, & Selvin, 2001; Spinath, Harlaar et al., 2004).

People who are mildly retarded differ from other people in three important ways (Campione, Brown, & Ferrara, 1982):

1. They perform certain mental operations more slowly, such as retrieving information from long-term memory. When asked to repeat something they have learned, they are not as quick as a person of normal intelligence.

THE EAGLE HAS LANDED   ▲

In February 2000, Richard Keebler, 27, became an Eagle Scout in the Boy Scouts of America. His achievement was notable not only because a mere 4 percent of all Scouts ever reach this rank but also because Keebler has Down syndrome. As we come to better understand the potential, and not just the limitations, of mentally retarded people, their opportunities and their role in society will continue to expand.

cultural-familial mental retardation
Cases of mild retardation for which no environmental or genetic cause can be found.

TABLE 7.2   ■   CATEGORIES OF MENTAL RETARDATION

These categories are approximate. Especially at the upper end of the scale, many retarded persons can be taught to handle tasks well beyond what their IQs might suggest. Furthermore, IQ is not the only diagnostic criterion for retardation. Many people with IQs lower than 70 can function adequately in their everyday environment and so would not be classified as mentally retarded.

Level of Retardation	IQ Range	Characteristics
Mild	50–70	A majority of all the mentally retarded. Usually show no physical symptoms of abnormality. Individuals with higher IQs can marry, maintain a family, and work in unskilled jobs. Abstract reasoning is difficult for those with the lower IQs of this category. Capable of some academic learning to a sixth-grade level.
Moderate	35–49	Often lack physical coordination. Can be trained to take care of themselves and to acquire some reading and writing skills. Abilities of a 4- to 7-year-old. Capable of living outside an institution with their families.
Severe	20–34	Only a few can benefit from any schooling. Can communicate vocally after extensive training. Most require constant supervision.
Profound	Below 20	Mental age less than 3. Very limited communication. Require constant supervision. Can learn to walk, utter a few simple phrases, and feed themselves.

2. They simply know fewer facts about the world. It is likely that this deficiency is a consequence of the problem listed next.

3. They are not very good at using certain mental strategies that may be important in learning and problem solving. For example, they do not remember to rehearse material that must be held in short-term memory, even though they know how to do so.

Despite such difficulties, the intellectual abilities of mentally retarded people can be improved to some extent. One program that emphasized positive parent-child communications began when the children were as young as two and a half years old. It helped children with Down syndrome to eventually master reading skills at a second-grade level, providing the foundation for further achievement (Rynders & Horrobin, 1980; Turkington, 1987). However, designing effective programs for children who are retarded is complicated by the fact that learning does not depend on cognitive skills alone. It also depends on social and emotional factors, including where children learn. Much debate has focused on *mainstreaming*, the policy of teaching children with disabilities, including those who are retarded, in regular classrooms alongside children without disabilities. Is mainstreaming good for retarded children? A number of studies comparing the cognitive and social skills of children who have been mainstreamed and those who were separated show few significant differences overall. However, it does appear that students at higher ability levels may gain more from being mainstreamed than their less mentally able peers (Cole et al., 1991; Mills et al., 1998).

ACTIVE REVIEW ▶ Chapter 7

Thought, Language, *and* Intelligence

As noted in the introductory chapter, all of psychology's subfields are related to one another. Our discussion of group problem solving illustrates just one way that the topic of this chapter—thought, language, and intelligence—is linked to the subfield of social psychology, which is described

in the chapter by that name. The Linkages diagram shows ties to two other subfields, and there are many more ties throughout the book. Looking for linkages among subfields will help you see how they all fit together and help you better appreciate the big picture that is psychology.

linkages

Where are the brain's language centers? *(ans. on p. 67)*

Chapter 2
Biology and Behavior

How does motivation affect IQ scores? *(ans. on p. 283)*

Chapter 8
Motivation and Emotion

Do groups solve problems more effectively than individuals? *(ans. on p. 269)*

Chapter 14
Social Psychology

SUMMARY ▶

Basic Functions of Thought

▶ *What good is thinking, anyway?*

The five core functions of thought are describing, elaborating, deciding, planning, and guiding action. Many psychologists think of the components of this circle of thought as constituting an **information-processing system** that receives, represents, transforms, and acts on incoming stimuli. **Thinking,** then, is defined as the manipulation of mental representations by this system.

Mental Representations: The Ingredients of Thought

▶ *What are thoughts made of?*

Mental representations take the form of concepts, propositions, schemas, scripts, mental models, images, and cognitive maps. **Concepts** are categories of objects, events, or ideas with common properties. They may be formal or natural. *Formal concepts* are precisely defined by the presence or absence of certain features. *Natural concepts* are fuzzy; no fixed set of defining properties determines membership in a natural concept. A member of a natural concept that displays all or most of the concept's characteristic features is called a **prototype.**

Propositions are assertions that state how concepts are related. Propositions can be true or false. **Schemas** serve as generalized mental representations of concepts and generate expectations about them. **Scripts** are schemas about familiar sequences of events or activities. Experience creates accurate or inaccurate **mental models** that help guide our understanding of and interaction with the world. Mental **images** may also be manipulated when people think. **Cognitive maps** are mental representations of familiar parts of one's world.

Thinking Strategies

▶ *Do people always think logically?*

By combining and transforming mental representations, our information-processing system makes it possible for us to engage in **reasoning,** to solve problems, and to make decisions. **Formal reasoning** seeks

valid conclusions through the application of rigorous procedures. It is guided by **algorithms,** systematic methods that always reach a correct result (if there is one). To reach a sound conclusion, people should consider both the truth and falsity of their assumptions and whether the argument follows the rules of **logic.** Unfortunately, people are prone to logical errors.

People use **informal reasoning** to assess the validity of a conclusion based on the evidence supporting it. Errors in informal reasoning often stem from the use of **heuristics,** which are mental shortcuts or rules of thumb. Three important heuristics are the **anchoring bias** or **anchoring heuristic** (estimating the probability of an event by adjusting an earlier estimate), the **representativeness heuristic** (basing conclusions about whether something belongs in a certain class on how similar it is to other items in that class), and the **availability heuristic** (estimating probability by how available an event is in memory).

Problem Solving

▶ *What's the best way to solve a problem?*

Steps in problem solving include diagnosing the problem and then planning, executing, and evaluating a solution. Especially when solutions are not obvious, problem solving can be aided by incubation and the use of strategies such as means-end analysis (also called *decomposition*), working backward, and finding analogies.

Many of the difficulties that people experience in solving problems arise when they are dealing with hypotheses. People do not easily consider multiple hypotheses. Because of **mental sets,** they may stick to one hypothesis even when it is incorrect, and because of **functional fixedness,** they may miss opportunities to use familiar objects in unusual ways. People may be reluctant to revise or change hypotheses on the basis of new data, partly because **confirmation**

bias focuses their attention on evidence that supports their hypotheses. They may also fail to use the absence of symptoms or events as evidence in solving problems.

Some specific problems can be solved by computer programs developed by researchers in the field of **artificial intelligence (AI).** There are two approaches to AI. One focuses on programming computers to imitate the logical manipulation of symbols that occurs in human thought; the other (involving connectionist, or neural network, models) attempts to imitate the connections among neurons in the human brain.

Tests of **divergent thinking** are used to measure differences in **creativity.** In contrast, intelligence tests require **convergent thinking.** Although creativity and intelligence are not highly correlated, creative behavior requires a certain amount of intelligence, along with expertise in a creative field, skill at problem solving and divergent thinking, and motivation to pursue a creative endeavor for its own sake.

Decision Making

▶ *How can I become a better decision maker?*

Decisions are sometimes difficult because there are too many alternatives and too many features of each alternative to consider all at once. Furthermore, decisions often involve comparisons of subjective **utility,** not of objective value. Decision making is also complicated by the fact that the world is unpredictable, which makes decisions risky.

People should act in ways that maximize the **expected value** of their decisions. They often fail to do so because losses are perceived differently from gains of equal size and because people tend to overestimate the probability of rare events, underestimate the probability of frequent events, and feel overconfident about the accuracy of their forecasts. The gambler's fallacy leads people to believe that events in a random process are affected by previous events. People also make decisions aimed at goals other than maximizing expected value; these goals may be determined by personal and cultural factors.

Group decisions tend to show group polarization, the selection of more extreme outcomes than would have been chosen by the average group member. Group performance in problem solving and decision making can be effective, but depending on the problem and the people involved, it may be less efficient than when individuals work alone.

Language

► *How do babies learn to talk?*

Language consists of words or word symbols and rules for their combination—a **grammar.** Children develop grammar according to an orderly pattern. **Infant vocalizations,** such as **babblings,** come first, then a **one-word stage** of speech, and then two-word sentences. Next come three-word sentences and certain grammatical forms that appear in a somewhat predictable order. Once children learn certain regular verb forms and plural endings, they may overgeneralize rules. Children acquire most of the grammatical rules of their native language by the time they are five years old.

Both conditioning and imitation play a role in a child's acquisition of language, but neither can provide a complete explanation of how children acquire grammar. Humans may be biologically programmed to learn language. In any event, it appears that language must be learned during a certain critical period if normal language is to occur.

Testing Intelligence

► *How is intelligence measured?*

Intelligence refers to information-processing skills, problem-solving skills, and the capacity to adapt to changing environments. Binet's pioneering test of intelligence included questions that required reasoning and problem solving at varying levels of difficulty, graded by age. Terman developed a revision of Binet's test that became known as the **Stanford-Binet Intelligence Scale**; it included items designed to assess the intelligence of adults as well as that of children, and it became the model for

IQ tests. Early intelligence tests in the United States required not just cognitive ability but also knowledge of U.S. culture. Wechsler's intelligence tests remedied some of the deficiencies of earlier tests. Made up of subtests, including a verbal scale and also a performance scale with little verbal content, these tests allowed testers to obtain scores for different aspects of cognitive ability.

In schools, the Stanford-Binet and Wechsler tests are among the most popular individually administered intelligence tests. Both include subtests and provide scores for parts of the test as well as an overall score. A person's **intelligence quotient,** or **IQ,** is no longer the result of dividing mental age by actual age and multiplying by 100. It reflects instead how much the person's performance on the test deviates from the average performance of people in the same age group. An average performance is assigned an IQ of 100.

Evaluating Intelligence Tests

► *How good are intelligence tests?*

Tests are standardized, so the performance of different people can be compared; they also produce scores that can be compared with **norms.** A good test must have **statistical reliability,** which means that the results for each person are consistent, or stable. **Statistical validity** refers to the degree to which test scores are interpreted appropriately and used properly.

Intelligence tests are quite reliable and do a reasonable job of predicting academic and occupational success. However, these tests assess only some of the abilities that might be considered aspects of intelligence, and they may favor people who are most familiar with middle-class culture. Nonetheless, this familiarity is important for academic and occupational success in that culture.

Both genes and the environment influence IQs, and their effects interact. Genetic influences are reflected in the high correlation between IQs of identical twins raised in separate households and in the similarity between the IQs of children adopted at birth and those of their biological parents. The influence of the environment is revealed by the higher correlation of IQ between siblings who share the same environment than between those who do not and

by the effects of environmental changes such as adoption.

Different socioeconomic and ethnic groups have somewhat different average IQs. These differences appear to be due in part to noncognitive factors, such as differences in motivation, family support, educational opportunity, and other environmental conditions. An enriched environment sometimes raises preschool children's IQs. Despite their limitations, intelligence tests can help educators identify a student's strengths and weaknesses and offer the curriculum that will best serve that student.

Diversity in Intelligence

► *Is there more than one type of intelligence?*

Sternberg sees three types of intelligence: analytic, practical, and creative. He says that scores on tests of practical intelligence predict job success as well as traditional intelligence test scores do. According to Gardner, biology equips us with the capacities for several intelligences that can function with some independence—specifically, linguistic, logical-mathematical, spatial, musical, body-kinesthetic, intrapersonal, interpersonal, and naturalistic intelligences. Knowledge about cognitive abilities has been expanded by research on giftedness and mental retardation. People with very high IQs tend to be successful in life but are not necessarily geniuses. People are considered retarded if their IQs are below about 70 and if their communication and daily living skills are less than expected of people their age. In cases of **cultural-familial mental retardation,** no genetic or environmental causes are evident. Compared with people of normal intelligence, people who are retarded process information more slowly, know fewer facts, and are deficient at knowing and using mental strategies. Special teaching programs can, to some extent, improve the intellectual abilities of some people who are mentally retarded.

Put It in Writing

Try writing your own definition of *intelligence*. Make a list of at least seven behaviors or characteristics that you feel represent intelligence and then decide how they could best be tested in children and adults from your own culture and other cultures. Describe the kinds of difficulties you encountered in making your list and designing your assessment devices.

Personal Learning Activity

Consider a problem that you are facing at the moment or one that someone you know is facing. In accordance with the problem-solving section of this chapter, write down all the alternative solutions you can think of to solve this problem, then list the pros and cons of each option. Which alternative comes out on top? Does the alternative that seems best on paper also strike you as the best solution to try? Why or why not? *For additional projects, see the Personal Learning Activities in the corresponding chapter of the study guide that accompanies this book.*

Take Action to Learn More

Now that you have finished reading this chapter, how about exploring some of the ideas and information that you found most interesting? Here are some courses, books, films, and Internet resources to get you started. Enjoy!

Courses

Experimental Psychology
Cognitive Psychology
Psycholinguistics
Engineering Psychology (also called Human Factors)
Tests and Measurement (sometimes called Psychometrics)
Behavioral Genetics

Movies

Nell; Dances with Wolves; Clan of the Cave Bear. Language development.
The Day of the Dolphin; Gorillas in the Mist. Animal communication.
Apollo 13; The Negotiator; K-19: The Gods Must Be Crazy; The Widowmaker. Problem solving.
Blade Runner; Colossus: The Forbin Project; 2001: A Space Odyssey. Artificial intelligence.
My Left Foot. Assessment of ability.
Being There; Born Yesterday; Charly; Forrest Gump; Little Man Tate; Of Mice and Men; The Other Sister; Rain Man; Real Genius. Diversity of intelligence.
Cast Away; Tucker: The Man and His Dream. Problem solving, creativity, intelligence.
Searching for Bobby Fischer; Hilary and Jackie; Pi. Giftedness.

Books

GERD GIGERENZER, PETER M. TODD, AND ABC RESEARCH GROUP, *Simple Heuristics That Make Us Smart* (Oxford University Press, 2000). Research on and ideas for using mental shortcuts.
PETER BERNSTEIN, *Against the Gods: The Remarkable Story of Risk* (Wiley, 1998). History of efforts to understand risk and probability in decision making.
JAMES SUROWIECKI, *The Wisdom of Crowds: Why the Many Are Smarter Than the Few and How Collective Wisdom Shapes Business, Economies, Societies, and Nations.* (Doubleday, 2004). Presents theories and evidence for the value of group rather than individual decisions.
PHILIP TETLOCK, *Expert Political Judgment: How Good Is It? How Can We Know?* (Princeton University Press, 2006). Presents evidence that the judgment of even revered political experts is subject to the same flaws and pitfalls that plague the rest of us.
HOWARD GARDNER, *Intelligence Reframed: Multiple Intelligences for the 21st Century* (Basic Books, 1999). Theory of multiple intelligences.
NICHOLAS LEMANN, *The Big Test: The Secret History of American Meritocracy* (Farrar, Straus and Giroux, 1999). History of testing in the United States.
HANS EYSENCK, WITH DARRIN EVANS, *Test Your IQ* (Penguin, 1995). Self-testing.
STEVEN FATSIS, *Word Freak* (Houghton Mifflin, 2002). Inside the high-stakes world of professional Scrabble.

RICHARD HERRNSTEIN AND CHARLES MURRAY, *The Bell Curve* (Free Press, 1994). Controversial book about group differences in intelligence.
DANIEL SELIGMAN, *A Question of Intelligence: The IQ Debate in America* (Citadel Press, 1994). Nature, nurture, and IQ.
STEVEN FRASER, ED., *The Bell Curve Wars* (Basic Books, 1995). Essays critical of *The Bell Curve*.

The Web

***Essentials of Psychology* Book Companion Website**

www.cengage.com/psychology/bernstein

Visit the book companion website to access a wealth of resources, including chapter outlines, flashcards, web links, tutorial quizzes, and more!

CENGAGENOW™ Just what you need to know NOW! Spend time on what you need to master rather than on information you already have learned. Take a pre-test for this chapter, and CengageNOW will generate a personalized study plan based on your results. The study plan will identify the topics you need to review and direct you to online resources to help you master those topics. You can then take a post-test to help you determine the concepts you have mastered and what you will need to work on. Try it out! Go to www.cengage.com/login to sign in with an access code or to purchase access to this product.

Review of Key Terms ▶

Can you define each of the key terms in the chapter? Check your definitions against those on the pages shown in parentheses in the following list or in the Glossary at the end of the book.

algorithms (p. 255)
anchoring bias (anchoring heuristic) (p. 256)
artificial intelligence (AI) (p. 264)
availability heuristic (p. 257)
babblings (p. 271)
cognitive map (p. 254)
concepts (p. 251)
confirmation bias (p. 262)
convergent thinking (p. 266)
creativity (p. 265)

cultural-familial mental retardation, (p. 289)
divergent thinking (p. 265)
expected value (p. 267)
formal reasoning (p. 255)
functional fixedness (p. 261)
grammar (p. 270)
heuristics (p. 256)
images (p. 253)
infant vocalizations (p. 271)
informal reasoning (p. 256)
information-processing system (p. 249)
intelligence (p. 275)
intelligence quotient (IQ) (p. 275)
language (p. 270)
logic (p. 255)

mental models (p. 253)
mental set (p. 261)
norms (p. 278)
one-word stage (p. 272)
propositions (p. 252)
prototype (p. 252)
reasoning (p. 255)
representativeness heuristic (p. 257)
schemas (p. 252)
scripts (p. 253)
Stanford-Binet Intelligence Scale (p. 275)
statistical reliability (p. 278)
statistical validity (p. 279)
test (p. 278)
thinking (p. 249)
utility (p. 266)

MULTIPLE CHOICE ▶ Self Test

Select the best answer for each of the following questions. Then check your responses against the Answer Key at the end of the book.

1. Thinking is defined as the manipulation of _____.
   a. concepts.
   b. mental models.
   c. heuristics.
   d. mental representations.

2. While trying to describe an unusual bird he saw on his walk, Jarrod asks his friend to "think of a robin, but with blue tips on the wings and a tuft of hair on the head. That's what it looked like." Because "bird" is a _____ concept, Jarrod began with the image of a robin, which is the _____ of "bird." He hoped that his description would allow his friend to develop a _____ of the bird he saw.
   a. formal; concept; prototype
   b. natural; image; concept
   c. natural; prototype; mental model
   d. visual; mental model; script

3. Clint is frustrated. His uncle has been winning at checkers all night. During the next game he is going to base his strategy on an algorithm, not a heuristic. What problem will this strategy cause?
   a. Clint still may not win the game.
   b. Clint and his uncle may be playing the same game of checkers for a long time.
   c. Clint will be ignoring overall probabilities.
   d. The representativeness heuristic will bias Clint's choice of strategy.

4. Alicia agreed to go to dinner and a movie with Adam but was surprised and angry when Adam expected her to pay for her half of the evening's expenses. Adam and Alicia apparently had different _____ for what is supposed to happen on a date.
   a. mental models
   b. propositions
   c. images
   d. scripts

5. Stephanie has worked for hours on a biochemistry problem without success. She decides to put it aside and work on her psychology homework in the hope that a solution might occur to her while she is thinking about something else. Stephanie is trying the _____ strategy to solve her problem.
   a. decomposition
   b. incubation
   c. working backward
   d. analogies

6. Ebony wanted to leave a note for her husband but couldn't find a pen, so she wrote the note with her lipstick. Ebony was able to overcome the obstacle to problem solving called _____.
   a. absence of information
   b. multiple hypotheses
   c. confirmation bias
   d. functional fixedness

7. Dr. Sand is sure that Ahmed has appendicitis and as a result he pays more attention to test results that are consistent with appendicitis than to results that suggest a different problem. Dr. Sand has fallen victim to _____.
   a. functional fixedness
   b. a mental model
   c. confirmation bias
   d. the availability heuristic

8. While playing a dominos game, Richard drew a tile at random and got a "double blank," which costs the most points during the first two rounds. At the start of the third round, he says, "There is no way I will draw the double blank tile next time!" Richard is being influenced by _____.
   a. the gambler's fallacy
   b. loss aversion
   c. a disregard of negative evidence
   d. confirmation bias

9. The fact that children learning language sometimes make errors, such as saying "I goed" instead of "I went," has been used to suggest which of the following?
   a. There is a critical period in language development.
   b. Children are born with a knowledge of grammar.
   c. Children do not learn language entirely through imitation.
   d. Speech is learned mainly through imitation.

10. Children who spend their early years isolated from human contact and the sound of adult language are unable to develop adult language skills despite extensive training efforts later. This phenomenon provides evidence for the notion that _____.
    a. there is a critical period in language development
    b. children are born with a language acquisition device
    c. there are no fixed stages in language acquisition
    d. speech is acquired only through imitation

11. The earliest IQ test was developed to _____.
    a. identify children who needed special educational programs
    b. help the armed forces make appropriate assignments of recruits
    c. identify which immigrants were mentally defective and thus should not be allowed into the United States
    d. help employers decide which employees were most appropriate for the available jobs

12. "All monsters are ugly. The Creature from the Black Lagoon is a monster. Therefore, the Creature is ugly." Together, these three statements are an example of _____.
    a. a premise
    b. a proposition
    c. a natural concept
    d. formal reasoning

13. Jonah's parents are told that their son has an IQ of 100. According to the intelligence test scoring method used today, this means that Jonah _____.
    a. has a mental age that is higher than his chronological age
    b. scored higher than half the children in his age group
    c. can now be considered to be a gifted child
    d. shows about average skill at divergent thinking

14. Like all other applicants to medical school, Lavinia took the MCAT admission test. Later, researchers compared all the successful applicants' medical school grades with their MCAT scores. The researchers were obviously trying to measure the MCAT's _____.
    a. statistical reliability
    b. standardization
    c. statistical validity
    d. norms

15. When Jerrica first took the Handy Dandy Intelligence test, her score was 140. When she took the same test six weeks later, her score was only 102. If other people showed similarly changing score patterns, the Handy Dandy Intelligence test would appear to lack _____.
    a. statistical reliability   c. standardization
    b. statistical validity   d. norms

16. Research shows that today's standardized intelligence tests _____.
    a. have good reliability and reasonably good validity for predicting success in school
    b. do not do a good job of predicting success on the job
    c. are not correlated with performance on "real-life" tasks
    d. measure the full array of cognitive abilities

17. There are two sets of twins in the Mullis family. Louise and Lanie are identical twins; Andy and Adrian are not. According to research on heredity and intelligence, which pair of twins is likely to show the most similarity in IQs?
    a. Andy and Adrian, because they are male siblings.
    b. Andy and Adrian, because they are fraternal twins.
    c. Louise and Lanie, because they are female siblings.
    d. Louise and Lanie, because they are identical twins.

18. Rowena is mildly mentally retarded, but she is attending regular classes at a public school. Rowena most likely _____ and she will _____ from being mainstreamed.
    a. knows fewer facts about the world than others; benefit
    b. knows fewer facts about the world than others; not benefit
    c. learns just as fast as other children, but forgets it faster; not benefit.
    d. has little or no potential for employment; benefit.

19. Betsey took an intelligence test that included items requiring her to say what she would do if she were stranded in a large city with no money and how she would teach music to children who had no musical instruments. This test was most likely based on _____.
    a. Sternberg's triarchic theory of intelligence
    b. Gardner's concept of multiple intelligences
    c. Terman's giftedness theory
    d. the Wechsler Adult Intelligence Scale

20. Theresa Amabile identified cognitive and personality characteristics necessary for creativity. Which of the following is not one of these characteristics?
    a. A capacity for focusing on the most important element in a problem, which is tied to convergent thinking.
    b. Expertise in the field of endeavor, which is tied to learning.
    c. A set of creative skills, including the capacity for divergent thinking.
    d. The motivation to pursue creative work for internal reasons.

© John Gress/Reuters/Landov

8 Motivation *and* Emotion

Preview

When your alarm clock goes off in the morning do you jump out of bed, eager to face the day, or do you bury your head in the blankets, trying to avoid all that's ahead of you? Once you're out of bed, do you eat a big breakfast or do you just have coffee or tea, no matter how hungry you feel? As you leave home, do you notice your attractive neighbor and find yourself wondering whether the two of you might someday have a romantic relationship? Or if you're in a long-term relationship, do you find yourself thinking fond thoughts of your partner? Once you're at your job or on campus, do you always try to do your best or do you work just hard enough to get by? And how do you feel about your life? Are you generally happy? Do you sometimes worry or feel sad? In this chapter, we explore the physical, mental, and social factors that motivate behavior in areas ranging from eating to sexuality to achievement. We also examine what emotions are and how they are expressed.

W hen Tiger Woods won the British Open in July 2000, he became the youngest man to win all four tournaments that make up the Grand Slam in men's professional golf. He remains the world's best golfer today. Lance Armstrong, a bicyclist who had overcome cancer to win the Tour de France bicycle race in 1999, won it again every year for six more years. He then officially retired but returned to international cycling in 2008 to help promote the Global Cancer Campaign. Coming back from injury, tennis star Serena Williams captured the 2007 Australian Open. She had already won the 2002 and 2003 women's singles tennis championship at Wimbledon by winning in the finals against her sister, Venus Williams, which she won yet again in 2009. Venus herself won the Wimbledon title in 2000, 2001, 2005, 2007, and 2008.

Success did not come easily to these athletes; it took years of effort and unwavering determination. Why did they work so hard in the face of daunting challenges and tough competition to rise to the top of their fields? For that matter, what prompts any of us to excel, to perform acts of kindness, to look for food, to take dancing lessons, to go bungee jumping, to become violent, or to act in any other particular way? What makes some people go all out to reach a goal whereas others make only half-hearted efforts and quit at the first obstacle? These are all questions about **motivation,** the factors that influence the initiation, direction, intensity, and persistence of behavior (Reeve, 1996).

Like the study of *how* people and other animals behave and think, the puzzle of *why* they do so has intrigued psychologists for many decades. Part of the motivation for behavior is to feel certain emotions, such as the joy of finishing a race or becoming a parent. Motivation also affects emotion, as when hunger makes you more likely to become angry if people annoy you. In this chapter we review several aspects of motivation and the features and value of emotions. ■

Concepts and Theories of Motivation

▶ *Where does motivation come from?*

motivation The influences that account for the initiation, direction, intensity, and persistence of behavior.

Suppose that a woman works two jobs, never goes to parties, wears old clothes, drives an old car, eats food left behind by others, ignores charity appeals, and keeps her house at sixty degrees all winter. Why does she do these things? You could suggest a separate

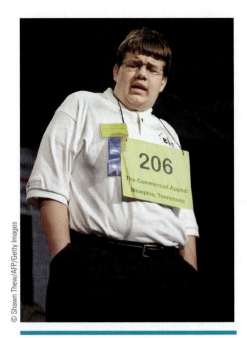

MOTIVATION AND EMOTION ▲

The link between motivation and emotion can be seen in many situations. For example, being motivated to win the U.S. National Spelling Bee creates strong emotions, as we see in this contestant as he struggles with a tough word. And the link works both ways. Often, emotions create motivation, as when anger leads a person to become aggressive toward a child or when love leads a person to provide for that child.

explanation for each of these behaviors: perhaps she likes to work hard, hates parties, doesn't care about new clothes and new cars, enjoys other people's leftovers, has no concern for the poor, and likes cold temperatures. Or you could suggest a **motive,** a reason or purpose that provides a single explanation for all these different behaviors. That unifying motive might be the woman's desire to save as much money as possible. This example illustrates the fact that motivation itself cannot be directly observed. We have to infer, or presume, that motivation is present on the basis of what we can observe.

Motivation helps explain why behavior changes over time. For example, many people are unable to lose weight, quit smoking, or get in shape until they have a heart attack or symptoms of some other serious health problem. At that point, they may suddenly be motivated to eat a healthier diet, give up tobacco, and exercise regularly (Keenan, 2009). In other words, a change in motivation can change a person's responses to stimuli such as ice cream, cigarettes, and health clubs.

Sources of Motivation

Human motivation stems from four main sources. First, we can be motivated by *physiological factors,* such as the need for food and water. Second, *emotional factors* can motivate behavior. Panic, fear, anger, love, and hatred can influence behavior ranging from selfless giving to brutal murder. *Cognitive factors* provide a third source of motivation. Your perceptions of the world, your beliefs about what you can do, and your expectations of how others will respond generate certain behaviors. For example, even the least musical contestants who try out for *American Idol* and other talent shows seem utterly confident in their ability to sing. Fourth, motivation can stem from *social factors,* including the influence of parents, teachers, siblings, friends, television, and other sociocultural forces. Have you ever bought a jacket or tried a particular hairstyle not because you liked it but because it was in fashion? This is just one example of how social factors can affect almost all human behavior.

Four main theories have been proposed to explain motivation. They include the instinct doctrine, drive reduction theory, arousal theory, and incentive theory. Each of these theories has proven helpful in accounting for some aspects of behavior.

Instinct Doctrine and Its Descendants

In the early 1900s, many psychologists explained motivation in terms of the **instinct doctrine,** which highlights the instinctive nature of behavior. **Instinctive behaviors** are automatic, involuntary, and unlearned behavior patterns consistently "released" or triggered by particular stimuli (Tinbergen, 1989). For example, the male stickleback fish instantly attacks when it sees the red underbelly of another male. Such behaviors in nonhuman species were originally called *fixed action patterns* because they are unlearned, genetically coded responses to specific "releaser" stimuli.

William McDougall (1908) argued that human behavior, too, is instinctive. He began by listing eighteen human instinctive behaviors that included self-assertion, reproduction, pugnacity (eagerness to fight), and gregariousness (sociability). Within a few years, McDougall and other theorists had named more than 10,000 instinctive behaviors, prompting one critic to suggest that his colleagues had "an instinct to produce instincts" (Bernard, 1924). The problem was that instincts had become meaningless labels that described behavior without explaining it. Saying that people gamble because of a gambling instinct or work hard because of a work instinct explains nothing about why these behaviors appear in some people and not others or about how they develop. Applying the instinct doctrine to human motivation also seemed problematic because people display few, if any, instinctive fixed-action patterns.

Today, psychologists continue to investigate the role played by inborn tendencies in human motivation. They have been stimulated partly by research on a number of human behaviors that are present at birth. Among these are the sucking, grasping, and other reflexes discussed in the human development chapter as well as certain facial expressions, such as grimacing at bitter tastes (Steiner et al., 2001). Further, as discussed

motive   A reason or purpose for behavior.

instinct doctrine   A view that behavior is motivated by automatic, involuntary, and unlearned responses.

instinctive behaviors   Innate, automatic dispositions to respond in particular ways to specific stimuli.

in the chapter on learning, humans appear to be biologically prepared to learn to fear snakes and other potential dangers (Öhman & Mineka, 2003). But psychologists' thinking about instinctive behavior is more sophisticated now than it was a century ago. They recognize that even though certain behaviors reflect inborn motivational tendencies, those behaviors may or may not actually appear, depending on each individual's experience. So although we might be biologically "programmed" to learn to fear snakes, that fear won't develop if we never see a snake. In other words, motivation can be influenced by inherited tendencies, but that doesn't mean that all motivated behavior is genetically determined.

Psychologists who take an evolutionary approach to behavior suggest that a wide range of behavioral tendencies have evolved because over the centuries they were adaptive for individual survival in particular circumstances. Those who possessed and expressed these adaptive predispositions were more likely than others to live to father or give birth to offspring. We are descendants of these human survivors. So to the extent that their behavioral predispositions were transmitted genetically, we should have inherited similar predispositions. Evolutionary psychologists also argue that many aspects of human social behavior—including helping, aggression, and the choice of sexual or marriage partners—are motivated by inborn factors, especially by the desire to maximize our genetic contribution to the next generation (Buss, 2004b). We may not be consciously aware of this desire (Geary, 2000), so you are more likely to hear someone say "I can't wait to have children" than to to hear them say "I want to pass on my genes."

By emphasizing the evolutionary roots of human behavior, modern versions of the instinct doctrine focus on the ultimate, long-term reasons behind much of what we do. The theories of motivation discussed next highlight influences that act as more immediate causes of behavior (Alcock, 2001).

Drive Reduction Theory

Like the instinct doctrine, the drive reduction theory of motivation emphasizes internal factors, but it focuses mainly on how these factors operate to maintain homeostasis. **Homeostasis** (pronounced "ho-me-oh-STAY-sis") is the tendency to make constant adjustments to maintain body temperature, blood pressure, and other physiological systems at a steady level, or *equilibrium*—much as a thermostat functions to maintain a constant temperature in a house.

According to **drive reduction theory,** any imbalances in homeostasis create **needs,** which are biological requirements for well-being. In responding to needs, the brain tries to restore homeostasis by creating a psychological state called **drive**—a feeling that prompts an organism to take action to fulfill the need and thus return to a balanced state. For example, if you have had nothing to drink for some time, the chemical balance of your bodily fluids will be disturbed, creating a physiological need for water. One consequence of this need is a drive—thirst—that motivates you to find and drink water. After you drink, the need for water is met, so the drive to drink is reduced. In other words, drives push people to satisfy needs, thus reducing the drives that have been created. This cycle is shown in Figure 8.1.

Early drive reduction theorists described two types of drives. **Primary drives** stem from physiological needs, such as the need for food or water. People do not have to learn these basic needs or the primary drives to satisfy them (Hull, 1951). Other drives, however, are learned through experience. These learned **secondary drives** motivate us to act as if we have unmet basic needs. For example, as people learn to associate money with the ability to buy things to satisfy primary drives for food, shelter, and so on, having money becomes a secondary drive. Having too little money then motivates many behaviors—from hard work to stealing—to obtain more funds.

Arousal Theory

Drive reduction theory can account for a wide range of motivated behaviors but not for all of them. Consider curiosity, for example. Monkeys, dogs, cats, and rats will work

Improve Your Grade
Tutorial: Homeostasis and Drive Reduction Theory

homeostasis The tendency for physiological systems to remain stable by constantly adjusting themselves in response to change.

drive reduction theory A theory that motivation arises from imbalances in homeostasis.

needs Biological requirements for well-being.

drive A physiological state that arises from an imbalance in homeostasis and prompts action to fulfill a need.

primary drives Drives that arise from basic biological needs.

secondary drives Stimuli that take on the motivational properties of primary drives through learning.

FIGURE 8.1 ■ DRIVE REDUCTION THEORY AND HOMEOSTASIS

The mechanisms of homeostasis, such as the regulation of body temperature or food and water intake, are often compared to thermostats. If the temperature in a house falls below the thermostat setting, the furnace comes on and brings the temperature up to that preset level, achieving homeostasis. When the temperature reaches the preset point, the furnace shuts off.

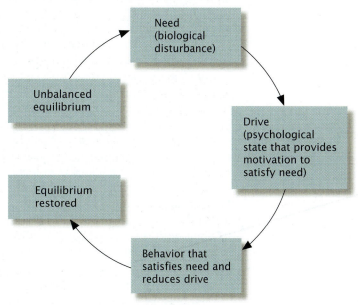

Need
(biological
disturbance)

Drive
(psychological
state that provides
motivation to
satisfy need)

Behavior that
satisfies need and
reduces drive

Equilibrium
restored

Unbalanced
equilibrium

© Andrew Shennan/Getty Images

AROUSAL AND PERSONALITY ▲

People whose ideal, or optimal, level of arousal is high are more likely to smoke, drink alcohol, engage in frequent sexual activity, listen to loud music, eat "hot" foods, and do other things that are stimulating, novel, and risky (Farley, 1986; Zuckerman, 1993). Those whose optimal level of arousal is lower tend to take fewer risks and behave in ways that are less stimulating. As discussed in the personality chapter, differences in optimal arousal may help shape other characteristics, such as whether we tend to be introverted or extraverted.

physiological arousal A general level of activation reflected in several physiological systems.

arousal theory A theory that people are motivated to maintain what is an optimal level of arousal for them.

hard simply to enter a new environment, especially if it is complex and full of novel objects to explore and manipulate (Loewenstein, 1994). And most people, too, can't resist checking out whatever is new and unusual. We go to the mall opening, watch builders work, surf the Internet, and travel the world just to see what there is to see. People also go out of their way to ride roller coasters, skydive, drive race cars, and do countless other things that do not reduce any known drive (Bergman & Kitchen, 2009; Hughes, 2007; Kaulfuss & Mills, 2008; Zuckerman, 1996).

In fact, these behaviors create an increase in **physiological arousal**—the body's general level of activation. Physiological arousal is reflected in heart rate, muscle tension, brain activity, blood pressure, and other bodily systems (Deschaumes et al., 1991; Plutchik & Conte, 1997). It is usually lowest during deep sleep, but physiological arousal can also be lowered by meditation, relaxation techniques, and various depressant drugs. Increases in arousal tend to occur in response to hunger, thirst, stimulant drugs, and stimuli that are intense, sudden, new, or unexpected. Because people sometimes try to reduce their arousal and sometimes try to increase it, some psychologists have suggested that motivation is tied to the regulation of physiological arousal.

Specifically, **arousal theory** suggests that we are motivated to behave in ways that keep or restore an ideal, or *optimal level*, of arousal (Hebb, 1955). Too much arousal can hurt performance, as when test anxiety interferes with some students' ability to recall what they have studied. Overarousal can also cause athletes to "choke" so badly that they miss an easy catch or a simple shot (Smith et al., 2000; Wright et al., 1995). Underarousal, too, can cause problems, as you probably know if you have ever tried to work, drive, or study when you are sleepy. So we try to increase arousal when it is too low and decrease it when it is too high. In simpler terms, we seek excitement when we're bored and relaxation when we're stressed or overstimulated.

In general, we perform best and may feel best when physiological arousal is moderate (Teigen, 1994), but people differ in the exact level of arousal that is optimal for them (Zuckerman, 1984). These differences in optimal arousal may stem from inherited differences in the nervous system (Bardo, Donohew, & Harrington, 1996; Berns et al., 2001; Eysenck, 1990a) and may motivate boldness, shyness, and many other personality traits and behavioral tendencies.

Incentive Theory

Instinct, drive reduction, and arousal theories of motivation all focus on internal processes that prompt people to behave in certain ways. In contrast, **incentive theory** emphasizes the role of external stimuli that motivate behavior. According to this view, people are pulled toward behaviors that offer positive incentives and pushed away from behaviors associated with negative incentives. In other words, differences in behavior from one person to another or from one situation to another can be traced to the incentives available and the value a person places on those incentives at the time. If you expect that some behavior (such as buying a lottery ticket) will lead to a valued outcome (winning money), you will be motivated to engage in that behavior. The value of incentives can be influenced by inborn physiological factors such as hunger and thirst as well as by cognitive and social factors that gain their power through learning. As an example of physiological influences, consider that food is a more motivating incentive when you are hungry than when you're full. As for cognitive and social influences, notice that the value of some things we eat—such as communion wafers or diet shakes—isn't determined by hunger or flavor but by what our culture has taught us about spirituality, health, or attractiveness. Perhaps you have also noticed that what early drive reduction theorists called *primary drives* reappear in incentive theory as unlearned influences on an incentive's value. *Secondary drives* reappear as learned influences on the value of incentives.

"In Review: Theories of Motivation" summarizes the theoretical approaches we have outlined. Each theory has helped to guide research on motivated behaviors such as eating, sex, and work, which we consider in the sections that follow.

Eating

 What makes me start eating and stop eating?

At first glance, eating seems to be a simple example of drive reduction theory at work. You get hungry when you haven't eaten for a while. Much as a car needs gasoline, you need fuel from food, so you eat. But what bodily mechanism acts as a "gauge" to signal the need for fuel? What determines which foods you eat, and how do you know when

> **incentive theory** A theory that people are pulled toward behaviors that offer positive incentives and pushed away from behaviors associated with negative incentives.

In Review

THEORIES OF MOTIVATION

THEORY	MAIN POINTS
Instinct doctrine	Innate biology produces instinctive behaviors.
Drive reduction	Behavior is guided by biological needs and learned ways of reducing drives that arise from those needs.
Arousal	People seek to maintain an optimal level of physiological arousal, which differs from person to person. Maximum performance occurs at optimal arousal levels.
Incentive	Behavior is guided by the lure of rewards and the threat of punishment. Cognitive factors influence expectations of the value of various rewards and the likelihood of attaining them.

1. The fact that some people like roller coasters and other scary amusement park rides has been cited as evidence for the _____ theory of motivation.
2. Evolutionary theories of motivation are modern outgrowths of theories based on _____.
3. The value of incentives can be affected by _____, _____, and _____ factors.

to stop? The answers to these questions involve complex interactions between the brain and the rest of the body (Pinel, Lehman, & Assand, 2002).

Signals for Hunger and Satiation

A variety of mechanisms operate to create **hunger,** the general state of wanting to eat, and **satiation** (pronounced "say-she-EH-shun"), the satisfaction of hunger. Satiation leads to **satiety** (pronounced "seh-TYE-a-tee"), a state in which we no longer want to eat.

Signals from the Gut   The stomach would seem to be a logical source of signals for hunger and satiation. You have probably felt "hunger pangs" from an "empty" stomach and felt "stuffed" after overeating. It is true that the stomach contracts during hunger pangs and that increased pressure within the stomach can reduce appetite (Cannon & Washburn, 1912; Houpt, 1994). But people who have lost their stomachs due to illness still get hungry and they still eat normal amounts of food (Janowitz, 1967). So stomach cues can affect eating, but they appear to operate mainly when you are very hungry or very full. The small intestine, too, is involved in the regulation of eating (Maljaars et al., 2008). It is lined with cells that detect the presence of nutrients and send neural signals to the brain about the need to eat (Capasso & Izzo, 2008).

Signals from the Blood   Still, the most important signals about the body's fuel level and nutrient needs are sent to the brain from the blood. The brain's ability to "read" blood-borne signals about the body's nutritional needs was discovered when researchers deprived rats of food for a long period and then injected some of the rats with blood from rats that had just eaten. When offered food, the injected rats ate little or nothing (Davis et al., 1969). Something in the injected blood of the well-fed animals apparently signaled the hungry rats' brains that there was no need to eat. What was that satiety signal? Research has shown that the brain constantly monitors both the level of *food nutrients* absorbed into the bloodstream from the stomach and the level of *hormones* released into the blood in response to those nutrients (Korner & Leibel, 2003).

The nutrients that the brain monitors include *glucose* (the main form of sugar used by body cells), *fatty acids* (from fat), and *amino acids* (from protein). When the level of blood glucose drops, eating increases sharply (Chaput & Tremblay, 2009; Mogenson, 1976). The brain also monitors hormone levels to regulate hunger and satiety. For example, when glucose levels rise, the pancreas releases *insulin*, a hormone that most body cells need in order to use the glucose they receive. Insulin itself may also provide a satiety signal by acting directly on brain cells (Brüning et al., 2000; Schwartz et al., 2000).

The hormone *leptin* (from the Greek word for "thin") also appears to provide a satiety signal to the brain (Farooqi et al., 2001; Margetic et al., 2002). Unlike glucose and insulin, whose satiety signals help us know when to end a particular meal, leptin appears to be involved mainly in the long-term regulation of body fat (Huang & Li, 2000). The process works like this: cells that store fat normally have genes that produce leptin. As the fat supply in these cells increases, leptin is released into the blood, helping to reduce food intake (Tamashiro & Bello, 2008). Mice with defects in these genes make no leptin and are obese (Bouret, Draper, & Simerly, 2004; Zhang et al., 1994). When these animals are given leptin injections, though, they rapidly lose weight and body fat but not muscle tissue (Forbes et al., 2001). Leptin injections can also produce the same changes in normal animals (Fox & Olster, 2000). Some cases of obesity in humans, too, have been linked to problems in leptin regulation (Considine et al., 1996; Müller et al., 2009). These research results initially raised hope that leptin might be a "magic bullet" for treating human obesity, but this is not the case. Although injections of leptin can help those rare individuals whose fat cells make no leptin (Baicy et al., 2007), this treatment is far less effective in people who are obese because they eat a high-fat diet (Gura, 1999; Heymsfield et al., 1999). In these far more common cases

hunger   The general state of wanting to eat.

satiation   The satisfaction of a need such as hunger.

satiety   The condition of no longer wanting to eat.

of obesity, the brain appears to have become less sensitive to leptin's satiety signals (Ahima & Flier, 2000; Lin et al., 2000; Lustig et al., 2004).

Hunger and the Brain

Many parts of the brain contribute to the control of eating. However, research has focused on regions of the hypothalamus that may play primary roles in detecting and reacting to the blood's signals about the need to eat. As shown in Figure 8.2, the hypothalamus influences both how much food is taken in and how quickly its energy is used, or metabolized.

Some regions of the hypothalamus detect leptin and insulin; these regions generate signals that either increase hunger and reduce energy expenditure or reduce hunger and increase energy expenditure. At least twenty neurotransmitters convey these signals to networks in various parts of the hypothalamus and in the rest of the brain (Cota et al., 2006; Woods et al., 2000).

Activity in a part of the neural network that passes through the *ventromedial nucleus* in the hypothalamus tells an animal that there is no need to eat. So if a rat's ventromedial nucleus is stimulated, the animal will stop eating (Kent et al., 1994). However, if the ventromedial nucleus is destroyed, the animal will eat much more than usual and maintain a much higher body weight.

In contrast, the *lateral hypothalamus* contains networks that tell an animal to start eating. So when the lateral hypothalamus is stimulated, rats begin to eat huge quantities, even if they have just had a large meal (Stanley et al., 1993). When the lateral hypothalamus is destroyed, however, rats stop eating almost entirely.

Decades ago, these findings led to the suggestion that these two hypothalamic regions interact to maintain some homeostatic level, or *set point,* based on food intake, body weight, or other eating-related signals (Powley & Keesey, 1970). According to this application of drive reduction theory, normal animals eat until their set point is

linkages

How does the brain know when we are hungry? *(a link to Biology and Behavior)*

FIGURE 8.2   ■   THE HYPOTHALAMUS AND HUNGER

Regions of the hypothalamus generate signals that either increase hunger and reduce energy expenditure, called *anabolic effects,* or reduce hunger and increase energy expenditure, called *catabolic effects.*
Adapted from Schwartz et al. (2000).

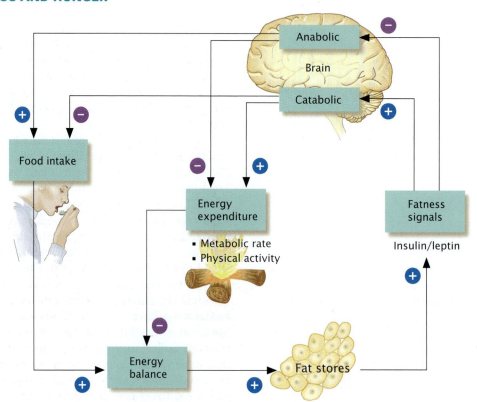

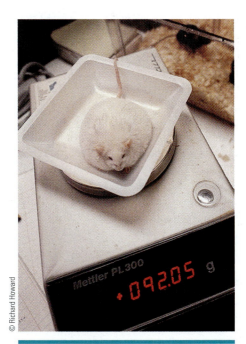

© Richard Howard

ONE FAT MOUSE ▲

After surgical damage to its ventromedial nucleus, this mouse ate enough to triple its body weight. Results such as this initially led many psychologists to conclude that food intake is regulated by a combination of "start-eating" signals from the lateral hypothalamus and "stop-eating" signals from the ventromedial nucleus. We now know that the regulation process is far more complex and involves more than just these two brain regions.

reached, then stop eating until desirable intake falls below the set point (Cabanac & Morrissette, 1992).

This theory turned out to be too simplistic. More recent research shows that the brain's control of eating involves more than just the interaction of a pair of "stop-eating" and "start-eating" areas (Winn, 1995). For example, the *paraventricular nucleus* in the hypothalamus also plays an important role. As with the ventromedial nucleus, stimulating the paraventricular nucleus reduces food intake. Damaging it causes animals to become obese (Leibowitz, 1992). In addition, hunger—and the eating of particular types of food—is related to the effects of various neurotransmitters on certain neurons in the brain. One of these neurotransmitters, called *neuropeptide Y,* stimulates increased eating of carbohydrates (Kishi & Elmquist, 2005; Kuo et al., 2007). Another one, *serotonin,* suppresses carbohydrate intake. *Galanin* motivates eating of high-fat food (Krykouli et al., 1990), and *enterostatin* reduces it (Lin et al., 1998). *Endocannabinoids* stimulate eating in general, especially the eating of tasty foods (DiPatrizio & Simansky, 2008; Mahler et al., 2007). They affect the same hypothalamic receptors as the active ingredient in marijuana does, which may account for "the munchies," a sudden hunger that marijuana use often creates (Cota et al., 2003; Di Marzo et al., 2001). *Peptide YY3–36* causes a feeling of fullness and reduced food intake (Batterham et al., 2002, 2003).

In other words, several brain regions and many brain chemicals regulate hunger and food selection. These internal regulatory processes are themselves affected by the physical environment (e.g., what foods are available), by learning experiences with particular foods, and, for humans, by social and cultural traditions about eating.

Flavor, Sociocultural Experience, and Food Selection

For example, eating is powerfully affected by the *flavor* of food—the combination of its taste and smell. In general, people eat more when differently flavored foods are served, as in a multicourse meal, than when only one food is served (Raynor & Epstein, 2001). Apparently the flavor of a food becomes less enjoyable as more of it is eaten (Swithers & Hall, 1994). In one study, participants rated how much they liked four kinds of food, then they ate one of the foods and rated all four again. The participants gave the food they had just eaten a lower rating the second time, whereas their liking increased for all the rest of the foods (Johnson & Vickers, 1993).

Eating is also affected by the appearance and smell of certain foods. These signals come to elicit conditioned physiological responses—including the secretion of saliva, digestive juices, and insulin—in anticipation of eating those foods (see the learning chapter for more on conditioned responses). So merely seeing a pizza on television may prompt you to order one. And if a delicious-looking cookie comes your way, you don't have to be hungry to start eating it. In fact, many people who have just pronounced themselves "full" after a huge holiday meal still manage to find room for an appetizing dessert. In other words, humans eat not just to satisfy nutritional needs but also because of *appetite,* the desire to experience enjoyment (Lundy, 2008; Stroebe et al., 2008).

Eating is stimulated by other kinds of signals, too. Do you usually eat while reading or watching television? If so, you may find that merely settling down with a book or your favorite show can trigger the desire to have a snack, even if you have just finished dinner! This happens partly because situations associated with eating in the past can become signals that stimulate eating in the future (Epstein et al., 2009). People also learn social rules and cultural traditions that influence eating. In North American culture, having lunch at noon, munching popcorn at movies, and eating hot dogs at ball games are common examples of how certain social situations can stimulate the eating of particular items at particular times. How much you eat may also depend on what others do. Politeness or custom might prompt you to try foods you would otherwise have avoided. Generally, the mere presence of others, even strangers, tends to increase food consumption. Most people consume 60 to 75 percent more food when they are with others than when eating alone (Clendenen, Herman, & Polivy, 1995),

BON APPETIT!   ▲

The definition of delicacy differs from culture to culture. At this elegant restaurant in Mexico, diners pay to feast on baby alligators, insects, and other dishes that some people from other cultures would not eat even if the restaurant paid *them*. To appreciate your own food culture, make a list of foods that are traditionally valued by your family or cultural group but that people from other groups do not (or might even be unwilling to) eat.

Learn BY **Doing**

obesity   A condition in which a person is severely overweight.

and the same effect has been observed in other species, from monkeys to chickens (Galloway et al., 2005; Keeling & Hurink, 1996).

Celebrations, holidays, vacations, and even daily family interactions often revolve around food and what some call a *food culture* (Rozin, 2007). Food use and selection varies widely across cultures. For example, chewing coca leaves is popular in the Bolivian highlands but illegal in the United States (Burchard, 1992). Many westerners regard insects called palm weevils as disgusting (Springer & Belk, 1994), but they are a delicacy for people in Papua New Guinea (Paoletti, 1995), and the beef those same westerners enjoy is morally repugnant to devout Hindus in India. Even within the same culture, different groups may have sharply contrasting food traditions. Squirrel brains won't be found on most dinner tables in the United States, but some people in the rural South consider them to be a tasty treat. In short, eating serves functions beyond nutrition—functions that help to remind us of who we are and with whom we identify.

Unhealthy Eating

Problems in the processes that regulate hunger and eating may cause *eating disorders* such as anorexia nervosa or bulimia and can result in a level of food intake that leads to obesity.

Obesity   The World Health Organization (WHO, 1998) defines **obesity** as a condition in which a person's body mass index, or BMI, is greater than 30. BMI is determined by dividing a person's weight (in kilograms) by the square of the person's height (in meters). So someone who is 5 feet 2 inches and weighs 164 pounds would be classified as obese, as would someone 5 feet 10 inches who weighs 207 pounds. BMI calculators are available at web sites such as http://www.nhlbisupport.com/bmi/. People whose BMI is 25 to 29.9 are considered to be overweight but not obese. (Keep in mind, though, that a given volume of muscle weighs more than the same volume of fat, so very muscular individuals may have an elevated BMI without being overweight.)

Using the BMI criterion, about 34 percent of adults in the United States are obese, as are about 16 percent of children and adolescents (Ogden et al., 2007; Ogden, Carroll, & Flegal, 2008). These percentages are even higher among the poor and members of some ethnic minority groups (Kumanyika, 2008). Obesity has become so common that commercial jets have to burn excess fuel to carry heavier loads, parents of obese young children have trouble finding car safety seats to fit them, and the funeral industry has to offer larger than normal coffins and order wider hearses (Dannenberg, Burton, & Jackson, 2004; St. John, 2003; Trifiletti et al., 2006). Though the problems of overweight and obesity are especially severe in the United States, they are growing worldwide. A recent analysis of data from 106 countries in Asia, Europe, South America, and Africa—comprising about 88 percent of the world's population—found that 23.2 percent of adults are overweight and another 10 percent are obese. Projections based on present trends suggest that by 2030, there will be over one *billion* obese people living in these countries (Kelly et al., 2008).

Obesity is a risk factor for physical health problems such as Type 2 diabetes, high blood pressure, certain cancers, liver and gall bladder disease, osteoarthritis, heart attack, and stroke (Baker, Olsen, & Sørensen, 2007; Bibbins-Domingo et al., 2007; Centers for Disease Control and Prevention, 2009b; Reeves et al., 2007). In the United States alone, obesity is blamed for about 300,000 deaths each year and for a predicted shortening of life expectancy in the twenty-first century (Adams et al., 2006; Flegel et al., 2005; Olshansky et al., 2005; Shimazu et al., 2009). Obesity, especially in adolescence, is also associated with the development of anxiety and depression (Anderson et al., 2007; Baumeister & Härter, 2007; BeLue, Francis, & Colaco, 2009; Kasen et al., 2008; Zhao et al., 2009), though it is not yet clear whether the relationship is causal, and if it is, which condition might be causing which problem (Atlantis & Baker, 2008; Scott et al., 2008).

The precise reasons for this obesity epidemic are unknown, but possible causes include big portion sizes at fast food outlets, a greater prevalence of high-fat foods, and less physical activity associated with both work and recreation (e.g., Adachi-Mejia et al., 2007; Slentz et al., 2004). These are important factors, because body weight is determined by a combination of food intake and energy output (Keesey & Powley, 1986). Obese people get more energy from food than their body metabolizes, or "burns up." The excess energy, measured in calories, is stored as fat. Obese people tend to eat above-average amounts of high-calorie tasty foods but below-average amounts of less tasty foods (Kauffman, Herman, & Polivy, 1995). Further, they may be less active than lean people, a pattern that often begins in childhood (Jago et al., 2005; Marshall et al., 2004; Strauss & Pollack, 2001). Spending long hours watching television or playing computer games is a major cause of the inactivity seen in overweight children (Adachi-Mejia et al., 2007; Cleland et al., 2008; Eisenmann et al., 2008).

In short, inadequate physical activity combined with overeating—especially of the high-fat foods so prevalent in most Western cultures—has a lot to do with obesity. But not everyone who is inactive and eats a high-fat diet becomes obese, and some obese people are as active as lean people, so other factors must also be involved (Blundell & Cooling, 2000; Parsons, Power, & Manor, 2005). Some people probably have a genetic predisposition toward obesity (Bouchard et al., 2007; Frayling et al., 2007; Loos et al., 2006; Su et al., 2008). For example, although most obese people have the genes to make leptin, they may not be sensitive to its weight-suppressing effects, perhaps because of differing genetic codes for leptin receptors in the hypothalamus. Brain-imaging studies also suggest that obese people's brains may be slower to "read" satiety signals coming from their blood, thus causing them to continue eating when leaner people would have stopped (Morton et al., 2006; Thorens, 2008). These genetic factors, along with the presence of viruses associated with the common cold and other infectious diseases (Dhurandhar et al., 2000; Vasilakopoulou & le Roux, 2007), may help explain obese people's tendency to eat more, accumulate fat, and feel hungrier than lean people.

Other explanations for obesity focus on factors such as learning from the examples set by parents who overeat (Hood et al., 2000), too little parental control over what and how much children eat (Johnson & Birch, 1994), and maladaptive reactions to stress. Many people do tend to eat more when under stress, a reaction that may be especially extreme among those who become obese (Dallman et al., 2003; Friedman & Brownell, 1995).

For most people, especially for people who are obese, it is a lot easier to gain weight than to lose it and keep it off (Jain, 2005; McTigue et al., 2003). The problem arises partly because our evolutionary ancestors—like nonhuman animals in the wild today—could not always be sure that food would be available. Those who survived lean times were the ones whose genes created tendencies to build and maintain fat reserves (e.g., Hara et al., 2000). These "thrifty genes" are adaptive in famine-plagued environments, but they can be harmful and even deadly in affluent societies in which overeating is unnecessary and in which doughnut shops and fast food restaurants are on every corner. Further, if people starve themselves to lose weight, their bodies may burn calories more slowly. This drop in metabolism saves energy and fat reserves and slows weight loss (Leibel, Rosenbaum, & Hirsch, 1995). Restricted eating also enhances activation of the brain's "pleasure centers" when a hungry person even looks at energy-rich foods (Siep et al., 2009), thus making restraint that much more difficult. It is no wonder, then, that health and nutrition experts warn that obese people (and others) should not try to lose a great deal of weight quickly by dramatically cutting food intake (Carels et al., 2008).

Researchers are constantly looking for safe and effective medications for the treatment of obesity. The drugs available today are designed to either suppress appetite or increase fat burning (Fernstrom & Choi, 2008; Kolonin et al., 2004; Loftus et al., 2000), and millions of people are already taking them (Neovius & Narbro, 2008). An even more radical approach to the problem of obesity is *bariatric surgery* (Hamad, 2004), which restructures the stomach and intestines so that less food energy is absorbed and stored (Hamad, 2004; Vetter et al., 2009). In the United States, bariatric surgery was performed on about 103,000 people in just one recent year (Santry, Gillen, & Lauderdale, 2005). Its popularity is growing, fueled in part by the examples of celebrities whose surgery resulted in dramatic weight loss. Still, due to its costs and risks—postoperative mortality rates range from 0.1 to 2 percent (Morino et al., 2007)—bariatric surgery is recommended only for extreme and life-threatening cases of obesity.

Though they might seem to offer relatively quick and easy options, neither medication nor surgery alone is likely to solve the problem of obesity. In fact, no single anti-obesity treatment is likely to be a safe, effective solution that works for everyone. To achieve the kind of gradual weight loss that is most likely to last, obese people are advised to make lifestyle changes in addition to (or instead of) seeking medical solutions. The most effective weight-loss programs include components designed to reduce food intake, change eating habits and attitudes toward food, and increase energy expenditure through regular exercise (Bray & Tartaglia, 2000; Stice & Shaw, 2004; Wadden et al., 2001). Exercise is especially important because it burns calories while raising metabolism instead of lowering it, as reducing food intake alone does (Binzen, Swan, & Manore, 2001; Curioni & Lourenço, 2005; Wadden et al., 2005).

Of course, the ultimate remedy for the obesity epidemic is prevention, which will require convincing parents and other caregivers to promote exercise and healthy eating habits in their children from an early age (Swinburn, 2009). There is a long way to go. A recent report from the Feeding Infants and Toddlers Study (Fox et al., 2004) found that the top vegetable choice of U.S. toddlers is french fries, that one in five babies eats candy every day, and that 44 percent of babies consume sugary drinks. Further, their preference for high-fat fast food is so well learned that, when children in one experiment were given identical foods wrapped either in plain paper or in paper bearing the logo of a popular fast food restaurant, they rated the restaurant-branded food as tasting better (Robinson et al., 2009). Changing these habits and preferences will not be easy, but the need to do so is obvious and urgent.

Anorexia Nervosa   In stark contrast to the problem of obesity is the eating disorder known as **anorexia nervosa** (pronounced "ann-or-EX-ee-ah nuhr-VO-suh"). It is characterized by some combination of self-starvation, self-induced vomiting, excessive exercise, and laxative use that results in weight loss to below 85 percent of normal (Kaye et al., 2000). Anorexia affects about 0.5 to 1 percent of young people in the United States, and it is a significant problem in many other industrialized nations as well (Currin, 2005; Hoek, 2006; Hudson et al., 2007). About 95 percent of those who suffer from anorexia are young females. Anorexics often feel hungry, and many are obsessed with food and its preparation yet they refuse to eat. Anorexic self-starvation causes serious, often irreversible, physical damage, including reduction in bone density that increases the risk of fractures (Grinspoon et al., 2000). The health dangers may be especially high in anorexic dancers, gymnasts, and other female athletes, who are at risk for stress fractures and heart problems (Davis & Kapstein, 2006; Sherman & Thompson, 2004). It is estimated that from 4 to 30 percent of those suffering severe anorexia eventually die of starvation, biochemical imbalances, or suicide; their death rate is twelve times higher than the death rate for other young women (Herzog et al., 2000; Millar et al., 2005; National Association of Anorexia Nervosa and Associated Disorders, 2002).

The appearance of anorexia has been attributed to a combination of factors, including genetic predispositions, hormonal and other biochemical imbalances, social influences, and psychological characteristics (Bulik et al., 2000, 2006; Jacobi et al., 2004; Kaye et al., 2000; Keel & Klump, 2003; Klump & Culbert, 2007; Procopio & Marriott, 2007; Ribases et al., 2005; Vink et al., 2001). Psychological factors that may contribute to the problem include a self-punishing, perfectionistic personality and a culturally reinforced obsession with thinness and attractiveness (American Psychological Association Task Force on the Sexualization of Girls, 2007; Cooley et al., 2008; Dittmar, Halliwell, & Ive, 2006; Dohnt & Tiggermann, 2006; Grabe, Ward, & Hyde, 2008; Moradi, Dirks, & Matteson, 2005). Anorexics appear to develop a fear of being fat, which they take to dangerous extremes (de Castro & Goldstein, 1995). Many anorexics continue to view themselves as fat or misshapen even as they are wasting away.

Drugs, hospitalization, and psychotherapy are all used to treat anorexia. In many cases, treatment brings recovery and the maintenance of normal weight (National Institutes of Health, 2001; Pike et al., 2003), but more effective treatment and early intervention methods are still needed. Prevention programs now being tested with

© Frank Trapper/Corbis

THIN IS IN   ▲

In Western cultures today, thinness is a much-sought-after ideal, especially among young women. This ideal is seen in fashion models as well as in Miss America pageant winners, whose body mass index has decreased from the "normal" range of 20 to 25 in the 1920s to an "undernourished" 18.5 in recent years (Rubinstein & Caballero, 2000; Voracek & Fisher, 2002). In the United States, 35 percent of normal-weight girls—and 12 percent of underweight girls!—begin dieting when they are as young as nine or ten. Correlational studies suggest that the efforts of many of these children to lose weight may have come in response to criticism from family members (Barr Taylor et al., 2006a; Schreiber et al., 1996); for some the result is anorexia.

anorexia nervosa   An eating disorder characterized by self-starvation and dramatic weight loss.

college women at high risk for developing anorexia are showing promising results (e.g., Barr Taylor et al., 2006b; Black Becker et al., 2008).

Bulimia   Like anorexia, bulimia (pronounced "bu-LEE-mee-uh") involves an intense fear of being fat, but the person may be thin, normal in weight, or even overweight. **Bulimia** (also referred to as *bulimia nervosa*) involves eating huge amounts of food (say, several boxes of cookies, a half-gallon of ice cream, and a bucket of fried chicken) and then getting rid of the food through self-induced vomiting or strong laxatives. These "binge-purge" episodes may occur as often as twice a day (Weltzin et al., 1995).

Bulimia shares many features with anorexia (Fairburn et al., 2008). For instance, most bulimics are female, and like anorexia, bulimia usually begins with a desire to be slender. However, bulimia and anorexia are quite different disorders (Eddy et al., 2008). For one thing, most bulimics see their eating habits as problematic, whereas most anorexics do not. In addition, bulimia is usually not life threatening (Thompson, 1996). It has consequences, however, that include dehydration, nutritional problems, and intestinal damage. Many bulimics develop dental problems from the acids associated with vomiting. Frequent vomiting and the insertion of objects to cause it can also damage the throat.

Estimates of the prevalence of bulimia in the United States range from 1 to 3 percent of adolescent and college-age women (National Institutes of Health, 2001; U.S. Surgeon General, 1999); a figure that has remained relatively stable since the early 1990s (Crowther et al., 2008). The combination of factors that contribute to bulimia includes perfectionism, low self-esteem, stress, a culturally encouraged preoccupation with being thin, and depression and other emotional problems. Problems in the brain's satiety mechanisms may also be involved (Crowther et al., 2001; Steiger et al., 2001; Stice, 2001; Stice & Fairburn, 2003; Smith et al., 2007; Zalta & Keel, 2006). Treatment for bulimia, which typically includes individual or group psychotherapy and sometimes antidepressant drugs, can help most bulimic people eat more normally (Herzog et al., 1999; Le Grange et al., 2007; Wilson et al., 1999).

For a summary of the processes involved in hunger and eating, see "In Review: Major Factors Controlling Hunger and Eating."

bulimia   An eating disorder that involves eating massive quantities of food, then eliminating it by self-induced vomiting or laxatives.

In Review

Major Factors Controlling Hunger and Eating

THEORY	STIMULATE EATING	INHIBIT EATING
Biological factors	Levels of glucose and insulin in the blood provide signals that stimulate eating. Neurotransmitters that affect neurons in different regions of the hypothalamus also stimulate food intake and influence hungers for specific kinds of foods, such as fats and carbohydrates. Stomach contractions are associated with subjective feelings of hunger, but they do not play a substantial role in the stimulation of eating.	Hormones released into the bloodstream produce signals that inhibit eating. Hormones such as leptin and insulin affect neurons in the hypothalamus and inhibit eating.
Nonbiological factors	Sights and smells of particular foods elicit eating because of prior associations. Family customs and social occasions often include norms for eating in particular ways.	Values in contemporary U.S. society encourage thinness and thus can inhibit eating.

?

1. People may eat when they are "full," suggesting that eating is not controlled by _____ alone.
2. People with _____ nervosa know that they have a problem; those with _____ tend not to.
3. The best strategy for lasting weight loss includes regular _____ as well as improved eating habits.

Sexual Behavior

▶ *How often does the average person have sex?*

Unlike food, sex is not necessary for an individual's survival, but it is obviously vital for improving the chances that an individual's genes will be represented in the next generation. The various factors that shape sexual motivation and behavior differ in strength across species. These factors often include physiology, learned behavior, and physical and social environments. For example, one species of desert bird requires adequate sex hormones, a suitable mate, and a particular environment before it engages in sexual behavior. As long as the dry season lasts, it shows no interest in sex, but within ten minutes of the first rainfall, the birds vigorously court and copulate.

Rainfall is obviously much less influential as a sexual trigger for humans. In fact, people show an amazing diversity of *sexual scripts,* or patterns of behavior that lead to sex. Surveys of college-age men and women have identified 122 specific acts, 34 different tactics, and 237 stated reasons surrounding their efforts to have sex (Greer & Buss, 1994; Meston & Buss, 2007). What actually happens during sex? The matter is exceedingly difficult to address scientifically, partly because most people are reluctant to allow researchers to observe their sexual behavior. Many won't even answer questions about their sexual practices. Yet having valid information about the nature of human sexual behavior is a vital first step for psychologists and other scientists who study such topics as individual differences in sexuality, gender differences in sexual motivation and behavior, sources of sexual orientation, disturbances of sexual functioning, and pathways through which AIDS and other sexually transmitted diseases reach new victims. This information can also help people think about their own sexual behavior in relation to trends in the general population.

Focus on RESEARCH

Tell Me About Your Sex Life

The first extensive studies of sexual behavior in the United States were completed in the 1950s and 1960s by Alfred Kinsey (Kinsey, Pomeroy, & Martin, 1948; Kinsey et al., 1953) and William Masters and Virginia Johnson (1966). In the Kinsey studies, volunteers answered questions about their sexual practices, whereas Masters and Johnson actually recorded volunteers' **sexual arousal,** their physiological responses during natural or artificial sexual stimulation in a laboratory. Together, these pioneering studies broke new ground in the exploration of human sexuality. However, the people who volunteered for them were probably not a representative sample of the adult population. So the results and the conclusions drawn from them might not apply to people in general. Further, the data are now so old that they may not reflect sexual practices today. Unfortunately, the results of more recent surveys, such as reader polls in *Cosmopolitan* and other magazines, are also flawed because the samples they use are not representative (Davis & Smith, 1990).

▶ **What was the researchers' question?**

Is it possible to gather data about sexual behavior that are more representative and therefore more applicable to people in general? A team of researchers at the University of Chicago believe it is, so they undertook the National Health and Social Life Survey,

the first extensive survey of sexual behavior in the United States since the Kinsey studies (Laumann et al., 1994).

▶ **How did the researchers answer the question?**

This survey included important design features that had been neglected in most other surveys of sexual behavior. First, the study did not depend on self-selected volunteers. The researchers sought out a particular sample of 3,432 people who ranged in age from 18 to 59. Second, the sample was carefully constructed so as to reflect the sociocultural diversity of the U.S. population in terms of gender, ethnicity, socioeconomic status, geographical location, and the like. Third, unlike previous surveys that had relied on mail-in responses from participants, the Chicago study was based on face-to-face interviews. This approach made it easier to ensure that the participants understood each question and allowed them to explain their responses. To encourage honesty, the researchers let participants answer some of the survey's questions anonymously by placing written responses in a sealed envelope.

▶ **What did the researchers find?**

For one thing, the researchers found that people in the United States have sex less often and with fewer partners than many had assumed. For most, sex occurs about once a week and only with the partner with whom they share a stable relationship. About a third of the participants reported having had sex only a few times (or not at all) in the preceding year. And, in contrast to various celebrities' splashy tales of dozens, even hundreds, of sexual partners per year, the average male survey participant had had only six sexual partners in his entire life. The average female respondent reported a lifetime total of two. Further, the survey data suggested that people in committed, one-partner relationships had the most frequent and the most satisfying sex. And although a wide variety of specific sexual practices were reported, the overwhelming majority of heterosexual couples said that they tend to engage mainly in penis-vagina intercourse. Many of these findings are consistent with the results of more recent surveys conducted by other researchers (e.g. National Center for Health Statistics, 2007).

▶ What do the results mean?

The Chicago survey challenges some of the cultural and media images of sexuality in the United States. In particular, it suggests that people in the United States may be more sexually conservative than one might think on the basis of magazine reader polls and the testimony of guests on daytime talk shows.

▶ What do we still need to know?

Many questions remain. The Chicago survey did not ask about some of the more controversial aspects of sexuality, such as the effects of pornography or the role in sexual activity of sexual fetishes such as shoes or other clothing. Had the researchers asked about such topics, their results might have painted a different picture. Further, because the Chicago survey focused on people in the United States, it told us little or nothing about the sexual practices, traditions, and values of people in the rest of the world.

The Chicago team has continued to conduct interviews and the results are beginning to fill in the picture about sexual behavior in the United States and around the world (Youm & Laumann, 2002). They have found, for example, that nearly one-quarter of U.S. women prefer to achieve sexual satisfaction without partners of either sex. And although people in the United States tend to engage in a wider variety of sexual behaviors than do those in Britain, people in the United States appear to be less tolerant of disapproved sexual practices (Laumann & Michael, 2000; Michael et al., 1998). They have found, too, that although sexual activity declines with advancing age, it by no means disappears. About 26 percent of people in the 75 to 85 age group—especially men—reported that they were still sexually active (Lindau et al., 2007).

Other researchers have found a number of consistent gender differences in sexuality. For example, men tend to have a stronger interest in and desire for sex than women, whereas women are more likely than men to associate sexual activity with love and to be affected by cultural and situational influences on sexual attitudes and behavior (Baumeister & Stillman, 2006; Diamond, 2008; Peplau, 2003).

The results of even the best survey methods—like those of the best of all other research methods—usually raise as many questions as they answer. When do people become interested in sex, and why? How do they choose to express these desires, and why? What determines their sexual likes and dislikes? How do learning and sociocultural factors modify the biological forces that seem to provide the raw material of human sexual motivation? These are some of the questions about human sexual behavior that a survey cannot easily or accurately explore (Benson, 2003).

The Biology of Sex

Observations in Masters and Johnson's laboratory led to important findings about the **sexual response cycle,** the pattern of physiological arousal before, during, and after sexual activity (see Figure 8.3). Masters and Johnson (1966) found that men show one primary pattern of sexual response and that women display at least three different patterns from time to time. In both men and women, the first, or *excitement,* phase begins with sexually stimulating input from the environment or from one's own thoughts. Further stimulation leads to intensified excitement in the second, or *plateau,* phase. If stimulation continues, the person reaches the third, or *orgasmic,* stage. Although orgasm lasts only a few seconds, it provides an intensely pleasurable release of physical and psychological tension. The *resolution* phase follows, during which the person returns to a state of relaxation. At this point, men enter a *refractory period,* during which they are temporarily unable to be aroused. Women are capable of immediately repeating the cycle if stimulation continues.

People's motivation to engage in sexual activity has biological roots in **sex hormones.** The female sex hormones are **estrogens** and **progestational hormones** (also called *progestins*); the main ones are *estradiol* and *progesterone.* The male hormones are **androgens;** the principal example is *testosterone.* Each sex hormone flows in the blood of both sexes, but males have relatively more androgens and women have relatively more estrogens and progestational hormones.

Sex hormones have both *organizing* and *activating* effects on the brain. The organizing effects are permanent changes in the brain that influence the brain's response to

sexual arousal Physiological arousal that arises from sexual contact or erotic thoughts.

sexual response cycle The pattern of arousal before, during, and after sexual activity.

sex hormones Chemicals in the blood that organize and motivate sexual behavior.

estrogens Feminine hormones that circulate in the bloodstream.

progestational hormones (progestins) Feminine hormones that circulate in the bloodstream.

androgens Masculine hormones that circulate in the bloodstream.

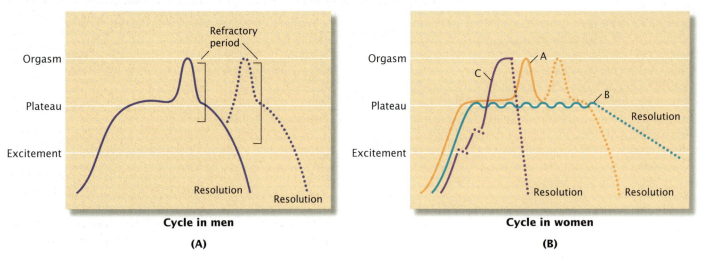

FIGURE 8.3   ■   THE SEXUAL RESPONSE CYCLE

Masters and Johnson (1966) found that men show one primary pattern of sexual response, depicted in Part A, and that women display at least three different patterns from time to time—labeled A, B, and C in Part B. For both men and women, sexual stimulation begins with the excitement phase, which is followed by intensified excitement in the plateau phase and the pleasurable release of tension in the orgasmic stage. During the resolution phase, both men and women return to a state of relaxation. Following resolution, men (but not women) enter a refractory phase, during which they are unresponsive to sexual stimulation.

hormones. The activating effects are temporary behavioral changes that last only as long as the level of a sex hormone is elevated, such as in the ovulation phase of the monthly menstrual cycle. In mammals, including humans, the organizing effects of hormones occur around the time of birth. It is then that certain brain areas are sculpted into a "female-like" or "male-like" pattern. For example, a brain area called *BnST* is generally larger in men than in women. Its possible role in some aspects of human sexuality was suggested by a study that compared the brains of men with a male gender identity to those of male-to-female transsexuals (genetic males who feel like women and may request surgery and hormone treatments to create more female-looking bodies). The BnST was larger in the male-identified men than in the transsexuals. In fact, the transsexuals' BnST was about the size usually seen in women (Zhou et al., 1995).

Rising levels of sex hormones during puberty activate increased sexual desire and interest in sexual behavior. Generally, estrogens stimulate females' sexual interest (Burleson, Gregory, & Trevarthen, 1995). Androgens raise males' sexual interest (Davidson, Camargo, & Smith, 1979), but they may also do so in females (Sherwin & Gelfand, 1987). The activating effects of hormones are also seen in reduced sexual motivation and behavior among people whose hormone-secreting ovaries or testes have been removed for medical reasons. Injections of hormones help restore these people's sexual interest and activity (Sherwin, Gelfand, & Brender, 1985).

Generally, hormones affect sexual desire, not the physical ability to have sex (Wallen & Lovejoy, 1993). This fact may explain why castration (removal of the testes) does not prevent sex crimes by male offenders. Men with low testosterone levels due to medical problems or castration show less sexual desire, but they still have erections in response to erotic stimuli (Kwan et al., 1983). So a sex offender treated by chemical or physical castration would be less likely to seek out sex, but he would still respond as before to his favorite sexual stimuli (Wickham, 2001).

Social and Cultural Factors in Sexuality

Human sexuality is shaped not only by hormones but also by a lifetime of learning and thinking. For example, children learn some of their sexual attitudes and behaviors as part of the development of *gender roles,* as described in the human development chapter. The specific attitudes and behaviors they learn depend partly on the nature of gender roles in their culture (Baumeister, 2000; Hyde & Durik, 2000; Peplau, 2003).

There are differences, too, in what women and men find sexually arousing. For example, in many cultures, men are far more interested in and responsive to erotic visual images than women are (Herz & Cahill, 1997; Symons, 1979). A biological basis for this difference was investigated in a study that scanned the brain activity of males and females while they looked at erotic photographs (Hamann et al., 2004). As expected, the men showed greater activity in the amygdala and hypothalamus than the women did. But even though there were gender differences in brain activity, the male and female participants rated the photos as equally attractive and sexually arousing. In another study, when men reported sexual arousal in response to erotic films, they showed signs of physiological arousal, too. For women, self-reports of sexual arousal were not strongly correlated with signs of physiological arousal (Chivers et al., 2004). Further, though men and women both show more sexual arousal to more intensely erotic films, the level of women's arousal may not depend as much as men's does on whether the actors are males or females (Chivers, Seto, & Blanchard, 2007).

These are just a few examples of the fact that sexuality is a product of a complex mixture of factors. Each person's learning history, cultural background, and perceptions of the world interact so deeply with such a wide range of physiological processes that—as in many other aspects of human behavior and mental processes—it is impossible to separate their influence on sexuality. Nowhere is this point clearer than in the case of sexual orientation.

Sexual Orientation

Sexual orientation refers to the nature of a person's enduring emotional, romantic, or sexual attraction to others (American Psychological Association, 2002a; Ellis & Mitchell, 2000). The most common sexual orientation is **heterosexuality,** in which the attraction is to members of the opposite sex. When attraction focuses on members of one's own sex, the orientation is called **homosexuality,** more specifically, gay (for men) and lesbian (for women). **Bisexuality** refers to the orientation of people who are attracted to members of both sexes. Sexual orientation involves feelings that may or may not be translated into corresponding patterns of sexual behavior (Pathela et al., 2006). For example, some people whose orientation is gay, lesbian, or bisexual may have sex only with opposite-sex partners. Similarly, people whose orientation is heterosexuality may have had one or more same-sex encounters.

In many cultures, heterosexuality has long been regarded as a moral norm and homosexuality has been seen as a disease, a disorder, or even a crime (Hooker, 1993). Yet attempts to alter the sexual orientation of gay men and lesbians—using psychotherapy, brain surgery, or electric shock—have usually been ineffective (American Psychiatric Association, 1999; King, Smith, & Bartlett, 2004). In 1973 the American Psychiatric Association dropped homosexuality from the *Diagnostic and Statistical Manual of Mental Disorders,* thus ending its official status as a mental disorder. The same change was made by the World Health Organization in its *International Classification of Diseases* in 1993, by Japan's psychiatric organization in 1995, and by the Chinese Psychiatric Association in 2001.

Nevertheless, some people still disapprove of homosexuality. Because gays, lesbians, and bisexuals are often the victims of discrimination and even hate crimes, many of them are reluctant to let their sexual orientation be known (Bernat et al., 2001; Meyer, 2003). It is difficult, therefore, to obtain an accurate picture of the mix of heterosexual, gay, lesbian, and bisexual orientations in a population. In the Chicago sex survey mentioned earlier, 1.4 percent of women and 2.8 percent of men identified themselves as exclusively gay or lesbian (Laumann et al., 1994). These figures are much lower than the 10 percent found earlier in Kinsey's studies. However, the Chicago survey's face-to-face interviews did not allow respondents to give anonymous answers to questions about sexual orientation. Some researchers suggest that if anonymous responses to those questions had been permitted, the prevalence figures for gay, lesbian, and bisexual orientations would have been higher (Bullough, 1995). In fact, studies that have allowed anonymous responding estimate that gay, lesbian, and bisexual people make up between 2 and 21 percent of the population in the United States, Canada, and Western Europe (Aaron et al., 2003; Bagley & Tremblay, 1998; Binson et al., 1995; Savin-Williams, 2006; Sell, Wells, & Wypij, 1995).

heterosexuality   Sexual desire or behavior that is focused on members of the opposite sex.

homosexuality   Sexual desire or behavior that is focused on members of one's own sex.

bisexuality   Sexual desire or behavior that is focused on members of both sexes.

Thinking CRITICALLY

What Shapes Sexual Orientation?

The question of where sexual orientation comes from is a topic of intense debate in scientific circles, on talk shows, in Internet chat rooms, and in everyday conversations.

▶ What am I being asked to believe or accept?

Some people believe that genes exert a major influence on our sexual orientation. According to this view, we do not learn a sexual orientation but rather are born with a strong predisposition to develop a particular orientation.

▶ Is evidence available to support the claim?

In 1995, a report by a respected research group suggested that one kind of sexual orientation—namely, that of gay men—is associated with a particular gene on the X chromosome (Hu et al., 1995). This finding was not supported by later studies (Rice et al., 1999), but a growing body of evidence from research in behavioral genetics suggests that genes might indeed influence sexual orientation in humans (Kendler et al., 2000; Pillard & Bailey, 1998). One study examined pairs of monozygotic male twins (whose genes are identical), pairs of dizygotic, or nonidentical, twins (whose genes are no more alike than those of any pair of brothers), and pairs of adopted brothers (who are genetically unrelated). To participate in this study, at least one brother in each pair had to be gay. As it turned out, the other brother was also gay or bisexual in 52 percent of the identical twin pairs but in only 22 percent of the nonidentical pairs and in just 11 percent of the adoptive pairs (Bailey & Pillard, 1991). Similar findings have been reported for male identical twins raised apart. In such cases, a shared sexual orientation cannot be due to the effects of a shared environment (Whitam, Diamond, & Martin, 1993). The few available studies of female sexual orientation have yielded similar results (Bailey & Benishay, 1993; Bailey, Dunne, & Martin, 2000).

Other evidence for the role of biological factors in sexual orientation comes from research on the impact of sex hormones. In adults, differences in the levels of these hormones are not generally associated with differences in sexual orientation. However, hormonal differences during prenatal development might be involved in the shaping of sexual orientation (Lalumière, Blanchard, & Zucker, 2000; Lippa, 2003; Williams et al., 2000), and the influences may differ for men and for women (Mustanski et al., 2002). For example, one study found that women—but not men—who had been exposed to high levels of androgens during their fetal development were much more likely to report bisexual or homosexual behaviors or fantasies than were their relatives of the same sex who had not been exposed (Hines, Brook, & Conway, 2004; Meyer-Bahlburg et al., 2008).

Another line of research focuses on the possibility that previous pregnancies might permanently affect a woman's hormones in ways that influence the sexual orientation of her next child (Blanchard, 2001). Some evidence for this hypothesis comes from a study showing that the more older biological brothers a man has, the higher is the probability he will have a homosexual orientation (Blanchard & Lippa, 2007; Bogaert, Blanchard, & Crosthwait, 2007). These results appear to reflect mainly hormonal rather than mainly environmental influences, because the number of *nonbiological* (adopted) brothers that the men had was not predictive of their sexual orientation. Further, because sexual orientation in women was not predicted by the number and gender of their older biological siblings, it was thought that the hormonal consequences of carrying male fetuses might only influence males' sexual orientation. The picture is not that simple, though. Other researchers have found that women's sexual orientation, too, is related to the number of older biological brothers they have (McConaghy et al., 2006), and still others have reported a relationship between men's sexual orientation and the number of older biological sisters they have (Francis, 2008; Vasey & VanderLaan, 2007). We don't yet know exactly how prenatal hormonal influences might operate to affect sexual orientation, but studies of nonhuman animals have found that such influences alter the structure of the hypothalamus, a brain region known to underlie some aspects of sexual functioning (Swaab & Hofman, 1995).

Finally, a biological basis for sexual orientation is suggested by the fact that sexual orientation is not predicted by environmental factors. For example, the sexual orientation of children's caregivers has little or no effect on those children's own orientation. Several studies have shown that children adopted by homosexual parents are no more or less likely to display a homosexual orientation than are children raised by heterosexual parents (Anderssen, Amlie, & Ytteroy, 2002; Bailey et al., 1995; Tasker & Golombok, 1995).

▶ Can that evidence be interpreted another way?

Like all correlational data, correlations between genetics and sexual orientation are open to alternative interpretations. As discussed in the introductory chapter, a correlation describes the strength and direction of the relationship between two variables, but it does not guarantee that one variable actually influences the other. Consider again the data showing that the brothers who shared the most genes (identical twins) were also most likely to share a gay orientation. What they shared was probably not a "gay gene" but rather a set of genes that influenced the boys' activity levels, emotionality, aggressiveness, and the like. One example is gender conformity/nonconformity in childhood, the tendency for children to either conform or not conform to the behaviors, interests, and appearance that are typical for their gender in their culture (Bailey, Dunne, & Martin, 2000; Knafo, Iervolino, & Plomin, 2005). Such general aspects of their temperaments or personalities in childhood—and other people's reactions to them—could influence the emergence in later life of a particular sexual orientation (Bem, 2000). In other words, sexual orientation could arise as a reaction to the way people respond to a genetically determined but nonsexual aspect of personality. The influence of prenatal hormone levels could also influence

A COMMITTED RELATIONSHIP, WITH CHILDREN ▶

Like heterosexual relationships, gay and lesbian relationships can be brief and stormy or stable and long lasting (Kurdek, 2005). These gay men are committed to each other for the long haul, as evidenced by their decision to adopt two children together. The strong role of biological factors in sexual orientation is seen in research showing that these children's orientation will not be influenced much, if at all, by that of their adoptive parents (Anderssen, Amlie, & Ytteroy, 2002; Patterson, 2004; Stacey & Biblarz, 2001; Tasker & Golombok, 1995).

© Erin Patrice O'Brien

sexual orientation by shaping aggressiveness or other nonsexual aspects of behavior.

It is also important to look at behavioral genetics evidence for what it can tell us about the role of *environmental* factors in sexual orientation. When we read a study showing that 52 percent of the time, both members of identical-twin pairs have a gay, lesbian, or bisexual orientation, it is easy to ignore the fact that the sexual orientation of the twin pair members *differed* in 48 percent of the cases. Viewed in this way, the results suggest that genes do not tell the entire story of sexual orientation. In other words, it is not determined by unlearned, genetic forces alone. As described in the chapter on biology and behavior, the brains and bodies we inherit are quite responsive to environmental influences. In fact, the behaviors we engage in and the experiences we have often result in physical changes in the brain and elsewhere (Wang et al., 1995). For example, physical changes

occur in the brain's synapses as we form new memories. So differences seen in the brains of adults with differing sexual orientations could be the effect, not the cause, of their behavior or experiences.

▶ *What evidence would help to evaluate the alternatives?*

Much more evidence is needed regarding the role of genes in shaping sexual orientation. We also have a lot to learn about the extent to which genes and hormones shape physical and psychological characteristics that lead to various sexual orientations. In studying these topics, researchers will want to learn more about the genetic makeup, mental style, and behavioral characteristics of people with different sexual orientations. Are there personality characteristics associated with particular sexual orientations? If so, do those characteristics have a strong genetic component?

To what extent are heterosexuals, gays, lesbians, and bisexuals similar—and different—in terms of biases, coping skills, developmental histories, and the like (Bailey, Dunne, & Martin, 2000)? The more we learn about sexual orientation in general, the easier it will be to interpret data relating to its origins.

Yet even classifying sexual orientation is not simple, because people do not always fall into sharply defined categories (Savin-Williams, 2006; Thompson & Morgan, 2008; Worthington, et al., 2008). Should a man who identifies himself as gay be considered bisexual because he occasionally has heterosexual daydreams? What sexual orientation label would be appropriate for a 40-year-old woman who experienced a few lesbian encounters in her teens but has engaged in exclusively heterosexual sex since then? Progress in understanding the origins of sexual orientation would be enhanced by a generally accepted system for describing and defining all facets of exactly what is meant by the term *sexual orientation* (Klein, 1990; Stein, 1999).

▶ *What conclusions are most reasonable?*

The evidence available so far suggests that genetic factors, probably operating via prenatal hormones, create differences in the brains of people with different sexual orientations. However, the manner in which a person expresses a genetically influenced sexual orientation will be profoundly shaped by what that person learns through social and cultural experiences (Bancroft, 1994). In short, as is true of other psychological phenomena, sexual orientation reflects the complex interplay of both genetic and nongenetic mechanisms—of both nature and nurture.

Sexual Function Disturbances

The biological, social, and psychological factors that shape human sexual behavior can also contribute to **sexual function disturbances,** which are problems in a person's desire for or ability to have satisfying sexual activity (Goldstein & Rosen, 2002). For men, a common problem is *erectile disorder,* a persistent inability to have or maintain an erection adequate for sex. Physical causes—such as fatigue, diabetes, high blood pressure, the use of alcohol or other drugs, and perhaps even genetics—account for some cases (Fischer et al., 2004; Heiman, 2002). Psychological causes such as anxiety are also common (Everaerd & Laan, 1994). As its name implies, *premature ejaculation* is a recurring tendency to ejaculate during sex sooner than the man or his partner desires.

For women, the most common sexual function disturbance is *sexual arousal disorder* (once called *frigidity*), which involves a recurring inability to become aroused during sexual activity (Phillips, 2000; Wilson et al., 1996). Sexual arousal disorder can stem from inadequate genital stimulation, hormonal imbalances, insufficient vaginal lubrication, or inadequate blood flow to the clitoris (Anastasiadis et al., 2002; Mansfield, Voda, & Koch, 1995; Wilson et al., 1996). However, it is also often tied to psychological factors such as guilt or self-consciousness, which can affect men as well as women (Davidson & Moore, 1994; Laan et al., 1993).

Many people experience episodes of at least one of these problems at some point in their lives (Heiman, 2002; Laumann, Paik, & Rosen, 1999; West et al., 2008), but these episodes are considered dysfunctions only if they become a persistent and distressing obstacle to sexual functioning (American Psychiatric Association, 1994; Mercer et al., 2003). Fortunately, most sexual function disturbances can be overcome through psychotherapy, medication, or both (Braunstein et al., 2005; de Silva, 1994). For example, Viagra, Cialis, and other drugs that affect blood flow in the penis are effective in treating many cases of erectile disorder.

Achievement Motivation

▶ *Why do some people try harder than others to succeed?*

This sentence was written at 6 A.M. on a beautiful Sunday in June. Why would someone get up that early to work on a weekend? Why do people take their work seriously and try to do the best that they can? People work hard partly due to *extrinsic motivation,* a desire for external rewards such as money. But work and other human activities also reflect *intrinsic motivation,* a desire for internal satisfaction (Deci et al., 2001).

The next time you visit someone's home or office, notice the mementos displayed there. Perhaps there are framed diplomas and awards, trophies and ribbons, and photos

sexual function disturbances Problems with sexual motivation, arousal, or orgasmic response.

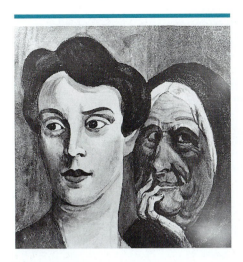

FIGURE 8.4 ■ ASSESSING ACHIEVEMENT MOTIVATION

This picture is similar to those included in the Thematic Apperception Test, or TAT (Morgan & Murray, 1935). The strength of people's achievement motivation is inferred from the stories they tell about TAT pictures. A response like "The young woman is hoping that she will be able to make her grandmother proud of her" would be seen as reflecting high achievement motivation. *Source*: Murray (1971).

Reprinted by permission of the publishers from THEMATIC APPERCEPTION TEST by Henry A. Murray, Card 12F, Cambridge, Mass.: Harvard University Press, Copyright © 1943 by the President and Fellows of Harvard College, Copyright © 1971 by Henry A. Murray.

achievement motivation (need for achievement or n-Ach) The degree to which a person establishes specific goals, cares about meeting them, and experiences satisfaction by doing so.

of children and grandchildren. These badges of achievement affirm that a person has accomplished tasks that merit approval or establish worth. Much of human behavior is motivated by a desire for approval, admiration, and a sense of achievement—in short, for esteem—from others and from within. In this section, we examine two of the most common avenues to esteem: achievement in general and achievement in one's work.

Need for Achievement

Many athletes who already hold world records still train intensely; many people who have built multimillion-dollar businesses still work fourteen-hour days. What motivates these people? One answer is **achievement motivation** (also called the *need for achievement*, abbreviated *n-Ach*) (Murray, 1938). People with high achievement motivation seek to master tasks—such as sports, business ventures, occupational skills, intellectual puzzles, or artistic creation—and feel intense satisfaction from doing so. They work hard at striving for excellence, enjoy themselves in the process, and take great pride in achieving at a high level.

Individual Differences How do people with strong achievement motivation differ from others? To find out, researchers gave children a test to measure their need for achievement (Figure 8.4 shows a test for adults) and then asked them to play a ring-toss game. Most of the children who scored low on the need-for-achievement test stood either so close to the ring-toss target that they couldn't fail or so far away that they could not succeed. In contrast, children scoring high on the need-for-achievement test stood at a moderate distance from the target, making the game challenging but not impossible (McClelland, 1958).

Experiments with adults and children suggest that people with high achievement needs tend to set challenging but realistic goals. They actively seek success, take risks when necessary, can wait for rewards, and are intensely satisfied when they do well (Mayer & Sutton, 1996). Yet if they feel they have tried their best, people with high achievement motivation are not too upset by failure. Those with low achievement motivation also like to succeed, but instead of joy, success tends to bring them relief at having avoided failure (Winter, 1996). Indeed, there is some evidence that the differing emotions—such as anticipation versus worry—that accompany the efforts of people with high and low achievement motivation can affect how successful those efforts will be (Pekrun et al., 2009).

Differences in achievement motivation also appear in the kinds of goals people seek in achievement-related situations (Molden & Dweck, 2000). Some tend to adopt *learning goals*. When they play golf, take piano lessons, work at problems, go to school, and engage in other achievement-oriented activities, they do so mainly to get better at those activities. They realize that they may not yet have the skills necessary to achieve at a high level, so they tend to learn by watching others and to struggle with problems on their own rather than asking for help (Mayer & Sutton, 1996). When they do seek help, people with learning goals are likely to ask for explanations, hints, and other forms of task-related information, not for quick, easy answers that remove the challenge from the situation. In contrast, people who adopt *performance goals* are usually more concerned with demonstrating the competence they believe they already possess. They tend to seek information about how well they have performed compared with others rather than about how to improve their performance (Butler, 1998). When they seek help, it is usually to ask for the "right answer" rather than for tips on how to find the answer themselves. Because their primary goal is to display competence, people with performance goals tend to avoid new challenges if they are not confident that they will be successful, and they tend to quit in response to failure (Grant & Dweck, 2003; Weiner, 1980). Those with learning goals tend to be more persistent and less upset when they don't immediately perform well (Niiya, Crocker, & Bartmess, 2004).

Development of Achievement Motivation Achievement motivation develops in early childhood under the influence of both genetic and environmental factors.

HELPING THEM DO THEIR BEST ▶

Learning-oriented goals are especially appropriate in classrooms, where students typically have little knowledge of the subject matter. This is why most teachers tolerate errors and reward gradual improvement. They do not usually encourage performance goals, which emphasize doing better than others and demonstrating immediate competence (Reeve, 1996). Still, to help students do their best in the long run, teachers may also promote performance goals. The proper combination of both kinds of goals may be more motivating than either kind alone (Barron & Harackiewicz, 2001).

© Mary Kate Denny/PhotoEdit

As described in the personality chapter, children inherit general behavioral tendencies, such as impulsiveness and emotionality, and these tendencies may support or undermine the development of achievement motivation. The motivation to achieve is also shaped by what children learn from watching and listening to others, especially their parents. Evidence for the influence of parental teachings about achievement comes from a study in which young boys were given a task so difficult that they were sure to fail. Fathers whose sons scored low on achievement motivation tests often became annoyed as they watched their boys work on the task, discouraged them from continuing, and interfered or even completed the task themselves (Rosen & D'Andrade, 1959). A much different response pattern emerged among parents of children who scored high on tests of achievement motivation. Those parents tended to (1) encourage the child to try difficult tasks, especially new ones; (2) give praise and other rewards for success; (3) encourage the child to find ways to succeed rather than merely complaining about failure; and (4) prompt the child to go on to the next, more difficult challenge (McClelland, 1985). Parents' influence on achievement reaches well beyond their physical presence. Research with adults shows that even the slightest cues that bring a parent to mind can boost some people's efforts to achieve a goal (Shah, 2003) and that college students—especially those who have learning goals—feel closer to their parents while taking exams (Moller et al., 2008).

More general cultural influences also affect the development of achievement motivation. Subtle messages about a culture's view of the importance and value of achievement often appear in the books children read, the stories they hear, and the programs they see on television. Does the story's main character work hard and overcome obstacles, thus creating expectations of a payoff for persistence? Or does a lazy main character drift aimlessly and then win the lottery, suggesting that rewards come randomly, regardless of effort? And if the main character succeeds, is it the result of personal effort, as is typical of stories in individualist cultures? Or is success based on ties to a cooperative and supportive group, as is typical of stories in collectivist cultures? These themes appear to act as blueprints for reaching one's goals. It is not surprising, then, that ideas about achievement motivation differ from culture to culture. In one study, individuals from Saudi Arabia and from the United States were asked to comment on short stories describing people succeeding at various tasks. Saudis tended to see the people in the stories as having succeeded because of the help they got from others, whereas Americans tended to attribute success to the internal characteristics of each story's main character (Zahrani & Kaplowitz, 1993).

► Children raised in environments that support the development of strong achievement motivation tend not to give up on difficult tasks—even if all the king's horses and all the king's men do!

"Maybe they didn't try hard enough."

In short, achievement motivation is strongly influenced by social and cultural learning experiences and by the beliefs about oneself that these experiences help create. People who come to believe in their ability to achieve are more likely to do so than those who expect to fail (Dweck, 1998; Greven et al., 2009; Wigfield & Eccles, 2000).

Achievement and Success in the Workplace

In the workplace, there is usually more concern with employees' motivation to work hard during business hours than with their general level of achievement motivation. In fact, employers tend to set up jobs in accordance with their ideas about how intrinsic and extrinsic motivations combine to shape employees' performance (Riggio, 1989). Employers who see workers as lazy, dishonest, and lacking in ambition tend to offer highly structured, heavily supervised jobs. They give the employees little say in deciding what to do or how to do it. These employers assume that workers are motivated mainly by extrinsic rewards—especially money. So they are often surprised when some employees are dissatisfied with their jobs and show little motivation to work hard, in spite of good pay and benefits (Diener & Seligman, 2004; Igalens & Roussel, 1999).

If good pay and benefits alone don't bring job satisfaction and the desire to excel on the job, what does? In Western cultures low worker motivation appears to come largely from negative thoughts and feelings about having little or no control over the work environment (Rosen, 1991). Compared with those in highly structured jobs, workers tend to be happier, more satisfied, and more productive if they are (1) encouraged to participate in decisions about how work should be done; (2) given problems to solve, without being told how to solve them; (3) taught more than one skill; (4) given individual responsibility; and (5) given public recognition, not just money, for good performance (Fisher, 2000).

Allowing people to set and achieve clear goals is one way to increase both job performance and job satisfaction (Abramis, 1994). Goals that most effectively maintain work motivation have three features (Katzell & Thompson, 1990). First, they are personally meaningful. When a memo from a high-level administrator tells employees that their goal should be to increase production, they tend to feel unfairly burdened and not particularly motivated to meet the goal. Second, effective goals are specific and concrete (Locke & Latham, 2002). The goal of "doing better" is usually not a strong motivator. A specific target, such as increasing sales by 10 percent, is a far more motivating goal. It is there for all to see, and it is easy to determine whether, and when, the goal has been reached. Finally, goals are most effective if management supports the

GOAL SETTING AND ACHIEVEMENT MOTIVATION

Clear and specific goals motivate the most persistent of achievement efforts on the job and in other areas, too (Locke & Latham, 2002). These women are more likely to stick with their exercise program if they are pursuing the goal of "losing twenty pounds" or "doing aerobics three times a week" rather than the vague goal of "getting in shape." Similarly, you are more likely to keep reading this chapter if your goal is to "read the motivation section of the motivation and emotion chapter today" than if it is to "do some studying." Clarifying your goal makes it easier to know when you have reached it and when it is time to take a break. Without clear goals, a person can be more easily distracted by fatigue, boredom, or frustration and more likely to give up before completing a task.

well-being (subjective well-being)
A cognitive judgment of satisfaction with life, the frequent experiencing of positive moods and emotions, and the relatively infrequent experiencing of unpleasant moods and emotions.

workers' own goal setting, offers special rewards for reaching goals, and gives encouragement for renewed efforts after failure (Kluger & DeNisi, 1998).

To summarize, motivating jobs offer personal challenges, independence, and both intrinsic and extrinsic rewards. They provide enough satisfaction for people to feel excitement and pleasure in working hard. They inspire workers to be passionate about their work, not merely driven by it (Burke & Fiksenbaum, 2009). For employers, the rewards are more productivity, less absenteeism, and fewer resignations (Ilgen & Pulakos, 1999).

Achievement and Well-Being

Some people believe that the more they achieve and the more money and other material goods they have as a result, the happier they will be. Do you agree? Researchers studying *positive psychology* (Seligman et al., 2005; Sheldon & King, 2001) have become increasingly interested in the systematic study of what it actually takes to achieve happiness, or, more formally, well-being (Lyubomirsky, 2001). **Well-being** (also known as **subjective well-being**) is a combination of a cognitive judgment of satisfaction with life, the frequent experiencing of positive moods and emotions, and the relatively infrequent experiencing of unpleasant moods and emotions (Eid & Larsen, 2008; Fredrickson & Losada, 2005; Urry et al., 2004).

Research on well-being indicates that as you might expect, people living in extreme poverty or in war-torn or politically chaotic countries are less happy than people in better circumstances. And people everywhere react to good or bad events with corresponding changes in mood. As described in the chapter on health, stress, and coping, for example, severe or long-lasting stressors—such as the death of a loved one—can lead to psychological and physical problems. But although events do have an impact, the depressing or elevating effects of major changes, such as being promoted or fired or even being imprisoned, seriously injured, or disabled tend not to last as long as we might think they would (Abrantes-Pais, et al., 2007). In other words, how happy you are may have less to do with what happens to you than you might expect (Bonanno, 2004; Gilbert & Wilson, 1998; Kahneman et al., 2006; Lyubomirsky, 2001; Riis et al., 2005).

Most event-related changes in mood subside within days or weeks, and most people then return to their previous level of happiness (Suh, Diener, & Fujita, 1996). Even when events create permanent changes in circumstances, most people adapt by changing their expectancies and goals, not by radically and permanently changing their baseline level of happiness. For example, people may be thrilled after getting a big salary increase, but as they get used to having more money, the thrill fades, and they may eventually feel just as underpaid as before. In fact, although there are exceptions (Fujita & Diener, 2005; Lucas, 2007), most people's level of well-being tends to be remarkably stable throughout their lives. This stable baseline may be related to temperament, or personality, and it has been likened to the homeostatic processes that maintain body temperature or weight (Lykken, 1999). And like many other aspects of temperament, our baseline level of happiness may be influenced by genetics. Twin studies have shown, for example, that individual differences in happiness are more strongly associated with inherited personality characteristics than with environmental factors such as money, popularity, or physical attractiveness (Lykken, 1999; Tellegen et al., 1988).

Beyond inherited tendencies, the things that appear to matter most in generating happiness are close social ties (such as friends and a satisfying marriage or partnership), religious faith, and having the resources necessary to make progress toward one's goals (Diener, 2000; Myers, 2000). So you don't have to be a smart, rich, physically attractive high achiever to be happy, and it turns out that most people in Western cultures are relatively happy (Diener & Diener, 1995; Gow et al., 2005).

These results are consistent with the views expressed over many centuries by philosophers, psychologists, and wise people in all cultures (e.g., Ekman et al., 2005). As discussed in the personality chapter, for example, Abraham Maslow (1970) noted that when people in Western cultures experience unhappiness and psychological problems, those problems can often be traced to a *deficiency orientation*. He said that these people tend to seek happiness by trying to acquire the goods and status they don't have—but think they need—rather than by appreciating life itself and the material and nonmaterial riches they already have. Others have amplified this point, suggesting that our efforts to get more of the things we think will bring happiness may actually contribute to unhappiness if what we get is never "enough" (Diener & Seligman, 2004; Luthar & Latendresse, 2005; Nickerson et al., 2003; Srivastava, Locke, & Bartol, 2001). Indeed, the old saying that "life is a journey, not a destination" suggests that we are more likely to find happiness by experiencing full engagement in what we are *doing*—a state that some positive psychologists call *flow* (Hektner, Schmidt, & Csikszentmihalyi, 2007)—rather than by focusing on what we are or are not *getting*.

Relations and Conflicts Among Motives

● *Which motives move me most?*

It is far too early to tell whether research on well-being will help channel people's achievement motivation toward a more balanced set of goals, but there is no doubt that people will continue striving to meet whatever needs they perceive to be important. What are those needs?

Maslow's Hierarchy

Maslow (1970) suggested that human behavior is influenced by a hierarchy, or ranking, of five classes of needs, or motives (see Figure 8.5). He said that needs at the lowest level of the hierarchy must be at least partially satisfied before people can be motivated by the ones at higher levels. From the bottom to the top of Maslow's hierarchy, these five motives are as follows:

1. *Physiological,* such as the need for food, water, oxygen, and sleep.
2. *Safety,* such as the need to be cared for as a child and to have a secure income as an adult.
3. *Belongingness and love,* such as the need to be part of groups and to participate in affectionate sexual and nonsexual relationships.
4. *Esteem,* such as the need to be respected as a useful, honorable individual.
5. *Self-actualization,* which means reaching one's full potential. People motivated by this need explore and enhance relationships with others; follow interests for intrinsic pleasure rather than for money, status, or esteem; and are concerned with issues affecting all people, not just themselves.

FIGURE 8.5 ■ MASLOW'S HIERARCHY OF MOTIVES

Abraham Maslow saw human motives as organized in a hierarchy in which motives at lower levels come before those at higher levels. According to this view, self-actualization is the essence of mental health, but Maslow recognized that only rare individuals, such as Mother Teresa or Martin Luther King, Jr., approach full self-actualization. Take a moment to consider which level of Maslow's hierarchy you are focused on at this point in your life. Which level do you ultimately hope to reach?

Source: Adapted from Maslow (1943).

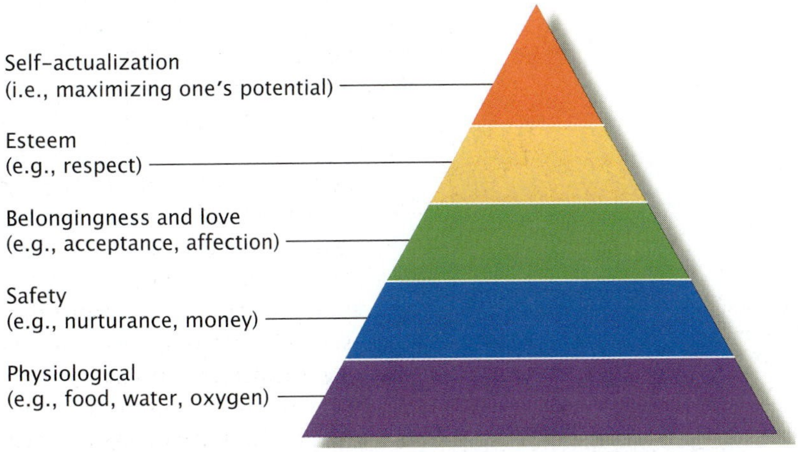

Self-actualization
(i.e., maximizing one's potential)

Esteem
(e.g., respect)

Belongingness and love
(e.g., acceptance, affection)

Safety
(e.g., nurturance, money)

Physiological
(e.g., food, water, oxygen)

Maslow's hierarchy has been very influential over the years, partly because the needs associated with basic survival and security do generally take precedence over those related to self-enhancement or personal growth (Baumeister & Leary, 1995; Oishi et al., 1999). But critics see the hierarchy as too simplistic (Hall, Lindzey, & Campbell, 1998; Neher, 1991). It doesn't predict or explain, for example, the motivation of people who starve themselves to draw attention to political or moral causes. Further, people may not have to satisfy one kind of need before addressing others; we can seek to satisfy several needs at once. Finally, the ordering of needs within the survival/security and enhancement/growth categories differs from culture to culture, suggesting that there may not be a single, universal hierarchy of needs.

To address some of the problems in Maslow's theory, Clayton Alderfer (1969) proposed *existence, relatedness, growth (ERG) theory,* which places human needs into just three categories: *existence needs* (such as for food and water), *relatedness needs* (e.g., for social interactions and attachments), and *growth needs* (such as for developing one's capabilities). Unlike Maslow, Alderfer doesn't assume that these needs must be satisfied in a particular order. Instead, he sees needs in each category as rising and falling from time to time and from situation to situation. When a need in one area is fulfilled (or even if it is frustrated), a person will be motivated to pursue some other needs. For example, if a breakup frustrates relatedness needs, a person might focus on existence or growth needs by eating more or volunteering to work late.

linkages

Can motivational conflicts cause stress? *(a link to Health, Stress, and Coping)*

Linkages

Conflicting Motives and Stress

As in the case of hunger strikes, in which the desire to promote a cause is pitted against the desire to eat, human motives can sometimes conflict. The usual result is some degree of discomfort. For example, imagine that you are alone and bored on a Saturday night and you think about going out for a snack. What are your motives? Hunger might play a part, and so might the prospect of the increased physiological arousal that a change of scene will provide. Even sexual motivation might be involved, as you consider the chances of meeting someone exciting in the convenience store. But safety-related motives may also kick in: Is your neighborhood safe enough for you to go out alone? Even an esteem motive might come into play, making you hesitate to be seen on your own on a weekend night.

These are just a few of the motives that may shape a trivial decision. When the decision is more important, the number and strength of motivational pushes and pulls are often greater, creating far more internal conflict and indecision. There are four basic types of motivational conflicts (Elliott, 2008; Miller, 1959):

1. **Approach-approach conflicts.** When we must choose only one of two desirable activities—say, going to a movie or to a concert—an *approach-approach conflict* exists.
2. **Avoidance-avoidance conflicts.** An *avoidance-avoidance conflict* arises when we must select one of two undesirable alternatives. Someone forced either to sell the family home or to declare bankruptcy faces an avoidance-avoidance conflict.
3. **Approach-avoidance conflicts.** If someone you dislike had tickets to your favorite group's sold-out concert and invited you to come along, what would you do? When a particular event or activity has both attractive and unattractive features, an *approach-avoidance* conflict is created.
4. **Multiple approach-avoidance conflicts.** Suppose you must choose between two jobs. One offers a high salary with a well-known company but requires long working hours and relocation to a miserable climate. The other boasts advancement opportunities, fringe benefits, and a better climate, but it doesn't pay as much and involves an unpredictable work schedule. This is an example of

a *multiple approach-avoidance conflict,* in which two or more alternatives each have both positive and negative features. Such conflicts are especially difficult to resolve, partly because the features of each option may not be easy to compare. For example, how many dollars a year does it take to compensate you for living in a bad climate?

The difficulties associated with resolving each of these conflicts can create stress, a topic explored in the chapter on health, stress, and coping. Most people who have motivational conflicts are tense, irritable, and more vulnerable than usual to physical and psychological problems. These reactions are especially likely when no choice is obviously "right," when varying motives have approximately equal strength, and when a choice can have serious consequences (as in decisions about marrying, splitting up, or placing an elderly parent in a nursing home). Some people may spend a long time agonizing over these conflicts, whereas others may make a choice quickly, impulsively, and thoughtlessly, simply to end the discomfort of uncertainty. Even after resolving the conflict on the basis of careful thought, people may continue to experience stress responses, such as worrying about whether they made the right decision or blaming themselves for bad choices. These and other consequences of conflicting motives can even lead to depression or other serious disorders.

© Myrleen Ferguson Cate/PhotoEdit

A STRESSFUL CONFLICT ▲

Think back to when you were deciding which college to attend. Was the decision easy and obvious or did it create a motivational conflict? If there was a conflict, was it an approach-approach, approach-avoidance, or multiple approach-avoidance conflict? What factors were most important in deciding how to resolve the conflict, and what emotions and signs of stress did you experience during and after the decision-making process?

Learn BY Doing

The emotions associated with motivational conflicts provide just one example of the close links between motivation and emotions. Motivation can intensify emotions, as when hunger leads a normally calm person to angrily complain about slow service at a restaurant. But emotions can also create motivation. Happiness, for example, is an emotion that people want to feel (e.g., Bryant & Veroff, 2006), so they engage in whatever behaviors—studying, artwork, investing, beachcombing—they think will achieve it. Similarly, as an emotion that most people want to avoid, anxiety motivates many behaviors, from leaving the scene of an accident to avoiding poisonous snakes. But sometimes, as when facing a stressful job interview or agreeing to a painful medical procedure, people are motivated to endure anxiety or other unpleasant emotions because they believe that doing so will eventually lead to a desired goal (Tamir, 2009). Let's take a closer look at emotions.

The Nature of Emotions

▶ *How do feelings differ from thoughts?*

Everyone seems to agree that joy, sorrow, anger, fear, love, and hate are emotions. However, it is often hard to identify the shared features that make these experiences emotions rather than, say, thoughts or impulses.

Defining Characteristics

Most psychologists in Western cultures tend to see emotions as organized psychological and physiological reactions to changes in our relationship to the world. These reactions are partly private, or *subjective,* experiences and partly measurable patterns of behavior and physiological arousal. The subjective experience of emotions has several characteristics:

1. Emotions are usually *temporary.* In other words, they tend to have relatively clear beginnings and ends and a relatively short duration. Moods, by contrast, tend to last longer.
2. Emotional experience can be *positive,* as in joy, or *negative,* as in sadness. It can also be a mixture of both, as in the bittersweet feelings of watching one's child leave for the first day of kindergarten (Larsen et al., 2004).
3. Emotions can vary in intensity. You can feel pleased, happy, or ecstatic. You can also feel mildly disappointed, sad, or deeply depressed.

WINNERS AND LOSERS ▶
Emotional experiences depend in part on our interpretation of situations and how those situations relate to our goals. A single event—the announcement of the results of this wrestling match—triggered drastically different emotional reactions in the contestants, depending on whether they perceived it as making them the winner or the loser.

4. Emotional experience is triggered partly by thoughts, especially by a *mental assessment* of how a situation relates to your goals. The same event can bring on different emotions depending on what it means to you. An exam score of 75 percent may thrill you if your best previous score had been 50 percent, but it may upset you if you had never before scored below 90 percent.

5. Emotional experience *alters thought processes,* often by directing attention toward some things and away from others. Negative emotions tend to narrow attention, and positive emotions tend to broaden it (Fredrickson et al., 2008). Anxiety about terrorism, for example, narrows our attention to focus on potential threats in airports and other public places (Craske, 1999; Yovel & Mineka, 2005).

6. Emotional experience brings on an *action tendency,* a motivation to behave in certain ways. Grieving parents' anger, for example, might motivate them to harm their child's killer. But for John Walsh, whose son was kidnapped and murdered, grief led him to help prevent such crimes by creating *America's Most Wanted,* a TV show dedicated to bringing criminals to justice.

7. Emotional experiences are *passions* that you feel, whether you want to or not. You do have some control over emotions, though, because they depend partly on how you interpret situations (Gross, 2001). For example, you can reduce your emotional reaction to a car accident by reminding yourself that no one was hurt and that you are insured. Still, you can't just *decide* what emotions you experience; instead, you "fall in love" or "explode in anger" or are "overcome by grief."

In other words, the subjective aspects of emotions are experiences that are both triggered by the thinking self and felt as happening to the self. The extent to which we are "victims" of our passions versus rational controllers of our emotions is a central dilemma of human existence.

The objectively measurable aspects of emotions include learned and innate *expressive displays* and *physiological responses.* Expressive displays—such as a smile or a frown—communicate feelings to others. Physiological responses—changes in heart rate, for example—provide the biological adjustments needed to perform actions generated by the emotional experience. If you throw a temper tantrum, for instance, your heart must deliver additional oxygen and fuel to your muscles.

In summary, **emotions** are temporary experiences with positive, negative, or mixed qualities. People experience emotions with varying intensity as happening to

emotions Temporary positive or negative experiences that are felt as happening to the self, that are generated partly by interpretation of situations, and that are accompanied by learned and innate physical responses.

the self, generated in part by a mental assessment of situations, and accompanied by both learned and innate physical responses. Through emotions, whether they mean to or not, people communicate their internal states and intentions to others. Emotions often disrupt thinking and behavior, but they also trigger and guide thinking and organize, motivate, and sustain behavior and social relations (Izard, 2007).

The Biology of Emotions

The biological systems described in the chapter on biology and behavior play a major role in emotions. In the *central nervous system*, numerous brain areas are involved in the generation of emotions as well as in our experience of those emotions (Barrett & Wager, 2006). The *autonomic nervous system* gives rise to many of the physiological changes associated with emotional arousal.

Brain Mechanisms Although many questions remain, researchers have described three main aspects of how emotions are processed in the brain. First, it appears that activity in the *limbic system,* especially in the *amygdala,* is central to emotions (Kensinger & Corkin, 2004; Phelps & LeDoux, 2005; see Figure 2.9 in the chapter on biology and behavior). Normal functioning in the amygdala appears critical to the ability to learn emotional associations, recognize emotional expressions, and perceive emotionally charged words (Anderson & Phelps, 2001; Suslow et al., 2006; Whalen et al., 2004). For example, victims of a disease that destroys only the amygdala are unable to judge other people's emotional states by looking at their faces (Adolphs, Tranel, & Damasio, 1998).

A second aspect of the brain's involvement in emotions is seen in its control over our emotional and nonemotional facial expressions (Rinn, 1984). Take a moment to

Learn BY Doing look in a mirror, and put on your best fake smile. The voluntary facial movements you just made, like all voluntary movements, are controlled by the brain's *pyramidal motor system,* a system that includes the motor cortex. However, a smile that expresses genuine happiness is involuntary. That kind of smile, like the other facial movements associated with emotions, is governed by the *extrapyramidal motor system,* which depends on areas beneath the cortex. Brain damage can disrupt either system (see Figure 8.6). People with pyramidal motor system damage show normal facial expressions during genuine emotion, but they cannot fake a smile. In contrast, people with damage to the extrapyramidal system can pose facial expressions at will, but they remain straight-faced even when feeling genuine joy or profound sadness (Hopf, Muller, & Hopf, 1992).

A third aspect of the brain's role in emotions is revealed by research on the two sides, or hemispheres, of the cerebral cortex. For example, after suffering damage to the right, but not the left, hemisphere, people no longer laugh at jokes, even though they can still understand their words, the logic (or illogic) underlying them, and their punch lines (Critchley, 1991). Further, when people are asked to name the emotions shown in slides of facial expressions, blood flow increases in the right hemisphere more than in the left hemisphere (Gur, Skolnic, & Gur, 1994). But smiling while experiencing a positive emotion is correlated with greater activity in the *left* side of the brain (Davidson et al., 1990). When an area of one patient's left hemisphere was stimulated, she began to smile, then laugh (Fried et al., 1998). She attributed her emotional expression to the situation ("You guys are just so funny . . . standing around"). Similarly, brain-imaging studies conducted while sports fans watched their favorite team in action have revealed greater activation in the left hemisphere when the team is winning and more activation in the right hemisphere when the team is losing (Park et al., 2009).

The fact that different brain areas appear to be involved in displaying and experiencing positive and negative emotions (Harmon-Jones, 2004; Harmon-Jones & Sigelman, 2001; Heller, 1993) makes it difficult to map the exact roles the two hemispheres play in emotions (Root, Wong, & Kinsbourne, 2006; Vingerhoets, Berckmoes, & Stroobant, 2003). Generally, however, most aspects of emotions—the experiencing of negative emotion, the perception of any emotion exhibited in faces or other stimuli,

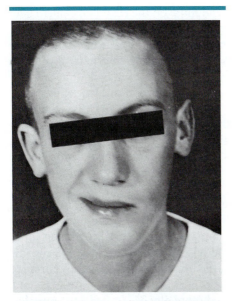

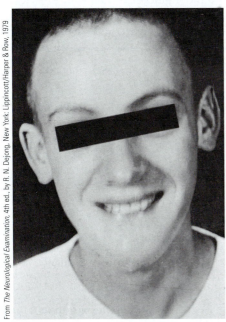

From *The Neurological Examination*, 4th ed., by R. N. Dejong, New York: Lippincott/Harper & Row, 1979

FIGURE 8.6 ■ CONTROL OF VOLUNTARY AND EMOTIONAL FACIAL MOVEMENTS

This man has a tumor in his motor cortex that prevents him from voluntarily moving the muscles on the left side of his face. In the top photograph he is trying to smile in response to instructions from the examiner. He cannot smile on command, but he can smile with happiness, as the bottom photograph shows, because the movements associated with genuine emotion are controlled by the extrapyramidal motor system, which is beneath the motor cortex.

and the facial expression of any emotion—depend more on the right hemisphere than on the left (Heller, Nitschke, & Miller, 1998; Kawasaki et al., 2001).

If the right hemisphere is relatively dominant in emotions, which side of the face would you expect to be somewhat more involved in expressing emotions? If you said the left side, you are correct, because, as described in the chapter on biology and behavior, movements of each side of the body are controlled by the opposite side of the brain.

Mechanisms of the Autonomic Nervous System   The autonomic nervous system (ANS) triggers many of the physiological changes that accompany emotions (Vernet, Robin, & Dittmar, 1995; see Figure 8.7). If your hands get cold and clammy when you are nervous, it is because the ANS has increased perspiration and decreased the blood flow in your hands.

As described in the chapter on biology and behavior, the ANS carries information between the brain and most organs of the body—the heart and blood vessels, the digestive system, and so on. Each of these organs is active on its own, but input from the ANS can increase or decrease that activity. By doing so, the ANS coordinates the functioning of these organs to meet the body's general needs and prepare the body for change (Porges, Doussard, & Maita, 1995). If you are aroused to take action, such as running to catch a bus, you need more glucose to fuel your muscles.

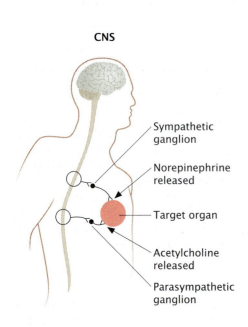

CNS

Sympathetic ganglion

Norepinephrine released

Target organ

Acetylcholine released

Parasympathetic ganglion

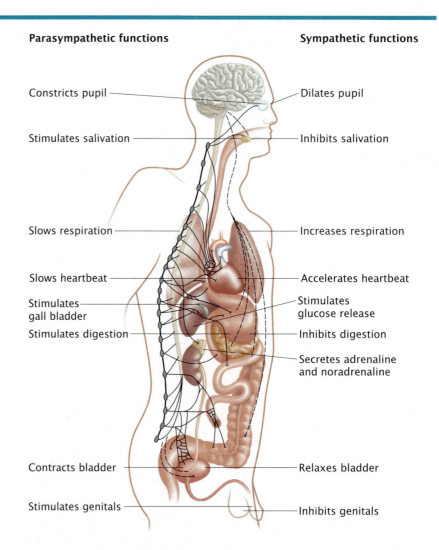

Parasympathetic functions

Constricts pupil

Stimulates salivation

Slows respiration

Slows heartbeat

Stimulates gall bladder

Stimulates digestion

Contracts bladder

Stimulates genitals

Sympathetic functions

Dilates pupil

Inhibits salivation

Increases respiration

Accelerates heartbeat

Stimulates glucose release

Inhibits digestion

Secretes adrenaline and noradrenaline

Relaxes bladder

Inhibits genitals

FIGURE 8.7 ■ **THE AUTONOMIC NERVOUS SYSTEM**

Emotional responses involve activation of the autonomic nervous system, which is organized into sympathetic and parasympathetic subsystems. Which of the bodily responses shown here do you associate with emotional experiences?

Learn BY Doing

The ANS frees needed energy by stimulating the secretion of glucose-generating hormones and promoting blood flow to the muscles.

Figure 8.7 shows that the autonomic nervous system is organized into two parts: the sympathetic nervous system and the parasympathetic nervous system. Emotions can activate either part, both of which send axon fibers to each organ in the body. Generally, the sympathetic and parasympathetic fibers have opposite effects on these *target organs.* Axons from the **parasympathetic nervous system** release the neurotransmitter *acetylcholine* onto target organs, leading to activity related to the protection, nourishment, and growth of the body. Axons from the **sympathetic nervous system** release a different neurotransmitter, *norepinephrine,* onto target organs, helping prepare the body for vigorous activity. When one part of the sympathetic system is stimulated, other parts are activated "in sympathy" with it (Gellhorn & Loofbourrow, 1963). The result is the **fight-or-flight reaction,** a pattern of increased heart rate and blood pressure, rapid or irregular breathing, dilated pupils, perspiration, dry mouth, increased blood sugar, "goose bumps," and other changes that help prepare the body to confront or run from a threat.

You cannot consciously experience the brain mechanisms that alter the activity of your autonomic nervous system. This is why most people cannot exert direct, conscious control over blood pressure or other aspects of ANS activity. However, you can do things that have indirect effects on the ANS. For example, to create autonomic arousal of your sex organs, you might imagine an erotic situation. To raise your blood pressure, you might hold your breath or strain your muscles. And to lower your blood pressure, you can lie down, relax, and think calming thoughts.

Theories of Emotion

▶ *Are emotions in the heart, in the head, or both?*

Are the physiological responses associated with emotions enough to create an emotional experience? Or are those responses the *result* of emotional experiences that begin in the brain? And how do our mental interpretations of events affect our emotional reactions to them? For over a century now, psychologists have worked at finding the answers to these questions. In the process, they have developed a number of theories that explain emotions mainly in terms of biological or cognitive factors. The main biological theories are those of William James and Walter Cannon. The most prominent cognitive theories are those of Stanley Schachter and Richard Lazarus. Let's review these theories, along with some research designed to evaluate them.

James's Peripheral Theory

Suppose you are camping in the woods when a huge bear approaches your tent in the middle of the night. You would no doubt be afraid and run for your life, but would you run because you're afraid or are you afraid because you run? This was the example and the question posed by William James, one of the first psychologists to offer a formal account of how physiological responses relate to emotional experience. He argued that you are afraid because you run. Your running and the physiological responses associated with it, he said, follow directly from your perception of the bear.

At first, James's claim sounds ridiculous; it would be silly to run from something unless you already feared it. James concluded otherwise after examining his own mental processes. He decided that once you strip away all physiological responses—such as changes in heart rate, breathing, and other peripheral nervous system activity—nothing remains of the experience of an emotion (James, 1890). Without these responses, he said, you would feel no fear, because it is the experiencing of physiological responses that creates fear and other emotions. The same argument was made by Carle Lange, a Danish physician, so James's view is sometimes called the *James-Lange theory* of emotion. It is also known as a *peripheral theory* of emotion, because it emphasizes activity

parasympathetic nervous system The subsystem of the autonomic nervous system that typically influences activity related to the protection, nourishment, and growth of the body.

sympathetic nervous system The subsystem of the autonomic nervous system that readies the body for vigorous activity.

fight-or-flight reaction Physical reactions triggered by the sympathetic nervous system that prepare the body to fight or flee a threatening situation.

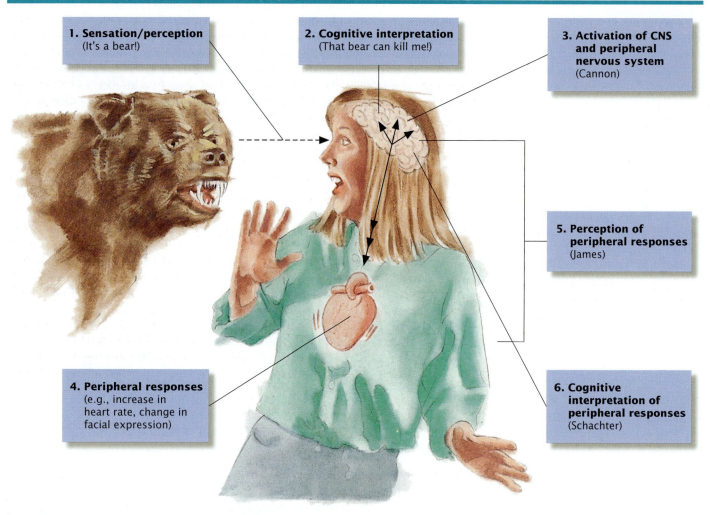

1. Sensation/perception
(It's a bear!)

2. Cognitive interpretation
(That bear can kill me!)

3. Activation of CNS and peripheral nervous system
(Cannon)

5. Perception of peripheral responses
(James)

4. Peripheral responses
(e.g., increase in heart rate, change in facial expression)

6. Cognitive interpretation of peripheral responses
(Schachter)

FIGURE 8.8 ■ COMPONENTS OF EMOTION

Emotion is associated with activity in the brain as well as with responses elsewhere in the body (called peripheral responses) and with cognitive interpretations of events. Emotion theorists have argued about which of these components are essential for emotion. William James emphasized the perception of peripheral responses, such as changes in heart rate. Walter Cannon asserted that emotion could occur entirely within the brain. Stanley Schachter emphasized cognitive factors, including how we interpret events and label peripheral responses.

in the peripheral nervous system, not in the central nervous system, as the main cause of emotional experience.

Observing Peripheral Responses   Figure 8.8 outlines the components of emotional experience, including those emphasized by James. First, perception affects the cerebral cortex. The brain interprets a situation and automatically directs a particular set of physiological changes, such as increased heart rate, sinking stomach, perspiration, and certain patterns of blood flow. It is when we become *aware* of this pattern of bodily changes, said James, that we experience an emotion. According to this view, each particular emotion is created by a particular pattern of physiological responses.

Notice that according to James's theory, emotional experience is not generated by the brain alone. There is no special "emotion center" in the brain where the firing of neurons creates a direct experience of emotion. If this theory is accurate, it might account for the difficulty we sometimes have in knowing our true feelings: we must figure out what emotions we feel by perceiving small differences in specific physiological response patterns (Katkin, Wiens, & Öhman, 2001).

Evaluating James's Theory   Research shows that certain emotional states are indeed associated with particular patterns of autonomic changes (Damasio et al., 2000; Keltner & Buswell, 1996; Sinha & Parsons, 1996). For example, blood flow to the hands and feet increases in association with anger and decreases in association with fear (Levenson, Ekman, & Friesen, 1990). So fear involves "cold feet"; anger does not.

A pattern of activity associated with disgust includes increased muscle activity but no change in heart rate. And when people mentally relive different kinds of emotional experiences, they show different patterns of autonomic activity (Ekman, Levenson, & Friesen, 1983). These emotion-specific patterns of physiological activity have been found in widely different cultures (Levenson et al., 1992). Further, people who are more keenly aware of physiological changes in their bodies are likely to experience emotions more intensely than those who are less aware of such changes (Schneider, Ring, & Katkin, 1998; Wiens, Mezzacappa, & Katkin, 2000). It has even been suggested that the "gut feelings" that cause us to approach or avoid certain situations might be the result of physiological changes that are perceived without conscious awareness (Bechara et al., 1997; Damasio, 1994; Katkin, Wiens, & Öhman, 2001; Winkielman & Berridge, 2004).

Different patterns of autonomic activity are also related to specific emotional facial expressions. In one study, research participants were asked to make a series of facial movements that, when combined, would create the appearance of sadness, fear, happiness, anger, or some other emotion (Levenson, Ekman, & Friesen, 1990). Making these movements led to autonomic changes that resembled those normally accompanying emotions (see Figure 8.9). In addition, almost all of the participants reported feeling the emotion associated with the expression they had created, even though they couldn't see their own expressions and didn't realize that they had made an "emotional" face.

Other studies have confirmed these results (Schnall & Laird, 2003) and have also shown that emotional feelings can be eased by relaxing facial muscles (Duclos & Laird, 2001). To get an idea of how facial expressions can alter as well as communicate emotion, look at a photograph of someone whose face is showing a strong emotion and try

FIGURE 8.9 ■ PATTERNS OF PHYSIOLOGICAL CHANGE ASSOCIATED WITH DIFFERENT EMOTIONS

In this experiment, facial movements characteristic of different emotions produced different patterns of change in (A) heart rate; (B) peripheral blood flow, as measured by finger temperature; (C) skin conductance; and (D) muscle activity (Levenson, Ekman, & Friesen, 1990). For example, making an angry face caused heart rate and finger temperature to rise, whereas making a fearful face raised heart rate but lowered finger temperature.
Source: Levenson, Ekman, & Friesen (1990)

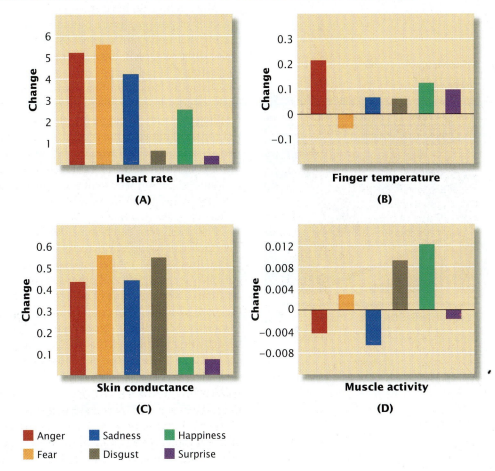

your best to imitate it. Did this create in you the same feelings and autonomic responses that the other person appears to be experiencing?

A variation on James's theory, called the *facial feedback hypothesis,* suggests that involuntary facial movements provide enough information about activity in the rest of the body to create an emotional experience (Ekman & Davidson, 1993). If so, it would help to explain how posed facial expressions create the emotions normally associated with them. Try taking advantage of this notion in your own life. The next time you want to cheer yourself up, it might help to smile—even though you don't feel like it (Fleeson, Malanos, & Achille, 2002)!

Lie Detection   James's view that different patterns of physiological activity are associated with different emotions forms the basis for the lie detection industry. If people experience anxiety or guilt when they lie, specific patterns of physiological activity accompanying these emotions should be detectable on instruments, called *polygraphs,* that record heart rate, breathing rate, perspiration, and other autonomic responses (Granhag & Stromwall, 2004; Iacono & Patrick, 2006).

To identify the perpetrator of a crime using the *control question test,* a polygraph tester might ask questions specific to the crime, such as "Did you stab someone on May 31, 2009?" Responses to such *relevant questions* are then compared with responses to *control questions,* such as "Have you ever lied to get out of trouble?" Innocent people might have lied at some time in the past and might feel guilty when asked about it, but they should have no reason to feel guilty about what they did on May 31, 2009. Accordingly, an innocent person should have a stronger emotional response to control questions than to relevant questions (Rosenfeld, 1995). Another approach, called the *directed lie test,* compares a person's physiological reactions when asked to lie about something and when telling what is known to be the truth. Finally, the *guilty knowledge test* seeks to determine whether a person reacts in a notable way to information about a crime that only the guilty party would know (Ben-Shakhar, Bar-Hillel, & Kremnitzer, 2002).

Most people do have emotional responses when they lie, but statistics about the accuracy of polygraphs are difficult to obtain. Estimates vary widely, from those suggesting that polygraphs detect 90 percent of guilty, lying individuals (Gamer et al., 2006; Honts & Quick, 1995; Kircher, Horowitz, & Raskin, 1988; Raskin, 1986) to those suggesting that polygraphs mislabel as many as 40 percent of truthful, innocent persons as guilty liars (Ben-Shakhar & Furedy, 1990; Saxe & Ben-Shakhar, 1999). Obviously, the results of a polygraph test are not determined entirely by whether a person is telling the truth. What people think about the act of lying and about the value of the test can also influence the accuracy of its results. For example, people who believe that lying is acceptable and who don't believe in the power of polygraphs are not likely to display emotion-linked physiological responses while lying during the test. However, an innocent person who believes in such tests and who thinks that "everything always goes wrong" might show a large fear response when asked about a crime, thus wrongly indicating "guilt" (Lykken, 1998b).

Polygraphs can catch some liars, but most researchers agree that a guilty person can "fool" a polygraph lie detector and that some innocent people can be mislabeled as guilty (Ruscio, 2005). After reviewing the relevant research literature, a panel of distinguished psychologists and other scientists in the United States expressed serious reservations about the value of polygraph tests in detecting deception and argued against their use as evidence in court or in employee screening and selection (Committee to Review the Scientific Evidence on the Polygraph, 2003). Scientists are working on other lie-detecting techniques that focus on brain activity and other measures that do not depend on a link between deception and autonomic nervous system responses (Bhatt et al., 2009; Lee et al., 2009).

© Bob Daemmrich

SEARCHING FOR THE TRUTH   ▲

Polygraph tests are not foolproof, though they may intimidate people who believe that they are. In one small town where the police could not afford a polygraph, a guilty suspect confessed his crime when a "lie detector" consisting of a kitchen colander was placed on his head and attached by wires to a copy machine (Shepherd, Kohut, & Sweet, 1989).

Cannon's Central Theory

James said that the experience of emotions depends on feedback from physiological responses occurring outside the brain, but Walter Cannon disagreed (Cannon, 1927).

According to Cannon, you feel fear at the sight of a wild bear even before you start to run because emotional experience starts in the brain—specifically, in the thalamus, the brain structure that relays information from most sense organs to the cortex.

According to Cannon's *central theory* of emotions (called the *Cannon-Bard theory,* in recognition of Philip Bard's contribution), information about emotional situations goes first to the thalamus. The thalamus then sends signals to the autonomic nervous system and—at the same time—to the cerebral cortex, where the emotion becomes conscious. So when you see a bear, the brain receives sensory information about it, interprets that information as a bear, and instantly creates the experience of fear while at the same time sending messages to your heart, lungs, and legs to get you out of the situation. According to Cannon's theory, then, there is a *direct,* central-nervous-system experience of emotion, whether or not the brain receives feedback about responses in other parts of the body (see Figure 8.8).

Updating Cannon's Theory   Later research indicates that the thalamus is not the "seat" of emotion, as Cannon had suggested. Still, the thalamus is indeed involved in some aspects of emotional processing (Lang, 1995). For example, studies of humans and laboratory animals show that the emotion of fear is generated by connections from the thalamus to the amygdala (Anderson & Phelps, 2000; LeDoux, 1995). The implication is that strong emotions can sometimes bypass the cortex without requiring conscious thought to activate them. This process helps explain why people find it so difficult to overcome an intense fear, or phobia, even though they may consciously know the fear is irrational.

An updated version of Cannon's theory suggests that in humans and other animals, activity in specific brain areas is experienced as either enjoyable or aversive and produces the feelings of pleasure or discomfort associated with emotion. In humans, these areas have extensive connections throughout the brain (Fossati et al., 2003). As a result, the representation of emotions in the brain probably involves activity in widely distributed neural circuits, not just in a narrowly localized emotion "center" (Derryberry & Tucker, 1992).

Cognitive Theories

Suppose you are about to be interviewed for your first job or go out on a blind date or take your first ride in a hot-air balloon. In such situations, it is not always easy to be sure of what you are feeling. Is it fear, excitement, anticipation, worry, happiness, dread, or what? Stanley Schachter suggested that the emotions we experience every day are shaped partly by how we interpret the arousal we feel. His cognitive theory of emotions is known as the *Schachter-Singer theory* in recognition of the contributions of Jerome Singer. The theory took shape in the early 1960s, when many psychologists were raising questions about the validity of James's theory of emotion. Schachter argued that the theory was essentially correct, but required a few modifications (Cornelius, 1996).

According to the Schachter-Singer theory, emotions result from a combination of feedback from the body's responses and our interpretation of what caused those responses. So cognitive interpretation comes into play twice: first when you perceive the situation that leads to bodily responses and again when you interpret those responses as a particular emotion (see Figure 8.8). Schachter said that a given pattern of physiological responses can be interpreted in many different ways and so might give rise to many different emotions. According to Schachter, then, the emotion you experience when that bear approaches your campsite might be fear, excitement, astonishment, or surprise, depending on how you label your bodily reactions to seeing it (Schachter & Singer, 1962).

Schachter also said that how we label arousal depends on **attribution,** the process of identifying the cause of some event. We attribute our physiological arousal to different emotions depending on the information we have about the situation. For example, if you are watching the final seconds of a close ball game, you might attribute your racing heart, rapid breathing, and perspiration to excitement. But you might attribute the same physiological reactions to anxiety if you are waiting for a big exam to begin. Schachter predicted that our emotional experiences will be less intense if we attribute

attribution   The process of explaining the cause of some event.

LABELING AROUSAL ▶

Schachter's cognitive theory of emotion predicts that these people will attribute their physiological arousal to the game they are watching and will label their emotion "excitement." Further, as described in the chapter on health, stress, and coping, the emotions they experience will also depend partly on their cognitive interpretation of the outcome (Lazarus & Folkman, 1984). Those who see their team's defeat as a disaster will experience more negative emotions than those who think of it as a challenge to improve.

arousal to a nonemotional cause. So if you notice your heart pounding before an exam but say to yourself, "Sure my heart's pounding—I just drank five cups of coffee!" then you should feel "wired" from caffeine rather than afraid or worried. This prediction has received some support (Mezzacappa, Katkin, & Palmer, 1999; Sinclair et al., 1994), but other aspects of Schachter's theory have not.

Few researchers today fully accept the Schachter-Singer theory, but it did stimulate an enormous amount of valuable research, including research on **excitation-transfer theory.** This theory focuses on a phenomenon in which physiological arousal from one experience carries over to affect emotions in an independent situation (Reisenzein, 1983; Zillmann, 1984). For example, people who have been aroused by physical exercise become angrier when provoked and experience more intense sexual feelings around an attractive person than do people who have been less physically active (Allen et al., 1989). Physiological arousal from fear, like arousal from exercise, can also enhance emotions, including sexual feelings. One study of this transfer took place in Canada, near a deep river gorge. The gorge could be crossed either by a shaky swinging bridge or by a more stable wooden structure. A female researcher asked men who had just crossed each bridge to respond to a questionnaire which included pictures from the TAT, the projective test described in Figure 8.4. The amount of sexual content in the stories these men wrote about the pictures was much higher among those who met the woman after crossing the more dangerous bridge compared to those who had crossed the stable bridge. Furthermore, they were more likely to rate the researcher as attractive and to attempt to contact her afterward (Dutton & Aron, 1974). When the person giving out the questionnaire was a male, however, the type of bridge crossed had no impact on sexual imagery. You might be wondering whether the men who crossed the dangerous bridge were simply more adventurous than other men regarding both bridge crossing and heterosexual encounters. To check this possibility, the researchers repeated the study, but with one change. This time, the woman approached the men farther down the trail, long after physiological arousal from the bridge crossing had subsided. Now the apparently adventurous men were no more likely than others to rate the woman as attractive. So it was probably excitation transfer, not differing amounts of adventurousness, that produced the original result.

Schachter focused on the way we interpret our bodily responses to events. Other cognitive theorists have argued that it is our interpretations of events themselves that are most important in shaping emotional experiences. For example, as we mentioned earlier, a person's emotional reaction to receiving exam results can depend partly on whether the score is seen as a sign of improvement or as a disaster. According to Richard Lazarus's (1966, 1991) *cognitive appraisal theory* of emotion, these differing reactions can be best explained by how we think exam scores, job interviews, blind dates, bear

excitation-transfer theory The theory that physiological arousal that stems from one situation is carried over to and enhances emotional experience in an independent situation.

sightings, and other events will affect our personal well-being. According to Lazarus, the process of cognitive appraisal, or evaluation, begins when we decide whether or not an event is relevant to our well-being; that is, do we even care about it? If we don't, as might be the case when an exam doesn't count toward our grade, we are unlikely to have an emotional experience when we get the results. If the event is relevant to our well-being, we will probably have a significant emotional reaction to it. That reaction will be positive or negative, said Lazarus, depending on whether we interpret the event as advancing our personal goals or blocking our progress. The *specific* emotion we experience depends on our individual goals, needs, standards, expectations, and past experiences. As a result, a second-place finisher in a marathon race might experience bitter disappointment at having "lost," whereas someone at the back of the pack may be thrilled just to have completed the race alive (Larsen et al., 2004).

More recently, researchers have developed cognitive theories of emotion that depart from Schachter's in some new directions. In the *conceptual act model* of emotion, for instance, *core affect*—pleasant or unpleasant feelings—is distinguished from *emotion*. According to this model, emotion results when we impose on a feeling a *category label* (e.g. guilt, shame, anger, or resentment) that our cultural and language training has taught us to use (Barrett et al., 2007). Models like this one are valuable because they incorporate research on language and culture in an effort to better understand the labeling processes involved in human emotional experience.

"In Review: Theories of Emotion" summarizes key elements of the theories we have discussed. Research on these theories suggests that both bodily responses (including facial responses) and the cognitive interpretation of those responses add to emotional experience. So does cognitive appraisal of events themselves. In addition,

Improve Your Grade
Tutorial: Three Theories of Emotion

In Review

THEORIES OF EMOTIONS

THEORY	SOURCE OF EMOTIONS	EXAMPLE
James-Lange	Emotions are created by awareness of specific patterns of peripheral (autonomic) responses.	Anger is associated with increased blood flow in the hands and feet; fear is associated with decreased blood flow in these areas.
Cannon-Bard	The brain generates direct experiences of emotions.	Stimulation of certain brain areas can create pleasant or unpleasant emotions.
Cognitive (Schachter-Singer, Lazarus)	Cognitive interpretation of events and of physiological reactions to events shapes emotional experiences.	Autonomic arousal can be experienced as anxiety or excitement, depending on how it is labeled. A single event can lead to different emotions, depending on whether it is perceived as threatening or challenging.

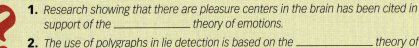

1. Research showing that there are pleasure centers in the brain has been cited in support of the _____ theory of emotions.

2. The use of polygraphs in lie detection is based on the _____ theory of emotions.

3. The process of attribution is most important to _____ theories of emotions.

WHAT ARE THEY FEELING? ▲

People's emotions are usually "written on their faces." Jot down what emotions you think these people are feeling, and then look at the answer shown at the bottom of page 336 to see how well you "read" their emotions.

Learn BY Doing

the brain can apparently generate emotional experience independent of physiological arousal. So emotions are probably both in the heart and in the head (including the face). The most basic emotions probably occur directly within the brain, whereas the many shades of emotions probably arise from attributions, categorization, and other cognitive interpretations of physiological responses (Barrett et al., 2007).

The issue of which, if any, component of emotion is primary remains a topic of lively debate. Each of the emotion theories we have discussed has helped psychological scientists better understand how the various components interact to produce emotional experience. Cognitive appraisal theories have been especially useful in studying and treating stress-related emotional problems (see the chapters on health, stress, and coping; psychological disorders; and treatment of psychological disorders).

Communicating Emotion

❯ *Which emotional expressions are innate and which are learned?*

So far, we have described emotions and how people experience them. Let's now consider how people communicate emotions to one another.

One way they do this is, of course, through words. Some people describe their feelings relatively simply and mainly in terms of pleasantness or unpleasantness; others include information about the intensity of their emotions (Barrett, 1995; Barrett et al., 2001, 2007). In general, women are more likely than men to talk about their emotions and the complexity of their feelings (Barrett et al., 2000; Kring & Gordon, 1998). Humans also communicate emotion through the movement and posture of their bodies (de Gelder et al., 2004; Hadjikhani & de Gelder, 2003), through their tone of voice, and especially through their facial movements and expressions.

Imagine a woman watching television. You can see her face but not what she sees on the screen. She might be deep in complex thought, perhaps comparing her investment decisions with those of the experts being interviewed on CNBC. Or she might be thinking of nothing at all as she loses herself in a rerun of *Seinfeld*. In other words, you can't tell much about what she is thinking just by looking at her. But if the TV program creates an emotional experience, you will be able to make a reasonably accurate guess about which emotion she is feeling based on her facial expressions. The human face can create thousands of different expressions, and people—especially females—are good at detecting them (McClure, 2000; Zajonc, 1998). Observers can see even very small facial movements: a twitch of the mouth can carry a lot of information (Ambadar, Schooler, & Cohn, 2005). Are emotional facial expressions innate or are they learned? And how are they used in communicating emotion?

Innate Expressions of Emotion

Charles Darwin observed that some facial expressions seem to be universal (Darwin, 1872). He proposed that these expressions are genetically determined, passed on biologically from one generation to the next. The facial expressions seen today, said Darwin, are those that have been most effective over the centuries for telling others something about how a person is feeling. If someone is scowling with teeth clenched, for example, you will probably assume that the person is angry. And you will be unlikely to choose that particular moment to ask for a loan (Marsh, Ambady, & Kleck, 2005).

Infants provide one source of evidence that some facial expressions are innate. Newborns do not have to be taught to grimace in pain, to smile in pleasure, or to blink when startled (Balaban, 1995). Even blind infants, who cannot imitate adults' expressions, show the same emotional expressions as do sighted infants (Goodenough, 1932).

A second line of evidence for innate facial expressions comes from studies showing that for the most basic emotions, people in all cultures show similar facial responses to similar emotional stimuli (Hejmadi, Davidson, & Rozin, 2000; Matsumoto & Willingham, 2006; Zajonc, 1998). Participants in these studies looked at photographs of people's faces and then tried to name the emotion each person was feeling. The pattern of facial

THE UNIVERSAL SMILE ▶

The idea that some emotional expressions are inborn is supported by the fact that the facial movement pattern we call a smile is related to happiness, pleasure, and other positive emotions in cultures throughout the world.

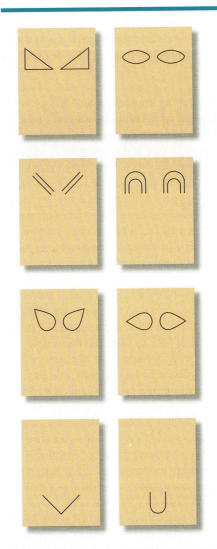

FIGURE 8.10 ■ **ELEMENTS OF CEREMONIAL FACIAL MASKS THAT CONVEY THREAT**

Certain geometric patterns are common to threatening masks in many cultures. "Scary" Halloween pumpkins tend to include these patterns, too. When people in various cultures were asked which member of each of these pairs was more threatening, they consistently chose those containing triangular and diagonal elements (shown here on the left). Cover this caption, then ask a few friends to try the same task. How many of them chose the elements on the left as being more threatening?

Learn BY Doing

movements we call a smile, for example, is universally related to positive emotions. Sadness is almost always accompanied by slackened muscle tone and a "long" face. Likewise, in almost all cultures, people contort their faces in a similar way when shown something they find disgusting. And a furrowed brow is frequently associated with frustration or unpleasantness (Ekman, 1994).

Anger is also linked with a facial expression recognized by almost all cultures. One study examined the ceremonial masks seen in 18 Western and non-Western cultures (Aronoff, Barclay, & Stevenson, 1988). In all these cultures, angry, threatening masks contained similar elements, such as triangular eyes and diagonal lines on the cheeks. In particular, angular and diagonal elements carry the impression of threat (see Figure 8.10).

Social and Cultural Influences on Emotional Expression

Not all basic emotional expressions are innate or universal (Ekman, 1993). Some are learned through contact with a particular culture, and all of them, even innate expressions, are flexible enough to change as necessary in the social situations in which they occur (Fernández-Dols & Ruiz-Belda, 1995). For example, facial expressions become more intense and change more frequently when people are imagining social scenes as opposed to solitary scenes (Fridlund et al., 1990). Similarly, facial expressions in response to odors tend to be more intense when others are watching than when people are alone (Jancke & Kaufmann, 1994).

Further, although some basic emotional facial expressions are recognized by all cultures (Hejmadi, Davidson, & Rozin, 2000), even these can be interpreted differently depending on body language and environmental cues. For example, research participants interpreted a particular expression as disgust when it appeared on the face of a person who was holding a dirty diaper, but that same expression was seen as anger when it was digitally superimposed on a person in a fighting stance (Aviezer et al., 2008). There is even a certain degree of cultural variation when it comes to recognizing some emotions (Russell, 1995). In one study, Japanese and North American people agreed about which facial expressions signaled happiness, surprise, and sadness, but they frequently disagreed about which faces showed anger, disgust, and fear (Matsumoto & Ekman, 1989). Members of cultures such as the Fore of Papua New Guinea agree even less with people in Western cultures on the labeling of facial expressions (Russell, 1994). People from different cultures may also differ in the way they interpret emotions expressed by tone of voice (Mesquita & Frijda, 1992). An example is provided by a study showing that Taiwanese participants were best at recognizing a sad tone of voice, whereas Dutch participants were best at recognizing happy tones (Van Bezooijen, Otto, & Heenan, 1983).

People learn how to express certain emotions in ways specified by cultural rules. Suppose you say, "I just bought a new car," and all your friends stick their tongues out at you. In North America, this display probably means they are envious or resentful. But in some regions of China, it expresses surprise.

Even smiles can vary as people learn to use them to communicate certain feelings. Paul Ekman and his colleagues categorized seventeen types of smiles, including "false smiles," which fake enjoyment, and "masking smiles," which hide unhappiness. They called the smile that occurs with real happiness the *Duchenne smile* (pronounced "do-SHEN"), after the French researcher who first noticed a difference between spontaneous, happy smiles and posed smiles. A genuine Duchenne smile includes contractions of the muscles around the eyes (creating a distinctive wrinkling of the skin in these areas) as well as contractions of the muscles that raise the lips and cheeks. Few people can successfully contract the muscles around the eyes during a posed smile, so this feature can be used to distinguish "lying smiles" from genuine ones (Frank, Ekman, & Friesen, 1993).

Learning About Emotions   The effects of learning are seen in a child's growing range of emotional expressions. Although infants begin with a set of innate emotional responses, they soon learn to imitate facial expressions and use them to express a wide range of emotions. In time, these expressions become more precise and personalized, so that a particular expression conveys a clear message to anyone who knows that person well.

If facial expressions become too personalized, however, no one will know what the expressions mean and they will fail to bring responses from others. Operant shaping, described in the chapter on learning, probably helps keep emotional expressions within certain limits. If you could not see other people's facial expressions or observe their responses to yours, you might show fewer, or less intense, facial signs of emotion. In fact, as congenitally blind people grow older, their facial expressions tend to become less animated (Izard, 1977).

As children grow, they learn an *emotion culture*—rules that govern what emotions are appropriate in what circumstances and what emotional expressions are allowed. These rules can vary between genders and from culture to culture (LaFrance, Hecht, & Paluck, 2003; Matsumoto et al., 2005; Tsai, Levenson, & McCoy, 2006). For example, TV news cameras showed that men in the U.S. military being deployed to a war zone tended to keep their emotions in check as they said goodbye to wives, girlfriends, and parents. However, many male soldiers in Italy—where mother-son ties are particularly strong—wailed with dismay and wept openly as they left. In a laboratory study, when viewing a distressing movie with a group of peers, Japanese students exerted much more control over their facial expressions than did North American students. When they watched the film while alone, however, the Japanese students' faces showed the same emotional expressions as those of the North American students (Ekman, Friesen, & Ellsworth, 1972).

Emotion cultures also shape how people describe and categorize feelings, resulting in both similarities and differences across cultures (Russell, 1991). At least five of the seven basic emotions listed in an ancient Chinese book called the *Li Chi*—joy, anger, sadness, fear, love, disliking, and liking—are considered primary emotions by most Western theorists. Yet although English has more than 500 emotion-related words, some emotion words in other languages have no English meaning. The Czech word *litost* apparently has no English word equivalent: "It designates a feeling that is the synthesis of many others; grief, sympathy, remorse, and an indefinable longing. . . . Litost is a state of torment caused by a sudden insight into one's own miserable self" (Russell, 1991). The Japanese word *ijirashii* also has no English equivalent; it describes the feeling of seeing a praiseworthy person overcoming an obstacle (Russell, 1991).

Similarly, other cultures have no equivalent for some English emotion words. Many cultures do not see anger and sadness as different, for example. The Ilongot, a headhunting group in the Philippines, have only one word, *liget*, for both anger and grief (Russell, 1991). Tahitians have different words for forty-six types of anger but no word for sadness and, apparently, no concept of it. One westerner described a Tahitian

---

The photo on page 334 shows the wife and daughter of a U.S. Marine helicopter pilot waving goodbye as he departs for duty in a war zone. Their emotions probably included sadness, anxiety, worry, dread, uncertainty, hope, and perhaps anger.

man as being sad over separation from his wife and child. The man himself said that he felt *pe'a pe'a*—a general word for feeling ill, troubled, or fatigued—and did not attribute it to the separation.

Social Referencing   Facial expressions, tone of voice, body postures, and gestures can do more than communicate emotion. They can also influence other people's behavior, especially people who are not sure what to do. An inexperienced chess player, for instance, might reach out to move the queen, catch sight of a spectator's pained expression, and infer that another move would be better. The process of letting another person's emotional state guide our own behavior is called *social referencing* (Campos, 1980). This process begins early; even three-month-old infants will look in the direction in which an adult's eyes have moved (Hood, Willen, & Driver, 1998).

The visual-cliff studies described in the sensation and perception chapter have been used to create an uncertain situation for infants. To reach its mother, an infant in these experiments must cross the visual cliff. If the apparent drop-off is very small or very large, there is no doubt about what to do. One-year-olds crawl across in the first case and stay put in the second case. However, if the apparent drop-off is just large enough (say, two feet) to create uncertainty, the infant relies on its mother's facial expressions to decide what to do. In one study, mothers were asked to make either a fearful or a joyful face. When the mothers made a fearful face, no infant crossed the glass floor. But when they made a joyful face, most infants crossed (Sorce et al., 1981). Here is yet another example of the adaptive value of sending, and receiving, emotional communications.

ACTIVE REVIEW ▶ Chapter 8

Motivation *and* Emotion

As noted in the introductory chapter, all of psychology's subfields are related to one another. Our discussion of motivational conflicts and stress illustrates just one way that the topic of this chapter, motivation and emotion, is linked to the subfield of health psychology, discussed in the chapter

on health, stress, and coping. The Linkages diagram shows ties to two other subfields, and there are many more ties throughout the book. Looking for linkages among subfields will help you see how they all fit together and help you better appreciate the big picture that is psychology.

linkages

How does the brain know when we're hungry? *(ans. on p. 304)*

Can motivational conflicts cause stress? *(ans. on p. 322)*

Why do some people take more risks than others? *(ans. on p. 435)*

Chapter 2
Biology and Behavior

Chapter 10
Health, Stress, and Coping

Chapter 11
Personality

SUMMARY ▶

Motivation refers to factors that influence the initiation, direction, intensity, and persistence of behavior. Emotions and motivation are often linked: motivation can influence emotions, and people are often motivated to seek certain emotions.

Concepts and Theories of Motivation

◗ *Where does motivation come from?*

Focusing on a *motive* often reveals a single theme within apparently diverse behaviors. The many sources of motivation fall into four categories: biological factors, emotional factors, cognitive factors, and social factors.

An early argument held that motivation is based on *instinctive behaviors*—automatic, involuntary, and unlearned action patterns consistently "released" by particular stimuli. Modern versions of the *instinct doctrine* are seen in evolutionary accounts of helping, aggression, mate selection, and other aspects of social behavior. *Drive reduction theory* is based on *homeostasis,* a tendency to maintain equilibrium in a physical or behavioral process. When disruption of equilibrium creates *needs* of some kind, people are motivated to reduce the resulting *drives* by behaving in some way that satisfies the needs and restores balance. *Primary drives* are unlearned; *secondary drives* are learned. According to the *arousal theory* of motivation, people are motivated to behave in ways that maintain a level of *physiological arousal* that is optimal for their functioning. Finally, *incentive theory* highlights behaviors that are motivated by attaining desired stimuli (positive incentives) and avoiding undesirable ones (negative incentives). Each of these theories has contributed to our understanding of the basis for various kinds of motivated behavior.

Eating

◗ *What makes me start eating and stop eating?*

Eating is controlled by a complex mixture of learning, culture, and biochemistry. The desire to eat (*hunger*) and the satisfaction (*satiation*) of that desire (*satiety*) that leads us to stop eating,

depend on signals from the gut and from blood-borne substances such as glucose, fatty acids, amino acids, insulin, and leptin. Activity in the ventromedial nucleus of the hypothalamus results in satiety, whereas activity in the lateral hypothalamus results in hunger. Other areas of the hypothalamus, such as the paraventricular nucleus, are also involved. Further, several neurotransmitters act in various regions of the hypothalamus to motivate the eating of certain types of foods. Eating may also be influenced by the flavor of food and by the pleasure it can bring. Food selection is influenced by many factors, including social contexts and cultural traditions.

Obesity has been linked to overconsumption of certain kinds of foods, low energy metabolism, genetic factors, and even viruses. People suffering from *anorexia nervosa* starve themselves. Those who suffer from *bulimia* engage in binge eating, followed by purging through self-induced vomiting or laxatives.

Sexual Behavior

◗ *How often does the average person have sex?*

Sexual motivation and behavior result from a rich interplay of biology and culture. Sexual stimulation produces a *sexual response cycle,* a predictable physiological pattern of *sexual arousal* before, during, and after sexual activity. *Sex hormones,* which include male hormones (*androgens*) and female hormones (*estrogens* and *progestational hormones,* or progestins), occur in different relative amounts in both sexes. They can have organizing effects, which create physical differences in the brain, and activating effects, which temporarily increase the desire for sex.

Gender-role learning, educational experiences, media influences, and family dynamics are examples of cultural factors that can bring about variations in sexual attitudes and behaviors. Sexual orientation—*heterosexuality, homosexuality* (gay or lesbian), or *bisexuality*—is increasingly viewed as a sociocultural variable

that affects many other aspects of behavior and mental processes. Although undoubtedly shaped by a lifetime of learning, sexual orientation appears to have strong biological roots.

Common male **sexual *function disturbances*** include erectile disorder and premature ejaculation. Females may experience such problems as sexual arousal disorder.

Achievement Motivation

◗ *Why do some people try harder than others to succeed?*

People gain esteem from achievement in many areas, including the workplace. The motive to succeed is called *achievement motivation,* or the *need for achievement.* Individuals with high achievement motivation strive for excellence, persist despite failures, and set challenging but realistic goals.

Workers are most satisfied when they are working toward their own goals and getting concrete feedback. Jobs that offer clear and specific goals, a variety of tasks, individual responsibility, and other intrinsic rewards are the most motivating. People tend to have a characteristic level of happiness, or *well-being,* that is not necessarily related to the attainment of money, status, or other material goals.

Relations and Conflicts Among Motives

◗ *Which motives move me most?*

People's behavior reflects many motives, some of which may be in conflict. Maslow proposed a hierarchy of five types of human motives, from meeting basic physiological needs to attaining self-actualization. Motives at the lowest levels, according to Maslow, must be at least partially satisfied before people can be motivated by higher level goals. Alderfer's three-level version does not assume that needs are met in a particular order.

Four types of motivational conflict have been identified: approach-approach, avoidance-avoidance, approach-avoidance, and multiple approach-avoidance conflicts. These conflicts act as stressors, and people caught in them often experience physical and psychological problems.

The Nature of Emotions

▶ *How do feelings differ from thoughts?*

Emotions are temporary experiences with negative or positive qualities that are felt with some intensity as happening to the  self, are generated in part by interpretation of a situation, and are accompanied by both learned and innate physical responses.

Several brain mechanisms are involved in emotions, including the amygdala in the limbic system. The expression of emotions through involuntary facial movement is controlled by the extrapyramidal motor system. Voluntary facial movements are controlled by the pyramidal motor system. The brain's right and left hemispheres play somewhat different roles in emotions. In addition to specific brain mechanisms, both the **sympathetic nervous system** and the **parasympathetic nervous system,** which are divisions of the autonomic nervous system, are involved in physiological changes that accompany emotional activation. The **fight-or-flight reaction,** for example, follows from activation of the sympathetic nervous system.

Theories of Emotion

▶ *Are emotions in the heart, in the head, or both?*

James said that pe-  ripheral physiological responses are the primary source of emotions and that awareness of these responses creates emotional experience. James's peripheral theory is supported by evidence that, at least for several basic emotions, physiological responses are distinguishable enough for emotions to be generated in this way. Distinct facial expressions are linked to particular patterns of physiological change.

Cannon's central theory of emotions proposes that emotional experience is independent of bodily responses and that there is a direct experience of emotions based on activity of the central nervous system. Updated versions of this theory suggest that various parts of the central nervous system may be involved in different emotions and different aspects of emotional experience. Some pathways in the brain, such as the pathway from the thalamus to the amygdala, allow strong emotions to occur before conscious thought can take place. Specific parts of the brain appear to be responsible for the feelings of pleasure or pain in emotions.

Cognitive theories of emotions include the Schachter-Singer theory. It suggests that physiological responses are primary sources of emotion but that interpretation of these responses in light of the situation is required to label the emotion. This interpretation process depends on **attribution.** Attributing arousal from one situation to stimuli in another situation is explained by **excitation-transfer theory**, which suggests that

physiological arousal stemming from one situation can intensify the emotion experienced in a second situation. Other cognitive theorists such as Lazarus have argued that emotional experience is significantly affected by how we interpret events themselves, not just by how we interpret physiological responses to those events.

Communicating Emotion

▶ *Which emotional expressions are innate, and which are learned?*

In humans, emo-  tions can be communicated by words, voice tones, postures, bodily movements, and facial movements and expressions. Darwin suggested that certain facial expressions of emotions are innate and universal and that these expressions evolved because they effectively communicate one creature's emotional condition to other creatures. Some facial expressions of basic emotions do appear to be innate, and certain facial movements are universally associated with certain emotions.

Other emotional expressions are learned, and even innate expressions are modified by learning and social contexts. As children grow, they learn an emotion culture, the rules of emotional expression appropriate to their culture. Accordingly, the same emotion may be communicated by different facial expressions in different cultures. Especially in ambiguous situations, one person's emotional expressions may serve to guide another person's behavior, a phenomenon called **social referencing.**

Learn BY Doing ▶

Put It in Writing

Write a page or two about what goals you hope to achieve in life, what motivates you to strive for them, and how important it is for you to reach them. In light of our discussion about achievement and well-being, consider the question of whether reaching your goals will make you happy and contented or leave you always wanting more.

Personal Learning Activity

Videotape a session in which you ask a friend four questions, such as "Who was the best teacher you ever had?" "What's the strangest thing

that ever happened to you?" "What is your most surprising talent?" or "Where would you most like to live?" Ask your friend to give truthful answers to two of these questions but to lie as convincingly as possible while answering the other two. Now play the tape for a group of people and ask them to say which answers are true and which are lies. How well did your participants do? If they are like most people, they probably were right about half the time on this lie detection task (DePaulo, 1994). Did the participants' accuracy differ depending on whether or not they knew the person on the tape? If so, why do you think this was so? *For additional projects, see the Personal Learning Activities in the corresponding chapter of the study guide that accompanies this text.*

Take Action to Learn More ▶

Now that you have finished reading this chapter, how about exploring some of the ideas and information that you found most interesting? Here are some courses, books, films, and Internet resources to get you started. Enjoy!

Courses

Health Psychology
Motivation and Emotion
Human Sexuality
Personality
Industrial and Organizational Psychology

Movies

A Mighty Wind; Chocolat; It's a Wonderful Life; Patch Adams; Waitress; When Harry Met Sally. Emotions.

The Bishop's Wife; The Edge; Entrapment; Holiday; The Milagro Beanfield War; The Shadow; The Truth About Cats and Dogs. Motivational conflict.

The Heidi Chronicles. Secondary drives.

Being BAWSI; Super Size Me; Two Angry Moms. Diet and obesity.

As Good As It Gets; The Birdcage; Boys Don't Cry; La Cage aux Folles; Southern Comfort; Closer; Normal; Venus Boyz; Wild Reeds; Wilde. Sexual orientation.

Bach's Fight for Freedom; Best in Show; Cool Runnings; Dead Poets Society; Endurance; Fame; The Family Man; Rudy; Waiting for Guffman; Wall Street. Achievement motivation.

Books

GELSEY KIRKLAND, *Dancing on My Grave* (Doubleday, 1987). Eating disorders.

JOYCE MURDOCH AND DEB PRICE, *Courting Justice: Gay Men and Lesbians v. the Supreme Court* (Basic Books, 2001). Homosexuality and the law.

LILLIAN RUBIN, *Intimate Strangers: Men and Women Together* (Harper, 1983). Gender differences in intimacy and sexuality.

DAVID C. EDWARDS, *Motivation and Emotion: Evolutionary, Physiological, Cognitive, and Social Influences* (AltaMira Press, 1998). A basic introduction to the field of motivation and emotion.

STEVEN PINKER, *The Blank Slate: The Modern Denial of Human Nature* (Viking Press, 2002). Wide-ranging description of evolutionary and genetic explanations of motivation.

DAVID GOLDSTEIN (ED.), *The Management of Eating Disorders and Obesity* (Humana Press, 2005). A summary of research on and treatment of eating disorders.

WILLIAM H. MASTERS, VIRGINIA E. JOHNSON, AND ROBERT C. KOLODNY, *Heterosexuality* (Grammercy Press, 1998). An overview of sexuality between males and females.

ALDERT VRIJ, *Detecting Lies and Deceit: The Psychology of Lying and Implications for Professional Practice* (Wiley, 2000). A summary of various approaches.

DAVID LYKKEN, *Happiness: The Nature and Nurture of Joy and Contentment* (Griffin, 2000). A summary of research on the "happiness set point" and other aspects of well-being.

ANTONIA DAMASIO, *Looking for Spinoza* (Harcourt, 2003). A discussion of emotions as bodily sensations.

The Web

Essentials of Psychology Book Companion Website

www.cengage.com/psychology/bernstein

Visit the book companion website to access a wealth of resources, including chapter outlines, flashcards, web links, tutorial quizzes, and more!

CENGAGENOW™ Just what you need to know NOW! Spend time on what you need to master rather than on information you already have learned. Take a pre-test for this chapter, and CengageNOW will generate a personalized study plan based on your results. The study plan will identify the topics you need to review and direct you to online resources to help you master those topics. You can then take a post-test to help you determine the concepts you have mastered and what you will need to work on. Try it out! Go to www.cengage.com/login to sign in with an access code or to purchase access to this product.

Review of Key Terms ▶

Can you define each of the key terms in the chapter? Check your definitions against those on the pages shown in parentheses in the following list or in the Glossary at the end of the book.

achievement motivation (p. 317)
androgens (p. 311)
anorexia nervosa (p. 308)
arousal theory (p. 301)
attribution (p. 331)
bisexuality (p. 313)
bulimia (p. 309)
drive (p. 300)
drive reduction theory (p. 300)

emotions (p. 324)
estrogens (p. 311)
excitation-transfer theory (p. 332)
fight-or-flight reaction (p. 327)
heterosexuality (p. 313)
homeostasis (p. 300)
homosexuality (p. 313)
hunger (p. 303)
incentive theory (p. 302)
instinct doctrine (p. 299)
instinctive behaviors (p. 299)
motivation (p. 298)
motive (p. 299)
needs (p. 300)

obesity (p. 306)
parasympathetic nervous system (p. 327)
physiological arousal (p. 301)
primary drives (p. 300)
progestational hormones (p. 311)
satiation (satiety) (p. 303)
secondary drives (p. 300)
sex hormones (p. 311)
sexual arousal (p. 311)
sexual function disturbances (p. 316)
sexual response cycle (p. 311)
sympathetic nervous system (p. 327)
well-being (subjective well-being) (p. 320)

MULTIPLE-CHOICE ▶ Self Test

Select the best answer for each of the following questions. Then check your responses against the Answer Key at the end of the book.

1. Although most researchers do not believe in instinct theories of motivation, psychologists who advocate _____ theory argue that many aspects of human behavior are motivated by efforts to pass on our genes to the next generation.

   a. drive reduction
   b. evolutionary
   c. arousal
   d. incentive

2. Steve is cold, so he turns up the thermostat in his house. As soon as it starts to get too warm, the thermostat shuts off the furnace. This process is similar to the biological concept of _____.

   a. homeostasis
   b. secondary drive
   c. incentive
   d. arousal

3. Lisbeth and Harriet work as instructors in an exercise class. After class, Lisbeth prefers to go home and read quietly, whereas Harriet is ready to party. Which theory of motivation *best* explains the difference between these two women?

   a. Drive reduction
   b. Instinct
   c. Evolutionary
   d. Arousal

4. Monica wants her daughter to get high grades, so she offers her $10 for each A that she earns and $5 for each B. Monica appears to believe in the _____ theory of motivation.

   a. drive reduction
   b. incentive
   c. evolutionary
   d. arousal

5. Ahmed is desperate to lose weight. To keep from eating, he buys an electrical device that allows him to stimulate various areas of his brain. Which areas should he stimulate if he wants his brain to help him reduce food intake?

   a. Ventromedial nucleus and paraventricular nucleus
   b. Lateral hypothalamus and ventromedial nucleus
   c. Lateral hypothalamus and paraventricular nucleus
   d. Thalamus and pineal gland

6. Ronia is on a diet—again! She is *most* likely to eat less food if she _____.

   a. eats only with friends, never alone
   b. eats only one or two kinds of food at each meal
   c. changes her food culture
   d. focuses on the flavor of what she eats

7. Dr. Stefan is working in the emergency room when a very dehydrated young woman comes in. She is of normal weight, but a medical exam reveals nutritional imbalances and intestinal damage. The woman is *most* likely suffering from _____.

   a. anorexia nervosa
   b. bulimia
   c. lateral hypothalamic disorder
   d. ventromedial disorder

8. The University of Chicago's National Health and Social Life Survey found that people in the United States _____.

   a. are more sexually active than previously thought
   b. have sex more often if they are not in an exclusive relationship
   c. have sex less often and with fewer people than previously thought
   d. do not enjoy sex very much

9. According to the Thinking Critically section of this chapter, sexual orientation is *most* likely influenced by _____.

   a. prenatal hormones
   b. genetic factors
   c. sociocultural learning
   d. all of the above

10. Edwina wants her son, Egbert, to develop high achievement motivation and to be successful in life. According to research on the need for achievement, Edwina should do all of the following *except* _____.

    a. encourage Egbert to try difficult tasks
    b. encourage Egbert to avoid failure at all costs
    c. give praise and rewards for success
    d. read achievement-oriented stories to him

11. Liang wants his employees to work hard. As a psychologist specializing in motivation, you tell Liang that the *best* way to increase employee performance is to _____.

    a. increase their pay and benefits
    b. allow them to set their own goals
    c. remind them regularly of the need to do better
    d. keep all tasks as simple as possible

12. According to Maslow, which of the following would you *most* likely do first if you were shipwrecked on a desert island?

    a. Look for food and fresh water
    b. Look for firewood
    c. Start keeping a diary
    d. Build a place to live

13. Jill would like to send her son to an expensive private school, but this would create a financial hardship for her. Jill is faced with a(n) _____ motivational conflict.

    a. approach-approach
    b. avoidance-avoidance
    c. approach-avoidance
    d. multiple approach-avoidance

14. Which of the following is *not* a characteristic associated with emotion? They _____.

    a. tend to last a relatively short time
    b. can be triggered by thoughts
    c. are always intense
    d. can motivate behavior

15. When people are afraid to do something, they are said to have "cold feet." The fact that fear is associated with decreased blood flow to the feet and hands supports _____ theory of emotion.
    a. James's peripheral
    b. Cannon's central
    c. Schachter's cognitive
    d. Lazarus's cognitive

16. After she finished a vigorous workout, Lydia saw Thaddeus walk into the gym and instantly fell in love. This is an example of _____, which is consistent with _____ theory of emotion.
    a. social referencing; James's
    b. social referencing; Schachter's
    c. excitation transfer; James's
    d. excitation transfer; Schachter's

17. When Yatsira saw someone trying to open her car door while she was stopped at a light, her heart raced and at the exact same time she felt fear. This is *most* consistent with _____ theory of emotion.
    a. James's
    b. Cannon's
    c. Schachter's
    d. Lazarus's

18. As Jarrod got older, he learned that he could not express his anger by throwing his toys. Jarrod is learning _____.
    a. to use facial feedback
    b. Darwin's universal rules
    c. to use social referencing
    d. his emotion culture

19. Suppose that Dick, Sally, Harry, and Tommy, the space aliens on the TV show *Third Rock from the Sun,* first came to earth in your backyard. They tell you they want to learn how to communicate their emotions so that humans will understand them. What should you focus on teaching them?
    a. Body postures
    b. Facial movements
    c. Hand gestures
    d. Voice inflections

20. Sam is unsure how to react to a comment from one of his friends, so he glances at his girlfriend, Diane, to see what her reaction is. In doing so, he is using _____.
    a. facial feedback
    b. social referencing
    c. attribution
    d. excitation transfer

© LWA Dann Tardif/Jupiterimages

9 Human Development

A colt begins walking within an hour of being born, but it typically takes a human baby about a year to reach this milestone—a year in which the baby also first smiles, eats solid food, learns to recognize familiar people and objects, and gets ready to talk, to name just a few accomplishments. Four years later, the child is entering school, where learning, development, and change continue. Ten years after that, the adolescent is still changing and developing, becoming more independent and mature with each passing day. In young adulthood, change and development take the form of decisions about jobs, families, and relationships—and the effects of these decisions echo throughout adulthood. Development occurs in late adulthood too, as the person adjusts to the joys and challenges of growing older. Developmental psychologists explore how people change and grow over the course of the life-span.

© Najlah Feanny/Corbis Saba

A DEADLY CHILD ▲

Andrew Golden was barely out of diapers when he was given camouflage clothing and taught to fire a hunting rifle. In March 1998, at the age of 11, he and a 13-year-old friend, Mitchell Johnson, used their rifles to kill four classmates and a teacher at their elementary school in Jonesboro, Arkansas. Many youngsters learn to hunt; what led these two to commit murder? Researchers in developmental psychology study the genetic and environmental factors that underlie violent aggression and many other patterns of behavior and mental processes.

developmental psychology The psychological specialty that documents the course of people's social, emotional, moral, and intellectual development over the life-span.

Over the past several years, the tragedy of shooting sprees in schools has plagued all too many towns and cities in the United States and Canada, and we continue to hear news of the thwarted mass murder plots of disgruntled students (Logue, 2008; Moser, 2008). Though the number of school homicides has been dropping, this trend is of little solace to the friends and families of the students or teachers who have died or been injured in these horrific events. Why do these things happen? In each case, the killers were boys ranging in age from six to eighteen. Had they watched too many violent movies and television shows? Were their actions the fault of a "gun culture" that allows children access to firearms? Had they been victims of abuse and neglect? Were their parents too strict—or not strict enough? Did they come from "broken homes" or witness physical violence between family members? Did they behave violently because they were going through a difficult "stage," because they had not been taught right from wrong, because they wanted to impress their peers, because males are more aggressive in general, or because their brains were "defective"? Or were they just "bad kids"?

Developmental psychologists try to find answers to questions like these. They explore the times when certain kinds of behavior first appear, how those behaviors change with age, and whether the changes are sudden or gradual. They look into how development in one area, such as moral reasoning, relates to development in other areas, such as aggressive behavior. Developmental psychologists attempt to discover whether everyone develops at the same rate and if they do not, whether slow starters ever catch up to early bloomers. They ask how and why some children develop into well-adjusted, socially competent, caring individuals whereas others become murderers or why some adolescents go on to win honors in college and others drop out of high school. They seek to explain how development through infancy, childhood, and adolescence is affected by both genetics and the environment. They analyze the extent to which development is a product of what we arrive with at birth (our inherited, biological *nature*) and the extent to which it is a product of what the world provides (the nurture of the environment). And of course, they also study the development that occurs over the years of adulthood and try to determine how these changes are related to earlier abilities and the events of life. In short, **developmental psychology** is concerned with the course and causes of developmental changes over a person's entire lifetime.

This chapter focuses on many of these changes, beginning with the physical and biological changes that take place from the moment of conception to the moment of birth. ■

Exploring Human Development

▶ *What does "genetic influence" mean?*

Arguments about how nature and nurture affect development can be traced back through centuries of philosophy. In essays published in the 1690s, the British empiricist philosopher John Locke argued for the importance of nurture. He believed that what happens in childhood has a profound and permanent effect on the individual. Empiricists saw the newborn as a blank slate, or *tabula rasa*. Adults write on that slate, said Locke, as they teach children about the world and how to behave in it. About seventy years later, Jean-Jacques Rousseau (pronounced "roo-SOH"), a French philosopher, argued just the opposite, claiming that children are capable of discovering how the world operates and how they should behave without instruction from adults. According to Rousseau, children should be allowed to grow as nature commands, with little guidance or pressure from parents.

The first American psychologist to investigate systematically the role of nature in behavior was Arnold Gesell (pronounced "geh-ZELL"). In the early 1900s, Gesell made many observations of children of all ages. He found that motor skills, such as standing and walking, picking up a cube, and throwing a ball, develop in a fixed sequence of stages in all children, as illustrated in Figure 9.1. Gesell argued that the order of the stages and

FIGURE 9.1 ■ MOTOR DEVELOPMENT

When did you start walking? The left end of each bar indicates the age at which 25 percent of infants were able to perform a particular behavior; 50 percent of the babies were performing the behavior at the age indicated by the vertical line in the bars; the right end indicates the age at which 90 percent could do so (Frankenberg & Dodds, 1967). Although different infants, especially in different cultures, achieve milestones of motor development at slightly different ages, all infants—regardless of their ethnicity, social class, or temperament—achieve them in the same order.

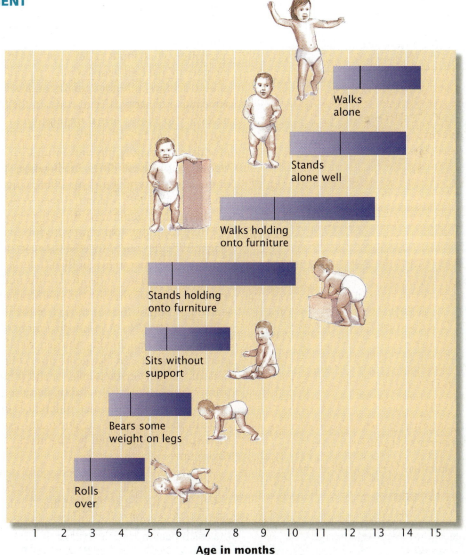

Walks alone

Stands alone well

Walks holding onto furniture

Stands holding onto furniture

Sits without support

Bears some weight on legs

Rolls over

1 2 3 4 5 6 7 8 9 10 11 12 13 14 15

Age in months

the age at which they appear are determined by nature and are relatively unaffected by nurture. Only under extreme conditions, such as famine, war, or poverty, he claimed, are children thrown off their biologically programmed timetable. This type of natural growth or change, which unfolds in a fixed sequence relatively independent of the environment, is called **maturation.** The broader term *development* encompasses not only maturation but also the behavioral and mental processes that are influenced by learning.

John B. Watson disagreed with Gesell's views. He argued that the environment, not nature, molds and shapes development. As described in the introductory chapter, Watson founded the behaviorist approach to psychology. In the early 1900s he began conducting experiments with children. From these experiments Watson inferred that children learn *everything,* from skills to fears. In his words, "There is no such thing as an inheritance of capacity, talent, temperament, mental constitution and characteristics. These things . . . depend on training that goes on mainly in the cradle" (Watson, 1925, pp. 74–75).

It was the Swiss psychologist Jean Piaget (pronounced "p-ah-ZHAY") who first suggested that nature and nurture work together and that their influences are inseparable and interactive. Through a series of books published from the 1920s until his death in 1980, Piaget's ideas influenced the field of developmental psychology more than those of any other person before or since (Flavell, 1996).

Understanding Genetic Influence

Most developmental psychologists now accept Piaget's idea that both nature and nurture contribute to development. Guided by research in **behavioral genetics,** the study of how genes affect behavior, they explore how genes and the environment influence specific aspects of development. Their studies have demonstrated that nature and nurture jointly contribute to development in two ways. First, nature and nurture operate together to make all people *similar* in some respects. For example, nature influences all of us to achieve milestones of motor development in the same order and at roughly the same rate. But supportive nurture, in the form of proper nutrition and exercise, is also necessary to allow normal maturation to unfold. Second, nature and nurture operate together to make each person *unique.* The nature of inherited genes and the nurture of widely different family and cultural environments produce differences among individuals in athletic abilities, intelligence, speech patterns, personality, and many other dimensions (Brendgen et al., 2008; Ducci & Goldman, 2008; Gregory et al., 2009; Haddad et al., 2008; Malouff, Rooke, & Schutte, 2008; South & Krueger, 2008).

Behavioral geneticists are concerned with the *differences* between individuals or groups of individuals, not with the characteristics of a single individual. Consider height. Whether raised together or apart, identical twins (who have identical genes) are much more similar in height than fraternal twins (who share no more genes than other siblings) or unrelated individuals. This finding suggests that height is more strongly influenced by genes than by the environment. Does this mean that a person who is six feet tall grew, say, four of those feet because of genes and the other two feet because of environment? No. It means that more of the variability in height that we see among people can be explained by the genetic differences among them than by the environmental differences. In fact, genes do account for about 80 to 95 percent of the variability in height. So if a person is taller or shorter than average, genetic factors are probably the primary cause. We say "probably" because genetic influences on height refer only to the origins of average individual differences in the population. So even though the differences in people's heights are due mainly to genetic factors, a particular person's shorter than normal height could be due mainly to an early illness or other growth-stunting environmental factors.

To see how the logic of behavioral genetics applies to conclusions about psychological characteristics, suppose a researcher discovered that a certain personality trait is 50 percent heritable. This finding would mean that approximately half of the *differences between people* on that trait can be explained by genetic factors. It would not mean that each person inherits half of the trait and gets the other half from environmental

maturation   Natural growth or change triggered by biological factors independent of the environment.

behavioral genetics   The study of the effect of genes on behavior.

influences. In other words, the results of behavioral genetics research allow us to draw general conclusions about the influence of nature and nurture on certain characteristics, but those conclusions do not necessarily apply to the origins of a *particular person's* characteristics. Keep in mind, too, that the effects of genes on our traits and behaviors are not always simple or fixed. Complex traits such as intelligence and personality are influenced by many genes as well as by many environmental factors. So genetic influence means just that: *influence* (Malouff, Rooke, & Schutte, 2008; Plomin et al., 2002; South & Krueger, 2008). Genes can affect a trait without completely determining whether that trait will actually appear in a particular individual.

Genes and the Environment

The relative contributions of nature and nurture differ for specific aspects of development, but their influences on all human characteristics are forever intertwined. They are also mutually influential. Just as the environment encourages or discourages the expression of an individual's inherited characteristics, those inherited characteristics determine the individual's environment to some extent. In short, heredity creates predispositions that interact with the immediate environment, including family, teachers, books, and computers (Caspi et al., 2002). This interaction is what produces developmental outcomes. Let's now consider how it all begins.

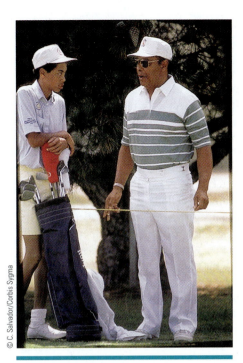

A TIGER IN TRAINING ▲

The development of human behavior is shaped by both heredity and environment—by nature and nurture. The joint and inseparable influence of these two factors in development is perfectly illustrated in the case of professional golfer Tiger Woods, shown here as a youngster with his father, who not only provided some of Tiger's genes but also served as his golf teacher.

Beginnings

▶ *Why should pregnant women stay away from tobacco and alcohol?*

Nowhere are the intertwined contributions of heredity and environment clearer than during the eventful nine months before birth, when a single fertilized egg develops into a functioning newborn infant.

Prenatal Development

The process of development begins when sperm from a father-to-be fertilizes the egg of a mother-to-be and forms a brand-new cell. Most human cells contain 46 **chromosomes** (pronounced "KROH-muh-sohmz"), arranged in 23 matching pairs. Each chromosome is made up of thousands of **genes,** the biochemical units of heredity that govern the development of an individual. Genes, in turn, are composed of **deoxyribonucleic acid (DNA).** (*Deoxyribonucleic* is pronounced "dee-OKS-ee-rye-boh-noo-KLAY-ic.") The DNA in genes provides coded messages that serve as blueprints for constructing every aspect of a physical human being, including eye color, height, blood type, inherited disorders, and the like. All of this information fits in less space than the period that ends this sentence.

New cells in the body are constantly being produced by the division of existing cells. Most of the body's cells divide through a process called *mitosis* (pronounced "mye-TOH-sis"), in which the cell's chromosomes duplicate themselves so that each new cell contains copies of the 23 pairs of chromosomes in the original cell.

A different kind of cell division occurs when a male's sperm cells and a female's egg cells, called *ova,* are formed. This process is called *meiosis* (pronounced "mye-OH-sis"). In meiosis, the chromosome pairs are not copied. Instead, they are randomly split and rearranged, leaving each new sperm and egg cell with just one member of each chromosome pair, or 23 *single* chromosomes. No two of these special new cells are quite the same, and none contains an exact copy of the person who produced it. So, at conception, when a male's sperm penetrates, or *fertilizes,* the female's ovum, a truly new cell is formed. The fertilized cell, called a *zygote,* carries the usual 23 pairs of chromosomes, but half of each pair comes from the mother and half from the father. The zygote represents a unique heritage—a complete genetic code for a new person that combines randomly selected aspects from both parents. The zygote divides first into copies of itself;

chromosomes Structures in every biological cell that contain genetic information in the form of genes.

genes Hereditary units, located on chromosomes, that contain biological instructions inherited from both parents, providing the blueprint for physical development.

deoxyribonucleic acid (DNA) The molecular structure of a gene that provides the genetic code.

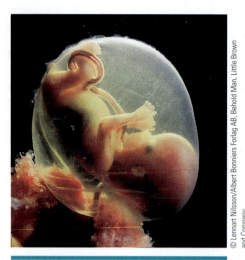

© Lennart Nilsson/Albert Bonniers Forlag AB, Behold Man, Little Brown and Company

A FETUS AT TWELVE WEEKS   ▲

In this photo of a fetus at three months after conception, the umbilical cord and placenta are clearly visible. At this point in prenatal development, the fetus can kick its legs, curl its toes, make a fist, turn its head, squint, open its mouth, swallow, and take a few "breaths" of amniotic fluid.

then it divides and redivides into the billions of specialized cells that form a complete new human being.

Stages of Prenatal Development   The first two weeks after conception are called the *germinal stage* of development. By the end of this stage, the cells of the dividing zygote have formed an **embryo** (pronounced "EM-bree-oh"). Next comes the *embryonic stage* of development, during which the embryo quickly forms a heart, nervous system, stomach, esophagus, and ovaries or testes. By two months after conception, when the embryonic stage ends, the embryo looks decidedly human, with eyes, ears, nose, jaw, mouth, and lips. The tiny arms have elbows, hands, and stubby fingers and the legs have knees, ankles, and toes.

The seven-month period remaining until birth is called the *fetal stage* of prenatal development. During this stage, the various organs grow and start to function. By the end of the third month, the **fetus** can kick, make a fist, turn its head, open its mouth, swallow, and frown. In the sixth month, the eyelids, which have been sealed, open. The fetus is now capable of making sucking movements and has taste buds, eyebrows, eyelashes, and a well-developed grasp.

By the end of the seventh month, the organ systems, though immature, are all functional. In the eighth and ninth months, the fetus can respond to light and touch and it can hear what is going on outside. It can also learn. When it hears its mother's familiar voice, its heart beats a little faster, but the heart slows if the fetus hears a stranger (Kisilevsky et al., 2003).

Prenatal Risks   During prenatal development, a spongy organ called the *placenta* appears and attaches itself to the mother's uterus through an *umbilical cord*. (The cord is detached at birth, but you can see where yours was by looking at your navel.) The placenta sends nutrients from the mother to the developing baby and carries away wastes. It also screens out many potentially harmful substances, including most bacteria. This screening is imperfect, however: gases, viruses, nicotine, alcohol, and other drugs can pass through. Severe damage can occur if the baby's mother takes certain drugs, is exposed to certain toxic substances such as mercury, or has certain illnesses while organs are forming in the embryonic stage (Koger, Schettler, & Weiss, 2005).

Harmful external substances that invade the womb and result in birth defects are called **teratogens** (pronounced "tuh-RAT-uh-jens"). Teratogens are especially damaging in the embryonic stage, because it is a **critical period** in prenatal development, a time during which certain kinds of growth must occur if development is to proceed normally. If the heart, eyes, ears, hands, and feet do not appear during the embryonic stage, they cannot form later on. If they form incorrectly, the defects will be permanent. So even before a mother knows she is pregnant, she may accidentally damage her infant by exposing it to teratogens. For example, a baby whose mother has rubella (German measles) during the third or fourth week after conception has a 50 percent chance of being blind, deaf, or mentally retarded or of having a malformed heart. If the mother has rubella later in the pregnancy, after the infant's eyes, ears, brain, and heart have formed, the likelihood that the baby will have one of these defects is much lower. Later, during the fetal stage, teratogens affect the baby's size, behavior, intelligence, and health rather than the formation of organs and limbs.

Of special concern today are the effects of drugs on infants' development (e.g., Eroglu et al., 2008; Forcelli, & Heinrichs, 2008; Gendle et al., 2004; James et al., 2007; Jones, 2006; Weiss, St. Jonn-Seed, & Harris-Muchell, 2007). Pregnant women who use substances such as cocaine create a substantial risk for their fetuses, which do not yet have the enzymes necessary to break down the drugs. "Cocaine babies" or "crack babies" may be born premature, underweight, tense, and fussy (Inciardi, Surratt, & Saum, 1997; Tronick et al., 2005). They may also suffer delayed physical growth and motor development (Richardson, Goldschmidt, & Larkby, 2007) and are more likely to have behavioral and learning problems (Bada et al., 2007; Singer et al., 2001; Singer et al., 2002; Tan-Laxa et al., 2004). They may display slower-than-normal cognitive processing, too (Mayes et al., 2005), but other aspects of their cognitive abilities are

embryo   The developing individual from two weeks to two months after fertilization.

fetus   The developing individual from the third month after conception until birth.

teratogens   Harmful substances, such as alcohol and other drugs, that can cause birth defects.

critical period   An interval during which certain kinds of growth must occur if development is to proceed normally.

A RARE MULTIPLE BIRTH ▲

When Nadya Suleman delivered eight babies on January 26, 2009, it was only the second time that octuplets have been known to survive for more than a few hours. The infants remained at severe risk though, because they were premature and underweight (the heaviest was 3 pounds, 4 ounces, and the lightest only 1 pound, 8 ounces).

not necessarily different from those of any baby born into an impoverished environment (Behnke et al., 2006; Frank et al., 2001; Jones, 2006). How well these children ultimately do in school depends on how supportive that environment turns out to be (Bennett, Bendersky, & Lewis, 2008; Messinger et al., 2004).

Alcohol is another dangerous teratogen, because it interferes with infants' brain development (Avaria et al., 2004; Sayal et al., 2009). Almost half the children born to expectant mothers who abuse alcohol will develop **fetal alcohol syndrome,** a pattern of defects that includes mental retardation and malformations of the face (Jenkins & Culbertson, 1996). Pregnant women who drink as little as a glass or two of wine a day can harm their infants' intellectual functioning (Willford, Leech, & Day, 2006). Those who engage in bouts of heavy drinking triple the odds that their child will develop alcohol-related problems by the age of 21 (Baer et al., 2003). The effects of prenatal exposure to alcohol might be even more severe when combined with the effects of other environmental toxins, such as air pollution (Mancinelli, Binetti, & Ceccanti, 2007).

Smoking, too, can affect the developing fetus. Smokers' babies often suffer from respiratory problems, irritability, and attention problems, and they are at greater risk for nicotine addiction in adolescence and adulthood (Buka, Shenassa, & Niaura, 2003; Law et al., 2003; Linnet et al., 2005; Wakschlag et al., 2006). Worse, they may be born prematurely, and they are usually underweight. Babies who are premature and/ or underweight—for whatever reason—are likely to have cognitive, emotional, and behavioral problems that continue throughout their lives (Bhutta et al., 2002; Ginzel et al., 2007; Jefferis, Power, & Hertzman, 2002).

Defects due to teratogens are most likely to appear when the negative effects of nature and nurture combine. The worst-case scenario is one in which a genetically vulnerable infant receives a strong dose of a damaging substance during a critical period of prenatal development. The risk of low birth weight and behavioral and psychological difficulties in later life is also increased for children whose mothers were under significant stress during the first six months of pregnancy (Huizink, Mulder, & Buitelaar, 2004; Khashan et al., 2008; Van den Bergh & Marcoen, 2004) or who got the flu during that period (Brown et al., 2005).

Fortunately, mental or physical problems resulting from all harmful prenatal factors affect fewer than 10 percent of the babies born in Western nations. The vast majority of fetuses arrive at the end of their nine-month gestation averaging a healthy seven pounds and ready to continue a normal course of development in the world.

The Newborn

Determining what newborns can see, hear, or do is one of the most fascinating and frustrating challenges for researchers in developmental psychology. Babies are extremely difficult to study because they sleep about 70 percent of the time. When they are not sleeping, they are drowsy, crying, awake and active, or awake and inactive. It is only when they are in this latter state, which is infrequent and lasts only a few minutes, that researchers can assess the infants' abilities.

To do so, psychologists show infants objects or pictures and record where they look and for how long. They film the infants' eye movements and note changes in heart rates, sucking rates, brain waves, bodily movements, and skin conductance (a measure of perspiration that accompanies emotion) when objects are shown or sounds are made. From studies using these techniques, researchers have pieced together a fair picture of what infants can see and hear (Kellman & Arterberry, 2006).

Vision and Other Senses   Infants can see at birth, but their vision is blurry. Researchers estimate that newborns have 20/300 eyesight. In other words, an object 20 feet away looks as clear as it would if viewed from 300 feet by an adult with normal vision. The reason infants' vision is so limited is that their eyes and brains still need time to grow and develop. Newborns' eyes are smaller than those of adults, and the cells in their foveas—the area in each eye on which images are focused—are fewer and far less sensitive. Their eye movements are slow and jerky. And pathways connecting

fetal alcohol syndrome   A pattern of defects found in babies born to women who drink heavily during pregnancy.

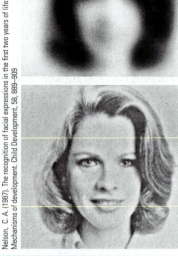

Nelson, C. A. (1987). The recognition of facial expressions in the first two years of life: Mechanisms of development. Child Development, 58, 889–909

A BABY'S-EYE VIEW OF THE WORLD ▲

The top photograph simulates what a mother looks like to her infant at three months of age. Although their vision is blurry, infants particularly seem to enjoy looking at faces.

reflexes Simple, involuntary, unlearned behaviors directed by the spinal cord without instructions from the brain.

the eyes to the brain are still inefficient, as is the processing of visual information within the brain.

Although infants cannot see small objects across the room, they can see large objects up close—the distance at which most interactions with caregivers take place. Infants look longest at moving objects, especially those that have large elements, clear contours, and a lot of contrast—all of which are features of the human face (Farroni et al., 2005; Turati, 2004).

Newborns actively use their senses to explore the world around them. At first they attend to sights and sounds for only short periods, but gradually their attention span lengthens and their exploration becomes more systematic. In the first two months, they focus only on the edges of objects, but after two months of age, they scan whole objects (Banks & Salapatek, 1983). Then, when they see an object, they get all the information they can from it before going on to something new (Hunter & Ames, 1988). Newborns stare at human faces longer than at other figures (Valenza et al., 1996). They are particularly interested in eyes, as shown in their preference for faces that are looking directly at them (Farroni et al., 2002).

At two or three days of age, newborns can hear soft voices and notice differences between tones about one note apart on the musical scale (Aslin, Jusczyk, & Pisoni, 1998). In addition, they turn their heads toward sounds (Clifton, 1992). But their hearing is not as sharp as that of adults' until well into childhood. This condition is not merely a hearing problem; it also reflects an inability to listen selectively to some sounds over others (Bargones & Werner, 1994). As infants grow, they develop sensory capacities and the skill to use them.

Infants pay special attention to speech. When they hear someone talking, they open their eyes wider and search for the speaker. Infants also prefer certain kinds of speech. They like rising tones spoken by women or children (Sullivan & Horowitz, 1983). They also like high-pitched, exaggerated, and expressive speech. In other words, they like to hear the "baby talk" used by most adults in all cultures when talking to babies. They even seem to learn language faster when they hear baby talk (Thiessen, Hill, & Saffran, 2005).

Newborns also like certain smells and tastes better than others. When given something sweet to drink, they suck longer and slower, pause for shorter periods, and smile and lick their lips (Ganchrow, Steiner, & Daher, 1983). When they smell their mother's breast, newborns become quiet, open their eyes, and try to suck (Doucet et al., 2007). Within a few days after birth, breastfed babies prefer the odor of their own mother's breast milk to that of another mother (Porter et al., 1992).

Reflexes and Motor Skills   In the first weeks and months after birth, babies show involuntary, unlearned reactions called **reflexes.** These swift, automatic movements occur in response to external stimuli. Figure 9.2 illustrates the *grasping reflex,* one of more than 20 reflexes that have been observed in newborn infants. Another is the *rooting reflex,* whereby the infant turns its mouth toward a finger or nipple that touches its cheek. And the newborn exhibits the *sucking reflex* in response to anything that touches its lips. Many of these reflexive behaviors evolved because they help infants survive. The absence of reflexes in a newborn signals problems in brain development. So does a failure of reflexes to disappear during the first three or four months, when brain development allows the infant to control muscles voluntarily.

Voluntary control permits the development of motor skills, allowing the infant to roll over, sit up, crawl, stand, and walk. Until a few years ago, most developmental psychologists accepted Gesell's view that except under extreme environmental conditions, these motor abilities occur spontaneously as the central nervous system and muscles mature. Research demonstrates, however, that maturation does not tell the whole story, even in normal environments (Thelen, 1995).

Consider the fact that many babies today aren't learning to crawl on time—or at all. Why? One reason has to do with the "Back to Sleep" campaign, which was launched in 1995 in an effort to prevent sudden infant death syndrome (see the chapter on consciousness). This public health campaign urges parents to put babies to sleep on

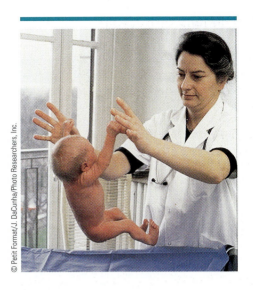

FIGURE 9.2 ■ REFLEXES IN THE NEWBORN

When a finger is pressed into a newborn's palm, the grasping reflex causes the infant to hold on tightly enough to suspend its entire weight. And when a newborn is held upright over a flat surface, the stepping reflex leads to walking movements.

their backs rather than face down. The campaign has been successful, but researchers have discovered that many babies who were never placed on their tummies went directly from sitting to toddling, skipping the crawling stage but reaching all other motor milestones on schedule (Kolata & Markel, 2001). In contrast, the "Prone to Play" campaign, which began in 2001, advised parents to place their babies in a prone (face down) position when awake in order to encourage play and learning. Babies of parents who followed this advice did show earlier than expected skill at rolling, crawling on their abdomens, and crawling on all fours, but their ability to walk did not appear unusually early (Kuo et al., 2008).

Observation of infants as they learn to crawl has shown that it does not happen suddenly. It takes the development of enough muscle strength to support the abdomen—and some active experimentation—to get the job done. Six infants in one study tried various crawling techniques—moving backward, moving one limb at a time, using the arms only, and so on (Freedland & Bertenthal, 1994). After a week or two of trial and error, all six infants arrived at the same method: moving the right arm and left leg together, then the left arm and right leg. This pattern turned out to be the most efficient way of getting around quickly without tipping over. Such observations suggest that as maturation increases infants' strength, they try out various motor patterns and select the ones that work best (Nelson, 1999).

In other words, motor development results from a combination of maturation and experience. It is not the result of an entirely automatic sequence that is genetically etched in the brain. Yet again, we see that nature and nurture influence each other. The brain controls developing behavior, but its own development is affected by experience, including efforts to build motor skills.

Infancy and Childhood: Cognitive Development

▶ *How do babies think?*

In less than 10 years, a tiny infant becomes a person who can read a book, write a poem, and argue logically for access to the family's new computer. What leads to the dramatic shifts in thinking, knowing, and remembering that occur between early infancy and later childhood? Researchers studying *cognitive development* try to answer this question.

The Development of Knowledge: Piaget's Theory

Foremost among these researchers was Jean Piaget, who dedicated his life to a search for the origins of intelligence and the factors that lead to changes in knowledge over the life-span. Piaget was the first to chart the journey from the simple reflexes of the newborn to the complex understandings of the adolescent. Although his theory turned out to be incomplete (and in some respects incorrect), his ideas about cognitive development are still guiding research (Fischer & Hencke, 1996; Shayer, 2008; Zittoun et al., 2007).

Intensive observations of infants (including his own) and extensive interviews with children led Piaget to propose that cognitive development proceeds in a series of distinct stages, or periods. He believed that all children's thinking goes through the same stages, in the same order, without skipping. (Table 9.1 outlines these stages.) According to Piaget, the thinking of infants is different from the thinking of children, which in turn is different from that of adolescents. He said that children are not just miniature adults and that they are not dumber than adults, they just think in completely different ways at different stages of development. In other words, entering each stage involves a *qualitative* change from whatever preceded it, much as a caterpillar is transformed into a butterfly.

TABLE 9.1 ■ PIAGET'S PERIODS OF COGNITIVE DEVELOPMENT

According to Piaget, a predictable set of features characterizes each period of children's cognitive development. The ages associated with the stages are approximate; Piaget realized that some children move through the stages slightly faster or slower than others.

Period	Activities and Achievements
Sensorimotor	Infants discover aspects of the world through their sensory impressions, motor activities, and coordination of the two.
Birth–2 years	They learn to differentiate themselves from the external world. They learn that objects exist even when they are not visible and that these objects are independent of the infants' own actions. Infants gain some appreciation of cause and effect.
Preoperational	Children cannot yet manipulate and transform information in logical ways, but they now can think in images and symbols.
2–4 years 4–7 years	They become able to represent something with something else, acquire language, and play games of pretend. Intelligence at this stage is said to be intuitive because children cannot make general, logical statements.
Concrete operational	Children can understand logical principles that apply to concrete external objects.
7–11 years	They can appreciate that certain properties of an object remain the same, despite changes in appearance, and they can sort objects into categories. They can appreciate the perspective of another viewer. They can think about two concepts (such as longer and wider) at the same time.
Formal operational	Only adolescents and adults can think logically about abstractions, can speculate, and can consider what might or what ought to be.
Over 11 years	They can work in probabilities and possibilities. They can imagine other worlds, especially ideal ones. They can reason about purely verbal or logical statements. They can relate any element or statement to any other, manipulate variables in a scientific experiment, and deal with proportions and analogies. They can reflect on their own activity of thinking.

Building Blocks of Development   To explain how infants and children move to ever higher stages of understanding and knowledge, Piaget introduced the concept of *schemas* as the basic units of knowledge, the building blocks of intellectual development. As noted in other chapters, **schemas** are the generalizations that form as people experience the world. Schemas, in other words, organize past experiences and provide a framework for understanding future experiences.

At first, infants form simple schemas. For example, a sucking schema combines their experiences of sucking into images of what objects can be sucked on (bottles, fingers, pacifiers) and what kinds of sucking can be done (soft and slow, speedy and vigorous). Later, children form more complex schemas, such as a schema for tying a knot or making a bed. Still later, adolescents form schemas about what it is to be in love.

Two related processes guide this development: assimilation and accommodation. In **assimilation,** infants and children take in information about new objects by trying out existing schemas and finding schemas that the new objects will fit. They *assimilate* the new objects into their existing schemas. So when an infant is given a squeaker toy, he will suck on it, thus assimilating it into the sucking schema he has developed with his bottle and pacifier. In the same way, a toddler who sees a butterfly for the first time may assimilate it into her "birdie" schema because, like a bird, it's colorful and it flies. Now suppose an older toddler encounters a large dog. How she assimilates this new experience depends on her existing schema of dogs. If she has had positive experiences with the family dog, she will have a positive schema, and, expecting the dog to behave like her pet, she will greet it happily. In other words, past experiences affect what and how children think about new ones.

Sometimes, like Cinderella's stepsisters squeezing their oversized feet into the glass slipper, people distort information about a new object to make it fit an existing schema. When squeezing won't work, though, people are forced to change, or *accommodate,* their schemas to the new objects. In **accommodation,** the person tries out familiar schemas on a new object, finds that the schemas cannot be made to fit the object, and

schemas   Mental representations of what we know and expect about the world.

assimilation   The process of taking in new information about objects by using existing schemas on objects that fit those schemas.

accommodation   The process of modifying schemas as an infant tries out familiar schemas on objects that do not fit them.

changes the schemas so that they will fit (see Figure 9.3). So when the infant discovers that the squeaker toy is more fun when it makes a noise, he accommodates his sucking schema and starts munching on the squeaker instead. When the toddler realizes that butterflies are not birds because they don't have beaks and feathers, she accommodates her "birdie" schema to include two kinds of "flying animals"—birds and butterflies. And if the child with the positive "doggie" schema meets a snarling stray, she discovers that her original schema does not extend to all dogs and refines it to distinguish between friendly dogs and aggressive ones.

Sensorimotor Development   Piaget (1952) called the first stage of cognitive development the **sensorimotor period,** a time when mental activity is confined to schemas about sensory functions, such as seeing and hearing, and schemas about motor skills, such as grasping and sucking. Piaget believed that during the sensorimotor stage, infants can form schemas only of objects and actions that are present—things they can see, hear, or touch. They cannot think about absent objects, he said, because they cannot act on them. For infants, then, thinking is doing. They do not lie in the crib thinking about their mother or their teddy bear, because they are not yet able to form schemas that are *mental representations* of objects and actions that are not present.

The sensorimotor period ends when infants do become able to form such mental representations. At that point, they can think about objects or actions when the objects are not visible or the actions are not occurring. This milestone, according to Piaget, frees the child from the here and now of the sensory environment. It allows for the development of thought. One sign of this milestone is the child's ability to find a hidden object. This behavior reflects the infant's knowledge that an object exists even if it cannot be seen, touched, or sucked. Piaget called this knowledge **object permanence.**

Piaget believed that before infants acquire knowledge of object permanence, they do not search for objects that are placed out of sight. For infants, out of sight is literally out of mind. He said that evidence of object permanence begins to appear when infants are four to eight months old. At this age, for the first time, they can recognize a familiar object even if part of it is hidden: they know it's their bottle even if they can see only the nipple peeking out from under the blanket. Infants now have some primitive mental representations of objects. If an object is completely hidden, however, they will not search for it.

Several months later, infants will search briefly for a hidden object, but their search is random and ineffective. Not until they are about 18 to 24 months old, said Piaget, do infants appear able to picture and follow events in their minds. They look for the object in places other than where they saw it last, sometimes in entirely new places. According to Piaget, their concept of object permanence is now fully developed. They have a mental representation of the object that is completely separate from their immediate perception of it.

New Views of Infants' Cognitive Development   In the years since Piaget's death, psychologists have found new ways to measure what is going on in infants' minds. They use infrared photography to record infants' eye movements, time-lapse photography to detect slight hand movements, special equipment to measure infants' sucking rates, and computer technology to track and analyze it all. Their research shows that infants know a lot more—and know it sooner—than Piaget ever thought they did (Onishi & Baillargeon, 2005).

For example, it turns out that infants in the sensorimotor period are doing more than just sensing and moving; they are thinking as well (Saxe, Tzelnic, & Carey, 2007; Sobel & Kirkham, 2006). They are not just experiencing isolated sights and sounds but combining these experiences. In one study, for example, infants were shown two different videotapes at the same time, while the soundtrack for only one of them came from a speaker placed between the two TV screens. The infants tended to look at the video that went with the soundtrack—at a toy bouncing in synch with a tapping sound, at Dad's face when his voice was on the audio, or at an angry face when an angry voice was heard (Soken & Pick, 1992). Infants remember, too. Babies as young as two to

© George S. Zimbel 2009

FIGURE 9.3 ■
ACCOMMODATION

Because the bars of the crib are in the way, this child discovers that her schema for grasping and pulling objects toward her will not work. So she adjusts, or accommodates, her schema to achieve her goal.

sensorimotor period According to Piaget, the first stage of cognitive development, when the infant's mental activity is confined to sensory perception and motor skills.

object permanence The knowledge that an object exists even when it is not in view.

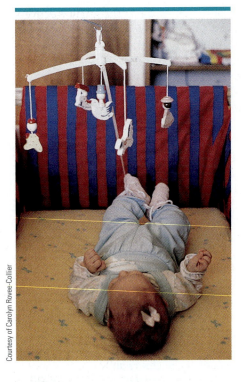

Courtesy of Carolyn Rovee-Collier

FIGURE 9.4 ■ INFANT MEMORY

This infant has learned to move a mobile by kicking her left foot, which is connected to the mobile by a ribbon. Even a month later, the baby will show recognition of this particular mobile by kicking more vigorously when she sees it than when she sees another one.

THE FAMILY CIRCUS®   **By Bil Keane**

Family Circus © Bil Keane, Inc. King Features Syndicate

"I think the moon likes us. It keeps on followin' us."

▲ During the second half of the preoperational period, according to Piaget, children believe that inanimate objects are alive and have intentions, feelings, and consciousness.

three months of age can recall a mobile that was hung over their crib a few days before (Rovee-Collier, 1999; see Figure 9.4).

Young babies even seem to have a sense of object permanence. Piaget required infants to demonstrate object permanence by making effortful responses, such as removing a cover that had been placed over an object. Today, researchers recognize that finding a hidden object under a cover requires several abilities: mentally representing the hidden object, figuring out where it might be, and pulling off the cover. Piaget's tests did not allow for the possibility that infants know a hidden object still exists but don't yet have the skill to find it. When researchers have created situations in which infants merely have to stare to indicate that they know where an object is hidden, even infants under the age of one have demonstrated this cognitive ability, especially when the object is a familiar one (Baillargeon, 2008; Bertenthal, Longo, & Kenny, 2007; Hespos & Baillargeon, 2001; Shinskey & Munakata, 2005). And when experimenters simply turn off the lights in a room, infants as young as five months of age may reach for now-unseen objects in the dark (Clifton et al., 1991).

Developmental psychologists generally agree that infants develop some mental representations earlier than Piaget suggested. However, they disagree about whether this knowledge is "programmed" in infants (Spelke et al., 1992), whether it develops quickly through interactions with the world (Baillargeon, 1995, 2008), or whether it is constructed by combining old schemas into new ones (Fischer & Bidell, 1991).

Preoperational Development   According to Piaget, the **preoperational period** follows the sensorimotor stage of development. During the first half of this period, he observed, children begin to understand, create, and use *symbols* that represent things that are not present. They draw, pretend, and talk.

Using and understanding symbols opens up a new world for two- to four-year-olds. At two, for the first time, children are able to play "pretend." They make their fingers "walk" or "shoot" and use a spoon to make a bridge. By the age of three or four, children can symbolize complex roles and events as they play "house," "doctor," or "superhero." They also can use drawing symbolically: pointing to their scribble, they might say, "This is Mommy and Daddy and me going for a walk."

During the second half of the preoperational stage, according to Piaget, four- to seven-year-olds begin to make intuitive guesses about the world as they try to figure out how things work. However, Piaget observed that they cannot tell the difference between imagination and reality. For example, children in this age range might claim that dreams are real and take place outside of themselves as "pictures on the window," "a circus in the room," or "something from the sky." And they believe that inanimate objects are alive and have intentions, feelings, and consciousness: "Clouds go slowly because they have no legs"; "Flowers grow because they want to"; and "Empty cars feel lonely." Children in the preoperational period are also *egocentric,* meaning that they assume that their own view of the world is shared by everyone else. (This helps explain why they stand between you and the TV screen and assume you can still see it or ask "What's this?" as they look at a picture book in the back seat of the car you're driving.)

Children's thinking at this stage is so dominated by what they can see and touch for themselves that they do not realize something is the same if its appearance is changed. In one study, preoperational children thought that a cat wearing a dog mask was actually a dog because that's what it looked like (DeVries, 1969). These children do not yet have what Piaget called **conservation,** the ability to recognize that important properties of a substance or a person remain the same despite changes in shape or appearance.

In a test of conservation, Piaget showed children water from each of two equal-sized glasses being poured into either a tall, thin glass or a short, wide one. They were then asked if one glass contained more water than the other. Children at the preoperational stage of development said that one glass (usually the taller one) contained more. They were dominated by the evidence of their eyes. If the glass looked bigger, then they thought it contained more.

Children at this stage do not understand the logic of *reversibility*—that if you just poured the water from one container to another, you can pour it back into the original

TESTING FOR CONSERVATION ▶

If you know a child who is between the ages of four and seven, get parental permission to test the child for what Piaget called *conservation*. Show the child two identical lumps of clay and ask which lump is bigger. The child will probably say they are the same. Now roll one lump into a long "rope" and again ask which lump is bigger. If the child says that they are still the same, this is evidence of conservation. If the child sees the longer one as bigger, conservation has not yet developed—at least not for this task. The older the child, the more likely it is that conservation will appear, but some children display conservation much earlier than Piaget thought was possible.

Learn BY Doing

online study center

Improve Your Grade
Tutorial: Preoperational Inability to Conserve Matter

preoperational period   According to Piaget, the second stage of cognitive development, during which children begin to understand, create, and use symbols that represent things that are not present.

conservation   The ability to recognize that the important properties of substances or objects, such as quantity, volume, or weight, remain constant despite changes in shape, length, or position.

concrete operations   According to Piaget, the third stage of cognitive development, during which children can learn to count, measure, add, and subtract.

formal operational period   According to Piaget, the fourth stage of cognitive development, characterized by the ability to engage in hypothetical thinking.

container and it will be the same amount. Nor do they understand the concept of *complementarity*—that one glass is taller but narrower and the other is shorter but wider. They focus on only one dimension at a time—the most obvious or important one—and make their best guess. In fact, Piaget named this stage *preoperational* because children at this stage do not yet understand logical mental *operations* such as reversibility and complementarity.

Concrete and Formal Operational Thought   At around the age of six or seven, Piaget observed, children do develop conservation. When this happens, they enter what he called the stage of **concrete operations.** Now, he said, they can count, measure, add, and subtract. Their thinking is no longer dominated by the appearance of things. They can use simple logic and perform simple mental manipulations and mental operations on things. They can sort objects into classes (such as tools, fruit, and vehicles) or series (such as largest to smallest) by systematic searching and ordering.

Still, concrete operational children can perform their logical operations only on real, concrete objects, such as sticks, glasses, tools, and fruit—not on abstract concepts, such as justice or freedom. They can reason only about what *is*, not about what is *possible*. The ability to think logically about abstract ideas comes in the next stage of cognitive development, as children enter adolescence. This new stage is called the **formal operational period,** and it is marked by the ability to engage in hypothetical thinking, including the imagining of logical consequences. For example, adolescents who have reached this level can consider various strategies for finding a part-time job and recognize that some methods are more likely to succeed than others. They can form general concepts and understand the impact of the past on the present and the present on the future. They can question social institutions, think about the world as it might be and ought to be, and consider the consequences and complexities of love, work, politics, and religion. They can think logically and systematically about symbols and propositions.

Piaget explored adolescents' formal operational abilities by asking them to perform science experiments that involved forming and investigating hypotheses. Research indicates that only about half the people in Western cultures ever reach the formal operational level necessary to succeed in Piaget's experiments (Kuhn & Franklin, 2006). People who have not studied science and math at a high school level are less likely to

THINKING ABOUT THE FUTURE ▶
Once they have reached the formal operational stage, many young people become involved in politics because for the first time, they can think about the consequences of differing approaches to government and which approach might support their emerging ideals.

do well in those experiments (Keating, 1990). In adulthood, people are more likely to use formal operations for problems based on their own occupations; this is one reason that people who think logically at work may still become victims of a home-repair or investment scam (Cialdini, 2001).

Modifying Piaget's Theory

Piaget's observations and demonstrations of children's cognitive development are vivid and fascinating. He was right in pointing out that significant shifts in children's thinking occur with age and that thinking becomes more systematic, consistent, and integrated as children get older. His idea that children are active explorers and constructors of knowledge, not passive recipients of input from the environment, influenced our contemporary views of child development. Piaget's work also inspired other psychologists to test his findings and theory with experiments of their own. The results of these experiments suggest that Piaget's theory needs some modification.

What needs to be modified most is Piaget's notion of developmental stages. Several studies have shown that changes from one stage to the next are less consistent and global than Piaget described them. For example, three-year-olds can sometimes make the distinction between physical and mental events; they know the characteristics of real dogs versus pretend dogs (Woolley, 1997). And they are not always egocentric. In one study, children of this age knew that a white card, which looked pink to them because they were wearing rose-colored glasses, looked white to someone who was not wearing the glasses (Liben, 1978). Preoperational children can even succeed at conservation tasks if they are allowed to count the number of objects or have been trained to focus on relevant dimensions such as number, height, and width (Gelman & Baillargeon, 1983).

Taken together, these studies suggest that children's knowledge and mental strategies develop at different ages in different areas and in "pockets" rather than at global levels of understanding. Knowledge in particular areas is demonstrated sooner in children who are given specific experience in those areas or who are faced with very simple questions and tasks. In other words, children's reasoning depends not only on their general level of development but also on (1) how easy the task is; (2) how familiar they are with the objects involved; (3) how well they understand the language being used; and (4) what experiences they have had in similar situations (Siegal, 1997). Research has also shown that the level of a child's thinking varies from day to day and may even shift when the child solves the same problem twice in the same day (Siegler, 1994).

In summary, psychologists now tend to think of cognitive development as occurring in rising and falling "waves" rather than in fixed stages characterized by permanent shifts from one way of thinking to another (Siegler, 2006). Children appear to systematically try out many different solutions to problems and gradually come to select the best of them.

Information Processing During Childhood

An alternative to Piaget's theory of cognitive development is based on the concept of information processing described in the chapters on memory and thought, language, and intelligence. The **information-processing** approach to development describes cognitive activities in terms of how people take in information, use it, and remember it. Developmental psychologists taking this approach focus on gradual quantitative changes in children's mental capacities rather than on qualitative advances or stages in development.

Research by these psychologists demonstrates that as children get older, their information-processing skills gradually get better (Munakata, 2006). Older children have longer attention spans. They take in information and shift their attention from one task to another more rapidly. (This is how they manage to do their homework while watching TV.) They are also more efficient in processing information once it is received (Miller & Vernon, 1997). Children's memory storage capacity also improves (Riggs et al., 2006; Schneider & Bjorklund, 1998). Preschoolers can keep only two or three pieces of information in mind at the same time; older children can hold four or five. And compared with younger children, older children are better at choosing problem-solving strategies that fit the task they are facing (Siegler, 2006).

We don't yet know exactly what causes these increases in children's attention, information-processing, and memory capacities. A full explanation will undoubtedly include both nature (specifically, maturation of the brain; Bell & Wolfe, 2007; Richmond & Nelson, 2007) and nurture (including increased familiarity with the information that is to be processed and memorized). Researchers have noticed that the cognitive abilities of children improve dramatically when they are dealing with familiar rather than unfamiliar material. In one experiment, Mayan children in Mexico lagged behind their age-mates in the United States on standard memory tests of pictures and

linkages

Why does memory improve during childhood? (a link to Memory)

information processing The process of taking in, remembering or forgetting, and using information.

nouns. But they did a lot better when researchers gave them a more familiar task, such as recalling miniature objects in a model of a Mayan village (Rogoff & Waddell, 1982).

Better memorization strategies may also help account for the improvement in children's memories. To a great extent, children learn these strategies in school. They learn how to memorize and how to study. They learn to repeat information over and over to help fix it in memory, to place information into categories, and to use other memory aids to help them remember.

After about age seven, schoolchildren are also better at remembering more complex and abstract information. Their memories are more accurate, extensive, and well organized. The knowledge they have accumulated allows them to draw more inferences and integrate new information into a more complete network of facts. (See "In Review: Milestones of Cognitive Development in Infancy and Childhood.")

In Review

MILESTONES OF COGNITIVE DEVELOPMENT IN INFANCY AND CHILDHOOD

AGE*	ACHIEVEMENT	DESCRIPTION
3–4 months	Maturation of senses	Immaturities that limit the newborn's vision and hearing are overcome.
	Voluntary movement	Reflexes disappear, and infants begin to gain voluntary control over their movements.
12–18 months	Mental representation	Infants can form images of objects and actions in their minds.
	Object permanence	Infants understand that objects exist even when out of sight.
18–24 months	Symbolic thought	Young children use symbols to represent things that are not present in their pretend play, drawing, and talk.
4 years	Intuitive thought	Children reason about events, real and imagined, by guessing rather than by engaging in logical analysis.
6–7 years	Concrete operations; Conservation	Children can apply simple logical operations to real objects. For example, they recognize that important properties of a substance, such as number or amount, remain constant despite changes in shape or position.
7–8 years	Information processing	Children can remember more information; they begin to learn strategies for memorization.

1. Research in cognitive development suggests that children form mental representations _____ than Piaget thought they did.

2. Recognizing that changing the shape of clay doesn't change the amount of clay is evidence of a cognitive ability called _____.

3. The appearance of object permanence signals the end of the _____ period.

*These ages are approximate; they indicate the order in which children first reach these milestones of cognitive development rather than the exact ages.

linkages

What happens to our memories of infancy? *(a link to Memory)*

Linkages

Development and Memory

The ability to remember facts, figures, pictures, and objects improves as we get older and more expert at processing information. But take a minute right now and try to recall anything that happened to you when you were, say, one year old. Most people can accurately recall a few memories from age five or six but remember virtually nothing from before the age of three (Bauer, 2006; Bruce, Dolan, & Phillips-Grant, 2000; Davis, Gross, & Hayne, 2008).

Psychologists have not yet found a fully satisfactory explanation for this "infantile amnesia." Some have suggested that young children lack the memory encoding and storage processes described in the chapter on memory. Yet children of two or three can clearly recall experiences that happened weeks or even months earlier (Bauer, 2006; Cleveland & Reese, 2008). Others suggest that infantile amnesia occurs because very young children lack a sense of self. Because they don't even recognize themselves in the mirror, they may not have a framework for organizing memories about what happens to them (Howe, 2003). However, this explanation would hold for only the first two years or so, because after that children do recognize their own faces and even their taped voices (Legerstee, Anderson, & Schaffer, 1998).

Another possibility is that early memories, though "present," are implicit rather than explicit. As mentioned in the memory chapter, *implicit memories* form automatically and can affect our emotions and behavior even when we do not consciously recall them. However, children's implicit memories of their early years, like their explicit memories, are quite limited. One study found that when 10-year-old children were shown photographs of preschool classmates they hadn't seen in five years, the children had little implicit or explicit memory of them (Newcombe & Fox, 1994). In contrast, adults can correctly identify 90 percent of photographs of high-school classmates they have not seen for 30 years (Bahrick, Bahrick, & Wittlinger, 1975).

Other explanations of infantile amnesia suggest that our early memories are lost because in early childhood we don't yet have the language skills to talk about—and thus solidify—those memories. This possibility was explored in a study in which two- to three-year-old children played with a machine that supposedly could shrink toys (Simcock & Hayne, 2002). Six months later, they were asked what they remembered about this event. If they had not yet developed language at the time they played with the machine, the children were able to say little or nothing about the experience when asked about it later. However, most of these same children could correctly identify pictures of the machine and act out what they had done with it. It appears that they had memories of the event that could be recalled nonverbally but not in words (Richardson & Hayne, 2007). Another possibility is that early experiences tend to be fused into *generalized event representations*, such as "going to Grandma's" or "playing at the beach," so it becomes difficult to remember any specific event.

Some researchers believe that adults have difficulty accessing early memories because when they were very young children they lacked the emotional knowledge necessary for interpreting, representing, organizing, and retrieving information about the events they experience (Wang, 2008). Still other researchers believe that infantile amnesia is due partly to the ways that people are asked about their early memories and that specialized questioning techniques might allow retrieval of early memories that are normally unavailable (Jack & Hayne, 2007).

Research on hypotheses such as these may someday unravel the mystery of infantile amnesia (Nelson & Fivush, 2004; Newcombe et al., 2000; Wang, 2006).

Culture and Cognitive Development

To explain cognitive development, Piaget focused on the physical world of objects. Russian psychologist Lev Vygotsky (pronounced "vah-GOT-skee") focused on the social world of people. He viewed cognitive abilities as the product of cultural history. The child's mind, said Vygotsky, grows through contact with other minds. It is through interaction with parents, teachers, and other representatives of their culture that children acquire the ideas of that culture (Vygotsky, 1991).

Vygotsky's followers have studied the effects of the social world on children's cognitive development—especially how participation in social routines affects children's developing knowledge of the world (Gauvain, 2001). In Western societies, those routines include shopping, eating at McDonald's, going to birthday parties, and attending religious services. In other cultures they might include helping to make pottery, going hunting, and weaving baskets (Larson & Verma, 1999). Quite early, children develop mental representations, called *scripts,* for these activities (see the chapter on thought, language, and intelligence). By the time they are three, children can describe routine activities quite accurately. Scripts, in turn, affect children's knowledge and understanding of cognitive tasks. For example, in cultures in which pottery making is important, children display conservation about the mass of objects sooner than children do in other cultures (Gardiner & Kosmitzki, 2005).

Children's cognitive abilities are also influenced by the language of their culture. Korean and Chinese children, for instance, show exceptional ability at adding and subtracting large numbers (Miller et al., 1995). As third-graders, they do three-digit problems in their heads (such as 702 minus 125) that their peers in the United States labor over or fail to solve. The difference seems traceable in part to the clear and explicit words that Asian languages use for the numbers from 11 to 19. In English, the meaning of the words *eleven* and *twelve,* for instance, is not as clear as the Asian *ten-one* and *ten-two.* Moreover, Asians use the abacus and the metric system of measurement, both of which are structured around the number 10. Korean math textbooks emphasize this tens structure by presenting the ones digits in red, the tens in blue, and the hundreds in green. Above all, for children in Asian cultures, educational achievement, especially in mathematics, is encouraged at home and strongly encouraged in school (Naito & Miura, 2001). In short, children's cognitive development is affected in ways large and small by the culture they live in (Cole, 2006; Tomasello, 2000).

BABIES AT RISK ▶

The cognitive development of infants raised in this understaffed Russian orphanage will be permanently impaired if they are not given far more stimulation in the orphanage or, better yet, adopted into a loving family before they're six months of age (Beckett et al., 2006; Kreppner et al., 2007). It's likely that they'll suffer from reduced brain metabolism and reduced activity in regions associated with higher cognitive functions, memory, and emotion (Nelson, 2007).

© Josef Polleross/The Image Works

WHEN DOES STIMULATION BECOME OVERSTIMULATION? ▶

A child's cognitive development is enhanced by a stimulating environment, but can there be too much stimulation? In the face of an avalanche of electronic media aimed specifically at babies and toddlers, some people are beginning to wonder (Zimmerman & Christakis, 2007; Zimmerman, Christakis, & Neltzoff, 2007). These stimulating media include computer "lapware," such as this baby is enjoying, videos and DVDs for even the tiniest infants, and, of course, television programs such as *Teletubbies*. Many babies in Western countries are immersed in electronic media for hours each day. In the United States, more than 25 percent of children under two have a TV set in their rooms, and one third of them have videos in the "Baby Einstein" series (Lewin, 2003; Vandewater et al., 2007). We don't yet know how all this well-intentioned electronic stimulation is affecting young children because we don't yet have enough evidence on which to base conclusions.

Individual Variations in Cognitive Development

Even within a single culture, some children are mentally advanced, whereas others lag behind their peers. Why? As already suggested, heredity is an important factor, but experience also plays a role. To explore how significant that role is, psychologists have studied the cognitive development of children raised in many different environments.

Cognitive development is seriously delayed if children are raised in environments where they are deprived of the everyday sights, sounds, and feelings provided by pictures and books, by conversation and loving interaction with family members, and even by television, radio, and the Internet. Children subjected to this kind of severe deprivation show significant impairment in intellectual development by the time they are two or three years old. "Genie" was one such child. When rescued at age 14, she weighed only fifty-nine pounds. The only things she could say were "stop it" and "no more." Investigators discovered that she had spent her life confined to a small bedroom, harnessed to a potty chair during the day and caged in a crib at night. She had not been permitted to hear or make many sounds. Although scientists and therapists worked intensively with Genie in the years after her discovery, she never learned to speak in complete sentences, and she remains in an adult care facility.

Cognitive development may also be impaired by less extreme conditions of deprivation, including the neglect, malnourishment, noise, and chaos that occur in some homes. A study of the effects of poverty found that by the time they were five years old, children raised in poverty scored nine points lower on IQ tests than did children in families whose incomes were at twice the poverty level—even after the researchers had controlled for all other family variables, such as family structure and parents' education (Duncan, Brooks-Gunn, & Klebanov, 1994). These differences continue as poor children enter school. Children who remain in poverty have lower IQs and poorer school achievement (McLoyd, 1998; Siegler, 2003; Stipek & Ryan, 1997): they have more learning disabilities (Bigelow, 2006), they are less engaged in school (Teachman, 2008), and they score lower on neurocognitive tests (Farah et al., 2006). One study of more than 10,000 children found that the economic status of the family into which a child is born is a much better predictor of the child's later cognitive development than are physical risk factors such as low birth weight (Jefferis, Power, & Hertzman, 2002). It is no wonder then that lower average IQs are seen in countries where higher numbers of children are living in poverty (Weiss, 2007).

In families with incomes above the poverty line, too, children's cognitive development is related to their surroundings and experiences. Parents can often make the difference between a child's getting A's or getting C's. To help children achieve those A's, adults can expose them from the early years to a variety of interesting materials and experiences—though not so many that the child is overwhelmed. Children's cognitive development is also enhanced when parents read and talk to them, encourage and help them explore, and actively teach them (Gottfried, 1997; Raikes et al., 2006)—in short, when they provide both support and challenge for their children's talents (Yeung, Linver, & Brooks-Gunn, 2002).

To improve the cognitive skills of children who do not get these kinds of stimulation, developmental psychologists have provided some children with extra lessons, educational materials, and contact with caring adults. In the United States, the most comprehensive effort to provide this kind of help has been made through Project Head Start, a federally funded preschool program for poor children. Many smaller, more intensive programs have also been established by state and local agencies. In a variety of such programs, children's cognitive abilities have been enhanced (Love et al., 2005; Ramey, Ramey, & Lanzi, 2006), and some effects can last into adulthood (Campbell, Pungello et al., 2001). Music lessons can also promote children's cognitive development, especially verbal memory (Ho, Cheung, & Chan, 2003; Rauscher et al., 1997; Schellenberg, 2004). Access to the Internet, too, has been related to improved reading scores and school grades among poor children (Jackson et al., 2006). Online and stand-alone electronic games, although they are no substitute for adult attention, can provide opportunities for school-age children to develop problem-solving skills (Blumberg, Rosenthal, & Randall, 2008; de Freitas & Griffiths, 2007), hone spatial skills that can help improve their performance in math and science (Canada & Goering, 2008; Green & Bavelier, 2003; Greenfield, 1994), and possibly even enhance their physical fitness (Hayes & Silberman, 2007; Trout & Christie, 2007).

Infancy and Childhood: Social and Emotional Development

▶ *How do infants become attached to their caregivers?*

Life for the child is more than learning about objects, doing math problems, and getting good grades. It is also about social relationships and emotional reactions. From the first months onward, infants are sensitive to those around them (Mumme & Fernald, 2003), and they are both attracted by and attractive to other people—especially parents and other caregivers.

PLAYING THEIR WAY TO FITNESS? ▶

Some researchers claim that people can improve their physical fitness by using video games that simulate athletic activity (Baumann, 2007; Light, 2008). Others have found that the amount of exercise involved in playing these games is not enough to help stem the rising tide of childhood obesity (Graves et al., 2008).

© John Morrison/PhotoEdit

FORMING A BOND ▲

Mutual eye contact, exaggerated facial expressions, and shared "baby talk" are an important part of the early social interactions that promote an enduring bond of attachment between parent and child.

During the first hour or so after birth, mothers gaze into their infants' eyes and give them gentle touches (Klaus & Kennell, 1976). This is the first opportunity for the mother to display her *bond* to her infant—an emotional tie that begins even before the baby is born (Feldman et al., 2007). Psychologists once believed that this immediate contact was critical—that the mother-infant bond would never be strong if the opportunity for early interaction was missed. Research has revealed, however, that such interaction is a luxury, not a requirement for a close relationship (Myers, 1987). Mothers and fathers, whether biological or adoptive, gradually form close attachments to their infants by interacting with them day after day.

As the mother gazes at her baby, the baby is gazing back. By the time infants are two days old, they recognize—and like—their mother's face. They will suck more vigorously to see a videotaped image of her face than to see that of a stranger (Walton, Bower, & Bower, 1992). Soon, they begin to respond to the mother's facial expressions as well. By the time they are a year old, children use their mothers' emotional expressions to guide their own behavior in uncertain situations (Hertenstein & Campos, 2004; Saarni, 2006). If the mother looks frightened when a stranger approaches, for example, the child is more likely to avoid the stranger. Research on infants' brain activity suggests that they pay particular attention to fear and other negative emotions in adults (Carver & Vaccaro, 2007). This tendency helps to explain why, as described in the chapter on learning, observation of other people's reactions can sometimes lead to the development of fears and even phobias.

Infants communicate feelings as well as recognize them. Before they can speak a word, infants use gestures to show their caregivers that they are feeling happy, mad, sad, scared, sleepy, or cold (Vallotton, 2008).

Individual Temperament

From the moment infants are born, they differ from one another. Some are happy, active, and vigorous; they splash, thrash, and wriggle. Others lie still most of the time. Some infants approach new objects with enthusiasm; others turn away or fuss. Some infants whimper; others kick, scream, and wail. Characteristics such as these make up the infant's temperament. **Temperament** refers to the infant's individual style and frequency of expressing needs and emotions; it is constitutional, biological, and genetically based. Although temperament mainly reflects nature's contribution to the beginning of an individual's personality, it can also be affected by the prenatal environment, including—as noted earlier—the mother's smoking and drug use during pregnancy. The stress experienced by the mother after her baby's birth also affects the baby's temperament. Research indicates that breastfed infants who ingest more of the stress-related hormone cortisol tend to have more fearful temperaments (Glynn et al., 2007). And if mothers of babies with negative temperaments continue to experience stress, the babies tend to express even more negative emotion during the next five years (Pesonen et al., 2008).

In some of the earliest research on infant temperament, Alexander Thomas and Stella Chess (1977) found three main temperament patterns. *Easy babies,* the most common kind, get hungry and sleepy at predictable times, react to new situations cheerfully, and seldom fuss. *Difficult babies* are irregular and irritable. Those in the third group, *slow-to-warm-up babies,* react warily to new situations but eventually come to enjoy them.

Traces of early temperamental characteristics weave their way throughout childhood (Komsi et al., 2008; Rothbart, 2007). Easy infants usually stay easy (Zhou et al., 2004) and tend not to develop conduct problems (Lahey et al., 2008); difficult infants often remain difficult, sometimes developing attention and aggression problems in childhood (Else-Quest et al., 2006; Miner & Clarke-Stewart, 2008). Timid toddlers tend to become shy preschoolers, restrained and inhibited eight-year-olds, and somewhat anxious teenagers (Roberts, Caspi, & Moffitt, 2001). However, in temperament, as in cognitive development, nature interacts with nurture (Jaffari-Bimmel et al., 2006). Events and influences that occur between infancy and adulthood can help to stabilize an individual's temperament or shift its development in one direction or the other.

temperament An individual's basic, natural disposition that is evident from infancy.

One source of influence suggested by Thomas and Chess (1977) is the degree to which an infant's temperament matches the parents' personal styles and what they want and expect from their baby. When the match is a good one, parents tend to support and encourage the infant's behavior, thus increasing the chances that temperamental qualities will be stable. Consider the temperament patterns of Chinese American and European American children. At birth, Chinese American infants are calmer, less changeable, less excitable, and more easily comforted when upset than European American infants (Kagan et al., 1994). This tendency toward self-control is powerfully reinforced by the Chinese culture. Compared with European American parents, Chinese parents are less likely to reward and stimulate infants' babbling and smiling and more likely to maintain close control of their young children. The children, in turn, are more dependent on their mothers and less likely to play by themselves. They are less vocal, noisy, and active than European American children (Smith & Freedman, 1983), and as preschoolers they show far more impulse control, including the ability to wait their turn (Sabbagh et al., 2006).

These temperamental differences between children in different ethnic groups illustrate the combined contributions of nature and nurture. Mayan infants, for example, are relatively inactive from birth. The Zinacantecos, a Mayan group in southern Mexico, reinforce this innate predisposition toward restrained motor activity by tightly wrapping their infants and by nursing at the slightest sign of movement (Greenfield & Childs, 1991). This combination of genetic predisposition and cultural reinforcement is adaptive. Quiet infants do not kick off their covers at night, which is important in the cold highlands where they live. Inactive infants are able to spend long periods on their mothers' backs as the mothers work. And infants who do not begin to walk until they can understand some language do not wander into the open fire at the center of the house. This adaptive interplay of innate and cultural factors in the development of temperament operates in all cultures.

Nature and nurture combine to influence individual differences within cultures, too. A variety of studies show that children are more likely to display aggressiveness, anxiety, depression, or academic and social problems if they have suffered the "double whammy" of starting life with a difficult temperament and then being raised in a harsh, insensitive, unsupportive, or anxiety-provoking family environment (Miner & Clarke-Stewart, 2008; Paulussen-Hoogeboom et al., 2008; Stright, Gallagher, & Kelley, 2008). For example, children who had both timid temperaments and mothers who were unsupportive, negative, or depressed were more likely to remain fearful, to be socially withdrawn, to have more negative moods, and to have difficulty controlling their negative emotions (Feng et al., 2008; Gilissen et al., 2008; Hane et al., 2008). However, if a difficult or shy baby is lucky enough to have patient parents who allow their baby to respond to new situations and changes in daily routines at a more relaxed pace, the baby is likely to become less difficult or shy over time.

The Infant Grows Attached

As infants and caregivers respond to one another in the first year, the infant begins to form an **attachment**—a deep, affectionate, close, and enduring relationship—to these important figures. **Attachment theory** was first developed by John Bowlby, a British psychoanalyst who drew attention to the importance of attachment after he observed children who had been orphaned in World War II. These children's depression and other emotional scars led Bowlby to propose a theory about the importance of developing a strong attachment to one's primary caregivers—a tie that normally keeps infants close to those caregivers and, therefore, safe (Bowlby, 1973). Soon after Bowlby first described his theory, researchers in the United States began to investigate how such attachments are formed and what happens when they fail to form or are broken by loss or separation. The most dramatic of these studies was conducted with monkeys by Harry Harlow.

Motherless Monkeys—and Children   Harlow (1959) separated newborn monkeys from their mothers and raised them in cages containing two artificial mothers. One "mother" was made of wire with a rubber nipple from which the infant could get

attachment   A deep, affectionate, close, and enduring relationship with a person with whom a baby has shared many experiences.

attachment theory   The idea that children form a close attachment to their earliest caregivers and that this attachment pattern can affect aspects of the children's later life.

FIGURE 9.5 ■ WIRE AND TERRY CLOTH "MOTHERS"

These are the two types of artificial mothers used in Harlow's research. Although baby monkeys received milk from the wire mother, they spent most of their time with the terry cloth version, and they clung to it when frightened.
Source: Baillargeon (1992).

milk (see Figure 9.5). It provided food but no physical comfort. The other artificial mother had no nipple but was made of soft, comfortable terry cloth. If attachments form entirely because caregivers provide food, the infants would be expected to prefer the wire mother. In fact, they spent most of their time with the terry cloth mother. And when they were frightened, the infants immediately ran to their terry cloth mother and clung to it. Harlow concluded that the monkeys were motivated by the need for comfort. The terry cloth mother provided feelings of softness and cuddling, which were things the infants needed when they sensed danger.

Harlow also investigated what happens when attachments do not form. He isolated some monkeys from all social contact from birth. After a year of this isolation, the monkeys showed dramatic disturbances. When visited by normally active, playful monkeys, they withdrew to a corner, huddling or rocking for hours. These monkeys' problems continued into adulthood. As adults, they were unable to have normal sexual relations. When some of the females became pregnant through artificial means, their maternal behaviors were woefully inadequate. In most cases, these mothers ignored their infants. When the infants became distressed, the mothers physically abused and sometimes even killed them.

Tragically, humans who spend their first few years without a consistent caregiver react in a similar manner. At Romanian and Russian orphanages in which many children were neglected by institutional caregivers, visitors discovered that the children, like Harlow's deprived monkeys, were withdrawn and engaged in constant rocking (Holden, 1996). These effects tend to remain even after the children are adopted. In one study, researchers observed the behavior of four-year-old children who had been in a Romanian orphanage for at least eight months before being adopted (Chisholm, 1997). Compared with children who had been adopted before they were four months old, the late-adopted children were found to have many more serious problems. Depressed or withdrawn, they stared blankly, demanded attention, and could not control their tempers. Although they interacted poorly with their adoptive mothers, they were friendly with strangers, usually trying to cuddle and kiss them. At age six, a third of late-adopted children still showed no preference for their parents or any tendency to look to them when stressed (Rutter, O'Connor, & ERA Study Team, 2004). Neuroscientists suggest that the dramatic problems seen in isolated monkeys—as well as in humans—are the result of developmental brain dysfunction and damage brought on by a lack of touch and body movement in infancy (Wismer Fries et al., 2005; Prescott, 1996).

Forming an Attachment Fortunately, most infants do have a consistent caregiver, usually the mother, to whom they can form an attachment. They learn to recognize her and are able to distinguish her from a stranger at an early age. Some infants vocalize more to their mothers than to a stranger when they are only three months old. By the age of six or seven months, infants show signs of preferring the mother to anyone else. They crawl after her, call out to her, hug her, climb into her lap, and protest when she leaves (Ainsworth & Marvin, 1995). Babies who recognize and prefer their mothers even earlier—at three months—may be especially bright. One study found that such babies eventually achieve higher-than-average grades in high school, score higher on college entrance exams, and complete more years of education (Roe, 2001).

Infants also develop attachments to their fathers, but usually a little later (Lamb, 1997). Father-infant interaction is also less frequent than mother-infant interaction, and most studies show that it has a somewhat different nature (Parke, 2002). Mothers tend to feed, bathe, dress, cuddle, and talk to their infants, whereas fathers are more likely to play with, jiggle, and toss them, especially sons.

Variations in Attachment The amount of closeness and contact the infant seeks with either mother or father depends to some extent on the infant. Babies who are ill, tired, or slow to warm up may require more closeness. Closeness also depends to some extent on the parent. An infant whose parent has been absent or unresponsive is likely to need more closeness than one whose parent is accessible and responsive.

THINKING CRITICALLY

Does Day Care Harm the Emotional Development of Infants?

With about 60 percent of mothers of infants and young children in the United States working outside the home, concern has been expressed about how daily separations from their mothers might affect the children, especially the infants (Clarke-Stewart & Allhusen, 2005). Some have argued that putting infants in day care with a baby-sitter or in a day-care center damages the quality of the mother-infant relationship and increases the babies' risk for psychological problems later on (Gallagher, 1998).

▶ What am I being asked to believe or accept?

The claim is that daily separations created by day care damage the formation of an attachment between the mother and infant and harm the infant's emotional development.

▶ Is evidence available to support the claim?

There is clear evidence that separation from the mother is painful for young children. If separation lasts a week or more, children who have formed an attachment to their mother tend to protest, then become apathetic and mournful, and finally seem to lose interest in the missing mother (Robertson & Robertson, 1971). But day care does not involve such lasting separations. Research has shown that infants who are in day care do form attachments to their mothers. In fact, they prefer their mothers to their daytime caregivers (Lamb & Ahnert, 2006).

Are these attachments as secure as the attachments formed by infants whose mothers do not work outside the home? Researchers have examined this question by comparing how infants react to brief separations from their mothers in the Strange Situation. A review of about 20 studies done in the 1980s revealed that infants in full-time day care were somewhat more likely to be classified as insecurely attached. About 36 percent of them were classified as insecure; only 29 percent of the infants who were not in full-time day care were counted as insecure (Clarke-Stewart, 1989). These results appear to support the suggestion that day care harms infants' attachments to their mothers.

▶ Can that evidence be interpreted another way?

Perhaps factors other than day care could explain the difference between infants in day care and those at home with their mothers.

Improve Your Grade
Tutorial: Strange Situation Test and Attachment

attachment behavior Actions such as crying, smiling, vocalizing, and gesturing that help bring an infant into closer proximity to its caretaker.

Researchers have studied the differences in infants' **attachment behavior** in a special situation that simulates the natural comings and goings of parents and infants—the so-called *Strange Situation* (Ainsworth et al., 1978). Testing occurs in an unfamiliar playroom where the infant interacts with the mother and an unfamiliar woman in brief episodes: the infant plays with the mother and the stranger, the mother leaves the baby with the stranger for a few minutes, the mother and the stranger leave the baby alone in the room briefly, and the mother returns to the room.

Videotapes of these sessions show that most infants display a *secure attachment* to the mother in the Strange Situation (Thompson, 2006). In the unfamiliar room, the infant uses the mother as a home base, leaving her side to explore and play but returning to her periodically for comfort or contact. Securely attached children can tolerate the brief separation from their mothers, but they are always happy to see them return, and they are always receptive to the mothers' offers of contact. These mother-child pairs, researchers have found, tend to have harmonious interactions from the earliest months. The mothers themselves tend to be sensitive and responsive (DeWolff & van IJzendoorn, 1997).

Some infants, however, form *insecure attachments*. If the relationship is *avoidant*, the infant avoids or ignores the mother when she approaches or when she returns after the brief separation. If the relationship is *ambivalent*, the infant is upset when the mother leaves, but when she returns the child acts angry and rejects the mother's efforts at contact; when picked up, the child squirms to get down. If the relationship is *disorganized*, the infant's behavior is inconsistent, disturbed, and disturbing; the child may begin to cry again after the mother has returned and provided comfort or may reach out for the mother while looking away from her (Moss et al., 2004).

The nature of a child's attachment to caregivers can have long-term and far-reaching effects (NICHD Early Child Care Research Network, 2006b). For example, unless it is disrupted by the loss of a parent, abuse by a family member, chronic depression in the mother, or some other severe negative event (Weinfield, Sroufe, & Egeland, 2000), an infant's secure attachment continues into young adulthood—and probably throughout life (Hamilton, 2000; Mattanah, Hancock, & Brand, 2004; Waters et al., 2000). A secure

One such factor could be the method that was used to assess attachment. Infants in these studies were judged insecure if they did not run to their mothers after a brief separation in the Strange Situation. But maybe infants who experience daily separations from their mothers during day care feel more comfortable in the Strange Situation and therefore seek out less closeness with their mothers. A second factor concerns the possible differences between the infants' mothers. Perhaps mothers who value independence in themselves and in their children are more likely to be working and to place their children in day care, whereas mothers who emphasize closeness with their children are more likely to stay home.

▶ *What evidence would help evaluate the alternatives?*

Finding insecure attachment to be more common among the infants of working mothers does not, by itself, demonstrate that day care is harmful. To judge the effects of day care, we must consider other measures of emotional adjustment as well. If infants in day care showed consistent signs of impaired emotional relations in other situations (at home, say) and with other caregivers (such as the father), this evidence would support the argument that day care harms children's emotional development. Another useful method would be to statistically control for differences in the behavior and attitudes of parents who do and do not put their infants in day care and then look for differences in their children.

In fact, this research design has already been employed. In 1990, the U.S. government funded a study of infant day care in ten sites around the country. The psychological and physical development of more than 1,300 randomly selected infants was tracked from birth through age three. The results available so far show that when factors such as parents' education, income, and attitudes were statistically controlled, infants in day care were no more likely to have emotional problems or to be insecurely attached to their mothers than infants not in day care. However, in cases in which infants were placed in poor-quality day care with caregivers who were insensitive and unresponsive and in which mothers were insensitive to their babies' needs at home, the infants were less likely to develop a secure attachment to their mothers (Belsky et al., 2007; NICHD Early Child Care Research Network, 2005, 2006a).

▶ *What conclusions are most reasonable?*

Based on available evidence, the most reasonable conclusion appears to be that day care by itself does not lead to insecure attachment. But if that day care is of poor quality, it can worsen a risky situation at home and increase the likelihood that infants will have problems forming a secure attachment to their mothers. The U.S. government study is still under way, and the children's progress is being followed into adolescence.

attachment to the mother is also reflected in relationships with other people. Children who are securely attached receive more positive reactions from other children when they are toddlers (Fagot, 1997) and have better relations with peers in middle childhood and adolescence (Carlson, Sroufe, & Egeland, 2004; Schneider, Atkinson, & Tardif, 2001; Thompson, 2006). In school, teachers like them more, expect more of them, and rate them as more competent (Diener et al., 2008).

Patterns of child care and attachment vary widely in different parts of the world. In northern Germany, for example, where parents are quite strict, the proportion of infants who display avoidant attachments is much higher than in the United States (Spangler, Fremmer-Bombik, & Grossman, 1996). Kibbutz babies in Israel, who sleep in infant houses away from their parents, are relatively likely to show insecure attachments and other related problems (Aviezer et al., 1999). In Japan, where mothers are expected to be completely devoted to their children and are seldom apart from them, even at night, children develop an attachment relationship that emphasizes harmony and union (Rothbaum, Pott et al., 2000). These attachment patterns differ from the secure type that is most common in the United States: with their parents' encouragement, U.S. children balance closeness and proximity with exploration and autonomy.

In all countries, the likelihood that children will develop a secure attachment depends on the mother's attentiveness; if the mother is sensitive and responsive to the baby's needs and signals, a secure attachment is more likely; if she is rejecting or neglecting, the child's attachment is more likely to be insecure (Bakermans-Kranenburg, van IJzendoorn, & Juffer, 2008; Nievar & Becker, 2008).

Relationships with Parents and Peers

Erik Erikson (1968) saw the first year of life as a time when infants develop a feeling of trust (or mistrust) about the world. According to his theory, an infant's first year represents the first of eight stages of lifelong psychosocial development (see Table 9.2). Each stage focuses on an issue, or "crisis," that is especially important at that time of life. Erikson believed that the ways that people resolve these crises shape their personalities

© Lawrence Migdale/Getty Images

THE EFFECTS OF DAY CARE ▲

Parents are understandably concerned that leaving their infants in a day-care center all day long might interfere with the mother-infant attachment or with other aspects of the child's development. Research shows that most infants in day care do form healthy bonds with their parents but that if children spend many hours in day care between infancy and kindergarten, they are more likely to have behavior problems in school, such as talking back to the teacher or getting into fights with other children (NICHD Early Child Care Research Network, 2001, 2006b). Some employers try to help parents build attachments with their infants by providing on-site day care or allowing employees to keep their babies in their offices while working (Armour, 2008). These policies help parents and their children stay in contact throughout the day, but do you think they might create any problems in the workplace?

socialization   The process by which parents, teachers, and others teach children the skills and social norms necessary to be well-functioning members of society.

TABLE 9.2   ■   ERIKSON'S STAGES OF PSYCHOSOCIAL DEVELOPMENT

In each of Erikson's stages of development, a different psychological issue presents a new crisis for the person to resolve. The person focuses attention on that issue and by the end of the period has worked through the crisis and resolved it either positively, in the direction of healthy development, or negatively, hindering further psychological development.

Age	Central Psychological Issue or Crisis
First Year	**Trust versus mistrust** Infants learn to trust that their needs will be met by the world, especially by the mother—or they learn to mistrust the world.
Second year	**Autonomy versus shame and doubt** Children learn to exercise will, make choices, and control themselves—or they become uncertain and doubt that they can do things by themselves.
Third to fifth year	**Initiative versus guilt** Children learn to initiate activities and enjoy their accomplishments, acquiring direction and purpose—or, if they are not allowed initiative, they feel guilty for their attempts at becoming independent.
Sixth year through puberty	**Industry versus inferiority** Children develop a sense of industry and curiosity and are eager to learn—or they feel inferior and lose interest in the tasks before them.
Adolescence	**Identity versus role confusion** Adolescents come to see themselves as unique and integrated persons with an ideology—or they become confused about what they want out of life.
Early adulthood	**Intimacy versus isolation** Young people become able to commit themselves to another person—or they develop a sense of isolation and feel they have no one in the world but themselves.
Middle age	**Generativity versus stagnation** Adults are willing to have and care for children and to devote themselves to their work and the common good—or they become self-centered and inactive.
Old age	**Integrity versus despair** Older people enter a period of reflection, becoming assured that their lives have been meaningful and becoming ready to face death with acceptance and dignity—or they are in despair about their unaccomplished goals, failures, and ill-spent lives.

---

and social relationships. Resolving a crisis in a positive way provides the foundation for characteristics such as trust, independence, initiative, or industry. But if the crisis is not resolved positively, according to Erikson, the person will be psychologically troubled and cope less effectively with later crises. In Erikson's theory, trusting caregivers during infancy forms the bedrock for all future social and emotional development.

After children have formed strong emotional attachments to their parents, their next psychological task is to develop a more independent relationship with them. In Erikson's theory, this task is reflected in the second stage (again, see Table 9.2). Children begin to exercise their wills, to develop some independence from their parents, and to begin activities on their own. According to Erikson, children who are not allowed to exercise their wills or start their own activities will feel uncertain about doing things for themselves and guilty about seeking independence. The extent to which parents allow or encourage their children's independence is related to their parenting style.

Parenting Styles   Most parents try to channel children's impulses into socially accepted outlets and teach them the skills and rules needed to function in their society. Cultural values strongly shape this **socialization** process. Parents in Hispanic cultures of Mexico, Puerto Rico, and Central America, for example, tend to be influenced by the collectivist tradition discussed in the introductory chapter, in which family and community interests are emphasized over individual goals. Children in these cultures are expected to respect and obey their elders, and they are taught to do less of the questioning, negotiating, and arguing that is encouraged—or at least tolerated—in many middle-class European American families (Greenfield, Suzuki, & Rothstein-Fisch, 2006; Parke & Buriel, 2006).

European American parents tend to employ one of four distinct **parenting styles** (Baumrind, 1991; Maccoby & Martin, 1983). **Authoritarian parents** tend to be strict, punishing, and unsympathetic. They value obedience from children and try to curb the children's wills and shape their children's behavior to meet a set standard. They do not encourage independence. They are detached and seldom praise their youngsters. In contrast, **permissive parents** give their children complete freedom and provide little discipline. **Authoritative parents** fall between these two extremes. They reason with their children, encouraging give and take. They allow children increasing responsibility as they get older and better at making decisions. They are firm but understanding. They set limits but also encourage independence. Their demands are reasonable, rational, and consistent. **Uninvolved parents** are indifferent to their children. They invest as little time, money, and effort in their children as possible, focusing on their own needs before their children's. These parents often fail to monitor their children's activities, particularly when the children are old enough to be out of the house alone.

Research shows that these parenting styles are consistently related to young children's social and emotional development (Eisenberg, Fabes, & Spinrad, 2006; Parke & Buriel, 2006; Thompson, 2006). Authoritarian parents tend to have children who are unfriendly, distrustful, and withdrawn. The children of permissive parents tend to be immature, dependent, and unhappy; they are likely to have tantrums or to ask for help when they encounter even slight difficulties. Children raised by authoritative parents tend to be friendly, cooperative, self-reliant, and socially responsible.

Other researchers have found that authoritative parenting styles are associated with additional positive outcomes, including better school achievement, greater popularity, and better psychological adjustment to parental divorce (Hetherington & Clingempeel, 1992; Hinshaw et al., 1997; Steinberg et al., 1994). In contrast, children of authoritarian parents are more likely to cheat, to display aggression and other behavioral problems, and to be less likely to experience guilt or accept blame after doing something wrong (Eisenberg, Fabes, & Spinrad, 2006; Paulussen-Hoogeboom et al., 2008).

The results of all these parenting studies are interesting, but they are limited in several ways. First, they are based on correlations, which, as discussed in the introductory chapter, do not prove causation. Finding consistent correlations between parents' and children's behavior does not establish that the parents are *creating* the differences seen in their children. Even evidence that differences between the children of authoritative and nonauthoritative parents tend to increase over time can only show that parents' socialization styles *might* have a direct influence on children's behavior (Steinberg et al., 1994). It is also possible, for example, that parents' behavior might be shaped to some extent by their children. Children's temperament, size, and appearance may influence the way parents treat them (Bugental & Grusec, 2006) and may alter the effects of parenting styles (Zhou et al., 2004).

Second, some developmental psychologists suggest that it is not the parents' socialization practices that influence children but rather how the children perceive the discipline they receive—as stricter or more lenient than what an older sibling received, for example (Reiss et al., 2000). In fact, research shows that the effects of parents' socialization can differ depending on their children's temperament (Kochanska, Aksan, & Joy, 2007). A third limitation of parenting studies is that the correlations between parenting styles and children's behavior, though statistically significant, are usually not terribly strong (Ho, Bluestein, & Jenkins, 2008). Expected outcomes do not always appear. For example, Baumrind (1971) found a small group of "harmonious" families in which discipline was never observed, yet the children were thriving.

In all likelihood, it is the "fit" between parenting style and children's characteristics that affects children the most. There is no universally "best" style of parenting (Parke & Buriel, 2006). So authoritative parenting, which is so consistently linked with positive

parenting style The varying patterns of behavior—ranging from permissive to authoritarian—that parents display as they interact with and discipline their children.

authoritarian parents Parents who are firm, punitive, and unsympathetic.

permissive parents Parents who give their children complete freedom and lax discipline.

authoritative parents Parents who reason with their children and are firm but understanding.

uninvolved parents Parents who invest as little time, money, and effort in their children as possible.

© David Grossman/Photo Researchers, Inc.

CHILDREN'S FRIENDSHIPS ▲

Although relationships with peers may not always be this friendly, they are often among the closest and most positive in a child's life. Friends are more interactive than nonfriends; they smile and laugh together more, pay closer attention to equality in their conversations, and talk about mutual goals. Having at least one close friend in childhood predicts good psychological functioning later on (Laursen et al., 2007; Parker et al., 2001).

outcomes in European American families, is not related to better school performance among African American or Asian American youngsters (Kim & Rohner, 2002; Steinberg, Dornbusch, & Brown, 1992). And frequent spankings in the first two years increases the risk of behavior problems by school age for European American children, but not for African American and Hispanic American children (Slade & Wissow, 2004). One possible reason for these differing patterns is that disciplinary styles can have different meanings in different cultures (Ho, Bluestein, & Jenkins, 2008). When Chinese American parents use authoritarian discipline—which they do to a greater extent than European American parents—their goal is usually to "train" (*chiao shun*) and "govern" (*guan*) children so that they will know what is expected of them (Chao, 1994). By contrast, European American parents who use authoritarian discipline are more likely to do so to "break the child's will." In other words, each parenting style must be evaluated in its cultural context.

Some people have suggested that parenting styles are a less significant influence on children's social development than are the influences they encounter outside the home, especially peer influences (Harris, 1995, 1998). Research evidence does not justify dismissing the impact of parenting styles, but there is no denying the impact of peer influences either (Collins et al., 2000; Leventhal & Brooks-Gunn, 2000).

Relationships with Peers   Social development over the years of childhood spans an ever-enlarging social world that broadens to include siblings, playmates, and classmates. Psychologists have observed that from a remarkably early age—as young as one year—children are interested in the behavior of other children (usually their siblings) and that by the time they are a year and a half old, they know how to hurt or comfort other children (Rubin, Bukowski, & Parker, 2006).

It takes time for children to learn how to interact with other children. Two-year-olds in Western cultures are only able to exchange or fight over toys. By the time they are three, they can use toys to get a response from peers. At age four, children converse about the toys they are playing with, and at the end of the preschool period, they are able to share toys and tasks cooperatively. This kind of play is important because it shows children how to communicate what they are feeling and gives them the chance to form their first friendships (Dunn & Hughes, 2001; Rubin, Bukowski, & Parker, 2006).

In the school years, peer interaction becomes more complex and structured as children play games with rules, play on teams, tutor each other, and cooperate—or compete—in achieving goals. The school years are also the time when friends become important and friendships become long lasting (Hartup & Stevens, 1997). At this age, the most important aspects of friendship are companionship and fun; psychological intimacy does not enter the picture until children become teenagers (Parker et al., 2001).

Social Skills

The changes in peer interactions and relationships over the years of childhood reflect children's increasing social competence and understanding. Social skills, like cognitive skills, must be learned (Rubin et al., 2006).

One important social skill is the ability to engage in sustained, responsive interactions with peers. These interactions require cooperation, sharing, and taking turns—behaviors that first appear in the preschool years. A second social skill that children learn is the ability to detect and correctly interpret other people's emotional signals. Much as children's school performance depends on processing academic information, their social performance depends on processing information about other people (Slomkowski & Dunn, 1996). A related set of social skills involves the ability to feel what another person is feeling, or something close to it (*empathy*), and to respond with comfort or help if the person is in distress.

Children whose social skills allow them to understand another person's perspective, appreciate how that person might be feeling, and offer sympathy, cooperation, and help tend to be the most popular members of a peer group (Izard et al., 2001; Rubin et al., 2006). Children without these skills tend to be rejected or neglected;

they may become bullies or the victims of bullies. Parents, other adults, and even older siblings can help their children develop these skills by engaging them in lots of "pretend" play and other prosocial activities and by encouraging them to express their emotions constructively (Eisenberg, Fabes, & Spinrad, 2006; Ladd, 2005; Lopes et al., 2005).

Focus on RESEARCH

Exploring Developing Minds

Children's ability to make sense of other people's behavior depends on their ability to understand the thinking that underlies other people's actions. Critical to this understanding is the recognition that what other people think is sometimes incorrect. For more than 20 years, researchers have argued that children under four years of age cannot understand other people's mental states because they do not yet have a "theory of mind." This argument was based on studies that asked children questions about other people's beliefs (e.g., Baron-Cohen, Leslie, & Frith, 1985). In one study, children were brought to a laboratory, one at a time, and shown a simple little drama starring two dolls, "Sally" and "Anne." First, Sally puts a marble in her basket and then leaves the stage. While Sally is away, Anne takes the marble out of Sally's basket and puts it into her own box. Then Sally returns to get her marble, and each child is asked where Sally will look for her marble. To correctly predict that Sally will look in the basket where she last saw the marble, the children would have to recognize that Sally has a false belief about its location. Even though they know where the marble really is, they will have to be able to "read Sally's mind," realize what she must be thinking, and say "she will look in her basket." However, most children under the age of four ignore the fact that Sally thinks the marble is still in her basket and say that she will look in Anne's box.

▶ What was the researcher's question?

Renee Baillargeon (pronounced "by-ar-ZHAN") wondered, though, whether the inability of these young children to recognize what others are thinking reflected a true lack of a "theory of mind" or was the result of using research methods that were not sensitive enough to detect its existence. So her research question was whether more specialized research methods might reveal that even children under four can understand that the behavior they see in others is affected by the other people's mental states, including false beliefs and false perceptions.

▶ How did the researcher answer the question?

Instead of requiring children to answer questions about other people's behavior, Baillargeon used a more creative and potentially more sensitive method to probe young children's knowledge. Specifically, she showed infants various events and then carefully measured the amount of time they spent looking at them. She reasoned that infants' tendency to look longer at certain events indicates that those events violate their expectations about the world.

Baillargeon used this method to measure the ability of 15-month-old infants to predict where a woman would look for a toy,

depending on whether she had a true or a false belief about the toy's location (Onishi & Baillargeon, 2005). Each infant first watched the woman play with a toy watermelon slice for a few seconds, then hide it inside a green box. Next, the woman watched the toy being moved from the green box to a yellow box. Then she left the scene, and while she was gone the toy was put back into the green box. When she came back, she looked for the toy by reaching either into the green box or the yellow box. Baillargeon reasoned that if the infants expected the woman to search for the toy on the basis of her false belief that it was still in the yellow box, they would look longer at her if she violated their expectation by searching in the green box instead. This longer looking would convey the message that "Hey, how could she know the toy had been moved? I expected her to look where she last saw it!" But if, as earlier studies had found, the infants really had no "theory of mind," they would ignore the woman's false belief and expect her to look in the green box where they knew the toy now lay. If she met this expectation, they would not pay any special attention to her action.

▶ What did the researcher find?

The results of this study showed that, contrary to what would be expected from previous research, the infants looked reliably longer when the woman looked for the toy in the green box.

▶ What do the results mean?

These results support the view that despite lots of earlier research evidence to the contrary, infants under the age of four do have a "theory of mind." When evaluated using the right kinds of research methods, these children demonstrate an ability to recognize that other people have beliefs and perceptions that can be false, that those beliefs and perceptions can differ from the child's own, and that these mental states affect the other person's behavior.

▶ What do we still need to know?

Among other things, it would be good to know more about the extent of infants' understanding of mental states. Does it appear in other situations? Baillargeon has conducted a series of studies to begin to explore this question. In one of these, infants viewed a scene in which a woman looked for a doll with blue pigtails. She could look in either a plain box or in a box that had a blue tuft of hair sticking out from under its lid (Song & Baillargeon, 2008). The infants knew that the doll was in the plain box, but they stared longer when the woman looked in that box first; this meant that they expected her to be misled by the blue tuft of hair and to falsely perceive it as belonging to the doll. In another study, Baillargeon investigated whether infants know that new information can correct an adult's false belief (Song et al., 2008). In this case, infants watched an adult hide a ball in a box while another adult looked on. After the first adult left the scene, the second adult moved the ball from the box to a cup. When the first adult returned, the second adult told her "The ball is in the cup!" Infants stared longer if despite this corrective information, the adult searched for the ball in the box. Those who saw her reach for the cup did not pay

special attention, suggesting that the infants expected her to do so once her false belief had been corrected.

What mental states besides beliefs and perceptions can infants understand? Do they also realize that other people's behavior can be influenced by goals, intentions, emotions, and even by the fairness or unfairness of a situation? How soon after birth does a "theory of mind" develop? These are among the dozens of additional questions that remain for future research in this fascinating area of developmental psychology (Woodward, 2009).

linkages

Who teaches boys to be men and girls to be women? *(a link to Learning)*

Gender Roles

An important aspect of understanding other people is knowing about social roles, including those linked to being male or female. All cultures establish expectations about **sex roles**—also known as **gender roles**—which are the general patterns of work, appearance, and behavior associated with being a man or a woman. Gender roles appear in every culture, but they are more pronounced in some cultures than in others. One analysis revealed, for example, that where smaller differences in social status exist between males and females, gender-role differences are smaller as well (Wood & Eagly, 2002). In North America, some roles—such as homemaker and firefighter—have traditionally been tied to gender, although these traditions are weakening. Research by Deborah Best suggests that although children show gender-role expectations earliest in Muslim countries (where the differences in roles are perhaps most extreme), children in all 25 countries she studied eventually developed them (Best, 1992; Williams & Best, 1990).

Gender roles appear and persist because they are deeply rooted in both nature and nurture. Small physical and behavioral differences between the sexes appear early on and tend to increase over the years. For example, girls tend to speak and write earlier and to be better at grammar and spelling than boys (Halpern, 1997). Girls are also able to read emotional signals at younger ages than boys (Dunn et al., 1991) and to ask for help as well as offer it (Benenson & Koulnazarian, 2008). Their play also tends to be

LEARNING GENDER ROLES ▶

In every culture, socialization by parents and others typically encourages the interests, activities, and other characteristics traditionally associated with a child's own gender.

gender roles (sex roles) Patterns of work, appearance, and behavior that society associates with being male or female.

© Superstudio/The Image Bank/Getty Images

more orderly. Boys tend to be more skilled than girls at manipulating objects, constructing three-dimensional forms, and mentally manipulating complex figures and pictures (Choi & Silverman, 2003; Newhouse, Newhouse, & Astur, 2007). They are more physically active and aggressive and are more inclined to hit obstacles or people (Baillargeon et al., 2007; Card et al., 2008; Ostrov, 2006). They play in larger groups and spaces and enjoy noisier, more strenuous physical games (Fabes, Martin, & Hanish, 2003; Rose & Rudolph, 2006).

Biological Factors   A biological contribution to these and other male-female differences is supported by many different types of evidence. Research in behavioral genetics shows that genes exert a moderate influence on the appearance of gender-typed behaviors (Iervolino et al., 2005). Sex differences are evident at very early ages (Baillargeon et al., 2007). Researchers have found differences in anatomy, hormones, and brain organization and functioning (Auyeung et al., 2009; Geary, 1999; Ruble, Martin, & Berenbaum, 2006). A biological basis for male-female differences is also supported by cross-cultural research that shows consistency in gender patterns despite differing socialization (Simpson & Kenrick, 1997). In virtually every culture, for example, males are more violent than females. Research with nonhuman primates has found sex differences that parallel those seen in human children. For example, young female animals preferred playing with dolls and young males preferred playing with a toy car (Alexander & Hines, 2002; Williams & Pleil, 2008).

Social Factors   There is no doubt, though, that socialization also influences gender roles, partly by exaggerating whatever sex differences may already exist (Hyde, 2005, 2007). From the moment they are born, boys and girls are treated differently. Adults usually play more gently with, and talk more to, infants they believe to be girls than infants they believe to be boys (Culp, Cook, & Housley, 1983). They often shower their daughters with dolls and tea sets, their sons with trucks and tools. They tend to encourage boys to achieve, compete, and explore; to control their feelings; to be independent; and to assume personal responsibility. They more often encourage girls to be expressive, nurturing, reflective, dependent, domestic, obedient, and unselfish (Ruble, Martin, & Berenbaum, 2006). In short, parents, teachers, and television role models consciously or accidentally pass on their ideas about "appropriate" behaviors for boys and girls (Parke & Buriel, 2006; Ruble et al., 2006). They also convey information about gender-appropriate interests. For example, sixth-grade girls and boys express equal interest in science and earn the same grades. Yet parents underestimate their daughters' interest in science, believe that science is difficult for them, and are less likely to give them scientific explanations when working on a physics task (Tenenbaum & Leaper, 2003).

Children also pick up ideas about gender-appropriate behavior from their peers (Martin & Fabes, 2001; Rose & Rudolph, 2006). For example, boys tend to be better than girls at computer or video games (Greenfield, 1994). However, this difference stems partly from the fact that boys encourage and reward each other for skilled performance at these games more than girls do (Law, Pellegrino, & Hunt, 1993). Children are also more likely to play with children of the same sex and in gender-typical ways on the playground than they are in private, at home, or in the classroom (Luria, 1992). An analysis of 143 studies of sex differences in aggression showed that boys acted significantly and consistently more aggressively than girls, but especially so when they knew they were being watched (Hyde, 1986). Among girls, aggression is less obvious; it is usually "relational aggression" that shows up in nasty words, not punching (Crick et al., 2004).

In short, social and cultural training tends to support and amplify any biological predispositions that distinguish boys and girls. Gender roles reflect a mix of nature and nurture. (Gender roles and other elements of early development are summarized in "In Review: Social and Emotional Development During Infancy and Childhood.")

In Review

Social and Emotional Development During Infancy and Childhood

AGE	RELATIONSHIPS WITH PARENTS	RELATIONSHIPS WITH OTHER CHILDREN	SOCIAL UNDERSTANDING
Birth–2 years	Infants form an attachment to the primary caregiver.	Play focuses on toys, not on other children.	Infants respond to emotional expressions of others.
2–4 years	Children become more independent and no longer need their parents' constant attention.	Toys are a way of eliciting responses from other children.	Young children can recognize emotions of others.
4–10 years	Parents actively socialize their children.	Children begin to cooperate, compete, play games, and form friendships with peers.	Children learn social rules (such as politeness) and roles (such as being a male or female).

1. *As part of their social development, children learn _____, which tell them what patterns of appearance and behavior are associated with being male or female.*
2. *Teaching children to talk quietly in a restaurant is part of the process called _____.*
3. *Strict rules and the threat of punishment are typical of _____ parenting.*

The efforts of some parents to deemphasize gender roles in their children's upbringing may be helping to reduce the size of sex differences in areas such as verbal and quantitative skills. However, the evolutionary approach to psychology suggests that other sex differences are unlikely to change much. These differences include males' greater ability to visualize the rotation of objects in space and females' greater ability to read facial expressions (Quinn & Liben, 2008). Evolutionary psychologists see these differences as deeply rooted reflections of gender-related hunting versus child-rearing duties that were adaptive eons ago for the survival of both sexes (Buss, 2004a). Others have suggested that such differences result from prenatal exposure to male or female hormones that shape brain development in different ways (Halpern, 1997). Still others see gender differences as reflecting social inequality, not just biological destiny (Wood & Eagly, 2002). Whatever the cause of gender differences, it is important to remember that most of them are quite small (Hyde, 2005).

Adolescence

▶ *What threatens adolescents' self-esteem?*

The years of middle childhood usually pass smoothly as children busy themselves with schoolwork, hobbies, friends, and clubs. But in adolescence, things change dramatically. All adolescents undergo significant changes in size, shape, and physical capacities. In Western cultures, many adolescents also experience huge changes in their social lives, reasoning abilities, and views of themselves.

The Challenges of Change

A sudden spurt in physical growth is a visible signal that adolescence has begun. This growth spurt peaks at about age 12 for girls and at about age 14 for boys (Tanner, 1978; see Figure 9.6). Suddenly, adolescents find themselves in new bodies. At around the peak of the growth spurt, menstruation begins in females and live sperm are produced in males. This condition of being able to reproduce is called **puberty.**

puberty   The condition of being able, for the first time, to reproduce.

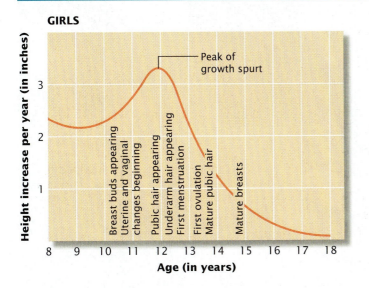

GIRLS

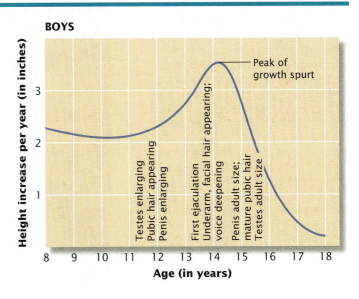

BOYS

FIGURE 9.6 ■ PHYSICAL CHANGES IN ADOLESCENCE

At about ten and a half years of age, girls begin their growth spurt, and by age twelve, they are taller than their male peers. When boys, at about twelve and a half years of age, begin their growth spurt, they usually grow faster and for a longer period of time than girls. Adolescents may grow as much as five inches a year. The development of sexual characteristics accompanies these changes in height. The ages at which these changes occur vary considerably across individuals, but the sequence of changes is the same.

In Western cultures, *early adolescence* (the period from age 11 to 14 or so) is filled with challenges. Sexual interest stirs and there are opportunities to smoke, drink alcohol, and take other drugs (Patton et al., 2004; Reyna & Farley, 2006). Adolescents tend to spend more time with peers than with family, to be more influenced by peers, and to take more risks and seek out more novel sensations than either younger children or adults do (Gardner & Steinberg, 2005; Steinberg, 2007, 2008). Much of this behavior seems to be due to the different rates at which parts of the adolescent brain develop. The impulse control areas in the prefrontal cortex complete their development long after the emotional and reward-related areas of the limbic system do (Casey, Getz, & Galvan, 2008; Steinberg, 2007, 2008). All this change can be disorienting. Adolescents—especially early-maturing girls—may experience bouts of depression and other psychological problems (Ge, Conger, & Elder, 2001; Ohring, Graber, & Brooks-Gunn, 2002).

Some of these problems appear as adolescents begin to face challenges to their *self-esteem*, their sense of being worthy, capable, and deserving of respect (Harter, 2006). Adolescents are especially vulnerable if other stressors occur at the same time (DuBois et al., 1992; Kling et al., 1999). The switch from elementary school to middle school is particularly challenging. Declining grades are especially likely among students who were already having trouble in school or who don't have confidence in their own abilities (Rudolph et al., 2001). But grades do not affect self-esteem in all teens; many base their self-esteem primarily on what others think of them or on other social factors that might affect their feelings of self-worth (Crocker & Wolfe, 2001).

The changes and pressures of adolescence are often played out at home. Many teenagers become discontented with their parents' rules and values, leading to arguments over everything from taking out the garbage to who left the gallon of milk on top of the refrigerator. Serious conflicts may lead adolescents—especially those who do not feel close to their parents—to serious problems, including running away, pregnancy, stealing, taking drugs, or even suicide (Blum, Beuhring, & Rinehart, 2000; Goldstein, Davis-Kean, & Eccles, 2005). Fortunately, although the bond with parents weakens during the transition from early to mid-adolescence, most adolescents and young adults maintain reasonably good relationships with their parents (van Wel, ter Bogt, & Raaijmakers, 2002). In fact, research suggests that although most parents and teachers seem to believe that adolescence is a time of "storm and stress" in Western cultures (Hines & Paulson, 2007), more than half of today's teens find early adolescence relatively trouble free (Arnett, 1999, 2007); only about 15 percent of the adolescents studied experience serious turmoil.

© Charles Gulling/zefa/Corbis

DIGITAL CONNECTIONS ▶

Adolescents spend more time on line and more often use instant messaging and other electronic communication technologies than either adults or children (Valkenburg & Peter, 2009). They most often use the Internet to communicate with their network of friends (Valkenburg & Peter, 2007a) and find that this enhances both their friendships and their sense of well-being (Valkenburg & Peter, 2007b). About a third believe that online communication is more effective than in-person conversation for disclosing intimate personal information. Because this technology is relatively new, we do not yet know what (if any), long-term effects it might have on adolescents' cognitive functioning, such as planning, thinking flexibly and abstractly, learning rules, initiating appropriate actions and inhibiting inappropriate ones, and focusing attention on relevant information.

Love and Sex in Adolescence   Surveys suggest that nearly half of 15-year-olds and 70 percent of 18-year-olds in North America have romantic relationships (Carver, Joyner, & Udry, 2003). Approximately half of adolescents between ages 15 and 19 say they have had sexual intercourse, about 55 percent have engaged in oral sex, and roughly 10 percent have tried anal sex (Melby, 2008; National Center for Chronic Disease Prevention and Health Promotion, 2002). Teens who have sex differ from those who do not in a number of ways. They hold less conventional attitudes and values and they are more likely to smoke, use alcohol and other drugs (National Center on Addiction and Substance Abuse, 2004), be aggressive, and have attention problems in school (Schofield et al., 2008). They also spend more unsupervised time after school (Cohen et al., 2002), they are more likely to belong to peer groups with socially deviant behavioral norms (diNoia, & Schinke, 2008), and they are more likely to have sexually active best friends (Jaccard, Blanton, & Dodge, 2005). Their parents tend to be less educated, less likely to exert control over them, and less likely to talk openly with them. The typical pairing of sexually active heterosexual teens is a "macho" male and a "girly" female (Udry & Chantala, 2003). Adolescents who displayed poor self-control skills as children are the ones most likely to take greater sexual risks, such as having multiple partners and not using condoms (Atkins, 2008; Raffaelli & Crockett, 2003).

Too often, sexual activity leads to declining interest in academic achievement and in school generally (Frisco, 2008), as well as to sexually transmitted diseases, and unplanned and unwanted pregnancies. Teenagers have the highest rates of sexually transmitted diseases (such as gonorrhea, chlamydia, human papillomavirus, and pelvic inflammatory disease) of any age group (National Center for Health Statistics, 2000; Ross, 2002). Each year, roughly half of the 19 million reported cases of sexually transmitted diseases occur in adolescents (Malhotra, 2008); these cases include about one fourth of all teenage girls (Contemporary Sexuality, 2008; Hampton, 2008). One-fifth of all AIDS cases start in adolescence. Teenage pregnancy rates declined between 1991 and 2005, but began to rise again in 2006 (Centers for Disease Control and Prevention, 2009a); the latest figures suggest that nearly 750,000 teenage girls in the United States get pregnant before they reach age 19 and about 435,000 of them become teenage mothers (Malhotra, 2008; Martin et al., 2009). The teens most likely to become pregnant are those with little confidence in themselves or in their educational futures (Young et al., 2004). To combat the problems associated with teenage pregnancy, some communities have begun to use innovative methods, such as San Francisco's SEXINFO, which allows adolescents to get information about sex, contraception, STDs, and other topics by text messaging (Levine, McCright et al., 2008).

MOTHERS TOO SOON? ▲

More than half of the U.S. adolescents who become pregnant elect to keep their babies and become single mothers. In 2008, 18 girls at Gloucester High School in Massachusetts reportedly decided to get pregnant as a group. They told reporters that they wanted to have someone to love them unconditionally and that they wanted to raise their children together (Gibbs, 2008; Kingsbury & McLeod, 2008). Like other unmarried teenage mothers, these girls and their children are likely to face special academic, social, and other problems.

A teenage pregnancy can create problems for the mother, the baby, and others in the family. Teenage parents tend to be less positive and stimulating with their children than older parents and are more likely to abuse them (Brooks-Gunn & Chase-Lansdale, 2002). The children of teenage parents, in turn, are more likely to develop behavior problems and to do poorly in school than those whose parents are older (Moffitt, 2002; National Center for Health Statistics, 2000). For this reason, support programs for teenage mothers have been developed, and a number of them have reported some success in three areas: alleviating the mothers' symptoms of depression, increasing the mothers' parenting capabilities, and achieving the mothers' educational goals (Cox et al., 2008; Sadler et al., 2007).

Identity and Development of the Self

In many less economically developed nations today (and in the United States in the nineteenth century), early adolescence ends at around age 14. This age marks the onset of adulthood—a time when work, parenting, and grown-up responsibilities begin. In modern North America, the transition from childhood to adulthood often lasts well into the twenties. Adolescents spend a lot of time being students or trainees. This lengthened adolescence has created special problems—among them, the matter of finding or forming an identity.

Forming a Personal and Ethnic Identity   Preschool children asked to describe themselves often mention a favorite or habitual activity: "I watch TV" or "I play in the yard." At eight or nine, children identify themselves by giving facts such as their sex, age, name, physical appearance, and likes and dislikes. They may still describe themselves in terms of what they do, but they now include how well they do it compared with other children. Then, at about age eleven, children begin to describe themselves in terms of social relationships, personality traits, and other general, stable psychological characteristics such as "smart" or "friendly" (Sakuma, Endo, & Muto, 2000; Shaffer, 1999). These changes in the way children and adolescents describe themselves suggest changes in the way they think about themselves. As they become more self-conscious, they gradually develop a personal identity as unique individuals.

Their personal identity may be affected by their **ethnic identity**—the part of a person's identity that reflects the racial, religious, or cultural group to which the person belongs (French et al., 2006). In melting-pot nations such as the United States, some members of ethnic minorities may identify with their ethnic group—Chinese, Mexican, or Italian, for example—even more than with their national citizenship. Children are aware of ethnic cues such as skin color before they reach the age of three. Minority-group children notice these cues earlier than other children and prefer to play with children from their own group (Milner, 1983). In high school, most students hang out with members of their own ethnic group. They tend not to know classmates in other ethnic groups well, seeing them more as members of those groups than as individuals (Steinberg, Dornbusch, & Brown, 1992). A positive ethnic identity contributes to self-esteem, partly because seeing their own group as superior makes people feel good about themselves and is associated with more positive attitudes about education (Fiske, 1998; Fuligni, Witkow, & Garcia, 2005). Adolescents with a strong ethnic identity are less likely to become delinquents, especially if they are from ethnic minorities (Bruce & Waelde, 2008), and they are more likely to do better academically (Adelabu, 2008). As described in the chapter on social psychology, the same processes that create ethnic identity can also sow the seeds of ethnic prejudice, but such prejudice is not inevitable. Adolescents who regularly interact with members of other ethnic groups usually become less prejudiced adults (Phinney, Ferguson, & Tate, 1997), and those who have achieved a secure ethnic identity of their own have more positive attitudes toward—and more mature ways of thinking about—other cultural groups (Phinney, Jacoby, & Silva, 2007).

ethnic identity   The part of a person's identity that reflects the racial, religious, or cultural group to which that person belongs.

Facing the Identity Crisis   Identity formation is the central task of adolescence in Erikson's theory of psychosocial development. According to Erikson (1968), events of late adolescence—graduating from high school, going to college, and forming new

HANGING OUT, SEPARATELY ▶

Ethnic identity is that part of our personal identity that reflects the racial, religious, or cultural group to which we belong. Ethnic identity often leads people to interact mainly with others who share that same identity. To what extent is this true of you? You can get a rough idea by jotting down the ethnicity of all the people you chose to spend time with over the past week or so.

© Spencer Grant/PhotoEdit

relationships—challenge the adolescent's self-concept and trigger an **identity crisis** (see Table 9.2). In this crisis, the adolescent must develop the self-image of a unique person by pulling together self-knowledge acquired during childhood. If infancy and childhood brought trust, autonomy, and initiative, according to Erikson, adolescents will resolve the identity crisis positively and develop feelings of self-confidence and competence. If infancy and childhood resulted in feelings of mistrust, shame, guilt, and inferiority, adolescents will be confused about their identity and goals.

In Western cultures there is some limited empirical support for Erikson's ideas about the identity crisis. In late adolescence, young people do consider alternative identities (Waterman, 1982). They may "try out" being rebellious, studious, or detached as they attempt to resolve questions about sexuality, self-worth, industriousness, and independence, but late adolescence is also a time when many people become more aware of their obligations to their families (Fuligni & Pedersen, 2002). By the time they are 21, about half of the adolescents studied have resolved the identity crisis in a way that is consistent with their self-image and the historical era in which they are living. They enter young adulthood with self-confidence. They are basically the same people they were when they entered adolescence, but they now have more mature attitudes and behavior, more consistent goals and values, and a clearer idea of who they are (Savin-Williams & Demo, 1984). For those who fail to resolve identity issues—either because they avoided the identity crisis by accepting the identity their parents set for them or because they postponed dealing with the crisis and remain uncommitted and lacking in direction—there are often problems ahead (Lange & Byrd, 2002).

Moral Development

Adolescents are able to develop an identity partly because, according to Piaget's theory, they have entered the *formal operational period,* which allows them to think logically and reason about abstract concepts. Adolescents often find themselves applying these advanced cognitive skills to questions of morality.

Kohlberg's Stages of Moral Reasoning   To examine how people think about morality, psychologists have asked them to say how they would resolve moral dilemmas and to describe the reasoning behind their choices. Perhaps the most famous of these is the "Heinz dilemma," in which people must decide whether a man named

identity crisis   The phase during which an adolescent attempts to develop an integrated self-image as a unique person by pulling together self-knowledge acquired during childhood.

TABLE 9.3 ■ KOHLBERG'S STAGES OF MORAL DEVELOPMENT

Kohlberg's stages of moral reasoning describe differences in how people think about moral issues. Here are some examples of answers that people at different stages of development might give to the "Heinz dilemma" described in the text. This dilemma is more realistic than you might think. In 1994, a man was arrested for robbing a bank after being turned down for a loan to pay for his wife's cancer treatments.

Stage	What Is Right?	Should Heinz Steal the Drug?
Preconventional		
1	Obeying and avoiding punishment from a superior authority	"Heinz should not steal the drug because he will be jailed."
2	Making a fair exchange, a good deal	"Heinz should steal the drug because his wife will repay him later."
Conventional		
3	Pleasing others and getting their approval	"Heinz should steal the drug because he loves his wife and because she and the rest of the family will approve."
4	Doing your duty, following rules and social order	"Heinz should steal the drug for his wife because he has a duty to care for her," or "Heinz should not steal the drug because stealing is illegal."
Postconventional		
5	Respecting rules and laws but recognizing that they may have limits	"Heinz should steal the drug because life is more important than property."
6	Following universal ethical principles such as justice, reciprocity, equality, and respect for human life and rights	"Heinz should steal the drug because of the principle of preserving and respecting life."

Heinz should steal a rare and unaffordably expensive drug in order to save his wife from cancer.

By posing moral dilemmas such as this one, Lawrence Kohlberg found that the reasons given for moral choices change systematically and consistently with age (Kohlberg & Gilligan, 1971). Young children make moral judgments that differ from those of older children, adolescents, or adults. Kohlberg proposed that moral reasoning develops in six stages, which are summarized in Table 9.3. These stages, he said, are not tightly linked to a person's chronological age. Instead, there is a range of ages for reaching each stage, and not everyone reaches the highest level.

Stage 1 and Stage 2 moral judgments, which are most typical of children under the age of nine, tend to be selfish in nature. Kohlberg called this level of moral reasoning **preconventional** because it is not based on the conventions or rules that usually guide social interactions in society. People at this level of **moral development** are mainly concerned with avoiding punishment or following rules when it is to their own advantage. At the **conventional** level of moral reasoning, Stages 3 and 4, people care about other people. They think that morality consists of following rules and conventions such as duty to the family, to marriage vows, and to the country. The moral reasoning of children and adolescents from nine to nineteen is most often at this level. Stages 5 and 6 represent the highest level of moral reasoning, which Kohlberg called **postconventional** because it occurs after conventional reasoning. Moral judgments at this level are based on personal standards or universal principles of justice, equality, and respect for human life, not just on the demands of authority figures or society. People who have reached this level view rules and laws as arbitrary but respect them because they protect human welfare. They believe that individual rights can sometimes justify violating these laws if the laws become destructive. People do not usually reach this level until sometime after the end of adolescence. Stage 6 is seen only rarely, in extraordinary individuals. Studies of Kohlberg's stages have generally supported the sequence he proposed (Turiel, 2006).

Limitations of Kohlberg's Stages   Do Kohlberg's stages appear across cultures? In general, yes. Forty-five studies in 27 cultures from Alaska to Zambia showed that people do tend to make upward progress through Kohlberg's stages, without reversals

preconventional reasoning   Moral reasoning that is not based on the conventions or rules that guide social interactions in a society.

moral development   The growth of an individual's understanding of the concepts of right and wrong.

conventional reasoning   Moral reasoning that reflects a concern about other people as well as the belief that morality consists of following rules and conventions.

postconventional reasoning   Moral reasoning that reflects moral judgments based on personal standards or universal principles of justice, equality, and respect for human life.

(Snarey, 1987). Stages 5 and 6, however, did not always appear. Further, the moral judgments made in some cultures do not always fit neatly into Kohlberg's stages. For example, some people in collectivist cultures, such as Papua New Guinea, Taiwan, and Israeli kibbutzim, explained their answers to moral dilemmas by pointing to the importance of the community. And people in India included in their moral reasoning the importance of acting in accordance with one's caste (social class) and with maintaining personal purity (Shweder et al., 1994). As in other areas of cognitive development, culture plays a significant role in shaping moral judgments.

Gender may also play a role. Carol Gilligan (1982, 1993) has suggested that Kohlberg's research documented mainly the abstract, impersonal concept of justice typically seen in males. When Gilligan asked people about moral conflicts, the majority of men focused on justice, but only half of the women did. The other half focused on caring. This finding supports Gilligan's belief that for North American females, the moral ideal is to protect enduring relationships and fulfill human needs. This difference between men and women has not been found consistently, however (Jaffee & Hyde, 2000). In fact, it appears that males and females are capable of using either approach to moral reasoning (Johnston, 1988). The tendency for females to focus on caring more than males do and for males to focus on justice more than females do appears most clearly when they are resolving hypothetical moral dilemmas (Turiel, 2006). When resolving real-life moral issues, both men and women focus more on caring than on justice (Walker, 1995).

Taken together, the results of research in different countries and with both genders suggest that moral ideals are not absolute and universal. Moral development is apparently an adaptation to the moral world and the specific situations in which people find themselves (Bersoff, 1999). Formal operational reasoning may be necessary for people to reach the highest level of moral reasoning, but formal operational reasoning alone is not sufficient. To some extent, at the highest levels, moral reasoning is a product of culture and history, of situations, and of people's emotions and goals in those situations (Krebs & Denton, 2005; Turiel, 2006).

Adulthood

> *What developmental changes occur in adulthood?*

Development does not end with adolescence. Adults too go through transitions and experience physical, cognitive, and social changes. It has been suggested that adulthood emerges as early as age 18 (Arnett, 2000), but for our purposes, adulthood can be divided into three periods: *early adulthood* (ages 20 to 39), *middle adulthood* (ages 40 to 65), and *late adulthood* (beyond age 65).

Physical Changes

In early adulthood, physical growth continues. Shoulder width, height, and chest size increase and people continue to develop their athletic abilities. By their mid-thirties nearly everyone shows some hearing impairment, but for most people, the years of early adulthood are the prime of life.

In middle adulthood, other physical changes slowly emerge. The most common of these involve the further loss of sensory sharpness (Fozard et al., 1977). People become less sensitive to light, less accurate at perceiving differences in distance, and slower and less able at seeing details. Increased farsightedness is common among people in their forties, and they may need glasses to correct for it. In their late forties or early fifties, women generally experience *menopause,* the shutdown of reproductive capability. Estrogen and progesterone levels drop and the menstrual cycle eventually ceases.

Most people are well into late adulthood before their bodily functions show noticeable impairment. However, inside the body, bone mass is dwindling and the risk of heart disease is increasing. Men shrink about an inch in height and women about two inches as their posture changes and cartilage disks between the spinal vertebrae become thinner. Older adults tend to go to sleep earlier but may find it harder to sleep through the night without awakening to use the bathroom (Park et al., 2002). Hardening of the arteries and a buildup of fat deposits on the artery walls may lead to heart disease. The digestive system slows down and becomes less efficient. Both digestive disorders and heart disease sometimes result from problems of diet—too little fluid, too little fiber, too much fat—and inactivity. In addition, the brain shrinks during late adulthood. The few reflexes that remained after infancy, such as the knee-jerk reflex, weaken or disappear. The flow of blood to the brain slows. As in earlier years, many of these changes can be delayed or diminished by a healthy diet and exercise (Brach et al., 2003; Larson et al., 2006; Seeman & Chen, 2002).

Cognitive Changes

Adulthood is marked by increases as well as decreases in cognitive abilities. Reaction times become slower and more variable (Deary & Der, 2005), and although abilities that involve intensive information processing begin to decline in early adulthood, those that depend on accumulated knowledge and experience increase and don't begin to decline until old age, and some individuals never experience this decline. In fact, older adults may function as well as or better than younger adults in situations that tap their long-term memories and well-learned skills (Park et al., 2002; Park & Gutchess, 2006). The experienced teacher may deal with an unruly child more skillfully than the new teacher, and the senior lawyer may understand the implications of a new law better than the recent graduate. Their years of accumulating and organizing information can make older adults practiced, skillful, and wise.

Early and Middle Adulthood   Until age 60 at least, important cognitive abilities improve. During this period, adults do better on tests of vocabulary, comprehension, and general knowledge—especially if they use these abilities in their daily lives or engage in enriching activities such as travel or reading (Park, 2001). Young and middle-aged adults learn new information and new skills and remember old information and hone old skills. In fact, it is in their forties through their early sixties that people tend to put in the best performance of their lives on complex mental tasks such as reasoning, verbal memory, and vocabulary (Willis & Schaie, 1999).

The nature of thought may also change during adulthood. Adult thought is often more complex and adaptive than adolescent thought (Labouvie-Vief, 1992). Unlike adolescents, adults see both the possibilities and the problems in every course of action—in deciding whether to start a new business, back a political candidate, move to a new place, or change jobs. Middle-aged adults are more expert than adolescents or young adults at making rational decisions and at relating logic and abstractions to actions, emotions, social issues, and personal relationships (Tversky & Kahneman, 1981). As they appreciate these relationships, their thought becomes more global, more concerned with broad moral and practical issues (Labouvie-Vief, 1982). It has been suggested that the achievement of these new kinds of thinking reflects a stage of cognitive development that goes beyond Piaget's formal operational period (Lutz & Sternberg, 1999). In this stage, people's thinking becomes *dialectical,* which means they understand that knowledge is relative, not absolute. They realize that what is considered as wise today might have been thought foolish in times past. They see life's contradictions as an inevitable part of reality, and they tend to weigh various solutions to problems rather than just accepting the first one that springs to mind.

Late Adulthood   It is not until late in adulthood, after the age of 65 or so that some intellectual abilities decline noticeably (Craik & Salthouse, 2008). Generally, these are abilities that require intense mental effort, such as rapid and flexible manipulation of ideas and symbols, and active thinking and reasoning (Baltes, 1993, 1994; Bugg et al., 2006; Finkel et al., 2003; Gilmore, Spinks, & Thomas, 2006; see Figure 9.7). Older adults do just as well as younger ones at tasks they know well, such as naming familiar

FIGURE 9.7   ■   MENTAL ABILITIES OVER THE LIFE-SPAN

Mental abilities collectively known as "fluid" intelligence—speed and accuracy of information processing, for example—begin to decline quite early in adult life. Changes in these biologically based aspects of thinking are usually not noticeable until late adulthood, however. "Crystallized" abilities learned over a lifetime—such as reading, writing, comprehension of language, and professional skills—decline too, but later and at a slower pace (Finkel et al., 2007; Li et al., 2004).
Source: Adapted from Baltes (1994).

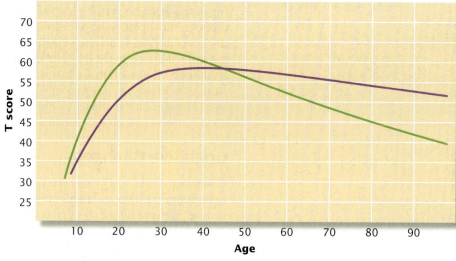

Crystallized intelligence

Fluid intelligence

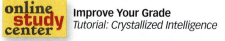
Improve Your Grade
Tutorial: Crystallized Intelligence

objects (Radvansky, 1999). However, when asked to perform an unfamiliar task or solve a complex problem they have not seen before, older adults are generally slower and less effective than younger ones (Craik & Rabinowitz, 1984). When faced with complex problems, older people apparently suffer from having too much information to sift through (Gazzaley et al., 2005). They have trouble considering, choosing, and executing solutions (Arenberg, 1982; Peters et al., 2007). As people age, they grow less efficient at organizing the elements of a problem and at holding and mentally manipulating more than one idea at a time. They have difficulty doing tasks that require them to divide their attention between two activities and are slower at shifting their attention back and forth between those activities (Smith et al., 2001; Wecker et al., 2005). If older adults have enough time, though, and can separate the two activities, they can perform just as well as younger adults (Hawkins, Kramer, & Capaldi, 1993).

Usually, the loss of intellectual abilities is slow and need not cause severe problems (Bashore & Ridderinkhof, 2002). A study of older adults in Sweden (Nilsson, 1996) showed, for example, that their memory problems were largely confined to *episodic memory* (e.g., remembering what they had for lunch yesterday) rather than *semantic memory* (remembering general information, such as the capital of Italy). In other words, everyday abilities that involve verbal processes are likely to remain intact into advanced old age (Freedman, Aykan, & Martin, 2001).

The risk of cognitive decline is significantly lower for people who are healthy and psychologically flexible and who have a high level of education, income, and occupation. Environmental factors are important, too (Reynolds et al., 2005). Cognitive decline is slower among those who eat a healthy diet (Morris et al., 2006), live in an intellectually stimulating atmosphere with mentally able spouses or companions (Albert et al., 1995; Chodosh et al., 2002; Shimamura et al., 1995) and who had high IQ and activity levels in adolescence (Fritsch et al., 2005). Continued mental exercise—such as doing puzzles, painting, and having intellectually stimulating conversations with friends—can also help older adults think and remember effectively and creatively (Schooler, 2007; Verghese et al., 2003, 2006; Wilson, Beckett et al., 2002). Practice at memory and other information-processing tasks may even lead to some improvement in skills already impaired by old age and disuse (Erickson et al., 2007; Kramer & Willis, 2002; Rapp, Brenes, & Marsh, 2002; Tranter & Koutstaal, 2008). Maintaining physical fitness through dancing or other forms of aerobic exercise has been associated with better maintenance of skills on a variety of mental tasks, including those involving

STAYING ALERT, STAYING ACTIVE, STAYING ALIVE ▶

Sisters Alcantara, Claverine, and Nicolette of the School Sisters of Notre Dame convent were in their eighties or nineties when this photo was taken. They stayed alert by reading, solving puzzles, playing cards, and participating in vocabulary quizzes. The nuns at this convent are participating in a study of aging and the brain.

reaction time, reasoning, and divided attention (Abbott et al., 2004; McAuley, Kramer, & Colcombe, 2004; Weuve et al., 2004). And a life full of organized activities and opportunities to interact with a lots of different people—not just family members—seems best for preventing decline in communication abilities (Keller-Cohen et al., 2004).

The greatest threat to cognitive abilities in late adulthood is Alzheimer's disease. As the disease progresses, it leaves even the brightest minds incapable. Victims become emotionally flat, then disoriented, then mentally vacant. They usually die prematurely. The average duration of the disease, from onset to death, is seven years. But the age of onset and rate of decline depends on a number of factors, such as intelligence (Rentz et al., 2004), gender (Molsa, Marttila, & Rinne, 1995), and education (Mortimer, Snowdon, & Markesbery, 2003). Highly intelligent people show clinical signs of Alzheimer's later than the general population does. Women and people of either gender who are well educated and/or mentally active in old age deteriorate more slowly (Wilson et al., 2007b).

Social Changes

Adulthood is a time when changes occur in social relationships and positions. These changes do not come in neat, predictable stages but instead follow various paths, depending on individual experiences. Transitions—such as divorcing, being fired, going back to school, remarrying, losing a spouse to death, being hospitalized, getting arrested, moving back home, or retiring—are just a few of the turning points that can redirect a person's life path and lead to changes in personality (Caspi & Shiner, 2006; Roberts, Helson, & Klohnen, 2002).

Early Adulthood Men and women in Western cultures usually enter the adult world in their twenties. The process may begin with an "emerging adulthood" period during which they explore life's possibilities through education, dating, and travel before they settle into stable adult roles and responsibilities (Arnett, 2000; Roisman et al., 2004). They decide on an occupation (or at least take a job) and become preoccupied with their careers (Srivastava et al., 2003). They also become more agreeable—warm, generous, and helpful (Srivastava et al., 2003); more controlled and confident; more socially dominant, conscientious, and emotionally stable; and less angry and alienated (Roberts, Caspi, & Moffitt, 2001; Roberts, Walton, & Viechtbauer, 2006; Roberts & Mroczek, 2008). Nevertheless, by age 25 about 20 percent of young adults are still living with their parents, and just under half are still financially dependent

(Cohen et al., 2003). It is in their twenties, too, that young adults become more concerned with matters of romantic love. Having reached the sixth of Erikson's stages of psychosocial development noted in Table 9.2 (intimacy versus isolation), they begin to focus on forming mature relationships based on sexual intimacy, friendship, or mutual intellectual stimulation. The result may be marriage or some other form of committed relationship.

Just how willing and able people are to make intimate commitments may depend on their earlier attachment relationships (Birnbaum et al., 2006; Roisman, 2007; Treboux, Crowell, & Waters, 2004). Researchers have discovered that young adults' views of intimate relationships parallel the patterns of infant attachment that we described earlier (Campbell et al., 2005; Horowitz, Rosenberg, & Bartholomew, 1993). If their view reflects a secure attachment, they tend to feel valued and worthy of support and affection; they develop closeness easily. They have relationships characterized by joy, trust, and commitment. If their view reflects an insecure attachment, however, they tend to be preoccupied with relationships and may feel misunderstood, underappreciated, and worried about being abandoned. Their relationships are often negative, obsessive, and jealous. Alternatively, they may be aloof and unable to trust or to commit themselves to a partner. Overall, young adults whose parents have been accepting and supportive tend to develop warm and supportive romantic relationships (Conger et al., 2000; Dresner & Grolnick, 1996; Overbeek et al., 2007).

For many young adults, the experience of becoming parents represents entry into a major new developmental phase often accompanied by personal, social, and occupational changes (Palkovitz, Copes, & Woolfolk, 2001). This milestone usually comes earlier for young adults from lower income backgrounds, who are more likely to be in full-time employment and less likely to be living at home (Cohen et al., 2003). Often, satisfaction with the marriage or partnership declines once a baby is born (Doss et al., 2009; Gilbert, 2006), and about half of all marriages break under the strain (National Center for Health Statistics, 2001). Young mothers may experience particular dissatisfaction—especially if they resent the constraints infants bring, if they see their careers as important, if the infants are temperamentally difficult, if the partnerships are not strong, and if the partners are not supportive (Harwood, McLean, & Durkin, 2007; Shapiro, Gottman, & Carrere, 2000). When the father does not do his share of caring for the baby, both mothers and fathers are dissatisfied (Levy-Shiff, 1994). The ability of young parents to provide adequate care for their babies is related to their own attachment histories. New mothers whose attachments to their own mothers were secure tend to be more responsive to their infants and the infants, in turn, are more likely to develop secure attachments to them (Adam, Gunnar, & Tanaka, 2004; Behrens, Hesse, & Main, 2007; van IJzendoorn, 1995).

The challenges of young adulthood are complicated by the nature of family life today (Halpern, 2005). Forty years ago, about half of North American households consisted of married couples in their twenties and thirties—a breadwinner husband and a homemaker wife—raising at least two children together. This description now applies to only about 23.5 percent of households (Frey, 2003). Parents are older now because young adults are delaying marriage longer and waiting longer to have children. Many are having children without marrying or choosing to raise children on their own (Weinraub, Horvath, & Gringlas, 2002). Those who divorce face many unanticipated stressors, including money problems, changes in living circumstances and working hours, loneliness, anxiety, and, for custodial parents, a dramatic increase in housework and child-care tasks (Clarke-Stewart & Brentano, 2006). In short, the changes seen in families and family life over the past several decades have made it more challenging than ever to successfully navigate the years of early adulthood.

Middle Adulthood At around age 40, people go through a *midlife transition* during which they may rethink and modify their lives and relationships. Many feel invigorated and liberated; some may feel upset and have a "midlife crisis" (Beck, 1992; Levinson et al., 1978). The contrast between youth and middle age may be especially upsetting for men who matured early in adolescence and were sociable and athletic rather

BUILDING MONUMENTS ▶
Middle adulthood tends to be a time when people become deeply committed to building personal monuments, either by raising children or through achievements outside the home. This graduating parent seems to have accomplished both goals.

than intellectual (Block, 1971). Women who chose a career over a family now hear the biological clock ticking out their last childbearing years. Women who have had children, however, become more independent and confident and more oriented toward achievement and events outside the family (Helson & Moane, 1987). For both men and women, the emerging sexuality of their teenage children, the emptiness of the nest as children leave home, or the declining health of a parent may precipitate a crisis.

Following the midlife transition, the middle years of adulthood are often a time of satisfaction and happiness (Mroczek & Spiro, 2005). Many people become concerned with producing something that will outlast them—usually through parenthood and/or job achievements (Sheldon & Kasser, 2001; Zucker, Ostrove, & Stewart, 2002). Erikson called this concern the crisis of **generativity** because people are focused on producing or generating something. If people do not resolve this crisis, he suggested, they stagnate.

THE "SANDWICH" GENERATION ▶
During their midlife transition, many people feel "sandwiched" between generations—pressured by the social, emotional, and financial needs of their children on one side and the needs of their aging parents on the other (Keene & Prokos, 2007; Wujcik, 2008).

generativity The concern of adults in their forties with generating something enduring.

"When I was your age, I was an adult."

▲ Most people in their sixties want their offspring to be independent, so they may have mixed feelings toward children who continue to need financial support during an extended period of "emerging adulthood" (Pillemer & Suitor, 2002).

STILL GOING STRONG   ▲

At the age of 79, actor and Academy Award–winning director Clint Eastwood is a famous example of the many people whose late adulthood is healthy and vigorous. And he is not slowing down. His acting remains as riveting as ever, and the films he directs continue to attract huge audiences and critical acclaim.

terminal drop   A sharp decline in mental functioning that tends to occur in late adulthood, a few months or years before death.

In their fifties, most people become grandparents (Smith & Drew, 2002), though they may find it hard to believe they are no longer young (Karp, 1991). At this age, spending lots of time caring for young grandchildren can be stressful and may even increase the risk of heart disease (Lee, Colditz et al., 2003). One study of more than 7,000 adults suggested that the degree of happiness and healthiness people experience during middle adulthood depends on how much control they feel they have over their work, finances, marriages, children, and sex lives as well as how many years of education they completed and what kind of jobs they have (Azar, 1996).

Late Adulthood   Most people between 65 and 75 years of age think of themselves as middle-aged, not old (Neugarten, 1977). They are active and influential politically and socially, and they often are physically vigorous. Ratings of life satisfaction and self-esteem are, on average, as high in old age as during any other period of adulthood (Ben-Zur, 2002; Charles, Mather, & Carstensen, 2003; Hamarat et al., 2002). Men and women who have been employed usually retire from their jobs during this period. They adjust most easily to retirement if they view it as a choice (Swan, 1996).

Today, more people than ever are reaching old age. In fact, those over 75 make up the fastest-growing segment of the population, a group that is 25 times larger than it was a century ago. Today, 77,000 people in the United States are over 100, and the Census Bureau predicts that number will rise to 834,000 by 2050 (Volz, 2000). Old age is not necessarily a time of loneliness and desolation, but it is a time when people generally become more inward looking, cautious, and conforming (Reedy, 1983). It is a time when people develop coping strategies that increasingly take into account the limits of their control; people in this age group begin to accept what they cannot change, such as chronic health problems (Brandtstadter & Renner, 1990). Although they interact with others less frequently, older adults enjoy these interactions more (Carstensen, 1997).

Compared to younger adults, positive events account for a larger proportion of older people's memories (Mather & Carstensen, 2005), and older adults report less anger in response to interpersonal conflicts than do younger adults (Charles & Carstensen, 2008). In late adulthood, people find relationships more satisfying, supportive, and fulfilling than they did earlier in life. As they sense that time is running out, they value positive interactions and become selective about their social partners. As long as they have a network of at least three close relatives or friends, they are usually content.

The many changes associated with adolescence and adulthood are summarized in "In Review: Milestones of Adolescence and Adulthood."

Death and Dying

With the onset of old age, people become aware that death is approaching. They watch as their friends disappear. They may feel their health failing, their strength waning, and their intellectual capabilities declining. A few years or a few months before death, some people experience a sharp decline in mental functioning known as **terminal drop** (Small & Bäckman, 1999; Wilson et al., 2007a).

The awareness of impending death brings about the last psychological crisis, according to Erikson's theory. During this stage, people evaluate their lives and accomplishments and see them as meaningful (leading to a feeling of integrity) or meaningless (leading to a feeling of despair). They tend to become more philosophical and reflective. They attempt to put their lives into perspective. They revisit old memories, resolve past conflicts, and integrate past events. They may also become more interested in the religious and spiritual side of life. This "life review" may trigger anxiety, regret, guilt, and despair; the risk of suicide does increase with age (Anderson & Conwell, 2002). But it may also help people face their own deaths and the deaths of friends and relatives with a feeling of peace and acceptance (Lieberman & Tobin, 1983).

Even the actual confrontation with death does not have to bring despair and depression. When death finally is imminent, old people strive for a death with dignity, love, affection, physical contact, and no pain (Schulz, 1978). As they think about death,

In Review

Milestones of Adolescence and Adulthood

AGE	PHYSICAL CHANGES	COGNITIVE CHANGES	SOCIAL EVENTS AND PSYCHOLOGICAL CHANGES
Early adolescence (11–15 years)	Puberty brings reproductive capacity and marked bodily changes.	Formal operations and principled moral reasoning become possible for the first time. (This occurs only for some people.)	Social and emotional changes result from growing sexual awareness; adolescents experience mood swings, physical changes, and conflicts with parents.
Late adolescence (16–19 years)	Physical growth continues.	Formal operations and principled moral reasoning become more likely.	An identity crisis accompanies graduation from high school.
Early adulthood (20–39 years)	Physical growth continues.	Increases continue in knowledge, problem-solving ability, and moral reasoning.	People choose a job and often a mate; they may become parents.
Middle adulthood (40–65 years)	Size and muscle mass decrease; fat increases; eyesight declines; reproductive capacity in women ends.	Thought becomes more complex, adaptive, and global.	Midlife transition may lead to change; for most, the middle years are satisfying.
Late adulthood (over 65 years)	Size decreases; organs become less efficient.	Reasoning, mathematical ability, comprehension, novel problem solving, and memory may decline.	Retirement requires adjustments; people look inward; awareness of death precipitates life review.

1. The greatest threat to cognitive abilities in late adulthood is _____ disease.
2. Adolescents' _____ identity may be more defining than their national citizenship.
3. Not stealing because "I might get caught" reflects the _____ stage of moral reasoning.

they are comforted by their religious faith, their achievements, and the love of their friends and family.

Longevity Facing death with dignity and openness helps people complete the life cycle with a sense of life's meaningfulness, but most of us want to live as long as possible. How can we do so? Research suggests that longevity is greater in women and in people who do not have a history of heavy drinking or smoking. Longevity is also related to personality characteristics such as conscientiousness as a child (Friedman et al., 1995a) and curiosity as an adult (Swan & Carmelli, 1996). People with higher IQs and faster reaction times tend to live longer, too (Deary & Der, 2005), as do those who typically experienced happiness, enthusiasm, contentment, and other forms of *positive affect* during adulthood (Cohen & Pressman, 2006). Adults who had more positive self-perceptions when they were in their fifties and sixties lived seven and a half years longer than those with less positive self-perceptions. This factor was more predictive of longevity than were health problems such as high blood pressure, high cholesterol, smoking, lack of exercise, or being overweight (Levy et al., 2002). Still, people who restrict their caloric intake, engage in regular physical and mental exercise, and have a sense of control over important aspects of their lives are likely to live longer (Krause & Shaw, 2000; Manini et al., 2006; Yaffe et al., 2001). So eat your veggies, stay physically fit, and continue to think actively—not just to live longer later but also to live better now.

Human Development

As noted in the introductory chapter, all of psychology's subfields are related to one another. Our discussion of infantile amnesia illustrates just one way that the topic of this chapter, human development, is linked to the subfield of memory, which is discussed in the chapter on memory.

The Linkages diagram shows ties to two other subfields, and there are many more ties throughout the book. Looking for linkages among subfields will help you see how they all fit together and help you better appreciate the big picture that is psychology.

linkages

What happens to our memories of infancy? *(ans. on p. 359)*

How do we learn to speak? *(ans. on p. 273)*

Are childhood traits related to how long we live? *(ans. on p. 411)*

Chapter 6
Memory

Chapter 7
Thought, Language, and Intelligence

Chapter 10
Health, Stress, and Coping

SUMMARY ▶

Developmental psychology is the study of the course and causes of systematic, sequential, age-related changes in mental abilities, social relationships, emotions, and moral understanding over the life-span.

Exploring Human Development

▶ *What does "genetic influence" mean?*

A central question in developmental psychology concerns the relative influences of nature and nurture. Gesell stressed nature in his theory of development, proposing that development is *maturation*—the natural unfolding of abilities with age. Watson took the opposite

view, claiming that development is learning, as shaped by the external environment. In his theory of cognitive development, Piaget described how nature and nurture work together. Today we accept the notion that both nature and nurture affect development and ask not whether but how and to what extent each contributes. Research in *behavioral genetics* shows that complex traits, such as intelligence and personality, are influenced by many genes as well as by many environmental factors.

Beginnings

▶ *Why should pregnant women stay away from tobacco and alcohol?*

Development begins with the union of an ovum and a sperm to form a zygote, which develops into an *embryo*. *Genes*, which consist of *deoxyribonucleic acid (DNA)*, make up the *chromosomes* that are in each body cell. The embryonic stage is a *critical period* for development, a time when certain organs must develop properly or they never will. The development of organs at this stage is permanently affected by harmful *teratogens* such as tobacco, alcohol, or other drugs. After the embryo develops into a *fetus*, adverse conditions may harm the infant's size, behavior, intelligence, or health. Babies born to women who drink heavily are at risk for *fetal alcohol syndrome*.

Newborns have limited but effective senses of vision, hearing, taste, and smell. They exhibit many *reflexes*—swift, automatic responses to external stimuli. Motor development proceeds as the nervous system matures and muscles grow and as the infant experiments with and selects the most efficient movement patterns.

Infancy and Childhood: Cognitive Development

▶ *How do babies think?*

Cognitive development refers to the development of thinking, knowing, and remembering. According to Piaget, *schemas* are modified through the complementary processes of *assimilation* (fitting new objects or events into existing schemas) and *accommodation* (changing schemas when new objects will not fit existing schemas). During the *sensorimotor period,* infants progress from using only their senses and simple reflexes to forming mental representations of objects and actions. As a result, the child becomes capable of thinking about objects that are not present. The ability to recognize that objects continue to exist even when they are hidden from view is what Piaget called *object permanence*. During the *preoperational period,* children can use symbols, but they do not have the ability to think logically and rationally. Their understanding of the world is intuitive. When children develop the ability to think logically about concrete objects, they enter the period of *concrete operations*. At this time they can solve simple problems and have a knowledge of *conservation,* recognizing that, for example, the amount of a substance is not altered when its shape changes. The *formal operational period* begins in adolescence and allows thinking and logical reasoning about abstract ideas.

Today, developmental psychologists believe that new levels of cognition do not appear in sharply separated stages of global understanding but emerge more gradually and that children's reasoning can be affected by factors such as task difficulty and degree of familiarity with the objects and language involved.

Psychologists who explain cognitive development in terms of *information processing* have documented age-related improvements in children's attention, their abilities to explore and focus on features of the environment, and their memories. "Infantile amnesia" leaves us with virtually no memory of events from before the age of three. Several explanations have been suggested, but this phenomenon is not yet fully understood.

The specific content of cognitive development, including the development of scripts, depends on the cultural context in which children live. How fast children develop cognitive abilities depends to some extent on how stimulating and supportive their environments are. Children growing up in poverty are likely to have delayed or impaired cognitive abilities.

Infancy and Childhood: Social and Emotional Development

▶ *How do infants become attached to their caregivers?*

From the early months onward, infants and their caregivers respond to each other's emotional expressions. Most infants can be classified as having easy, difficult, or slow-to-warm-up *temperaments*. Whether they retain these temperamental styles depends to some extent on their parents' expectations and demands. According to *attachment theory*, infants form a deep form a deep, long-lasting emotional *attachment* to their mothers or other primary caregivers. Their *attachment behavior* may reflect secure or insecure attachment, depending. The process of *socialization* begins as parents teach their children the skills and rules needed in their culture, using *parenting styles* described as *authoritarian, permissive, authoritative,* or *uninvolved*. Among European American parents, those with authoritative styles tend to have more competent and cooperative children. Patterns of socialization depend on the culture and conditions in which parents find themselves.

Over the childhood years, interactions with peers evolve into cooperative and competitive encounters and friendships become more important. Changes in children's relationships are based in part on their growing social competence. Children become increasingly able to interpret and understand social situations and emotional signals. They also learn social rules and roles, including those related to gender. *Gender roles,* also known as *sex roles,* are based both on biological differences between the sexes and on implicit and explicit socialization by parents, teachers, and peers.

Adolescence

▶ *What threatens adolescents' self-esteem?*

Adolescents undergo significant changes not only in size, shape, and physical capacity but also, typically, in their social lives, reasoning abilities, and views of themselves. *Puberty* brings about physical changes that lead to psychological changes. Early adolescence is a period of shaky self-esteem. It is also a time when conflict with parents is likely to arise and when closeness with friends and conformity to peer group norms are likely to emerge. Later adolescence focuses on finding an answer to the question Who am I? Events such as graduating from high school and going to college challenge the adolescent's self-concept, precipitating an *identity crisis*. To resolve this crisis, the adolescent must develop an integrated self-image as a unique person, an image that often includes *ethnic identity*. *Moral development* progresses from *preconventional* to *conventional* and (possibly) *postconventional* stages. Principled moral judgment—shaped by gender and culture—becomes possible for the first time.

Adulthood

▶ *What developmental changes occur in adulthood?*

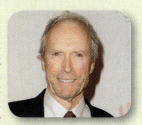

Physical, cognitive, and social changes occur throughout adulthood. During middle adulthood, changes begin that include decreased sharpness of the senses, increased risk of heart disease, and declining fertility. Nevertheless, most people do not experience major health problems until late adulthood.

The cognitive changes that occur in early and middle adulthood are generally positive, including improvements in reasoning and problem-solving ability. In late adulthood, some intellectual abilities decline—especially those involved in tasks that are unfamiliar, complex, or difficult. Other abilities, such as recalling facts or making wise decisions, tend not to decline.

In their twenties, young adults make choices about occupations and form intimate commitments. By the end of their thirties, they settle down and decide what is important. They become concerned with *generativity*—with producing something that will outlast them. Sometime around age forty, adults experience a midlife transition, which may or may not be a crisis. The forties and fifties are often a time of satisfaction. In their sixties, people contend with the issue of retirement. They generally become more inward looking, cautious, and conforming. In their seventies, eighties, and beyond, people confront their own mortality. They may become more philosophical and reflective as they review their lives. A few years or months before death, many experience a sharp decline in mental functioning known as **terminal drop**. Still, they strive for a death with dignity, love, and no pain.

Death is inevitable, but healthy diets, exercise, conscientiousness and curiosity, and a sense of control over one's life are associated with living longer and happier lives. Older adults feel better and live longer if they receive attention from other people, maintain an open attitude toward new experiences, and keep their minds active.

Put It in Writing

Write a short paper describing some aspects of your development over the past five years. Include comments on physical changes as well as changes in your thoughts, feelings, and behavior. Imagine yourself in another five years and describe what further changes you expect in your physical condition, lifestyle, relationships, ideas, emotional state, and behavior. Compare the changes that have taken place in your life with those we have described in this chapter for the average person of your age.

Personal Learning Activity

Ask several of your friends about the way their parents raised them, especially about how strict or permissive they were in providing discipline. Take notes on these interviews and then try to categorize your friends' parents as authoritarian, permissive, authoritative, or uninvolved. (You might try categorizing your own parents as well.) Was it easy to decide which category to use in each case? Do you think that additional categories are necessary to describe parenting styles? Do you think that your friends' personalities reflect the effects of the parenting styles described in this chapter? *For additional projects, see the Personal Learning Activities in the corresponding chapter of the study guide that accompanies this book.*

Take Action to Learn More ▶

Now that you have finished reading this chapter, how about exploring some of the ideas and information that you found most interesting? Here are some courses, books, films, and Internet resources to get you started. Enjoy!

Courses

Infancy
Child Development
Adolescence
Life-Span Development
Social Development
Cognitive Development
Death and Dying

Movies

Antwone Fisher; Radio Flyer. Overcoming abuse and abandonment.
Grumpy Old Men; On Golden Pond; Cocoon; Space Cowboys; Wrestling Ernest Hemingway; Driving Miss Daisy; The Whales of August. Aging.
About Schmidt; Father of the Bride. Aging; Erikson's stage of generativity versus stagnation.
The War; Pop and Me. Parenting styles.
The Scent of a Woman; Do the Right Thing; Schindler's List. Moral development, moral reasoning, and moral action.

Billy Elliot; Kissing Jessica Stein. Gender issues.
Lord of the Flies. Nature versus nurture.
Stand by Me; A Christmas Story; My Life as a Dog. Childhood.
Parenthood. Child rearing.
Little Man Tate; Searching for Bobby Fischer; What's Eating Gilbert Grape. Raising special children.
October Sky; American Graffiti; Revenge of the Nerds; Ferris Bueller's Day Off; The Breakfast Club; My Life in Pink; Rushmore. Adolescence.
Dead Poets Society; Harold and Maude; Hancock; Kung Fu Panda. Identity.
To Sir with Love; St. Elmo's Fire; Good Will Hunting; Reality Bites; Clerks; Chasing Amy. Young adulthood.
The Big Chill; American Beauty; Same Time, Next Year. Adulthood.
City Slickers. Midlife transition.
The Color Purple. Development of self-esteem.

Books

Deborah Blum, *Love at Goon Park: Harry Harlow and the Science of Affection* (Perseus, 2002). Study of Harlow's famous research.

Sampson Davis, George Jenkins, and Rameck Hunt, *The Pact: Three Young Men Make a Promise and Fulfill a Dream* (Penguin/Putnam, 2002). How three young men overcame their disadvantaged backgrounds and became doctors.

Lawrence J. Friedman, *Identity's Architect: A Biography of Erik H. Erikson* (Scribner's, 1999). Focusing on Erikson's own identity crisis.

Thomas Hine, *The Rise and Fall of the American Teenager* (Avon, 1999). Social and cultural history of adolescence.

Jeffrey W. Trawick-Smith, *Early Childhood Development: A Multicultural Perspective* (Prentice Hall, 1999). Introduction to cultural influences on development.

Alison Gopnik, Andrew N. Meltzoff, and Patricia K. Kuhl, *The Scientist in the Crib: Minds, Brains, and How Children Learn* (William Morrow, 1999). Readable summary of research in cognitive development.

Richard Shulz and Timothy A. Salthouse, *Adult Development and Aging: Myths and Emerging Realities* (Prentice Hall, 1998). The title says it all.

Rachel Simmons, *Odd Girl Out: The Hidden Culture of Aggression in Girls* (Harcourt

Books, 2002). Study of girls' relational aggression.

ROBIN KARR-MORSE AND MEREDITH S. WILEY, *Ghosts from the Nursery: Tracing the Roots of Violence* (Grove/Atlantic, 1999). How biological predispositions may lead to violence.

ROBERT KAREN, *Becoming Attached: First Relationships and How They Shape Our Capacity to Love* (Oxford University Press, 1995). Emotional development.

The Web

Essentials of Psychology **Book Companion Website**

www.cengage.com/psychology/bernstein

Visit the book companion website to access a wealth of resources, including chapter outlines, flashcards, web links, tutorial quizzes, and more!

CENGAGENOW™ Just what you need to know NOW! Spend time on what you need to master rather than on information you already have learned. Take a pre-test for this chapter, and CengageNOW will generate a personalized study plan based on your results. The study plan will identify the topics you need to review and direct you to online resources to help you master those topics. You can then take a post-test to help you determine the concepts you have mastered and what you will need to work on. Try it out! Go to www.cengage.com/login to sign in with an access code or to purchase access to this product.

Review of Key Terms ▶

Can you define each of the key terms in the chapter? Check your definitions against those on the pages shown in parentheses in the following list or in the Glossary at the end of the book.

accommodation (p. 352)
assimilation (p. 352)
attachment (p. 364)
attachment behavior (p. 366)
attachment theory (p. 364)
authoritarian parents (p. 369)
authoritative parents (p. 369)
behavioral genetics (p. 346)
chromosomes (p. 347)
concrete operations (p. 355)
conservation (p. 355)
conventional reasoning (p. 379)

critical period (p. 348)
deoxyribonucleic acid (DNA) (p. 347)
developmental psychology (p. 344)
embryo (p. 348)
ethnic identity (p. 377)
fetal alcohol syndrome (p. 349)
fetus (p. 348)
formal operational period (p. 355)
gender roles (p. 372)
generativity (p. 385)
genes (p. 347)
identity crisis (p. 378)
information processing (p. 357)
maturation (p. 346)
moral development (p. 379)
object permanence (p. 353)
parenting styles (p. 369)

permissive parents (p. 369)
postconventional reasoning (p. 379)
preconventional reasoning (p. 379)
preoperational period (p. 355)
puberty (p. 374)
reflexes (p. 350)
schemas (p. 352)
sensorimotor period (p. 353)
sex roles (p. 372)
socialization (p. 368)
temperament (p. 363)
teratogens (p. 348)
terminal drop (p. 386)
uninvolved parents (p. 369)

MULTIPLE-CHOICE ▶ Self Test

Select the best answer for each of the following questions. Then check your response against the Answer Key at the end of the book.

1. Ralph read an article that described intelligence as 50 percent heritable. Ralph can reasonably conclude that
   a. half of his intelligence came from his genes and half from his environment.
   b. about half of the variation in intelligence among groups of people can be accounted for by genetic influences.
   c. about half of a person's intelligence can be changed by environmental influences.
   d. about half the population got their intelligence from their genes alone.

2. When she became pregnant, Alyse was advised to quit smoking, but she didn't. Her baby is likely to be born _____.
   a. mentally retarded   **c.** underweight
   b. with facial deformities **d.** with an irritable temperament

3. When they brought their newborn, Tyrone, home from the hospital, his parents always laid him on his back, especially at night. As Tyrone grew, he began to roll over, sit up, pull himself up on furniture, and walk. He skipped the crawling stage. Tyrone's physical development is the result of _____.
   a. behavioral genetics alone
   b. maturation alone
   c. environmental influences alone
   d. maturation and environmental influences

4. Keshawn is one month old. He is most likely to look longest at

   _____.
   a. small figures on the wallpaper
   b. a ribbon hanging above his crib
   c. colorful figures
   d. a nearby human face

5. At six months of age, Jacob still demonstrates the grasping and rooting reflexes. This could signal that Jacob

a. has advanced motor skills.

b. has muscles that cannot support his body.

c. has a problem with brain development.

d. needs less environmental stimulation than the average baby.

6. When two-year-old Jesse sees a scuba diver emerge on the beach, he says "Big fish!" According to Piaget, Jesse used _____ to try to understand the new stimulus of a scuba diver.

a. assimilation

b. accommodation

c. object permanence

d. conservation

7. Adriana is crying because her teddy bear, Boyd, has fallen off the table and landed face down. She insists that her mother put a bandage on Boyd's nose. According to Piaget's theory, Adriana is most likely in the stage of _____ cognitive development.

a. sensorimotor

b. preoperational

c. concrete operational

d. formal operational

8. Renee Baillargeon's research focused on infants' understanding about the mental states of other people and how those states affect behavior. Baillargeon found that infants under the age of four

a. looked longer at "possible" events that they had experienced many times.

b. looked longer at events that violated their expectations about other people's beliefs.

c. do not yet have a "theory of mind" and thus are unable to anticipate what others might do.

d. can recognize the effects of people's true beliefs but are unable to recognize the effects of false beliefs.

9. According to research on information processing and memory, when you try to recall your first birthday, you are likely to

a. recall a general schema of "birthday" as well as details about your first one.

b. be unable to recall anything about your first birthday due to infantile amnesia.

c. recall information about your first birthday if you are shown pictures of yourself taken that day.

d. recall information about the birthday if you hear a tape recording of your party.

10. Tara is a difficult baby. She is irritable, sleeps at irregular intervals, and cries at unpredictable times. According to research on temperament, Tara will most likely

a. outgrow her difficult temperament and become an easier child.

b. remain difficult in childhood and may display aggressiveness.

c. develop a dependent relationship with her parents.

d. become independent and especially successful in school.

11. Harlow's research with infant monkeys and artificial mothers demonstrated that

a. infant monkeys become attached to the "mothers" that feed them.

b. infant monkeys become attached to the "mothers" that provide contact comfort.

c. attachment is entirely innate and has no learned component.

d. "mothering" is instinctive and has no learned component.

12. When young Habib's mother drops him off at the day care center, he always cries when she leaves. When his mother returns and lifts him up, Habib tries to squirm away. Habib is demonstrating a(n) _____ attachment to his mother.

a. secure

b. anxious insecure

c. avoidant insecure

d. ambivalent insecure

13. Sam and Alex are 16 and want to drive to a rock concert in a big city that is five hours away. Sam's parents explain that it is too dangerous for him to drive that distance and to be in a major city without an adult. They offer to drive him and Alex to the concert. Alex's parents tell him that it is no problem if he wants to drive their car and stay in the city overnight. According to Baumrind's research, Sam's parents are displaying a(n) _____ style of parenting, whereas Alex's parents are displaying a(n) _____ style.

a. authoritative; authoritarian

b. authoritarian; authoritative

c. authoritative; permissive

d. authoritarian; permissive

14. Pat is seven years old and lives in the midwestern United States. Pat learned to speak early and writes well. Pat is able to "read" people's emotional reactions by watching their faces. From this information we can conclude that Pat is most likely _____.

a. female

b. male

c. African American

d. Asian American

15. Ludmilla recently graduated from high school but can't decide whether to attend a local community college or work full time. She doesn't know what career she would like to pursue, and she is also uncertain whether she should stay with her current boyfriend. According to Erikson, Ludmilla is most likely experiencing the psychosocial crisis characterized by _____.

a. trust versus mistrust

b. initiative versus guilt

c. identity versus role confusion

d. integrity versus despair

16. Louise is 16 and having a difficult time with adolescence. She became sexually active two years ago and doesn't worry about using condoms or other safe sex practices. Louise is most likely to

a. hold conventional attitudes and values and feel ashamed of herself.

b. avoid smoking and drinking alcohol.

c. have average or better grades at school.

d. have parents who are not highly educated.

17. Jeanine and Helen are in a drugstore when Jeanine suggests that they steal some candy. Helen says that they should not steal the candy because they might get caught and put into jail. According to Kohlberg's theory, Helen is at the _____ stage of moral reasoning.

 a. preconventional
 b. conventional
 c. postconventional
 d. universal

18. In the past ten years Vernon has gained weight, especially around the middle. He also now needs glasses. If he is typical of most people his age, Vernon has most likely reached _____.

 a. adolescence
 b. early adulthood
 c. middle adulthood
 d. late adulthood

19. Verna is 50 years old. Based on developmental research, we would assume that Verna

 a. has less general knowledge than younger people.
 b. has a more limited vocabulary than younger people.
 c. understands that knowledge is relative, not absolute.
 d. is experiencing a slow but steady decay of all of her cognitive skills.

20. Patrice is 80 years old and has recently been unable to understand what she reads. She can't make sense of her checkbook, even though she was once an expert accountant. Her health is deteriorating, and her strength is waning. Patrice is most likely experiencing _____.

 a. cognitive dissonance
 b. terminal drop
 c. the crisis of initiative versus guilt
 d. androgyny

© Andrew Councill/Aurora Photos

10 Health, Stress, *and* Coping

Preview

In North America, people are living longer than ever. In fact, those over 75 constitute the fastest-growing age group in the United States. Will you eventually join them? To some extent, the answer lies in your genes, but how long you live is also determined in large measure by how you behave, how you think, and what stressors you face. Health care psychologists explore how illness and death are related to these behavioral, psychological, and social factors, and they apply their research to preventing illness and promoting health. They develop programs to help people make lifestyle changes that can lower their risk of illness and premature death. And they study how stress affects people's mental and physical health. Of particular importance is the immune system's response to stress. In this chapter, you will learn about several kinds of stressors, how people respond to them, and the relationship between stress reactions and illness. You will also discover what you can do to protect your own health and change risky behaviors that may affect it.

I n Bangor, Maine, where snow and ice have paralyzed the community, Angie's headache gets worse as her four-year-old daughter and six-year-old son start bickering again. The day-care center and elementary school are closed, so Angie must stay home from her job at the grocery store. She probably couldn't have gotten there anyway, because the buses have stopped running. During the latest storm the power went out, and the house is now almost unbearably cold; the can of spaghetti Angie opens is nearly frozen. Worry begins to creep into her head: "If I can't work, how will I pay for rent and day care?" Her parents have money problems, too, so they can't offer financial help, and her ex-husband rarely makes his child support payments. On top of everything else, Angie is coming down with the flu.

How do people manage such adversity, and what are its consequences for the individual? Psychologists who study questions such as these have established a specialty known as **health care psychology** (also called **health psychology**), "a field within psychology devoted to understanding psychological influence on how people stay healthy, why they become ill, and how they respond when they do get ill" (Taylor, 1999, p. 4). ■

Health Psychology

⊙ *What do health care psychologists do?*

The themes underlying health care psychology date back to ancient times. For thousands of years, in many cultures around the world, people have believed that their mental state, their behavior, and their health are linked. Today, there is scientific evidence to support this belief (Antoni & Lutgendorf, 2007; Schneiderman, 2004; Taylor, 2002). We now know that the stresses of life influence health through their impact on psychological and physical processes. Researchers have also associated anger, hostility, pessimism, depression, and hopelessness with the appearance of physical illnesses. Traits such as optimism are associated with good health. Similarly, poor health has been linked to behavioral factors such as lack of exercise, eating too much fat and sugar, smoking, and abuse of alcohol and other drugs (Freedman et al., 2006; Mente et al., 2009;

health care psychology (health psychology)   A field focused on understanding how psychological factors affect health and illness and which interventions help maintain health and combat illness.

TABLE 10.1 ■ LIFESTYLE BEHAVIORS THAT AFFECT THE LEADING CAUSES OF DEATH IN THE UNITED STATES

This table shows five of the leading causes of death in the United States today and behavioral factors that contribute to their development (Centers for Disease Control and Prevention, 2008; Jemal et al., 2005).

Cause of Death	Excessive Alcohol Consumption	Tobacco Smoking	Unhealthy Diet	Inadequate Exercise	Inadequate Sleep
Heart Disease	X	X	X	X	X
Cancer	X	X	X		X
Stroke	X	X	X	?	X
Lung disease		X			X
Accidents and injury	X	X			X

Source: Data from Centers for Disease Control and Prevention (2008).

van Dam et al., 2008; Vollset, Tverdal, & Gjessing, 2006). Good health has been associated with behaviors such as adequate exercise and following medical advice.

Health psychology has become increasingly prominent in North America, in part because of changing patterns of illness. Until the middle of the twentieth century, acute infectious diseases such as influenza, tuberculosis, and pneumonia were the major causes of illness and death in the United States and Canada. With these deadly diseases now tamed, chronic illnesses—such as coronary heart disease, cancer, and diabetes—have joined stroke, accidents, and injury as the leading causes of disability and death (Heron, 2007). Compared with acute diseases, these chronic diseases develop more slowly and are more strongly associated with people's psychological makeup, lifestyle, and environment (Centers for Disease Control and Prevention, 2008; see Table 10.1). The psychological and behavioral factors that contribute to these illnesses can be changed by intervention programs such as those that promote nonsmoking, exercise, and healthy eating (e.g., Bazzano et al., 2003; Kraus et al., 2002). In fact, about half the deaths in the United States today are due to preventable health-risk behaviors (Greenland et al., 2003; Khot et al., 2003; Mokdad et al., 2004). Worldwide, the number of deaths caused by health-damaging behaviors is expected to double by 2015 (World Health Organization, 2008).

Yet as few as 3 percent of people in the United States follow a lifestyle that includes maintaining a healthy weight, getting regular exercise, eating a healthy diet, getting eight hours of sleep, and not smoking (Reeves & Rafferty, 2005). One goal of health psychology is to help people understand the role they can play in controlling their own health and life expectancy (Nash et al., 2003; Nicassio, Meyerowitz, & Kerns, 2004). For example, health care psychologists have been active in educating people about the warning signs of cancer, heart disease, and other serious illnesses; encouraging them to engage in self-examinations; and emphasizing the importance of seeking medical attention while lifesaving treatment is still possible. Health care psychologists also study and help people understand the role stress plays in physical health and illness. And clinical health care psychologists help individuals cope as effectively as possible with cancer, diabetes, heart disease, and many other kinds of serious illness.

Understanding Stress and Stressors

▶ *How do psychological stressors affect physical health?*

You have probably heard that death and taxes are the only two things guaranteed in life. If there is a third, it surely must be stress. Stress is woven into the fabric of life. No matter how wealthy, powerful, attractive, or happy you might be, stress happens.

It comes in many forms: a difficult exam, an automobile accident, standing in a long line, reading about frightening world events, or just having a day when everything goes wrong. Some stress experiences, such as waiting to be with that special person, can be stimulating, motivating, and even desirable, but when circumstances begin to exceed our ability to cope with them, the result can be stress that creates physical, psychological, and behavioral problems. Stress in the workplace, for example, costs U.S. businesses more than $150 billion each year as a result of employee absenteeism, reduced productivity, and health care costs (Chandola, Brunner, & Marmot, 2006; Sauter et al., 1999; Schwartz, 2004; Spector, 2002).

Stress is the negative emotional and physiological process that occurs as individuals try to adjust to or deal with stressors. **Stressors,** in turn, are environmental circumstances (such as exams or accidents) that disrupt or threaten to disrupt people's daily functioning and cause people to make adjustments. **Stress reactions** are the physical, psychological, and behavioral responses (such as nervousness, nausea, or fatigue) that occur in the face of stressors (Taylor, 2002).

Some of us are more strongly affected by stressors than others, and we may be more strongly affected on some occasions than on others. Why? As described in more detail later, several *mediating factors* influence the relationship between people and their environments. These mediating factors include (1) the extent to which we can *predict* and *control* our stressors; (2) how we *interpret* the threat involved; (3) the *social support* we get; and (4) our *skills* for coping with stress. Mediating factors can either minimize or magnify a stressor's impact. In other words, as shown in Figure 10.1, stress is not a specific event but a transaction between people and their environments. It is a *process* in which the nature and intensity of our responses depend on what stressors occur and how they are affected by factors such as the way we think about them and how much confidence we have in our coping skills and resources.

Psychological Stressors

Most of our stressors have both physical and psychological components. Because these components overlap, it is often difficult to separate them for analysis. For example, students are challenged by psychological demands to do well in their courses as well as by physical fatigue resulting from a heavy load of classes and maybe a job and family responsibilities, too. So although we focus here on psychological stressors, remember that physical stressors almost always accompany them.

Any event that forces a person to change or adapt can be a psychological stressor. Even pleasant events can be stressful. For example, a vacation is supposed to be relaxing and a wedding is supposed to be wonderful, but both can also be exhausting. And a promotion that brings higher pay can also bring new pressures (Schaubroeck, Jones, & Xie, 2001). Still, it is usually unpleasant circumstances that produce the most adverse psychological and physical effects (e.g., Kiecolt-Glaser et al., 2005). These circumstances include catastrophic events, life changes and strains, chronic stressors, and daily hassles.

stress The process of adjusting to circumstances that disrupt or threaten to disrupt a person's daily functioning.

stressors Events or situations to which people must adjust.

stress reactions Physical and psychological responses to stressors.

FIGURE 10.1   ■   THE PROCESS OF STRESS

Stressful events, stress reactions, and stress mediators are all important components of the stress process. Notice that the process involves many two-way relationships. For example, if a person has effective coping skills, stress responses will be less severe. Having milder stress responses can act as a "reward" that strengthens those skills. Further, as coping skills (such as refusing unreasonable demands) improve, certain stressors (such as a boss's unreasonable demands) may become less frequent.

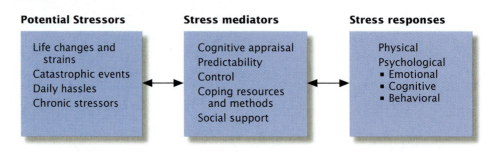

Potential Stressors	Stress mediators	Stress responses
Life changes and strains Catastrophic events Daily hassles Chronic stressors	Cognitive appraisal Predictability Control Coping resources and methods Social support	Physical Psychological ■ Emotional ■ Cognitive ■ Behavioral

COPING WITH CATASTROPHE ▶

Catastrophic events such as terrorism, explosions, hurricanes, and plane crashes are stressors that can be psychologically devastating for victims, their families, and rescue workers. As was the case in the wake of the shootings that killed 33 people at Virginia Tech University in 2007, health psychologists and other professionals provide on-the-spot counseling and follow-up sessions to help people deal with the consequences of trauma.

© AP Photo/Charles Dharapak

Catastrophic events are sudden, unexpected, potentially life-threatening experiences or traumas. Physical or sexual assault, military combat, natural disasters, terrorist attacks, and accidents fall into this category. *Life changes* and *strains* include divorce, illness in the family, difficulties at work, moving to a new house, and other circumstances that create demands to which people must adjust (see Table 10.2). *Chronic stressors*—those that continue over a long period of time—include such circumstances as living under the threat of terrorism, having a serious illness, being unable to earn a decent living, residing in a neighborhood with a high crime rate, being the victim of discrimination, and even enduring years of academic pressure. Finally, *daily hassles* involve irritations, pressures,

---

TABLE 10.2 ■ THE UNDERGRADUATE STRESS QUESTIONNAIRE

Here are some items from the Undergraduate Stress Questionnaire (Crandall, Priesler, & Aussprung, 1992), which asks students to indicate whether various stressors have occurred in their lives during the previous week.

Has this stressful event happened to you at any time during the last week? If it has please check the space next to it. If it has not please leave it blank.
_____ 1. Assignments in all classes due the same day
_____ 2. Having roommate conflicts
_____ 3. Lack of money
_____ 4. Trying to decide on major
_____ 5. Can't understand your professor
_____ 6. Stayed up late writing a paper
_____ 7. Sat through a boring class
_____ 8. Went into a test unprepared
_____ 9. Parents getting divorced
_____ 10. Incompetence at the registrar's office

Source: Crandall, Priesler, & Aussprung (1992).

and annoyances that may not be major stressors by themselves but whose effects add up to become significant (Almeida, 2005; Evans & Wener, 2006). The frustrations of daily commuting in heavy traffic, for example, can become so intense for some drivers that they display a pattern of aggression called "road rage."

Measuring Stressors

Which stressors are the most harmful? To study stress more precisely, psychologists have tried to measure the impact of particular stressors. In 1967, Thomas Holmes and Richard Rahe (pronounced "ray") pioneered the effort to find a standard way of measuring the stress in a person's life. Working on the assumption that both positive and negative changes produce stress, they asked a large number of people to rate—in terms of *life-change units,* or *LCUs*—the amount of change and demand for adjustment caused by events such as divorcing, being fired, retiring, losing a loved one, or becoming pregnant. On the basis of these ratings, Holmes and Rahe (1967) created the *Social Readjustment Rating Scale,* or *SRRS.* People taking the SRRS receive a stress score equal to the sum of the LCUs for all the stressful events they have recently experienced. Numerous studies have shown that people scoring high on the SRRS and other life-change scales are more likely to suffer physical illness, mental disorder, or other problems than those with lower scores (e.g., Monroe, Thase, & Simons, 1992).

Other researchers wondered, though, whether life changes alone tell the whole story about the impact of stressors. Accordingly, some investigators have used face-to-face interviews to more precisely measure stressors and their impact (e.g., Dohrenwend et al., 1993). Others developed scales such as the *Life Experiences Survey,* or *LES* (Sarason, Johnson, & Siegel, 1978), which measure not just which life events occurred but also people's perceptions of how positive or negative the events were and how well they were able to cope with the events. The LES also allows respondents to write in and rate any stressors they have experienced that are not on the printed list. This individualized approach can capture the differing impact and meaning that certain experiences might have for men compared with women and for members of various cultural groups. Divorce, for example, may have different meanings to people of different religious backgrounds. And members of some ethnic groups may experience prejudice and discrimination that is not felt by other groups (Lewis et al., 2006; Matthews et al., 2005; Merritt et al., 2006; Yip, Gee, & Takeuchi, 2008).

Stress Responses

 How do people react to stressors?

Physical and psychological stress reactions often occur together, especially as stressors become more intense. Furthermore, one type of stress response can set off a stress response in another dimension. For example, a physical stress reaction such as mild chest pains might trigger the psychological stress response of worrying about a heart attack. Still, it is useful to consider each category of stress responses one at a time.

Physical Responses

If you have experienced a near-accident or some other sudden, frightening event, you know that the physical responses to stressors include rapid breathing, increased heartbeat, sweating, and, a little later, shakiness. These reactions make up a general pattern known as the *fight-or-flight syndrome.* As described in the chapters on biology and behavior and on motivation and emotion, this syndrome prepares the body to either face or flee an immediate threat. Once the danger passes, fight-or-flight responses subside (Gump et al., 2005).

When stressors are longer lasting or recovery from stressors is slow, however, the fight-or-flight syndrome is only the beginning of a longer sequence of reactions.

FIGURE 10.2 ■ THE GENERAL ADAPTATION SYNDROME

Hans Selye found that physical reactions to stressors include an initial alarm reaction followed by resistance and then exhaustion. During the alarm reaction, the body's resistance to stress temporarily drops below normal as it absorbs a stressor's initial impact. Resistance increases and then levels off in the resistance stage, but it ultimately declines if the exhaustion stage is reached.
Source: Adapted from Selye (1975).

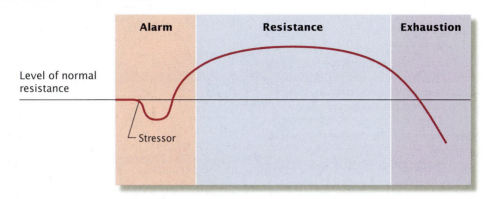

Improve Your Grade
Tutorial: Physical Reactions to Stressors—General Adaptation Syndrome

Observation of animals and humans led Hans Selye (pronounced "SELL-yay") to suggest that this extended sequence of physical stress responses occurs in a consistent pattern. He called this sequence the **general adaptation syndrome,** or **GAS** (Selye, 1956, 1976). The GAS occurs in three stages (see Figure 10.2), and it is activated by efforts to adapt to any stressor, whether it is physical or psychological.

The first stage, called the *alarm reaction,* involves some version of the fight-or-flight syndrome. The alarm reaction to a mild stressor, such as an overheated room, might be no more than changes in heart rate, respiration, and perspiration that help the body regulate its temperature. More severe stressors prompt more dramatic alarm reactions, rapidly mobilizing the body's adaptive energy, much as a burglar alarm alerts the police to take action (Kiecolt-Glaser et al., 1998).

Alarm reactions are controlled by the sympathetic nervous system through organs and glands that make up the *sympatho-adreno-medullary (SAM) system.* As shown on the right side of Figure 10.3, stressors trigger a process that begins when the brain's hypothalamus activates the sympathetic branch of the autonomic nervous system (ANS), which stimulates the medulla (inner part) of the adrenal glands. The adrenals, in turn, secrete *catecholamines* (pronounced "kat-uh-KOH-luh-meens")—especially adrenaline and noradrenaline—which circulate in the bloodstream, activating the liver, kidneys, heart, lungs, and other organs. The result is increased blood pressure, muscle tension, and blood sugar, along with other physical changes needed to cope with stressors. Even brief exposure to a stressor can produce major changes in these coordinated regulatory body systems (Cacioppo et al., 1995).

As shown on the left side of Figure 10.3, stressors also activate the *hypothalamic-pituitary-adrenocortical (HPA) system,* in which the hypothalamus stimulates the pituitary gland in the brain. The pituitary, in turn, secretes hormones such as adrenocorticotropic hormone (ACTH). Among other things, ACTH stimulates the cortex (outer surface) of the adrenal glands to secrete *corticosteroids*; these hormones release the body's energy supplies and fight inflammation. The pituitary gland also triggers the release of *endorphins,* which are some of the body's natural painkillers.

Together, these stress systems generate the energy needed to cope with an emergency. The more stressors there are and the longer they last, the more resources the body must spend in responding to them. If the stressors persist, the *resistance stage* of the GAS begins. Here, obvious signs of the initial alarm reaction fade as the body settles in to resist the stressor on a long-term basis. The drain on adaptive energy is less during the resistance stage compared with the alarm stage, but the body is still working hard to cope with stress.

This continued campaign of biochemical resistance is costly. It slowly but surely uses up the body's reserves of adaptive energy. The body then enters the third GAS stage, known as *exhaustion.* In extreme cases, such as prolonged exposure to freezing temperatures, the result is death. More commonly, the exhaustion stage brings signs

general adaptation syndrome (GAS)
A three-stage pattern of responses triggered by the effort to adapt to stressors.

FIGURE 10.3 ■ ORGAN SYSTEMS INVOLVED IN THE GAS

Stressors produce a variety of physiological responses that begin in the brain and spread to organs throughout the body. For example, the pituitary gland triggers the release of painkilling endorphins. It also stimulates the release of corticosteroids, which help resist stress but also tend to suppress the immune system. Some of these substances may interact with sex hormones to create different physical stress responses and coping methods in men and women (Taylor, Klein et al., 2000; Taylor et al., 2006).

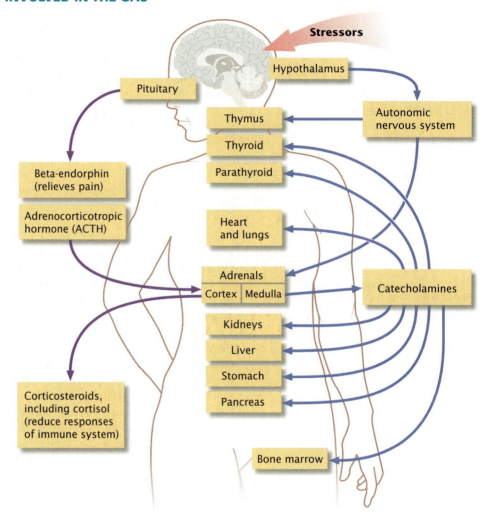

of physical wear and tear. Especially hard hit are the organ systems that were weak to begin with or that were heavily involved in the resistance process. For example, if adrenaline and cortisol (which help fight stressors during the resistance stage) remain elevated for an extended time, the result can be damage to the heart and blood vessels; suppression of the body's disease-fighting immune system; and vulnerability to illnesses such as heart disease, high blood pressure, arthritis, colds, and flu (e.g., Robles, Glaser, & Kiecolt-Glaser, 2005). Selye referred to illnesses caused or worsened by stressors as **diseases of adaptation.**

Psychological Responses

Selye's research focused mainly on the physiological aspects of stress responses, but stressors also create a variety of psychological responses, including changes in emotion and cognition (thinking) and accompanying changes in behavior.

Emotional Changes   The physical stress responses we have described are usually accompanied by emotional stress responses. If someone pulls out a gun and demands your money, you will most likely experience physiological changes, such as a spike in heart rate, but you will also feel some strong emotion—probably fear, maybe anger. In describing stress, people tend to say, "I was angry and frustrated!" rather than

diseases of adaptation   Illnesses caused or worsened by stressors.

"My heart rate increased and my blood pressure went up." In other words, they tend to mention changes in the emotions they are experiencing.

In most cases, emotional stress reactions fade soon after the stressors are gone. Even severe emotional stress responses ease eventually. However, if stressors continue for a long time or if lots of them occur in a short time, emotional stress reactions may persist. When people don't have a chance to recover their emotional equilibrium, they feel tense, irritable, short-tempered, or anxious and they may experience increasingly intense feelings of fatigue, depression, and hopelessness. These reactions can become severe enough to be diagnosed as major depressive disorder, generalized anxiety disorder, or other stress-related problems discussed in the chapter on psychological disorders.

Cognitive Changes

In 1995, in the busy, noisy intensive care unit of a London hospital, a doctor misplaced a decimal point while calculating the amount of morphine a one-day-old premature baby should receive. The child died of a massive overdose (Davies, 1999). Reductions in the ability to concentrate, think clearly, or remember accurately are typical cognitive stress reactions (Beilock & Carr, 2005; Cavenett & Nixon, 2006; Liston, McEwen, & Casey, 2009; Morgan et al., 2006). These problems appear partly because of *ruminative thinking,* the repeated intrusion of thoughts about stressful events (Lyubomirsky & Nolen-Hoeksema, 1995). Ruminative thoughts about relationship problems, for example, can seriously interfere with studying for a test. A related phenomenon is *catastrophizing,* which means dwelling on and overemphasizing the possible negative consequences of events. During exams, college students who are anxious about tests are likely to say to themselves, "I'm falling behind" or "Everyone is doing better than I am." As catastrophizing or ruminative thinking impairs memory and other aspects of cognitive functioning, resulting feelings of anxiety and other emotional arousal add to the total stress response, further hampering performance (Beilock et al., 2004; Mendl, 1999).

Overarousal created by stressors also tends to narrow the scope of attention, making it harder to scan the full range of possible solutions to complex problems (Craske, 1999). The result may be an increase in the problem-solving errors described in the chapter on thought, language, and intelligence. People under stress are more likely to cling to *mental sets,* which are well-learned (but not always efficient) approaches to problems. Stress may also intensify *functional fixedness,* the tendency to use objects for only one purpose. Victims of hotel fires, for example, sometimes die trapped in their rooms because in the stress of the moment, it did not occur to them to use the telephone or a piece of furniture to break a window.

Stressors may also impair decision making. Under stress, people who normally consider all aspects of a situation before making a decision may act impulsively and sometimes foolishly. High-pressure salespeople take advantage of this stress response by creating time-limited offers or by telling indecisive customers that others are waiting to buy the item they are considering (Cialdini, 2001).

Behavioral Responses

Clues about people's physical and emotional stress reactions come from changes in how they look, act, or talk. Strained facial expressions, a shaky voice, tremors, and jumpiness are common behavioral stress responses. Posture can also convey information about stress, a fact well known to skilled interviewers.

Even more obvious behavioral stress responses appear as people try to escape or avoid stressors. They may turn to alcohol, overeat (especially high-fat "comfort" foods) and either sleep too much or skimp on sleep in favor of late-night socializing. These tactics may provide some temporary relief, but they can also have negative health consequences (Cohen et al., 2009; Epel et al., 2004; Frone, 2008; Hamer, Molloy, & Stamatakis, 2008; King et al., 2008; Gangwisch et al., 2005). In the face of severe or long-lasting stress, some people quit their jobs, drop out of school, or even attempt suicide. In the month after Hurricane Katrina struck the U.S. Gulf Coast in 2005, for example, more than double the normal number of calls were placed from the affected area to the National Suicide Prevention Hotline, and stress-related mental health problems

© King World/Photofest

STRESS FOR $500, ALEX ▲

The negative effects of stress on memory, thinking, decision making, and other cognitive functions are often displayed by players on TV game shows such as *Jeopardy!* and *Who Wants to Be a Millionaire.* Under the intense pressure of time, competition, and the scrutiny of millions of viewers, contestants may miss questions that seem ridiculously easy to those calmly recalling the correct answers at home.

remained long after the storm's immediate effects abated (Breed, 2006; Kessler et al., 2008). Unfortunately, as discussed in the chapter on learning, escape and avoidance tactics deprive people of the opportunity to learn more adaptive ways of coping with stressful environments, including college (Cooper et al., 1992). Aggression is another common behavioral response to stressors. All too often, this response is directed at members of one's own family (Helmuth & McNulty, 2008; Polusny & Follette, 1995). So areas devastated by hurricanes and other natural disasters are likely to see not only an increase in suicides but also significant increases in reports of domestic violence (Curtis, Miller, & Berry, 2000).

linkages

When do stress responses become mental disorders? *(a link to Psychological Disorders)*

Linkages

Stress and Psychological Disorders

Physical and psychological stress responses sometimes appear together in patterns known as *burnout* and *posttraumatic stress disorder*. **Burnout** is an increasingly intense pattern of physical and psychological dysfunction in response to a continuous flow of stressors or to chronic stress (Maslach, 2003). As burnout nears, previously reliable workers or once-attentive spouses become indifferent, disengaged, impulsive, or accident prone. They miss work frequently, oversleep, perform their jobs poorly, abuse alcohol or other drugs, and become irritable, suspicious, withdrawn, and depressed (Fahrenkopf et al., 2008; Taylor, 2002). Burnout is particularly common among those who do "people work," such as teachers, doctors, and nurses, and those who perceive themselves as being treated unjustly by employers (Elovainio, Kivimäki, & Vahtera, 2002; Hoobler & Brass, 2006; Schultz & Schultz, 2002).

A different pattern of severe stress reactions is illustrated by the case of Mary, a 33-year-old nurse who was raped at knifepoint by an intruder in her apartment. In the weeks following this trauma, she was fearful about being alone and was preoccupied with thoughts about the attack and about the risk of it happening again. She installed additional locks on her doors and windows but experienced difficulty concentrating and could not immediately return to work. The thought of sex repelled her.

Mary suffered from **posttraumatic stress disorder (PTSD)**, a pattern of severe negative reactions following a traumatic event. Among the characteristic reactions are anxiety, irritability, jumpiness, inability to concentrate or work productively, sexual dysfunction, and difficulty in getting along with others. PTSD sufferers also experience sleep disturbances, intense startle responses to noise or other sudden stimuli, long-term suppression of their immune systems, and elevated risk of coronary heart disease (e.g., Goenjian et al., 2001; Guthrie & Bryant, 2005; Johnson, Westermeyer et al., 2002; Kawamura, Kim, & Asukai, 2001; Kubzansky et al., 2009). High-tech scanning techniques reveal that PTSD symptoms are accompanied by noticeable changes in brain functioning and even in brain structure (Kitayama et al., 2005). The most common feature of posttraumatic stress disorder is reexperiencing the trauma through nightmares or vivid memories. In rare cases, *flashbacks* occur in which the person behaves for minutes, hours, or days as if the trauma were occurring again.

Posttraumatic stress disorder is usually associated with events such as war, rape, terrorism, assault, or abuse in childhood (e.g., Dohrenwend et al., 2006; Galea, Ahern, et al., 2002; Galea, Resnick, et al., 2002; Goldberg & Garno, 2005; Shalev & Freedman, 2005; Shalev et al., 2006), but researchers believe that some PTSD symptoms can be triggered by any major stressor, such as a car accident, being stalked, or living in a community that is threatened by terrorism or serial killers (Ironson et al., 1997; Kamphuis & Emmelkamp, 2001; Schulden et al., 2006). PTSD usually appears immediately following a trauma, but full expression of its symptoms may not appear until weeks later (Andrews et al., 2007; Gilboa-Schechtman & Foa, 2001; Port, Engdahl, & Frazier, 2001). Many people affected by PTSD require

burnout   A pattern of physical and psychological dysfunctions in response to continuous stressors.

posttraumatic stress disorder (PTSD)   A pattern of adverse reactions following a traumatic event, commonly involving reexperiencing the event through nightmares or vivid memories.

LIFE HANGING IN THE BALANCE ▶

Symptoms of burnout and posttraumatic stress disorder often plague firefighters, police officers, emergency medical personnel, and others who are repeatedly exposed to time pressure, trauma, danger, and other stressors (Fullerton, Ursano, & Wang, 2004; Perrin et al., 2007). Posttraumatic stress disorder can also occur following a single catastrophic event. Surveys taken in the weeks and months following the terrorist attacks on the World Trade Center revealed that 7.5 percent of adults and 10.6 percent of children who lived near the devastated area experienced symptoms of PTSD; in many cases, these symptoms persisted for years (Farfel et al., 2008). PTSD symptoms were also widely reported by adult survivors of the massive tidal waves that devastated South and Southeast Asia in 2004 (DeLisi et al., 2003; Galea, Ahern, et al., 2002; Galea, Resnick, et al., 2002; Hoven et al., 2005; Simeon et al., 2003; van Griensven et al., 2006).

professional help, although some seem to recover without it (Bradley et al., 2005; Perkonigg et al., 2005). For most, improvement takes time; for nearly all, the support of family and friends is vital to recovery (Foa et al., 1999; Foa et al., 2005; LaGreca et al., 1996). For some people, though, PTSD never appears, even after severe trauma (Breslau et al., 2005). Some people, in fact, report enhanced psychological growth after surviving a trauma (Zoellner & Maercker, 2006). Researchers are working to discover what protective factors are operating in these individuals and whether those factors can be strengthened through PTSD treatment programs (Bonanno et al., 2007; Bonanno & Mancini, 2008; Haskett et al., 2006).

Stress is also thought to play a role in the development of many other psychological disorders, including depression, certain anxiety disorders, and schizophrenia (e.g., Cutrona et al., 2005). This point is emphasized in the chapter on psychological disorders, especially in relation to the *diathesis-stress model* of psychopathology. This model suggests that certain individuals may be predisposed to develop certain disorders but that whether or not these disorders actually appear depends on the frequency, nature, and intensity of the stressors the people encounter.

Stress Mediators

▶ *Why doesn't everyone react to stressors in the same way?*

The ways that particular people interact with particular stressors can be seen in many areas of life. The stress of combat, for example, is partly responsible for the errors in judgment and decision-making that lead to "friendly fire" deaths and injuries in almost every military operation (Adler, 1993). But not everyone in combat makes these mistakes. Why does stress disrupt the performance of some individuals and not others? And why does one individual survive and even thrive under the same circumstances that lead another to break down, give up, and burn out? The answer may lie in *psychobiological models,* which recognize the importance of psychological as well as biological factors in the stress process (Folkman et al., 2000; Suls & Rothman, 2004; Taylor, 2002). These models emphasize that (as shown in Figure 10.1) the impact of stressors depends not only on the stressors themselves but also on several important mediating factors (Bonanno, 2004, 2005; Kemeny, 2003; McEwen & Seeman, 1999).

How Stressors Are Perceived

As described in the chapter on sensation and perception, our view of the world depends partly on how we interpret sensory information. Similarly, our physical and psychological reactions to stressors depend somewhat on how we think about them, a process known as *cognitive appraisal*. A potential stressor usually has a stronger negative impact on people who perceive it as a threat than on people who see it as a challenge (Lazarus, 1999; Maddi & Khoshaba, 2005).

Evidence for the effects of cognitive factors on stress responses comes from surveys and experiments (e.g., Abelson et al., 2005). In one of the first laboratory demonstrations of these effects, Richard Lazarus gave differing instructions to three groups of students who were about to watch a film showing bloody industrial accidents (Lazarus et al., 1965). One group (the "intellectualizers") was instructed to remain mentally detached from the gruesome scenes; a second group (the "denial" group) was instructed to think of the scenes as unreal; and a third group (the "unprepared" group) was not told anything about the film. As Figure 10.4 shows, the intensity of physiological arousal during the film, as measured by sweat gland activity, depended on how the viewers were instructed to think about the film. The unprepared students were more upset than either of the other two groups. In a more recent study, students who were first trained to see the threatening aspects of information showed more emotional arousal to a stressful video than those who had been trained to see information as nonthreatening (Wilson et al., 2006). Similarly, physical and psychological symptoms associated with the stress of airport noise, of being diagnosed with a serious illness, of learning about toxins in local soil, or of living with terrorism threats are more common in people who engage in more catastrophic thinking about these problems (Bryant & Guthrie, 2005; Lerner et al., 2003; Matthies, Hoeger, & Guski, 2000; Speckhard, 2002). Those who hold a more optimistic outlook tend to show milder stress responses and better health outcomes (de Moor et al., 2006; Taylor, Kemeny et al., 2000; Taylor et al., 2003).

The influence of cognitive factors weakens somewhat as stressors become extreme. Still, even the impact of major stressors, such as a natural disaster or a divorce, may be less severe for those who think of them as challenges to be overcome. In other words, many stressful events are not inherently stressful; their impact depends partly on how

FIGURE 10.4 ■ COGNITIVE INFLUENCES ON STRESS RESPONSES

Richard Lazarus and his colleagues found that students' physiological stress reactions to a film showing bloody industrial accidents were affected by the way they thought about what they saw. Those who had been instructed to remain detached from the film (the "intellectualizers") or to think of it as unreal (the "denial" group) were less upset—as measured by sweat gland activity—than those in an "unprepared" group. These results were among the first to show that people's cognitive appraisal of stressors can affect their responses to those stressors. *Source*: Adapted from Lazarus et al. (1965).

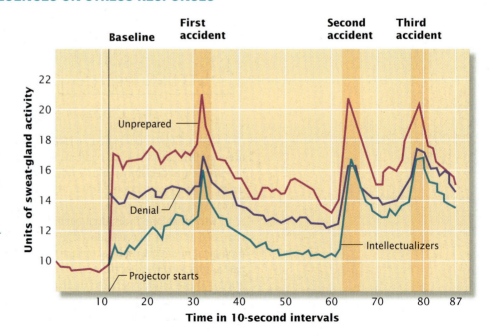

people perceive them. An important part of this appraisal is the degree to which the stressors are perceived to be predictable and controllable, or at least manageable.

Predictability and Control

Why is the threat of terrorism so terrorizing? For one thing, knowing that a stressor might occur but being uncertain whether or when it will occur tends to increase the stressor's impact (Lerner et al., 2003; Sorrentino & Roney, 2000). In other words, *unpredictable* stressors tend to have more impact than those that are predictable (Lazarus & Folkman, 1984; Pham, Taylor, & Seeman, 2001), especially when the stressors are intense and relatively brief. For example, people whose spouses have died suddenly tend to display more immediate disbelief, anxiety, and depression than those who have had weeks or months to prepare for the loss (Schulz et al., 2001; Swarte et al., 2003). However, predictability does not provide total protection against stressors. Research with animals shows that predictable stressors can be even more damaging than unpredictable ones if they occur over long periods of time (Abbott, Schoen, & Badia, 1984).

The *perception of control* also mediates the effects of stressors. If people feel they have some control over stressors, those stressors usually have less impact (e.g., Johnson & Krueger, 2005; Smith et al., 2008). For example, studies of several thousand employees in the United States, Sweden, and the United Kingdom have found that those who felt they had little or no control over their work environment were more likely to suffer heart disease and other health problems than workers with a high degree of perceived control over their work environment (Bosma et al., 1997; Cheng et al., 2000; Spector, 2002). And at many hospitals, it is now standard procedure to help patients manage or control the stress of emergency treatment or the side effects of surgery by providing preparatory information about what to expect during and after a medical procedure, teaching relaxation skills, and allowing patients to control the administration of their pain medication. These strategies have all been shown to help people heal faster and go home sooner (Broadbent et al., 2003; Chamberlin, 2000; Gordon et al., 2005; Kiecolt-Glaser et al., 1998; Ludwig-Rosenthal & Neufelf, 1988).

Simply *believing* that a stressor is controllable (even if it isn't) can also reduce its impact. This effect was demonstrated in a study in which participants with panic disorder inhaled a mixture of oxygen and carbon dioxide that typically causes a panic attack (Sanderson, Rapee, & Barlow, 1989). Half the participants were led to believe (falsely) that they could control the concentration of the mixture. Compared with those who believed that they had no control, significantly fewer of the "in-control" participants experienced full-blown panic attacks during the session, and their panic symptoms were fewer and less severe.

People who feel they have no control over negative events appear especially prone to physical and psychological problems. They often experience feelings of helplessness and hopelessness that in turn may promote depression or other mental disorders (Sarin, Abela, & Auerbach, 2005; Taylor & Aspinwall, 1996).

Coping Resources and Coping Methods

People usually suffer fewer ill effects from a stressor if they have adequate coping resources and effective coping methods. *Coping resources* include, among other things, the money and time to deal with stressful events. For example, the physical and psychological responses you experience if your car breaks down tend to be more negative if you are broke and pressed for time than if you have the money for repairs and the freedom to take a day off from work.

The impact of stressors can also be reduced by effective coping methods (Benight et al., 1999; Cote & Pepler, 2002; Poczwardowski & Conroy, 2002). Most of these methods can be classified as either problem focused or emotion focused. *Problem-focused* coping methods involve efforts to change or eliminate a source of stress, whereas *emotion-focused* techniques attempt to control the negative emotional consequences of stressors (Folkman et al., 1986). Some people use both kinds of coping. For example, you might

TABLE 10.3   ■   WAYS OF COPING

Coping is defined as cognitive and behavioral efforts to manage specific demands that people perceive as taxing their resources (Folkman et al., 1986). This table illustrates two major approaches to coping measured by Folkman and Lazarus's (1988) Ways of Coping Questionnaire: problem focused and emotion focused. Ask yourself which approach you usually take when faced with stressors. Now rank the coping skills under each major approach in terms of how often you tend to use each. Do you rely on just one or two or do you adjust your coping strategies to fit different kinds of stressors?

Learn BY Doing

Coping Skills	Example
Problem-focused coping	
Confronting	"I stood my ground and fought for what I wanted."
Seeking social support	"I talked to someone to find out more about the situation."
Planful problem solving	"I made a plan of action and I followed it."
Emotion-focused coping	
Self-controlling	"I tried to keep my feelings to myself."
Distancing	"I didn't let it get to me; I tried not to think about it too much."
Positive reappraisal	"I changed my mind about myself."
Accepting responsibility	"I realized I brought the problem on myself."
Escape/avoidance (wishful thinking)	"I wished that the situation would go away or somehow be over with."

Source: Adapted from Folkman et al. (1986).

deal with the problem of noise from a nearby factory by forming a community action group to push for tougher noise-reduction laws and at the same time calm your anger when noise occurs by mentally focusing on the group's efforts to improve the situation (Folkman & Moskowitz, 2000; Hatfield et al., 2002). Susan Folkman and Richard Lazarus (1988) devised a widely used questionnaire to assess the specific ways in which people cope with stressors; Table 10.3 shows some examples from their questionnaire.

Particularly when a stressor is difficult to control, it is sometimes helpful to fully express and think about the emotions you are experiencing in relation to the stressful event (Langens & Schüler, 2007; Low, Stanton, & Danoff-Burg, 2006; Niederhoffer & Pennebaker, 2002). The benefits of this coping strategy have been observed in many individuals whose religious beliefs or philosophy of life allow them to bring meaning to the experience of having cancer, the death of a loved one, or the devastation of natural disasters that might otherwise seem to be senseless tragedies (Heppner et al., 2006; Powell, Shahabi, & Thoreson, 2003; Tallman, Altmaier, & Garcia, 2007). Some individuals who use humor to help them cope also show better adjustment and milder physiological reactivity to stressful events (Martin, 2001; Moran, 2002).

Social Support

Has a good friend ever given you comfort and reassurance during troubled times? If so, you have experienced the value of *social support* in easing the impact of stressful events. Social support consists of emotional, tangible, or informational resources provided by other people. These people might help eliminate a stressor (by, say, fixing your car), suggest how to deal with the stressor (by recommending a good mechanic), or reduce a stressor's impact by providing companionship and reassurance (Sarason, Sarason, & Gurung, 1997). The people you can depend on for support make up your network of **social support** (Burleson, Albrecht, & Sarason, 1994).

The stress-reducing effects of social support have been documented in people dealing with a wide range of stressors, including cancer, stroke, military combat, loss of loved ones, natural disasters, arthritis, AIDS, and even ethnic discrimination (e.g., Antoni & Lutgendorf, 2007; Boden-Albala et al., 2005; Foster, 2000; Jason, Witter, & Torres-Harding, 2003; Penner, Dovidio, & Albrecht, 2001; Savelkoul et al., 2000; Weihs, Enright, & Simmens, 2008). Social support can have health benefits, too. For example, students who get emotional support from friends show better immune system functioning than those with less-adequate social support (Cohen & Herbert, 1996). This may be why people with strong social support are less vulnerable to colds and flu during exams and other periods of high academic stress (Kop et al., 2005; Pressman et al., 2005;

social support   The friends and social contacts on whom one can depend for help and support.

YOU'VE GOT A FRIEND ▶

Even when social support cannot eliminate stressors, it can help people, such as these cancer survivors, feel less anxious, more optimistic, more capable of control, and more willing to try new ways of dealing with stressors (Trunzo & Pinto, 2003). Those who provide support may feel better, too (Brown et al., 2003).

Taylor, Dickerson, & Klein, 2002). Having strong social support is also associated with faster recovery from surgery or illness, possibly because helpful friends and family members encourage patients to follow medical advice (Brummett et al., 2005; Grassi et al., 2000; Krohne & Slangen, 2005; Taylor, 2002). People in stronger social networks—especially those filled with happy people—tend to be happier than those in weaker networks and may even enjoy better mental functioning in old age (Barnes et al., 2004; Fowler & Christakis, 2008). According to some researchers, having inadequate social support can be as dangerous as smoking, obesity, or lack of exercise in that it nearly doubles a person's risk of dying from disease, suicide, or other causes (House, Landis, & Umberson, 1988a, 1988b; Kiecolt-Glaser & Newton, 2001; Rutledge et al., 2004).

Exactly how social support brings about its positive effects is not entirely clear. James Pennebaker (1995, 2000) has suggested that social support may help prevent illness by providing the person under stress with an opportunity to express pent-up thoughts and emotions. Pennebaker and other researchers suggest that keeping important things to yourself is itself a stressor (e.g., Dalgleish, Hauer, & Kuyken, 2008; Srivastava et al., 2009). In a laboratory experiment, for example, participants who were asked to deceive an experimenter showed elevated physiological arousal (Pennebaker & Chew, 1985). Further, if the spouses of people who die as the result of an accident or suicide do not or cannot confide their feelings to others they are especially likely to develop physical illness during the year following the death (Pennebaker & O'Heeron, 1984). Disclosing (even anonymously) the stresses and traumas one has experienced is associated with enhanced immune functioning, reduced physical symptoms, and decreased use of health services (Broderick, Junghaenel, & Schwartz, 2005; Campbell & Pennebaker, 2003; Epstein, Sloan, & Marx, 2005; Sloan, Marx, & Epstein, 2005). This may explain why support groups for a wide range of problems such as bereavement, overeating, and alcohol and drug abuse tend to promote participants' physical health (Taylor et al., 2002).

Research in this area is made more challenging by the fact that the relationship between social support and the impact of stressors is not a simple one. For one thing, the quality of social support can influence the ability to cope with stress, but the reverse may also be true: your ability to cope may determine the quality of the social support you receive (McLeod, Kessler, & Landis, 1992). People who complain endlessly about stressors but never do anything about them may discourage social support whereas those with an optimistic, action-oriented approach may attract support.

Second, *social support* refers not only to your relationships with others but also to the recognition that others care and will help (Demaray & Malecki, 2002). Some relationships in a seemingly strong social network can be stormy, fragile, or shallow, resulting in interpersonal conflicts that can have an adverse effect on health (Ben-Ari & Gil, 2002; Malarkey et al., 1994).

Third, having too much support or the wrong kind of support can be as bad as not having enough (Reynolds & Perrin, 2004). Dangerous behaviors such as smoking or overeating, for example, can be harder to give up if one's social support consists largely or entirely of smokers or overeaters (Christakis & Fowler, 2007). People whose friends and family overprotect them from stressors may actually put less energy into coping efforts or have less opportunity to learn effective coping strategies. And if the efforts of people in a social support network become annoying, disruptive, or interfering, they can increase stress and intensify psychological and physical problems (De Vogli, Chandola, & Marmot, 2007; Gleason et al., 2008; Newsom et al., 2008; Ruiz et al., 2006). It has even been suggested that among people under intense stress, the benefits of having a large social support network may be offset by the dangers of catching a cold or the flu from people in that network (Hamrick, Cohen, & Rodriguez, 2002).

Finally, the value of social support may depend on the kind of stressor being encountered. So although having a friend nearby might reduce the impact of some stressors, it might amplify the impact of others. In one study, participants who were about to make a speech experienced the task as more threatening—and showed stronger physical and psychological stress responses—when a friend was with them than when they were waiting alone (Stoney & Finney, 2000).

Stress, Personality, and Gender

The impact of stress on health appears to depend not only on how people think about particular stressors but also to some extent on how they think about and react to the world in general. For instance, stress-related health problems tend to be especially common among people whose "disease-prone" personalities lead them to (1) try to ignore stressors when possible; (2) perceive stressors as long-term, catastrophic threats that they brought on themselves; and (3) be pessimistic about their ability to overcome stressors (e.g., Penninx et al., 2001; Peterson et al., 1998; Segerstrom et al., 1998; Suinn, 2001).

Other cognitive styles, such as those characteristic of "disease-resistant" personalities, help insulate people from the ill effects of stress. These people tend to think of stressors as temporary challenges to be overcome, not catastrophic threats. And they don't constantly blame themselves for causing these stressors. One particularly important component of the "disease-resistant" personality seems to be *dispositional optimism*, the belief or expectation that things will work out positively (Folkman & Moskowitz, 2000; Pressman & Cohen, 2005; Rosenkranz et al., 2003; Taylor, Kemeny et al., 2000). Optimistic people tend to live longer (Giltay et al., 2004, 2006) and to have more resistance than pessimists to colds and other infectious diseases (Cohen et al., 2003a, 2003b; Pressman & Cohen, 2005), which helps explain why optimistic students experience fewer physical symptoms at the end of the academic term (Aspinwall & Taylor, 1992; Ebert, Tucker, & Roth, 2002). Optimistic coronary bypass surgery patients tend to heal faster and stay healthier than pessimists (Scheier et al., 1989, 1999) and perceive their quality of life following coronary surgery to be higher than do patients with less optimistic outlooks (Fitzgerald et al., 1993). And among HIV-positive men, dispositional optimism has been associated with lower psychological distress, fewer worries, and lower perceived risk of acquiring full-blown AIDS (Johnson & Endler, 2002; Taylor et al., 1992). These effects appear due in part to optimists' tendency to use challenge-oriented, problem-focused coping strategies that attack stressors directly, in contrast to pessimists' tendency to use emotion-focused coping strategies, such as denial and avoidance (Bosompra et al., 2001; Brenes et al., 2002; Moscowitz et al., 2009). They also tend to be happier than pessimists, a tendency associated not only with less intense and less dangerous physiological responses to stressors but also with greater success in life (e.g. Lyubomirsky, King, & Diener, 2005; Steptoe, Wardle, & Marmot, 2005).

Gender may also play a role in responses to stressors. In a review of 200 studies of stress responses and coping methods, Shelley Taylor and her colleagues found that males under stress tended to get angry, avoid stressors, or both, whereas females were more likely to help others and to make use of their social support (Taylor, Klein et al., 2000; Taylor et al., 2002). Further, in the face of equally intense stressors, men's physical responses tend to be more intense than women's (Stoney & Matthews, 1988). This is not true in every case, of course (Smith et al., 2008), but why should gender differences show up at all? Though the learning of gender roles that is discussed in the human development chapter surely plays a part (Eagly & Wood, 1999), Taylor proposes that women's "tend and befriend" style differs from the "fight or flight" pattern so often seen in men partly because of gender differences in how hormones combine under stress. Consider, for example, oxytocin (pronounced "ox-see-TOH-sin"), a hormone released in both sexes in response to social stressors (Taylor et al., 2006; Uvnas-Moberg, Arn, & Magnusson, 2005). Taylor suggests that oxytocin interacts differently with male and female sex hormones: in men it amplifies physical responses to stress but reduces those responses in women (Light et al., 2005). This gender difference could lead to the more intense emotional and behavioral stress responses typical of men, and it might be partly responsible for men's greater vulnerability to heart disease and other stress-related illnesses (Kajantie & Phillips, 2006). If that is the case, gender differences in stress responses may help explain why women in industrialized societies live an average of 5 to 10 years longer than men (Hoyert, Kung, & Smith, 2005; Kajantie, 2008). The role of gender-related hormones in responding to stress is supported by the fact that there are few (if any) gender differences in children's responses to stress. Those differences begin to appear only around adolescence, when sex hormone differences become pronounced (Allen & Matthews, 1997).

linkages

Are childhood traits related to how long we live? *(a link to Human Development)*

Focus on RESEARCH

Personality and Health

The way people think and act in the face of stressors, the ease with which they attract social support, and their tendency to be optimists or pessimists are but a few aspects of *personality*.

▶ **What was the researchers' question?**

Are there other personality characteristics that protect or threaten people's health? This was the question asked by Howard Friedman and his associates (Friedman, 2000; Friedman et al., 1995a, 1995b). In particular, they attempted to identify aspects of personality that increase the likelihood that people will die prematurely from heart disease, high blood pressure, or other chronic diseases.

▶ **How did the researchers answer the question?**

Friedman suspected that an answer might lie in the results of the Terman Life Cycle Study of Intelligence, which was named after Louis Terman, author of the Stanford-Binet intelligence test. As described in the chapter on thought, language, and intelligence, the study was originally designed to measure the long-term development of 1,528 gifted California children (856 boys and 672 girls), nicknamed the "Termites" (Terman & Oden, 1947).

Starting in 1921, and every five to ten years thereafter, Terman's research team gathered information about the Termites' personality traits, social relationships, stressors, health habits, and many other variables. The data were collected through questionnaires and interviews with the Termites themselves as well as with their teachers, parents, and other family members. By the early 1990s, about half of the Termites had died. It was then that Friedman realized that the Terman Life Cycle Study could shed light on the relationship between personality and health, because the personality traits identified in the Termites could be related to how long they lived. So he examined the Termites' death certificates, noting the dates and causes of death, and then looked for associations between their personalities and the length of their lives.

▶ **What did the researchers find?**

Friedman and his colleagues found that one of the most important predictors of long life was a dimension of personality known as *conscientiousness*, or social dependability (described in the personality chapter). Termites who in childhood had been seen as truthful, prudent, reliable, hard working, and humble tended to live longer than those whose parents and teachers had identified them as impulsive and lacking in self-control.

Friedman also examined the Terman Life Cycle Study for what it suggested about the relationship between health and social support. In particular, he compared Termites whose parents had divorced or who had been in unstable marriages themselves with those who grew up in stable homes and who had stable marriages. He discovered that people who had experienced parental divorce during childhood or who themselves had unstable marriages died an average of four years earlier than those whose close social relationships had been less stressful.

▶ **What do the results mean?**

Did these differences in personality traits and social support actually cause some Termites to live longer than others? Friedman's research is based mainly on correlational analyses, so it was difficult for the investigators to draw conclusions about what caused the relationships they observed. Still, Friedman and his colleagues searched the Terman data for clues to mechanisms through which personality and other factors might have exerted a causal influence on how long the Termites lived (Peterson et al., 1998). For example, they evaluated the hypothesis that conscientious, dependable Termites who lived socially stable lives might have followed healthier lifestyles than those who were more impulsive and socially stressed. They found that people in the latter group did, in fact, tend to eat less healthy diets and were more likely to smoke, drink to excess, or use drugs. But health behaviors alone did not fully account for their shorter average life spans. Another possible explanation is that conscientiousness and

stability in social relationships reflect a general attitude of caution that goes beyond eating right and avoiding substance abuse. Friedman found some support for this idea in the Terman data. Termites who were impulsive or low on conscientiousness were somewhat more likely to die from accidents or violence than those who were less impulsive.

▶ **What do we still need to know?**

The Terman Life Cycle Study does not provide final answers about the relationship between personality and health. However, it has generated some important clues and a number of intriguing hypotheses to be evaluated in research with more representative samples of participants. Some of that research has already taken place and tends to confirm Friedman's findings about conscientiousness (Hampson et al., 2006; Kern & Friedman, 2008; Roberts et al., 2009; Terracciano et al. 2008). Further, Friedman's decision to reanalyze a set of data on psychosocial development as a way of exploring issues in health care psychology stands as a fine example of how a creative researcher can pursue answers to complex questions that are difficult or impossible to study via controlled experiments.

In Review

STRESS RESPONSES AND STRESS MEDIATORS

CATEGORY	EXAMPLES
Responses	
Physical	The fight-or-flight syndrome involves increased heart rate, respiration, and muscle tension as well as sweating and dilated pupils. Activation of SAM and HPA systems releases catecholamines and corticosteroids. Organ systems involved in prolonged resistance to stressors eventually break down.
Psychological	*Emotional* examples include anger, anxiety, depression, and other emotional states. *Cognitive* examples include inability to concentrate or think logically, ruminative thinking, and catastrophizing. *Behavioral* examples include aggression and escape/avoidance tactics (including suicide attempts), and health-risk behaviors.
Mediators	
Appraisal	Thinking of a difficult new job as a challenge will create less discomfort than focusing on the threat of failure.
Predictability	A tornado that strikes without warning may have a more devastating emotional impact than a long-predicted hurricane.
Control	Repairing a disabled spacecraft may be less stressful for the astronauts doing the work than for their loved ones on earth, who can do nothing to help.
Coping resources and methods	Having no effective way to relax after a hard day may prolong tension and other stress responses.
Social support	Having no one to talk to about a rape or other trauma may amplify the negative impact of the experience.

1. *The friends and family we can depend on to help us deal with stressors are called our _____ network.*

2. *Fantasizing about winning money is a(n) _____-focused way of coping with financial stress.*

3. *Sudden, extreme stressors may cause psychological and behavioral problems known as _____.*

Our discussion of personality and other factors that can alter the impact of stressors should make it obvious that what is stressful for a given individual is not determined fully and simply by predispositions, coping styles, or situations (see "In Review: Stress Responses and Stress Mediators"). Even more important are interactions between the person and the situation, the mixture of each individual's coping resources with the specific characteristics of the situation encountered.

The Physiology and Psychology of Health and Illness

▶ *How does stress affect your immune system?*

Several studies mentioned so far show that people under stress are more likely than less-stressed people to develop infectious diseases. Other research shows that they are also more likely to experience flare-ups of the latent viruses responsible for oral herpes (cold sores) or genital herpes (Cohen & Herbert, 1996). In the following sections we focus on some of the ways that these and other illnesses are related to the impact of stress on the immune system and the cardiovascular system.

Stress, Illness, and the Immune System

On March 19, 1878, at a seminar at the Académie de Médecine in Paris, Louis Pasteur showed his distinguished audience three chickens. One bird had been raised normally and was healthy. A second bird had been intentionally infected with bacteria but given no other treatment; it was also healthy. The third chicken that Pasteur presented was dead. It had been infected with the same bacteria as the second bird but it had also been physically stressed by being exposed to cold temperatures; as a result, the bacteria had killed it (Kelley, 1985).

Research conducted since Pasteur's time has greatly expanded our knowledge about how stressors affect the body's reaction to disease. **Psychoneuroimmunology** is the field that examines the interaction of psychological and physiological processes that strengthen or weaken the body's ability to defend itself against disease (Ader, 2001).

The Immune System and Illness   The body's first line of defense against invading substances and microorganisms is the **immune system.** The immune system is perhaps as complex as the nervous system, and it contains as many cells as the brain (Guyton, 1991). Some of these cells are in organs such as the thymus and spleen, whereas others circulate in the bloodstream, entering tissues throughout the body. Components of the immune system kill or inactivate foreign or harmful substances in the body, such as viruses and bacteria (Simpson, Hurtley, & Marx, 2000). If our immune systems are impaired, we are left more vulnerable to colds, mononucleosis, and many other infectious diseases (Potter & Zautra, 1997). It is by disabling the immune system that the human immunodeficiency virus (HIV) leads to AIDS and leaves the HIV-infected person defenseless against other infections or cancers. The immune system can also become overactive, with devastating results. Many chronic, progressive diseases—including arthritis, diabetes, and lupus erythematosus—are now recognized as *autoimmune disorders.* In these cases, cells of the immune system begin to attack and destroy normal body cells (Oldenberg et al., 2000).

An important aspect of the human immune system is the action of the white blood cells, called *leukocytes* (pronounced "LU-koh-sites"). These cells are formed in the bone marrow and serve as the body's mobile defense units. Leukocytes are called to action when foreign substances are detected. Among the varied types of leukocytes are *B-cells,* which produce *antibodies* to fight foreign toxins; *T-cells,* which kill other cells; and *natural killer cells,* which destroy a variety of foreign organisms and are particularly important in fighting viruses and tumors. The brain can influence

linkages

Can stress give you the flu? *(a link to Biology and Behavior)*

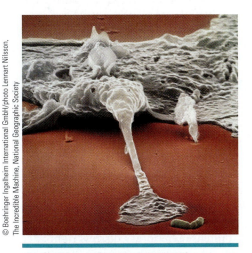

THE FIRST LINE OF DEFENSE ▲

A patrolling immune system cell sends out an extension known as a pseudopod (pronounced "SUE-doh-pod") to engulf and destroy a bacterial cell before alerting more defenders. These immune cells are able to squeeze out of the bloodstream and enter organs, where they destroy foreign cells.

psychoneuroimmunology   The field that examines the interaction of psychological and physiological processes affecting the body's ability to defend itself against disease.

immune system   The body's first line of defense against invading substances and microorganisms.

the immune system indirectly by altering the secretion of adrenal hormones, such as cortisol, that modify the circulation of T-cells and B-cells. The brain can also influence the immune system directly by making connections with the immune organs, such as the thymus, where T-cells and B-cells are stored (Felten et al., 1991; Maier & Watkins, 2000).

The Immune System and Stress   A wide variety of stressors can lead to suppression of the immune system. The effects are especially strong in the elderly (Penedo & Dahn, 2004), but they occur in everyone (Kiecolt-Glaser & Glaser, 2001; Kiecolt-Glaser et al., 2002). One study showed that as first-year law students participated in class, took exams, and experienced other stressful aspects of law school, they showed a decline in several measures of immune functioning (Segerstrom et al., 1998). Similarly, decreases in natural killer cell activity have been observed in both men and women following the deaths of their spouses (Irwin et al., 1987), and a variety of immune system impairments have been found in people suffering the effects of prolonged marital conflict, divorce, or extended periods of caring for elderly relatives (Cacioppo et al., 1998; Cohen et al., 2007; Kiecolt-Glaser et al., 2003, 2005; Vitaliano, Zhang, & Scanlan, 2003).

The relationship between stress and the immune system can be critical to people who are HIV positive but do not have AIDS. Because their immune systems are already fragile, further stress-related impairments could be life threatening. Research indicates that psychological stressors are associated with the progression of HIV-related illnesses (e.g., Antoni et al., 2000; Gore-Felton & Koopman, 2008). Unfortunately, people with HIV (and AIDS) face a particularly heavy load of immune-suppressing psychological stressors, including uncertainty about the future. A lack of perceived control and resulting depression and anxiety can further magnify their stress responses (e.g., Sewell et al., 2000).

Stress, Illness, and the Cardiovascular System

Earlier we mentioned the role of the sympatho-adreno-medullary (SAM) system in mobilizing the body's defenses during times of threat. Because the SAM system is linked to the cardiovascular system, its repeated activation in response to stressors has been linked to the development of coronary heart disease (CHD), high blood pressure (hypertension), and stroke (Krantz & McCeney, 2002). For example, adults in a nationwide sample who reported the strongest and longest-lasting worry about terrorism after the 9/11 attacks on New York City and Washington, D.C. were three times more likely than less worried people to develop heart problems over the next three years. Even those who reported the most intense temporary distress right after 9/11 were at elevated risk of developing heart problems over those same three years (Holman et al., 2008).

The link between CHD and physical stress responses appears especially close in people whose responses are especially strong (Andre-Petersson et al., 2001; Ming et al., 2004; Treiber et al., 2001). For example, among healthy young adult research participants, those whose blood pressure rose most dramatically in response to a mild stressor or a series of stressors were the ones most likely to develop hypertension later in life (Kasagi, Akahoshi, & Shimaoki, 1995; Light et al., 1999; Matthews et al., 2004).

As also mentioned earlier, these physical reactions to stressors—and the chances of suffering stress-related health problems—can depend partly on personality, especially on how people tend to think about stressors and about life in general. For example, the trait of *hostility*—especially when accompanied by irritability and impatience—has been associated with the appearance of coronary heart disease (Bunde & Suls, 2006; Day & Jreige, 2002; Krantz & McCeney, 2002; Smith et al., 2007).

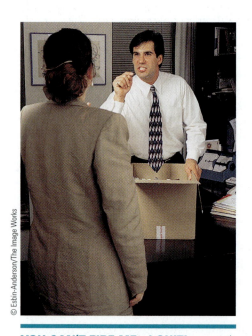

© Esbin-Anderson/The Image Works

YOU CAN'T FIRE ME—I QUIT!   ▲

For a time, researchers believed that anyone who displayed the pattern of aggressiveness, competitiveness, and nonstop work known as Type A behavior was at increased risk for heart disease (Friedman & Rosenman, 1974). More recent research, however, has led to the hypothesis that the danger lies not in these characteristics alone but in hostility, which is seen in some, but not all, Type A people.

Thinking CRITICALLY

Does Hostility Increase the Risk of Heart Disease?

Health care psychologists see hostility as characterized by suspiciousness, resentment, frequent anger, antagonism, and distrust of others (Krantz & McCeney, 2002; Williams, 2001). The identification of hostility as a risk factor for coronary heart disease and heart attack may be an important breakthrough in understanding these illnesses, which remain chief causes of death in the United States and most other Western nations. But is hostility as dangerous as health care psychologists suspect?

▶ **What am I being asked to believe or accept?**

Many researchers claim that individuals who display hostility increase their risk for coronary heart disease and heart attack (e.g., Bleil et al., 2004; Boyle et al., 2004). This risk, they say, is independent of other risk factors such as heredity, diet, smoking, and drinking.

▶ **Is evidence available to support the claim?**

There is evidence that hostility and heart disease are related, but scientists are still not sure about what causes the relationship. Some suggest that the risk of coronary heart disease and heart attack is elevated in hostile people because these people tend to be unusually reactive to stressors, especially when challenged. During interpersonal conflicts, for example, people predisposed to hostile behavior display not only overt hostility but also unusually large increases in blood pressure, heart rate, and other aspects of autonomic reactivity (Brondolo et al., 2003; Suls & Wan, 1993). In addition, it takes hostile individuals longer than normal to get back to their resting levels of autonomic functioning (Gerin et al., 2006). Like a driver who damages a car's engine by pressing the accelerator and applying the brakes at the same time, these "hot reactors" may create excessive wear and tear on the arteries of the heart as their increased heart rate forces blood through tightened vessels (Johnston, Tuomisto, & Patching, 2008). Increased sympathetic nervous system activation not only puts stress on the coronary arteries but also leads to surges of stress-related hormones from the adrenal glands. High levels of these hormones are associated with increases in cholesterol and other fatty substances that are deposited in arteries and contribute to coronary heart disease (Bierhaus et al., 2003; Stoney & Hughes, 1999; Stoney, Bausserman, et al., 1999; Stoney, Niaura, et al., 1999). Cholesterol levels do appear to be elevated in the blood of hostile people (Dujovne & Houston, 1991; Engebretson & Stoney, 1995).

Hostility may affect heart disease risk less directly as well, through its impact on social support. Some evidence suggests that hostile people get fewer benefits from social support (Lepore, 1995). Failing to use this support—and possibly offending potential supporters in the process—may intensify the impact of stressful events on hostile people. The result may be increased anger, antagonism, and, ultimately, additional stress on the cardiovascular system.

▶ **Can that evidence be interpreted another way?**

Studies suggesting that hostility causes coronary heart disease are not true experiments. Researchers cannot manipulate the independent variable by creating hostility in randomly selected people in order to assess its effects on heart health. Accordingly, we have to consider other possible explanations of the observed relationship between hostility and heart disease.

For example, some researchers suggest that higher rates of heart problems among hostile people are not due entirely to the impact of hostility on blood pressure, heart rate, and hormone surges. It may also be that a genetically determined tendency toward autonomic reactivity increases the likelihood of both hostility and heart disease (Cacioppo et al., 1998; Krantz et al., 1988). If this is the case, then the fact that hostility and coronary heart disease often appear in the same people might reflect not just the effects of hostility but also a third factor—autonomic reactivity—that contributes to both of them.

It has also been suggested that hostility may be only one of many traits linked to heart disease. Depressiveness, hopelessness, pessimism, anger, and anxiety may be involved, too (Frasure-Smith & Lespérance, 2005; Kubzansky, Davidson, & Rozanski, 2005; Nicholson, Fuhrer, & Marmot, 2005; Suls & Bunde, 2005).

▶ **What evidence would help to evaluate the alternatives?**

Research on the role these other traits may play in heart disease will be vital, and that work is now under way. One way to test whether hostile people's higher rates of heart disease are related specifically to their hostility or to a more general tendency toward intense physiological arousal is to examine how these individuals react to stress when they are not angry. Some researchers have done this by observing the physiological reactions of hostile people during the stress of surgery. One study found that even under general anesthesia, such people show unusually strong autonomic reactivity (Krantz & Durel, 1983). Because these patients were not conscious, it appears that oversensitivity to stressors, not hostile thinking, caused their exaggerated stress responses. This possibility is supported by research showing that compared with other people, individuals who have strong blood pressure responses to stressors also show different patterns of brain activity during stress (Gianaros et al., 2005).

▶ **What conclusions are most reasonable?**

Most studies continue to find that among generally healthy people, those who are hostile—especially men—are at greater risk for heart disease and heart attacks than other people (Chida & Steptoe, 2009; Krantz & McCeney, 2002; Stansfeld & Marmot, 2002). However, the picture is probably more complex than researchers first thought; it appears that many interacting factors affect the relationship between hostility and CHD.

A more elaborate psychobiological model may be required—one that takes into account that (1) some individuals may be biologically predisposed to react to stress with hostility and increased cardiovascular activity, each of which can contribute to heart disease; (2) hostile people help create and maintain stressors through aggressive thoughts and actions, which can provoke others to be aggressive; and (3) hostile people are more likely than others to smoke, drink to excess, overeat, fail to exercise, and engage in other heart-damaging behaviors.

We must also keep in mind that the relationship between heart problems and hostility may not be universal. Although this relationship appears to hold for women as well as men and for individuals in various ethnic groups (e.g., Davidson, Hall, & MacGregor, 1996; Nakano & Kitamura, 2001; Olson et al., 2005; Powch & Houston, 1996; Yoshimasu et al., 2002), final conclusions must await further research that examines the relationship between hostility and heart disease in other cultures.

Promoting Healthy Behavior

▶ *Who is most likely to adopt a healthy lifestyle?*

Health care psychologists are deeply involved in the development of smoking cessation programs, in campaigns to prevent young people from taking up smoking, in alcohol-education efforts, in the prevention of skin cancer through education about sun safety, and in the fight against the spread of HIV and AIDS (e.g., Albarracín et al., 2008; Buller, Buller, & Kane, 2005; Durantini et al., 2006; Morisky et al., 2006; Stice, Shaw, & Nathan, 2006). They have also helped promote early detection of disease. Encouraging women to perform breast self-examinations and men to do testicular self-examinations are just two examples of health care psychology programs that can save thousands of lives each year (Taylor, 2002). Health care psychologists have also explored the reasons behind some people's failure to follow doctors' orders that are vital to the control of diseases such as diabetes, heart disease, AIDS, and high blood pressure (Bartlett, 2002; Gonzalez et al., 2004). Understanding these reasons and finding ways to encourage better adherence to medical advice could speed recovery, prevent unnecessary suffering, and save many lives (Barclay et al., 2007; Simpson et al., 2006).

Efforts to reduce, eliminate, or prevent behaviors that pose health risks and to encourage healthy behaviors are called **health promotion** (Smith, Orleans, & Jenkins, 2004). For example, health care psychologists have developed programs that teach children as young as nine to engage in healthy behaviors and avoid health-risk behaviors. School systems now offer a variety of these programs, including those that give children and adolescents the skills necessary to turn down cigarettes, drugs, and unprotected sex. Health care psychologists also go into workplaces and communities with the goal of helping people adopt healthier lifestyles by altering diet, smoking, and exercise patterns. They teach stress-management techniques, too (Langenberg et al., 2000; Tuomilehto et al., 2001). These programs can create savings in future medical treatment costs (Blumenthal et al., 2002; Schneiderman et al., 2001) and better health for those who participate (Lisspers et al., 2005).

© Gustavo Gilabert/Corbis

DOCTOR'S ORDERS   ▲

Despite physicians' instructions, many patients fail to take their blood pressure medication and continue to eat an unhealthy diet. Noncompliance with medical advice is especially common when cultural values and beliefs conflict with that advice. Aware of this problem, health psychologists are developing culture-sensitive approaches to health promotion and disease prevention (Kazarian & Evans, 2001).

health promotion   The process of altering or eliminating behaviors that pose risks to health and, at the same time, fostering healthier behavior patterns.

Health Beliefs and Health Behaviors

Health care psychologists are also trying to understand the thought processes that lead people to engage in health-endangering behaviors and that can interfere with efforts to adopt healthier lifestyles (Klepp, Kelder, & Perry, 1995). Their research has led to intervention programs that seek to change these patterns of thinking or at least take them into account. In one study, for example, women who avoid thinking about the risks of breast cancer were more likely to get a mammogram screening after receiving health information that was tailored to their cognitive styles (Williams-Piehota et al., 2005).

This cognitive approach to health care psychology can be seen in various *health-belief models*. Irwin Rosenstock (1974) developed one of the most influential and extensively tested of these models (e.g., Aspinwall & Duran, 1999). He based his model on the assumption that people's decisions about health-related behaviors (such as smoking) are guided by four main factors:

1. Perceiving a *personal threat* of risk for getting a specific illness. (Do you believe that *you* will get lung cancer from smoking?)

© Reprinted by permission, Steve Kelley, *The Times-Picayune*, New Orleans

▲ As described in the chapter on thought, language, and intelligence, humans tend to underestimate the likelihood of common outcomes and to overestimate the likelihood of rare events. When this tendency causes people to ignore the dangers of smoking and other health-risk behaviors, the results can be disastrous.

Courtesy of the American Psychological Association

TAKING TIME OUT ▲

The workplace is the number-one source of stress for many people. On January 1, 2000, Raymond Fowler, who was then chief executive officer of the American Psychological Association, joined the ranks of those whose elevated blood pressure, heart problems, and other physical stress responses required a leave of absence from stressful jobs (Fowler, 2000). The National Institute for Occupational Safety and Health (1999) suggests a wide range of other behavioral coping options for stressed employees who cannot afford to take time off. You can view this advice online at http://www.cdc.gov/niosh/docs/99-101.

2. Perceiving the seriousness of the illness and the consequences of having it. (How serious do you think lung cancer is? What will happen to you if you get it?)
3. Believing that changing a particular behavior will reduce the threat. (Will stopping smoking prevent *you* from getting lung cancer?)
4. A comparison of the *perceived costs* of changing a health-risk behavior and the *benefits expected* from making that change. (Will the reduced risk of getting cancer in the future be worth the discomfort and loss of pleasure from not smoking?)

According to this health-belief model, the people most likely to quit smoking would be those who believe that they are at risk for getting cancer from smoking, that cancer is serious and life threatening, and that the benefits of reducing cancer risks are greater than the costs of quitting (McCaul et al., 2006).

Other cognitive factors are emphasized in other health-belief models. For example, people generally do not try to quit smoking unless they believe they can succeed. So *self-efficacy*, the belief that you are able to perform some behavior, is an additional consideration in making decisions about health behaviors (Armitage, 2005; Bandura, 1992; Dijkstra, DeVries, & Bakker, 1996). A related factor is the *intention* to engage in a healthy behavior (Albarracín et al., 2001; Schwarzer, 2001; Webb & Sheeran, 2006).

Health-belief models have been useful in predicting a variety of health behaviors, including exercise (McAuley, 1992), safe-sex practices (Fisher, Fisher, & Rye, 1995), adherence to doctors' orders (Bond, Aiken, & Somerville, 1992), and having routine vaccinations and mammograms (Brewer et al., 2007; Champion & Huster, 1995).

Changing Health Behaviors: Stages of Readiness

Changing health-related behaviors depends not only on a person's health beliefs but also on that person's readiness to change. According to James Prochaska and his colleagues, successful change occurs in five stages (Prochaska, DiClemente, & Norcross, 1992; Schumann et al., 2005):

1. *Precontemplation* The person does not perceive a health-related problem and has no intention of changing anytime soon.
2. *Contemplation* A problem behavior has been identified and the person is seriously thinking about changing it.
3. *Preparation* The person has a strong intention to change and has made specific plans to do so.
4. *Action* The person is engaging successfully in behavior change.
5. *Maintenance* The healthy behavior has continued for at least six months and the person is using newly learned skills to prevent relapse, or "backsliding."

These stages may actually overlap somewhat; for example, some "precontemplators" might actually be starting to contemplate change (Herzog & Blagg, 2007). The road from precontemplation through maintenance can be a bumpy one (Prochaska, 1994). Usually, people relapse and go through the stages repeatedly until they finally achieve stability in the healthy behavior they desire (Polivy & Herman, 2002). Smokers, for example, typically require three to four cycles through the stages over several years before they finally reach the maintenance stage (Piasecki, 2006).

Programs for Coping with Stress and Promoting Health

Improving people's stress-coping skills is an important part of health care psychologists' health promotion work (e.g., Keogh, Bond, & Flaxman, 2006). Let's consider a few specific procedures and programs associated with this effort.

Planning to Cope   Just as people with extra money in the bank have a better chance of weathering a financial crisis, those with effective coping skills have a better chance of escaping some of the more harmful effects of intense stress. Like family money, the ability to handle stress appears to come naturally—perhaps even genetically—to some people (Wilhelm et al., 2007), but coping strategies can also be learned. Programs for teaching these strategies include several stages, which are summarized in Table 10.4.

Bear in mind, though, that no single method of coping with stressors is right for everyone or every stressor. For example, denying the existence of an uncontrollable stressor may be fine in the short run but may lead to problems if no other coping method is used. Similarly, people who rely entirely on active, problem-focused coping might handle controllable stressors well but find themselves nearly helpless in the face of uncontrollable ones (Murray & Terry, 1999). The most successful stress managers may be those who can adjust their coping methods to the demands of changing situations and differing stressors (Taylor, 2002).

Developing Coping Strategies   Strategies for coping with stress can be cognitive, emotional, behavioral, or physical. *Cognitive coping strategies* involve changing the way we think. These changes include thinking more calmly, rationally, and constructively in the face of stressors and may lead to a more hopeful emotional outlook. For example, students with heavy course loads may experience anxiety, confusion, discouragement; lack of motivation; and the desire to run away from it all. Frightening, catastrophizing thoughts (such as "What if I fail?") magnify these stress responses. Cognitive coping strategies replace catastrophic thinking with thoughts that cast stressors as challenges, not threats. This substitution process is called *cognitive restructuring* (Lazarus, 1971; Meichenbaum, 1977). It involves first identifying upsetting thoughts (such as "I'll never figure this out!") and then developing and practicing more constructive thoughts to use when under stress (such as "All I can do is the best I can"). Cognitive coping doesn't eliminate stressors, of course, but it can help us to perceive them as less threatening and therefore less disruptive (Antoni et al., 2000; Chesney et al., 2003).

Finding social support is an effective *emotional coping strategy.* As mentioned earlier, feeling that you are cared about and valued by others can be a buffer against the ill

linkages

How can people manage stress?
(a link to Treatment of Psychological Disorders)

TABLE 10.4   ■   STEPS FOR COPING WITH STRESS

Many successful programs for systematically coping with stress guide people through several steps and are aimed at removing stressors that can be changed and improving responses to stressors that cannot be changed (Taylor, 2002).

Step	Task
1. Assessment	Identify the sources and effects of stress.
2. Goal setting	List the stressors and stress responses to be addressed. Designate which stressors can and cannot be changed.
3. Planning	List the specific steps to be taken to cope with stress.
4. Action	Implement coping plans.
5. Evaluation	Determine the changes in stressors and stress responses that have occurred as a result of coping methods.
6. Adjustment	Alter coping methods to improve results if necessary.

effects of stressors, which can lead to enhanced immune functioning (Kiecolt-Glaser & Newton, 2001) and quicker recovery from illness (Taylor, 2002).

Behavioral coping strategies involve changing behavior in order to minimize the negative impact of stressors. Time management is one example. If it seems that you are

Learn BY Doing

always pressed for time, consider developing a time management plan. The first step is to use a calendar or day planner to record how you spend each hour of each day in a typical week. Next, analyze the information to locate when and how you might be wasting time and how you might use your time more efficiently. Then set out a schedule for the coming week and stick to it. Make adjustments in subsequent weeks as you learn more realistic ways to manage your time. Time management can't create more time, but it can help control catastrophizing thoughts by providing reassurance that there is enough time for everything and a plan for handling all that you have to do.

Physical coping strategies can be used to alter the undesirable physical responses that occur before, during, or after the appearance of stressors. The most common physical coping strategy is some form of drug use. Prescription medications are sometimes an appropriate coping aid, especially when stressors are severe and acute, such as the sudden death of one's child. However, people who rely on prescribed or nonprescription drugs, including alcohol, to help them face stressors may come to believe that their ability to cope is due to the drug, not to their own skill. This belief can make people more and more psychologically dependent on the drug. Furthermore, the drug effects that blunt stress responses may also interfere with the ability to apply other coping strategies. The resulting loss of perceived control over stressors may make those stressors even more threatening and disruptive.

Nonchemical methods of reducing physical stress reactions and improving stress coping include progressive relaxation training (Bernstein, Borkovec, & Hazlette-Stevens, 2000; Scheufele, 2000), physical exercise (Anshel, 1996), biofeedback (Nestoriuc, Rief, & Martin, 2008; Sarafino & Goehring, 2000), and meditation and tai chi (Carlson et al., 2003; Davidson et al., 2003; Li et al., 2001), among others (Taylor, 2002).

"In Review: Methods for Coping with Stress" summarizes our discussion of methods for coping with stress.

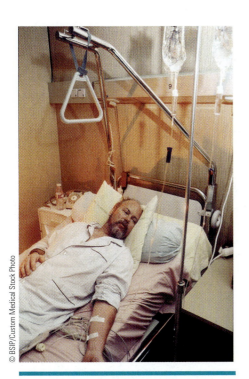

© BSIP/Custom Medical Stock Photo

DEALING WITH CHEMOTHERAPY ▲

Progressive relaxation training (Jacobson, 1938) involves briefly tensing groups of muscles throughout the body, one at a time, then releasing the tension and focusing on the resulting feelings of relaxation. It can be used to ease a variety of health-related problems, including the anxiety, physiological arousal, and nausea associated with cancer chemotherapy (Bernstein, Borkovec, & Hazlette-Stevens, 2000).

applying psychology

In Review

Methods for coping with stress

TYPE OF COPING METHOD	EXAMPLES
Cognitive	Thinking of stressors as challenges rather than as threats; avoiding perfectionism
Emotional	Seeking social support; getting advice
Behavioral	Implementing a time-management plan; where possible, making life changes to eliminate stressors
Physical	Progressive relaxation training; exercise; meditation

1. Catastrophizing thoughts are best overcome through _____ coping strategies.
2. The first step in coping with stress is to _____ the sources and effects of your stressors.
3. True or false: It is best to rely on only one good coping strategy. _____.

Health, Stress, *and* Coping

As noted in the introductory chapter, all of psychology's subfields are related to one another. Our discussion of how stressors can lead to the development of mental disorders illustrates just one way that the topic of this chapter—health, stress, and coping—is linked to the subfield of abnormal psychology, which is described

in the chapter on psychological disorders. The Linkages diagram shows ties to two other subfields, and there are many more ties throughout the book. Looking for linkages among subfields will help you see how they all fit together and help you better appreciate the big picture that is psychology.

linkages

Can stress give you the flu?
(ans. on p. 413)

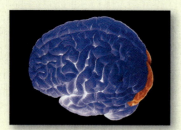

Chapter 2
Biology and Behavior

When do stress responses become mental disorders? *(ans. on p. 404)*

Chapter 12
Psychological Disorders

How does stress affect group decision making? *(ans. on p. 591)*

Chapter 14
Social Psychology

SUMMARY   ▶

Health Psychology

▶ *What do health care psychologists do?*

The development of **health care psychology** (or **health psychology)** was prompted by recognition of the link between stress and illness and of the role of behaviors such as smoking in increasing the risk of illness. Health care psychologists work to understand how psychological factors are related to physical disease and to help people behave in ways that prevent or minimize disease and promote health.

Understanding Stress and Stressors

▶ *How do psychological stressors affect physical health?*

The term *stress* refers in part to *stressors,* which are physical or psychological events and situations to which people must adjust. The term is

also used to refer to *stress reactions.* Most generally, however, stress is viewed as an ongoing, interactive process that takes place as people adjust to and cope with their environment. Psychological stressors include catastrophic events, life changes and strains, chronic stressors, and daily hassles. Stressors can be measured by tests such as the Social Readjustment Rating Scale (SRRS) and the Life Experiences Survey (LES), but scores on such tests provide only a partial picture of the stress in a person's life.

Stress Responses

◉ *How do people react to stressors?*

Responses to stressors can be physical and psychological. These stress responses can occur alone or in combination, and the appearance of one can often stimulate others.

Physical stress responses include changes in heart rate, respiration, and many other processes that are part of a pattern known as the *general adaptation syndrome,* or *GAS.* The GAS has three stages: alarm reaction, resistance, and exhaustion. The GAS helps people resist stress but if activated for too long it can lead to impairment of immune system functions as well as to physical illnesses; Selye called such illnesses *diseases of adaptation.*

Psychological stress responses can be emotional, cognitive, and behavioral. Anxiety, anger, and depression are among the most common emotional stress reactions. Cognitive stress reactions include ruminative thinking, catastrophizing, and disruptions in the ability to think clearly, remember accurately, and solve problems efficiently. Behavioral stress responses include irritability, aggression, absenteeism, engaging in health-damaging behaviors, and even suicide attempts. Severe or long-lasting stressors can lead to *burnout* or to psychological disorders such as *posttraumatic stress disorder (PTSD).*

Stress Mediators

◉ *Why doesn't everyone react to stressors in the same way?*

The key to understanding stress appears to lie in observing how particular people interact with specific stressors. Stressors are likely to have greater impact if an individual perceives them as threats or if they are unpredictable, uncontrollable, or unmanageable. The people most likely to react strongly to a stressor are those whose coping resources, coping methods, and *social support* are inadequate or perceived as inadequate.

The Physiology and Psychology of Health and Illness

◉ *How does stress affect your immune system?*

Psychoneuroimmunology is the field that examines the interaction of psychological and physiological processes that affect the body's ability to defend itself against disease. When a person is under stress, some of the hormones released from the adrenal glands, such as cortisol, reduce the effectiveness of the cells of the *immune system* (T-cells, B-cells, and natural killer cells) in combating foreign invaders, such as viruses and cancer cells.

People who are hostile appear to be at greater risk for heart disease than other people. The heightened reactivity to stressors that these people experience may damage their cardiovascular systems.

Promoting Healthy Behavior

◉ *Who is most likely to adopt a healthy lifestyle?*

The process of altering or eliminating health-risk behaviors and encouraging healthy behaviors is called *health promotion.* People's health-related behaviors are partly guided by their beliefs about health risks and what they can do about them.

The process of changing health-related behaviors appears to involve several stages, including precontemplation, contemplation, preparation, action, and maintenance. Understanding which stage people are in and helping them move through these stages is an important task in health care psychology.

To cope with stress, people must identify the stressors affecting them and develop a plan for coping with these stressors. Important coping skills include cognitive restructuring, acting to minimize the number or intensity of stressors, and using progressive relaxation training and other techniques for reducing physical stress reactions.

Learn BY Doing ▶

Put It in Writing

What is stress like for you? To help you understand the role of stress in your life, write a page or two describing a stressful incident that you had to face in the recent past. Identify what the stressors were and classify each of them as physical or psychological. List your physical, emotional, cognitive, and behavioral responses to these stressors, noting how long the responses lasted. Include a brief summary of how you coped with these stressors and how successful your coping efforts were. Some research suggests that writing about stressful experiences can help people deal with those experiences. Did this writing project have any such benefits for you? For more about writing and health, visit http://homepage.psy.utexas.edu/homepage/faculty/pennebaker/Home2000/WritingandHealth.html.

Personal Learning Activity

To get an idea of the differences in people's methods for coping with stress, create a one-paragraph story about a stressful situation (such as losing a job, having one's home destroyed by fire, working for an obnoxious boss, or being overburdened by schoolwork). Now show this description to ten people and ask each of them to tell you how they would cope with the situation if it happened to them. Classify each of their coping methods as problem focused or emotion focused. Did you notice any relationships between the kind of coping responses these people chose and their personal characteristics, such as age, gender, ethnicity, or experience with stress? If so, why do you think those relationships appeared? *For additional projects, see the Personal Learning Activities in the corresponding chapter of the study guide that accompanies this book.*

Take Action to Learn More ▶

Now that you have finished reading this chapter, how about exploring some of the ideas and information that you found most interesting? Here are some courses, books, films, and Internet resources to get you started. Enjoy!

Courses

Biological Psychology
Health Psychology
Stress Management
Stress and Coping

Movies

Black Hawk Down. General adaptation syndrome.

All That Jazz; Falling Down; Girlhood. Behavioral stress responses.

The Deer Hunter. Posttraumatic stress disorder.

Blue; Ikiru; My Flesh and Blood. Coping with disease.

Diary of a Mad Black Woman; Do the Right Thing; The Barbarian Invasions. Social support.

Women on the Verge of a Nervous Breakdown. Impact of a sudden stressor.

Glengarry Glen Ross; M*A*S*H; The Paper; Teachers. Effects of stress in the workplace.

Angela's Ashes. Impact of stress on development.

Saving Private Ryan. Individual differences in responses to traumatic stress.

Books

DAVID J. MAHONEY, *The Longevity Strategy: How to Live to 100 Using the Brain-Body Connection* (Wiley, 1998). The origins of longevity.

LANCE ARMSTRONG AND SALLY JENKINS, *It's Not About the Bike: My Journey Back to Life* (Berkley Books, 2001). Armstrong focuses on the origins of his survival of a deadly form of cancer.

LEWIS B. PULLER, *Fortunate Son* (Bantam, 1996). Son of a famous marine deals with posttraumatic stress and multiple amputations after the Vietnam War.

RICHARD SORRENTINO AND CHRISTOPHER RONEY, *The Uncertain Mind: Individual Differences in Facing the Unknown* (Psychology Press, 2000). Discusses the impact of uncertainty on physical and mental health.

TONY CASSIDY, *Stress, Cognition, and Health* (Routledge, 1999). Summarizes research on the effects of stress on thinking and physical well-being.

JERROLD GREENBERG, *Comprehensive Stress Management* (McGraw-Hill, 1999). Ideas for stress management.

ROBERT M. SAPOLSKY, *Why Zebras Don't Get Ulcers* (Owl Books, 2004). Describes the stress process, stress-related diseases, and coping skills.

JAMES W. PENNEBAKER, *Opening Up: The Healing Power of Expressing Emotions* (Guilford, 1997). Describes research on the benefits of self-disclosure.

The Web

Essentials of Psychology Book Companion Website

www.cengage.com/psychology/bernstein

Visit the book companion website to access a wealth of resources, including chapter outlines, flashcards, web links, tutorial quizzes, and more!

CENGAGENOW™   Just what you need to know NOW! Spend time on what you need to master rather than on information you already have learned. Take a pre-test for this chapter, and CengageNOW will generate a personalized study plan based on your results. The study plan will identify the topics you need to review and direct you to online resources to help you master those topics. You can then take a post-test to help you determine the concepts you have mastered and what you will need to work on. Try it out! Go to www.cengage.com/login to sign in with an access code or to purchase access to this product.

Review of Key Terms ▶

Can you define each of the key terms in the chapter? Check your definitions against those on the pages shown in parentheses in the following list or in the Glossary at the end of the book.

burnout (p. 404)
diseases of adaptation (p. 402)

general adaptation syndrome (GAS) (p. 401)
health care psychology (health psychology) (p. 396)
health promotion (p. 416)
immune system (p. 413)
posttraumatic stress disorder (PTSD) (p. 404)

psychoneuroimmunology (p. 413)
social support (p. 408)
stress (p. 398)
stress reactions (p. 398)
stressors (p. 398)

MULTIPLE-CHOICE ▶ Self Test

Select the best answer for each of the following questions. Then check your response against the Answer Key at the end of the book.

1. Health research statistics show that your great-grandparents' generation was most likely to die from _____ diseases, whereas your own generation is most likely to die from _____ diseases.
   a. infectious; infectious
   b. chronic; chronic
   c. infectious; chronic
   d. chronic; infectious

2. Stephanie married a wonderful guy, moved to a new city, and took a great new job, all in the same month. We would expect her to _____.
   a. display physical and/or psychological stress responses
   b. experience little stress, because these are all desirable changes
   c. experience little stress, because these are not chronic stressors
   d. experience physical stress responses only

3. Doug lives next to a family that includes several teenagers. He is forever reminding them not to run across his front lawn, their loud music often keeps him awake at night, and their cars are parked so that it is hard for him to back out of his driveway. These stressors can best be classified as _____ .
   a. life changes and strains
   b. traumatic
   c. catastrophic
   d. daily hassles

4. Aaron's sympathetic nervous system is engaged in the fight-or-flight syndrome. Which stage of the general adaptation syndrome (GAS) is he experiencing?
   a. Alarm
   b. Resistance
   c. Exhaustion
   d. Precontemplative

5. Bill and Ellen's car breaks down and it takes two hours for help to arrive. According to Shelley Taylor's research on stress and gender, Bill is likely to _____, and Ellen is likely to _____ .
   a. get angry; get angry, too
   b. be supportive of Ellen; be supportive of Bill
   c. get angry; seek and offer support
   d. seek and offer support; get angry

6. Enrico finds that no matter what else he is doing, he can't stop thinking about all the stressful events in his life. Enrico is experiencing _____ .
   a. catastrophizing
   b. ruminative thinking
   c. functional fixedness
   d. cognitive restructuring

7. Caitlin just failed her high school math test. She says to herself, "Mom is going to be furious with me! She will probably ground me, which means I won't be able to go to the prom. If I don't go to the prom, I will be a social outcast, and no one will talk to me. I'll never have any friends or find a partner, and no one will ever love me!" This is an example of _____ .
   a. cognitive restructuring
   b. catastrophizing
   c. posttraumatic stress disorder
   d. the fight-or-flight syndrome

8. Dr. Zarro finds that one of her patients, Juan, has a disease-resistant personality. This means that Juan is likely to _____ .
   a. ignore his stressors
   b. be optimistic
   c. blame himself for his stressors
   d. ruminate about his stressors

9. Shane, a veteran, occasionally experiences flashbacks involving vivid recollections of his wartime experiences. Flashbacks are associated with _____ .
   a. generalized anxiety disorder
   b. posttraumatic stress disorder
   c. the general adaptation syndrome
   d. the fight-or-flight syndrome

10. When Robin finds out he didn't get the promotion he had been hoping for, he tries to laugh it off. He goes out with friends and jokingly tells them that it is all for the best because the promotion would have forced him to buy a lot of new clothes. Robin is using _____ coping strategies.
    a. problem-focused
    b. social-focused
    c. emotion-focused
    d. posttraumatic

11. Postsurgery patients who are allowed to adjust their own levels of pain medication tend to use less medication than patients who must ask for it. This phenomenon is consistent with research showing that _____ .
    a. social support can mediate stress
    b. predictable stressors are easier to manage
    c. the perception of control reduces the impact of stressors
    d. thinking of stressors as threats amplifies their effects

12. Laton, the head of human resources at his company, knows that the employees have stressful jobs. He schedules group picnics and lunches to help employees get better acquainted. Laton is trying to ease the employees' stressors by _____ .
    a. promoting cognitive restructuring
    b. improving social support
    c. increasing employees' sense of control
    d. helping employees think of their stressors as challenges rather than threats

13. The Focus on Research section of this chapter described the relationship between personality and life expectancy. Researchers have found _____ .
    a. no relationship between the two
    b. that conscientiousness was associated with longer life
    c. that social relationships had no impact on longevity
    d. that impulsiveness was associated with longer life

14. Porter has a flu virus. Research on the immune system shows that Porter's _____ will be working to fight off this virus.
    a. B-cells
    b. T-cells
    c. natural killer cells
    d. macrophages

15. Fred is at high risk for coronary heart disease. As his friend, you tell him that current research suggests that he could lower his risk if he _____ .
    a. takes up fishing as a hobby
    b. works at being less hostile
    c. reduces his workload
    d. restructures his thinking about stress

16. When Larry finds out that he has arthritis, an autoimmune disease, he is very upset. His stress reactions are likely to be reduced *most* if Larry _____ .
    a. goes to a spa to try to ignore the situation
    b. keeps his worries to himself
    c. focuses all his attention on worrying about his medical condition
    d. joins an arthritis support group

17. According to Rosenstock's health-belief model, which of the following would *most* help Bridgit decide to quit smoking?

a. Perceiving a personal threat of getting cancer from her smoking

b. Knowing that smoking causes cancer

c. Knowing that quitting can lower people's risk of cancer

d. Carefully reading the statistics on smoking and health in general

18. Amanda is severely overweight. She knows that for her health's sake, she needs to limit her caloric intake, but she loves to eat and has made no specific plans to go on a diet. Amanda is at the _____ stage of readiness to change a health-risk behavior.

a. precontemplation

b. contemplation

c. preparation

d. maintenance

19. Sayumi is trying to control her stress. In response to a hurtful comment from a friend, Sayumi thinks to herself, "Don't jump to conclusions; he probably didn't mean it the way it sounded," instead of "That jerk! Who does he think he is?" Sayumi is using the coping strategy of _____.

a. cognitive restructuring

b. emotional restructuring

c. catastrophizing

d. contemplation

20. Loretta, a marriage counselor, finds her job very stressful. She has found that physical coping strategies help her the most. This means that Loretta most likely _____.

a. constantly reminds herself about the good she is doing

b. organizes a support group for therapists

c. practices progressive relaxation every evening

d. works on her time-management plan

© Royalty-free/Corbis

11 Personality

If you have ever been stuck in heavy traffic, you have probably noticed differences in how drivers deal with the situation. Some are tolerant and calm; others become so cautious that they worsen the congestion; still others react with such impatience and anger that they may trigger a shouting match or cause an accident. Variations in how people handle traffic jams and other frustrating situations reflect just one aspect of their *personality*—the consistent patterns of thinking, feeling, and behaving that make each person different from (and in some ways similar to) others. In this chapter, we examine four views of personality and review some of the personality tests psychologists have developed to measure and compare people's personalities. We also describe some of the ways that personality theory and research are being applied in areas such as diagnosing mental disorders and screening potential employees.

© Mary Evans/Sigmund Freud Copyrights/The Image Works

FOUNDER OF PSYCHOANALYTIC ▲
THEORY
Here is Sigmund Freud with his daughter, Anna, who became a psychoanalyst herself and eventually developed a revised version of her father's theories.

Take out your wallet, look through it, and select the four most important things you carry with you. One person we know picked a driver's license, a credit card, a friend's phone number, and a witty prediction from a fortune cookie. The driver's license describes his physical traits. The credit card represents information about his buying history and responsibility in paying debts. His friends provide support, affection, and intimacy. And the fortune cookie prediction says something about his wishes, beliefs, or hopes. In other words, the selected items form a crude personality sketch.

Learn BY **Doing**

There is no universally accepted definition, but psychologists generally view **personality** as the unique pattern of enduring thoughts, feelings, and actions that characterize a person. Personality research, in turn, seeks to understand how and why our consistent patterns of thinking, emotion, and behavior make each of us different in some ways and alike in others.

To gain a full understanding of just one individual's personality, a researcher would have to learn about many things, including the person's developmental experiences and cultural influences, genetic and other biological characteristics, perceptual and other information-processing habits and biases, typical patterns of emotional expression, and social skills. Psychologists also want to know about personality in general, such as how it develops and changes across the life span. They ask why some people are usually optimistic whereas others are usually pessimistic and whether people respond consistently or inconsistently from one situation to the next.

The specific questions psychologists ask and the methods they use to investigate personality often depend on which of the four main approaches to personality they take. These four are known as the *psychodynamic, trait, social-cognitive,* and *humanistic* approaches. ■

The Psychodynamic Approach

⊙ *How did paralyzed patients lead Freud to psychoanalysis?*

Some people think that personality reveals itself in behavior alone. A person with an "obnoxious personality," for example, shows it by acting obnoxiously. But is that all there is to personality? Not according to Sigmund Freud. As a physician in Vienna, Austria,

personality The pattern of psychological and behavioral characteristics by which each person can be compared and contrasted with other people.

FIGURE 11.1 ■ A FREUDIAN VIEW OF PERSONALITY STRUCTURE

According to Freud, some parts of the personality are conscious, whereas others are unconscious. Between these levels is the preconscious, which Freud saw as the home of memories and other material that we are not usually aware of but that we can easily bring into consciousness. *Source:* Adapted from Liebert & Spiegler (1994).

psychoanalytic theory Freud's view that human behavior and personality are determined largely by psychological factors, many of which are unconscious.

psychodynamic approach A view developed by Freud that emphasizes unconscious mental processes in explaining human thought, feelings, and behavior.

id According to Freud, a personality component containing basic instincts, desires, and impulses with which all people are born.

pleasure principle The operating principle of the id, which guides people toward whatever feels good.

ego According to Freud, the part of the personality that makes compromises and mediates conflicts between and among the demands of the id, the superego, and the real world.

reality principle The operating principle of the ego, which takes into account the constraints of the social world.

superego According to Freud, the component of personality that tells people what they should and should not do.

defense mechanisms Unconscious tactics that either prevent threatening material from surfacing or disguise it when it does.

during the 1890s, Freud specialized in treating "neurotic" disorders such as blindness or paralysis for which there was no physical cause and that hypnosis could often remove. One patient sleepwalked on legs that were paralyzed during the day. These cases led Freud to believe in *psychic determinism,* the idea that personality and behavior are determined more by psychological factors than by biological conditions or current events (Allen, 2006). He proposed that people may not know why they feel, think, or act the way they do because they are partly controlled by the unconscious portion of the personality—the part of which people are normally unaware (Funder, 2007). From these ideas Freud created **psychoanalytic theory,** a theory of personality that also led to a way of treating mental disorders. Freud's theory became the basis of the **psychodynamic approach** to personality, which assumes that various unconscious psychological processes interact to determine our thoughts, feelings, and behavior (Schultz & Schultz, 2009).

The Structure of Personality

Freud believed that people are born with basic needs or instincts—not only for food and water but also for sex and aggression (Schultz & Schultz, 2009). He believed that needs for love, knowledge, security, and the like arise from these more fundamental desires. He said that each of us has to find ways of meeting our needs in a world that often frustrates our efforts. Our personalities develop, said Freud, as we struggle with this task and are reflected in the way we satisfy a wide range of urges.

Id, Ego, and Superego Freud described the personality as having three major components: the id, the ego, and the superego (Allen, 2006; see Figure 11.1). The **id** represents the inborn, unconscious portion of the personality where life and death instincts reside. The *life instincts* promote positive, constructive behavior; the *death instincts* are responsible for human aggression and destructiveness (Carver & Scheier, 2004). The id operates on the **pleasure principle,** seeking immediate satisfaction of both kinds of instincts, regardless of society's rules or the rights and feelings of others. The hungry person who pushes to the front of the line at Burger King would be satisfying an id-driven impulse.

As parents, teachers, and others place ever greater restrictions on the expression of id impulses, a second part of the personality, called the *ego* (or "self"), emerges from the id. The **ego** is responsible for organizing ways to get what a person wants in the real world, as opposed to the fantasy world of the id. Operating on the **reality principle,** the ego makes compromises as the id's demands for immediate satisfaction run into the practical realities of the social world. The ego would influence that hungry person at Burger King to wait in line and think about what to order rather than risk punishment by pushing ahead.

As children gain experience with the rules and values of society, they tend to adopt them. This process of *internalizing* parental and cultural values creates the third component of personality. It is called the **superego,** and it tells us what we should and should not do. The superego becomes our moral guide, and it is just as relentless and unreasonable as the id in its demands to be obeyed. The superego would make the person at Burger King feel guilty for even thinking about violating culturally approved rules about waiting in line.

Conflicts and Defenses Freud described the inner clashes among id, ego, and superego as *intrapsychic,* or *psychodynamic, conflicts.* He believed that each individual's personality is shaped by the number, nature, and outcome of these conflicts. Freud said that the ego's main job is to prevent the anxiety or guilt that would arise if we became conscious of socially unacceptable id impulses, especially those that would violate the superego's rules (Engler, 2003; Westen et al., 2008). Sometimes the ego guides sensible actions, as when a parent asks for help because of impulses to abuse a child. However, the ego also uses **defense mechanisms,** which are unconscious tactics that protect against anxiety and guilt by either preventing threatening material from surfacing or disguising it when it does (Coifman et al., 2007; Cramer & Jones, 2007; Jurcevic, Urlic, & Vlastelica, 2005; Porcerelli et al., 2004; Rokach, 2008; see Table 11.1).

TABLE 11.1 ■ EGO DEFENSE MECHANISMS

According to Freud, defense mechanisms prevent anxiety or guilt in the short run, but they sap energy. Further, using them to avoid dealing with the source of problems can make those problems worse in the long run. Try listing some incidents in which you or someone you know might have used each of the defenses described here. What questions would a critical thinker ask to determine whether these behaviors were unconscious defense mechanisms or actions motivated by conscious intentions?

Defense Mechanism	Description
Repression	Unconsciously pushing threatening memories, urges, or ideas from conscious awareness: a person may experience loss of memory of unpleasant events.
Rationalization	Attempting to make actions or mistakes seem reasonable: the reasons or excuses given (e.g., "I spank my children because it is good for them") sound rational, but they are not the real reasons for the behavior.
Projection	Unconsciously attributing one's own unacceptable thoughts or impulses to another person: instead of recognizing that "I hate him," a person may feel that "He hates me."
Reaction formation	Defending against unacceptable impulses by acting opposite to them: sexual interest in a married co-worker might appear as strong dislike instead.
Sublimation	Converting unacceptable impulses into socially acceptable actions and perhaps symbolically expressing them: sexual or aggressive desires may appear as artistic creativity or devotion to athletic excellence.
Displacement	Deflecting an impulse from its original target to a less threatening one: anger at one's boss may be expressed through hostility toward a clerk, a family member, or even the dog.
Denial	Simply discounting the existence of threatening impulses: a person may vehemently deny ever having had even the slightest degree of physical attraction to a person of the same sex.
Compensation	Striving to make up for unconscious impulses or fears: a business executive's extreme competitiveness might be aimed at compensating for unconscious feelings of inferiority.

▶ Which of Freud's ego defense mechanisms is operating here? (Check the answer at the bottom of page 430).

© Scott Adams/Dist. By United Feature Syndicate, Inc.

Stages of Personality Development

Freud proposed that during childhood, personality evolves through several stages of **psychosexual development.** Failure to resolve the conflicts that appear at any of these stages can leave a person *fixated*—that is, unconsciously preoccupied with the area of pleasure associated with that stage. Freud believed that the stage at which a person became fixated in childhood can be seen in the person's adult personality characteristics.

The Oral Stage   In Freud's theory, a child's first year or so is called the **oral stage** because the mouth—which infants use to eat and to explore everything from toys to their own hands and feet—is the center of pleasure during this period. Personality problems arise, said Freud, when oral needs are either neglected or overindulged. For example, early or late weaning from breastfeeding or bottle feeding may leave a child fixated at the oral stage. The resulting adult characteristics may range from overeating or childlike dependence (late weaning) to the use of "biting" sarcasm (early weaning).

THE ORAL STAGE ▶

According to Freud, personality develops in a series of psychosexual stages. At each stage, a different part of the body becomes the primary focus of pleasure. This baby would appear to be in the oral stage.

psychosexual development In Freud's psychodynamic theory, personality development in which internal and external conflicts focus on particular issues during particular periods or stages.

oral stage The first of Freud's psychosexual stages, in which the mouth is the center of pleasure; occurs during the first year of life.

anal stage The second of Freud's psychosexual stages, in which the focus of pleasure shifts from the mouth to the anus; occurs during the second year of life.

phallic stage The third of Freud's psychosexual stages, in which the focus of pleasure shifts to the genital area; lasts from approximately age three to age five.

Oedipal complex The notion that young boys' impulses involve sexual feelings for the mother and the desire to eliminate the father.

Electra complex The notion that young girls develop an attachment to the father and compete with the mother for the father's attention.

latency period The fourth of Freud's psychosexual stages, in which sexual impulses become dormant and the child focuses on education and other matters; usually begins during the fifth year of life.

The Anal Stage   The **anal stage** occurs during the second year, when the child's ego develops to cope with parental demands for socially appropriate behavior. For example, in most Western cultures, toilet training clashes with the child's freedom to have bowel movements at will. Freud said that if toilet training is too harsh or begins too early, it can produce an anal fixation that leads, in adulthood, to stinginess or excessive neatness (symbolically withholding feces). If toilet training is too late or too lax, however, the result could be a kind of anal fixation that is reflected in adults who are disorganized or impulsive (symbolically expelling feces).

The Phallic Stage   According to Freud, between the ages of three and five the focus of pleasure shifts to the genital area. Because he emphasized the psychosexual development of boys, Freud called this period the **phallic stage** (*phallus* is another word for penis). It is during this stage, he claimed, that the boy experiences sexual feelings for his mother and a desire to eliminate, or even kill, his father, with whom the boy competes for the mother's affection. Freud called this set of impulses the **Oedipal complex** because it reminded him of the plot of the classical Greek play *Oedipus Rex*. (In the play, Oedipus unknowingly kills his father and marries his mother.) The boy's fantasies create so much fear, however, that the ego represses his incestuous desires and leads him to "identify" with his father and try to be like him. In the process, the child's superego begins to develop.

According to Freud, a girl begins the phallic stage with a strong attachment to her mother. However, when she realizes that boys have penises and girls don't, she supposedly develops *penis envy* and transfers her love to the father. (This sequence has been called the **Electra complex** because it echoes the plot of *Electra*, another classical Greek play, but Freud never used this term.) To avoid her mother's disapproval, the girl identifies with and imitates her, thus forming the basis for her own superego.

Freud believed that unresolved conflicts during the phallic stage create a fixation that is reflected in many kinds of adult problems. These problems can include difficulties with authority figures and an inability to maintain a stable love relationship.

The Latency Period   As the phallic stage draws to a close and its conflicts are coped with by the ego, there is an interval of psychological peace. During this **latency period,** which lasts through childhood, sexual impulses stay in the background as the youngster focuses on education, same-sex peer play, and the development of social skills.

The Genital Stage   During adolescence, when sexual impulses reappear at the conscious level, the genitals again become the focus of pleasure. Thus begins what Freud called the **genital stage,** which lasts for the rest of the person's life. The quality of relationships and the degree of fulfillment experienced during this final stage, he claimed, are influenced by how intrapsychic conflicts were resolved during the earlier stages.

Variations on Freud's Personality Theory

Freud's ideas—especially those concerning infantile sexuality and the Oedipal complex—were (and still are) controversial. Even many of Freud's followers did not entirely agree with him. Some of these followers are known as *neo-Freudian* theorists because they maintained many of the basic ideas in Freud's theory but developed their own approaches. Others are known as *ego psychologists* because their theories focus more on the ego than on the id (Hergenhahn & Olson, 2007; Larsen & Buss, 2005).

Jung's Analytic Psychology   Carl Jung (pronounced "YOONG") was the most prominent of Freud's early followers to chart his own theoretical course. Jung (1916) argued that people are born with a general life force that (in addition to a sex drive) includes a drive for creativity, for growth-oriented resolution of conflicts, and for the productive blending of basic impulses with real-world demands. Jung did not identify specific stages in personality development. He suggested instead that people gradually develop differing degrees of *introversion* (a tendency to reflect on one's own experiences) or *extraversion* (a tendency to focus on the social world) along with differing tendencies to rely on specific psychological functions, such as thinking or feeling. The combination of these tendencies and functions, said Jung (1933), creates personalities that show distinctive and predictable patterns of behavior.

Other Neo-Freudian Theorists   Alfred Adler, once a loyal follower of psychoanalysis, came to believe that the power behind the development of personality comes not from id impulses but from an innate desire to overcome infantile feelings of helplessness and gain some control over the environment. Other prominent neo-Freudians emphasized social relationships in the development of personality. Some, including Erik Erikson, Erich Fromm, and Harry Stack Sullivan, argued that once biological needs are met, the attempt to meet social needs (to feel protected, secure, and accepted, for example) is the main force that shapes personality. According to these theorists, the strategies that people use to meet social needs, such as dominating other people or being dependent on them, become core features of their personalities.

The first feminist personality theorist, Karen Horney (pronounced "HORN-eye"), challenged Freud's view that women's lack of a penis causes them to envy men and feel inferior to them. Horney (1937) argued that it is men who envy women. Realizing that they cannot bear children, males see their lives as having less meaning and substance than women's. Horney called this condition *womb envy,* and she felt that it led men to belittle women. She believed that when women feel inferior, it is because of cultural factors—such as the personal and political restrictions that men have placed on them—not because of penis envy (Hergenbahn & Olson, 2007; Larsen & Buss, 2005).

Contemporary Psychodynamic Theories

Today, some of the most influential psychodynamic approaches to personality focus on *object relations*—that is, on how early relationships, particularly with their parents, affect how people perceive and relate to other people later in life (Pervin, Cervone, & John, 2005; Westen et al., 2008) According to object relations theorists, early relationships between infants and their love objects (usually the mother and other primary caregivers) are vital influences on the development of personality (Greenberg & Mitchell, 1983; Klein, 1975; Kohut, 1984; Sohlberg & Jansson, 2002). These relationships,

genital stage   The fifth and last of Freud's psychosexual stages, when sexual impulses begin to appear at the conscious level; begins during adolescence.

The defense mechanism illustrated in the cartoon on page 428 is displacement.

they say, shape our thoughts and feelings about social relationships in later life (Westen et al., 2008).

A close cousin of object relations theory is called *attachment theory* because it focuses specifically on the early attachment process that we describe in the chapter on human development. Ideally, infants form a secure bond, or attachment, to their mothers, gradually tolerate separation from this "attachment object," and eventually develop the ability to relate to others as independent, secure individuals (Ainsworth & Bowlby, 1991). Attachment theorists have studied how variations in the nature of this early bond are related to differences in self-image, identity, security, and social relationships in adolescence, adulthood, and even old age (Consedine & Magai, 2003; Mattanah, Hancock, & Brand, 2004; Shaver & Mikulincer, 2005; Simpson et al., 2007). In one study, women who had been securely attached in childhood were more likely to have happy marriages than women whose childhood attachments had been insecure (Klohnen & Bera, 1998). Other researchers found that people who had had insecure attachments showed much stronger physiological stress reactions to interpersonal conflicts than did people whose attachments had been secure (Powers et al., 2006). In yet another study, people with insecure early attachments were less likely than those with secure attachments to be helpful when they encountered a person in distress (Mikulincer & Shaver, 2005). Further evidence along these lines comes from a long-term study of children diagnosed with severe heart disease. That study found that the children whose mothers had not been securely attached to their own mothers tended to show greater evidence of anxiety and other emotional difficulties in the years following the diagnosis than did those whose mothers had been more securely attached (Berant, Mikulincer, & Shaver, 2008). In short, attachment theorists suggest that people who miss the opportunity to become securely attached may suffer significant disturbances in their later relationships (Aizawa, 2002), including in relationships with their own children.

Evaluating the Psychodynamic Approach

Freud's personality theory is probably the most comprehensive and influential psychological theory ever proposed. His ideas have shaped a wide range of psychotherapy techniques (see the chapter on treatment of psychological disorders) and stimulated the development of several personality assessments, including the projective personality measures described later in this chapter. Some of Freud's ideas have received support from research on cognitive processes (Andersen & Chen, 2002). It appears, for example, that people employ several of the defense mechanisms Freud described (Cramer, 2003, 2007), although these may not always operate at an unconscious level. There is also evidence that our thoughts and actions can be influenced by events and experiences that we don't recall (Andersen & Chen, 2002; Andersen & Miranda, 2000; Bargh & Morsella, 2008; Dijksterhuis et al., 2008; Ferguson & Bargh, 2004; Kihlstrom, 2008) and possibly by emotions we don't consciously experience (Winkielman & Berridge, 2004). Some researchers believe that unconscious processes may even affect our health (Goldenberg et al., 2008).

However, Freud's theories have several weaknesses. For one thing, his conclusions about personality are based almost entirely on case studies of a few individuals. As discussed in the introductory chapter, conclusions drawn from case studies may not apply to people in general. Freud's sample of cases was certainly not representative of people in general. Most of his patients were upper-class Viennese women who not only had psychological problems but (like most people in some other social classes) were raised in a society that considered the discussion of sex to be uncivilized. Second, Freud's theory reflected Western European and North American cultural values, which may or may not be helpful in understanding people in other cultures (Feist & Feist, 2002). For example, the concepts of ego and self that are so central to Freud's personality theory are based on the self-oriented values of individualist cultures and thus may be less descriptive of personality development in collectivist cultures, such as those of Asia and South America (Matsumoto, 2000; Morling & Kitayama, 2008).

Freud's conclusions may have been distorted by other biases as well. Some Freud scholars believe he might have (perhaps unconsciously) modified reports of what happened during therapy to better fit his theory (Esterson, 2001; Powell & Boer, 1995; Schultz & Schultz, 2005, 2009). He may also have asked leading questions that influenced patients to "recall" events from their childhoods that never happened (Esterson, 2001). Today, as described in the memory chapter, there are similar concerns that some patients who recover allegedly repressed memories about childhood sexual abuse may actually be reporting false memories implanted by their therapists (Loftus, 2004; Loftus, Garry, & Hayne, 2008).

Freud's focus on male psychosexual development and his notion that females envy male anatomy have also been attacked. In the tradition of Horney, some contemporary neo-Freudians have proposed theories that focus specifically on the psychosexual development of women (Sayers, 1991; Yonke & Barnett, 2001).

Finally, as judged by modern standards, Freud's theory is not very scientific. His definitions of *id, ego, unconscious conflict,* and other concepts lack the precision required for scientific measurement and testing (Pervin, Cervone, & John, 2005). Further, his belief that unconscious desires drive most human behavior ignores evidence showing that much of that behavior goes beyond impulse gratification. For example, the conscious drive to attain personal, social, and spiritual goals is an important determinant of behavior, as is learning from others. Some of the weaknesses in Freudian theory have been addressed by those who seek to subject psychodynamic principles and theories to empirical tests (e.g., Betan et al., 2005; Roffman & Gerber, 2008; Wegner, Wenzlaff, & Kozak, 2004; Westen, 2005), but the psychodynamic approach to personality remains less popular today than it was in past decades (Allen, 2006; Carver & Scheier, 2004; Funder, 2007).

The Trait Approach

▶ *What personality traits are most basic?*

You could probably describe the personality of someone you know well with just a few statements. For example, you might say,

> He's a really caring person, and very outgoing. He's generous with his time, and he works very hard at everything he does. Yet sometimes I think he also lacks self-confidence. He always gives in to other people's demands because he wants to be accepted by them.

In other words, most people describe others by referring to the kind of people they are ("outgoing"); to the thoughts, feelings, and actions that are most typical of them ("caring," "lacks self-confidence"); or to their needs ("wants to be accepted"). Together, these statements describe **personality traits**—the tendencies that help direct how a person usually thinks and behaves (Pervin, Cervone, & John, 2005).

The trait approach to personality makes three main assumptions:

1. Personality traits are relatively stable, and therefore predictable, over time. So a gentle person tends to stay that way day after day, year after year (Cervone & Pervin, 2008; Costa & McCrae, 2002).
2. Personality traits are relatively stable across situations, and they can explain why people act in predictable ways in many different situations. A person who is competitive at work will probably also be competitive on the tennis court or at a party (Roberts et al., 2007).
3. People differ in how much of a particular personality trait they possess; no two people are exactly alike on all traits. The result is an endless variety of unique personalities.

In short, psychologists who take the **trait approach** see personality as a combination of stable internal characteristics that people display consistently over time and across situations (Pervin, Cervone, & John, 2005). Trait theorists seek to measure the relative strength of the many personality characteristics that they believe are present in everyone (see Figure 11.2).

personality traits A set of stable characteristics that people display over time and across situations.

trait approach A perspective on personality that views it as the combination of stable characteristics that people display over time and across situations.

FIGURE 11.2 ■ TWO PERSONALITY PROFILES

Trait theory describes personality in terms of the strength of particular dimensions, or traits. Here are trait profiles for Rodney, an inner-city social worker, and James, a sales clerk. Compared with James, Rodney is about equally industrious, more generous, and less nervous, extraverted, and aggressive. Just for fun, mark this figure to indicate how strong you think you are on each of the listed traits. Trait theorists suggest that it should be easy for you to do these ratings because, they say, virtually everyone displays a certain amount of almost any personality characteristic.
Source: Costa & McCrae (1992).

Learn BY **Doing**

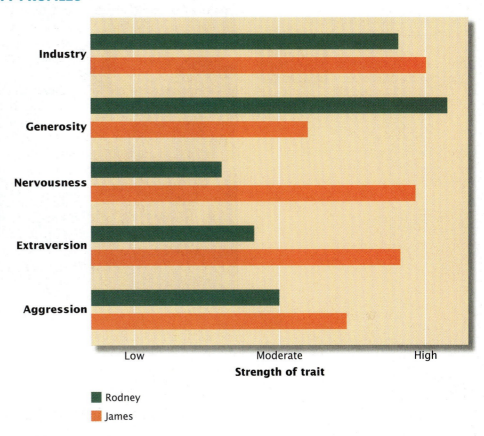

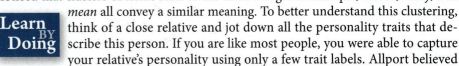

Early Trait Theories

Today's trait theories of personality are largely based on the work of Gordon Allport and Raymond Cattell. (The contributions of another early trait theorist, Hans Eysenck, are discussed later.) Allport spent 30 years searching for the traits that combine to form personality. When he looked at the nearly 18,000 dictionary terms that can be used to describe human behavior (Allport & Odbert, 1936; John, Naumann, & Soto, 2008), he noticed that clusters of terms refer to the same thing. For example, *hostile, nasty,* and *mean* all convey a similar meaning. To better understand this clustering, **Learn** BY **Doing** think of a close relative and jot down all the personality traits that describe this person. If you are like most people, you were able to capture your relative's personality using only a few trait labels. Allport believed that the set of labels that describe a particular person reflects that person's *central traits*—those that are usually obvious to others and that organize and control behavior in many different situations. Central traits are roughly equivalent to the descriptive terms used in letters of recommendation (*reliable* or *distractible*, for example) that are meant to tell what can be expected from a person most of the time (Schultz & Schultz, 2005, 2009). Allport also believed that people possess *secondary traits*—those that are more specific to certain situations and control far less behavior. "Dislikes crowds" is an example of a secondary trait.

Allport's research helped lay the foundation for modern research on personality traits. His focus on the uniqueness of each personality made it difficult to draw conclusions about the structure of personality in general (Barenbaum & Winter, 2008), but some researchers today continue to employ a modern version of Allport's approach (e.g., Caldwell, Cervone, & Rubin, 2008). In contrast, British psychologist Raymond Cattell was interested in the personality traits that people share. He used a mathematical technique called factor analysis to study which traits are correlated with

SELECTING A JURY   ▶

Some psychologists employ trait theories of personality in advising prosecution or defense attorneys about which potential jurors are most likely to be sympathetic to their side of a court case.

applying psychology

one another. Factor analysis can reveal, for example, whether people who are moody are also likely to be anxious, rigid, and unsociable. Cattell found sixteen clusters of traits that he believed make up the basic dimensions, or factors, of personality (Cattell, Eber, & Tatsuoka, 1970).

The Five Factor Personality Model

Building on the work of Allport and Cattell, today's trait theorists use factor-analysis to bring the structure of personality into even sharper focus. The results of their research have led many of these theorists to conclude that personality is organized around just five basic factors (McCrae & Costa, 2004, 2008). The components of this **Five Factor,** or **Big Five, Personality Model** have been given slightly different labels by different researchers, but the most widely used names are *openness, conscientiousness, extraversion, agreeableness,* and *neuroticism* (see Table 11.2). The fact that some version of the Big Five factors reliably appear in many countries and cultures—including Canada, China, the Czech Republic, Germany, Greece, Finland, India, Japan, Korea, the Philippines, Poland, Turkey, and Zimbabwe (Allik & McCrae, 2004; Ashton et al., 2004; McCrae et al., 2004;

TABLE 11.2   ■   DIMENSIONS OF THE FIVE FACTOR PERSONALITY MODEL

Here is a list of the adjectives that define the Big Five personality factors. You can more easily remember these factors by noting that the first letters of their names spell the word *ocean*.

Dimension	Defining Descriptors
Openness	Artistic, curious, imaginative, insightful, original, wide interests, unusual thought processes, intellectual interests
Conscientiousness	Efficient, organized, planful, reliable, thorough, dependable, ethical, productive
Extraversion	Active, assertive, energetic, outgoing, talkative, gesturally expressive, gregarious
Agreeableness	Appreciative, forgiving, generous, kind, trusting, noncritical, warm, compassionate, considerate, straightforward
Neuroticism	Anxious, self-pitying, tense, emotionally unstable, impulsive, vulnerable, touchy, prone to worry

Source: Adapted from McCrae & John (1992).

ANIMAL PERSONALITIES ▶

The idea that personality can be described in terms of five main dimensions seems to hold for some animals as well as humans. The five animal dimensions differ from (but are still related to) human traits. For example, hyenas differ among themselves in terms of dominance, excitability, agreeableness (toward people), sociability (toward each other), and curiosity. Some of these same traits have been observed in a wide variety of other species, including sheep, langurs, orangutans, chipmunks, and chimpanzees (Gosling, 2001; King, Weiss, & Farmer, 2005; Konecná et al., 2008; Martin & Réale, 2008; Michelana et al., 2009; Weiss, King, & Perkins, 2006). Dog and cat lovers often report such traits in their pets, too (Gosling, Kwan, & John, 2003; Lee, Ryan, & Kreiner, 2007; Ley, Bennett, & Coleman, 2009).

© Robert Caputo/Aurora Photos

linkages

Why do some people take more risks than others? *(a link to Motivation and Emotion)*

Five Factor Personality Model (Big Five Personality Model) A view based on studies using factor analysis that suggests the existence of five basic components of human personality: openness, conscientiousness, extraversion, agreeableness, and neuroticism.

McCrae & Costa, 2006; Saucier et al., 2005; Yamagata et al., 2006)—provides evidence that these factors may indeed represent the most important components of human personality (McCrae, Terracciano, & Profiles of Cultures Project, 2005).

Many trait theorists consider the emergence of the Five Factor Personality Model to be a major breakthrough in examining the personalities of all people, regardless of where they live or the nature of their economic, social, and cultural backgrounds (Carver & Scheier, 2004; John, Naumann, & Soto, 2008) The model also allows researchers to precisely describe the similarities and differences in people's personalities and to explore how these factors are related to everything from personality disorders and political beliefs to substance abuse, academic performance, happiness, and a sense of well-being (Brummett et al., 2006; DeNeve, 1999; Diener, 2000; Lynam & Widiger, 2001; Roberts & Bogg, 2004; Noftle & Shaver, 2006; Noftle & Robins, 2007; Poropat, 2009; Van Hiel & Merviedle, 2004).

Biological Trait Theories

Some personality theorists are interested not only in which traits form the core of human personality but also in why people differ on these traits. Their research suggests that differences in traits might be due to biological factors.

Eysenck's Biological Trait Theory   The biological basis for personality was emphasized in the work of British psychologist Hans Eysenck (pronounced "EYE-sink"). Like other trait theorists who helped lay the groundwork for the Five Factor Personality Model, Eysenck used factor analysis to study personality. His research led him to focus on two main personality dimensions known as *introversion-extraversion* and *emotionality-stability* (Eysenck, 1990a, 1990b):

1. *Introversion-extraversion.* Extraverts are sociable and outgoing, enjoy parties and other social activities, take risks, and love excitement and change. Introverts tend to be quiet, thoughtful, and reserved, enjoying solitary pursuits and avoiding excitement and social involvement.
2. *Emotionality-stability* (also often called *neuroticism*). At one extreme of this dimension are people who exhibit such characteristics as moodiness, restlessness, worry, anxiety, and other negative emotions. People at the opposite end are calm, even-tempered, relaxed, and emotionally stable.

According to Eysenck, personality can be described in terms of where a person falls along these two dimensions. For example, an introverted but stable person is likely to be controlled and reliable. An introverted but emotional person is likely to be rigid and anxious (see Figure 11.3).

FIGURE 11.3 ■ EYSENCK'S PERSONALITY DIMENSIONS

According to Eysenck, varying degrees of emotionality-stability and introversion-extraversion combine to produce predictable trait patterns. The traits appearing in the four sections created by crossing these two personality dimensions roughly define the four basic temperaments identified centuries ago by the ancient Greek physician Hippocrates: melancholic (sad), choleric (hot-tempered), phlegmatic (slow and lethargic), and sanguine (optimistic). Which section of the figure do you think best describes your personality traits? How about those of a friend or a relative? Did you find it any easier to place other people's personalities in a particular section than it was to place your own personality? If so, why do you think that might be?
Source: Eysenck & Rachman (1965).

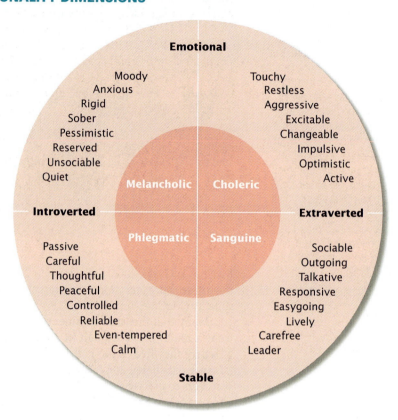

Eysenck argued that the variations in personality characteristics that we see among individuals can be traced to inherited differences in their nervous systems, especially in their brains. These biological differences, he said, create differences in people's typical levels of physiological arousal and in their sensitivity to stress and other environmental stimulation. For example, people who inherit a nervous system that normally operates below some ideal level of arousal will always be on the lookout for excitement, change, and social contact in order to increase their arousal. As a result, they will be *extraverted*. In contrast, people whose nervous system is normally "overaroused" will tend to avoid excitement, change, and social contact in order to reduce arousal to their ideal level. In short, they will be *introverted*. What about the emotionality-stability dimension? Eysenck said that people who fall toward the stability side have nervous systems that are relatively insensitive to stress; those who are more emotional have nervous systems that react more strongly to stress.

Gray's Reinforcement Sensitivity Theory Jeffrey Gray, another British psychologist, agrees with Eysenck about the two basic dimensions of personality but offers a different explanation of the biological factors underlying them (Corr, 2002; Gray, 1991). According to Gray's *reinforcement sensitivity theory*, differences among people along the dimensions of introversion-extraversion and emotionality-stability originate in the brain regions that influence how sensitive people are to different kinds of events. These regions are called the behavioral approach system and the flight or freeze system (Pickering & Gray, 1999). The *behavioral approach system*, or *BAS*, affects people's sensitivity to rewards and their motivation to seek these rewards. The BAS has been called a "go" system because it is responsible for how impulsive or uninhibited a person is. The *flight or freeze system*, or *FFS*, affects how sensitive people are to punishment (Smillie, Pickering, & Jackson, 2006). Gray sees extraverts as having a sensitive reward system (BAS) and an insensitive punishment system (FFS). Introverts are just the opposite: they are relatively insensitive to rewards but highly sensitive to punishment. Emotionally unstable people are much more sensitive to both rewards and punishments than are those who are emotionally stable.

Gray's theory has its critics (e.g., Jackson, 2003; Matthews, 2008), but it is now more widely accepted than Eysenck's theory—primarily because it is supported by data from other researchers (e.g., Revelle, 2008) and because it is consistent with what neuroscientists have learned about brain structures and neurotransmitters and how they operate (Buckholtz et al., 2008; Franken, Muris, & Georgieva, 2006; Larsen & Buss, 2005; Reuter et al., 2006; Wacker, Chavanon, & Stemmler, 2006).

Thinking CRITICALLY

Are Personality Traits Inherited?

Gray's reinforcement sensitivity theory is one of several biologically oriented explanations of the origins of personality traits (e.g., Zuckerman, 2004). A related approach involves exploring the role of genetics in these traits (Bouchard, 2004; Ebstein, 2006; Kreuger & Johnson, 2008; Shifman et al., 2008; Weiss, Bates, & Luciano, 2008). For example, consider a pair of identical twins who had been separated at five weeks of age and did not meet again for 39 years. Both men drove Chevrolets, chain-smoked the same brand of cigarettes, had divorced a woman named Linda, were remarried to a woman named Betty, had sons named James Allan, had dogs named Toy, enjoyed similar hobbies, and had served as sheriff's deputies (Tellegen et al., 1988).

● What am I being asked to believe or accept?

Cases like this have helped focus the attention of behavioral geneticists on the possibility that some core aspects of personality might be partly or even largely inherited (Bouchard, 2004; Ebstein, 2006; Johnson et al., 2004; Noblett & Coccaro, 2005; South & Krueger, 2008; Vernon, Martin et al., 2008; Vernon, Villani et al., 2008).

● Is evidence available to support the claim?

Some of the evidence for this assertion comes from the many familiar cases in which children seem to "have" their parents' or grandparents' bad temper, generosity, or shyness. More systematic studies have also found moderate but significant correlations between children's personality test scores and those of their parents and siblings (Davis, Luce, & Kraus, 1994; DeYoung, Quilty, & Peterson, 2007; Loehlin, 1992; Loehlin et al., 1998).

Even stronger evidence comes from studies conducted around the world that compared identical twins raised together, identical twins raised apart, nonidentical twins raised together, and nonidentical twins raised apart (Grigorenko, 2002; Yamagata et al., 2006). Whether they are raised apart or together, identical twins (who have exactly the same genes) tend to be more alike in personality than nonidentical twins (whose genes are no more similar than those of other siblings). This research also shows that identical twins are more alike than nonidentical twins in general temperament, such as how active, sociable, anxious, and emotional they are (Pickering & Gray, 1999; Borkenau et al., 2002, 2006; Wolf et al., 2004; Yamagata et al., 2006). On the basis of such twin studies, behavioral geneticists have concluded that about 50 percent of the differences among people in terms of personality traits are due to genetic factors (Caspi, Roberts, & Shiner, 2005; Kreuger et al., 2008).

● Can that evidence be interpreted another way?

Family resemblances in personality could reflect inheritance or social influence. So an obvious alternative interpretation of this evidence might be that family similarities come not from common genes but from a common environment. Children learn many rules, skills, and behaviors by watching parents, siblings, and others; perhaps they learn their personalities as well (Funder, 2007). And the fact that nontwin siblings are less alike than twins may well result from what is called a *nonshared environment* (Plomin, 2004). Nonshared factors include, for example, a child's place in the family birth order, differences in the way parents treat each of their children, and accidents, illnesses, or events that alter a particular child's life or health (Paulhus, Trapnell, & Chen, 1999). Nontwins are more likely than twins, especially identical twins, to be affected by these nonshared environmental factors.

● What evidence would help to evaluate the alternatives?

One way to evaluate the idea that personality is inherited would be to locate genes that are associated with certain personality characteristics (Ebstein, 2006). Genetic differences have already been tentatively associated with certain behavior disorders, but most behavioral genetics researchers doubt that there are direct links between particular genes and particular personality traits (Caspi, Roberts, & Shiner, 2005; Kreuger & Johnson, 2008; Reif & Lesch, 2003).

Another way to evaluate the role of genes in personality is to study people in infancy, before the environment has had a chance to exert its influence. If the environment were entirely responsible for personality, newborns should be essentially alike. However, as discussed in the chapter on human development, infants show immediate differences in activity level, sensitivity to the environment, the tendency to cry, and interest in new stimuli (Rothbart & Derryberry, 2002). These differences in *temperament* suggest biological and perhaps genetic influences.

To evaluate the relative contributions of nature and nurture beyond infancy, psychologists have examined the personality characteristics of adopted children. If adopted children are more like their biological than their adoptive parents, this suggests the influence of heredity in personality. If they are more like their adoptive families, a strong role for environmental factors in personality is suggested. In actuality, adopted children's personalities tend to resemble the personalities of their biological parents and siblings more closely than they do those of the families in which they are raised (Kreuger & Johnson, 2008; Plomin et al., 1998).

Further research will determine more clearly what aspects of the environment are most important in shaping personality (Turkheimer & Waldron, 2000). So far, the evidence suggests that personality is not influenced very strongly by elements of the shared environment—such as socioeconomic status—that equally affect all children in the same family. However, nonshared environmental influences, at home and elsewhere, appear to be very important in personality development (Harris, 2000; Loehlin, Neiderhiser, & Reiss, 2003). We need to know more about the exact impact on personality development of nonshared environmental factors that may be different for twins and nontwin siblings.

▶ *What conclusions are most reasonable?*

Even those researchers, such as Robert Plomin, who support genetic theories of personality caution that we should not replace "simple-minded environmentalism" with the equally incorrect view that personality is almost completely biologically determined (Plomin & Crabbe, 2000). It is pointless to talk about heredity *versus* environment as causes of personality, because nature and nurture always intertwine to exert joint and simultaneous influences (Dodge, 2004; Johnson, McGue, & Krueger, 2005; Kreuger & Johnson, 2008).

With this caution in mind, we would be well advised to draw only tentative conclusions about the origins of personality

differences. The evidence available so far suggests that genetic influences do appear to contribute significantly to the differences among people in many personality traits (DeYoung et al., 2007; Plomin & Crabbe, 2000; Vernon et al., 2008; Yamagata et al., 2006). As noted earlier, however, there is no evidence of a specific gene for any specific personality trait (Kreuger & Johnson, 2008). The genetic contribution to personality most likely comes as genes influence people's nervous systems and general predispositions toward certain temperaments (Arbelle et al., 2003; Ebstein, 2006; Grigorenko, 2002). Temperamental factors (e.g., emotionality and sociability) then interact with environmental factors, such as family experiences, to produce specific features of personality (Caspi et al., 2005). For example, a child's ability to control or regulate emotions appears to be strongly determined by heredity. Children who are less able to regulate their emotions might play less with other children, withdraw more from social interactions, and thereby fail to learn important social skills (Eisenberg, Champion & Ma, 2004; Eisenberg, Fabes, & Murphy, 1995). These experiences and tendencies, in turn, might foster the self-consciousness and shyness seen in introverted personalities.

Notice, though, that genetic predispositions toward particular personality characteristics may or may not be expressed in behavior, depending on whether the environment supports or stifles them. Changes in genetically predisposed traits are not only possible but may actually be quite common as children grow (Cacioppo et al., 2000). So even though there is a strong genetic basis for shyness, many children learn to overcome this tendency and become quite outgoing (Leary, 2001; Rowe, 1997). In summary, rather than inheriting specific traits, people appear to inherit the behavioral and emotional raw materials out of which their personalities are shaped by the world.

FAMILY RESEMBLANCE ▶

Do children inherit personality traits in the same direct way as they inherit facial features, coloration, and other physical characteristics? Research in behavioral genetics suggests that personality is the joint product of genetically influenced behavioral tendencies and the environmental conditions each child encounters.

© Bruce Plotkin/Getty Images

Evaluating the Trait Approach

The trait approach, and especially the Five Factor Personality Model, tends to dominate contemporary research in personality. Yet there are several problems and weaknesses associated with this approach.

For one thing, trait theories seem better at describing people than at understanding them. It is easy to say, for example, that Marilyn is nasty because she has a strong hostility trait; but other factors, such as the way people treat her, could also be responsible. In other words, trait theories say a lot about how people behave, but they don't always explain why (Mischel, 2004a, 2004b). Nor do trait theories say much about how traits are related to the thoughts and feelings that precede, accompany, and follow behavior. Do introverts and extraverts decide to act as they do? Can they behave otherwise? And how do they feel about their actions and experiences (Cervone & Shoda, 1999)? Some personality psychologists are linking their research with that of cognitive psychologists in an effort to better understand how thoughts and emotions influence, and are influenced by, personality traits (Shoda & LeeTiernan, 2002). And as noted earlier, other psychologists are studying the role played by genes, brain structures, and neurotransmitters in the individual differences we see among people's personality traits (e.g., Canli, 2008; Netter, 2006).

The trait approach has also been criticized for offering a short list of traits that provides, at best, a fixed and rather shallow description of personality that fails to capture how traits combine to form a complex and dynamic individual (Block, 2001; Funder, 2001, 2007). There are questions, too, about whether there really are exactly five core dimensions of personality. Some evidence suggests, for example, that there might be a sixth dimension known as *honesty and humility* (Lee, Ogunfowora, & Ashton, 2005). Whatever the number turns out to be, some doubt that these dimensions are exactly the same in all cultures (Benet-Martinez & Oishi, 2008). Finally, even if some version of the Five Factor Personality Model proves to be correct and universal, its factors are not all-powerful. Situations, too, affect behavior. For example, people high in extraversion are not always sociable. Whether they behave sociably depends, in part, on where they are and who else is present.

In fairness, early trait theorists such as Allport acknowledged the importance of situations in influencing behavior, but it is only recently that consideration of interactions between people and situations has become an important part of trait-based approaches to personality. This change is largely the result of research conducted by psychologists who have taken a social-cognitive approach to personality, which we describe next.

The Social-Cognitive Approach

▶ *Do we learn our personalities?*

To social-cognitive researchers, psychodynamic theories place too much emphasis on unconscious forces in personality and trait theories presume more consistency in people's behavior than there really is. In contrast, researchers who take a **social-cognitive approach** see personality as the full set of behaviors that people have acquired through *learning* and that they then display in particular situations (Mischel & Shoda, 2008). Some aspects of this approach reflect the view of traditional behaviorists, namely that all behavior is learned through classical and operant conditioning (see the chapter on learning). However, the social-cognitive approach expands that view by emphasizing (1) the role played by *learned patterns of thinking* in guiding behavior; and (2) the fact that personality is learned in social situations as people observe and interact with other people (Bandura & Walters, 1963; Cervone & Pervin, 2008; Funder, 2007). The social-cognitive approach is sometimes called the *social-learning approach* because it defines personality as the sum of the behaviors and cognitive habits that develop as people learn through experience in the social world. Social-cognitive

social-cognitive approach An approach that views personality as a label that summarizes the unique patterns of thinking and behavior that a person learns.

theorists are interested in how our thinking affects our behavior as well as how our behavior and its consequences affect our thinking and our future actions (Mischel & Shoda, 2008; Shoda & Mischel, 2006).

Prominent Social-Cognitive Theories

Julian Rotter, Albert Bandura, and Walter Mischel have presented the most influential social-cognitive personality theories.

Rotter's Expectancy Theory   Julian Rotter (1982) argued that learning creates cognitions known as *expectancies* and that these expectancies guide behavior. He suggested that a person's decision to engage in a behavior is determined by (1) what the person expects to happen following the behavior; and (2) the value the person places on the outcome. For example, people spend a lot of money on new clothes to wear at job interviews because past learning leads them to expect that doing so will help get them the job and they place a high value on having the job. To Rotter, then, behavior is shaped by the positive or negative consequences it brings and by the expectancy that a particular behavior will be rewarded or punished (Mischel, Shoda, & Smith, 2004).

Personality researchers influenced by Rotter have suggested that in addition to learning expectancies about particular behaviors in particular situations, we also learn more general expectancies, especially about how life's rewards and punishments are controlled (e.g., Phares, 1976). Some people (called *internals*) come to expect that events are controlled mainly by their own efforts. These people assume, for example, that what they achieve and the rewards they get are determined by what they themselves do. Others (*externals*) tend to expect events to be controlled by external forces over which they have no control. So when externals succeed, they tend to believe that their success was based on chance or luck.

Research on differences in generalized expectancies does show that they are correlated with differences in behavior. For example, when threatened by a hurricane or other natural disaster, internals—in accordance with their belief that they can control what happens to them—are more likely than externals to buy bottled water and make other preparations (Sattler, Kaiser, & Hittner, 2000). Internals tend to work harder than externals at staying physically healthy and as a result may be healthier (Stürmer, Hasselbach, & Amelang, 2006). We know, for example, that children with an internal control orientation are less likely than externals to become obese in later life (Gale, Batty, & Deary, 2008). Internals are less likely to drink alcohol or if they do drink, are less likely to drive while intoxicated (Cavaiola & Desordi, 2000). They are also more careful with money (Lim, Teo, & Loo, 2003). As college students, internals tend to be better informed about their courses and about what they need to do to get a high grade than externals are. This may help to account for why internals tend to get better grades and graduate sooner (Dollinger, 2000; Hall, Smith, & Chia, 2008).

Bandura and Reciprocal Determinism   In his social-cognitive theory, Albert Bandura (1999, 2006) sees personality as shaped by the ways that thoughts, behavior, and the environment interact and influence one another. He points out that whether people learn through direct experience with rewards and punishments or through watching what happens to others, their behavior creates changes in their environment. Observing these changes, in turn, affects how they think, which then affects their behavior and so on in a constant web of mutual influence that Bandura calls *reciprocal determinism* (see Figure 11.4).

An especially important cognitive element in this system of mutual influence is perceived **self-efficacy**, the learned expectation of success. Bandura says that what we do and what we try to do are largely controlled by our perceptions or beliefs about the chances of success at a particular task or problem. People with a high degree of perceived self-efficacy believe that they can successfully perform a behavior regardless of past failures or current obstacles. So the higher your perceived self-efficacy is in a particular situation or task, the greater your actual accomplishments in that situation

self-efficacy   According to Bandura, the learned expectation of success in given situations.

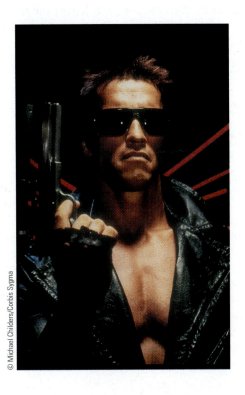

B = Behavior

E = The external environment

P = Personal factors, such as thoughts, feelings, and biological events

FIGURE 11.4 ■ RECIPROCAL DETERMINISM

Bandura's notion of reciprocal determinism suggests that thoughts, behavior, and the environment are constantly affecting each other. For example, a person's hostile thoughts might lead to hostile behavior, which generates even more hostile thoughts. At the same time, the hostile behavior offends others, thus creating a threatening environment that causes the person to think and act in even more negative ways. As increasingly negative thoughts alter the person's perceptions of the environment, that environment seems to be more threatening than ever (e.g., Bushman et al., 2005).

or task are likely to be (Coutinho & Neuman, 2008; Jawahar et al., 2008; Pearson, 2008; Zimmerman & Schunk, 2003). For example, going into a job interview believing that you have the skills for the job may help you to get the job. (Perhaps you recall the classic children's story *The Little Engine That Could:* Trying to get up a steep hill, the scared little engine starts by saying "I think I can, I think I can" and ends up saying "I know I can, I know I can." And it did.)

According to Bandura, self-efficacy interacts with expectancies about the outcome of behavior in general and the result of this interplay helps shape a person's psychological well-being (Bandura, 1997; Maddux & Gosselin, 2003). So if a person has low self-efficacy and expects that nothing anyone does has much effect on the world, apathy may result. But if a person with low self-efficacy believes that *other* people are enjoying the benefits of their efforts, the result may be self-criticism and depression.

Mischel's Cognitive/Affective Theory   Social-cognitive theorists argue that learned beliefs, feelings, and expectancies characterize each individual and make that individual different from other people. Walter Mischel calls these characteristics *cognitive person variables.* He believes that they outline the dimensions along which individuals differ (Mischel & Shoda, 1999, 2008).

According to Mischel, the most important cognitive person variables are (1) *encodings* (the person's beliefs about the environment and other people); (2) *expectancies* (including self-efficacy and what results the person expects will follow from various behaviors); (3) *affects* (feelings and emotions); (4) *goals and values* (the things a person believes in and wants to achieve); and (5) *competencies and self-regulatory plans* (the things the person can do and the ability to thoughtfully plan behaviors (Mischel & Shoda, 1999; Shoda & Mischel, 2006).

To predict how a person might behave in a particular situation, says Mischel, we need to know about these cognitive person variables and about the features of that situation. In short, the person and the situation interact to produce behavior. Mischel's ideas have been called an "if-then" theory because he proposes that *if* people encounter a particular situation, *then* they will engage in the characteristic behaviors (called *behavioral signatures*) that they typically show in this situation (Kammrath, Mendoza-Denton, & Mischel, 2005).

THE IMPACT OF SITUATIONS ▶

Like the rest of us, Arnold Schwarzenegger behaves differently in different situations, including when acting in his Terminator movies and when serving as the governor of California. Mischel's theory of personality emphasizes that the interaction between particular people and specific situations are vitally important in determining behavior.

Mischel was once highly critical of the trait approach to personality, but now he sees his own theory as generally consistent with that approach. In fact, the concept of behavioral signatures is quite similar to the concept of traits. However, Mischel still argues that trait theorists underestimate the power of situations to alter behavior and do not pay enough attention to the cognitive and emotional processes that underlie people's overt actions. Despite their remaining differences, most advocates of the trait and social-cognitive approaches are now focusing on the similarities between their views (Cervone, 2005; Fleeson, 2004; Funder, 2008). This search for similarities between the trait approach and the social-cognitive approach has helped clarify the relationship between personal and situational variables and how they affect behavior under various conditions. Many of the conclusions that have emerged are consistent with Bandura's concept of reciprocal determinism:

1. Personal dispositions (which include traits and cognitive person variables) influence behavior only in relevant situations. The trait of anxiousness, for example, may predict anxiety, but mainly in situations in which an anxious person feels threatened.
2. Personal dispositions can lead to behaviors that alter situations that in turn promote other behaviors. For example, a hostile child can trigger aggression in others and thus start a fight.
3. People choose to be in situations that are in accord with their personal dispositions. Introverts, for instance, are likely to choose quiet environments, whereas extraverts tend to seek out livelier, more social circumstances.
4. Personal dispositions are more important in some situations than in others. Where many different behaviors would be appropriate—at a picnic, for example—what people do can usually be predicted from their dispositions (extraverts will probably play games and socialize while introverts will probably watch from the sidelines). However, in situations such as a funeral, where fewer options are socially acceptable, personal dispositions will not differentiate one person from another; everyone is likely to be quiet and somber.

Today, social-cognitive theorists are attempting to discover how person variables develop, how they relate to stress and health, and how they interact with situational variables to affect behavior.

Evaluating the Social-Cognitive Approach

The social-cognitive approach to personality is valuable because it blends behavioral learning theories with concepts from cognitive psychology and applies them to such socially important topics as aggression, the effects of mass media on children, and the development of techniques that enhance personal control over behavior. Social-cognitive principles have also been translated into cognitive-behavioral treatment procedures (O'Donohue, Fisher, & Hayes, 2003; see the chapter on treatment of psychological disorders).

The social-cognitive approach has not escaped criticism, however. Psychodynamic theorists point out that social-cognitive theories leave no role for unconscious thoughts and feelings in determining behaviors (e.g., Westen et al., 2008). Some advocates of trait theory complain that social-cognitive theorists have focused more on explaining why traits are unimportant than on why situations are important and argue that they have failed to identify what it is about specific situations that brings out certain behaviors (Friedman & Schustack, 2003; Funder, 2001, 2008). Finally, some critics feel that the social-cognitive approach cannot capture the complexities, richness, and uniqueness that are inherent in human personality (Carver & Scheier, 2004). For these critics, a far more attractive alternative is offered by the humanistic approach to personality.

The Humanistic Approach

 Is everyone basically good?

Unlike theories that emphasize the instincts and learning processes that humans seem to share with other animals, the **humanistic psychology** approach to personality focuses on mental capabilities that set humans apart: self-awareness, creativity, planning, decision making, and responsibility. Those who adopt the *humanistic approach* view human behavior as motivated mainly by an innate drive toward growth that prompts us all to fulfill our own unique potential and thus to achieve an ideal condition known as **self-actualization** (Goldstein, 1939). And like the planted seed whose natural potential is to become a flower, people are seen as naturally inclined toward goodness, creativity, love, and joy. Humanistic psychologists also believe that to explain people's actions, it is more important to understand their view of the world than their instincts, traits, or learning experiences. To humanists, that world view is a bit different for each of us, and it is this unique *phenomenology* (pronounced "feh-nah-men-AHL-oh-gee"), or way of perceiving and interpreting the world, that shapes personality and guides behavior (Kelly, 1980). Because of its emphasis on the importance of looking at people's perceptions, this approach to personality is also sometimes called the *phenomenological approach.*

Prominent Humanistic Theories

The most prominent humanistic theories of personality are those of Carl Rogers and Abraham Maslow.

Rogers's Self Theory   In his extensive writings, Carl Rogers (1961, 1970, 1980) emphasized the **actualizing tendency**, which he described as an innate inclination toward growth and fulfillment that motivates all human behavior (Raskin & Rogers, 2001). To Rogers, personality is the expression of that actualizing tendency as it unfolds in each person's uniquely perceived reality (Allen, 2006).

The centerpiece of Rogers's theory is the *self,* the part of experience that a person identifies as "I" or "me." According to Rogers, those who accurately experience the self—with all its preferences, abilities, fantasies, shortcomings, and desires—are on the road to self-actualization. The progress of those whose experiences of the self become distorted, however, is likely to be slowed or stopped.

Rogers saw personality development beginning early, as children learn to need the approval, or *positive regard,* of others. Evaluations by parents, teachers, and others soon begin to affect children's self-evaluations. When these evaluations by others are in agreement with a child's own self-evaluations, the child reacts in a way that matches, or is *congruent* with, self-experience. The child not only feels the other person's positive regard but also evaluates the self as "good" for having earned approval. This positive self-experience becomes part of the **self-concept**, which is the way one thinks of oneself. Unfortunately, things may not always go so smoothly. If a pleasurable self-experience is evaluated negatively by others, the child must either do without their positive regard or reevaluate the experience. So a little boy who is teased by his father for having fun playing with dolls might adopt a distorted self-experience—deciding, perhaps, that "I don't like dolls" or that "Feeling good is bad."

In other words, said Rogers, personality is shaped partly by the actualizing tendency and partly by other people's evaluations. In this way, people come to like what they are "supposed" to like and to behave as they are "supposed" to behave. This socialization process helps people get along in society, but it often requires that they suppress their self-actualizing tendencies and distort their experiences. Rogers argued that psychological discomfort, anxiety, or mental disorder can result when the feelings people experience or express are *incongruent,* or at odds, with their true feelings.

Incongruence is likely, Rogers said, when parents and teachers lead children to believe that their personal worth depends on displaying the "right" attitudes, behaviors, and values. These **conditions of worth** are created whenever *people* are evaluated

---

humanistic psychology   The school of psychology in which human behavior is viewed as being controlled by the decisions that people make about their lives based on their perceptions of the world.

self-actualization   The reaching of one's fullest potential; the complete realization of a person's talents, faculties, and abilities.

actualizing tendency   An innate inclination toward growth and fulfilment that motivates all human behavior.

self-concept   The way one thinks of oneself.

conditions of worth   According to Rogers, circumstances in which an individual experiences positive regard from others only when displaying certain behaviors or attitudes.

"Just remember, son, it doesn't matter whether you win or lose—unless you want Daddy's love."

▲ Parents are not usually this obvious about creating conditions of worth, but according to Rogers, the message gets through in many more subtle ways.

instead of their behavior. For example, parents who find their child drawing on the wall are not likely to say, "I love you, but I don't approve of this behavior." They are more likely to shout, "Bad boy!" or "Bad girl!" This reaction suggests that the child is lovable and worthwhile only when well behaved. As a result, the child's self-experience is not "I like drawing on the wall but Mom and Dad don't approve," but instead, "Drawing on the wall is bad and I am bad if I like it, so I don't like it." The child may eventually show overly neat and tidy behaviors that do not reflect the real self but rather are part of an ideal self that is dictated by the parents.

As with Freud's concept of superego, conditions of worth are first set up by external pressure but eventually become part of the person's belief system. To Rogers, then, rewards and punishments are important in personality development not just because they shape behavior but also because they so easily create distorted self-perceptions and incongruence.

Maslow's Growth Theory   Like Rogers, Abraham Maslow (1954, 1971a, 1971b) viewed personality as the expression of a basic human tendency toward growth and self-actualization. In fact, Maslow believed that self-actualization is not just a human capacity but a human need; as described in the chapter on motivation and emotion, he placed self-actualization as the highest in a hierarchy of needs. Yet, said Maslow, people are often distracted from seeking self-actualization because they are focusing on needs that are lower in the hierarchy.

Maslow saw most people as controlled by a *deficiency orientation,* a preoccupation with perceived needs for material things. Ultimately, he said, deficiency-oriented people come to see life as a meaningless exercise in disappointment and boredom and they may begin to behave in problematic ways. For example, in an attempt to satisfy the need for love, many people focus on what love can give them (security), not on what they can give to someone else. This deficiency orientation may lead a person to be jealous and to focus on what is missing in relationships; as a result, the person will never truly experience love or security.

In contrast, people with a *growth orientation* do not focus on what is missing but draw satisfaction from what they have, what they are, and what they can do. This orientation opens the door to what Maslow called *peak experiences,* in which people feel joy, and even ecstasy, in the mere fact of being alive, being human, and knowing that they are utilizing their fullest potential.

SEEKING SELF-ACTUALIZATION ▶

According to Rogers, conditions of worth can make it harder for children to become aware of and accept those aspects of themselves that conflict with their parents' values. Many people find that their progress toward self-actualization is enhanced by associating with those whose positive regard for them does not depend on their displaying any particular set of behaviors.

THE JOYS OF A GROWTH ORIENTATION ▶

According to Maslow's theory of personality, the key to personal growth and fulfillment lies in focusing on what we have, not on what we don't have or on what we have lost. Rachel Barton Pine could have let the accident that took her leg destroy her career as a concert violinist and with it, her joy in life—but she didn't. You can find out more about her life in music at http://www.rachelbartonpine.com.

Evaluating the Humanistic Approach

The humanistic approach to personality is consistent with the way many people view themselves. It gives a central role to immediate experience and emphasizes each person's uniqueness. The best-known application of the humanistic approach is the client-centered therapy of Carl Rogers, which is discussed in the chapter on treatment of psychological disorders. The humanistic approach has also inspired other therapies as well as short-term personal-growth experiences such as sensitivity training and encounter groups that are designed to help people become more aware of themselves and the way they relate to others (e.g., Cain & Seeman, 2002). It has also led to programs designed to teach parents how to avoid creating conditions of worth while maximizing their children's potential. Further, the humanistic approach is consistent with the rapidly growing field of *positive psychology,* which, as described in the chapter on motivation and emotion, focuses on well-being and other positive aspects of human thought and feelings (Diener, 2003; Fredrickson & Cohn, in press; Peterson, 2006a; Seligman, 2002; Snyder & Lopez, 2006).

Yet to some, the humanistic approach is naive, romantic, and unrealistic. Are people all as inherently good and "growth oriented" as this approach suggests? Critics wonder about that, and they also fault humanists for paying too little attention to the role of inherited characteristics, learning, situational influences, and unconscious motivation in shaping personality. Further, the idea that personality development is directed only by an innate growth potential is seen by many as an oversimplification. So, too, is the humanistic assumption that all human problems stem from blocked self-actualization. Personality researchers also see many humanistic concepts as too vague to be tested empirically. Accordingly, the humanistic approach has not been popular among those who conduct empirical research to learn about personality (Friedman & Schustack, 2003). That view may begin to change, though, as an explosion of research in positive psychology leads to new humanistically oriented theories that better lend themselves to empirical evaluation (e.g., Burton et al., 2006; Fredrickson & Cohn, in press; Waugh et al., in press).

Finally, humanists' tendency to define ideal personality development in terms of personal growth, independence, and self-actualization has been criticized for emphasizing culture-specific concepts about mental health that may not apply outside North America and other Western cultures (Heine, 2003; Heine & Buchtel, 2009). As discussed in the next section, the foundations of humanistic self theories may be in direct conflict with the values of non-Western collectivist cultures.

In Review

MAJOR APPROACHES TO PERSONALITY

APPROACH	BASIC ASSUMPTIONS ABOUT BEHAVIOR	TYPICAL RESEARCH METHOD
Psychodynamic	Determined by largely unconscious intrapsychic conflicts	Case studies
Trait	Determined by traits or needs	Analysis of tests for basic personality dimensions
Social-cognitive	Determined by learning, cognitive factors, and specific situations	Analysis of interactions between people and situations
Humanistic	Determined by innate growth tendency and individual perception of reality	Studies of relationships between perceptions and behavior

?

1. Tests that measure the Five Factor Model's dimensions of personality are based on the _____ approach to personality.
2. The role of learning is most prominent in the _____ approach to personality.
3. Object relations and attachment theories are modern variants on _____ personality theories.

"In Review: Major Approaches to Personality" summarizes key features of the humanistic approach and those of the other approaches we have described. Which approach is most accurate? There is no simple answer to that question, partly because each approach emphasizes different aspects of personality. Accordingly, it has been suggested that a full understanding of the origins and development of personality will come only by recognizing the roles of all the factors that various approaches have shown to be important. Some psychologists are working on theoretical models that take this promising integrative approach (Mayer, 2005; McAdams & Pals, 2006).

linkages

Does culture determine personality?
(a link to Human Development)

Linkages

Personality, Culture, and Human Development

In many Western cultures, people encourage others to "stand up for yourself" or to "blow your own horn" in order to "get what you have coming to you." In middle-class North America, the values of achievement and personal distinction are taught to children, particularly male children, very early in life (Kitayama, Duffy, & Uchida, 2007). North American children are encouraged to feel special, to have self-esteem, and to feel good about themselves, partly because these characteristics are associated with happiness, popularity, and superior performance in school.

▶ The goal of esteem building is clear these days in many children's activities at school and in some team sports, too, which are designed either to eliminate competition or (as in this case) assure that everyone feels like winners. The same goal is reflected in day-care centers, summer camps, and other children's programs with names such as Starkids, Little Wonders, Superkids, and Precious Jewels.

"We lost!"

Whether self-esteem is the cause or the result of these good outcomes (Baumeister et al., 2003), children who learn and display these values tend to receive praise for doing so.

As a result of this cultural training, many people in North America and Europe develop personalities that are largely based on a sense of high self-worth. In a study by Hazel Markus and Shinobu Kitayama (1991), for example, 70 percent of a sample of U.S. students believed that they were superior to their peers. In addition, 60 percent believed that they were in the top 10 percent on a wide variety of personal attributes! This tendency toward self-enhancement is evident as early as age four.

Many Western personality theorists see a sense of independence, uniqueness, and self-esteem as fundamental to mental health. As noted in the chapter on human development, for example, Erik Erikson included the emergence of personal identity and self-esteem as part of normal psychosocial development. Middle-class North Americans who fail to value and strive for independence, self-promotion, and unique personal achievement may be seen as having a personality disorder, some form of depression, or other psychological problems.

Are these ideas based on universal truths about personality development or do they reflect the values of the cultures that generated them? It is certainly clear that people in many non-Western cultures develop personal orientations that are quite different from those of North Americans and Europeans (Heine & Buchtel, 2009; Lehman, Chiu, & Schaller, 2004). In China and Japan, for example, an independent, unique self is not emphasized (Ho & Chiu, 1998). Children there are encouraged to develop and maintain pleasant, respectful relations with others and not to stand out from the crowd, because doing so might make others seem inferior by comparison. In fact, the Japanese word for "different" (tigau) also means "wrong" (Kitayama & Markus, 1992). So whereas children in the United States hear that "the squeaky wheel gets the grease" (meaning that you don't get what you want unless you ask for it), Japanese children are warned that "the nail that stands up gets pounded down" (meaning that it is not a good idea to draw attention to yourself). From a very young age, they are taught to be modest, to play down the value

CULTURE AND PERSONALITY ▶

In individualist cultures, most children learn early that personal distinction is valued by parents, teachers, and peers. In collectivist cultures, having a strong sense of self-worth may be seen as less important. In other words, the features of "normal" personality development vary from culture to culture. Make a list of the core values you have learned. Which of them are typical of individualist cultures, which are typical of collectivist cultures, and which reflect a combination of both?

of personal contributions, and to appreciate the joy and value of group work (Kitayama & Uchida, 2003).

In contrast to the *independent* self system common in individualist cultures such as Great Britain, Switzerland, and the United States, cultures with a more collectivist orientation (such as Brazil, China, Japan, and Nigeria) promote an *interdependent* self system through which people see themselves as a fraction of the social whole. Each person has little or no meaningful definition without reference to the group. These differences in self systems may produce differences in what gives people a sense of well-being and satisfaction (Tsai, Knutson, & Fung, 2006). For example, in the United States, a sense of well-being is usually associated with having *positive* attributes, such as intelligence, creativity, competitiveness, persistence, and so on. In Japan and other Asian countries, feelings of well-being are more likely to be associated with having no *negative* attributes (Eliot et al., 2001). Studies of thousands of people all over the world indicate that in collectivist cultures, life satisfaction is associated with having social approval and harmonious relations with others. In individualist cultures, life satisfaction is associated with having high self-esteem and good feelings about one's own life (Uchida et al., 2001).

Because cultural factors shape ideas about how the ideal personality develops, it is important to evaluate various approaches to personality in terms of how well they apply to cultures other than the one in which they were developed (Church, 2001; Cross & Markus, 1999; McCrae, 2001; Nye et al., 2008; Van de Vijver & Leung, 2001). Their applicability to males and females must be considered as well. Even within North American cultures, for example, there are gender differences in the development of self-esteem. Females tend to show an interdependent self system, achieving their sense of self and self-esteem from attachments to others. By contrast, males' self-esteem tends to develop in relation to personal achievement, in a manner more in keeping with an independent self system (Cross & Madson, 1997). Cross-gender and cross-cultural differences in the nature and determinants of a sense of self highlight the widespread effects of gender and culture on the development of many aspects of human personality (Matsumoto, Yoo, & Nakagawa, 2008; Zakriski, Wright, & Underwood, 2005).

Focus on RESEARCH

Personality Development over Time

Psychologists have long been interested in how people's personalities differ, but they also want to know why those differences appear. Some search for the source of personality differences by looking at infants' differing temperaments. As noted in the chapter on human development, temperament is reflected in the unlearned, generalized patterns of emotional expression and other behavior that humans display from birth (Buss, 1997).

▶ What was the researchers' question?

Can young children's temperaments predict their personality characteristics and behaviors as adults?

▶ How did the researchers answer the question?

To try to answer this question, Avshalom Caspi and his colleagues conducted a longitudinal study that assessed the same people at several different times in their lives (Caspi, 2000; Caspi & Silva, 1995; Caspi et al., 1997; Caspi et al., 1995; Caspi, Harrington et al., 2003). The research sample included all the children born in Dunedin, New Zealand, between April 1972 and March 1973—a total of about 1,000 people. When these children were three years old, research assistants observed them in a standard situation and rated them on a number of dimensions, including the degree to which they showed explosive or uncontrolled behavior, interacted easily with others, or acted withdrawn and unresponsive. These observations were used to place each child into one of five temperament categories: *undercontrolled* (irritable, impatient, emotional), *inhibited* (shy, fearful, easily distracted), *confident* (eager to perform, responsive to questions), *reserved* (withdrawn, uncomfortable), and *well adjusted* (friendly, well controlled). The children were observed and categorized again when they were five, seven, and nine years old. If it occurs to you that seeing a child at one point in life might bias an observer's ratings of that child later on, you are right. To ensure that ratings would not be influenced by this kind of observer bias, the researchers arranged for different people to make the ratings at each point in time. These ratings indicated that the children's temperaments stayed about the same over the years from age three to age nine.

When the research participants were twenty-one, they were interviewed about their involvement in risky and unhealthy behaviors, such as excessive drinking, violent criminal activities, unprotected sex, and unsafe driving habits. To avoid bias, the interviewers were given no information about the participants' childhood temperaments. At age twenty-six, the participants took a standard personality test and were rated by friends on the Big Five personality dimensions.

▶ What did the researchers find?

Several significant differences were found in the personality test results of the five original temperament groups. For example, the average test scores of 26-year-olds who had been classified as "undercontrolled" in childhood showed that they were more alienated, uninhibited, and stressed than the other temperament groups. Further, people who had been classified as "confident" or "well adjusted" as children tended to be better adjusted and more extraverted at twenty-six than people who had been classified as "inhibited" or "reserved." These findings held true for males and females alike.

There were also small but significant correlations between childhood temperament and risky behavior in young adulthood. For example, "undercontrolled" children were about twice as likely as others to develop personalities that are associated with violence, excessive drinking, and other health-endangering behaviors (Caspi, Harrington et al., 2003).

▶ What do the results mean?

The results of this research provide support for a hypothesis long endorsed by personality psychologists, namely that we can make relatively accurate predictions about people's personalities and behaviors as adults if we know about their temperaments as children (e.g. Glenn et al., 2007; Pulkki-Råback et al., 2005; Schwartz et al., 2003). But as critical thinkers, we must be careful not to overstate the strength of these results. Although the correlations between temperament and personality and between temperament and various problematic behaviors were statistically significant, they were also relatively small. In other words, not all children classified as "undercontrolled" at age three turned out to be aggressive or violent at eighteen. So it is more accurate to say that personality may be influenced and shaped by temperament but not completely determined by it (Clark & Watson, 2008; Roberts, Walton, & Viechtbauer, 2006).

▶ What do we still need to know?

Valuable as it is, this study leaves a number of unanswered questions about the relationship between temperament and personality (Roberts & DelVecchio, 2000). For example, why is there a connection between temperament as a child and personality as an adult? The link is probably a complex one involving both nature and nurture (Hampson, 2008). Caspi and his colleagues (1989) offered one explanation that draws heavily on social-cognitive theories, especially Bandura's notion of reciprocal determinism. They proposed that long-term consistencies in behavior result from the mutual influence that temperament and environmental events have on one another. For example, people may put themselves in situations that reinforce their temperament. So undercontrolled people might choose to spend time with people who accept (and even encourage) rude or impolite behavior. When such behavior brings negative reactions, the world seems that much more hostile and the undercontrolled people become even more aggressive and negative. Caspi and his colleagues see the results of their studies as evidence that this process of mutual influence between personality and situations can continue over a lifetime (Caspi, Harrington et al., 2003).

Assessing Personality

▶ *How do psychologists measure personality?*

Suppose you are an industrial and organizational psychologist whose job is to ensure that your company hires only honest, cooperative, and hardworking employees. How would you know which candidates had these characteristics? There are four basic methods of assessing and describing personality (Funder, 2007): *life outcomes* (such as records of education, income, or marital status), *situational tests* (observations of behavior in situations designed to measure personality), *observer ratings* (judgments about a person made by friends or family; Oltmanns & Turkheimer, 2009), and *self-reports* (responses to interviews and personality test items). Data gathered through these methods assist in employee selection, in the diagnosis of psychological disorders, in making predictions about a convict's or mental patient's dangerousness, in choosing astronaut candidates best suited to space travel, and in other situations involving risky decisions (Kramer, Bernstein, & Phares, 2009; Meyer et al., 2001).

Life outcomes, observer ratings, and situational tests make it possible to directly assess many aspects of personality and behavior, including how often, how effectively, and how consistently various actions occur. *Interviews* provide information about personality from the person's own point of view. Some interviews are *open-ended,* meaning that questions are tailored to the intellectual level, emotional state, and special needs of the person being assessed. Others are *structured,* meaning that the interviewer asks a fixed set of questions about specific topics in a particular order. Structured interviews are routinely used in personality research because they are sure to cover matters of special interest to the researcher.

Personality tests offer a way to gather self-report information that is more standardized and economical than interviews. To be useful, however, a personality test must be reliable and valid. As described in the chapter on thought, language, and intelligence, *reliability* refers to how stable or consistent the results of a test are; *validity* reflects the degree to which test scores are interpreted appropriately and used properly in making inferences about people. The many personality tests available today are traditionally classified as either *projective* or *nonprojective.*

Projective Personality Measures

Projective personality measures contain items or tasks that are ambiguous, meaning that they can be perceived in many different ways. People taking projective tests might be asked to draw a house, a person, a family, or a tree; to fill in the missing parts of incomplete pictures or sentences; to say what they associate with particular words; or to report what they see in a drawing or picture. Projective techniques are sometimes used in personality research, but they are far more popular among psychodynamically oriented clinical psychologists, who use them to assess psychological disorders (Wood et al., 2003). These psychologists believe that people's responses to projective tests are guided by unconscious needs, motives, fantasies, conflicts, thoughts, and other hidden aspects of personality.

One widely used projective test, called the *Thematic Apperception Test,* or *TAT,* is described in the chapter on motivation and emotion as a measure of need for achievement. Henry Murray and Christina Morgan developed this test to assess the needs they saw as the basis of personality. Another well-known projective test, the *Rorschach Inkblot Test,* features a series of ten inkblots similar to the one in Figure 11.5. The respondent is asked to tell what the blot might be and then to explain why.

Those who support projective testing claim that using ambiguous test items makes it difficult for respondents to detect what is being measured and what the "best" answers would be. They argue, therefore, that these tests can measure aggressive and

projective personality measures Personality tests made up of relatively unstructured stimuli in which responses are seen as reflecting the individuals' unconscious needs, fantasies, conflicts, thought patterns, and other aspects of personality.

FIGURE 11.5 ■ THE RORSCHACH INKBLOT TEST

People taking the Rorschach test are shown ten patterns similar to this one and asked to tell what the blot looks like and why. Try jotting down what you see in the blot and why and then compare your responses to those of some friends. Most methods of scoring this test focus on (1) what part of the blot the person responds to; (2) what details, colors, or other features determine each response; (3) the content of responses (such as seeing animals, maps, or body parts); and (4) the popularity or commonness of the responses.

Learn BY Doing

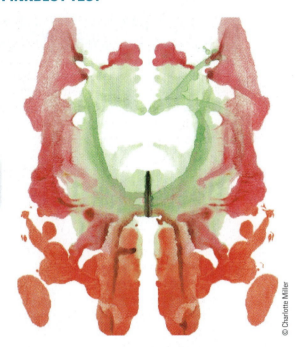

© Charlotte Miller

sexual impulses and other personality features that people might be able to conceal in their responses to a nonprojective personality measure. Advocates of projective measures also point to specific cases in which projective tests have shown acceptable reliability and validity, such as in the assessment of achievement motivation with the TAT (Grønnerød, 2003; Meyer, Mihura, & Smith, 2005; Schultheiss, 2008; Schultheiss & Rohde, 2002).

Nonetheless, most researchers agree that projective personality measures, especially the Rorschach, are substantially less reliable and valid than the nonprojective personality measures described next (Garb et al., 2005; Hunsley, Lee, & Wood, 2003). In fact, because of their generally poor ability to predict behavior, projective measures often add little information about people beyond what might be inferred from interviews or other sources (Hunsley, Lee, & Wood, 2003).

Nonprojective Personality Measures

Nonprojective personality measures, also known as *objective personality measures,* ask clear questions about a person's thoughts, feelings, or behavior (such as "Do you like parties?"). The answers are used to draw conclusions about the individual's personality. These self-report tests are usually set up in a multiple-choice or true-false format that allows them to be given to many people at once, much like the academic tests used in many classrooms. And as in the classroom, nonprojective personality measures can be scored by machine and then compared with the responses of other people. So before interpreting your score on a nonprojective personality measure of extraversion, for example, a psychologist would compare it to a *norm,* or the average score of thousands of others of your age and gender. You would be considered unusually extraverted only if you scored well above that norm.

Some nonprojective personality measures focus on one particular trait, such as optimism (Carver & Scheier, 2002). Others measure a small group of related traits, such as empathy and social responsibility (Penner, 2002; Penner & Orom, in press). Still other nonprojective tests measure the strength of a wider variety of traits to reveal general psychological functioning. For example, the *Neuroticism Extraversion*

nonprojective personality measures
Tests that list clear, specific questions, statements, or concepts to which people are asked to respond.

TABLE 11.3   ■   SAMPLE SUMMARY OF RESULTS FROM THE NEO-PI-R

The NEO-PI-R assesses the Big Five personality dimensions. In this example of the results a person might receive, the five factors scored are (from the top row to the bottom row) neuroticism, extraversion, openness, agreeableness, and conscientiousness. Because people with different NEO profiles tend to have different psychological problems, this test has been used to aid in the diagnosis of personality disorders (Trull & Sher, 1994).

Compared with the responses of other people, your responses suggest that you can be described as:

☐ Sensitive, emotional, and prone to experience feelings that are upsetting.	☒ Generally calm and able to deal with stress but you sometimes experience feelings of guilt, anger, or sadness.	☐ Secure, hardy, and generally relaxed even under stressful conditions.
☐ Extraverted, outgoing, active, and high-spirited. You prefer to be around people most of the time.	☐ Moderate in activity and enthusiasm. You enjoy the company of others but you also value privacy.	☒ Introverted, reserved, and serious. You prefer to be alone or with a few close friends.
☐ Open to new experiences. You have broad interests and are very imaginative.	☐ Practical but willing to consider new ways of doing things. You seek a balance between the old and the new.	☒ Down-to-earth, practical, traditional, and pretty much set in your ways.
☐ Compassionate, good-natured, and eager to cooperate and avoid conflict.	☒ Generally warm, trusting, and agreeable, but you can sometimes be stubborn and competitive.	☐ Hardheaded, skeptical, proud, and competitive. You tend to express your anger directly.
☒ Conscientious and well organized. You have high standards and always strive to achieve your goals.	☐ Dependable and moderately well organized. You generally have clear goals but are able to set your work aside.	☐ Easygoing, not very well organized, and sometimes careless. You prefer not to make plans.

linkages

Can personality tests be used to diagnose mental disorders? *(a link to Psychological Disorders)*

Openness Personality Inventory, Revised, or *NEO-PI-R* (Costa & McCrae, 1992) is designed to measure the Big Five personality traits described earlier. Table 11.3 shows how the test's results are presented. The NEO-PI-R is quite reliable (Viswesvaran & Ones, 2000), and people's scores on its various scales have been successfully used to predict a number of criteria, including performance on specific jobs and overall career success (Barrick & Mount, 1991; Conte & Gintoft, 2005; Siebert & Kraimer, 2001; Zhao & Seibert, 2006), social status (Anderson et al., 2001), and the likelihood that a person will engage in criminal activities and risky sexual behaviors (Clower & Bothwell, 2001; Miller et al., 2004).

When the goal of personality assessment is to diagnose psychological disorders, the most commonly used nonprojective measure is the *Minnesota Multiphasic Personality Inventory,* better known as the *MMPI* (Butcher & Rouse, 1996). This 556-item true-false test was developed during the 1930s at the University of Minnesota by Starke Hathaway and J. C. McKinley. It has since been revised and updated in the MMPI-2 (National Computer Systems, 1992).

The MMPI is organized into ten groups of items called *clinical scales.* Certain patterns of responses to the items on these scales have been associated with people who display particular psychological disorders or personality characteristics. The MMPI and MMPI-2 also contain four *validity scales.* Responses to these scales detect whether respondents are distorting their answers, misunderstanding the items, or being uncooperative. For example, someone who responds "true" to items such as "I never get angry" may not be giving honest answers to the test as a whole.

To interpret the meaning of MMPI results, a person's scores on the ten clinical scales are plotted as a *profile* (see Figure 11.6). This profile is then compared with the profiles of people who are known to have certain personality characteristics or problems. It is presumed that people taking the MMPI share characteristics with people whose profiles are most similar to their own. So although a high score on a particular clinical scale, such as depression, might suggest a problem in that area,

FIGURE 11.6 ■ THE MMPI: CLINICAL SCALES AND SAMPLE PROFILES

A score of 50 on the MMPI's clinical scales is average. Scores at or above 65 mean that responses on that scale are more extreme than at least 95 percent of the normal population. The red line represents the profile of Kenneth Bianchi, the "Hillside Strangler," who murdered thirteen women in the late 1970s. His profile is characteristic of a shallow person with poor self-control and little personal insight who is sexually preoccupied and unable to reveal himself to others. The profile in green comes from a more normal man, but it is characteristic of someone who is self-centered, passive, and unwilling to accept personal responsibility for his behavior and who, when under stress, complains of numerous vague physical symptoms. The clinical scales abbreviated in the figure are as follows:

1. Hypochondriasis (Hs; concern with bodily functions and symptoms).
2. Depression (D; pessimism, hopelessness, slowed thinking).
3. Hysteria (Hy; use of physical or mental symptoms to avoid problems).
4. Psychopathic deviate (Pd; disregard for social customs, emotional shallowness).
5. Masculinity/femininity (Mf; interests associated with a particular gender).
6. Paranoia (Pa; delusions, suspiciousness).
7. Psychasthenia (Pt; worry, guilt, anxiety).
8. Schizophrenia (Sc; bizarre thoughts and perceptions).
9. Hypomania (Ma; overactivity, excitement, impulsiveness).
10. Social introversion (Si; shy, insecure).

Source: Form for use with the MMPI-2™ test as published and copyrighted by the Regents of the University of Minnesota. All rights reserved. "MMPI-2" and "Minnesota Multiphasic Personality Inventory-2" are trademarks owned by the Regents of the University of Minnesota.

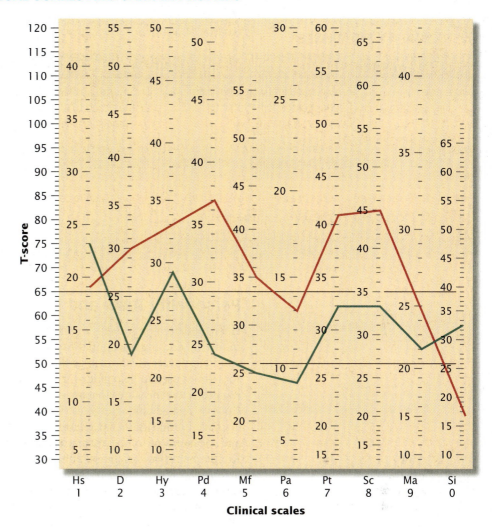

interpreting the MMPI usually focuses on the overall pattern in the clinical scale scores—particularly on the combination of two or three scales on which a person's scores are unusually high.

There is considerable evidence for the reliability and validity of MMPI clinical scales (Forbey & Ben-Porath, 2008), but even the latest editions of the test are far from perfect measurement tools (Carr, Moretti, & Cue, 2005; Munley, 2002; Rouse, 2007). The validity of MMPI interpretations may be particularly suspect when—because of cultural factors—the perceptions, values, and experiences of the test taker differ significantly from those of the test developers and the people with whom the respondent's results are compared. So although an MMPI profile might look like that of someone with a mental disorder, the profile might actually reflect the culture-specific way the person interpreted the test items, not a psychological problem (Butcher, 2004; Groth-Marnat, 1997). Even though the MMPI-2 uses comparison norms that represent a more culturally diverse population than did those of the original MMPI, psychologists must still be cautious when interpreting the profiles of people who identify with minority subcultures (Butcher, 2004.)

"In Review: Personality Measures" summarizes the characteristics of projective and nonprojective personality tests and some of their advantages and disadvantages.

In Review

PERSONALITY MEASURES

TYPE OF TEST	CHARACTERISTICS	ADVANTAGES	DISADVANTAGES
Projective	Ambiguous stimuli create maximum freedom of response; scoring is relatively subjective	"Correct" answers not obvious; designed to tap unconscious impulses; flexible use	Reliability and validity lower than those of nonprojective tests
Nonprojective	Paper-and-pencil format; quantitatively scored	Efficiency, standardization	Subject to deliberate distortion

1. Projective personality measures are based on the _____ approach to personality.

2. The NEO-PI-R and the MMPI-2 are examples of _____ tests.

3. Most personality researchers use _____ tests in their work.

Personality Tests and Employee Selection

How good are nonprojective personality measures at selecting people for jobs? Most industrial and organizational psychologists see them as valuable tools for selecting good employees. Tests such as the MMPI (and even some projective measures) are sometimes used to help guide hiring decisions, but large organizations usually choose nonprojective measures that are designed to measure the Big Five personality dimensions or related characteristics (Borman et al., 1997; Costa, 2001). Several researchers have found significant relationships between scores on the Big Five dimensions and measures of job performance and effective leadership (Hirschfeld et al., 2008; Kieffer, Schinka, & Curtiss, 2004; Lim & Ployhart, 2004; Motowidlo, Brownlee, & Schmit, 2008; Silverthorne, 2001). A more general review of studies involving thousands of people has shown that nonprojective personality measures are of value in helping businesses reduce theft, absenteeism, and other disruptive employee behaviors (Berry, Sackett, & Wiemann, 2007; Hogan, 2006; Ones & Viswesvaran, 2001; Ones, Viswesvaran, & Schmidt, 2003).

Still, personality tests are far from perfect predictors of workplace behavior. Many of them measure traits that may be too general to predict specific aspects of job performance (Berry, Sackett, & Wiemann, 2007; Furnham, 2001). In fact, features of the work situation are often better predictors of employee behavior than are personality measures (Mumford et al., 2001). Further, some employees see personality measures as an invasion of their privacy. They worry that test results in their personnel files might later be misinterpreted and hurt their chances for promotion or for employment by other companies. Lawsuits have resulted in a ban on the use of personality tests in the selection of U.S. federal employees. Concerns about privacy and other issues surrounding personality testing have led the American Psychological Association and related organizations to publish joint ethical standards relating to procedures for the development, distribution, and use of all psychological tests (American Educational Research Association, American Psychological Association, & National Council on Measurement in Education, 1999; American Psychological Association, 2002b). The goal is not only to improve the reliability and validity of tests but also to ensure that their results are properly used and do not infringe on individuals' rights (Turner et al., 2001).

ACTIVE REVIEW ▶ Chapter 11

Personality

As noted in the introductory chapter, all of psychology's subfields are related to one another. Our discussion of personality, culture, and human development illustrates just one way that the topic of this chapter, personality, is linked to the subfield of developmental psychology, which is described in the chapter on human

development. The Linkages diagram shows ties to two other subfields, and there are many more ties throughout the book. Looking for linkages among subfields will help you see how they all fit together and help you better appreciate the big picture that is psychology.

linkages

How do you know if a personality test (or any other kind of test) is any good? *(ans. on p. 278)*

Does culture determine personality? *(ans. on p. 446)*

Can therapy change personality? *(ans. on p. 526)*

Chapter 7
Thought, Language, and Intelligence

Chapter 9
Human Development

Chapter 13
Treatment of Psychological Disorders

SUMMARY ▶

Personality refers to the unique pattern of psychological and behavioral characteristics by which each person can be compared and contrasted with other people. The four main theoretical approaches to personality are the psychodynamic, trait, social-cognitive, and humanistic approaches.

The Psychodynamic Approach

▶ *How did paralyzed patients lead Freud to psychoanalysis?*

The **psychodynamic approach,** pioneered by Freud, assumes that personality arises out of unconscious psychological processes that interact to determine our thoughts, feelings, and behavior. According to Freud's **psychoanalytic theory,** personality has three components—the **id,** which operates according to the **pleasure**

principle; the **ego,** which operates according to the **reality principle;** and the **superego,** which internalizes society's rules and values. The ego uses **defense mechanisms** to prevent unconscious conflicts among these components from becoming conscious and causing anxiety or guilt.

Freud proposed that the focus of conflict changes as the child passes through stages of **psychosexual development.** These include the **oral stage,** the **anal stage,** the **phallic stage** (during which the **Oedipal complex** or the **Electra complex** occurs), the **latency period,** and the **genital stage.**

Many of Freud's followers developed new theories that differed from his. Among these

theorists were Jung, Adler, and Horney. They tended to downplay the role of instincts and the unconscious, emphasizing instead the importance of conscious processes, ego functions, and social and cultural factors. Horney also challenged the male-oriented nature of Freud's original theory.

Current psychodynamic theories reflect the neo-Freudians' emphasis on family and social relationships. According to object relations and attachment theorists, personality development depends mainly on the nature of early interactions between individuals and their caregivers.

The psychodynamic approach is reflected in many forms of psychotherapy, but critics fault the approach for its lack of a scientific base and for its view of human behavior as driven by forces that are difficult or impossible to measure.

The Trait Approach

▶ *What personality traits are most basic?*

The **trait approach** assumes that personality is made up of stable internal **personality traits** that appear at varying strengths  in different people and guide their thoughts, feelings, and behavior. Allport believed that personality is created by a small set of central traits and a larger number of secondary traits in each individual. Allport studied unique patterns of traits, whereas later researchers such as Cattell used factor analysis to explore common traits or core dimensions of personality. Most recently, these factor analyses have identified five basic dimensions of personality, collectively referred to as the **Five Factor**, or **Big Five, Personality Model.** These dimensions—openness, conscientiousness, extraversion, agreeableness, and neuroticism—have been found in many different cultures and may arise partly from inherited differences in temperament and other biological factors that provide the raw materials from which each personality is molded by experience. These biological factors are the focus of trait theories proposed by Eysenck and by Gray.

The trait approach has been criticized for being better at describing personality than at explaining it, for failing to consider mechanisms that motivate behavior, and for under-emphasizing the role of situational factors. Nevertheless, the trait approach—particularly the Five Factor Personality Model—currently dominates the field.

The Social-Cognitive Approach

▶ *Do we learn our personalities?*

The **social-cognitive approach** assumes that personality is a set of unique patterns of thinking and behavior that a person acquires through  learning and then displays in particular situations. The social-cognitive approach has expanded on traditional behavioral approaches by emphasizing the role of cognitive factors, such as observational learning, in personality development.

Rotter's theory focuses on expectancies that guide behavior, and it generated interest in assessing general beliefs about whether rewards occur because of personal efforts (internal control) or chance (external control). Bandura believes that personality develops largely through cognitively mediated learning, including observational learning. He sees personality as reciprocally determined by interactions among cognition, environmental stimuli, and behavior. **Self-efficacy**—the belief in one's ability to accomplish a given task—is an important determinant of behavior. Mischel emphasizes the importance of situations and their interactions with cognitive person variables in determining behavior. According to Mischel, we must look at both cognitive person variables and situational variables in order to understand human consistencies and inconsistencies.

The social-cognitive approach has led to new forms of psychological treatment and many other applications. However, critics of this approach consider even its latest versions to be incapable of capturing all the unlearned factors that some psychologists see as important in personality.

The Humanistic Approach

▶ *Is everyone basically good?*

The **humanistic psychology** approach, also called the *phenomenological approach,* is based on the assumption that personality is deter-  mined by the unique ways that each individual views the world. These perceptions form a personal version of reality and guide people's behavior as they strive to reach **self-actualization**, their fullest potential.

Rogers believed that personality development is driven by an innate **actualizing tendency** but also that one's **self-concept** is shaped by social evaluations. He proposed that the **conditions of worth** parents and others impose interfere with personal growth and can lead to psychological problems. Maslow saw self-actualization as the highest in a hierarchy of needs. Personality development is healthiest, he said, when people have a growth orientation rather than a deficiency orientation.

The humanistic approach has been used in certain forms of psychotherapy, in parent

training, and in group experiences designed to enhance personal growth. This approach has considerable popularity, but it has been faulted for being too idealistic, for failing to explain personality development, for being vague and unscientific, and for underplaying cultural differences in "ideal" personalities.

Many people in the individualist cultures of North America and Europe are taught to believe in the importance of self-worth and personal distinction. This independent self system contrasts with the interdependent self system that is often fostered in collectivist cultures, in which the self is defined mainly in relation to family or other groups. Contrasting definitions of the self in different cultures and among males versus females tend to exert differing influences on the development of personality.

Research suggests that temperament in childhood may influence personality development into adulthood.

Assessing Personality

▶ *How do psychologists measure personality?*

Personality is usually assessed through some combination of life outcomes, observer ratings, situational tests, and  self-reports. To be useful, personality assessments must be both reliable and valid.

Based on psychodynamic theories, **projective personality measures** present ambiguous stimuli in an attempt to tap unconscious personality characteristics. Two popular projective tests are the TAT and the Rorschach. In general, projective personality measures are less reliable and valid than nonprojective personality measures.

Nonprojective personality measures, also known as objective measures, usually present clear, direct items; their scores can be compared with group norms. The NEO-PI-R and the MMPI are examples of nonprojective personality measures.

Nonprojective personality measures are often used to identify which people are best suited for certain occupations. Although such tests can be helpful in this regard, those who use them must be aware of the tests' limitations and take care not to violate the rights of test respondents.

Put It in Writing

Choose a well-known person who interests you. It could be a rock star; an actor; a television personality; a political, religious, or business figure; or even a famous criminal. Write a one-paragraph description of this individual's personality traits as they seem to you. Now continue by writing a page or two about how you think the development of these traits would be explained by psychodynamic, biological trait, social-cognitive, and humanistic personality theories.

Personal Learning Activity

To get an idea of the problems involved in scoring projective personality tests, try creating your own projective test that contains pictures, drawings, or other stimuli that can be interpreted in many different ways. Administer your test to some friends and record their responses to each stimulus (in writing or on tape). How will you decide what your friends' responses tell you about their personalities? Do you think your conclusions about their personalities were affected mainly by their test responses or by what you already knew about them? Now give your test to someone you don't know. Was it easier or harder to draw conclusions about this person's personality? How will you know if your conclusions about this new person are correct, or valid? *For additional projects, see the Personal Learning Activities in the corresponding chapter of the study guide that accompanies this book.*

Take Action to Learn More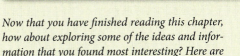

Now that you have finished reading this chapter, how about exploring some of the ideas and information that you found most interesting? Here are some courses, books, films, and Internet resources to get you started. Enjoy!

Courses

Personality Psychology
Personality Research Methods
Personality Theories
History and Systems of Psychology

Movies

A Christmas Carol; My Life as a Dog; Good Will Hunting; Unforgiven; The Cider House Rules. Personality development.
Desk Set; My Man Godfrey; Freedom Writers; Kung Fu Panda; Hoop Dreams. Self-efficacy.
Freud. Development of psychoanalytic theory.
To Sir, with Love; Pygmalion; All That Jazz; Cyrano; Roxanne; The Truth About Cats & Dogs; Girl, Interrupted; Bridget Jones's Diary. Effect of conditions of worth; development of self-concept.
Harold and Maude; 10 Questions for the Dalai Lama; Cool Runnings; October Sky; Gandhi. Self-actualization.

Raiders of the Lost Ark; Indiana Jones and the Kingdom of the Crystal Skull; Indiana Jones and the Last Crusade; Adrenaline Rush: The Science of Risk. Personality factors associated with risk-taking.
The Shadow; Dr. Jekyll and Mr. Hyde. Different aspects of the personality.

Books

DAVID C. FUNDER ET AL., eds., *Studying Lives Through Time* (American Psychological Association, 1996). Famous studies in personality and development.
HARRY STACK SULLIVAN, *The Interpersonal Theory of Psychiatry* (Norton, 1968). Sullivan's neo-Freudian theory.
FRANK J. SULLOWAY, *Born to Rebel: Birth Order, Family Dynamics and Creative Lives* (Vintage, 1997). Psychodynamics in personality development.
DUANE P. SCHULTZ AND SYDNEY E. SCHULTZ, *Theories of Personality* (Brooks-Cole, 2009). Summary of personality theories.
STELLA CHESS AND M. D. ALEXANDER, *Temperament: Theory and Practice* (Brunner/Mazel, 1996). Differences in temperament.
EDWARD CHANG AND LAWRENCE SANNA, *Virtue, Vice, and Personality: The Complexity of*

Behavior (American Psychological Association, 2003). Readable chapters on how cultural factors alter evaluation of personality traits.

The Web

Essentials of Psychology Book Companion Website

www.cengage.com/psychology/bernstein

Visit the book companion website to access a wealth of resources, including chapter outlines, flashcards, web links, tutorial quizzes, and more!

CENGAGENOW™ Just what you need to know NOW! Spend time on what you need to master rather than on information you already have learned. Take a pre-test for this chapter, and CengageNOW will generate a personalized study plan based on your results. The study plan will identify the topics you need to review and direct you to online resources to help you master those topics. You can then take a post-test to help you determine the concepts you have mastered and what you will need to work on. Try it out! Go to www.cengage.com/login to sign in with an access code or to purchase access to this product.

Review of Key Terms ▶

Can you define each of the key terms in the chapter? Check your definitions against those on the pages shown in parentheses in the following list or in the Glossary at the end of the book.

actualizing tendency (p. 443)
anal stage (p. 429)

Big Five Personality Model (p. 435)
conditions of worth (p. 443)
defense mechanisms (p. 427)
ego (p. 427)
Electra complex (p. 429)
Five Factor Personality Model (p. 435)
genital stage (p. 430)

humanistic psychology (p. 443)
id (p. 427)
latency period (p. 429)
nonprojective personality measures (p. 451)
Oedipal complex (p. 429)
oral stage (p. 429)

MULTIPLE-CHOICE ▶ Self-Test

Select the best answer for each of the following questions. Then check your responses against the Answer Key at the end of the book.

1. When psychologists talk about the unique pattern of enduring psychological and behavioral characteristics by which each person can be compared and contrasted with other people, they are referring to _____.
   a. motivation
   b. personality
   c. reciprocal determinism
   d. conditions of worth

2. As Jared is jostled by a passerby he thinks, "I'd like to hit that guy!" Freud would say that this impulse comes from Jared's _____, which operates on the _____ principle.
   a. id; pleasure
   b. id; reality
   c. ego; pleasure
   d. ego; reality

3. Nine-year-old Jeffrey has just bounded into the room with his latest artistic creation. He chatters about his friends at school and how much he likes reading and working math problems. According to Freud, Jeffrey is most likely in the _____ stage of psychosexual development.
   a. oral
   b. anal
   c. phallic
   d. latency

4. Elizabeth's therapist suggests that Elizabeth's inability to trust her boyfriend could stem from her parents' neglecting her when she was a child. This therapist most likely follows the _____ theory of personality.
   a. reciprocal deterministic
   b. social-cognitive
   c. humanistic
   d. object relations

5. Oscar strives to be the best at everything he does. He believes that he is successful because he is intelligent, works hard, and never gives up. Oscar most likely has a(n) _____ self system.
   a. independent
   b. interdependent
   c. reciprocal
   d. growth-oriented

6. Which of the following is not a common criticism of Freud's psychodynamic approach to personality?
   a. His sample of patients was small and unrepresentative of the general population.
   b. His theory reflects Western European and North American cultural values.
   c. The theory was not developed scientifically and thus is subject to bias.
   d. The theory was not comprehensive and has had little influence on psychology.

7. Rajeem believes that he is unique because no one else has exactly the same combination of internal characteristics (such as high intelligence, low sociability, average creativity) that he does. In other words, Rajeem believes in the _____ approach to personality.
   a. psychodynamic
   b. trait
   c. social-cognitive
   d. humanistic

8. A politician is described by her critics as dishonest, intelligent, industrious, extraverted, aggressive, generous, and charming. This method of describing personality most closely matches _____ model of personality.
   a. Eysenck's biological trait
   b. Rotter's expectancy
   c. Allport's trait
   d. the Five Factor

9. Tamerika has been described as high on openness (very curious and imaginative), low in conscientiousness (disorganized and unproductive), high in extraversion (very active, talkative, and energetic), high in agreeableness (generous, kind, and trusting), and high in neuroticism (impulsive, touchy, and vulnerable). This description reflects _____ model of personality
   a. Eysenck's biological trait
   b. Rotter's expectancy
   c. Allport's trait
   d. the Five Factor

10. David is very sociable and tends to seek out situations in which other people are appreciative of his work and his jokes. He is usually happy and loves to try new activities, such as bungee jumping. According to Gray, David has an active _____ system.
    a. external control
    b. internal control
    c. behavioral approach
    d. flight or freeze system

11. According to the Thinking Critically section of this chapter, research on the question of whether or not personality is inherited concludes that _____.
    a. there are specific genes for specific personality traits
    b. there are genetic predispositions toward particular personality characteristics
    c. the environment is the strongest influence on personality development
    d. personality is essentially determined by the age of six months

12. Sandy believes that if she works hard, she will be rewarded. So when she gets a D on her psychology test, she decides that she didn't study hard enough. When she wins the "Outstanding Senior of the Month" award, she believes that she earned it. According to one type of social-cognitive personality theory, Sandy would be described as _____.

   a. internal
   b. external
   c. deficiency oriented
   d. growth oriented

13. Darma was standing in line at a movie theater, thinking about how her boyfriend had dumped her, when she was accidentally shoved from behind. She shouted "Hey! Back off, you jerks!" This prompted angry comments from the people behind her, which made Darma even angrier, so she refused to move forward in line. This case is an example of _____.

   a. conditions of worth
   b. growth orientation
   c. reciprocal determinism
   d. internal locus of control

14. At college basketball games, Melinda jumps up and down and yells and screams continuously. Otherwise, however, she is a quiet person who chooses peaceful environments without much social stimulation. She finds that when she is around other people, they often become quiet, too. Melinda's personality can best be explained by _____ theory.

   a. psychodynamic
   b. Allport's trait
   c. Rotter's expectancy
   d. Mischel's person-situation

15. Rolf believes that his children's personalities are shaped by the way he rewards and punishes them. His wife, Jena, believes that the children were born with an innate drive toward growth and that their personalities are shaped by their unique perceptions of the world. Rolf's beliefs most closely match the _____ approach to personality, and Jena's most closely match the _____ approach.

   a. psychodynamic; trait
   b. social-cognitive; trait
   c. social-cognitive; humanistic
   d. psychodynamic; humanistic

16. When Lizzie finger-paints on the wall, her mother gets angry and shouts, "You are a very bad girl!" Rogers would say that Lizzie's mother is creating _____.

   a. growth-oriented development
   b. deficiency-orientated development
   c. conditions of worth
   d. psychodynamic conflicts

17. Ruben is preoccupied with what is missing from his life. He has a good job and just got a raise, but he still feels underpaid. He has a great wife, but he wishes she were more attractive. He bought a new car, but he just saw a better one that has become his latest obsession. Maslow would say that Ruben is controlled by _____.

   a. growth orientation
   b. deficiency orientation
   c. conditions of worth
   d. self-actualization

18. Which of the following techniques would a psychodynamic psychologist be most likely to use to assess personality?

   a. Behavioral observations
   b. Nonprojective personality measures
   c. Measurements of physiological activity
   d. Projective personality measures

19. Paul is an undercontrolled eight-year-old who regularly has tantrums. The longitudinal study described in this chapter's Focus on Research section would suggest that, when Paul is an adult, he will most likely _____.

   a. join the military or live in some other highly structured environment
   b. have outgrown his lack of control
   c. be more aggressive than most other men
   d. keep jobs longer than most other men

20. Peggy is responsible for hiring new employees for her company. To guide her selections, she decides to use _____, which have been shown to have value in screening out employees who are likely to be unreliable or dishonest.

   a. structured interviews
   b. nonprojective personality measures
   c. projective personality measures
   d. life outcome measures

© Marcus Mok/Getty Images

12 Psychological Disorders

Preview

A man sits alone in a restaurant booth, giving his order to a waitress. But when she leaves, he continues talking and laughing as though someone were sitting with him. When his lunch arrives, he thanks the waitress, then continues his "conversation." Later, he pays his bill, leaves a tip, and walks outside, chatting to his invisible companion all the while. Is this person crazy or just eccentric? When does oddness become abnormality? When does sadness become depression? What are psychological disorders? In this chapter, we describe the major categories of psychological disorders, discuss some of their possible causes, consider how they have been explained over the centuries, and examine their role in the insanity defense.

J osé is a 55-year-old electronics technician. A healthy and vigorous father of two adult children, he was recently forced to take medical leave because of a series of sudden, uncontrollable panic attacks in which dizziness, a racing heart, sweating, and other terrifying symptoms made him fear that he was about to die. José is suffering from a psychological disorder, also called a *mental disorder* or *psychopathology*. **Psychopathology** involves patterns of thought, emotion, and behavior that are maladaptive, disruptive, or uncomfortable either for the person affected or for others.

Psychological disorders appear in every country in the world, and the number of people who are affected is staggering (King et al., 2008; Stein et al., 2008; World Health Organization, 2009). Surveys reveal that in any given year in the United States alone, about 60 million people, or about 30 percent of the adult population, have displayed some form of mental disorder and that as many as 48 percent have experienced a disorder at some point in their lives (Bjil et al., 2003; Kessler, Berglund, Demier et al., 2005; Kessler, Chiu et al., 2005; Narrow et al., 2002; National Institute of Mental Health, 2008a; see Figure 12.1). In addition, about 20 percent of U.S. children display a significant mental disorder in any given year (Costello et al., 2003; U.S. Surgeon General, 2009). These rates of mental disorder have remained steady in recent years and are seen in all segments of U.S. society. As described later, though, some disorders are more prevalent in males or females or in certain ethnic groups (Beals et al., 2005; Peterson et al., 1993). The overall prevalence rates may actually be higher than the survey percentages suggest, because major studies have examined fewer than half of all known psychological disorders. In short, psychological disorders are enormously costly in terms of human suffering, wasted potential, economic burden, and lost resources (Insel, 2008; Kessler, Chiu et al., 2006, 2008; Stewart et al., 2003). ■

Defining Psychological Disorders

▶ *How do psychologists define abnormal behavior?*

A woman's husband dies. In her grief, she stays in bed all day, weeping, refusing to eat, at times holding "conversations" with him. In India, a Hindu holy man on a pilgrimage rolls along the ground for more than 1,000 miles of deserts and mountains, in all kinds of weather, until he reaches the sacred place he seeks. A British artist randomly scratches parked cars as part of his "creative process" (Telegraph Correspondent,

psychopathology Patterns of thinking and behaving that are maladaptive, disruptive, or uncomfortable for the affected person or for others.

FIGURE 12.1 ■ INCIDENCE OF SPECIFIC PSYCHOLOGICAL DISORDER

Several large-scale surveys of adults in the United States revealed that about 30 percent of them experience some form of mental disorder in any given year and that almost half of them have displayed a disorder at some time in life. The data shown here summarize these findings by category of disorder. The same general patterns appear among the more than 400 million people worldwide who suffer from some form of psychological disorder (King et al., 2008; World Health Organization, 2009).

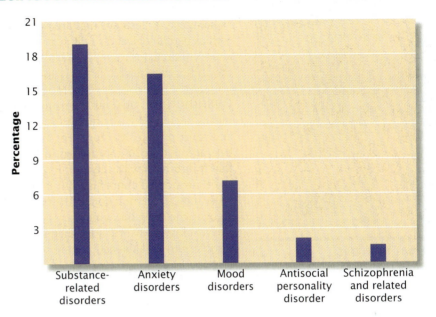

2005). Eight percent of U.S. adults surveyed say they have seen a UFO (CNN/Time, 1997), and hundreds claim to have been abducted by space aliens (Clancy, 2005). These examples and countless others raise the question of where to draw the line between normality and abnormality, between eccentricity and mental disorder.

What Is Abnormal?

There are several criteria for judging whether a person's thinking, emotions, or behaviors are abnormal. Each criterion has value but also some flaws.

Deviance If we define *normality* as what most people do, then the criterion for abnormality becomes *statistical infrequency,* or that which is deviant, meaning unusual or rare. By this criterion, the few people who believe that space aliens steal their thoughts would be judged as abnormal; the many people who worry about becoming victims of crime or terrorism would not. But statistical infrequency alone is a poor criterion for abnormality because it would define as abnormal any rare quality or characteristic, including creative genius or world-class athletic ability. Further, the infrequency criterion implies that conformity with the majority is normal, so equating rarity with abnormality may result in the oppression of nonconformists who express unusual or unpopular views or ideas. Finally, just how rare must a behavior be in order to call it "abnormal"? The dividing line is not easy to locate.

A related criterion for abnormality is the violation of social norms, the cultural rules that tell us how we should and shouldn't behave in various situations, especially in relation to others. According to this *norm violation* criterion, when people behave in ways that are unusual enough or disturbing enough to violate social norms, they may be described as abnormal. However, norm violation alone is an inadequate measure of abnormality. For one thing, some norm violations are better characterized as eccentric or illegal than as abnormal. People who seldom bathe or who stand too close during conversation violate social norms, but are they abnormal or merely annoying? Further, whose norms are we talking about? Social norms vary across cultures, subcultures, and historical eras, so certain behaviors that qualify as abnormal in one part of the world might be perfectly acceptable elsewhere (Giosan, Glovsky, & Haslam, 2001; Phelan et al., 2000).

Distress Abnormality can also be described in terms of *personal suffering.* In fact, experiencing distress is the criterion that people often use in deciding that their

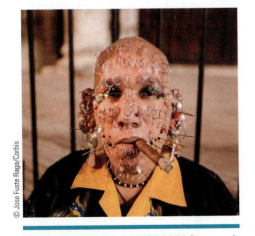

IS THIS PERSON ABNORMAL? Whether unusual individuals are labeled "abnormal" and perhaps given treatment for psychological disorders depends on a number of factors, including how abnormality is defined by the culture in which they live, who is most directly affected by their behavior, and how much distress they suffer or cause.

© Jose Fuste Raga/Corbis

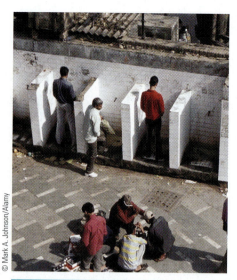

SITUATIONAL FACTORS IN DEFINING ABNORMALITY

Men in Delhi, India, can take advantage of outdoor urinals like this one. In some countries, it is even acceptable for men to urinate against buildings on city streets. In the United States and many other places, though, males who urinate anywhere other than the relative privacy of a men's room are considered to be deviant and might even be arrested for indecent exposure. In other words, situational factors can determine whether a particular behavior is labeled "normal" or "abnormal." Make a list of the reasons you would give for, or against, calling these men "abnormal." Which criteria for abnormality did you use?

Learn BY Doing

psychological problems are severe enough to require treatment. But personal suffering alone is not an adequate criterion for abnormality. For one thing, it does not take into account the fact that people are sometimes distressed about characteristics (such as being gay or lesbian) that are not mental disorders. Second, some people display serious psychological disorders but experience little or no distress. Those who sexually abuse children, for example, create far more distress in victims and their families than they suffer themselves.

Dysfunction   A final criterion for abnormality is *impaired functioning*, which means having difficulty in fulfilling appropriate and expected roles in family, social, and work-related situations. For example, it is normal for people to experience sadness at one time or another, but if their sadness becomes so intense or long-lasting that it interferes with their ability to hold a job or care for their children, it is likely to be considered abnormal. But it isn't quite fair to call someone abnormal just because they are dysfunctional. Their dysfunction might be caused by physical illness, by an overwhelming but temporary family problem, or by a variety of things other than a psychological disorder. Further, some people who display significant psychological disorders are still able to function reasonably well at school, at work, or at home.

Behavior in Context: A Practical Approach

Obviously, no single criterion fully defines abnormality. So mental health practitioners and researchers tend to adopt a *practical approach* that combines aspects of all the criteria we've described. They consider the *content* of behavior (that is, what the person does), the sociocultural *context* in which the person's behavior occurs, and the *consequences* of the behavior for that person and for others.

They recognize, too, that the definition of behavior that is "appropriate," "expected," and "functional" depends on age, gender, culture, and the particular situation and historical era in which people live. For example, a short attention span and unemployment are considered normal in a two-year-old but inappropriate and problematic in an adult. In some countries, expressing certain emotions is considered more appropriate for women than for men. So kisses, tears, and long embraces are common when women in North America greet each other after a long absence; men tend to simply shake hands or hug briefly. And because of cultural differences, hearing a dead relative's voice calling from the afterlife would be more acceptable in certain American Indian tribes than among, say, the families of suburban Toronto. Situational factors are important as well. Falling to the floor and "speaking in tongues" is considered appropriate and even desirable during the worship services of some religious groups; but the same behavior would be seen as inappropriate (and possibly a sign of disorder) in a college classroom. Finally, judgments about behavior are shaped by changes in social trends and cultural values. At one time, the American Psychiatric Association listed homosexuality as a mental disorder, but it dropped this category from its official list of disorders in 1973. In taking this step, it was responding to changing views of sexual orientation prompted in part by the political and educational efforts of gay and lesbian rights groups.

In summary, it is difficult (and probably impossible) to define a specific set of behaviors that everyone, everywhere, will agree constitutes abnormality. Instead, the practical approach sees abnormality as including those patterns of thought, behavior, and emotion that lead to suffering and significantly impair people's ability to function as expected within their culture (Wakefield, 1992).

Explaining Psychological Disorders

▶ *What causes abnormality?*

It is one thing to define psychological disorders; it is quite another to explain them. Centuries ago, explanations of abnormal behavior focused on gods or demons. Disordered people were seen either as innocent victims of evil spirits or as social or moral

AN EXORCISM ▶

The exorcism being performed by this Buddhist monk in Thailand is designed to cast out the evil forces that are seen as causing this child's disorder. Supernatural explanations of mental disorder remain influential among religious groups in many cultures and subcultures around the world (Fountain, 2000). Awareness of this influence in the United States and Europe has increased recently after cases in which people have died during exorcism rituals (e.g., Christopher, 2003; Radford, 2005).

deviants suffering supernatural punishment. In Europe during the late Middle Ages, for example, it was widely believed that people who engaged in threatening or unusual behavior were controlled by the devil or other evil beings. Supernatural explanations of psychological disorders are still invoked today in many cultures around the world, including certain ethnic and religious subcultures in North America (Glazer et al., 2004; Legare & Gelman, 2008). Other explanations have focused on mental incompetence, weak character, personal choices, illness or other physical problems, faulty learning, and difficult social conditions.

Each explanation of psychological disorders tends to influence a society's attitudes and responses toward the people who display them (Fontaine, 2009). Where disorder is seen as a sign that a person is evil, that person may be the target of anger and punishment, but in societies in which the cause of disorder is thought to be demonic possession, the person may be the object of sympathy and might be offered an exorcism ceremony. If abnormality is viewed as a personal decision to behave in odd ways, those who do so are likely to be avoided, isolated, and ignored, but if psychological problems are assumed to be caused by illness or learned habits, troubled people are likely to receive drugs or to be offered programs designed to teach less troublesome behaviors.

The Biopsychosocial Approach

Today, most mental health researchers in Western cultures attribute the appearance of psychopathology to three main causes: biological factors, psychological processes, and sociocultural contexts. For many decades, there was controversy over which of these three causes was most important, but it is now widely agreed that they can all be important. Most researchers have adopted a **biopsychosocial approach** in which mental disorders are seen as caused by the combination and interaction of biological, psychological, and sociocultural factors, each of which contributes in varying degrees to particular problems in particular people (Andrews, 2008; Krueger & Markon, 2006).

Biological Factors   The biological factors thought to be involved in causing mental disorders include physical illnesses and disruptions or imbalances of bodily processes. This view of psychological disorder has a long history. For example, Hippocrates, a physician in ancient Greece, said that psychological disorders result from imbalances among four *humors,* or bodily fluids (blood, phlegm, black bile, and yellow bile).

biopsychosocial approach   An explanation for mental disorders that sees them as the result of a combination of biological, psychological, and sociocultural factors.

In ancient Chinese cultures, psychological disorders were seen as arising from an imbalance of *yin* and *yang,* the dual forces of the universe flowing in the physical body.

As the biologically oriented view gained prominence in Western cultures after the Middle Ages, special hospitals for the insane were established throughout Europe. Treatment in these early *asylums* consisted mainly of physical restraints, laxative purges, bleeding of "excess" blood, and induced vomiting. Cold baths, fasts, and other physical discomforts were also used in efforts to "shock" patients back to normality.

The biologically oriented view, sometimes called the *medical model,* also gave rise to the concept of abnormality as *mental illness.* Today the medical model is now more properly called the *neurobiological model* because it explains psychological disorders in terms of particular disturbances in the anatomy and chemistry of the brain and in other biological processes, including genetic influences (e.g., Kendler, 2005; Plomin & McGuffin, 2003; Williams, 2008). Neuroscientists and others who employ a neurobiological model investigate these disorders as they would investigate any physical illness, seeing problematic symptoms stemming primarily from an underlying illness that can be diagnosed, treated, and cured. This model is widely accepted in Western cultures today; most people tend to seek medical doctors and hospitals for the diagnosis and treatment of psychological disorders (Wang et al., 2006).

Psychological Processes   The biological factors we have described are constantly influencing and being influenced by a variety of psychological processes, such as our wants, needs, and emotions; our learning experiences; and our way of looking at the world. The roots of the *psychological model* of mental disorders can be found in ancient Greek literature and drama dealing with *psyche,* or mind, and especially with the problems people experience as they struggle to resolve inner conflicts or to overcome the effects of stressful events.

These ideas took center stage in the late 1800s, when Sigmund Freud challenged the assumption that psychological disorders had only physical causes. As described in the chapter on personality, Freud viewed psychological disorders as resulting mainly from the effects of unresolved, mostly unconscious clashes between people's inborn impulses and the limits placed on those impulses by the environment. These conflicts, he said, begin early in childhood. Today's versions of this *psychodynamic approach* focus less on instinctual urges and more on the role of attachment and other early interpersonal relationships, but they retain the basic idea that internal conflicts can cause psychological disorders (Bienenfeld, 2005; Levy & Ablon, 2009; Schultz & Schultz, 2005).

VISITING BEDLAM ▶

As shown in William Hogarth's portrayal of "Bedlam" (slang for a hospital in London formerly known as St. Mary Bethlehem), most asylums of the 1700s were little more than prisons. Notice the well-dressed visitors. In those days, the public could buy tickets to look at mental patients, much as people go to the zoo today.

"The Interior of Bedlam," from A Rake's Progress by William Hogarth, 1763

linkages

Are psychological disorders learned behaviors? *(a link to Learning)*

linkages

How do societies define what is abnormal? *(a link to Social Psychology)*

sociocultural perspective An approach to explaining mental disorder that emphasizes the role of factors such as gender and age, physical situations, cultural values and expectations, and historical era.

sociocultural factors Characteristics or conditions that can influence the appearance and form of maladaptive behavior, such as gender, age, and marital status; physical, social, and economic situations; and cultural values, traditions, expectations, and opportunities.

Other theories discussed in the personality chapter suggest other psychological processes that contribute to the appearance of mental disorders. For example, *social-cognitive* theorists, also known as *social-learning* theorists, see most psychological disorders as the result of past learning and current situations. These theorists say that just as people learn to avoid touching hot stoves after being burned by one, bad experiences in school or a dental office can "teach" people to fear such places. Social-cognitive theorists also emphasize the effects of expectancies and other mental processes (e.g., Johnson-Laird, Mancini, & Gangemi, 2006). They see depression, for example, as stemming from negative events, such as losing a job, and from learned patterns of thoughts about these events, such as "I never do anything right."

According to the *humanistic,* or phenomenological, approach to personality, behavior disorders appear when a person's natural tendency toward healthy growth is blocked, usually by a failure to be aware of and to express true feelings. When this happens, the person's perceptions of reality become distorted. The greater the distortion, the more serious the psychological disorder.

Sociocultural Context Together, neurobiological and psychological factors can go a long way toward explaining many forms of mental disorder. Still, they focus mainly on causes residing within the individual. The **sociocultural perspective** on disorder suggests that we cannot fully explain all forms of psychopathology without also looking outside the individual—especially at the social and cultural factors that form the context, or background, of abnormal behavior. Looking for causes of disorders in this *sociocultural context* means paying attention to **sociocultural factors** such as gender, age, and marital status; the physical, social, and economic situations in which people live; and the cultural values, traditions, and expectations in which they are immersed (Appignanesi, 2009; Lim, 2006; Martinez-Taboas, 2005). Sociocultural context influences not only what is and is not labeled "abnormal" but also who displays what kind of disorder.

Consider gender, for instance. The greater tolerance in many cultures for open expression of emotional distress among women but not men may contribute to the fact that women report higher rates of depression than men do (Hightower, 2005; Whiffen, 2006; Wupperman & Neumann, 2006). Similarly, the view held in many cultures that excessive alcohol consumption is less appropriate for women than for men is a sociocultural factor that may set the stage for rates of alcohol abuse that are higher in men than women (Helzer et al., 1990).

Sociocultural factors also influence the form that abnormality takes (Kyrios et al., 2001). For example, depression is considered a *culture-general* disorder because it appears virtually everywhere in the world. However, specific symptoms tend to differ depending on a person's cultural background (Hopper & Wanderling, 2000). In Western cultures, in which the emotional and physical components of disorders are generally viewed separately, symptoms of depression tend to revolve around despair and other signs of emotional distress (Kleinman, 1991). But in China and certain other Asian cultures, in which emotional and physical experiences tend to be viewed as one, depressed people are as likely to report stomach or back pain as to complain of sadness (Karasz, 2005; Kleinman, 2004; Parker, Gladstone, & Chee, 2001; Ryder et al., 2008).

There are also *culture-specific* forms of disorder. For instance, Puerto Rican and Dominican Hispanic women sometimes experience *ataques de nervios* ("attacks of nerves"), a unique way of reacting to stress that includes heart palpitations, shaking, shouting, nervousness, depression, and possibly fainting or seizure-like episodes (Baer et al., 2003; Keough, Timpano, & Schmidt, 2009; Spiegel, 1994). In Asia, Khmer refugees sometimes suffer from panic-related fainting spells known as *kyol goeu* (Hinton, Um, & Ba, 2001). And genital retraction syndromes are occasionally observed in a number of places around the world. Called *koro* in Southeast Asia, southern China, and Malaysia, the disorder appears as a fear that the penis will shrivel, retract into the body, and cause death (Dzokoto & Adams, 2005; Garlipp, 2008). These disorders usually appear in men, but in females the fear relates to shriveling of the breasts.

In short, sociocultural factors create differing social roles, stressors, opportunities, and experiences for people who differ in age, gender, and cultural traditions.

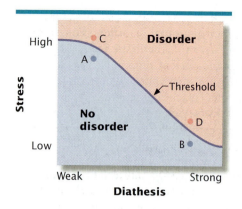

FIGURE 12.2 ■ DIATHESIS, STRESS, AND DISORDER

The diathesis-stress model's explanations suggest that psychological disorders can result from many combinations of predisposition and stress. Point D shows disorder stemming from a strong predisposition and relatively little stress. At Point C, disorder resulted from a weak predisposition but a lot of stress. Points A and B represent blends of diathesis and stress that are not potent enough to trigger disorder.

They also help shape the disorders and symptoms to which certain categories of people are prone. Any attempt to fully explain psychological disorders must take these sociocultural factors into account.

The Diathesis-Stress Model as an Integrative Explanation

The biopsychosocial approach is currently the most comprehensive and influential way of explaining psychological disorders. It is prominent partly because it encompasses so many important causal factors, including biological imbalances, genetically inherited characteristics, brain damage, psychological traits, socioculturally influenced learning experiences, stressful life events, and many more.

But how do all these factors actually interact to create disorder? Most researchers who study psychopathology believe that inherited characteristics, biological processes, learning experiences, and sociocultural forces combine to create a predisposition, or *diathesis* (pronounced "dye-ATH-uh-sis"), for psychological disorders. Whether or not a person eventually develops symptoms of disorder, they say, depends on the nature and amount of stress the person encounters (Elwood et al., 2009; Turner & Lloyd, 2004). For example, a person may have inherited a biological tendency toward depression or may have learned depressing patterns of thinking, but these predispositions might not result in a depressive disorder unless the person is faced with a severe financial crisis or suffers the loss of a loved one. If major stressors don't occur or if the person has good stress-coping skills, depressive symptoms may never appear or may be relatively mild (Canli et al., 2006).

So according to the **diathesis-stress model**, biological, psychological, and sociocultural factors can predispose us toward disorder, but it takes a certain amount of stress to actually trigger it. For those with a strong diathesis, relatively mild stress might be enough to create a problem. Those whose predisposition is weaker might not show signs of disorder until stress becomes extreme or prolonged (see Figure 12.2). Another way to think about the diathesis-stress model is in terms of *risk*: The more risk factors for a disorder a person has—whether they take the form of genetic tendencies, personality traits, cultural traditions, or stressful life events—the more likely it is that the person will display a form of psychological disorder associated with those risk factors.

Table 12.1 shows how a particular case of psychopathology might be explained by various biopsychosocial factors and how it might be summarized in terms of

TABLE 12.1 ■ EXPLAINING PSYCHOPATHOLOGY

Here are the factors that would be highlighted by the biopsychosocial approach in the case of José, the man described at the beginning of this chapter. At the bottom is a summary of how these factors might be combined within a diathesis-stress framework.

Explanatory Domain	Possible Contributing Factors
Neurobiological/medical	José may have organic disorders (e.g., a genetic tendency toward anxiety, a brain tumor, an endocrine dysfunction, or a neurotransmitter imbalance).
Psychological: psychodynamic	José has unconscious conflicts and desires. Instinctual impulses are breaking through ego defenses into consciousness, causing panic.
Psychological: social-cognitive	José interprets physical stress symptoms as signs of serious illness or impending death. His panic is rewarded by the reduction in work stress when he stays home.
Psychological: humanistic	José fails to recognize his genuine feelings about work and his place in life, and he fears expressing himself.
Sociocultural	A culturally based belief that "a man should not show weakness" amplifies the intensity of stress reactions and delays José's decision to seek help.
Diathesis-stress summary	José has a biological (possibly genetic) predisposition to be overly responsive to stressors. The stress of work and extra activity exceeds his capacity to cope and triggers panic as a stress response.

diathesis and stress. Later, you'll see these same biopsychosocial factors combined within a diathesis-stress framework to explain a number of other psychological disorders.

 **Improve Your Grade**
Tutorial: Disorder Categories

Classifying Psychological Disorders

 How many psychological disorders have been identified?

Although definitions of abnormality differ within and across cultures, there does seem to be a set of behavior patterns that roughly defines the range of most abnormality in most cultures. The majority of these behavior patterns qualify as disorders because they result in impaired functioning, a main criterion of the practical approach to defining abnormality. It has long been the goal of those who study abnormal behavior to classify these patterns into a set of diagnostic categories. Ideally, establishing these categories should make it easier to diagnose which disorder a particular person is displaying and thus which treatment method would be most appropriate.

Diagnoses are also important for research on the causes of psychopathology. If researchers can accurately classify people into particular disorder categories, they will have a better chance of spotting genetic features, biological abnormalities, cognitive processes, and environmental experiences that people in the same category might share. Finding that people in one category share a set of features that differs from those shared by people in other categories could provide clues about which features are related to the development of each disorder.

In 1952 the American Psychiatric Association published the first edition of what has become the "official" North American diagnostic classification system, the *Diagnostic and Statistical Manual of Mental Disorders (DSM)*. Each edition of the *DSM* has included more categories. The latest editions, the *DSM-IV* and the *DSM-IV-TR* (text revision), include more than 300 specific diagnostic labels (American Psychiatric Association, 1994, 2000). Mental health professionals outside North America diagnose mental disorders using classification systems that appear in the tenth edition of the World Health Organization's *International Classification of Diseases (ICD-10)* and its companion volume, the second edition of the *International Classification of Impairments, Disabilities and Handicaps (ICIDH-2)*. To facilitate international communication about—and cross-cultural research on—psychopathology, the *DSM-IV* was designed to be compatible with these manuals, and efforts are under way to remove inconsistencies existing between the systems (Cottler & Grant, 2007; Löwe et al., 2008; Widiger et al., 2006).

A Classification System: The *DSM-IV*

The *DSM-IV* describes the patterns of thinking, emotion, and behavior that define various mental disorders. For each disorder, the *DSM-IV* provides specific criteria outlining the conditions that must be present before a person is given that diagnostic label. In keeping with the biopsychosocial approach, diagnosticians using *DSM-IV* can evaluate troubled people on five dimensions, or *axes*. (*Axes* is the plural of *axis* and is pronounced "AX-eez"). Together, these axes provide a broad picture of each person's biological and psychological problems and of any sociocultural context factors that might contribute to them. As shown in Table 12.2, mental disorders such as schizophrenia or depression are recorded on Axis I, whereas evidence of personality disorders or mental retardation is noted on Axis II. Any medical conditions that might be important in understanding the person's cognitive, emotional, or behavioral problems are listed on Axis III. On Axis IV, the diagnostician notes any psychosocial or environmental problems (such as the loss of a loved one, physical or sexual abuse, discrimination, unemployment, poverty, homelessness, inadequate health care, or conflict with religious or cultural traditions) that are important for understanding the person's

diathesis-stress model An approach that recognizes the roles of predispositions and situational factors in the appearance of psychological disorders.

TABLE 12.2 ■ *THE DIAGNOSTIC AND STATISTICAL MANUAL OF MENTAL DISORDERS (DSM) OF THE AMERICAN PSYCHIATRIC ASSOCIATION*

Axis I of the fourth edition (*DSM-IV*) lists the major categories of mental disorders. Personality disorders and mental retardation are listed in Axis II.

Axis I (Clinical Syndromes)

1. ***Disorders usually first diagnosed in infancy, childhood, or adolescence.*** Problems such as hyperactivity, childhood fears, conduct disorders, frequent bed-wetting or soiling, and other problems in normal social and behavioral development. Includes autistic spectrum disorders (severe impairment in social, behavioral, and language development) as well as learning disorders.

2. ***Delirium, dementia, and amnesic and other cognitive disorders.*** Problems caused by physical deterioration of the brain due to aging, disease, drugs or other chemicals, or other possible unknown causes. These problems can appear as an inability to "think straight" (delirium) or as loss of memory and other intellectual functions (dementia).

3. ***Substance-related disorders.*** Psychological, behavioral, physical, social, or legal problems caused by dependence on or abuse of a variety of chemical substances, including alcohol, heroin, cocaine, amphetamines, painkillers, hallucinogens, marijuana, and tobacco.

4. ***Schizophrenia and other psychotic disorders.*** Severe conditions characterized by abnormalities in thinking, perception, emotion, movement, and motivation that greatly interfere with daily functioning. Problems involving false beliefs (delusions).

5. ***Affective disorders*** (also called ***mood disorders***). Severe disturbances of mood, especially depression, overexcitement (mania), or alternating episodes of each extreme (as in bipolar disorder).

6. ***Anxiety disorders.*** Specific fears (phobias), panic attacks, generalized feelings of dread, rituals of thought and action (obsessive-compulsive disorder) aimed at controlling anxiety, and problems caused by traumatic events, such as rape or military combat (see the chapter on health, stress, and coping for more on posttraumatic stress disorder).

7. ***Somatoform disorders.*** Physical symptoms such as paralysis and blindness that have no physical cause. Unusual preoccupation with physical health or with nonexistent physical problems (hypochondriasis, somatization disorder, somatoform pain disorder).

8. ***Factitious disorders.*** False mental disorders that are intentionally produced to satisfy some psychological need.

9. ***Dissociative disorders.*** Psychologically caused problems of consciousness and self-identification—e.g., loss of memory (amnesia) or the development of more than one identity (multiple personality).

10. ***Sexual and gender identity disorders.*** Problems of (a) finding sexual arousal through unusual objects or situations (like shoes or exposing oneself); (b) unsatisfactory sexual activity (sexual dysfunction; see the chapter on motivation and emotion); or (c) identifying with the opposite gender.

11. ***Eating disorders.*** Problems associated with eating too little (anorexia nervosa) or binge eating followed by self-induced vomiting (bulimia). (See the chapter on motivation and emotion.)

12. ***Sleep disorders.*** Severe problems involving the sleep-wake cycle, especially an inability to sleep well at night or to stay awake during the day. (See the chapter on consciousness.)

13. ***Impulse control disorders.*** Compulsive gambling, stealing, or fire setting.

14. ***Adjustment disorders.*** Failure to adjust to or deal well with such stressors as divorce, financial problems, family discord, or other unhappy life events.

Axis II (Personality Disorders and Mental Retardation)

1. ***Personality disorders.*** Diagnostic labels given to individuals who may or may not receive an Axis I diagnosis but who show lifelong behavior patterns that are unsatisfactory to them or that disturb other people. These patterns may involve unusual suspiciousness, unusual ways of thinking, self-centeredness, shyness, overdependency, excessive concern with neatness and detail, or overemotionality, among others.

2. ***Mental retardation.*** As described in the chapter on thought, language, and intelligence, the label of "mental retardation" is applied to individuals whose measured IQ is less than about 70 and who fail to display the skills of daily life, communication, and other tasks expected of people their age.

---

psychological problems. Finally, on Axis V, the person is rated (from 100 down to 1) on current psychological, social, and occupational functioning. Here is a sample *DSM-IV* diagnosis for someone who received labels on all five axes:

Axis I: Major depression, single episode; alcohol abuse.

Axis II: Dependent personality disorder.

Axis III: Alcoholic cirrhosis of the liver.

Axis IV: Problems with primary support group (death of spouse).

Axis V: Global assessment of functioning = 50.

Notice that *neurosis* and *psychosis* are no longer listed in the *DSM*, because they are not specific enough. However, some mental health professionals still sometimes use these terms as shorthand descriptions. *Neurosis* refers to conditions in which some form of anxiety is the major characteristic. *Psychosis* refers to conditions involving more extreme problems that leave people "out of touch with reality" or unable to function on a daily basis. The disorders once listed under these headings now appear in various Axis I categories in the *DSM-IV*.

ANXIETY AND DEPRESSION ▲

People who experience anxiety disorders—particularly panic disorder, generalized anxiety disorder, or posttraumatic stress disorder—are likely to display some other mental disorder as well, most often depression (Kaufman & Charney, 2000; Roy-Byrne et al., 2000). Accordingly, the next edition of the *DSM* may include *mixed anxiety-depression disorder*, a new category to describe people whose symptoms of anxiety and depression combine to impair their daily functioning (Das-Munshi et al., 2008).

Further changes in the diagnostic system will surely appear in the *DSM-V,* a new edition of the *DSM* currently under development for publication in 2012 (Beutler & Malik, 2002; Helzer & Hudziak, 2002; Maj et al., 2002; McHugh, 2005). For example, because it is common for certain kinds of disorders, such as anxiety and depression, to appear together, *DSM-V* diagnoses may include some labels that designate "mixed" disorders (Das-Munshi et al., 2008). A variety of other suggestions have been made, such as a new category for disorders characterized primarily by obsessive-compulsive symptoms (Hollander, Braum, & Simeon, 2008; Huprich, 2009). One popular proposal is to organize the *DSM-V* around symptom clusters or symptom dimensions rather than around specific diagnostic categories (Widiger & Lowe, 2008). The idea behind this *dimensional approach* would be to create a set of symptom "building blocks" that could be combined in many different ways so as to better recognize and describe the precise nature of each person's problems (Bell, Sowers, & Thompson, 2008; Hankin et al., 2005; Krueger & Markon, 2006; Krueger, Watson, & Barlow, 2005; Markon, Krueger, & Watson, 2005; Widiger & Samuel, 2005). Other proposals for the *DSM-V* include basing diagnoses on the results of brain imaging and the analysis of people's genetic characteristics (Kiviniemi, 2008).

To broaden the diagnostic process even further, some researchers have suggested that mental health professionals should consider not just people's weaknesses and problems but also their character strengths, virtues, prosocial values, and other psychological resources upon which they can potentially build during treatment. Some researchers in the field of *positive psychology* have even offered comprehensive lists of human strengths and values from which diagnosticians can choose (Baumgardner & Crothers, 2009; Park, Peterson, & Seligman, 2004; Peterson, 2006b).

Evaluating the Diagnostic System

How good is the current diagnostic system? One way to evaluate the *DSM-IV* is to consider *interrater reliability,* the degree to which different mental health professionals agree on what diagnostic label a particular person should have. Reviews of research show that the reliability of the *DSM-IV* is acceptable or high for some disorders but not others. For instance, interrater agreement is strong on Axis I categories such as anxiety disorders, affective disorders, some childhood disorders, and schizophrenia (Brown et al., 2001; Jakobsen et al., 2005; Keenan et al., 2007; Simpson et al., 2002), but is much lower for other categories, such as somatoform disorders and Axis II personality disorders (Mayou et al., 2005; Shedler & Westen, 2004; Westen, Shedler, & Bradley, 2006; Wollert, 2007). Overall, interrater agreement appears highest when diagnosis is based on structured interviews that systematically address each area of functioning and provide uniform guidelines for interpreting people's responses (Brown et al., 2001; Rogers, 2003; Widiger & Sanderson, 1995).

Do diagnostic labels give accurate information that guides correct inferences about people? This *validity* question is difficult to answer because accuracy can be judged in different ways. A diagnosis could be evaluated, for example, on how well it predicts a person's future behavior or perhaps on whether the person is helped by treatment that has helped others in the same diagnostic category. Still, evidence does support the validity of most criteria in the *DSM-IV* (Clark, Watson, & Reynolds, 1995; Deep-Soboslay et al., 2006; Keenan & Wakschlag, 2004; Kim-Cohen et al., 2005; Langenbucher & Nathan, 2006; Simon & von Korff, 2006; Vieta & Phillips, 2007). Validity is likely to improve even more as diagnostic labels—and the diagnostic system—are refined in the *DSM-V* to reflect what researchers are learning about the characteristics, causes, courses, and cultural factors involved in various disorders.

The diagnostic system is far from perfect, however (Beutler & Malik, 2002; Kendell & Jablensky, 2003; Krueger & Markon, 2006; Nestadt et al., 2005). First, people's problems often do not fit neatly into a single category. For example, a person may suffer both anxiety and depression. Second, the same symptom (such as difficulty sleeping) can appear as part of more than one disorder. Third, although the *DSM-IV* provides many useful diagnostic criteria, some of them—such as "clinically significant impairment"—are open to a certain amount of interpretation. When mental health professionals must decide for themselves whether a particular person's symptoms are severe enough to warrant a particular diagnosis, personal bias can creep into the system (Kim & Ahn, 2002; Widiger & Clark, 2000). All of these factors may lead to misdiagnosis in some cases. Concern over this possibility has grown as the nations of North America and Western Europe have become increasingly multicultural. Diagnosticians in these countries are encountering more and more people whose cultural backgrounds they may not fully understand and whose behavior they may misinterpret.

Some people whose behavior differs enough from cultural norms to cause annoyance feel that society should tolerate their "neurodiversity" instead of giving them a diagnostic label (Harmon, 2004). In the same vein, Thomas Szasz (pronounced "zaws") and other critics argue that the entire process of labeling people instead of describing problems is dehumanizing because it ignores people's strengths and the features that make each case unique (Caplan, 1995; Kutchins & Kirk, 1997; Snyder & Lopez, 2006, 2007; Szasz, 2003; Wampold, Ahn, & Coleman, 2001). Calling people "schizophrenics" or "alcoholics," he says, may actually encourage the behaviors associated with these labels, undermine the confidence of clients and therapists about a person's chances for improvement, and may even force people—especially those who hold noncomformist or politically unpopular views—to undergo treatment (Szasz, 1972, 2009). Though most mental health professionals disagree with Szasz on this last point, his arguments are worth noting because psychiatric diagnosis has indeed been used in the past and even in some countries today to suppress social dissent or unpopular beliefs and lifestyles.

In summary, it is unlikely that any diagnostic system will ever satisfy everyone. No shorthand label can fully describe a person's problems or predict exactly how that person will behave. All that can be reasonably expected of a diagnostic system is that it provide informative general descriptions of the types of problems displayed by people who have been placed in various categories (First et al., 2004).

Thinking CRITICALLY

Is Psychological Diagnosis Biased?

Some researchers and clinicians worry that problems with the reliability and validity of the diagnostic system are due partly to bias in its construction and use. They point out, for example, that if the criteria for diagnosing a certain disorder were based on research that focused on only one gender, one ethnic group, or one age group, those criteria might not apply to other groups. Moreover, diagnosticians, like other people, hold expectations and make assumptions about males versus females and about individuals from differing cultures or ethnic groups. These cognitive biases could color their judgments and might lead them to apply diagnostic criteria in ways that are slightly but significantly different from one case to the next (Bjorklund, 2006; Garb, 1997; Hartung & Widiger, 1998; Poland & Caplan, 2004).

▶ What am I being asked to believe or accept?

Here we focus on ethnicity as a possible source of bias in diagnosing psychopathology. It is of special interest because there is evidence that like social class and gender, ethnicity is an important sociocultural factor in the development of mental disorder. The assertion to be considered is that clinicians in the United States base their diagnoses partly on a client's ethnic background and more specifically that bias affects these clinicians' diagnoses of African Americans.

▶ Is evidence available to support the claim?

Several facts suggest the possibility of ethnic bias in psychological diagnosis. For one thing, African Americans receive the diagnosis of schizophrenia more frequently than European Americans do (Barnes, 2004; Kilbourne et al., 2004; Minsky et al., 2003). One study found that certain kinds of odd symptoms tend to be diagnosed as a mood disorder in European Americans but as schizophrenia in African Americans (Neighbors et al., 2003). Further, relative to their presence in the general population, African Americans are overrepresented in public mental hospitals, where the most serious forms of disorder are seen, and underrepresented in private hospitals and outpatient clinics, where less severe problems are treated (Barnes, 2004; Snowden & Cheung, 1990; U.S. Surgeon General, 1999). African Americans are also more likely than European Americans to be discharged from mental hospitals without a definite diagnosis, suggesting that clinicians have more difficulty in diagnosing their disorders (Sohler & Bromet, 2003). Emergency room physicians, too, appear less likely to recognize psychiatric disorders in African American patients than in patients from other groups (Kunen et al., 2005).

There is also evidence that members of ethnic minorities, including African Americans, are underrepresented in research on psychopathology (Iwamasa, Sorocco, & Koonce, 2002). This lack of minority representation may leave clinicians less aware of sociocultural factors that could influence diagnosis. For example, they might more easily misinterpret an African American's unwillingness to trust a European American diagnostician as evidence of paranoid symptoms (Whaley, 2001).

▶ Can that evidence be interpreted another way?

Differences among ethnic groups in diagnosis or treatment do not automatically indicate bias based on ethnicity. Perhaps there are real differences in psychological functioning among different ethnic groups. If African Americans are exposed to more risk factors for disorder, including poverty, violence, and other major stressors than other groups are, they could be especially vulnerable to more serious forms of mental disorder (Plant & Sachs-Ericsson, 2004; Turner & Lloyd, 2004). And poverty, not diagnostic bias, could be responsible for the fact that African Americans are more often seen at less expensive public hospitals than at more expensive private ones. Finally, there is no guarantee that diagnostic criteria would be significantly different if more African Americans had been included in psychopathology research samples.

▶ What evidence would help to evaluate the alternatives?

So do African Americans actually display more signs of mental disorder than other groups do, or do diagnosticians just perceive them as more disordered? One way of approaching this question is to conduct experiments in which diagnosticians assign labels to clients on the basis of case histories, test scores, and the like. In some studies, the cases are selected so that pairs of clients show about the same amount of disorder but one member of the pair is described as European American and the other as African American. In other studies, the same case materials, described as representing either African American or European American clients, are presented to different diagnosticians. Bias in diagnosis would be suggested if, for example, the clinicians saw patients who were described as African American as more seriously disordered than others.

Most studies of this type have found little or no ethnic bias (e.g., Angold et al., 2002; Garb, 1997; Littlewood, 1992). These results are difficult to interpret, however, because the diagnosticians may be aware of the purpose of the study and so may go out of their way to be unbiased (Abreu, 1999; Gushue, 2004). In fact, researchers *have* found evidence of some diagnostic bias against African Americans when clinicians were unaware of the purpose of the research (e.g., Baskin, Bluestone, & Nelson, 1981; Jones, 1982). But bias can result in underdiagnosis as well as overdiagnosis. One review of research found that African American children exhibited more signs of hyperactivity disorder than European American children did yet were given that diagnosis less often (Miller, Nigg, & Miller, 2009). In another study, socially disruptive African American youngsters were less likely than disruptive European American adolescents to be diagnosed with conduct disorder (Pottick et al., 2007). These results suggest that some diagnosticians might believe

that a certain amount of overactivity, inattention, and misbehavior is to be expected of African Americans and that this behavior is therefore "normal" for them.

Bias has also appeared in studies aimed at identifying the factors that influence clinicians' diagnostic judgments following extensive interviews with patients. For example, one hospital study found that in arriving at their diagnoses, psychiatrists were more likely to attribute hallucinations and paranoid thinking to African American patients than to non–African American patients and they were more likely to attribute symptoms of depressive disorders to non–African Americans (Trierweiler et al., 2000). As noted earlier, these differences could reflect ethnic differences in the rate of disorder in the population. However, when people were interviewed in their own homes as part of large-scale mental health surveys, the diagnosis of schizophrenia was given only slightly more often to African Americans than to European Americans (Robins & Regier, 1991; Snowden & Cheung, 1990). So the presence of ethnic bias is suggested, at least for some diagnoses, for patients who are evaluated in mental hospitals but not necessarily for those who are interviewed in their own homes (Trierweiler et al., 2000, 2005).

▶ What conclusions are most reasonable?

Just as the *DSM-IV* is imperfect, so are the people who use it. As described in the chapters on social psychology and on thought, language, and intelligence, cognitive biases and stereotypes affect human thinking to some extent in virtually every social situation. It is not surprising, then, that they operate in diagnosis as well. Diagnostic bias does not necessarily reflect deliberate discrimination, however. At least one study has shown that like the processes of prejudice discussed in the social psychology chapter, diagnostic bias based on ethnicity can operate unconsciously, without the diagnostician's being aware of it (Abreu, 1999). So no matter how precisely researchers specify the criteria for assigning diagnostic labels, biases and stereotypes are likely to threaten the objectivity of the diagnostic process (Funtowicz & Widiger, 1999; Poland & Caplan, 2004; Trierweiler et al., 2000).

Minimizing diagnostic bias requires a better understanding of it. Hope Landrine (1991) suggests that diagnosticians should focus more intently than ever on the fact that their concepts of "normality" and "abnormality" are affected by sociocultural values that a given client might not share (Kales et al., 2006; Trierweiler et al., 2005). Steven Lopez (1989) argues that mental health professionals must become more aware that the same cognitive shortcuts and biases that affect everyone else's thinking and decision making can impair their own clinical judgments. In fact, future research on memory, problem solving, decision making, social attributions, and other aspects of culture and cognition may turn out to hold the key to reducing bias in the diagnosis of psychological disorders. Meanwhile, perhaps the best way to counteract clinicians' cognitive shortcomings is to teach them to base their diagnoses solely on standard diagnostic criteria and decision rules rather than relying on their (potentially biased) clinical impressions (Akin & Turner, 2006; Kramer, Bernstein, & Phares, 2009).

We do not have space to cover all the *DSM-IV* categories, so we focus on several of the most prevalent and socially significant examples. As you read, try not to catch "medical student's disease." Just as medical students often think that they have the symptoms of every illness they read about, some psychology students worry that certain aspects of their behavior (or that of a relative or friend) might reflect a mental disorder. This phenomenon has recently been labeled *cyberchondria* (Harding et al., 2008; Lewis, 2006; Markoff, 2008) because people's worries so often stem from their unguided use of the Internet to learn about psychiatric disorders (Al-Shammary et al., 2007; Lewis, 2006; Trotter & Morgan, 2008). Just remember that everyone has problems sometimes. Before deciding that you or someone you know has a serious disorder or needs psychological help, consider whether the content, context, and functional impairment associated with the behavior would qualify it as abnormal according to the criteria of the practical approach.

TABLE 12.3 ■ SOME PHOBIAS

Phobia, the Greek word for "morbid fear," refers to *Phobos*, the Greek god of terror. The names of most phobias begin with the Greek word for the feared object or situation.

Name	Feared Stimulus
Acrophobia	Heights
Aerophobia	Flying
Claustrophobia	Enclosed places
Cynophobia	Dogs
Entomophobia	Insects
Gamophobia	Marriage
Gephyrophobia	Crossing a bridge
Hematophobia	Blood
Kenophobia	Empty rooms
Melissophobia	Bees
Ophidiphobia	Snakes
Xenophobia	Strangers

Anxiety Disorders

 What is a phobia?

If you have ever been tense before an exam, a date, or a job interview, you have some idea of what anxiety feels like. Increased heart rate, sweating, rapid breathing, dry mouth, and a sense of dread are all common features of anxiety. Brief episodes of moderate anxiety are a normal part of life for most people. But when anxiety is so intense and long-standing that it disrupts a person's daily functioning, it is called an **anxiety disorder.**

Types of Anxiety Disorders

Here, we discuss four types of anxiety disorders: *phobia, generalized anxiety disorder, panic disorder,* and *obsessive-compulsive disorder.* Another type, called *posttraumatic stress disorder,* is described in the chapter on health, stress, and coping. Together, these are the most common psychological disorders in North America; about 29 percent of the U.S. population will have an anxiety disorder at some point in their lives (Kessler et al., 2009).

Phobia   An intense, irrational fear of an object or situation that is not likely to be dangerous is called a **phobia.** Even though people who experience phobias may realize that their fears are groundless, their efforts to avoid some object or event greatly interfere with daily life. Thousands of phobias have been described; some of them are listed in Table 12.3.

The *DSM-IV* classifies phobias into three subtypes: specific phobias, social phobias, and agoraphobia. **Specific phobias** are fear and avoidance of heights, blood, animals, automobile or air travel, and other specific stimuli and situations. In the United States and other developed nations, they are the most prevalent of the anxiety disorders, affecting 9 to 10 percent of adults and children (Hollander & Simeon, 2008; Kessler, Demler et al., 2005; National Institute of Mental Health, 2006). Here is an example:

> *Mr. L., a 50-year-old office worker, became terrified whenever he had to drive over a bridge. For years, he avoided bridges by taking roundabout ways to and from work and he refused to be a passenger in anyone else's car, in case they used a bridge. Even these inconvenient strategies failed when Mr. L. was transferred to a job requiring frequent automobile trips, many of which were over bridges. He refused the transfer and lost his job.*

Social phobias involve anxiety about being criticized by others or acting in a way that is embarrassing or humiliating. The anxiety is so intense and persistent that it impairs the person's normal functioning. Common social phobias include fear of public speaking or performance ("stage fright"), fear of eating in front of others, and fear of using public rest rooms (Gren-Landell et al., 2009; Kleinknecht, 2000). *Generalized*

anxiety disorder   A condition in which intense feelings of fear and dread are long-standing or disruptive.

phobia   An anxiety disorder that involves strong, irrational fear of an object or situation that does not objectively justify such a reaction.

specific phobias   Phobias that involve fear and avoidance of specific stimuli and situations such as heights, blood, and specific animals.

social phobias   Strong, irrational fears related to social situations.

social phobia is a more severe form of social phobia in which fear occurs in virtually all social situations (Jacobs et al., 2009; Mineka & Zinbarg, 2006; Noyes & Hoehn-Saric, 2006; Williams et al., 2005). Sociocultural factors can alter the form of social phobias. For example, in Japan, where cultural training emphasizes group-oriented values and goals, a common social phobia is *tai-jin kyofu sho,* fear of embarrassing those around you (Kleinknecht, 1994).

Agoraphobia is a strong fear of being away from a safe place, such as home; of being away from a familiar person, such as a spouse or close friend; or of being in crowds or in other situations that are difficult to leave. People who suffer from agoraphobia prefer to stay at home, thus avoiding the intense anxiety associated with shopping, driving, or using public transportation. Many individuals who display agoraphobia have a history of panic attacks, which we describe later (Fava et al., 2008; Kessler, Chiu et al., 2006). In Western cultures, agoraphobia is more often reported by women, many of whom are totally homebound by the time they seek help. Although agoraphobia occurs less frequently than specific phobias (affecting about 0.8 percent of the U.S. population, versus 9 percent for specific phobias), it is the phobia that most often leads people to seek treatment—mainly because it so severely disrupts everyday life (National Institute of Mental Health, 2006).

Generalized Anxiety Disorder   Strong and long-lasting anxiety that is not focused on any particular object or situation marks **generalized anxiety disorder.** Because the problem occurs in virtually all situations and because the person cannot pinpoint its source, this disorder is sometimes called *free-floating anxiety* and is essentially a disorder of worry (Fisher & Wells, 2009). For weeks at a time, the person feels anxious and preoccupied, sure that some disaster is about to occur. The person becomes jumpy and irritable and cannot sleep soundly. Fatigue, inability to concentrate, and physiological signs of anxiety are also common. Generalized anxiety disorder affects about 3 percent of the U.S. population in any given year and about 6 percent of the population at some point in their lives (Hollander & Simeon, 2008; Kessler, Berglund, & Demier et al., 2005). It is more common in women, often accompanying other problems such as depression or substance abuse (Wittchen & Hoyer, 2001).

Panic Disorder   For some people, anxiety takes the form of **panic disorder.** Like José, whom we met at the beginning of this chapter, people suffering from panic disorder experience recurrent, terrifying *panic attacks* that seem to come without warning or obvious cause. These attacks are marked by intense heart palpitations, pressure or pain in the chest, sweating, dizziness, and feeling faint. Often, victims believe they are having a heart attack. They may worry so much about having panic episodes that they limit their activities to avoid possible embarrassment. In fact, it is the fear of experiencing panic attacks that may lead to agoraphobia as the person begins to fear and avoid places where help won't be available should panic recur (Grant et al. 2006; National Institute of Mental Health, 2006). Panic disorder may last for many years, during which periods of improvement may be followed by recurrence. As many as 30 percent of the U.S. population have experienced at least one panic attack within the past year, but full-blown panic disorder is seen in only about 2 to 3 percent of the population in any given year (Hollander & Simeon, 2008; Kessler, Chiu et al., 2006). Here is one example:

> *Geri, a 32-year-old nurse, had her first panic attack while driving on a freeway. Afterward, she would not drive on freeways. Her next attack occurred while she was with a patient and a doctor in a small examining room. A sense of impending doom flooded over her, and she burst out of the office and into the parking lot, where she felt immediate relief. From then on, fear of another attack made it impossible for her to tolerate any close quarters, including crowded shopping malls. She eventually quit her job because of terror of the examining rooms.*

Obsessive-Compulsive Disorder   Anxiety is also at the root of **obsessive-compulsive disorder (OCD),** which affects about 1 percent of the U.S. population in any given year and about 2 to 3 percent of the world population at some time in their lives

agoraphobia   A strong fear of being alone or away from the safety of home.

generalized anxiety disorder   A condition that involves long-lasting anxiety that is not focused on any particular object or situation.

panic disorder   Anxiety in the form of severe panic attacks that come without warning or obvious cause.

obsessive-compulsive disorder (OCD)   An anxiety disorder in which a person becomes obsessed with certain thoughts or feels a compulsion to do certain things.

© Abe Rezny/The Image Works

A CLEANING COMPULSION ▲

Obsessive-compulsive disorder is diagnosed when a culturally expected degree of cleanliness turns into an obsessive preoccupation with germs and a life-disrupting compulsion to clean things. Learning and stress appear to play the major role in shaping and triggering this and other anxiety disorders, but biological factors, including genetically inherited characteristics and problems in certain neurotransmitter systems, may result in an oversensitive nervous system and a predisposition toward anxiety.

obsessions   Persistent, upsetting, and unwanted thoughts that interfere with daily life and may lead to compulsions.

compulsions   Repetitive behaviors that interfere with daily functioning but are performed in an effort to prevent dangers or events associated with obsessions.

(Matthews, 2009; National Institute of Mental Health, 2006). People displaying this disorder are plagued by persistent, upsetting, and unwanted thoughts—called **obsessions**—that often focus on the possibility of infection, contamination, or doing harm to themselves or others. They don't actually carry out harmful acts, but the obsessive thoughts motivate repetitive behaviors—called **compulsions**—that the person believes will prevent infection, aggressive acts, or other events associated with the obsessions (Noyes & Hoehn-Saric, 2006). Common compulsions include rituals such as checking locks; repeating words, images, or numbers; counting things; or arranging objects "just so." Obsessions and compulsions are much more intense than the familiar experience of having a thought or tune running "in the back of your mind" or rechecking a door to see that it is locked. In OCD, the obsessions and compulsions are intense, disturbing, and often strange intrusions that can severely impair daily activities. (The *DSM-IV* defines compulsions as taking up more than one hour a day.) Many of those who display OCD recognize that their thoughts and actions are irrational, but they still experience severe anxiety if they try to interrupt their obsessions or give up their compulsive rituals.

Causes of Anxiety Disorders

As with all the forms of psychopathology we consider, the exact causes of anxiety disorders are a matter of some debate. However, there is good evidence that biological, psychological, and social factors all contribute. The exact nature and combination of causal factors varies from one anxiety disorder to the next. For example, the brain regions involved in panic disorder are not identical to those involved in obsessive-compulsive disorder, and the learning experiences that contribute to specific phobias may differ from those that contribute to agoraphobia.

Biological Factors   Most anxiety disorders appear to run in families (Bolton et al., 2006; Grabe et al., 2006; Stewart et al., 2007), suggesting that these disorders are influenced by a genetic predisposition (Hettema et al., 2003, 2005; Maron et al., 2005). This influence is seen in the fact that if one identical twin has an anxiety disorder, the other twin (who shares the same genes) is more likely to also have an anxiety disorder than is the case in nonidentical twin pairs (Bolton et al., 2006; Kendler, Jacobson et al., 2002). Some inherited predispositions may be rather specific. One study found that identical twins are more likely than other siblings to share phobias about small animals and social situations but not about heights or enclosed spaces (Skre et al., 2000). The degree of genetic influence in anxiety disorders is moderate, however (Hollander & Simeon, 2008), and varies among disorders. For instance, genes appear to play a stronger role in early-onset panic disorder and generalized anxiety disorder than in specific phobias (Bolton et al., 2006; Distel et al., 2008; Neumeister et al., 2004).

Many researchers are trying to identify the specific genes or gene combinations involved in anxiety disorders. For example, a number of genes have been suggested as contributing to OCD, including two variations of the SLlC6A4 gene (Saiz et al., 2008). This work is difficult, though, because the mere presence of a gene doesn't necessary predict the appearance of a disorder. Rather, as described in our discussion of *epigenetics* in the opening chapter of this book, genes are often "switched on" or "switched off" by environmental triggers. The genes or gene combinations that may be involved in anxiety disorders may exert their influence through their effects on the brain's neurotransmitter systems, which are discussed in the chapter on biology and behavior. For instance, excessive activity of norepinephrine circuits in certain parts of the brain has been linked with panic disorder, and dysregulation of serotonin has been associated with obsessive-compulsive disorder and social phobia (Lanzenberger et al., 2007). The role of these neurotransmitters is also suggested by the fact that medications that affect them are often effective in the treatment of OCD and other anxiety disorders (Bartz & Hollander, 2006).

Psychological and Environmental Factors   Biological predispositions combine with environmental stressors and psychological factors—especially cognitive processes and learning—to bring about most anxiety disorders (Hudson & Rapee, 2009;

Mineka & Zinbarg, 2006; Moses & Barlow, 2006; Wilcox et al., 2008). To see the effects of environmental stressors, one need only look at the dramatic rise in cases of posttraumatic stress disorder following natural disasters or terrorist attacks (Galea, Ahern et al., 2002; Galea, Resnick et al., 2002; Hoven et al., 2005). The impact of learning can be seen in families in which parents don't socialize much, tend to be suspicious of others, and exaggerate life's everyday dangers. These parents might unwittingly promote social anxiety in their children—especially in those born with a tendency toward shyness—by influencing them to interpret social situations as threatening. Abuse or other traumatic childhood experiences also increase the risk of developing an anxiety disorder, particularly panic disorder (Brook & Schmidt, 2008; Safren et al., 2002).

Learned ways of thinking play their part, too. Many people suffering from anxiety disorders exaggerate dangers in their environment, thereby creating an unrealistic expectation that bad things are going to happen (Brook & Schmidt, 2008; Wenzel et al., 2006; Wilson et al., 2006). In addition, they tend to underestimate their own capacity for dealing with threatening events, thus triggering anxiety and desperation when feared events do occur (Beck & Emery, 1985). Their lack of perceived control, in turn, can lead these people to avoid or overreact to threatening situations (Wells & Matthews, 2006; White et al., 2006). Consider the development of a panic attack. Unexplained symptoms of physical arousal may set the stage for a panic attack, but it is the person's sensitivity to and cognitive interpretation of those symptoms that can determine whether or not the attack actually develops (Hollander & Simeon, 2008; Lim & Kim, 2005). In the chapter on health, stress, and coping we describe a study in which patients with panic disorder breathed air rich in carbon dioxide. Some were told that they could control the amount of carbon dioxide they were inhaling by turning a dial on a control panel. Others were told they could not control it. In fact, the dial had no effect for either group, but the patients who believed they had control were far less likely to have a full-blown panic attack (Rapee et al., 1992; Sanderson, Rapee, & Barlow, 1989). In another study, patients with panic disorder who inhaled carbon dioxide in the presence of a person they associated with safety were significantly less fearful than patients whose "safe person" was not present (Carter et al., 1995). These and other research results suggest that cognitive factors play an important role in panic disorder as well as in specific phobias, social phobias, generalized anxiety disorder, and OCD (Kolassa et al., 2009; Purdon, 2009; White et al., 2006).

linkages

Can we learn to become "abnormal"? *(a link to Learning)*

Linkages

Anxiety Disorders and Learning

Money troubles, illness, final exams, unhappy relationships, and other problems often create upsetting thoughts. And upsetting thoughts create worry and anxiety, especially for people who are under stress or feel incapable of dealing with their problems. As these thoughts become more persistent, anxiety increases. If doing something such as cleaning the kitchen temporarily relieves the anxiety, that action may be strengthened through the process of negative reinforcement (see the chapter on learning). But cleaning can't eliminate the obsessive thoughts, so when they return, the cleaning may begin again. Eventually, cleaning or other actions may become compulsive, endlessly repeated rituals that keep the person trapped in a vicious circle of anxiety (Barlow, 1988). Based on this kind of analysis, social-cognitive theorists see obsessive-compulsive disorder as a learned pattern sparked by distressing thoughts and maintained by operant conditioning (Abramowitz et al., 2006).

They also see phobias as based in part on the principles of learning, especially classical conditioning and observational learning. The object of the phobia becomes a conditioned aversive stimulus through association with a traumatic event that acts as

BIOLOGICAL PREPAREDNESS ▶

Being predisposed to learn to fear snakes and other potentially dangerous stimuli makes evolutionary sense. Like other animals, humans who rapidly learn a fear response to objects or situations that they see frightening their parents or peers are more likely to survive to pass on their genes to the next generation. Are there things you are especially afraid of? If so, list them and make a note of how you think these fears developed. How many of them appear to have "survival value"?

Learn BY Doing

an unconditioned stimulus (Olatunji, 2006; Stein, 2006). Fear of dogs, for example, may result from a dog attack. Observing or hearing about other people's bad experiences can produce the same result: most people who fear flying have never been in a plane crash. Once the fear is learned, avoidance of the feared object or situation prevents the person from finding out that the fear is exaggerated. This cycle of avoidance helps explain why many fears do not disappear on their own.

Why are phobias involving snakes and spiders so common, even though people are seldom harmed by them? And why are there so few cases of phobias about electrical shocks, even though lots of people receive accidental shocks? The answer may be that people are *biologically prepared* to learn to fear and avoid things that had the potential to harm their evolutionary ancestors (Canu, 2008; Öhman & Mineka, 2001, 2003; Skre et al., 2000). This idea is supported by laboratory research (Hamm, Vaitl, & Lang, 1989). In one study, a group of Swedish psychologists created conditioned fear reactions to certain stimuli by associating photographs of those stimuli with electrical shocks (Öhman, Dimberg, & Öst, 1985). Their volunteer participants developed approximately equal conditioned anxiety reactions to photos of houses, human faces, and snakes. Later, however, when the participants were shown the photos alone, their conditioned reaction to snakes remained long after their response to houses and faces had faded. Similar results have also been obtained in experiments with monkeys (Mühlberger et al., 2006; Zinbarg & Mineka, 1991). These results suggest that anxiety disorders probably arise through the combined effects of genetic predispositions and learning.

Somatoform Disorders

▶ *Can mental disorder cause blindness?*

somatoform disorders Psychological problems in which a person shows the symptoms of some physical (somatic) disorder for which there is no physical cause.

conversion disorder A somatoform disorder in which a person appears to be (but actually is not) blind, deaf, paralyzed, or insensitive to pain.

A young athlete was suffering fainting spells that prevented her from competing in track and field events. Doctors found no physical problems, and it was only after a program of stress management that her symptoms disappeared and she was able to rejoin her team (Lively, 2001). Sometimes people show symptoms of a *somatic,* or bodily, disorder even though there is nothing physically wrong. When psychological problems take somatic form, they are called **somatoform disorders.** The classic example of a somatoform disorder is **conversion disorder,** a condition in which a person appears to be (but is not) blind, deaf, paralyzed, or insensitive to pain in various parts of the

FIGURE 12.3 ■ GLOVE ANESTHESIA

In a form of conversion disorder called *glove anesthesia*, lack of feeling stops abruptly at the wrist (Part B). But as indicated by the overlapping colors in Part A, the nerves of the hand and arm blend, so if they were actually impaired, part of the arm would also lose sensitivity. Other neurologically impossible symptoms of conversion disorder include sleepwalking at night on legs that are "paralyzed" during the day.

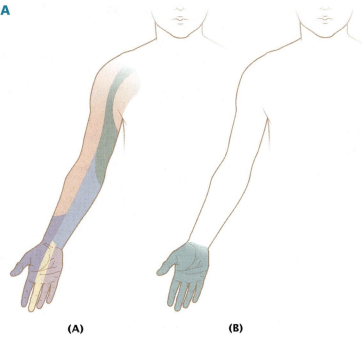

(A)   (B)

body. (An earlier term for this disorder was *hysteria*.) Conversion disorders are rare, accounting for only about 2 percent of diagnoses (American Psychiatric Association, 2000; Eifert, Zvolensky, & Louis, 2008). Although they can occur at any point in life, they usually appear in adolescence or early adulthood.

Conversion disorders differ from true physical disabilities in several ways. First, they tend to appear when a person is under severe stress. Second, they often help reduce that stress by enabling the person to avoid unpleasant situations. Third, the symptoms may be physiologically impossible or improbable, as Figure 12.3 illustrates. Finally, the person may show remarkably little concern about what most people would think was a rather serious problem. One college student, for example, experienced visual impairment that began each Sunday evening and became total blindness by Monday morning. Her vision would begin to return on Friday evenings and was fully restored in time for weekend social activities. She expressed no particular concern over her condition (Holmes, 1991). In such cases, the visual system remains intact, but the person appears to be unaware of the sensory information that the brain is still processing (Ballmaier & Schmidt, 2005; Blake, 1998; Halligan & David, 1999; Harvey, Stanton, & David, 2006).

Another type of somatoform disorder is **hypochondriasis** (pronounced "hye-poh-kon-DRY-a-sis"), a strong, unjustified fear that one has or might get cancer, heart disease, AIDS, or some other serious medical problem. In some ways, hypochondriasis is like an anxiety disorder in that it includes elements of phobia, panic, and obsessive-compulsive disorder. Some people with hypochondriasis fear that they will contract a terrible disease; the majority are convinced that they already have one. The fear prompts frequent visits to doctors and reports of numerous symptoms. Their preoccupation with illness often leads people with hypochondriasis to become "experts" on their most feared diseases, sometimes by endlessly searching health-related Internet websites (Taylor & Asmundson, 2008). In a related condition called **somatization disorder,** individuals make dramatic but vague reports about a multitude of physical problems rather than any specific illness. **Somatoform pain disorder** is marked by complaints of severe, often constant pain (typically in the neck, chest, or back) with no physical cause. In **body dysmorphic disorder,** the person is intensely distressed about an imagined abnormality of the skin, hair, face, or other bodily area. They may become preoccupied with the imagined deformity or imperfection, avoid social contacts, become dysfunctional, and even seek unnecessary corrective surgery (Veale, 2009).

hypochondriasis   A strong, unjustified fear of physical illness.

somatization disorder   A psychological problem in which a person has numerous physical complaints without verifiable physical illness.

somatoform pain disorder   A somatoform disorder marked by complaints of severe, often constant pain with no physical cause.

body dysmorphic disorder   A somatoform disorder characterized by intense distress over imagined abnormalities of the skin, hair, face, or other areas of the body.

A number of biological, psychological, and social factors have been suggested as contributing to somatoform disorders. Some cases, for example, may be related to childhood experiences in which a person learns that symptoms of physical illness bring special attention and care (Abramowitz & Braddock, 2006; Barsky et al., 1994). Others, including conversion disorder, may be triggered by severe stressors (Ballmaier & Schmidt, 2005; Ovsiew, 2006; Spiegel, 1994). Cognitive factors come into play, too. When given information about their health, people who display hypochondriasis are strongly biased to focus on threat-confirming information but to ignore reassuring information (Eifert, Zvolensky, & Louis, 2008). Abnormal serotonin functioning has also been associated with hypochondriasis, and various combinations of neurochemical and social skill deficits appear to accompany conversion disorder and body dysmorphic disorder (Brodino et al., 2008; Eifert, Zvolensky, & Louis, 2008).

Based on such findings, many researchers have adopted a diathesis-stress approach to explaining somatoform disorders. The results of their work suggest that certain people may have biological and psychological traits that make them especially vulnerable to somatoform disorders, particularly when combined with a history of physical illness. Among these traits are self-consciousness and oversensitivity to physical sensations. If such people experience a number of long-lasting stressors, intense emotional conflicts, or severe traumas, they are more likely than others to display physical symptoms in association with negative emotional arousal.

Sociocultural factors may also shape some somatoform disorders. In many Asian, Latin American, and African cultures, it is not unusual for people to experience severe headaches and other physical symptoms in association with psychological or interpersonal conflicts. In North America such conflicts are more likely to be accompanied by anxiety or depression (Brislin, 1993). Genetic factors appear to play only a minor role in somatoform disorders.

Dissociative Disorders

▶ *What disorders create sudden memory loss?*

Have you ever been driving all day on a boring highway and suddenly realized that you had almost no memory of what happened during the past half-hour? This common experience does not signal a mental disorder, but when disruptions in a person's memory, consciousness, or identity are more intense and long-lasting, they are known as **dissociative disorders.** These disruptions can come on gradually, but they usually occur suddenly and last from a few hours to many years. Consider the case of John, a 30-year-old computer executive. When his wife announced that she was leaving him to live with his younger brother, John did not go to work the next day. In fact, his whereabouts were unknown until two weeks later, when he was arrested for public drunkenness and assault in a city more than 300 miles away. The police discovered that during those two weeks, John had lived under a different name at a cheap hotel and worked selling tickets at a pornographic movie theater. He did not know his real name or his home address, couldn't explain how he got to his new location, and could not remember much about the previous two weeks.

John displayed a disorder known as a **fugue reaction** or **dissociative fugue** (pronounced "fewg"), a sudden loss of personal memory and the adoption of a new identity in a new place. A related disorder called **dissociative amnesia** also involves sudden loss of memory about personal information but the person does not leave home or create a new identity. These conditions are rare, but they tend to attract intense publicity because they are so dramatic.

The most famous dissociative disorder is **dissociative identity disorder (DID),** known in earlier editions of the *DSM* (and still commonly called) *multiple personality disorder (MPD)*. A person with DID appears to have more than one identity, each

dissociative disorders Conditions involving sudden and usually temporary disruptions in a person's memory, consciousness, or identity.

fugue reaction (dissociative fugue) A psychological disorder involving sudden loss of memory and the assumption of a new identity in a new locale.

dissociative amnesia A psychological disorder marked by a sudden loss of memory for one's own name, occupation, or other identifying information.

dissociative identity disorder (DID) A dissociative disorder in which a person appears to have more than one identity, each of which behaves in a different way.

"Would it be possible to speak with the personality that pays the bills?"

▲ Debate and skepticism about the nature and origins of dissociative identity disorder are not confined to professional journals. This drawing appeared in *The New Yorker* magazine.

of which speaks and acts in a different way. Each personality seems to have its own memories, wishes, and (often conflicting) impulses. Here is a case example:

> *Mary, a pleasant and introverted 35-year-old social worker, was referred to a psychiatrist for hypnotic treatment of chronic pain. At an early interview she mentioned the odd fact that though she had no memory of using her car after coming home from work, she often found that it had been driven 50 to 100 miles overnight. It turned out that she also had no memory of large parts of her childhood. Mary rapidly learned self-hypnosis for pain control, but during one hypnotic session, she suddenly began speaking in a hostile manner. She told the doctor her name was Marian and that it was "she" who had been taking long evening drives. She also called Mary "pathetic" for "wasting time" trying to please other people. Eventually, six other identities emerged, some of whom told of having experienced parental abuse in childhood. (Spitzer et al., 1994)*

There is a great deal of controversy over how dissociative disorders develop. Psychodynamic theorists see massive repression of traumatic events as the basis for creating "new personalities" who act out otherwise unacceptable impulses or recall otherwise unbearable memories (Maldonado & Spiegel, 2008; Ross, 1997). Social-cognitive theorists focus on the fact that everyone is capable of behaving in different ways depending on circumstances (e.g., rowdy in a bar, quiet in a museum). In rare cases, they say, this variation can become so extreme that a person feels like and is perceived by others as a "different person." Further, sudden memory loss or unusual behavior may be rewarded if they allow a person to escape unpleasant situations, responsibilities, or punishment for misbehavior (Lilienfeld & Lynn, 2003; Lilienfeld et al., 2009).

Evaluating these hypotheses has been difficult, partly because dissociative disorders have been so rare. Recently, however, DID has been diagnosed more frequently, either because clinicians are looking for it more carefully or because the conditions leading to it are more widespread. Research available so far suggests four conclusions. First, memory loss and other forms of dissociation are genuine phenomena and (as seen in fugue reactions) can sometimes be extreme. Second, many people displaying DID have experienced events they would like to forget or avoid. The majority (some clinicians believe all) have suffered severe, unavoidable, persistent abuse in childhood (Foote et al., 2006; Kihlstrom, 2005). Third, like Mary, most of these people appear to be skilled at self-hypnosis, through which they can induce a trance-like dissociative state. Fourth, most found that they could escape the trauma of abuse (at least temporarily) by creating "new personalities" to deal with stress (Spiegel, 1994; van der Hart et al., 2005). However, not all abused children display DID, and there is evidence that some cases of DID may be triggered by media stories or by suggestions therapists have made to clients (Lindsay et al., 2004; McHugh, 2009).

This evidence has led some skeptics to question the existence of multiple personalities (Acocella, 1998; Merckelbach, Devilly, & Rassin, 2002). Others suggest that the increased incidence of dissociative identity disorder may simply reflect its status as a culturally approved method of expressing distress (Hacking, 1995; Spanos, 1994). In fact, concerns such as these were partly responsible for the change in designation in the *DSM* from *multiple personality disorder* to *dissociative identity disorder*. The authors of *DSM-IV* wanted to downplay the idea that people harbor multiple personalities that can easily be "contacted" through hypnosis or related techniques. The new name was chosen to suggest, instead, that dissociation, or separation, between one's memories and other aspects of identity can be so dramatic that people experiencing it may come to believe that they have more than one personality (Gleaves, May, & Cardena, 2001; Kong, Allen, & Gilsky, 2008; Spiegel, 1994). They point to research showing, for example, that people who display DID may be more aware than they think they are of the memories and actions of each apparent identity (Allen, 2002; Allen & Iacono, 2001; Canaris, 2008).

Research on the existence and effects of repressed memories (discussed in the memory chapter) is sure to have an impact on our understanding of (and the controversy over) the causes of dissociative identity disorder. ("In Review: Anxiety, Somatoform, and Dissociative Disorders" presents a summary of our discussion of these topics.)

In Review

ANXIETY, SOMATOFORM, AND DISSOCIATIVE DISORDERS

DISORDER	SUBTYPES	MAJOR SYMPTOMS
Anxiety disorders	Phobias	Intense, irrational fear of objectively nondangerous situations or things leading to disruptions of behavior.
	Generalized anxiety disorder	Excessive anxiety not focused on a specific situation or object; free-floating anxiety.
	Panic disorder	Repeated attacks of intense fear involving physical symptoms such as faintness, dizziness, and nausea.
	Obsessive-compulsive disorder	Persistent ideas or worries accompanied by ritualistic behaviors performed to neutralize anxiety-driven thoughts.
Somatoform disorders	Conversion disorder	A loss of physical ability (e.g., sight, hearing) that is related to psychological factors.
	Hypochondriasis	Preoccupation with or belief that one has serious illness in the absence of any physical evidence.
	Somatization disorder	Wide variety of somatic complaints that occur over several years and are not the result of a known physical disorder.
	Somatoform pain disorder	Preoccupation with pain in the absence of physical reasons for the pain.
Dissociative disorders	Dissociative amnesia Fugue reaction (dissociative fugue)	Sudden, unexpected loss of memory that may result in a person relocating and assuming a new identity.
	Dissociative identity disorder (multiple personality disorder)	Appearance within the same person of two or more distinct identities, each with a unique way of thinking and behaving.

1. *Concern that it may be triggered by media stories or therapists' suggestions has made _____ the most controversial of the dissociative disorders.*

2. *A person who sleepwalks but is not able to walk when awake is showing signs of _____.*

3. *Panic disorder sometimes leads to another anxiety disorder called _____.*

Affective Disorders

▶ *How common is depression?*

Everyone's mood, or *affect*, tends to rise and fall from time to time. However, when people experience long periods of extreme moods such as wild elation or deep depression, when they shift from one extreme to another, and especially when their moods are not consistent with the events around them, they are said to show an **affective disorder** (also called a **mood disorder**). We describe two main types: depressive disorders and bipolar disorders.

Depressive Disorders

Depression can range from occasional, normal "down" periods to episodes severe enough to require hospitalization. A person suffering **major depression** (also called **major depressive disorder**) feels sad and overwhelmed for weeks or months, typically losing interest in activities and relationships and taking pleasure in nothing (Coryell et al., 1993; Getzfeld, 2006; Rapaport et al., 2005; Sloan, Strauss, & Wisner, 2001). Exaggerated feelings of inadequacy, worthlessness, hopelessness, or guilt are common.

affective disorder (mood disorder)
A condition in which a person experiences extremes of moods for long periods, shifts from one extreme mood to another, and experiences moods that are inconsistent with events.

major depression (major depressive disorder)   A condition in which a person feels sad and hopeless for weeks or months, often losing interest in all activities and taking pleasure in nothing.

Despite the person's best efforts, anything from conversation to bathing can become an unbearable, exhausting task. Changes in eating habits resulting in weight loss or weight gain often accompany major depression. There may also be disturbed sleeping or excessive sleeping. Problems in working, concentrating, making decisions, and thinking clearly are also common, as are symptoms of an accompanying anxiety disorder (Andreescu et al., 2007; Zimmerman, McDermut, & Mattia, 2000). In extreme cases, depressed people may express false beliefs, or **delusions,** worrying, for example, that government agents are planning to punish them. Major depression may come on suddenly or gradually. It may consist of a single episode, but it more commonly appears in repeated depressive periods. Here is a case example:

> *Mr. J. was a fifty-one-year-old industrial engineer. . . . Since the death of his wife five years earlier, he had been suffering from continuing episodes of depression marked by extreme social withdrawal and occasional thoughts of suicide. . . . He drank, and when thoroughly intoxicated would plead to his deceased wife for forgiveness. He lost all capacity for joy. . . . Once a gourmet, he now had no interest in food and good wine. . . and could barely manage to engage in small talk. As might be expected, his work record deteriorated markedly. Appointments were missed and projects haphazardly started and left unfinished. (Davison & Neale, 1990, p. 221)*

Depression is not always so extreme. In a less severe pattern of depression, called **dysthymic disorder,** the person shows the sad mood, lack of interest, and loss of pleasure associated with major depression but less intensely and for a longer period. (The duration must be at least two years to qualify as dysthymic disorder.) Mental and behavioral disruptions are also less severe. People exhibiting dysthymic disorder rarely require hospitalization.

Major depression occurs at some time in the lives of about 17 percent of people in North America and Europe; in any given year, about 9.5 percent of these populations are experiencing the disorder (Edwards & Glick, 2008; Hasin et al., 2005; Kessler, Chiu et al., 2005). Unfortunately, depression is becoming more common, both in the United States and elsewhere. The World Health Organization estimates that if current trends continue, depression will become the second leading cause of disability and premature death in developed economies (Moussavi et al., 2007; World Health Organization Mental Health Survey Consortium, 2004). The incidence of the disorder varies considerably across cultures and subcultures, however. For example, it occurs at much higher rates in urban Ireland than in urban Spain (Judd et al., 2002). There are gender differences in some cultures, too. North American and European women are two to three times more likely than men to experience major depression (Kessler, Chiu et al., 2005), but this difference does not appear in the less economically developed countries of the Middle East, Africa, and Asia (Ayuso-Mateos et al., 2001; Culbertson, 1997). Depression can occur at any age, but it peaks in late adolescence to young adulthood and again during old age (Cross-National Collaborative Group, 2002; Durand & Barlow, 2006; Fassler & Dumas, 1997; Sowdon, 2001).

Suicide and Depression Suicide is associated with a variety of psychological disorders, but it is most closely tied to depression and other affective disorders (Balázs et al., 2006). In fact, thinking about suicide is a symptom of depressive disorders. When suicidal thoughts combine with hopelessness about the future, which is another depressive symptom, a suicide attempt is much more likely to occur. Indeed, the rate of suicide among those with major depression is 3.4 percent overall, but 7 percent for males and as high as 15 percent for those who have been hospitalized for depression (Brown et al., 2000; Dawe, 2008).

About 33,000 people in the United States commit suicide each year, or about one every 17 minutes, and ten to twenty times that many people attempt it (Centers for Disease Control and Prevention, 2004; Dawe, 2008). This puts the U.S. suicide rate at about 11 per 100,000 individuals, making suicide the eleventh leading cause of death. Worldwide, the suicide rate is as high as 25 per 100,000 in some northern European countries, China, and Japan and as low as 6 per 100,000 in countries with stronger

delusions False beliefs, such as those experienced by people suffering from schizophrenia or severe depression.

dysthymic disorder A pattern of depression in which the person shows the sad mood, lack of interest, and loss of pleasure associated with major depression but to a lesser degree and for a longer period.

religious prohibitions against suicide, such as Greece, Italy, Ireland, and the nations of the Middle East (Lamar, 2000; Ono et al., 2008; Phillips, Li, & Zhang, 2002; World Health Organization, 2003).

Suicide rates differ considerably depending on sociocultural factors such as age, gender, and ethnicity (Centers for Disease Control and Prevention, 2002b; Oquendo et al., 2001). In the United States, suicide is most common among people 65 and older, especially males (Centers for Disease Control and Prevention, 2004). However, since 1950, suicide among adolescents has tripled. And though the rate has begun to level off in the last decade (Centers for Disease Control and Prevention, 2006), it is still the third leading cause of death, after accidents and homicides, among 15- to 24-year-olds (Centers for Disease Control and Prevention, 2002a, 2006). Suicide is the second leading cause of death among college students; about 10,000 try to kill themselves each year and about 1,000 actually do so. These figures are much higher than for young people in general but much lower than for the elderly. Women attempt suicide three times as often as men, but men are four times as likely to actually kill themselves (Centers for Disease Control and Prevention, 2006). The gender difference is even greater among people who have been diagnosed with depression. In this group, the male suicide rate of 65 per 100,000 is ten times higher than the rate for women (Blair-West et al., 1999; Centers for Disease Control and Prevention, 1999b). The suicide rate for men who are 85 or older is 55 per 100,000; which is more than ten times higher than for women in this age group (Centers for Disease Control and Prevention, 2004).

Suicide rates also differ across ethnic groups (see Figure 12.4). Among males in the United States, for example, the overall rate for American Indians is 19.1 per 100,000, compared with 19.4 for European Americans, 9.7 for Asian Americans, 10.7 for Hispanic Americans, and 10.4 for African Americans. The same pattern of ethnic differences appears among women, though the actual rates are much lower (Centers for Disease Control and Prevention, 2002a).

Surveys indicate that at some time in their lives, about 14 percent of persons will have suicidal thoughts and that at sometime during the previous year, about 3 percent of all adults and as many as 10 percent of college students will have thought about committing suicide (Brener, Hassan, & Barrios, 1999; Dawe, 2008; Kessler, Berglund, Borges et al., 2005). Predicting who will actually do so is difficult, but the results of hundreds of research studies provide some guidance. In the United States, at least,

FIGURE 12.4   ■   SUICIDE RATES BY GENDER AND ETHNICITY

The suicide rates among ethnic groups in the United States vary widely. In 2002, more teenagers and young adults died from suicide than from cancer, heart disease, AIDS, birth defects, stroke, pneumonia and influenza, and chronic lung disease *combined* (National Center for Health Statistics, 2004).
Source: Centers for Disease Control and Prevention (2002b).

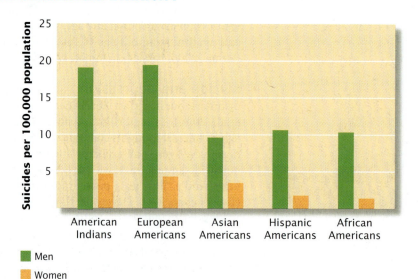

suicide is most likely among European American males, especially those who are older than 45, single or divorced, and living alone. Extended unemployment increases the suicide risk for this group (Joska & Stein, 2008; Inoue et al., 2006). The risk is also heightened among people diagnosed with an affective disorder, anxiety disorder, or schizophrenia (Boardman & Healy, 2001; Khan et al., 2002; Rihmer, 2001). Among the elderly, suicide is most common in males who suffer depression over health problems (e.g., Brown, Bongar, & Cleary, 2004). The risk is higher, too, in people who have made a specific plan, given away possessions, and are impulsive (Centers for Disease Control and Prevention, 2004; Corruble, Damy, & Guelfi, 1999). A previous suicide attempt may not always be a good predictor of eventual suicide, because such attempts may have been help-seeking gestures, not failed efforts to die (Nock & Kessler, 2006). In fact, although about 10 percent of unsuccessful attempters try again and succeed, most people who commit suicide had made no prior attempts (Clark & Fawcett, 1992).

It is often said that people who talk about suicide will never try it. This is a myth (Shneidman, 1987). Those who say they are thinking of suicide are much more likely than other people to try suicide. In fact, most suicides are preceded by some kind of warning, whether direct ("I think I'm going to kill myself") or vague ("Sometimes I wonder if life is worth living"). Failure to recognize or respond to warning signs is a common phenomenon (Valuck et al., 2007). So although not everyone who threatens suicide follows through, if you suspect that someone you know is thinking about suicide, encourage the person to contact a mental health professional or a crisis hotline. If the danger is immediate, make the contact yourself and ask for advice about how to respond. Many suicide attempts—including those triggered by other suicides in the same town or school—can be prevented by social support and other forms of help for people at high risk (Centers for Disease Control and Prevention, 2004; Mann et al., 2005). For more information, visit suicide-related websites, such as that of the American Association of Suicidology (www.suicidology.org).

Bipolar Disorders

The alternating appearance of two emotional extremes, or poles, characterizes the **bipolar disorders.** In these disorders, episodes of depression alternate with **mania,** which is an extremely agitated and usually elated emotional state. During periods of mania, people tend to be overly optimistic, boundlessly energetic, certain of having extraordinary powers and abilities, and bursting with all sorts of ideas. They are irritated by anyone who tries to reason with them or "slow them down," and they may make impulsive and unwise decisions, including spending their life savings on foolish schemes; they can even become a danger to themselves or to others (Goldberg & Burdick, 2008; Kessler, Berglund, & Demier et al., 2005; National Institute of Mental Health, 2006).

There are two versions of bipolar disorder, known as bipolar I and bipolar II. In *bipolar I disorder,* episodes of mania may alternate with periods of deep depression (Ghaemi, 2008). Sometimes periods of relatively normal mood separate these extremes (Tohen et al., 2003). This pattern has also been called *manic depression.* Compared with major depression, bipolar disorder is rare. It occurs in only about 1 percent of adults, and it affects men and women about equally. Another 1 percent of adults display *bipolar II disorder,* in which major depressive episodes alternate with episodes known as *hypomania,* which are less severe than the manic phases seen in bipolar I disorder.

Slightly more common is a pattern of milder mood swings known as **cyclothymic personality** (also called **cyclothymic disorder),** the bipolar equivalent of dysthymic disorder. Like major depression, bipolar disorders are extremely disruptive to a person's ability to work or maintain social relationships (Goldberg, Harrow, & Grossman, 1995), and they are often accompanied by anxiety disorders or substance abuse (Andreescu et al., 2007; Freeman, Freeman, & McElroy, 2002; Ghaemi, 2008). "In Review: Affective Disorders" summarizes the main types of affective disorders.

bipolar disorder A condition in which a person alternates between the two emotional extremes of depression and mania.

mania An elated, active emotional state.

cyclothymic personality (cyclothymic disorder) An affective disorder characterized by an alternating pattern of mood swings that is less extreme than that of bipolar disorder.

In Review

AFFECTIVE DISORDERS

TYPE	TYPICAL SYMPTOMS	RELATED FEATURES
Major depression (major depressive disorder)	Deep sadness, feelings of worthlessness, changes in eating and sleeping habits, loss of interest and pleasure	Lasts weeks or months; may occur in repeating episodes; severe cases may include delusions
Dysthymic disorder	Similar to major depression but less severe and longer lasting	Hospitalization usually not necessary
Bipolar disorder	Alternating extremes of mood from deep depression to mania and back	Manic episodes include impulsivity, unrealistic optimism, high energy, severe agitation
Cyclothymic personality (Cyclothymic disorder)	Similar to bipolar disorder, but less severe	Hospitalization usually not necessary

?

1. The risk of suicide is associated with _____ more than with any other symptom of disorder.
2. Cyclothymic personality is the bipolar version of _____.
3. Women are _____ likely than men to try suicide, but men are _____ likely to succeed.

Causes of Affective Disorders

Research on the causes of affective disorders has focused on biological, psychological, and sociocultural risk factors. The more of these risk factors people have, the more likely they are to experience an affective disorder.

Biological Factors   The role of genetics is well established by twin studies and family studies showing that affective disorders tend to run in families (Cho et al., 2005; Goodwin & Jamison, 2007; Hayden & Nurnberger, 2006; Kendler et al., 2006; Kieseppä et al., 2004; Weissman et al., 2005). For example, bipolar disorder is much more likely to be seen in both members of genetically identical twin pairs than in genetically nonidentical twins (Smoller, 2008). Family studies also show that those who are closely related to people with bipolar disorder are more likely than others to develop the disorder themselves (Althoff et al., 2005; Serretti et al., 2009). Major depression, too, is more likely to occur in both members of identical twins than in both members of nonidentical twins (Klein et al., 2001; Levinson, 2006). Findings such as these suggest that genetic influences tend to be stronger for affective disorders (especially for bipolar I disorder and severe, early-onset depression) than for most other disorders. And researchers have already identified certain genetic variations that affect vulnerability to affective disorders (Detera-Wadleigh & McMahon, 2004; Hariri et al., 2005; Jacobs et al., 2006; Joska & Stein, 2008; Smoller, 2008; Wilhelm et al., 2006). Still, it is important to recognize that genetic variations alone probably do not cause affective disorders. Rather, genes appear to act in combination with other biological, psychological, and environmental factors. Researchers in the field of epigenetics are investigating how genes associated with affective disorders can be "turned on" or "turned off" by these psychological and environmental factors (Butcher, Mineka, & Hooley, 2010; Levinson et al., 2007).

linkages

Are some psychological disorders inherited? *(a link to Biology and Behavior)*

Other biological factors that may contribute to affective disorders include structural abnormalities or malfunctions in regions of the brain involved in mood, imbalances in the brain's neurotransmitter systems, malfunctioning of the endocrine system, disruption of biological rhythms, and underdevelopment in the frontal lobes, hippocampus, or other brain areas (Blumberg et al., 2003; Butcher et al., 2010; Geuze, Vermetten, & Bremner, 2005; Jacobs, 2004; Jans et al., 2007; MacQueen et al., 2005; Milak et al., 2005; Munn et al., 2007; Shankman et al., 2007; Staley et al., 2006; Strakowski, DelBello, & Adler, 2005). All of these conditions may themselves be influenced by genetics.

As for the role of neurotransmitters, decades ago norepinephrine, serotonin, and dopamine were implicated when scientists discovered that drugs capable of altering these substances also relieved affective disorders. However, the precise nature of the relationship between neurotransmitters and affective disorders is still not fully understood (Martinot et al., 2001; Schloss & Williams, 1998; U.S. Surgeon General, 1999).

Affective disorders have also been related to malfunctions of the endocrine system, especially the subsystem involved in the body's responses to stress (see the chapter on health, stress, and coping). For example, research shows that as many as 70 percent of depressed people secrete abnormally high levels of the stress hormone cortisol (Dinan, 2001; Posener et al., 2000). Studies of identical twins also suggest that higher levels of cortisol are associated with depression (Dinan, 2001; Wichers et al., 2008).

The cycles of mood swings seen in bipolar disorders and in recurring episodes of major depression suggest that affective disorders may be related to stressful triggering events (Miklowitz & Alloy, 1999). They may also be related to disturbances in the body's biological clock, which is described in the chapter on biology and behavior (Goodwin & Jamison, 1990; Monteleone & Maj, 2008). This second possibility seems especially likely to apply to the 15 percent of depressed people who consistently experience a calendar-linked pattern of depressive episodes known as *seasonal affective disorder (SAD)*. During months of shorter daylight, these people slip into severe depression, accompanied by irritability and excessive sleeping (Durand & Barlow, 2006). Their depression tends to lift as daylight hours increase (Faedda et al., 1993). Disruption of biological rhythms is also suggested by the fact that many depressed people tend to have trouble sleeping, partly because during the day their biological clocks may be telling them it is the middle of the night. Resetting the biological clock through methods such as sleep deprivation or light stimulation has relieved depression in many cases (Golden et al., 2005; Lewy et al., 2006; Terman et al., 2001).

TREATING SAD ▶

Seasonal affective disorder (SAD) can often be relieved by exposure to full-spectrum light for as little as a couple of hours a day (Terman & Terman, 2005).

© Dan McCoy/Rainbow

Psychological and Social Factors   Researchers have come to recognize that the biological factors involved in affective disorders always operate in combination with psychological and social factors (Jacobs, 2004). As mentioned earlier, the very nature of depressive symptoms can depend on the culture in which a person lives. Biopsychosocial explanations for affective disorders also emphasize the impact of anxiety, negative thinking; other psychological and emotional responses triggered by stressful events such as trauma; and the impact of cultural factors (Kendler, Hettema et al., 2003; Kendler, Kuhn, & Prescott, 2004; Rice et al., 2006; Steunenberg et al., 2006). For example, the higher rate of depression among females—especially among poor ethnic-minority single mothers—has been attributed to their greater exposure to stressors of all kinds (Brown & Moran, 1997; Miranda & Green, 1999; Nolen-Hoeksema, 2006; Whiffen, 2006). Environmental stressors affect men, too (Bierut et al., 1999), which may be one reason that gender differences are smaller in countries in which men and women face equally stressful lives. Still, differing stressors may not be the only source of these gender differences (Kendler, Thornton, & Prescott, 2001).

A number of social-cognitive theories suggest that the way people think about their stressors can increase or decrease the likelihood of affective disorders. One of these theories is based on the *learned helplessness* research described in the chapter on learning. Just as animals become inactive and appear depressed when they have no control over negative events (El Yacoubi et al., 2003), humans may experience depression as a result of feeling incapable of controlling their lives, especially the stressors confronting them (Alloy et al., 2008; Klein & Seligman, 1976; Seligman, 1991). But most of us have limited control, so why aren't we all depressed? The ways that people learn to think about events in their lives may hold the key. For example, Aaron Beck's (1967, 1976, 2008) cognitive theory of depression suggests that depressed people develop mental habits of (1) blaming themselves when things go wrong; (2) focusing on and exaggerating the negative side of events; and (3) jumping to overly generalized, pessimistic conclusions. Such cognitive habits, says Beck, are errors that lead to depressing thoughts and other symptoms of depression (Beck & Beck, 1995). Depressed people, in fact, do tend to think about significant negative events in ways that are likely to increase or prolong their depression (Gotlib & Hammen, 1992; Gotlib et al., 2004; Strunk, Lopez, & DeRubeis, 2006).

Severe, long-lasting depression is especially likely among people who blame their lack of control or other problems on a permanent, generalized lack of personal competence rather than on a temporary mistake or some external cause (Seligman et al., 1988). This *negative attributional style* may be another important cognitive factor in depression (Alloy et al., 2006; Ball et al., 2008; Hankin, Fraley, & Abela, 2005; Hunt & Forand, 2005). Are depressed people's unusually negative beliefs about themselves actually helping cause their depression or are they merely symptoms of it? A number of studies have assessed the attributional styles of large samples of nondepressed people and then kept in touch with them to see whether individuals with negative self-beliefs are more likely to become depressed when stressors occur. These longitudinal studies suggest that a negative attributional style is, in fact, a risk factor for depression, not just a result of being depressed (Alloy et al., 2006; Evans et al., 2005; Keenan et al., 2008). In one study, for example, adolescents who held strong negative self-beliefs were more likely than other youngsters to develop depression when faced with stress later in life (Lewinsohn, Joiner, & Rohde, 2001).

Social-cognitive theorists also suggest that whether depression continues or worsens depends in part on how people respond once they start to feel depressed. Those who continuously think about negative events, about why they occur, and even about being depressed are likely to feel more and more depressed (Just & Alloy, 1997; McMurrich & Johnson, 2008; Rimes & Watkins, 2005; Sarin, Abela, & Auerbach, 2005). According to Susan Nolen-Hoeksema (1990, 2001), this *ruminative style* is especially characteristic of women and may help explain gender differences in the frequency of depression. When men start to feel sad, she says, they tend to use a *distracting style*. In other words, they engage in activity that distracts them from their concerns and helps bring them out of their depressed mood (Hankin & Abramson, 2001; Just & Alloy, 1997; Nolen-Hoeksema, Morrow, & Frederickson, 1993).

Notice that social-cognitive explanations of depression are consistent with the diathesis-stress model's explanation of disorder (Hankin & Abramson, 2001). These explanations suggest that certain cognitive styles serve as a predisposition (or diathesis) that makes a person vulnerable to depression, which is made even more likely by stressors. As suggested in the chapter on health, stress, and coping, the depressing effects of these stressors are likely to be magnified by lack of social support, inadequate coping skills, and the presence of other stressful conditions, such as poverty (e.g., Belik et al., 2007; Stice, Ragan, & Randall, 2004).

Given the number and complexity of biological, psychological, social, and situational factors potentially involved in causing affective disorders, the diathesis-stress approach appears to be an especially appropriate guide to future research (Kendler, Gardner, & Prescott, 2006). Indeed, researchers are attempting to integrate the various factors into predictive and causal models. For instance, Kenneth Kendler and his colleagues have described specific sets of risk factors for depression in women that appear at five developmental stages, including childhood, early adolescence, late adolescence, adulthood, and in the year preceding the diagnosis of depression (Kendler, Gardner, & Prescott, 2006). Aaron Beck, too, has begun to sketch out how genetic and neurochemical pathways might interact with cognitive variables to promote and maintain depression (Beck, 2008). Others are attempting to integrate the vast amount of research on how cognitive variables influence the development and maintenance of bipolar disorder (Goldberg & Burdick, 2008). In the final analysis, it may turn out that each subtype of affective disorder is caused by a unique combination of factors. The challenge for researchers is to identify these subtypes and map out their causal ingredients.

Schizophrenia

 Is schizophrenia the same as "split personality"?

Here is part of a letter that arrived in the mail several years ago:

> *Dear Sirs:*
> *Pertaining to our continuing failure to prosecute violations of minor's rights to sovereign equality which are occurring in gestations being compromised by the ingestation of controlled substances, . . . the skewing of androgyny which continues in female juveniles even after separation from their mother's has occurred, and as a means of promulflagitating my paying Governor Hickel of Alaska for my employees to have personal services endorsements and controlled substance endorsements, . . . the Iraqi oil being released by the United Nations being identified as Kurdistanian oil, and the July, 1991 issue of the Siberian Review spells President Eltsin's name without a letter y.*

The disorganization and strange content of this letter suggest that its writer might be displaying **schizophrenia** (pronounced "skit-so-FREE-nee-uh"), a pattern of severely disturbed thinking, emotion, perception, and behavior that seriously impairs the ability to communicate and relate to others and disrupts most other aspects of daily functioning (Freedman, 2003). Schizophrenia is one of the most severe and disabling of all mental disorders. Its core symptoms are seen virtually everywhere in the world, in about 1 to 2 percent of the population (American Psychiatric Association, 2000; National Institute of Mental Health, 2006). In the United States, it appears about equally in various ethnic groups, but like most disorders, it tends to be diagnosed more frequently in economically disadvantaged populations. Schizophrenia is seen about equally in men and women, although in women it may appear later in life, be less severe, and respond better to treatment (Aleman, Kahn, & Selten, 2003; American Psychiatric Association, 2000).

Schizophrenia tends to develop in adolescence or early adulthood. In about three out of four cases, symptoms appear gradually over a period of years; in other cases, the onset is more rapid. Longitudinal studies suggest that about 40 percent of people diagnosed with schizophrenia improve with treatment and are able to function reasonably well; the

schizophrenia A pattern of severely disturbed thinking, emotion, perception, and behavior that constitutes one of the most serious and disabling of all mental disorders.

rest continue to display symptoms that permanently impair their functioning (Harrow & Jobe, 2005). It has been estimated that 10 to 13 percent of homeless individuals suffer from schizophrenia (Fischer & Breakey, 1991; Olfson et al., 1999; Timms, 2005).

One of the best predictors of the outcome of schizophrenia is *premorbid adjustment,* the level of functioning a person had achieved before schizophrenia symptoms first appeared. Improvement is more likely in those who had reached higher levels of education and occupation and who had established supportive relationships with family and friends (Keshaven et al., 2005; Rabinowitz et al., 2002).

Symptoms of Schizophrenia

The main problems seen in people displaying schizophrenia relate to thinking—both how they think and what they think (Heinrichs, 2005). Indeed, the very word *schizophrenia,* or "split mind," refers to the oddities of schizophrenic thinking, including a splitting of normally integrated mental processes, such as thoughts and feelings. So the person may giggle while talking about sad events and claiming to feel unhappy. Contrary to common usage, schizophrenia does not refer to the "split personality" seen in dissociative identity disorder (multiple personality disorder), discussed earlier in this chapter.

Schizophrenic thought and language are often disorganized. *Neologisms,* or new words, that in schizophrenia are usually nonsensical and have meaning only to the person speaking them, are common. The word "promulflagitating" in the preceding letter is one example. That letter also illustrates *loose associations,* the tendency for one thought to be logically unconnected or only loosely connected to the next. In the most severe cases, thought becomes just a jumble known as *word salad.* For example, one patient was heard to say, "Upon the advisability of held keeping, environment of the seabeach gathering, to the forest stream, reinstatement to be placed, poling the paddleboat, of the swamp morass, to the forest compensation of the dunce" (Lehman, 1967, p. 627).

The content of schizophrenic thinking is also disturbed. Often it includes a bewildering assortment of *delusions* (false beliefs), especially *delusions of persecution.* Some patients believe that space aliens or government agents are trying to steal their internal organs, and they may interpret everything from TV commercials to casual hand gestures as part of the plot. Delusions that such common events are somehow related to oneself are called *ideas of reference. Delusions of grandeur* may also appear; one young man was convinced that the president of the United States was trying to contact him for advice. Other types of delusions include (1) *thought broadcasting,* in which patients believe that their thoughts can be heard by others; (2) *thought blocking* or *thought withdrawal,* the belief that someone is either preventing thoughts or "stealing" them as they appear; and (3) *thought insertion,* the belief that other people's thoughts are appearing in one's own mind. Some patients believe that their behavior is being controlled by others; in one case, a man claimed that the CIA had placed a control device in his brain. Such delusions tend to be deeply entrenched and resistant to change, no matter how strong the evidence against them (Minzenberg et al., 2008; Woodward et al., 2006).

Hallucinations, or false perceptions, are common in schizophrenia, often emerging as voices. These voices may sound like an overheard conversation or they may urge the person to do or not to do things. Sometimes they comment on, narrate, or (most often) criticize the person's actions. Hallucinations can also involve the experience of nonexistent sights, smells, tastes, and touch sensations. The brain areas activated during hallucinations are related to those that respond to real sights and sounds (Alerman & Larøi, 2008; Shergill et al., 2000).

People with schizophrenia often report that they cannot focus their attention. They may feel overwhelmed by stimulation as they try to attend to everything at once. Various perceptual disorders may also appear. The person may feel detached from the world and see other people as flat cutouts. The body may feel like a machine or parts of it may seem to be dead or rotting. Emotional expression is often muted—a pattern called *flat affect.* But when schizophrenics do display emotion, it is often exaggerated or inappropriate. For example, they may cry for no apparent reason or fly into a rage in response to a simple question.

linkages

Do people perceive hallucinations as real sensory events? *(a link to Sensation and Perception)*

hallucinations False or distorted perceptions of objects or events.

Some people with schizophrenia are quite agitated, constantly fidgeting, grimacing, or pacing the floor in ritualized patterns. Others become so withdrawn that they move very little. Lack of motivation and poor social skills, deteriorating personal hygiene, and an inability to function in everyday situations are other common characteristics of schizophrenia.

Categorizing Schizophrenia

The *DSM-IV* lists five major subtypes of schizophrenia: paranoid, disorganized, catatonic, undifferentiated, and residual. These subtypes are summarized in Table 12.4.

Researchers have also made other useful distinctions among various forms of schizophrenia. One of these distinctions involves the presence of positive vs. negative symptoms. Disorganized thoughts, delusions, and hallucinations are sometimes called *positive symptoms* of schizophrenia, because they appear as undesirable *additions* to a person's mental life (Iancu et al., 2005; Racenstein et al., 2002). In contrast, the absence of pleasure and motivation, lack of emotion, social withdrawal, reduced speech, and other deficits seen in schizophrenia are sometimes called *negative symptoms,* because they appear to *subtract* elements from normal mental life (Batki et al., 2008; Nicholson & Neufeld, 1993). Many patients exhibit both positive and negative symptoms, but when the negative symptoms are stronger, schizophrenia generally has a more severe course, including long-term disability and relative lack of response to treatment (e.g., Milev et al., 2005; Prikryl et al., 2006; Racenstein et al., 2002). Yet another way of categorizing schizophrenic symptoms focuses on whether they are *psychotic* (e.g., hallucinations or delusions), *disorganized* (e.g., incoherent speech, chaotic behavior, or inappropriate affect), or *negative* (e.g., lack of speech or motivation). The fact that, like positive and negative symptoms, these dimensions of schizophrenia are to some extent independent from one another suggests to some researchers that each symptom cluster or dimension may ultimately be traceable to different causes. For this reason, schizophrenia is often referred to as the *schizophrenia spectrum,* in recognition of the fact that each cluster may develop differently and require different treatments (Tsuang, Stone, & Faraone, 2000). The schizophrenia spectrum also includes other diagnoses that share features with schizophrenia. For example, people diagnosed with *schizoaffective disorder* show symptoms of both schizophrenia and depression. *Schizophreniform disorder* is characterized by schizophrenia-like symptoms that do not last as long as those typically seen in schizophrenia.

TABLE 12.4 ■ SUBTYPES OF SCHIZOPHRENIA

These traditional categories of schizophrenia convey some useful information, but subtype labels are not always accurate. Some symptoms of schizophrenia appear in more than one subtype, and people first placed in one subtype might later display characteristics of another. These concerns, plus the fact that subtypes in the *DSM-IV* may not be linked to different causal factors, have led researchers to develop additional ways of categorizing schizophrenia, such as whether positive or negative symptoms are most prominent in a given case (Villalta-Gil et al., 2006).

Type	Frequency	Prominent Features
Paranoid schizophrenia	40 percent of people with schizophrenia; appears late in life (after age 25–30)	Delusions of grandeur or persecution; anger; anxiety; argumentativeness; extreme jealousy; onset often sudden; signs of impairment may be subtle
Disorganized schizophrenia	5 percent of all people with schizophrenia; high prevalence in homeless population	Delusions, hallucinations, incoherent speech, facial grimaces, inappropriate laughter/giggling, neglected personal hygiene, loss of bladder/bowel control
Catatonic schizophrenia	8 percent of all people with schizophrenia	Disordered movement, alternating between total immobility (stupor) and wild excitement. In stupor, the person does not speak or attend to communication
Undifferentiated schizophrenia	40 percent of all people with schizophrenia	Patterns of disordered behavior, thought, and emotion that do not fall easily into any other subtype
Residual schizophrenia	Varies	Applies to people who have had prior episodes of schizophrenia but are not currently displaying symptoms

© Grunnitus/Photo Researchers, Inc.

CATATONIC STUPOR ▲

The symptoms of schizophrenia often occur in characteristic patterns. This woman's lack of motivation and other negative symptoms of schizophrenia are severe enough that she appears to be in a catatonic stupor. Such patients may become rigid or, as in this case, show a waxy flexibility that allows them to be "posed" in virtually any position. Diagnosticians using the traditional subtype system would probably label her as displaying catatonic schizophrenia.

Causes of Schizophrenia

The search for causes of schizophrenia has been more intense than for any other psychological disorder. The findings so far confirm one thing for certain: as with other disorders, biological, psychological, and sociocultural factors combine to cause or worsen all forms of schizophrenia (Sullivan, Kendler, & Neale, 2003).

Biological Factors   Research in behavioral genetics shows that schizophrenia runs in families (Asarnow et al., 2001; Dubertret et al., 2004). If one person in a family is diagnosed with schizophrenia, the risk that another family member will receive the same diagnosis increases in proportion with their genetic similarity (Kasper & Papadimitriou, 2009). Even if they are adopted by families that do not have schizophrenia, the children of parents with schizophrenia are ten times more likely to develop schizophrenia than adopted children whose biological parents do not have schizophrenia (Kety et al., 1994; Tienari et al., 2003). Still, even though identical twins have virtually identical genes, the appearance of schizophrenia in one of them does not guarantee that the other will be diagnosed as well. In fact, the rate of shared diagnosis is only about 50 percent, which suggests that genetics alone cannot explain the disorder. Further, it is unlikely that a single gene transmits schizophrenia (Minzenberg et al., 2008; Plomin & McGuffin, 2003). Rather, several genes on several chromosome pairs are probably involved. Researchers are currently focusing on genes known as the 5-HT-sub(5A) receptor gene, DTNBP1, RGS4, and a 7 neuronal nicotinic receptor subunit (CHRNA7). These genetic factors may combine with other genetic and nongenetic factors to cause the disorder (DeRosse et al., 2006; Fan et al., 2006; Law, Cotton, & Berger, 2006; Levitt et al., 2006; Vazza et al., 2007).

The search for biological factors in schizophrenia also focuses on a number of abnormalities in the structure, functioning, and chemistry of the brain that tend to appear in people with schizophrenia (e.g., Andrews et al., 2006; Neves-Pereira et al., 2005; Tamminga & Holcomb, 2005). For example, brain imaging studies have compared schizophrenia patients with other mental patients. Many patients with schizophrenia (especially those who display mostly negative symptoms) have less tissue in areas of the brain that are involved in emotional expression, thinking, and information processing—functions that are disordered in schizophrenia (Behrendt, 2006; Conklin & Iacono, 2002; Csernansky et al., 2004; Ettinger et al., 2007; Highley et al., 2003; Javitt & Kantrowitz, 2009; Selemon et al., 2003; Velakoulis et al., 2006). There is also evidence that worsening symptoms are associated with continued tissue loss in these areas (Ho et al., 2003). Patients with mainly positive symptoms tend to have essentially normal-looking brains (Andreasen, 1997).

Researchers are also investigating the possibility that abnormalities in brain chemistry—especially in neurotransmitter systems that use dopamine—play a role in causing or intensifying the symptoms of schizophrenia (Javitt & Kantrowitz, 2009; Seeman et al., 2005). Because drugs that block the brain's dopamine receptors often reduce the hallucinations, disordered thinking, and other positive symptoms of schizophrenia, some investigators speculate that schizophrenia results from excess dopamine. Other research suggests that excessive activity in dopamine systems may be related to the appearance of these positive symptoms (Buchsbaum et al., 2006; Winterer, 2006). However, the relationship between dopamine and schizophrenia may be more complex than that (Albert et al., 2002; Carlsson & Lecrubier, 2004). For example, it may be that changes in the ratio of dopamine to other neurochemicals, particularly in the region of the thalamus, are involved in the difficulties experienced by people with schizophrenia in distinguishing genuine sights and sounds from those produced by neural "noise" within the brain (Buchsbaum et al., 2006; Winterer, 2006).

Some researchers are integrating genetic and environmental explanations for schizophrenia by looking for *neurodevelopmental* abnormalities (e.g., Meyer et al., 2005; Rapoport, Addington, & Frangou, 2005). Perhaps, they say, some forms of schizophrenia arise from disruptions in brain development during the period from before birth through childhood, when the brain is growing and its various functions are maturing. For instance, prenatal exposure to physical trauma, flu, or other infections is associated with increased risk for developing schizophrenia (AbdelMalik et al., 2003; Brown et al., 2004, 2005; Malaspina et al., 2001). It may be that the expression of a genetically transmitted predisposition for brain abnormality is enhanced by environmental stressors such as maternal drug use during pregnancy, complications during birth, and childhood malnutrition (Sørenson et al., 2003; National Institute of Mental Health, 2008b). Neurodevelopmental factors may help explain why children of parents with schizophrenia tend to show cognitive and intellectual problems associated with brain abnormalities (Ashe, Berry, & Boulton, 2001; Cannon et al., 1994; McGlashan & Hoffman, 2000; Neumann et al., 1995).

Psychological and Sociocultural Factors Psychological factors alone are not considered to be primary causes of schizophrenia (Bassett et al., 2001), but psychological processes and sociocultural influences can contribute to the appearance of schizophrenia and influence its course (Kealy, 2005; Vahia & Cohen, 2009). Among the factors cited are dysfunctional cognitive habits, the stress of urban living, being an immigrant, and exposure to stressful family communication patterns (Mueser & Jeste, 2009; van Os et al., 2008). For example, individuals with schizophrenia who live with relatives who are critical, unsupportive, or emotionally overinvolved are especially likely to relapse following improvement (Hooley, 2004; Nomura et al., 2005; Rosenfarb et al., 2000; Wearden et al., 2000). Family members' negative attitudes may be a source of stress that actually increases the chances that disruptive or odd behaviors will persist or worsen (Rosenfarb et al., 1995). Keep in mind, though, that the strange and often disturbing behavior of a family member with schizophrenia can place tremendous strain on the rest of the family, making it harder for them to remain helpful and supportive (Kymalainen et al., 2006; Rosenfarb, Bellack, & Aziz, 2006). In any case, patients who are helped to cope with the potentially damaging influences we have described tend to have better long-term outcomes (Bustillo et al., 2001; Velligan et al., 2000).

Vulnerability Theory All the causal theories of schizophrenia we have outlined are consistent with the diathesis-stress approach, which assumes that stress activates a person's predisposition for disorder. ("In Review: Schizophrenia" summarizes these theories, as well as the symptoms of schizophrenia.) In fact, a diathesis-stress framework forms the basis for the *vulnerability theory* of schizophrenia (Cornblatt & Erlenmeyer-Kimling, 1985; Zubin & Spring, 1977). This theory suggests that (1) vulnerability to schizophrenia is mainly biological; (2) different people have differing degrees of vulnerability; (3) vulnerability is influenced partly by genetic influences on development and partly by abnormalities that arise from environmental risk factors; and (4) psychological components, such as exposure to poor parenting, a high-stress environment, or inadequate coping skills, may help determine whether schizophrenia actually appears and may also influence the course of the disorder (Walker & Diforio, 1998; Wearden et al., 2000).

Many different blends of vulnerability and stress can lead to schizophrenia. People whose genetic characteristics or prenatal experiences leave them vulnerable to developing schizophrenia may be especially likely to do so if they are later exposed to learning experiences, family conflicts, or other stressors that trigger and maintain schizophrenic patterns of thought and action. Those same experiences and stressors would not be expected to lead to schizophrenia in people who are less vulnerable to developing the disorder. In other words, schizophrenia is a highly complex disorder—probably more than one disorder (Kirkpatrick et al., 2001; Lenzenweger, McLachlan, & Rubin, 2007; Tsuang, Stone, & Faraone, 2000)—whose origins appear to lie in numerous biological, psychological, and sociocultural domains, some of which are yet to be discovered.

In Review

SCHIZOPHRENIA

ASPECT	KEY FEATURES
Common Symptoms	
Disorders of thought	Disturbed content, including delusions; disorganization, including loose associations, neologisms, and word salad
Disorders of perception	Hallucinations or false perceptions; poorly focused attention
Disorders of emotion	Flat affect; inappropriate tears, laughter, or anger
Possible Causes	
Biological	Genetics; abnormalities in brain structure; abnormalities in dopamine systems; neurodevelopmental problems
Psychological and sociocultural	Learned maladaptive behavior; disturbed patterns of family communication

?

1. The _____ approach forms the basis of the vulnerability theory of schizophrenia.
2. Hallucinations are _____ symptoms of schizophrenia; lack of emotion is a _____ symptom.
3. Patients with schizophrenia who were able to finish school are _____ likely to show improvement.

Personality Disorders

▶ *Which personality disorder often leads to crime?*

Personality disorders are long-standing, inflexible ways of behaving that are not so much severe mental disorders as dysfunctional styles of living (Clarkin, 2006; Shea et al., 2002). These disorders affect all areas of functioning and from childhood or adolescence on create problems for those who display them and for others (Cohen, 2008; Millon & Davis, 1996). Some psychologists view personality disorders as interpersonal strategies (Kiesler, 1996) or as extreme, rigid, and maladaptive expressions of personality traits (Widiger, 2008).

The ten personality disorders found on Axis II of the *DSM-IV* are grouped into three clusters that share certain features (see Table 12.5). The *odd-eccentric* cluster includes paranoid, schizoid, and schizotypal personality disorders. People diagnosed as having *schizotypal personality disorder,* for example, display some of the peculiarities seen in schizophrenia but are not disturbed enough to be labeled as having schizophrenia. The *anxious-fearful* cluster includes dependent, obsessive-compulsive, and avoidant personality disorders. The *avoidant personality disorder,* for example, is similar to social phobia in the sense that persons labeled with this disorder tend to be "loners" with a long-standing pattern of avoiding social situations and of being particularly sensitive to criticism or rejection. Finally, the *dramatic-erratic* cluster includes the histrionic, narcissistic, borderline, and antisocial personality disorders. The main characteristics of *narcissistic personality disorder,* for example, are an exaggerated sense of self-importance, extreme sensitivity to criticism, a constant need for attention, and a tendency to arrogantly overestimate personal abilities and achievements.

The most serious, costly, and intensively studied personality disorder is **antisocial personality disorder**. It is marked by a long-term pattern of irresponsible, impulsive, unscrupulous, and sometimes criminal behavior, beginning in childhood or early adolescence. In the nineteenth century, the pattern was called *moral insanity* because the people displaying it appear to have no morals or common decency. Later, people in this category

personality disorders Long-standing, inflexible ways of behaving that become styles of life that create problems, usually for others.

antisocial personality disorder A long-term, persistent pattern of impulsive, selfish, unscrupulous, even criminal behavior.

TABLE 12.5 ■ PERSONALITY DISORDERS

Here are brief descriptions of the ten personality disorders listed on Axis II of the *DSM-IV*.

Type	Typical Features
Paranoid	Suspiciousness and distrust of others, all of whom are assumed to be hostile
Schizoid	Detachment from social relationships; restricted range of emotion
Schizotypal	Detachment from and great discomfort in social relationships; odd perceptions, thoughts, beliefs, and behaviors
Dependent	Helplessness, excessive need to be taken care of, submissive and clinging behavior, difficulty in making decisions
Obsessive-compulsive	Preoccupation with orderliness, perfection, and control
Avoidant	Inhibition in social situations, feelings of inadequacy, oversensitivity to criticism
Histrionic	Excessive emotionality and preoccupation with being the center of attention, emotional shallowness, overly dramatic behavior
Narcissistic	Exaggerated ideas of self-importance and achievements, preoccupation with fantasies of success, arrogance
Borderline	Lack of stability in interpersonal relationships, self-image, and emotion; impulsivity; angry outbursts; intense fear of abandonment; recurring suicidal gestures
Antisocial	Shameless disregard for and violation of other people's rights

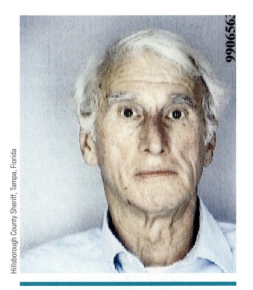

Hillsborough County Sheriff, Tampa, Florida

A CLASSIC CASE OF ANTISOCIAL PERSONALITY DISORDER ▲

Alfred Jack Oakley meets women through personal ads, claiming to be a millionaire movie producer, pilot, and novelist. In reality, he is a penniless con artist who uses his smooth-talking charm to gain the women's trust so he can steal from them. In January 2000, after being convicted of stealing a Florida woman's Mercedes, Oakley complimented the prosecutor's skills and the jury's wisdom and claimed remorse. The judge appeared to see through this ploy ("I don't believe there is a sincere word that ever comes out of your mouth"), but it was still effective enough to get Oakley probation instead of jail time!

were called *psychopaths* or *sociopaths.* The current "antisocial personality" label more accurately portrays them as troublesome but not "insane" by the legal standards we discuss later. About 3 percent of men and about 1 percent of women in the United States fall into this diagnostic category (American Psychiatric Association, 2000; Hodgins, 2007).

At their least troublesome, these people are a nuisance. They are often charming, intelligent "fast talkers" who borrow money and fail to return it; they are arrogant, selfish manipulators who "con" people into doing things for them, usually by lying and taking advantage of the decency and trust of others. At their most troublesome, people with this disorder are criminals, sometimes violent ones. Persistent violent offenders, most of whom have antisocial personality disorder, make up less than 5 percent of the male population, but they commit over 50 percent of violent crimes (Hodgins, 2007). A hallmark of those displaying antisocial personality is a lack of anxiety, remorse, or guilt, whether they have wrecked a borrowed car or killed an innocent person (Gray et al., 2003; Hare, 1993). No method has yet been found for permanently altering the behavior of these people (Rice, 1997). Research suggests that the best hope for dealing with them is to identify their antisocial personalities early, before the most treatment-resistant traits are fully developed (Compton et al., 2005; Crawford, Cohen, & Brooks, 2001; Lynam, 1996; Stoff, Breiling, & Maser, 1997).

There are numerous theories about the causes of antisocial personality. Some research suggests a genetic predisposition (Arseneault et al., 2003; Larsson, Andershed, & Lichtenstein, 2006; Slutske et al., 2001), possibly in the form of abnormal brain development, impaired neurological functioning, or chronic underarousal of both the autonomic and central nervous systems (Dolan & Park, 2002; Fung et al., 2005; Kiehl et al., 2006; Narayan et al., 2007; Raine et al., 2000, 2005). This underarousal may render people less sensitive to punishment and more likely to seek excitement than is normally the case (Birbaumer et al., 2005; Verona et al., 2004). Broken homes, rejection by parents, poor discipline, lack of good parental models, lack of attachment to early caregivers, impulsivity, conflict-filled childhoods, and poverty have all been suggested as psychological and sociocultural factors that contribute to the development of antisocial personality disorder (Caspi et al., 2004; Lahey et al., 1995; Raine, Brennan, & Mednick, 1994; Tremblay et al., 1994). The biopsychosocial approach suggests that antisocial personality disorder results when these psychosocial and environmental conditions combine with a genetic predisposition to low arousal and the sensation seeking and impulsivity associated with it (Gray et al., 2003).

Focus on RESEARCH

Exploring Links Between Child Abuse and Antisocial Personality Disorder

One of the most prominent environmental factors associated with the more violent forms of antisocial personality disorder is the experience of abuse in childhood (MacMillan et al., 2001). However, most of the studies that have found a relationship between childhood abuse and antisocial personality disorder were based on potentially biased reports (Monane, Leichter, & Lewis, 1984; Rosenbaum & Bennett, 1986). People with antisocial personalities—especially those with criminal records—are likely to make up stories of abuse in order to shift the blame for their behavior onto others. Even if their reports were accurate, however, most of these studies didn't compare the abuse histories of antisocial people with those of a control group from similar backgrounds who did not become antisocial. This research design flaw makes it almost impossible to separate the effects of reported child abuse from the effects of poverty or other factors that might also have contributed to the development of antisocial personality disorder.

▶ What was the researcher's question?

Can childhood abuse cause antisocial personality disorder? To help answer this question and to correct some of the flaws in earlier studies, Cathy Widom (1989) used a *prospective* research design, first finding cases of childhood abuse and then looking for the effects of that abuse on adult behavior.

▶ How did the researcher answer the question?

Widom began by identifying 416 adults whose backgrounds included official records of their having been physically or sexually abused before the age of eleven. She then explored the stories of these people's lives as told in police and school records as well as in a two-hour diagnostic interview. To reduce experimenter bias and distorted reporting, Widom ensured that the interviewers did not know the purpose of the study and that the respondents were told only that the study's purpose was to talk to people who had grown up in an urban area of the midwestern United States in the late 1960s and early 1970s. Widom also selected a comparison group of 283 people who had no histories of abuse but who were similar to the abused sample in terms of age, gender, ethnicity, hospital of birth, schools attended, and area of residence. Her goal was to obtain a nonabused control group that had been exposed to approximately the same environmental risk factors and socioeconomic conditions as the abused children.

▶ What did the researcher find?

First, Widom (1989) tested the hypothesis that exposure to abuse in childhood is associated with criminality and/or violence in later life. She found that 26 percent of the abused youngsters went on to commit juvenile crimes, 29 percent were arrested as adults, and 11 percent committed violent crimes. These percentages were significantly higher than the figures for the nonabused group.

The correlations between criminality and abuse were higher for males than for females and higher for African Americans than for European Americans. And overall, victims of physical abuse were more likely to commit violent crimes as adults than were victims of sexual abuse.

Next, Widom tested the hypothesis that childhood abuse is associated with the development of antisocial personality disorder (Luntz & Widom, 1994). She found that the abused group did show a significantly higher rate of antisocial personality disorder (13.5 percent) than did the comparison group (7.1 percent). The apparent role of abuse in antisocial personality disorder was particularly pronounced in men, and it remained strong even when other factors—such as age, ethnicity, and socioeconomic status—were accounted for in the statistical analyses. One other factor—failure to graduate from high school—was also strongly associated with the appearance of antisocial personality, whether or not childhood abuse had occurred.

▶ What do the results mean?

Widom's research supported earlier studies in finding an association between childhood abuse and criminality, violence, and antisocial personality disorder. Further, although her study did not permit a firm conclusion that abuse alone causes antisocial personality disorder, the data from its prospective design added strength to the argument that abuse may be an important causal factor (Widom, 2000). This interpretation is supported by the results of research by other investigators (Dudeck et al., 2007; Jaffee et al., 2004). Finally, Widom's work offers yet another reason (as if more reasons were needed) why it is so important to prevent the physical and sexual abuse of children. The long-term consequences of such abuse can be tragic not only for its immediate victims but also for those victimized by the criminal actions and antisocial behavior of some abused children as they grow up (Weiler & Widom, 1996; Widom, Czaja, & Dutton, 2008).

▶ What do we still need to know?

Widom's results suggest that child abuse can have a broad range of effects, all of which can derail normal childhood development. It is not yet clear, though, how abuse combines with other risk factors such as genetics or differences in neurocognitive functioning. More research is obviously needed to discover whether antisocial personality disorder stems from abuse itself, from one of the factors accompanying it, or from some specific combination of known and still-unknown risk factors. The importance of combined and interacting risk factors is suggested by the fact that abuse is often part of a larger pool of experiences, such as exposure to deviant models, social rejection, poor supervision, and various stressful events. Until we understand how all these potentially causal pieces fit together, we will not fully understand the role childhood abuse plays in the chain of events leading to antisocial personality disorder.

We need to know more, too, about why such a small percentage of the abused children in Widom's sample displayed violence, criminal behavior, and antisocial personality disorder. These results raise the question of which genetic characteristics or environmental experiences serve to protect children from at least some of the devastating effects of abuse (Flores, Cicchetti, & Rogosch, 2005; Rind, Tromovitch, & Bauserman, 1998; Widom et al., 2007). An understanding of what these protective elements are might go a long way toward the development of programs to prevent antisocial personality disorder.

A Sampling of Other Psychological Disorders

▶ *How do children's disorders differ from adults' disorders?*

The disorders described so far represent some of the most prevalent and socially disruptive psychological problems encountered in cultures around the world. Several others are mentioned in other chapters. In the chapter on consciousness, for example, we discuss insomnia, night terrors, and other sleep disorders; mental retardation is covered in the chapter on thought, language, and intelligence; sexual dysfunctions are mentioned in the chapter on motivation and emotion; and posttraumatic stress disorder is described in the chapter on health, stress, and coping. Here we consider two other significant psychological problems: disorders of childhood and substance-related disorders.

Psychological Disorders of Childhood

The physical, cognitive, emotional, and social changes that occur in childhood—and the stress associated with them—can create or worsen psychological disorders in children. Stress can do the same in adults, but childhood disorders are not just miniature versions of adult psychopathology. Because children's development is still incomplete and because their capacity to cope with stress is limited, children are often vulnerable to special types of disorders. The *DSM-IV* lists over two dozen Axis I disorders seen in infants, children, and adolescents, but the majority of childhood behavior problems can be placed in two broad categories: externalizing disorders and internalizing disorders (Phares, 2008).

The *externalizing*, or *undercontrolled*, category includes behaviors that disturb people in the child's environment. Lack of control shows up as *conduct disorders* in about 9.5 percent of children and adolescents (mostly boys) and appears most frequently at around 11 or 12 years of age (Nock et al., 2006). Conduct disorders are characterized by a relatively stable pattern of aggression, disobedience, destructiveness, and other obnoxious behaviors (Kalb & Loeber, 2003; Lahey et al., 1995). Often these behaviors involve criminal activity, and they may signal the development of antisocial personality disorder (Lahey et al., 2005). There may be a genetic predisposition toward externalizing disorders that begin in childhood and progress into adulthood (Larsson, Andershed, & Lichtenstein, 2006). For example, many children who display conduct disorder have parents who display antisocial personality disorder (Gelhorn et al., 2005). Children who are temperamentally inclined toward high activity levels are at greater risk for externalizing disorders (Mesman & Koot, 2000). There is no doubt, though, that parental and peer influences as well as academic problems at school also help shape the antisocial behavior of these children (Laird et al., 2001; Scourfield et al., 2004; Shaw et al., 2001).

Another kind of externalizing problem, *attention deficit hyperactivity disorder (ADHD)*, is seen in 3 to 7 percent of children, mainly boys (and in about 4 percent of adults, mainly men; Kessler, Adler et al., 2006). An ADHD diagnosis is given to children who are more impulsive, more inattentive, or both, than other children their age (Nigg, 2001; Wolraich et al., 2005). Many of these children also have great difficulty sitting still or otherwise controlling their physical activity. They appear to be less able

© PureStock RF/Getty Images

ACTIVE OR HYPERACTIVE? ▲

Normal behavior for children in one culture might be considered hyperactive in other cultures. Do people in the same culture disagree on what is hyperactive? To find out, ask two or three friends to join you in observing a group of children at a playground, a schoolyard, a park, or some other public place. Ask your friends to privately identify which children they would label as "hyperactive" and then count how many of their choices agree with yours and with others in your group.

Learn BY Doing

than other children to recognize emotions in others and to regulate their own emotions (Da Fonseca et al., 2009). Their impulsiveness and lack of self-control contribute to significant impairments in learning and to an astonishing ability to annoy and exhaust those around them. Children diagnosed with ADHD also tend to perform poorly on tests of attention, memory, decision making, and other information-processing tasks. As a result, ADHD is being increasingly viewed as a neurological condition rather than just "bad" behavior (Halperin & Schulz, 2006; Konrad et al., 2006; Krain & Castellanos, 2006; Ollendick & Prinz, 2002; Sergeant, Geurts, & Oosterlaan, 2002).

ADHD may result from a genetic predisposition. Some studies suggest that the genes involved may be those that regulate dopamine, a neurotransmitter important in the functioning of the attention system (Gilden & Marusich, 2009; Waldman & Gizer, 2006). Other factors, such as brain damage, poisoning from lead or other household substances, and low birth weight may also play causal roles (Hudziak et al., 2005; Linnet et al., 2003; Mick et al., 2002; Sergeant, Geurts, & Oosterlaan, 2002; Spencer, 2002). In some cases, problems in parenting may increase the risk for ADHD (Clarke et al., 2002). Exactly how all these factors might combine is still not clear. Also uncertain is exactly what constitutes hyperactivity. Cultural standards about acceptable activity levels in children vary, so a "hyperactive" child in one culture might be considered merely "active" in another. In fact, when mental health professionals from four cultures used the same rating scale to judge hyperactivity in a videotaped sample of children's behavior, the Chinese and Indonesians rated the children as significantly more hyperactive than did their U.S. and Japanese colleagues (Jacobson, 2002; Mann et al., 1992). And as mentioned earlier, there is evidence that African American children are diagnosed with ADHD only about two thirds as often as European American children even when they have at least as many symptoms (Miller, Nigg, & Miller, 2009). Such findings remind us that sociocultural factors can be important determinants of what is expected or acceptable and thus what is considered abnormal.

The second broad category of child behavior problems involves *internalizing,* or *overcontrol.* Children in this category experience significant distress, especially depression and anxiety, and may be socially withdrawn. Those displaying *separation anxiety disorder,* for example, constantly worry that they will be lost, kidnapped, or injured or that some harm may come to a parent (usually the mother). The child clings desperately to the parent and becomes upset or sick at the prospect of separation. Refusal to go to school (sometimes called "school phobia") is often the result. Children who are temperamentally shy or withdrawn are at higher risk for internalizing disorders, but these disorders are also associated with environmental factors, including rejection by peers and (especially for girls) being raised by a single parent (Phares, 2008; Prinstein & La Greca, 2002).

A few childhood disorders, such as *pervasive developmental disorders,* do not fall into either the externalizing or internalizing category. Children diagnosed with these disorders show severe deficits in communication and impaired social relationships. They also often show repetitive patterns of behavior (such as spinning objects) and unusual preoccupations and interests (American Psychiatric Association, 2000). The disorders in this group, also known as *autistic spectrum disorders* (Filipek et al., 1999; Rutter & Schopler, 1992; U.S. Surgeon General, 1999), share many of these core symptoms, although the severity of the symptoms may vary (Çeponien et al., 2003; Constantino & Todd, 2003). Estimates of the prevalence of autistic spectrum disorders vary from 30 to 60 children per 10,000 (a rate of about 0.3 percent to 0.6 percent); the most recent data suggest rates nearer the high end of this range (Williams et al., 2008) About half of these children suffer *autistic disorder,* which can be the most severe disorder of the group. The earliest signs of autistic disorder usually occur within the first 30 months after birth; these babies show little or no evidence of forming an attachment to their caregivers. Language development is seriously disrupted in most of these children; half of them never learn to speak at all. However, those who display "high functioning autism" or a less severe autistic spectrum disorder called *Asperger's disorder* are able to function adaptively and, in some cases, independently as adults (e.g., Grandin, 1996).

Possible biological roots of autistic disorder include genetic factors (Freitag, 2007; Gupta & State, 2007; Segurado et al., 2005; Skaar et al., 2005; Vorstman et al.,

2006) or neurodevelopmental abnormalities that affect language and communication (Baron-Cohen, Knickmeyer, & Belmonte, 2005; Belmonte et al., 2004; Courchesne et al., 2001; Grossberg & Seidman, 2006; Minshew & Williams, 2007). Researchers studying these biological factors have recently become interested in the activity of *mirror neurons* in the brain. As described in the chapter on biology and behavior, these neurons are activated when we see other people's actions, such as smiling, frowning, or showing disgust. Because they are in the areas of our own brain that control these same actions, activity in mirror neurons help us understand how the other person might be feeling and to empathize with those feelings. The functioning of mirror neurons appears disturbed in people with autism, which may help explain why these individuals seem to operate with little appreciation for what others might be thinking or feeling (Welsh et al., 2009; Williams et al., 2006). The once-popular hypothesis that autistic disorder is caused by cold and unresponsive parents has been rejected by the results of contemporary research.

Disorders of childhood differ from adult disorders not only because the patterns of behavior are distinct but also because their early onset disrupts development. To take just one example, children whose separation anxiety causes spotty school attendance may not only fall behind academically but also may fail to form the relationships with other children that promote normal social development (Wood, 2006). Some children never make up for this deficit. They may drop out of school and risk a life of poverty, crime, and violence. Moreover, children depend on others to get help for their psychological problems, but all too often those problems may go unrecognized or untreated. For some, the long-term result may be adult forms of mental disorder.

Substance-Related Disorders

Childhood disorders, especially externalizing disorders, often lead to substance-related disorders in adolescence and adulthood. The *DSM-IV* defines **substance-related disorders** as the use of psychoactive drugs for months or years in ways that harm the user or others. These disorders create major political, economic, social, and health problems worldwide. The substances involved most often are alcohol and other depressants (such as barbiturates), opiates (such as heroin), stimulants (such as cocaine or amphetamines), and hallucinogenic drugs (such as LSD). About half of the world's population uses at least one psychoactive substance, and about two thirds of U. S. citizens report that alcohol or drug addiction has affected them, their families, or their close friends (Leamon, Wright, & Myrick, 2008).

One effect of using some substances (including alcohol, heroin, and amphetamines) is **addiction,** a physical need for the substance. The *DSM-IV* calls addiction *physiological dependence.* Even when the use of a drug does not create physical addiction, some people may overuse, or *abuse,* it because the drug gives them temporary self-confidence, enjoyment, or relief from tension. The *DSM-IV* defines *substance abuse* as a pattern of use that causes serious social, legal, or interpersonal problems. In other words, people can become psychologically dependent on psychoactive drugs without becoming physiologically addicted to them. People who are psychologically dependent on a drug often have problems that are at least as serious as those of people who are addicted and that may be even more difficult to treat. In the consciousness chapter, we describe how consciousness is affected by a wide range of psychoactive drugs. Here, we focus more specifically on the problems associated with the use and abuse of alcohol, heroin, and cocaine.

Alcohol Use Disorders

According to recent national surveys in the United States, 7.6 percent of the adult population abuse alcohol or are dependent on it in any given year, and 14 percent of adults have suffered these problems at some time in their lives (Leamon, Wright, & Myrick, 2008). *Alcohol abuse* is characterized by a pattern of continuous or intermittent drinking that may lead to *alcohol dependence,* an addiction that almost always causes severe social, physical, and other problems (U.S. Department of Health and Human Services

substance-related disorders Problems involving the use of psychoactive drugs for months or years in ways that harm the user or others.

addiction Development of a physical need for a psychoactive drug.

Office of Applied Studies, 2003). Males outnumber females in this category by a ratio of about three to one, although the problem is on the rise among women and teenagers of both genders (Grucza et al., 2008). Abuse is greater among European Americans and American Indians than among African Americans and Hispanics; it is lowest among Asians (Chassin, Pitts, & Prost, 2002; Grant et al., 2004). Prolonged overuse of alcohol can result in life-threatening liver damage, reduced cognitive abilities, vitamin deficiencies that can lead to severe and permanent memory loss, and a host of other physical ailments (Hommer et al., 2001; Pfefferbaum et al., 2001). Alcohol dependence and abuse, commonly referred to as **alcoholism,** are serious problems. They are involved in 40 to 50 percent of all automobile accidents, murders, and rapes (Butcher et al., 2010). Alcohol abuse also figures prominently in child abuse and in elevated rates of hospitalization and absenteeism from work. Children growing up in families in which one or both parents abuse alcohol are at increased risk for developing a host of mental disorders, including substance-related disorders (Hoffmann & Cerbone, 2002; Odgers et al., 2008). And as described in the chapter on human development, children of mothers who abused alcohol during pregnancy may be born with fetal alcohol syndrome. In short, alcohol abuse and dependence carry a staggering cost in terms of personal suffering, medical expenditures, lost productivity, and shortened lifespans.

The biopsychosocial approach suggests that alcohol abuse stems from a combination of genetically influenced characteristics (including inherited aspects of temperament such as impulsivity and emotionality) and what people learn in their social and cultural environments (Elkins et al., 2006; Kendler, Jacobson et al., 2003; Petry, 2001; Sher et al., 1991; Wall et al., 2001). For example, the children of people with alcoholism are more likely than others to develop alcoholism themselves, and if the children are identical twins, both are at increased risk for alcoholism, even when raised apart (Volk et al., 2007). It is still unclear just what might be inherited or which genes are involved. One possibility involves inherited abnormalities in the brain's neurotransmitter systems or in the body's metabolism of alcohol (Martinez et al., 2005; Nurnberger et al., 2001; Petrakis et al., 2004). Males with alcoholism do tend to be less sensitive than other people to the effects of alcohol—a factor that may contribute to greater consumption (Pollack, 1992; Schuckit, 1998). Now that the human genome has been decoded, researchers are focusing on specific chromosomes as the possible location of genes that predispose people to—or protect them from—the development of alcoholism (Cheng et al., 2004; National Institute on Alcohol Abuse and Alcoholism, 2000, 2001; Wall et al., 2005). However, the genetics of addiction are highly complex; there is probably not a single gene for alcoholism (Crabbe, 2002). As with other disorders, many genes interact with each other and with environmental events, including parental influences (Duncan et al., 2006; Kaufman et al., 2007; Rhee et al., 2003). One study found that (as expected) the sons of identical twins were at elevated risk for alcoholism if their father had alcoholism but not if it was the father's identical twin who had alcoholism (Jacob et al., 2003). In these cases, something in the boys' nonalcoholic family environment had apparently moderated whatever genetic tendency toward alcoholism they might have inherited.

Youngsters typically learn to drink by watching their parents and their peers. The observations help shape their expectations, such as that alcohol will make them feel good and help them cope with stressors (Chassin, Pitts, & Prost, 2002; Schell et al., 2005). But alcohol use can become abuse and perhaps addiction if drinking is a person's main coping strategy (National Institute on Alcohol Abuse and Alcoholism, 2001). The importance of learning is supported by evidence that alcoholism is more common among ethnic and cultural groups in which frequent drinking tends to be socially approved (such as the Irish and English) than among groups in which all but moderate drinking tends to be discouraged (such as Jews, Italians, and Chinese; Gray & Nye, 2001; Wilson et al., 1996). Moreover, different forms of social support for drinking can result in different consumption patterns within a cultural group. For example, one study found significantly more drinking among Japanese men living in Japan (where social norms for male drinking are most permissive) compared with Japanese men living in Hawaii or California, where excessive drinking is less strongly supported (Kitano et al., 1992).

alcoholism   A pattern of continuous or intermittent drinking that may lead to addiction and that almost always causes severe social, physical, and other problems.

Heroin and Cocaine Dependence   Like alcoholics, those who are addicted to heroin or cocaine suffer many serious health problems as a result of both the drugs themselves and the poor eating and health habits related to use of those drugs. The risk of death from overdose, contaminated drugs, AIDS (contracted through shared needles), or suicide is also always present. Drug dependence tends to be more prevalent among males, especially young males (Compton et al., 2007; Warner et al., 1995).

Addiction to heroin and cocaine appears in about 4 percent of the adult population in the United States (Compton et al., 2005) and is mainly a biological process brought about by the physical effects of the drugs (Kalivas & Volkow, 2005; Phillips et al., 2003). Explaining why people first use these drugs is more complicated. Beyond the obvious and immediate pleasure these drugs provide, the causes of initial drug use are less well established than the reasons for alcohol abuse. One line of theorizing suggests that there might be a genetic tendency toward behavioral compulsions that predisposes some people to abuse many kinds of drugs (Crabbe, 2002; National Institute on Alcohol Abuse and Alcoholism, 2000). One study supporting this idea found a link between alcoholism in biological parents and drug abuse in the sons they had given up for adoption (Cadoret et al., 1995). The same study also found a link between antisocial personality traits in biological parents and antisocial acts—including drug abuse—in the sons they had put up for adoption. A number of psychological and environmental factors have been proposed as promoting initial drug use (Alessi et al., 2002; Brems & Namyniuk, 2002; Hoffmann & Cerbone, 2002). These include seeing parents use drugs, being abused in childhood, using drugs to cope with stressors or to ease anxiety or depression, associating drug use with pleasant experiences, seeking popularity, caving in to peer pressure, and thrill seeking (Alessi et al., 2002; Baker et al., 2004; Dube et al., 2003; Putnam, 2003; Reed, Anthony, & Breslau, 2007). Research has not yet established why continued drug use occurs in some people and not in others, but, again, it is likely that a biological predisposition interacts with psychological processes and stressors that play out their roles in specific social and cultural contexts (Kendler et al., 2003; Kreek et al., 2005).

Mental Illness and the Law

▶ *Can insanity protect criminals from punishment?*

Have you wondered why the word *insanity* doesn't appear in our definition of *mental disorder* or in the the *DSM-IV* categories we have described? The reason is that *insanity* is a legal term, not a psychiatric diagnosis. For example, in 1984 John Hinckley, Jr., was found *not guilty by reason of insanity* for his attempted assassination of President Ronald Reagan. This verdict reflected U.S. laws and rules that protect people with severe psychological disorders when they are accused of crimes (Cassel & Bernstein, 2007). Many other countries around the world have similar laws (Ahn-Redding, 2008).

This protection takes two forms. First, under certain conditions, people designated as mentally ill may be protected from prosecution. If at the time of trial individuals accused of crimes are unable to understand the proceedings and charges against them or help in their own defense, they are declared *mentally incompetent* to stand trial. When that happens, defendants are sent to a mental institution until they are judged to have become mentally competent. If they are still not competent after some specified period—two years, in most cases—a defendant may be ruled permanently ineligible for trial and either committed to a mental institution or released. Release is rare, however, because competency to stand trial requires only minimal mental abilities. If drugs can produce even temporary mental competence, the defendant will usually go to trial.

Second, the mentally ill may be protected from punishment. In most U.S. states, defendants may be judged not guilty by reason of insanity if at the time of the crime mental illness prevented them from (1) understanding what they were doing; (2) knowing that what they were doing was wrong; and (3) resisting the impulse to do wrong.

ASSESSMENT OF MENTAL COMPETENCE ▶

Andrea Yates admitted to drowning her five children in the bathtub of her Houston, Texas, home in 2001. She had twice tried to kill herself in previous years, and she was reportedly depressed at the time of the murders. Accordingly, she pleaded not guilty by reason of insanity. The first legal step in deciding her fate was to confine her in a mental institution to assess her mental competency to stand trial. Following testimony of psychologists who examined her, she was found competent and ultimately sentenced to life in prison. Her conviction was overturned on appeal, though, and at a second trial in 2006, she was found not guilty by reason of insanity and committed to a mental hospital.

applying psychology

© AP Photo

The first two of these criteria relate to a person's ability to think clearly and are called the *M'Naghton rule,* for the defendant in the 1843 case that established it. The third criterion, which relates to the defendant's emotional state during a crime, is known as the *irresistible impulse test.* All three criteria were combined in a rule proposed by the American Law Institute in 1962—a rule that is now followed in about one third of U.S. states.

After the Hinckley verdict, the U.S. Congress passed the Insanity Defense Reform Act, which eliminated the irresistible impulse criterion from the definition of insanity in federal cases. About 75 percent of the U.S. states have passed similar or related reform laws (Giorgi-Guarnieri et al., 2002); in about half the states, these laws require the use of some version of the narrower M'Naghton rule (American Psychiatric Association, 2003). Whatever criteria are used, when defendants plead insanity, judges and juries must decide whether or not a defendant should be held responsible for criminal acts. Defendants who are judged not guilty by reason of insanity and who still display a psychological disorder are usually required to receive treatment, typically through commitment to a hospital, until judged to be cured or no longer dangerous. Thirteen U.S. states have laws allowing jurors to find defendants *guilty but mentally ill.* These defendants are supposed to receive treatment while in prison, though they seldom do (Cassel & Bernstein, 2007).

Critics of insanity rules complain that these rules allow criminals to "get away with murder." Actually, such outcomes are rare. Insanity pleas occur in only 1 out of every 200 felony cases in the United States, and they are successful in only 2 of every 1,000 attempts (American Psychiatric Association, 2003; Silver, Cirincione, & Steadman, 1994). Even the few defendants found not guilty by reason of insanity in the United States are usually hospitalized for two to nine times as long as they would have spent in prison had they been found guilty (Silver, 1995; Steadman, 1993). John Hinckley, Jr., has been in Saint Elizabeth's Hospital in Washington, D.C., since 1982, and in spite of his annual efforts to be released and court approval for longer visits with his mother outside the hospital, he is unlikely to be freed anytime soon.

In summary, society is constantly seeking the proper balance between protecting the rights of defendants and protecting society from dangerous criminals. In the process, the sociocultural values that shape our views about what is abnormal also influence judgments about the extent to which abnormality should relieve people of responsibility for criminal behavior.

Chapter 12

Psychological Disorders

As noted in the introductory chapter, all of psychology's subfields are related to one another. Our discussion of how mental disorders might be learned illustrates just one way that the topic of this chapter, psychological disorders, is linked to the subfield of learning, which is discussed in the chapter by that name. The Linkages diagram shows ties to two other subfields, and there are many more ties throughout the book. Looking for linkages among subfields will help you see how they all fit together and help you better appreciate the big picture that is psychology.

linkages

Are some psychological disorders inherited? *(ans. on p. 486)*

Can we learn to become "abnormal"? *(ans. on p. 477)*

Can personality tests be used to diagnose mental disorders? *(ans. on p. 452)*

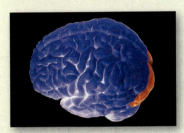

Chapter 2
Biology and Behavior

Chapter 5
Learning

Chapter 11
Personality

SUMMARY ▶

Psychopathology involves patterns of thinking, feeling, and behaving that are maladaptive, disruptive, or distressing, either for the person affected or for others.

Defining Psychological Disorders

 How do psychologists define abnormal behavior?

Some psychological disorders show considerable similarity across cultures, but the definition of *abnormality* is largely determined by social and cultural factors. The criteria for judging abnormality include *deviance* (statistical infrequency and norm violations), *distress* (personal suffering), and *dysfunction*. Each of these criteria is flawed to some extent. The practical approach, which considers the content, context, and consequences of behavior, emphasizes the question of whether people show impaired functioning in fulfilling the roles appropriate for particular people in particular settings, cultures, and historical eras.

Explaining Psychological Disorders

 What causes abnormality?

At various times and places, abnormal behavior has been attributed to the action of gods or the devil. Mental health professionals in Western cultures rely on a *biopsychosocial approach,* which attributes mental disorders to the interaction of biological, psychological, and *sociocultural factors*. Biological factors, such as brain chemistry, are highlighted by the medical or *neurobiological model* of disorder. The *psychological model* focuses on processes such as inner conflicts, maladaptive learning experiences, or blocked personal growth. The *sociocultural perspective* helps explain disorder by focusing on the social relations, social support and cultural and subcultural factors that form the context of abnormality. *The diathesis-stress model* suggests that biological, psychological, and sociocultural characteristics create predispositions for disorder that are translated into symptoms in the face of sufficient amounts of stress.

Classifying Psychological Disorders

▶ *How many psychological disorders have been identified?*

The dominant system for classifying abnormal behavior in North America is the fourth edition of the *Diagnostic and Statistical Manual of Mental Disorders (DSM-IV and DSM-IV-TR)* of the American Psychiatric Association. It includes more than 300 specific categories of mental disorder that can be described using five dimensions, or axes. Diagnosis helps identify the features, causes, and most effective methods of treating various psychological disorders. Research on the reliability and validity of the *DSM-IV* shows that it is a useful but not perfect classification system.

Anxiety Disorders

▶ *What is a phobia?*

Long-standing and disruptive patterns of anxiety characterize *anxiety disorders.* The most prevalent type of anxiety disorder is *phobia,* a category that includes *specific phobias, social phobias,* and *agoraphobia.* Other anxiety disorders are *generalized anxiety disorder,* which involves nonspecific anxiety; *panic disorder,* which brings unpredictable attacks of intense anxiety; and *obsessive-compulsive disorder (OCD),* which is characterized by uncontrollable repetitive thoughts called *obsessions* and ritualistic actions called *compulsions.*

The most influential explanations of anxiety disorders suggest that they may develop when a biological predisposition for strong anxiety reactions combines with fear-enhancing thought patterns and learned anxiety responses. Many anxiety disorders appear to develop in accordance with the principles of classical and operant conditioning and with those of observational learning. People may be biologically prepared to learn fear of certain objects and situations.

Somatoform Disorders

▶ *Can mental disorder cause blindness?*

Somatoform disorders appear as physical problems that have no apparent physical cause or as intense preoccupation with physical illness or deformity. They include *conversion disorder,* which involves problems such as blindness, deafness, and paralysis that have no apparent physical cause; *hypochondriasis,* an unjustified concern over being or becoming ill; *somatization disorder,* in which the person complains of numerous unconfirmed physical complaints; *somatoform pain disorder,* in which pain is felt in the absence of a physical cause; and *body dysmorphic disorder,* in which there is intense distress over imagined abnormalities of the skin, hair, face, or other bodily areas.

Dissociative Disorders

▶ *What disorders create sudden memory loss?*

Dissociative disorders involve rare conditions such as *fugue reactions* and *dissociative amnesia,* both of which involve sudden and severe memory loss, and *dissociative identity disorder (DID),* or multiple personality disorder, in which a person appears to have two or more identities. There is considerable controversy about the origins of dissociative identity disorder.

Affective Disorders

▶ *How common is depression?*

Affective disorders, also known as *mood disorders,* are quite common and involve extreme moods that may be inconsistent with events. *Major depression (major depressive disorder)* is marked by feelings of inadequacy, worthlessness, and guilt; in extreme cases, *delusions* may also occur. *Dysthymic disorder* includes similar but less severe symptoms that persist for a long period. Suicide is often related to these disorders. Alternating periods of depression and *mania* characterize *bipolar disorders;* there are more intense manic phases in *bipolar I disorder* than in *bipolar II disorder.* These disorders are also known as manic depression. *Cyclothymic personality* or *cyclothymic disorder,* an alternating pattern of less extreme mood swings, is a slightly more common variant.

Affective disorders have been attributed to biological causes such as genetic inheritance, disruptions in neurotransmitter and endocrine systems, and irregularities in biological rhythms. These interact with stressors and psychological factors such as maladaptive patterns of thinking.

A predisposition toward some of these disorders may be inherited, although their appearance is probably determined by a diathesis-stress process.

Schizophrenia

▶ *Is schizophrenia the same as "split personality"?*

Schizophrenia is perhaps the most severe and puzzling disorder of all. Among its symptoms are problems in thinking, perception (often including *hallucinations*), attention, emotion, movement, motivation, and daily functioning. Positive symptoms of schizophrenia include hallucinations or disordered speech; negative symptoms can include withdrawal, immobility, and the absence of affect.

Genetic influences, neurotransmitter problems, abnormalities in brain structure and functioning, and neurodevelopmental abnormalities are biological factors implicated in schizophrenia. Psychological factors such as maladaptive learning experiences and disturbed family interactions can affect the severity and course of this disorder. Diathesis-stress explanations, including vulnerability theory, provide a promising framework for research into the multiple causes of schizophrenia.

Personality Disorders

▶ *Which personality disorder often leads to crime?*

Personality disorders are long-term patterns of maladaptive behavior that are not always associated with discomfort for the person with the disorder but may be disturbing to others. These include odd-eccentric types (paranoid, schizoid, and schizotypal personality disorders), anxious-fearful types (dependent, obsessive-compulsive, and avoidant personality disorders), and dramatic-erratic types (histrionic, narcissistic, borderline, and antisocial personality disorders). *Antisocial personality disorder* is marked by impulsive, irresponsible, and unscrupulous behavior patterns that often begin in childhood. Childhood abuse may be related to the appearance of this potentially dangerous personality disorder.

A Sampling of Other Psychological Disorders

▶ *How do children's disorders differ from adults' disorders?*

Childhood psychological disorders can be categorized as externalizing conditions (such as conduct disorders or attention deficit hyperactivity disorder) and internalizing disorders, in which children show overcontrol and experience distress (as in separation anxiety disorder). Pervasive developmental disorders do not fall into either category and include the autistic spectrum disorders. In autistic disorder, which can be the most severe of these, children show no interest in or attachment to others.

Substance-related disorders involving alcohol and other drugs affect millions of people. *Addiction* to and psychological dependence on these substances contribute to disastrous personal and social problems, including physical illnesses, accidents, and crime. Genetic factors probably create a predisposition for *alcoholism,* but learning, cultural traditions, and other nonbiological processes are also important. Stress reduction, imitation, thrill seeking, and social maladjustment have been proposed as important factors in drug addiction, as has genetic predisposition; but the exact causes of initial use of these drugs are unknown.

Mental Illness and The Law

▶ *Can insanity protect criminals from punishment?*

"Insanity" is a legal term, not a psychiatric diagnosis. Current rules protect people accused of crimes from prosecution or punishment if they are declared mentally incompetent at the time of their trials or if they were legally insane at the time of their crimes. Defendants judged not guilty by reason of insanity and who still display a psychological disorder are usually required to receive treatment until they are judged to be cured or no longer dangerous. Those found guilty but mentally ill are supposed to receive treatment in prison.

Put It in Writing

Think about something you have seen someone do recently that you considered truly abnormal. Now write a page describing what happened and the specific rules or criteria—such as statistical infrequency, norm violation, personal suffering, or impaired functioning—that you used in deciding that this person's behavior qualifies as abnormal. Include a statement about whether you think this person should be treated for his or her behavior problem and why. Predict the degree to which this behavior would be considered abnormal by other people in your culture. Finally, tell whether and why people in other cultures might have a different view of the case.

Personal Learning Activity

To what extent do people agree on what is abnormal? To find out, ask at least 20 friends, family members, teachers, classmates in other courses, casual acquaintances, and maybe even some strangers to read your description of the behavior you diagnosed as abnormal in the Put It in Writing exercise. (Show them only the description, not your comments.) Ask these people to tell you whether they think the behavior is normal, merely odd, or seriously abnormal and whether they think the person is in need of treatment. Analyze the results in terms of how many of these people agreed with your diagnosis and with one another. Did you notice any trends in their responses based on age, gender, educational status, or cultural background? What do your results say about how easy or difficult it is to precisely define abnormality? *For additional projects, see the Personal Learning Activities in the corresponding chapter of the study guide that accompanies this book.*

Take Action to Learn More ▶

Now that you have finished reading this chapter, how about exploring some of the ideas and information that you found most interesting? Here are some courses, books, films, and Internet resources to get you started. Enjoy!

Courses

Abnormal Psychology
Child Psychopathology
Psychology and the Law

Movies

A Beautiful Mind; People Say I'm Crazy; Pink Floyd: The Wall; The Ruling Class; 12 Monkeys. Schizophrenia.
Boys Don't Cry; Flawless; Normal. Gender identity disorder.
The Fisher King. Psychosis, depression, substance abuse, avoidant personality disorder.
Mercury Rising; Rain Man. Autism.

The Hours; Ordinary People; The House of Sand and Fog. Depression and suicidality.
The Silence of the Lambs; The Talented Mr. Ripley; In Cold Blood; Natural Born Killers; Dahmer; Girl Interrupted. Antisocial personality disorder.
Copycat. Agoraphobia.
Blue Sky. Borderline personality disorder; substance abuse.

One Flew over the Cuckoo's Nest. Life in a state mental hospital of the 1960s.

The Three Faces of Eve; Sybil; Identity. Dissociative identity disorder.

Adaptation; Vertigo. Anxiety disorders.

As Good as It Gets; The Aviator. Obsessive-compulsive disorder.

Coffee and Cigarettes; Days of Wine and Roses; Leaving Las Vegas; Permanent Midnight; Trainspotting; 21 Grams; 25th Hour. Substance abuse and addiction.

Man on the Moon; Fast, Cheap, and Out of Control. Defining abnormality.

The Exorcism of Emily Rose. Supernatural explanations of abnormality.

Anatomy of a Murder. Use of the insanity defense in a murder case.

Cyrano de Bergerac; Roxanne. Body dysmorphic disorder.

Hollywood Ending; The Secret of Dr. Kildare. Conversion disorder.

Bartleby. Schizoid personality disorder.

The Birdcage. Histrionic personality disorder.

Books

Robert Spitzer et al., *DSM-IV Casebook: A Learning Companion to the Diagnostic and Statistical Manual of Mental Disorders* (American Psychiatric Press, 1994). A case-book illustrating the disorders listed in the *DSM-IV*.

Karen Eriksen and Victoria Kress, *Beyond the DSM Story: Ethical Quandaries, Challenges, and Best Practices* (Sage, 2005). A summary of the *DSM* and its problems and alternative approaches.

Larry Beutler and Mary Malik, *Rethinking the DSM: A Psychological Perspective* (American Psychological Association, 2002). A critical analysis of the standard diagnostic system.

William Styron, *Darkness Visible* (Vintage, 1992). Depression, suicidality.

Sylvia Plath, *The Bell Jar* (Harper & Row, 1971). Major depression, suicidality.

Kay Redfield Jamison, *An Unquiet Mind: A Memoir of Moods and Madness* (Vintage, 1997). A psychiatrist writes about her own bipolar disorder.

Patty Duke, *A Brilliant Madness* (Bantam, 1993). Bipolar disorder.

Sally Bedell Smith, *Diana: In Search of Herself—Portrait of a Troubled Princess* (Signet, 2000). Eating disorders, depression, borderline personality disorder.

Vaslav Nijinsky, *The Diary of Vaslav Nijinsky* (Farrar, Straus and Giroux, 1999). Insight into schizophrenia from one of Eugen Bleuler's most famous patients, the Russian ballet dancer.

Jerald J. Kriesman and Hal Straus, *I Hate You—Don't Leave Me: Understanding the Borderline Personality* (Avon, 1991). Descriptions and explanations of borderline behaviors, focusing on conflicted relationships.

Lewis B. Pullen, *Fortunate Son* (Bantam, 1996). Posttraumatic stress disorder.

Judith Rapoport, *The Boy Who Couldn't Stop Washing* (New American Library, 1997). Obsessive-compulsive disorder.

Karlene K. Hale, *Being There: Profiles of Mental Illness* (Dilligaf, 1997). Case studies of mental disorder.

Clark R. Clipson and Jocelyn M. Steer, *Case Studies in Abnormal Psychology* (Houghton Mifflin, 1998). More case studies.

Joan Acocella, *Creating Hysteria: Women and Multiple Personality Disorder* (Jossey-Bass, 1999). A description of the influence of culture and other social forces in shaping dissociative identity disorder.

Meyer Glantz and Christine Hartel, eds., *Drug Abuse: Origins and Interventions* (American Psychological Association, 2000). Information that challenges various myths about drug abuse.

The Web

Essentials of Psychology Book Companion Website

www.cengage.com/psychology/bernstein

Visit the book companion website to access a wealth of resources, including chapter outlines, flashcards, web links, tutorial quizzes, and more!

CENGAGENOW™   Just what you need to know NOW! Spend time on what you need to master rather than on information you already have learned. Take a pre-test for this chapter, and CengageNOW will generate a personalized study plan based on your results. The study plan will identify the topics you need to review and direct you to online resources to help you master those topics. You can then take a post-test to help you determine the concepts you have mastered and what you will need to work on. Try it out! Go to www.cengage.com/login to sign in with an access code or to purchase access to this product.

Review of Key Terms ▶

Can you define each of the key terms in the chapter? Check your definitions against those on the pages shown in parentheses in the following list or in the Glossary at the end of the book.

addiction (p. 499)
affective disorder (mood disorder) (p. 482)
agoraphobia (p. 475)
alcoholism (p. 500)
antisocial personality disorder (p. 494)
anxiety disorder (p. 474)
biopsychosocial approach (p. 465)
bipolar disorder (p. 485)
body dysmorphic disorder (p. 479)
compulsions (p. 476)
conversion disorder (p. 478)

cyclothymic personality (cyclothymic disorder) (p. 485)
delusions (p. 483)
diathesis-stress model (p. 469)
dissociative amnesia (p. 480)
dissociative disorders (p. 480)
dissociative identity disorder (DID) (p. 480)
dysthymic disorder (p. 483)
fugue reaction (dissociative fugue) (p. 480)
generalized anxiety disorder (p. 475)
hallucinations (p. 490)
hypochondriasis (p. 479)
major depression (major depressive disorder) (p. 482)
mania (p. 485)

obsessions (p. 476)
obsessive-compulsive disorder (OCD) (p. 475)
panic disorder (p. 475)
personality disorders (p. 494)
phobia (p. 474)
psychopathology (p. 462)
schizophrenia (p. 489)
social phobias (p. 474)
sociocultural factors (p. 467)
sociocultural perspective (p. 467)
somatization disorder (p. 479)
somatoform disorders (p. 478)
somatoform pain disorder (p. 479)
specific phobias (p. 474)
substance-related disorders (p. 499)

MULTIPLE-CHOICE ▶ Self Test

Select the best answer for each of the following questions. Then check your responses against the Answer Key at the end of the book.

1. According to the statistics on psychopathology, _____ percent of people in the United States experience a mental disorder in their lifetimes.
   a. less than 5 percent
   b. approximately 25 percent
   c. almost 50 percent
   d. over 75 percent

2. Babette, a successful opera singer, believes that aliens could snatch her at any time if she isn't wearing her lucky charm. She is constantly worried and insists that the stage be rimmed with foil to ward off evil spirits. According to which criterion of abnormality would Babette *not* be considered abnormal?
   a. Statistical
   b. Norm violation
   c. Practical
   d. Personal suffering

3. Herman murdered a man who bumped into him in a bar. In order to be found not guilty by reason of insanity, the jury would have to find that he _____.
   a. was under the influence of alcohol when he committed the crime
   b. is currently insane
   c. was insane when he committed the crime
   d. knew the crime was wrong but did it anyway

4. Roberta and Rhonda are identical twins who inherited identical predispositions for depression. Roberta has lived an easy life and has not developed any depressive symptoms. Rhonda, who has been divorced and lost several jobs over the years, has been diagnosed with major depression. The difference between these twins is most consistent with the _____ approach to abnormality.
   a. neurobiological   c. sociocultural
   b. psychological   d. diathesis-stress

5. Dr. Kramer is evaluating a patient brought in for psychiatric treatment. In his report he indicates that his global assessment of the patient's functioning is about 30 on a 100-point scale. Dr. Kramer is using _____ to evaluate the patient.
   a. the M'Naghton rule
   b. norm violation criteria
   c. insanity criteria
   d. the *DSM-IV*

6. Kat stopped going to classes because of worry that she will embarrass herself by saying something silly. She takes her meals to her dorm room so that no one will see her eat. According to the *DSM-IV*, Kat is probably displaying _____.
   a. agoraphobia
   b. simple phobia
   c. generalized anxiety disorder
   d. social phobia

7. Terraba had a difficult time driving to work. Every time she went over a bump she had to drive back around to make sure that she had not run over anything. This occurred ten or twelve times each day, so Terraba was always late for everything. Terraba appears to be suffering from _____.
   a. specific phobia
   b. panic attacks
   c. obsessive-compulsive disorder
   d. generalized anxiety disorder

8. Conversion disorder is characterized by _____.
   a. impairment of movement or sensory ability with no apparent physical cause
   b. severe pain with no apparent physical cause
   c. fear of becoming seriously ill
   d. frequent, vague complaints of physical symptoms

9. Tomas has been suffering severe back pain for several weeks, but extensive medical tests reveal no physical problem. Tomas appears to be displaying _____.
   a. somatoform pain disorder
   b. hypochondriasis
   c. paranoid schizophrenia
   d. somatization disorder

10. When Jennifer, a newspaper reporter, disappeared while covering a crime story that put her under constant threat, everyone assumed she had been kidnapped. But she was found several months later, now married and calling herself Emily, working as a waitress in a city 1,000 miles from her home. She had no memory of her previous life, even after being reunited with her parents. Jennifer would most likely be diagnosed as displaying _____.
    a. fugue reaction
    b. dissociative identity disorder
    c. dissociative amnesia
    d. schizophrenia

11. Over the past three months, Barb has been feeling very sad; she has been sleeping as much as 15 hours a day and has gained thirty pounds. Debbie, too, feels very low, but she can barely sleep and has lost both her appetite and 15 pounds. Both Barb and Debbie have symptoms of _____.
    a. obsessive-compulsive disorder
    b. major depression
    c. bipolar disorder
    d. hypochondriasis

12. Suicide is closely tied to depression. Studies of suicide in the United States have found that _____.
    a. people who talk about suicide typically don't attempt suicide
    b. older males who are living alone are the most likely to commit suicide
    c. suicide rates are about the same across ethnic groups and gender
    d. depressed women almost never actually attempt suicide

13. Carlisle has been very depressed. He can't face his responsibilities and often spends days at a time in bed. A psychologist who adopts the social-cognitive approach would be most likely to see this depression as caused by Carlisle's _____ .

  a. attributional style
  b. brain chemicals
  c. unconscious conflicts
  d. blocked growth tendencies

14. As you sit down next to a messy-looking man on a bus, he says, "Ohms vibrate orange and dishwrings obvious dictionary." As he continues talking in this manner, you begin to suspect that he is displaying _____ , a _____ symptom of _____ .

  a. anxiety; negative; obsessive-compulsive disorder
  b. thought disorder; positive; schizophrenia
  c. thought disorder; negative; schizophrenia
  d. flat affect; negative; depression

15. Juan can't explain why, but he worries constantly that something terrible is going to happen to him. This vague feeling of impending doom is associated with a diagnosis of _____ .

  a. conversion disorder
  b. specific phobia
  c. social phobia
  d. generalized anxiety disorder

16. Forty-year-old Richard believes that he was ordered by God to save the world. He is suspicious of other people because he thinks they want to prevent him from fulfilling his mission. He is un-able to keep a job because he is angry and argumentative most of the time. Richard would most likely be diagnosed as displaying

  _____ .

  a. affective disorder
  b. dissociative identity disorder
  c. paranoid schizophrenia
  d. catatonic schizophrenia

17. Al is charming and intelligent, but he has always been irresponsible, impulsive, and unscrupulous. None of his girlfriends knows he is dating other women. He borrows money from friends and doesn't pay them back. He doesn't care about anyone else, including his family. Al would probably be diagnosed as displaying _____ personality disorder.

  a. antisocial
  b. narcissistic
  c. passive-aggressive
  d. inadequate

18. Cathy Widom's research study, discussed in the Focus on Research section of this chapter, found that there was a relationship between antisocial personality disorder and _____ .

  a. narcissistic personality disorder
  b. schizophrenia
  c. high intelligence
  d. being abused in childhood

19. Angelo drinks alcohol until he passes out. Unable to hold a job or take care of himself, Angelo is diagnosed as having a substance-related disorder. Research on alcoholism suggests that Angelo's problems are caused by _____ .

  a. a single inherited gene
  b. a culture that did not tolerate drinking
  c. alcoholic parents
  d. a combination of genetic and environmental factors

20. Aaron is an infant who shows no signs of attachment to his parents. He dislikes being held and doesn't smile or laugh. Aaron's symptoms are most consistent with _____ .

  a. infantile schizophrenia
  b. autistic disorder
  c. antisocial personality disorder
  d. an externalizing disorder of childhood

13 Treatment *of* Psychological Disorders

Preview

In old Hollywood movies, such as *The Dark Past* or *The Three Faces of Eve*, troubled people find instant cures when a psychotherapist helps them discover an unconscious memory that holds the key to their psychological disorder. Somewhat more realistic versions of psychotherapy have been presented in movies and television shows such as *Good Will Hunting* and *The Sopranos*. Yet even these portrayals do not convey what psychotherapy is really like, and even the best of them tell only part of the story of how psychological disorders can be treated. In this chapter we describe a wide range of treatment options, including methods based on psychodynamic, humanistic, behavioral, and biological theories of psychological disorders. We also consider research on the effectiveness of treatment and methods for preventing disorders.

I n the chapter on psychological disorders, we described José, an electronics technician who had to take medical leave from his job because of his panic attacks. After four months of diagnostic testing turned up no physical problems, José's physician suggested that he see a psychologist. José resisted at first, insisting that his condition was not "just in his head," but he eventually began psychological treatment. Within a few months, his panic attacks had ceased and José had returned to all his old activities. After the psychologist helped him reconsider his workload, José decided to take early retirement from his job in order to pursue more satisfying work at his home-based computer business.

José's case is by no means unique. During any given year in the United States alone, about 15 percent of adults and about 21 percent of children and adolescents are receiving some form of treatment for psychological disorders, including substance abuse problems (Druss et al., 2007; Kessler et al., 2005; Wang et al., 2005). This treatment can be expensive, but its cost is made up for by the savings it creates (Insel, 2008). Compared with untreated patients, those who receive treatment typically need fewer mental and physical health services later on (American Psychological Association, 2009; Jordan et al., 2008; Schoenbaum, Sherbourne, & Wells, 2005).

The most common targets of treatment in adults are problems involving anxiety, mood, impulse control, substance abuse, or some combination of these (Druss et al., 2007; Kessler et al., 2005). Many people also seek treatment for problems that are not officially diagnosed as disorders, such as relationship conflicts or difficulties associated with grief, divorce, retirement, or other life transitions. Among children, the most common treatment targets are hyperactivity, oppositional behavior, anxiety, and mood disorders (Phares, 2008).

In this chapter, we describe a variety of treatment methods, most of which are based on the theories of stress and coping, personality, and psychological disorders reviewed in the chapters on those topics. First, we examine the basic features common to all forms of treatment. Then we discuss approaches that rely on **psychotherapy**, the treatment of psychological disorders through psychological methods, such as talking about problems and exploring new ways of thinking and acting. Next, we consider biological approaches to treatment, which depend mainly on prescription drugs and other physical therapies. (Many clients receive these drugs in addition to psychotherapy during the course of psychological treatment.) ■

psychotherapy   The treatment of psychological disorders through psychological methods, such as analyzing problems, talking about possible solutions, and encouraging more adaptive ways of thinking and acting.

Basic Features of Treatment

▶ *What features do all treatment techniques have in common?*

All treatments for psychological disorders share certain basic features—not only with one another but also with efforts to help the physically ill (Frank, 1978; Wampold, 2007). These common features include a *client* or *patient,* a *therapist* or other agent who is accepted as capable of helping the client, and a *special therapeutic relationship* between the client and the therapist. In addition, all forms of treatment are based on some *theory* about the causes of the client's problems (Dumont & Corsini, 2000). The presumed causes can range from magic spells to infections and everything in between (Corey, 2008). These theories form the basis of *treatment procedures* for dealing with the client's problems. Traditional healers combat supernatural forces with ceremonies and prayers, medical doctors treat chemical imbalances with drugs, and psychologists focus on altering psychological processes through psychotherapy.

People can receive treatment as inpatients or outpatients. *Inpatients* are treated in a hospital or other residential institution. They are institutionalized because their impairments are severe enough to create a threat to their own well-being or that of others. Depending on their level of functioning, inpatients may stay in the hospital for a few days or weeks or (in rare cases) several years. Their treatment almost always includes prescription drugs. *Outpatients* receive psychotherapy and/or prescription drugs while living in the community. Compared with inpatients, outpatients tend to have fewer and less severe symptoms of disorder and to function better in social and occupational situations (Hybels et al., 2008; Pottick et al., 2008).

Those who provide psychological treatment are a diverse group (Robiner, 2006). **Psychiatrists** are medical doctors who complete specialty training in the treatment of mental disorders. Like other physicians, they are authorized to prescribe drugs for the relief of psychological problems. **Psychologists** who offer psychotherapy have usually completed a doctoral degree in clinical or counseling psychology, often followed by additional specialized training. Except in Louisiana and New Mexico, psychologists in the United States are not authorized to prescribe drugs, though this privilege may eventually be granted to specially trained psychologists elsewhere (Heiby, DeLeon, & Anderson, 2008). Other therapy providers include *clinical social workers, marriage*

MEDIEVAL TREATMENT METHODS ▶

Methods used to treat psychological disorders have always been related to the presumed causes of those disorders. In medieval times, when abnormal behavior was associated with demonic possession, physician-priests tried to make the victim's body an uncomfortable place for evil spirits. In this depiction, demons are shown fleeing as an afflicted person's head is placed in an oven.

psychiatrists Medical doctors who have completed special training in the treatment of mental disorders.

psychologists In the area of treatment, therapists with advanced training in clinical or counseling psychology.

Stock Montage

and family therapists, and *licensed professional counselors,* all of whom typically hold a master's degree in their respective fields. They provide treatment in many settings, including hospitals, clinics, and private practice. *Psychiatric nurses, substance abuse counselors,* members of the clergy working as *pastoral counselors,* and a host of *paraprofessionals* also provide therapy services, often as part of a hospital or outpatient treatment team (Kramer, Bernstein, & Phares, 2009).

The overall goal of treatment is to help troubled people change their thinking, feelings, and behavior in ways that relieve discomfort, promote happiness, and improve functioning as parents, students, employees, and the like. More specific goals and the methods chosen to reach them are included in a treatment plan that the therapist and client develop together. The details of this plan depend on the nature of the client's problems, preferences, and financial circumstances and on the time available for treatment (Johnson, 2003). They depend, too, on the therapist's training and qualifications, theoretical leanings, and methodological preferences and the degree to which the therapist is guided by the results of experimental research on treatment. Later, we discuss drugs and other biological treatments. For now, however, let's consider several forms of psychotherapy, each of which is based on psychodynamic, humanistic, behavioral, or cognitive behavioral explanations of mental disorder.

Although we describe different approaches in separate sections, keep in mind that the majority of mental health professionals describe themselves as *eclectic* therapists. In other words, they might lean toward one set of treatment methods, but when working with particular clients or particular problems they may employ other methods as well (Magnavita, 2006; Norcross & Goldfried, 2005).

Psychodynamic Psychotherapy

▶ *How did Freud get started as a therapist?*

The field of formal psychotherapy began in the late 1800s when, as described in the personality chapter, Sigmund Freud established the psychodynamic approach to personality and mental disorders. Freud's method of treatment, **psychoanalysis,** was aimed at understanding unconscious conflicts and how they affect clients. Almost all forms of psychotherapy reflect some of Freud's ideas, including (1) his one-on-one treatment method; (2) his search for relationships between an individual's life history and current problems; (3) his emphasis on thoughts, emotions, and motivations in treatment; and (4) his focus on the client-therapist relationship. We describe Freud's original methods first and then consider some more recent treatments that are rooted in his psychodynamic approach.

Classical Psychoanalysis

Classical psychoanalysis developed mainly out of Freud's medical practice. He was puzzled by patients who suffered from blindness, paralysis, or other disabilities that had no physical cause (see our discussion of *conversion disorders* in the chapter on psychological disorders). Freud tried to cure these patients with hypnotic suggestions, but he found this method to be only partially and temporarily successful. Later, he asked hypnotized patients to recall events that might have caused their symptoms. Eventually, however, he stopped using hypnosis and merely had patients lie on a couch and report whatever thoughts, memories, or images came to mind. Freud called this process *free association.*

Freud's "talking cure" produced surprising results. He was struck by how many patients reported childhood memories of sexual abuse, usually by a parent or other close relative (Esterson, 2001). Was child abuse rampant in Vienna, or were his patients' reports distorted by psychological factors? Freud concluded that these reports of childhood seduction probably reflected unconscious impulses and fantasies, not reality. He also concluded that his patients' physical symptoms were based on unconscious conflicts about those fantasies. So psychoanalysis came to focus on exploring the unconscious and resolving the conflicts raging within it.

psychoanalysis   A method of psychotherapy that seeks to help clients gain insight into and work through unconscious thoughts and emotions presumed to cause psychological problems.

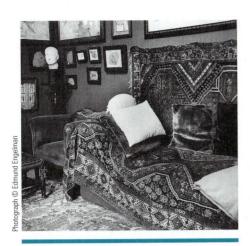

FREUD'S CONSULTING ROOM ▲

During psychoanalytic sessions, Freud's patients lay on this couch, free associating or describing dreams and events in their lives, while he sat in the chair behind them. According to Freud, even apparently trivial actions may carry messages from the unconscious. Forgetting a dream or missing a therapy appointment might reflect a client's unconscious resistance to treatment. Even accidents may be meaningful. The waiter who spills hot soup on an older male customer might be seen as acting out unconscious aggressive impulses against a father figure.

Classical psychoanalytic treatment involves the use of free association, dream analysis, and analysis of the client's reactions to the therapist (called *transference*) to help the client gain insight into problems. Clients are first encouraged to recognize unconscious thoughts and emotions. Then they are encouraged to discover, or *work through*, the many ways those unconscious elements continue to motivate maladaptive thinking and behavior in everyday life. The treatment may require as many as three to five sessions per week, usually over several years. Generally, the psychoanalyst remains compassionate but neutral as the client slowly develops insight into how past conflicts have shaped current problems (Gabbard, 2004).

Contemporary Variations on Psychoanalysis

Classical psychoanalysis is still practiced, but not nearly as much as it was several decades ago (Gabbard, 2004; Kaner & Prelinger, 2007). The decline is due in part to the growth of several alternative forms of treatment, including variations on classical psychoanalysis (e.g., Roseborough, 2006; Russ, 2006; Stricker, 2006). Many of these variations were developed by neo-Freudian theorists. As noted in the personality chapter, these theorists placed less emphasis than Freud did on the past and on unconscious impulses driven by the id. They focused instead on the role played by social relationships in clients' problems and on how the power of the ego can be harnessed to solve them. Psychotherapists who adopt various neo-Freudian treatment methods tend to take a much more active role than classical analysts do, in particular by directing the client's attention to evidence of certain conflicts in social relationships.

Many of these methods have come to be known as *short-term psychodynamic psychotherapy* because they aim to provide benefits in far less time than is required in classical psychoanalysis (Davanloo, 1999; Levenson, 2003; Rawson, 2003, 2006). In a particularly popular short-term psychodynamic approach known as *object relations therapy*, the powerful need for human contact and support takes center stage (Greenberg & Mitchell, 2006). Object relations therapists believe that most of the problems for which clients seek treatment ultimately stem from their relationships with others, especially their mothers or other early caregivers. (The term *object* usually refers to a person who has emotional significance for the client.) Accordingly, these therapists work to create a nurturing relationship in which the client's problems can be understood and corrected (Kahn & Rachman, 2000; Wallerstein, 2002). This relationship provides a "second chance" for the client to receive the support that might have been missing in infancy and to counteract some of the consequences of maladaptive early attachment

A PLAY THERAPY SESSION ▶

Modern versions of psychoanalytic treatment include fantasy play and other techniques that make the approach more useful with children. A child's behavior and comments while playing with puppets representing family members, for example, are seen as a form of free association that the therapist hopes will reveal important unconscious material, such as fear of abandonment (Booth & Lindaman, 2000; Carlson, Watts, & Maniacci, 2006).

applying psychology

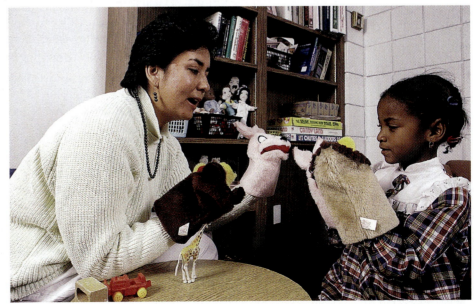

patterns. For example, object relations therapists take pains to show that they will not abandon their clients, as might have happened to these people in the past. *Interpersonal therapy,* too, is rooted partly in neo-Freudian theory (Sullivan, 1954). Often used in cases of depression, it focuses on helping clients explore and overcome the problematic effects of interpersonal events that occur after early childhood, such as the loss of a loved one, conflicts with a parent or a spouse, job loss, or social isolation (Mufson et al., 2004; Stuart & Robertson, 2003; Weissman, Markowitz, & Kierman, 2007).

With their focus on interpersonal relationships rather than instincts, their emphasis on clients' potential for self-directed problem solving, and their reassurance and emotional supportiveness, contemporary variants on classical psychoanalysis have helped the psychodynamic approach retain its influence among mental health professionals (Kaner & Prelinger, 2007; Stiles et al., 2006).

Humanistic Psychotherapy

▶ *Why won't some therapists give advice?*

Whereas some therapists revised Freud's ideas, others developed radical new therapies based on the humanistic approach to personality, which we describe in the personality chapter. *Humanistic psychologists,* sometimes called *phenomenologists,* emphasize the ways people interpret the events in their lives. They view people as capable of consciously controlling their own actions and taking responsibility for their decisions. Most humanistic therapists believe that human behavior isn't motivated by inner conflicts but by an innate drive toward growth that is guided by the way people perceive their world. Disordered behavior, they say, reflects a blockage in natural growth brought on by distorted perceptions or lack of awareness about feelings. Accordingly, humanistic (or phenomenological) therapy operates on the following assumptions:

1. Treatment is an encounter between equals, not a "cure" given by an expert. It is a way to help clients restart their natural growth and feel and behave in a more genuine way.
2. Clients will improve on their own, given the right conditions. These ideal conditions promote clients' awareness, acceptance, and expression of their feelings and perceptions.
3. Ideal conditions in therapy can best be established through a therapeutic relationship in which clients are made to feel accepted and supported as human beings, no matter how problematic or undesirable their behavior may be. It is the client's experience of this relationship that brings beneficial changes. (Notice that this assumption is shared with object relations and some other forms of brief psychodynamic therapy.)
4. Clients must remain responsible for choosing how they will think and behave.

Of the many humanistically oriented treatments in use today, the most influential are client-centered therapy, developed by Carl Rogers, and Gestalt therapy, developed by Frederick and Laura Perls (Cain & Seeman, 2002; Patterson, 2000; Woldt & Toman, 2005).

Client-Centered Therapy

Carl Rogers was trained in psychodynamic therapy methods during the 1930s, but he soon began to question their value. He especially disliked being a detached expert whose task is to "figure out" the client. Eventually convinced that a less formal approach would be more effective, Rogers allowed his clients to decide what to talk about and when to talk about it, without direction, judgment, or interpretation by the therapist (Raskin & Rogers, 2005). This approach, now called **client-centered therapy** or **person-centered therapy,** relies on the creation of a relationship that reflects three intertwined therapist attitudes: unconditional positive regard, empathy, and congruence.

client-centered therapy (person-centered therapy)   A type of therapy in which the client decides what to talk about and when without direction, judgment, or interpretation from the therapist.

Unconditional Positive Regard   The attitude Rogers called **unconditional positive regard** consists of treating the client as a valued person, no matter what. This attitude is communicated through the therapist's willingness to listen without interrupting and to accept what is said without evaluating it. The therapist doesn't have to approve of everything the client says but must accept it as reflecting that client's view of the world. Because Rogerian therapists trust clients to solve their own problems, they rarely give advice (Merry & Brodley, 2002). Doing so, said Rogers, would send clients an unspoken message that they are incompetent, making them less confident and more dependent on help.

Empathy   In addition, the client-centered therapist tries to see the world as the client sees it. In other words, the therapist tries to develop **empathy,** an emotional understanding of what the client might be thinking and feeling. Client-centered therapists convey empathy by showing that they are actively listening to the client. Like other skillful interviewers, they make eye contact with the client, nod in recognition as the client speaks, and give other signs of careful attention. They also use *reflection,* a paraphrased summary of the client's words that emphasizes the feelings and meanings that appear to go along with them. Reflection confirms that the therapist has understood what the client has said, conveys the therapist's interest in hearing it, and helps the client to be more clearly aware of the thoughts and feelings that he or she has just expressed. Here is an example:

> *Client:*   *This has been such a bad day. I've felt ready to cry any minute, and I'm not even sure what's wrong!*
>
> *Therapist:*   *You really do feel so bad. The tears just seem to well up inside, and I wonder if it is a little scary to not even know why you feel this way.*

Notice that in rephrasing the client's statements, the therapist reflected back not only the obvious feelings of sadness but also the fear in the client's voice. Most clients respond to empathic reflection by elaborating on their feelings. This client went on to say, "It *is* scary, because I don't like to feel in the dark about myself. I have always prided myself on being in control."

Empathic listening tends to be so effective in promoting self-understanding and awareness that it is used across a wide range of therapies (Corsini & Wedding, 2005; Miller & Rollnick, 2002). Even beyond the realm of therapy, people who are thought of as easy to talk to are usually "good listeners" who reflect back the important messages they hear from others.

unconditional positive regard   In client-centered therapy, the therapist's attitude that expresses caring for and acceptance of the client as a valued person.

empathy   In client-centered therapy, the therapist's attempt to appreciate how the world looks from the client's point of view.

A CLIENT-CENTERED THERAPY GROUP ▶

Carl Rogers (shown here in shirtsleeves) believed that people in successful client-centered therapy become more self-confident, more aware of their feelings, more accepting of themselves, more comfortable and genuine with other people, more reliant on self-evaluation than on the judgments of others, and more effective and relaxed.

applying psychology

Congruence   Rogerian therapists also try to convey **congruence** (sometimes called *genuineness*) by acting in ways that are consistent with their feelings during therapy. For example, if they are confused by what a client has said, they say so instead of trying to pretend that they always understand everything. When the therapist's unconditional positive regard and empathy are genuine, the client is able to see that relationships can be built on openness and honesty. Ideally, this experience will help the client become more congruent, or genuine, in other relationships.

Gestalt Therapy

Another form of humanistic treatment was developed by Frederick S. (Fritz) Perls and his wife, Laura Perls. A European psychoanalyst, Frederick Perls was greatly influenced by Gestalt psychology. (As noted in the chapter on sensation and perception, Gestalt psychologists emphasized the idea that people actively organize their perceptions of the world.) As a result, he believed that (1) people create their own versions of reality; and (2) people's natural psychological growth continues only as long as they perceive, remain aware of, and act on their true feelings. Growth stops and symptoms of mental disorder appear, said Perls, when people are not aware of all aspects of themselves (Perls, 1969; Perls, Hefferline, & Goodman, 1951).

Like client-centered therapy, **Gestalt therapy** seeks to create conditions in which clients can become more unified, self-aware, and self-accepting and thus ready to grow again. However, Gestalt therapists use more direct and dramatic methods than do Rogerians. Often working with groups, Gestalt therapists prod clients to become aware of feelings and impulses that they have disowned and to discard feelings, ideas, and values that are not really their own. For example, the therapist or other group members might point out inconsistencies between what clients say and how they behave. Gestalt therapists pay particular attention to clients' gestures and other forms of "body language" that appear to conflict with what the clients are saying (Kepner, 2001). The therapist may also ask clients to engage in imaginary dialogues with other people, with parts of their own personalities, and even with objects (Elliott, Watson, & Goldman, 2004a, 2004b). Like a shy person who can be socially outgoing only while at a costume party, clients often find that these dialogues help them get in touch with and express their feelings (Woldt & Toman, 2005).

Over the years, client-centered and other forms of humanistic therapy have declined in popularity (Norcross, Hedges, & Castle, 2002), but Carl Rogers's contributions to psychotherapy remain significant. In particular, many other treatment approaches have incorporated his emphasis on the importance of the therapeutic relationship in bringing about change (Kirschenbaum & Jourdan, 2005).

Behavior Therapy and Cognitive Behavior Therapy

▶ *Can we learn to conquer fears?*

Psychodynamic and humanistic approaches to therapy assume that if clients gain insight or self-awareness about underlying problems, the symptoms created by those problems will disappear. Behavior therapists emphasize a different kind of self-awareness: they help clients think about psychological problems as *learned behaviors* that can be changed without first searching for hidden meanings or unconscious causes (Miltenberger, 2007; Spiegler & Guevremont, 2009). For example, suppose you have a panic attack every time you leave home and find relief only when you return. Making excuses when friends invite you out temporarily eases your anxiety but does nothing to solve the problem. Could you reduce your fear without first searching for what it might mean or represent? Behavior therapists say yes. So instead of focusing on the possible meaning of your anxiety, they would begin by helping you identify the

congruence   In client-centered therapy, a consistency between the way therapists feel and the way they act toward clients.

Gestalt therapy   A form of treatment that seeks to create conditions in which clients can become more unified, more self-aware, and more self-accepting.

learning principles that have served to create and maintain it. They would then guide you in learning more adaptive responses in anxiety-provoking situations.

These goals are based on the behavioral approach to psychology in general and on the social-cognitive approach to personality and disorder in particular. As described in the personality chapter, social-cognitive theorists see learning as the basis of both normal personality and most behavior disorders. According to this perspective, disordered behavior and thinking are examples of the maladaptive thoughts and actions that the client has developed through the processes described in the chapter on learning. For example, fear of leaving home (agoraphobia) would be seen by behavior therapists as stemming from classically conditioned associations between being away from home and having panic attacks. The problem is partly maintained, they say, through operant conditioning: Staying home and making excuses for doing so is rewarded by reduced anxiety.

Some behavior therapists also emphasize that fears and other problems are maintained by what we think about situations and about ourselves. As discussed later, these *cognitive behavior* therapists focus their treatment efforts on changing maladaptive thoughts as well as problematic behaviors. In short, behavior therapists believe that if problems can be created through prior learning experiences, they can be eliminated through new learning experiences. So whether phobias and other problems are based on events in childhood or were learned more recently, behavior therapists address them by arranging for their clients to have beneficial new experiences.

The notion of applying learning principles in order to change troublesome overt behavior has its roots in the work of John B. Watson, Ivan Pavlov, and others who studied the learned nature of fear in the 1920s. It stems, too, from B. F. Skinner's research on the impact of reward and punishment on behavior. In the late 1950s and early 1960s, researchers began to use classical conditioning, operant conditioning, and observational learning techniques in a systematic way to create treatment programs designed to eliminate fears, improve the behavior of disruptive schoolchildren and mental patients, and deal with many other problems (Plaud, 2003; Ullmann & Krasner, 1965). By 1970, behavioral treatment had become a popular alternative to psychodynamic and humanistic methods (Martin & Pear, 2006). The most notable features of behavioral treatment include the following:

1. Development of a productive therapist-client relationship. As in other therapies, this relationship enhances clients' confidence that change is possible and makes it easier for them to speak openly and to cooperate in and benefit from treatment (Creed & Kendall, 2005; Lejuez et al., 2005; Wilson, 1995).
2. A careful listing of the behaviors and thoughts to be changed (Umbreit et al., 2006). This assessment and the establishment of specific treatment goals sometimes replace the formal diagnosis used in some other therapy approaches. So instead of treating "depression" or "obsessive-compulsive disorder," behavior therapists work to change the specific thoughts, behaviors, and emotional reactions that lead people to receive these diagnostic labels.
3. A therapist who acts as a teacher/assistant by providing learning-based treatments, giving "homework" assignments, and helping the client make specific plans for dealing with problems rather than just talking about them (Kazantizis et al., 2005).
4. Continuous monitoring and evaluation of treatment and constant adjustments to any procedures that do not seem to be effective (Farmer & Nelson-Gary, 2005). (Because ineffective procedures are soon altered or abandoned, behavioral treatment tends to be one of the briefer forms of therapy.)

Behavioral treatment can take many forms. By tradition, those that rely mainly on classical conditioning principles are usually referred to as **behavior therapy.** Those that focus on operant conditioning methods are usually called **behavior modification.** And behavioral treatment that focuses on changing thoughts as well as overt behaviors is called **cognitive behavior therapy.** These methods, especially cognitive behavior therapy, have become increasingly influential in recent years (Durlak, 2006).

behavior therapy Treatments that use classical conditioning principles to change behavior.

behavior modification Treatments that use operant conditioning methods to change behavior.

cognitive behavior therapy Behavioral treatment methods that help clients change the way they think as well as the way they behave.

Techniques for Modifying Behavior

The most commonly used behavioral treatment methods include systematic desensitization therapy, modeling, positive reinforcement, extinction, aversion conditioning, and punishment.

Systematic Desensitization Therapy   Joseph Wolpe (1958) developed one of the first behavioral methods for helping clients overcome phobias and other forms of anxiety. Called **systematic desensitization therapy,** it is a treatment in which the client visualizes a series of anxiety-provoking stimuli while remaining relaxed. Wolpe believed that this process gradually weakens the learned association between anxiety and the feared object until the fear disappears.

Wolpe first helped his clients learn to relax, often using the *progressive relaxation training* procedures described in the chapter on health, stress, and coping. While relaxed, clients would be asked to imagine the easiest item on a *desensitization hierarchy,* a list of increasingly fear-provoking situations (see Table 13.1). As treatment progressed, clients imagined each item in the hierarchy, one at a time, moving to a more difficult item only after learning to imagine the previous one without distress. Wolpe found that once clients could remain calm as they imagined being in feared situations, they were better able to actually deal with those situations later on.

It turns out, though, that desensitization can be especially effective when it slowly and carefully presents clients with real, rather than imagined, hierarchy items (Bouton, 2000; Choy, Fyer, & Lipsitz, 2007; Marks, 2002; McGlynn et al., 1999; Tryon, 2005). This *in vivo,* or "real life," desensitization was once difficult to arrange or control, especially in treating fear of heights, highway driving, or flying for example. Recently, however, *virtual reality graded exposure* has made it possible for clients to "experience" vivid and precisely graduated versions of feared situations without actually being exposed to the real thing. In one early study of this approach, clients who feared heights wore a virtual reality helmet that gave the impression of standing on bridges of gradually increasing heights, on outdoor balconies on higher and higher floors, and in a glass elevator as it slowly rose 49 stories (Rothbaum et al., 1995). The same technology has been used successfully in the treatment of fears caused by spiders, dentists, air travel, social interactions, and posttraumatic stress disorder (Anderson, Rothbaum, & Hodges, 2003; Choi et al., 2001; Dittman, 2005; Gershon et al., 2002; Glantz, Rizzo, & Graap, 2003; Maltby, Kirsch, & Mayers, 2002; North, North, & Burwick, 2008; Rothbaum, 2006; Rothbaum et al, 1999, 2002; Rothbaum, Hodges, 2000; Wiederhold & Wiederhold, 2005; Winerman, 2005).

linkages

Can people learn their way out of a disorder? *(a link to Learning)*

© Virtual Reality Medical Center

VIRTUAL DESENSITIZATION ▲

This client fears heights. She is wearing a virtual reality display that creates the visual experience of being in a glass elevator, which, under the therapists' careful control, seems to gradually rise higher and higher. After learning to tolerate these realistic images without anxiety, clients are better able to fearlessly face the situations they once avoided.

applying psychology

  Improve Your Grade
Tutorial: Phobia Treatments

systematic desensitization therapy
A behavioral method for treating anxiety in which clients visualize a graduated series of anxiety-provoking stimuli while remaining relaxed.

TABLE 13.1 ■ **A DESENSITIZATION HIERARCHY**

Desensitization hierarchies are lists of increasingly fear-provoking stimuli or situations that clients visualize while using relaxation methods to remain calm. Here are a few items from the beginning and the end of a hierarchy that was used to help a client overcome fear of flying.

1. You are reading a newspaper and notice an ad for an airline.

2. You are watching a television program that shows a group of people boarding a plane.

3. Your boss tells you that you need to take a business trip by air.

4. You are in your bedroom packing your suitcase for your trip.

.

.

.

12. Your plane begins to move as you hear the flight attendant say, "Be sure your seat belt is securely fastened."

13. You look at the runway as the plane is readied for takeoff.

14. You look out the window as the plane rolls down the runway.

15. You look out the window as the plane leaves the ground.

modeling A behavioral therapy method in which desirable behaviors are demonstrated for clients.

assertiveness training A set of methods for helping clients learn to express their feelings and stand up for their rights in social situations.

positive reinforcement Presenting a positive reinforcer (reward) after a desired response.

token economy program A system for improving the behavior of clients in institutions by rewarding desirable behaviors with tokens that can be exchanged for various rewards.

extinction The gradual disappearance of a conditioned response.

flooding An exposure technique for reducing anxiety that keeps a client in a feared but harmless situation.

implosive therapy An exposure technique in which clients are helped to imagine being kept in a feared but harmless situation.

© Rick Wilking/Reuters/Landov

TREATING FEAR THROUGH FLOODING ▲

Flooding is designed to extinguish anxiety by allowing it to occur without the harmful consequences the person dreads. These clients' fear of flying is obvious here, just before takeoff, but it is likely to diminish during and after an uneventful flight. Like other behavioral treatments, flooding is based on the idea that phobias and other psychological disorders are learned and can thus be "unlearned." Some therapists prefer more gradual exposure methods similar to those of in vivo desensitization, which start with situations that are lower on the client's fear hierarchy (Back et al., 2001; Fava et al., 2001; Fritzler, Hecker, & Losee, 1997).

applying psychology

Modeling

Therapists often teach clients desirable behaviors by first demonstrating those behaviors. In **modeling** treatments, the client learns important skills by watching other people perform desired behaviors (Bidwell & Rehfeldt, 2004). For example, modeling can teach fearful clients how to respond fearlessly and confidently. In one case study, a therapist showed a spider-phobic client how to calmly kill spiders with a fly swatter and then gave her the assignment of practicing this skill at home with rubber spiders (MacDonald & Bernstein, 1974). This combination of fearless demonstrations and firsthand practice, called *participant modeling,* is one of the most powerful treatments for fear (e.g., Bandura, Blanchard, & Ritter, 1969; Zinbarg & Griffith, 2008).

Modeling is also a major part of *assertiveness training* and *social skills training,* which help clients learn how to deal with people more comfortably and effectively. Social skills training has been used to help children interact more effectively with peers, to help social-phobic singles make conversation on dates, and to help rebuild mental patients' ability to have normal conversations with people outside a hospital setting (Al-Kubaisy & Jassim, 2003; Dowd, 2005; Lin et al., 2008). In **assertiveness training,** the therapist helps clients learn to express their feelings and stand up for their rights in social situations (Alberti & Emmons, 2008; Ballou, 1995; Patterson, 2000). Assertiveness training is often done in groups and involves both modeling and role playing of specific situations. For example, group assertiveness training has helped wheelchair-bound adults and learning-disabled students more comfortably handle the socially awkward situations in which they sometimes find themselves (Eamon, 2008).

Positive Reinforcement

Behavior therapists also use **positive reinforcement** to alter problematic behaviors and teach new skills in cases ranging from childhood tantrums and juvenile delinquency to schizophrenia and substance abuse (Lussier et al., 2006). Employing operant conditioning principles, they set up *contingencies,* or rules, that specify the behaviors to be strengthened through reinforcement. In one pioneering study, children with autistic disorder, who typically speak very little, were given grapes, popcorn, or other items they liked in return for saying "please," "thank you," and "you're welcome" while exchanging crayons and blocks with a therapist. After the therapist modeled the desired behavior by saying the appropriate words at the appropriate times, the children began to say these words on their own. Their use of language also began to appear in other situations, and, as shown in Figure 13.1, the new skills were still evident six months later (Matson et al., 1990).

When working with severely retarded or disturbed clients in institutions or with unruly juveniles in residential facilities, behavior therapists sometimes establish a **token economy program,** which is a system for reinforcing desirable behaviors with points or coin-like tokens that can be exchanged later for snacks, access to television, or other rewards (Kazdin, 2008; LePage et al., 2003; Matson & Moisjoli, 2009; Seegert, 2003). The goal is to shape more adaptive behavior patterns that will persist outside the institution (Moore et al., 2001; Paul, 2000; Paul, Stuve, & Cross, 1997).

Extinction

Just as reinforcing desirable behaviors can make them more likely to occur, failing to reinforce undesirable behaviors can make them less likely to occur, a process known as **extinction.** Treatment methods that use extinction change behavior slowly but offer a valuable way of reducing inappropriate behavior in children and adolescents and in retarded or seriously disturbed adults. For example, a client who gets attention by disrupting a classroom, damaging property, or violating hospital rules might be placed in a quiet, boring "time out" room for a few minutes to eliminate reinforcement for misbehavior (Kaminski et al., 2008; Kazdin, 2008).

Extinction is also the basis of a fear-reduction treatment called **flooding,** in which clients are kept in a feared but harmless situation and are not permitted to use their normally rewarding escape strategies (O'Donohue, Fisher, & Hayes, 2003). (In a related method called **implosive therapy,** the therapist helps the client to vividly imagine being in the feared situation by describing it at length and in great detail.) The client is flooded with fear at first, but after an extended period of exposure to the feared stimulus (a frog, say) without experiencing pain, injury, or any other dreaded result, the

FIGURE 13.1 ■ POSITIVE REINFORCEMENT FOR AN AUTISTIC CHILD

During each pretreatment baseline period, an autistic child rarely said "please," "thank you," or "you're welcome," but the child began to make such statements once the therapist demonstrated them, then reinforced the child when he said them. Did modeling and reinforcement actually cause the change? Probably, because each type of response did not start to increase until the therapist began demonstrating it. *Source*: Matson et al. (1990).

applying psychology

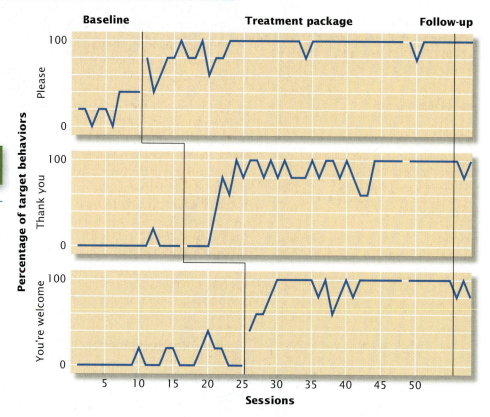

association between the feared stimulus and the fear response gradually weakens and the conditioned fear response is extinguished (Basoglu, Livanou, & Salcioglu, 2003; Harris & Goetsch, 1990; McNally, 2007; Öst et al., 2001). In one early study, 20 clients who feared needles were exposed for two hours to the sight and feel of needles, including by having mild finger pricks, harmless injections, and blood samplings (Öst, Hellström, & Kåver, 1992). Afterward, all except one client were able to have a blood sample drawn without experiencing significant anxiety. (Because they continuously expose clients to feared stimuli, flooding, implosion, and other similar methods are also called *exposure techniques*.)

Aversion Therapy Some unwanted behaviors, such as excessive gambling or using addictive drugs, can become so habitual and temporarily rewarding that they must be made less attractive if a client is to have any chance of giving them up. Methods for reducing the appeal of certain stimuli are known as *aversion therapy*. The name reflects the fact that these methods rely on a classical conditioning process called **aversion conditioning** to associate shock, nausea, or other physical or psychological discomfort with stimuli, thoughts, or actions the client needs to stop or avoid (e.g., Bordnick et al., 2004).

Because aversion conditioning is unpleasant and uncomfortable, because it may not work with all clients (Flor et al., 2002), and because its effects are often temporary, most behavior therapists use this method relatively rarely, only when it is the best treatment choice, and only long enough to allow the client to learn more appropriate alternative behaviors.

Punishment Sometimes the only way to eliminate a dangerous or disruptive behavior is to punish it with an unpleasant but harmless stimulus, such as a shouted "No!" or a mild electric shock. Unlike aversion conditioning, in which the unpleasant

aversion conditioning A method for reducing unwanted behaviors by using classical conditioning principles to create a negative response to some stimulus.

stimulus occurs along with the behavior that is to be eliminated (a classical conditioning approach), **punishment** is an operant conditioning technique; it presents the unpleasant stimulus *after* the undesirable response occurs.

Before using electric shock or other forms of punishment, behavior therapists are required by ethical and legal guidelines to ask themselves several important questions: Have all other methods failed? Would the client's life be in danger without treatment? Has an ethics committee reviewed and approved the procedures? Has the adult client or a close relative of a child client agreed to the treatment (Kazdin, 2008)? When the answer to these questions is yes, punishment can be an effective, sometimes life-saving, treatment—as in the case illustrated in Figure 5.12 in the chapter on learning. As with extinction and aversion conditioning, punishment works best when it is used just long enough to eliminate undesirable behavior and is combined with other behavioral methods designed to reward more appropriate behavior.

Cognitive Behavior Therapy

Like psychodynamic and humanistic therapists, most behavior therapists recognize that depression, anxiety, and many other behavior disorders can stem from how clients think about themselves and the world. And like other therapists, most behavior therapists try to change clients' troublesome ways of thinking, not just their overt behavior. Unlike other therapists, however, behavior therapists rely on learning principles to help clients change the way they think. Their methods are known collectively as *cognitive behavior therapy* (Barlow, 2007; Beck, 2005; Beck, Freeman, & Davis, 2007). Suppose, for example, that a client has good social skills but suffers intense anxiety around other people. In a case like this, social skills training would obviously be unnecessary. Instead, the behavior therapist would use cognitive behavioral methods designed to help the client identify habitual thoughts (such as "I shouldn't draw attention to myself") that create awkwardness and discomfort in social situations. Once these cognitive obstacles are brought to light, the therapist describes new and more adaptive ways of thinking and encourages the client to learn and practice them. As these cognitive skills develop (e.g., "I have as much right to give my opinion as anyone else"), it becomes easier and more rewarding for clients to let these new thoughts guide their behavior (Beck, 2005).

Rational-Emotive Behavior Therapy

One prominent form of cognitive behavior therapy is **rational-emotive behavior therapy (REBT),** which was developed by Albert Ellis (1962, 1993, 1995, 2004a, 2004b; Ellis & MacLaren, 2005). REBT aims first at identifying unrealistic and self-defeating thoughts, such as "I must be loved or approved of by everyone" or "I must always be competent to be worthwhile." After the client learns to recognize such thoughts as these and to see how they can cause problems, the therapist uses suggestions, encouragement, and logic to help the client replace maladaptive thoughts with more realistic and beneficial ones. The client is then given "homework" assignments to try these new ways of thinking in everyday situations. Here is part of an REBT session with a woman who suffered from panic attacks. She has just said that it would be "terrible" if she had an attack in a restaurant and that people "should be able to handle themselves!"

Therapist: *The reality is that . . . "shoulds" and "musts" are the rules that other people hand down to us, and we grow up accepting them as if they are the absolute truth, which they most assuredly aren't.*

Client: *You mean it is perfectly okay to, you know, pass out in a restaurant?*

Therapist: *Sure!*

Client: *But . . . I know I wouldn't like it to happen.*

Therapist: *I can certainly understand that. It would be unpleasant, awkward, inconvenient. But it is illogical to think that it would be terrible, or . . . that it somehow bears on your worth as a person.*

punishment   The presentation of an aversive stimulus or the removal of a pleasant one following some behavior.

rational-emotive behavior therapy (REBT)   A treatment that involves identifying illogical, self-defeating thoughts that clients have learned, then helping clients replace these thoughts with more realistic and beneficial ones.

ALBERT ELLIS ▲

Rational-emotive behavior therapy (REBT) focuses on altering the self-defeating thoughts that Ellis believed underlie people's behavior disorders. Ellis argued, for example, that students do not get upset because they fail a test but because they have learned to believe that failure is a disaster that indicates they are worthless. Many of Ellis's ideas have been incorporated into various forms of cognitive behavior therapy, and they helped Ellis himself to deal rationally with the health problems he encountered prior to his death in 2007 (Ellis, 1997).

Client: *What do you mean?*

Therapist: *Well, suppose one of your friends calls you up and invites you back to that restaurant. If you start telling yourself, "I might panic and pass out and people might make fun of me and that would be terrible," . . . you might find you are dreading going to the restaurant, and you probably won't enjoy the meal very much.*

Client: *Well, that is what usually happens.*

Therapist: *But it doesn't have to be that way. . . . The way you feel, your reaction . . . depends on what you choose to believe or think, or say to yourself.* (Masters et al., 1987)

Cognitive behavior therapists use many techniques related to REBT to help clients learn to think in more adaptive ways. Techniques aimed at replacing upsetting thoughts with alternative thinking patterns are described by behaviorists as *cognitive restructuring* (Lazarus, 1971; Moore, Zoellner, & Bittinger, 2004). They help clients plan calming thoughts to use during exams, tense conversations, and other anxiety-provoking situations. These thoughts might include "OK, stay calm, you can handle this. Just focus on the task, and don't worry about being perfect." Sometimes, these techniques are expanded to include *stress inoculation training,* in which clients imagine being in a stressful situation and then practice newly learned cognitive skills to remain calm (Meichenbaum, 2003; Sheehy & Horan, 2004).

Beck's Cognitive Therapy   Behavior therapists seek a different kind of cognitive restructuring when they use Aaron Beck's **cognitive therapy** (Beck, 1976, 1995, 2005; Beck, Freeman, & Davis, 2007). Beck's treatment approach is based on the idea that certain psychological problems—especially those related to depression and anxiety but also those related to personality disorders and schizophrenia (Beck et al., 2007; Beck et al., 2008)—can be traced partly to errors in logic (e.g., "If I fail my driver's test the first time, I will never pass it") and false beliefs (e.g., "Everyone ignores me"). Beck says that over time, these learned *cognitive distortions* occur so quickly and automatically that the client never stops to consider that they might not be true (see Table 13.2).

Cognitive therapy takes an active, organized, problem-solving approach in which therapists first help clients learn to identify the errors in logic, false beliefs, and other cognitive distortions that precede anxiety, depression, conduct problems, eating disorders, and other psychological problems (Beck & Rector, 2005; Drinkwater & Stewart, 2002; Fairburn, 2008; Hendricks & Thompson, 2005; Pardini & Lochman, 2003; Turkington, Kingdon, & Weiden, 2006). Then, much as in the five-step critical thinking system illustrated throughout this book, these thoughts and beliefs are considered as hypotheses to be tested, not as "facts" to be uncritically accepted (Hatcher, Brown, & Gariglietti, 2001). In other words, the therapist and client become a team of "investigators" as they plan ways to test beliefs such as "I'm no good around the house." For example, they might agree on tasks that the client will attempt as "homework"—such as cleaning the basement, hanging a picture, or cutting the grass. Success at accomplishing even one of these tasks provides concrete evidence to challenge a false belief about incompetence that has supported feelings of depression or anxiety, thus helping to reduce them (Beck et al., 1992; Mullin, 2000).

As described in the chapter on psychological disorders, however, depression, anxiety, and some other disorders may not be due entirely to specific thoughts or beliefs about specific situations. Sometimes they stem from a more general cognitive style that leads people to expect that the worst will always happen to them and to assume that negative events occur because they are completely and permanently incompetent and worthless (Beck & Alford, 2009). So cognitive behavior therapists also work with clients to develop more optimistic ways of thinking and to reduce their tendency to blame themselves for negative outcomes (Persons, Davidson, & Tompkins, 2001). In some cases, cognitive restructuring is combined with skill training, techniques for managing anxiety, and practice in using logical thinking, all of which are designed to

cognitive therapy An organized problem-solving approach in which the therapist actively collaborates with clients to help them notice how certain negative thoughts precede anxiety and depression.

help clients experience success and develop confidence in situations in which they had previously expected to fail (Bryant et al., 2008).

Group, Family, and Couples Therapy

▶ *How does group psychotherapy differ from individual therapy?*

The one-on-one methods of psychodynamic, humanistic, and behavioral treatment we have described are often adapted for use with groups of clients or family units (Petrocelli, 2002; Rosen, Stukenberg, & Saeks, 2001; Scheidinger, 2004; Thorngren & Kleist, 2002).

Group Psychotherapy

Group psychotherapy refers to the treatment of several clients under the guidance of a therapist who encourages helpful interactions among group members. Many groups are organized around one type of problem (such as alcoholism) or one type of client (such as adolescents). In most cases, a group of six to twelve clients meets with their therapist at least once a week for about two hours. All group members agree to hold confidential everything that occurs within group sessions.

Group psychotherapy offers features that are not found in individual treatment (Marmarosh, Holtz, & Schottenbauer, 2005; Ogrondniczuk & Piper, 2003; Yalom, 2005). First, it allows the therapist to observe clients interacting with one another. Second, groups encourage their members to talk about themselves and explore their feelings. As they listen to each other, clients often feel less alone because they realize that many people are struggling with difficulties at least as severe as their own. This realization tends to raise each client's expectations for improvement, a factor that is important in all forms of treatment. Third, group members can boost one another's self-confidence and self-acceptance as they come to trust and value one another. Fourth, clients learn from one another. They share ideas for solving problems and give one another honest feedback about their attitudes and behavior. Fifth, perhaps through mutual modeling, the group experience makes clients more sensitive to other people's needs, motives, and messages. Finally, group psychotherapy allows clients to try out new skills in a supportive environment. So although the procedures and techniques employed in group psychotherapy may reflect any one (or more than one) of the theoretical orientations we have described in relation to individual therapy (Bieling,

group psychotherapy Psychotherapy involving six to twelve unrelated individuals.

TABLE 13.2 ■ SOME EXAMPLES OF NEGATIVE THINKING

Here are just a few examples of the kinds of thoughts that cognitive behavior therapists believe to be at the root of anxiety, depression, and other behavior problems. After reading this list, try writing an alternative thought that clients could use to replace each of these ingrained cognitive habits. Then jot down a "homework assignment" that you would recommend to help clients challenge each maladaptive statement and thus develop new ways of thinking about themselves.

"I shouldn't draw attention to myself."

"I will never be any good at this."

"It would be so awful if I don't know the answer."

"Everyone is smarter than I am."

"Nobody likes me."

"I should be able to do this job perfectly."

"What if I panic?"

"I'll never be happy."

"I should have accomplished more by this point in my life."

McCabe, & Antony, 2006), the impact of the treatment is thought to be enhanced by the nature and strength of the group itself.

Family and Couples Therapy

As its name implies, **family therapy** involves treatment of two or more individuals from the same family. One of these, often a troubled adolescent or child, is the initially identified client. Whether family therapy is based on psychodynamic, humanistic, or cognitive behavioral approaches, the family is usually considered as a functioning unit known as a *family system*. As with group psychotherapy, the family therapy format gives the therapist an excellent view of how the initially identified client interacts with others, thus providing a basis for discussion of topics that are important to each family member. And as with group psychotherapists, family therapists usually have special training that helps them understand how the problems of individual family members affect and are affected by problems in the complex interactions taking place within the family system as a whole (Cox & Paley, 2003; Nichols, 2007; Williams, 2005). Ultimately, the client in family therapy is the family itself, and treatment involves as many members as possible. In fact, the goal of family therapy is not just to ease the identified client's problems but also to create greater harmony and balance within the family by helping each member understand family interaction patterns and the problems they create (Blow & Timm, 2002; Goldenberg & Goldenberg, 1995).

In **couples therapy,** improving communication between partners is one of the most important targets of treatment (Christensen et al., 2004; Gurman, 2008). Discussions in couples therapy sessions typically focus on identifying the miscommunication or lack of communication that interferes with the couples' happiness and intimacy and improving their ability to interact more positively and productively. Often the sessions revolve around learning to abide by certain "rules for talking," such as those listed in Table 13.3. For some therapists, helping couples become closer also means helping them express emotions more honestly and be more accepting of one another (Shadish & Baldwin, 2005; Wood et al., 2005). Some therapists even offer preventive treatment to couples who are at risk for relationship problems (Gottman, Gottman, & Declaire, 2006; Jacobson et al., 2000; Laurenceau et al., 2004). ("In Review: Approaches to Psychological Treatment" summarizes key features of the main approaches to treatment that we have discussed so far.)

family therapy A type of treatment involving two or more clients from the same family.

couples therapy A form of therapy that focuses on improving communication between partners.

TABLE 13.3 ■ **SOME "RULES FOR TALKING" IN COUPLES THERAPY**

Many forms of couples therapy help partners improve communication through establishing rules such as these. Think about your own experience in relationships or your observations of couples as they interact, and then write down some rules you would add to this list. Why do you think it would be important for couples to follow the rules on your list?

Learn BY Doing

1. Always begin with something positive when stating a problem.

2. Use specific behaviors rather than derogatory labels or overgeneralizations to describe what is bothersome about the other person.

3. Make connections between those specific behaviors and feelings that arise in response to them (e.g., "It makes me sad when you . . .").

4. Admit your own role in the development of the problem.

5. Be brief; don't lecture or harangue.

6. Maintain a focus on the present or the future; don't review all previous examples of the problem or ask "why" questions such as "Why do you always . . .?"

7. Talk about observable events; don't make inferences about them (e.g., say "I get angry when you interrupt me" rather than "Stop trying to make me feel stupid").

8. Paraphrase what your partner has said and check out your own perceptions of what was said before responding. (Note that this suggestion is based on the same principle as Rogers's empathic listening.)

In Review

APPROACHES TO PSYCHOLOGICAL TREATMENT

DIMENSION	CLASSICAL PSYCHOANALYTIC	CONTEMPORARY PSYCHODYNAMIC	HUMANISTIC	BEHAVIORAL/ COGNITIVE BEHAVIORAL
Nature of the human being	Driven by sexual and aggressive urges	Driven by the need for human relationships	Has free will, choice, and capacity for self-actualization	Is a product of social learning and conditioning; behaves on the basis of past experience
Therapist's role	Neutral; helps client explore meaning of free associations and other material from the unconscious	Active; develops relationship with client as a model for other relationships	Facilitates client's growth; some therapists are active, some are nondirective	Teacher/trainer who helps client replace undesirable thoughts and behaviors; active, action oriented
Focus	Unresolved unconscious conflicts from the distant past	Understanding the past but focusing on current relationships	Here and now; focus on immediate experience	Current behavior and thoughts; may not need to know original causes to create change
Goals	Psychosexual maturity through insight; strengthening of ego functions	Correction of effects of failures of early attachment; development of satisfying intimate relationships	Expanded awareness; fulfilment of potential; self-acceptance	Changes in thinking and behaving in particular classes of situations; better self-management
Typical methods	Free association; dream analysis, analysis of transference	Analysis of interpersonal relationships, including the client-therapist relationship	Reflection-oriented interviews designed to convey unconditional positive regard, empathy, and congruence; exercises to promote self-awareness	Systematic desensitization therapy, flooding, implosive therapy, modeling, assertiveness and social skills training, positive reinforcement, extinction, aversion conditioning, punishment, cognitive restructuring

1. *Object relations therapy and interpersonal therapy are both contemporary examples of the _____ approach to psychological treatment.*
2. *Imagining increasingly fear-provoking stimuli is a _____ treatment method called _____.*
3. *Reflection is an interviewing technique associated mainly with the _____ approach to treatment.*

Evaluating Psychotherapy

▶ *How effective is psychotherapy?*

Some years ago, a consumer magazine's survey suggested that most clients believe that psychotherapy is effective (Consumer Reports, 1995; Seligman, 1996), but confirming that effectiveness through experimental research has proven to be challenging and controversial (Dawes, 1994; DeRubeis & Crits-Christoph, 1998; Laurenceau, Hayes, & Feldman, 2007; Norcross, Beutler, & Levant, 2005; Seligman, 1995; Weisz, Weersing, & Henggeler, 2005; Westen, Novotny, & Thompson-Brenner, 2004).

Can therapy change personality?
(a link to Personality)

The value of psychotherapy was first widely questioned in 1952, when British psychologist Hans Eysenck reviewed studies in which thousands of clients had received either traditional psychodynamic therapy, various other therapies, or no treatment. To the surprise and dismay of many therapists, Eysenck (1952) found that the percentage of clients who improved following any kind of psychotherapy was actually lower than among people who received no treatment.

Critics argued that Eysenck was wrong (e.g., Bergin, 1971; de Charms, Levy, & Wertheimer, 1954; Luborsky, 1972). They claimed that he had ignored studies supporting the value of psychotherapy and had misinterpreted the data. In fact, when some of these critics reviewed treatment successes and failures themselves, they concluded that psychotherapy tends to be *more* helpful than no treatment (e.g., Bergin, 1971).

Debate over Eysenck's findings and the contradictory reports that followed them highlight several reasons why it is so hard to answer the apparently simple question of whether psychotherapy works. For one thing, there is the problem of how to measure improvement in psychotherapy. Should we focus on psychological test results, behavioral observations, interviews, or a combination of all three? Different measurements may tell somewhat different stories about improvement, making it difficult for researchers to compare or combine the results of different studies and draw conclusions about the overall effectiveness of treatment (De Los Reyes & Kazdin, 2006; Krause, 2005; Sass, Twohig, & Davies, 2004).

The question of effectiveness is further complicated by the broad range of clients, therapists, and treatments involved in psychotherapy. Clients differ in the problems they present, in their motivation to solve their problems, and in the amount of stress and social support present in their environments. Therapists differ, too, not only in skill, experience, and personality but also in which of the hundreds of available treatment procedures they decide to use and for how long (Barkham et al., 2006; Feltham, 2000; Wampold, 2005). In addition, differences in the nature and quality of the client-therapist relationship from one case to another can significantly alter the course of treatment, the clients' faith in the procedures, and the clients' willingness to cooperate (Lambert & Barley, 2001; Norcross, 2002; Zuroff & Blatt, 2006). Because clients' responses to psychotherapy can be influenced by all of these factors, results from any particular treatment evaluation study might not tell us much about how well different therapists using different methods would do with other kinds of clients and problems (Kazdin, 1994; Roth & Fonagy, 2005).

In short, the question of whether psychotherapy "works" is difficult (if not impossible) to answer scientifically in a way that applies to all therapies for all disorders. However, several research reviews (Galatzer-Levy et al., 2000; Kazdin & Weisz, 2003; Leichsenring, Rabung, & Leibing, 2004; Nathan & Gorman, 2007; Shadish et al., 2000) have demonstrated that in general psychotherapy does work (see Figure 13.2).

FIGURE 13.2 ■ **AN ANALYSIS OF PSYCHOTHERAPY'S EFFECTS**

These curves show the results of one large-scale analysis of the effects of psychotherapy. Notice that on average, people who received therapy were better off than 80 percent of troubled people who did not. The overall effectiveness of psychotherapy has also been confirmed in a more recent analysis of 90 treatment outcome studies (Shadish et al., 2000).
Source: Data from Smith, Glass, & Miller (1980).

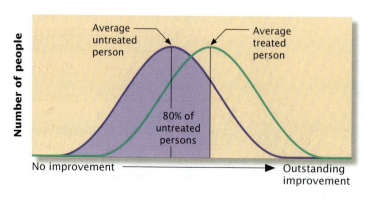

Thinking CRITICALLY

Are All Forms of Therapy Equally Effective?

As you might imagine, most therapists agree that psychotherapy is effective and most believe that the theoretical approach and treatment methods *they* use work better than those of other therapists (Mandelid, 2003).

▷ What am I being asked to believe or accept?

They can't all be right, of course, and some researchers claim that they are all wrong. These researchers argue that in fact, various theories of behavior disorder and the specific treatment methods based on them don't have much to do with the success of psychotherapy. All approaches, they say, are equally effective. This has been called the "Dodo Bird Verdict," named after the *Alice in Wonderland* creature who when called on to judge who had won a race answered, "Everybody has won and all must have prizes" (Duncan, 2002; Luborsky, Singer, & Luborsky, 1975).

▷ Is evidence available to support the claim?

Some evidence does suggest that there are no significant differences in the overall effectiveness of psychodynamic, humanistic, and behavioral therapies. Statistical analyses that combine the results of a large number of therapy studies show that the three approaches are associated with about the same degree of success (Luborsky et al., 2002; Luborsky, Rosenthal, & Diguer, 2003; Shadish et al., 2000; Weisz, McCarty, & Valeri, 2006).

▷ Can that evidence be interpreted another way?

It is possible, however, that evidence in favor of the Dodo Bird Verdict is based on statistical methods that cannot detect genuine differences among treatments. A statistical analysis that averages the results of many different studies might not reveal important differences in the impact of particular treatments for particular problems (Beutler, 2002; Carroll, 2002; Eysenck, 1978; Rounsaville & Wilson, 1985). Suppose, for example, that Therapy A works better than Therapy B in treating anxiety but that Therapy B works better than Therapy A in cases of depression. If you combined the results

of treatment studies with both kinds of clients, the average effects of each therapy would be about the same, making it appear that the two treatments are about equally effective. Differences among the effects of specific treatment procedures might also be overshadowed by the beneficial *common factors* almost all forms of therapy share—such as the support of the therapist, the hope and expectancy for improvement that therapy creates, and the trust that develops between client and therapist (Barber et al., 2000; Greenberg, Constantino, & Bruce, 2006; Kazantzis, Lampropoulos, & Deane, 2005; Martin, Garske, & Davis, 2000; Vocisano et al., 2004). Therapists whose personal characteristics can motivate clients to change might promote that change no matter what specific therapeutic methods they use (Norcross, 2002).

▷ What evidence would help to evaluate the alternatives?

Debate over the question of whether all forms of psychotherapy are about equally effective on the average is likely to continue, but to many researchers, it is the wrong question. They argue that is pointless to compare the effects of psychodynamic, humanistic, and behavioral methods in general. It is more important, they say, to address what Gordon Paul called the "ultimate question" about psychotherapy: "What treatment, by whom, is most effective for this individual with that specific problem, under what set of circumstances?" (Paul, 1969, p. 44).

▷ What conclusions are most reasonable?

Statistical analyses show that various treatment approaches appear about equally effective overall. But this does not mean that every psychotherapy experience will be equally helpful. Potential clients must realize that the success of their treatment can still be affected by how severe their problems are, by the quality of the therapeutic relationship they form with a therapist, by their motivation to change, and by the appropriateness of the therapy methods chosen for their problems (Goldfried & Davila, 2005).

---

linkages

Does psychotherapy work? *(a link to Introduction to the Science of Psychology)*

evidence based practice The selection of treatment methods based mainly on empirical evidence of their effectiveness.

Like those seeking treatment, many clinical psychologists are eager for more specific scientific evidence about the effectiveness of particular therapies for particular kinds of clients and disorders. These empirically oriented clinicians are concerned that all too often, therapists' choices of therapy methods depend more heavily on personal preferences or current trends than on scientific evidence of effectiveness (Lynn, Lilienfeld, & Lohr, 2003; Nathan, Stuart, & Dolan, 2000; Norcross, Beutler, & Levant, 2005; Tavris, 2003). They believe that advocates of any treatment—whether it is object relations therapy or systematic desensitization therapy—must demonstrate that its benefits are the result of the treatment itself and not just of the passage of time, the effects of repeated assessment, the client's motivation and personal characteristics, or other confounding factors (Chambless & Hollon, 1998). In other words, these clinicians advocate **evidence based practice,** in which practitioners make decisions about which methods to use based mainly on the results of empirical evidence about the effectiveness of those methods. A movement toward evidence based practice has also appeared in the medical and dental professions (Borry, Schotsmans, & Dierickx, 2006; Niederman & Richards, 2005).

Empirically oriented clinicians also want to see evidence that the benefits of treatment are clinically significant. To be *clinically significant,* therapeutic changes must be great enough to make the feelings and actions of treated clients similar to those of people who have not experienced these clients' disorders (Crits-Christoph et al., 2008; Kazdin, 2003; Kendall & Choudhury, 2003). The need to demonstrate clinical significance has become more important than ever as increasingly cost-conscious clients and their health insurance companies decide whether and how much to pay for various psychotherapy services (Levant, 2005; Makeover, 2004; Nelson & Steele, 2006). The most scientific way to evaluate treatment effects is through studies in which clients are randomly assigned to various treatments or control conditions and their progress is measured objectively.

Focus on RESEARCH

Which Therapies Work Best for Which Problems?

To help clinicians select treatment methods on the basis of this kind of empirical evidence, the American Psychological Association's Clinical Psychology Division, also known as the Society of Clinical Psychology, created a task force on effective psychotherapies that is now called the Committee on Science and Practice (Sanderson, 2003; Task Force on Promotion and Dissemination of Psychological Procedures, 1995).

▶ What was the researchers' question?

The question addressed by this task force was "What therapies have proven themselves most effective in treating various kinds of psychological disorders?"

▶ How did the researchers answer the question?

Working with other empirically oriented clinical psychologists, members of this task force examined the outcomes of thousands of well-controlled experiments that evaluated psychotherapy methods used to treat mental disorder, marital distress, and health-related behavior problems in children, adolescents, and adults (Baucom et al., 1998; Chambless & Ollendick, 2001; Compas et al., 1998; DeRubeis & Crits-Christoph, 1998; Foley, 2004; Kazdin & Weisz, 1998; Kendall & Chambless, 1998).

▶ What did the researchers find?

The task force found that a number of treatments—known as **empirically supported therapies,** or **ESTs**—have been validated by controlled experimental research (Chambless & Ollendick, 2001; DeRubeis & Crits-Christoph, 1998; Kendall & Chambless, 1998; Norcross, 2001, 2002). Table 13.4 contains some examples of these therapies. Notice that the treatments identified as effective for particular problems in adult clients are mainly behavioral, cognitive, and cognitive behavioral methods (Norcross, Beutler, & Levant, 2005), but that a few psychodynamic therapies (e.g., interpersonal therapy and brief dynamic therapy) also made the list (Chambless & Ollendick, 2001; Svartberg, Stiles, & Seltzer, 2004).

▶ What do the results mean?

The authors of the report on empirically supported therapies and those who support their efforts claim that by relying on analysis of experimental research, they have scientifically evaluated various treatments and generated a list of methods from which consumers—and clinicians who want to conduct an evidence based practice—can choose with confidence when facing specific disorders (e.g., Hunsley & Rumstein-McKean, 1999; Kendall & Chambless, 1998). Therapists are even being urged to follow *treatment manuals* stemming from this research to help them deliver empirically supported therapies exactly as they were intended (Addis, 1997; Addis & Krasnow, 2000; Wade, Treat, & Stuart, 1998). The state of Kansas was the first in the United States to formally encourage the use of empirically supported treatments for children (Roberts, 2002).

Not everyone agrees with the conclusions and recommendations of the APA task force. Critics note, first, that treatments missing from the latest list of ESTs haven't necessarily been discredited. Some of those treatments might not yet have been studied or validated in relation to the efficacy criteria selected by the task force. These critics also have doubts about the value of some of those criteria. They point to research showing that had the task force used different outcome criteria, it might have reached different (and perhaps less optimistic) conclusions about the value of some empirically supported treatments (Bradley et al., 2005; Thompson-Brenner, Glass, & Westen, 2003). There is concern, too, about the wisdom of categorizing treatments as either "supported" or "unsupported." These simple either-or judgments seem reassuring but may fail to give a complete picture of the impact of various treatments on various clients with various problems (Krause & Lutz, 2006; Westen & Bradley, 2005). Critics argue further that the list of empirically supported therapies is based on research that may not be relevant to clinicians working in the real world of clinical practice. They note that experimental studies of psychotherapy have focused mainly on relatively brief treatments for highly specific disorders, even though most clients' problems tend to be far

TABLE 13.4 ■ EXAMPLES OF EMPIRICALLY SUPPORTED THERAPIES FOR SELECTED DISORDERS

Treatments listed as "efficacious and specific" (pronounced "effeh-KAY-shus") were shown to be superior to no treatment or to an alternative treatment in at least two experiments in which clients were randomly assigned to various treatment conditions. These experiments are called *randomized clinical trials*, or RCTs. Also included in this category are treatments supported by scientific outcome measures from a large number of carefully conducted case studies. Treatments listed as "probably efficacious" are supported by at least one RCT or by a smaller number of rigorously evaluated case studies. Those listed as "possibly efficacious" are supported by a mixture of data, generally from case studies or other nonexperimental studies (Chambless & Ollendick, 2001). More information about these ESTs is available at http://www.apa.org/divisions/div12/rev_est/. Other reviews of empirical research are aimed at identifying potentially harmful therapies (Lilienfeld, 2007).

Problem	Efficacious and Specific	Probably Efficacious	Possibly Efficacious
Major depression	Behavior therapy Cognitive behavior therapy Interpersonal therapy	Brief dynamic therapy	
Specific phobia	Exposure therapy	Systematic desensitization therapy	
Agoraphobia/panic disorder	Cognitive behavior therapy	Couples training + exposure therapy	
Generalized anxiety disorder	Cognitive behavior therapy	Applied relaxation therapy	
Obsessive-compulsive disorder	Exposure therapy + response prevention	Cognitive therapy Family-assisted exposure therapy + response prevention + relaxation	Rational emotive behavior therapy + exposure therapy
Posttraumatic stress disorder		Exposure Stress inoculation Cognitive therapy + stress inoculation + exposure	Structured psychodynamic treatment
Schizophrenia	Behavioral family therapy	Family systems therapy Social skills training Supportive group therapy	Cognitive therapy (for delusions)
Alcohol abuse and dependence	Community reinforcement	Cue exposure therapy Behavioral marital therapy + anti-alcohol drug disulfiram Social skills training (with inpatients)	
Opiate abuse and dependence		Behavior therapy Brief dynamic therapy Cognitive therapy	
Marital discord	Behavioral marital therapy	Insight-oriented marital therapy	

Source: Chambless & Ollendick (2001).

more complex (Westen & Bradley, 2005). These studies focus, too, on the therapeutic procedures used rather than on the characteristics and interactions of therapists and clients (Cornelius-White, 2002; Garfield, 1998; Hilliard, Henry, & Strupp, 2000; Westen et al., 2004). This emphasis on procedure in these studies is a problem, critics say, because the outcome of therapy in these experiments might have been affected strongly by client-therapist factors, such as whether the random pairing of clients and therapists resulted in a match or a mismatch on certain personal characteristics. In real clinical situations, clients and therapists are not usually paired up at random (Goldfried & Davila, 2005; Hill, 2005; Hohman & Shear, 2002). Finally, because therapists participating in experimental research were required to follow standard treatment manuals, they were not free to adapt treatment methods to the needs of particular clients, as they normally would do (Garfield, 1998). Perhaps, say critics, when there is less experimental control over the treatment situation, all therapies really are about equally effective, as suggested by the statistical analyses of outcome research we mentioned earlier (Shadish et al., 2000; Smith, Glass, & Miller, 1980).

In short, critics reject the empirically supported therapies list as a useful guide. In fact, some see it as an incomplete and ultimately misleading document (Westen & Bradley, 2005). They also worry that widespread use of treatment manuals would make psychotherapy mechanical and less effective and would discourage therapists from developing new treatment methods (Addis & Krasnow, 2000; Beutler, 2000; Garfield, 1998).

Partly in response to these concerns, it has been suggested that the evidence in evidence based practice should come not just from randomized clinical trials but also from less rigorous studies of therapy and the therapeutic relationship and from clinicians' experiences in real-world treatment settings. This idea was formalized in an APA task force policy statement that says, in part, that "evidence-based practice in psychology . . . is the integration of the best available research with clinical expertise in the context of patient characteristics, culture, and preferences" (American Psychological Association Presidential Task Force on Evidence-Based Practice, 2006, p. 273). The contrast between this view and the one that defines effective psychotherapy in terms of ESTs illustrates the gap that remains between those who would base treatment decisions mainly on the outcome of controlled experimental research (Hunsley, 2007) and those who feel that the guidance provided by research results must be interpreted and adjusted in light of clinical judgment and experience (Zeldow, 2009).

▶ **What do we still need to know?**

It remains to be seen if clinicians and researchers will be able to come together to bridge the gap between them in a way that makes the best use of both domains of knowledge in the service of clients' welfare (e.g., Barlow, 2006; Becker et al., 2009; Castonguay & Beutler, 2005; Fago, 2009; Shapiro, 2009). Still, the effort to identify empirically supported treatments and to develop evidence based practice in clinical psychology (Levant, 2005) represent important steps in responding to Paul's (1969) "ultimate question" about psychotherapy: "What treatment, by whom, is most effective for this individual with that specific problem, under what set of circumstances?" We still have a long way to go to answer all aspects of Paul's complex question, but empirically oriented clinical psychologists are determined to do so.

Though the combinations of treatment methods and therapist and client characteristics that are best suited to solving particular psychological problems have not yet been mapped out, a few notable trends have emerged. For example, when differences in the effectiveness of different treatments do show up in comparative studies of adult psychotherapy, they tend to reveal a small to moderate advantage for behavioral and cognitive behavioral methods, especially in the treatment of phobias and certain other anxiety disorders (Butler et al., 2006; Craske & Barlow, 2008; Eddy et al., 2004; Hollon, Stewart, & Strunk, 2006; Schnurr et al., 2007) and in the prevention and treatment of eating disorders (Hendricks & Thompson, 2005; Stice & Shaw, 2004). The same overall trend also holds true in the treatment of child and adolescent clients (Carr, 2009; Kendall et al., 2008; Weisz, Doss, & Hawley, 2005).

Further, the client-therapist relationship seems to play a significant role in the success of many forms of treatment (Brown & O'Leary, 2000; Constantino et al., 2005; Horvath, 2005; Karver et al., 2006; Martin, Garske, & Davis, 2000; Messer & Wampold, 2002; Uwe, 2005; Zuroff & Blatt, 2006). Certain people seem to be particularly effective in forming productive human relationships. Even without formal training, these people can sometimes be as helpful as professional therapists because of personal qualities that are inspiring, healing, and soothing to others (Hill & Lent, 2006; Ronnestad & Ladany, 2006). These qualities may help account for the success of many kinds of therapy.

In summary, the Dodo Bird Verdict is probably incorrect, and it is certainly incomplete. Although different treatments can be equally effective in addressing some disorders, empirical research shows that for other disorders certain therapies are more effective than others. That research provides valuable guidelines for matching treatments to disorders, but it doesn't guarantee success. The outcome of any given case will also be affected by characteristics of the client, characteristics of the therapist, and the nature of the therapeutic relationship that develops between them (e.g., Hill, 2005; Sherer & Schreibman, 2005). The challenge now is to combine research on empirically supported therapy methods with research on the common factors they share and create a picture of the effectiveness of psychotherapy methods that is based on both sets of data (Messer, 2004; Westen & Bradley, 2005). Such a comprehensive view would be a useful guide for clinicians practicing today and an ideal training model for the clinicians of tomorrow.

Given what is known so far, potential clients are well advised to choose a treatment approach and a therapist based on (1) suggestions from empirical research about the best treatment for their particular problem; (2) the treatment approach, methods, and goals the person finds comfortable and appealing; (3) information about the potential therapist's "track record" of clinically significant success with a particular method for treating

empirically supported therapies (ESTs) Treatments for psychological disorders whose effectiveness has been validated by controlled experimental research.

problems similar to those the person faces; and (4) the likelihood of forming a productive relationship with the therapist. This last consideration assumes special importance when the client and the therapist do not share similar social or cultural backgrounds.

Sociocultural Factors in Therapy

Sociocultural differences between clients and therapists—in religious faith, gender, age, ethnicity, sexual orientation, socioeconomic background, and the like—can sometimes create miscommunication or mistrust (Seeley, 2006). If it does, their working relationship and the clients' motivation to change may both be impaired (Jones, Botsko, & Gorman, 2003; Pachankis & Goldfried, 2004; Vasquez, 2007). Suppose, for example, that a therapist suggests that a client's insomnia is a reaction to stress but the client is sure that it comes as punishment for having offended a long-dead ancestor. That client may not easily accept a treatment based on the principles of stress management (Wohl, 1995). Similarly, a therapist who believes that people should confront and overcome life's problems might run into trouble when treating clients whose cultural or religious training encourages the calm acceptance of such problems (Sue et al., 2009). In such cases, the result may be much like two people singing a duet using the same music but different lyrics (Martinez et al., 2005; Martinez-Taboas, 2005).

In the United States, cultural clashes may be partly to blame for the underuse of or withdrawal from mental health services by recent immigrants and by African Americans, Asian Americans, Hispanic Americans, American Indians, and members of other minority populations (Dingfelder, 2005; Duran et al., 2005; Gone, 2004; Neighbors et al., 2007; Sanders et al., 2004; Thurston & Phares, 2008; Wang et al., 2005). Accordingly, major efforts are under way to ensure that such differences do not impede the delivery of treatment to anyone who wants or needs it (Richards & Bergin, 2000). Virtually every mental health training program in North America is seeking to recruit more students from traditionally underserved minority groups to eventually make it easier to match clients with therapists from similar cultural backgrounds (e.g., Kersting, 2004; Meredith & Baker, 2007; Rogers & Molina, 2006). In the meantime, many minority clients are likely to encounter a therapist from a differing background, so researchers have also examined the value of matching therapeutic techniques with clients' culturally based expectations and preferences (Jones, Botsko, & Gorman, 2003; Li & Kim, 2004; Muñoz & Mendelson, 2005).

Today, psychotherapists are more sensitive than ever to the cultural values of particular groups and the difficulties that can impair intercultural communication (Ali,

PREPARING FOR THERAPY ▶

Special pretreatment orientation programs may be offered to clients who because of sociocultural factors are unfamiliar with the rules and procedures of psychotherapy. These programs provide a preview of what psychotherapy is, how psychotherapy can help, and what the client is expected to do to make it more effective (Reis & Brown, 2006; Swartz, Zuckoff et al., 2007).

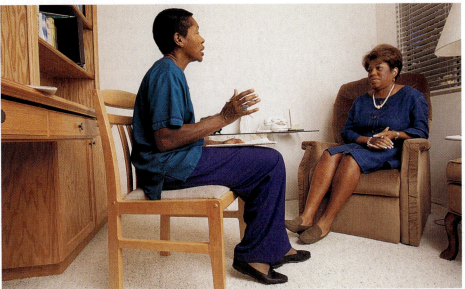

© Spencer Grant/PhotoEdit

Liu, & Humedian, 2004; Hays & Iwamasa, 2006; Hwang, 2006; LaRoche & Martin, 2005; Martinez et al., 2005; Sue et al., 2009; Weisman, 2005). Some U.S. states now require psychologists to complete courses on the role of cultural factors in therapy before they can qualify for licenses (Rehm & DeMers, 2006). Similar cultural diversity training is also required for all graduate students in clinical and counseling psychology training programs accredited by the American Psychological Association (Commission on Accreditation, 2008; Kersting, 2004; Smith, Constantine et al., 2006). This special training helps clinicians and graduate students appreciate, for example, that it is considered impolite in some cultures to make eye contact with a stranger. Armed with this information, a therapist is more likely to realize that clients from those cultures are not necessarily depressed, lacking in self-esteem, or overly submissive just because they look at the floor during an interview.

There is no guarantee that ethnic matching or cultural diversity training for therapists will improve treatment results (McCabe, 2002; Shin et al., 2005), but there is some evidence that it can help (e.g., Constantine, 2002; Razali, Aminah, & Umeed, 2002; Sue et al., 2009). And although it is unrealistic to expect all therapists to be equally effective with clients of all sociocultural backgrounds, cultural diversity training offers a way to improve their *cultural competence,* an extension of Carl Rogers's concept of empathy. When therapists appreciate the client's view of the world, it is easier for them to set goals that are in harmony with that view (Dyche & Zayas, 2001; Pedersen & Draguns, 2002; Stuart, 2004; Ulrich, Richards, & Bergin, 2000). Minimizing misunderstanding and miscommunication is one of the many ethical obligations that therapists assume when working with clients (Tomes, 1999). Let's consider some others.

Rules and Rights in the Therapeutic Relationship

Treatment can be an intensely emotional experience, and the relationship established with a therapist can profoundly influence a client's life. Professional ethics and common sense require the therapist to ensure that this relationship does not harm the client. For example, the American Psychological Association's *Ethical Principles of Psychologists and Code of Conduct* forbids a sexual relationship between therapist and client during treatment and for at least two years afterward because of the severe harm it can cause the client (American Psychological Association, 2002b; Behnke, 2004). Even after two years have passed, therapists may not ethically pursue a sexual relationship with a former client unless they can demonstrate that the relationship is not exploitative or otherwise harmful to that client. Laws in some U.S. states prohibit therapists from *ever* having a sexual relationship with a former client, and these laws take precedence over the APA's code of conduct.

The APA's ethical standards also require therapists to keep strictly confidential everything a client says in therapy. Confidentiality is one of the most important features of a successful therapeutic relationship. It allows the client to reveal unpleasant or embarrassing impulses, behaviors, or events without fear that this information will be repeated to anyone else. Professionals do sometimes consult with one another about a client, but each is required not to reveal information to outsiders (including members of an adult client's family) without the client's consent. The APA's code of ethics even includes standards for protecting confidentiality for the growing number of clients who seek psychological services via *telehealth* or *e-health* channels, which include telephone, video conferencing, e-mail, or other Internet links (Andersson, 2009; American Psychological Association, 2002b; Barnett & Scheetz, 2003; Christensen, Griffiths, & Jorm, 2004; Fisher & Fried, 2003; Mohr et al., 2005; Ruskin et al., 2004). One of these standards requires therapists to inform clients that others might be able to gain access to their e-mail messages and that no formal client-therapist relationship exists in e-mail exchanges.

Professional standards about confidentiality are backed up in most U.S. states and in federal courts by laws that recognize that information revealed in therapy (like information given to a priest, a lawyer, or a physician) is privileged communication. This means that a therapist can refuse—even in court—to answer questions about a client or to provide personal notes or recordings from therapy sessions. Only under special circumstances can therapists be legally required to violate confidentiality (Donner et al., 2008). These circumstances include those in which (1) a client is so severely disturbed or suicidal that hospitalization is needed; (2) a client uses his or her mental condition and history of therapy as part of his or her defense in a civil or criminal trial; (3) the therapist must defend against a client's charge of malpractice; (4) a client reveals information about sexual or physical abuse of a child who is still under the age of 18; and (5) the therapist believes a client may commit a violent act against a specific person.

Biological Treatments

▶ *Is electric shock still used to treat disorders?*

So far, we have described psychological approaches to the treatment of mental disorders. But biological treatments are also available, primarily through psychiatrists and other medical doctors, who often work in cooperation with psychologists. Today, biological treatments for psychological problems mainly involve the prescribing of psychoactive drugs. In the mid-1900s, however, the most common biological treatment for severe psychological problems was the use of electric shock to create seizures.

Electroconvulsive Shock Therapy

In the 1930s, a Hungarian physician named Ladislaus von Meduna used a drug to induce convulsions in people with schizophrenia. He believed—incorrectly—that because schizophrenia and epilepsy rarely occur in the same person, epileptic-like seizures might combat schizophrenia. In 1938, Italian physicians Ugo Cerletti and Lucio Bini created seizures by passing an electric current through the brains of people with schizophrenia. During the next twenty years or so, this procedure, called **electroconvulsive shock therapy (ECT or EST)** or **electroshock therapy,** became a routine treatment for schizophrenia, depression, and sometimes mania. Although many patients improved at first, in many cases their problems reappeared. The benefits of ECT also had to be weighed against side effects such as memory loss, confusion, speech disorders, and, in some cases, death due to cardiac arrest (Lickey & Gordon, 1991; Shiwach, Reid, & Carmody, 2001).

In an effort to make ECT safer, doctors now give patients an anesthetic so that they are unconscious before the shock is delivered and a muscle relaxant to prevent bone fractures during convulsions. Also, the shock now lasts only about half a second and is usually delivered to only one side of the brain (Sackeim et al., 2000). Finally, in contrast to the dozens of treatments administered decades ago, patients now receive only about six to twelve shocks, one approximately every two days (Shorter & Healy, 2007).

Although we still don't know for sure how and why ECT works (Greenberg & Kellner, 2005; Shorter & Healy, 2007), it is being performed more frequently in the United States than coronary bypass operations, appendectomies, and tonsillectomies (Mathew, Amiel, & Sackeim, 2005). It is administered mainly to patients suffering severe depression (and occasionally to manic patients) who do not respond to medication (Daly et al., 2001; de Macedo-Soares et al., 2005; Rasmussen, 2003). ECT can be effective in such cases—especially when followed up with medication—and it does not appear to cause brain damage, even when administered repeatedly (e.g., Anghelescu et al., 2001; Dwork et al., 2004; Kellner et al., 2005, 2006; Sackeim et al., 2001). Nevertheless, researchers are looking for even safer methods of inducing seizures. Among the techniques being investigated are *magnetic seizure therapy (MST),* which administers timed pulses of magnetic energy (Lisanby, 2004), and a related but less intense procedure called *repetitive transcranial magnetic stimulation (rTMS;* Jorge et al., 2008; O'Reardon et al., 2007). *Deep brain stimulation (DBS)* does not cause seizures but requires the placement of electrodes in the brain to provide continuous pulses of electricity to a particular target area. Some researchers suggest that DBS may be of value in

The Medical History Museum of the University of Zurich

HOSPITAL RESTRAINTS ▲

Here are examples of the chains, straitjackets, belts, and covered bathtubs that were used to restrain disruptive patients in North American and European mental hospitals in the 1800s and well into the 1900s. These devices were gentle compared with some of the methods endorsed in the late 1700s by Benjamin Rush. Known as the father of American psychiatry, Rush advocated curing patients by frightening or disorienting them— for example, by placing them in a coffin-like box that was then briefly immersed in water. *Source*: The Museum of the History of Medicine of the University of Zurich, accessed online at http://www.nobel.se/medicine/articles/moniz/.

electroconvulsive shock therapy (electroshock therapy; ECT, EST)
A brief electric shock administered to the brain, usually to reduce severe depression that does not respond to drug treatments.

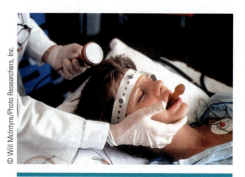

© Will McIntyre/Photo Researchers, Inc.

ELECTROCONVULSIVE SHOCK THERAPY ▲

Estimates of the number of people receiving ECT each year in the United States range from 30,000 to over 100,000 (Hermann et al., 1995; Mathew, Amiel, & Sackeim, 2005). A survey in the United Kingdom suggests that about 12,000 patients a year are receiving ECT (U.K. Statistical Bulletin, 1999). Because of its dramatic and potentially dangerous nature, the use of ECT remains controversial (Breggin, 2007). Critics want it outlawed, but proponents say the benefits of ECT for certain patients outweigh its potential dangers.

severe cases of depression and obsessive-compulsive disorder that are unresponsive to other treatments (Hardesty & Sackeim, 2007; Malone et al., 2009). Nevertheless, ECT and related brain stimulation procedures continue to be controversial (Breggin, 2007).

Psychoactive Drugs

The use of ECT declined after the 1950s, in part because psychoactive drugs had begun to emerge as more convenient and effective treatment alternatives. In the chapters on biology and behavior and on consciousness, we discuss the effects of psychoactive drugs on neurotransmitter systems, autonomic activity, emotions, thinking, and behavior. Here, we describe their role in combating schizophrenia, depression, mania, and anxiety.

Neuroleptic Drugs   **Neuroleptic drugs,** which are also called *antipsychotics*, dramatically reduce the intensity of psychotic symptoms such as hallucinations, delusions, paranoid suspiciousness, disordered thinking, and confused speech in many mental patients, especially those with schizophrenia. The most widely used antipsychotic drugs are the *phenothiazines* (pronounced "fee-noh-THIGH-uh-zeens"), of which the first, chlorpromazine (marketed as Thorazine in the United States and as Largactil in Canada and the United Kingdom), has been especially popular. Another neuroleptic drug, haloperidol (Haldol), is about as effective as the phenothiazines, but it creates less sedation (Julien, 2005). Patients who do not respond to one type of neuroleptic may respond to the other (Schatzberg, Cole, & DeBattista, 2007). Between 60 and 70 percent of psychiatric patients receiving these drugs show improvement, though fewer than 30 percent respond well enough to live successfully on their own.

Neuroleptic drugs have side effects ranging from dry mouth and dizziness to symptoms similar to those of Parkinson's disease, including muscle rigidity, restlessness, tremors, and slowed movement. Some of these side effects can be treated with medication, but at least 25 percent of patients who take chlorpromazine or haloperidol for several years develop an irreversible movement disorder. This disorder, called *tardive dyskinesia (TD),* causes uncontrollable, repetitive actions, often including twitching of the face, flailing of the arms and legs, and thrusting of the tongue.

Among a newer generation of antipsychotic drugs (also called *atypical neuroleptics*) is clozapine (Clozaril), which has effects like those of the phenothiazines but is less likely to cause movement disorders except at high doses (Louzá & Bassitt, 2005; Rochon et al., 2005). Although no more effective overall than the phenothiazines, clozapine has helped many patients who did not respond to the phenothiazines or haloperidol (Green & Patel, 1996; Rabinowitz et al., 2001). Unfortunately, taking clozapine carries a slight risk of developing a fatal blood disease called *agranulocytosis* (Ginsberg, 2006), which means that weekly blood tests are required to detect early signs of this disease. These tests greatly increase the cost and inconvenience of using clozapine (Meltzer, 1997), so it is usually prescribed only for patients who have not responded well to other medications and are willing to have their blood drawn frequently.

Several other atypical neuroleptics have been introduced recently, including risperidone (Risperdal), olanzapine (Zyprexa), quetiapine (Seroquel), ziprasidone (Geodon), and, most recently, aripiprazole (Abilify). These medications are expensive, but they have fewer side effects than clozapine and they do not seem to cause agranulocytosis (Schatzberg et al., 2007). Like clozapine, they also appear to reduce the "negative" symptoms of schizophrenia, such as lack of emotion, social withdrawal, and reduced speech (e.g., Fleischhacker & Widschwendter, 2006; Kane et al., 2003; Kapur, Sridhar, & Remington, 2004; Lieberman et al., 2003; Potkin et al., 2003). There is some doubt, though, whether these newest atypical neuroleptics are significantly more effective than older drugs, partly because 60 to 80 percent of patients may stop taking them because of weight gain, nervous tics, and other bothersome side effects (Lieberman et al., 2005; Miyamoto et al., 2005; Swartz, Perkins et al., 2007).

Antidepressant drugs   Soon after antipsychotic drugs appeared, they were joined by **antidepressant drugs,** a class of medications that is now widely prescribed for relieving the symptoms of depression (Schatzberg et al., 2007; Thomson Healthcare,

neuroleptic drugs   Drugs that relieve the symptoms of schizophrenia or other severe forms of psychological disorder. Also called antipsychotics.

antidepressant drugs   Drugs that reduce depression.

A NATURAL CURE?
An herbal remedy from a plant called *St. John's wort* has become a popular nonprescription treatment for depression. One of its active ingredients, *hypericin*, is thought to affect neurotransmitters in the brain much as Prozac or Zoloft does. One double-blind, placebo controlled study showed St. John's wort to be no more effective than a placebo for treating major depression (Hypericum Depression Trial Study Group, 2002), though others have shown it to be as effective as Prozac in cases of milder depression (e.g. Hammerness, Basch, & Ulbricht, 2003; Szegedi et al., 2005). Final conclusions about the safety and effectiveness of St. John's wort must await the results of further research (National Center for Complementary and Alternative Medicine, 2008).

2007). There are several types of antidepressant drugs. The *monoamine oxidase inhibitors (MAOIs)* are used to treat many cases of depression, especially with clients who also experience anxiety and panic (Julien, 2005). The *tricyclic antidepressants (TCAs)* are another popular type. The TCAs have been prescribed more frequently than MAOI drugs because they seem to work somewhat better and have fewer side effects. However, overdoses of TCAs can be fatal, as can taking TCAs and drinking alcohol at the same time (Nutt, 2005a).

The most prominent of several newer antidepressant drugs is fluoxetine (Prozac). Introduced in 1986, fluoxetine quickly became the most widely used antidepressant drug in North America. Its popularity is due to the fact that it is about as effective as older drugs and in most cases has fewer and milder side effects—mainly weight gain, sexual dysfunction, and gastrointestinal problems (Cookson & Duffett, 1998; Nutt, 2005a; Patten et al., 2005). An improved version of Prozac, R-fluoxetine, has now been developed (Norman & Olver, 2004), and other, even newer antidepressants also show promise. These include bupropion (Wellbutrin), venlafaxine (Effexor), nefazodone (Serzone), escitalopram (Lexapro), and duloxetine (Cymbalta; Brambilla et al., 2005; Hirschfeld & Vornik, 2004; Schatzberg et al., 2007; Zimmerman et al., 2005).

About 50 to 60 percent of patients who take antidepressant drugs show improved mood, greater physical activity, increased appetite, and better sleep (Hollon, Thase, & Markowitz, 2002). Escitalopram (Lexapro) seems to be particularly effective for clients with severe depression (Montgomery et al., 2007). Overall, though, only about 10 to 20 percent of people suffering the most severe psychotic depression show this same amount of improvement. It has long been assumed that the effects of antidepressant drugs were due to the chemical action of their active ingredients, but there is some doubt about this assumption. An analysis of clinical trial data submitted to the U.S. Food and Drug Administration by the makers of six widely prescribed antidepressant drugs showed that in 57 percent of the trials, antidepressant drugs did only a little better than placebo medications ("sugar pills") at relieving depression (Kirsch et al., 2002; Kirsch, Scoboria, & Moore, 2002). Defenders of antidepressant medications argue that even relatively small effects are better than none (e.g., Thase, 2002), whereas critics contend that those effects are too small to matter, especially when viewed in light of these drugs' high cost and potential adverse side effects (Breggin, 2008; Moncrieff & Kirsch, 2005; Wampold et al., 2005).

Lithium and Anticonvulsants The mineral salt lithium carbonate, when taken regularly, prevents both the depression and the mania associated with bipolar disorder in some patients (Baldessarini & Tondo, 2000; Geddes et al., 2004; Schatzberg et al., 2007). Without lithium, the typical patient with bipolar disorder has a manic episode about every fourteen months and a depressive episode about every seventeen months (American Psychiatric Association, 2000); with lithium, attacks of mania occur as rarely as every nine years (Geddes et al., 2004). The lithium dosage must be exact and carefully controlled, however, because taking too much can cause vomiting, nausea, tremor, fatigue, slurred speech, and, with severe overdoses, coma or death (Johnson, 2002). Combining lithium with other mood stabilizing drugs, such as carbamazepine, has shown enhanced benefits but also more adverse side effects (Baethge et al., 2005).

In recent years, anticonvulsant drugs such as divalproex and lamotrigine (Epival/Depakote; Lamictal) have been used as an alternative to lithium in treating mania (e.g., Daban et al., 2006; Delbello et al., 2006; Goodwin, Bowden, & Calabrese, 2004; McElroy, Zarate, & Cookson, 2004). Compared with lithium, these drugs cause fewer side effects, are less dangerous at higher doses, and are easier to regulate (Bowden, 2000; Bowden et al., 2003; Schatzberg et al., 2007). However, their long-term benefits in reducing mania and the risk of suicide are not as well established, so lithium is still considered the treatment of choice against which others are measured (Baldessarini et al., 2002; Calabrese et al., 2005; Capriani et al., 2005; Carney & Goodwin, 2005; McAllister-Williams, 2006).

Tranquilizing Drugs (Anxiolytics) During the 1950s, a new class of drugs called *tranquilizers* was shown to reduce mental and physical tension and the symptoms of anxiety. The first of these drugs, meprobamate (Miltown or Equanil), acts somewhat like barbiturate sleeping pills, meaning that overdoses can cause sleep and even death. Because they do not pose this danger, the benzodiazepines—particularly chlordiazepoxide (Librium) and diazepam (Valium)—became the worldwide drug treatment of choice for anxiety (Blackwell, 1973). Today, these and other anti-anxiety drugs, now called **tranquilizing drugs,** or **anxiolytics** (pronounced "ang-zee-oh-LIT-ix"), are the most widely prescribed and used of all legal drugs (Stevens & Pollack, 2005). Anxiolytics have an immediate calming effect and are quite useful in treating the symptoms of generalized anxiety and posttraumatic stress disorder.

One of the benzodiazepines, alprazolam (Xanax), has become especially popular for the treatment of panic disorder and agoraphobia (Verster & Volkerts, 2004). But benzodiazepines can have bothersome side effects, such as sleepiness, lightheadedness, and impaired memory and thinking. Combining these drugs with alcohol can be fatal, and continued use can lead to tolerance and physical dependence (Chouinard, 2004). Further, suddenly discontinuing benzodiazepines after heavy or long-term use can cause severe withdrawal symptoms, including seizures and anxiety attacks (Lemoine et al., 2006; Rickels et al., 1993).

The tranquilizing drug called buspirone (BuSpar) provides an alternative anxiety treatment that eliminates some of these problems (Lickey & Gordon, 1991; Stahl, 2002; Wagner et al., 2003). Its effects do not occur for days or weeks after treatment begins, but buspirone can ultimately equal diazepam in reducing generalized anxiety (Gorman, 2003; Rickels & Rynn, 2002; U.S. Surgeon General, 1999). Further, it does not seem to promote dependence, it causes less interference with thinking, and it does not interact dangerously with alcohol.

Because depression often accompanies anxiety, antidepressant drugs such as fluoxetine (Prozac), paroxetine (Paxil), clomipramine (Anafranil), fluvoxamine (Luvox), and sertraline (Zoloft) are also used in treating anxiety-related problems such as panic disorder, social phobia, obsessive-compulsive disorder, and posttraumatic stress disorder (e.g., Gorman, 2003; Julien, 2005; Nutt, 2005b; Rickels et al., 2003). Table 13.5 lists the effects and side effects of some of the psychoactive drugs we have described.

Human Diversity and Drug Treatment

Drug treatments are designed to benefit everyone in the same way, but it turns out that the same psychoactive drug dose can have significantly different effects in each sex and in people from various ethnic groups (e.g., Esel et al., 2005; Lambert & Norman, 2008; Seeman, 2004). For example, compared with Asians, Caucasians must take significantly higher doses of the benzodiazepines, haloperidol, clozapine, lithium, and possibly the tricyclic antidepressants in order to obtain equally beneficial effects (Hull et al., 2001; Ng et al., 2005). In addition, African Americans may show a faster response to tricyclic antidepressants than European Americans and may respond to lower doses of lithium (Chaudhry et al., 2008). There is also some evidence that, compared with European Americans, African Americans and Hispanic Americans might require higher doses of antipsychotic drugs to get the same benefits (Citrome et al., 2005). Some of these ethnic differences are thought to be related to genetically regulated differences in drug metabolism, whereas others may be due to dietary practices and other sociocultural factors (Bakare, 2008).

Males and females may respond in about the same way to tricyclic antidepressants (Wohlfarth et al., 2004), but women may maintain higher blood levels of these and other therapeutic psychoactive drugs and may show better response to neuroleptic drugs (Hildebrandt et al., 2003; Salokangas, 2004). They also may be more vulnerable to adverse effects such as tardive dyskinesia (Yarlagadda et al., 2008). These gender differences in drug response appear less related to estrogen than to other hormonal or body-composition differences between men and women, such as the ratio of body fat to muscle (Dawkins & Potter, 1991; Salokangas, 2004). Continued research on these and other dimensions of human diversity will undoubtedly lead to more effective and safer drug treatments for everyone (Thompson & Pollack, 2001).

tranquilizing drugs (anxiolytics) Drugs that reduce tension and symptoms of anxiety.

TABLE 13.5 ■ A SAMPLING OF PSYCHOACTIVE DRUGS USED FOR TREATING PSYCHOLOGICAL DISORDERS

Psychoactive drugs have been successful in dramatically reducing the symptoms of many psychological disorders. Critics point out that drugs can have troublesome side effects, however, and that they may create dependence, especially after years of use (e.g., Breggin, 2008). They note, too, that drugs do not "cure" mental disorders (National Institute of Mental Health, 1995), that their effects are not always strong (Kirsch et al., 2002), and that temporary symptom relief may make some patients less likely to seek a permanent solution to their psychological problems.

For Schizophrenia: Neuroleptic Drugs (Antipsychotics)

Chemical Name	Trade Name	Effects and Side Effects
Chlorpromazine	Thorazine	Reduce hallucinations, delusions, incoherence, jumbled thought processes; but may cause movement-disorder side effects, including tardive dyskinesia
Haloperidol	Haldol	
Clozapine	Clozaril	Reduces psychotic symptoms; causes no movement disorders but increases risk of serious blood disease
Risperidone	Risperdal	Reduces positive and negative psychotic symptoms without risk of blood disease
Ziprasidone	Geodon	Reduces positive and negative psychotic symptoms without causing weight gain
Aripiprazole	Abilify	Reduces positive and negative psychotic symptoms without weight gain and with few side effects

For Affective (Mood) Disorders: Antidepressant Drugs and Mood Elevators

Tricyclics

Imipramine	Tofranil	Act as antidepressants but also have antipanic action; cause sleepiness and other moderate side effects; potentially dangerous if taken with alcohol
Amitriptyline	Elavil, Amitid	

Other Antidepressant Drugs

Fluoxetine	Prozac	Have antidepressant, antipanic, and anti-obsessive action
Clomipramine	Anafranil	
Fluvoxamine	Luvox	
Sertraline	Zoloft	
Escitalopram	Lexapro	

Other Drugs

Lithium carbonate	Carbolith, Lithizine	Calms mania and reduces mood swings of bipolar disorder; overdose harmful, potentially deadly
Divalproex	Depakote	Is effective against mania with fewer side effects
Lamotrigine	Lamictal	Is effective in delaying relapse in bipolar disorder; most benefits associated with depression

For Anxiety Disorders: Tranquilizing Drugs (Anxiolytics)

Benzodiazepines

Chlordiazepoxide	Librium	Act as potent anxiolytics for generalized anxiety, panic, stress; extended use may cause physical dependence and withdrawal syndrome if abruptly discontinued
Diazepam	Valium	
Alprazolam	Xanax	Also has antidepressant effects; often used in agoraphobia; has high dependence potential
Clonazepam	Klonopin	Often used in combination with other anxiolytics for panic disorder

Other Anti-Anxiety Agents

Buspirone	BuSpar	Has slow-acting anti-anxiety action; no known dependence problems

Drugs and Psychotherapy

Despite their widespread success in the treatment of psychological disorders, psychoactive drugs do have some drawbacks. As we have seen, some of them can result in physical or psychological dependence, and their side effects can range from minor problems such as the thirst and dry mouth caused by some antidepressant drugs to movement disorders such as tardive dyskinesia caused by some neuroleptic drugs. Although the most serious of these side effects are relatively rare, some are irreversible, and it is impossible to predict in advance who will develop them. For example, although a clear causal link has not yet been confirmed (Gibbons et al., 2005; Simon et al.,

▶ There is widespread concern that psychiatrists, and especially general practitioners, rely too heavily on drugs to deal with psychological problems, partly because of drug ads that fuel consumer demand (Albee, 2002; Breggin, 2008; Olfson et al., 2006; Zuvekas, Vitiello, & Nordquist, 2006). In one case, for example, increasing doses of medication failed to stop a paranoid schizophrenia patient's repeated escapes from a mental hospital. The problem was solved without drugs, though, after a psychologist discovered that the man's escapes were motivated by his fear of calling his mother on "bugged" hospital phones, and he was allowed to use a telephone at a nearby shopping mall (Rabasca, 1999).

"I medicate first and ask questions later."

2006; Wheeler et al., 2008), the U.S. National Institute of Mental Health (NIMH) and regulatory agencies in Canada and Britain have issued warnings about the danger of suicidal behavior in children and adolescents who are given Prozac and similar antidepressant drugs (Bridge et al., 2007; Breggin, 2008; Gualtieri & Johnson, 2006; Hammad, Laughren, & Racoosin, 2006; Jureidini et al., 2004; Martinez et al., 2005; National Institute of Mental Health, 2004; Olfson, Marcus, & Shaffer, 2006; Vitiello & Swedo, 2004; Whittington, Kendall, & Pilling, 2005). There is concern, too, about whether psychoactive drugs are as effective as they appear to be, especially in research sponsored by the drug companies that make them (Heres et al., 2006; Moncrieff & Kirsch, 2005; Turner et al., 2008).

With these issues in mind, many clinicians and clients wonder which is better: drugs or psychotherapy. Can they be combined effectively? A considerable amount of research is being conducted to address these questions.

Although occasionally a study shows that one form of treatment or the other is more effective, neither drugs nor psychotherapy has been shown to be clearly superior overall for treating problems such as anxiety disorders and major depressive disorder (Smits, O'Cleirigh, & Otto, 2006; Thase et al., 2007). For example, several studies of treatment for severe depression have found that behavior therapy, cognitive behavior therapy, and interpersonal psychotherapy can be as effective as an antidepressant drug (Butler et al., 2006; DeRubeis et al., 2005; Dimidjian et al., 2006; Hollon, Thase, & Markowitz, 2002; March et al., 2004). The effects of cognitive behavior therapy have also equaled drug effects in the treatment of phobias (Clark et al., 2003; Davidson et al., 2004; Otto et al., 2000; Thom, Sartory, & Jöhren, 2000), panic disorder (Barlow, 2007; Mitte, 2005a), generalized anxiety disorder (Mitte, 2005b), and obsessive-compulsive disorder (Kozak, Liebowitz, & Foa, 2000). Further, the dropout rate from psychotherapy may be lower than from drug therapies, and the benefits of many kinds of psychotherapy may last longer than those of drug therapies (e.g., Casacalenda, Perry, & Looper, 2002; Hollon, Stewart, & Strunk, 2006; Segal, Gemar, & Williams, 2000; Thom, Sartory, & Jöhren, 2000).

What about combining drugs and psychotherapy? Research suggests that doing so can sometimes be helpful (Hofmann et al., 2006; Miklowitz, 2007; Winston, Been, & Serby, 2005). Combined treatment is recommended in cases of bipolar disorder (Miklowitz, 2008; Otto, Bruce, & Deckersbach, 2005) and produces slightly better results than either psychotherapy or drugs alone in people suffering from severe, long-term depression (Hegerl, Plattner, & Moller, 2004). The combination of drugs and psychotherapy has been also shown to be more effective than either method alone in treating attention deficit hyperactivity disorder, childhood anxiety disorders, obsessive-compulsive disorder, alcoholism, stammering, compulsive sexual behavior, and panic disorder (Barlow, 2007; Keller et al., 2000; March et al., 2004; Roy-Byrne et al., 2005; Walkup et al., 2008). The combined approach may be especially useful for clients who are initially too distressed to benefit much from psychotherapy. A related approach that has already been shown to be successful with clients who had been taking drugs for panic disorder and depression is the use of psychotherapy to prevent relapse and to make further progress as drug treatment is discontinued (e.g., Bruce, Spiegel, & Hegel, 1999; Dobson et al., 2008; Klein et al., 2004; Lam et al., 2003). Preliminary evidence also suggests that a drug called D-cycloserine might be helpful in preventing the reappearance of fears being extinguished through exposure techniques or other forms of behavior therapy (Choy, Fyer, & Lipsitz, 2007; Davis et al., 2005, 2006; Hofmann et al., 2006; Norberg, Krystal, & Tolin, 2008).

However, many other studies have found little advantage in combining drugs and psychotherapy (e.g., Davidson et al., 2004; Elkin, 1994; Nemeroff et al., 2003; Spiegel & Bruce, 1997). One early study compared the effects of a form of in vivo desensitization called *gradual exposure* and an anti-anxiety drug (Xanax) in the treatment of agoraphobia. Clients who received gradual exposure alone showed better short- and long-term benefits than those who received either the drug alone or a combination of the drug and gradual exposure (Echeburua et al., 1993). Other studies, too, have found that combining drugs and psychotherapy may produce surprisingly little added benefit (e.g., Elkin, 1994; Spiegel & Bruce, 1997).

Perhaps the most conservative strategy for treating most cases of anxiety and depression is to begin with cognitive or interpersonal psychotherapy (which have no major negative side effects) and then to add or switch to drug treatment if psychotherapy alone is ineffective (Jacobs et al., 2004; Schatzberg et al., 2005). Often clients who do not respond to one method will be helped by the other (Heldt et al., 2006). Someday research may offer better guidelines about which clients should be treated with psychotherapy alone, medication alone, or a combination of the two (Hollon et al., 2005).

linkages

How do psychoactive drugs work?
(a link to Biology and Behavior)

Improve Your Grade
Tutorial: Different Drug Effects.

Linkages

Biology, Behavior, and the Treatment of Psychological Disorders

As described in the chapter on biology and behavior, human feelings, thoughts, and actions—whether normal or abnormal—are ultimately the result of biological processes, especially those involving neurotransmitters and their receptors in the brain. Because different neurotransmitters are especially prominent in particular circuits or regions of the brain, altering the functioning of particular neurotransmitter systems will have relatively specific psychological and behavioral effects.

Let's consider some of the ways that therapeutic psychoactive drugs affect neurotransmitters and their receptors. Some therapeutic drugs cause neurons to fire, whereas others reduce, or inhibit, firing. For example, benzodiazepines (e.g., Valium and Xanax) exert their anti-anxiety effects by helping the inhibitory neurotransmitter GABA bind to receptors and thus suppress neuron firing. This increased inhibitory effect acts as a sort of braking system that slows the activity of GABA-sensitive neurons involved in the experience of anxiety. However, benzodiazepines also slow the action of all neural systems that use GABA, including those associated with motor activity and mental processing, which are spread throughout the brain. The result is the decreased motor coordination and clouded thinking that appear as the side effects of the benzodiazepines. Research suggests that it might soon be possible to develop drugs that will bind only to certain kinds of GABA receptors and thus greatly reduce these side effects (Gorman, 2005; Löw et al., 2000; Stahl, 2002).

linkages

How do drugs help people who suffer from schizophrenia? *(a link to Biology and Behavior)*

Other therapeutic drugs are receptor antagonists (see Figure 4.8 in the consciousness chapter), acting to block the receptor site normally used by a particular neurotransmitter. The phenothiazines and haloperidol, for example, exert their antipsychotic effects by blocking receptors for dopamine, a neurotransmitter that is important for movement, as described in the chapter on biology and behavior. Blocking dopamine seems to normalize the jumbled thinking of many schizophrenia patients, but it can create severe disorders—including tardive dyskinesia—in the movement systems that are also controlled by dopamine.

Some psychoactive drugs exert their therapeutic influence by increasing the amount of a neurotransmitter available to act on receptors. This effect usually occurs because the drug slows a process called *reuptake* by which the neurotransmitter would normally return to the brain cell from which it was released. The tricyclic antidepressants, for example, operate by slowing the reuptake of norepinephrine. Prozac, Anafranil, and some other antidepressant drugs are called *selective serotonin reuptake inhibitors (SSRIs)* because they slow the reuptake of serotonin. Others, such as Effexor, slow the reuptake of both serotonin and norepinephrine.

Community Psychology

▶ *How can we prevent psychological disorders?*

It has long been argued that even if psychologists and psychiatrists knew exactly how to treat every psychological problem, there would never be enough mental health professionals to help everyone in need (Albee, 1968, 2006). A recent study by the World Health Organization found, for example, that even individuals with severe mental health problems often do not receive the psychological services they need (Wang et al., 2007). The study revealed, too, that the treatment situation is especially dire in poorer countries where only about 11 percent of psychologically troubled individuals had received treatment for their disorders. In "high income" countries such as the United States and Belgium, the figure was about 60 percent. Even that percentage is too low, though, and recognition of the treatment access problem helped fuel the rise of **community psychology,** which seeks to treat people in their local communities and work for social changes that can prevent psychological disorders.

One aspect of community psychology, the *community mental health movement,* appeared during the 1960s as an attempt to make treatment available to people in their own communities. As antipsychotic drugs became available and as concern grew that patients were not improving (and might be getting worse) after years of confinement in mental hospitals, thousands of these patients were released. The plan was for them to receive drugs and other mental health services in newly funded community mental health centers. This *deinstitutionalization* process spared patients the boredom and isolation of the hospital environment, but the mental health services available in the community never matched the need for them (Leff, 2006). Some former hospital patients and many people whose disorders might once have sent them to mental hospitals are now living in halfway houses and other community-based facilities where they receive *psychosocial rehabilitation.* These community support services are not designed to "cure" them but to help them cope with their problems and develop the social and occupational skills necessary for semi-independent living (Coldwell & Bender, 2007; Cook et al., 2005; Liberman et al., 1998; Talbott, 2004). But too many others with severe psychological disorders did not receive or respond to rehabilitation and are to be found enduring the dangers of homelessness on city streets or of confinement in jails and prisons (Luhrmann, 2008; Teplin et al., 2005; U.S. Department of Health and Human Services, 2001b).

Community psychology also attempts to prevent psychopathology by addressing unemployment, poverty, overcrowded substandard housing, and other stressful social situations that may put vulnerable people at greater risk for some disorders (Tucker & Herman, 2002; Weissberg, Kumpfer, & Seligman, 2003; Xue et al., 2005). Less ambitious

community psychology A mental health approach whose goal is to minimize or prevent psychological disorders by promoting social change and making treatment methods more accessible to those who normally have little or no access to psychological services.

COMMUNITY MENTAL HEALTH EFFORTS ▶

Professional and nonprofessional staff members at community mental health centers provide traditional therapy and mental health education as well as walk-in facilities and hotlines for people who are suicidal or in crisis because of rape or domestic violence. They also offer day treatment to former mental patients, many of whom are homeless.

applying psychology

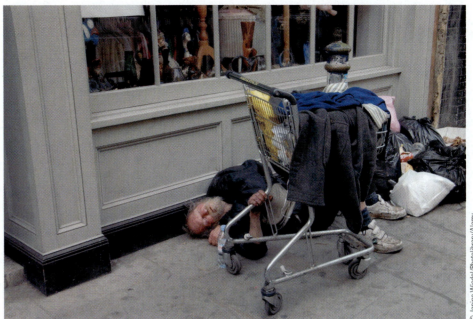

but perhaps even more significant are efforts to detect psychological problems in their earliest stages and keep those problems from becoming worse (e.g., Bond & Hauf, 2004; President's New Freedom Commission on Mental Health, 2003; Sanders et al., 2000). Some examples include prevention of depression and suicide (Beardslee et al., 2003; Cuijpers et al., 2008; Freres et al., 2002; Gillham et al., 2007; Horowitz & Garber, 2006; Lynch et al., 2005; Oyama et al., 2004; Spence, Sheffield, & Donovan, 2005); programs (including Project Head Start) that help preschoolers whose backgrounds hurt their chances of doing well in school and put them at risk for failure and delinquency (Foster et al., 2006; Reid, Webster-Stratton, & Baydar, 2004; Shaw et al., 2006; Tremblay et al., 1995); and identification of children who are at risk for disorder because of parental divorce or because they are rejected or victimized at school (e.g., Frey et al., 2005; Greenberg et al., 1999; Martinez & Forgatch, 2001). Other interventions are designed to head off anxiety disorders or schizophrenia in children and adults (McGorry et al., 2002; Neil & Christensen, 2009; Rapee et al., 2005); to prevent domestic violence and child abuse (Duggan et al., 2004; Whitaker et al., 2006), and to promote health consciousness in ethnic minority communities (Borg, 2002).

Further, community psychology supports the notion that nonprofessionals—including the relatives and friends of troubled clients—can be enlisted in efforts to combat psychological disorders (e.g., Bright, Baker, & Neimeyer, 1999). This idea is compatible with and has encouraged the development of *self-help* or *mutual-help* organizations. Self-help groups, such as Alcoholics Anonymous (AA), are made up of people who share some problematic experience and want to help one another. Millions of people in the United States and Canada take part each year in face-to-face or Internet-based self-help groups for alcohol and drug addiction, childhood sexual abuse, pain, depression, anxiety, cancer, HIV/AIDS, overeating, overspending, bereavement, compulsive gambling, schizophrenia, and many other problems (Barlow et al., 2000; Dittman, 2004; Norcross et al., 2000; Swindle et al., 2000; Zuckerman, 2003).

Lack of reliable data makes it difficult to assess the value of many self-help programs, but available information suggests that active members may obtain some moderate improvement in their lives (Kelly, 2003; Mains & Scogin, 2003; Moos et al., 2001). Some professional therapists view these groups with suspicion; others encourage clients to participate in them as part of their treatment or as a first step toward more formal treatment (Haaga, 2000; Salzer, Rappaport, & Segre, 1999). This recommendation is especially likely for clients with problems such as eating disorders, alcoholism, and other substance-related disorders (Guimon, 2004; Knack, 2009; Scheidinger, 2004).

ACTIVE REVIEW   ▶ Chapter 13

Treatment of Psychological Disorders

As noted in the introductory chapter, all of psychology's subfields are related to one another. Our discussion of the psychopharmacology of drug treatment illustrates just one way that the topic of this chapter, treatment of psychological disorders, is linked to the subfield of biological psychology, which is described

in the chapter on biology and behavior. The Linkages diagram shows ties to two other subfields, and there are many more ties throughout the book. Looking for linkages among subfields will help you see how they all fit together and help you better appreciate the big picture that is psychology.

linkages

How do psychoactive drugs work?
(ans. on p. 539)

Chapter 2
Biology and Behavior

Can people learn their way out of a disorder? *(ans. on p. 518)*

Chapter 5
Learning

How can people manage stress?
(ans. on p. 418)

Chapter 10
Health, Stress, and Coping

SUMMARY   ▶

Basic Features of Treatment

 What features do all treatment techniques have in common?

 **Psychotherapy** for psychological disorders is usually based on psychodynamic, humanistic, or behavioral theories of personality and behavior disorder. Many therapists employ elements of more than one approach. The biological approach uses drugs and other physical treatment methods.

All forms of treatment include a client, a therapist, a theory of behavior disorder, a set of treatment procedures suggested by the theory, and a special relationship between the client and therapist. Therapy may be offered to inpatients and outpatients in many different settings by

psychologists, psychiatrists, and other helpers. The goal of treatment is to help people change their thinking, feelings, and behavior so that they will be happier and function better.

Psychodynamic Psychotherapy

 How did Freud get started as a therapist?

 Psychodynamic psychotherapy began with Freud's *psychoanalysis,* which seeks to help clients gain insight into unconscious conflicts and impulses and then to explore how those factors have created disorders. Exploration of the

unconscious is aided by the use of free association, dream interpretation, and related methods. Some variations on psychoanalysis retain most of Freud's principles but are typically shorter in duration and tend to stress social and interpersonal factors, such as early relationships with caregivers.

Humanistic Psychotherapy

 Why won't some therapists give advice?

 Humanistic psychotherapy helps clients become more aware of discrepancies between their feelings and their behavior. According to the humanistic approach, these discrepancies are at the root of behavior disorders

and can be resolved by the client once they are brought to light in the context of a genuine, trusting relationship with the therapist.

Therapists using Rogers's **client-centered therapy,** also known as **person-centered therapy,** help mainly by adopting attitudes toward the client that express **unconditional positive regard, empathy,** and **congruence.** These attitudes create a nonjudgmental atmosphere that makes it easier for clients to be open and honest with the therapist, with themselves, and with others. One way of creating this atmosphere is through reflection. Therapists employing the **Gestalt therapy** of Fritz and Laura Perls use more active techniques than Rogerian therapists, often pointing out inconsistencies between what clients say and how they behave.

Behavior Therapy

▶ *Can we learn to conquer fears?*

Behavior therapy and **behavior modification** apply learning principles to eliminate undesirable behavior patterns and strengthen more desirable alternatives. The methods they employ include **systematic desensitization therapy, modeling, assertiveness training** and social skills training, **positive reinforcement** (sometimes within a **token economy program**), **extinction** techniques (such as **flooding** or **implosive therapy**), **aversion conditioning,** and **punishment**.

Many behavior therapists also employ **cognitive behavior therapy** to help clients alter the way they think as well as the way they behave. Among the specific cognitive behavioral methods are **rational-emotive behavior therapy (REBT),** cognitive restructuring, stress inoculation training, and **cognitive therapy**.

Group, Family, and Couples Therapy

▶ *How does group psychotherapy differ from individual therapy?*

Therapists of all theoretical persuasions offer **group psychotherapy, family therapy,** and **couples therapy.** These forms of treatment take advantage of relationships in the group, family, or couple to enhance the effects of treatment.

Evaluating Psychotherapy

▶ *How effective is psychotherapy?*

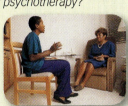

Research has found that clients who receive psychotherapy are better off than most clients who receive no treatment but that no single approach is uniformly better than all others for all clients and problems. Still, some methods appear effective enough in the treatment of particular disorders to have been listed as **empirically supported therapies (ESTs)** that can guide **evidence based practice**. The outcome of treatment is also affected by the characteristics of the client and the therapist and the relationship that develops between them. More research is needed to discover all the combinations of therapists, clients, and treatments ideally suited to treating particular psychological problems. Several factors, including personal preferences, must be considered when choosing a form of treatment and a therapist. The effects of cultural differences in the values and goals of therapist and client have also attracted increasing attention. In all forms of treatment and under all but the most exceptional circumstances, the client's rights include the right to confidentiality.

Biological Treatments

▶ *Is electric shock still used to treat disorders?*

Biological treatment methods seek to relieve psychological disorders by physical, rather than psychological, means. **Electroconvulsive shock therapy** (abbreviated as **ECT** or **EST),** also known as **electroshock therapy**, involves passing an electric current through the patient's brain, usually in an effort to relieve severe depression. Today, the most prominent form of biological treatment involves psychoactive drugs, including those with **antipsychotic (neuroleptic), antidepressant,** or **tranquilizing (anxiolytic)** effects. Psychoactive drugs appear effective in many cases, but critics point out that a number of undesirable side effects are associated with these drugs. Drugs may be no more effective than some forms of psychotherapy for many people. Combining drugs and psychotherapy may help in some cases and in the treatment of certain disorders, but their joint effect may be no greater than the effect of either one alone.

Community Psychology

▶ *How can we prevent psychological disorders?*

The realization that there will never be enough therapists to treat all who need help prompted the development of **community psychology**. Community mental health programs and efforts to prevent mental disorders are the two main elements of community psychology. The growth of self-help or mutual-help organizations is compatible with the goals of community psychology.

Learn **BY** Doing ▶

Put It in Writing

Imagine that you have decided to get help for depression, anxiety, or some other psychological problem. Using what you have learned in this chapter, write a page describing what approach to treatment you would prefer and why. Tell whether you would choose that approach for all kinds of problems or whether your choice would depend on the nature of the problem. Finally, list the characteristics of your ideal therapist and say why you think those characteristics might lead to successful treatment.

Personal Learning Activity

To get a better idea of how practicing therapists choose their treatment methods, ask a local psychologist, psychiatrist, or counselor (at the student counseling center on campus, perhaps) to meet with you for a short research interview. Ask this person what treatment approach and methods he or she prefers, how this preference developed, and what convinces him or her to continue using these methods. Write a summary of what you learned in this interview, and don't forget to include your impressions of whether this therapist's choice of treatment methods depends mainly on personal experience, empirical research evidence, or a combination of both. *For additional projects, see the Personal Learning Activities in the corresponding chapter of the study guide that accompanies this book.*

Take Action to Learn More ▶

Now that you have finished reading this chapter, how about exploring some of the ideas and information that you found most interesting? Here are some courses, books, films, and Internet resources to get you started. Enjoy!

Courses

Clinical Psychology
Methods of Psychotherapy
Psychopharmacology
Behavior Modification
Community Psychology

Movies

Analyze This; Analyze That; Good Will Hunting; Shock Corridor; Vertigo. Hollywood portrayals of psychotherapy.
Beautiful Dreamers; Girl, Interrupted; House of Fools; Manic; One Flew over the Cuckoo's Nest; The Snake Pit. Institutional treatment.
A Beautiful Mind. Biological treatment of schizophrenia.
A Clockwork Orange. Aversion therapy.
I Never Promised You a Rose Garden. Psychodynamic treatment for schizophrenia.
Antwone Fisher; Equus; Ordinary People. Psychotherapy.

Books

Peter Wyden, *Conquering Schizophrenia: A Father, His Son, and a Medical Breakthrough*

(Knopf, 1998). A father searches for a cure for his son with schizophrenia.
Ken Kesey, *One Flew over the Cuckoo's Nest* (New American Library, 1989). The book from which the award-winning movie was adapted.
Michael Winerip, *9 Highland Road* (Vintage, 1995). The aftermath of deinstitutionalization.
Peter Kramer, *Listening to Prozac* (Penguin, 1997). Psychotropic antidepressant medications.
Susan Sheehan, *Is There No Place on Earth for Me?* (Vintage, 1983). Inadequate treatment for a woman with schizophrenia.
Raymond J. Corsini and Danny Wedding, *Current Psychotherapies,* 6th ed. (Peacock, 2001). A comparison of numerous approaches to psychotherapy.
Frank Dumont and Raymond J. Corsini, eds., *Six Therapists and One Client* (Springer, 2000). Therapists representing six different treatment methods describe how they would help the same client.
W. S. Appleton, *Prozac and the New Antidepressants: What You Need to Know About Prozac, Zoloft, Paxil, Luvox, Wellbutrin, Effexor, Serzone, Vestra, Celexa, St. John's Wort, and Others* (rev. ed.; Plume Books, 2000). A summary of modern drug treatment options for depression.
T. M. Luhrmann, *Of Two Minds: The Growing Disorder in American Psychiatry* (Knopf, 2000). Summary of the conflict between

biological and psychological approaches to treatment.
Christina Hoff Summers and Sally Satel, *One Nation Under Therapy: How the Helping Culture Is Eroding Self-Reliance* (St. Martin's Press, 2005). Argues that people have become overly dependent on psychotherapy and drugs to solve their problems.

The Web

Essentials of Psychology **Book Companion Website**

www.cengage.com/psychology/bernstein

Visit the book companion website to access a wealth of resources, including chapter outlines, flashcards, web links, tutorial quizzes, and more!

CENGAGENOW™ Just what you need to know NOW! Spend time on what you need to master rather than on information you already have learned. Take a pre-test for this chapter, and CengageNOW will generate a personalized study plan based on your results. The study plan will identify the topics you need to review and direct you to online resources to help you master those topics. You can then take a post-test to help you determine the concepts you have mastered and what you will need to work on. Try it out! Go to www.cengage.com/login to sign in with an access code or to purchase access to this product.

Review of Key Terms ▶

Can you define each of the key terms in the chapter? Check your definitions against those on the pages shown in parentheses in the following list or in the Glossary at the end of the book.

antidepressant drugs (p. 534)
anxiolytics (see tranquilizing drugs) (p. 536)
assertiveness training (p. 519)
aversion conditioning (p. 520)

behavior modification (p. 517)
behavior therapy (p. 517)
client-centered therapy (person-centered therapy) (p. 514)
cognitive behavior therapy (p. 517)
cognitive therapy (p. 522)
community psychology (p. 540)
congruence (p. 515)
couples therapy (p. 524)

electroconvulsive shock therapy (ECT, EST) (p. 533)
electroshock therapy (p. 533)
empathy (p. 515)
empirically supported therapies (ESTs) (p. 530)
evidence based practice (p. 527)
extinction (p. 519)
family therapy (p. 524)

MULTIPLE-CHOICE ▶ Self Test

Select the best answer for each of the following questions. Then check your responses against the Answer Key at the end of the book.

1. Claudia's therapist asks her to talk about whatever thoughts, memories, or ideas come into her mind. He asks her not to "edit" any of her thoughts. This technique is called _____ and is part of _____ therapy.

a. reflection; psychodynamic
b. reflection; humanistic
c. free association; psychodynamic
d. free association; humanistic

2. Vicki tells Dr. Denter, her therapist, that she is very happy in her marriage. Dr. Denter points out that as she says this, she is clenching her fist. He asks her to have a dialogue with herself by "becoming" her fist and saying what it would say to her. Dr. Denter is most likely a _____ therapist.

a. Gestalt
b. psychodynamic
c. behavior
d. cognitive

3. Melinda is a licensed clinical psychologist, which means she probably has _____.

a. a doctoral degree in psychology
b. a psychodynamic approach to therapy
c. the right to prescribe drugs in all but two U.S. states
d. a medical degree

4. A primary aim of classical psychoanalysis is to _____.

a. help clients get in touch with their current feelings
b. help clients gain insight into their unconscious conflicts
c. replace clients' problematic behaviors with more desirable behaviors
d. teach clients new ways of thinking

5. Dr. Margent listens as her client, Eric, talks at length about his problems at work, including the fact that he hates the job, often sneaks out early, sometimes ignores his manager's instructions, and generally avoids working hard. Dr. Margent doesn't interrupt or criticize him but often rephrases what he says to be sure she understands it. Dr. Margent is using methods most closely associated with _____ therapy.

a. psychodynamic
b. behavioral
c. client-centered
d. cognitive-behavioral

6. Carl's therapist is helping him overcome his fear of heights by imagining increasingly frightening images while he is relaxed. The therapist is using methods known as _____.

a. assertion training
b. systematic desensitization therapy
c. flooding
d. modeling

7. Shanobi is tearfully telling a friend that she is depressed and does not know why. Her friend says, "You seem so unhappy, and maybe a bit scared, too." The friend's response is most like which method used in client-centered therapy?

a. Sympathy
b. Empathy
c. Reflection
d. Actualization

8. Rebecca is convinced that she will never get the promotion she wants because she "is just not good at job interviews." Her therapist asks her to close her eyes and say the first thing that comes into her mind as she thinks about her job. He also asks Rebecca for details of the dreams she has been having lately. Rebecca's therapist appears to prefer the _____ approach to treatment.

a. behavioral
b. cognitive behavioral
c. Gestalt
d. psychodynamic

9. Brandon complains that he has an intense need to touch all four walls of any room he enters for the first time. His therapist suggests that Brandon might have learned this compulsive behavior because it helped him avoid anxiety. The therapist appears to favor the _____ approach to treatment.

a. psychodynamic
b. humanistic
c. behavioral
d. neurobiological

10. Your friend Rallo is considering entering psychotherapy, but he wonders if it will help. Based on the research you read about in this chapter, you tell Rallo that _____.

a. therapy does not help the average client
b. therapy helps the average client
c. humanistic therapies are most effective overall
d. there is no experimental research on the effectiveness of therapy

11. According to the American Psychological Association's *Ethical Principles of Psychologists and Code of Conduct,* a therapist may reveal information learned about a client during therapy if _____.
    a. the client's employer requests this information in confidence
    b. the client drops out of therapy
    c. the client is suicidal and needs immediate hospitalization
    d. the therapist feels it will do no harm

12. Juanita is trying to influence her state legislature to pass laws that will help prevent psychological problems caused by malnutrition, overcrowding, and homelessness. She is most likely a _____ psychologist.
    a. behavioral
    b. community
    c. humanistic
    d. psychodynamic

13. Rafer's intense fear of spiders greatly interferes with his job as a forest ranger. His therapist suggests that he stay in a room full of harmless spiders until he feels no further anxiety. This therapy technique is known as _____.
    a. flooding
    b. punishment
    c. systematic desensitization therapy
    d. aversion conditioning

14. Sally constantly tells herself that she is "worthless" and "will never succeed at anything." Her therapist helps her practice new thoughts such as "I'm as good as the next person" and "I am going to try my best." Her therapist is using the technique of _____, which is part of _____ therapy.
    a. free association; psychodynamic
    b. reflection; humanistic
    c. stress inoculation; behavioral
    d. cognitive restructuring; cognitive behavior

15. Lucinda is experiencing severe depression that leaves her unable to enjoy life. She has not responded to psychotherapies or medication. Lucinda would be a candidate for _____.
    a. neuroleptic drugs
    b. ECT
    c. aversion conditioning
    d. cognitive restructuring

16. Therapeutic drugs can work in many ways, but *not* by _____.
    a. increasing the amount of neurotransmitters released in the brain
    b. decreasing the amount of neurotransmitters released in the brain
    c. blocking the action of neurotransmitters in the brain
    d. changing the kind of neurotransmitters released by neurons in the brain

17. An important common element in the success of many forms of psychotherapy is _____.
    a. the client-therapist relationship
    b. randomly assigning therapists to clients
    c. having a therapist trained in a variety of therapeutic methods
    d. having appropriate assessment methods to measure outcomes

18. When prescribing neuroleptic drugs for schizophrenia, psychiatrists must consider that patients may _____.
    a. become addicted to them
    b. become insensitive to them after an extended period of time
    c. develop side effects such as tardive dyskinesia
    d. experience hallucinations after extensive use

19. Jon's therapist has prescribed anxiolytics for him. Jon is probably being treated for _____.
    a. depression
    b. an anxiety disorder
    c. schizophrenia
    d. somatoform disorder

20. Which of the following is *not* an advantage of group psychotherapy?
    a. It allows the therapist to observe clients interacting with one another.
    b. Clients learn from one another.
    c. Clients improve more quickly.
    d. Clients feel less alone.

© Tim Pannell/Corbis

14 Social Psychology

If you are like most people, there is probably at least one thing you do in private that you would never do when someone else is around. The tendency to behave differently when others are present is just one aspect of social psychology. This chapter describes many other ways that the presence and behavior of other people affect our own thoughts and actions and how we, in turn, affect the thoughts and actions of others. It explores how perception, learning, memory, thinking, and emotion occur in relation to other people; how people think about themselves and others; why we may like one person but dislike another; how people form and change attitudes; and why and how we judge other people, sometimes in biased ways. Social pressure, ranging from unspoken social rules to commands for obedience, is another concern of social psychologists. The chapter also reviews some of the helpful, cooperative, competitive, and aggressive ways in which people behave toward one another in the workplace and in other social situations. Finally, it considers group decision making and other group processes.

The death toll in the September 11, 2001, attacks on the World Trade Center and the Pentagon exceeded 3,000, the largest number of people to die violently on American soil in a single day since 1862, during the U.S. Civil War. Almost all of the questions that can be asked about this horrendous tragedy and about terrorism in general relate to human behavior. For example, what could lead people to kill themselves and thousands of innocent people in the name of political or religious beliefs? Why did hundreds of firefighters, police officers, emergency medical workers, and others enter the World Trade Center's burning towers to save the lives of others while risking (and ultimately losing) their own? Why did some of the people who were fleeing the damaged buildings return to their offices after hearing an announcement telling them to do so? Is there any reason to hope that the hatred, distrust, and extremism that brought about this disaster can someday be reduced or eliminated?

We may never have final answers to such questions as these, but some partial answers may lie in the study of **social psychology,** the scientific investigation of how people's thoughts and feelings influence their behavior toward others and how the behavior of others influences people's own thoughts, feelings, and behavior. In this chapter, we focus on several topics in social psychology, including **social cognition,** the mental processes associated with how people perceive and react to other individuals and groups (Fiske & Taylor, 2008), and group and interpersonal behaviors such as conformity, aggression, and helping. One important aspect of social cognition is how it affects the way we see ourselves.

social psychology   The subfield of psychology that explores the effects of the social world on the behavior and mental processes of individuals and groups.

social cognition   Mental processes associated with people's perceptions of and reactions to other people.

Social Influences on the Self

▶ *How do we compare ourselves with others?*

Each of us lives in both a personal and a social world. This means that although you experience your thoughts and feelings as your own, they have been strongly influenced by other people.

The thoughts, feelings, and beliefs about what characteristics you have and who you are make up your **self-concept.** Although your self-concept is unique to you, it is a product of your social and cultural environment. In the chapters on human development and personality, we describe how each individual develops within a cultural context and how collectivist and individualist cultures emphasize different core values and encourage contrasting definitions of the self. As you will see in this chapter, culture also provides the context for **self-esteem,** the evaluations you make of your worth as a human being (Crocker et al., 2006). Let's look at how self-esteem develops.

Social Comparison

People spend a lot of time thinking about themselves, trying to evaluate their own perceptions, opinions, values, abilities, and so on (Epstude & Mussweiler, 2009; Mussweiler, 2003). Decades ago, Leon Festinger (1954) noted that self-evaluation involves two distinct types of questions: those that can be answered by taking objective measurements and those that cannot. You can determine your height or weight by measuring it, but for other types of questions—about your creativity or attractiveness, for example—there are no objective criteria. In these cases, according to Festinger's theory of **social comparison,** people evaluate themselves in relation to others. When you use others as a basis for evaluating how intelligent, athletic, interesting, or attractive you are, you are engaging in social comparison (Buunk et al., 2005).

Who serves as your basis of comparison? Festinger said that people usually look to others who are similar to themselves. For example, if you are curious about how good you are at swimming or science, you will probably compare yourself with people who are at about your own level of experience and ability, not with Olympic champions or Nobel Prize winners (Major, Sciacchtinano, & Crocker, 1993). The categories of people you feel you belong to and usually compare yourself with are called your **reference groups.**

The performance of individuals in your reference groups can affect your self-esteem (Seta, Seta, & McElroy, 2006). For example, if being good at science is important to you, knowing that someone in your reference group always scores much higher than you on science tests can lower your self-esteem. To protect their self-esteem and make themselves feel better, people sometimes compare themselves with those who are not as good, a strategy called *downward social comparison.* They may also sometimes engage in *upward social comparison,* in which they compare themselves with people who are doing much better than they are (Buunk et al., 2007). At first glance, this might not seem sensible, but upward social comparison can create optimism about improving our own situations (Buunk & Oldersma, 2001; Buunk et al., 2007). We may tell ourselves "If they can do it, so can I!" Or we might tell ourselves that the superior performer is not really similar enough to be in our reference group (Mussweiler, 2003) or even that the ability in question is not that important to us (Alicke et al., 1997).

An unfavorable comparison of your own status with that of others can produce **relative deprivation**—the belief that whatever you are getting, it is less than what you deserve (Kassin, Fein, & Markus, 2008). The concept of relative deprivation explains why a movie star who is paid $5 million per film feels abused if a costar is receiving $10 million. It also explains the far more common situation in which employees become dissatisfied when they see themselves as underpaid or underappreciated in comparison to their coworkers (Feldman & Turnley, 2004; Tougas, et al., 2005). Relative deprivation can create depression and anxiety (Taylor & Lobel, 1989), and when large groups of people experience relative deprivation, political unrest may follow. The turmoil usually starts after the members of an oppressed group experience some improvement in their lives and begin to compare their circumstances with those of people in other groups (Moghaddam, 2008). This improvement brings higher expectations about what they deserve. It is likely, for example, that resentment over U.S. prosperity and global influence plays a role in creating the hatred that leads some people to engage in terrorist attacks against the United States (Plous & Zimbardo, 2004; Pyszczynski, Rothschild, & Abdollahi, 2008).

self-concept The way one thinks of oneself.

self-esteem The evaluations people make about their worth as human beings.

social comparison Using other people as a basis of comparison for evaluating oneself.

reference groups Categories of people with whom individuals compare themselves.

relative deprivation The sense that one is not getting all that one deserves.

Focus on RESEARCH

Self-Esteem and the Ultimate Terror

Why is self-esteem so important to so many people? An intriguing answer to this question comes from the *terror management theory* proposed by Jeff Greenberg, Tom Pyszczynski, and Sheldon Solomon. This theory is based on the notion that humans are the only creatures capable of thinking about the future and realizing that we will all eventually die. Terror management theory suggests that humans cope with anxiety, including the terror that thoughts about death might bring, by developing a variety of self-protective psychological strategies. One of these is the effort to establish and maintain high self-esteem (Greenberg, Solomon, & Arndt, 2008; Pyszczynski et al., 2004).

▶ What was the researchers' question?

In one series of experiments, Greenberg and his colleagues (1992) asked whether high self-esteem would, in fact, serve as a buffer against anxiety—specifically, the anxiety brought on by thoughts about death and pain.

▶ How did the researchers answer the question?

About 150 students at several North American universities participated in one of three studies, each of which followed a similar format. The first step was to temporarily alter the participants' self-esteem. To do so, the researchers gave the students feedback about a personality or intelligence test they had taken earlier in the semester. Half the participants received positive feedback designed to increase their self-esteem. The other half received feedback that was neutral—it was neither flattering nor depressing. (Measurement of the students' self-esteem showed that the positive feedback actually did create higher self-esteem than the neutral feedback.) In the next phase of each experiment, the researchers used either a film about death or the (false) threat of a mild electric shock to provoke some anxiety in half the participants in the positive-feedback group and half the participants in the neutral-feedback group. The amount of anxiety created was measured by the participants' self-reports or by monitoring galvanic skin resistance (GSR), a measure of perspiration in their skin that reflects anxiety-related physiological arousal (Dawson, Schell, & Filion, 2000).

▶ What did the researchers find?

Self-reports and GSR measures revealed that participants in all three experiments were significantly less upset by an anxiety-provoking experience (the death film or the threat of shock) if they had first received esteem-building feedback about their previous test performance.

▶ What do the results mean?

The researchers concluded that their results support the notion that self-esteem can act as a buffer against anxiety and other negative feelings. This conclusion would help explain why people are so eager to maintain or enhance their self-esteem (Tesser, 2001): we don't like to feel anxious, and increased self-esteem reduces most people's anxiety.

▶ What do we still need to know?

These results certainly support terror management theory, but by themselves they are not broad enough to confirm all of its assumptions. For example, the theory also predicts that when people are sensitized to the threat of death, they will seek to protect themselves by suppressing thoughts of death and also by doing things that increase the approval and support of others in the society in which they live. Consistent with this prediction, people have been found to make larger contributions to charity after they have been made more aware of their own mortality (Jonas et al., 2002). Similarly, dramatic increases in volunteering for charity work occurred after the events of September 11, 2001 (Penner, Brannick, et al., 2005).

But which strategies are people most likely to use, and why? Are some strategies more or less likely to be adopted at different times in a person's life or among people in certain cultures? And what forms of self-esteem are most important in different cultures? So far, most of the research on terror management theory has been done in individualistic cultures such as North America, where self-esteem is largely based on personal accomplishments. However, terror management theory has also been supported by preliminary studies in China, Japan, aboriginal Australia, and other collectivist cultures in which feelings of self-worth tend to be more closely tied to the performance and status of the groups to which people belong (Halloran & Kashima, 2004; Heine, Harihara, & Niiya, 2002; Tam, Chiu, & Lau, 2007; Wakimoto, 2006). It will take many more experiments to test all the predictions derived from the theory.

Social Identity Theory

Stop reading for a moment and complete the following sentence: I am a(n) _____. Some people fill in the blank using characteristics such as "hard worker," "good sport," or some other aspect of their *personal* identity. However, many others identify themselves using a word or phrase that refers to their nationality, gender, or religion (Lee & Yoo, 2004). These latter responses reflect **social identity,** our beliefs about the groups to which we belong.

social identity   The beliefs we hold about the groups to which we belong.

Our social identity is therefore a part of our self-concept (Brewer, 2008; Tropp & Wright, 2001; Vignoles et al., 2006).

Our social or group identity permits us to feel part of a larger whole (Ashmore et al., 2004). Its importance is seen in the pride people feel when a member of their family graduates from college or when a local team wins a big game (Burris, Branscombe, & Klar, 1997). In wars between national, ethnic, or religious groups, individuals sacrifice and sometimes die for the sake of their group identity. A group identity is also one reason people donate money to those in need, support friends in a crisis, and display other forms of assistance. As we shall see later, however, defining ourselves in terms of a group identity can foster an "us versus them" mentality that sets the stage for prejudice, social discrimination, intergroup conflict, and even terrorism (Brewer & Pierce, 2005).

Social Perception

> *Do we perceive people and objects in similar ways?*

There is a story about a company president who was having lunch with a man being considered for an executive position. When the man salted his food without first tasting it, the president decided not to hire him. The reason, she explained, was that the company had no room for a person who acted before collecting all relevant information. The candidate lost his chance because of the president's **social perception,** the processes through which people interpret information about others, form impressions of them, and draw conclusions about the reasons for their behavior. In this section we examine how and why social perception influences our thoughts, feelings, and actions.

The Role of Schemas

The perception of people follows many of the same laws that govern the perception of objects, including the Gestalt principles discussed in the chapter on sensation and perception (Cloutier, Mason, & Macrae, 2005). Consider Figure 14.1. Consistent with Gestalt principles, most people would describe it as "a square with a notch in one side," not as eight straight lines (Woodworth & Schlosberg, 1954). The reason is that they interpret new information using the mental representations, or **schemas,** that they already have about squares (Fiske & Taylor, 2008). In other words, they interpret this diagram as a square with a slight modification.

Schemas about people, too, can affect our perception of them. For one thing, schemas influence what we pay attention to and what we ignore. We tend to process information about the other person more quickly if it confirms our beliefs about that person's gender or ethnic group, for example, than if it violates those beliefs (Smith & Oueller, 2001). Second, schemas influence what we remember about others. In one study, if people thought a woman they saw in a videotape was a waitress, they recalled that she had a beer with dinner and owned a TV set. Those who thought she was a librarian remembered that she was wearing glasses and liked classical music (Cohen, 1981). Finally, schemas affect our judgment about the behavior of others (Moskowitz, 2005). Thomas Hill and his colleagues (1989) found that participants' ratings of male and female friends' sadness were influenced not only by the friends' actual behavior but also by the participants' general schemas about how much sadness men versus women experience.

In other words, through top-down processing (discussed in the chapter on sensation and perception), our schemas about people influence our perceptions of them. And just as schemas help us read sentences that contain words with missing letters, they also allow us to efficiently "fill in the blanks" about people. Our schemas tell us, for example, that someone wearing a store uniform or name tag is likely to know where merchandise is located, so we usually approach that person for assistance. Accurate schemas help us categorize people quickly and respond appropriately in social

linkages

Do we sometimes perceive people the same way we perceive objects?
(a link to Sensation and Perception)

FIGURE 14.1 ■ A SCHEMA-PLUS-CORRECTION

People who see an object like this tend to use a preexisting mental representation (their schema of a square) and then correct or modify it in some way (here, with a notch).

social perception The processes through which people interpret information about others, draw inferences about them, and develop mental representations of them.

schemas Mental representations about people and social situations.

MAY I HELP YOU? ▶

Schemas help us quickly categorize people and respond appropriately to them, but schemas can also create narrowmindedness and, as we shall see later, social prejudice. If this woman does not fulfill your schema—your mental representation—of how carpenters are supposed to look, you might be less likely to ask her advice on your home improvement project. One expert carpenter who manages the hardware department of a large home improvement store told us that most customers walk right past her in order to ask the advice of one of her less-experienced male clerks.

situations, but if schemas are incorrect they can create false expectations and errors in judgment about people that can lead to narrowmindedness and even prejudice.

First Impressions

Our schemas about people act as lenses that alter our first impressions of them. Those impressions, in turn, affect both our later perceptions of their behavior and our reactions to it. First impressions are formed quickly, usually change slowly, and typically have a long-lasting influence. No wonder they are so important in the development of social relations (Brehm, Kassin, & Fein, 2005). How do people form impressions of other people? And why are these impressions so resistant to change?

Forming Impressions   Think about your first impression of a close friend. It was probably formed quickly, because existing schemas create a tendency to automatically

assume a great deal about a person on the basis of limited information (Smith & Quellar, 2001). One study found that people were able to make judgments about how trustworthy and competent a person was after seeing that person's face for only a tenth of a second (Willis & Todorov, 2006). First impression judgments become much more accurate after as little as one minute of exposure to a new person (Carney, Colvin, & Hall, 2007), but they are not influenced by appearance alone. An ethnic name, for example, might have caused you to draw inferences about your friend's religion, food preferences, or temperament. Clothing or hairstyle might have led you to make assumptions about political views or taste in music. These inferences and assumptions may or may not be accurate. How many turned out to be true in your friend's case?

One schema has a particularly strong influence on first impressions: We tend to assume that the people we meet have attitudes and values similar to our own (Hoyle, 1993). So all else being equal, we are inclined to like other people. However, even a small amount of negative information can change our minds. Why? The main reason is that most of us don't expect other people to act negatively toward us. When unexpectedly negative behaviors do occur, they capture our attention and lead us to believe that these behaviors reflect something negative about the other person (Taylor, Peplau, & Sears, 2006). The result is that negative information attracts more attention and carries more weight than positive information in shaping first impressions (Smith & Mackie, 2007; Vaish, Grossmann, & Woodward, 2008).

▶ Noticeable features or actions help shape our impressions of others. Those impressions may or may not be correct.

Lasting Impressions   Does your friend seem the same today as when you first met? First impressions can change, but the process is usually slow. One reason is that negative first impressions may cause us to avoid certain people, thus reducing our exposure to new information that might change our view of them (Denrell, 2005). Further, most people want to keep their social environment simple and easy to understand (Kenrick, Neuberg, & Cialdini, 2007). We cling to our beliefs about the world, often using our schemas to preserve a reality that fits our expectations. Holding on to existing impressions appears to be part of this effort. If your friend recently violated your expectations by being impatient, your view of her probably did not change much, if at all. In fact, you may have acted to preserve your impression of her by thinking something like "She is not herself today." In other words, impressions change slowly because the meaning we give to new information about people is shaped by what we already know or believe about them (Kenrick, Neuberg, & Cialdini, 2007).

Self-Fulfilling Prophecies   Another reason first impressions tend to be stable is that we often do things that cause others to confirm our impressions (Franzoi, 2003; Madon et al., 2004). If teachers expect particular students to do poorly in mathematics, those students may sense this expectation, exert less effort, and perform below

SELF-FULFILLING PROPHECIES IN THE CLASSROOM ▶
If teachers inadvertently spend less time helping children who at first seem "dull," those children may not learn as much, thus fulfilling the teachers' expectations. If the girls in the back row have not impressed this teacher as being bright, how likely do you think it is that they will be called on?

their ability level. And if mothers expect their young children to eventually abuse alcohol, they are more likely to do so than the children of mothers who didn't convey that expectation (Madon et al., 2006). When, without our awareness, schemas cause us to subtly lead people to behave in line with our expectations, a **self-fulfilling prophecy** is at work.

Self-fulfilling prophecies also help maintain judgments about groups. If you assume that members of a certain ethnic group are a threat, you might be defensive or even hostile when you meet a member of that group. That person might react to your behavior with hostility and anger. These reactions fulfill your prophecy and strengthen the impressions that created it (Kenrick, Neuberg, & Cialdini, 2005).

Explaining Behavior: Attribution

So far, we have examined how people form impressions about other people's characteristics. But our perceptions of others also include our explanations of their behavior. People tend to form ideas about why people (including themselves) behave as they do and about what behavior to expect in the future (Brehm, Kassin, & Fein, 2005). Psychologists use the term **attribution** to describe the process we go through to explain the causes of behavior (including our own).

Suppose a classmate borrows your notes but fails to return them. You could attribute this behavior to many causes, from an emergency situation to selfishness. Which of these explanations you choose is important, because it will help you *understand* your classmate's behavior, *predict* what will happen if this person asks to borrow something in the future, and decide how to *control* the situation should it arise again. Similarly, whether a person attributes a partner's nagging to temporary stress or to loss of affection can influence whether that person will work on the relationship or end it.

People usually attribute behavior in a particular situation to either internal causes (characteristics of the person) or external causes (characteristics of the situation). For example, if you thought your classmate's failure to return your notes was due mainly to lack of consideration or laziness, you would be making an *internal attribution*. If you thought that the oversight was due mainly to preoccupation with a family crisis, you would be making an *external attribution*. Similarly, if you failed an exam, you could explain it by concluding that you're not very smart (internal attribution) or that your work schedule left you too little time to study (external attribution). The attribution that you make, in turn, might determine how much you study for the next exam or even whether you decide to stay in school.

Biases in Attribution

Most people are usually logical in their attempts to explain behavior (Trope, Cohen, & Alfieri, 1991). However, they are also prone to *attributional biases,* or errors, that can distort their view of behavior (Baumeister & Bushman, 2008).

The Fundamental Attribution Error   North American psychologists have paid special attention to the **fundamental attribution error,** a tendency to overattribute the behavior of others to internal factors (Fiske & Taylor, 2008). Imagine that you hear a student give an incorrect answer in class. You will probably attribute this behavior to an internal cause and infer that the person is not very smart. In doing so, however, you might be ignoring possible external factors (such as lack of study time).

A related attributional bias is called the *ultimate attribution error.* Through this error, the positive actions of people from a different ethnic or social group are attributed to external causes, such as easy opportunities, whereas their negative actions are attributed to internal causes, such as dishonesty (Pettigrew, 1979). The ultimate attribution error also causes people to see good deeds done by those in their own group as due to kindness or other internal factors and bad deeds as stemming from external causes, such as unemployment. In this way, the ultimate attribution error helps create and maintain people's negative views of other groups and positive views of their own group (Fiske, 1998).

Improve Your Grade
Tutorial: Fundamental Attribution Error

self-fulfilling prophecy   A process in which an initial impression causes us to bring out behavior in another that confirms the impression.

attribution   The process of explaining the causes of people's behavior, including our own.

fundamental attribution error   A bias toward attributing the behavior of others to internal factors.

WHY ARE THEY HELPING? ▶
Attributional biases are more common in some cultures than others. In one study, students in an individualist culture were more likely than those in a collectivist culture to explain acts of helping as being due to internal causes such as kindness or the enjoyment of helping (Miller & Bersoff, 1994).

These attributional biases may not be universal (Miyamoto & Kitayama, 2002). For example, research suggests that the fundamental attribution error and the ultimate attribution error are less likely to appear among people in collectivist cultures such as India, China, Japan, and Korea than among people in the individualist cultures of North America and Europe (Heine & Buchtel, 2009). And even within individualist cultures, some people hold a stronger individualist orientation than others. So some people in these cultures are more likely than others to make attribution errors (Miller, 2001; Vandello & Cohen, 1999).

Other Attributional Biases   The tendency to make internal attributions is much less pronounced when people explain their own behavior. In fact, people tend to show the **actor-observer effect:** that is, we often attribute other people's behavior to internal causes but attribute our own behavior to external factors, especially when our behavior is inappropriate or inadequate (Baumeister, 1998). For example, when Australian students were asked why they sometimes drive too fast, they focused on circumstances, such as being late, but saw other people's dangerous driving as a sign of aggressiveness or immaturity (Harré, Brandt, & Houkamau, 2004). Similarly, when you are driving too slowly, the reason is that you are looking for an address, not that you are a big loser like that jerk who crawled along in front of you yesterday.

The actor-observer effect occurs mainly because people have different kinds of information about their own behavior and the behavior of others. When *you* are in some situation—giving a speech, perhaps—the information most available to you is likely to be external and situational, such as the temperature of the room and the size of the audience. You also have a lot of information about other external factors, such as the amount of time you had to prepare your talk or the upsetting conversation that occurred this morning. If your speech is disorganized and boring, you can easily attribute it to one or all of these external causes. But when you observe someone else, the most obvious information in the situation is *that person*. You do not know what happened to the person last night or this morning, so you are likely to attribute the quality of the performance to stable, internal characteristics (Moskowitz, 2005).

Of course, people do not always attribute their own behavior to external forces. In fact, whether they do so often depends on whether the outcome is positive or negative. In one study, when people were asked what they saw as the cause of their good and bad experiences when shopping online, they tended to take personal credit for positive

actor-observer effect   The tendency to attribute other people's behavior to internal causes while attributing one's own behavior to external causes.

outcomes (such as finding bargains) but to blame the computer for problems such as receiving the wrong merchandise (Moon, 2003). In other words, these people showed a **self-serving bias,** the tendency to take personal credit for success but to blame external causes for failure. This bias has been found in almost all cultures, but as with the fundamental attribution error, it is usually more pronounced among people from individualistic Western cultures than among those from collectivist Eastern cultures (Mezulis et al., 2004).

The self-serving bias occurs, in part, because people are motivated to maintain their self-esteem, and ignoring negative information about themselves is one way to do so. If you just failed an exam, it is painful to admit that the exam was fair. Like the other attributional biases we have discussed, self-serving bias helps people think about their failures and shortcomings in ways that protect their self-esteem (Dunning et al., 2003; Gilbert et al., 2004; Tesser, 2001). These self-protective cognitive biases can help us temporarily escape from unpleasant thoughts and feelings, but they may also create a distorted view of reality that can lead to other problems. One such problem is *unrealistic optimism,* the tendency to believe that good things (such as financial success or having a gifted child) are likely to happen to you but that bad things (such as accidents or illness) are not (Lin & Raghubir, 2005). Unrealistic optimism tends to persist even when there is strong evidence against it, and it can lead to potentially harmful behaviors. For example, people who are unrealistically optimistic about their health may not bother to exercise, may ignore information about how to prevent heart disease, or may underestimate the risks of engaging in unsafe sex (Dillard, McCaul, & Klein, 2006; Radcliffe & Klein, 2002; Taylor et al., 1992). ("In Review: Some Biases in Social Perception" summarizes the common cognitive biases discussed here.)

In Review

Some Biases in Social Perception

BIAS	DESCRIPTION
Importance of first impression	Ambiguous information is interpreted in line with a first impression and the initial schema is recalled better and more vividly than any later correction to it. Actions based on this impression may elicit behavior that confirms it.
Fundamental attribution error	The tendency to overattribute the behavior of others to internal factors.
Actor-observer bias	The tendency for actors to attribute their own behavior to external causes and for observers to attribute the behavior of others to internal factors.
Self-serving bias	The tendency to attribute one's successes to internal factors and one's failures to external factors.
Unrealistic optimism	The tendency of people to believe that good things will happen to them but that bad things will not.

?

1. The fundamental attribution error appears to be somewhat less likely to occur among people in _____ cultures.
2. First impressions form _____, but change _____.
3. If you believed that immigrants' successes are due to government help but that their failures are due to laziness, you would be committing the _____ error.

self-serving bias   The tendency to attribute one's successes to internal characteristics while blaming one's failures on external causes.

Attitudes

> ▶ *Do attitudes always determine behavior?*

Our views about health, safety, or any other topic reflect our *attitudes*. Social psychologists have studied this aspect of social cognition longer and more intensely than any other. An **attitude** is the tendency to think, feel, or act positively or negatively toward objects in our environment (Albarracín, Johnson, & Zanna, 2005). Attitudes play an important role in guiding how we react to other people, what causes and politicians we support, which products we buy, and countless other daily decisions.

The Structure of Attitudes

Social psychologists have long viewed attitudes as having three components (Fabrigar, MacDonald, & Wegener, 2005). The *cognitive* component is a set of beliefs about the attitude object. The emotional, or *affective,* component includes feelings about the object. And the *behavioral* component is the way people act toward the object. If these three components were always in harmony, we would be able to predict people's behavior toward the homeless, for example, on the basis of the thoughts or feelings they express, and vice versa. This is often not the case, however (Schwarz & Bohner, 2001). Many people's charitable thoughts and sympathetic emotions regarding the homeless are never translated into actions aimed at helping them.

What determines whether people's behavior will be consistent with the cognitive and affective components of their attitudes? Several factors are important. For one thing, behavior is more likely to be consistent with attitude when people see the attitude as important and relevant to their lives (Kenrick, Neuberg, & Cialdini, 2007; Skitka, Bauman, & Sargis, 2005). Attitude-behavior consistency is also more likely when the behavioral component of the attitude is in line with a *subjective norm,* our view of how the important people in our lives want us to act. If there is a conflict between what we want to do and what a subjective norm tells us we should do, we may end up behaving in ways that are inconsistent with our attitudes (Ajzen & Gilbert-Cote, 2008). For example, someone who believes that the rights of gay men and lesbians should be protected might not go out and campaign for this cause because doing so would upset valued family members or co-workers who are strongly against it. Third, attitude-consistent behavior is more likely when people have *perceived control,* a belief that they can actually perform the behavior (Ajzen & Fishbein, 2005). The cognitive and emotional components of your attitude toward the homeless might be positive, but if you don't believe you can do anything to help them, you are not likely to even try. Finally, *direct experience* with the object of an attitude increases the likelihood of attitude-consistent behavior (Glasman & Albarracín, 2006; Kenrick, Neuberg, & Cialdini, 2005). So you might be more likely to actively support and perhaps even participate in efforts to help the homeless if you have come to know a homeless person on your campus than if you have only read about their plight.

Forming Attitudes

People's attitudes about objects begin to appear in early childhood and continue to emerge throughout life. How do these attitudes form? Genetics may have a certain amount of influence on some attitudes (Abrahamson, Baker, & Caspi, 2002; Verweij et al., 2008), but social learning—what children learn from their parents and others—appears to play the major role in attitude formation. Children learn not only the names of objects but also what they should believe and feel about them and how they should act toward them. For example, a parent may teach a child not only that snakes are reptiles but also that they should be feared and avoided. So as children learn concepts such as "reptile" or "work," they learn attitudes about those concepts, too (Bohner & Schwarz, 2001).

A REMINDER ABOUT POVERTY ▲

Photographs such as this one are used by fund-raising organizations to remind us of the kind thoughts and charitable feelings we have toward needy people and other worthy causes. As a result, we may be more likely to behave in accordance with the cognitive and affective components of our attitudes and make a donation to these causes. Browse through several newspapers and popular magazines and calculate the percentage of such photos you find in ads for charitable organizations.

Learn BY Doing

© David Woo/Stock, Boston

attitude A tendency toward a particular cognitive, emotional, or behavioral reaction to objects in one's environment.

Classical and operant conditioning can also shape positive or negative attitudes (Baron, Byrne, & Branscombe, 2006). Advertisers pair up enjoyable music, soothing colors, or sexy images with the products they try to sell (Pratkanis & Aronson, 2001; Walther & Langer, 2008), and parents, teachers, and peers reward children for stating particular views. The *mere-exposure effect* is influential as well. All else being equal, attitudes toward an object become more positive the more frequently people are exposed to the object. In one study, for example, after European American college students were repeatedly exposed to pictures of Asians and Blacks, their liking for new pictures of Asians and Blacks increased (Zebrowitz, White, & Wieneke, 2008). This mere-exposure effect helps explain why commercials and political ads are aired over and over and why some rock bands won't include new songs in a live concert until their fans have repeatedly heard and come to like the recorded versions.

Changing Attitudes

The nearly $100 billion a year spent on advertising in the United States alone provides just one example of how people constantly try to change our attitudes. Stop for a moment and make a list of other examples, starting, perhaps, with the persuasive messages of groups concerned with abortion or gun control or recycling—and don't forget about friends who want you to think the way they do.

Two Routes to Attitude Change   Whether a persuasive message succeeds in changing attitudes depends mainly on three factors: (1) the person communicating the message; (2) the content of the message; and (3) the audience who receives it (Johnson, Maio, & Smith-McLallen, 2005). The **elaboration likelihood model** of attitude change—illustrated in Figure 14.2—provides a framework for understanding when and how these factors affect attitude change (Petty & Briñol, 2008). The model is based on the idea that persuasive messages can change people's attitudes through one of two main routes.

The first is called the *peripheral route* because when it is activated, we devote little attention to the central content of the persuasive message. We tend to be affected instead by peripheral, or surrounding, persuasion cues, such as the confidence, attractiveness, or other characteristics of the person who delivers the message. These persuasion cues influence attitude change even though they may have nothing to do with the logic or accuracy of the message itself. Commercials in which movie stars or other attractive nonexperts endorse pain relievers or denture cleaners are designed to encourage the peripheral route to attitude change.

By contrast, when the *central route* to attitude change is activated, the core content of the message becomes more important than the communicator's characteristics in determining attitude change. A person following the central route uses logical steps—such as those outlined in the Thinking Critically sections of this book—to analyze the

elaboration likelihood model   A model of attitude change suggesting that people can change their attitudes through a central route (by considering an argument's content) or through a peripheral route (by relying on irrelevant persuasion cues).

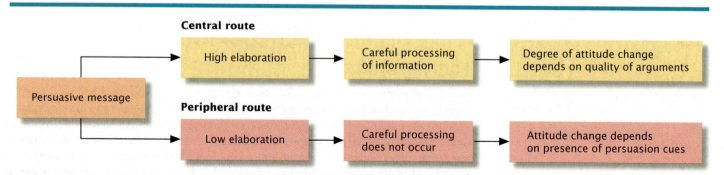

FIGURE 14.2   ■   THE ELABORATION LIKELIHOOD MODEL OF ATTITUDE CHANGE

The central route to attitude change involves carefully processing and evaluating a message's content (high elaboration). The peripheral route involves little processing and evaluation of message content (low elaboration) and relying instead on persuasion cues such as the attractiveness of the person making the argument (Cacioppo, Petty, & Crites, 1993).

content of the persuasive message, including the validity of its claims, whether it leaves out pertinent information, alternative interpretations of evidence, and so on.

What determines which route people will follow? Personal involvement with the content of a message is an important factor. The elaboration likelihood model predicts that the more personally involving a topic is, the more likely it is that the central route will be activated (Fabrigar, MacDonald, & Wegener, 2005; Holbrook et al., 2006). Suppose, for example, that you hear someone arguing for the cancellation of all student loans in Chile. This message might persuade you through the peripheral route if it comes from someone who looks attractive and sounds intelligent. However, if the message proposes eliminating student loans at your own school, you are more likely to follow the central route. You might still be persuaded, but only if the logic of the message is clear and convincing. This is why celebrity endorsements tend to be more effective when the products being advertised are relatively unimportant to the audience.

Persuasive messages are not the only means of changing attitudes. Another approach is to get people to act in ways that are inconsistent with their attitudes in the hope that they will adjust those attitudes to match their behavior. Often, such adjustments do occur. Cognitive dissonance theory attempts to explain why.

Cognitive Dissonance Theory Leon Festinger's (1957) classic **cognitive dissonance theory** holds that people want their thoughts, beliefs, and attitudes to be in harmony with one another and with their behavior. When people experience inconsistency, or *dissonance*, among these elements, they become anxious and are motivated to make them more consistent (Elliot & Devine, 1994; Olson & Stone, 2005). For example, someone who believes that "smoking is dangerous" but who must also admit that "I smoke" would be motivated to reduce the resulting dissonance. Because it is often difficult to change behavior, people usually reduce cognitive dissonance by changing attitudes that are inconsistent with the behavior. So rather than quit smoking, the smoker might decide that smoking is not so dangerous after all.

In one of the first studies of cognitive dissonance, Festinger and his colleague Merrill Carlsmith asked people to turn pegs in a pegboard, a very dull task (Festinger & Carlsmith, 1959). Later, some of these people were asked to persuade a person who was waiting to participate in the study that the task was "exciting and fun." Some were told that they would be paid $1 to tell this lie. Others were promised $20. After they had talked to the waiting person, their attitudes toward the dull task were measured. Figure 14.3 shows and explains the surprising results. The people who were paid just $1 to lie liked the dull task more than those who were paid $20 (Festinger & Carlsmith, 1959).

Hundreds of other experiments have also found that when people publicly engage in behaviors that are inconsistent with their privately held attitudes, they are likely to change their attitudes to be consistent with their behavior (Cooper, Mirabile, & Scher, 2005; Stone & Cooper, 2001). These experiments have found that attitude-behavior inconsistency is likely to change attitudes when (1) the inconsistency causes some distress or discomfort in a person; and (2) changing attitudes will reduce that discomfort. But why should attitude-behavior inconsistency cause discomfort in the first place? There is considerable debate among attitude researchers about this question (Harmon-Jones & Harmon-Jones, 2007; Wood, 2000).

Currently, the most popular of several possible answers is that discomfort results when people's positive self-concept (e.g., "I am honest") is threatened by recognizing that they have done something inconsistent with that self-concept. For example, if they have encouraged another person to do something that they themselves didn't believe in or that they themselves wouldn't do, this inconsistency makes most people feel uncomfortable. So they change their attitudes to reduce or eliminate the discomfort (Stone, 2003; Stone & Cooper, 2001; Stone & Fernandez, 2008). In other words, if people can persuade themselves that they really believe in what they have said or done, the inconsistency disappears, their positive self-concept is restored, and they can feel good about themselves again.

The circumstances that lead to cognitive dissonance may be different in the individualist cultures of Europe and North America than in collectivist cultures such as those in Japan and China. In individualist cultures, dissonance typically arises from

Improve Your Grade
Tutorial: Cognitive Dissonance Theory

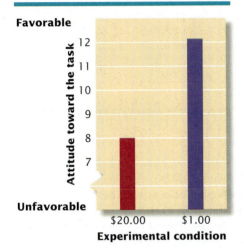

High justification (low dissonance)
Low justification (high dissonance)

FIGURE 14.3 ■ COGNITIVE DISSONANCE AND ATTITUDE CHANGE

According to cognitive dissonance theory, the $20 that people were given to say that a boring task was enjoyable provided them with a clear justification for lying. Having been paid to lie, they should experience little dissonance between what they said and what they felt about the task. And indeed, their attitude toward the task did not change much. However, people who received only $1 had little justification to lie and reduced their dissonance mainly by displaying a more positive attitude toward the task. *Source*: Festinger & Carlsmith (1959).

cognitive dissonance theory A theory that attitude change is driven by efforts to reduce tension caused by inconsistencies between attitudes and behaviors.

In Review

FORMING AND CHANGING ATTITUDES

TYPE OF INFLUENCE	DESCRIPTION
Social learning and conditioning	Attitudes are usually formed through observing how others behave and speak about an attitude object as well as through classical and operant conditioning.
Elaboration likelihood model	People change attitudes through either a central or peripheral route, depending on factors such as personal involvement.
Cognitive dissonance	Holding inconsistent cognitions can motivate attitude change.

1. According to the elaboration likelihood model, people are more likely to pay close attention to the content and logic of a persuasive message if the _____ route to attitude change has been activated.

2. Holding attitudes that are similar to those of your friends illustrates the importance of _____ in attitude formation.

3. According to cognitive dissonance theory, we tend to reduce conflict between attitudes and behaviors by changing our _____.

behaving in a manner inconsistent with one's own beliefs because this behavior causes self-doubt. But in collectivist cultures, dissonance typically arises when such behavior causes the person to worry about one's reputation with others (Kitayama et al., 2004). Cultural values also operate in shaping dissonance-reducing strategies. For example, people from individualistic cultures can reduce the unpleasant feelings that accompany dissonance by affirming their value as unique individuals, whereas people from collectivist cultures can reduce the same kind of feelings by affirming the value of the groups to which they belong (Hoshino-Browne et al., 2005). ("In Review: Forming and Changing Attitudes" summarizes some of the main processes through which attitudes are formed and changed.)

Prejudice and Stereotypes

▶ *How does prejudice develop?*

All of the principles behind impression formation, attribution, and attitudes come together in prejudice and stereotypes. **Stereotypes** are the perceptions, beliefs, and expectations a person has about members of some group. They are schemas about entire groups of people (Fiske & Taylor, 2008). Usually, they involve the false assumption that all members of a group share the same characteristics. The characteristics that make up the stereotype can be positive, but more often they are negative. The most prevalent and powerful stereotypes focus on observable personal attributes, particularly ethnicity, gender, and age (Operario & Fiske, 2001).

The stereotypes people hold can be so ingrained that their effects on behavior can be automatic and unconscious (Banaji, Lemm, & Carpenter, 2001; Blair, Judd, & Fallman, 2004; Dovidio et al., 2009; Sue et al., 2007). In one study, for example, European American and African American participants played a video game in which white or black men suddenly appeared on a screen holding an object that might be

linkages

Can subconscious processes alter our reaction to people? *(a link to Consciousness)*

stereotypes   False assumptions that all members of some group share the same characteristics.

a weapon (Correll et al., 2002; see Figure 14.4). The participants had to immediately "shoot" armed men but not unarmed ones. Under this time pressure, participants' errors were not random. If they "shot" an unarmed man, he was more likely to be black than white; when they failed to "shoot" an armed man, he was more likely to be white than black. These differences appeared in both European American and African American participants, but was most pronounced among those who held the strongest cultural stereotypes about blacks.

Stereotyping often leads to **prejudice,** which is a positive or negative attitude toward an individual based simply on that individual's membership in some group (Dion, 2003; Maio et al., in press). The word *prejudice* means "prejudgment." Many theorists believe that prejudice, like other attitudes, has cognitive, affective, and behavioral components. Stereotyped thinking is the cognitive component of prejudicial attitudes. The hatred, admiration, anger, and other feelings people have about stereotyped groups constitute the affective component. The behavioral component of prejudice involves **social discrimination,** which is differing treatment of individuals who belong to different groups.

Theories of Prejudice and Stereotyping

Prejudice and stereotyping may occur for several reasons. Let's consider three explanatory theories, each of which has been supported by research and accounts for many instances of stereotyping and prejudice.

Motivational Theories   For some people, prejudice meets certain needs and increases their sense of security. This idea was first proposed by Theodor W. Adorno and his associates more than 50 years ago (Adorno et al., 1950) and was elaborated more recently by Bob Altemeyer (1996, 2004; Altemeyer & Hunsberger, 2005). These researchers suggest that prejudice is especially likely among people who display a personality trait called *authoritarianism.* According to Altemeyer, authoritarianism is composed of three main elements: (1) acceptance of conventional or traditional values; (2) willingness to unquestioningly follow the orders of authority figures; and (3) an inclination to act aggressively toward individuals or groups identified by authority figures as threats to the person's values or well-being. In fact, people with an authoritarian orientation tend to view the world as a threatening place (Sibley, Wilson, & Duckitt, 2007). One way to protect themselves from the threats they perceive all around them is to strongly identify with people like themselves—their *in-group*—and to reject, dislike, and maybe even punish people who are members of *out-groups,* groups that are different from their own (Thomsen, Green, & Sidanius, 2008). Looking down on and discriminating against members of these out-groups—such as gay men and lesbians, African Americans, or Muslims, for example—may help authoritarian people feel safer and better about themselves (Duckitt, 2006).

Another motivational explanation of prejudice involves the concept of social identity discussed earlier. Recall that whether or not they display authoritarianism, most people are motivated to identify with their in-group and tend to see it as better than other groups (Brewer & Pierce, 2005). As a result, members of an in-group often see all members of out-groups as less attractive and less socially acceptable than members of the in-group and may thus treat them badly (Jackson, 2002). In other words, prejudice may result when people's motivation to enhance their own self-esteem causes them to disrespect other people.

Cognitive Theories   Stereotyping and prejudice may also result from the thought processes that people use in dealing with the world. There are so many other people, so many situations in which we meet them, and so many behaviors that others might display that we cannot possibly attend to and remember them all. Therefore, people must use schemas and other cognitive shortcuts to organize and make sense of their social world (Moskowitz, 2005). Often these cognitive processes provide accurate and useful summaries of other people, but sometimes they lead to inaccurate stereotypes.

For example, one effective way to deal with social complexity is to group people into *social categories.* Rather than remembering every detail about everyone we have

© Joshua Correll

FIGURE 14.4 ▬ THE IMPACT OF STEREOTYPES ON BEHAVIOR

When these men suddenly appeared on a video screen, participants were supposed to "shoot" them but only if they appeared to be armed (Correll et al., 2002). Stereotypes about whether white men or black men are more likely to be armed significantly affected the errors made by participants in firing their video game "weapons." Similar results appeared in a sample of police officers, although they were not as quick as civilians were to "shoot" an unarmed black man (Correll et al. 2002). Cover these photos with a pair of index cards, then ask a few friends to watch as you show each photo, one at a time, for just an instant, before covering it again. Then ask your friends to say whether either man appeared to be armed. Was one individual more often seen as armed? If so, which one?

Learn BY Doing

prejudice   A positive or negative attitude toward people in certain groups.

social discrimination   Differential treatment of people in certain groups; the behavioral component of prejudice.

SCHEMAS AND STEREOTYPES ▶

The use of schemas to assign certain people to certain categories can be helpful when deciding who is a customer and who is a store employee, but it can also lead to inaccurate stereotypes. After the September 11, 2001, terrorist attacks on New York and Washington, D.C., many people began to think of all Muslims as potential terrorists and to discriminate against them. This false assumption and the problems it has created for Muslims in the United States was one of the many awful side effects of the terrorist attacks.

© Bonnie Kamin/PhotoEdit

ever encountered, we tend to put other people into categories such as doctor, senior citizen, Republican, student, Italian, and the like (Dovidio, Kawakami, & Gaertner, 2000). To further simplify perception of these categories, we tend to see group members as being quite similar to one another. This tendency can be seen in the fact that members of one ethnic group may find it harder to distinguish among specific faces in other ethnic groups than in their own (Anthony, Cooper, & Mullen, 1992; Michel et al., 2006). People also tend to assume that all members of a different group hold the same beliefs and values and that those beliefs and values differ from those of their own group (Dion, 2003). Finally, because particularly noticeable stimuli tend to draw a lot of attention, rude behavior by even a few members of an easily identified ethnic group may lead people to see an *illusory correlation* between rudeness and ethnicity (Meiser & Hewstone, 2006). As a result, they may incorrectly believe that all members of that group are rude.

Learning Theories   Like other attitudes, prejudice can be learned. Some prejudice is learned as a result of personal conflicts with members of different groups, but people also develop negative attitudes toward groups with whom they have had little or no contact. Learning theories suggest that children can pick up prejudices just by watching and listening to parents, peers, and others (Rohan & Zanna, 1996; Taylor, Peplau, & Sears, 2006). There may even be a form of biopreparedness (described in the learning chapter) that makes us especially likely to learn to fear people who are strangers or who look different from us (Kelly et al., 2007; Olson et al., 2001). Movies and television also portray ethnic or other groups in ways that teach stereotypes and prejudice (Brehm, Kassin, & Fein, 2005; Jost & Hamilton, 2005). One study revealed that local news coverage often gives the impression that African Americans are responsible for a higher percentage of crimes than is actually the case (Romer, Jamieson, & deCoteau, 1998). No wonder so many young children know about the supposed negative characteristics of other ethnic groups, sometimes long before they ever meet people in those groups (Baron & Banaji, 2006; Quintana, 1998).

Reducing Prejudice

One clear implication of the cognitive and learning theories of prejudice and stereotyping is that members of one group are often ignorant or misinformed about the characteristics of people in other groups (Dovidio, Gaertner, & Kawakami, 2003). Before 1954, for example, most black and white schoolchildren in the United States

FIGHTING ETHNIC PREJUDICE ▲

Negative attitudes about members of ethnic groups are often based on negative personal experiences or on the negative experiences and attitudes people hear about from others. Cooperative contact between equals can help promote mutual respect and reduce ethnic prejudice.

contact hypothesis The idea that stereotypes and prejudice toward a group will diminish as contact with the group increases.

knew very little about one another because they went to separate schools. Then the Supreme Court declared that segregated public schools should be prohibited. In doing so, the court created a real-life test of the **contact hypothesis,** which states that stereotypes and prejudice toward a group will decrease as contact with that group increases (Pettigrew & Tropp, 2006).

Did the desegregation of U.S. schools confirm the contact hypothesis? In a few schools, integration was followed by a decrease in prejudice, but in most places, either no change occurred or prejudice actually increased (Oskamp & Schultz, 1998). However, these results did not necessarily disprove the contact hypothesis. In-depth studies of schools with successful desegregation suggested that contact alone was not enough. Integration reduced prejudice only when certain social conditions were created (Pettigrew & Tropp, 2006). First, members of the two groups had to be of roughly equal social and economic status. Second, school authorities had to promote cooperation and interdependence between ethnic groups by having members of the two groups work together on projects that required reliance on one another to achieve success. Third, the contact between group members had to occur on a one-on-one basis. It was only when *individuals* got to know each other that the errors contained in stereotypes became apparent. Finally, the members of each group had to be seen as typical and not unusual in any significant way. When these four conditions were met, the children's attitudes toward one another became more positive.

Elliot Aronson (Aronson & Patnoe, 2000) describes a teaching strategy called the *jigsaw technique* that helps create these conditions. Children from several ethnic groups must work together on a team to complete a task, such as writing a report about a famous person in history. Each child learns a separate piece of information about this person, such as place of birth or greatest achievement, then provides this information to the team (Aronson, 1990). Studies show that children from various ethnic groups who take part in the jigsaw technique and other cooperative learning experiences display substantial reductions in prejudice toward other groups (e.g., Aronson, 1997). The success reported in these studies has greatly increased the popularity of cooperative learning exercises in U.S. classrooms. Such exercises may not eliminate all aspects of ethnic prejudice in children, but they seem to be a step in the right direction.

Can friendly, cooperative, interdependent contact reduce the more entrenched forms of prejudice seen in adults? It may. One study found that the prejudicial attitudes of first-year college students weakened more if their roommate was from a different ethnic group rather than from the students' own ethnic group (Shook & Fazio, 2008). Another showed that when equal-status adults from different ethnic groups work jointly toward a common goal, bias and distrust can be reduced, particularly among those in ethnic majority groups (Tropp & Pettigrew, 2005). This is especially true if they come to see themselves as members of the same group rather than as belonging to opposing groups (Dovidio, Kawakami, & Gaertner, 2000; Fiske, 2000; Gaertner & Dovidio, 2008). The challenge to be met in creating such cooperative experiences in the real world is that the participants must be of equal status, a challenge made more difficult in many countries by the status differences that still exist between ethnic groups (Dixon, Durrheim, & Tredoux, 2007; Kenworthy et al., 2006).

In the final analysis, contact can provide only part of the solution to the problems of stereotyping, prejudice, and social discrimination. To reduce ethnic prejudice, we must develop additional techniques to address the social cognitions and perceptions that lie at the core of bigotry and hatred toward people who are different from ourselves (Amodio & Devine, 2009; Bigler & Liben, 2007). Altering these mental processes will be difficult because, as we saw earlier, they can operate both consciously and unconsciously, causing even those who do not see themselves as prejudiced to discriminate against individuals who are different (Banaji, Lemm, & Carpenter, 2001; Uleman, Blader, & Todorov, 2005). However, recent research suggests that it may be possible to change even unconscious forms of stereotyping and prejudice (Kawakami, Dovidio, & van Kamp, 2005; Plant & Peruche, 2005; Wheeler & Fiske, 2005).

Interpersonal Attraction

▶ *What factors affect who likes whom?*

Research on prejudice suggests some of the reasons why people may come to dislike or even hate other people. An equally fascinating aspect of social cognition is why people like or love other people. Folklore tells us that "opposites attract" but also that "birds of a feather flock together." Each statement is partly true, but neither is entirely accurate in all cases. We begin our coverage of interpersonal attraction by discussing the factors that draw people toward one another. We then examine how liking sometimes develops into more intimate relationships.

Keys to Attraction

Whether you like someone or not depends partly on situational factors and partly on personal characteristics.

The Environment   One of the most important determinants of attraction is simple physical proximity (Berscheid & Reis, 1998; Kassin, Fein, & Markus, 2008). As long as you do not initially dislike a person, your liking for that person will increase with additional contact (Brehm, Kassin, & Fein, 2005). This proximity phenomenon—another example of the *mere-exposure effect* mentioned earlier—helps account for why next-door neighbors are usually more likely to become friends than people who live farther from one another. Chances are, most of your friends are people you met as neighbors, co-workers, or classmates (Liben-Nowell et al., 2005).

The circumstances under which people first meet also influence attraction. You are much more likely to be attracted to a stranger if you meet in comfortable (as opposed to uncomfortable) physical conditions. Similarly, if you receive a reward in the presence of a stranger, the chances are greater that you will like that stranger, even if the stranger is not the one giving the reward (Clark & Pataki, 1995). In one study, for example, an experimenter judged one person's creativity while another person watched. Compared with those who received a negative evaluation, participants who were evaluated positively tended to like the observer more (Griffitt & Guay, 1969). At least among strangers, then, liking can occur through associating someone with something pleasant.

Similarity   People also tend to like those they perceive as similar to themselves on variables such as age, religion, smoking or drinking habits, or being a "morning" or "evening" person (Buston & Emlen, 2003; Rushton & Bons, 2005; Smith & Mackie, 2007). Similarity in attitudes is another important influence on attraction (Brehm, Kassin, & Fein, 2005; Taylor, Peplau, & Sears, 2006).

An especially good predictor of liking is similarity in attitudes about mutual acquaintances, because in general, people prefer relationships that are *balanced*. As illustrated in Figure 14.5, if Meagan likes Abigail, the relationship is balanced as long as they agree on their evaluation of a third person, regardless of whether they like or dislike that third person. However, the relationship will be imbalanced if Meagan and Abigail disagree on their evaluation of a third person.

One reason why we like people whose attitudes are similar to our own is that we expect such people to think highly of us (Condon & Crano, 1988). It's hard to say, though, whether attraction is a cause or an effect of similarity. For example, you might like someone because his attitudes are similar to yours, but it is also possible that as a result of liking him, your attitudes will become more similar to his (Davis & Rusbult, 2001). Even if your own attitudes do not change, you may change your perceptions of the liked person's attitudes such that those attitudes now seem more similar to yours (Brehm, 1992).

Physical Attractiveness   Physical characteristics are another important factor in attraction, particularly in the early stages of a relationship (Smith & Mackie, 2007). From preschool through adulthood, physical attractiveness is a key to popularity

PROXIMITY AND LIKING ▲

Research on environmental factors in attraction suggests that, barring bad first impressions, the more often we make contact with someone—as neighbors, classmates, or co-workers, for example—the more we tend to like that person. Does this principle apply in your life? To find out, think about how and where you met each of your closest friends. If you can think of cases in which proximity did not lead to liking, what do you think interfered with the formation of friendship?

Learn BY **Doing**

© Michelle D. Bridwell/PhotoEdit

FIGURE 14.5 ■ BALANCED AND IMBALANCED RELATIONSHIPS

Here are some common examples of balanced and imbalanced relationships among three people. The plus and minus signs refer to liking and disliking, respectively. Balanced relationships are comfortable and harmonious; imbalanced ones often bring conflict.

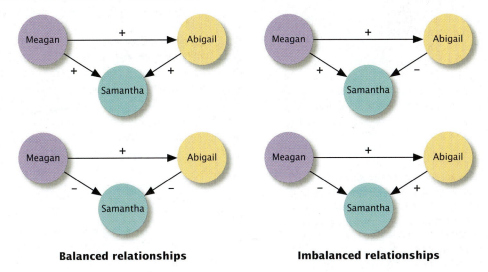

Balanced relationships   **Imbalanced relationships**

with members of both sexes (Langlois et al., 2000; Lemly, 2000). Consistent with the **matching hypothesis** of interpersonal attraction, however, people tend to date, marry, or form other committed relationships with those who are similar to themselves in physical attractiveness (Yela & Sangrador, 2001). One possible reason for this outcome is that although people tend to be most attracted to those with the greatest physical appeal, they also want to avoid being rejected by such individuals. So it may be compromise, not preference, that leads people to pair off with those who are roughly equivalent to themselves in physical attractiveness (Carli, Ganley, & Pierce-Otay, 1991; Lee et al., 2008).

Intimate Relationships and Love

There is much about intimate relationships that psychologists do not and may never understand, but they are learning all the time (Reis & Aron, 2008). For example, evolutionary psychologists suggest that men and women employ different strategies to ensure the survival of their genes and that each gender looks for different attributes in a potential mate (Buss, 2004a; Kenrick, Neuberg, & Cialdini, 2005; Li & Kenrick, 2006; Schmitt, 2003). The physical appearance of a partner tends to be more important to men than to women, whereas the partner's intelligence tends to be more important to women than to men (Buss, 2004b; see Figure 14.6).

Intimate Relationships Eventually, people who are attracted to each other usually become *interdependent,* which means that the thoughts, emotions, and behaviors of one person affect the thoughts, emotions, and behaviors of the other (Rusbult, Arriaga, & Agnew, 2001; Rusbult & Van Lange, 2003). Interdependence is one of the defining characteristics of intimate relationships (Agnew et al., 1998).

Another key component of successful intimate relationships is *commitment,* which is the extent to which each person is psychologically attached to the relationship and wants to remain in it (Amodio & Showers, 2005; Rusbult & Van Lange, 1996). People feel committed to a relationship when they are satisfied with the rewards they receive from it, when they have invested significant tangible and intangible resources in it, and when they have few attractive alternative relationships available to them (Bui, Peplau, & Hill, 1996; Lydon et al., 2008).

Analyzing Love Although some people think love is simply a strong form of liking, recent research suggests that romantic love and liking are quite separate emotions, at

matching hypothesis The notion that people are most likely to form committed relationships with others who are similar to themselves in physical attractiveness.

FIGURE 14.6 ■ SEX DIFFERENCES IN DATE AND MATE PREFERENCES

According to evolutionary psychologists, men and women have developed different strategies for selecting sexual partners (Buss, 2004b; Kenrick, Neuberg, & Cialdini, 2005; Li & Kenrick, 2006; Schmitt, 2003). These psychologists say that women became more selective than men because they can have relatively few children and want a partner who is best able to help support those children. Here are some data that support this idea. When asked about the intelligence of people they would choose for one-night stands, dating, and sexual relationships, women preferred much smarter partners than men did. Only when the choices concerned steady dating and marriage did the men's preference for bright partners equal that of the women (Eastwick & Finkel, 2008). Critics of the evolutionary approach explain such sex differences as reflecting learned social norms and expectations of the way men and women should behave (Eagly & Wood, 1999; Miller, Putcha-Bhagavatula, & Pedersen, 2002). *Source*: Kenrick et al. (1993).

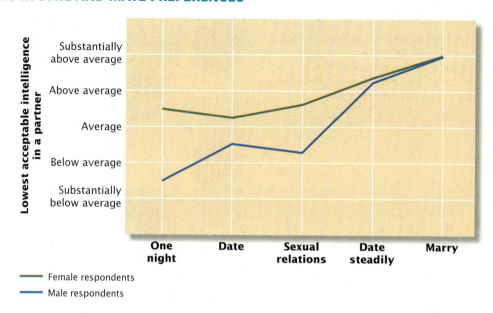

least in the sense that they are associated with differing patterns of brain chemistry and brain activity (Aron et al., 2005; Emanuele et al., 2006). And although romantic love and sexual desire are often experienced together, they too seem to be separate emotions associated with different patterns of physiological arousal (Diamond, 2004). Further, most theorists agree that there are several different types of love (Brehm, Kassin, & Fein, 2005; Kassin, Fein, & Markus, 2008). One widely accepted view distinguishes between passionate (romantic) love and companionate love (Hendrick & Hendrick, 2003). *Passionate love* is intense, arousing, and marked by both strong physical attraction and deep emotional attachment. Sexual feelings are intense, and thoughts of the other intrude on each person's awareness frequently. *Companionate love* is less arousing but psychologically more intimate. It is marked by mutual concern for the welfare of the other and a willingness to disclose personal information and feelings. People who experience companionate love seem especially satisfied with their lives (Brehm, Kassin, & Fein, 2005; Hendrick & Hendrick, 2003; Kim & Hatfield, 2004).

Robert Sternberg (2009) has offered an even broader analysis of love. According to his *triangular theory,* the three basic components of love are passion, intimacy, and commitment (see Figure 14.7). Various combinations of these components result in various types of love. For example, Sternberg suggests that *romantic love* involves a high degree of passion and intimacy yet lacks substantial commitment to the other person. *Companionate love* is marked by a great deal of intimacy and commitment but little passion. *Consummate love* is the most complete and satisfying. It is the most complete because it includes a high level of all three components. It is the most satisfying because the relationship is likely to fulfill many of the needs of each partner. Recently, Sternberg has created a "duplex theory" of love by pairing his triangular theory with a second one that focuses on love as a story. This second theory focuses on the fact that in Western cultures, at least, it appears that the success of a relationship depends not just on its perceived characteristics but also on the degree to which those characteristics fit each partner's ideal story of love, such as that of a prince and princess, a pair of business partners, or whatever (Sternberg, 2009).

Cultural factors have a strong influence on the way people think about love and marriage. In North America and the United Kingdom, for example, the vast majority of people believe that they should love the person they marry. By contrast, in India and Pakistan, about half the people interviewed in a survey said they would marry someone they did not love if that person had other qualities that they desired (Levine et al., 1995).

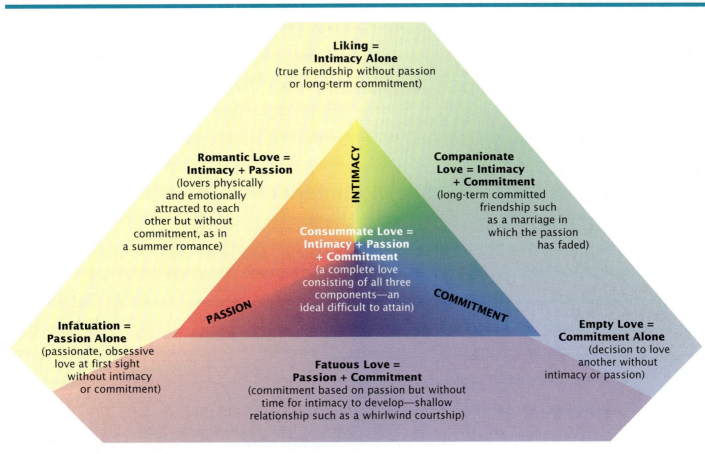

FIGURE 14.7 ■ A TRIANGULAR THEORY OF LOVE

According to Sternberg (2009), different types of love result when the three basic components in his triangular theory occur in different combinations. The size of the triangle of love increases as love increases, and its shape is determined by the relative strength of each basic component. The perfectly balanced triangle shown here illustrates a relationship in which all three components are of about equal strength.
Source: Sternberg (1988a).

In Russia, only 40 percent of respondents said that they married for love. Most reported marrying because of loneliness, shared interests, or an unplanned pregnancy (Baron & Byrne, 1994). Many such cultural differences in the role of love in marriage are likely to continue, but others seem to be disappearing (Hatfield & Rapson, 2006).

Strong and Weak Marriages Long-term research on successful and unsuccessful marriages suggests that premarital attitudes, feelings, and perceptions can predict marital success. For example, couples who have a close, intimate relationship; similar attitudes; and realistic views of each other's strengths and weaknesses when they are dating are more likely than other couples to remain married (Hill & Peplau, 1998; Neff & Karney, 2005).

Among married couples, women—but not men—generally tend to be more satisfied with their marriages when the partners talk a lot about the relationship (Acitelli, 1992). Partners in successful marriages also tend to share each other's view of themselves and the other, even if that view is a negative one (Swann, De La Ronde, & Hixon, 1994). The perception that the relationship is fair and equitable also increases marital satisfaction (Grote & Clark, 2001). After the birth of a first child, for example, many wives find that they have much more work caring for the child than they had anticipated. If their husbands do not share this work to the degree their wives expected, marital satisfaction tends to decrease (Doss et al., 2009; McNulty & Karney, 2004).

One particularly interesting line of research suggests that even brief observations of couples' interactions can predict whether couples will divorce and when (Driver & Gottman, 2004). Among couples who divorced relatively soon after marriage, the partners tended to express both positive and negative feelings toward one another, but they were unable to control the way they expressed these feelings, especially the negative ones. Communication became increasingly hurtful and eventually broke down

(Driver et al., 2003). A different picture emerged, however, in couples who divorced after many years of marriage. These people did not necessarily express negative emotions toward one another. They simply became less and less likely to communicate *any* feelings. The increasing emotional distance between the spouses created a sense of isolation that eventually led to divorce (Gottman & Levenson, 2002). These findings can help us understand why people in a long (and apparently strong) marriage might suddenly announce that they are divorcing—and why they may remain friends afterward. These people may still like each other but no longer love each other (Gottman & Levenson, 2000; Huston et al., 2001).

Social Influence

 What social rules shape our behavior?

So far, we have considered social cognition, the mental processes associated with people's perceptions of, and reactions to, other people. Let's now explore *social influence,* the process through which individuals and groups directly and indirectly influence a person's thoughts, feelings, and behavior. Research has shown, for example, that suicide rates increase following well-publicized suicides (Romer, Jamieson, & Jamieson, 2006) and that murder rates increase after well-publicized homicides (Jamieson, Jamieson, & Romer, 2003). Do these correlations mean that media coverage of violence triggers similar violence? As described in the chapter on learning, televised violence can play a causal role in aggressive behavior, but there are other reasons to believe that murders or suicides stimulate imitators when they become media events. For one thing, many of the people who kill themselves after a widely reported suicide are similar to the original victim in some respect (Cialdini, 2007). For example, after German television reported a story about a young man who committed suicide by jumping in front of a train, there was a dramatic increase in the number of young German men who committed suicide in the same way (Schmidtke & Hafner, 1988). This phenomenon—known as "copycat" violence—illustrates the effects of social influence.

Social Norms

The most common yet the most subtle form of social influence is communicated through social norms. **Social norms** are learned, socially based rules that tell people what they should or should not do in various situations (Cialdini & Goldstein, 2004). Parents, teachers, members of the clergy, peers, and other agents of culture transmit these social norms. Because of the power of social norms, people often follow them automatically. In North America and Britain, for example, social norms tell us that we should get in line to buy a movie ticket rather than crowd around the box office window. They also lead us to expect that others will do the same. By informing people of what is expected of them and others, social norms make social situations clearer, more predictable, and more comfortable (Schultz et al., 2007).

One particularly powerful social norm is *reciprocity,* the tendency to respond to others as they have acted toward you (Cialdini & Goldstein, 2004). Restaurant servers often take advantage of this social norm by leaving some candy with the bill. Customers who receive this gift tend to reciprocate by leaving a larger tip than customers who don't get candy (Strohmetz et al., 2002). The reciprocity norm probably exists in every culture, but other social norms are not universal (Miller, 2001). For instance, people around the world differ greatly in terms of the physical distance they keep between themselves and others while talking. People from South America usually stand much closer to each other than do people from North America. And as suggested in the chapter on psychological disorders, behavior that is considered normal and friendly in one culture may be seen as offensive or even abnormal in another.

The social influence exerted by social norms creates orderly social behavior. But social influence can also lead to a breakdown in order. For example, **deindividuation**

social norms Learned, socially based rules that prescribe what people should or should not do in various situations.

DEINDIVIDUATION ▶

Robes, hoods, and group rituals help create deindividuation in these members of the Ku Klux Klan by focusing their attention on membership in their organization and its values. The hoods also hide their identities, which reduces their sense of personal responsibility and accountability and makes it easier for them to engage in hate crimes and other cowardly acts of bigotry. Deindividuation operates in other groups, too, ranging from lynch mobs and terrorist cells to political protesters and urban rioters. Through deindividuation, people appear to become "part of the herd," and they may do things that they might not do on their own (Spears et al., 2001).

© David Leeson/The Image Works

is a psychological state in which a person becomes "submerged in the group" and loses the sense of individuality (Cialdini & Goldstein, 2004). When people experience deindividuation, they become emotionally aroused and feel intense closeness with their group. This increased awareness of group membership may lead people to follow the group's social norms, even if those norms promote antisocial behavior (Spears et al., 2001). Normally mild-mannered adults may throw rocks at police during political protests, and youngsters who would not ordinarily commit hate crimes have done so as part of gangs. Such behavior becomes more extreme as people feel less identifiable. An analysis of newspaper accounts of lynchings in the United States over a 50-year period showed that larger lynch mobs were more savage and vicious than smaller ones (Mullen, 1986). Deindividuation provides an example of how, given the right circumstances, quite normal people can engage in destructive, even violent behavior.

Conformity and Compliance

When people change their behavior or beliefs to match those of other members of a group, they are said to conform. **Conformity** occurs as a result of unspoken group pressure, real or imagined (Cialdini & Goldstein, 2004). You probably have experienced group pressure when everyone around you stands to applaud a performance that you thought was not particularly great. You may conform by standing as well, though no one told you to do so; the group's behavior creates a silent but influential pressure to follow suit. **Compliance,** in contrast, occurs when people adjust their behavior because of a request. The request can be clear and direct, such as "Please do me a favor," or it can be more subtle, as when someone simply looks at you in a way that lets you know that the person needs a favor.

Conformity and compliance are usually generated by spoken or unspoken social norms. In a classic experiment, Muzafer Sherif (1937) charted the formation of a group norm by taking advantage of a visual illusion: if you look at a fixed point of light in a pitch-dark room, the light will appear to move. Estimates of how far the light seems to move tend to stay the same over time if an observer is alone. But when Sherif tested several people at once, asking each person to say aloud how far the light moved on repeated trials, their estimates tended to converge; they had established a group norm. Even more important, when individuals who had been in the group were later tested alone, they continued to be influenced by this norm.

deindividuation A psychological state occurring in group members that results in loss of individuality and a tendency to do things not normally done when alone.

conformity Changing one's behavior or beliefs to match those of others, generally as a result of real or imagined (though unspoken) group pressure.

compliance Adjusting one's behavior because of a direct request.

Standard line

(A)

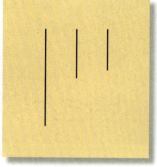

Test lines

(B)

FIGURE 14.8 ■ TYPES OF STIMULUS LINES USED IN EXPERIMENTS BY ASCH

Participants in Asch's experiments saw a new set of lines like these in each trial. The middle line in Part B matches the one in Part A, but when several of Asch's assistants claimed that a different line matched, so did many of the participants. Try re-creating this experiment with four friends. Secretly ask three of them to say that the test line on the left matches the standard line, then show this drawing to all four. Did the fourth person conform to the group norm? If not, do you think it was something about the person, the length of the incorrect line chosen, or both that led to nonconformity? Would conformity be more likely if the first three people had chosen the test line on the right? (Read on for more about this possibility.)

Improve Your Grade
Tutorial: Conformity and the Asch experiment

In another classic experiment, Solomon Asch (1956) explored what people do when faced with a norm that is obviously wrong. The participants in this experiment saw a standard line like the one in Figure 14.8(A); then they saw a display like that in Figure 14.8(B). Their task was to pick out the line in the display that was the same length as the one they had first been shown.

Each participant performed this task in a small group of people who posed as fellow participants but who were actually the experimenter's assistants. There were two conditions. In the control condition, the real participant responded first. In the experimental condition, the participant did not respond until after the other people did. The experimenter's assistants chose the correct response in 6 trials, but in the other 12 trials they all gave the same, obviously incorrect response. So in 12 trials, each participant was confronted with a "social reality" created by a group norm that conflicted with the physical reality created by what the person could clearly see. Only 5 percent of the participants in the control condition ever made a mistake during this easy perceptual task. However, among participants who heard the assistants' incorrect responses before giving their own, about 70 percent made at least one error by conforming to the group norm. An analysis of 133 studies conducted in 17 countries reveals that conformity in Asch-type situations has declined somewhat in the United States since the 1950s but that it still occurs. It is especially likely in collectivist cultures, where conformity to group norms is emphasized (Cialdini et al., 2001).

Why Do People Conform?   Why did so many people in Asch's experiment give incorrect responses when they were capable of near-perfect performance? One possibility, called *public conformity,* is that they didn't really believe in their responses but gave them simply because it was the socially desirable thing to do. Another possibility is that the participants experienced *private acceptance.* Perhaps they used the other people's responses as a guide, became convinced that their own perceptions were wrong, and actually changed their minds. Which possibility is more likely? Morton Deutsch and Harold Gerard (1955) reasoned that if people still conformed even when the other group members couldn't hear their response, then Asch's findings must reflect private acceptance, not just public conformity. Actually, although conformity does decrease when people respond privately, it doesn't disappear (Deutsch & Gerard, 1955). So people sometimes say things in public that they don't believe in, but hearing other people's responses also appears to influence their private beliefs (Moscovici, 1985).

Why are group norms so powerful? Research suggests several influential factors (Cialdini & Goldstein, 2004). First, people are motivated to be correct, and group norms provide information about what is right and wrong. This factor may help explain why some extremely disturbed or distressed people consider stories about suicide to be "social proof" that self-destruction is a reasonable way out of their problems (Cialdini, 2007). Second, people want others to like them, so they may seek favor by conforming to the social norms that those others have established. Third, conforming to group norms may increase a person's sense of self-worth, especially if the group is valued or has high prestige (Cialdini & Goldstein, 2004). The process may occur without our awareness (Lakin & Chartrand, 2003). For example, observations of interviews by television talk show host Larry King revealed that he tended to imitate the speech patterns of high-status guests but not low-status ones (Gregory & Webster, 1996). Finally, social norms affect the distribution of social reward and punishment (Cialdini, 1995). From childhood on, people in many cultures learn that going along with group norms is good and earns rewards. (These positive outcomes presumably help compensate for not always saying or doing exactly what we please.) People also learn that breaking a norm may bring punishments ranging from scoldings for small transgressions to imprisonment for violation of social norms that have been translated into laws.

When Do People Conform?   People do not always conform to group influence. In the Asch studies, for example, nearly 30 percent of the participants did not go along with the assistants' obviously wrong judgments. Countless experiments have probed the question of what combinations of people and circumstances do and do not lead to conformity.

MASS CONFORMITY ▲

The faithful who gather at Mecca, at the Vatican, and at other holy places around the world exemplify the power of religion and other social forces to produce conformity to group norms.

For example, *ambiguity*, or uncertainty, is important in determining how much conformity will occur. As the features of a situation become less clear, people rely more and more on others' opinions and conformity to a group norm becomes increasingly likely (Cialdini & Goldstein, 2004). You can demonstrate this aspect of conformity on any street corner. First, create an ambiguous situation by having several people look at the sky or the top of a building. When passersby ask what is going on, be sure everyone excitedly reports seeing something interesting but fleeting—perhaps a faint flashing light or a tiny, shiny high-flying object. If you are especially successful, conforming newcomers will begin persuading other passersby that there is something fascinating to be seen.

Learn BY Doing

If ambiguity contributes so much to conformity, though, why did so many of Asch's participants conform to a judgment that was clearly wrong? The answer has to do with the *unanimous* nature of the group's judgment and the number of people expressing that judgment. Specifically, people experience intense pressure to conform as long as the rest of the group all agree with each other. If even one other person in the group disagrees with the majority view, conformity drops greatly. When Asch (1951) arranged for just one assistant to disagree with the others, fewer than 10 percent of the real participants conformed. Once unanimity is broken, it becomes much easier to disagree with the majority, even if the other nonconformist does not agree with the person's own view (Turner, 1991).

Conformity also depends on the *size of the majority*. Asch (1955) demonstrated this phenomenon by varying the number of assistants in the group from one to fifteen. Conformity to incorrect social norms grew as the number of people in the group increased. However, most of the growth in conformity occurred as the size of the majority rose from one to about three or four members. This effect probably occurs because pressure to conform has already reached a peak after someone has heard three or four people agree. Hearing more people confirm the majority view has little additional social impact (Latané, 1981).

Conformity can also occur through *minority influence,* by which a minority of group members influence the behavior or beliefs of the majority (Crano & Prislin, 2006; Kenrick, Neuberg, & Cialdini, 2005). This phenomenon is less common than majority influence, but when members of a numerical minority are established group members, agree with one another, and persist in their views, they can be influential (Martin, Gardikiotis, & Hewstone, 2002; Mucchi-Faina & Pagliaro, 2008).

Perhaps because the views of a numerical minority are examined especially carefully by the rest of the group (Martin & Hewstone 2003), minority-influenced change often takes a while to occur. And these changes may involve only a moderate adjustment of the majority view (Alvaro & Crano, 1997; Crano & Chen, 1998).

Does gender affect conformity? Early research suggested that women conform more than men, but the gender difference stemmed mainly from the fact that the tasks used in those studies were often more familiar to men than to women. This fact is important because people are especially likely to conform when they are faced with an unfamiliar situation (Cialdini & Goldstein, 2004). No male-female differences in conformity have been found in research using materials that are equally familiar to both genders (Maupin & Fisher, 1989). So why do some people still perceive women as more conforming than men despite evidence to the contrary? Part of the answer may lie in their perception of the relative social status of men and women. People who think of women as having lower social status than men in most social situations are likely to see women as easier to influence, even though men and women conform equally often (Eagly, 1987).

Creating Compliance   In the experiments just described, the participants experienced psychological pressure to conform to the views or actions of others even though no one specifically asked them to do so. In contrast, *compliance* involves changing what you say or do because of a direct request.

How is compliance brought about? Many people believe that the direct approach is always best: if you want something, ask for it. But salespeople, political strategists, social psychologists, and other experts have learned that often the best way to get something is to ask for something else. Three examples of this strategy are the foot-in-the-door technique, the door-in-the-face procedure, and the lowball approach.

The *foot-in-the-door technique* works by getting a person to agree to small requests and then working up to larger ones. In the original experiment on this strategy, homeowners were asked to do one of two things. Some were asked to allow a large, unattractive "Drive Carefully" sign to be placed on their front lawns. About 17 percent of the people approached in this way complied with the request. In the foot-in-the-door condition, however, homeowners were first asked only to sign a petition supporting laws aimed at reducing traffic accidents. Several weeks later, when a different person asked these same homeowners to put the "Drive Carefully" sign on their lawns, 55 percent of them complied (Freedman & Fraser, 1966).

Why should the granting of small favors lead to granting larger ones? First, people are usually far more likely to comply with a request that doesn't cost much in time, money, effort, or inconvenience. Second, complying with a small request makes people think of themselves as being committed to the cause or issue involved (Burger & Guadagno, 2003). In the study just described, participants who signed the petition might have thought, "I must care enough about traffic safety to do something about it." Compliance with the higher-cost request (displaying the sign) increased because it was consistent with these people's self-perceptions and past actions (Burger & Guadagno, 2003).

The foot-in-the-door technique can be amazingly effective. Steven Sherman (1980) created a 700 percent increase in the rate at which people volunteered to work for a charity simply by first getting them to say that in a hypothetical situation they would volunteer if asked. For some companies, the foot in the door is a request that potential customers merely answer a few questions; the request to buy something comes later. Others offer a small gift, or "door opener," as salespeople call it. Acceptance of the gift not only gives the salesperson a foot in the door but also may activate the reciprocity norm: many people who get something for free feel obligated to reciprocate by buying something, especially if the request to do so is delayed for a while (Cialdini, 2007; Guadagno et al., 2001).

The *door-in-the-face procedure* offers a second effective way of obtaining compliance (Cialdini, 2001; Pascual & Guéguen, 2005; Turner et al., 2007). This strategy begins with a request for a favor that is likely to be refused. The person making the request then concedes that this favor was too much to ask and substitutes a lesser alternative, which is what the person really wanted in the first place! Because the person appears

PROMOTING COMPLIANCE ▲

Have you ever been asked to sign a petition favoring some political, social, or economic cause? Supporters of these causes know that people who comply with this small request are the best people to contact later with requests to do more. Complying with larger requests is made more likely because it is consistent with the signer's initial commitment to the cause. If you were contacted after signing a petition, did you agree to donate money or become a volunteer?

applying psychology

willing to compromise and because the second request seems small in comparison with the first one, it is more likely to be granted than if it had been made at the outset. The door-in-the-face strategy is at the heart of bargaining among political groups and between labor and management (Ginges et al., 2007).

The third technique, called the *lowball approach,* is commonly used by car dealers and other businesses (Cialdini, 2001). The first step in this strategy is to get people to say that they will do something, such as purchase a car. Once this commitment is made, the cost of fulfilling it is increased, often because of an "error" in computing the car's price. Why do buyers end up paying much more than originally planned for "lowballed" items? Apparently, once people commit themselves to do something, they feel obligated to follow through, especially when the initial commitment was made in public and when the person who obtained that commitment also makes the higher-cost request (Burger & Cornelius, 2003).

Obedience

▶ *How far will people go in obeying authority?*

Compliance involves a change in behavior in response to a request. In the case of **obedience,** the behavior change comes in response to a *demand* from an authority figure (Blass, 2004). In the 1960s, Stanley Milgram developed a laboratory procedure at Yale University to study obedience. For his first experiment, he used newspaper ads to find 40 male volunteer participants. They ranged in age from 20 to 50, lived in the local community, and included professionals, white-collar businessmen, and unskilled workers (Milgram, 1963).

Imagine you are one of the people who answered the ad. When you arrive for the experiment, you join a 50-year-old man who has also volunteered and has been scheduled for the same session. The experimenter explains that the purpose of the experiment is to examine the effects of punishment on learning. One of you—the "teacher"—will help the "learner" remember a list of words by administering an electric shock whenever the learner makes a mistake. Then the experimenter turns to you and asks you to draw one of two cards out of a hat. Your card says, "TEACHER." You think to yourself that this must be your lucky day.

Now the learner is taken into another room and strapped into a chair, and, as illustrated in Figure 14.9, electrodes are attached to his arm. You are shown a shock generator with 30 switches. The experimenter explains that the switch on the far left administers a mild, 15-volt shock and that each succeeding switch increases the shock by 15 volts. The one on the far right delivers 450 volts. The far left section of the shock generator is labeled "Slight shock." Looking across the panel, you see "Moderate shock," "Very strong shock," and at the far right, "Danger—severe shock." The last two switches are ominously labeled "XXX." The experimenter explains that you, the teacher, will begin by reading a list of word pairs to the learner. Then you will go through the list again, presenting just one word of each pair. The learner will have to say which word went with it. After the first mistake, you are to throw the switch to deliver 15 volts of shock. Each time the learner makes another mistake, you are to increase the shock by 15 volts.

You begin, following the experimenter's instructions. But after the learner makes his fifth mistake and you throw the switch to give him 75 volts, you hear a loud moan. At 90 volts, the learner cries out in pain. At 150 volts, he screams and asks to be let out of the experiment. You look to the experimenter, who says, "Proceed with the next word."

No shock was actually delivered in Milgram's experiments. The learner was always an employee of the experimenter, and the moans and other sounds of pain came from a prerecorded tape. But you do not know that. What would you do in this situation? Suppose you continue and eventually deliver 180 volts. The learner screams that he cannot stand the pain any longer and starts banging on the wall. The experimenter says, "You have no other choice; you must go on." Would you continue? Would you keep going even when the learner begged to be let out of the experiment and then

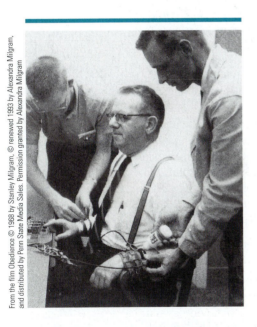

FIGURE 14.9 ■ STUDYING OBEDIENCE IN THE LABORATORY

In this photograph from Milgram's original experiment, a man is being strapped into a chair with electrodes on his arm. Although participants in the experiment didn't know it, the man was actually the experimenter's research assistant and received no shock.

obedience Changing behavior in response to a demand from an authority figure.

FIGURE 14.10 ■ **RESULTS OF MILGRAM'S OBEDIENCE EXPERIMENT**

When Milgram asked a group of college students and a group of psychiatrists to predict how participants in his experiment would respond, they estimated that fewer than 2 percent would go all the way to 450 volts. In fact, 65 percent of the participants did so. What do you think you would have done in this situation?
Source: Milgram (1963).

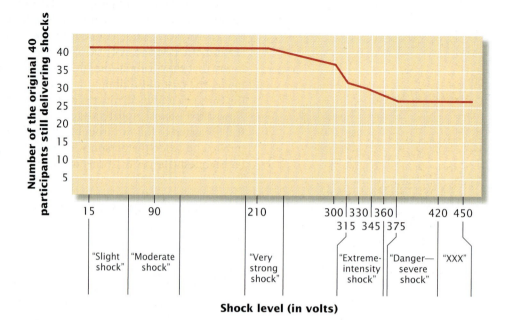

fell silent? Would you administer 450 volts of potentially deadly shock to an innocent stranger just because an experimenter demanded that you do so?

Figure 14.10 shows that only 5 participants in Milgram's experiment stopped before 300 volts and that 26 out of 40 (65 percent) went all the way to the 450-volt level. The decision to continue was difficult and stressful for the participants. Many protested repeatedly. But each time the experimenter told them to continue, they did so. Here is a partial transcript of what a typical participant said:

[After throwing the 180-volt switch]: *He can't stand it. I'm not going to kill that man in there. Do you hear him hollering? He's hollering. He can't stand it. What if something happens to him? I'm not going to get that man sick in there. He's hollering in there. Do you know what I mean? I mean, I refuse to take responsibility. He's getting hurt in there. . . . Too many left here. Geez, if he gets them wrong. There are too many of them left. I mean, who is going to take responsibility if anything happens to that gentleman?*

[After the experimenter accepts responsibility]: *All right. . . .*

[After administering 240 volts]: *Oh, no, you mean I've got to keep going up the scale? No sir, I'm not going to kill that man. I'm not going to give him 450 volts.*

[After the experimenter says, "The experiment requires that you go on"]: *I know it does, but that man is hollering in there, sir.*

This participant administered shock up to 450 volts (Milgram, 1974).

Factors Affecting Obedience

Milgram had not expected so many people to deliver such apparently intense shocks. Was there something about his procedure that produced this high level of obedience? To find out, Milgram and other researchers varied the original procedure in a number of ways. The overall level of obedience to an authority figure was usually quite high, but the degree of obedience was affected by several aspects of the situation and procedure.

Experimenter Status and Prestige One possibility is that the experimenter's status as a Yale University professor helped produce high levels of obedience in Milgram's original experiment (Blass & Schmitt, 2001). To test the effects of status and prestige, Milgram rented an office in a rundown building in Bridgeport, Connecticut. He then placed a newspaper ad for research sponsored by a private firm. There was

PROXIMITY AND OBEDIENCE ▲

Milgram's research showed that close physical proximity to an authority figure is one of several factors that can enhance obedience to authority (Rada & Rogers, 1973). This proximity principle is used in the military, where no one is ever far away from the authority of a higher-ranking person.

no mention of Yale. In all other ways, the experimental procedure was identical to the original.

Under these less impressive circumstances, the level of obedience dropped, but not as much as Milgram expected: 48 percent of the participants continued to the maximum level of shock, compared with 65 percent in the original study. Milgram concluded that people are willing to obey orders to do great harm to another person even when the authority making the demand is not especially reputable or prestigious.

The Behavior of Other People   To study how the behavior of fellow participants might affect obedience, Milgram (1965) created a situation in which there appeared to be three teachers. Teacher 1 (in reality, a research assistant) read the words to the learner. Teacher 2 (another research assistant) stated whether or not the learner's response was correct. Teacher 3 (the actual participant) was to deliver shock when the learner made mistakes. At 150 volts, when the learner began to complain that the shock was too painful, Teacher 1 refused to participate any longer and left the room. The experimenter asked him to come back, but he refused. The experimenter then instructed Teachers 2 and 3 to continue by themselves. The experiment continued for several more trials. However, at 210 volts, Teacher 2 said that the learner was suffering too much and also refused to participate further. The experimenter then told Teacher 3 (the actual participant) to continue the procedure. In this case, only 10 percent of the participants (compared with 65 percent in the original study) continued to deliver shock all the way up to 450 volts. In other words, as research on conformity would suggest, the presence of others who disobey appears to be the most powerful factor in reducing obedience.

The Behavior of the Learner   A recent reanalysis of data from Milgram's obedience studies (Packer, 2008) found that although the supposedly shocked learner's increasingly intense expressions of pain had no effect on whether the participants disobeyed the experimenter, the learner's stated desire to be released from the experiment did affect disobedience. In fact, among those participants who refused to continue to shock the learner, almost 37 percent of them disobeyed at the 150 volt level, which was when the learner first said he wanted to be released from the experiment. So it appears that perceiving a victim's pain does not reduce obedience to authority but being reminded of a victim's right to be released from the experiment does.

Personality Characteristics   Were the participants in Milgram's original experiment heartless creatures who would have given strong shocks even if there had been no pressure on them to do so? Quite the opposite; most of them were nice people who were influenced by experimental situations to behave in apparently antisocial ways. In a later demonstration of the same phenomenon, college students playing the role of prison guards behaved with aggressive heartlessness toward other students who were playing the role of prisoners (Zimbardo, 1973). A more recent illustration of this phenomenon occurred among some U.S. soldiers who were assigned to guard or interrogate prisoners in Afghanistan and Iraq.

Still, not everyone is equally obedient to authority. For example, people who display what we described earlier as *authoritarianism* are more likely than others to obey an experimenter's instructions to shock the learner (Blass, 2000). Support for this idea comes from findings that German soldiers who may have obeyed orders to kill Jews during World War II displayed more authoritarianism than other German men of the same age and background (Steiner & Fahrenberg, 2000). In contrast, a recent study that repeated Milgram's experimental procedures (Burger, 2009) found that the participants who were less likely to obey orders to harm the learner were also the ones who were concerned about others and predisposed to have *empathy*—that is, to understand or experience another person's emotional state (Davis, 1994).

Evaluating Obedience Research

Milgram's obedience studies were conducted 40 years ago. How relevant are they today? Consider this fact: the U.S. Federal Aviation Administration attributes some commercial airplane accidents to what it calls "captainitis." In this phenomenon, the pilot of an airliner makes an obvious error but none of the other crew members are willing to challenge the captain's authority by pointing out the error. As a result, planes have crashed and people have died (Kanki & Foushee, 1990). Captainitis might have been operating aboard the nuclear submarine USS *Greeneville* on February 9, 2001, when, as it surfaced off the coast of Hawaii, it struck and sank a Japanese fishing boat, killing nine people. A navy board of inquiry found that crew members had been reluctant to challenge their captain's order to surface, even though they felt he had not checked carefully enough for other vessels in the area (Myers, 2001). Obedience to authority may also have operated during the World Trade Center attack on September 11, 2001, when some people returned to their offices after hearing an ill-advised public address announcement telling them to do so. Most of these people died as a result.

These tragic events suggest that Milgram's findings are still relevant and important (Blass, 2004). Similar kinds of obedience have been observed in experiments conducted in many countries, from Europe to the Middle East, with female as well as male participants (Burger, 2009). In short, people may be as likely to obey orders today as they were when Milgram conducted his research (Blass, 2004, 2009; Burger, 2009). Nevertheless, there is still debate over the ethics and meaning of Milgram's work. (For a summary of Milgram's results, plus those of studies on conformity and compliance, see "In Review: Types of Social Influence.")

In Review

TYPES OF SOCIAL INFLUENCE

TYPE	DEFINITION	KEY FINDINGS
Conformity	A change in behavior or beliefs to match those of others	In cases of ambiguity, people develop a group norm and then adhere to it.
		Conformity occurs because people want to be right, because they want to be liked by others, and because conformity to group norms is usually reinforced.
		Conformity usually increases with the ambiguity of the situation as well as with the unanimity and size of the majority.
Compliance	Adjusting one's behavior because of a direct request	Compliance increases with the foot-in-the-door technique, which begins with a small request and works up to a larger one.
		The door-in-the-face procedure can also be used. After making a large request that is denied, the person substitutes a less extreme alternative that was desired all along.
		The lowball approach also elicits compliance. An oral commitment for something is first obtained, then the person claims that only a higher-cost version of the original request will suffice.
Obedience	A change in behavior in response to an explicit demand, typically from an acknowledged authority figure	People may inflict great harm on others when an authority demands that they do so.
		Even when people obey orders to harm another person, they often agonize over the decision.
		People are most likely to disobey orders to harm someone else when they see another person disobey.

1. *Joining the end of a ticket line is an example of _____, whereas forming two lines when a theater employee requests it is an example of _____.*

2. *Seeing someone disobey a questionable order makes people _____ likely to obey the order themselves.*

3. *Pricing your used car for more than you expect to get then agreeing to reduce it to make a sale is an example of the _____ approach to gaining compliance.*

linkages

Is it ethical to deceive people to learn about their social behavior?
(a link to Introduction to the Science of Psychology)

MAY I TAKE YOUR ORDER? ▲

In February 2004, the managers of four fast food restaurants in Boston, Massachusetts, received calls from someone claiming to be a police detective on the trail of a robbery suspect. The caller said the suspect might be one of the restaurant's employees and told the managers to strip search all of them for evidence of guilt. The calls turned out to be hoaxes, but every manager obeyed this bizarre order, apparently because it appeared to come from a legitimate authority. In two similar cases, residents of a special needs school were given unnecessary electric shock treatments on telephoned orders from a hoaxer and hospital nurses obeyed medical treatment orders given by a teenager who claimed he was a doctor (Associated Press, 2007a; Kenrick, Neuberg, & Cialdini, 2005).

aggression (aggressive behavior)
An act that is intended to harm another person.

Questions About Ethics   Although the "learners" in Milgram's experiment suffered no discomfort, the participants did. Milgram (1963) observed participants "sweat, stutter, tremble, groan, bite their lips, and dig their fingernails into their flesh" (p. 375). Against the potential harm inflicted by Milgram's experiments stand the potential gains. For example, people who learn about Milgram's work often take his findings into account when deciding how to act in social situations (Sherman, 1980). But even if social value has come from Milgram's studies, a question remains: Was it ethical for Milgram to treat his participants as he did?

In the years before his death in 1984, Milgram defended his experiments (e.g., Milgram, 1977). He argued that the way he dealt with his participants after the experiment prevented any lasting harm. For example, he explained to them that the learner did not experience any shock; in fact, the learner came in and chatted with each participant. On a later questionnaire, 84 percent of the participants said that they had learned something important about themselves and that the experience had been worthwhile. Milgram argued, therefore, that the experience was actually a positive one. Still, the committees charged with protecting human participants in research today would be unlikely to approve Milgram's experiments as they were originally done, and less controversial ways to study obedience have now been developed (Blass, 2004; Elms, 2009).

Questions About Meaning   Do Milgram's dramatic results mean that most people are putty in the hands of authority figures and that most of us would blindly follow inhumane orders from our leaders? Some critics have argued that Milgram's results cannot be interpreted in this way because his participants knew they were in an experiment and may simply have been playing a cooperative role. If so, the social influence processes identified in his studies may not explain obedience in the real world today (Berkowitz, 1999).

Most psychologists believe, however, that Milgram demonstrated a basic truth about human behavior—namely, that under certain circumstances people are capable of unspeakable acts of brutality toward other people. Sadly, examples abound. And one of the most horrifying aspects of human inhumanity—whether it is the Nazis' campaign of genocide against Jews 60 years ago or the campaigns of terror under way today—is that the perpetrators are not necessarily demented, sadistic fiends. Most of them are normal people who have been prompted by economic, political, or religious influences and the persuasive power of their leaders to behave in a demented and fiendish manner (Moghaddam, 2005).

In short, inhumanity can occur even without pressure to obey. A good deal of people's aggressiveness toward other people appears to come from within. Let's now consider human aggressiveness and some of the circumstances that influence its expression.

Aggression

▶ *Are people born aggressive?*

Aggressive behavior, more commonly known as **aggression,** is any action intended to harm another person. It is all too common. More than 1.3 million violent crimes are committed each year in the United States alone, including more than 90,000 rapes and 17,000 murders (Federal Bureau of Investigation, 2008). In fact, homicide is the third leading cause of death for people in the United States between the ages of 15 and 24 (Heron, 2007). One of the most disturbing aspects of these figures is that about 85 percent of all murder victims knew their assailants and that over 70 percent of rapists were romantic partners, friends, relatives, or acquaintances of their victims (U.S. Department of Justice, 2007). Further, as many as one-third of married people and a significant proportion of dating couples in the United States have engaged in aggressive acts toward each other that range from pushing, shoving, and slapping to beatings and the threatened or actual use of weapons (Cornelius & Resseguie, 2007; Durose et al., 2005).

Why Are People Aggressive?

Sigmund Freud proposed that aggression is an instinctive biological urge that builds up in everyone and must be released. Evolutionary psychologists offer a different view, suggesting that in prehistoric times, aggression helped people compete for mates, thus ensuring the survival of their genes in the next generation (Malamuth & Addison, 2001). Through natural selection, they say, aggressive tendencies have been passed on through countless generations.

Evolutionary theories of aggression are popular, but even evolutionary theorists recognize that "nature" alone cannot fully account for aggression. "Nurture," in the form of environmental factors, also plays a large role in when and why people are aggressive. We know this partly because there are large differences in aggression from culture to culture. The murder rate in Colombia, for example, is more than 10 times higher than it is in the United States, and the U.S. murder rate is almost twice as high as the rate in either Canada or the United Kingdom (United Nations Office on Drugs and Crime, 2007). These data suggest that even if aggressive *impulses* are universal, the appearance of aggressive *behavior* reflects the influence of both nature and nurture (Malamuth & Addison, 2001). No equation can predict exactly when people will be aggressive, but years of research have revealed a number of important biological, learning, and environmental factors that combine in various ways to produce aggression in various situations.

Genetic and Biological Mechanisms

There is strong evidence for hereditary influences on aggression, especially in animals (Cairns, Gariepy, & Hood, 1990). In one study, the most aggressive members of a large group of mice were interbred and then the most aggressive of their offspring were interbred. After this procedure was followed for 25 generations, the resulting animals would immediately attack any mouse put in their cage. Continuous inbreeding of the least aggressive members of the original group produced animals that were so nonaggressive that they would refuse to fight even when attacked (Lagerspetz & Lagerspetz, 1983). Research that rated the aggressiveness of human twins who had been raised together or apart suggests that there is a genetic component to aggression in people as well (Hudziak et al., 2003; Vierikko et al., 2006). However, other research suggests that people do not necessarily inherit the tendency to be aggressive. Instead, they may inherit certain aspects of temperament (such as impulsiveness) or certain aspects of brain chemistry that in turn make aggression more likely (Eisenberger et al., 2007; Hennig et al., 2005).

Several parts of the brain influence aggression (Anderson & Bushman, 2002a). One of these is the limbic system, which includes the amygdala, the hypothalamus, and related areas. Damage to these structures may produce *defensive aggression*, which includes aggressiveness to stimuli that are not usually threatening or a decrease in the responses that normally inhibit aggression (Coccaro, 1989; Eichelman, 1983; Siever, 2008). The cerebral cortex may also be involved in aggression (Pietro et al., 2000).

Hormones such as *testosterone*—the masculine hormone that is present in both sexes—may also play an important role in aggression (Dabbs & Dabbs, 2001; Herman, Ramsey, & van Honk, 2008; van Bokhoven et al., 2006). Experiments have shown that aggressive behavior increases or decreases dramatically with the amount of testosterone in an animal's body (Klinesmith, Kasser, & McAndrew, 2006; Pope, Kouri, & Hudson, 2000; Yates, 2000). Among criminals, those who commit violent crimes have higher levels of testosterone than those whose crimes are nonviolent. And among murderers, those with higher levels of testosterone are more likely than others to have planned their crimes before committing them (Dabbs, Riad, & Chance, 2001).

Testosterone may have its most significant and durable influence through its impact on early brain development. One natural test of this hypothesis occurred when pregnant women were given testosterone in an attempt to prevent miscarriage. As a result, their children were exposed to high doses of testosterone during prenatal development. Figure 14.11 shows that these children grew up to be more aggressive than their same-sex siblings who were not exposed to testosterone during prenatal development (Reinisch, Ziemba-Davis, & Sanders, 1991).

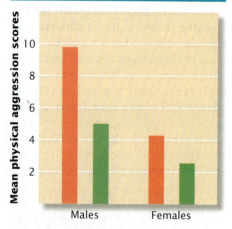

Mean physical aggression scores

■ Participants exposed to high doses of testosterone during prenatal development

■ Unexposed participants

FIGURE 14.11 ■ TESTOSTERONE AND AGGRESSION

In the study illustrated here, the children of women who had taken testosterone during pregnancy to prevent miscarriage became more aggressive than the mothers' other children of the same sex who had not been exposed to testosterone during prenatal development. This outcome appeared in both males' and females' development (Reinisch, Ziemba-Davis, & Sanders, 1991).

More recent research with both animals and humans has linked low levels of the neurotransmitter serotonin with high levels of impulsive aggression (Carver, Johnson, & Joorman, 2008). It is not yet clear whether serotonin levels are primarily a cause or a consequence of aggression, but it is most likely they are both (Kassin, Fein, & Markus, 2008).

Drugs that affect the central nervous system also affect the likelihood that a person will act aggressively. Even relatively small amounts of alcohol, for example, can greatly increase some people's aggressiveness. Canadian researchers have found that in almost 70 percent of the acts of aggression they studied, the aggressors had been drinking alcohol. And the more alcohol the aggressors consumed, the more aggressive they were (Wells, Graham, & West, 2000). No one knows exactly why alcohol increases aggression, but research suggests that the drug may affect areas of the brain that normally inhibit aggressive responses (Bartholow & Heinz, 2006; Graham et al., 2006; Lau, Pihl, & Peterson, 1995).

Learning and Cultural Mechanisms   Biological factors may increase or decrease the likelihood of aggression, but cross-cultural research makes it clear that learning also plays a role. Aggressive behavior is much more common in individualist than in collectivist cultures, for example (Oatley, 1993). Cultural differences in the expression of aggression appear to stem in part from differing cultural values (Cohen, 1998). For example, the Utku (an Inuit culture) view aggression in any form as a sign of social incompetence. In fact, the Utku word for "aggressive" also means "childish" (Oatley, 1993). The effects of culture on aggression can also be seen in the fact that the amount of aggression in a given culture changes over time as cultural values change (Matsumoto, 2000).

In addition, people learn many aggressive responses by watching others (Bingheimer, Brennan, & Earls, 2005; Bushman & Anderson, 2001). Children, in particular, learn and perform many of the aggressive responses they see modeled by others. Bandura's Bobo-doll experiments, which are described in the chapter on learning, provide impressive demonstrations of the power of observational learning. The significance of observational learning is also highlighted by studies described in that chapter on the effects of televised violence. For example, the amount of violent content eight-year-olds watch on television predicts aggressiveness in these children even 15 years later (Bushman & Huesmann, 2006; Huesmann et al., 2003). Fortunately, not everyone who sees aggression becomes aggressive. Individual differences in temperament, the modeling of nonaggressive behavior by parents, and other factors can reduce the effects of violent television. Nevertheless, observational learning, including the learning that comes through exposure to violent television and violent video and computer games, does play a significant role in the development and display of aggressive behavior (Anderson & Murphy, 2003; Bushman & Anderson, 2001; Konijn, Bijvank, & Bushman, 2007).

FOLLOWING ADULT EXAMPLES ▶

Learning to express aggression is especially easy for children who live in countries plagued by war or sectarian violence because they see aggressive acts modeled for them all too often.

© Mario Tama/Getty Images

Reward or punishment can also alter the frequency of aggressive acts. People become more aggressive when rewarded for aggressiveness and less aggressive when punished for aggression (Geen, 1998). In short, a person's life experiences, including culturally transmitted teachings, combine with daily rewards and punishments to influence whether, when, and how aggressive acts occur (Baron & Richardson, 1994; Bettencourt et al., 2006).

When Are People Aggressive?

In general, people are more likely to be aggressive when they are both physically aroused and experiencing a strong emotion such as anger (Anderson & Bushman, 2002a). People tend either to lash out at those who make them angry or to displace, or redirect, their anger toward children, pets, or other defenseless targets. However, aggression can also be made more likely by other forms of emotional arousal. One emotion that has long been considered to be a major cause of aggression is *frustration*, which occurs when we are prevented from reaching some goal.

Frustration and Aggression   Suppose that a friend interrupts your studying for an exam by asking to borrow a book. If things have been going well that day and you are feeling confident about the exam, you will probably be friendly and helpful. But what if you are feeling frustrated because your friend's visit was the fifth interruption in the last hour? Under these emotional circumstances, you may react aggressively, perhaps snapping at your startled visitor for bothering you.

Your aggressiveness in this situation would be predicted by the **frustration-aggression hypothesis,** which suggests that frustration leads to aggression (Dollard et al., 1939). Research on this hypothesis has shown that it is too simple and too general, however. For one thing, frustration sometimes produces depression and withdrawal, not aggression (Berkowitz, 1998). In addition, not all aggression is preceded by frustration (Berkowitz, 1994).

After many years of research, Leonard Berkowitz suggested that the frustration-aggression hypothesis be modified in two ways. First, he proposed that it may be stress in general, not just frustration, that is involved in aggression. Stress, he said, produces a readiness for aggression that may or may not be translated into aggressive behavior (Berkowitz, 1998). Once this readiness exists, however, aggression can be more easily triggered by stimuli in the environment. The triggering stimuli might be guns or knives, televised scenes of people arguing, violent song lyrics, or other cues associated with aggression. In other words, neither stress alone nor environmental cues alone are enough to set off aggression. When combined, however, they often do. Support for this aspect of Berkowitz's theory has been quite strong (Anderson & Bushman, 2002a).

Second, Berkowitz argues that the direct cause of most kinds of aggression is negative feelings, or *negative affect* (Berkowitz, 1998). Research suggests that the more negative affect people experience, regardless of what caused it, the stronger is their readiness to be aggressive. Participants in one study experienced negative affect caused by the pain of immersing their hands in ice water. They became more aggressive than participants in a control group whose hands were in water of room temperature (Berkowitz, 1998).

Generalized Arousal   Imagine that you've just jogged three miles. You are hot, sweaty, and out of breath, but you aren't angry. Still, the physiological arousal caused by jogging may increase the probability that you will become aggressive if, say, a passerby shouts an insult (Zillmann, 1988). Why? The answer lies in a phenomenon described in the chapter on motivation and emotion: arousal from one experience may carry over to a new situation, producing what is called *excitation transfer*. So the physiological arousal caused by jogging may intensify your reaction to an insult (Harrison, 2003).

By itself, however, arousal does not lead to aggression. It is most likely to produce aggression when a situation presents some reason, opportunity, or target for aggression (Zillmann, 2003). In one study, for example, people engaged in two minutes of vigorous exercise. Then they had the opportunity to deliver electric shock to another person. The participants chose to give high levels of shock only if they had first been

frustration-aggression hypothesis
A proposition stating that frustration always leads to some form of aggressive behavior.

insulted (Zillmann, Katcher, & Milavsky, 1972). Apparently, the arousal resulting from the exercise made aggression more likely; the insult "released" it. These findings are in keeping with the notion that aggression is caused not by internal impulses alone or by particular situations alone but by the interaction of the two (Klinesmith, Kasser, & McAndrew, 2006).

Thinking CRITICALLY

Does Pornography Cause Aggression?

In both men and women, sexual stimulation produces strong, generalized physiological arousal, especially in the sympathetic nervous system. If arousal in general can make a person more likely to be aggressive (given a reason, opportunity, and target), could stimuli that create sexual arousal be dangerous? In particular, does viewing or reading pornographic material make people more likely to be aggressive? Prior to the mid-1980s, several scholars had concluded that there was no evidence for an overall relationship between any type of antisocial behavior and mere exposure to pornographic material (Donnerstein, 1984). However, in 1986 the U.S. Attorney General's Commission on Pornography reexamined the question and concluded that pornography is dangerous.

▶ What am I being asked to believe or accept?

Specifically, the commission proposed that there is a cause-effect link between exposure to erotic material and several forms of antisocial behavior, including sexually related violent crimes.

▶ Is evidence available to support the claim?

The commission cited several types of evidence in support of its conclusion. First, there was the testimony of men convicted of sex crimes. Rapists, for example, are unusually heavy users of pornography, and they often say that they were aroused by erotic material immediately before committing a rape (Silbert & Pines, 1984). Similarly, child molesters often view child pornography immediately before committing their crimes (Marshall, 1989).

In addition, the commission cited experimental evidence that men who are most aroused by aggressive themes in pornography are also the most potentially sexually aggressive. One study, for example, showed that men who said they could commit a rape became sexually aroused by scenes of rape and less aroused by scenes of mutually consenting sex; this was not true for men who said they could never commit a rape (Malamuth & Check, 1983).

Perhaps the strongest evidence cited by the commission, however, came from excitation transfer studies. In one experiment, male participants were told that a person in another room (actually an employee of the experimenter) would be performing a learning task and that they were to administer an electric shock every time the person made a mistake. The intensity of shock could be varied (as in the Milgram studies, no shock actually reached the employee), but participants were told that changing the intensity would not affect the speed of learning. So the shock intensity (and presumed pain) that they chose to administer was considered to be a measure of aggression. Before the learning trials began, some participants watched a film in which several men had sex with the same woman. These participants' aggressiveness during the learning experiment was greater than that of men who did not watch the film (Donnerstein, 1984).

▶ Can that evidence be interpreted another way?

The commission's interpretation of all this evidence was questioned for several reasons. First, critics argued that some of the evidence should be given little weight. In particular, how much should we rely on what convicted sex offenders say? Their testimony may reflect self-serving attempts to lay the blame for their crimes on pornography. These reports cannot establish that exposure to pornography causes aggression. In fact, it may be that pornography partially *satisfies* sex offenders' aggressive impulses rather than creating them (Aronson, Wilson, & Akert, 2005). Similarly, the fact that potential rapists are most aroused by rape-oriented material may show only that they prefer violence-oriented pornography, not that such materials created their impulse to rape.

What about the evidence from excitation transfer studies? To interpret these studies, you need to know that the pornography that led to increased aggression contained violence as well as sex. The sexual activity depicted was painful for or unwanted by the woman. So the higher levels of aggression that followed viewing these films could have been due to the transfer of sexual arousal, the effects of observing violent behavior, or the effects of seeing sex combined with violence (Donnerstein, Slaby, & Eron, 1995).

Several careful experiments have found that highly arousing sexual themes do not produce aggression in and of themselves. When men in excitation transfer studies experience pleasant arousal by viewing a film depicting nudity or mutually consenting sexual activity, they are actually less aggressive than when they viewed no film or a neutral film (Lord, 1997). In short, excitation transfer studies might be interpreted as showing that aggressiveness is influenced by portrayals of sexual violence but not by watching other kinds of sexually arousing material.

▶ What evidence would help to evaluate the alternatives?

Two types of evidence are needed to better understand the effects of pornography on aggression. First, because pornography can include sexual acts, aggressive acts, or both, the effects of each of these components must be more carefully examined. Second, factors affecting men's reactions to pornography, particularly pornography that involves violence, must be more clearly understood. Work is in progress on each of these fronts.

Whether specifically paired with sexual activity or not, aggressive themes do appear to increase subsequent aggression (Bushman & Anderson, 2001). Research has focused on *aggressive pornography,* which contains both sexual themes and scenes of violence against women (Malamuth, Addison, & Koss, 2000). In laboratory experiments, males have been shown to administer stronger electric shocks to females after viewing aggressive pornographic films than after viewing nonpornographic films. Yet there was no parallel increase in aggression against other men, suggesting that aggressive pornography creates an increase in aggressiveness that is specifically directed toward women (Aronson, Wilson, & Akert, 2005). Similarly, viewing aggressive pornography in which a rape victim appears to be aroused by the aggression usually leads males to become less sympathetic toward the victim and more tolerant of aggressive acts toward women (Donnerstein & Linz, 1995). Sexually explicit films that do not contain violence have no effects on attitudes toward rape (Linz, Donnerstein, & Penrod, 1987).

Are all men who are exposed to aggressive pornography equally likely to become rapists? The evidence available so far suggests that the answer is no (Seto, Maric, & Barbaree, 2001). Whether aggressive pornography alters men's behavior and attitudes toward women depends to some extent on the men. For example, one study of about 2,700 men in the United States collected data on their sexual aggressiveness, their use of pornography, their history of sexual promiscuity, and their feelings of hostility toward women (Malamuth, 1998). Among men low in promiscuity and hostility, viewing pornography had little or no impact on sexual aggression, but among men who were high in promiscuity and hostility, pornography dramatically increased the chances that these men would engage in sexual aggression. In fact, 72 percent of the men who were high in all three factors—use of pornography, promiscuity, and hostility—had actually engaged in sexually aggressive acts (see Figure 14.12). Viewing pornography appears to have similar effects on convicted sex offenders who have been placed on probation or released on parole, and the effects are especially pronounced among those who had committed the most serious sex crimes (Kingston et al., 2008)

▶ What conclusions are most reasonable?

The attorney general's commission appeared to ignore numerous studies showing that the relationship between sexual arousal and aggression is neither consistent nor simple (Seto, Marick, & Barbaree, 2001). Analysis of this relationship reveals that it is important to distinguish between pornography in general and aggressive pornography in particular. Aggressive pornography can lead to violence against women, especially in men who are already inclined to abuse and exploit them. So there is reason for concern over the impact of sexual violence commonly seen on television and in movies, especially in "slasher" films. Remarkably, such films are sometimes given less restrictive ratings ("R" or even "PG-13") than films that are nonviolent but erotic.

The effects of nonaggressive pornography are more complicated. For most men, it has little or no impact on their behavior toward women. But among men who are inclined to abuse and exploit women, exposure to a lot of pornography might increase the chances that they would act on their abusive impulses (Malamuth, Addison, & Koss, 2000; Seto, Marick, & Barbaree, 2001). In summary, pornography is probably not, by itself, a major cause of violence against women. In combination with other factors, however, pornography—especially aggressive pornography—can play a role in sexual aggression.

FIGURE 14.12 ■ PORNOGRAPHY AND SEXUAL AGGRESSION

Extensive exposure to pornography does not, by itself, increase most men's sexual aggressiveness. Such aggressiveness is much more likely, however, among men who not only view or read a lot of pornography but also are hostile toward women and are sexually promiscuous (Malamuth, 1998).

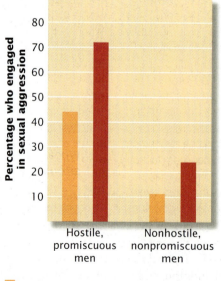

Percentage who engaged in sexual aggression

Hostile, promiscuous men   Nonhostile, nonpromiscuous men

■ Small amount of pornography watched
■ Large amount of pornography watched

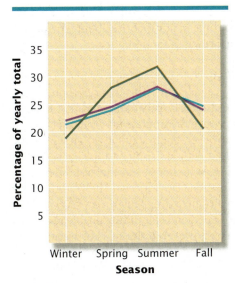

Season

— Rape
— Murder
— Other violent crime

FIGURE 14.13 ■ TEMPERATURE AND AGGRESSION

Studies from around the world indicate that aggressive behaviors are most likely to occur during the hottest months of the year. These studies support the hypothesis that environmental factors can affect aggression (Anderson et al., 2000).

environmental psychology The study of the effects of the physical environment on people's behavior and mental processes.

assistance (helping behavior) Any act that is intended to benefit another person.

altruism An unselfish concern for another's welfare.

Environmental Influences on Aggression The link between stress, arousal, and the likelihood of aggressive behavior suggests that stressful environmental conditions can create enough arousal to make aggressive behavior more likely (Anderson, 2001). This possibility is one of the research topics in **environmental psychology,** the study of the relationship between people's physical environment and their behavior (Bell et al., 2000). One aspect of the environment that clearly affects social behavior is the weather, especially temperature. High temperatures are a source of stress: as Figure 14.13 indicates, murder and other violent crimes are most likely to occur during the hottest months of the year (Anderson et al., 2000).

Living arrangements also influence aggressiveness. Compared with the tenants of crowded apartment buildings, those in buildings with relatively few residents are less likely to behave aggressively (Bell et al., 2000). This difference appears to be due in part to how people feel when they are crowded. Crowding tends to create physiological arousal and make people tense, uncomfortable, and more likely to experience negative feelings (Oskamp & Schultz, 1998). This arousal and tension can influence people to like one another less and to be more aggressive (Ray et al., 1982).

Altruism and Assistance

▶ *What motivates people to help one another?*

Like all acts of terrorism, the attacks on the World Trade Center and the Pentagon in September 2001 were horrifying examples of human behavior at its worst. But like all tragedies, they drew responses that provide inspiring examples of human behavior at its best. For example, Michael Benfante and John Cerqueira were working in the World Trade Center when one of the hijacked planes struck their building. They headed for a stairwell, but they did not just save themselves. Although it slowed their own escape, they chose to carry Tina Hansen, a wheelchair-bound co-worker, down 68 flights of stairs to safety. Acts of selflessness and sacrifice were common that day and in the days and weeks and months that followed. Police officers, medical personnel, search-and-rescue specialists, and just ordinary people came to New York from all over the United States to help clear wreckage, look for survivors, and recover bodies. More than $1 billion in donations to the Red Cross and other charity organizations poured in to help victims, and volunteering in general more than tripled in the weeks following the attacks (Penner, Dovidio, et al., 2005).

All of these actions are examples of **assistance,** or **helping behavior,** which is defined as any act that is intended to benefit another person. Assistance can range from picking up dropped packages to donating a kidney. Closely related to assistance is **altruism,** an unselfish concern for another's welfare (Penner, Dovidio, et al., 2005). Let's consider some of the reasons behind assistance and altruism, along with some of the conditions under which people are most likely to help others.

Why Do People Help?

The tendency to assist others begins early in life, although at first it is not automatic. Children have to learn to be helpful (Eisenberg & Fabes, 1998). In most cultures, very young children usually help others only when they are asked to do so or are offered a reward (Grusec, Davidov, & Lundell, 2002). Still, observational studies have shown that many children as young as 18 months will spontaneously act to help a friend, a family member, or even a stranger (Warneken & Tomasello, 2006; Zahn-Waxler et al., 1992). As they grow older, children use assistance to gain social approval and their efforts at helping become more elaborate. The role of social influence in the development of assistance is seen as children follow the examples set by people around them. In addition, children are usually praised and given other rewards for helpfulness but are scolded for selfishness. Eventually most children come to believe that being helpful is good and that they are good when they are helpful. By the late teens, people often

© Ellen Senisi/The Image Works

A YOUNG HELPER ▲

Even before their second birthday, some children offer assistance to those who are hurt or crying by snuggling, patting, or offering food or even their own teddy bears. Their helpful actions are shaped by the norms established by their families and the broader culture (Grusec & Goodnow, 1994).

arousal: cost-reward theory   A theory which describes the decision to provide assistance as motivated by efforts to reduce the unpleasant arousal people feel when confronted with a suffering victim while also considering the costs involved.

bystander effect   A phenomenon in which the chances that someone will help in an emergency decrease as the number of people present increases.

assist others even when no one is watching and no one will know that they did so (Grusec, Davidov, & Lundell, 2002). There are three major theories about why people help even when they cannot expect any external rewards for doing so.

Arousal: Cost-Reward Theory   One approach to explaining why people help is called the **arousal: cost-reward theory** (Piliavin et al., 1981). This theory proposes that people find the sight of a victim distressing and anxiety-provoking and that this experience motivates them to do something to reduce the unpleasant arousal (Dovidio et al., 2006). Before rushing to a victim's aid, however, the bystander will first evaluate two aspects of the situation: the costs associated with assisting and the costs (to the bystander and the other person) of not assisting. Whether or not the bystander actually assists depends on the outcome of this evaluation (Dovidio et al., 1991). If the costs of assisting are low (as when helping someone pick up a dropped grocery bag) and the costs of not assisting are high (as when the other person is physically unable to do this alone), the bystander will almost certainly help. However, if the costs of assisting are high (as when helping someone lift a heavy box into a car) and the costs of not assisting are low (as when the other person is obviously strong enough to do the job alone), the bystander is unlikely to offer help. One of the strengths of the arousal: cost-reward theory is that it is broad enough to explain several factors that affect assistance.

The first of these factors is the *clarity of the need for help* (Dovidio et al., 1991). In a laboratory study of this factor, undergraduate students waiting alone in a campus building saw what appeared to be an accident involving a window washer. The man screamed as he and his ladder fell to the ground, then he clutched his ankle and groaned in pain. All the students looked out of the window to see what had happened, but only 29 percent of them did anything to help. Other students witnessed the same "accident" but with one important added element: the man said he was hurt and needed help. In this case, more than 80 percent of the participants came to his aid (Yakimovich & Saltz, 1971). Why so many? Apparently, this one additional cue eliminated any uncertainty about whether assistance was needed. The man's more obvious need for assistance served to raise the perceived costs of not helping him, thus making helping more likely.

If this laboratory study seems unrealistic, consider the March 2000 case of a 62-year-old woman in Darby, Pennsylvania. She was walking to the grocery store when she was pushed from behind by an attacker. She fended him off and then did her shopping as usual. It was only when she got home and her daughter saw the handle of a knife protruding from her back that she realized that the assailant had stabbed her! No one in the grocery store said anything to her about the knife, let alone offered to help. Why? The most likely explanation is that the woman did nothing to suggest that assistance was necessary.

The *presence of others* also has a strong influence on the tendency to help. Somewhat surprisingly, however, their presence tends to make assistance less likely (Garcia et al., 2002). For example, on June 23, 2007, in a Wichita, Kansas, convenience store, a 27-year-old woman who had been stabbed after an argument lay ignored by passersby as she bled to death. Surveillance video shows five other shoppers stepping over her, including one who stopped only long enough to take a picture with a cell phone (Associated Press, 2007b). Whenever such cases are publicized, journalists and social commentators express dismay about the cold, uncaring attitudes that seem to exist among people who live in big cities.

That description may apply to some people, but research stimulated by such cases has revealed a social phenomenon that offers a different explanation of why those passersby in Wichita took no action to help. This phenomenon, called the **bystander effect,** can be described as follows: the chance that someone will help in an emergency usually decreases as the number of people present increases (Garcia et al., 2002). Why does the bystander effect occur? One explanation is that each witness assumes someone else will take responsibility for helping the victim. This *diffusion of responsibility* among all the witnesses leaves each witness feeling less obligated to help and thus lowers the perceived cost of not helping (Dovidio & Penner, 2001).

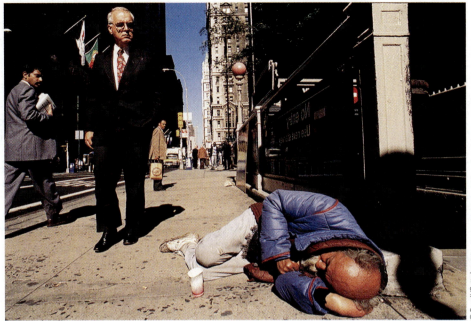

DIFFUSION OF RESPONSIBILITY ▶

Does the man on the sidewalk need help? The people walking by him are probably not sure, and they might assume that if he does need help, someone else will assist him. Research on factors affecting helping (e.g., Flynn & Lake, 2008) suggests that if you are ever in need of help, especially in a crowd, it is important not only to clearly ask for help but also to tell a specific onlooker to take specific action (e.g., "You, in the yellow shirt, please call an ambulance!").

The degree to which the presence of other people will suppress the tendency to help may depend on who those other people are. When they are strangers, perhaps poor communication interferes with assistance. Many people have difficulty speaking to strangers, particularly in an emergency, and without speaking, they have difficulty knowing what the others intend to do. According to this logic, if people are with friends rather than strangers, they should be less embarrassed, more willing to discuss the problem, and more likely to help.

In a study designed to test this idea, an experimenter left a research participant in a waiting room, either alone, with a friend, with a stranger, or with a stranger who was actually the experimenter's assistant (Latané & Rodin, 1969). The experimenter then stepped behind a curtain into an office. For a few minutes, she could be heard opening and closing the drawers of her desk, shuffling papers, and so on. Then there was a loud crash and she screamed, "Oh, my god—my foot, I—I can't move it. Oh, my ankle—I can't get this—thing off me." Then the participant heard her groan and cry.

Would the participant go behind the curtain to offer assistance? Once again, people were most likely to help if they were alone. When one other person was present, participants were more likely to communicate with one another and offer help if they were friends than if they were strangers. When the stranger was the experimenter's assistant—who had been instructed not to assist—very few participants offered to help. Other studies have confirmed that bystanders' tendency to help increases when they know one another (Rutkowski, Gruder, & Romer, 1983).

Research suggests that the *personality of the helper* also plays a role in helping. Some people are simply more likely to assist than others. Consider, for example, the Christians who risked their lives to save Jews from the Nazi Holocaust during World War II. Researchers interviewed these rescuers many years later and compared their personalities with those of people who had a chance to save Jews but did not do so (Fagin-Jones & Midlarsky, 2007; Oliner & Oliner, 1988). The rescuers were found to have more empathy, more concern about others, a greater sense of responsibility for their own actions, and greater confidence that their efforts would succeed. Louis Penner and his associates (Penner, 2002; Penner & Finkelstein, 1998) have found that these kinds of personality traits predict a broad range of assistance, from how quickly bystanders intervene in an emergency to how much time volunteers spend assisting AIDS patients. Consistent with the arousal: cost-reward theory, these personality characteristics are correlated with people's estimates of the costs of assisting and not assisting. For example, empathic individuals usually estimate the costs of not assisting as high, and people who are confident about their ability to assist usually rate the costs of assisting as low (Penner et al., 1995).

Valuable as it is, the arousal: cost-reward theory cannot account for all aspects of assistance. For instance, it cannot easily explain why environmental factors affect helping behavior. Research conducted in several countries has shown that people in urban areas are generally less helpful than those in rural areas (Aronson, Wilson, & Akert, 2005; Dovidio et al., 2006). Why? The explanation probably has more to do with the stressors found in cities than with city living itself. One study of 24 U.S. cities showed that the greater a city's size and density (number of people per square mile), the less likely people were to help others. Helping was also much less likely in cities where stressful economic conditions were greatest (Levine, Reysen, & Ganz, 2008). Previous studies of cities in the United States, the United Kingdom, the Middle East, and Africa had also found that people's tendency to help was more strongly related to the population density where they lived than to the overall size of their city (Hedge & Yousif, 1992; Levine et al., 1994; Yousif & Korte, 1995). The higher the density, the less likely people were to assist others. Why should stress make people less helpful? Two explanations have been suggested. The first is that stressful environments create bad moods—and generally speaking, people in bad moods are less likely to help (Forgas, Dunn, & Granland, 2008; Salovey, Mayer, & Rosenhan, 1991). A second possibility is that noise, crowding, and other urban stressors create too much stimulation. To reduce this stimulation, people may pay less attention to their surroundings, including less attention to individuals who need assistance.

Empathy-Altruism Helping Theory   There are also situations in which matters of cost are not the major cause of a decision to help or not help. A second approach to explaining helping behavior considers some of these situations. This second approach is embodied in the **empathy-altruism helping theory,** which maintains that people are more likely to engage in altruistic, or unselfish, assistance—even at a high cost—if they feel empathy toward the person in need (Batson, 1998). In one experiment illustrating this phenomenon, students listened to a tape-recorded interview in which a young woman told how her parents had died in an automobile accident, leaving no life insurance (Batson et al., 1997). She said that she was trying to take care of her younger brother and sister while going to college but that time and money were so tight that she might have to quit school or give up her siblings for adoption. None of this was true, but the participants were told that it was. Before hearing the tape, half the participants were given information about the woman that would increase their empathy for her; the other half were not. After listening to the tape, all participants were asked to help the woman raise money for herself and her siblings. Consistent with the empathy-altruism helping theory, more participants in the empathy group offered to help than did those in the control group.

Were the students who offered assistance in this experiment being utterly unselfish or could there have been other reasons for their apparent altruism? This is a hotly debated question. Some researchers dispute the claim that this study illustrated truly altruistic helping. They suggest instead that people help in such situations for more selfish reasons, such as relieving the distress they experienced after hearing of the woman's problems (Maner et al., 2002). The final verdict on this question is not yet in.

Evolutionary Theory   The evolutionary approach to psychology offers a third way to explain helping behavior. According to this approach, many human social behaviors are a reflection of actions that contributed to the survival of our prehistoric ancestors (Buss, 2003). At first glance, it might not seem reasonable to apply evolutionary theory to assistance and altruism, because helping others at the risk of our own well-being does not appear adaptive. If we die while trying to save others, it will be their genes, not ours, that will survive. In fact, according to Darwin's concept of the "survival of the fittest," helpers—and their genes—should have disappeared long ago. Today's evolutionary theorists suggest, however, that Darwin's thinking about natural selection focused too much on the survival of the fittest *individuals* and not enough on the

empathy-altruism helping theory   A theory suggesting that people assist others because they feel empathy toward them.

survival of their genes in *others.* Accordingly, the concept of survival of the fittest has been replaced by the concept of *inclusive fitness,* the survival of one's genes in future generations (Hamilton, 1964; Kruger, 2003). Because we share genes with our relatives, helping—or even dying for—a cousin, a sibling, or (above all) our own child increases the likelihood that at least some of our genetic characteristics will be passed on to the next generation through the beneficiary's future reproduction (Rachlin & Jones, 2008). So *kin selection,* or helping a relative survive, may produce genetic benefits for the helper even if it provides no personal benefits (Kruger, 2003).

There is considerable evidence that kin selection occurs among birds, squirrels, and other animals. The more closely the animals are related, the more likely they are to risk their lives for one another. Studies in a wide variety of cultures show the same pattern of helping behavior among humans (Buss, 2003). For example, people in the United States are three times as likely to donate a kidney to a relative as to a nonrelative (Borgida, Conner, & Monteufel, 1992). (See "In Review: Assistance" for a summary of the major reasons why people help and the conditions under which they are most likely to do so.)

Cooperation, Competition, and Conflict

Helping is one of several ways that people *cooperate* with one another. **Cooperation** is any type of behavior that involves people working together to attain a goal

---

In Review

Assistance

THEORY	BASIC PREMISE	IMPORTANT VARIABLES
Arousal: cost-reward	People assist others in order to reduce the unpleasant arousal caused by another person's distress. They attempt to minimize the costs of doing this.	Factors that affect the costs of assisting and of not assisting
Empathy-altruism	People sometimes assist others for unselfish reasons if they feel empathy for a person in need. They are motivated by a desire to increase another person's well-being.	The amount of empathy that one person feels for another
Evolutionary	People assist relatives because it increases the chances that the helper's genes will survive in future generations.	The biological relationship between the helper and the recipient of help

1. *If you could save only one person from a burning house, the _____ theory of assistance would predict that it would be your own child rather than, say, a grandparent.*

2. *Are you more likely to receive assistance in a nearly empty bus or in a crowded bus terminal?*

3. *People who have empathy for others are _____ likely to be helpful.*

---

cooperation Any type of behavior in which people work together to attain a goal.

(Penner, Dovidio, et al., 2005). For example, several law students might form a study group to help one another pass the bar exam. But people also compete with others for limited resources. Those same students might later try to outdo one another to be chosen for a single job opening at a top law firm. **Competition** exists whenever individuals try to reach a goal while denying others access to that goal. Finally, there is **conflict,** which occurs when a person or group believes that another person or group interferes with the attainment of a goal. When the law students become attorneys and represent opposing parties in a trial, they will be in conflict with one another. One way that psychologists have learned about all three of these phenomena is by studying social dilemmas (Weber, Kopelman, & Messick, 2004).

Social dilemmas are situations in which an action that is most rewarding for each individual will create problems for everyone if it is adopted by all others in the situation (Dawes & Messick, 2000). For instance, during a drought, individual homeowners are better off in the short run by watering their lawns as often as necessary to keep them from dying, but if everyone ignores local water restrictions, there will be no drinking water for anyone in the long run. Social dilemmas reflect conflicts between the interests of the individual and those of the group and between short-term and long-term interests (Schroeder, 1995). Are people from collectivist cultures (which emphasize cooperation) less likely to act competitively or selfishly in social dilemma situations? In general, they may be, but interpersonal conflict in such situations still appears to some extent in all cultures (Smith & Bond, 1999).

Group Processes

▶ *What makes a good leader?*

Although Western industrialized cultures tend to emphasize individuals over groups, the fact remains that most important decisions and efforts by governments and businesses in those cultures and elsewhere are made by groups, not individuals (Kerr & Tindale, 2004). Sometimes groups function very well. Perhaps you recall the extraordinary teamwork by engineers, emergency workers, and volunteers that led to the dramatic rescue of nine men trapped in a flooded Pennsylvania coal mine in July 2002. At other times, though, groups have been known to make bad (or even disastrous) decisions. To begin to understand why, let's consider some of the social psychological processes that often occur in groups to alter the behavior of individuals and the quality of their collective efforts.

The Presence of Others

In 1897, in what was probably the first social psychological experiment ever conducted, Norman Triplett demonstrated that an individual's behavior is affected by the mere presence of other people. Triplett found that bicycle racers went much faster when another racer was nearby than when they were simply racing against time. This effect occurred even when the cyclists were not competing against each other. There was something about the presence of another person—not just competition—that made riders go faster.

The term **social facilitation** describes circumstances in which the presence of other people can improve performance (Aiello & Douthitt, 2001). This improvement does not always occur, however. In fact, having other people present sometimes hurts performance, a process known as **social interference.** For decades, these results seemed contradictory; then Robert Zajonc (pronounced "ZYE-onze") suggested that both effects could be explained by one process: arousal.

The presence of other people, said Zajonc, increases a person's general level of arousal or motivation (Zajonc, 1965). Why? One reason is that being watched by others increases our sense of being evaluated, producing worry that in turn increases emotional arousal (Penner & Craiger, 1992). Arousal increases the tendency to perform

competition   Any type of behavior in which individuals try to attain a goal while denying others access to that goal.

conflict   What occurs when a person or group believes that another person or group interferes with the attainment of a goal.

social dilemmas   Situations in which actions that produce rewards for one individual will produce negative consequences for all if they are adopted by everyone.

social facilitation   A phenomenon in which the presence of others improves a person's performance.

social interference   A reduction in performance due to the presence of other people.

© AP Photo/Kirsty Wigglesworth

SOCIAL FACILITATION ▶

Premier athletes like Serena Williams, shown here winning the 2009 women's singles championship at Wimbledon, are able to perform at their best even though large crowds are present. In fact, the crowds probably help them do well, because the presence of others tends to increase arousal, which enhances the performance of familiar and well-learned skills, such as tennis strokes. However, arousal created by an audience tends to interfere with the performance of unfamiliar and poorly developed skills. This is one reason that professional athletes who show flawless grace in front of thousands of fans are likely to freeze up or blow their lines in front of a small production crew when trying for the first time to tape a TV ad or a public service announcement.

those behaviors that are most *dominant*—the ones you know best. This tendency can either help or hinder performance. When you are performing an easy, familiar task, such as riding a bike, increased arousal due to the presence of others should allow you to ride even faster than normal. But when a task is hard or unfamiliar—such as trying new dance steps or playing a newly learned piano piece in front of an audience—the most dominant responses may be incorrect and cause performance to suffer. In other words, the impact of other people on performance depends on whether the task is easy or difficult.

What if a person is not merely in the presence of others but is working with them on some task? In these situations, people often exert less effort than when performing alone, a phenomenon called **social loafing** (Liden et al., 2004). Whether the task is pulling on a rope, clapping as loudly as possible, or working together on a class project, people tend to work harder when alone than with others (Price, Harrison, & Gavin, 2006). Research in industrial and organizational psychology suggests that social loafing is most likely when large groups work on the same task (making each member's contribution harder to evaluate), when the group is not closely knit, and when members feel they are not being rewarded according to their performance (Hoigaard & Ingvaldeson, 2006; Liden et al., 2004; Szymanski, Garczynski, & Harkins, 2000). Social loafing is less likely when group members like each other and identify with the group and its goals (Hoigaard, Säfvenbom, & Tonnessen, 2006). It is also reduced when harder-working members of a group punish the social loafers with criticism or other negative consequences (Barclay, 2006).

In Western cultures, social loafing appears in groups of all sorts, from volunteer committees to search parties. It is much less likely among people in Eastern cultures such as those in China and Japan. In fact, in these collectivist cultures, working in a group usually produces *social striving*—defined as greater individual effort when working in a group (Matsumoto, 2000). This difference in the effects of group membership on individual efforts probably reflects the high value that collectivist cultures place on coordinated and cooperative group activities.

Group Leadership

The role of group leaders is especially important when social loafing and other obstacles threaten to impair the effectiveness of group efforts. A good leader can help a group pursue its goals, but a bad one can get in the way of a group's functioning

social loafing Exerting less effort when performing a group task than when performing the same task alone.

(Kaiser, Hogan, & Craig, 2008). What makes a good leader? Psychologists once thought that the personalities of good and bad leaders were about the same, but we now know that certain personality traits often distinguish effective from ineffective leaders. For example, using tests similar to those that measure the Big Five traits described in the personality chapter, Colin Silverthorne (2001) examined the characteristics of leaders in the United States, Thailand, and China. He found that effective leaders in all three countries tended to score high on agreeableness, emotional stability, extraversion, and conscientiousness. Other researchers have found that in general, effective leaders are intelligent, success oriented, flexible, and confident (Chemers, Watson, & May, 2000; Foti & Hauenstein, 2007).

Having particular personality traits does not guarantee good leadership ability, however. People who are effective leaders in one situation may be ineffective in another (Chemers, 2000; Ng, Ang, & Chan, 2008). The reason is that effective leadership also depends on the characteristics of the group members, the task at hand, and, most important, the interaction between these factors and the leader's style (Yun, Faraj, & Sims, 2005).

For many years, leadership research focused on two main types of leaders. The first, called **task-motivated leaders,** provide close supervision, lead by giving orders, and generally discourage group discussion (Yukl & Van Fleet, 1992). Their style may make them unpopular. The second, called **relationship-motivated leaders,** provide loose supervision, ask for group members' ideas, and are generally concerned with subordinates' feelings. They are usually well liked by the group, even when they must discipline a group member (Brehm, Kassin, & Fein, 2005). More recently, additional leadership styles have been identified. One of these styles is seen in *transactional leaders,* whose actions depend on the actions of those they lead. They reward those who behave as the leader wishes and they correct or punish those who don't. There are also *transformational* or *charismatic leaders* (Bass & Riggio, 2006). These people concentrate on creating a vision of the group's goals, inspiring others to pursue that vision, and giving their followers reason to respect and admire them.

Do men or women make better leaders? Research by Alice Eagly and her colleagues at first found that overall, men and women are equally capable leaders. It also looked as though men tend to be more effective when success requires a task-motivated leader and that women tend to be more effective when success requires a more relationship-motivated leader. In other words, it appeared that people of each gender tend to be most effective when they are acting in a manner consistent with gender-role traditions (Eagly & Karau, 1991; Eagly, Karau, & Makhijani, 1995). Perhaps the reason was that some people did not like female leaders who act in a "masculine" manner or occupy leadership positions traditionally held by men (Eagly, Makhijani, & Klonsky, 1992).

A somewhat different picture of gender and leadership has emerged from Eagly's more recent research. For one thing, she found that females are generally more likely than males to display a transformational leadership style. Further, when women display a transactional style, they tend to be more encouraging than transactional male leaders, focusing more on using rewards rather than punishments to modify group members' behaviors. Finally, and in contrast to earlier findings, Eagly's results now suggest that women may be slightly more effective leaders overall than men (Eagly, Johannesen-Schmidt, & van Engen, 2003).

Groupthink

The emphasis on group decisions in most large organizations is based on the belief that several people working together will make better decisions than will individuals working alone. As noted in the chapter on thought, language, and intelligence, this belief is generally correct, yet under certain circumstances groups have been known to make amazingly bad decisions (Kerr & Tindale, 2004). Consider, for example, the fact that, in 1986, administrators at the National Aeronautics and Space Administration (NASA) ignored engineers' warnings about the effects of cold weather and decided to launch the space shuttle *Challenger.* The spacecraft exploded 73 seconds after liftoff, killing

task-motivated leaders   Leaders who provide close supervision, lead by giving directions, and generally discourage group discussion.

relationship-motivated leaders   Leaders who provide loose supervision, ask for group members' ideas, and are generally concerned with subordinates' feelings.

all aboard. After analyzing these and other disastrous decisions, Irving Janis (1989) proposed that they can be attributed to a phenomenon called *groupthink*. **Groupthink** occurs, he said, when group members are unable to realistically evaluate the options available to them or to fully consider the potential negative consequences of the option they are about to choose.

Groupthink is particularly likely when four conditions exist: (1) the decision is not based on all the facts at hand; (2) group members all share certain biases; (3) members who express disagreement with the majority view are punished or even ejected from the group; and (4) the group leader puts pressure on the members to reach agreement. This last condition appeared to play a crucial role in the U.S. government's decision to support a disastrously unsuccessful invasion of Cuba by anti-Castro Cubans in 1961. Before the final decision was made, several advisers were told that President John F. Kennedy had made up his mind to support the invasion and that it was time to "close ranks with the president." This situation created enormous pressure for conformity (May & Zelikow, 1997).

Some researchers have questioned the prevalence and dangers of groupthink (e.g., Aldag & Fuller, 1993; Park, 2000), but because it does sometimes occur, other researchers have worked on developing techniques to help groups avoid it (Galinsky & Kray, 2004; Kray & Galinsky, 2003).

One way to avoid groupthink is to teach group members to imagine all the negative outcomes of each course of action they are considering. Another is to designate someone to play the "devil's advocate," a person who constantly challenges the group's emerging decision and forces everyone to consider all the facts and other decisions that are possible (Risen, 1998). Yet another technique is to encourage diverse opinions by allowing people to express them anonymously. For example, group members might communicate by e-mail on networked computers that hide the sender's identity. Research suggests that allowing groups to discuss decision options without knowing who is saying what stimulates logical debate and makes it easier for people to disagree with the group (O'Brien, 1991).

linkages

How does stress affect group decision making? *(a link to Health, Stress, and Coping)*

linkages

Can we "see" prejudice in the brain? *(a link to Biology and Behavior)*

groupthink   A pattern of thinking that renders group members unable to evaluate realistically the wisdom of various options and decisions.

social neuroscience   A specialty that focuses on the influence of social processes on biological processes and on the influence of biological processes on social psychological phenomena.

Linkages

Biological and Social Psychology

Research in social psychology was once thought to be entirely separate from research on the biological processes that underlie social behavior (Winkielman, Berntson, & Cacioppo, 2001). Social psychologists believed it was impossible to reduce complex social psychological processes to the firing of neurons or the secretion of hormones. For their part, biological psychologists, more commonly known as *neuroscientists*, viewed the study of social psychology as having little, if any, relevance to the understanding of, say, behavioral genetics or the functioning of the nervous system. Recently, however, scientists in both subfields have begun to take a closer look at each other's research and at how their subfields are linked. The result has been the emergence of a new specialty called **social neuroscience** or *social cognitive neuroscience* (Adolphs, 2003; Heatherton, Macrae, & Kelley, 2004; Mitchell, 2008; Ochsner, 2004). This new specialty focuses on the influence of social processes on biological processes and on the influence of biological processes, including genetics, on social psychological phenomena (e.g. Bielsky et al., 2005; Robinson, Fernald, & Clayton, 2008; Thompson et al., 2006).

There are many reasons to believe that this approach will be valuable. For example, the chapter on health, stress, and coping contains numerous examples of how social stressors can have health-related biological consequences. Health psychologists have also found that the availability and quality of a person's social support network can affect biological processes ranging from blood pressure to the healing of wounds (Gouin et al., 2008; Kiecolt-Glaser et al., 1998; Loving, Heffner, & Keicolt-Glaser, 2006; Robles & Kiecolt-Glaser, 2003). In addition, as discussed in the chapter on psychological disorders, some problems in social behavior can result from the interaction of environmental stressors with genetic influences. One study compared the amount of antisocial behavior displayed by men who either had or had not suffered the stress of parental abuse in childhood. Antisocial behavior was much more common among men who had been abused, but this behavior was most common among abused men who also had inherited characteristics associated with antisocial behaviors (Caspi et al., 2002).

Researchers are beginning to identify the biological aspects of many social processes. One example can be seen in studies of how the amygdala—a brain structure involved in emotion—is related to the stereotyping and prejudice discussed earlier in this chapter (Eberhardt, 2005). Researchers found that European Americans who were prejudiced against African Americans showed significantly more amygdala activity when looking at pictures of black people than when looking at pictures of white people (Cunningham et al., 2004; Hart et al., 2000; Phelps et al., 2000).

In short, social cognitive neuroscience shows great promise for creating a better understanding of the linkages among social, cognitive, and biological phenomena as well as a better understanding of complex social and physiological processes.

ACTIVE REVIEW　▶　Chapter 14

Social Psychology

As noted in the introductory chapter, all of psychology's subfields are related to one another. Our discussion of social neuroscience illustrates just one way that the topic of this chapter, social psychology, is linked to the subfield of biological psychology, which is discussed in the chapter on biology and behavior. The Linkages diagram shows ties to two other subfields, and there are many more ties throughout the book. Looking for linkages among subfields will help you see how they all fit together and help you better appreciate the big picture that is psychology.

linkages

Can we "see" prejudice in the brain? *(ans. on p. 591)*

Do groups solve problems more effectively than individuals? *(ans. on p. 269)*

How do societies define what is abnormal? *(ans. on p. 467)*

Chapter 2
Biology and Behavior

Chapter 7
Thought, Language, and Intelligence

Chapter 12
Psychological Disorders

SUMMARY ▶

Social cognition, the mental processes through which people perceive and react to others, is one aspect of **social psychology,** the study of how people influence and are influenced by other people. Through social cognition, each person creates a unique perception of reality.

Social Influences on the Self

◐ *How do we compare ourselves with others?*

People's social and cultural environments affect their thoughts and feelings about themselves, including their **self-concept** and their **self-esteem.** When people have no objective criteria by which to judge themselves, they look to others as the basis for **social comparison.** Such comparison can affect self-evaluation or self-esteem. Categories of people that are regularly used for social comparison are known as **reference groups.** Comparison with reference groups sometimes produces **relative deprivation,** which in turn can cause personal and social turmoil.

A person's **social identity** is formed from beliefs about the groups to which the person belongs. Social identity affects the beliefs we hold about ourselves, our self-concept. Social identity permits people to feel that they are part of a larger group, generating loyalty and sacrifice from group members but also potentially creating bias and social discrimination toward people who are not members of the group.

Social Perception

◐ *Do we perceive people and objects in similar ways?*

Social perception concerns the processes by which people interpret information about others, form impressions of them,

and draw conclusions about the reasons for their behavior. **Schemas,** the knowledge about people and social situations that we carry into social interactions, affect what we pay attention to, what we remember, and how we judge people and events.

First impressions are formed easily and quickly, in part because people apply existing schemas to their perceptions of others. First impressions change slowly because once we form an impression about another person, we try to maintain it. Schemas, however, can create **self-fulfilling prophecies,** leading us to act in ways that bring out behavior in others that is consistent with our expectations of them.

Attribution is the process of explaining the causes of people's behavior, including our own. Observers tend to attribute behavior to causes that are either internal or external to the actor. Attributions are also affected by biases that systematically distort our view of behavior. The most common attributional biases are the **fundamental attribution error** (and its cousin, the ultimate attribution error), the **actor-observer effect,** and the **self-serving bias.** Personal and cultural factors can affect the extent to which people exhibit these biases.

Attitudes

◐ *Do attitudes always determine behavior?*

An **attitude** is the tendency to respond positively or negatively to a particular object. Attitudes affect a wide range of behaviors.

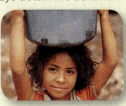

Most social psychologists see attitudes as composed of three components: cognitive components (beliefs), affective components (feelings), and behavioral components (actions). However, it is often difficult to predict a specific behavior from a person's beliefs or feelings about an object. Cognitive theories suggest that the likelihood of attitude-behavior consistency depends on the importance of the attitude, subjective social norms, perceived control over the behavior, and prior direct experience with the attitude object.

Attitudes can be learned through modeling as well as through classical or operant conditioning. They are also subject to the mere-exposure effect: all else being equal, people develop greater liking for a new object the more often they are exposed to it.

The effectiveness of a persuasive message in changing attitudes is influenced by the characteristics of the person who communicates the message, by its content, and by the audience receiving it. The **elaboration likelihood model** suggests that attitude change can occur through either the peripheral or the central route, depending on a person's ability to carefully consider an argument and their motivation for doing so. Accordingly, different messages will produce attitude change under different circumstances. Another approach is to change a person's behavior in the hope that attitudes will be adjusted to match the behavior. **Cognitive dissonance theory** holds that if inconsistency between attitude and behavior creates discomfort related to a person's self-concept, the attitude may change in order to reduce the conflict.

Prejudice and Stereotypes

◐ *How does prejudice develop?*

Stereotypes often lead to **prejudice** and **social discrimination.** Motivational theories of prejudice suggest that some people have a need

to dislike people who differ from themselves. This need may stem from the trait of authoritarianism as well as from a strong social identity with one's in-group. In either case, feeling superior to members of out-groups helps these people feel better about themselves. As a result, in-group members tend to discriminate against out-groups. Cognitive theories suggest that people categorize others into groups in order to reduce social complexity. Learning theories maintain that stereotypes, prejudice, and discriminatory behaviors can be learned from parents, peers, and the media. The **contact hypothesis** proposes that intergroup contact can reduce prejudice and lead to more favorable attitudes toward the stereotyped group, but only if the contact occurs under specific conditions, such as equal status between groups.

Interpersonal Attraction

◐ *What factors affect who likes whom?*

Interpersonal attraction is affected by many variables. Physical proximity is important because it allows people to meet. The situation

in which they meet is important because positive or negative aspects of the situation tend to be associated with the other person. Characteristics of the other person are also important. Attraction tends to be greater when two people share similar attitudes and personal characteristics. Physical appearance plays a role in attraction; initially, attraction is strongest to those who are most physically attractive. But for long-term relationships, the **matching hypothesis** applies: people tend to choose others whose physical attractiveness is about the same as theirs.

Two key components of successful intimate relationships are interdependence and mutual commitment. Sternberg's triangular theory suggests that love is a function of three components:

passion, intimacy, and commitment. Varying combinations of these three components create qualitatively different types of love. Marital satisfaction depends on communication, the perception that the relationship is equitable, the couple's ability to deal effectively with conflict and anger, and agreement on important issues in the marriage.

Social Influence

▶ *What social rules shape our behavior?*

Social norms establish the rules for what should and should not be done in a particular situation. One particularly powerful norm is reciprocity, the tendency to respond to others as they have acted toward us. *Deindividuation* is a psychological state in which people temporarily lose their individuality, their normal inhibitions are relaxed, and they may perform aggressive or illegal acts that they would not do otherwise.

When behavior or beliefs change as the result of unspoken or implicit group pressure, *conformity* has occurred. When the change is the result of a request, *compliance* has occurred. People tend to follow the normative responses of others, and groups create norms when none already exist. People sometimes display public conformity without private acceptance; at other times, the responses of others have an impact on private beliefs. People conform because they want to be right, because they want to be liked, and because they tend to be rewarded for conformity. People are most likely to conform when the situation is unclear as well as when others in the group are in unanimous agreement. Up to a point, conformity usually increases as the number of people holding the majority view grows larger. Effective strategies for creating compliance include the foot-in-the-door technique, the door-in-the-face procedure, and the lowball approach.

Obedience

▶ *How far will people go in obeying authority?*

Obedience involves complying with an explicit demand from an authority figure. Research by Milgram indicates that obedience is likely even when obeying an authority appears to result in pain and suffering for another person. Obedience declines when the status of the authority figure declines, when others are observed

to disobey, and if a victim asks to be released. Some people are more likely to obey orders than others. Because participants in Milgram's studies experienced considerable stress, the experiments have been questioned on ethical grounds. Nevertheless, his research showed that people do not have to be psychologically disordered to inflict pain on others.

Aggression

▶ *Are people born aggressive?*

Aggression is an act intended to harm another person. Freud saw aggression as due partly to instincts. More recent theories attribute aggressive tendencies to genetic and evolutionary factors, brain dysfunctions, and hormonal influences. Learning is also important; people learn to display aggression by watching others and by being rewarded for aggressive behavior. There are wide cultural differences in the occurrence of aggression.

A variety of emotional factors play a role in aggression. The *frustration-aggression hypothesis* suggests that frustration can lead to aggression, particularly in the presence of cues that invite or promote aggression. Arousal from sources unrelated to aggression, such as exercise, can also make aggressive responses more likely, especially if aggression is already a dominant response in that situation. Research in *environmental psychology* suggests that factors such as high temperature and crowding increase the likelihood of aggressive behavior, particularly among people who are already angry.

Altruism and Assistance

▶ *What motivates people to help one another?*

Humans often display *assistance (helping behavior)* and *altruism*. There are three major theories of why people assist others. According to the *arousal: cost-reward theory*, people help in order to reduce the unpleasant arousal they experience when others are in distress. Their specific reaction to a suffering person depends on the costs associated with helping or not helping. Assistance is most likely when the need for help is clear and when diffusion of responsibility is not created by the presence of other people—a phenomenon called the *bystander*

effect. Environmental and personality factors also affect willingness to assist others. The *empathy-altruism helping theory* suggests that assistance can be truly unselfish if the helper feels empathy for the person in need. Finally, evolutionary theory suggests that humans have an innate tendency to assist others, especially relatives, because doing so increases the likelihood that family genes will survive.

Cooperation is any type of behavior in which people work together to attain a goal; *competition* exists whenever individuals try to attain a goal while denying others access to that goal. Interpersonal or intergroup *conflict* occurs when one person or group believes that another stands in the way of reaching some goal. Psychologists study conflict by observing behavior in *social dilemmas,* situations in which behavior that benefits individuals in the short run may spell disaster for an entire group in the long run.

Group Processes

▶ *What makes a good leader?*

People's behavior is affected by the mere presence of other people. By enhancing one's most likely behavior in a situation, the presence of others sometimes creates *social facilitation* (which improves performance) and sometimes creates *social interference* (which impairs performance). When people work in groups, they often exert less effort than when alone, a phenomenon called *social loafing*. Effective group leaders tend to score high on emotional stability, agreeableness, and conscientiousness. In general, they are also intelligent, success oriented, flexible, and confident. *Task-motivated leaders* provide close supervision, lead by giving orders, and generally discourage group discussion. *Relationship-motivated leaders* provide loose supervision, ask for group members' ideas, and are generally concerned with subordinates' feelings. Transactional leaders focus on rewarding or correcting group members' performance, and transformational leaders tend to lead by example, thus inspiring good performance.

When *groupthink* occurs, decisions are not based on all the facts, group members share certain biases, dissenting members' views are rejected, and the group leader pressures members to reach agreement.

A new specialty called *social neuroscience* focuses on the influence of social processes on biological processes and on the influence of biological processes on social psychological phenomena.

Put It in Writing

A survey reveals that first-graders from various ethnic groups in a local school hold prejudiced attitudes toward one another. Imagine that you have been hired to develop a program to help these children become less prejudiced and more accepting of members of other ethnic groups. Write a one-page description of two or three classroom activities that would help you accomplish this goal and tell why you think they would do so. Do you think these activities could be successful in eliminating all prejudiced thinking in the children? Why or why not?

Personal Learning Activity

Research mentioned in this chapter suggests that the physical appearance of a partner tends to be more important to men, whereas a partner's intelligence tends to be more important to women. If that is true, what qualities would you hypothesize that men versus women will say they are looking for when they place ads for a partner in a personal column or web site? Develop a research plan to test your hypothesis and then collect some data by reading and analyzing personal ads in your local newspaper or on a web site for singles. Was your hypothesis supported? Did gender differences in the content of the ads appear more often, less often, or about equally in ads placed by heterosexuals, homosexuals, and bisexuals? Write a brief report of your findings, and summarize what you think they can and cannot say about the factors that attract people to each other. *For additional projects, see the Personal Learning Activities in the corresponding chapter of the study guide that accompanies this book.*

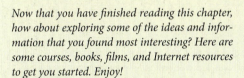

Take Action to Learn More ▶

Now that you have finished reading this chapter, how about exploring some of the ideas and information that you found most interesting? Here are some courses, books, films, and Internet resources to get you started. Enjoy!

Courses

Social Psychology
Social Conflict
Marriage and Family
Social Cognition
Interpersonal Processes
Prejudice and Social Discrimination

Movies

Being There; My Man Godfrey. First impressions, social roles, and attribution.
The Birdcage; Desk Set; Holiday; The Gunfighter; Victor/Victoria. Social roles and stereotypes.
Best in Show; The Big Chill; My Big Fat Greek Wedding; Peter's Friends; Pygmalion; The Last of the Mohicans. Reference groups.
Snow Falling on Cedars; Ray; Rosewood; A Patch of Blue; Trading Places. Stereotypes, prejudice, and social discrimination.
The Adventures of Robin Hood; The Breakfast Club; Cool Runnings; The Defiant Ones; Remember the Titans. Prejudice and the contact hypothesis.
The Gods Must Be Crazy; Higher Learning; Revenge of the Nerds; Legally Blonde. Cultural diversity and stereotypes.
A Clockwork Orange; Gangs of New York; Mississippi Burning. Deindividuation; aggression.
Schindler's List; THX 1138. Obedience, compliance.

Dune; Evita; Ghandhi; Mr. Smith Goes to Washington. Leadership

Books

Henry Louis Gates, Jr., *Colored People: A Memoir* (Vintage, 1994). Growing up black in segregated West Virginia.
James Goodman, *Stories of Scottsboro* (Vintage, 1994). Prejudice and social discrimination lead to wrongful rape convictions of young black men in Alabama in 1931.
Elliot Aronson, *Nobody Left to Hate* (W. H. Freeman, 2000). A social psychologist explores the social roots of the Columbine school massacre.
Alex Kotlowitz, *The Other Side of the River: A Story of Two Towns, a Death, and America's Dilemma* (Doubleday, 1998). A story of social discrimination in law enforcement and prejudice in a town that is racially and geographically divided.
John Gray, *Men Are from Mars, Women Are from Venus* (HarperCollins, 1993). Interpersonal relationships.
Hans-Werner Bierhoff, *Prosocial Behaviour* (Psychology Press, 2002). An introductory overview of research on helping and altruism.
Charles Stangor, ed., *Stereotypes and Prejudice: Essential Readings* (Psychology Press, 2000). A collection of research articles on prejudice.
Robert Cialdini, *Influence: Science and Practice* (Addison-Wesley, 2001). Summary of research on influence and how it is applied in everyday life.

Russell Geen and Edward Donnerstein, eds., *Human Aggression: Theory, Research, and Implications for Social Policy* (Academic Press, 1998). Readings on the origins of and factors in aggression.
Malcolm Gladwell, *The Tipping Point: How Little Things Can Make a Big Difference* (Back Bay Books, 2002). Describes how concepts from social psychology can help explain the development of popular fads and trends.

The Web

Essentials of Psychology Book Companion Website

www.cengage.com/psychology/bernstein

Visit the book companion website to access a wealth of resources, including chapter outlines, flashcards, web links, tutorial quizzes, and more!

CENGAGENOW™ Just what you need to know NOW! Spend time on what you need to master rather than on information you already have learned. Take a pre-test for this chapter, and CengageNOW will generate a personalized study plan based on your results. The study plan will identify the topics you need to review and direct you to online resources to help you master those topics. You can then take a post-test to help you determine the concepts you have mastered and what you will need to work on. Try it out! Go to www.cengage.com/login to sign in with an access code or to purchase access to this product.

Review of Key Terms ▶

Can you define each of the key terms in the chapter? Check your definitions against those on the pages shown in parentheses in the following list or in the Glossary at the end of the book.

actor-observer effect (p. 555)
aggression (aggressive behavior; p. 577)
altruism (p. 583)
arousal: cost-reward theory (p. 584)
assistance (helping behavior) (p. 583)
attitude (p. 557)
attribution (p. 554)
bystander effect (p. 584)
cognitive dissonance theory (p. 559)
competition (p. 588)
compliance (p. 569)
conflict (p. 588)

conformity (p. 569)
contact hypothesis (p. 563)
cooperation (p. 587)
deindividuation (p. 568)
elaboration likelihood model (p. 558)
empathy-altruism helping theory (p. 586)
environmental psychology (p. 583)
frustration-aggression hypothesis (p. 580)
fundamental attribution error (p. 554)
groupthink (p. 591)
matching hypothesis (p. 565)
obedience (p. 573)
prejudice (p. 561)
reference groups (p. 549)
relationship-motivated leaders (p. 590)
relative deprivation (p. 549)
schemas (p. 551)

self-concept (p. 549)
self-esteem (p. 549)
self-fulfilling prophecy (p. 554)
self-serving bias (p. 556)
social cognition (p. 548)
social comparison (p. 549)
social dilemmas (p. 588)
social discrimination (p. 561)
social facilitation (p. 588)
social identity (p. 550)
social interference (p. 588)
social loafing (p. 589)
social neuroscience (p. 591)
social norms (p. 568)
social perception (p. 551)
social psychology (p. 548)
stereotypes (p. 560)
task-motivated leaders (p. 590)

MULTIPLE-CHOICE ▶ Self Test

Select the best answer for each of the following questions. Then check your responses against the Answer Key at the end of the book.

1. Jack took an entry-level job after completing college with honors and having his senior research paper published. Now Jack is depressed because the older people around him make more money than he does and are more advanced in their careers. Jack is experiencing _____.
   a. cognitive dissonance
   b. relative deprivation
   c. social facilitation
   d. a self-fulfilling prophecy

2. One of the assumptions of terror management theory is that _____.
   a. having high self-esteem helps reduce the impact of thoughts about death
   b. people who engage in terrorism have antisocial personalities
   c. it is better to dwell on negative thoughts than avoid them
   d. people cope better with terrifying thoughts when they do not seek social support

3. When Rowland first met Jacob, Jacob wasn't feeling well and threw up on Rowland's shoes. According to research on first impressions, we would expect Rowland to _____.
   a. feel sorry for Jacob and thus have a positive first impression of him
   b. develop a negative impression of Jacob because of the negative first experience with him
   c. have an initial negative impression that will become positive later, no matter what Jacob does
   d. have a positive first impression of Jacob because he is a male

4. Gena is in a bad mood because she is convinced that she won't like her blind date, Pat. When Pat arrives, he is outgoing and considerate, but Gena is short-tempered and rude to him. Soon Pat becomes irritable and ends the date early. Gina's prediction that she wouldn't have a good time came true mainly because of _____.
   a. cognitive dissonance
   b. prejudice
   c. a self-fulfilling prophecy
   d. the fundamental attribution error

5. "I earned an A on my history test because I studied hard and I'm smart, but I failed my philosophy test because its questions were poorly worded and the teacher doesn't like me." This statement is an example of _____.
   a. the actor-observer effect
   b. the fundamental attribution error
   c. a self-fulfilling prophecy
   d. a self-serving bias

6. Richard is listening to a student government leader suggest that professors on campus should stop giving grades. Richard is most likely to be convinced if the speaker _____.
   a. introduces a famous celebrity who supports this idea
   b. circulates a petition in support of the idea
   c. presents evidence that eliminating grades does not hurt students' job prospects
   d. is personable and funny

7. Rachel and Matteus listen to a boring lecture. Afterward, Rachel is offered $100 and Matteus is offered $1 to tell the lecturer's next class that the lecture was interesting and fun. Both agree to do so. According to cognitive dissonance theory, we would expect real attitude change about the lecture to occur in _____.

  a. Rachel, but not Matteus
  b. Matteus, but not Rachel
  c. both Rachel and Matteus
  d. neither Rachel nor Matteus

8. In an attempt to reduce prejudice between ethnic groups at Lincoln School, the principal asks members of all groups to help build a new playground. Prejudice would be most likely to decrease as a result if _____.

  a. teams from each ethnic group competed to see which could work the fastest
  b. one member of each group was appointed to a committee to lead the project
  c. members of all the groups worked together in teams to complete various parts of the playground
  d. members of each ethnic group wore the same kind of T-shirt

9. Rhona, a pretty woman with conservative political views, has just moved into an apartment building on campus. All else being equal, which neighbor will Rhona probably like the most?

  a. Jill, whose hair color, height, and weight are similar to Rhona's
  b. Shauna, president of the Young Conservatives club
  c. Patrice, president of the Young Liberals club
  d. Yolanda, who comes from Rhona's home town

10. Giorgio and Louisa share their thoughts, hopes, and daily worries. They plan to stay married throughout their lifetime, and they enjoy an active and satisfying sex life. According to Sternberg's theory, Giorgio and Louisa are experiencing _____ love.

  a. consummate
  b. companionate
  c. temporary
  d. romantic

11. When her best friend stopped by with a Christmas gift, Jen was upset because she had nothing to give in return. Jen was uncomfortable because she had _____.

  a. experienced deindividuation
  b. engaged in social loafing
  c. made the ultimate attribution error
  d. violated the reciprocity norm

12. In Harper Lee's novel *To Kill a Mockingbird,* an angry mob tries to lynch a prisoner. The prisoner's attorney, Atticus Finch, and his young daughter, "Scout," talk to the crowd, calling people by name, and reminding them that they know their families. Soon the mob disperses, no longer a faceless crowd but a group of identifiable individuals. Atticus and Scout disrupted the phenomenon of _____.

  a. diffusion of responsibility
  b. deindividuation
  c. situational ambiguity
  d. social facilitation

13. Shawn's teacher doesn't keep track of her students' performance in groups, so Shawn does not put as much effort into his group project as he does into his individual project. Shawn is exhibiting _____.

  a. a self-serving bias
  b. social facilitation
  c. social loafing
  d. diffusion of responsibility

14. Keyonna thought that the play she had just seen was boring, but everyone else seemed to like it. At the closing curtain, the audience gave the actors a standing ovation. Keyonna stood up and applauded too, even though she didn't believe the actors deserved it. Keyonna's behavior in this situation is an example of _____.

  a. conformity
  b. compliance
  c. obedience
  d. a self-fulfilling prophecy

15. Colleen knows she should take a day off from work to study for a big exam, but she also knows her boss won't like it. So she first asks for the entire week off. When the boss refuses, she asks for the one day off instead and he agrees. Colleen used the _____ approach to gain her boss's compliance.

  a. foot-in-the-door
  b. door-in-the-face
  c. lowball
  d. peripheral

16. Which of the following is not a major factor in determining whether or not a person will obey an order?

  a. The status of the authority figure giving the order.
  b. The personality characteristics of the person receiving the order.
  c. The presence of another person who disobeys the order.
  d. The gender of the person given the order.

17. Leonard is upset because he just can't get his new iPod to work. When his roommate comes home and accidentally knocks over Leonard's glass of lemonade, Leonard becomes abusive, screaming at his roommate and throwing books and pillows at him. This is an example of the _____ theory of aggression.

  a. frustration-aggression
  b. generalized arousal
  c. authoritarian
  d. biological

18. While shopping, Lenora falls and breaks her ankle. She is most likely to receive help from a stranger if she _____.

  a. is in a quiet area where only a few people saw her fall
  b. is in the midst of a large crowd
  c. is in a large city
  d. doesn't ask for help

19. Which of the following summarizes the evolutionary view of assistance?

  a. People feel good when they help others.
  b. People help others in order to improve the chance that some of their genes will survive in future generations.
  c. People are motivated to protect others if the costs of helping are outweighed by the benefits.
  d. People are helpful because it improves everyone's chances of survival.

20. When groups fail to consider all the facts and all their options, when they share similar biases, and when they are pressured to reach an agreement, they often make poor decisions because of a phenomenon called _____.

  a. deindividuation
  b. groupthink
  c. social facilitation
  d. social interference

Statistics in Psychological Research

Understanding and interpreting the results of psychological research depend on *statistical analyses,* the methods for describing and drawing conclusions from data. The introductory chapter introduced some terms and concepts associated with these analyses. *Descriptive statistics* are the numbers that psychologists use to describe and present their data. *Inferential statistics* are the mathematical procedures they use to draw conclusions from data and to make inferences about what the data mean. Here, we present more details about these statistical analyses that will help you to evaluate research results.

Describing Data

To illustrate our discussion, let's imagine a hypothetical experiment about the effects of rewards on performance. The experimenter presents a set of mathematics problems to two groups of people. Each group must solve the problems within a fixed time. For each correct answer, the low-reward group is paid ten cents. The high-reward group gets one dollar. The hypothesis to be tested is the **null hypothesis**, the assertion that the independent variable manipulated by the experimenter will have no effect on the dependent variable measured by the experimenter. In this case, the null hypothesis is that the size of the reward (the independent variable) will not affect performance on the mathematics task (the dependent variable).

Assume that the experimenter has obtained a sample of participants, assigned them randomly to the two groups, and done everything possible to avoid the influence of confounding variables and other research problems discussed in the introductory chapter. The experiment has been run, and the researcher now has the data, a list of the number of correct answers given by each participant in each group. Now comes the first task of statistical analysis. We must describe the data in a way that makes them easy to understand.

The Frequency Histogram

The simplest way to describe the data is to draw up something like Table 1, in which all the numbers are simply listed. After examining the table, you might notice that the high-reward group seems to have done better than the low-reward group. But the difference is not immediately obvious. It might be even harder to see if more participants had been involved or if the scores included three-digit numbers. A more satisfactory way of presenting the same data is in a picture-like graphic known as a frequency **histogram** (see Figure 1).

Construction of a histogram is simple. First, divide the scale for measuring the dependent variable (in this case, the number of correct solutions) into a number of categories, or "bins." The bins in our example are 1–2, 3–4, 5–6, 7–8, and 9–10. Next, sort the raw data into the appropriate bin. (For example, the score of a participant who had 5 correct answers would go into the 5–6 bin, a score of 8 would go into the 7–8 bin, and so on.) Finally, for each bin, count the number of scores in that bin, and draw a bar up to the height of that number on the vertical axis of the graph. The set of bars makes up the frequency histogram. Figure 1 shows a histogram comparing the scores of the

null hypothesis A testable statement that the independent variable manipulated by an experimenter will have no effect on the dependent variable being measured by the experimenter.

histogram A pictorial presentation of how often each possible score on a dependent variable occurs in a set of research data.

TABLE 1 ■ A SIMPLE DATA SET

Here are the test scores obtained by thirteen participants performing under low-reward conditions and thirteen participants performing under high-reward conditions.

Low Reward	High Reward
4	6
6	4
2	10
7	10
6	7
8	10
3	6
5	7
2	5
3	9
5	9
9	3
5	8

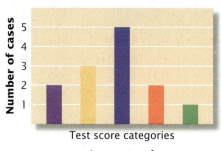

Low reward

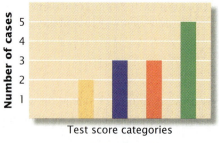

High reward

Color	Range	Color	Range	Color	Range
■	1–2	■	5–6	■	9–10
■	3–4	■	7–8		

FIGURE 1 ■ A HISTOGRAM

The height of each bar of a histogram represents the number of scores falling within each range of score values. The pattern formed by these bars gives a visual image of how research results are distributed.

high-reward group and the low-reward group. Now the difference between groups that was difficult to see in Table 1 becomes clearly visible. More people in the high-reward group obtained high scores than in the low-reward group.

Histograms and other "pictures" of data are useful for visualizing and better understanding the "shape" of research data. But in order to analyze data statistically, we need to use other ways of handling the numbers that make up these graphic presentations. For example, before we can tell whether two histograms are different statistically or just visually, the data they represent must be summarized using descriptive statistics.

Descriptive Statistics

The four basic categories of descriptive statistics do the following: (1) count the number of observations made; (2) summarize the typical value of a set of data; (3) summarize the spread, or variability, in a set of data; and (4) express the correlation between two sets of data, using the correlation coefficient described in the introductory chapter.

N The easiest statistic to compute, abbreviated as N, simply describes the number of observations that make up the data set. In Table 1, for example, $N = 13$ for each group, or 26 for the entire data set. Simple as it is, N plays a very important role in more sophisticated statistical analyses.

Measures of Central Tendency It is apparent in Figure 1 that there is a difference in the pattern of scores between the two groups. But how much of a difference? What is the typical value, the *central tendency*, that represents each group's performance? There are three measures that capture this typical value: the mode, the median, and the mean. The *mode* is the value or score that occurs most frequently in the data set. The *median* is the halfway point in a set of data; half the scores fall above the median, and half fall below it. The *mean* is the arithmetic average. To find the mean, add the values of all the scores and divide by the number of scores *(N)*.

Measures of Variability The variability (or spread or dispersion) of a set of data is often just as important as its central tendency. This variability can be quantified

► Statistics can be valuable for describing research results, but critical thinking demands that we evaluate them carefully before drawing conclusions about what they mean. Knowing this pointy-haired executive's tendency toward uncritical thinking, you can bet that Dogbert's impressive-sounding restatement of the definition of median will win him an extension of his pricey consulting contract.

by measures known as the *range* and the *standard deviation.* The range is simply the difference between the highest and the lowest values in a data set. For the data in Table 1, the range for the low-reward group is $9 - 2 = 7$; for the high-reward group, the range is $10 - 3 = 7$. The standard deviation, or SD, describes the average difference between each score and the mean of the data set.

The Normal Distribution   In most subfields in psychology, when researchers collect many measurements and plot their data in histograms, the pattern that results often resembles that shown for the low-reward group in Figure 1. That is, the majority of scores tend to fall in the middle of the distribution, whereas fewer and fewer scores occur as one moves toward the extremes. As more and more data are collected, and as smaller and smaller bins are used (perhaps containing only one value each), the histogram tends to smooth out until it resembles the bell-shaped curve known as the **normal distribution,** or normal curve, which is shown in Figure 2. When a distribution of scores follows a truly normal curve, its mean, median, and mode all have the same value. Furthermore, if the curve is normal, we can use its standard deviation to describe how any particular score stands in relation to the rest of the distribution.

The distribution of IQ scores shown in Figure 2 provides an example. They are distributed in a normal curve, with a mean, median, and mode of 100 and a standard deviation (SD) of 16. In such a distribution, half of the population will have an IQ

FIGURE 2 ■ THE NORMAL DISTRIBUTION

Many kinds of research data approximate the shape of the normal curve, in which most scores fall toward the center of the range.

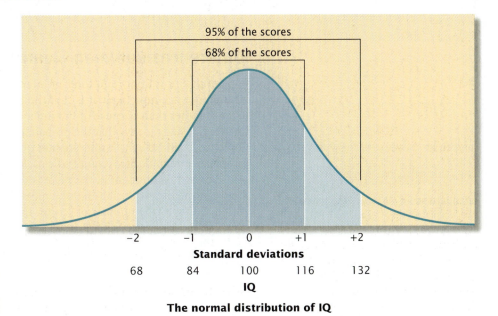

The normal distribution of IQ

normal distribution   A smooth, bell-shaped curve representing a set of data in which most scores occur in the middle of the possible range, with fewer and fewer scores occurring toward the extremes of the range.

above 100, and half will have one below 100. The shape of the true normal curve is such that 68 percent of the area under it lies within 1 standard deviation above and below the mean. In terms of IQ, this means that 68 percent of the population has an IQ somewhere between 84 (100 minus 16) and 116 (100 plus 16). Of the remaining 32 percent of the population, half falls more than 1 SD above the mean, and half falls more than 1 SD below the mean. Thus, 16 percent of the population has an IQ above 116, and 16 percent scores below 84.

The normal curve is also the basis for percentiles. A **percentile** score indicates the percentage of people or observations that fall at or below a given score in a normal distribution. In Figure 2, for example, the mean score (which is also the median) lies at a point below which 50 percent of the scores fall. Thus, the mean of a normal distribution is at the 50th percentile. What does this mean for IQ? If you score 1 SD above the mean, your score is at a point above which only 16 percent of the population falls. This means that 84 percent of the population (100 percent minus 16 percent) must be below that score. So this IQ score is at the 84th percentile. A score at 2 SDs above the mean is at the 97.5 percentile, because 97.5 percent of the scores are below it in a normal distribution.

Scores may also be expressed in terms of their distance in standard deviations from the mean, producing what are called **standard scores.** A standard score of 1.5, for example, is 1.5 standard deviations from the mean.

Inferential Statistics

It can be hard to understand the meaning of research results summarized in descriptive statistics alone. Is a correlation between college grade-point averages and the eating of certain foods large enough to support the hypothesis that diet is important for mental functioning? Is the difference in the effects of two different kinds of psychotherapy large enough to recommend one over the other? The answers to questions such as these are based largely on the results of analyses that use inferential statistics.

Consider again the descriptive statistics from our rewards experiment. They tell us that the performances of the high- and low-reward groups differ, but there is some uncertainty. Is the difference large enough to be important? Does it represent a real effect or a fluke? The researcher would like to have some measure of confidence that the difference between groups did not occur by chance alone. **Inferential statistics** use certain rules to estimate the likelihood that a particular correlation or a particular difference between groups was due to chance. If that likelihood is small enough, the researcher can usually conclude that the correlation or difference is *statistically significant.*

Differences Between Means: The *t* Test

One of the most important tools of inferential statistics is the *t* test. It allows the researcher to ask how likely it is that the difference between two means occurred by chance rather than because of the independent variable. When the *t* test or another inferential statistic says that the probability of chance effects is small enough (usually less than 5 percent), the results are said to be *statistically significant.* Conducting a *t* test of statistical significance requires the use of three descriptive statistics.

The first component of the *t* test is the size of the observed effect, the difference between the means. Recall that the mean is calculated by summing a group's scores and dividing by the number of scores. In the example shown in Table 1, the mean of the high-reward group is 94/13, or 7.23, and the mean of the low-reward group is 65/13, or 5. Thus the difference between the means for the high- and low-reward groups is $7.23 - 5 = 2.23$.

Second, the standard deviation of scores in each group must be known. If the scores in the groups are quite variable, their standard deviations will be large, indicating that chance may have played a large role in producing the results. If the scores

percentile A way of stating what percentage of scores in a data set fall at or below a certain score.

standard score A way of stating how many standard deviations separate a particular score from the mean of all the scores in a data set.

inferential statistics A form of statistical analysis designed to provide a measure of confidence about how likely it is that a certain result appeared by chance.

within each group are all very similar, however, their standard deviations will be small, which suggests that the participants in each group reacted in about the same way to the rewards they were given. Thus, the difference between groups is more likely to be significant when each group's standard deviation is small. In Table 1, some people in the low-reward group actually did better on the math test than some in the high-reward group. If variability is high enough that the scores of two groups overlap, the difference between group means, though large, may not be statistically significant.

Third, we need to take the sample size, N, into account. The larger the number of participants or observations, the more likely it is that a given difference between means is significant. This is so because with larger samples, random factors within a group will have less impact on the group's mean. The unusual performance of a few people who were sleepy or anxious or hostile, for example, will likely be canceled out by the scores of the more representative majority of people. The same effect of sample size can be seen in coin tossing. If you toss a quarter 5 times, you might not be too surprised if heads come up 80 percent of the time. But if you get 80 percent heads after 100 tosses, you might begin to suspect that this is probably not due to chance alone. Some other effect, perhaps some bias in the coin, is probably producing the results. For the same reason, a relatively small correlation coefficient—between diet and grades, say—might be statistically significant if it was based on 50,000 students. As the number of participants increases, it becomes less likely that the correlation reflects the influence of a few oddball cases.

To summarize, as the difference between the means gets larger, as N increases, and as standard deviations get smaller, t increases. This increase in t raises the researcher's confidence in the significance of the difference between means.

Beyond the *t* Test

Many experiments in psychology are considerably more complex than simple comparisons between two groups. They often involve three or more experimental and control groups. Some experiments also include more than one independent variable. For example, suppose we were interested not only in the effect of reward size on performance but also in the effect of problem difficulty. We might then create six groups whose members would perform easy, moderate, or difficult problems under low- or high-reward conditions.

In an experiment like this, the results might be due to the size of the reward, the difficulty of the problem, or the combined effects (known as the *interaction*) of the two. Analyzing the size and source of these effects is typically accomplished through procedures known as *analysis of variance*. The details of analysis of variance are beyond the scope of this book, but note that, as in the *t* test, the statistical significance of each effect is influenced by differences between means, standard deviation, and sample size.

For more detailed information about how analysis of variance and other inferential statistics are used to understand and interpret the results of psychological research, consider taking courses in research methods and statistical or quantitative methods.

Multiple-Choice Self-Test Questions

Chapter 1 ■ Introduction to the Science of Psychology

1A The first research laboratory in psychology was established to study consciousness *(p. 10)*.   **2C** A community psychologist would believe that low-income families who live in crowded conditions are more likely to need mental health services *(p. 5)*.   **3B** Someone who believes that human behavior is influenced by genetic inheritance, unconscious motivations, and environmental influences exemplifies the multiple perspectives of the eclectic approach *(p. 14)*.   **4C** An educational psychologist studies what teachers actually do when they are teaching students to read *(p. 5)*.   **5A** Behaviorists say that people think and behave in ways that have previously been rewarded *(pp. 12–13)*.   **6C** In collectivist cultures, people tend to think of themselves as part of a family or work group *(p. 18)*.   **7D** Recognition of a smile is a behavior that cross-cultural psychologists find to be similar around the world *(p. 19)*.   **8D** "What am I being asked to believe or accept?" is the first of five critical thinking questions discussed in this chapter *(pp. 22–23)*.   **9D** An operational definition defines a variable so that it can be measured. In this case the score on the mood survey is the operational definition of mood *(p. 24)*.   **10C** Case studies are used to collect descriptive data *(pp. 26–27)*.   **11D** Before using survey results to support a hypothesis, we must be sure that the questions are properly worded, the sample used is representative of the population of interest, and the responses are not biased by efforts to appear "socially acceptable" *(pp. 27–28)*.   **12A** When research results are statistically significant it means that the probability that the results occurred by chance is extremely small *(pp. 38–39)*.   **13D** To avoid the possibility that experimenter bias may confound the results of an experiment aimed at testing a hypothesis, a researcher should use a double-blind study *(pp. 33–34)*.   **14A** In an experiment, the outcome behavior being measured (such as memory) is the dependent variable *(p. 31)*.   **15B** In an experiment, the group that receives the "treatment" or intervention is the experimental group *(p. 31)*.   **16B** Using a true experiment to try to scientifically study this problem would pose the greatest ethical problems for Jose because it is not ethical to purposely create abusive conditions for children *(pp. 39–40)*.   **17B** The number closest to ±1.00 is the strongest correlation coefficient *(pp. 29–30)*.   **18D** A correlation coefficient can tell us the strength, direction, and existence of a relationship between two variables, but not its cause *(pp. 29–30)*.   **19C** To select participants for a study such as smoking habits of a group of students, you would use a representative sample *(p. 34)*.   **20D** All are good reasons for ethical behavior *(pp. 39–40)*.

Chapter 2 ■ Biology and Behavior

1D The nucleus of a cell provides genetic information, and the mitochondria keep a stable chemical environment *(p. 49)*.   **2C** Malfunctions of serotonin systems contribute to depression, and malfunctions in dopamine systems contribute to Parkinson's disease *(p. 74)*.   **3A** Overactivity of glutamate, which occurs when oxygen is cut off from neurons in the brain, can result in a stroke *(p. 75)*.   **4B** Functional magnetic resonance imaging (fMRI) combines the advantages of PET and MRI and is capable of detecting changes in blood flow and blood oxygen that reflect ongoing changes in the activity of neurons *(pp. 56–57)*.   **5C** The somatic system carries information to and from the central nervous system *(p. 54)*.   **6D** The sympathetic nervous system is less active, and the parasympathetic system is more active, now that Kalli is relaxing *(p. 54)*.   **7A** Some simple behaviors like reflexes occur automatically via the spinal cord and without instructions from the other portion of the central nervous system, the brain *(pp. 55–56)*.   **8A** A neuron's action potential shoots down its axon with greater speed when the axon is coated in myelin *(pp. 50–51)*.   **9A** The medulla, located in the hindbrain, helps to regulate heart rate, blood pressure, and breathing *(p. 61)*.   **10D** If the reticular formation fibers in Lily's hindbrain were damaged, she would go into a coma *(p. 61)*.   **11A** The cerebellum is that part of the hindbrain that controls finely coordinated movements *(p. 62)*.   **12B** Defects in the hippocampus have been found in people with Alzheimer's disease *(p. 64)*.   **13A** The sensory system provides information about the environment *(pp. 53–54)*.   **14C** The sensory cortex in the occipital lobe receives information concerning vision *(p. 65)*.   **15A** Voluntary movements are controlled by neurons in the motor cortex, located in the frontal lobe *(pp. 65–66)*.   **16A** Damage to Broca's area creates difficulties in speaking *(p. 67)*.   **17A** The left hemisphere of the brain is specialized for language *(pp. 67–69)*.   **18A** Brain imaging research reveals that imagining practicing movements causes changes in the motor cortex *(p. 71)*.   **19A** Neurons secrete neurotransmitters across synapses and endocrine organs release hormones into the blood stream *(pp. 51, 77)*.   **20A** Glands release hormones such as cortisol into the bloodstream *(p. 78)*.

Chapter 3 ■ Sensation and Perception

1A Perception is the process of using information and your understanding of the world so that messages from the senses become meaningful experiences *(p. 85)*.   **2B** Transduction is the process of converting incoming energy into neural activities *(p. 85)*.   **3A** The described procedure defines absolute threshold *(p. 86)*.   **4B** Expecting a stimulus to occur lowers the response criterion *(p. 86)*.   **5B** According to Weber's law, the lighter the objects being compared, the smaller the weight difference needed to detect a change in weight *(pp. 87–88)*.   **6B** When a star is faint, it is more easily seen by looking slightly away from where the star is expected to be *(p. 91)*.   **7D** The trichromatic theory proposes that combining three primary colors can produce any other color *(pp. 93–94)*.   **8A** According to the gate control theory, input from other skin senses can come into the spinal cord at the same time the pain gets there and "take over" the pathways that the pain impulses would have used *(p. 108)*.   **9C** Constant loud noise causes hair cell damage, literally ripping off hair cells from his inner ear, resulting in nerve deafness *(p. 99)*.   **10D** Unlike other senses, our sense of smell does not send its messages through the thalamus *(pp. 103–104)*.   **11A** Your blind spot is located where the optic nerve leaves the eyeball (p. 92). **12D** Nutritional state and temperature can both contribute to food's flavor (p. 102). **13C** The Stroop task is difficult because one must divide attention between the meaning of the word and the color of the word. Without knowing the meaning of the word, there is no divided attention (p. 130). **14A** Kinesthesia gives us knowledge of the position of our body parts (p. 106). **15B** Stroboscopic motion is an illusion in which lights or images flashed in rapid succession are perceived as moving (p. 118). **16B** People moving at the same speed, in a sense having a "common fate," are perceived as a group (p. 115). **17B** Interposition is the depth perception cue that operates on this basis (p. 116). **18B** Looming is a motion cue such that objects increasingly fill the retinal space as they get closer (p. 118). **19B** Bottom-up processing involves basic sensory feature analysis, including the sensation of changes in salt level (p. 123). **20A** Covert orienting involves a shift of attention that isn't easily observed (pp. 128–129).

Chapter 4 ■ Consciousness

1A Mental processing of bodily processes, such as the brain regulating blood pressure, occur at the nonconscious level, and some people are able to learn to control these processes through biofeedback (p. 139). **2C** Dr. Eplort will most likely sleep about the same as he did before (p. 149). **3C** Zandra's preference for the Rembrandt paintings was most likely affected by priming (p. 141). **4B** Edie's success depends on her expectation that the messages will help her (pp. 141–142). **5D** Mitch's responses to marijuana were most likely due to learned expectations (p. 159). **6C** Leroy was most likely in stage 4 sleep, the deepest stage of slow-wave sleep (p. 145). **7C** Alan is most likely suffering from REM behavior disorder, a condition that allows dreams to be acted out (p. 148). **8A** SIDS (sudden infant death syndrome) has been greatly reduced in the United States by the "back to sleep" program, which advises parents to have their babies sleep face up (p. 148). **9B** Disruptions of your circadian rhythm can make you grouchy and less productive. Melatonin has been used to maintain these circadian rhythms (p.150). **10C** It is non-REM sleep that researchers believe is important for restoring the body and brain's energy stores for the next day's activity; the other three responses are functions of REM sleep (p. 150). **11D** According to the activation-synthesis theory, dreams are meaningless, random byproducts of REM sleep (p. 153). **12C** People susceptible to hypnosis are able to focus and redistribute their attention on the hypnotist (pp. 153–154). **13C** Hypnosis has been used to help people reduce nausea from chemotherapy, surgical bleeding, and pain (p. 155). **14A** Research on meditation has shown that meditators report a decrease in stress-related problems and anxiety (p. 156). **15A** Agonists are drugs that bind to a receptor and mimic the effects of the neurotransmitter that normally fits that receptor (p. 157). **16A** Drug tolerance is a condition in which increasingly larger drug doses are required to produce the same effect (p. 158). **17D** Since alcohol's physiological effects involve dopamine, dopamine agonists can reduce cravings and withdrawal effects (pp. 159–161). **18C** Caffeine is a stimulant, which does not cause hallucinations (p. 162). **19B** Opiates relieve pain and cause sleep (p. 163). **20B** Marijuana disrupts memory function and reduces creativity (pp. 164–165).

Chapter 5 ■ Learning

1C The expression "Once burned, twice shy" reflects a change in knowledge (or behavior) due to experience (p. 172). **2B** After repeated pairings with a stimulus that already triggers a reflexive response, the conditioned stimulus alone elicits the reflexive-like response (pp. 174–175).

3B Extinction is the gradual disappearance of a conditioned response when the UCS is eliminated (p. 175). **4A** The law of effect predicts that Kim will be more likely to date Brad because he is associated with a positive outcome, her enjoyment of the movie (p. 181). **5D** Najla has developed a phobia through classical conditioning (pp. 178–180). **6A** The idea that knowledge is located in many areas throughout the brain rather than in one particular place is a basic assumption of neural network theories (p. 191). **7A** Stimulus generalization is a process in which a conditioned response is triggered by stimuli similar to the original conditioned stimulus (pp. 175–176). **8C** For survival reasons, people are biologically prepared to link taste signals with illness (p. 177). **9A** Extinction occurs because the behavior is no longer being rewarded (p. 175). **10B** Operant conditioning involves learning that behaviors have consequences (pp. 181–182). **11B** Negative reinforcement strengthens behavior that is followed by the removal of an unpleasant event or stimulus (p. 182). **12B** Once avoidance conditioning is learned, avoidance can be a difficult habit to break (pp. 182–184). **13D** A discriminative conditioned stimulus signals that a reward will occur if a certain response is given (p. 184). **14D** Shaping is the process of reinforcing successive approximations to the target behavior (p. 185). **15B** Jamey must exhibit a fixed number of behaviors while Susan must work a variable amount of time (p. 187). **16D** They are all problems with using punishment (pp. 189–191). **17B** Learned helplessness occurs when people learn they are unable to control circumstances or outcomes (p. 194). **18C** Latent learning is learning that is not demonstrated when it is first learned (pp. 195–196). **19D** Najla has learned from the experience of watching others pet a dog (p. 198). **5C** Group work is not really helpful for everything. Practice is. It's more likely to be active learning. (pp. 202–203).

Chapter 6 ■ Memory

1A Acoustic codes represent information as sequences of sounds, such as a tune or a rhyme (p. 211). **2B** Episodic memory is a person's recall of a specific event that happened while that person was present; explicit memory involves the processes through which people try to remember something (p. 212). **3C** Implicit memories are not purposefully recalled but do influence behavior (p. 212). **4B** Maintenance rehearsal is a method of keeping information in short-term memory by repeating it (p. 213). **5B** The transfer-appropriate processing model of memory suggests that a critical factor in memory is how the encoding process matches up with what is later retrieved (p. 213). **6C** Selective attention allows Reepal to focus on the most important information (p. 216). **7B** Unrehearsed information stays in short-term memory for about eighteen seconds (p. 218). **8A** Chunking involves grouping information into meaningful units that can be stored (pp. 217–218). **9C** Semantic memory contains general knowledge not linked to a specific event (pp. 222–224). **10C** Ebbinghaus found that most forgetting occurs during the first nine hours after learning, and especially during the first hour (p. 230). **11D** The serial position curve predicts that first items (primacy effect) and last items (recency effect) will be best remembered.(p. 220). **12A** State-dependent memory is memory that is helped or hindered by similarities or differences in a person's internal state during learning versus recall (p. 222). **13C** The tip-of-the-tongue phenomenon represents the retrieval of incomplete knowledge (pp. 223–224). **14C** In the process of constructive memory, people use generalized knowledge, or schemas, to fill in gaps in the information they encode and retrieve (pp. 224–225). **15C** Recent use of DNA evidence has revealed that many people in prison for serious crimes did not commit those crimes (pp. 227–229). **16C** As Ebbinghaus discovered, relearning takes much less time than original learning. This difference represents the savings from one learning to the next learning (pp. 231–232). **17C** Proactive inhibition occurs when old information disrupts the learning of new information *(p. 231)*. **18A** Spontaneous generalizations are produced by PDP networks *(p. 226)*. **19B** Anterograde amnesia is the inability to form new long-term memories following a brain injury *(p. 237)*. **20A** The method of loci involves mentally placing objects in various spots in a familiar location (locus) *(p. 239)*.

Chapter 7 ■ Thought, Language, and Intelligence

1D Thinking is part of an information processing system that manipulates mental representations *(p. 249)*. **2C** A natural concept has no fixed set of defining characteristics but a prototype possesses most of its characteristic features *(p. 251)*. **3B** Basing his strategy on an algorithm would require Clint to evaluate every possible move and countermove *(p. 255)*. **4D** Scripts are mental representations of familiar sequences of activity *(p. 253)*. **5B** Setting aside a difficult problem, hoping for a solution to occur while working on something else, is called incubation *(p. 258)*. **6D** Functional fixedness occurs when a person fails to use a familiar object in a novel way to solve a problem *(pp. 261–262)*. **7C** Confirmation bias is a strong tendency to confirm rather than refute the preferred hypothesis, even in the face of strong evidence against the hypothesis *(pp. 262–263)*. **8A** The gambler's fallacy has led Richard to believe that the probability of a random event will change over time *(p. 268)*. **9C** Incorrect words or word endings are not likely to have been reinforced. They are overgeneralizations of a language rule the child has learned *(pp. 271–273)*. **10A** A critical period is a limited window of opportunity for language learning. If the critical period is missed, normal language development will not occur *(p. 273)*. **11A** Alfred Binet designed the first IQ test to identify children with special educational needs *(p. 275)*. **12D** Formal reasoning is based on the rules of logic *(p. 255)*. **13B** The average score obtained by people at each age level is assigned the IQ value of 100 with half of the scores lower than 100 and half higher than 100 *(p. 277)*. **14C** If the scores from this pre-employment test predict future performance on the job, the test is statistically valid for the purpose of employee selection *(p. 279)*. **15A** A statistically reliable test yields consistent and stable scores over time *(p. 278)*. **16A** IQ tests appear to be most valid for assessing aspects of intelligence that are related to school work *(p. 279)*. **17D** The highest correlation is likely to be found between the identical twins' scores *(pp. 279–280)*. **18A** Individuals with mild mental retardation will have most difficulty with academic material and abstract reasoning but are able to learn new material *(pp. 289–290)*. **19A** This test was most likely based on Sternberg's triarchic theory of intelligence which proposes three types of intelligences: creative, analytic, and practical *(p. 286)*. **20A** Creative people are internally motivated, have a set of creative skills, use divergent thinking, and have expertise in the field of pursuit *(pp. 265–266)*.

Chapter 8 ■ Motivation and Emotion

1B The evolutionary approach suggests that adaptive behaviors that promote the survival of the species reflect inborn motivations to pass on genes *(p. 380)*. **2A** Homeostasis is the tendency to maintain physiological systems at a steady, stable level by adjusting to changes *(p. 300)*. **3D** Arousal theory states that people are motivated to behave in ways that maintain an individual, optimal level of arousal *(pp. 300–301)*. **4B** Incentive theory states that behavior is goal directed to obtain positive stimuli and avoid negative stimuli *(p. 302)*. **5A** When stimulated, the ventromedial nucleus tells Ahmed that there is no need

to eat *(p. 304)*. **6B** Research shows that we tend to eat less when given only one food than when given several choices of food *(p. 305)*. **7B** Although bulimics can maintain normal weight, they may experience dehydration and other symptoms *(p. 309)*. **8C** The Chicago survey found that people in the United States have sex less frequently and with fewer partners than was earlier believed *(pp. 310–311)*. **9D** According to the Thinking Critically section of this chapter, sexual orientation is most likely influenced by prenatal hormones, genetic factors and sociocultural learning *(pp. 314–316)*. **10B** Edwina will encourage her son to try difficult tasks, praise his efforts, and help him learn from his mistakes *(p. 318)*. **11B** Studies have shown that allowing people to set and achieve clear goals is one way to increase job performance *(p. 319)*. **12A** Physiological needs, including those for food and water, come first in Maslow's hierarchy *(p. 321)*. **13C** an approach-avoidance conflict arises when we must decide whether to do something that has both positive and negative consequences. *(p. 322)*. **14C** Emotions can vary in intensity from ecstatic to mildly disappointed *(p. 324)*. **15A** James's theory states that we experience emotions only by perceiving our physiological response to an event *(p. 328)*. **16D** Excitation transfer occurs when arousal from an experience carries over to a different situation. This is consistent with Schachter's theory of emotion *(p. 332)*. **17B** Cannon's theory maintains that emotional experience originates in the thalamus and simultaneously triggers physiological arousal and cognitive awareness *(pp. 330–331)*. **18D** As children grow up, they learn an emotional culture, which are rules that govern what emotions are appropriate, in what situations, and what expressions are allowed *(p. 336)*. **19B** Human emotions are communicated mainly through facial movements and expressions *(p. 325)*. **20B** In allowing Diane's emotional state to guide his behavior, Sam is using social referencing *(p. 337)*.

Chapter 9 ■ Human Development

1B Behavioral genetics is concerned with the differences between groups of individuals, not with the characteristics of a single individual *(p. 346)*. **2C** Smokers' babies are usually underweight *(p. 349)*. **3D** Tyrone's physical development is the result of maturation and environmental influences *(p. 346)*. **4D** Newborns visually prefer novelty and shapes that resemble human faces *(p. 350)*. **5C** With normal brain development, grasping and rooting reflexes should have disappeared by 6 months of age *(p. 350)*. **6A** Assimilation is the process of taking in information that adds to an existing schema *(p. 352)*. **7B** Adriana is probably four to six years old; she is in the preoperational stage *(pp. 354–355)*. **8B** Babies stare longer when they see events that violate their expectations about other people's beliefs. *(pp. 353–354)*. **9B** We are unlikely to recall anything about our first year due to infantile amnesia *(p. 359)*. **10B** Difficult babies tend to remain difficult into childhood *(p. 364)*. **11B** Harlow's attachment studies demonstrate that infant monkeys form attachments based on contact comfort needs *(pp. 364–365)*. **12D** With ambivalent insecure attachment, the child sometimes prefers and sometimes rejects the primary caregiver *(pp. 364–365)*. **13C** Authoritative parents are sympathetic but firm; permissive parents give lots of freedom *(p. 369)*. **14A** Girls tend to speak and write earlier and are able to read emotional signals at younger ages than boys *(p. 372)*. **15C** Ludmilla is still confused about her identity *(p. 375)*. **16D** Teens who have sex tend to have parents who are less educated and less likely to exert control over them than teens who do not have sex *(p. 376)*. **17A** People at the Stage 1 (preconventional) level of moral reasoning are concerned with avoiding punishment *(p. 376)*. **18C** These changes occur mainly in middle adulthood *(pp. 380–381)*. **19C** Up until at least age sixty, people's thinking becomes dialectical, which means they understand that knowledge is relative, not absolute *(p. 381)*. **20B** Terminal drop is the decline in mental functioning that occurs in the months or years preceding death *(p. 386)*.

Chapter 10 ■ Health, Stress, and Coping

1C Your great-grandparents' generation was most likely to die from infectious diseases, whereas your own generation is most likely to die from chronic diseases (p. 397). **2A** The more stressors Lila has, the more physical, psychological, and behavioral responses she will probably experience (p. 398). **3D** Daily hassles involve irritations, pressures, and annoyances that may not be major stressors by themselves but whose effects add up to become significant (pp. 399–400). **4A** The first stage of the GAS, the alarm reaction, involves some version of the fight-or-flight syndrome (p. 407). **5C** Males under stress tended to get angry, avoid stressors, or both, whereas females are more likely to help others and to make use of their social support network (p. 411). **6B** Rumination is continuously thinking about negative events and it tends to intensify negative emotional states (p. 403). **7B** Catastrophizing involves the exaggeration of negative consequences (p. 403). **8B** People with disease-resistant personalities tend to think of stressors as temporary challenges to be overcome, not catastrophic threats (p. 410). **9B** Flashbacks are associated with posttraumatic stress disorder (pp. 404–405). **10C** Emotion-focused coping strategies include denial and avoidance (pp. 407–408). **11C** Perceived control over stressful events helps reduce their negative effects (p. 407). **12B** Laton is trying to improve the employees' social support (p. 408). **13B** People who are impulsive or low on conscientiousness are more likely to die from accidents or violence (p. 411). **14C** Natural killer cells of the immune system have antiviral properties and help prevent tumors (p. 413). **15B** Hostility is a risk factor in heart disease (pp. 415–416). **16D** Social support is a mediating factor on stress (pp. 418–419). **17A** Personalizing the risk of danger to the individual should increase the likelihood of behavioral change (pp. 416–417). **18B** Being aware of a problem behavior and thinking about changing it occur during the contemplation stage of readiness to alter a health-related behavior (p. 417). **19A** Sayumi is using the coping strategy of cognitive restructuring, or changing her thinking about an event or person (p. 418). **20C** Progressive relaxation trains a person to physically relax muscles, thus reducing heart rate and blood pressure (p. 419).

Chapter 11 ■ Personality

1B Personality is defined as a person's unique pattern of enduring psychological and behavioral characteristics (p. 426). **2A** The id contains the life and death instincts, is impulsive and pleasure seeking (p. 427). **3D** During the latency period, which lasts from about age five until puberty, an individual's focus is on education and social development (p. 429). **4B** Object relations theory sees today's problems as reflecting the impact of early relationships with caregivers and other significant people in a child's life (p. 428). **5A** Oscar's belief reflects an independent self system often seen in individualist cultures (p. 429). **6D** Although based on a small, culturally biased sample and not scientifically derived, Freud's theory is comprehensive and has profoundly affected psychology (p. 431). **7B** Trait theory assumes that personality traits are relatively stable, consistent, and predictable (p. 432). **8C** Allport believed that personality can be described using about seven central traits (pp. 433–434). **9D** Trait theorists have identified five (called "the five factor") main factors that make up personality (p. 434). **10C** According to Gray, people with an active behavioral approach system tend to experience positive emotions (p. 436). **11B** Twin studies suggest that there are genetic predispositions toward particular personality traits and temperament (p. 437). **12A** Internals expect outcomes and events to be controlled mainly by their own efforts (p. 440). **13C** Reciprocal determinism is a mutually influential interaction among cognitive patterns, the environment, and behavior (p. 440). **14D** According to Mischel, person variables and situation variables are important in explaining particular behaviors (pp. 441–442). **15C** Social-cognitive theories describe personality as patterns of thought and behavior that are learned though experience in social situations (p. 439). **16C** Conditions of worth are created when "people" are evaluated instead of their behavior (p. 443). **17B** A preoccupation with perceived need for material things and a devaluation of what one does have, reflects a deficiency orientation (p. 444). **18D** Unconscious needs, motives, and conflicts supposedly guide responses to the relatively unstructured stimuli of projective personality measures (p. 450). **19C** Research has found that those rated as ill-tempered as children are more likely to be aggressive in adulthood (pp. 449–450). **20B** Nonprojective personality measures are often used by potential employers to screen out employees who are likely to be unreliable or dishonest (p. 454).

Chapter 12 ■ Psychological Disorders

1C Approximately 48 percent of the population in the United States have experienced a mental disorder at some point in their lives (p. 462). **2C** The practical approach defines abnormality based on the content, context, and consequence of behavior (p. 463). **3C** To be found not guilty by reason of insanity, they jury would have to find that Herman was insane at the time he committed the crime (p. 501). **4D** The diathesis-stress approach attributes abnormal behavior to the interaction of stress with biological, environmental, and psychological predispositions (p. 468). **5D** The global assessment of functioning is one evaluation axis of the DSM IV (p. 469). **6D** Social phobias involve anxiety about being criticized by others or acting in a way that is embarrassing or humiliating (p. 474). **7C** OCD involves an obsession with particular thoughts or images, which motivates repetitive, uncontrollable behaviors called compulsions (p. 475). **8A** Conversion disorder involves functional impairment with no physical cause (p. 478). **9A** Severe pain in the absence of any physical problem is symptomatic of somatoform pain disorder (p. 479). **10A** Fugue reaction is disorder that includes a sudden loss of personal memory and the adoption of a new identity in a new place (p. 480). **11B** Sleep changes and weight gain or loss are typical of major depression (p. 483). **12B** Depressed women, certain ethnic groups, males over forty-five and living alone, and those who talk about suicide do tend to be at elevated risk for committing suicide (p. 484). **13A** Attribution is the process of explaining the causes of one's own and other's behavior; social-cognitive theorists see a depressive attributional style as partly responsible for depression (p. 488). **14B** Schizophrenia is characterized by abnormality in thinking, writing, speaking, affect, perception and attention, and personal identity. Positive symptoms are undesirable additions to a person's mental life (p. 489). **15D** Strong and long-lasting anxiety that is not focused on any particular object or situation marks generalized anxiety disorder (p. 475). **16C** The most common symptoms of paranoid schizophrenia include delusions of grandeur or persecution, which are often accompanied by anger, anxiety, or jealousy (p. 490). **17A** People diagnosed with antisocial personality disorder display impulsive, selfish, unscrupulous behavior and have few morals or deep feelings for others (p. 494). **18D** The more violent forms of antisocial personality disorder are associated with the experience of abuse in childhood (p. 496). **19D** Studies have shown that genetics and what people learn in their social and cultural environment play a role in alcoholism (p. 500). **20B** Children with autistic disorder usually show little attachment, poor eye contact, and asocial behavior (p. 498).

Chapter 13 ■ Treatment of Psychological Disorders

1C As a part of psychodynamic therapy, the client reports all feelings, thoughts, memories, and images that come to mind in free association (*p. 512*). **2A** Gestalt therapy uses role playing, among other techniques, to help clients become more self-aware and self-accepting (*p. 516*). **3A** Licensed clinical psychologists generally hold a doctoral degree in clinical or counseling psychology (*p. 511*). **4B** Psychoanalysis focuses on revealing and working through unconscious conflicts (*p. 512*). **5C** Client-centered therapists use reflection, a paraphrased summary of the client's words that emphasizes the feelings and meanings that appear to go along with them (*p. 514*). **6B** systematic desensitization therapy is a behavioral method for treating anxiety in which clients visualize a graduated series of anxiety-provoking stimuli while remaining relaxed (*p. 518*). **7C** By paraphrasing what Shanobi has said, her friend is responding in a manner consistent with reflection (*p. 515*). **8D** Psychodynamic therapists seek to help clients gain insight by recognizing and understanding unconscious thoughts and emotions (*p. 512*). **9C** Behavioral therapists see compulsive behaviors as learned habits (*p. 517*). **10B** Although there is much controversy about the effectiveness of therapy, there are therapies that have been empirically found to help clients. And over all, those seeking therapy get better more often than those who do not (*pp. 527–528*). **11C** Confidentiality is a critical aspect of therapy that can be violated only under special circumstances, as when the therapist believes the client's life is in danger (*p. 533*). **12B** Community psychologists are concerned with promoting social changes that prevent psychological problems (*pp. 540–541*). **13A** Flooding is a behavior therapy technique that places a client in a feared but harmless situation to extinguish the fear (*p. 519*). **14D** Cognitive restructuring, which is a part of cognitive behavior therapy seeks to replace stress-producing thoughts with more constructive ones. (*p. 522*). **15B** ECT involves passing electric current through the brain to treat depression when other treatments have failed (*p. 533*). **16D** Therapeutic psychoactive drugs may alter the functioning of particular neurotransmitter systems but they cannot change the type of neurotransmitters released into the brain (*p. 534*). **17A** One of the most important elements of success with any therapy is the client-therapist relationship, which involves trust, disclosure, and empathy (*p. 530*). **18C** Neuroleptics are those that can reduce psychotic symptoms but some of these drugs can cause severe side effects (*p. 534*). **19B** Anxiolytics are drugs that reduce anxiety and tension (*p. 536*). **20C** Simultaneous treatment of several clients has many positive features, but client improvement is not more rapid with this technique than with others (*p. 523*).

Chapter 14 ■ Social Psychology

1B Jack is experiencing relative deprivation, comparing himself to others around him (*p. 549*). **2A** An experiment conducted by Greenberg et al. revealed that participants were significantly less upset by an anxiety-provoking experience if they had first received esteem-building feedback about their previous test performance (*p. 550*). **3B** The first impression is formed quickly and is difficult to change (*pp. 552*). **4C** The change in her date's behavior was probably due to a self-fulfilling prophecy (*p. 554*). **5D** A self-serving bias is the tendency to take credit for success and blame external causes for failures (*p. 556*). **6C** Richard will more likely be persuaded by evidence from the presenter (central route) since he is personally involved in the content of the presenter's message (*p. 558*). **7B** The amount of money Matteus received was too small to justify lying about what he thought about the lecture, so he changed his attitude toward the lecture, thus making his attitude consistent with his behavior (*p. 559*). **8C** The contact hypothesis suggests that stereotypes and prejudices can be reduced through cooperation and interdependence (*p. 563*). **9B** People tend to like others who have attitudes similar to their own, especially attitudes about other people (*p. 564*). **10A** Intimacy, commitment, and passion are characteristic of consummate love (*p. 566*). **11D** A particularly powerful norm is reciprocity, the tendency to respond to others as they have acted toward you (*p. 568*). **12B** Deindividuation occurs when people in a group temporarily lose their individuality and behave in ways they otherwise would not (*p. 569*). **13C** Shawn is exhibiting social loafing by not putting in as much effort as other group members (*p. 589*). **14A** Conformity results from unspoken group pressure (*p. 569*). **15B** Colleen used the door-in-the-face procedure, first asking for an unrealistic favor, then a smaller one (*p. 572*). **16D** The gender of the person giving the order is not a major factor determining whether someone will obey the order (*p. 575*). **17A** According to frustration-aggression hypothesis, frustration produces a readiness to respond aggressively, which can later be environmentally triggered (*p. 580*). **18A** The presence of others actually tends to suppress helping behavior so the fewer people who witness Lenora's fall, the better chance she will have that one of them will help her (*p. 585*). **19B** According to the evolutionary view, people display helping behaviors to improve the chances that some of their genes will survive in future generations (*p. 586*). **20B** Groupthink impairs a group's ability to realistically evaluate options and their own decisions (*p. 590*).

Chapter 15 ■ Industrial and Organizational Psychology

1A I/O psychologists conduct research on behavior and mental processes in the workplace (*p. 600*). **2C** The information from a job analysis of the position is used to guide decisions about whom to hire (*p. 602*). **3A** A job-oriented approach describes the tasks involved in doing a job (*p. 602*). **4B** A job analysis identifies the KSAOs required for a specific position (*pp. 603–604*). **5C** KSAOs are attributes or characteristics necessary to successfully perform a job (*p. 602*). **6C** Research has consistently shown that structured interviews are far more effective than unstructured interviews in leading to good hiring decisions (*p. 604*). **7A** Assessment centers are used primarily to determine an individual's suitability for a position and are often used to hire or promote managers (*p. 604*). **8D** Performance appraisals are used for all of these purposes (*pp. 606–607*). **9C** A theoretical criterion is a general statement of what we mean by good or poor performance (*p. 605*). **10A** Subjective measures of job performance take the form of judgments about various aspects of an employee's work (*p. 606*). **11C** A critical incident provides an example of what is considered to be effective or ineffective behavior by an employee (*p. 607*). **12B** The most valuable training programs are those that teach knowledge or skills that can be applied or transferred to the workplace (*p. 612*). **13C** Massed training is less expensive and disruptive to employees' work schedules but people do not retain as much after massed training as they do after distributed or distributed training (*p. 613*). **14B** I/O psychologists usually conduct a training needs assessment, design the training, and evaluate the training but do not usually deliver the training (*p. 611*). **15D** In Maslow's theory the need for water is a physiological need; in Alderfer's theory it is an existence need (*p. 615*). **16B** The facet approach to job satisfaction presumes that employees can be satisfied with some aspects of their jobs, but dissatisfied with others (*p. 616*). **17B** Knowing that salary and pay raise decisions are made in a fair way can be more important to job satisfaction than to the amount of money employees receive (*p. 618*). **18A** Employees steal more from their employers than do shoplifters (*p. 621*). **19B** A work team is a special kind of workgroup in which the members' activities depend on one another; each person has a specialized task, and everyone is working toward a common goal *(p. 625).* **20A** Leader-member exchange theory suggests that most leaders tend to adopt different styles with different kinds of subordinates *(p. 627).*

Chapter 16 ■ Neuropsychology

1A The experimental neuropsychologist's aim is to add to our knowledge of brain functioning among people in general, whereas the clinical neuropsychologist's aim is to use this knowledge to try to understand the problems that appear in particular individuals *(p. 637).* **2C** Phrenology originated from the idea that particular brain areas, indicated by corresponding bumps in the skull just above them, controlled particular aspects of mental life *(p. 638).* **3B** Broca's area was identified when people experiencing language difficulties were found to have left frontal brain lesions *(p. 639).* **4A** Lesion analysis is research conducted by experimental neuropsychologists in an attempt to understand localization of function by looking at the results of brain damage *(p. 640).* **5A** The neuropsychologist evaluating Damian will most likely give him a battery of psychometric tests and compare his scores to established norms *(p. 637).* **6C** A cardiovascular accident is the loss of blood supply to some part of the brain, resulting in disruption of some aspect of behavior or mental processes *(pp. 643–644).* **7D** Neurodegenerative disease affects a particular kind of brain cell, or cells in a particular part of the brain, causing them to be the first to stop working properly *(pp. 644–645).* **8D** Patients with Korsakoff's syndrome are prone to creating false memories *(p. 647).* **9B** People with delirium enter alternating periods of abnormally impaired consciousness and abnormally elevated levels of consciousness *(p. 648).* **10C** Anosognosia is a disorder of consciousness in which a person has difficulty becoming aware of the loss of neurological function *(p. 649).* **11C** The pathway leading toward the ventrolateral temporal lobe has been called the "what" system because the cortical regions along this pathway help us to decide what it is that we are seeing *(p. 651).* **12D** Prosopagnosia is a condition in which a person can no longer recognize faces, even their own *(p. 652).* **13A** Hemineglect is a condition, usually occurring after a cardiovascular accident, that involves difficulty in seeing, responding to, or acting on information coming from either the right, or more often, the left side of the world *(p. 652).* **14A** In the study cited, patients exhibiting hemineglect were not found to have visual deficits that explained their symptoms *(pp. 652–653).* **15B** People who suffer damage to Broca's area display Broca's aphasia, which is seen mainly in the loss of language fluency *(pp. 654–655).* **16A** People with Wernicke's aphasia can still speak fluently and effortlessly, but what they say sounds like gibberish *(p. 655).* **17C** Alexia without agraphia is a neurological deficit in which people have difficulty reading the letters that they themselves wrote *(p. 640).* **18D** Alfreda is most likely experiencing aprosodia, a condition whereby she has lost the ability to use tone of voice to express meaning *(p. 656).* **19A** Dementia is a neuropsychological disorder in which there are significant and disruptive impairments in memory, as well as in perceptual ability, language, or learned motor skills *(p. 657).* **20C** Research on Alzheimer's disease has found that patient's with Alzheimer's have a different brain pathology than those experiencing normal aging *(p. 658).*

The questions at the bottom of each chapter's In Review charts are listed here, followed in parentheses by the correct answers. The questions are grouped under each chapter's title and by the name and page number of the In Review chart in which they appear. The answer key for the optional Industrial and Organizational Psychology and Neuropsychology chapters appears in blue.

Chapter 1 ▬ Introduction to the Science of Psychology

The Development of Psychology (p. 13)

1. Darwin's theory of evolution had an especially strong influence on _____ism and _____ism. (*functionalism; behaviorism*)
2. Which school of psychological thought was founded by a European medical doctor? _____ (*Psychoanalysis*)
3. In the history of psychology, _____ was the first school of thought to appear. (*structuralism*)

Approaches to Psychology (p. 17)

1. Teaching people to be less afraid of heights reflects the _____ approach. (*behavioral*)
2. Charles Darwin was not a psychologist, but his work influenced the _____ approach to psychology. (*evolutionary*)
3. Assuming that people inherit mental disorders suggests a _____ approach. (*biological*)

Methods of Psychology (p. 35)

1. The _____ method is most likely to use a double-blind design. (*experimental*)
2. Research on a new treatment method is most likely to begin with _____. (*case studies*)
3. Studying language by listening to people in public places is an example of _____ research. (*naturalistic observation*)

Chapter 2 ▬ Biology and Behavior

Neurons, Neurotransmitters, and Receptors (p. 52)

1. For one neuron to communicate with another, a _____ has to cross the _____ between them. (*neurotransmitter; synapse*)
2. The nervous system's main functions are to _____, _____, and _____ information. (*receive; process; act on*)
3. The two main types of cells in the nervous system are _____ and _____. (*neurons; glial cells*)

Organization of the Brain (p. 66)

1. The oldest part of the brain is the _____. (*hindbrain*)
2. Cells that operate as the body's twenty-four-hour "time clock" are found in the _____. (*hypothalamus*)

3. Memory problems seen in Alzheimer's disease are related to shrinkage of the _____ (*hippocampus*)

Classes of Neurotransmitters (p. 76)

1. The main neurotransmitter for slowing, or inhibiting, brain activity is _____. (*GABA*)
2. A group of neurons that use the same neurotransmitter is called a _____. (*neurotransmitter system*)
3. Which neurotransmitter's activity causes brain damage during a stroke? _____ (*glutamate*)

Chapter 3 ▬ Sensation and Perception

Seeing (p. 95)

1. The ability to see in very dim light, depends on photoreceptors called _____. (*rods*)
2. Color afterimages are best explained by the _____ theory of color vision. (*opponent-process*)
3. Nearsightedness and farsightedness occur when images are not focused on the eye's _____. (*retina*)

Hearing (p. 101)

1. Sound energy is converted to neural activity in an inner ear structure called the _____. (*cochlea [or basilar membrane]*)
2. Hearing loss due to damage to hair cells or the auditory nerve is called _____. (*nerve deafness*)
3. How high or low a sound sounds is called _____ and is determined by the _____ of a sound wave. (*pitch; frequency*)

Smell and Taste (p. 105)

1. The flavor of food arises from a combination of _____ and _____. (*taste; smell*)
2. Emotion and memory are linked especially closely to our sense of _____. (*smell*)
3. Perfume ads suggest that humans are affected by _____ that increase sexual attraction. (*pheromones*)

Body Senses (p. 112)

1. Gate control theory offers an explanation of why we sometimes do not feel _____. (*pain*)
2. Professional dancers look at the same spot as long as possible during repeated spins. They are trying to avoid the dizziness caused when the sense of _____ is overstimulated. (*equilibrium*)
3. Without your sense of _____, you would not be able to swallow food without choking. (*touch*)

Principles of Perceptual Organization and Constancy (p. 121)

1. The movement we see in movies, videos, and DVDs is due to a perceptual illusion called _____. *(the stroboscopic illusion)*
2. People who have lost an eye also lose the depth cue called _____. *(retinal disparity)*
3. The grouping principle of _____ allows you to identify objects seen through a picket fence. *(closure)*

Mechanisms of Pattern Recognition (p. 125)

1. Your ability to read a battered old sign that has some letters missing is a result of _____ processing. *(top-down)*
2. When stimulus features match the stimuli we are looking for, _____ takes place. *(recognition)*
3. Schemas can create a _____ that makes us more likely to perceive stimuli in a particular way. *(perceptual set)*

Chapter 4 ■ Consciousness

Sleep and Sleep Disorders (p. 152)

1. Jet lag occurs because of a disruption in a traveler's _____. *(circadian rhythms [or sleep-wake cycle])*
2. The importance of non-REM sleep is suggested by its appearance _____ in the night. *(early)*
3. The safest sleeping position for babies is _____. *(face up)*

Major Classes of Psychoactive Drugs (p. 165)

1. Physical dependence on a drug is a condition more commonly known as _____. *(addiction)*
2. Drugs that act as antagonists _____ the interaction of neurotransmitters and receptors. *(block)*
3. Drug effects are determined partly by what we learn to _____ the effects to be. *(expect)*

Chapter 5 ■ Learning

Basic Processes of Classical Conditioning (p. 179)

1. If your conditioned fear of spiders is triggered by the sight of other creatures that look like spiders, you are demonstrating stimulus _____. *(generalization)*
2. Because of _____, we are more likely to learn a fear of snakes than a fear of cars. *(biopreparedness)*
3. Feeling sad upon hearing a song associated with a long-lost relationship illustrates _____. *(spontaneous recovery)*

Reinforcement and Punishment (p. 192)

1. Taking an aspirin can relieve headache pain, so people learn to do so through the process of _____ reinforcement. *(negative)*
2. The "walk" sign that tells people it is safe to cross the street is an example of a _____ stimulus. *(discriminative conditioned)*
3. Response rates tend to be higher under _____ schedules of reinforcement than under _____ schedules. *(ratio; interval)*

Chapter 6 ■ Memory

Models of Memory (p. 215)

1. The value of elaborative rehearsal over maintenance rehearsal has been cited as evidence for the _____ model of memory. *(levels-of-processing)*

2. Deliberately trying to remember something means using your _____ memory. *(explicit)*
3. Playing the piano uses _____ memory. *(procedural)*

Storing New Memories (p. 221)

1. If you looked up a phone number but forgot it before you could call it, the information was probably lost from _____ memory. *(short-term)*
2. The capacity of short-term memory is about _____ to _____ items. *(five; nine)*
3. Encoding is usually _____ in short-term memory and _____ in long-term memory. *(acoustic; semantic)*

Factors Affecting Retrieval from Long-Term Memory (p. 223)

1. Stimuli called _____ help you recall information stored in long-term memory. *(retrieval cues)*
2. If it is easier to remember something in the place where you learned it, you have _____ memory. *(context-dependent)*
3. The tendency to remember the last few items in a list is called the _____ effect. *(recency)*

Improving Your Memory (p. 241)

1. Using mnemonic strategies and the PQ4R system to better remember course material are examples of the value of _____ rehearsal. *(elaborative)*
2. "Cramming" illustrates _____ practice that usually leads to _____ long-term retention than _____ practice. *(massed; poorer [or less]; distributed)*
3. To minimize forgetting, you should review lecture notes _____ after a lecture ends. *(immediately [or as soon as possible])*

Chapter 7 ■ Thought, Language, and Intelligence

Ingredients of Thought (p. 254)

1. Thinking is the manipulation of _____. *(mental representations)*
2. Arguments over what is "fair" occur because "fairness" is a _____ concept. *(natural)*
3. Your _____ of "hotel room" would lead you to expect yours to include a bathroom. *(schema)*

Solving Problems (p. 263)

1. People stranded without water could use their shoes to collect rain, but they may not do so because of an obstacle to problem solving called _____. *(functional fixedness)*
2. Because of the _____ heuristic, once sellers set a value on their house, they may refuse to take much less for it. *(anchoring)*
3. If you tackle a massive problem one small step at a time, you are using an approach called _____. *(decomposition or means-end analysis)*

Influences on IQ (p. 283)

1. Intelligence is influenced by both _____ and _____. *(heredity; environment)*
2. Children living in poverty tend to have _____ IQs than those in middle-class families. *(lower)*
3. IQs of children whose parents encourage learning tend to be _____ than those of children whose parents do not. *(higher)*

Chapter 8 ■ Motivation and Emotion

Theories of Motivation (p. 302)

1. The fact that some people like roller coasters and other scary amusement park rides has been cited as evidence for the _____ theory of motivation. *(optimal arousal)*
2. Evolutionary theories of motivation are modern outgrowths of theories based on _____.
3. The value of incentives can be affected by _____, _____ , and _____ factors. *(physiological [or biological]; cognitive; social)*

Major Factors Controlling Hunger and Eating (p. 309)

1. People may eat when they are "full," suggesting that eating is not controlled by _____ alone. *(hunger)*
2. People with _____ know that they have a problem; those with _____ nervosa tend not to. *(bulimia; anorexia)*
3. The best strategy for lasting weight loss includes regular _____, as well as improved eating habits. *(exercise)*

Theories of Emotion (p. 333)

1. Research showing that there are pleasure centers in the brain has been cited in support of the _____ theory of emotions. *(Cannon-Bard)*
2. The use of polygraphs in lie detection is based on the _____ theory of emotions. *(James-Lange)*
3. The process of attribution is most important to _____ theories of emotions. *(cognitive)*

Chapter 9 ■ Human Development

Milestones of Cognitive Development in Infancy and Childhood (p. 358)

1. Research in cognitive development suggests that children form mental representations _____ than Piaget thought they did. *(earlier)*
2. Recognizing that changing the shape of clay doesn't change the amount of clay is evidence of a cognitive ability called _____. *(conservation)*
3. The appearance of object permanence signals the end of the _____ period. *(sensorimotor)*

Social and Emotional Development During Infancy and Childhood (p. 374)

1. As part of their social development, children learn _____, which tell them what patterns of appearance and behavior are associated with being male or female. *(gender roles)*
2. Teaching children to talk quietly in a restaurant is part of the process called _____. *(socialization)*
3. Strict rules and the threat of punishment are typical of _____ parenting. *(authoritarian)*

Milestones of Adolescence and Adulthood (p. 387)

1. The greatest threat to cognitive abilities in late adulthood is _____ disease. *(Alzheimer's)*
2. Adolescents' _____ identity may be more defining than their national citizenship. *(ethnic)*
3. Not stealing because "I might get caught" reflects the _____ stage of moral reasoning. *(preconventional)*

Chapter 10 ■ Health, Stress, and Coping

Stress Responses and Stress Mediators (p. 412)

1. The friends and family we can depend on to help us deal with stressors are called our _____ network. *(social support)*
2. Fantasizing about winning money is a(n) _____-focused way of coping with financial stress. *(emotion)*
3. Sudden, extreme stressors may cause psychological and behavioral problems known as _____. *(posttraumatic stress disorder)*

Methods for Coping with Stress (p. 419)

1. Catastrophizing thoughts are best overcome through _____ coping strategies. *(cognitive)*
2. The first step in coping with stress is to _____ the sources and effects of your stressors. *(identify)*
3. True or false: It is best to rely on only one good coping strategy. _____ *(False?)*

Chapter 11 ■ Personality

Major Approaches to Personality (p. 446)

1. Tests that measure the Five Factor Model's dimensions of personality are based on the _____ approach to personality. *(trait)*
2. The role of learning is most prominent in the _____ approach to personality. *(social-cognitive)*
3. Object relations and attachment theories are modern variants on _____ personality theories. *(psychodynamic)*

Personality Tests (p. 454)

1. Projective personality measures are based on the _____ approach to personality. *(psychodynamic)*
2. The NEO-PI-R and the MMPI-2 are examples of _____ tests. *(nonprojective)*
3. Most personality researchers use _____ tests in their work. *(nonprojective)*

Chapter 12 ■ Psychological Disorders

Anxiety, Somatoform, and Dissociative Disorders (p. 482)

1. Concern that it may be triggered by media stories or therapists' suggestions has made _____ the most controversial of the dissociative disorders. *(dissociative identity disorder)*
2. A person who sleepwalks but is not able to walk when awake is showing signs of _____. *(conversion disorder)*
3. Panic disorder sometimes leads to another anxiety disorder called _____. *(agoraphobia)*

Affective Disorders (p. 486)

1. The risk of suicide is associated with _____ more than with any other symptom of disorder. *(depression)*
2. Cyclothymic personality is the bipolar version of _____. *(dysthymic disorder)*
3. Women are _____ likely than men to try suicide, but men are _____ likely to succeed. *(more; more)*

Schizophrenia (p. 494)

1. The _____ approach forms the basis of the vulnerability theory of schizophrenia. *(diathesis-stress)*

2. Hallucinations are _____ symptoms of schizophrenia; lack of emotion is a _____ symptom. *(positive; negative)*
3. Patients with schizophrenia who were able to finish school are _____ likely to show improvement. *(more)*

Chapter 13 ■ Treatment of Psychological Disorders

Approaches to Psychological Treatment *(p. 525)*

1. Object relations therapy and interpersonal therapy are both contemporary examples of the _____ approach to psychological treatment. *(psychodynamic)*
2. Imagining increasingly fear-provoking stimuli is a _____ treatment method called _____. *(behavioral; systematic desensitization)*
3. Reflection is an interviewing technique associated mainly with the _____ approach to treatment. *(humanistic [or nondirective])*

Chapter 14 ■ Social Psychology

Some Biases in Social Perception *(p. 556)*

1. The fundamental attribution error appears to be somewhat less likely to occur among people in _____ cultures. *(collectivist)*
2. First impressions form _____, but change _____. *(quickly; slowly)*
3. If you believed that immigrants' successes are due to government help but that their failures are due to laziness, you would be committing the _____ error. *(ultimate attribution error)*

Forming and Changing Attitudes *(p. 560)*

1. According to the elaboration likelihood model, people are more likely to pay close attention to the content and logic of a persuasive message if the _____ route to attitude change has been activated. *(central)*
2. Holding attitudes that are similar to those of your friends illustrates the importance of _____ in attitude formation *(learning)*
3. According to cognitive dissonance theory, we tend to reduce conflict between attitudes and behaviors by changing our _____. *(attitudes)*

Types of Social Influence *(p. 576)*

1. Joining the end of a ticket line is an example of _____, whereas forming two lines when a theater employee requests it is an example of _____. *(conformity; compliance)*
2. Seeing someone disobey a questionable order makes people _____ likely to obey the order themselves. *(less)*
3. Pricing your used car for more than you expect to get, then agreeing to reduce it to make a sale, is an example of the _____ approach to gaining compliance. *(door-in-the-face)*

Assistance *(p. 587)*

1. If you could save only one person from a burning house, the _____ theory of assistance would predict that it would be your own child rather than, say, a grandparent. *(evolutionary)*

2. Are you more likely to receive assistance in a nearly empty bus or a crowded bus terminal? _____. *(A nearly empty bus)*
3. People who have empathy for others are _____ likely to be helpful. *(more)*

Chapter 15 ■ Industrial/Organizational Psychology

Assessing People, Jobs, and Job Performance *(p. 608)*

1. Lists of critical incidents are contained in _____-focused employee rating forms. *(behavior)*
2. A potential employer might use a two-day _____ to measure your skill at the job you want. *(assessment center)*
3. In general, _____ interviews are more useful in employee selection than _____ interviews. *(structured; unstructured)*

Recruiting, Selecting, and Training Employees *(p. 614)*

1. Employees tend to remember more from a training program when it is set up on a _____ rather than a _____ schedule. *(distributed; massed)*
2. Depending on "walk-in" applications is usually acceptable when hiring _____ level employees. *(low)*
3. Assuring that your hiring criteria actually predict employees' job performance requires a _____. *(validation study)*

Chapter 16 ■ Neuropsychology

Foundations of Neuropsychology *(p. 641)*

1. A person who studies individual patients to determine what kind of brain damage each one happens to have is called a _____. *(clinical neuropsychologist)*
2. The case of "Tan" helped to establish the principle of _____. *(localization of function)*
3. In alexia without agraphia, the brain areas that control reading and writing are intact but cannot interact. This condition is called a _____. *(disconnection syndrome)*

Mechanisms of Brain Dysfunction *(p. 645)*

1. The brain floats in a bath of _____ inside the skull. *(cerebrospinal fluid)*
2. The brain needs a constant flow of fresh _____ all the time. *(blood)*
3. Cerebrovascular accidents rank as the number _____ cause of death in the United States. *(three)*

Major Neuropsychological Problems *(p. 660)*

1. A patient who has become forgetful but has no problems in other areas of cognitive function may be said to have _____. *(mild cognitive impairment)*
2. A dementia patient whose hippocampus is relatively intact and can still form new memories probably has _____ dementia. *(vascular)*
3. A patient with thiamine deficiency who is forgetful but makes up memories and believes they are real probably has _____. *(Korsakoff's syndrome)*

REFERENCES

Entries that appear in blue refer to the optional Industrial and Organizational Psychology or Neuropsychology chapters.

Aaron, D. J., Chang, Y.-F., Markovic, N., & LaPorte, R. E. (2003). Estimating the lesbian population: A capture-recapture approach. *Journal of Epidemiology and Community Health, 57,* 207–209.

Abad, V. C., & Guilleminault, C. (2004). Review of rapid eye movement behavior sleep disorders. *Current Neurology and Neuroscience Reports, 4,* 157–163.

Abbott, B. B., Schoen, L. S., & Badia, P. (1984). Predictable and unpredictable shock: Behavioral measures of aversion and physiological measures of stress. *Psychological Bulletin, 96,* 45–71.

Abbott, R. D., White, L. R., Ross, G. W., Masaki, K. H., Curb, J. D., & Petrovitch, H. (2004). Walking and dementia in physically capable elderly men. *Journal of the American Medical Association, 292,* 1447–1453.

AbdelMalik, P., Husted, J., Chow, E. W., & Bassett, A. S. (2003). Childhood head injury and expression of schizophrenia in multiply affected families. *Archives of General Psychiatry, 60,* 231–236.

Abelson, J. L., Liberzon, I., Young, E. A., & Khan, S. (2005). Cognitive modulation of the endocrine stress response to a pharmacological challenge in normal and panic disorder subjects. *Archives of General Psychiatry, 62,* 668–675.

Abraham, W. C. (2006). Memory maintenance: The changing nature of neural mechanisms. *Current Directions in Psychological Science, 15,* 5–8.

Abrahamson, A. C., Baker, L. A., & Caspi, A. (2002). Rebellious teens? Genetic and environmental influences on the social attitudes of adolescents. *Journal of Personality and Social Psychology, 83,* 1392–1408.

Abramis, D. J. (1994). Work role ambiguity, job satisfaction, and job performance: Meta-analyses and review. *Psychological Reports, 75,* 1411–1433.

Abramowitz, J. S., & Braddock, A. E. (2006). Hypochondriasis: Conceptualization, treatment, and relationship to obsessive-compulsive disorder. *Psychiatric Clinics of North America, 29,* 503–519.

Abramowitz, J. S., Khandker, M., Nelson, C. A., Deacon, B. J., & Rygwall, R. (2006). The role of cognitive factors in the pathogenesis of obsessive-compulsive symptoms: A prospective study. *Behaviour Research and Therapy, 44,* 1361–1374.

Abrams, D. I., Jay, C. A., Shade, S. B., Vizoso, H., Reda, H., Press, S., Kelly, M. E., Rowbotham, M. C., & Petersen, K. L. (2007). Cannabis in painful HIV-associated sensory neuropathy. *Neurology, 68,* 515–521.

Abrantes-Pais, F. de N., Friedman, J. K., Lovallo, W. R., & Ross, E. D. (2007). Psychological or physiological: Why are tetraplegic patients content? *Neurology, 69,* 261–267.

Abreu, J. M. (1999). Conscious and unconscious African American stereotypes: Impact on first impression and diagnostic ratings by therapists. *Journal of Consulting and Clinical Psychology, 67,* 387–393.

Acitelli, L. K. (1992). Gender differences in relationship awareness and marital satisfaction among young married couples. *Personality and Social Psychology Bulletin, 18,* 102–110.

Acker, T., & Acker, H. (2004). Cellular oxygen sensing need in CNS function: Physiological and pathological implications. *Journal of Experimental Biology, 207*(Pt. 18), 3171–3188.

Ackerman, P. L. (2007). New developments in understanding skilled performance. *Current Directions in Psychological Science, 16,* 235–239.

Acocella, J. (1998, April 6). The politics of hysteria. *New Yorker,* pp. 64–79.

Adachi-Mejia, A. M., Longacre, M. R., Gibson, J. J., Beach, M. L., Titus-Ernstoff, L. T., & Dalton, M. A. (2007). Children with a TV in their bedroom at higher risk for overweight. *International Journal of Obesity, 31,* 644–651.

Adair, J. C., Gilmore, R. L., Fennell, E. B., Gold, M., & Heilman, K. M. (1995). Anosognosia during intracarotid barbiturate anesthesia: Unawareness or amnesia for weakness. *Neurology, 45*(2), 241–243.

Adam, E. K., Gunnar, M. R., & Tanaka, A. (2004). Adult attachment, parent emotion, and observed parenting behavior: Mediator and moderator models. *Child Development, 75,* 110–122.

Adams, K. F., Schatzkin, A., Harris, T. B., Kipnis, V., Mouw, T., Ballard-Barbash, R., et al. (2006). Overweight, obesity, and mortality in a large prospective cohort of persons 50 to 71 years old. *New England Journal of Medicine, 355,* 763–778.

Adams, W. J., Graf, E. W., & Ernst, M. O. (2004). Experience can change the "light from above" prior. *Nature Neuroscience, 7,* 1057–1058.

Addis, D. R., Wong, A. T., & Schacter, D. L. (2007). Remembering the past and imagining the future: common and distinct neural substrates during event construction and elaboration. *Neuropsychologia, 45,* 1363–1377.

Addis, M. E. (1997). Evaluating the treatment manual as a means of disseminating empirically validated psychotherapies. *Clinical Psychology: Science and Practice, 4,* 1–11.

Addis, M. E., & Krasnow, A. D. (2000). A national survey of practicing psychologists' attitudes toward psychotherapy treatment manuals. *Journal of Consulting and Clinical Psychology, 68,* 331–339.

Adelabu, D. H. (2008). Future time perspective, hope, and ethnic identity among African American adolescents. *Urban Education, 43,* 347–360.

Ader, R. (2001). Psychoneuroimmunology. *Current Directions in Psychological Science, 10,* 94–98.

Adler, T. (1993, March). Bad mix: Combat stress, decisions. *APA Monitor,* p. 1.

Adolphs, R. (2003). Investigating the cognitive neuroscience of social behavior. *Neuropsychologia, 41,* 119–126.

Adolphs, R., Tranel, D., & Damasio, A. R. (1998). The human amygdala in social judgment. *Nature, 393*(6684), 470–474.

Adolphs, R., Tranel, D., Koenigs, M., & Damasio, A. R. (2005). Preferring one taste over another without recognizing either. *Nature Neuroscience, 8,* 860–861.

Adorno, T. W., Frenkel-Brunswik, E., Levinson, D. J., & Sanford, R. N. (1950). *The authoritarian personality.* New York: Harper & Row.

Agarwal, D. P. (1997). Molecular genetic aspects of alcohol metabolism and alcoholism. *Pharmacopsychiatry, 30*(3), 79–84.

Aggarwal, R., Cheshire, N., & Darzi, A. (2008). Endovascular simulation-based training. *Surgeon, 6*(4), 196–197.

Agnew, C. R., Van Lange, P. A. M., Rusbult, C. E., & Langston, C. A. (1998). Cognitive interdependence: Commitment and the mental representation of close relationships. *Journal of Personality and Social Psychology, 74,* 939–954.

Aharonov, R., Segev, L., Meilijson, I., & Ruppin, E. (2003). Localization of function via lesion analysis. *Neural Computation, 15*(4), 885–913.

Ahima, R. S., & Flier, J. S. (2000). Leptin. *Annual Review of Physiology, 62,* 413–437.

Ahn-Redding, H. (2008). *The insanity defense the world over.* Lanham, MD: Lexington Books.

Aiello, J. R., & Douthitt, E. A. (2001). Social facilitation from Triplett to electronic performance monitoring. *Group Dynamics, 5,* 163–180.

Aiken, L. R. (1994). *Psychological testing and assessment* (8th ed.). Boston: Allyn & Bacon.

Ainsworth, M. D. S., Blehar, M. D., Waters, E., & Wall, S. (1978). *Patterns of attachment: A psychological study of the Strange Situation.* Hillsdale, NJ: Erlbaum.

Ainsworth, M. D. S., & Bowlby, J. (1991). An ethological approach to personality development. *American Psychologist, 46,* 333–341.

Ainsworth, M. D. S., & Marvin, R. S. (1995). On the shaping of attachment theory and research: An interview with Mary D. S. Ainsworth (Fall 1994). *Monographs of the Society for Research in Child Development, 60,* 3–21.

Aizawa, N. (2002). Grandiose traits and hypersensitive traits of the narcissistic personality. *Japanese Journal of Educational Psychology, 50,* 215–224.

Ajzen, I., & Fishbein, M. (2005). The influence of attitudes on behavior. In D. Albarracín, B. T. Johnson, & M. P. Zanna (Eds.), *Handbook of attitudes* (pp. 173–221). Mahwah, NJ: Erlbaum.

Ajzen, I., & Gilbert-Cote, N. (2008). Attitudes and the prediction of behavior. In W. Crano, & R. Prislin (Eds.), *Attitudes and attitude change* (pp. 289–311). New York: Psychology Press.

Akerstedt, T. (2007). Altered sleep/wake patterns and mental performance. *Physiology and Behavior, 90,* 209–218.

Akin, W. M., & Turner, S. M. (2006). Toward understanding ethnic and cultural factors in the interviewing process. *Psychotherapy: Theory, Research, Practice, Training, 43,* 50–64.

Akins, C. K., & Zentall, T. R. (1998). Imitation in Japanese quail: The role of reinforcement of demonstrator responding. *Psychonomic Bulletin and Review, 5,* 694–697.

Albarracín, D., Durantini, M. R., Allison, E., Gunnoe, J. B., & Leeper, J. (2008). Beyond the most willing audiences: A meta-intervention to increase exposure to HIV-prevention programs by vulnerable populations. *Health Psychology, 27,* 638–644.

Albarracín, D., Johnson, B. T., Fishbein, M., & Muellerleile, P. A. (2001). Theories of reasoned action and planned behavior as models of condom use: A meta-analysis. *Psychological Bulletin, 127,* 142–161.

Albarracín, D., Johnson, B. T., & Zanna, M. P. (Eds.). (2005). *Handbook of attitudes.* Mahwah, NJ: Erlbaum.

Albee, G. W. (1968). Conceptual models and manpower requirements in psychology. *American Psychologist, 23,* 317–320.

Albee, G. W. (2002). Just say no to psychotropic drugs! *Journal of Clinical Psychology, 58,* 635–648.

Albee, G. W. (2006). Historical overview of primary prevention of psychopathology. *Journal of Primary Prevention, 27,* 449–456.

Albers, M. W., Tabert, M. H., & Devanand, D. P. (2006). Olfactory dysfunction as a predictor of neurodegenerative disease. *Current Neurology and Neuroscience Reports, 6,* 379–386.

Albert, K. A., Hemmings, H. C., Adamo, A. I. B., Potkin, S. G., Akbarian, S., Sandman, C. A. (2002). Evidence for decreased DARPP-32 in the prefrontal cortex of patients with schizophrenia. *Archives of General Psychiatry, 59,* 705–712.

Albert, M. S., Savage, C. R., Blazer, D., Jones, K., Berkman, L., & Seeman, T. (1995). Predictors of cognitive change in older persons: MacArthur studies of successful aging. *Psychology and Aging, 10,* 578–589.

Alberti, R., & Emmons, M. (2008). *Your perfect right: Assertiveness and equality in your life and relationships* (9th ed.). Atascadero, CA: Impact Publishers.

Alberto, P. A., Troutman, A. C., & Feagin, J. R. (2002). *Applied behavior analysis for teachers* (6th ed.). Englewood Cliffs, NJ: Prentice Hall.

Albus, H., Vansteensel, M. J., Michel, S., Block, G. D., & Meijer, J. H. (2005). A GABAergic mechanism is necessary for coupling dissociable ventral and dorsal regional oscillators within the circadian clock. *Current Biology, 15,* 886–893.

Alcock, J. (2001). *Animal behavior: An evolutionary approach* (7th ed.). Sunderland, MA: Sinauer.

Aldag, R. J., & Fuller, S. R. (1993). Beyond fiasco: A reappraisal of the groupthink phenomenon and a new model of group decision processes. *Psychological Bulletin, 113,* 533–552.

Alderfer, C. P. (1969). An empirical test of a new theory of human needs. *Organizational Behavior and Human Performance, 4,* 142–175.

Aldridge, J. W. (2005). Interpreting correlation as causation? *Science, 308*(5724), 954.

Aleman, A., Kahn, R. S., & Selten, J.-P. (2003). Sex differences in the risk of schizophrenia: Evidence from meta-analysis. *Archives of General Psychiatry, 60,* 565–571.

Alerman, A., & Larøi, F. (2008). *Hallucinations: The science of idiosyncratic perception.* Washington, DC: American Psychological Association.

Alessi, S. M., Roll, J. M., Reilly, M. P., & Johanson, C.-E. (2002). Establishment of a diazepam preference in human volunteers following a differential- conditioning history of placebo versus diazepam choice. *Experimental and Clinical Psychopharmacology, 10,* 77–83.

Alexander, G. M., & Hines, M. (2002). Sex differences in response to children's toys in non-human primates (*Cercopithecus aethiops sabaeus*). *Evolution and Human Behavior, 23,* 467–479.

Alexander, K. W., Quas, J. A., Goodman, G. S., Ghetti, S., Edelstein, R. S., Redlich, A. D., et al. (2005). Traumatic impact predicts long-term memory for documented child sexual abuse. *Psychological Science, 16,* 33–40.

Ali, R., Liu, W. M., & Humedian, M. (2004). Islam 101: Understanding the religion and therapy implications. *Professional Psychology: Research and Practice, 35,* 635–642.

Alicke, M., LoSchiavo, F. M., Zerbst, J., & Zhang, S. (1997). The person who outperforms me is a genius: Maintaining perceived competence in upward social comparisons. *Journal of Personality and Social Psychology, 73,* 781–789.

Alison, L., Kebbell, M., & Lewis, P. (2006). Considerations for experts in assessing the credibility of recovered memories of child sexual abuse: The importance of maintaining a case-specific focus. *Psychology, Public Policy, and Law, 12,* 419–441.

Alkire, M. T., Hudetz, A. G., & Tononi, G. (2008). Consciousness and anesthesia. *Science, 322,* 876–880.

Al-Kubaisy, T. F., & Jassim, A. L. (2003). The efficacy of assertive training in the acquisition of social skills in Iraqi social phobics. *Arab Journal of Psychiatry, 14,* 68–72.

Allen, B. P. (2006). *Personality theories: Development, growth, and diversity* (5th ed.). Boston, MA: Pearson.

Allen, J. B., Kenrick, D. T., Linder, D. E., & McCall, M. A. (1989). Arousal and attraction: A response-facilitation alternative to misattribution and negative- reinforcement models. *Journal of Personality and Social Psychology, 57,* 261–270.

Allen, J. J. B. (2002). The role of psychophysiology in clinical assessment: ERPs in the evaluation of memory. *Psychophysiology, 39,* 261–280.

Allen, J. J. B., & Iacono, W. G. (2001). Assessing the validity of amnesia in dissociative identity disorder: A dilemma for the DSM and the courts. *Psychology, Public Policy and Law, 7,* 311–344.

Allen, M. T., & Matthews, K. A. (1997). Hemodynamic responses to laboratory stressors in children and adolescents: The influences of age, race and gender. *Psychophysiology, 34,* 329–339.

Allen, S. R., & Thorndike, R. M. (1995). Stability of the WPPSI-R and WISC-III factor structure using cross-validation of covariance structure models. *Journal of Psychoeducational Assessment, 13,* 3–20.

Alliger, G. M., & Dwight, S. A. (2000). A meta-analytic investigation of the susceptibility of integrity tests to faking and coaching. *Educational and Psychological Measurement, 60,* 59–72.

Allik, J., & McCrae, R. R. (2004). Toward a geography of personality traits: Patterns of profiles across 36 cultures. *Journal of Cross-Cultural Psychology, 35,* 13–28.

Alloy, L. B., Abramson, L. Y., Cogswell, A., Hughes, M. E., & Iacoviello, B. M. (2008). Cognitive vulnerability to depression: Implications for prevention. In M. T. Tsuang, W. S. Stone, & M. J. Lyons (Eds.) *Recognition and prevention of major mental and substance use disorders* (pp. 97–113). Arlington, VA: American Psychiatric Publishing.

Alloy, L. B., Abramson, L. Y., Whitehouse, W. G., Hogan, M. E., Panzarella, C., & Rose, D. T. (2006). Prospective incidence of first onsets and recurrences of depression in individuals at high and low cognitive risk for depression. *Journal of Abnormal Psychology, 115,* 145–156.

Allport, G. W., & Odbert, H. S. (1936). Trait names: A psycholexical study. *Psychological Monographs, 47*(1, Whole No. 211).

Almeida, D. M. (2005). Resilience and vulnerability to daily stressors assessed via diary methods. *Current Directions in Psychological Science, 14,* 64–68.

Al-Shammary, N., Awan, S., Butt, K., & Yoo, J. (2007). Internet use before consultation with a health professional. *Primary Health Care, 17*(10), 18–21.

Alston, J. H. (1920). Spatial condition of the fusion of warmth and cold in heat. *American Journal of Psychology, 31,* 303–312.

Altemeyer, B. (1996). *The authoritarian specter.* Cambridge: Harvard University Press.

Altemeyer, B. (2004). Highly dominating, highly authoritarian personalities. *Journal of Social Psychology, 144,* 421–447.

Altemeyer, B., & Hunsberger, B. (2005). Fundamentalism and authoritarianism. In R. Paloutzian & C. Park (Eds.), *Handbook of the psychology of religion and spirituality* (pp. 378–393). New York: Guilford Press.

Althoff, R. R., Faraone, S. V., Rettew, D. C., Morley, C. P., & Hudziak, J. J. (2005). Family, twin, adoption, and molecular genetic studies of juvenile bipolar disorder. *Bipolar Disorders, 7,* 598–609.

Altman, L. K. (2000, April 10). Company developing marijuana for medical uses. *New York Times.* Retrieved December 13, 2004, from http://www.mapinc.org/ drugnews/v00/n474/ a01.html.

Aluja-Fabregat, A., & Torrubia-Beltri, R. (1998). Viewing of mass media violence, perception of violence, personality and academic achievement. *Personality and Individual Differences, 25,* 973–989.Amaro, E., Jr., & Barker, G. J. (2006). Study design in fMRI: Basic principles. *Brain and Cognition, 60,* 220–232.

Alvarez, K., Salas, E., & Garofano, C. M. (2004). An integrated model of training evaluation and effectiveness. *Human Resource Development and Review, 3,* 385–416.

Alvaro, E. M., & Crano, W. D. (1997). Indirect minority influence: Evidence for leniency in source evaluation and counterargumentation. *Journal of Personality and Social Psychology, 72,* 949–964.

Alzheimer's Association. (2007). *Alzheimer's disease facts and figures: 2007* [Statistical abstract]. Retrieved February 1, 2009, from http://www.alz.org/national/documents/ Report_2007FactsAndFigures.pdf.

Alzheimer's Association. (2009). 2009 Alzheimer's disease facts and figures. *Alzheimer's & Dementia: The Journal of the Alzheimer's Association, 5*(3), 234–70.

Amabile, T. M. (1996). *Creativity in context: Update to "The Social Psychology of Creativity."* Boulder, CO: Westview.

Amabile, T. M. (2001). Beyond talent: John Irving and the passionate craft of creativity. *American Psychologist, 56,* 333–336.

Amabile, T. M., Hennessey, B. A., & Grossman, B. S. (1986). Social influences on creativity: The effects of contracted-for reward. *Journal of Personality and Social Psychology, 50,* 14–23.

Ambadar, Z., Schooler, J. W., & Cohn, J. F. (2005). Deciphering the enigmatic face. *Psychological Science, 16,* 403–410.

Amedi, A., Merabet, L. B., Bermpohl, F., & Pascual-Leone, A. (2005). The occipital cortex in the blind. *Current Directions in Psychological Science, 14,* 306–311.

American Educational Research Association, American Psychological Association, & National Council on Measurement in Education. (1999). *Standards for educational and psychological testing.* Washington, DC: American Educational Research Association.

American Psychiatric Association. (1994). *Diagnostic and statistical manual of mental disorders* (4th ed.). Washington, DC: American Psychiatric Association.

American Psychiatric Association. (1999). Position statement on psychiatric treatment and sexual orientation. *American Journal of Psychiatry, 156,* 1131.

American Psychiatric Association. (2000). *Diagnostic and statistical manual of mental disorders* (4th ed., text rev.). Washington DC: Author.

American Psychiatric Association. (2003). *The insanity defense.* Retrieved May 26, 2004, from http://www.psych.org/public_info/insanity.cfm.

American Psychological Association. (1993). *Violence and youth: Psychology's response.* Washington: DC: American Psychological Association.

American Psychological Association. (2002a). *Answers to your questions about sexual orientation and homosexuality.* Retrieved December 13, 2004, from http://www.apa.org/pubinfo/ answers.html#whatis.

American Psychological Association. (2002b). Ethical principles of psychologists and code of conduct. *American Psychologist, 57,* 1060–1073.

American Psychological Association. (2009). Medical cost offset. In *Resources for practicing psychologists: The practice directorate.* Retrieved April 23, 2009, from http://www.apa.org/ practice/offset3.html.

American Psychological Association Committee on Animal Research and Ethics. (2006). *Research with animals in psychology.* Retrieved January 15, 2009, from http://www.apa.org/science/animal2.html.

American Psychological Association Presidential Task Force on Evidence-Based Practice. (2006). Evidence-based practice in psychology. *American Psychologist, 61,* 271–285.

American Psychological Association Task Force on the Sexualization of Girls. (2007). *Report of the APA Task Force on the Sexualization of Girls.* Washington, DC: American Psychological Association.

Amodio, D. M., & Devine, P. G. (2009). On the functions of implicit prejudice and stereotyping: Insights from social neuroscience. In R. E. Petty, R. H. Fazio, & P. Briñol (Eds.), *Attitudes: Insights from the new wave of implicit measures* (pp. 192–229). Hillsdale, NJ: Erlbaum.

Amodio, D. M., Harmon-Jones, E., Devine, P. G., Curtin, J. J., Hartley, S. L., & Covert, A. E. (2004). Neural signals for the detection of unintentional race bias. *Psychological Science, 15,* 88–93.

Amodio, D. M., Jost, J. T., Master, S. L., & Yee, C. M. (2007). Neurocognitive correlates of liberalism and conservatism. *Nature Neuroscience, 10,* 1246–1247.

Amodio, D. M., & Showers, C. J. (2005). "Similarity breeds liking" revisited: The moderating role of commitment. *Journal of Social and Personal Relationships, 22,* 817–836.

Anastasi, A., & Urbina, S. (1997). *Psychological testing* (7th ed.). Upper Saddle River, NJ: Prentice Hall.

Anastasiadis, A. G., Davis, A. R., Salomon, L., Burchardt, M., & Shabsigh, R. (2002). Hormonal factors in female sexual dysfunction. *Current Opinion in Urology, 12,* 503–507.

Andersen, S. M., & Chen, S. (2002). The relational self: An interpersonal social-cognitive theory. *Psychological Review, 109,* 619–645.

Andersen, S. M., & Miranda, R. (2000). Transference: How past relationships emerge in the present. *Psychologist, 13,* 608–609.

Anderson, A., & Conwell, Y. (2002). Doctors study why elderly so prone to suicide. *American Journal of Geriatric Psychiatry.* Retrieved June 7, 2009, from http://www.stopgettingsick.com/templates/news_template.cfm/6086.

Anderson, A. K., & Phelps, E. A. (2000). Expression without recognition: Contributions of the human amygdala to emotional communication. *Psychological Science, 11,* 106–111.

Anderson, A. K., & Phelps, E. A. (2001). Lesions of the human amygdala impair enhanced perception of emotionally salient events. *Nature, 411,* 305–309.

Anderson, B. L. (2004). The role of occlusion in the perception of depth, lightness, and opacity. *Psychological Review, 110,* 785–801.

Anderson, C., John, O. P., Keltner, D., & Kring, A. M. (2001). Who attains social status? Effects of personality and physical attractiveness in social groups. *Journal of Personality and Social Psychology, 81,* 116–132.

Anderson, C. A. (2001). Heat and violence. *Current Directions in Psychological Science, 10,* 33–38.

Anderson, C. A. (2004). And update on the effects of playing violent video games. *Journal of Adolescence, 27,* 113–122.

Anderson, C. A., Anderson, K. B., Dorr, N., DeNeve, K. M., & Flanagan, M. (2000). Temperature and aggression. In M. Zanna (Ed.), *Advances in experimental social psychology* (Vol. 32, pp. 63–133). New York: Academic Press.

Anderson, C. A., Berkowitz, L., Donnerstein, E., Huesmann, L. R., Johnson, J. D., Linz, D., et al. (2003). The influence of media violence on youth. *Psychological Science in the Public Interest, 4,* 81–110.

Anderson, C. A., & Bushman, B. J. (2001). Effects of violent video games on aggressive behavior, aggressive cognition, aggressive affect, physiological arousal, and prosocial behavior: A meta-analytic review of the scientific literature. *Psychological Science, 12,* 353–359.

Anderson, C. A., & Bushman, B. J. (2002a). Human aggression. *Annual Review of Psychology, 53,* 27–51.

Anderson, C. A., & Bushman, B. J. (2002b). Media violence and the American public revisited. *American Psychologist, 57,* 448–450.

Anderson, C. A., & Dill, K. E. (2000). Video games and aggressive thoughts, feelings, and behavior in the laboratory and in life. *Journal of Personality and Social Psychology, 78,* 772–790.

Anderson, C. A., Lindsay, J. J., & Bushman, B. J. (1999). Research in the psychological laboratory: Truth or triviality? *Current Directions in Psychological Science, 8,* 3–9.

Anderson, C. A., & Murphy, C. R. (2003). Violent video games and aggressive behavior in young women. *Aggressive Behavior, 29,* 423–429.

Anderson, C. A., Sakamoto, A., Gentile, D. A., Ihori, N., Shibuya, A. Yukawa, S., Naito, M., & Kobayashi, K. (2008). Longitudinal effects of violent video games on aggression in Japan and the United States. *Pediatrics, 122,* 1067–1072.

Anderson, J. R. (2000). *Cognitive psychology and its implications* (5th ed). New York: Worth.

Anderson, J. R., Bothell, D., Byrne, M. D., Douglass, S., Lebiere, C., & Qin, Y. (2004). An integrated theory of the mind. *Psychological Review, 111,* 1036–1060.

Anderson, M. C., & Green, C. (2001). Suppressing unwanted memories by executive control. *Nature, 410,* 366–369.

Anderson, M. C., Ochsner, K. N., Kuhl, B., Cooper, J., Robertson, E., Gabrieli, S. W., et al. (2004). Neural systems underlying the suppression of unwanted memories. *Science, 303,* 232–235.

Anderson, P., Rothbaum, B. O., & Hodges, L. F. (2003). Virtual reality exposure in the treatment of social anxiety. *Cognitive and Behavioral Practice, 10*(3), 240–247.

Anderson, S. E., Cohen, P., Naumova, E. N., Jacques, P. F., & Must, A. (2007). Adolescent obesity and risk for subsequent major depressive disorder and anxiety disorder: Prospective evidence. *Psychosomatic Medicine 69,* 740–747.

Anderssen, N., Amlie, C., & Ytteroy, E. A. (2002). Outcomes for children with lesbian or gay parents: A review of studies from 1978 to 2000. *Scandinavian Journal of Psychology, 43,* 335–351.

Anderson, G. (2009). Using the Internet to provide cognitive behaviour therapy. *Behaviour Research and Therapy, 47,* 175–180.

Ando, Y., Kitayama, H., Kawaguchi, Y., & Koyanagi, Y. (2008). Primary target cells of herpes simplex virus type 1 in the hippocampus. *Microbes & Infection, 10*(14/15), 1514–1523.

Andreasen, N. C. (1997). Linking mind and brain in the study of mental illnesses: A project for a scientific psychopathology. *Science, 275,* 1586–1593.

Andreasen, N. C., & Pierson, R. (2008). The role of the cerebellum in schizophrenia. *Biological Psychiatry, 64,* 81–88.

Andreescu, C., Lenze, E. J., Dew, M. A., Begley, A. E., Mulsant, B. H., et al. (2007). Effect of comorbid anxiety on treatment response and relapse risk in late-lefe depression. *British Journal of Psychiatry, 190,* 344–349.

Andre-Petersson, L., Engstroom, G., Hagberg, B., Janzon, L., Steen, G., Lane, D. A., et al. (2001). Adaptive behavior in stressful situations and stroke incidence in hypertensive men: Results from prospective cohort study "Men Born in 1914" in Malmo, Sweden. *Stroke, 32,* 1712–1720.

Andrew, D., & Craig, A. D. (2001). Spinothalamic lamina I neurons selectively sensitive to histamine: A central neural pathway for itch. *Nature Neuroscience, 4,* 72–77.

Andrews, B., Brewin, C., Ochera, J., Morton, J., Bekerian, D. A., Davies, G. M., & Mollon, P. (2000). The timing, triggers, and quality of recovered memories in therapy. *British Journal of Clinical Psychology, 39,* 11–26.

Andrews, B., Brewin, C. R., Philpott, R., & Stewart, L. (2007). Delayed-onset posttraumatic stress disorder: A systematic review of the evidence. *American Journal of Psychiatry, 164,* 1319–1326.

Andrews, J., Wang, L., Csernansky, J. G., Gado, M. H., & Barch, D. M. (2006). Abnormalities of thalamic activation and cognition in schizophrenia. *American Journal of Psychiatry, 163,* 463–469.

Andrews, L. B. (2008). The psychiatric interview and mental status examination. In R. E. Hales, S. C. Yudofsky, & G. O. Gabbard (Eds) *Textbook of psychiatry.* (pp. 3–17). Washington, DC: American Psychiatric Publishing.

Angelaki, D. E., & Cullen, K. E. (2008). Vestibular system: The many faces of a multimodal sense. *Annual Review of Neuroscience, 31,* 125–150.

Anghelescu, I., Klawe, C. J., Bartenstein, P., & Szegedi, A. (2001). Normal PET after long-term ETC. *American Journal of Psychiatry, 158,* 1527.

Angold, A., Erkanli, A., Farmer, E. M. Z., Fairbank, J. A., Burns, B. J., Keeler, G., & Costello, E. J. (2002). Psychiatric disorder, impairment, and service use in rural African American and white youth. *Archives of General Psychiatry, 59,* 893–901.

Annenberg Public Policy Center. (1999). *The 1999 state of children's television report: Programming for children over broadcast and cable television.* Washington, DC: Annenberg Public Policy Center.

Annenberg Public Policy Center. (2000). *Media in the home: The fifth annual survey of parents and children 2000.* Washington, DC: Annenberg Public Policy Center.

Anrep, G. V. (1920). Pitch discrimination in the dog. *Journal of Physiology, 53,* 367–385.

Anshel. (1996). Coping styles among adolescent competitive athletes. *Journal of Social Psychology, 136,* 311–323.

Anthony, M., & Bartlett, P. L. (1999). *Neural network learning: Theoretical foundations.* Cambridge, UK: Cambridge University Press.

Anthony, T., Cooper, C., & Mullen, B. (1992). Cross-racial facial identification: Five studies of sex differences in facial prominence. *Personality and Social Psychology Bulletin, 18,* 296–301.

Antoni, M. H., Cruess, D. G., Cruess, S., Lutgendorf, S., Kumar, M., Ironson, G., et al. (2000). Cognitive-behavioral stress management intervention effects on anxiety, 24-hr urinary norepinephrine output, and t-cytotoxic/suppressor cells over time among symptomatic HIV-infected gay men. *Journal of Consulting and Clinical Psychology, 68,* 31–45.

Antoni, M. H., & Lutgendorf, S. (2007). Psychosocial factors and disease progression in cancer. *Current Directions in Psychological Science, 16,* 42–46.

Antrobus, J. (2001). Rethinking the fundamental process of dream and sleep mentation production: Defining new questions that avoid the distraction of REM versus NREM comparisons. *Sleep and Hypnosis, 3,* 1–8.

APA Office of Ethnic Minority Affairs. (2000). *Guidelines for research in ethnic minority communities.* Washington, DC: American Psychological Association.

Appignanesi, L. (2009). *Mad, bad, and sad: A history of women and mind doctors.* New York, NY: W. W. Norton.

Aquino, K., Tripp, T. M., & Bies, R. J. (2006). Getting even or moving on? Power, procedural justice, and types of offense as predictors of revenge, forgiveness, reconciliation, and avoidance in organizations. *Journal of Applied Psychology, 91,* 653–668.

Arbelle, S., Benjamin, J., Golin, M., Kremer, I., Belmaker, R. H., & Ebstein, R. P. (2003). Relation of shyness in grade school children to the genotype for the long form of the serotonin transporter promoter region polymorphism. *American Journal of Psychiatry, 160,* 671–676.

Arenberg, D. (1982). Changes with age in problem solving. In F. I. M. Craik & S. Trehub (Eds.), *Aging and cognitive processes* (pp. 221–236). New York: Plenum.

Arkes, H. R., & Ayton, P. (1999). The sunk cost and Concorde effects: Are humans less rational than lower animals? *Psychological Bulletin, 125,* 591–600.

Arle, J. E., & Shils, J. L. (2008). Motor cortex stimulation for pain and movement disorders. *Neurotherapeutics, 5*(1), 37–49.

Armitage, C. J. (2005). Can the theory of planned behavior predict the maintenance of physical activity? *Health Psychology, 24,* 235–245.

Armour, S. (2008, March 31). Day care's new frontier: Your baby at your desk. *USA Today.*

Armstrong, L. E. (2006). Nutritional strategies for football: Counteracting heat, cold, high altitude, and jet lag. *Journal of Sports Sciences, 24*(7), 723–740.

Arndt, J., Greenberg, J., Pyszczynski, T., & Solomon, S. (1997). Subliminal exposure to death-related stimuli increases defense of the cultural worldview. *Psychological Science, 8,* 379–385.

Arnedt, J. T., Owens, J., Crouch, M., Stahl, J., & Carskadon, M. A. (2005). Neurobehavioral performance of residents after heavy night call vs after alcohol ingestion. *Journal of the American Medical Association, 294,* 1025–1033.

Arnett, J. J. (1999). Adolescent storm and stress, reconsidered. *American Psychologist, 54,* 317–326.

Arnett, J. J. (2000). Emerging adulthood: A theory of development from the late teens through the twenties. *American Psychologist, 55,* 469–480.

Arnett, J. J. (2007). Suffering, selfish, slackers? Myths and reality about emerging adults. *Journal of Youth & Adolescence, 36*(1), 23–29.

Aron, A., Fisher, H. E., Mashek, D. J. Strong, G., Li, H.-F., & Brown, L. L. (2005). Reward, motivation and emotion systems associated with early-stage intense romantic love. *Journal of Neurophysiology, 94,* 327–337.

Aronoff, J., Barclay, A. M., & Stevenson, L. A. (1988). The recognition of threatening stimuli. *Journal of Personality and Social Psychology, 54,* 647–655.

Aronson, E. (1990). Applying social psychology to desegregation and energy conservation. *Personality and Social Psychology Bulletin, 16,* 118–132.

Aronson, E. (1997). *The jigsaw classroom.* New York: Longman.

Aronson, E. (1999). *The social animal* (8th ed.). New York: Worth/Freeman.

Aronson, E., & Patnoe, S. (1997). *The jigsaw classroom: Building cooperation in the classroom* (2nd ed.). New York: Addison Wesley Longman.

Aronson, E., Wilson, T. D., & Akert, R. M. (2005). *Social psychology* (5th ed.). Upper Saddle River, NJ: Prentice Hall.

Arseneault, L., Cannon, M., Witton, J., & Murray, R. M. (2004). Causal association between cannabis and psychosis: Examination of the evidence. *British Journal of Psychiatry, 184,* 110–117.

Arterberry, M. E., Craton, L. G., & Yonas, A. (1993). Infants' sensitivity to motion-carried information for depth and object properties. In C. Granrud (Ed.), *Visual perception and cognition in infancy. Carnegie Mellon symposia on cognition* (pp. 215–234). Hillsdale, NJ: Erlbaum.

Arthur, W., Jr., Day, E. A., McNelly, T. L., & Edens, P. S. (2003). A meta-analysis of the criterion-related validity of assessment center dimensions. *Personnel Psychology, 56,* 125–154.

Arvey, R. D., Bouchard, T. J., Segal, N. L., & Abraham, L. M. (1989). Job satisfaction: Environmental and genetic components. *Journal of Applied Psychology, 74,* 187–192.

Asarnow, R. F., Nuechterlein, K. H., Fogelson, D., Subotnik, K. L., Payne, D. A., Russell, A. T., et al. (2001). Schizophrenia and schizophrenia-spectrum personality disorders in the first-degree relatives of children with schizophrenia: The UCLA family study. *Archives of General Psychiatry, 58,* 581–588.

Asch, S. E. (1951). Effects of group pressure upon the modification and distortion of judgments. In H. Guetzkow (Ed.), *Groups, leadership, and men* (pp. 177–190). Pittsburgh, PA: Carnegie Press.

Asch, S. E. (1955). Opinions and social pressure. *Scientific American, 193,* 31–35.

Asch, S. E. (1956). Studies of independence and conformity: A minority of one against a unanimous majority. *Psychological Monographs, 70,* 1–70.

Ashcraft, M. H. (2006). *Cognition* (4th ed.). Upper Saddle River, NJ: Prentice Hall.

Ashe, P. C., Berry, M. D., & Boulton, A. A. (2001). Schizophrenia, a neurodegenerative disorder with neurodevelopmental antecedents. *Progress in Neuro- Psychopharmacology and Biological Psychiatry, 25,* 691–707.

Ashmore, R. D., Deaux, K., McLaughlin-Volpe, T. (2004). An organizing framework for collective identity: Articulation and significance of multidimensionality. *Psychological Bulletin, 130,* 80–114.

Ashton, M. C., Lee, K., Perugini, M., Szarota, P., de Vries, R. E., Di Blas, L., et al. (2004). A six-factor structure of personality-descriptive adjectives: Solutions from psycholexical studies in seven languages. *Journal of Personality and Social Psychology, 86,* 356–366.

Askew, C., & Field, A. P. (2008). The vicarious learning pathway to fear 40 years on. *Clinical Psychology Review, 28,* 1249–1265.

Aslin, R. N., Jusczyk, P. W., & Pisoni, D. B. (1998). Speech and auditory processing during infancy: Constraints on and precursors to language. In W. Damon (Ed.), *Handbook of child psychology* (5th ed., pp. 147–198). New York: Wiley.

Aspinwall, L. G., & Duran, R. E. F. (1999). Psychology applied to health. In A. M. Stec & D. A. Bernstein (Eds.), *Psychology: Fields of application* (pp. 17–38). Boston: Houghton Mifflin.

Aspinwall, L. G., & Taylor, S. E. (1992). Modeling cognition adaptation: A longitudinal investigation of the impact of individual differences and coping on college adjustment and performance. *Journal of Personality and Social Psychology, 63,* 989–1003.

Assefi, N. P., Sherman, K. J., Jacobsen, C., Goldberg, J., Smith, W. R., & Buchwald, D. (2005). A randomized clinical trial of acupuncture compared with sham acupuncture in fibromyalgia. *Annals of Internal Medicine, 143,* 10–19.

Assefi, S. L., & Garry, M. (2003). Absolut® memory distortions: Alcohol placebos influence misinformation effect. *Psychological Science, 14,* 77–80.

Associated Press. (2007a). Officials investigating prank call that led to shock treatments at special needs school. December 18.

Associated Press. (2007b). Kansas store video captures five shoppers stepping over dying stabbing victim. July 3.

Associated Press. (2002, March 9). Odds and ends. *Naples Daily News.* Retrieved August 27, 2003, from http://www.nctimes.net/news/2002/20020313/ wwww.html.

Associated Press. (2003, January 10). Man to get $900,000 for 20 years spent in prison for rape he did not commit. *Naples Daily News.*

Associated Press. (2004, November 1). *Genetic disorder deprives kindergartner of natural alarms.* Retrieved September 26, 2006, from http://www.msnbc.msn. com/ id/6379795/.

Associated Press. (2007, August 1). Rate of accidents not affected by phase of the moon, study finds. Retrieved August 1, 2007 from http://www.foxnews.com.

Associated Press. (2007, December 17). Excellent driving, now pull over: California cops to reward motorists with $5 Starbucks cards.

Astin, J. A. (2004). Mind-body therapies for the management of pain. *Clinical Journal of Pain, 20,* 27–32.

Aston-Jones, G., & Cohen, J. D. (2005). An integrative theory of locus coeruleus-norepinephrine function: Adaptive gain and optimal performance. *Annual Review of Neuroscience, 28,* 403–450.

Atance, C. M., & O'Neill, D. K. (2001). Episodic future thinking. *Trends in Cognitive Science, 5,* 533–539.

Atkins, R. (2008). The association of childhood personality on sexual risk taking during adolescence. *Journal of School Health, 78*(11), 594–600.

Atkinson, J. (2006, August). Shake it off. *GQ: Gentlemen's Quarterly, 76*(8), 87–92.

Atkinson, R. C., & Shiffrin, R. M. (1968). Human memory: A proposed system and its control processes. In K. Spence (Ed.), *The psychology of learning and motivation* (Vol. 2, pp. 89–195). New York: Academic Press.

Atlantis, E., & Baker, M. (2008). Obesity effects on depression: Systematic review of epidemiological studies. *International Journal of Obesity, 32,* 881–891.

Atran, S., Medin, D. L., & Ross, N. O. (2005). The cultural mind: Environmental decision making and cultural modeling within and across populations. *Psychological Review, 112,* 744–776.

Audero, E., Coppi, E., Mlinar, B., Rossetti, T., Caprioli, A., Al Banchaabouchi, M., Corradetti, R., & Gross, C. (2008). Sporadic autonomic dysregulation and death associated with excessive serotonin autoinhibition. *Science, 321,* 130–133.

Auyeung B., Baron-Cohen, S., Ashwin, E., Knickmeyer, R., Taylor, K., Hackett, G., & Hines, M. (2009). Fetal testosterone predicts sexually differentiated childhood behavior in girls and in boys. *Psychological Science, 20,* 144–148.

Avaria, M., Mills, J. L., Kleinsteuber, K., Aros, S., Conley, M. R., Cox, C., et al. (2004). Peripheral nerve conduction abnormalities in children exposed to alcohol in utero. *Journal of Pediatrics, 144,* 338–343.

Avidan, M. S., Zhang, L., Burnside, B. A., Finkel, K. J., Searleman, A. C., Selvidge, J. A., Saager, L., Turner, M. S., Rao, S., Bottros, M., Hantler, C., Jacobsohn, E., & Evers, A. S. (2008). Anesthesia awareness and the bispectral index. *New England Journal of Medicine, 358,* 1097–1108.

Aviezer, H., Hassin, R. R., Ryan, J., Grady, C., Susskind, J., Anderson, A., Moscovitch, M., & Bentin, S. (2008). Angry, disgusted, or afraid? Studies on the malleability of emotion perception. *Psychological Science, 19*(7), 724–732.

Aviezer, O., Sagi, A., Joels, T., & Ziv, Y. (1999). Emotional availability and attachment representations in kibbutz infants and their mothers. *Developmental Psychology, 35,* 811–821.

Axtell, R. (Ed.). (1998). *Gestures: The do's and taboos of body language around the world.* Hoboken, NJ: Wiley.

Ayache, D., Corre, A., Can Prooyen, S., & Elbaz, P. (2003). Surgical treatment of otosclerosis in elderly patients. *Otolaryngological Head and Neck Surgery, 129,* 674–677.

Ayas, N. T., Barger, L. K., Cade, B. E., Hashimoto, D. M., Rosner, B., Cronin, J. W., et al. (2006). Extended work duration and the risk of self-reported percutaneous injuries in interns. *Journal of the American Medical Association, 296,* 1055–1062.

Ayas, N. T., FitzGerald, J. M., Fleetham, J. A., White, D. P., Schulzer, M., Ryan, C. F., et al. (2006). Cost-effectiveness of continuous positive airway pressure therapy for moderate to severe obstructive sleep apnea/hypopnea. *Archives of Internal Medicine, 166,* 977–984.

Ayuso-Mateos, J. L., Vazquez-Barquero, J. L., Dowrick, C., Lehtinen, V., Dalgard, O. S., Casey, P., et al. (2001). Depressive disorders in Europe: Prevalence figures fromt he ODIN study. *British Journal of Psychiatry, 179,* 308–316.

Azar, B. (1996, November). Project explores landscape of midlife. *APA Monitor,* p. 26.

Babinski, J. (1914). Contribution a l'etude dies troubles mentaux dans l'hemiplegie organique cerebrale (anosognosia). *Reveu Neurologie (Paris), 27,* 845–847.

Bacharach, V. R., & Baumeister, A. A. (1998). Direct and indirect effects of maternal intelligence, maternal age, income, and home environment on intelligence of preterm, low-birth-weight children. *Journal of Applied Developmental Psychology, 19,* 361–375.

Bach-Mizrachi, H., Underwood, M. D., Kassir, S. A., Bakalian, M. J., Sibille, E., Tamir, H., et al. (2006). Neuronal tryptophan hydroxylase mRNA expression in the human dorsal and median raphe nuclei: Major depression and suicide. *Neuropsychopharmacology: Official Publication of the American College pf Neuropsychopharmacology, 31,* 814–824.

Back, S. E., Dansky, B. S., Carroll, K. M., Foa, E. B., & Brady, K. T. (2001). Exposure therapy in the treatment of PTSD among cocaine-dependent individuals: Description of procedures. *Journal of Substance Abuse Treatment, 21,* 35–45.

Backman, L., & Nilsson, L. (1991). Effects of divided attention on free and cued recall of verbal events and action events. *Bulletin of the Psychonomic Society, 29,* 51–54.

Bada, H. S., Das, A., Bauer, C. R., Shankaran, S., Lester, B., LaGasse, L., et al. (2007). Impact of prenatal cocaine exposure on child behavior problems through school age. *Pediatrics, 119,* 348–359.

Baddeley, A. (1982). *Your memory: A user's guide.* New York: Macmillan.

Baddeley, A. (1992). Working memory. *Science, 255,* 556–559.

Baddeley, A. (1998). *Human memory: Theory and practice.* Boston: Allyn & Bacon.

Baddeley, A. D. (2003). Working memory: Looking back and looking forward. *Nature Reviews Neuroscience, 4,* 829–839.

Baer, J. S., Sampson, P. D., Barr, H. M., Connor, P. D., & Streissguth, A. P. (2003). A 21-year longitudinal analysis of the effects of prenatal alcohol exposure on young adult drinking. *Archives of General Psychiatry, 60,* 377–385.

Baethge, C., Baldessarini, R. J., Mathiske-Schmidt, K., Hennen, J., Berghofer, A., et al. (2005). Long-term combination therapy versus monotherapy with lithium and carbamazepine in 46 bipolar I patients. *Journal of Clinical Psychiatry, 66,* 174–182.

Bagley, C., & Tremblay, P. (1998). On the prevalence of homosexuality and bisexuality, in a random survey of 750 men aged 18–27. *Journal of Homosexuality, 36,* 1–18.

Bahrick, H. P., Bahrick, P. O., & Wittlinger, R. P. (1975). Fifty years of memory for names and faces: A cross-cultural approach. *Journal of Experimental Psychology: General, 104,* 54–75.

Bahrick, H. P., & Hall, L. K. (1991). Lifetime maintenance of high school mathematics content. *Journal of Experimental Psychology: General, 120,* 20–33.

Bahrick, H. P., Hall, L. K., Noggin, J. P., & Bahrick, L. E. (1994). Fifty years of language maintenance and language dominance in bilingual Hispanic immigrants. *Journal of Experimental Psychology: General, 123,* 264–283.

Baicy, K., London, E. D., Monterosso, J. Wong, M.-L., Delibasi, T., Sharma, A., & Licinio, J. (2007). Leptin replacement alters brain response to food cues in genetically leptin-deficient adults. *Proceedings of the National Academies of Science, 104,* 18276–18279.

Bailey, J. M., & Benishay, D. S. (1993). Familial aggregation of female sexual orientation. *American Journal of Psychiatry, 150,* 272–277.

Bailey, J. M., Bobrow, D., Wolfe, M., & Mikach, S. (1995). Sexual orientation of adult sons of gay fathers. *Developmental Psychology, 31*(1), 124–129.

Bailey, J. M., Dunne, M. P., & Martin, N. G. (2000). Genetic and environmental influences on sexual orientation and its correlates in an Australian twin sample. *Journal of Personality and Social Psychology, 78,* 524–536.

Bailey, J. M., & Pillard, R. C. (1991). A genetic study of male sexual orientation. *Archives of General Psychiatry, 48,* 1086–1096.

Baillargeon, R. (1992). A model of physical reasoning in infancy. In C. Rovee-Collier & L. P. Lipsett (Eds.), *Advances in infancy research.* Norwood, NJ: Ablex.

Baillargeon, R. (1995). Physical reasoning in infancy. In M. S. Gazzaniga (Ed.), *The cognitive neurosciences* (pp. 181–204). Cambridge, MA: MIT Press.

Baillargeon, R. (2008). Innate ideas revisited: For a principle of persistence in infants' physical reasoning. *Perspectives on Psychological Science, 3*(1), 2–13.

Baillargeon, R. H., Zoccolillo, M., Keenan, K., Côté, S., Pérusse, D., Wu, H.-X., Boivin, M., & Tremblay, R. E. (2007). Gender differences in physical aggression: A prospective population-based survey of children before and after 2 years of age. *Developmental Psychology, 43,* 13–26.

Bajo, M., Crawford, E. F., Roberto, M., Madamba, S. G., & Siggins, G. R. (2006). Chronic morphine treatment alters expression of N-methyl-D-aspartate receptor subunits in the extended amygdala. *Journal of Neuroscience Research, 83,* 532–537.

Bakare, M. O. (2008). Effective therapeutic dosage of antipsychotic medications in patients with psychotic symptoms: Is there a racial difference? *BMC Research Notes, 1,* 25.

Baker, J. L., Olsen, L. W., & Sørensen, T. I. A. (2007). Childhood body-mass index and the risk of coronary heart disease in adulthood. *The New England Journal of Medicine, 357,* 2229–2237.

Baker, M. C. (2002). *The atoms of language: The mind's hidden rules of grammar.* New York: Basic Books.

Baker, T. B., Piper, M. E., McCarthy, D. E., & Majeskie, M. R. (2004). Addiction motivation reformulated: An affective processing model of negative reinforcement. *Psychological Review, 111,* 33–51.

Bakermans-Kranenburg, M. J., van IJzendoorn, M. H., & Juffer, F. (2008). Less is more: Meta-analytic arguments for the use of sensitivity-focused interventions. In F. Juffer, M. J. Bakermans-Kranenburg, & M. H. van IJzendoorn (Eds.), *Promoting positive parenting: An attachment-based intervention* (pp. 59–74). New York: Taylor & Francis Group/Lawrence Erlbaum Associates.

Balaban, M. T. (1995). Affective influences on startle in five-month-old infants: Reactions to facial expressions of emotion. *Child Development, 66*(1), 28–36.

Balat, O., Balat, A., Ugur, M. G., & Pence, S. (2003). The effect of smoking and caffeine on the fetus and placenta in pregnancy. *Clinical and Experimental Obstetrics and Gynecology, 30,* 57–59.

Balázs, J., Benazzi, F., Rihmer, Z., Annamaria, A., Akiskal, K. K., et al. (2006). The close link between suicide attempts and mixed (bipolar) depression: Implications for suicide prevention. *Journal of Affective Disorders, 91,* 133–138.

Baldessarini, R. J., & Tondo, L. (2000). Does lithium treatment still work? Evidence of stable responses over three decades. *Archives of General Psychiatry, 57,* 187–190.

Baldessarini, R. J., Tondo, L., Hennen, J., Viguera, A. C. (2002). Is lithium still worth using? An update of selected research. *Harvard Review of Psychiatry, 10,* 59–75.

Baldock, M. R. J., Mathias, J., McLean, J., & Berndt, A. (2007). Visual attention as a predictor of on-road driving performance of older drivers. *Australian Journal of Psychology, 59*(3), 159–168.

Baldwin, T. T., & Ford, J. K. (1988). Transfer of training: A review and directions for future research. *Personnel Psychology, 41,* 63–105.

Balfour, D. J. (2002). The neurobiology of tobacco dependence: A commentary. *Respiration, 69,* 7–11.

Ball, H. A., McGuffin, P., & Farmer, A. E. (2008). Attributional style and depression. *British Journal of Psychiatry, 192,* 275–278.

Ballmaier, M., & Schmidt, R. (2005). Conversion disorder revisited. *Functional Neurology, 20,* 105–113.

Ballou, M. (1995). Assertiveness training. In M. Ballou (Ed.), *Psychological interventions: A guide to strategies* (pp. 125–136). Westport, CT: Praeger.

Baltes, B. B., Briggs, T. E., Huff, J. W., Wright, J. A., & Neumann, G. A. (1999). Flexible and compressed workweek schedules: A meta-analysis of their effects on work-related criteria. *Journal of Applied Psychology, 84,* 496–513.

Baltes, B. B., & Heydens-Gahir, H. A. (2003). Reduction of work–family conflict through the use of selection, optimization, and compensation behaviors. *Journal of Applied Psychology, 88,* 1005–1018.

Baltes, P. B. (1993). The aging mind: Potential and limits. *The Gerontologist, 33,* 580–594.

Baltes, P. B. (1994, August). *Life-span developmental psychology: On the overall landscape of human development.* Address presented at the annual meeting of the American Psychological Association, Los Angeles.

Baltes, P. B., & Smith, J. (2008). The fascination of wisdom: Its nature, ontogeny, and function. *Perspectives on Psychological Science, 3,* 56–64.

Balzer, W. K., & Sulsky, L. M. (1992). Halo and performance appraisal research: A critical examination. *Journal of Applied Psychology, 77,* 975–985.

Banaji, M., Lemm, K. M., & Carpenter, S. J. (2001). The social unconscious. In A. Tesser & N. Schwarz (Eds.), *Blackwell handbook of social psychology: Intraindividual processes* (pp. 134–158). Oxford, UK: Blackwell.

Bancroft, J. (1994). Homosexual orientation: The search for a biological basis. *British Journal of Psychiatry, 164,* 437–440.

Bandura, A. (1965). Influence of a model's reinforcement contingencies on the acquisition of imitative responses. *Journal of Personality and Social Psychology, 1,* 589–595.

Bandura, A. (1992). Self-efficacy mechanism in psychobiologic functioning. In R. Schwarzer (Ed.), *Self-efficacy: Thought control of action* (pp. 355–394). Washington, DC: Hemisphere.

Bandura, A. (1997). *Self-efficacy: The exercise of control.* New York: Freeman.

Bandura, A. (1999). Social cognitive theory of personality. In L. Pervin & O. John (Eds.), *Handbook of personality: Theory and research* (2nd ed., pp. 154–196). New York: Guilford.

Bandura, A. (2006). Toward a psychology of human agency. *Perspectives on Psychological Science, 1,* 164–180.

Bandura, A., Blanchard, E. B., & Ritter, B. (1969). The relative efficacy of desensitization and modeling approaches for inducing behavioral, affective, and attitudinal changes. *Journal of Personality and Social Psychology, 13,* 173–199.

Bandura, A., Ross, D., & Ross, S. A. (1963). Imitation of film-mediated aggressive models. *Journal of Abnormal and Social Psychology, 66,* 3–11.

Bandura, A., & Walters, R. H. (1963). *Social learning and personality development.* New York: Holt, Rinehart & Winston.

Banich, M. T. (2004). *Cognitive neuroscience and neuropsychology.* Boston: Houghton Mifflin.

Banich, M. T., & Heller, W. (1998). Evolving perspectives on lateralization of function. *Current Directions in Psychological Science, 7,* 1–2.

Banker, R. D., Field, J. M., Schroeder, R. G., & Sinha, K. K. (1996). Impact of work teams on manufacturing performance: A longitudinal field study. *Academy of Management Journal, 39,* 867–890.

Banks, M. S., & Salapatek, P. (1983). Infant visual perception. In P. H. Mussen (Ed.), *Handbook of child psychology: Vol. 2. Infancy and developmental psychobiology* (pp. 435–571). New York: Wiley.

Bantick, S. J., Wise, R. G., Ploghaus, A., Clare, S., Smith, S. M., & Tracey, I. (2002). Imaging how attention modulates pain in humans using functional MRI. *Brain, 125,* 310–319.

Bar, M., & Biederman, I. (1998). Subliminal visual priming. *Psychological Science, 9,* 464–469.

Barber, J. P., Connolly, M. B., Crits-Christoph, P., Gladis, L., & Siqueland, L. (2000). Alliance predicts patients' outcome beyond in-treatment change in symptoms. *Journal of Consulting & Clinical Psychology, 68*, 1027–1032.

Barclay, J. R., Bransford, J. D., Franks, J. J., McCarrell, N. S., & Nitsch, K. (1974). Comprehension and semantic flexibility. *Journal of Verbal Learning and Verbal Behavior, 13*, 471–481.

Barclay, P. (2006). Reputational benefits for altruistic punishment. *Evolution and Human Behavior, 27*, 325–344.

Barclay, T. R., Hinkin, C. H., Castellon, S. A., Mason, K. I., Reinhard, M. J., Marion, S. D., et al. (2007). Age-associated predictors of medication adherence in HIV-positive adults: health beliefs, self-efficacy, and neurocognitive status. *Health Psychology, 26*, 40–49.

Bardo, M. T., Donohew, R. L., & Harrington, N. G. (1996). Psychobiology of novelty-seeking and drug-seeking behavior. *Behavioral Brain Research, 77*(1–2), 23–43.

Barenbaum, N., & Winter, D. (2008). History of modern personality theory and research. In O. John, R. Robins, & L. Pervin (Eds.), *Handbook of personality: Theory and research* (3rd ed., pp. 3–28). New York: Guilford.

Barger, L. K., Cade, B. E., Ayas, N. T., Cronin, J. W., Rosner, B., Speizer, F. E., et al. (2005). *New England Journal of Medicine, 352*, 125–134.

Bargh, J., & Morsella, E. (2008). The unconscious mind. *Perspectives on Psychological Science, 3*, 73–79.

Bargones, J. Y., & Werner, L. A. (1994). Adults listen selectively; infants do not. *Psychological Science, 5*, 170–174.

Barkham, M., Connell, J., Stiles, W. B., Miles, J. N. V., Margison, F., Evans, C., et al. (2006). Dose-effect relations and responsive regulation of treatment duration: The good enough level. *Journal of Consulting and Clinical Psychology, 74*, 160–167.

Barling, J., Dupré, K. E., & Kelloway, E. K. (2009). Predicting workplace aggression and violence. *Annual Review of Psychology, 60*, 671–692.

Barling, J., & Frone, M. R. (Eds.). (2004). *The psychology of workplace safety.* Washington, DC: APA Books.

Barling, J., Weber, T., & Kelloway, E. K. (1996). Effects of transformational leadership training on attitudinal and financial outcomes: A field experiment. *Journal of Applied Psychology, 81*, 827–832.

Barlow, D. H. (1988). *Anxiety and its disorders: The nature and treatment of panic and anxiety.* New York: Guilford.

Barlow, D. H. (2006). Psychotherapy and psychological treatments: The future. *Clinical Psychology: Science and Practice, 13*, 216–220.

Barlow, D. H. (2007). *Clinical handbook of psychological disorders.* New York: Guilford.

Barlow, D. H., Gorman, J. M., Shear, M. K., & Woods, S. W. (2000). Cognitive- behavioral therapy, imipramine, or their combination for panic disorder: A randomized controlled trial. *Journal of the American Medical Association, 283*, 2529–2536.

Barnes, A. (2004). Race schizophrenia, and admission to state psychiatric hospitals. *Administration and Policy in Mental Health, 31*, 241–252.

Barnes, L. L., Mendes de Leon, C. F., Wilson, R. S., Bienias, J. L., & Evans, D. A. (2004). Social resources and cognitive decline in a population of older African Americans and whites. *Neurology, 63*, 2322–2326.

Barnes, S. M., Lynn, S. J., & Pekala, R. J. (2009). Not all group hypnotic suggestibility scales are created equal: Individual differences in behavioral and subjective responses. *Consciousness and Cognition, 18*, 255–265.

Barnes-Farrell, J. L., Davies-Schuls, K., McGonagle, A., Walsh, B., Di Milia, L., Fischer, F. M., Hobbs, B. B., Kaliterna, L., & Tepas, D. (2008). What aspects of shiftwork influence off-shift well-being of healthcare workers? *Applied Ergonomics, 39*, 589–596.

Barnett, J. E., & Scheetz, K. (2003). Technological advances and telehealth: Ethics, law, and the practice of psychotherapy. *Psychotherapy: Theory, Research, Practice, and Training, 40*, 86–93.

Barnier, A. J. (2002). Posthypnotic amnesia for autobiographical episodes: A laboratory model of functional amnesia? *Psychological Science, 13*, 232–237.

Barnier, A. J., & McConkey, K. M. (1998). Posthypnotic responding away from the hypnotic setting. *Psychological Science, 9*, 256–262.

Baron, A. S., & Banaji, M. R. (2006). The development of implicit attitudes. *Psychological Science 17*, 53–58.

Baron, J. C. (2005). How healthy is the acutely reperfused ischemic penumbra? *Cerebrovascular Disease, 20*(Suppl. 2), 25–31.

Baron, R. A., & Byrne, D. (1994). *Social psychology: Understanding human interaction* (7th ed.). Boston: Allyn & Bacon.

Baron, R. A., Byrne, D., & Branscombe, N. R. (2006). *Social psychology* (11th ed.). Boston: Allyn & Bacon.

Baron, R. A., & Richardson, D. C. (1994). *Human aggression* (2nd ed.). New York: Plenum.

Baron, R. N., Branscombe, N., & Byrnne, D. (2008). *Social psychology* (12th ed.). Boston, MA: Allyn & Bacon.

Baron-Cohen, S., Knickmeyer, R. C., & Belmonte, M. K. (2005). Sex differences in the brain: Implications for explaining autism. *Science, 310*, 819–823.

Baron-Cohen, S., Leslie, A. M., & Frith, U. (1985). Does the autistic child have a "theory of mind"? *Cognition, 21*, 37–46.

Barr Taylor, C., Bryson, S., Celio Doyle, A. A., Luce, K. H., Cunning, D., Abascal, L. B., et al. (2006a). The adverse effect of negative comments about weight and shape from family and siblings on women at high risk for eating disorders. *Pediatrics, 118*, 731–738.

Barr Taylor, C., Bryson, S., Luce, K. H., Cunning, D., Celio Doyle, A. A., Abascal, L. B., et al. (2006b). Prevention of eating disorders in at-risk college-age women. *Archives of General Psychiatry, 63*, 881–888.

Barres, B. A. (2008). The mystery and magic of glia: A perspective on their roles in health and disease. *Neuron, 60*(3), 430–440.

Barrett, L. F. (1995). Valence focus and arousal focus: Individual differences in the structure of affective experience. *Journal of Personality and Social Psychology, 69*, 153–166.

Barrett, L. F., Lane, R. D., Sechrest, L., & Schwartz, G. E. (2000). Sex differences in emotional awareness. *Personality and Social Psychology Bulletin, 26*, 1027–1035.

Barrett, L. F., Mesquita, B., Ochsner, K. N., & Gross, J. J. (2007). The experience of emotion. *Annual Review of Psychology, 58*, 373–403.

Barrett, L. F., & Wager, T. D. (2006). The structure of emotion. *Current Directions in Psychological Science, 15*, 79–83.

Barrick, M. R., & Mount, M. K. (1991). The Big Five personality dimensions and job performance: A meta-analysis. *Personnel Psychology, 44*, 1–26.

Barriera-Viruet, H., Sobeih, T. M., Daraiseh, N., & Salem, S. (2006). Questionnaires vs observational and direct measurements: A systematic review. *Theoretical Issues in Ergonomics Science, 7*(3), 261–284.

Barron, K. E., & Harackiewicz, J. M. (2001). Achievement goals and optimal motivation: Testing multiple goal models. *Journal of Personality and Social Psychology, 80*, 706–722.

Barsalou, L. W. (1993). Flexibility, structure, and linguistic vagary in concepts: Manifestations of a compositional system of perceptual symbols. In A. F. Collins, S. E. Gathercole, M. A. Conway, & P. E. Morris (Eds.), *Theories of memory* (pp. 29–102). Hillsdale, NJ: Erlbaum.

Barsky, A. J., Wool, C., Barnett, M. C., & Cleary, P. D. (1994). Histories of childhood trauma in adult hypochondriacal patients. *American Journal of Psychiatry, 151*, 397–401.

Bartels, A., & Zeki, S. (2000). The neural basis of romantic love. *Neuroreport, 11*, 3829–3834.

Bartholow, B. D., & Heinz, A. (2006). Alcohol and aggression without consumption: Alcohol cues, aggressive thoughts, and hostile perception bias. *Psychological Science, 17*, 30–37.

Bartlett, J. A. (2002). Addressing the challenges of adherence. *Journal of Acquired Immune Deficiency Syndrome, 29*(Suppl. 1), S2–S10.

Barton, J. J., Cherkasova, M. V., Press, D. Z., Intriligator, J. M., & O'Connor, M. (2004). Perceptual functions in prosopagnosia. *Perception, 33*(8), 939–956.

Barton, J., & Folkard, S. (1991). The response of day and night nurses to their work schedules. *Journal of Occupational Psychology, 64*, 207–218.

Barton, J. J., Press, D. Z., Keenan, J. P., & O'Connor, M. (2002). Lesions of the fusiform face area impair perception of facial configuration in prosopagnosia. *Neurology, 58*(1), 71–78.

Bartoshuk, L. M. (1991). Taste, smell, and pleasure. In R. C. Bollef (Ed.), *The hedonics of taste* (pp. 15–28). Hillsdale, NJ: Erlbaum.

Bartoshuk, L. M. (2000). Comparing sensory experiences across individuals: Recent psychophysical advances illuminate genetic variation in taste perception. *Chemical Senses, 25*, 447–460.

Bartoshuk, L. M., Fast, K., & Snyder, D. J. (2005). Differences in our sensory worlds: Invalid comparisons with labeled scales. *Current Directions in Psychological Science, 14*, 122–125.

Bartoshuk, L. M., & Wolfe, J. M. (1990). Conditioned taste aversion in humans: Are there olfactory versions? *Chemical Senses, 15*, 551.

Bartz, J. A., & Hollander, E. (2006). Is obsessive-compulsive disorder an anxiety disorder? *Progress in Neuro-Psychopharmacology & Biological Psychiatry, 30*, 338–352.

Bashore, T. R., & Ridderinkhof, K. R. (2002). Older age, traumatic brain injury, and cognitive slowing: Some convergent and divergent findings. *Psychological Bulletin, 128*, 151–198.

Baskin, D., Bluestone, H., & Nelson, M. (1981). Ethnicity and psychiatric diagnosis. *Journal of Clinical Psychology, 37*, 529–537.

Basoglu, M., Livanou, M., & Salcioglu, E. (2003). A single session with an earthquake simulator for traumatic stress in earthquake survivors. *American Journal of Psychiatry, 160*, 788–790.

Bass, B. M., Avolio, B. J., Jung, D. I., & Berson, Y. (2003). Predicting unit performance by assessing transformational and transactional leadership. *Journal of Applied Psychology, 88*, 207–218.

Bass, E., & Davis, L. (1994). *The courage to heal* (3rd ed.). New York: Harper Perennial Library.

Bass, B. M., & Riggio, R. E. (2006). *Transformational leadership* (2nd ed.). Mahwah, NJ: Erlbaum.

Bassett, A. S., Chow, E. W. C., O'Neill, S., & Brzustowicz, L. M. (2001). Genetic insights into the neurodevelopmental hypothesis of schizophrenia. *Schizophrenia Bulletin, 27*, 417–430.

Bassetti, C. L. (2007). Differential diagnosis and management of non-psychiatric acute confusional states. *Schweizer Archiv für Neurologie und Psychiatrie, 158*(8), 368–378.

Basu, S., Chapman, G. B., & Galvani, A. P. (2008). Integrating epidemiology, psychology, and economics to achieve HPV vaccination targets. *Proceedings of the National Academy of Sciences, 105*(48), 19018–19023.

Bates, E. (1993, March). *Nature, nurture, and language development.* Paper presented at the biennial meeting of the Society for Research in Child Development, New Orleans.

Batki, S. L., Leontieva, L., Dimmock, J. A., & Ploutz-Snyder, R. (2008). Negative symptoms are associated with less alcohol use, craving, and "high" in alcohol dependent patients with schizophrenia. *Schizophrenia Research, 105*, 201–207.

Batson, C. D. (1998). Altruism and prosocial behavior. In D. Gilbert, S. T. Fiske, & G. Lindzey (Eds.), *Handbook of social psychology* (Vol. 2, 4th ed., pp. 282–316). Boston: McGraw-Hill.

Batson, C. D., Sager, K., Garst, E., & Kang, M. (1997). Is empathy-induced helping due to self-other merging? *Journal of Personality and Social Psychology, 73*, 495–509.

Batterham, R. L., Cohen, M. A., Ellis, S. M., Le Roux, C. W., Withers, D. J., Frost, G. S., et al. (2003). Inhibition of food intake in obese subjects by peptide YY3-36. *New England Journal of Medicine, 349,* 941–948.

Batterham, R. L., Cowley, M. A., Small, C. J., Herzog, H., Cohen, M. A., Dakin, C. L., et al. (2002). Gut hormone PYY3-36 physiologically inhibits food intake. *Nature, 418,* 650–654.

Baucom, D. H., Shoham, V., Mueser, K. T., Daiuto, A. D., & Stickle, T. R. (1998). Empirically supported couple and family interventions for marital distress and adult mental health problems. *Journal of Consulting and Clinical Psychology, 66,* 53–88.

Bauer, P. J. (2006). Event memory. In W. Damon & R. M. Lerner (Series Eds.) & D. Kuhn & R. Siegler (Vol. Eds.), *Handbook of child psychology: Vol. 2. Cognition, perception, and language* (6th ed., pp. 373–345). New York: Wiley.

Bauer, R. M., & Demery, J. A. (2003). Agnosia. In K. M. Heilman & E. Valenstein (Eds.), *Clinical neuropsychology* (4th ed.). New York: Oxford.

Bauer, T. N., & Green, S. G. (1996). Development of leader-member exchange: A longitudinal test. *Academy of Management Journal, 39,* 1538–1567.

Baumann, M. (2007). Slimming down with Wii sports. *Information Today, 24*(4), 47.

Baumann, S., Meyer, M., & Jäncke, L. (2008). Enhancement of auditory-evoked potentials in musicians reflects an influence of expertise but not selective attention. *Journal of Cognitive Neuroscience, 20*(12), 2238–2249.

Baumeister, H., & Härter, M. (2007). Mental disorders in patients with obesity in comparison with healthy probands. *International Journal of Obesity, 31,* 1155–1164.

Baumeister, R., & Bushman, B. (2008). *Social psychology and human nature.* Belmont, CA: Wadsworth.

Baumeister, R. F. (1998). The self. In D. Gilbert, S. T. Fiske, & G. Lindzey (Eds.), *Handbook of social psychology* (Vol. 1, 4th ed., pp. 680–740). Boston: McGraw-Hill.

Baumeister, R. F. (2000). Gender differences in erotic plasticity: The female sex drive as socially flexible and responsive. *Psychological Bulletin, 126,* 347–374.

Baumeister, R. F., Campbell, J. D., Krueger, J. I., & Vohs, K. D. (2003). Does high self-esteem cause better performance, interpersonal success, happiness, or healthier lifestyles? *Psychological Science in the Public Interest, 4,* 1–44.

Baumeister, R. F., & Leary, M. R. (1995). The need to belong: Desire for interpersonal attachments as a fundamental human motivation. *Psychological Bulletin, 117*(3), 497–529.

Baumeister, R. F., & Stillman, T. (2006). Erotic plasticity: Nature, culture, gender, and sexuality. In McAnulty, R. D., Burnette, M. M. (Eds.), *Sex and sexuality: Vol 1. Sexuality today: Trends and controversies* (pp. 343–359). Westport, CT, US: Praeger Publishers/Greenwood Publishing Group.

Baumgardner, S. R., & Crothers, M. K. (2009). *Positive psychology.* Upper Saddle River, NJ: Prentice Hall/Pearson.

Baumrind, D. (1971). Current patterns of parental authority. *Developmental Psychology Monographs, 4*(1, part 2).

Baumrind, D. (1991). Effective parenting during the early adolescent transition. In P. A. Cowan & E. M. Hetherington (Eds.), *Family transition* (pp. 111–163). Hillsdale, NJ: Erlbaum.

Baumrind, D., Larzelere, R. E., & Cowan, P. A. (2002). Ordinary physical punishment: Is it harmful? Comment on Gershoff. *Psychological Bulletin, 128,* 580–589.

Bayley, P. J., Hopkins, R. O., & Squire, L. R. (2003). Successful recollection of remote autobiographical memories by amnesic patients with medial temporal lobe lesions. *Neuron, 38,* 135–144.

Bazzano, L. A., He, J., Ogden, L. G., Loria, C. M., & Whelton, P. K. (2003). Dietary fiber intake and reduced risk of coronary heart disease in US men and women. *Archives of Internal Medicine, 163,* 1897–1904.

Beals, J., Novins, D. K., Whitesell, N. R., Spicer, P., Mitchell, C. M., & Manson, S. M. (2005). Prevalence of mental disorders and utilization of mental health services in two American Indian reservation populations: Mental health disparities in a national context. *American Journal of Psychiatry, 162,* 1723–1732.

Beardslee, W. R., Gladstone, T. R. G., Wright, E. J., & Cooper, A. B. (2003). A family-based approach to the prevention of depressive symptoms in children at risk: Evidence of parental and child change. *Pediatrics, 112,* 119–131.

Beatty, J. (1995). *Principles of behavioral neuroscience.* Dubuque: Brown and Benchmark.

Beauchamp-Turner, D. L., & Levinson, D. M. (1992). Effects of meditation on stress, health, and affect. *Medical Psychotherapy: An International Journal, 5,* 123–131.

Beaulieu, D. (2003). *Eye movement integration therapy: The comprehensive clinical guide.* Williston, VT: Crown House.

Beaumont, M., Batejat, D., Pierard, C., Coste, O., Doireau, P., Van Beers, P., et al. (2001). Slow release caffeine and prolonged (64-h) continuous wakefulness: effects on vigilance and cognitive performance. *Journal of Sleep Research, 10*(4), 265.

Beaumont, M., Batejat, D., Pierard, C., Van Beers, P., Denis, J. B., Coste, O., et al. (2004). Caffeine or melatonin effects on sleep and sleepiness after rapid eastward transmeridian travel. *Journal of Applied Physiology, 96,* 50–58.

Bech, B. H., Nohr, E. A., Vaeth, M., Henriksen, T. B., & Olsen, J. (2005). Coffee and fetal death: A cohort study with prospective data. *American Journal of Epidemiology, 162,* 983–990.

Bechara, A., Damasio, H., Tranel, D., & Damasio, A. R. (1997). Deciding advantageously before knowing the advantageous strategy. *Science, 275,* 1293–1295.

Beck, A. T. (1967). *Depression: Clinical, experimental and theoretical aspects.* New York: Harper & Row.

Beck, A. T. (1976). *Cognitive therapy and the emotional disorders.* New York: International Universities Press.

Beck, A. T. (1995). Cognitive therapy: A 30-year retrospective. In S. O. Lilienfeld (Ed.), *Seeing both sides: Classic controversies in abnormal psychology* (pp. 303–311). Pacific Grove, CA: Brooks/Cole. (Original work published 1991.)

Beck, A. T. (2008). The evolution of the cognitive model of depression and its neurobiological correlates. *American Journal of Psychiatry, 165,* 969–977.

Beck, A. T., & Alford, B. A. (2009). *Depression: Causes and treatment.* Philadelphia, PA: University of Pennsylvania Press.

Beck, A. T., & Emery, G. (1985). *Anxiety disorders and phobias: A cognitive perspective.* New York: Basic Books.

Beck, A. T., Freeman, A., & Davis, D. D. (2007). *Cognitive therapy of personality disorders.* New York: Guilford.

Beck, A. T., & Rector, N. A. (2005). Cognitive approaches to schizophrenia: Theory and therapy. *Annual Review of Clinical Psychology, 1,* 577–606.

Beck, A. T., Rector, N. A., Stolar, N., & Grant, P. (2008). *Schizophrenia: Cognitive theory, research, and therapy.* New York: Guilford.

Beck, A. T., Sokol, L., Clark, D., Berchick, R., & Wright, F. (1992). A crossover study of focused cognitive therapy for panic disorder. *American Journal of Psychiatry, 149,* 778–783.

Beck, J. S. (2005). *Cognitive therapy for challenging problems: What to do when the basics don't work.* New York: Guilford.

Beck, M. (1992, December 7). The new middle age. *Newsweek,* 50–56.

Becker, C. B., Stice, E., Shaw, H., & Woda, S. (2009). Use of empirically supported interventions for psychopathology: Can the participatory approach move us beyond the research-to-practice gap? *Behaviour Research and Therapy, 47,* 265–274.

Beckett, C., Maughan, B., Rutter, M., Castle, J., Colvert, E., Groothues, C., et al. (2006). Do the effects of early severe deprivation on cognition persist into early adolescence? Findings from the English and Romanian adoptees study. *Child Development, 77,* 696–711.

Behnke, M., Eyler, F. D., Warner, T. D., Garvan, C. W., Hou, W., & Wobie, K. (2006). Outcome from a prospective, longitudinal study of prenatal cocaine use: Preschool development at 3 years of age. *Journal of Pediatric Psychology, 31*(1), 41–49.

Behnke, S. (2004, December). Sexual involvements with former clients: A delicate balance of core values. *Monitor on Psychology,* 76–77.

Behrendt, R. (2006). Dysregulation of thalamic sensory "transmission" in schizophrenia: Neurochemical vulnerability to hallucinations. *Journal of Psychopharmacology, 20,* 356–372.

Behrens, K. Y., Hesse, E., & Main, M. (2007). Mothers' attachment status as determined by the Adult Attachment Interview predicts their 6-year-olds' reunion responses: A study conducted in Japan. *Developmental Psychology, 43,* 1553–1567.

Beilock, S. L., & Carr, T. H. (2005). When high-powered people fail: Working memory and "choking under pressure" in math. *Psychological Science, 16,* 101–105.

Beilock, S. L., Kulp, C. A., Holt, L. E., & Carr, T. H. (2004). More on the fragility of performance: Choking under pressure in mathematical problem solving. *Journal of Experimental Psychology: General, 133,* 584–600.

Beirne, R. O., Zlatkova, M. B., & Anderson, R. S. (2005). Changes in human short-wavelength-sensitive and achromatic resolution acuity with retinal eccentricity and meridian. *Visual Neuroscience, 22,* 79–86.

Beisel, K., Hansen, L., Soukup, G., & Fritzsch, B. (2008). Regenerating cochlear hair cells: Quo vadis stem cell. *Cell and Tissue Research, 333*(3), 373–379.

Bekinschtein, T., Tiberti, C., Niklison, J., Tamashiro, M., Ron, M., Carpintiero, S., et al. (2005). Assessing level of consciousness and cognitive changes from vegetative state to full recovery. *Neuropsychological Rehabilitation, 15*(3–4), 307–322.

Belik, S., Cox, B. J., Murray, B. S., Asmundson, G. J. G., & Sareen, J. (2007). Traumatic events and suicidal behavior: Results from a National Mental Health Survey. *Journal of Nervous and Mental Disease, 195,* 342–350.

Belin, P., Zatorre, R. J., & Ahad, P. (2002). Human temporal-lobe response to vocal sounds. *Brain Research and Cognitive Brain Research, 13,* 17–26.

Bell, B. E., & Loftus, E. F. (1989). Trivial persuasion in the courtroom: The power of (a few) minor details. *Journal of Personality and Social Psychology, 56,* 669–679.

Bell, C. C., Sowers, W., & Thompson, K. S. (2008). American Association of Community Psychiatrists' views on general features of DSM-IV. *Psychiatric Services, 59,* 687–690.

Bell, M. A., & Wolfe, C. D. (2007). Changes in brain functioning from infancy to early childhood: Evidence from EEG power and coherence working memory tasks. *Developmental Neuropsychology, 31*(1), 21–38.

Bell, P. A., Greene, T. C., Fisher, J. D., & Baum, A. (2000). *Environmental psychology* (5th ed.). Belmont, CA: Wadsworth.

Bellaby, P. (2003). Communication and miscommunication of risk: Understanding UK parents' attitudes to combined MMR vaccination. *British Medical Journal, 327,* 725–728.

Belli, R. F., & Loftus, E. F. (1996). The pliability of autobiographical memory: Misinformation and the false memory problem. In D. C. Rubin (Ed.), *Remembering our past: Studies in autobiographical memory* (pp. 157–179). New York: Cambridge University Press.

Belmonte, M. K., Cook, E. H., Jr, Anderson, G. M., Rubenstein, J. L., Greenough, W. T., Beckel-Mitchener, A., et al. (2004). Autism as a disorder of neural information processing: Directions for research and targets for therapy. *Molecular Psychiatry, 9,* 646–663.

Belsky, J., Vandell, D. L., Burchinal, M., Clarke-Stewart, K. A., McCartney, K., Owen, M. T., & The NICHD Early Child Care Research Network. (2007). Are there long-term effects of early child care? *Child Development, 74*, 681–701.

BeLue, R., Francis, L. A., & Colaco, B. (2009). Mental health problems and overweight in a nationally representative sample of adolescents: effects of race and ethnicity. *Pediatrics, 123*, 697–702.

Bem, D. J. (2000). Exotic becomes erotic: Interpreting the biological correlates of sexual orientation. *Archives of Sexual Behavior, 29*(6), 531–548.

Ben-Ari, A., & Gil, S. (2002). Traditional support systems: Are they sufficient in a culturally diverse academic environment? *British Journal of Social Work, 32*, 629–638.

Benecke, M. (1999). Spontaneous human combustion: Thoughts of a forensic biologist. *Skeptical Inquirer, 22*, 47–51.

Benedetti, F. G. (2007). Placebo and endogenous mechanisms of analgesia. *Handbook of Experimental Pharmacology,177*, 393–413.

Benedetti, F., Arduino, C., & Amanzio, M. (1999). Somatotopic activation of opioid systems by target-directed expectations of analgesia. *Journal of Neuroscience, 19*, 3639–3648.

Benenson, J. F., & Koulnazarian, M. (2008). Sex differences in help-seeking appear in early childhood. *British Journal of Developmental Psychology, 26*, 163–169.

Bener, A., Al Maadidb, M. G. A., Özkanc, T., Al-Bastb, D. A. E., Diyabb, K. N., & Lajunenc, T. (2008). The impact of four-wheel drive on risky driver behaviours and road traffic accidents. *Transportation Research Part F: Traffic Psychology and Behaviour, 11*, 324–333.

Benet-Martinez V., & Oishi, S. (2008). Culture and personality. In O. John, R. Robins, & L. Pervin (Eds.), *Handbook of personality: Theory and research* (3rd ed., pp. 542–567). New York: Guilford.

Benham, G., Woody, E. Z., Wilson, K. S., & Nash, M. R. (2006). Expect the unexpected: Ability, attitude, and responsiveness to hypnosis. *Journal of Personality and Social Psychology, 91*, 342–350.

Benight, C. C., Swift, E., Sanger, J., Smith, A., & Zeppelin, D. (1999). Coping self-efficacy as a mediator of distress following a natural disaster. *Journal of Applied Social Psychology, 29*, 2443–2464.

Benjamin, L. T., Jr. (2000). The psychology laboratory at the turn of the 20th century. *American Psychologist, 55*, 318–321.

Benjamin, L. T., Jr., & Baker, D. (2004). *From séance to science: A history of the profession of psychology in America.* Belmont, CA: Wadsworth.

Bennett, D. S., Bendersky, M., & Lewis, M. (2008). Children's cognitive ability from 4 to 9 years old as a function of prenatal cocaine exposure, environmental risk, and maternal verbal intelligence. Developmental Psychology, 44, 919–928.

Bennett, H. L., Giannini, J. A., & Davis, H. S. (1985). Nonverbal response to intraoperational conversation. *British Journal of Anaesthesia, 57*, 174–179.

Bennett, K. K., & Elliott, M. (2002). Explanatory style and health: Mechanisms linking pessimism to illness. *Journal of Applied Social Psychology, 32*, 1508–1526.

Bennett, R. J., & Robinson, S. L. (2000). Development of a measure of workplace deviance. *Journal of Applied Psychology, 85*, 349–360.

Ben-Shakhar, G., & Furedy, J. J. (1990). *Theories and applications in the detection of deception: A psychophysiological and international perspective.* New York: Springer-Verlag.

Ben-Shakhar, G., Bar-Hillel, M., & Kremnitzer, M. (2002). Trial by polygraph: Reconsidering the use of the guilty knowledge technique in court. *Law & Human Behavior, 26*, 527–541.

Benson, D. F., & Geschwind, N. (1971). Aphasia and related cortical disturbances. In A. B. Baker & L. H. Baker (Eds.) *Clinical neurology.* New York: Harper & Row.

Benson, E. (2003). Sex: The science of sexual arousal. *Monitor on Psychology, 34*, 50.

Benson, H. (1975). *The relaxation response.* New York: Morrow.

Bentin, S., DeGutis, J. M., D'Esposito, M., & Robertson, L. C. (2007). Too many trees to see the forest: Performance, event-related potential, and functional Magnetic Resonance Imaging manifestations of integrative congenital prosopagnosia. *Journal of Cognitive Neuroscience, 19*(1), 132–146.

Ben-Zur, H. (2002). Coping, affect and aging: The roles of mastery and self-esteem. *Personality & Individual Differences, 32*(2), 357–372.

Berant, E., Mikulincer, M., & Shaver, P. R. (2008). Mothers' attachment style, their mental health, and their children's emotional vulnerabilities: A 7-year study of children with congenital heart disease. *Journal of Personality, 76*, 31–65.

Berdahl, J. L., & Moore, C. (2006). Workplace harassment: Double jeopardy for minority women. *Journal of Applied Psychology, 91*, 426–436.

Beresford, J., & Blades, M. (2006). Children's identification of faces from lineups: The effects of lineup presentation and instructions on accuracy. *Journal of Applied Psychology, 91*, 1102–1113.

Beresford, T. P., Arciniegas, D. B., Alfers, J., Clapp, L., Martin, B., Du, Y., Liu, D., Shen, D., & Davatzikos, C. (2006). Hippocampus volume loss due to chronic heavy drinking. *Alcoholism, Clinical and Experimental Research, 30*, 1866–1870.

Bergin, A. E. (1971). The evaluation of therapeutic outcomes. In A. E. Bergin & S. L. Garfield (Eds.), *Handbook of psychotherapy and behavior change: An empirical analysis* (pp. 217–270). New York: Wiley.

Bergman, T., J., Kitchen, D. M. (2009). Comparing responses to novel objects in wild baboons (*Papio ursinus*) and geladas (*Theropithecus gelada*). *Animal Cognition, 12*(1), 63–73.

Berkowitz, L. (1994). Is something missing? Some observations prompted by the Cognitive-neoassociationist view of anger and emotional aggression. In L. R. Huesmann (Ed.), *Human aggression: Current perspectives* (pp. 35–60). New York: Plenum.

Berkowitz, L. (1998). Affective aggression: The role of stress, pain, and negative affect. In R. G. Geen & E. Donnerstein (Eds.), *Human aggression* (pp. 49–72). San Diego: Academic Press.

Berkowitz, L. (1999). Evil is more than banal: Situationism and the concept of evil. *Personality and Social Psychology Review, 3*, 246–253.

Bernard, L. L. (1924). *Instinct.* New York: Holt, Rinehart & Winston.

Bernardin, H. J., & Beatty, R. W. (1984). *Performance appraisal: Assessing human behavior at work.* Boston: Kent.

Bernat, J. A., Calhoun, K. S., Adams, H. E., & Zeichner, A. (2001). Homophobia and physical aggression toward homosexual and heterosexual individuals. *Journal of Abnormal Psychology, 110*, 179–187.

Berns, G. S., McClure, S. M., Pagnoni, G., & Montague, P. R. (2001). Predictability modulates human brain response to reward. *Journal of Neuroscience, 21*, 2793–2798.

Bernstein, D. A. (1970). The modification of smoking behavior: A search for effective variables. *Behaviour Research and Therapy, 8*, 133–146.

Bernstein, D. A., Borkovec, T. D., & Hazlett-Stevens, H. (2000). *Progressive relaxation training: A manual for the helping professions* (2nd ed.). New York: Praeger.

Bernstein, D. M., & Loftus, E. F. (2009). The consequences of false memories for food preferences and choices. *Perspectives on Psychological Science, 4*, 135–139.

Bernstein, D. M., & Roberts, B. (1995). Assessing dreams through self-report questionnaires: Relation with past research and personality. *Dreaming: Journal of the Association for the Study of Dreams, 5*, 13–27.

Bernstein, I. L. (1978). Learned taste aversions in children receiving chemotherapy. *Science, 200*, 1302–1303.

Berry, C. M., Ones, D. S., & Sackett, P. R. (2007). Interpersonal deviance, organizational deviance, and their common correlates: A review and meta-analysis. *Journal of Applied Psychology, 92*, 409–423.

Berry, C. M., Sackett, P. R., & Wiemann, S. (2007). A review of recent developments in integrity test research. *Personnel Psychology, 60*, 271–301.

Berry, J. W., & Bennett, J. A. (1992). Cree conceptions of cognitive competence. *International Journal of Psychology, 27*, 73–88.

Berscheid, E., & Reis, H. T. (1998). Attraction and close relationships. In D. Gilbert, S. T. Fiske, & G. Lindzey (Eds.), *Handbook of social psychology* (Vol. 2, 4th ed., pp. 193–281). Boston: McGraw-Hill.

Bersoff, D. M. (1999). Why good people sometimes do bad things: Motivated reasoning and unethical behavior. *Personality and Social Psychology Bulletin, 25*, 28–39.

Bertau, C., Anderson, N., & Salgado, J. F. (2005). The predictive validity of cognitive ability tests: A UK meta-analysis. *Journal of Occupational and Organizational Psychology, 78*, 387–409.

Bertenthal, B. I., Longo, M. R., & Kenny, S. (2007). Phenomenal permanence and the development of predictive tracking in infancy. *Child Development, 78*(1), 350–363.

Berti, A., Ladavas, E., & Corti, M. D. (1996). Anosognosia for hemiplegia, neglect dyslexia, and drawing neglect: Clinical findings and theoretical implications. *Journal of the International Neuropsychological Association, 2*, 426–440.

Best, D. (1992, June). *Cross-cultural themes in developmental psychology.* Paper presented at workshop on cross-cultural aspects of psychology. Western Washington University, Bellingham.

Best, J. B. (1999). *Cognitive psychology* (5th ed.). Belmont, CA: Brooks/Cole.

Bestmann, S., Ruff, C. C., Blankenburg, F., Weiskopf, N., Driver, J., & Rothwell, J. C. (2008). Mapping causal interregional influences with concurrent TMS-fMRI. *Experimental Brain Research, 191*(4), 383–402.

Betan, E., Heim, A. K., Conklin, C. Z., & Westen, D. (2005). Countertransference phenomena and personality pathology in clinical practice: An empirical investigation. *American Journal of Psychiatry, 162*, 890–898.

Betch, T., Hoffman, K., Hoffrage, U., & Plessner, H. (2003). Intuition beyond recognition: When less familiar events are liked more. *Experimental Psychology, 50*, 49–54.

Bettencourt, B. A., Talley, A., Benjamin, A. J., & Valentine, J. (2006). Personality and aggressive behavior under provoking and neutral conditions: A meta-analytic review. *Psychological Bulletin. 132*, 751–777.

Beutler, L. E. (2000). David and Goliath: When empirical and clinical standards of practice meet. *American Psychologist, 55*, 997–1007.

Beutler, L. E. (2002). The dodo bird is extinct. *Clinical Psychology: Science and Practice, 9*, 30–34.

Beutler, L. E., & Malik, M. L. (Eds.). (2002). *Rethinking DSM: A psychological perspective.* Washington, DC: American Psychological Association.

Beyerstein, B. L. (1999). Pseudoscience and the brain: Tuners and tonics for aspiring superhumans. In S. Della Sala (Ed.), *Mind myths: Exploring popular assumptions about the mind and brain* (pp. 59–82). Chichester, UK: Wiley.

Bhatt, R. S., & Bertin, E. (2001). Pictorial cues and three-dimensional information processing in early infancy. *Journal of Experimental Child Psychology, 80*, 315–332.

Bhatt, S., Mbwana, J., Adeyemo, A., Sawyer, A. Hailu, A., & VanMeter, J. (2009). Lying about facial recognition: An fMRI study. *Brain and Cognition, 69*, 382–390.

Bhopal, R., Vettini, A., Hunt, S., Wiebe, S., Hanna, L., & Amos, A. (2004). Review of prevalence data in, and evaluation of methods for cross cultural adaptation of, UK surveys on tobacco and alcohol in ethnic minority groups. *British Medical Journal, 328*, 76.

Bhutta, A. T., Cleves, M. A., Casey, P. H., Cradock, M. M., & Anand, K. J. S. (2002). Cognitive and behavioral outcomes of school-aged children who were born preterm. *Journal of the American Medical Association, 288*, 728–737.

Bhutta, M. F. (2007). Sex and the nose: Human pheromonal responses. *Journal of the Royal Society of Medicine, 100*(6), 268–274.

Bibbins-Domingo, K., Coxson, P., Pletcher, M. J., Lightwood, J., & Goldman, L. (2007). Adolescent overweight and future adult coronary heart disease. *The New England Journal of Medicine, 357*, 2371–2379.

Bickis, M., Kelly, I. W., & Byrnes, G. (1995). Crisis calls and temporal and lunar variables: A comprehensive study. *Journal of Psychology, 129*, 701–711.

Bidwell, M. A., & Rehfeldt, R. A. (2004). Using video modeling to teach a domestic skill with an embedded social skill to adults with severe mental retardation. *Behavioral Interventions, 19*, 263–274.

Bieling, P. J., McCabe, R. E., & Antony, M. M. (2006). *Cognitive-behavioral therapy in groups.* New York: Guilford.

Bielsky, I. F., Hu, S.-B., Ren, X., Terwilliger, E. F., & Young, L. J. (2005). The V1a Vasopressin receptor is necessary and sufficient for normal social recognition: A gene replacement study. *Neuron, 47*, 503–513.

Bienenfeld, D. (2005). *Psychodynamic theory for clinicians.* New York: Lippincott Williams & Wilkins.

Bierhaus, A., Wolf, J., Andrassy, M., Rohleder, N., Humpert, P. M., Petrov, D., et al. (2003). A mechanism converting psychosocial stress into mononuclear cell activation. *Proceedings of the National Academy of Sciences, 100*, 1920–1925.

Bierut, L. J., Heath, A. C., Bucholz, K. K., Dinwiddie, S. H., Madden, P. A., Statham, D. J., et al. (1999). Major depressive disorder in a community-based twin sample: Are there different genetic and environmental contributions for men and women? *Archives of General Psychiatry, 56*, 557–563.

Bierut, L. J., Stitzel, J. A., Wang, J. C., Hinrichs, A. L., Grucza, R. A., Xuei, X., Saccone, N. L., Saccone, S. F., Bertelsen, S., Fox, L., Horton, W. J., Breslau, N., Budde, J., Cloninger, C. R., Dick, D. M., Foroud, T., Hatsukami, D., Hesselbrock, V., Johnson, E. O., Kramer, J., Kuperman, S., Madden, P. A. F., Mayo, K., Nurnberger, J., Jr., Pomerleau, O., Porjesz, B., Reyes, O., Schuckit, M., Swan, G., Tischfield, J. A., Edenberg, H. J., Rice, J. P., & Goate, A. M. (2008). Variants in nicotinic receptors and risk for nicotine dependence. *American Journal of Psychiatry, 165*, 1163–1171.

Bies, R. J., Tripp, T. M., & Kramer, R. M. (1997). At the breaking point: Cognitive and social dynamics of revenge in organizations. In R. A. Giacalone & J. Greenberg (Eds.), *Antisocial behavior in organizations* (pp. 18–36). Thousand Oaks, CA: Sage.

Biever, C. (2009, January 3). Interview: Inside the savant mind. *New Scientist, 200*(2688), 40–41.

Bigelow, B. J. (2006). There's an elephant in the room: The impact of early poverty and neglect on intelligence and common learning disorders in children adolescents, and their parents. *Developmental Disabilities Bulletin, 34*, 177–215.

Bigler, R., & Liben, L. (2007). Developmental intergroup theory: Explaining and reducing children's social stereotyping and prejudice. *Current Directions in Psychological Science, 16*, 162–166.

Bikbaev, A., & Manahan-Vaughan, D. (2008). Relationship of hippocampal theta and gamma oscillations to potentiation of synaptic transmission. *Frontiers in Neuroscience, 2*(1), 56–63.

Binet, A., & Simon, T. (1905). Methodes nouvelles pour le diagnostic du niveau intellectuel des anormaux. *L'Annee Psychologique, 11*, 191–244.

Binet, A., & Simon, T. (1908). The development of intelligence in the child. *L'Annee Psychologique, 14*, 1–94.

Bingheimer, J. B., Brennan, R. T., & Earls, F. J. (2005). Firearm violence exposure and serious violent behavior. *Science, 308*, 1323–1326.

Binson, D., Michaels, S., Stall, R., Coates, T. J., Gagnon, J. H., & Catania, J. A. (1995). Prevalence and social distribution of men who have sex with men: United States and its urban centers. *Journal of Sex Research, 32*(3), 245–254.

Binsted, G., Brownell, K., Vorontsova, Z., Heath, M., & Saucier, D. (2007). Visuomotor system uses target features unavailable to conscious awareness. *Proceedings of the National Academies of Science, 104*, 12669–12672.

Binzen, C. A., Swan, P. D., & Manore, M. M. (2001). Postexercise oxygen consumption and substrate use after resistance exercise in women. *Medicine and Science in Sports and Exercise, 33*, 932–938.

Birbaumer, N., Veit, R., Lotze, M., Erb, M., Hermann, C., Grodd, W., & Flor, H. (2005). Deficient fear conditioning in psychopathy: A functional magnetic resonance imaging study. *Archives of General Psychiatry, 62*, 799–805.

Birch, H. G. (1945). The relation of previous experience to insightful problem solving. *Journal of Comparative Psychology, 38*, 367–383.

Birnbaum, G. E., Reis, H. T., Mikulincer, M., Gillath, O., & Orpaz, A. (2006). When sex is more than just sex: Attachment orientations, sexual experience, and relationship quality. *Journal of Personality & Social Psychology, 91*, 929–943.

Bisiach, E., Capitani, E., & Tansini, E. (1979). Detection from left and right hemifields on single and double simultaneous stimulation. *Perceptual and Motor Skills, 48*(3, Pt. 1), 960.

Bisiach, E., Luzzatti, C., & Perani, D. (1979). Unilateral neglect, representational schema and consciousness. *Brain, 102*(3), 609–618.

Bisiach, E., Vallar, G., Perani, D., Papagano, C., & Berti, A. (1986). Unawareness of disease following lesions of the right hemisphere: Anosognosia for hemiplegia and anosognosia for hemianopia. *Neuropsychologia, 24, 471–482.*

Bisson, J. I. (2007). Eye movement desensitisation and reprocessing reduces PTSD symptoms compared with fluoxetine at six months post-treatment. *Evidence-Based Mental Health, 10*(4), 118.

Bjil, R. V., de Graaf, R., Hiripi, E., Kessler, R. C., Kohn, R., Offord, D. R., et al. (2003). The prevalence of treated and untreated mental disorders in five countries. *Health Affairs, 22*, 122–133.

Bjork, R. A. (1999). Assessing our own competence: Heuristics and illusions. In D. Gopher & A. Koriat (Eds.), *Attention and performance XVII. Cognitive regulation of performance: Interaction of theory and application* (pp. 435–459). Cambridge: MIT Press.

Bjork, R. A. (2001, March). How to succeed in college: Learn how to learn. *American Psychological Society Observer, 14*, 9.

Bjork, R. A., & Linn, M. C. (2006, March). The science of learning and the learning of science: Introducing desirable difficulties. *American Psychological Society Observer, 19*, 29, 39.

Bjorklund, D. F., & Green, B. L. (1992). The adaptive nature of cognitive immaturity. *American Psychologist, 47*, 46–54.

Bjorklund, P. (2006). No man's land: Gender bias and social constructivism in the diagnosis of borderline personality disorder. *Issues in Mental Health Nursing, 27*, 3–23.

Black Becker, C., Bull, S., Smith, L. M., Ciao, A. C. (2008). Effects of being a peer-leader in an eating disorder prevention program: can we further reduce eating disorder risk factors? *Eating Disorders, 16*(5), 444–459.

Blackwell, B. (1973). Psychotropic drugs in use today. *Journal of the American Medical Association, 225*, 1637–1641.

Blagrove, M. (1996). Problems with the cognitive psychological modeling of dreaming. *Journal of Mind and Behavior, 17*, 99–134.

Blair, I. V., Judd, C. M., & Fallman, J. L. (2004). The automaticity of race and Afrocentric facial features in social judgments. *Journal of Personality and Social Psychology, 87*, 763–778.

Blair, P. S., Sidebotham, P., Berry, P. J., Evans, M., & Fleming P. J. (2006). Major epidemiological changes in sudden infant death syndrome: A 20-year population-based study in the UK. *Lancet, 367*, 314–319.

Blair-West, G. W., Cantor, C. H., Mellsop, G. W., & Eyeson-Annan, M. L. (1999). Lifetime suicide risk in major depression: Sex and age determinants. *Journal of Affective Disorders, 53*, 171–178.

Blaisdell, A. P., Sawa, K., & Leising, K. J. (2006). Causal reasoning in rats. *Science, 311*, 1020–1022.

Blake, J., & de Boysson-Bardies, B. (1992). Patterns in babbling: A cross-linguistic study. *Journal of Child Language, 19*, 51–74.

Blake, R. (1998). What can be "perceived" in the absence of visual awareness? *Current Directions in Psychological Science, 6*, 157–162.

Blakeslee, S. (2000, January 4). A decade of discovery yields a shock about the brain. *New York Times.*

Blakeslee, S. (2001, August 28). Therapies push injured brains and spinal cords into new paths. *New York Times.*

Blanchard, P. N., & Thacker, J. W. (2007). *Effective training: Systems, strategies, and practices.* Upper Saddle River, NJ: Pearson Prentice Hall.

Blanchard, R. (2001). Fraternal birth order and the maternal immune hypothesis of male homosexuality. *Hormones and Behavior, 40*(2), 105–114.

Blanchard, R., & Lippa, R. A. (2007). Birth order, sibling sex ratio, handedness, and sexual orientation of male and female participants in a BBC Internet Research Project. *Archives of Sexual Behavior, 36*(2), 163–176.

Blascovich, J., Spencer, S. J., Quinn, D., & Steele, C. (2001). African Americans and high blood pressure: The role of stereotype threat. *Psychological Science, 12*, 225–229.

Blass, T. (2000). The Milgram paradigm 35 years later: Some things we know about obedience to authority. In T. Blass (Ed.), *Current perspectives on the Milgram paradigm* (pp. 35–59). Mahwah, N.J: Erlbaum.

Blass, T. (2004). *The man who shocked the world: The life and legacy of Stanley Milgram.* New York: Basic Books.

Blass, T. (2009). From New Haven to Santa Clara: A historical perspective on the Milgram obedience experiments. *American Psychologist, 64*, 37–45.

Blass, T., & Schmitt, C. (2001). The nature of perceived authority in the Milgram paradigm: Two replications. *Current Psychology: Developmental, Learning, Personality, Social, 20*, 115–121.

Bleck, T. P., & Klawans, H. L. (1986). Neurologic emergencies. *Medical Clinics of North America, 70*(5), 1167–1184.

Bleil, M. E., McCaffery, J. M., Muldoon, M. F., Sutton-Tyrrell, K., & Manuck, S. B. (2004). Anger-related personality traits and carotid artery atherosclerosis in untreated hypertensive men. *Psychosomatic Medicine, 66*, 633–639.

Bloch, M. H., Landeros-Weisenberger, A., Rosario, M., C., Pittenger, C., & Leckman, J. F. (2008). Meta-analysis of symptoms structure of obsessive-compulsive disorder. *American Journal of Psychiatry, 165*, 1532–1542.

Block, J. (2001). Millennial contrarianism: The Five-Factor approach to personality description 5 years later. *Journal of Research in Personality, 35*, 98–107.

Block, J. A. (1971). *Lives through time.* Berkeley: Bancroft Books.

Block, R. I., & Ghoneim, M. M. (1993). Effects of chronic marijuana use on human cognition. *Psychopharmacology, 110*(1–2), 219–228.

Blood, A. J., & Zatorre, R. J. (2001). Intensely pleasurable responses to music correlate with activity in brain regions implicated in reward and emotion. *Proceedings of the National Academy of Sciences, 98,* 11818–11823.

Bloom, L. (1995). *The transition from infancy to language: Acquiring the power of expression.* New York: Cambridge University Press.

Bloomgarden, A., & Calogero, R. M. (2008). A randomized experimental test of the efficacy of EMDR treatment on negative body image in eating disorder inpatients. *Eating Disorders, 16*(5), 418–427.

Blow, A. J., & Timm, T. M. (2002). Promoting community through family therapy: Helping clients develop a network of significant social relationships. *Journal of Systematic Therapies, 21,* 67–89.

Blum, R. W., Beuhring, T., & Rinehart, P. M. (2000). *Protecting teens: Beyond race, income and family structure.* Minneapolis, MN: Center for Adolescent Health, University of Minnesota.

Blumberg, F. C., Rosenthal, S. F., & Randall, J. D. (2008, July). Impasse-driven learning in the context of video games. *Computers in Human Behavior, 24*(4), 1530–1541.

Blumberg, H. P., Leung, H.-C., Skudlarski, P., Lacadie, C. M., Fredericks, C. A., Harris, B. C., et al. (2003). A functional magnetic resonance imaging study of bipolar disorder: State- and trait-related dysfunction in ventral prefrontal cortices. *Archives of General Psychiatry, 60,* 601–609.

Blumberg, M. S., & Lucas, D. E. (1994). Dual mechanisms of twitching during sleep in neonatal rats. *Behavioral Neuroscience, 108*(6), 1196–1202.

Blume, E. S. (1998). *Secret survivors: Uncovering incest and its aftereffects in women.* New York: Ballantine.

Blumenthal, J. A., Babyak, M., Wei., J., O'Conner, C., Waugh, R., Eisenstein, E., et al. (2002). Usefulness of psychosocial treatment of mental stress-induced myocardial ischemia in men. *American Journal of Cardiology, 89,* 164–168.

Blundell, J. E., & Cooling, J. (2000). Routes to obesity: Phenotypes, food choices, and activity. *British Journal of Nutrition, 83,* S33–S38.

Boake, C., Yeates, K. O., & Donders, J. (2002). Association of postdoctoral programs in clinical neuropsychology: Update and new directions. *Clinical Neuropsychology, 16*(1), 1–6.

Boardman, A. P., & Healy, D. (2001). Modeling suicide risk in affective disorders. *European Psychiatry, 16,* 400–405.

Bob, P. (2008). Pain, dissociation and subliminal self-representations. *Consciousness and Cognition, 17,* 355–369.

Boden, M. A. (2006). *Computer models of mind.* Cambridge, UK: Cambridge University Press.

Boden-Albala, B., Litwak, E., Elkind, M. S., Rundek, T., & Sacco, R. L. (2005). Social isolation and outcomes post stroke. *Neurology, 64,* 1888–1892.

Bodian, S. (1999). *Meditation for dummies.* Indianapolis: IDG Books Worldwide.

Boehning, D., & Snyder, S. H. (2003). Novel neural modulators. *Annual Review of Neuroscience, 26,* 105–131.

Bogaert, A. F., Blanchard, R., & Crosthwait, L. (2007). Interaction of birth order, handedness, and sexual orientation in the Kinsey interview data. *Behavioral Neuroscience, 121*(5), 845–853.

Bohner, G., & Schwarz, N. (2001). Attitudes persuasion and behavior. In A. Tesser & N. Schwarz (Eds.), *Blackwell handbook of social psychology: Intraindividual processes* (pp. 413–435). Oxford, UK: Blackwell.

Bolla, K. I., Brown, K., Eldreth, D., Tate, K., & Cadet, J. L. (2002). Dose-related neurocognitive effects of marijuana use. *Neurology, 59,* 1337–1343.

Bolton, D., Eley, T. C., O'Connor, T. G., Perrin, S., & Rabe-Hesketh, S., et al. (2006). Prevalence and genetic and environmental influences on anxiety disorders in 6-year-old twins. *Psychological Medicine, 36,* 335–344.

Bomze, H. M., Bulsara, K. R., Iskandar, B. J., Caroni, P., & Skene, J. H. (2001). Spinal axon regeneration evoked by replacing two growth cone proteins in adult neurons. *Nature Neuroscience, 4,* 38–43.

Bonanno, G. A. (2004). Loss, trauma, and human resilience: Have we underestimated the human capacity to thrive after extremely aversive events? *American Psychologist, 59,* 20–28.

Bonanno, G. A. (2005). Resilience in the face of potential trauma. *Current Directions in Psychological Science, 14,* 135–138.

Bonanno, G. A., Galea, S., Bucciarelli, A., & Vlahov, D. (2007). What predicts psychological resilience after disaster? The role of demographics, resources, and life stress. *Journal of Consulting and Clinical Psychology, 75,* 671–682.

Bonanno, G. A., & Mancini, A. D. (2008). The human capacity to thrive in the face of potential trauma. *Pediatrics, 121,* 369–375.

Bonci, A., Bernardi, G., Grillner, P., & Mercuri, N. B. (2003). The dopamine- containing neuron: Maestro or simple musician in the orchestra of addiction? *Trends in Pharmacological Science, 24,* 172–177.

Bond, F. W., & Bunce, D. (2003). The role of acceptance and job control in mental health, job satisfaction, and work performance. *Journal of Applied Psychology, 88,* 1057–1067.

Bond, A., Aiken, L., & Somerville, S. (1992). The Health Beliefs Model and adolescents with insulin-dependent diabetes mellitus. *Health Psychology, 11,* 190–198.

Bond, L. A., & Hauf, A. M. C. (2004). Taking stock and putting stock in primary prevention: Characteristics of effective programs. *Journal of Primary Prevention, 24,* 199–221.

Bonner, R. (2001, August 24). Death row inmate is freed after DNA test clears him. *New York Times.*

Bonwell, C. C., & Eison, J. A. (1991). *Active learning: Creating excitement in the classroom.* Washington, DC: George Washington University.

Bordnick, P. S., Elkins, R. L., Orr, T. E., Walters, P., & Thyer, B. A. (2004). Evaluating the relative effectiveness of three aversion therapies designed to reduce craving among cocaine abusers. *Behavioral Interventions, 19,* 1–24.

Borg, M. B., Jr. (2002). The Avalon Garden Men's Association: A community health psychology case study. *Journal of Health Psychology, 7,* 345–357.

Borgida, E., Conner, C., & Monteufel, L. (1992). Understanding living kidney donors: A behavioral decision-making perspective. In S. Spacapan & S. Oskamp (Eds.), *Helping and being helped* (pp. 183–212). Newbury Park, CA: Sage.

Borkardt, J. J., Smith, A. R., Reeves, S. T., Weinstein, M., Kozel, F. A., Nahas, Z., Shelley, N., Branham, R. K., Thomas, K. J., and George, M. S. (2007). Fifteen minutes of left prefrontal repetitive transcranial magnetic stimulation acutely increases thermal pain thresholds in healthy adults. *Pain Research Management, 12*(4), 287–290.

Borkenau, P., Riemann, R., Angleitner, A., & Spinath, F. M. (2002). Similarity of childhood experiences and personality resemblance in monozygotic and dizygotic twins: A test of the equal environments assumption. *Personality & Individual Differences, 33,* 261–269.

Borkenau, P., Riemann, R., Spinath, F. M., & Angleitner, A. (2006). Genetic and environmental influences on person [MUL] situation profiles. *Journal of Personality, 74,* 1451–1479.

Borman, W. C., Hanson, M. A., & Hedge, J. W. (1997). Personnel selection. *Annual Review of Psychology, 48,* 299–337.

Borman, W. C., Penner, L. A., Allen T. D., & Motowidlo, S. (2001). Personality predictors of citizenship performance. *International Journal of Selection and Assessment, 9,* 52–69.

Borry, P., Schotsmans, P., & Dierickx, K. (2006). Evidence-based medicine and its role in ethical decision-making. *Journal of Evaluation in Clinical Practice, 12,* 306–311.

Borsutzky, S., Fujiwara, E., Brand, M., & Markowitsch, H. J. (2008). Confabulations in alcoholic Korsakoff patients. *Neuropsychologia, 46*(13), 3133–3143.

Bosma, H., Marmot, M. G., Hemingway, H., Nicholson, A. C., Brunner, E., & Stansfeld, S. A. (1997). Low job control and risk of coronary heart disease in Whitehall II (prospective cohort) study. *British Medical Journal, 314,* 558–565.

Bosompra, K., Ashikaga, T., Worden, J. K., & Flynn, B. S. (2001). Is more optimism associated with better health? Findings from a population-based survey. *International Quarterly of Community Health Education, 20,* 29–58.

Botwinick, J. (1961). Husband and father-in-law: A reversible figure. *American Journal of Psychology, 74,* 312–313.

Bouchard, L., Tremblay, A., Bouchard, C., & Perusse, L. (2007). Contribution of several candidate gene polymorphisms in the determination of adiposity changes: Results from the Quebec family study. *International Journal of Obesity, 31,* 891–899.

Bouchard, T. J. (1999). Genes, environment, and personality. In S. J. Ceci & W. M. Williams (Eds.), *The nature-nurture debate: The essential readings* (pp. 97–103). Malden, MA: Blackwell.

Bouchard, T. J., & McGue, M. (1981). Familial studies of intelligence: A review. *Science, 212*(4498), 1055–1059.

Bouchard, T. J., Jr. (2004). Genetic influence on human psychological traits: A survey. *Current Directions in Psychological Science, 13,* 148–151.

Bourassa, M., & Vaugeois, P. (2001). Effects of marijuana use on divergent thinking. *Creativity Research Journal, 13,* 411–416.

Bouret, S. G., Draper, S. J., & Simerly, R. B. (2004). Trophic action of leptin on hypothalamic neurons that regulate feeding. *Science, 304,* 108–110.

Bouton, M. E. (1993). Context, time, and memory retrieval in the interference paradigms of Pavlovian learning. *Psychological Bulletin, 114,* 80–99.

Bouton, M. E. (2000). A learning theory perspective on lapse, relapse, and the maintenance of behavior change. *Health Psychology, 19,* 57–63.

Bouton, M. E. (2002). Context, ambiguity, and unlearning: Sources of relapse after behavioral extinction. *Biological Psychiatry, 52,* 976–986.

Bouton, M., Mineka, S., & Barlow, D. (2001). A modern learning theory perspective on the etiology of panic disorder. *Psychological Review, 107,* 4–32.

Bouvier, S. E., & Engel, S. A. (2006). Behavioral deficits and cortical damage loci in cerebral achromatopsia. *Cerebral Cortex, 16*(2), 183–191.

Bowden, C. L. (2000). Efficacy of lithium in mania and maintenance therapy of bipolar disorder. *Journal of Clinical Psychiatry, 61,* 35–40.

Bowden, C. L., Calabrese, J. R., Sachs, G., Yatham, L. N., Asghar, S. A., Hompland, M., et al. (2003). A placebo-controlled 18-month trial of lamotrigine and lithium maintenance treatment in recently manic or hypomanic patients with bipolar I disorder. *Archives of General Psychiatry, 60,* 392–400.

Bower, G. H. (1981). Mood and memory. *American Psychologist, 36,* 129–148.

Bower, J. M., & Parsons, L. M. (2003). Rethinking the "lesser brain." *Scientific American, 289,* 50–57.

Bowlby, J. (1973). *Attachment and loss: Vol. 2. Separation.* New York: Basic Books.

Boxer, A. L., & Miller, B. L. (2005). Clinical features of frontotemporal dementia. *Alzheimer Disease and Associated Disorders, 19*(Suppl. 1), S3–S6.

Boyd, S. T. (2006). The endocannabinoid system. *Pharmacotherapy, 26*(12 Pt. 2), 218S–221S.

Boyer, J. L., Harrison, S., & Ro, T. (2005). Unconscious processing of orientation and color without primary visual cortex. *Proceedings of the National Academy of Sciences, 102,* 16875–16879.

Boyles, S. (2008, October 14). Phiten necklace: Red Sox secret weapon? Some athletes are true believers in the power of titanium. Retrieved January 15, 2009, from http://www.webmd.com/pain-management/news/20081014/phiten-necklace-red-sox-secret-weapon.

Boyle, S. H., Williams, R. B., Mark, D. B., Brummett, B. H., Siegler, I. C., Helms, M. J., & Barefoot, J. C. (2004).Hostility as a predictor of survival in patients with coronary artery disease. *Psychosomatic Medicine, 66,* 629–632.

Brach, J. S., FitzGerald, S., Newman, A. B., Kelsey, S., Kuller, L., VanSwearingen, J. M., & Kriska, A. M. (2003). Physical activity and functional status in community-dwelling older women. *Archives of Internal Medicine, 163,* 2565–2571.

Bradley, R., Greene, J., Russ, E., Dutra, L., & Westen, D. (2005). A multidimensional meta-analysis of psychotherapy for PTSD. *American Journal of Psychiatry, 162,* 214–227.

Bradley-Johnson, S., Graham, D. P., & Johnson, C. M. (1986). Token reinforcement on WISC-R performance for white, low-socioeconomic, upper and lower elementary-school-age students. *Journal of School Psychology, 24,* 73–79.

Bradshaw, G. L. (1993a). Why did the Wright brothers get there first? Part 1. *Chemtech, 23*(6), 8–13.

Bradshaw, G. L. (1993b). Why did the Wright brothers get there first? Part 2. *Chemtech, 23*(7), 16–22.

Brainerd, C. J., & Reyna, V. F. (2005). *The science of false memory.* New York: Oxford University Press.

Brainerd, C. J., Reyna, V. F., Wright, R., & Mojardin, A. H. (2003). Recollection rejection: False memory editing in children and adults. *Psychological Review, 110,* 762–784.

Brambilla, P., Cipriani, A., Hotopf, M., & Barbul, C. (2005). Side-effect profile of fluoxentine in comparison with other SSRIs, tricyclic, and newer antidepressants: A meta-analysis of clinical trial data. *Pharmacopsychiatry, 38,* 69–77.

Brandimonte, M. A., Hitch, G. J., & Bishop, D. V. M. (1992). Influence of short-term memory codes on visual image processing: Evidence from image transformation tasks. *Journal of Experimental Psychology: Learning, Memory, and Cognition, 18,* 157–165.

Brandtstadter, J., & Renner, G. (1990). Tenacious goal pursuit and flexible goal adjustment: Explication and age-related analysis of assimilative and accommodative strategies of coping. *Psychology and Aging, 5,* 58–67.

Brannick, M., & Levine, E. (2002). *Job analysis.* Thousand Oaks: CA: Sage.

Brannick, M. T., Levine, E. L., & Morgeson, F. P. (Eds.) (2007). *Job and work analysis, second edition: Methods, research, and applications for human resource management.* Thousand Oaks, CA: Sage.

Bransford, J. D., & Johnson, M. K. (1972). Contextual prerequisites for understanding: Some investigations of comprehension and recall. *Journal of Verbal Learning and Verbal Behavior, 11,* 717–726.

Brasher, E. E., & Chen, P. Y. (1999). Evaluation of success criteria in job search: A process perspective. *Journal of Occupational and Organizational Psychology, 72,* 57–70.

Braun, A. E., Balkin, T. J., & Wesensten, N. J. (1998). Dissociated pattern of activity in visual cortices and their projections during human rapid eye movement sleep. *Science, 279,* 91–95.

Braver, T. S., Reynolds, J. R., & Donaldson, D. I. (2003). Neural mechanisms of transient and sustained cognitive control during task switching. *Neuron, 39,* 713–726.

Bray, G. A., & Tartaglia, L. A. (2000). Medicinal strategies in the treatment of obesity. *Nature, 404,* 672–677.

Breed, A. G. (2006, January 28). Stress from Katrina is called "recipe for suicide." *Naples Daily News,* p. 4A.

Brefczynski-Lewis, J. A., Lutz, A., Schaefer, H. S., Levinson, D. B., & Davidson, R. J. (2007). Neural correlates of attentional expertise in long-term meditation practitioners. *Proceedings of the National Academies of Science, 104,* 11483–11488.

Breggin, P. R. (2007). *Brain-disabling treatments in psychiatry: Drugs, electroshock, and the psychopharmaceutical complex* (2nd ed.). New York: Springer Publishing.

Breggin, P. R. (2008). *Medication madness: True stories of mayhem, murder, and suicide caused by psychiatric drugs.* New York: St. Martin's Press.

Brehm, S. (1992). *Intimate relationships.* New York: McGraw-Hill.

Brehm, S., Kassin, S., & Fein, S. (1999). *Social psychology* (4th ed., Table 6.4). Boston: Houghton Mifflin.

Brehm, S., Kassin, S., & Fein, S. (2005). *Social psychology* (6th ed.). Boston, MA: Houghton-Mifflin.

Breier, J. I., Adair, J. C., Gold, M., Fennell, E. B., Gilmore, R. L., & Heilman, K. M. (1995). Dissociation of anosognosia for hemiplegia and aphasia during left-hemisphere anesthesia. *Neurology, 45,* 65–67.

Brelsford, J. W. (1993). Physics education in a virtual environment. In *Proceedings of the 37th Annual Meeting of the Human Factors and Ergonomics Society.* Santa Monica, CA: Human Factors.

Bremner, J. D., Shobe, K. K., & Kihlstrom, J. F. (2000). False memories in women with self-reported childhood sexual abuse. *Psychological Science, 11,* 333–337.

Bremner, J. D., Vythilingam, M., Vermetten, E., Caccarino, V., & Charney, D. S. (2004). Deficits in hippocampal and anterior cingulate functioning during verbal declarative memory encoding in midlife major depression. *American Journal of Psychiatry, 161,* 637–645.

Bremner, J. D., Vythilingam, M., Vermetten, E., Southwick, S. M., McGlashan, T., Nazeer, A., et al. (2003). MRI and PET study of deficits in hippocampal structure and function in women with childhood sexual abuse and posttraumatic stress disorder. *American Journal of Psychiatry, 160,* 924–932.

Brems, C., & Namyniuk, L. (2002). The relationship of childhood abuse history and substance use in an Alaska Sample. *Substance Use and Misuse, 37,* 473–494.

Brendgen, M., Boivin, M., Vitaro, F., Bukowski, W. M., Dionne, G., Tremblay, R. E., & Pérusse, D. (2008). Linkages between children's and their friends' social and physical aggression: Evidence for a gene-environment interaction? *Child Development, 79*(1), 13–29.

Brener, N. D., Hassan, S. S., & Barrios, L. C. (1999). Suicidal ideation among college students in the United States. *Journal of Consulting and Clinical Psychology, 67,* 1004–1008.

Brenes, G. A., Rapp, S. R., Rejeski, W. J., & Miller, M. E. (2002). Do optimism and pessimism predict physical functioning? *Journal of Behavioral Medicine, 25,* 219–231.

Brennan, F. X., & Charnetski, C. J. (2000). Explanatory style and Immunoglobulin A (IgA). *Integrative Physiological & Behavioral Science, 35,* 251–255.

Brennen, T., Baguley, T., Bright, J., & Bruce, V. (1990). Resolving semantically induced tip-of-the-tongue states for proper nouns. *Memory & Cognition, 18,* 339–347.

Brenner, R. A., Trumble, A. C., Smith, G. S., Kessler, E. P., & Overpeck, M. D. (2001). Where children drown, United States, 1995. *Pediatrics, 108,* 85–89.

Brenner, R. P. (2005). The interpretation of the EEG in stupor and coma. *Neurologist, 11*(5), 271–284.

Breslau, N., Lucia, V. C., & Alvarado, G. F. (2006). Intelligence and other predisposing factors in exposure to trauma and posttraumatic stress disorder: A follow-up study at age 17 years. *Archives of General Psychiatry, 63,* 1238–1245.

Breslau, N., Reboussin, B. A., Anthony, J. C., & Storr, C. L. (2005). The structure of posttraumatic stress disorder: Latent class analysis in 2 community samples. *Archives of General Psychiatry, 62,* 1343–1351.

Breteler, M. H., Hilberink, S. R., Zeeman, G., & Lammers, S. M. (2004). Compulsive smoking: The development of a Rasch homogeneous scale of nicotine dependence. *Addiction and Behavior, 29,* 199–205.

Brewer, J. B., Zhao, Z., Desmond, J. E., Glover, G. H., & Gabriel, J. D. E. (1998). Making memories: Brain activity that predicts how well visual experience will be remembered. *Science, 281,* 1185–1187.

Brewer, M. B. (2008). Social identity and close relationships. In J. Forgas & J. Fitness (Eds.), *Social relationships: Cognitive, affective, and motivational processes. The Sydney symposium of social psychology* (pp. 167–183). New York: Psychology Press.

Brewer, M. B., & Pierce, K. P. (2005). Social identity complexity and outgroup tolerance. *Personality and Social Psychology Bulletin, 31,* 428–437.

Brewer, N. T., Chapman, G. B., Gibbons, F. X., Gerrard, M., McCaul, K. D., & Weinstein, N. D. (2007). *Health Psychology, 26,* 136–145.

Brewer, W. F. (1977). Memory for the pragmatic implications of sentences. *Memory & Cognition, 5,* 673–678.

Brewer, W. F., & Treyens, J. C. (1981). Role of schemata in memory for places. *Cognitive Psychology, 13,* 207–230.

Bridge, J. A., Iyengar, S., Salary, C. B., Barbe, R. P., Birmaher, B., Pincus, H. A., et al. (2007). Clinical response and risk for reported suicidal ideation and suicide attempts in pediatric antidepressant treatment: A meta-analysis of randomized controlled trials. *Journal of the American Medical Association, 297,* 1683–1696.

Brigham, C. C. (1923). *A study of American intelligence.* Princeton, NJ: Princeton University Press.

Bright, J. I., Baker, K. D., & Neimeyer, R. A. (1999). Professional and paraprofessional group treatments for depression: A comparison of cognitive-behavioral and mutual support interventions. *Journal of Consulting and Clinical Psychology, 67,* 491–501.

Brinkhaus, B., Witt, C. M., Jena, S., Linde, K., Streng, A., Wagenpfeil, S., et al. (2006). Acupuncture in patients with chronic low back pain: A randomized controlled trial. *Archives of Internal Medicine, 166,* 450–457.

Brislin, R. (1993). *Understanding culture's influence on behavior.* Fort Worth: Harcourt, Brace, Jovanovich.

British Medical Association. (2000). *Acupuncture: Efficacy, safety, and practice.* London: Harwood Academic.

Broadbent, E., Petrie, K. J., Alley, P. G., & Booth, R. J. (2003). Psychological stress impairs early wound repair following surgery. *Psychosomatic Medicine, 65,* 865–869.

Broca, P. (1861). Remargues sur le siege de la faculte de la porle articulee, suives d'une observation d'aphemie (perte de parole). *Bulletin Societie Anatomie, 36,* 330–357.

Broca, P. (1865). Sur la faculté du langage articulé. *Bulletin Societe Anthropologie Paris, 6,* 337–393.

Brock, J. W., Farooqui, S. M., Ross, K. D., & Payne, S. (1994). Stress-related behavior and central norepinephrine concentrations in the REM sleep-deprived rat. *Physiology and Behavior, 55*(6), 997–1003.

Broderick, J. E., Junghaenel, D. U., & Schwartz, J. E. (2005). Written emotional expression produces health benefits in fibromyalgia patients. *Psychosomatic Medicine, 67,* 326–34.

Brodino, N., Lanati, N., Barale, F., Martinelli, V., Politi, P., et al. (2008). Decreased NT-3 plasma levels and platelet serotonin content in patients with hypochondriasis. *Journal of Psychosomatic Research, 65,* 435–439.

Brody, A. L., Mandelkern, M. A., London, E. D., Olmstead, R. E., Farahi, J., Scheibal, D., et al. (2006). Cigarette smoking saturates brain alpha 4 beta 2 nicotine acetylcholine receptors. *Archives of General Psychiatry, 63,* 907–915.

Brody, N. (2003). Construct validation of the Sternberg Triarchic Abilities Test: Comment and reanalysis. *Intelligence, 31,* 319–330.

Brody, N., & Ehrlichman, H. (1998). *Personality psychology: The science of individuality.* Upper Saddle River, NJ: Prentice Hall.

Brondolo, E., Rieppi, R., Erickson, S. A., Bagiella, E., Shapiro, P. A., McKinley, P., & Sloan, R. P. (2003). Hostility, interpersonal interactions, and ambulatory blood pressure. *Psychosomatic Medicine, 65,* 1003–1011.

Brook, C. A., & Schmidt, L. A. (2008). Social anxiety disorder: A review of environmental factors. *Neuropsychiatric Disease and Treatment, 4,* 123–143.

Brooks-Gunn, J., & Chase-Lansdale, P. L. (2002). Adolescent parenthood. In M. H. Bornstein (Ed.), *Handbook of parenting* (2nd ed.). Mahwah, NJ: Erlbaum.

Brown, A. L., Campione, J. C., Webber, L. S., & McGilly, K. (1992). Interactive learning environments: A new look at assessment and instruction. In B. Gifford & M. C. O'Connor (Eds.), *Changing assessments: Alternative views of aptitude, achievement, and instruction* (pp. 121–212). Boston: Kluwer.

Brown, A. S. (1991). A review of the tip-of-the-tongue experience. *Psychological Bulletin, 109,* 204–233.

Brown, A. S. (2004). *The déjà vu experience.* New York: Psychology Press.

Brown, A. S., & Nix, L. A. (1996). Age-related changes in the tip-of-the-tongue experience. *American Journal of Psychology, 109,* 79–91.

Brown, A. S., Begg, M. D., Gravenstein, S., Schaefer, C. A., Wyatt, R. J., Bresnahan, M., et al. (2005). Serologic evidence of prenatal influenza in the etiology of schizophrenia. *Obstetrical and Gynecological Survey, 60,* 77–78.

Brown, A. S., Schaefer, C. A., Quesenberry, C. P., Jr., Liu, L., Babulas, V. P., & Susser, E. S. (2005). Maternal exposure to toxoplasmosis and risk of schizophrenia in adult offspring. *American Journal of Psychiatry, 162,* 767–773.

Brown, C. (2003, January 31). The man who mistook his wife for a deer. *New York Times Magazine.*

Brown, G. K., Beck, A. T., Steer, R. A., & Grisham, J. R. (2000). Risk factors for suicide in psychiatric outpatients: A 20-year prospective study. *Journal of Consulting and Clinical Psychology, 68,* 371–377.

Brown, G. W., & Moran, P. M. (1997). Single mothers, poverty and depression. *Psychological Medicine, 27,* 21–33.

Brown, J. (1958). Some tests of the decay theory of immediate memory. *Quarterly Journal of Experimental Psychology, 10,* 12–21.

Brown, L. M., Bongar, B., & Cleary, K. M. (2004). A profile of psychologists' views of critical risk factors for completed suicide in older adults. *Professional Psychology: Research and Practice, 35,* 90–96.

Brown, P. D., & O'Leary, K. D. (2000). Therapeutic alliance: Predicting continuance and success in group treatment for spouse abuse. *Journal of Consulting and Clinical Psychology, 68,* 340–345.

Brown, R. A. (1973). *First language.* Cambridge: Harvard University Press.

Brown, R., & Kulik, J. (1977). Flashbulb memories. *Cognition, 5,* 73–99.

Brown, R., & McNeill, D. (1966). The "tip-of-the-tongue" phenomenon. *Journal of Verbal Learning and Verbal Behavior, 5,* 325–337.

Brown, S. L., Nesse, R. M., Vinokur, A. D., & Smith, D. M. (2003). Providing social support may be more beneficial than receiving it: Results from a prospective study of mortality. *Psychological Science, 14,* 320–327.

Brown, T., DiNardo, P. A., Lehman, C., & Campbell, L. A. (2001). Reliability of DSM-IV anxiety and mood disorders: Implications for classification of emotional disorders. *Journal of Abnormal Psychology, 110,* 49–58.

Browne, K. D., & Hamilton-Giachritsis, C. (2005). The influence of violent media on children and adolescents: A public health approach. *Lancet, 365,* 702–710.

Bruce, D., Dolan, A., & Phillips-Grant, K. (2000). On the transition from childhood amnesia to the recall of personal memories. *Psychological Science, 11,* 360–364.

Bruce, E., & Waelde, L. C. (2008). Relationships of ethnicity, ethnic identity, and trauma symptoms to delinquency. *Journal of Loss & Trauma, 13,* 395–405.

Bruce, T. J., Spiegel, D. A., & Hegel, M. T. (1999). Cognitive-behavioral therapy helps prevent relapse and recurrence of panic disorder following Alpazolam discontinuation: A long-term follow-up of the Peoria and Dartmouth studies. *Journal of Consulting and Clinical Psychology, 67,* 151–156.

Bruck, M., Cavanagh, P., & Ceci, S. J. (1991). Fortysomething: Recognizing faces at one's 25th reunion. *Memory and Cognition, 19,* 221–228.

Brüning, J. C., Gautam, D., Burks, D. J., Gillette, J., Schubert, M., Orban, P. C., et al. (2000). Role of brain insulin receptor in control of body weight and reproduction. *Science, 289,* 2122–2125.

Bruff, D. (2009). *Teaching with classroom response systems: Creating active learning environments.* San Francisco: Jossey-Bass.

Brummett, B. H., Babyak, M. A., Williams, R. B., Barefoot, J. C., Costa, P. T., & Siegler, I. C. (2006). NEO personality domains and gender predict levels and trends in body mass index over 14 years during midlife *Journal of Research in Personality, 40,* 222–236.

Brummett, B. H., Mark, D. B., Siegler, I. C., Williams, R. B., Babyak, M. A., Clapp-Channing, N. E., & Barefoot, J. C. (2005). Perceived social support as a predictor of mortality in coronary patients: Effects of smoking, sedentary behavior, and depressive symptoms. *Psychosomatic Medicine, 67,* 40–45.

Brun, A. (2007). Identification and characterization of frontal lobe degeneration: Historical perspective on the development of FTD. *Alzheimer Disease & Associated Disorders, 21*(4), S3-s4.

Brunvald, J. H. (1989). *Curses! Broiled again! The hottest urban legends going.* New York: Norton.

Brush, D. H., Moch, M. K., & Pooyan, A. (1987). Individual demographic differences and job satisfaction. *Journal of Occupational Behaviour, 8,* 139–155.

Bryant, F. B., & Veroff, J. (2006). *The process of savoring: A new model of positive experience.* Mahwah, NJ: Erlbaum.

Bryant, R. A., & Guthrie, R. M. (2005). Maladaptive appraisals as a risk factor for posttraumatic stress. *Psychological Science, 16,* 749–752.

Bryant, R. A., & Mallard, D. (2003). Seeing is believing: The reality of hypnotic hallucinations. *Consciousness and Cognition, 12,* 219–230.

Bryant, R. A., & McConkey, K. M. (1989). Hypnotic blindness: A behavioral and experiential analysis. *Journal of Abnormal Psychology, 98,* 71–77.

Bryant, R. A., Moulds, M. L., Guthrie, R. M., Dang, S. T., Mastrodomenico, J., Nixon, R. D. V., et al. (2008). A randomized controlled trial of exposure therapy and cognitive restructuring for posttraumatic stress disorder. *Journal of Consulting and Clinical Psychology, 76,* 695–703.

Buccino, G., Vogt, S., Ritzl, A., Fink, G. R., Zilles, K., Freund, H. J., et al. (2004). Neural circuits underlying imitation learning of hand actions: An event-related fMRI study. *Neuron, 42,* 323–334.

Buchsbaum, M. S., Christian, B. T., Lehrer, D. S., Narayanan, T. K., Shi, B., et al. (2006). D2/D3 dopamine receptor binding with (F-18) fallypride in thalamus and cortex of patients with schizophrenia. *Schizophrenia Research, 85,* 232–244.

Buckholtz, J. W., Callicott, J. H., Kolachana, B., Hariri, A. R., Goldberg, T. E., Genderson, M., Egan, M. F., Mattay, V. S., Weinberger, D. R., & Meyer-Lindenberg, A. (2008). Genetic variation in MAOA modulates ventromedial prefrontal circuitry mediating individual differences in human personality. *Molecular Psychiatry, 13,* 313–324.

Budney, A. J., Hughes, J. R., Moore, B. A., & Novy, P. L. (2001). Marijuana abstinence effects in marijuana smokers maintained in their home environment. *Archives of General Psychiatry, 58,* 917–924.

Budney, A. J., Moore, B. A., Vandrey, R. G., & Hughes, J. R. (2003). The time course and significance of cannabis withdrawal. *Journal of Abnormal Psychology, 112,* 393–402.

Büssing, A., & Höge, A. (2004). Aggression and violence against home care workers. *Journal of Occupational Health Psychology, 9,* 206–219.

Bugental, D. B., & Grusec, J. E. (2006). Socialization processes. In W. Damon & R. M. Lerner (Series Eds.) & N. Eisenberg (Vol. Ed.), *Handbook of child psychology: Vol. 3. Social, emotional, and personality development* (6th ed.). New York: Wiley.

Bugg, J. M., Zook, N. A., DeLosh, E. L., Davalos, D. B., & Davis, H. P. (2006). Age differences in fluid intelligence: Contributions of general slowing and frontal decline. *Brain and Cognition, 62*(1), 9–16.

Bui, K.-V. T., Peplau, L. A., & Hill, C. T. (1996). Testing the Rusbult model of relationship commitment and stability in a 15-year study of heterosexual couples. *Personality and Social Psychology Bulletin, 22,* 1244–1257.

Buka, S. L., Shenassa, E. D., & Niaura, R. (2003). Elevated risk of tobacco dependence among offspring of mothers who smoked during pregnancy: A 30-year prospective study. *American Journal of Psychiatry, 160,* 1978–1984.

Bulevich, J. B., Roediger, H. L., Balota, D. A., & Butler, A. C. (2006). Failures to find suppression of episodic memories in the think/no-think paradigm. *Memory and Cognition, 34,* 1569–1577.

Bulik, C. M., Sullivan, P. F., Tozzi, F., Furberg, H., Lichtenstein, P., & Pedersen, N. L. (2006). Prevalence, heritability, and prospective risk factors for anorexia nervosa. *Archives of General Psychiatry, 63,* 305–312.

Bulik, C. M., Sullivan, P. F., Wade, T. D., & Kendler, K. S. (2000). Twin studies of eating disorders: A review. *International Journal of Eating Disorders, 27,* 1–20.

Bulkeley, K., & Kahan, T. L. (2008). The impact of September 11 on dreaming. *Consciousness and Cognition, 17,* 1248–1256.

Buller, D. B., Buller, M. K., & Kane, I. (2005). Web-based strategies to disseminate a sun safety curriculum to public elementary schools and state-licensed child-care facilities. *Health Psychology, 24,* 470–476.

Buller, D. J. (2005). *Adapting minds: Evolutionary psychology and the persistent quest for human nature.* Cambridge, MA: MIT Press.

Bullough, V. L. (1995, August). Sex matters. *Scientific American,* 105–106.

Bunde, J., & Suls, J. (2006). A quantitative analysis of the relationship between the Cook-Medley hostility scale and traditional coronary artery disease risk factors. *Health Psychology, 25,* 493–500.

Burchard, R. E. (1992). Coca chewing and diet. *Current Anthropology, 33*(1), 1–24.

Burger, J. M. (2009). Replicating Milgram: Would people still obey today? *American Psychologist, 64,* 1–11.

Burger, J. M., & Cornelius, T. (2003). Raising the price of agreement: Public commitment and the lowball compliance procedure. *Journal of Applied Social Psychology, 33,* 923–934.

Burger, J. M., & Guadagno, R. E. (2003). Self-concept clarity and the foot-in-the-door procedure. *Basic and Applied Social Psychology, 25,* 79–86. Burish, T., & Jenkins, R. (1992). Effectiveness of biofeedback and relaxation training in reducing the side effects of cancer chemotherapy. *Health Psychology, 11,* 17–23.

Burke, R. J., & Fiksenbaum, L. (2009). Work motivations, work outcomes, and health: Passion versus addiction. *Journal of Business Ethics, 84*(Suppl. 2), 257–263.

Burleson, B. R., Albrecht, T. L., & Sarason, I. G. (Eds.). (1994). *Communication of social support: Messages, interactions, relationships, and community.* Thousand Oaks, CA: Sage.

Burleson, M. H., Gregory, W. L., & Trevarthen, W. R. (1995). Heterosexual activity: Relationship with ovarian function. *Psychoneuroendocrinology, 20*(4), 405–421.

Burns, A., Bernabei, R., Bullock, R., Jentoft, A. J. C., Frölich, L., Hock, C., Raivio, M., Triau, E. Vandewoude, M. Wimo, A., Came, E. Van Baelen, B., Hammond, G. L., van Oene, J. C., & Schwalen, S. (2009). Safety and efficacy of galantamine (Reminyl) in severe Alzheimer's disease (the SERAD study): a randomised, placebo-controlled, double-blind trial. *Lancet Neurology, 8*(1), 39–47.

Burr, D. C., Morrone, C., & Fiorentini, A. (1996). Spatial and temporal properties of infant colour vision. In F. Vital-Durand, J. Atkinson, & O. J. Braddick (Eds.), *Infant vision* (pp. 63–77). Oxford: Oxford University Press.

Burris, C. T., Branscombe, N. R., & Klar, Y. (1997). Maladjustment implications of self and group gender-role discrepancies: An ordered-discrepancy model. *European Journal of Social Psychology, 27*, 75–95.

Burton, A. M., Wilson, S., Cowan, M., & Bruce, V. (1999). Face recognition in poor-quality video: Evidence from security surveillance. *Psychological Science, 10*, 243–248.

Burton, K. D., Lydon, J. E., D'Alessandro, D. U., & Koestner, R. (2006). The differential effects of intrinsic and identified motivation on well-being and performance: Prospective, experimental, and implicit approaches to self-determination theory. *Journal of Personality and Social Psychology, 91*, 750–762.

Bushman, B. J. (1998). Priming effects of media violence on the accessibility of aggressive constructs in memory. *Personality and Social Psychology Bulletin, 24*, 537–545.

Bushman, B. J., & Anderson, C. A. (2001). Media violence and the American public: Scientific facts versus media misinformation. *American Psychologist, 56*, 477–489.

Bushman, B. J., & Anderson, C. A. (2009). Comfortably numb: Desensitizing effects of violent media on helping others. *Psychological Science, 20*, 273–277.

Bushman, B. J., & Huesmann, L. R. (2000). Effects of televised violence on aggression. In D. Singer & J. Singer (Eds.), *Handbook of children and the media* (pp. 223–254). Thousand Oaks, CA: Sage.

Bushman, B. J., & Huesmann, L. R. (2006). Short-term and long-term effects of violent media on aggression in children and adults. *Archives of Pediatrics & Adolescent Medicine, 160*, 348–352.

Bushman, B. J., Bonacci, A. M., Pedersen, W. C., Vasquez, E. A., & Miller, N. (2005). Chewing on it can chew you up: Effects of rumination on triggered displaced aggression. *Journal of Personality and Social Psychology, 88*, 969–983.

Buss, A. H. (1997). Evolutionary perspectives on personality traits. In R. Hogan, J. Johnson, & S. Briggs (Eds.), *Handbook of personality psychology* (pp. 345–366). San Diego: Academic Press.

Buss, D. M. (2003). *The evolution of desire: Strategies of human mating.* New York: Basic Books.

Buss, D. M. (2004a). *Evolutionary psychology: The new science of the mind* (2nd ed.). Boston: Allyn & Bacon.

Buss, D. M. (2004b). *The evolution of desire: Strategies of human mating.* New York: Basic Books.

Buss, D. M. (2009). The great struggles of life: Darwin and the emergence of evolutionary psychology. *American Psychologist, 64*, 140–148.

Bustillo, J. R., Lauriello, J., Horan, W. P., & Keith, S. J. (2001). The psychosocial treatment of schizophrenia: An update. *American Journal of Psychiatry, 158*, 163–175.

Buston, P. M., & Emlen, S. T. (2003). Cognitive processes underlying human mate choice: The relationship between self-perception and mate preference in Western society. *Proceedings of the National Academy of Sciences, 100*, 8805–8810.

Butcher, J. N. (2004). Personality assessment without borders: Adaptation of the MMPI-2 across cultures. *Journal of Personality Assessment, 83*(2), 90–104.

Butcher, J. N., & Rouse, S. V. (1996). Personality: Individual differences and clinical assessment. *Annual Review of Psychology, 47*, 87–111.

Butcher, J. N., Mineka, S., & Hooley, J. M. (2010). *Abnormal psychology* (14th ed.). Boston: Allyn & Bacon.

Butler, A. C., Chapman, J. E., Forman, E. M., & Beck, A. T. (2006). The empirical status of cognitive-behavioral therapy: A review of meta-analyses. *Clinical Psychology Review, 26*, 17–31.

Butler, R. (1998). Information seeking and achievement motivation in middle childhood and adolescence: The role of conceptions of ability. *Developmental Psychology, 35*, 146–163.

Butters, N. (1981). The Wernicke-Korsakoff syndrome: A review of psychological, neuropathological and etiological factors. *Currents in Alcohol, 8*, 205–232.

Buunk, A. P., Cohen-Schotanus, J., & van Nek, R. H. (2007). Why and how people engage in social comparison while learning social skills in groups. *Group Dynamics: Theory, Research, and Practice, 11*, 140–152.

Buunk, A. P., Peiró, J. M., & Griffioen, C. (2007). A positive role model may stimulate career-oriented behavior. *Journal of Applied Social Psychology, 37*, 1489–1500.

Buunk, B., & Oldersma, F. L. (2001). Social comparisons and close relationships. In G. Fletcher & M. Clark (Eds.), *Blackwell handbook of social psychology: Interpersonal processes* (pp. 388–408). Oxford, UK: Blackwell.

Buunk, B. P., Zurriaga, R., Peiró, J. M., Nauta, A., & Gonsalvez, I. (2005). Social comparisons at work as related to a cooperative social climate and to individual differences in social comparison orientation. *Applied Psychology: An International Review, 54*, 61–80.

Buxhoeveden, D. P., Switala, A. E., Roy, E., Litaker, M., & Casanova, M. F. (2001). Morphological differences between minicolumns in human and nonhuman primate cortex. *American Journal of Physical Anthropology, 115*, 361–371.

Byrne, U. T. E., Ross, J. M., Faull, R. L. M., & Dragunow, M. (2009). High-throughput quantification of Alzheimer's disease pathological markers in the post-mortem human brain. *Journal of Neuroscience Methods, 176*(2), 298–309.

Cabanac, M., & Morrissette, J. (1992). Acute, but not chronic, exercise lowers the body weight set-point in male rats. *Physiology and Behavior, 52*(6), 1173–1177.

Cabeza, R., Rao, S. M., Wagner, A. D., Mayer, A. R., & Schacter, D. L. (2001). Can medial temporal lobe regions distinguish true from false? An event-related functional MRI study of veridical and illusory recognition memory. *Proceedings of the National Academy of Sciences, 98*, 4805–4810.

Cabot, P. J. (2001). Immune-derived opioids and peripheral antinociception. *Clinical and Experimental Pharmacology and Physiology, 28*, 230–232.

Caccamo, A., Fisher, A., & LaFerla, F. M. (2009). M1 Agonists as a Potential Disease-Modifying Therapy for Alzheimer's Disease. *Current Alzheimer Research, 6*(2), 112–117.

Cacioppo, J. T., & Decety, J. (2009). What are the brain mechanisms on which psychological processes are based? *Perspectives on Psychological Science, 4*, 10–18.

Cacioppo, J. T., Berntson, G. G., Sheridan, J. F., & McClintock, M. K. (2000). Multilevel integrative analyses of human behavior: Social neuroscience and the complementing nature of social and biological approaches. *Psychological Bulletin, 126*, 829–843.

Cacioppo, J. T., Malarkey, W. B., Kiecolt-Glaser, J. K., Uchino, B. N., Sgoutas-Emch, S. A., Sheridan, J. F., et al. (1995). Heterogeneity in neuroendocrine and immune responses to brief psychological stressors as a function of autonomic cardiac activation. *Psychosomatic Medicine, 57*, 154–164.

Cacioppo, J. T., Petty, R. E., & Crites, S. L. (1993). Attitude change. In V. S. Ramachandran (Ed.), *Encyclopedia of human behavior* (pp. 261–270). San Diego: Academic Press.

Cacioppo, J. T., Poehlmann, K. M., Kiecolt-Glaser, J. K., Malarkey, W. B., Burleson, M. H., Berntson, G. G., & Glaser, R. (1998). Cellular immune responses to acute stress in female caregivers of dementia patients and matched controls. *Health Psychology, 17*, 182–189.

Cadinu, M., Maass, A., Rosabianca, A., & Kiesner, J. (2005). Why do women underperform under stereotype threat? *Psychological Science, 16*, 572–578.

Cadoret, R. J., Yates, W. R., Troughton, E., Woodworth, G., & Stewart, M. A. (1995). Adoption study demonstrating two genetic pathways to drug abuse. *Archives of General Psychiatry, 52*, 42–52.

Caggiano, V., Fogassi, L., Rizzolatti, G., Thier, P., & Casile, A. (2009). Mirror neurons differentially encode the peripersonal and extrapersonal space of monkeys. *Science, 324*, 403–406.

Cahill, S. P., Carrigan, M. H., & Frueh, B. C. (1999). Does EMDR work? And if so, why?: A critical review of controlled outcome and dismantling research. *Journal of Anxiety Disorders, 13*, 5–33.

Cahn, B. R., & Polich, J. (2006). Meditation states and traits, EEG, ERP, and neuroimaging studies. *Psychological Bulletin, 132*, 180–211.

Cain, D. J., & Seeman, J. (Eds.). (2002). *Humanistic psychotherapies: Handbook of research and practice.* Washington, DC: APA Books.

Cairns, R. B., Gariepy, J., & Hood, K. E. (1990). Development, microevolution, and social behavior. *Psychological Review, 97*, 49–65.

Calabrese, J. R., Shelton, M. D., Rapport, D. J., Youngstrom, E. A., Jackson, K., Bilali, S., et al. (2005). A 20-month, double-blind, maintenance trial of lithium versus divalproex in rapid-cycling bipolar disorder. *American Journal of Psychiatry, 162*, 2152–2161.

Caldwell, T. L., Cervone, D., & Rubin, L. H. (2008). Explaining intra-individual variability in social behavior through idiographic assessment: The case of humor. *Journal of Research in Personality 42*, 1229–1242.

Campbell, F. A., Pungello, E. P., Miller-Johnson, S., Burchinal, M., & Ramey, C. T. (2001). The development of cognitive and academic abilities: Growth curves from an early childhood educational experiment. *Developmental Psychology, 37*, 231–242.

Campbell, L., Simpson, J. A., Boldry, J., & Kashy, D. A. (2005). Perceptions of conflict and support in romantic relationships: The role of attachment anxiety. *Journal of Personality and Social Psychology, 88*, 510–531.

Campbell, R., & Capek, C. (2008). Seeing speech and seeing sign: Insights from a fMRI study. *International Journal of Audiology, 47*(Suppl. 2), S3–S9.

Campbell, R. S., & Pennebaker, J. W. (2003). The secret life of pronouns: Flexibility in writing style and physical health. *Psychological Science, 14*, 60–65.

Campion, M. A., & Campion, J. E. (1987). Evaluation of an interviewee skills training program in a natural field experiment. *Personnel Psychology, 40*, 676–691.

Campion, M. A., Palmer, D. K., & Campion, J. E. (1997). A review of structure in the selection interview. *Personnel Psychology, 50*, 655–702.

Campione, J. C., Brown, A. L., & Ferrara, R. A. (1982). Mental retardation and intelligence. In R. J. Sternberg (Ed.), *Handbook of human intelligence* (pp. 392–490). Cambridge: Cambridge University Press.

Campos, J. J. (1980). Human emotions: Their new importance and their role in social referencing. *Research and Clinical Center for Child Development, 1980–81 Annual Report*, 1–7.

Canada, D., & Goering, D. (2008). Deep thoughts on the river crossing game. *Mathematics Teacher, 101*(9), 632–639.

Canaris, J. (2008). An analysis of the efficacy of extinction as an intervention in the modification of switching in patients with dissociative identity disorder. *Dissertation Abstracts International: Section B: Sciences and Engineering*, p. 3255.

Candia, V., Rosset-Llobet, J., Elbert, T., & Pascual-Leone, A. (2005). Changing the brain through therapy for musicians' hand dystonia. *Annals of the New York Academy of Sciences, 1060,* 335–342.

Canli, T. (2008). Toward a "molecular psychology" of personality. In O. John, R. Robins, & L. Pervin (Eds.), *Handbook of personality: Theory and research* (3rd ed., pp. 311–327). New York: Guilford.

Canli, T., Qui, M., Omura, K., Congdon, E., Haas, B. W., Amin, Z., et al. (2006). Neural correlates of epigenesist. *Proceedings of the National Academy of Sciences, 103,* 16033–16038.

Cann, A., & Ross, D. A. (1989). Olfactory stimuli as context cues in human memory. *American Journal of Psychology, 102,* 91–102.

Cannon, C. P. (2005). The endocannabinoid system: A new approach to control cardiovascular disease. *Clinical Cornerstone, 7*(2–3), 17–26.

Cannon, T. D., Zorrilla, L. E., Shtasel, D., Gur, R. E., Gur, R. C., Marco, E. J., Moberg, P., & Price, A. (1994). Neuropsychological functioning in siblings discordant for schizophrenia and healthy volunteers. *Archives of General Psychiatry, 51,* 651–661.

Cannon, W. B. (1927). *Bodily changes in pain, hunger, fear and rage—An account of recent researches into the function of emotional excitement.* New York: Appleton.

Cannon, W. B., & Washburn, A. L. (1912). An explanation of hunger. *American Journal of Physiology, 29,* 444–454.

Canu, W. H. (2008). An experimental learning activity demonstrating normal and phobic anxiety. *Teaching of Psychology, 35,* 22–25.

Capasso, R., Izzo, A. A. (2008). Gastrointestinal regulation of food intake: General aspects and focus on anandamide and oleoylethanolamide. *Journal of Neuroendocrinology, 20*(Suppl. 1), 39–46.

Caplan, D. (2003a). Aphasic syndromes. In K. M. Heilman & E. Valenstein (Eds.), *Clinical neuropsychology* (4th ed.). New York: Oxford.

Caplan, D. (2003b). Syntactic aspects of language disorders. In K. M. Heilman & E. Valenstein (Eds.), *Clinical neuropsychology* (4th ed.). New York: Oxford University Press.

Caplan, L. R. (2004). Clinical diagnosis of patients with cerebrovascular disease. *Primary Care, 31*(1), 95–109.

Caplan, L. R. (2005). Stroke. *Review of Neurological Disorders, 2,* 223–225.

Caplan, P. J. (1995). *They say you're crazy. How the world's most powerful psychiatrists decide who's normal.* Reading, MA: Addison-Wesley.

Capriani, A., Pretty, H., Hawton, K., & Geddes, J. R. (2005). Lithium in the prevention of suicidal behavior and all-cause mortality in patients with mood disorders: A systematic review of randomized trials. *American Journal of Psychiatry, 162,* 1805–1819.

Capron, C., & Duyme, M. (1989). Assessment of effects of socio-economic status on IQ in a full cross-fostering study. *Nature, 340,* 552–553.

Capron, C., & Duyme, M. (1996). Effect of socioeconomic status of biological and adoptive parents on WISC-R subtest scores of their French adopted children. *Intelligence, 22,* 259–276.

Caputo, M., Monastero, R., Mariani, E., Santucci, A., Mangialasche, F., Camarda, R., Senin, U., & Mecocci, P. (2008). Neuropsychiatric symptoms in 921 elderly subjects with dementia: a comparison between vascular and neurodegenerative types. *Acta Psychiatrica Scandinavica, 117*(6), 455–464.

Caramazza, A., & Hillis, A. E. (1991). Lexical organization of nouns and verbs in the brain. *Nature, 349,* 788–790.

Card, N. A., Stucky, B. D., Sawalani, G. M., & Little, T. D. (2008). Direct and indirect aggression during childhood and adolescence: A meta-analytic review of gender differences, intercorrelations, and relations to maladjustment. *Child Development, 79,* 1185–1229.

Cardinali, D. P., Bortman, G. P., Liotta, G., Perez Lloret, S., Albornoz, L. E., Cutrera, R. A., et al. (2002). A multifactorial approach employing melatonin to accelerate resynchronization of sleep-wake cycle after a 12 time-zone westerly transmeridian flight in elite soccer athletes. *Journal of Pineal Research, 32,* 41–46.

Cardon, L. R., & Fulker, D. W. (1993). Genetics of specific cognitive abilities. In R. Plomin & G. McClearn (Eds.), *Nature, nurture, and psychology* (pp. 99–120). Washington, DC: American Psychological Association.

Cardon, L. R., Fulker, D. W., DeFries, J. C., & Plomin, R. (1992). Multivariate genetic analysis of specific cognitive abilities in the Colorado Adoption Project at age 7. *Intelligence, 16,* 383–400.

CARE Study Group. (2008). Maternal caffeine intake during pregnancy and risk of fetal growth restriction: A large prospective observational study. *British Medical Journal, 337,* a2332.

Carels, R. A., Young, K. M., Coit, C., Clayton, A. M., Spencer, A., & Hobbs, M. (2008). Can following the caloric restriction recommendations from the Dietary Guidelines for Americans help individuals lose weight? *Eating Behaviors, 9,* 328–335.

Carli, L. L. (1999). Cognitive reconstruction, hindsight, and reactions to victims and perpetrators. *Personality and Social Psychology Bulletin, 25,* 966–979.

Carli, L. L., Ganley, R., & Pierce-Otay, A. (1991). Similarity and satisfaction in romantic relationships. *Personality and Social Psychology Bulletin, 17,* 419–426.

Carlson, E. A., Sroufe, L. A., & Egeland, B. (2004). The construction of experience: A longitudinal study of representation and behavior. *Child Development, 75,* 66–83.

Carlson, J., Watts, R. E., & Maniacci, M. (2006). Play therapy. In J. Carlson, R. E. Watts, & M. Maniacci (Eds.), *Adlerian therapy: Theory and practice* (pp. 227–248). Washington, DC: American Psychological Association.

Carlson, L. E., Speca, M., Patel, K. D., & Goodey, E. (2003). Mindfulness-based stress reduction in relation to quality of life, mood, symptoms of stress, and immune parameters in breast and prostate cancer outpatients. *Psychosomatic Medicine, 65,* 571–581.

Carlsson, A., & Lecrubier, Y. (Eds.). (2004). *Progress in dopamine research schizophrenia.* New York: Taylor & Francis.

Carmichael, L. L., Hogan, H. P., & Walter, A. A. (1932). An experimental study of the effect of language on the reproduction of visually perceived form. *Journal of Experimental Psychology, 15,* 73–86.

Carney, D. R., Colvin, C. R., & Hall, J. A. (2007). A thin slice perspective on the accuracy of first impressions. *Journal of Research in Personality, 41,* 1054–1072.

Carney, S. M., & Goodwin, G. M. (2005). Lithium—A continuing story in the treatment of bipolar disorder. *Acta Psychiatricia Scandinavica, 111,* 7–12.

Carpenter, J. T. (2004). EMDR as an integrative psychotherapy approach: Experts explore the paradigm prism. *Psychotherapy Research, 14,* 135–136.

Carr, A. (2009). The effectiveness of family therapy and systemic interventions for child-focused problems. *Journal of Family Therapy, 31,* 3–45.

Carr, G. D., Moretti, M. M., & Cue, B. J. H. (2005). Evaluating parenting capacity: Validity problems with the MMPI-2, PAI, CAPI, and ratings of child adjustment. *Professional Psychology: Research and Practice, 36,* 188–196.

Carraher, T. N., Carraher, D., & Schliemann, A. D. (1985). Mathematics in the streets and in the schools. *British Journal of Developmental Psychology, 3,* 21–29.

Carroll, J., Neitz, M., Hofer, H., Neitz, J., & Williams, D. R. (2004). Functional photoreceptor loss revealed with adaptive optics: An alternate cause of color blindness. *Proceedings of the National Academy of Sciences, 101,* 8461–8466.

Carstensen, L. (1997, August). *Psychology and the aging revolution: Changes in social needs and social goals across the lifespan.* Paper presented at the annual convention of the American Psychological Association.

Carter, M. M., Hollon, S. D., Carson, R., & Shelton, R. C. (1995). Effects of a safe person on induced distress following a biological challenge in panic disorder with agoraphobia. *Journal of Abnormal Psychology, 104,* 156–163.

Cartwright, R. D. (1978). *A primer on sleep and dreaming.* Reading, MA: Addison-Wesley.

Cartwright, R. D. (1993). Who needs their dreams? The usefulness of dreams in psychotherapy. *Journal of the American Academy of Psychoanalysis, 21*(4), 539–547.

Carver, C. S., Johnson, S. L., & Joormann, J. (2008). Serotonergic function, two-mode models of self-regulation, and vulnerability to depression: What depression has in common with impulsive aggression. *Psychological Bulletin, 134,* 912–943.

Carver, C., & Scheier, M. (2004). *Perspectives on personality* (5th ed.). Boston, MA: Pearson.

Carver, C. S., & Scheier, M. F. (2002). The hopeful optimist. *Psychological Inquiry, 13,* 288–290.

Carver, K., Joyner, K., & Udry, J. R. (2003). National estimates of adolescent romantic relationships. In P. Florsheim (Ed.), *Adolescent romantic relations and sexual behavior: Theory, research, and practical implications* (pp. 23–56). Mahwah, NJ: Erlbaum.

Carver, L. J., & Vaccaro, B. G. (2007). 12-month-old infants allocate increased neural resources to stimuli associated with negative adult emotion. *Developmental Psychology, 43,* 54–69.

Casacalenda, N., Perry, J. C., & Looper, K. (2002). Remission in major depressive disorder: A comparison of pharmacotherapy, psychotherapy, and control conditions. *American Journal of Psychiatry, 159,* 1354–1360.

Casagrande, M., Violani, C., Lucidi, F., Buttinelli, E., & Bertini, M. (1996). Variations in sleep mentation as a function of time of night. *International Journal of Neuroscience, 85,* 19–30.

Casbon, T. S., Curtin, J. J., Lang, A. R., & Patrick, C. J. (2003). Deleterious effects of alcohol intoxication: Diminished cognitive control and its behavioral consequences. *Journal of Abnormal Psychology, 112,* 476–487.

Case, L., & Smith, T. B. (2000). Ethnic representation in a sample of the literature of applied psychology. *Journal of Consulting and Clinical Psychology, 68,* 1107–1110.

Casey, B. J., Galvan, A., & Hare, T. A. (2005). Changes in cerebral functional organization during cognitive development. *Current Opinion in Neurobiology, 15,* 239–244.

Casey, B. J., Getz, S., & Galvan, A. (2008, March). The adolescent brain. *Developmental Review, 28*(1), 62–77.

Caspi, A. (2000). The child is the father of man: Personality continuities from childhood to adulthood. *Journal of Personality and Social Psychology, 78,* 158–172.

Caspi, A., & Shiner, R. L. (2006). Personality development. In W. Damon & R. M. Lerner (Series Eds.) & N. Eisenberg (Vol. Ed.), *Handbook of child psychology: Vol. 3. Social, emotional, and personality development* (6th ed., pp. 300–365). New York: Wiley.

Caspi, A., & Silva, P. A. (1995). Temperamental qualities at age 3 predict personality traits in young adulthood: Longitudinal evidence from a birth cohort. *Child Development, 66,* 468–498.

Caspi, A., Begg, D., Dickson, N., Harrington, H., Langley, J., Moffitt, T. E., & Silva, P. A. (1997). Personality differences predict health-risk behaviors in young adulthood: Evidence from a longitudinal study. *Journal of Personality and Social Psychology, 73,* 1052–1063.

Caspi, A., Bem, D. J., & Elder, G. H., Jr. (1989). Continuities and consequences of interactional styles across the life course. *Journal of Personality, 57,* 375–406.

Caspi, A., Harrington, H., Milne, B., Amell, J. W., Theodore, R. F., & Moffitt, T. E. (2003). Children's behavioral styles at age 3 are linked to their adult personality traits at age 26. *Journal of Personality, 71,* 495–513.

Caspi, A., Henry, B., McGee, R. O., Moffitt, T. E., & Silva, P. A. (1995). Temperamental origins of child and adolescent behavior problems: From age 3 to Age 15. *Child Development, 66,* 55–68.

Caspi, A., McClay, J., Moffitt, T. E., Mill, J., Martin, J., Craig, I. W., et al. (2002). Role of genotype in the cycle of violence in maltreated children. *Science, 297,* 851–854.

Caspi, A., Moffitt, T. E., Morgan, J., Rutter, M., Taylor, A., Arseneault, L., et al. (2004). Maternal expressed emotion predicts children's antisocial behavior problems: Using monozygotic-twin differences to identify environmental effects on behavioral development. *Developmental Psychology, 40*, 149–161.

Caspi, A., Roberts, B. W., & Shiner, R. L. (2005). Personality development: Stability and change. *Annual Review of Psychology, 56*, 453–484.

Caspi, A., Sugden, K., Moffitt, T. E., Taylor, A., Craig, I. W., Harrington, H., et al. (2003). Influence of life stress on depression: Moderation by a polymorphism in the 5-HTT gene. *Science, 301*, 386–389.

Cassel, E., & Bernstein, D. A. (2007). *Criminal behavior* (2nd ed.). Mahwah, NJ: Erlbaum.

Castonguay, L. G., & Beutler, L. E. (Eds.) (2005). *Principles of therapeutic change that work.* New York: Oxford University Press.

Castro, L., & Toro, M. A. (2004).The evolution of culture: From primate social learning to human culture. *Proceedings of the National Academy of Sciences, 101*, 10235–10240.

Cattell, R. B., Eber, H. W., & Tatsuoka, M. (1970). *Handbook for the sixteen personality factor questionnaire (16PF).* Champaign, IL: Institute for Personality Testing.

Cavaiola, A. A., & Desordi, E. G. (2000). Locus of control in drinking driving offenders and nonoffenders. *Alcoholism Treatment Quarterly, 18*, 63–73.

Cavenett, T., & Nixon, D. V. (2006). The effect of arousal on memory for emotionally-relevant information: A study of skydivers. *Behaviour Research and Therapy, 44*, 1461–1469.

Ceci, S. J., Huffman, M. L. C., Smith, E., & Loftus, E. F. (1994). Repeatedly thinking about a non-event: Source misattributions among preschoolers. *Consciousness and Cognition, 3*, 388–407.

Centers for Disease Control and Prevention. (1999b). *Suicide deaths and rates per 100,000.* Retrieved December 7, 2004, from http://www.cdc.gov/ncipc/data/us9794/suic.htm.

Centers for Disease Control and Prevention. (2001). Deaths: Preliminary data for 2000. *National Vital Statistics Reports, 49*, 1–40.

Centers for Disease Control and Prevention. (2002a). *Suicide and self-inflicted injury.* Retrieved June 30, 2009, from http://www.cdc.gov/nchs/fastats/suicide.htm.

Centers for Disease Control and Prevention. (2002b). *Table 46: Death rates for suicide, according to sex, race, Hispanic origin, and age: United States, selected years 1950–2003.* Retrieved July 1, 2009, from http://www.ncbi.nlm.nih.gov/books/bv.fcgi?rid=healthus05.table.394.

Centers for Disease Control and Prevention. (2004). Web-based injury statistics query and reporting system (WISQARS). Retrieved December 7, 2004, from http://www.cdc.gov/ncipc/wisqars.

Centers for Disease Control and Prevention. (2006). WISQARS website and "Fatal Injury Reports." Retrieved February 8, 2006, from http://www.cdc.gov/ncipc/wisqars/.

Centers for Disease Control and Prevention. (2008). Deaths: Final Data for 2005. *National Vital Statistics Reports, 56*, 1–121.

Centers for Disease Control and Prevention. (2009a). Overweight and obesity: Introduction. Retrieved June 10, 2009, from http://www.cdc.gov/nccdphp/dnpa/obesity.

Centers for Disease Control and Prevention. (2009b). Preventing teen pregnancy: An update in 2009. Retrieved June 10, 2009, from http://www.cdc.gov/reproductivehealth/AdolescentReproHealth/AboutTP.htm#b.

Centerwall, L. (1990). Controlled TV viewing and suicide in countries: Young adult suicide and exposure to television. *Social Psychiatry and Social Epidemiology, 25*, 149–153.

Centonze, D., Picconi, B., Baunez, C., Borrelli, E., Pisani, A., Bernardi, G., & Calabresi, P. (2002). Cocaine and amphetamine depress striatal GABAergic synaptic transmission through D2 dopamine receptors. *Neuropsychopharmacology, 26*, 164–175.

Cepeda, N. J., Vul, E., Rohrer, D., Wixted, J. T., & Pashler, H. (2008). Spacing effects in learning: A temporal ridgeline of optimal retention. *Psychological Science, 19*, 1095–1102.

Çeponien, R., Lepisto, T., Shesakova, A., Vanhala, R., Alku, P., Naatanen, R., & Yaguchi, K. (2003). Speech-sound-selective auditory impairment in children with autism: They can perceive but do not attend. *Proceedings of the National Academy of Sciences, 100*, 5567–5572.

Cervone, D. (2005). Personality architecture: Within-person structures and processes. *Annual Review of Psychology, 56*, 423–452.

Cervone, D., & Pervin, L. A. (2008). *Personality theory and research* (10th ed.). Hoboken, NJ: Wiley.

Cervone, D., & Shoda, Y. (1999). *The coherence of personality: social cognitive bases of consistency, variability, and organization.* New York: Guilford.

Cha, J. H., Farrell, L. A., Ahmed, S. F., Frey, A., Hsiao-Ashe, K. K., Young, A. B., et al. (2001). Glutamate receptor dysregulation in the hippocampus of transgenic mice carrying mutated human amyloid precursor protein. *Neurobiological Disorders, 8*, 90–102.

Chamberlin, J. (2000). Easing children's psychological distress in the emergency room. *Monitor on Psychology, 31*, 40–42.

Chamberlin, J. (2000). Easing children's psychological distress in the emergency room. *Monitor on Psychology, 31*, 40–42.

Chambless, D. L., & Hollon, S. D. (1998). Defining empirically supported therapies. *Journal of Consulting and Clinical Psychology, 66*, 7–18.

Chambless, D. L., & Ollendick, T. H. (2001). Empirically supported psychological treatments. *Annual Review of Psychology, 52*, 685–716.

Champagne, F. A. (2009). Beyond nature vs. nurture: Philosophic insights from molecular biology. *Association for Psychological Science Observer, 22*, 3, 27–28.

Champion, V., & Huster, G. (1995). Effect of interventions on stage of mammography adoption. *Journal of Behavioral Medicine, 18*, 159–188.

Chan, D. (2005). Current directions in personnel selection research. *Current Directions in Psychological Science, 14*, 220–223.

Chan, J. C. K., Thomas, A. K., & Bulevich, J. B. (2009). Recalling a witnessed event increases eyewitness suggestibility: The reversed testing effect. *Psychological Science, 20*, 66–73.

Chandola, T., Brunner, E., & Marmot, M. (2006). Chronic stress at work and the metabolic syndrome: Prospective study. *British Medical Journal, 332*, 521–525.

Chandrashekar, J., Hoon, M. A., Ryba, N. J., & Zuker, C. S. (2006). The receptors and cells for mammalian taste. *Nature, 444*(7117), 288–294.

Chang, E. F., & Merzenich, M. M. (2003). Environmental noise retards auditory cortical development. *Science, 300*, 498–502.

Chao, R. K. (1994). Beyond parental control and authoritarian parenting style: Understanding Chinese parenting through the cultural notion of training. *Child Development, 65*, 1111–1119.

Chapman, D. Z., & Zweig, D. I. (2005). Developing a nomological network for interview structure: Antecedents and consequences of the structured selection interview. *Personnel Psychology, 58*, 673–702.

Chapman, G. B., & Coups, E. J. (2006). Emotions and preventive health behavior: Worry, regret, and influenza vaccination. *Health Psychology, 25*(1), 82–90.

Chapman, S., & Morrell, S. (2000). Barking mad? Another lunatic hypothesis bites the dust. *British Medical Journal, 321*, 1561–1563.

Chaput, J.-P., & Tremblay, A. (2009). The glucostatic theory of appetite control and the risk of obesity and diabetes. *International Journal of Obesity, 33*, 46–53.

Charles, S. T., & Carstensen, L. L. (2008). Unpleasant situations elicit different emotional responses in younger and older adults. *Psychology and Aging, 23*, 495–504.

Charles, S. T., Mather, M., & Carstensen, L. L. (2003). Aging and emotional memory: The forgettable nature of negative images for older adults. *Journal of Experimental Psychology: General, 132*, 310–324.

Charleton, T., Gunter, B., & Coles, D. (1998). Broadcast television as a cause of aggression? Recent findings from a naturalistic study. *Emotional and Behavioral Difficulties, 3*, 5–13.

Chase, T. N. (1998). The significance of continuous dopaminergic stimulation in the treatment of Parkinson's disease. *Drugs, 55*(Suppl. 1), 1–9.

Chassin, L., Pitts, S. C., & Prost, J. (2002). Binge drinking trajectories from adolescence to emerging adulthood in a high-risk sample: Predictors and substance abuse outcomes. *Journal of Consulting and Clinical Psychology, 70*, 67–78.

Chaudhry, I. B., Neelam, K., Duddu, V., & Husain, N. (2008). Ethnicity and psychopharmacology. *Journal of Psychopharmacology, 22*, 673–680.

Chemers, M. M. (2000). Leadership research and theory: A functional integration. *Group Dynamics, 4*, 27–43.

Chemers, M. M., Watson, C. B., & May, S. T. (2000). Dispositional affect and leadership effectiveness: A comparison of self-esteem, optimism, and efficacy. *Personality and Social Psychology Bulletin, 26*, 267–277.

Chen, J., Magavi, S. S. P., & Macklis, J. D. (2004). Neurogenesis of corticospinal motor neurons extending spinal projections in adult mice. *Proceedings of the National Academy of Sciences, 101*, 16357–16362.

Cheng, A. T. A., Gau, S.-F., Chen, T. H. H., Chang, J.-C., & Chang, Y.-T. (2004). A 4-year longitudinal study on risk factors for alcoholism. *Archives of General Psychiatry, 61*, 184–191.

Cheng, L.-C., Tavazoie, M., & Doetsch, F. (2005). Stem cells: From epigenetics to microRNAs. *Neuron, 46*, 363–367.

Cheng, Y., Kawachi, I., Coakley, E. H., Schwartz, J., & Colditz, G. (2000). Association between psychosocial work characteristics and health functioning in American women: Prospective study. *British Medical Journal, 320*, 1432–1436.

Chesney, M. A., Chambers, D. B., Taylor, J. M., Johnson, L. M., & Folkman, S. (2003). Coping effectiveness training for men living with HIV: Results from a randomized clinical trial testing a group-based intervention. *Psychosomatic Medicine, 65*, 1038–1046.

Chida, Y., & Steptoe, A. (2009). The association of anger and hostility with future coronary heart disease. *Journal of the American College of Cardiology, 53*, 936–946.

Chisholm, L. (1997, June). Trauma at an early age inhibits ability to bond. *APA Monitor*, 11.

Chivers, M. L., Rieger, G., Latty, E., & Bailey, J. M. (2004). A sex difference in the specificity of sexual arousal. *Psychological Science, 15*, 736–744.

Chivers, M. L., Seto, M. C., & Blanchard, R. (2007). Gender and sexual orientation differences in sexual response to sexual activities versus gender of actors in sexual films. *Journal of Personality and Social Psychology, 93*, 1108–1121.

Cho, H. J., Meira-Lima, I., Cordeiro, Q., Michelon, L., Sham, P., Vallada, H., et al. (2005). Population-based and family-based studies on the serotonin transporter gene polymorphisms and bipolar disorder: A systematic review and meta-analysis. *Molecular Psychiatry, 10*, 771–781.

Chodosh, J., Reuben, D. B., Albert, M. S., & Seeman, T. E. (2002). Predicting cognitive impairment in high-functioning community-dwelling older persons: MacArthur studies of successful aging. *Journal of the American Geriatrics Society, 50*(6), 1051–1060.

Choi, J., & Silverman, I. (2003). Processes underlying sex differences in route-learning strategies in children and adolescents. *Personality and Individual Differences, 34*, 1153–1166.

Choi, Y. H., Jang, D. P., Ku, J. H., Shin, M. B., & Kim, S. I. (2001). Short-term treatment of acrophobia with virtual reality therapy (VRT): A case report. *CyberPsychology and Behavior, 4*, 349–354.

Chomsky, N. (1965). *Aspects of the theory of syntax.* Cambridge, MA: MIT Press.

Chomsky, N. (1986). *Knowledge of language: Its nature, origin, and use.* New York: Praeger.

Chouinard, G. (2004). Issues in the clinical use of benzodiazepines: Potency, withdrawal, and rebound. *Journal of Clinical Psychiatry, 65*(Suppl. 5), 7–21.

Choy, Y., Fyer, A. J., & Lipsitz, J. D. (2007). Treatment of specific phobia in adults. *Clinical Psychology Review, 27*, 266–286.

Christakas, D. A., & Zimmerman, F. J. (2007). Violent television viewing during preschool is associated with antisocial behavior during school age. *Pediatrics, 120*, 993–999.

Christakis, N. A., & Fowler, J. R. (2007). The spread of obesity in a large social network over 32 years. *New England Journal of Medicine, 357*, 370–379.

Christensen, A., Atkins, D. C., Berns, S., Wheeler, J., Baucom, D. H., & Simpson, L. E. (2004). Traditional versus integrative behavioral couple therapy for significantly and chronically distressed married couples. *Journal of Consulting and Clinical Psychology, 72*, 176–191.

Christensen, H. C., Schüz, J., Kosteljanetz, M., Poulsen, H. S., Boice, J. D., Jr., McLaughlin, J. K., & Johansen, C. (2005). Cellular telephones and risk for brain tumors: A population-based, incident case-control study. *Neurology, 64*, 1189–1195.

Christensen, H., Griffiths, K. M., & Jorm, A. F. (2004). Delivering interventions for depression by using the Internet: Randomized controlled trial. *British Medical Journal, 328*, 265.

Christensen, M. S., Kristiansen, L., Rowe, J. B., & Nielsen, J. B. (2008). Action-blindsight in healthy subjects after transcranial magnetic stimulation. *Proceedings of the National Academies of Science, 105*, 1353–1357.

Christopher, K. (2003). Autistic boy killed during exorcism. *Skeptical Inquirer, 27*(6), 11.

Chu, J. (1994). Active learning in epidemiology and biostatistics. *Teaching and Learning in Medicine, 6*, 191–193.

Chua, H. F., Boland, J. E., & Nisbett, R. E. (2005). Cultural variation in eye movements during scene perception. *Proceedings of the National Academy of Sciences, 102*, 12629–12633.

Chugani, H. T., & Phelps, M. E. (1986). Maturational changes in cerebral function in infants determined by 18FDG positron emission tomography. *Science, 231*, 840–843.

Church, A. T. (2001). Personality measurement in cross-cultural perspective. *Journal of Personality, 69*(6), 979–1006.

Churchland, P. M. (1989). *A neurocomputational perspective: The nature of mind and the structure of science.* Cambridge, MA: MIT Press.

Cialdini, R. (2007). *Influence: Sciences and Practice* (5th ed.). New York: Allyn & Bacon.

Cialdini, R. B. (1995). Principles and techniques of social influence. In A. Tesser (Ed.), *Advanced social psychology* (pp. 257–282). New York: McGraw-Hill.

Cialdini, R. B. (2001). *Influence: Science and practice* (4th ed.). Boston: Allyn & Bacon.

Cialdini, R. B., & Goldstein, N. J. (2004). Social influence: Compliance and conformity. *Annual Review of Psychology, 55*, 591–621.

Cialdini, R. B., Wosinska, W. B., Barrett, D. W., Butner, J., & Gornik-Durose, M. (2001). The differential impact of two social influence principles on individualists and collectivists in Poland and the United States. In W. Wosinska, R. B. Cialdini, D. W. Barrett, & J. Reykowski (Eds.), *The practice of social influence in multiple cultures: Applied social research* (pp. 33–50). Mahwah, NJ: Erlbaum.

Ciccocioppo, R., Martin-Fardon, R., & Weiss, F. (2004). Stimuli associated with a single cocaine experience elicit long-lasting cocaine-seeking. *Nature Neuroscience, 7*, 495–496.

Ciccocioppo, R., Sanna, P. P., & Weiss, F. (2001). Cocaine-predictive stimulus induces drug-seeking behavior and neural activation in limbic brain regions after multiple months of abstinence: Reversal by D1 antagonists. *Proceedings of the National Academy of Sciences, 98*, 1976–1981.

Cicogna, P. C., Occhioneroa, M., Natalea, V., & Espositoa, M. J. (2006). Bizarreness of size and shape in dream images. *Consciousness and Cognition, 16*, 381–390.

Cilia, R., Siri, C., Marotta, G., Isaias, I. U., De Gaspari, D., Canesi, M., Pezzoli, G., & Antonini, A. (2008). Functional abnormalities underlying pathological gambling in Parkinson disease. *Archives of Neurology, 65*, 1604–1611.

Ciocca, V. (2008). The auditory organization of complex sounds. *Frontiers in Bioscience, 13*, 148–169.

Citrome, L., Jaffe, A., Levine, J., & Lindenmayer, J. (2005). Dosing of quetiapine in schizophrenia: How clinical practice differs from registration studies. *Journal of Clinical Psychiatry, 66*, 1512–1516.

Clancy, S. A. (2005). *Abducted: How people come to believe they were kidnapped by aliens.* Cambridge, MA: Harvard University Press.

Clancy, S. A., McNally, R. J., Schacter, D. L., Lenzenweger, M. F., & Pitman, R. K. (2002). Memory distortion in people reporting abduction by aliens. *Journal of Abnormal Psychology, 111*, 455–461.

Clancy, S. A., Schacter, D. L., McNally, R. J., & Pittman, R. K. (2000). False recognition in women reporting recovered memories of sexual abuse. *Psychological Science, 11*, 26–31.

Clark, A., Oswald, A., & Warr, P. (1996). Is job satisfaction U-shaped in age? *Journal of Occupational and Organizational Psychology, 69*, 57–81.

Clark, D. C., & Fawcett, J. (1992). Review of empirical risk factors for evaluation of the suicidal patient. In B. Bongar (Ed.), *Suicide: Guidelines for assessment, management, and treatment* (pp. 16–48). New York: Oxford University Press.

Clark, D. M., Ehlers, A., McManus, F., Hackmann, A., Fennell, M., Campbell, H., et al. (2003). Cognitive therapy versus fluoxetine in generalized social phobia: A randomized placebo-controlled trial. *Journal of Consulting and Clinical Psychology, 71*, 1058–1067.

Clark, E. V. (1983). Meanings and concepts. In P. H. Mussen, J. H. Flavell, & E. M. Markman (Eds.), *Handbook of child psychology: Vol. 3. Cognitive development* (4th ed., pp. 787–840). New York: Wiley.

Clark, E. V. (1993). *The lexicon in acquisition.* Cambridge: Cambridge University Press.

Clark, L. A., & Watson, D. (2008). Temperament: An organizing paradigm for trait psychology. In O. John, R. Robins, & L. Pervin (Eds.), *Handbook of personality: Theory and research* (3rd ed., pp. 265–286). New York: Guilford.

Clark, L. A., Watson, D., & Reynolds, S. (1995). Diagnosis and classification of psychopathology: Challenges to the current system and future directions. *Annual Review of Psychology, 46*, 121–153.

Clark, M. S., & Pataki, S. P. (1995). Interpersonal processes influencing attraction and relationships. In A. Tesser (Ed.), *Advanced social psychology* (pp. 283–332). New York: McGraw-Hill.

Clarke, L., Ungerer, J., Chahoud, K., Johnson, S., Stiefel, I. (2002). Attention deficit hyperactivity disorder is associated with attachment insecurity. *Clinical Child Psychology and Psychiatry, 7*, 179–198.

Clarke-Stewart, A., & Allhusen, V. (2005). *What we know about childcare.* Cambridge, MA: Harvard University Press.

Clarke-Stewart, A., & Brentano, C. (2006). *'Til divorce do us part: Causes and consequences of marital separation for children and adults.* New Haven, CT: Yale University Press.

Clarke-Stewart, K. A. (1989). Infant day care: Maligned or malignant? *American Psychologist, 44*, 266–273.

Clarkin, J. F. (2006). Conceptualization and treatment of personality disorders. *Psychotherapy Research, 16*, 1–11.

Clay, R. A. (2000). Often, the bells and whistles backfire. *Monitor on Psychology, 31*, 64–65.

Cleland, V., Crawford, D., Baur, L. A., Humel, C., Timperio, A., & Salmon, J. (2008). A prospective examination of children's time spent outdoors, objectively measured physical activity and overweight. *International Journal of Obesity, 32*, 1685–1693.

Clendenen, V. I., Herman, C. P., & Polivy, J. (1995). Social facilitation of eating among friends and strangers. *Appetite, 23*, 1–13.

Cleveland, E. S., & Reese, E. (2008). Children remember early childhood: Long-term recall across the offset of childhood amnesia. *Applied Cognitive Psychology, 22*(1), 127–142.

Clifton, R. K. (1992). The development of spatial hearing in human infants. In L. A. Werner & E. W. Rubel (Eds.), *Developmental psychoacoustics* (pp. 135–157). Washington, DC: American Psychological Association.

Clifton, R. K., Rochat, P., Litovsky, R., & Perris, E. (1991). Object representation guides infants' reaching in the dark. *Journal of Experimental Psychology: Human Perception and Performance, 17*, 323–329.

Cloutier, J., Mason, M. F., & Macrae, C. N. (2005). The perceptual determinants of person construal: Reopening the social-cognitive toolbox. *Journal of Personality and Social Psychology, 88*, 885–894.

Clower, C. E., & Bothwell, R. K. (2001). An exploratory study of the relationship between the Big Five and inmate recidivism. *Journal of Research in Personality, 35*, 231–237.

CNN/Time. (1997). Poll: U.S. hiding knowledge of aliens. *CNN/Time.* Retrieved December 13, 2004, from http://www-cgi.cnn.com/US/9706/15/ufo.poll/index.html.

Coccaro, E. F. (1989). Central serotonin and impulsive aggression. *British Journal of Psychiatry, 155*, 52–62.

Cocchini, G., Beschin, N., Cameron, A., Fotopoulou, A., & Della Sala, S. (2009). Anosognosia for motor impairment following left brain damage. *Neuropsychology, 23*, 223–230.

Cofer, L. F., Grice, J., Palmer, D., Sethre-Hofstad, L., & Zimmermann, K. (1992, June 20–22). *Evidence for developmental continuity of individual differences in morningness-eveningness.* Paper presented at the annual meeting of the American Psychological Society, San Diego, CA.

Cohen, A. (2009). Many forms of culture. *American Psychologist, 64*, 194–204.

Cohen, C. E. (1981). Person categories and social perception: Testing some boundaries of the processing effects of prior knowledge. *Journal of Personality and Social Psychology, 40*, 441–452.

Cohen, D. (1998). Culture, social organization, and patterns of violence. *Journal of Personality and Social Psychology, 75*, 408–419.

Cohen, F., Kemeny, M. E., Zegans, L. S., Johnson, P., Kearney, K. A., & Strites, D. P. (2007). Immune function declines with unemployment and recovers after stressor termination. *Psychosomatic Medicine, 69*, 225–234.

Cohen, N. J., & Corkin, S. (1981). The amnesic patient H. M.: Learning and retention of a cognitive skill. *Neuroscience Abstracts, 7*, 235.

Cohen, N. J., & Squire, L. R. (1980). Preserved learning and retention of pattern analyzing skills in amnesia: Dissociation of knowing how and knowing that. *Science, 210*, 207–210.

Cohen, P. (2008). Child development and personality disorder. *Psychiatric Clinics of North America, 31*, 477–493.

Cohen, S., & Herbert, T. B. (1996). Health psychology: Psychological factors and physical disease from the perspective of human psychoneuroimmunology. *Annual Review of Psychology, 47*, 113–142.

Cohen, S., & Pressman, S. D. (2006). Positive affect and health. *Current Directions in Psychological Science, 15*, 122–125.

Cohen, S., Doyle, W. J., Alper, C. M., Janicki-Deverts, D., & Turner, R. B. (2009). Sleep habits and susceptibility to the common cold. *Archives of Internal Medicine, 169*, 62–67.

Cohen, S., Doyle, W. J., Turner, R. B., Alper, C. M., & Skoner, D. P. (2003a). Emotional style and susceptibility to the common cold. *Psychosomatic Medicine, 65*, 652–657.

Cohen, S., Doyle, W. J., Turner, R., Alper, C. M., & Skoner, D. P. (2003b). Sociability and susceptibility to the common cold. *Psychological Science, 14*, 389–395.

Coifman, K. G., Bonanno, G. A., Ray, R. D., & Gross, J. J. (2007). Does repressive coping promote resilience? Affective-autonomic response discrepancy during bereavement. *Journal of Personality & Social Psychology, 92*(4), 745–758.

Colak, A., Soy, O., Uzun, H., Aslan, O., Barut, S., Belce, A., et al. (2003). Neuroprotective effects of GYKI 52466 on experimental spinal cord injury in rats. *Journal of Neurosurgery, 98,* 275–281.

Coldwell, C. M., & Bender, W. S. (2007). The effectiveness of assertive community treatment for homeless populations with severe mental illness: A meta-analysis. *American Journal of Psychiatry, 164,* 393–399.

Cole, K. N., Mills, P. E., Dale, P. S., & Jenkins, J. R. (1991). Effects of preschool integration for children with disabilities. *Exceptional Children, 58,* 36–45.

Cole, M. (2006). Culture and cognitive development in phylogenetic, historical, and ontogenetic perspective. In W. Damon & R. M. Lerner (Series Eds.) & D. Kuhn & R. Siegler (Vol. Eds.), *Handbook of child psychology: Vol. 2. Cognition, perception, and language* (6th ed., pp. 636–686). New York: Wiley.

Coleman, D. (1992). Why do I feel so tired? Too little, too late. *American Health, 11*(4), 43–46.

Collins, R. L., Elliott, M. N., Berry, S. H., Kanouse, D. E., Kunkel, D., Hunter, S. B., et al. (2004). Watching sex on television predicts adolescent initiation of sexual behavior. *Pediatrics, 114,* e280–e289.

Collins, W. A., Maccoby, E. E., Steinberg, L., Hetherington, E. M., & Bornstein, M. H. (2000). Contemporary research on parenting: The case for nature and nurture. *American Psychologist, 55,* 218–232.

Colloca, L., & Benedetti, F. (2005). Placebos and painkillers: Is mind as real as matter? *Nature Reviews Neuroscience, 6,* 545–552.

Colom, R., & Flores-Mendoza, C. E. (2007). Intelligence predicts scholastic achievement irrespective of SES factors: Evidence from Brazil. *Intelligence, 35,* 243–251.

Colombo, M., D'Amato, M. R., Rodman, H. R., & Gross, C. G. (1990). Auditory association cortex lesions impair auditory short-term memory in monkeys. *Science, 247,* 336–338.

Commission on Accreditation. (2008). *Guidelines and principles for accreditation of programs in professional psychology.* Washington, DC: American Psychological Association.

Committee to Review the Scientific Evidence on the Polygraph. (2003). *The polygraph and lie detection.* Washington, DC: National Academies Press.

Compas, B. E., Haaga, D. A. F., Keefe, F. J., Leitenberg, H., & Williams, D. A. (1998). Sampling of empirically supported psychological treatments from health psychology: Smoking, chronic pain, cancer, and bulimia nervosa. *Journal of Consulting and Clinical Psychology, 66,* 89–112.

Compton, W. M., Conway, K. P., Stinson, F. S., Colliver, J. D., & Grant, B. F. (2005). Prevalence, correlates, and comorbidity of DSM-IV antisocial personality syndromes and alcohol and specific drug use disorders in the United States: Results from the national epidemiologic survey on alcohol and related conditions. *Journal of Clinical Psychiatry, 66,* 677–685.

Compton, W. M., Thomas, Y. F., Stinson, F. S., & Grant, B. F. (2007). Prevalence, correlates, disability, and comorbidity of DSM-IV drug abuse and dependence in the United States: Results from the National Epidemiologic Survey on Alcohol and Related Conditions. *Archives of General Psychiatry, 164,* 566–576.

Condic, M. L. (2001). Adult neuronal regeneration induced by transgenic integrin expression. *Journal of Neuroscience, 21,* 4782–4788.

Condon, J. W., & Crano, W. D. (1988). Inferred evaluation and the relationship between attitude similarity and interpersonal attraction. *Journal of Personality and Social Psychology, 54,* 789–797.

Cone, E. J., Fant, R. V., Rohay, J. M., Caplan, Y. H., Ballina, M., Reder, R. F., et al. (2004). Oxycodone involvement in drug abuse deaths: II. Evidence for toxic multiple drug-drug interactions. *Journal of Analytical Toxicology, 28,* 616–624.

Conel, J. L. (1939/1967). *The postnatal development of the human cerebral cortex* (Vols. 1, 8). Cambridge, MA: Harvard University Press.

Conger, R. D., Cui, M., Bryant, C. M., & Elder, G. H. (2000). Competence in early adult romantic relationships: A developmental perspective on family influences. *Journal of Personality and Social Psychology, 79*(2), 224–237.

Conklin, H. M., & Iacono, W. G. (2002). Schizophrenia: A neurodevelopmental perspective. *Current Directions in Psychological Science, 11,* 33–37.

Connor, L. T., Balota, D. A., & Neely, J. H. (1992). On the relation between feeling of knowing and lexical decision: Persistent subthreshold activation of topic familiarity? *Journal of Experimental Psychology: Learning, Memory, and Cognition, 18,* 544–554.

Conrad, R. (1964). Acoustic confusions in immediate memory. *British Journal of Psychology, 55,* 75–84.

Consedine, N. S., & Magai, C. (2003). Attachment and emotion experience in later life: The view from emotions theory. *Attachment and Human Development, 5,* 165–187.

Considine, R., V., Sinha, M. K., Heiman, M. L., Kriauciunas, A., et al. (1996). Serum immunoreactive-leptin concentrations in normal-weight and obese humans. *New England Journal of Medicine, 334*(5), 292–295.

Constantine, M. G. (2002). Predictors of satisfaction with counseling: Racial and ethnic minority clients' attitudes toward counseling and ratings of their counselors' general and multicultural competence. *Journal of Counseling Psychology, 49,* 255–263.

Constantino, J. N., & Todd, R. D. (2003). Autistic traits in the general population: A twin study. *Archives General Psychiatry, 60,* 524–530.

Constantino, M. J., Arnow, B. A., Blasey, C., & Agras, W. S. (2005). The association between patient characteristics and the therapeutic alliance in cognitive- behavioral and interpersonal therapy for bulimia nervosa. *Journal of Consulting and Clinical Psychology, 73,* 203–211.

Consumer Reports. (1995, November). Mental health: Does therapy help? *Consumer Reports,* pp. 734–739.

Conte, J. M., & Gintoft, J. N. (2005). Polychronicity, big five personality dimensions, and sales performance. *Human Performance, 18,* 427–444.

Contemporary Sexuality. (2008, May). CDC: One in four teens has an STI. *Contemporary Sexuality, 42*(5), 11–12.

Cook, J. A., Leff, H. S., Blyler, C. R., Gold, P. B., Goldberg, R. W., Mueser, K. T., et al. (2005). Results of a multisite randomized trial of supported employment interventions for individuals with severe mental illness. *Archives of General Psychiatry, 62,* 505–512.

Cook, N. D., Yutsudo, A., Fujimoto, N., & Murata, M. (2008). Factors contributing to depth perception: Behavioral studies on the reverse perspective illusion. *Spatial Vision, 21*(3–5), 397–405.

Cookson, J., & Duffett, R. (1998). Fluoxetine: Therapeutic and undesirable effects. *Hospital Medicine, 59,* 622–626.

Cooley, E., Toraya, T., Wanga, M. C., & Valdeza, N. N. (2008). Maternal effects on daughters' eating pathology and body image. *Eating behaviors, 9,* 52–61.

Cooper, A., Gomez, R., & Buck, E. (2008). The relationships between the BIS and BAS, anger and responses to anger. *Personality and Individual Differences, 44*(2), 403–413.

Cooper, J., Mirabile, R., & Scher, S. J. (2005). Actions and attitudes: The theory of cognitive dissonance. In T. Brock & M. Green (Eds.), *Persuasion: Psychological insights and perspectives* (2nd ed., pp. 63–79). Thousand Oaks, CA: Sage Publications, Inc.

Cooper, L. N. (2007). On the problem of consciousness. *Neural Networks, 20*(9), 1057–1058.

Cooper, M. L., Russell, M., Skinner, J. B., Frone, M. R., & Mudar, P. (1992). Stress and alcohol use: The moderating effects of gender, coping, and alcohol expectancies. *Journal of Abnormal Psychology, 101,* 139–152.

Corbetta, M., Miezin, F. M., Dobmeyer, S., Shulman, G. L., & Petersen, S. E. (1991). Selective and divided attention during visual discriminations of shape, color, and speed: Functional anatomy by positron emission tomography. *Journal of Neuroscience, 11,* 2383–2402.

Corden, B., Critchley, H. D., Skuse, D., & Dolan, R. J. (2006). Fear recognition ability predicts differences in social cognitive and neural functioning in men. *Journal of Cognitive Neuroscience, 18,* 889–897.

Cordery, J. L., Mueller, W. S., & Smith, L. M. (1991). Attitudinal and behavioral effects of autonomous group working: A longitudinal field study. *Academy of Management Journal, 34,* 464–476.

Coren, S. (1999). Psychology applied to animal training. In A. Stec & D. Bernstein (Eds.), *Psychology: Fields of application.* Boston: Houghton Mifflin.

Coren, S., & Girgus, J. S. (1978). *Seeing is deceiving: The psychology of visual illusions.* Hillsdale, NJ: Erlbaum.

Corey, G. (2008). *Theory and practice of counseling and psychotherapy* (8th ed.). Belmont, CA: Brooks/Cole.

Cork, R. C., Kihlstrom, J. F., & Hameroff, S. R. (1992). Explicit and implicit memory dissociated by anesthetic technique. *Society for Neuroscience Abstracts, 22,* 523.

Corkin, S. (2002). What's new with the amnesic patient H. M.? *Nature Reviews. Neuroscience, 3*(2), 153–160.

Cornblatt, B., & Erlenmeyer-Kimling, L. E. (1985). Global attentional deviance in children at risk for schizophrenia: Specificity and predictive validity. *Journal of Abnormal Psychology, 94,* 470–486.

Cornelius, R. R. (1996). *The science of emotion.* Upper Saddle River, NJ: Prentice Hall.

Cornelius, T. L., & Resseguie, N. (2007). Primary and secondary prevention programs for dating violence: A review of the literature. *Aggression and Violent Behavior, 12,* 364–375.

Cornelius-White, J. H. D. (2002). The phoenix of empirically supported therapy relationships: The overlooked person-centered bias. *Psychotherapy: Theory, Research, Practice, Training, 39,* 219–222.

Corr, P. J. (2002). J. A. Gray's reinforcement sensitivity theory: Tests of the joint subsystem hypothesis of anxiety and impulsivity. *Personality and Individual Differences, 33,* 511–532.

Corrao, G., Zambon, A., Conti, V., Nicotra, F., La Vecchia, C., Fornari, C., Cesana, G., Contiero, P., Tagliabue, G., Nappi, R. E., & Merlino, L. (2008). Menopause hormone replacement therapy and cancer risk: An Italian record linkage investigation. *Annals of Oncology: Official Journal of the European Society for Medical Oncology/ESMO, 19*(1), 150–155.

Correll, J., Park, B., Judd, C. M., & Wittenbrink, B. (2002). The police officer's dilemma: Using ethnicity to disambiguate potentially threatening individuals. *Journal of Personality and Social Psychology, 83,* 1314–1329.

Corruble, E., Damy, C., & Guelfi, J. D. (1999). Impulsivity: A relevant dimension in depression regarding suicide attempts. *Journal of Affective Disorders, 53,* 211–215.

Corsini, R. J., & Wedding, W. (Eds.). (2005). *Current psychotherapies* (7th ed.). Belmont, CA: Thomson Brooks/Cole.

Corwin, M. J., Lesko, S. M., Heeren, T., Vezina, R. M., Hunt, C. E., Mandell, F., et al. (2003). Secular changes in sleep position during infancy: 1995–1998. *Pediatrics, 111,* 52–60.

Coryell, W., Scheftner, W., Keller, M., Endicott, J., Maser, J., & Klerman, G. (1993). The enduring consequences of mania and depression. *American Journal of Psychiatry, 150,* 720–727.

Coslett, H. B., & Lie, E. (2008b). Simultanagnosia: Effects of semantic category and repetition blindness. *Neuropsychologia, 46*(7), 1853–1863.

Coslett, H. B., & Lie, G. (2008a). Simultanagnosia: When a rose is not red. *Journal of Cognitive Neuroscience, 20*(1), 36–48.

Coslett, H. B., & Saffran, E. (1991). Simultanagnosia: To see but not two see. *Brain, 114* (Pt. 4), 1523–1545.

Costa, P. (2001, June). *New insights on personality and leadership provided by the five-factor model.* Paper presented at Annual Convention of American Psychological Society, Toronto, Canada.

Costa, P. T., & McCrae, R. R. (2002). Looking backwards: Changes in mean levels of personality traits from 80 to 12. In D. Cervone & W. Mischel (Eds.), *Advances in personality science* (pp. 196–217). New York: Guilford Press.

Costa, P. T., Jr., & McCrae, R. (1992). *Revised NEO Personality Inventory: NEO PI and NEO Five-Factor Inventory (NEO FFI: Professional Manual).* Odessa, FL: Psychological Assessment Resources.

Costello, E. J., Mustillo, S., Erkanli, A., Keeler, G., & Angold, A. (2003). Prevalence and development of psychiatric disorders in childhood and adolescence. *Archives of General Psychiatry, 60,* 837–844.

Cota, D., Marsicano, G., Lutz, B., Vicennati, V., Stalla, G. K., Pasquali, R., & Pagotto, U. (2003). Endogenous cannabinoid system as a modulator of food intake. *International Journal of Obesity, 27,* 289–301.

Cota, D., Proulx, K., Smith, K. A. B., Kozma, S. C., Thomas, G., Woods, S. C., et al. (2006). Hypothalamic mTOR signaling regulates food intake. *Science, 312,* 927–930.

Cotanche, D. A. (1997). Hair cell regeneration in the avian cochlea. *Annals of Otology, Rhinology,and Laryngology Supplement, 168,* 9–15.

Cote, J. K., & Pepler, C. (2002). A randomized trial of a cognitive coping intervention for acutely ill HIV-positive men. *Nursing Research, 51,* 237–244.

Cottler, L. B., & Grant, B. F. (2007). Characteristics of nosologically informative data sets that address key diagnostic issues facing the DSM-V and ICD-11 substance use disorders workgroups. In J. B. Saunders, M. A. Schuckit, P. J. Sirovatka, & Reiger, D. A. (Eds.) *Diagnostic issues in substance use disorders: Refining the research agenda for DSM-V. Advancing the research agenda for DSM-V.* (pp. 285–302). Washington, DC: American Psychiatric Association.

Courchesne, E., Karns, C. M., Davis, H. R., Ziccardi, R., Carper, R. A., Tigue, Z. D., et al. (2001). Unusual brain growth patterns in early life in patients with autistic disorder: An MRI study. *Neurology, 57,* 245–254.

Coutinho, S. A., & Neuman, G. (2008). A model of metacognition, achievement goal orientation, learning style and self-efficacy. *Learning Environments Research, 11*(2), 131–151.

Cowan, C. A., Atienza, J., Melton, D. A., & Eggan, K. (2005). Nuclear reprogramming of somatic cells after fusion with human embryonic stem cells. *Science, 309,* 1369–1373.

Cowan, D. T., Allan, L. G., Libretto, S. E., & Griffiths, P. (2001). Opiod drugs: A comparative survey of therapeutic and "street" use. *Pain, 2,* 193–203.

Cowan, N. (1988). Evolving concepts of memory storage, selective attention, and their mutual constraints within the human information-processing system. *Psychological Bulletin, 104,* 163–191.

Cowan, N. (2008). Working memory. In N. J. Salkind (Ed.), *Encyclopedia of educational psychology* (Vol. 2, pp. 1015–1016). London: Sage Publications.

Cowey, A. (1994). Cortical visual areas and the neurobiology of higher visual processes. In M. J. Farah & G. Ratcliff (Eds.), *The neurophysiology of high-level vision: Collected tutorial essays* (pp. 3–31). Hillsdale, NJ: Erlbaum.

Cox, J. E., Buman, M., Valenzuela, J., Joseph, N. P., Mitchell, A., & Woods, E. R. (2008). Depression, parenting attributes, and social support among adolescent mothers attending a teen tot program. *Journal of Pediatric & Adolescent Gynecology, 21*(5), 275–281.

Cox, M. J., & Paley, B. (2003). Understanding families as systems. *Current Directions in Psychological Science, 12,* 193–196.

Crabbe, J. C. (2002). Alcohol and genetics: new models. *American Journal of Medical Genetics, 114,* 969–974.

Craig, A. D. (2009). How do you feel—now? The anterior insula and human awareness. *Nature Reviews Neuroscience, 10*(1), 59–70.

Craig, A. D., & Bushnell, M. C. (1994). The thermal grill illusion: Unmasking the burn of cold pain. *Science, 265,* 252–254.

Craik, F. I. M., & Lockhart, R. S. (1972). Levels of processing: A framework for memory research. *Journal of Verbal Learning and Verbal Behavior, 11,* 671–684.

Craik, F. I. M., & Rabinowitz, J. C. (1984). Age differences in the acquisition and use of verbal information. In H. Bouma & D. G. Bouwhuis (Eds.), *Attention and performance* (Vol. 10, pp. 471–499). Hillsdale, NJ: Erlbaum.

Craik, F. I. M., & Salthouse, T. A. (2008). *The handbook of aging and cognition* (3rd ed.). New York: Psychology Press.

Cramer, P. (2003). Personality change in later adulthood is predicted by defense mechanism use in early adulthood. *Journal of Research in Personality, 37,* 76–104.

Cramer, P. (2007). Longitudinal study of defense mechanisms: Late childhood to late adolescence. *Journal of Personality, 75,* 1–24.

Cramer, P., & Jones, C. J. (2007). Defense mechanisms predict differential lifespan change in self-control and self-acceptance. *Journal of Research in Personality, 41*(4), 841–855.

Cramer, S. C. (2008). Repairing the human brain after stroke: I. Mechanisms of recovery. *Annals of Neurology, 63*(3), 272–287.

Crandall, C. S., Preisler, J. J., & Aussprung, J. (1992). Measuring life event stress in the lives of college students: The Undergraduate Stress Questionnaire (USQ). *Journal of Behavioral Medicine, 15,* 627–662.

Crano, W. D., & Chen, X. (1998). The leniency contract and persistence of majority and minority influence. *Journal of Personality and Social Psychology, 74,* 1437–1450.

Crano, W. D., & Prislin, R. (2006). Attitudes and persuasion. *Annual Review of Psychology, 57,* 345–374.

Craske, M. G. (1999). *Anxiety disorders: Psychological approaches to theory and treatment.* Boulder, CO: Westview Press.

Craske, M. G., & Barlow, D. H. (2008). Panic disorder and agoraphobia. In D. H. Barlow (Ed.), *Clinical handbook of psychological disorders: A step-by-step treatment manual* (4th ed., pp. 1–64). New York: Guilford.

Crawford, H. J., Brown, A. M., & Moon, C. E. (1993). Sustained attentional and disattentional abilities: Differences between low and highly hypnotizable persons. *Journal of Abnormal Psychology, 102*(4), 534–543.

Crawford, T. N., Cohen, P., & Brooks, J. S. (2001). Dramatic-erratic personality disorder symptoms: II. Developmental pathways from early adolescence to adulthood. *Journal of Personality Disorders, 15,* 336–350.

Creed, T. A., & Kendall, P. C. (2005). Therapist alliance-building behavior within a cognitive-behavioral treatment for anxiety in youth. *Journal of Counseling and Clinical Psychology, 73,* 498–505.

Creery, D., & Mikrogianakis, A. (2004). Sudden infant death syndrome. *Clinical Evidence, 12,* 545–555.

Crespi, B. (2008). Genomic imprinting in the development and evolution of psychotic spectrum conditions. *Biological Reviews, 83*(4), 441–493.

Crick, N. R., Ostrov, J. M., Appleyard, K., Jansen, E. A., & Casas, J. F. (2004). Relational aggression in early childhood: "You can't come to my birthday party unless. . . ." In M. Putallaz & K. L. Bierman (Eds.), *Aggression, antisocial behavior, and violence among girls: A developmental perspective* (pp. 71–89). New York: Guilford Press.

Critchley, E. M. (1991). Speech and the right hemisphere. *Behavioural Neurology, 4*(3), 143–151.

Crits-Christoph, P., Gibbons, M. B. C., Ring-Kurtz, S., Gallop, R., Stirman, S., Present, J., Temes, C., & Goldstein, L. (2008). Changes in positive quality of life over the course of psychotherapy. *Psychotherapy: Theory, Research, Practice, Training, 45,* 419–430.

Crocker, J., & Wolfe, T. (2001). Contingencies of self-worth. *Psychological Review, 108,* 593–623.

Crocker, J., Brook, A. T., Niiya, Y., & Villacorta, M. (2006). The pursuit of self-esteem: Contingencies of self-worth and self-regulation. *Journal of Personality, 74,* 1749–1771.

Croen, L. A., Grether, J. K., & Selvin, S. (2001). The epidemiology of mental retardation of unknown cause. *Pediatrics, 107,* 86.

Cronbach, L. J. (1990). *Essentials of psychological testing* (5th ed.). New York: Harper & Row.

Cronbach, L. J. (1996). Acceleration among the Terman males: Correlates in midlife and after. In C. P. Benbow & D. J. Lubinski (Eds.), *Intellectual talent: Psychometric and social issues* (pp. 179–191). Baltimore: Johns Hopkins University Press.

Cross, S. E., & Madson, L. (1997). Models of the self: Self-construals and gender. *Psychological Bulletin, 122,* 5–37.

Cross, S. E., & Markus, H. R. (1999). The cultural constitution of personality. In L. Pervin & O. John (Eds.), *Handbook of personality research* (2nd ed., pp. 378–398). New York: Guilford.

Cross-National Collaborative Group. (2002). The changing rate of major depression: Cross-national comparisons. *Journal of the American Medical Association, 268,* 3098–3105.

Crowther, J. H., Armey, M., Luce, K. H., Dalton, G. R., & Leahey, T. (2008). The point prevalence of bulimic disorders from 1990 to 2004. *International Journal of Eating Disorders, 41*(6), 491–497.

Crowther, J. H., Sanftner, J., Bonifazi, D. Z., & Shepherd, K. L. (2001). The role of daily hassles in binge eating. *International Journal of Eating Disorders, 29,* 449–454.

Cruz, A., & Green, B. G. (2000). Thermal stimulation of taste. *Nature, 403,* 889–892.

Csernansky, J. G., Schindler, M. K., Splinter, N. R., Wang, L., Gado, M., Selemon, L. D., et al. (2004). Abnormalities of thalamic volume and shape in schizophrenia. *American Journal of Psychiatry, 161,* 896–902.

Cuijpers, P., van Straten, A., Smit, F., Mihalopoulos, C., & Beekman, A. (2008). Preventing the onset of depressive disorders: A meta-analytic review of psychological interventions. *American Journal of Psychiatry, 165,* 1272–1280.

Culbertson, F. M. (1997). Depression and gender. An international review. *American Psychologist, 52,* 25–31.

Cullen, M. J., Hardison, C. M., & Sackett, P. R. (2004). Using SAT-grade and ability-job performance relationships to test predictions derived from stereotype threat theory. *Journal of Applied Psychology, 89,* 220–230.

Cullen, M. J., Waters, S. D., & Sackett, P. R. (2006). Testing stereotype threat theory predictions for math-identified and non-math-identified students by gender. *Human Performance, 19*(4), 421–440.

Culp, R. E., Cook, A. S., & Housley, P. C. (1983). A comparison of observed and reported adult-infant interactions: Effects of perceived sex. *Sex Roles, 9,* 475–479.

Cummings, B. J., Uchida, N., Tamaki, S. J., Salazar, D. L., Hooshmand, M., Summers, R., et al. (2005). Human neural stem cells differentiate and promote locomotor recovery in spinal cord-injured mice. *Proceedings of the National Academy of Sciences, 102,* 14069–14074.

Cummings, J. L. (2003). Toward a molecular neuropsychiatry of neurodegenerative diseases. *Annals of Neurology, 54*(2), 147–154.

Cummings, J. L. (2004). Alzheimer's disease. *New England Journal of Medicine, 351,* 56–67.

Cumsille, P. E., Sayer, A. G., & Graham, J. W. (2000). Perceived exposure to peer and adult drinking as predictors of growth in positive alcohol expectancies during adolescence. *Journal of Consulting and Clinical Psychology, 68,* 531–536.

Cunningham, W. A., Johnson, M. K., Raye, C. L., Gatenby, J. C., Gore, J. C., & Banaji, M. R. (2004). Separable neural components in the processing of black and white faces. *Psychological Science, 15,* 806–813.

Curioni, C. C., & Lourenço, P. M. (2005). Long-term weight loss after diet and exercise: A systematic review. *International Journal of Obesity, 29,* 1168–1174.

Curran, H. V., & Monaghan, L. (2001). In and out of the K-hole: A comparison of the acute and residual effects of ketamine in frequent and infrequent ketamine users. *Addiction, 96,* 749–760.

Currin, L., Schmidt, U., Treasure, J., & Jick, H. (2005). Time trends in eating disorder incidence. *British Journal of Psychiatry, 186,* 132–135.

Curry, D. T., Eisenstein, R. D., & Walsh, J. K. (2006). Pharmacologic management of insomnia: Past, present, and future. *Psychiatric Clinics of North America, 29,* 871–893.

Curtis, T., Miller, B. C., & Berry, E. H. (2000). Changes in reports and incidence of child abuse following natural disasters. *Child Abuse & Neglect, 24,* 1151–1162.

Cusack, K., & Spates, C. R. (1999). The cognitive dismantling of eye movement desensitization and reprocessing (EMDR) treatment of posttraumatic stress disorder (PTSD). *Journal of Anxiety Disorders, 13,* 87–99.

Cutrona, C. E., Russell, D. W., Brown, P. A., Clark, L. A., Hessling, R. M., & Gardner, K. A. (2005). Neighborhood context, personality, and stressful life events as predictors of depression among African American women. *Journal of Abnormal Psychology, 114,* 3–15.

Cvetek, R. (2008). EMDR treatment of distressful experiences that fail to meet the criteria for PTSD. *Journal of EMDR Practice and Research, 2*(1), 2–14.

Czeisler, C. A., Duffy, J. F., Shanahan, T. L., Brown, E. N., Mitchell, J. F., Rimmer, D. W., et al. (1999). Stability, precision, and near 24-hour period of the human circadian pacemaker. *Science, 284,* 2177–2181.

Czeisler, C. A., Walsh, J. K., Roth, T., Hughes, R. J., Wright, K. P., Kingsbury, L., et al. (2005). Modafinil for excessive sleepiness associated with shift-work sleep disorder. *New England Journal of Medicine, 353,* 476–486.

d'Ydewalle, G., & Rosselle, H. (1978). Text expectations in text learning. In M. M. Gruneberg, P. E. Morris, & R. N. Sykes (Eds.), *Practical aspects of memory.* Orlando, FL: Academic Press.

Da Fonseca, D., Seguier, V., Santos, A., Poinso, F., & Deruelle, C. (2009). Emotion understanding in children with ADHD. *Child Psychiatry and Human Development, 40,* 111–121.

Daban, C., Martínez-Arán, A., Torrent, C., Sánchez-Moreno, J., Goikolea, J. M., Benabarre, A., et al. (2006). Cognitive functioning in bipolar patients receiving lamotrigine: Preliminary results. *Journal of Clinical Psychopharmacology, 26,* 178–181.

Dabbs, J. M., Jr., Riad, J. K., & Chance, S. E. (2001). Testosterone and ruthless homicide. *Personality and Individual Differences, 31,* 599–603.

Dabbs, J., & Dabbs, M. G. (2001). *Heroes, rogues, and lovers: Testosterone and behavior.* New York: McGraw-Hill.

Daglish, M. R., & Nutt, D. J. (2003). Brain imaging studies in human addicts. *European Neuropsychopharmacology, 13,* 453–458.

Dale, P. S. (1976). *Language and the development of structure and function.* New York: Holt, Rinehart & Winston.

Daley, K. C. (2004). Update on sudden infant death syndrome. *Current Opinion in Pediatrics, 16,* 227–232.

Dalgleish, T., Hauer, B., & Kuyken, W. (2008). The mental regulation of autobiographical recollection in the aftermath of trauma. *Current Directions in Psychological Science, 17,* 259–263.

Dallman, M. F., Pecoraro, N., Akana, S. F., La Fleur, S. E., Gomez, F., Houshyar, H., et al. (2003). Chronic stress and obesity: A new view of "comfort food." *Proceedings of the National Academies of Science, 100,* 11696–11701.

Dalton, D. R., & Mesch, D. J. (1991). On the extent and reduction of avoidable absenteeism: An assessment of absence policy provisions. *Journal of Applied Psychology, 76,* 810–817.

Daly, J. J., Prudic, J., Devanand, D. P., Nobler, M. S., Mitchell, S., Lisanby, S. H., et al. (2001). ECT in bipolar and unipolar depression: Differences in speed of response. *Bipolar Disorders, 3,* 95–104.

Damasio, A. R. (1994). *Descartes' error.* New York: Putnam.

Damasio, A. R., Grabowski, T. J., Bechara, A., Damasio, H., Ponto, L. L. B., Parvizi, J., & Hichwa, R. D. (2000). Subcortical and cortical brain activity during the feeling of self-generated emotions. *Nature Neuroscience, 3,* 1049–1056.

Damos, D. (1992). *Multiple task performance.* London: Taylor & Francis.

Dannenberg, A. L., Burton, D. C., & Jackson, R. J. (2004). Economic and environmental costs of obesity: The impact on airlines. *American Journal of Preventive Medicine, 27,* 264–264.

Dansereau, F., Jr., Graen, G., & Haga, W. J. (1975). A vertical dyad linkage approach to leadership with formal organizations. *Organizational Behavior and Human Performance, 13,* 46–78.

Dapretto, M., Davies, M. S., Pfeifer, J. H., Scott, A. A., Sigman, M., Bookheimer, S. Y., et al. (2006). Understanding emotions in others: Mirror neuron dysfunction in children with autism spectrum disorders. *Nature Neuroscience, 9,* 28–30.

Dark, V. J., & Benbow, C. P. (1993). Cognitive differences among the gifted: A review and new data. In D. K. Detterman (Ed.), *Current topics in human intelligence* (Vol. 3, pp. 85–120). Norwood, NJ: Ablex.

Darkes, J., & Goldman, M. S. (1993). Expectancy challenge and drinking reduction. *Journal of Clinical and Consulting Psychology, 61,* 344–353.

Darwin, C. E. (1872). *The expression of the emotions in man and animals.* London: John Murray.

Dasgupta, A. M., Juza, D. M., White, G. M., & Maloney, J. F. (1995). Memory and hypnosis: A comparative analysis of guided memory, cognitive interview, and hypnotic hypermnesia. *Imagination, Cognition, and Personality, 14*(2), 117–130.

Das-Munshi, J., Goldberg, D., Bebbington, P. E., Bhugra, D. K., Brugha, T. S., Dewey, M. E., et al. (2008). Public health significance of mixed anxiety and depression: beyond current classification. *British Journal of Psychiatry, 192,* 171–177.

Dass, B., Olanow, C. W., & Kordower, J. H. (2006). Gene transfer of trophic factors and stem cell grafting as treatments for Parkinson's disease. *Neurology, 66,* S89–103.

Daus, C. S., Sanders, D. N., & Campbell, D. P. (1998). Consequences of alternative work schedules. In C. L. Cooper & I. T. Robertson (Eds.), *International review of industrial and organizational psychology 1998* (pp. 185–223). Chichester, UK: Wiley.

Davanloo, H. (1999). Intensive short-term dynamic psychotherapy-central dynamic sequence: Phase of challenge. *International Journal of Short-Term Dynamic Psychotherapy, 13,* 237–262.

Davidson, J. K., & Moore, N. B. (1994). Guilt and lack of orgasm during sexual intercourse: Myth versus reality in college women. *Journal of Sex Education and Therapy, 20*(3), 153–174.

Davidson, J. M., Camargo, C. A., & Smith, E. R. (1979). Effects of androgen on sexual behavior in hypogonadal men. *Journal of Clinical Endocrinological Metabolism, 48,* 955–958.

Davidson, J. R., Foa, E. B., Huppert, J. D., Keefe, F. J., Franklin, M. E., Compton, J. S., et al. (2004). Fluoxetine, comprehensive cognitive behavioral therapy, and placebo in generalized social phobia. *Archives of General Psychiatry, 61,* 1005–1013.

Davidson, K., Hall, P., & MacGregor, M. (1996). Gender differences in the relation between interview-derived hostility scores and resting blood pressure. *Journal of Behavioral Medicine, 19,* 185–201.

Davidson, P. R., & Parker, K. C. (2001). Eye movement desensitization and reprocessing (EMDR): A meta-analysis. *Journal of Consulting and Clinical Psychology, 69,* 305–316.

Davidson, R. J., Ekman, P., Saron, C., Senulis, J., & Friesen, W. V. (1990). Approach-withdrawal and cerebral asymmetry: Emotional expression and brain physiology: I. *Journal of Personality and Social Psychology, 58,* 330–341.

Davidson, R. J., Kabat-Zinn, J., Schumacher, J., Rosenkranz, M., Muller, D., Santorelli, S. F., et al. (2003). Alterations in brain and immune function produced by mindfulness meditation. *Psychosomatic Medicine, 65,* 564–570.

Davies, C. (1999, April 21). Junior doctor is cleared in baby overdose death. *London Daily Telegraph,* p. 2.

Davis, C., & Kapstein, S. (2006). Anorexia nervosa with excessive exercise: A phenotype with close links to obsessive-compulsive disorder. *Psychiatry Research, 142,* 209–217.

Davis, C., III, Aronson, J., & Salinas, M. (2006). Shades of threat: Racial identity as a moderator of stereotype threat. *Journal of Black Psychology, 32*(4), 399–417.

Davis, J. A., & Smith, T. W. (1990). *General social surveys, 1972–1990: Cumulative codebook.* Chicago: National Opinion Research Center.

Davis, J. D., Gallagher, R. J., Ladove, R. F., & Turansky, A. J. (1969). Inhibition of food intake by a humoral factor. *Journal of Comparative and Physiological Psychology, 67,* 407–414.

Davis, J. L., & Rusbult, C. (2001). Attitude alignment in close relationships. *Journal of Personality and Social Psychology, 81,* 65–84.

Davis, M. H. (1994). *Empathy: A social psychological approach.* Madison, WI: Brown and Benchmark.

Davis, M. H., Luce, C., & Kraus, S. J. (1994). The heritability of characteristics associated with dispositional empathy. *Journal of Personality, 60,* 369–391.

Davis, M., Myers, K. M., Ressler, K. J., & Rothbaum, B. O. (2005). Facilitation of extinction of conditioned fear by D-cycloserine. *Current Directions in Psychological Science, 14,* 214–219.

Davis, M., Ressler, K., Rothbaum, B. O., & Richardson, R. (2006). Effects of D-cycloserine on extinction: Translation from preclinical to clinical work. *Biological Psychiatry, 60,* 369–375.

Davis, N., Gross, J., & Hayne, H. (2008). Defining the boundary of childhood amnesia. *Memory, 16*(5), 465–474.

Davis, R. A., & Moore, C. C. (1935). Methods of measuring retention. *Journal of General Psychology, 12,* 144–155.

Davison, G. C., & Neale, J. M. (1990). *Abnormal psychology* (5th ed.). New York: Wiley.

Dawe, I. C. (2008). Suicide and homicide. In R. L. Glick, J. S. Berlin, A. B. Fishkind, & S. L. Zeller (Eds.). *Emergency psychiatry: Principles and practice* (pp. 149–159). Philadelphia: Wolters Kluwer Health/Lippincott Williams & Wilkins.

Dawes, R. M. (1994). *House of cards: Psychology and psychotherapy built on myth.* New York: Free Press.

Dawes, R. M. (1998). Behavioral decision making and judgment. In D. Gilbert, S. T. Fiske, & G. Lindzey (Eds.), *Handbook of social psychology* (Vol. 1, 4th ed., pp. 497–549). Boston: McGraw-Hill.

Dawes, R. M., & Messick, D. M. (2000). Social dilemmas. *International Journal of Psychology, 35,* 111–116.

Dawkins, K., & Potter, W. (1991). Gender differences in pharmacokinetics and pharmacodynamics of psychotropics: Focus on women. *Psychopharmacology Bulletin, 27,* 417–426.

Dawson, M., Schell, A. M., & Filion, D. L. (2000). The electodermal system. In J. Cacioppo, L. Tassinary, & G. Bernston (Eds.), *Handbook of psychophysiology* (2nd ed., pp. 200–222). New York: Cambridge University Press.

Dawson-Basoa, M., & Gintzler, A. R. (1997). Involvement of spinal cord delta opiate receptors in the antinociception of gestation and its hormonal simulation. *Brain Research, 757,* 37–42.

Day, A. L., & Jreige, S. (2002). Examining Type A behavior pattern to explain the relationship between job stressors and psychosocial outcomes. *Journal of Occupational Health Psychology, 7,* 109–120.

Dayan, K., Fox, S., & Kasten, R. (2008). The preliminary employment interview as a predictor of assessment center outcomes. *International Journal of Selection and Assessment, 16,* 102–111.

Dayan, K., Kasten, R., & Fox, S. (2002). Entry-level police candidate assessment center: An efficient tool or a hammer to kill a fly? *Personnel Psychology, 55,* 827–849.

de Araujo, I. E., Rolls, E. T., Kringelbach, M. L., McGlone, F., & Phillips, N. (2003). Taste-olfactory convergence, and the representation of the pleasantness of flavour, in the human brain. *European Journal of Neuroscience, 18,* 2059–2068.

de Castro, J. M., & Goldstein, S. J. (1995). Eating attitudes and behaviors pre- and postpubertal females: Clues to the etiology of eating disorders. *Physiology and Behavior, 58*(1), 15–23.

de Charms, R., Levy, J., & Wertheimer, M. (1954). A note on attempted evaluations of psychotherapy. *Journal of Clinical Psychology, 10,* 233–235.

de Freitas, S., & Griffiths, M. (2007). Online gaming as an educational tool in learning and training. *British Journal of Educational Technology, 38*(3), 535–537.

de Gelder, B., Snyder, J., Greve, D., Gerard, G., & Hadjikhani, N. (2004). Fear fosters flight: A mechanism for fear contagion when perceiving emotion expressed by a whole body. *Proceedings of the National Academy of Sciences, 101,* 16701–16706.

de Haan, M., Mishkin, M., Baldeweg, T., & Vargha-Khadem, F. (2006). Human memory development and its dysfunction after early hippocampal injury. *Trends in Neurosciences, 29*(7), 374–381.

de Houwer, A. (1995). Bilingual language acquisition. In P. Fletcher & B. MacWhinney (Eds.), *The handbook of child language* (pp. 219–250). Cambridge, MA: Blackwell.

De Los Reyes, A., & Kazdin, A. E. (2006). Conceptualizing changes in behavior in intervention research: The range of possible changes model. *Psychological Review, 113,* 554–583.

de Macedo-Soares, M. B., Moreno, R. A., Rigonatti, S. P., & Lafer, B. (2005). Efficacy of electroconvulsive therapy in treatment-resistant bipolar disorder: A case series. *Journal of ECT, 21,* 31–34.

de Moor, J. S., de Moor, C. A., Basen-Engquist, K., Kudelka, A., Bevers, M. W., & Cohen, L. (2006). Optimism, distress, health-related quality of life, and change in cancer antigen 125 among patients with ovarian cancer undergoing chemotherapy. *Psychosomatic Medicine, 68,* 555–562.

de Rios, M. D. (1989). Power and hallucinogenic states of consciousness among the Moche: An ancient Peruvian society. In C. A. Ward (Ed.), *Altered states of consciousness and mental health: A cross-cultural perspective* (pp. 285–299). Newbury Park, CA: Sage.

De Santi, S., Pirraglia, E., Barr, W., Babb, J., Williams, S., Rogers, K., Glodzik, L. Brys, M., Mosconi, L., Reisberg, B., Ferris, S., & de Leon, M. J. (2008). Robust and conventional neuropsychological norms: Diagnosis and prediction of age-related cognitive decline. *Neuropsychology, 22,* 469–484.

De Vogli, R., Chandola, T., & Marmot, M. G. (2007). Negative aspects of close relationships and heart disease. *Archives of Internal Medicine, 167,* 1951–1957.

Deary, I. J., & Der, G. (2005a). Reaction time, age, and cognitive ability: Longitudinal findings from age 16 to 63 years in representative population samples. *Aging, Neuropsychology, and Cognition, 12,* 187–215.

Deary, I. J., & Der, G. (2005b). Reaction time explains IQ's association with death. *Psychological Science, 16*(1), 64–69.

Deary, I. J., Whiteman, M. C., Starr, J. M., Whalley, L. J., & Fox, H. C. (2004). The impact of childhood intelligence on later life: Following up the Scottish mental surveys of 1932 and 1947. *Journal of Personality and Social Psychology, 86,* 130–147.

Death Penalty Information Center. (2009). *Innocence and the death penalty.* Washington, DC: Death Penalty Information Center. Retrieved May 17, 2009, from http://www.deathpenaltyinfo.org/innocence-and-death-penalty.

deCharms, R. C. (2008). Applications of real-time fMRI. *Nature Reviews Neuroscience, 9*(9), 720–729.

deCharms, R. C., Maeda, F., Glover, G. H., Ludlow, D., Pauly, J. M., Soneji, D., et al. (2005). Control over brain activation and pain learned by using real-time functional MRI. *Proceedings of the National Academy of Sciences, 102,* 18626–18631.

Deci, E. L., Koestner, R., & Ryan, R. M. (1999). The undermining effect is a reality after all—Extrinsic rewards, task interest, and self-determination: Reply to Eisenberger, Pierce, and

Cameron (1999) and Lepper, Henderlong, and Gingras (1999). *Psychological Bulletin, 125,* 692–700.

Deci, E. L., Koestner, R., & Ryan, R. M. (2001). A meta-analytic review of experiments examining the effects of extrinsic rewards on intrinsic motivation. *Psychological Bulletin, 125,* 627–668.

Deeprose, C., & Andrade, J. (2006). Is priming during anesthesia unconscious? *Consciousness and Cognition, 15,* 1–23.

Deep-Soboslay, A., Akil, M., Martin, C. E., Bigelow, L. B., Herman, M. M., et al. (2006). Reliability of psychiatric diagnosis in postmortem research. *Biological Psychiatry, 57,* 96–101.

Delamater, A. R. (2004). Experimental extinction in Pavlovian conditioning: Behavioural and neuroscience perspectives. *Quarterly Journal of Experimental Psychology, 57B,* 97–132.

Delbello, M. P., Kowatch, R. A., Adler, C. M., Stanford, K. E., Welge, J. A., Barzman, D. H., et al. (2006). A double-blind randomized pilot study comparing quetiapine and divalproex for adolescent mania. *Journal of the American Academy of Child & Adolescent Psychiatry, 45,* 305–313.

DeLeo, J. A. (2006). Basic science of pain. *Journal of Bone and Joint Surgery (American), 88*(Suppl. 2), 58–62.

DeLisi, L. E., Maurizio, A., Yost, M., Papparozzi, C. F., Fulchino, C., Katz, C. L., et al. (2003). A survey of New Yorkers after the Sept. 11, 2001, terrorist attacks. *American Journal of Psychiatry, 160,* 780–783.

Demaray, M. K., & Malecki, C. K. (2002). Critical levels of perceived social support associated with student adjustment. *School Psychology Quarterly, 17,* 213–241.

Dement, W. (1960). The effect of dream deprivation. *Science, 131,* 1705–1707.

Dement, W., & Kleitman, N. (1957). Cyclic variations in EEG during sleep and their relation to eye movements, body motility and dreaming. *Electroencephalography and Clinical Neurophysiology, 9,* 673–690.

Demerouti, E., Geurts, S. A. E., Bakker, A. B., & Euwema, M. (2004). The impact of shiftwork on work-home conflict, job attitudes, and health. *Ergonomics, 47,* 987–1002.

Demo, D. H., Allen, K. R., & Fine, M. A. (Eds.). (2000). *Handbook of family diversity.* New York: Oxford University Press.

Dempsey, P. G., McGorry, R. W., & Maynard, W. S. (2005). A survey of tools and methods used by certified professional ergonomists. *Applied Ergonomics, 36*(4), 489–503.

DeNeve, K. M. (1999). Happy as an extraverted clam? The role of personality for subjective well-being. *Current Directions in Psychological Science, 8,* 141–144.

Denrell, J. (2005). Why most people disapprove of me: Experience sampling in impression formation. *Psychological Review, 112,* 951–978.

Denton, G. (1980). The influence of visual pattern on perceived speed. *Perception, 9,* 393–402.

DePrince, A. P., & Freyd, J. J. (2004). Forgetting trauma stimuli. *Psychological Science, 15,* 488–492.

Derogowski, J. B. (1989). Real space and represented space: Cross-cultural perspectives. *Behavior and Brain Sciences, 12,* 51–73.

DeRosse, P., Funke, B., Burdick, K. E., Lencz, T., & Ekholm, J. M. (2006). Dysbindin genotype and negative symptoms of schizophrenia. *American Journal of Psychiatry, 163,* 532–534.

Derryberry, D., & Tucker, D. M. (1992). Neural mechanisms of emotion. *Journal of Consulting and Clinical Psychology, 60,* 329–338.

DeRubeis, R. J., & Crits-Christoph, P. (1998). Empirically supported individual and group psychological treatments for adult mental disorders. *Journal of Consulting and Clinical Psychology, 66,* 37–52.

DeRubeis, R. J., Hollon, S. D., Amsterdam, J. D., Shelton, R. C., Young, P. R., Salomon, R. M., et al. (2005). Cognitive therapy vs medications in the treatment of moderate to severe depression. *Archives of General Psychiatry, 62,* 409–416.

Deschaumes, M. C., Dittmar, A., Sicard, G., & Vernet, M. E. (1991). Results from six autonomic nervous system responses confirm "autonomic response specificity" hypothesis. *Homeostasis in Health and Disease, 33*(5–6), 225–234.

Deshpande, D. M., Kim, Y. S., Martinez, T., Carmen, J., Dike, S., Shats, I., et al. (2006). Recovery from paralysis in adult rats using embryonic stem cells. *Annals of Neurology, 60,* 32–44.

Detera-Wadleigh, S. D., & McMahon, F. J. (2004). Genetic association studies in mood disorders: Issues and promise. *International Review of Psychiatry, 16,* 301–310.

Deutsch, M., & Gerard, H. B. (1955). A study of normative and informative social influences on individual judgments. *Journal of Abnormal and Social Psychology, 51,* 629–636.

Devanand, D. P., Pradhaban, G., Liu, X., Khandji, A., De Santi, S., Segal, S., et al. (2007). Hippocampal and entorhinal atrophy in mild cognitive impairment: Prediction of Alzheimer's disease. *Neurology, 68,* 828–836.

Devenport, L. D. (1998). Spontaneous recovery without interference: Why remembering is adaptive. *Animal Learning and Behavior, 26,* 172–181.

Devi, G., & Quitschke, W. (1999). Alois Alzheimer, neuroscientist (1864–1915). *Alzheimer Disease and Associated Disorders, 13*(3), 132–137.

DeVries, R. (1969). Constancy of generic identity in the years three to six. *Monographs of the Society for Research in Child Development, 34*(3), 1–67.

DeWitt, L. A., & Samuel, A. G. (1990). The role of knowledge-based function in music perception. *Journal of Experimental Psychology: General, 119,* 123–144.

DeWolff, M. S., & van IJzendoorn, M. H. (1997). Sensitivity and attachment: A meta-analysis on parental antecedents of infant attachment. *Child Development, 68,* 571–591.

DeYoung, C. G., Quilty, L. C., & Peterson, J. B. (2007). Between facets and domains: 10 aspects of the Big Five. *Journal of Personality and Social Psychology, 93*(5), 880–896.

Dhurandhar, N. V., Israel, B. A., Kolesar, J. M., Mayhew, G. F., Cook, M. E., & Atkinson, R. L. (2000). Increased adiposity in animals due to a human virus. *International Journal of Obesity, 24,* 989–996.

Di Filippoa, M., Tozzi, A., Costa, C., Belcastro, V., Tantucci, M., Picconi, B., et al. (2008). Plasticity and repair in the post-ischemic brain. *Neuropharmacology, 55*(3), 353–362.

Di Marzo, V., Goparaju, S. K., Wang, L., Liu, J., Batkai, S., Jarai, Z., et al. (2001). Leptin-regulated endocannabinoids are involved in maintaining food intake. *Nature, 410,* 822–825.

Di Milia, L. (2006). Shift work, sleepiness, and long distance driving. *Transportation Research, 9,* 278–285.

Diakidoy, I. N., & Spanoudis, G. (2002). Domain specificity in creativity testing: A comparison of performance on a general divergent-thinking test and a parallel, content-specific test. *Journal of Creative Behavior, 36,* 41–61.

Diamond, L. M. (2004). Emerging perspectives on distinctions between romantic love and sexual desire. *Current Directions in Psychological Science, 13,* 116–119.

Diamond, L. M. (2008). *Sexual fluidity: Understanding women's love and desire.* Cambridge, MA: Harvard University Press.

Diana, M., Spiga, S., & Acquas, E. (2006). Persistent and reversible morphine withdrawal–induced morphological changes in the nucleus accumbens. *Annals of the New York Academy of Sciences, 1074,* 446–457.

Dickinson, A. (2001). Causal learning: Association versus computation. *Current Directions in Psychological Science, 10,* 127–132.

Diener, E. (2000). Subjective well-being: The science of happiness and a proposal for a national index. *American Psychologist, 55,* 34–43.

Diener, E. (2003). What is positive about positive psychology: The curmudgeon and Pollyanna. *Psychological Inquiry, 14,* 115–120.

Diener, E., & Diener, C. (1995). Most people are happy. *Psychological Science, 7,* 181–185.

Diener, E., & Seligman, M. E. P. (2004). Beyond money: Towards an economy of well-being. *Psychological Science in the Public Interest, 5,* 1–31.

Diener, M. L., Isabella, R. A., Behunin, M. G., & Wong, M. S. (2008). Attachment to mothers and fathers during middle childhood: Associations with child gender, grade, and competence. *Social Development, 17,* 84–101.

Dierdorff, E. C., & Ellington, K. J. (2008). It's the nature of the work: Examining behavior-based sources of work-family conflict across occupations. *Journal of Applied Psychology, 93,* 883–892.

Dijksterhuis, A., Bos, M. W., Nordgren, L. F., & van Baaren, R. B. (2006). On making the right choice: The deliberation-without-attention effect. *Science, 311,* 1005–1007.

Dijksterhuis, A., & Nordgren, L. F. (2006). A theory of unconscious thought. *Perspectives on Psychological Science, 1,* 95–109.

Dijksterhuis, A., Preston, J., Wegner, D. M., & Aarts, H. (2008). Effects of subliminal priming of self and God on self-attribution of authorship for events. *Journal of Experimental Social Psychology, 44,* 2–9.

Dijkstra, A., DeVries, H., & Bakker, M. (1996). Pros and cons of quitting, self-efficacy, and the stages of change in smoking cessation. *Journal of Consulting and Clinical Psychology, 64,* 758–763.

Dillard, A. J., McCaul, K. D., & Klein, W. M. P. (2006). Unrealistic optimism in smokers: Implications for smoking myth endorsement and self-protective motivation. *Journal of Health Communication, 11,* 93–102.

Dimidjian, S., Hollon, S. D., Dobson, K. S., Schmaling, K. B., Kohlenberg, R. J., Addis, M. E., et al. (2006). Randomized trial of behavioral activation, cognitive therapy, and antidepressant medication in the acute treatment of adults with major depression. *Journal of Consulting and Clinical Psychology, 74,* 658–670.

Dinan, T. G. (2001). Novel approaches to the treatment of depression by modulating the hypothalamic-pituitary-adrenal axis. *Human Psychopharmacology: Clinical and Experimental, 16,* 89–93.

Dingfelder, S. F. (2005, January). Closing the gap for Latino patients. *Monitor on Psychology,* 58–61.

diNoia, J., & Schinke, S. P. (2008). HIV risk-related attitudes, interpersonal influences, and intentions among at-risk urban, early adolescent girls. *American Journal of Health Behavior, 32*(5), 497–507.

Dion, K. (2003). Prejudice, racism and discrimination. In T. Millon & M. Lerner (Eds.) *Handbook of psychology: Volume 5: Personality and social psychology* (pp. 507–536). Hoboken, NJ: Wiley.

Dionne, V. E., & Dubin, A. E. (1994). Transduction diversity in olfaction. *Journal of Experimental Biology, 194,* 1–21.

DiPatrizio, N. V., & Simansky, K. J. (2008). Activating parabrachial cannabinoid CB-sub-1 receptors selectively stimulates feeding of palatable foods in rats. *Journal of Neuroscience, 28*(39), 9702–9709.

Distel, M. A., Vink, J. M., Willemsen, G., Middeldorp, C. M., Merckelbach, H. G. J., & Boomsma, D. I. (2008). Heritability of self-reported fear. *Behavioral Genetics, 38,* 24–33.

Dittmann, M. (2004, June). Alternative health care gains steam. *Monitor on Psychology,* 42–44.

Dittmann, M. (2005, July/August). When health fears hurt health. *Monitor on Psychology,* 100–103.

Dittmar, H., Halliwell, E., & Ive, S. (2006). Does Barbie make girls want to be thin? The effect of experimental exposure to images of dolls on the body image of 5- to 8-year-old girls. *Developmental Psychology, 42,* 283–292.

Dixon, J., Durrheim, K., & Tredoux, C. (2007). Intergroup contact and attitudes toward the principle and practice of racial equality. *Psychological Science, 18,* 867–872.

Dixon, J. B., Schachter, L. M., & O"Brien, P. E. (2005). Polysomnography before and after weight loss in obese patients with severe sleep apnea. *International Journal of Obesity, 29,* 1048–1054.

Dixon, M., Brunet, A., & Laurence, J.-R. (1990). Hypnotizability and automaticity: Toward a parallel distributed processing model of hypnotic responding. *Journal of Abnormal Psychology, 99,* 336–343.

D'Mello, R., & Dickenson, A. H. (2008). Spinal cord mechanisms of pain. *British Journal of Anesthesiology, 101*(1), 8–16.

Dobson, K. S., Hollon, S. D., Dimidjian, S., Schmaling, K. B., Kohlenberg, R. J., Gallop, R. J., Rizvi, S. L., Gollan, J. K., Dunner, D. L., & Jacobson, N. S. (2008). Randomized trial of behavioral activation, cognitive therapy, and antidepressant medication in the prevention of relapse and recurrence in major depression. *Journal of Consulting and Clinical Psychology, 76,* 468–477.

Dodd, M. L., Klos, K. J., Bower, J. H., Geda, Y. E., Josephs, K. A., & Ahlskog, J. E. (2005). Pathological gambling caused by drugs used to treat Parkinson disease. *Archives of Neurology, 62,* 1377–1381.

Dodge, K. A. (2004). The nature-nurture debate and public policy. *Merrill-Palmer Quarterly, 50,* 418–427.

Dohnt, H., & Tiggermann, M. (2006). The contribution of peer and media influences to the development of body satisfaction and self-esteem in young girls: A prospective study. *Developmental Psychology, 42,* 929–936.

Dohrenwend, B. P., Raphael, K. G., Schwartz, S., Stueve, A., & Skodol, A. (1993). The structured event probe and narrative rating method for measuring stressful life events. In L. Goldenberger & S. Breznitz (Eds.), *Handbook of stress: Theoretical and clinical aspects* (2nd ed.). New York: The Free Press.

Dohrenwend, B. P., Turner, J. B., Turse, N. A., Adams, B. G., Koenen, K. C., & Marshall, R. (2006). The psychological risks of Vietnam for U.S. veterans: A revisit with new data and methods. *Science, 313,* 979–982.

Dolan, M., & Park, I. (2002). The neuropsychology of antisocial personality disorder. *Psychological Medicine, 32,* 417–427.

Dollard, J., Doob, L., Miller, N., Mowrer, O. H., & Sears, R. R. (1939). *Frustration and aggression.* New Haven, CT: Yale University Press.

Dollinger, S. J. (2000). Locus of control and incidental learning: An application to college students. *College Student Journal, 34,* 537–540.

Domhoff, G. W. (1996). *Finding meaning in dreams: A quantitative approach.* New York: Plenum.

Domhoff, G. W. (1999). Drawing theoretical implications from descriptive empirical findings on dream content. *Dreaming, 9,* 201–210.

Domhoff, G. W. (2001). A new neurocognitive theory of dreams. *Dreaming: Journal of the Association for the Study of Dreams, 11,* 13–33.

Domino, E. F. (2003). Effects of tobacco smoking on electroencephalographic, auditory evoked and event related potentials. *Brain and Cognition, 53,* 66–74.

Domjan, M. (2005). Pavlovian conditioning: A functional perspective. *Annual Review of Psychology, 56,* 179–206.

Donnan, G. A., Fisher, M., Macleod, M., & Davis, S. M. (2008). Stroke. *Lancet, 371*(9624), 1612–1623.

Donner, M. B., VandeCreek, L., Gonsiorek, J. C., & Fisher, C. B. (2008). Balancing confidentiality: Protecting privacy and protecting the public. *Professional Psychology: Research and Practice, 39,* 369–376.

Donnerstein, E. (1984). Pornography: Its effects on violence against women. In N. M. Malamuth & E. Donnerstein (Eds.), *Pornography and sexual aggression.* New York: Academic Press.

Donnerstein, E., & Linz, D. (1995). The mass media: A role in injury causation and prevention. *Adolescent Medicine: State of the Art Reviews, 6,* 271–284.

Donnerstein, E., Slaby, R. G., & Eron, L. D. (1995). The mass media and youth aggression. In L. Eron, J. Gentry, & P. Schlegel (Eds.), *Reason to hope: A psychosocial perspective on violence and youth* (pp. 219–250). Washington, DC: American Psychological Association.

Donovan, J. J., & Radosevich, D. J. (1999). A meta-analytic review of the distribution of practice effect: Now you see it, now you don't. *Journal of Applied Psychology, 84,* 795–805.

Doody, R. S., Gavrilova, S. I., Sano, M., Thomas, R. G., Aisen, P. S., Bachurin, S. O., Seely, L., & Hung, D. (2008). Effect of dimebon on cognition, activities of daily living, behaviour, and global function in patients with mild-to-moderate Alzheimer's disease: a randomised, double-blind, placebo-controlled study. *Lancet, 372*(9634), 207–215.

Dordain, G., & Deffond, D. (1994). Pyridoxine neuropathies: Review of the literature. *Therapie, 49*(4), 333–337.

Doss, B. D., Rhoades, G. K., Stanley, S. M., & Markman, H. J. (2009). The effect of the transition to parenthood on relationship quality: An 8-year prospective study. *Psychological Bulletin, 96,* 601–619.

Doucet, S., Soussignan, R., Sagot, P., & Schaal, B. (2007). The "smellscape" of mother's breast: Effects of odor masking and selective unmasking on neonatal arousal, oral, and visual responses. *Developmental Psychobiology, 49,* 129–138.

Dovidio, J. F., Gaertner, S. L., & Kawakami, K. (2003). Intergroup contact: The past, present, and the future. *Group Processes and Intergroup Relations, 6,* 5–20.

Dovidio, J. F., Kawakami, K., & Gaertner, S. L. (2000). Reducing contemporary prejudice: Combating explicit and implicit bias ai the individual and intergroup level. In S. Oskamp (Ed.), *Reducing prejudice and discrimination* (pp. 137–163). Hillsdale, NJ: Erlbaum.

Dovidio, J. F., Kawakami, K., Smoak, N., & Gaertner, S. L. (2009). The roles of implicit and explicit processes in contemporary prejudice. In R. E. Petty, R. H. Fazio, & P. Brinol (Eds.), *Attitudes: Insights from the new implicit measures* (pp. 165–192). New York: Psychology Press.

Dovidio, J., Piliavin, J., Schroeder, D., & Penner, L. (2006). *The social psychology of prosocial behavior*. Mahwah, NJ: Lawrence Erlbaum.

Dovidio, J. F., & Penner, L. A. (2001). Helping and altruism. In G. Fletcher & M. Clark (Eds.), *Blackwell handbook of social psychology: Interpersonal processes* (pp. 162–195). Boston: Blackwell.

Dovidio, J. F., Piliavin, J. A., Gaertner, S. L., Schroeder, D. A., & Clark, R. D., III. (1991). The arousal: cost-reward model and the process of intervention: A review of the evidence. In M. Clark (Ed.), *Review of personality and social psychology: Vol. 12. Prosocial behavior* (pp. 86–118). Newbury Park, CA: Sage.

Dowd, J. T. (2005). *Teaching social skills to youth*. Boys Town, Nebraska: Boys Town Press.

Doyle, J. (2005). *True witness: Cops, courts, science, and the battle against misidentification.* New York: Palgrave Macmillan.

Drasbek, K. R., Christensen, J., & Jensen, K. (2006). Gamma-hydroxybutyrate—a drug of abuse. *Acta Neurologica Scandinavica, 114,* 145–156.

Dresner, R., & Grolnick, W. S. (1996). Constructions of early parenting, intimacy and autonomy in young women. *Journal of Social and Personal Relationships, 13,* 25–40.

Dreyfus, H. L., & Dreyfus, S. E. (1988). Making a mind versus modeling the brain: Intelligence back at a branchpoint. In S. R. Graubard (Ed.), *The artificial intelligence debate* (pp. 15–44). Cambridge: MIT Press.

Drinkwater, J., & Stewart, A. (2002). Cognitive behavior therapy for young people. *Current Opinion in Psychiatry, 15,* 377–381.

Driskell, J. E., Willis, R., & Copper, C. (1992). Effect of overlearning on retention. *Journal of Applied Psychology, 77,* 615–622.

Driver, J., Tabares, A., Shapiro, A., Nahm, E. Y., & Gottman, J. M. (2003). Interactional patterns in marital success and failure: Gottman laboratory studies. In F. Walsh (Ed.), *Normal family processes: Growing diversity and complexity* (3rd ed., pp. 493–513). New York: Guilford.

Driver, J. L., & Gottman, J. M. (2004). Daily marital interactions and positive affect during marital conflict among newlywed couples. *Family Process, 43,* 301–314.

Drucker-Colin, R., & Verdugo-Diaz, L. (2004). Cell transplantation for Parkinson's disease: Present status. *Cellular and Molecular Neurobiology, 24,* 301–316.

Druckman, D., & Bjork, R. A. (1994). *Learning, remembering, believing: Enhancing human performance.* Washington, DC: National Academy Press.

Drummond, S. P., Brown, G. G., Gillin, J. C., Stricker, J. L., Wong, E. C., & Buxton, R. B. (2000). Altered brain response to verbal learning following sleep deprivation. *Nature, 403,* 655–657.

Druss, B. G., Wang, P. S., Sampson, N. A., Olfson, M., Pincus, H. A., Wells, K. B., & Kessler, R. C. (2007). Understanding mental health treatment in persons without mental diagnoses: Results from the National Comorbidity Survey Replication. *Archives of General Psychiatry, 64,* 1196–1203.

Drzezga, A. (2008). Basic pathologies of neurodegenerative dementias and their relevance for state-of-the-art molecular imaging studies. *European Journal of Nuclear Medicine & Molecular Imaging, 35,* 4–11.

Duarte, N. T., Goodson, J. R., & Klich, N. R. (1993). How do I like thee? Let me appraise the ways. *Journal of Organizational Behavior, 14,* 239–249.

Dube, S. R., Felitti, V. J., Dong, M., Chapman, D. P., Giles, W. H., & Anda, R. F. (2003). Childhood abuse, neglect, and household dysfunction and the risk of illicit drug use: the adverse childhood experiences study. *Pediatrics, 111,* 564–572.

Dubertret, C., Hanoun, N., Ades, J., Hamon, M., & Gorwood, P. (2004). Family-based association studies between 5-HT-sub(5A) receptor gene and schizophrenia. *Journal of Psychiatric Research, 38,* 371–376.

Dubois, B. (2004). Amnestic MCI or prodromal Alzheimer's disease? *Lancet Neurology, 3*(4), 246–248.

DuBois, D. L., Felner, R. D., Brand, S., Adan, A. M., & Evans, E. G. (1992). A prospective study of life stress, social support, and adaptation in early adolescence. *Child Development, 63,* 542–557.

DuBreuil, S. C., Garry, M., & Loftus, E. F. (1998). Tales from the crib: Memories of infancy. In S. J. Lynn, & K. M. McConkey (Eds.), *Truth in memory* (pp. 137–160). New York: Guilford.

Dubrovsky, B. O. (2005). Steroids, neuroactive steroids and neurosteroids in psychopathology. *Progress in Neuropsychopharmacology and Biological Psychiatry, 29,* 169–192.

Ducci, F., & Goldman, D. (2008). Genetic approaches to addiction: Genes and alcohol. *Addiction, 103*(9), 1414–1428.

Duckitt, J. (2006). Differential effects of right-wing authoritarianism and social dominance orientation on outgroup attitudes and their mediation by threat from and competitiveness to outgroups. *Personality and Social Psychology Bulletin, 32,* 684–696.

Duclos, S. E., & Laird, J. D. (2001). The deliberate control of emotional experience through control of expressions. *Cognition and Emotion, 15,* 27–56.

Dudai, Y. (2004). The neurobiology of consolidations, or, how stable is the engram? *Annual Review of Psychology, 55,* 51–86.

Dudeck, M., Spitzer, C., Stopsack, M., Freyberger, H. J., & Barnow, S. (2007). Forensic inpatient male sexual offenders: The impact of personality disorders and childhood sexual abuse. *Journal of Forensic Psychiatry and Psychology, 18,* 494–506.

Dudley, N. M., Orvis, K. A., Lebeicki, J. E., & Cortina, J. M. (2006). A meta-analytic investigation of conscientiousness in the prediction of job performance: Examining the intercorrelations and the incremental validity of narrow traits. *Journal of Applied Psychology, 91,* 40–57.

Duggan, A., Fuddy, L., Burrell, L., Higman, S. M., McFarlane, E., Windham, A., et al. (2004). Randomized trial of a statewide home visiting program to prevent child abuse: Impact in reducing parental risk factors. *Child Abuse and Neglect, 28,* 623–643.

Dujovne, V., & Houston, B. (1991). Hostility-related variables and plasma lipid levels. *Journal of Behavioral Medicine, 14,* 555–564.

Dumont, F., & Corsini, R. J. (2000). *Six therapists and one client.* New York: Springer.

Duncan, A. E., Scherrer, J., Fu, Q., Bucholz, K. K., Heath, A. C., et al. (2006). Exposure to paternal alcoholism does not predict development of alcohol-use disorders in offspring: Evidence from an offspring-of-twins study. *Journal of Studies on Alcohol, 67,* 649–656.

Duncan, B. L. (2002). The legacy of Saul Rosenwieg: The profundity of the dodo bird. *Journal of Psychotherapy Integration, 12*(1), 32–57.

Duncan, G. J., Brooks-Gunn, J., & Klebanov, P. K. (1994). Economic deprivation and early childhood development. *Child Development, 65,* 296–318.

Dunlop, S. (2008). Activity-dependent plasticity: Implications for recovery after spinal cord injury. *Trends in Neurosciences, 31*(8), 410–418

Dunn, J., Brown, H., Slomkowski, C., Tesla, C., & Youngblade, L. (1991). Young children's understanding of other people's feelings and beliefs: Individual differences and their antecedents. *Child Development, 62,* 1352–1366.

Dunn, J., & Hughes, C. (2001). "I got some swords and you're dead!": Violent fantasy, antisocial behavior, friendship, and moral sensibility in young children. *Child Development, 72,* 491–505.

Dunning, D., Johnson, K., Ehrlinger, J., & Kruger, J. (2003). Why people fail to recognize their own incompetence. *Current Directions in Psychological Science, 12,* 83–87.

Duppils, G. S., & Wikblad, K. (2007). Patients' experiences of being delirious. *Journal of Clinical Nursing, 16*(5), 810–818.

Duran, B., Oetzel, J., Lucero, J., Jiang, Y., Novins, D. K., Manson, S., et al. (2005). Obstacles for rural American Indians seeking alcohol, drug, or mental health treatment. *Journal of Consulting and Clinical Psychology, 73,* 819–829.

Durand, M. V., & Barlow, D. H. (2006). *Essentials of abnormal psychology.* Belmont, CA: Thomson.

Durantini, M. R., Albarracin, D., Mitchell, A. L., Earl, A. N., & Gillette, J. C. (2006). Conceptualizing the influence of social agents of behavior change: A meta-analysis of the effectiveness of HIV-prevention interventionists for different groups. *Psychological Bulletin, 132,* 212–248.

Durka, P. J., Malinowska, U., Szelenberger, W., Wakarow, A., & Blinowska, K. J. (2005). High resolution parametric description of slow wave sleep. *Journal of Neuroscience Methods, 147,* 15–21.

Durlak, J. A. (2006). Cognitive-behavioral treatments. In R. T. Ammerman (Ed.), *Comprehensive handbook of personality and psychopathology* (Vol. 3, pp. 438–447). New York: Wiley.

Durose, M. R., Harlow, C. W., Langan, P. A., Motivans, M., Rantala, R. R., & Smith, E. L. (2005). *Family violence statistics.* Washington, DC: Bureau of Justice Statistics.

Dutton, D. G., & Aron, A. P. (1974). Some evidence for heightened sexual attraction under conditions of high anxiety. *Journal of Personality and Social Psychology, 30,* 510–517.

Dweck, C. S. (1998). The development of early self-conceptions: Their relevance for motivational processes. In J. Heckhausen & C. S. Dweck (Eds.), *Motivation and self-regulation across the life span.* New York: Cambridge University Press.

Dwork, A. J., Arango, V., Underwood, M., Iievski, B., Rosoklija, G., Sackeim, H. A., et al. (2004). Absence of histological lesions in primate models of ECT and magnetic seizure therapy. *American Journal of Psychiatry, 161,* 576–578.

Dyche, L., & Zayas, L. H. (2001). Cross-cultural empathy and training the contemporary psychotherapist. *Clinical Social Work Journal, 29,* 245–258.

Dyken, M. E., & Yamada, T. (2005). Narcolepsy and disorders of excessive somnolence. *Primary Care, 32,* 389–413.

Dzokoto, V. A., & Adams, G. (2005). Understanding genital-shrinking epidemics in West Africa: Koro, Juju, or mass psychogenic illness? *Culture, Medicine, and Psychiatry, 29,* 53–78.

Eagly, A. H. (1987). *Sex differences in social behavior: A social-role interpretation.* Hillsdale, NJ: Erlbaum.

Eagly, A. H., Johannesen-Schmidt, M. C., & van Engen, M. L. (2003). Transformational, transactional, and laissez-faire leadership styles: A meta-analysis comparing women and men. *Psychological Bulletin, 129,* 569–591.

Eagly, A. H., & Karau, S. J. (1991). Gender and the emergence of leaders: A meta-analysis. *Journal of Personality and Social Psychology, 60,* 685–710.

Eagly, A. H., Karau, S. J., & Makhijani, M. G. (1995). Gender and the effectiveness of leaders: A meta-analysis. *Psychological Bulletin, 117,* 125–145.

Eagly, A. H., Makhijani, M. G., & Klonsky, B. G. (1992). Gender and evaluation of leaders: A meta-analysis. *Psychological Bulletin, 111,* 3–22.

Eagly, A. H., & Wood, W. (1999). The orgins of sex diffrences in human behavior: Evolved dispositions versus social roles. *American Psychologist, 54,* 408–423.

Eamon, M. K. (2008). *Empowering vulnerable populations: Cognitive-behavioral interventions.* Chicago, IL: Lyceum Books.

Eastwick, P. W., & Finkel, E. J. (2008). Sex differences in mate preferences revisited: Do people know what they initially desire in a romantic partner? *Journal of Personality and Social Psychology, 94,* 245–264.

Eberhardt, J. L. (2005). Imaging race. *American Psychologist, 60,* 181–190.

Ebert, S. A., Tucker, D. C., & Roth, D. L. (2002). Psychological resistance factors as predictors of general health status and physical symptom reporting. *Psychology Health & Medicine, 7,* 363–375.

Ebstein, R. B. (2006). The molecular genetic architecture of human personality: Beyond self-report questionnaires. *Molecular Psychiatry, 11,* 427–445.

Eby, L. T., Casper, W. J., Lockwood, A., Bordeaux, C., & Brinley, A. (2005). Work and family research in IO/OB: Content analysis and review of the literature (1980–2002). *Journal of Vocational Behavior, 66,* 124–197.

Eccleston, C., & Crombez, G. (1999). Pain demands attention: A cognitive- affective model of the interruptive function of pain. *Psychological Bulletin, 125,* 356–366.

Echeburua, E., de Corral, P., Garcia Bajos, E., & Borda, M. (1993). Interactions between self-exposure and alprazolam in the treatment of agoraphobia without current panic: An exploratory study. *Behavioural and Cognitive Psychotherapy, 21,* 219–238.

Echo News. (2000). Car crash mum tells of fight to rebuild her life. March 17. Retrieved from May 17, 2009, at http://archive.echo-news.co.uk/2000/3/17/206088.html.

Eddy, K. T., Dorer, D. J., Franko, D. L., Tahilani, K., Thompson-Brenner, H., & Herzog, D. B. (2008). Diagnostic crossover in anorexia nervosa and bulimia nervosa: Implications for DSM-V. *American Journal of Psychiatry, 165,* 245–250.

Eddy, K. T., Dutra, L., Bradley, R., & Westen, D. (2004). A multidimensional meta-analysis of psychotherapy and pharmacotherapy for obsessive-compulsive disorder. *Clinical Psychology Review, 24,* 1011–1030.

Edelman, G. M. (2003). Naturalizing consciousness: A theoretical framework. *Proceedings of the National Academy of Sciences, 100,* 5520–5524.

Edinger, J. D., Wohlgemuth, W. K., Radtke, R. A., Marsh, G. R., & Quillian, R. E. (2001). Cognitive behavioral therapy for treatment of chronic primary insomnia. *American Medical Association, 285,* 1856–1864.

Edmond, T., & Rubin, A. (2004). Assessing the long-term effects of EMDR: Results from an 18-month follow-up study with adult female survivors of CSA. *Journal of Child Sexual Abuse, 13,* 69–86.

Edwards, B. J., Reilly, T., & Waterhouse, J. (2009). Zeitgeber-effects of exercise on human circadian rhythms: What are alternative approaches to investigating the existence of a phase-response curve to exercise? *Biological Rhythm Research, 40*(1), 53–69.

Edwards, C. D., & Glick, R. (2008). Depression. In R. L. Glick, J. S. Berlin, A. B. Fishkind, & S. L. Zeller (Eds.), *Emergency psychiatry: Principles and practice.* (pp. 175–187). Philedalphia: Wolters Kluwer/Lippincott, Williams & Wilkins.

Egner, T., Jamieson, G., & Gruzelier, J. (2005). Hypnosis decouples cognitive control from conflict monitoring processes of the frontal lobe. *Neuroimage, 27,* 969–978.

Eich, E. (1989). Theoretical issues in state dependent memory. In H. L. Roediger & F. I. M. Craik (Eds.), *Varieties of memory and consciousness.* Hillsdale, NJ: Erlbaum.

Eich, E., & Macaulay, D. (2000). Are real moods required to reveal mood-congruent and mood-dependent memory? *Psychological Science, 11,* 244–248.

Eich, E., & Macaulay, D. (2006). Cognitive and clinical perspectives on mood dependent memory. In Forgas, J. P. (Ed) *Affect in social thinking and behavior* (pp. 105–121). New York: Psychology Press.

Eich, E., & Metcalfe, J. (1989). Mood dependent memory for internal versus external events. *Experimental Psychology: Learning, Memory, and Cognition, 15,* 443–455.

Eich, J. E., Weingartner, H., Stillman, R. C., & Gillin, J. C. (1975). State dependent accessibility of retrieval cues in the retention of a categorized list. *Journal of Verbal Learning and Verbal Behavior, 14,* 408–417.

Eichelman, B. (1983). The limbic system and aggression in humans. *Neuroscience and Biobehavioral Reviews, 7,* 391–394.

Eickhoff, S. B., Dafotakis, M., Grefkes, C., Stöcker, T., Shah, N. J., Schnitzler, A., Zilles, K., & Siebler, M. (2008). fMRI reveals cognitive and emotional processing in a long-term comatose patient. *Experimental Neurology, 214*(2), 240–246.

Eid, M., & Larsen, R. J. (Eds.) (2008). *The science of subjective well-being.* New York, NY: Guilford Press.

Eifert, G. H., Zvolensky, M. J., & Louis, A. (2008). Somatoform disorders: Nature, psychological processes, and treatment strategies. In J. E. Maddux & B. A. Winstead (Eds.). *Psychopathology: Foundations for a contemporary understanding* (2nd ed., pp. 307–325). New York: Routledge/Taylor & Francis Group.

Einhorn, H., & Hogarth, R. (1982). Prediction, diagnosis and causal thinking in forecasting. *Journal of Forecasting, 1,* 23–36.

Eisenberg, M., Kobilo, T., Berman, D. E., & Dudai, Y. (2003). Stability of retrieved memory: Inverse correlation with trace dominance. *Science, 301,* 1102–1104.

Eisenberg, N., Champion, C., & Ma, Y. (2004). Emotion-related regulation: An emerging construct *Merrill-Palmer Quarterly, 50,* 236–259.

Eisenberg, N., & Fabes, R. A. (1998). Prosocial development. In W. Damon & N. Eisenberg (Eds.), *Handbook of child psychology: Vol. 3. Social, emotional, and personality development* (5th ed., pp. 701–778). New York: Wiley.

Eisenberg, N., Fabes, R. A., & Murphy, B. C. (1995). Relations of shyness and low sociability to regulation and emotionality. *Journal of Personality and Social Psychology, 68,* 505–518.

Eisenberg, N., Fabes, R. A., & Spinrad, T. L. (2006). Prosocial development. In W. Damon & R. M. Lerner (Series Eds.) & N. Eisenberg (Vol. Ed.), *Handbook of child psychology: Vol. 3. Social, emotional, and personality development* (6th ed.). New York: Wiley.

Eisenberger, N. I., Way, B. M., Taylor, S. E., Welch, W. T., & Lieberman, M. D. (2007). *Biological Psychiatry, 61,* 1100–1108.

Eisenmann, J. C., Bartee, R. T., Smith, D. T., Welk, G. J., & Fu, Q. (2008). Combined influence of physical activity and television viewing on the risk of overweight in US youth. *International Journal of Obesity, 32,* 613–618.

Eiser, A. S. (2005). Physiology and psychology of dreams. *Seminars in Neurology, 25,* 97–105.

Ekman, A., Lindholm, M. L., Lennmarken, C., & Sandin, R. (2004). Reduction in the incidence of awareness using BIS monitoring. *Acta Anaesthesiology Scandinavia, 48,* 20–26.

Ekman, P. (1993). Facial expression and emotion. *American Psychologist, 48,* 384–392.

Ekman, P. (1994). Strong evidence for universals in facial expressions: A reply to Russell's mistaken critique. *Psychological Bulletin, 115*(2), 268–287.

Ekman, P., & Davidson, R. J. (1993). Voluntary smiling changes regional brain activity. *Psychological Science, 4*(5), 342–345.

Ekman, P., Davidson, R. J., Ricard, M., & Alan, W. B. (2005). Buddhist and psychological perspectives on emotions and well-being. *Current Directions in Psychological Science, 14,* 59–63.

Ekman, P., Friesen, W. V., & Ellsworth, P. (1972). *Emotion in the human face: Guidelines for research and a review of findings.* New York: Pergamon Press.

Ekman, P., Levenson, R. W., & Friesen, W. V. (1983). Autonomic nervous system activity distinguishes among emotions. *Science, 221,* 1208–1210.

El Yacoubi, M., Bouali, S., Popa, D., Naudon, L., Leroux-Nicollet, I., Hamon, M., et al. (2003). Behavioral, neurochemical, and electrophysiological characterization of a genetic mouse model of depression. *Proceedings of the National Academy of Sciences, 100,* 6227–6232.

Eling, P. (2008). Cerebral localization in the Netherlands in the nineteenth century: Emphasizing the work of Aletta Jacobs. *Journal of the History of the Neurosciences, 17*(2), 175–194.

Eliot, A. J., Chirkov, V. I., Kim, Y., & Shelldon, K. M. (2001). A cross-cultural analysis of avoidance (relative to approach) personal goals. *Psychological Science, 12,* 505–510.

Elkin, I. (1994). The NIMH treatment of depression collaborative research program: Where we began and where we are. In A. E. Bergin & S. L. Garfield (Eds.), *Handbook of psychotherapy and behavior change* (pp. 114–139). New York: Wiley.

Elkins, I. J., King, S. M., McGue, M., & Iacono, W. G. (2006). Personality traits and the development of nicotine, alchohol, and illicit drug disorders: Prospective links from adolescence to young adulthood. *Journal of Abnormal Psychology, 115,* 26–39.

Elliot, A. J. (Ed.) (2008). *Handbook of approach and avoidance motivation* (pp. 273–288). New York, NY: Psychology Press.

Elliot, A. J., & Devine, P. G. (1994). On the motivational nature of cognitive dissonance: Dissonance as psychological discomfort. *Journal of Personality and Social Psychology, 67,* 382–394.

Elliot, S. N., Reynolds, C. R., & Kratochwill, T. R. (2006). *School psychology: Essentials of theory and practice.* Hoboken, NJ: Wiley.

Elliott, R., Watson, J. C., & Goldman, R. N. (2004a). Empty chair work for unfinished interpersonal issues. In R. Elliott & J. Watson (Eds.), *Learning emotion-focused therapy: The process-experiential approach to change* (pp. 243–265). Washington, DC: American Psychological Association.

Elliott, R., Watson, J. C., & Goldman, R. N. (2004b). Two-chair work for conflict splits. In R. Elliott & J. Watson (Eds.), *Learning emotion-focused therapy: The process-experiential approach to change* (pp. 219–241). Washington, DC: American Psychological Association.

Ellis, A. (1962). *Reason and emotion in psychotherapy.* New York: Lyle Stuart.

Ellis, A. (1993). Reflections on rational-emotive therapy. *Journal of Consulting and Clinical Psychology, 61,* 199–201.

Ellis, A. (1995). Rational emotive behavior therapy. In R. J. Corsini & D. Wedding (Eds.), *Current psychotherapies* (5th ed., pp. 162–196). Itasca, IL: Peacock.

Ellis, A. (1997). Using rational emotive behavior therapy techniques to cope with disability. *Professional Psychology: Research and Practice, 28,* 17–22.

Ellis, A. (2004a). Why I (really) became a therapist. *Journal of Rational-Emotive and Cognitive Behavior Therapy, 22*(2), 73–77.

Ellis, A. (2004b). Why rational emotive behavior therapy is the most comprehensive and effective form of behavior therapy. *Journal of Rational-Emotive and Cognitive Behavior Therapy, 22*(2), 85–92.

Ellis, A., & MacLaren, C. (2005). *Rational emotive behavior therapy* (2nd ed.). Manassas Park, VA: Impact Publishers.

Ellis, A. L., & Mitchell, R. W. (2000). Sexual orientation. In L. T. Szuchman & F. Muscarella (Eds.), *Psychological perspectives on human sexuality* (pp. 196–231). New York: Wiley.

Ellis, N. R. (1991). Automatic and effortful processes in memory for spatial location. *Bulletin of the Psychonomic Society, 29,* 28–30.

Elms, A. C. (2009). Obedience lite. *American Psychologist, 64,* 32–36.

Elofsson, U. O. E., von Schèele, B., Theorell, T., & Söndergaard, H. P. (2008). Physiological correlates of eye movement desensitization and reprocessing. *Journal of Anxiety Disorders, 22*(4), 622–634.

Elovainio, M., Kivimäki, M., & Vahtera, J. (2002). Organizational justice: Evidence on a new psychosocial predictor of health. *American Journal of Public Health, 92,* 105–108.

Else-Quest, N. M., Hyde, J. S., Goldsmith, H. H., & Van Hulle, C. A. (2006). Gender differences in temperament: A meta-analysis. *Psychological Bulletin, 132,* 33–72.

Elwood, L. S., Hahn, K. S., Olatunji, B. O., & Williams, N. L. (2009). Cognitive vulnerabilities to the development of PTSD: A review of four vulnerabilities and the proposal f an integrative vulnerability model. *Clinical Psychology Review, 29,* 87–100.

Emanuele, E., Politi, P., Bianchi, M., Minoretti, P., Bertona, M., & Geroldi, D. (2006). Raised plasma nerve growth factor levels associated with early-stage romantic love. *Psychoneuroendocrinology, 31,* 288–294.

Enblom, A., Hammar, M., Steineck, G., & Börjeson, S. (2008). Can individuals identify if needling was performed with an acupuncture needle or a non-penetrating sham needle? *Complementary Therapies in Medicine, 16*(5), 288–294.

Engebretson, T. O., & Stoney, C. M. (1995). Anger expression and lipid concentrations. *International Journal of Behavioral Medicine, 2,* 281–298.

Engen, T., Gilmore, M. M., & Mair, R. G. (1991). Odor memory. In T. V. Getchell et al. (Eds.), *Taste and smell in health and disease.* New York: Raven Press.

Engle, R. W., & Oransky, N. (1999). The evolution from short-term to working memory: Multi-store to dynamic models of temporary storage. In R. Sternberg (Ed.), *The nature of human cognition* (pp. 514–555). Cambridge: MIT Press.

Engler, B. (2003). *Personality theories: An introduction* (6th ed.). Boston: Houghton Mifflin.

Enoch, M. A. (2003). Pharmacogenomics of alcohol response and addiction. *American Journal of Pharmacogenomics, 3,* 217–232.

Epel, E., Jimenez, S., Brownell, K., Stroud, L., Stoney, C. M., & Niaura, R. (2004). Are stress eaters at risk for the metabolic syndrome? *Annals of the New York Academy of Sciences, 1032,* 208–210.

Epping-Jordan, M. P., Watkins, S. S., Koob, G. F., & Markou, A. (1998). Dramatic decreases in brain reward function during nicotine withdrawal. *Nature, 393,* 76–79.

Epstein, E. M., Sloan, D. M., & Marx, B. P. (2005). Getting to the heart of the matter: Written disclosure, gender, and heart rate. *Psychosomatic Medicine, 67,* 413–419.

Epstein, L. H., Temple, J. L., Roemmich, J. N., & Bouton, Mark E. (2009). Habituation as a determinant of human food intake. *Psychological Review, 116,* 384–407.

Epstein, R., Kirshit, C. E., Lanza, R. P., & Rubin, C. L. (1984). "Insight" in the pigeon: Antecedents and determinants of an intelligent performance. *Nature, 308,* 61–62.

Epstude, K., & Mussweiler, T. (2009). What you feel is how you compare: How comparisons influence the social induction of affect. *Emotion, 9,* 1–14.

Erdelyi, M. H. (1985). *Psychoanalysis: Freud's cognitive psychology.* San Francisco: Freeman.

Erez, A., Misangyi, V. F., Johnson, D. E., LePine, M. A., & Halverson, K. C. (2008). Stirring the hearts of followers: Charismatic leadership as the transferal of affect. *Journal of Applied Psychology, 93,* 602–616.

Erickson, K. I., Colcombe, S. J., Wadhwa, R., Scalf, P. E., Kim, J. S., et al. (2007). Training-induced plasticity in older adults: Effects of training on hemispheric asymmetry. *Neurobiology of Aging, 28,* 272–283.

Erickson, R. J., Nichols, L., & Ritter, C. (2000). Family influences on absenteeism: Testing an expanded process model. *Journal of Vocational Behavior, 57,* 246–272.

Ericsson, K. A., & Charness, N. (1994). Expert performance: Its structure and acquisition. *American Psychologist, 49,* 725–747.

Ericsson, K. A., & Simon, H. A. (1994). *Protocol analysis: Verbal reports as data* (Rev. ed.). Cambridge, MA: MIT Press.

Ericsson, K. A., & Staszewski, J. (1989). Skilled memory and expertise: Mechanisms of exceptional performance. In D. Klahr & K. Kotovsky (Eds.), *Complex information processing: The impact of Herbert A. Simon.* Hillsdale, NJ: Erlbaum.

Eriksen, S., & Jensen, V. (2006). All in the family? Family environment factors in sibling violence. *Journal of Family Violence, 21*(8), 497–507.

Erikson, E. H. (1968). *Identity: Youth and crisis.* New York: Norton.

Erikson, R., Goldthorpe, J. H., Jackson, M., Yaish, M., & Cox, D. R. (2005). On class differentials in educational attainment. *Proceedings of the National Academy of Sciences, 102,* 9730–9733.

Eriksson, P. S., Perfilieva, E., Bjork-Eriksson, T., Alborn, A. M., Nordborg, C., Peterson, D. A., & Gage, F. H. (1998). Neurogenesis in the adult human hippocampus. *Nature Medicine, 4,* 1313–1317.

Ernst, M., Matochik, J. A., Heishman, S. J., Van Horn, J. D., Jons, P. H., Henningfield, J. E., & London, E. D. (2001). Effect of nicotine on brain activation during performance of a working memory task. *Proceedings of the National Academy of Sciences, 98,* 4728–4733.

Eroglu, E., Gökçil, Z., Bek, S., Ulas, U. H., & Odabasi, Z. (2008). Pregnancy and teratogenicity of antiepileptic drugs. *Acta Neurologica Belgica, 108*(2), 53–57.

Eron, L. D., Huesmann, L. R., Lefkowitz, M. M., & Walder, L. O. (1972). Does television violence cause aggression? *American Psychologist, 27*(4), 253–263.

Esel, E., Ozsay, S., Tutus, A., Sofiuoglu, S., Kartaici, S., Bayram, F., et al. (2005). Effects of antidepressant treatment and of gender on serum leptin levels in patients with major depression. *Progress in Neuro-Psychopharmacology and Biological Psychiatry, 29,* 565–570.

Esterson, A. (2001). The mythologizing of psychoanalytic history: Deception and self-deception in Freud's account of the seduction theory episode. *History of Psychiatry, 12,* 329–352.

Ettinger, U., Picchioni, M., Landau, S., Matsumoto, K., van Haren, N. E., Marshall, N., et al. (2007). Magnetic resonance imaging of the thalamus and adhesio interthalamica in twins with schizophrenia. *Archives of General Psychiatry, 64,* 401–409.

Ettlin, T. M., Beckson, M., Benson, D. F., Langfitt, J. T., Amos, E. C., & Pineda, G. S. (1992). Prosopagnosia: A bihemispheric disorder. *Cortex, 28*(1), 129–134.

Evans, G. W. (2004). The environment of childhood poverty. *American Psychologist, 59,* 77–92.

Evans, G. W., & Wener, R. E. (2006). Rail commuting duration and passenger stress. *Health Psychology, 25,* 408–412.

Evans, J., Heron, J., Lewis, G., Araya, R., & Wolke, D. (2005). Negative self-schemas and the onset of depression in women: Longitudinal study. *British Journal of Psychiatry, 186,* 302–307.

Evans, J. A., Elliott, J. A., & Gorman, M. R. (2009). Dim nighttime illumination accelerates adjustment to timezone travel in an animal model. *Current Biology, 19*(4), R156–R157.

Everaerd, W., & Laan, E. (1994). Cognitive aspects of sexual functioning and dysfunctioning. *Sexual and Marital Therapy, 9,* 225–230.

Everitt, B. J., & Robbins, T. W. (2005). Neural systems of reinforcement for drug addiction: From actions to habits to compulsion. *Nature Neuroscience, 8,* 1481–1489.

Eysenck, H. J. (1952). The effects of psychotherapy: An evaluation. *Journal of Consulting Psychology, 16,* 319–324.

Eysenck, H. J. (1978). An exercise in mega-silliness. *American Psychologist, 33,* 517.

Eysenck, H. J. (1986). What is intelligence? In R. J. Sternberg & D. K. Detterman (Eds.), *What is intelligence? Contemporary viewpoints on its nature and definition.* Norwood, NJ: Ablex.

Eysenck, H. J. (1990a). Biological dimensions of personality. In L. A. Pervin (Ed.), *Handbook of personality: Theory and research* (pp. 244–276). New York: Guilford.

Eysenck, H. J. (1990b). Genetic and environmental contributions to individual differences: The three major dimensions of personality. *Journal of Personality, 58,* 245–261.

Eysenck, H. J., & Rachman, S. (1965). *The causes and cures of neurosis: An introduction to modern behavior therapy based on learning theory and the principle of conditioning.* San Diego: Knapp.

Eysenck, M. W., & Keane, M. T. (2005). *Cognitive psychology: A student's handbook* (5th ed.). East Sussex, UK: Psychology Press.

Fabes, R. A., Martin, C. L., & Hanish, L. D. (2003). Young children's qualities in same-, other-, and mixed-sex peer groups. *Child Development, 74,* 921–932.

Fabrigar, L. R., MacDonald, T. K., & Wegener, D. T. (2005). The structure of attitudes. In D. Albarracín, B. T. Johnson, & M. P. Zanna (Eds.), *Handbook of attitudes* (pp. 79–124). Mahwah, NJ: Erlbaum.

Faedda, G., Tondo, L., Teicher, M., Baldessarini, R., Gelbard, H., & Floris, G. (1993). Seasonal mood disorders: Patterns of seasonal recurrence in mania and depression. *Archives of General Psychiatry, 50,* 17–23.

Fagan, J. F. (2000). A theory of intelligence as processing. *Psychology, Public Policy, and Law, 26,* 168–179.

Fagan, J. F., & Detterman, D. K. (1992). The Fagan Test of Infant Intelligence: A technical summary. *Journal of Applied Developmental Psychology, 13,* 173–193.

Fagan, J. F., Holland, C. R., & Wheeler, K. (2007). The prediction, from infancy, of adult IQ and achievement. *Intelligence, 35,* 225–231.

Fagin-Jones, S., & Midlarsky, E. (2007). Courageous altruism : Personal and situational correlates of rescue during the Holocaust. *The Journal of Positive Psychology, 2,* 136–147.

Fago, David P. (2009). Comment: The evidence-based treatment debate: Toward a dialectical rapprochement. *Psychotherapy: Theory, Research, Practice, Training, 46,* 15–18.

Fagot, B. I. (1997). Attachment, parenting, and peer interactions of toddler children. *Developmental Psychology, 33,* 489–499.

Fahrenkopf, A. M., Sectish, T. C., Barger, L. K., Sharek, P. J., Lewin, D., Chiang, V. W., Edwards, S., Wiedermann, B. L., & Landrigan, C. P. (2008). Rates of medication errors among depressed and burnt out residents: prospective cohort study. *British Medical Journal, 336,* 488–491.

Fairburn, C. G. (Ed.). (2008). *Cognitive behavior therapy and eating disorders.* New York: Guilford.

Fairburn, C. G., Cooper, Z., Shafran, R., Wilson, G. T., & Barlow, D. H. (2008). Eating disorders: A transdiagnostic protocol. In Barlow, D. (Ed.), *Clinical handbook of psychological disorders: A step-by-step treatment manual* (4th ed., pp. 578–614). New York, NY: Guilford Press.

Fan, J., Ma, J., Li, X., Zhang, C., & Sun, W. (2006). Population-based and family-based association studies of an (AC)n dinucleotide repeat in a-7 nicotinic receptor subunit gene and schizophrenia. *Schizophrenia Research, 84,* 222–227.

Farah, M. J. (1996). Is face recognition "special"? Evidence from neuropsychology. *Behavioral Brain Research, 76*(1–2), 181–189.

Farah, M. J., McMullen, P. A., & Meyer, M. M. (1991). Can recognition of living things be selectively impaired? *Neuropsychologia, 29*(2), 185–193.

Farah, M. J., Shera, D. M., Savage, J. H., Betancourt, L., Giannetta, J. M., Brodsky, N. L., Malmud, E. K., & Hurt, H. (2006). Childhood poverty: Specific associations with neurocognitive development. *Brain Research, 1110,* 166–174.

Farfel, M., DiGrande, L., Brackbill, R., Prann, A., Cone, J., Friedman, S., Walker, D. J., Pezeshki, G., Thomas, P., Galea, S., Williamson, D., Frieden, T. R., & Thorpe, L. (2008). An overview of 9/11 experiences and respiratory and mental health conditions among World Trade Center health registry enrollees. *Journal of Urban Health, 85,* 880–909.

Farley, F. (1986). The big T in personality. *Psychology Today, 20,* 44–52.

Farmer, J. D., Patelli, P., & Zovko, I. I. (2005). The predictive power of zero intelligence in financial markets. *Proceedings of the National Academy of Sciences, 102,* 2254–2259.

Farmer, R. F., & Nelson-Gray, R. (2005). *Personality-guided behavior therapy.* Washington, DC: American Psychological Association.

Farooqi, I. S., Keogh, J. M., Kamath, S., Jones, S., Gibson, W. T., Trussel, R., et al. (2001). Metabolism: Partial leptin deficiency and human adiposity. *Nature, 414,* 34–35.

Farrell, D., & Stamm, C. L. (1988). Meta-analysis of the correlates of employee absence. *Human Relations, 41,* 211–227.

Farroni, T., Csibra, G., Simion, F., & Johnson, M. H. (2002). Eye contact detection in humans from birth. *Proceedings of the National Academy of Sciences, 99,* 9602–9605.

Farroni, T., Johnson, M. H., Menon, E., Zulian, L., Faraguna, D., & Csibra, G. (2005). Newborns' preference for face-relevant stimuli: Effects of contrast polarity. *Proceedings of the National Academy of Sciences, 102,* 17245–17250.

Fassler, D. G., & Dumas, L. S. (1997). *Help me, I'm sad: Recognizing, treating, and preventing childhood depression.* New York: Viking Press.

Fassler, O., Lynn, S. J., & Knox, J. (2008). Is hypnotic suggestibility a stable trait? *Consciousness and Cognition, 17,* 240–253.

Faulkner, M. (2001). The onset and alleviation of learned helplessness in older hospitalized people. *Aging & Mental Health, 5,* 379–386.

Fava, G. A., Grandi, S. Rafanelli, C., Ruini, C., Conti, S., & Bellurado, P. (2001). Long-term outcome of social phobia treated by exposure. *Psychological Medicine, 31,* 899–905.

Fava, G. A., Rafanelli, C., Tossani, E., & Grandi, S. (2008). Agoraphobia is a disease: A tribute to Sir Martin Roth. *Psychotherapy and Psychosomatics, 77,* 133–138.

Faymonville, M. E., Laureys, S., Degueldre, C., DelFiore, G., Luxen, A., Franck, G., et al. (2000). Neural mechanisms of antinociceptive effects of hypnosis. *Anesthesiology, 92,* 1257–1267.

Feder, B. J. (2004, May 31). Technology strains to find menace in the crowd. *The New York Times,* p. C1.

Federal Bureau of Investigation. (2008). *Crime in the United States, 2007.* Washington, DC: U.S. Department of Justice. Retrieved July 23, 2009, from http://www.fbi.gov/ucr/cius2007/data/table_01.html.

Feigin, V. L. (2003). Stroke epidemiology: A review of population based studies of incidence, prevalence, and case-fatality in the late 20th century. *Lancet Neurology, 2*(1), 43–53.

Feinberg, L., & Campbell, I. G. (1993). Total sleep deprivation in the rat transiently abolishes the delta amplitude response to darkness: Implications for the mechanism of the "negative delta rebound." *Journal of Neurophysiology, 70*(6) 2695–2699.

Feist, J., & Feist, G. J. (2002). *Theories of personality* (5th ed.). New York: McGraw-Hill.

Feit, R. (2003). LASIK results. *Ophthalmology Clinics of North America, 16*(1), 127–135.

Felder, R. M., & Brent, R. (2001). Effective strategies for cooperative learning. *Journal of Cooperation & Collaboration in College Teaching, 10,* 69–75.

Feldman, D. C., & Turnley, W. H. (2004). Contingent employment in academic careers: Relative deprivation among adjunct faculty. *Journal of Vocational Behavior, 64,* 284–307.

Feldman, R., Weller, A., Zagoory-Sharon, O., & Levine, A. (2007). Evidence for a neuroendocrinological foundation of human affiliation: Plasma oxytocin levels across pregnancy and the postpartum period predict mother-infant bonding. *Psychological Science, 18,* 965–970.

Felten, D. L., Cohen, N., Ader, R., Felten, S. Y., Carlson, S. L., & Roszman, T. L. (1991). Central neural circuits involved in neural-immune interactions. In R. Ader (Ed.), *Psychoneuroimmunology* (2nd ed.). New York: Academic Press.

Feltham, C. (2000). What are counselling and psychotherapy? In C. Feltham and I. Horton (Eds.), *Handbook of counselling and psychotherapy.* London: Sage.

Feng, X., Shaw, D. S., Kovacs, M., Lane, T., O'Rourke, F. E., & Alarcon, J. H. (2008). Emotion regulation in preschoolers: The roles of behavioral inhibition, maternal affective behavior, and maternal depression. *Journal of Child Psychology and Psychiatry, 49,* 132–141.

Fenn, K. M., Nusbaum, H. C., & Margoliash, D. (2003). Consolidation during sleep of perceptual learning of spoken language. *Nature, 425,* 614–616.

Fenson, L., Dale, P. S., Reznick, J. S., & Bates, E. (1994). Variability in early communicative development. *Monographs of the Society for Research in Child Development, 59,* 173.

Ferguson, C. J. (2002). Media violence: Miscast causality. *American Psychologist, 57,* 446–447.

Ferguson, M. J., & Bargh, J. A. (2004). How social perception can automatically influence behavior. *Trends in Cognitive Sciences, 8,* 33–39.

Fernández-Dols, J.-M., & Ruiz-Belda, M.-A. (1995). Are smiles a sign of happiness? Gold medal winners at the Olympic Games. *Journal of Personality and Social Psychology, 69,* 1113–1119.

Fernstrom, J. D., Choi, S. (2007). The development of tolerance to drugs that suppress food intake. *Pharmacology & Therapeutics, 117*(1), 105–122.

Ferrara, J. M., & Stacy, M. (2008). Impulse-control disorders in Parkinson's disease. *CNS Spectrums, 13*(8), 690–698.

Ferris, G. R., Judge, T. A., Rowland, K. M., & Fitzgibbons, D. E. (1994). Subordinate influence and the performance evaluation process: Test of a model. *Organizational and Human Decision Processes, 58,* 101–135.

Ferro, J. M. (2001). Hyperacute cognitive stroke syndromes. *Journal of Neurology, 248*(10), 841–849.

Feshbach, S., & Tangney, J. (2008). Television viewing and aggression: Some alternative perspectives. *Perspectives on Psychological Science, 3*(5), 387–389.

Festinger, L. (1954). A theory of social comparison processes. *Human Relations, 7,* 117–140.

Festinger, L. (1957). *A theory of cognitive dissonance.* Evanston, IL: Row, Petersen.

Festinger, L., & Carlsmith, J. M. (1959). Cognitive consequences of forced compliance. *Journal of Abnormal and Social Psychology, 58,* 203–210.

Fields, R. D. (2005). Making memories stick. *Scientific American, 292,* 74–81.

Filipek, P. A., Accardo, P. J., Barancek, G. T., Cook, E. H., Jr., Dawson, G., Gordon, B., et al. (1999). The screening and diagnosis of autistic spectrum disorders. *Journal of Autism and Developmental Disorders, 29,* 439–484.

Fincham, J. M., & Anderson, J. R. (2006). Distinct roles of the anterior cingulated and the prefrontal cortex in the acquisition and performance of a cognitive skill. *Proceedings of the National Academy of Sciences, 103,* 12941–12946.

Fine, I., Wade, A. R., Brewer, A. A., May, M. G., Goodman, D. F., Boynton, G. M., et al. (2003). Long-term deprivation affects visual perception and cortex. *Nature Neuroscience, 6,* 915–916.

Fink, J. N., & Caplan, L. R. (2003). Cerebrovascular cases. *Medical Clinics of North America, 87*(4), 755–770.

Finkel, D., Reynolds, C. A., McArdle, J. J., & Pedersen, N. L. (2007). Age changes in processing speed as a leading indicator of cognitive aging. *Psychology and Aging, 22*(3), 558–568.

Fiorentino, D. D. (2008). Cognition, but not sensation, mediates age-related changes in the ability to monitor the environment. *Psychology & Aging, 23*(3), 665–670.

First, M. B., Pincus, H. A., Levine, J. B., Williams, J. B. W., Ustun, B., & Peele, R. (2004). Clinical utility as a criterion for revising psychiatric diagnoses. *American Journal of Psychiatry, 161,* 946–954.

Fischer, K. W., & Bidell, T. (1991). Constraining nativist inferences about cognitive capacities. In S. Carey & R. Gelman (Eds.), *The epigenesis of mind: Essays on biology and cognition* (pp. 199–235). Hillsdale, NJ: Erlbaum.

Fischer, K. W., & Hencke, R. W. (1996). Infants' construction of actions in context: Piaget's contribution to research on early development. *Psychological Science, 7,* 204–209.

Fischer, M. E., Vitek, M. E., Hedeker, D., Henderson, W. G., Jacobsen, S. J., & Goldberg, J. (2004). A twin study of erectile dysfunction. *Archives of Internal Medicine, 164,* 165–168.

Fischer, M. J., & Massey, D. S. (2007). The effects of affirmative action in higher education. *Social Science Research, 36*(2), 531–549.

Fischer, P. J., & Breakey, W. R. (1991). The epidemiology of alcohol, drug, and mental disorders among homeless persons. *American Psychologist, 46,* 1115–1128.

Fischer, S., Hallschmid, M., Elsner, A. L., & Born, J. (2002). Sleep forms memory for finger skills. *Proceedings of the National Academy of Sciences, 99,* 11987–11991.

Fischoff, B., & MacGregor, D. (1982). Subjective confidence in forecasts. *Journal of Forecasting, 1,* 155–172.

Fisher, C. B., & Fried, A. L. (2003). Internet-mediated psychological services and the American Psychological Association ethics code. *Psychotherapy: Theory, Research, Practice, and Training, 40,* 103–111.

Fisher, C. D. (2000). Mood and emotion while working: Missing pieces of job satisfaction? *Journal of Organizational Behavior, 21,* 185–202.

Fisher, C. D. (2003). Why do lay people believe that satisfaction and performance are correlated? Possible sources of a commonsense theory. *Journal of Organizational Behavior, 24,* 753–777.

Fisher, C. M. (1982). Lacunar strokes and infarcts: A review. *Neurology, 32*(8), 871–876.

Fisher, C. M. (1989). Binswanger's encephalopathy: A review. *Journal of Neurology, 236*(2), 65–79.

Fisher, P. L., & Wells, A. (2009). Psychological models of worry and generalized anxiety disorder. In M. M. Antony & M. B. Stein (Eds.), *Oxford handbook of anxiety and related disorders* (pp. 225–237). New York: Oxford University Press.

Fisher, S. E. (2005). Dissection of molecular mechanisms underlying speech and language disorders. *Applied Psycholinguistics, 26,* 111–128.

Fisher, W. A., Fisher, J. D., & Rye, B. J. (1995). Understanding and promoting AIDS-preventive behavior: Insights from the theory of reasoned action. *Health Psychology, 14,* 255–264.

Fiske, A. P., Kitayama, S., Markus, H. R., & Nisbett, R. E. (1998). The cultural matrix of social psychology. In D. T. Gilbert, S. T. Fiske, & G. Lindzey (Eds.), *Handbook of social psychology* (Vol. 2, 4th ed., pp. 915–981). Boston: McGraw-Hill.

Fiske, S., & Taylor, S. (2008). *Social cognition, from brains to culture.* New York: McGraw-Hill.

Fiske, S. T. (1998). Stereotyping, prejudice, and discrimination. In D. Gilbert, S. T. Fiske, & G. Lindzey (Eds.), *Handbook of social psychology* (Vol. 2, 4th ed., pp. 357–414). Boston: McGraw-Hill.

Fiske, S. T. (2000). Interdependence and the reduction of prejudice. In S. Oskamp (Ed.), *Reducing prejudice and discrimination* (pp. 115–135). Mahwah, NJ: Erlbaum.

Fitch, W. T., & Hauser, M. D. (2004). Computational constraints on syntactic processing in a nonhuman primate. *Science, 303,* 377–380.

Fitzgerald, T. E., Tennen, H., Affleck, G. S., & Pransky, G. (1993). The relative importance of dispositional optimism and control appraisals in quality of life after coronary artery bypass surgery. *Journal of Behavioral Medicine, 16,* 25–43.

Flanagan, J. C. (1954). The critical incident technique. *Psychological Bulletin, 51,* 327–358.

Flavell, J. E., Azrin, N., Baumeister, A., Carr, E., Dorsey, M., Forehand, R., et al. (1982). The treatment of self-injurious behavior. *Behavior Therapy, 13,* 529–554.

Flavell, J. H. (1996). Piaget's legacy. *Psychological Science, 7,* 200–203.

Fleck, M. S., & Mitroff, S. R. (2007). Rare targets are rarely missed in correctable search. *Psychological Science, 18*(11), 943–947.

Fleeson, W. (2004). Moving personality beyond the person-situation debate: The challenge and the opportunity of within-person variability. *Current Directions in Psychological Science, 13,* 83–87.

Fleeson, W., Malanos, A. B., & Achille, N. M. (2002). An intraindividual process approach to the relationship between extraversion and positive affect: Is acting extraverted as "good" as being extraverted? *Journal of Personality & Social Psychology, 83,* 1409–1422.

Flegal, K. M., Graubard, B. I., Williamson, D. F., & Gail, M. H. (2005). Excess deaths associated with underweight, overweight, and obesity. *Journal of the American Medical Association, 293,* 1861–1867.

Fleischhacker, W. W., & Widschwendter, C. G. (2006). Treatment of schizophrenia patients: Comparing new-generation antipsychotics to each other. *Current Opinion in Psychiatry, 19,* 128–134.

Fleishman, E. A., & Harris, E. F. (1962). Patterns of leadership behavior related to employee grievances and turnover. *Personnel Psychology, 15,* 43–56.

Flor, H., Birbaumer, N., Herman, C., Ziegler, S., & Patrick, C. J. (2002). Aversive Pavlovian conditioning in psychopaths: Peripheral and central correlates. *Psychophysiology, 39,* 505–518.

Flores, E., Cicchetti, D., & Rogosch, F. A. (2005). Predictors of resilience in maltreated and nonmaltreated Latino children. *Developmental Psychology, 41,* 338–351.

Floyd, J. A. (2002). Sleep and aging. *Nursing Clinics of North America, 37,* 719–731.

Floyd, M. F., Spengler, J. O., Maddock, J. E., Gobster, P. H., & Suau, L. (2008). Environmental and social correlates of physical activity in neighborhood parks: An observational study in Tampa and Chicago. *Leisure Sciences, 30*(4), 360–375.

Flynn, F. J., & Lake, V. K. B. (2008). If you need help, just ask: Underestimating compliance with direct requests for help. *Journal of Personality and Social Psychology, 95,* 128–143.

Flynn, J. T. (1999). Searching for justice: The discovery of IQ gains over time. *American Psychologist, 54,* 5–20.

Foa, E. B., Cahill, S. P., Boscarino, J. A., Hobfoll, S. E., Lahad, M., McNally, R. J., et al. (2005). Social, psychological, and psychiatric interventions following terrorist attacks: Recommendations for practice and research. *Neuropsychopharmacology, 30,* 1806–1817.

Foa, E. B., Dancu, C. V., Hembree, E. A., Jaycox, L. H., Meadows, E. A., & Street, G. P. (1999). A comparison of exposure therapy, stress-inoculation training, and their combination for reducing posttraumatic stress disorder in female assault victims. *Journal of Consulting and Clinical Psychology, 67,* 194–200.

Fodor, J. A. (1983). Modularity of mind: An essay on faculty psychology. Cambridge, MA: MIT Press.

Foley, J. M. (2004). Empirically supported treatment endeavour: A successful future or inevitable debacle? *Clinical Psychologist, 8,* 29–38.

Folk, C. L., Remington, R. W., & Wright, J. H. (1994). The structure of attentional control: Contingent attentional capture by apparent motion, abrupt onset, and color. *Journal of Experimental Psychology: Human Perception and Performance, 20,* 317–329.

Folkman, S., & Lazarus, R. (1988). *Manual for the ways of coping questionnaire.* Palo Alto, CA: Consulting Psychologists Press.

Folkman, S., Lazarus, R., Dunkel-Shetter, C., DeLongis, A., & Gruen, R. (1986). Dynamics of a stressful encounter: Cognitive appraisal, coping, and encounter outcomes. *Journal of Personality and Social Psychology, 50,* 992–1003.

Folkman, S., Lazarus, R. S., Dunkel-Schetter, C., DeLongis, A., & Gruen, R. J. (2000). The dynamics of a stressful encounter. In E. T. Higgins & A. W. Kruglanski (Eds.), *Motivational science: Social and personality perspectives* (pp. 111–127). Hove, UK: Psychology Press.

Folkman, S., & Moskowitz, J. T. (2000). Stress, positive emotion, and coping. *Current Directions in Psychological Science, 9,* 115–118.

Fontaine, K. L. (2009). *Mental health nursing.* Upper Saddle River, NJ: Pearson/Prentice Hall.

Foote, B., Smolin, Y., Kaplan, M., Legatt, M. E., & Lipschitz, D. (2006). Prevalence of dissociative disorders in psychiatric outpatients. *American Journal of Psychiatry, 163,* 623–629.

Forbes, S., Bui, S., Robinson, B. R., Hochgeschwender, U., & Brennan, M. B. (2001). Integrated control of appetite and fat metabolism by the leptin- proopiommelanocortin pathway. *Proceedings of the National Academy of Sciences, 98,* 4233–4237.

Forbey, J. D., & Ben-Porath, Y. S. (2008). Empirical correlates of the MMPI-2 Restructures Clinical (RC) scales in a nonclinical setting. *Journal of Personality Assessment, 90,* 136–141.

Forcelli, P. A., & Heinrichs, S. C. (2008). Teratogenic effects of maternal antidepressant exposure on neural substrates of drug-seeking behavior in offspring. *Addiction Biology, 13*(1), 52–62.

Ford, M. T., Heinen, B. A., & Langkamer, K. L. (2007). Work and family satisfaction and conflict: A meta-analysis of cross-domain relations. *Journal of Applied Psychology, 92,* 57–80.

Forgas, J. P., Dunn, E., & Granland, S. (2008). Are you being served. . . ? An unobtrusive experiment of affective influences on helping in a department store. *European Journal of Social Psychology, 38,* 333–342.

Formisano, E., De Martino, F., Bonte, M., & Goebel, R. (2008). "Who" is saying "what?" Brain-based decoding of human voice and speech. *Science, 322*(5903), 970–973.

Fornaro, M., Gabrielli, F., Rasore, F., Pompei, F., & Fornaro, P. (2007). Phenomenological, subjective experience and neurobiological aspects of delirium. *Minerva Psichiatrica, 48*(3), 365–372.

Fossati, P., Hevenor, S. J., Graham, S. J., Grady, C., Keightley, M. L., Craik, F., & Mayberg, H. (2003). In search of the emotional self: An FMRI study using positive and negative emotional words. *American Journal of Psychiatry, 160,* 1938–1945.

Fosse, R., Stickgold, R., & Hobson, J. A. (2001). Brain-mind states: Reciprocal variation in thoughts and hallucinations. *Psychological Science, 12,* 30–36.

Foster, E. M., Jones, D., & the Conduct Problems Prevention Research Group. (2006). Can a costly intervention be cost-effective? An analysis of violence prevention. *Archives of General Psychiatry, 63,* 1284–1291.

Foster, M. D. (2000). Positive and negative responses to personal discrimination: Does coping make a difference? *Journal of Social Psychology, 140,* 93–106.

Foster, N. E., Thomas, E., Barlas, P., Hill, J. C., Young, J., Mason, E., & Hay, E. M. (2007). Acupuncture as an adjunct to exercise based physiotherapy for osteoarthritis of the knee: Randomised controlled trial. *British Medical Journal, 335,* 436.

Foti, R. J., & Hauenstein, N. M. A. (2007). Pattern and variable approaches in leadership emergence and effectiveness. *Journal of Applied Psychology, 92,* 347–355.

Foulkes, D. (1985). *Dreaming: A cognitive-psychological analysis.* Hillsdale, NJ: Erlbaum.

Fowler, J. R., & Christakis, N. A. (2009). Dynamic spread of happiness in a large social network: Longitudinal analysis over 20 years in the Framingham Heart Study. *British Medical Journal, 337,* a2533, 2008.

Fowler, R. D. (2000). A lesson in taking our own advice. *Monitor on Psychology, 31,* 9.

Fox, A. S., & Olster, D. H. (2000). Effects of intracerebroventricular leptin administration on feeding and sexual behaviors in lean and obese female zucker rats. *Hormones and Behavior, 37,* 377–387.

Fox, M. K., Pac, S., Devaney, B., & Jankowski, L. (2004). Feeding infants and toddlers study: What foods are infants and toddlers eating? *Journal of the American Dietetic Association, 104*(1 Suppl 1), s22–30.

Fox, P., Bain, P. G., Glickman, S., Carroll, C., & Zajicek, J. (2004). The effect of cannabis on tremor in patients with multiple sclerosis. *Neurology, 62,* 1105–1109.

Fox, S., Spector, P. E., & Miles, D. (2001). Counterproductive work behavior (CWB) in response to job stressors and organizational justice: Some mediator and moderator tests for autonomy and emotions. *Journal of Vocational Behavior, 59,* 291–309.

Fozard, J., Wolf, E., Bell, B., Farland, R., & Podolsky, S. (1977). Visual perception and communication. In J. Birren & K. Schaie (Eds.), *Handbook of the psychology of aging.* New York: Van Nostrand Reinhold.

Francis, A. M. (2008). Family and sexual orientation: The family-demographic correlates of homosexuality in men and women. *Journal of Sex Research, 45*(4), 371–377.

Frank, D. A., Augustyn, M., Knight, W. G., Pell, T., & Zuckerman, B. (2001). Growth, development, and behavior in early childhood following prenatal cocaine exposure: A systematic review. *Journal of the American Medical Association, 285,* 1613–1625.

Frank, J. S. (1978). *Psychotherapy and the human predicament.* New York: Schocken Books.

Frank, M. G., Ekman, P., & Friesen, W. V. (1993). Behavioral markers and recognizability of the smile of enjoyment. *Journal of Personality and Social Psychology, 64*(1), 83–93.

Franken, I. H. A., Muris, P., & Georgieva, I. (2006). Gray's model of personality and addiction. *Addictive Behaviors, 31,* 399–403.

Frankenberg, W. K., & Dodds, J. B. (1967). The Denver developmental screening test. *Journal of Pediatrics, 71,* 181–191.

Franzoi, S. (2003). *Social psychology* (3rd ed.). New York: McGraw-Hill.

Frasure-Smith, N., & Lespérance, F. (2005). Depression and coronary heart disease. *Current Directions in Psychological Science, 14,* 39–43.

Fratiglioni, L., & Qiu, C. (2009). Prevention of common neurodegenerative disorders in the elderly. *Experimental Gerontology, 44*(1–2), 46–50.

Frayling, T. M., Timpson, N. J., Weedon, M. N., Zeggini, E., Freathy R. M., Lindgren, C. M., Perry, J. R. B., Elliott, K. S., Lango, H., Rayner, N. W., Shields, B., Harries, L. W., Barrett, J. C., Ellard, S., Groves, C. J., Knight, B., Patch, A.-M., Ness, A. R., Ebrahim, S., Lawlor, D. A., Ring, S. M., Ben-Shlomo, Y., Jarvelin, M.-R., Sovio, U., Bennett, A. J., Melzer, D., Ferrucci, L., Loos, R. J. F., Barroso, I., Wareham, N. J., Karpe, F., Owen, K. R., Cardon, L. R., Walker, M., Hitman, G. A., Palmer, C. N. A., Doney, A. S. F., Morris, A. D., Davey-Smith, G. D., The Wellcome Trust Case Control Consortium, Hattersley, A. T., & McCarthy, M. I. (2007). A common variant in the FTO gene is associated with body mass index and predisposes to childhood and adult obesity. *Science, 316,* 889–894.

Fredrickson, B., L., & Cohn, M. A. (in press). Positive Emotions. In M. Lewis, J. M. Haviland-Jones, & L. F. Barrett (Eds). *Handbook of Emotions* (3rd ed.). NY: Guilford.

Fredrickson, B. L., Cohn, M. A., Coffey, K. A., Pek, J., & Finkel, S. M. (2008). Open hearts build lives: Positive emotions, induced through loving-kindness meditation, build consequential personal resources. *Journal of Personality and Social Psychology, 95*(5), 1045–1062.

Fredrickson, B. L., & Losada, M. F. (2005). Positive affect and the complex dynamics of human flourishing. *American Psychologist, 60,* 678–686.

Freed, C. R., Greene, P. E., Breeze, R. E., Tsai, W. Y., DuMouchel, W., Kao, R., et al. (2001). Transplantation of embryonic dopamine neurons for severe Parkinson's disease. *New England Journal of Medicine, 344,* 710–719.

Freedland, R. L., & Bertenthal, B. I. (1994). Developmental changes in interlimb coordination: Transition to hands-and-knees crawling. *Psychological Science, 5,* 26–32.

Freedman, D. M., Ron, E., Ballard-Barbash, R., Doody, M. M., & Linet, M. S. (2006). Body mass index and all-cause mortality in a nationwide U.S. cohort. *International Journal of Obesity, 30,* 822–829.

Freedman, J. L. (1992). Television violence and aggression: What psychologists should tell the public. In P. Suedfeld & P. E. Tetlock (Eds.), *Psychology and social policy.* New York: Hemisphere.

Freedman, J. L. (2002). *Media violence and its effect on aggression: Assessing the scientific evidence.* Toronto, Ontario, Canada: University of Toronto Press.

Freedman, J. L., & Fraser, S. C. (1966). Compliance without pressure: The foot-in-the-door technique. *Journal of Personality and Social Psychology, 4,* 195–202.

Freedman, R. (2003). Schizophrenia. *New England Journal of Medicine, 349,* 1738–1749.

Freedman, V. A., Aykan, H., & Martin, L. G. (2001). Aggregate changes in severe cognitive impairment among older Americans: 1993 and 1998. *Journal of Gerontology, 56B,* S100–S111.

Freeman, M. P., Freeman, S. A., & McElroy, S. L. (2002). The comorbidity of bipolar and anxiety disorders: Prevalence, psychobiology, and treatment issues. *Journal of Affective Disorders, 68,* 1–23.

Freitag, C. M. (2007). The genetics of autistic disorders and its clinical significance: A review of the literature. *Molecular Psychiatry, 12,* 2–22.

Fremgen, A., & Fay, D. (1980). Overextensions in production and comprehension: A methodological clarification. *Journal of Child Language, 7,* 205–211.

French, S. E., Seidman, E., Allen, L., & Aber, J. L. (2006). The development of ethnic identity during adolescence. *Developmental Psychology, 42,* 1–10.

Freres, D. R., Gillham, J. E., Reivich, K., & Shatte, A. J. (2002). Preventing depressive symptoms in middle school students: The Penn Resiliency Program. *International Journal of Emergency Mental Health, 4,* 31–40.

Frese, M., Beimel, S., & Schoenborn, S. (2003). Action training for charismatic leadership: Two evaluations of studies of a commercial training module on inspirational communication of a vision. *Personnel Psychology, 56,* 671–697.

Freud, S. (1900). The interpretation of dreams. In J. Strachey (Ed.), *The standard edition of the complete psychological works of Sigmund Freud* (Vol. 8). London: Hogarth Press.

Frey, K. S., Hirschstein, M. K., Snell, J. L., Edstrom, L. V. S., MacKenzie, E. P., & Broderick, C. J. (2005). Reducing playground bullying and supporting beliefs: An experimental trial of the steps to respect program. *Developmental Psychology, 41,* 479–491.

Frey, W. H. (2003). Married with children. *American Demographics, 25*(2), 17.

Fridlund, A., Sabini, J. P., Hedlund, L. E., Schaut, J. A., Shenker, J. I., & Knauer, M. J. (1990). Audience effects on solitary faces during imagery: Displaying to the people in your head. *Journal of Nonverbal Behavior, 14*(2), 113–137.

Fried, I., Wilson, C. L., MacDonald, K. A., & Behnke, E. J. (1998). Electric current stimulates laughter. *Nature, 391,* 650.

Fried, P. A., Watkinson, B., & Gray, R. (1992). A follow-up study of attentional behavior in 6-year-old children exposed prenatally to marijuana, cigarettes, and alcohol. *Neurotoxicity and Teratology, 14*(5), 299–311.

Fried, Y., & Ferris, G. R. (1987). The validity of the job characteristics model: A review and meta-analysis. *Personnel Psychology, 40,* 287–322.

Fried, Y., & Tiegs, R. B. (1995). Supervisors' role conflict and role ambiguity differential relations with performance ratings of subordinates and the moderating effect of screening ability. *Journal of Applied Psychology, 80,* 282–291.

Friedman, H. S. (2000). Long-term relations of personality and health: Dynamisms, mechanisms, tropisms. *Journal of Personality, 68,* 1089–1107.

Friedman, H. S., & Schustack, M. W. (2003). *Personality: Classic theories and modern research.* Boston: Allyn & Bacon.

Friedman, H. S., Tucker, J. S., Schwartz, J. E., Martin, L. R., Tomlinson-Keasey, C., Wingard, D. L., & Criqui, M. H. (1995a). Childhood conscientiousness and longevity: Health behaviors and cause of death. *Journal of Personality and Social Psychology, 68,* 696–703.

Friedman, H. S., Tucker, J. S., Schwartz, J. E., Tomlinson-Keasey, C., Martin, L. R., Wingard, D. L., & Criqui, M. H. (1995b). Psychosocial and behavioral predictors of longevity: The aging and death of the "Termites." *American Psychologist, 50,* 69–78.

Friedman, M., Ibrahim, H., Lee, G., & Joseph, N. J. (2003). Combined uvulopalatopharyngoplasty and radiofrequency tongue base reduction for treatment of obstructive sleep apnea/hypopnea syndrome. *Otolaryngological Head and Neck Surgery, 129,* 611–621.

Friedman, M. A., & Brownell, K. D. (1995). Psychological correlates of obesity: Moving to the next research generation. *Psychological Bulletin, 117*(1), 3–20.

Friedman, M., & Rosenman, R. H. (1974). *Type A behavior and your heart.* New York: Knopf.

Frisco, M. L. (2008). Adolescents' sexual behavior and academic attainment. *Sociology of Education, 81*(3), 284–311.

Fritsch, T., Smyth, K. A., McClendon, M. J., Ogrocki, P. K., Santillan, C., et al. (2005). Associations between dementia/mild cognitive impairment and cognitive performance and activity levels in youth. *Journal of the American Geriatrics Society, 53,* 1191–1196.

Fritzler, B. K., Hecker, J. E., & Losee, M. C. (1997). Self-directed treatment with minimal therapist contact: Preliminary findings for obsessive-compulsive disorder. *Behaviour Research and Therapy, 35,* 627–631.

Frizzell, J. P. (2005). Acute stroke: Pathophysiology, diagnosis, and treatment. *AACN Clinical Issues, 16*(4), 421–440.

Frodl, T., Meisenzahl, E. M., Zill, P., Baghai, T. Rujescu, D. Leinsinger, G., et al. (2004). Reduced hippocampal volumes associated with the long variant of the serotonin transporter polymorphism in major depression. *Archives of General Psychiatry, 61,* 177–183.

Frone, M. R. (2008). Are work stressors related to employee substance use? The importance of temporal context assessments of alcohol and illicit drug use. *Journal of Applied Psychology, 93,* 199–206.

Fu, Q., Fu, X., & Dienes, Z. (2008). Implicit sequence learning and conscious awareness. *Consciousness and Cognition, 17,* 185–202.

Fujita, F., & Diener, E. (2005). Life satisfaction set point: Stability and change. *Journal of Personality and Social Psychology, 88,* 158–164.

Fuligni, A. J., & Pedersen, S. (2002). Family obligation and the transition to young adulthood. *Developmental Psychology, 38*(5), 856–868.

Fuligni, A. J., Witknow, M., & Garcia, C. (2005). Ethnic identity and the academic adjustment of adolescents from Mexican, Chinese, and European backgrounds. *Developmental Psychology, 41,* 799–811.

Fullerton, C. S., Ursano, R. J., & Wang, L. (2004). Acute stress disorder, posttraumatic stress disorder, and depression in disaster or rescue workers. *American Journal of Psychiatry, 161,* 1370–1376.

Funder, D. (2001). Personality. *Annual Review of Psychology, 52,* 197–222.

Funder, D. (2008). Persons, situations, and person-situation interactions. In O. John, R. Robins, & L. Pervin (Eds.), *Handbook of personality: Theory and research* (3rd ed., pp. 568–582). New York: Guilford.

Funder, D. C. (2007). *The personality puzzle* (4th ed.). New York: W.W. Norton.

Fung, M. T., Raine, A., Loeber, R., Lynam, D. R., Steinhauer, S. R., Venables, P. H., et al. (2005). Reduced electrodermal activity in psychopathy-prone adolescents. *Journal of Abnormal Psychology, 114,* 187–196.

Funtowicz, M. N., & Widiger, T. A. (1999). Sex bias in the diagnosis of personality disorders: An evaluation of DSM-IV criteria. *Journal of Abnormal Psychology, 108,* 195–201.

Furey, M. L., Pietrini, P., & Haxby, J. V. (2000). Cholinergic enhancement and increased selectivity of perceptual processing during working memory. *Science, 290,* 2315–2319.

Furmark, T., Henningsson, S., Appel, L., Ahs, F., Linnman, C., Pissiota, A., et al. (2009). Genotype over-diagnosis in amygdala responsiveness: Affective processing in social anxiety disorder. *Journal of Psychiatry and Neuroscience, 34*(1), 30–40.

Furnham, A. (2001). Personality and individual differences in the workplace: Person-organization-outcome fit. In R. Hogan & B. Roberts (Eds.), *Personality psychology in the workplace* (pp. 223–251). Washington, DC: American Psychological Association.

Gabbard, G. O. (2004). *Long-term psychodynamic psychotherapy: A basic text.* Washington DC: American Psychiatric Association.

Gaertner, S. L., & Dovidio, J. F. (2008). Addressing contemporary racism: The common ingroup identity model. In C. Willis-Esqueda (Ed.), *Motivational aspects of prejudice and racism* (pp. 111–133). New York: Springer Science + Business Media.

Gagnon, J. F., Postuma, R. B., Mazza, S., Doyon, J., & Montplaisir, J. (2006). Rapid-eye-movement sleep behaviour disorder and neurodegenerative diseases. *Lancet Neurology, 5,* 424–432.

Gagnon, J. F., Postuma, R. B., & Montplaisir, J. (2006). Update on the pharmacology of REM sleep behavior disorder. *Neurology, 67,* 742–747.

Gais, S., Albouy, G., Boly, M., Dang-Vu, T. T., Darsaud, A., Desseilles, M., Rauchs, G., Schabus, M., Sterpenich, V., Vandewalle, G., Maquet, P., & Peigneux, P. (2007). Sleep transforms the cerebral trace of declarative memories. *Proceedings of the National Academies of Science, 104,* 18778–18783.

Gais, S., Lucas, B., & Born, J. (2006). Sleep after learning aids memory recall. *Learning & Memory, 13,* 259–262.

Galanter, E. (1962). Contemporary psychophysics. In R. Brown (Ed.), *New directions in psychology* (Vol. 1). New York: Holt, Rinehart, Winston.

Galatzer-Levy, R. M., Bachrach, H., Skolnikoff, A., & Waldron, S., Jr. (2000). *Does psychoanalysis work?* New Haven, CT: Yale University Press.

Galdeira, K. (2006, October). Phiten power. *Hawaii Business, 52*(4), 52–54.

Galdi, S., Arcuri, L., & Gawronski, B. (2008). Automatic mental associations predict future choices of undecided decision-makers. *Science, 321,* 1100–1102.

Gale, C., R., Batty, G., & Deary, I. J. (2008). Locus of control at age 10 years and health outcomes and behaviors at age 30 years: The 1970 British cohort study. *Psychosomatic Medicine, 70,* 397–403.

Galea, S., Ahern, J., Resnick H., Kilpatrick D., Bucuvalas M., Gold, J., & Vlahov, D. (2002). Psychological sequelae of the September 11 terrorist attacks in New York City. *New England Journal of Medicine, 346,* 982–987.

Galea, S., Ahern, J., Resnick H., Kilpatrick D., Bucuvalas M., Gold, J., & Vlahov, D. (2002). Psychological sequelae of the September 11 terrorist attacks in New York City. *New England Journal of Medicine, 346,* 982–987.

Galea, S., Resnick, H., Ahern, J., Gold, J., Bucuvalas, M., Kilpatrick, D., et al. (2002). Posttraumatic stress disorder in Manhattan, New York City, after the September 11th terrorist attacks. *Journal of Urban Health, 79,* 340–353.

Galinsky, A. D., & Kray, L. J. (2004). From thinking about what might have been to sharing what we know: The effects of counterfactual mind-sets on information sharing in groups. *Journal of Experimental Social Psychology, 40,* 606–618.

Gallagher, M. (1998, January 26). Day careless. *National Review, 50*(1), 37–43.

Gallagher, M., & Chiba, A. A. (1996). The amygdala and emotion. *Current Opinions in Neurobiology, 6*(2), 221–227.

Gallivan, J. P. Cavina-Pratesi, C., & Culham, J. C. (2009). Is that within reach? fMRI reveals that the human superior parieto-occipital cortex encodes objects reachable by the hand. *The Journal of Neuroscience, 29,* 4381–4391.

Gallo, D. A. (2006). *Associative illusions of memory.* New York: Psychology Press.

Galloway, A. T., Addessi, E., Fragaszy, D. M., & Visalberghi, E. (2005). Social facilitation of eating familiar food in tufted capuchins (*Cebus apella*): Does it involve behavioral coordination? *International Journal of Primatology, 26,* 181–189.

Gallup. (2007). U.S. workers remain largely satisfied with their jobs. November 27. Retrieved July 16, 2009, from http://www.gallup.com/poll/102898/US-Workers-Remain-Largely-Satisfied-Their-Jobs.aspx.

Galotti, K. M. (1999). *Cognitive psychology in and out of the laboratory* (2nd ed.). Belmont, CA: Brooks/Cole.

Galpin, A., Underwood, G., & Chapman, P. (2008). Sensing without seeing in comparative visual search. *Consciousness and Cognition, 17,* 672–687.

Galpin, A., Underwood, G., & Crundall, D. (2009). Change blindness in driving scenes. *Transportation Research Part F: Traffic Psychology and Behaviour, 12,* 179–185.

Gamer, M., Rill, H.-G., Vossel, G., & Gödert, H. W. (2006). Psychophysiological and vocal measures in the detection of guilty knowledge. *International Journal of Psychophysiology, 60,* 76–87.

Gamez, D. (2008). Progress in machine consciousness. *Consciousness and Cognition, 17,* 887–910.

Gan, T. J., Jiao, K. R., Zenn, M., & Georgiade, G. (2004). A randomized controlled comparison of electro-acupoint stimulation or ondansetron versus placebo for the prevention of postoperative nausea and vomiting. *Anesthesia and Analgesia, 99,* 1070–1075.

Ganai, S., Donroe, J. A., St. Louis, M. R., Lewis, G. M., & Seymour, N. E. (2007). Virtual-reality training improves angled telescope skills in novice laparoscopists. *American Journal of Surgery, 193*(2), 260–265.

Ganchrow, J. R., Steiner, J. E., & Daher, M. (1983). Neonatal facial expressions in response to different qualities and intensities of gustatory stimuli. *Infant Behavior and Development, 6,* 189–200.

Gangwisch, J. E., Malaspina, D., Boden-Albala, B., & Heymsfield, S. B. (2005). Inadequate sleep as a risk factor for obesity: Analysis of the NHANES I. *Sleep, 28,* 1289–1296.

Ganzel, B. L., Kim, P., Glover, G. H., & Temple, E. (2008). Resilience after 9/11: Multimodal neuroimaging evidence for stress-related change in the healthy adult brain. *NeuroImage, 40*(2), 788–795.

Garb, H. N. (1997). Race bias, social class bias, and gender bias in clinical judgment. *Clinical Psychology: Science and Practice, 4,* 99–120.

Garb, H. N., Wood, J. M., Lilienfeld, S. O., & Nezworski, T. (2005). Roots of the Rorschach controversy. *Clinical Psychology Review, 25,* 97–118.

Garbarino, S., Nobili, L., Beelke, M., De Carli, F., & Ferrillo, F. (2001). The contributing role of sleepiness in highway vehicle accidents. *Sleep: Journal of Sleep Research and Sleep Medicine, 24,* 203–206.

Garbutt, J. C., Kranzler, H. R., O'Malley, S. S., Gastfriend, D. R., Pettinati, H. M., Silverman, B. L., et al. (2005). Efficacy and tolerability of long-acting injectable naltrexone for alcohol dependence: A randomized controlled trial. *Journal of the American Medical Association, 293,* 1617–1625.

Garcia, J., & Koelling, R. A. (1966). Relation of cue to consequences in avoidance learning. *Psychonomic Science, 4,* 123–124.

Garcia, S. M., Weaver, K., Moskowitz, G. B., & Darley, J. M. (2002). Crowded minds: The implicit bystander effect. *Journal of Personality and Social Psychology, 83,* 843–853.

Gardiner, H. W., & Kosmitzki, C. (2005). *Lives across cultures: Cross-cultural human development* (3rd ed.). Needham Heights, MA: Allyn & Bacon.

Gardner, H. (1993). *Multiple intelligences: The theory in practice.* New York: Basic Books.

Gardner, H. (1999). Are there additional intelligences? The case for naturalist, spiritual, and existential intelligences. In J. Kane (Ed.), *Education, information and transformation: Essays on learning and thinking* (pp. 111–131). Englewood Cliffs, NJ: Prentice Hall.

Gardner, H. (2002). *Learning from extraordinary minds.* Mahwah, NJ: Erlbaum.

Gardner, M. (1988). *The second* Scientific American *book of mathematical puzzles and diversions.* Chicago: University of Chicago Press.

Gardner, M., & Steinberg, L. (2005). Peer influence on risk taking, risk preference, and risky decision making in adolescence and adulthood: An experimental study. *Developmental Psychology, 41,* 625–635.

Gardner, R., Heward, W. L., & Grossi, T. A. (1994). Effects of response cards on student participation and academic achievement: A systematic replication with inner-city students during whole-class science instruction. *Journal of Applied Behavior Analysis, 27,* 63–71.

Garfield, S. L. (1998). Some comments on empirically supported treatments. *Journal of Consulting and Clinical Psychology, 66,* 121–125.

Garlick, D. (2003). Integrating brain science research with intelligence research. *Current Directions in Psychological Science, 12,* 185–188.

Garlipp, P. (2008). Koro–a culture-bound phenomenon: Intercultural psychiatric implications. *German Journal of Psychiatry, 11,* 21–28.

Garry, M., & Gerrie, M. P. (2005). When photographs create false memories. *Current Directions in Psychological Science, 14,* 321–325.

Garry, M., & Polaschek, D. L. L. (2000). Imagination and memory. *Current Directions in Psychological Science, 9,* 6–10.

Garson, L. (2006). *Surviving Babylon: A journey through repressed memories of sexual abuse.* Atlanta, GA: Alexander Griffin Co.

Gasser, U. S., Rousson, V., Hentschel, F., Sattel, H., & Gasser, T. (2008). Alzheimer disease versus mixed dementias: An EEG perspective. *Clinical Neurophysiology, 119*(10), 2255–2259.

Gatewood, R. D., & Feild, H. S. (2001). *Human resource selection* (5th ed.). Fort Worth, TX: Harcourt.

Gaudiano, B. A., & Dalrymple, K. L. (2005). EMDR variants, pseudoscience, and the demise of empirically supported treatments? *PsycCRITIQUES, 50,* 8.

Gauvain, M. (2001). *The social context of cognitive development.* New York: Guilford.

Gauvreau, P., & Bouchard, S. (2008). Preliminary evidence for the efficacy of EMDR in treating generalized anxiety disorder. *Journal of EMDR Practice and Research, 2*(1), 26–40.

Gazzaley, A., Cooney, J. W., Rissman, J., & D'Esposito, M. (2005). Top-down suppression deficit underlies working memory impairment in normal aging. *Nature Neuroscience 8,* 1298–1300.

Gazzaniga, M. S., & LeDoux, J. E. (1978). *The integrated mind.* New York: Plenum.

Ge, X., Conger, R., & Elder, G. H. (2001). Pubertal transition, stressful life events, and the emergence of gender differences in adolescent depressive symptoms. *Developmental Psychology, 37,* 404–417.

Geary, D. C. (1999). Evolution and developmental sex differences. *Current Directions in Psychological Science, 8,* 115–120.

Geary, D. C. (2000). Evolution and proximate expression of human paternal investment. *Psychological Bulletin, 126,* 55–77.

Geddes, J. R., Burgess, S., Hawton, K., Jamison, K., & Goodwin, G. M. (2004). Long-term lithium therapy for bipolar disorder: Systematic review and meta-analysis of randomized controlled trials. *American Journal of Psychiatry, 161,* 217–222.

Geddes, L. (2008, June 7). Are autistic savants made not born? *New Scientist, 198*(2659), 10.

Geen, R. G. (1998). Aggression and antisocial behavior. In D. Gilbert, S. T. Fiske, & G. Lindzey (Eds.), *Handbook of social psychology* (Vol. 2, 4th ed., pp. 317–356). Boston: McGraw-Hill.

Gegenfurtner, K. R., & Kiper, D. C. (2003). Color vision. *Annual Review of Neuroscience, 26,* 181–206.

Gelabert-Gonzalez, M., & Fernandez-Villa, J. (2001). Mutism after posterior fossa surgery: Review of the literature. *Clinical Neurology & Neurosurgery, 103,* 111–114.

Gelhorn, H. L., Stallings, M. C., Young, S. E., Corley, R. P., Rhee, S. H., & Hewitt, J. K. (2005). Genetic and environmental influences on conduct disorder: symptom, domain and full-scale analyses. *Journal of Child Psychology and Psychiatry, 46,* 580–591.

Gellhorn, E., & Loofbourrow, G. N. (1963). *Emotions and emotional disorders.* New York: Harper & Row.

Gelmacher, D. S., Provenzano, G., McRae, T., Mastey, V., & Ieni, J. R. (2003). Donepezil is associated with delayed nursing home placement in patients with Alzheimer's disease. *Journal of the American Geriatric Society, 51*(7), 937–944.

Gelman, R., & Baillargeon, R. (1983). A review of some Piagetian concepts. In P. H. Mussen (Ed.), *Handbook of child psychology* (Vol. 3, pp. 167–230). New York: Wiley.

Gendle, M. H., White, T. L., Strawderman, M., Mactutus, C. F., Booze, R. M., Levitsky, D. A., & Strupp, B. J. (2004). Enduring effects of prenatal cocaine exposure on selective attention and reactivity to errors: Evidence from an animal model. *Behavioral Neuroscience, 118,* 290–297.

Gentilucci, M., & Dalla Volta, R. (2008). Spoken language and arm gestures are controlled by the same motor control system. *Quarterly Journal of Experimental Psychology, 61*(6), 944–957.

George, M. S., Anton, R. F., Bloomer, C., Teneback, C., Drobes, D. J., Lorberbaum, J. P., et al. (2001). Activation of prefrontal cortex and anterior thalamus in alcoholic subjects on exposure to alcohol-specific cues. *Archives of General Psychiatry, 58,* 345–352.

George, W. H., & Marlatt, G. A. (1986). The effects of alcohol and anger on interest in violence, erotica, and deviance. *Journal of Abnormal Psychology, 95,* 150–158.

Geraerts, E., Bernstein, D. M., Merckelbach, H., Linders, C., Raymaekers, L., & Loftus, E. F. (2008a). Lasting false beliefs and their behavioral consequences. *Psychological Science, 19,* 749–753.

Geraerts, E., Lindsay, D. S., Merckelbach, H., Jelicic, M., Raymaekers, L., Arnold, M. M., & Schooler, J. W. (2008b). Cognitive mechanisms underlying recovered-memory experiences of childhood sexual abuse. *Psychological Science, 20,* 92–98.

Geraerts, E., Schooler, J. W., Merckelbach, H., Jelicic, M., Hauer, B. J. A., & Ambadar, Z. (2007). The reality of recovered memories: Corroborating continuous and discontinuous memories of childhood sexual abuse. *Psychological Science, 18,* 564–568.

Geraerts, E., Smeets, E., Jelicic, M., Merckelbach, H., & van Heerden, J. (2006). Retrieval inhibition of trauma-related words in women reporting repressed or recovered memories of childhood sexual abuse. *Behaviour Research and Therapy, 44,* 1129–1136.

Gerbner, G., Morgan, M., & Signorielli, N. (1994). *Television violence profile no. 16: The turning point.* Philadelphia: Annenberg School for Communication.

Gerhart, B. (2005). The (affective) dispositional approach to job satisfaction: Sorting out the policy implications. *Journal of Organizational Behavior, 26,* 79–97.

Gerin, W., Davidson, K. W., Christenfeld, N. J. S., Goyal, T., & Schwartz, J. E. (2006). The role of angry rumination and distraction in blood pressure recovery from emotional arousal. *Psychosomatic Medicine, 68,* 64–72.

German, T. P., & Barrett, H. C. (2005). Functional fixedness in a technologically sparse culture. *Psychological Science, 16*(1), 1–5.

Gerschman, J. A., Reade, P. C., & Burrows, G. D. (1980). Hypnosis and dentistry. In G. D. Burrows & L. Dennerstein (Eds.), *Handbook of hypnosis and psychosomatic medicine.* New York: Elsevier.

Gershoff, E. T., & Bitensky, S. H. (2007). The case against corporal punishment of children: Converging evidence from social science research and international human rights law and implications for U.S. public policy. *Psychology, Public Policy, and Law, 13,* 231–272.

Gershon, J., Anderson, P., Graap, K., Zimand, E., Hodges, L., & Rothbaum, B. O. (2002). Virtual reality exposure therapy in the treatment of anxiety disorders. *The Scientific Review of Mental Health Practice, 1.* Retrieved October 12, 2002 from http://www.scientificmentalhealth.org/SRMHP/current.html.

Gerstner, C. R., & Day, D. V. (1997). Meta-analytic review of leader–member exchange theory: Correlates and construct issues. *Journal of Applied Psychology, 82,* 827–844.

Geschwind, N. (1968). Disconnexion syndromes in animals and man. *Brain, 88,* 237–294.

Getzfeld, A. R. (2006). *Essentials of abnormal psychology.* New York: Wiley.

Geuze, E., Vermetten, E., & Bremner, J. D. (2005). MR-based in vivo hippocampal volumetrics: 2. Findings in neuropsychiatric disorders. *Molecular Psychiatry, 10,* 160–184.

Gfeller, J. D. (1994). Hypnotizability enhancement: Clinical implications of empirical findings. *American Journal of Clinical Hypnosis, 37*(2), 107–116.

Ghaemi, S. N. (2008). *Mood disorders* (2nd ed.). Philadelphia: Wolters Kluwer Health/Lippincott, Williams & Wilkins.

Gianaros, P. J., May, J. C., Siegle, G. J., & Jennings, J. R. (2005). Is there a functional neural correlate of individual differences in cardiovascular reactivity? *Psychosomatic Medicine, 67,* 31–39.

Giancola, P. R., & Corman, M. D. (2007). Alcohol and aggression: A test of the attention-allocation model. *Psychological Science, 18,* 649–655.

Gibbons, R. D., Hur, K., Bhaumik, D. K., & Mann, J. J. (2005). The relationship between antidepressant use and rate of suicide. *Archives of General Psychiatry, 62,* 165–172.

Gibbs, N. (2008, July 7). Give the girls a break. *Time,* 36–36.

Gibson, E. J., & Walk, R. D. (1960). The visual cliff. *Scientific American, 202,* 64–71.

Gigerenzer, G. (2004). Dread risk, September 11, and fatal traffic accidents. *Psychological Science, 15,* 286–287.

Gilbert, D. T. (2006). *Stumbling on happiness.* New York: Knopf.

Gilbert, D. T., Morewedge, C. K., Risen, J. L., & Wilson, T. D. (2004). Looking forward to looking backward: The misprediction of regret. *Psychological Science, 15,* 346–350.

Gilbert, D. T., & Wilson, T. D. (1998). Miswanting: Some problems in the forecasting of future affective states. In J. P. Forgas (Ed.), *Feeling and thinking: The role of affect in social cognition* (pp. 178–197). New York: Cambridge University Press.

Gilbert, R., Salanti, G., Harden, M., & See, S. (2005). Infant sleeping position and the sudden infant death syndrome: A systematic review of observational studies and historical review of recommendations from 1940 to 2002. *International Journal of Epidemiology, 34,* 874–887.

Gilbert, S. (1997, August 20). Two spanking studies indicate parents should be cautious. *New York Times Magazine.*

Gilboa-Schechtman, E., & Foa, E. B. (2001). Patterns of recovery from trauma: The use of intraindividual analysis. *Journal of Abnormal Psychology, 110,* 392–400.

Gilden, D. L., & Marusich, L. R. (2009). Contraction of time in attention-deficit hyperactivity disorder. *Neruopsychology, 23,* 265–269.

Gilissen, R., Bakermans-Kranenburg, M. J., van IJzendoorn, M. H., & van der Veer, R. (2008). Parent-child relationship, temperament, and physiological reactions to fear-inducing film clips: Further evidence for differential susceptibility. *Journal of Experimental Child Psychology, 99,* 182–195.

Gillham, J. E., Reivich, K. J., Freres, D. R., Chaplin, T. M., Shatté, A. J., Samuels, B., et al. (2007). School-based prevention of depressive symptoms: A randomized controlled study of the effectiveness and specificity of the Penn Resiliency Program. *Journal of Consulting and Clinical Psychology, 75,* 9–19.

Gilligan, C. (1982). *In a different voice: Psychological theory and women's development.* Cambridge, MA: Harvard University Press.

Gilligan, C. (1993). Adolescent development reconsidered. In A. Garrod (Ed.), *Approaches to moral development: New research and emerging themes.* New York: Teachers College Press.

Gilmore, G. C., Spinks, R. A., & Thomas, C. W. (2006). Age effects in coding tasks: Componential analysis and test of the sensory deficit hypothesis. *Psychology and Aging, 21,* 7–18.

Gilmore, R. L., Heilman, K. M., Schmidt, R. P., Fennell, E. M., & Quisling, R. (1992). Anosognosia during Wada testing. *Neurology, 42*(4), 925–927.

Giltay, E. J., Geleijnse, J. M., Zitman, F. G., Hoekstra, T., & Schouten, E. G. (2004). Dispositional optimism and all-cause and cardiovascular mortality in a prospective cohort of elderly Dutch men and women. *Archives of General Psychiatry, 61,* 1126–1135.

Giltay, E. J., Kamphuis, M. H., Kalmijn, S., Zitman, F. G., & Kromhout, D. (2006). Dispositional optimism and the risk of cardiovascular death: The Zutphen elderly study. *Archives of Internal Medicine, 166,* 431–436.

Ginges, J., Atran, S., Medin, D., & Shikaki, K. (2007). Sacred bounds on rational resolution of violent political conflict. *Proceedings of the National Academy of Sciences, 104,* 7357–7360.

Ginsberg, D. L. (2006). Fatal agranulocytosis four years after clozapine discontinuation. *Primary Psychiatry, 13,* 32–33.

Ginzel, K. H., Maritz, G. S., Neuberger, M., Pauly, J. R., Polito, J. R., Schulte-Hermann, R., Slotkin, T. A., & Marks, D. F. (2007). Nicotine for the fetus, the infant and the adolescent? *Journal of Health Psychology, 12*(2), 215–224.

Giorgi-Guarnieri, D., Janofsky, J., Keram, E., Lawsky, S., Merideth, P., Mossman, D., et al. (2002). AAPL practice guideline for forensic psychiatric evaluation of defendants raising the insanity defense. *Journal of the American Academy of Psychiatry and the Law, 30*(Suppl. 2), S1–S40.

Giosan, C., Glovsky, V., & Haslam, N. (2001). The lay conception of "mental disorder": A cross-cultural study. *Transcultural Psychiatry, 38,* 317–332.

Givens, B. (1995). Low doses of ethanol impair spatial working memory and reduce hippocampal theta activity. *Alcoholism Clinical and Experimental Research, 19*(3), 763–767.

Gladwell, M. (2004, January 12). Big and bad. *New Yorker,* 28–33.

Gladwell, M. (2005). *Blink: The power of thinking without thinking.* New York: Little, Brown.

Glantz, K., Rizzo, A., & Graap, K. (2003). Virtual reality for psychotherapy: Current reality and future possibilities. *Psychotherapy: Theory, Research, Practice, and Training, 40,* 55–67.

Glanzer, M., & Cunitz, A. (1966). Two storage mechanisms in free recall. *Journal of Verbal Learning and Verbal Behavior, 5,* 351–360.

Glasman, L. R., & Albarracín, D. (2006). Forming attitudes that predict future behavior: A meta-analysis of the attitude-behavior relation. *Psychological Bulletin, 132,* 778–822.

Glassop, L. I. (2002). The organizational benefits of teams. *Human Relations, 55,* 225–249.

Glazer, M., Baer, R. D., Weller, S., de Alba, J. E. G., & Liebowitz, S. W. (2004). Susto and soul loss in Mexicans and Mexican Americans. *Cross-Cultural Research: The Journal of Comparative Social Science, 38,* 270–288.

Gleason, M. E. J., Iida, M., Shrout, P. E., & Bolger, N. (2008). Receiving support as a mixed blessing: Evidence for dual effects of support on psychological outcomes. *Journal of Personality and Social Psychology, 94,* 824–838.

Gleaves, D. H., May, M. C., & Cardena, E. (2001). An examination of the diagnostic validity of dissociative identity disorder. *Clinical Psychology Review, 21,* 577–608.

Gleitman, L., & Landau, B. (1994). *The acquisition of the lexicon.* Cambridge: MIT Press.

Glenn, A. L., Raine, A., Venables, P. H., & Mednick, S. A. (2007). Early temperamental and psychophysiological precursors of adult psychopathic personality. *Journal of Abnormal Psychology, 116*(3), 508–518.

Glover, J. A., Krug, D., Dietzer, M., George, B. W., & Hannon, M. (1990). "Advance" advance organizers. *Bulletin of the Psychonomic Society, 28,* 4–6.

Glummarra, M. J., Gibson, S. J., Georgiou-Karistianis, N., & Bradshaw, J. L. (2007). Central mechanisms in phantom limb perception: The past, present and future. *Brain Research Reviews, 54*(1), 219–232.

Glynn, L. M., Davis, E. P., Schetter, C. D., Chicz-DeMet, A., Hobel, C. J., & Sandman, C. A. (2007). Postnatal maternal cortisol levels predict temperament in healthy breastfed infants. *Early Human Development, 83,* 675–681.

Goenjian, A. K., Molina, L., Steinberg, A. M., Fairbanks, L. A., Alvarez, M. L., Goenjian, H. A., & Pynoos, R. S. (2001). Posttraumatic stress and depressive reactions among Nicaraguan adolescents after hurricane Mitch. *American Journal of Psychiatry, 158,* 788–794.

Gogtay, N., Giedd, J. N., Lusk, L., Hayashi, K. M., Greenstein, D., Vaituzis, A. C., Nugent, T. F., III, Herman, D. H., Clasen, L. S., Toga, A. W., Rapoport, J. L., & Thompson, P. M. (2004). Dynamic mapping of human cortical development during childhood through early adulthood. *Proceedings of the National Academy of Sciences, 101,* 8174–8179.

Gold, M. S. (1994). The epidemiology, attitudes, and pharmacology of LSD use in the 1990s. *Psychiatric Annals, 24*(3), 124–126.

Goldberg, J. F., & Burdick, K. E. (Eds.) (2008). *Cognitive dysfunction in bipolar disorder.* Washington, DC: American Psychiatric Association Publishing.

Goldberg, J. F., & Garno, J. L. (2005). Development of posttraumatic stress disorder in adult bipolar patients with histories of severe childhood abuse. *Journal of Psychiatric Research, 39,* 595–601.

Goldberg, J. F., Harrow, M., & Grossman, L. S. (1995). Course and outcome in bipolar affective disorder: A longitudinal follow-up study. *American Journal of Psychiatry, 152,* 379–384.

Goldblum, N. (2001). *The brain-shaped mind: A neural-network view: What the brain can tell us about the mind.* Cambridge: Cambridge University Press.

Golden, R. N., Gaynes, B. N., Ekstrom, R. D., Hamer, R. M., Jacobsen, F. M., Suppes, T., et al. (2005). The efficacy of light therapy in the treatment of mood disorders: A review and meta-analysis of the evidence. *American Journal of Psychiatry, 162,* 656–662.

Goldenberg, I., & Goldenberg, H. (1995). Family therapy. In R. J. Corsini & D. Wedding (Eds.), *Current psychotherapies* (5th ed.). Itasca, IL: Peacock.

Goldenberg, J. L., Arndt, J., Hart, J., & Routledge, C. (2008). Uncovering an existential barrier to breast self-exam behavior. *Journal of Experimental Social Psychology, 44,* 260–274.

Goldfried, M. R., & Davila, J. (2005). The role of relationship and technique in therapeutic change. *Psychotherapy: Theory, Research, Practice, Training, 42,* 421–430.

Goldman, M. S., Darkes, J., & Del Boca, F. K. (1999). Expectancy meditation of biopsychosocial risk for alcohol use and alcoholism. In I. Kirsch (Ed.), *How expectancies shape experience* (pp. 233–262). Washington, DC: American Psychological Association.

Goldstein, A. J., de Beurs, E., Chambless, D. L., & Wilson, K. A. (2000). EMDR for panic disorder with agoraphobia: Comparison with waiting list and credible attention-placebo control conditions. *Journal of Consulting and Clinical Psychology, 68*(6), 947–956.

Goldstein, E. B. (2002). *Sensation and perception* (6th ed.). Pacific Grove CA: Wadsworth.

Goldstein, I., & Rosen, R. C. (Eds.). (2002). Guest editors' introduction: Female sexuality and sexual dysfunction. *Archives of Sexual Behavior, 31,* 391.

Goldstein, I. L. (1993). *Training in organizations: Needs assessment, development, and evaluation* (3rd ed.). Monterey, CA: Brooks/Cole.

Goldstein, K. (1939). *The organism.* New York: American Book.

Goldstein, M. H., King, A. P., & West, M. J. (2003). Social interaction shapes babbling: Testing parallels between birdsong and speech. *Proceedings of the National Academy of Sciences, 100,* 8030–8035.

Goldstein, M. H., & Schwade, J. A. (2008). Social feedback to infants' babbling facilitates rapid phonological learning. *Psychological Science, 19,* 515–523.

Goldstein, S. E., Davis-Kean, P. E., & Eccles, J. S. (2005). Parents, peers, and problem behavior: A longitudinal investigation of the impact of relationship perceptions and characteristics on the development of adolescent problem behavior. *Developmental Psychology, 41,* 401–413.

Goltz, H. C., DeSouza, J. F. X., Menon, R. S., Tweed, D. B., & Vilis, T. (2003). Interaction of retinal image and eye velocity in motion perception. *Neuron, 39,* 569–576.

Gomez, R. L., Bootzin, R. R., & Nadel, L. (2006). Naps promote abstraction in language–learning infants. *Psychological Science, 17,* 670–674.

Gone, J. (2004). Mental health services for Native Americans in the 21st century United States. *Professional Psychology: Theory and Practice, 35,* 10–18.

Gonsalves, B., & Paller, K. A. (2000). Neural events that underlie remembering something that never happened. *Nature Neuroscience, 3,* 1316–1321.

Gonsalves, B. D., Kahn, I., Curran, T., Norman, K. A., & Wagner, A. D. (2005). Memory strength and repetition suppression: Multimodal imaging of medial temporal cortical contributions to recognition. *Neuron, 47,* 751–761.

Gonzalez, J. S., Penedo, F. J., Antoni, M. H., Duran, R. E., McPherson-Baker, S., Ironson, G., et al. (2004). Social support, positive states of mind, and HIV treatment adherence in men and women living with HIV/AIDS. *Health Psychology, 23,* 413–418.

Goodenough, F. L. (1932). Expression of the emotions in a blind-deaf child. *Journal of Abnormal and Social Psychology, 27,* 328–333.

Goodglass, H., & Kaplan, E. (1982). *The assessment of aphasia and related disorders* (2nd ed.). Philadelphia: Lea & Febiger.

Goodman, G. S., Ghetti, S., Quas, J. A., Edelstein, R. S., Alexander, K. W., Redlich, A. D., et al. (2003). A prospective study of memory for child sexual abuse: New findings relevant to the repressed-memory controversy. *Psychological Science, 14,* 113–118.

Goodwin, F. K., & Jamison, K. R. (Eds.). (1990). *Manic-depressive illness.* New York: Oxford University Press.

Goodwin, G. M., Bowden, C. L., & Calabrese, J. R. (2004). A pooled analysis of 2 placebo-controlled 18-month trials of lamotrigine and lithium maintenance in bipolar I disorder. *Journal of Clinical Psychiatry, 65*(3), 432–441.

Gordon, D. B., Dahl, J. L., Miaskowski, C., McCarberg, B., Todd, K. H., Paice, J. A., et al. (2005). American Pain Society recommendations for improving the quality of acute and cancer pain management: American Pain Society Quality of Care Task Force. *Archives of Internal Medicine, 165,* 1574–1580.

Gore-Felton, C., & Koopman, C. (2008). Behavioral mediation of the relationship between psychosocial factors and HIV disease progression. *Psychosomatic Medicine 70,* 569–574.

Gorman, J. M. (2003). Treating generalized anxiety disorder. *Journal of Clinical Psychiatry, 64*(Suppl. 2), 24–29. Gosling, S. D. (2001). From mice to men: What can we learn about personality from animal research? *Psychological Bulletin, 127,* 45–86.

Gorman, J. M. (2005). Benzodiazepines: Taking the good with the bad and the ugly. *CNS Spectrums, 10,* 14–15.

Gorter, R. W., Butorac, M., Cobian, E. P., & van der Sluis, W. (2005). Medical use of cannabis in the Netherlands. *Neurology, 64,* 917–919.

Gosling, S. D. (2008). Personality in non-human animals. *Social and Personality Psychology Compass, 2,* 985–1001.

Gosling, S. D., Kwan, V. S. Y., & John, O. P. (2003). A dog's got personality: A cross-species comparative approach to personality judgments in dogs and humans. *Journal of Personality and Social Psychology, 85,* 1161–1169.

Gosling, S. D., Vazire, S., Srivastava, S., & John, O. P. (2004). Should we trust web-based studies? A comparative analysis of six preconceptions about Internet questionnaires. *American Psychologist, 59,* 93–104.

Goss Lucas, S., & Bernstein, D. A. (2005). *Teaching psychology: A step by step guide.* Mahwah, NJ: Erlbaum.

Gotlib, I. H., & Hammen, C. L. (1992). *Psychological aspects of depression: Toward cognitive interpersonal integration.* Chichester, England: Wiley.

Gotlib, I. H., Krasnoperova, E., Yue, D. N., & Joorman, J. (2004). Attentional biases for negative interpersonal stimuli in clinical depression. *Journal of Abnormal Psychology, 113,* 127–135.

Gottfredson, L. S. (1997a). Mainstream science on intelligence: An editorial with 52 signatories, history, and bibliography. *Intelligence, 24,* 13–23.

Gottfredson, L. S. (1997b). Why g matters: The complexity of everyday life. *Intelligence, 24,* 79–132.

Gottfredson, L. S. (2004). Intelligence: Is it the epidemiologists' elusive "fundamental cause" of social class inequalities in health? *Journal of Personality and Social Psychology, 86,* 174–199.

Gottfredson, L. S., & Deary, I. J. (2004). Intelligence predicts health and longevity, but why? *Current Directions in Psychological Science, 13,* 1–4.

Gottfried, A. W. (1997, June). Parents' role is critical to children's learning. *APA Monitor,* 24.

Gottman, J. M., Gottman, J. S., & Declaire, J. (2006). *Ten lessons to transform your marriage.* New York: Crown Press.

Gottman, J. M., & Levenson, R. W. (2000). The timing of divorce: Predicting when a couple will divorce over a 14-year period. *Journal of Marriage and the Family, 62,* 737–745.

Gottman, J. M., & Levenson, R. W. (2002). A two-factor model for predicting when a couple will divorce: Exploratory analyses using 14-year longitudinal data. *Family Process, 41,* 83–96.

Gouin, J.-P., Kiecolt-Glaser, J. K., Malarkey, W. B., & Glaser, R. (2008). The influence of anger expression on wound healing. *Brain, Behavior, and Immunity, 22,* 699–708.

Gould, E., Beylin, A., Tanapat, P., Reeves, A., & Schors, T. J. (1999). Learning enhances adult neurogenesis in the hippocampal formation. *Nature Neuroscience, 2,* 260–265.

Gow, A. J., Whiteman, M. C., Pattie, A., Whalley, L., Starr, J., & Deary, I. J. (2005). Lifetime intellectual function and satisfaction with life in old age: Longitudinal cohort study. *British Medical Journal, 331,* 141–142.

Grabe, H. J., Ruhrmann, S., Ettelt, S., Buhtz, F., Hochrein, A., Schulze-Rauschenbach, S., et al. (2006). Familiality of obsessive-compulsive disorder in nonclinical and clinical subjects. *American Journal of Psychiatry, 163,* 1986–1992.

Grabe, H. J., Ward, L. M., & Hyde, J. S. (2008). The role of the media in body image concerns among women: A meta-analysis of experimental and correlational studies. *Psychological Bulletin, 134,* 460–476.

Graeber, M. B., & Mehraein, P. (1999). Reanalysis of the first case of Alzheimer's disease. *European Archives of Psychiatry and Clinical Neuroscience, 249*(Suppl. 3), 10–13.

Gräff, J., & Mansuy, I. M. (2008). Epigenetic codes in cognition and behaviour. *Behavioural Brain Research, 192*(1), 70–87.

Graham, K., Osgood, D. W., Wells, S., & Stockwell, T. (2006). To what extent is intoxication associated with aggression in bars? A multilevel analysis. *Journal of Studies on Alcohol, 67,* 382–390.

Grammer, K., Fink, B., & Neave, N. (2005). Human pheromones and sexual attraction. *European Journal of Obstetrics, Gynecology, and Reproductive Biology, 118,* 135–142.

Grandin, T. (1996). *Thinking in pictures: And other reports from my life with autism.* New York: Vintage Press.

Granhag, P.-A., & Stromwall, L. (2004). *The detection of deception in forensic contexts.* New York: Cambridge University Press.

Grant, B. F., Dawson, D. A., Stinson, F. S., Chou, S. P., Dufour, M. C., & Pickering, R. P. (2004). The 12-month prevalence and trends in DSM-IV alcohol abuse and dependence: United States, 1991–1992 and 2001–2002. *Drug and Alcohol Dependence, 74,* 223–234.

Grant, B. F., Hasin, D. S., Stinson, F. S., Dawson, D. A., Goldstein, R. B., Smith, S., Huang, B., & Saha, T. D. (2006). The epidemiology of DSM-IV panic disorder and agoraphobia in the United States: Results from the National Epidemiology survey on alcohol and related conditions. *Journal of Clinical Psychiatry, 67*(3), 363–374.

Grant, H., & Dweck, C. S. (2003). Clarifying achievement goals and their impact. *Journal of Personality and Social Psychology, 85,* 541–553.

Grant, J. E., & Kim, S. W. (2002). *Stop me because I can't stop myself: Taking control of impulsive behavior.* New York: McGraw-Hill.

Grassi, L., Rasconi, G., Pedriali, A., Corridoni, A., & Bevilacqua, M. (2000). Social support and psychological distress in primary care attenders. *Psychotherapy and Psychosomatics, 69,* 95–100.

Graves, L., Pack, A., & Abel, T. (2001). Sleep and memory: A molecular perspective. *Trends in Neurosciences, 24,* 237–243.

Graves, L., Stratton, G., Ridgers, N. D., & Cable, N. T. (2008). Energy expenditure in adolescents playing new generation computer games. *British Journal of Sports Medicine, 42*(7), 592–594.

Gray, J. A. (1991). Neural systems, emotions, and personality. In J. Madden, IV (Ed.), *Neurobiology of learning, emotion, and affect* (pp. 272–306). New York: Raven Press.

Gray, N., & Nye, P. S. (2001). American Indian and Alaska Native substance abuse: Co-morbidity and cultural issues. *American Indian and Alaska Native Mental Health Research, 10,* 67–84.

Gray, N. S., MacCulloch, M. J., Smith, J., Morris, M., & Snowden, R. J. (2003). Forensic psychology: Violence viewed by psychopathic murderers. *Nature, 423,* 497.

Gray-Little, B., & Hafdahl, A. R. (2000). Factors influencing racial comparisons of self-esteem: A quantitative review. *Psychological Bulletin, 126,* 26–54.

Graziano, M. (2006). The organization of behavioral repertoire in motor cortex. *Annual Review of Neuroscience, 29,* 105–134.

Graziano, M. S., Taylor, C. S., & Moore, T. (2002). Complex movements evoked by microstimulation of precentral cortex. *Neuron, 34,* 841–851.

Green, A. I., & Patel, J. K. (1996). The new pharmacology of schizophrenia. *Harvard Mental Health Letter, 13*(6), 5–7.

Green, C. S., & Bavelier, D. (2003). Action video game modifies visual selective attention. *Nature, 423,* 534–537.

Green, D. M., & Swets, J. A. (1966). *Signal detection theory and psychophysics.* New York: Wiley.

Greenberg, J. (2002). Who stole the money and when? Individual and situational determinants of employee theft. *Organizational Behavior and Human Decision Processes, 89,* 985–1003.

Greenberg, J. R., & Mitchell, S. A. (1983). *Object relations in psychoanalytic theory.* Cambridge, MA: Harvard University Press.

Greenberg, J. R., & Mitchell, S. A. (2006). *Object relations in psychoanalytic theory.* Cambridge, MA: Harvard University Press.

Greenberg, J., Solomon, S., & Arndt, J. (2008). A basic but uniquely human motivation: Terror management theory. In J. Shah & W. Gardner (Eds.), *Handbook of motivation science* (pp. 114–134). New York: Guilford Press.

Greenberg, J., Solomon, S., Pyszczynski, T., & Rosenblatt, A. (1992). Why do people need self-esteem? Converging evidence that self-esteem serves an anxiety-buffering function. *Journal of Personality and Social Psychology, 63,* 913–922.

Greenberg, M. T., Lengua, L. J., Coie, J. D., Pinderhughes, E. E., Bierman, K., Dodge, K. A., et al. (1999). Predicting developmental outcomes at school entry using a multiple-risk model: Four American communities. *Developmental Psychology, 35,* 403–417.

Greenberg, R. M., & Kellner, C. H. (2005). Electroconvulsive therapy: A selected review. *American Journal of Geriatric Psychiatry, 13,* 268–281.

Greenberg, R. P., Constantino, M. J., & Bruce, N. (2006). Are patient expectations still relevant for psychotherapy process and outcome? *Clinical Psychology Review, 26,* 657–678.

Greenfield, P. M. (1994). Video games as cultural artifacts. *Journal of Applied Developmental Psychology, 15,* 3–12.

Greenfield, P. M., & Childs, C. P. (1991). Developmental continuity in biocultural context. In R. Cohen & A. W. Siegel (Eds.), *Context and development* (pp. 135–159). Hillsdale, NJ: Erlbaum.

Greenfield, P. M., Suzuki, L. K., & Rothstein-Fisch, C. (2006). Cultural pathways through human development. In W. Damon & R. M. Lerner (Series Eds.) & K. A. Renninger & I. E. Sigel (Vol. Eds.), *Handbook of child psychology: Vol. 4. Child psychology in practice* (6th ed.). New York: Wiley.

Greenhaus, J. H., Parasuraman, S., & Wormley, W. M. (1990). Effects of race on organizational experiences, job performance evaluations, and career outcomes. *Academy of Management Journal, 33,* 64–86.

Greenland, P., Knoll, M. D., Stamler, J., Neaton, J. D., Dyer, A. R., Garside, D. B., & Wilson, P. W. (2003). Major risk factors as antecedents of fatal and nonfatal coronary heart disease events. *Journal of the American Medical Association, 290,* 891–897.

Greenwald, A. G., & Banaji, M. R. (1995). Implicit social cognition: Attitudes, self-esteem, and stereotypes. *Psychological Review, 102,* 4–27.

Greenwald, A. G., Klinger, M. R., & Schuh, E. S. (1995). Activation by marginally perceptible ("subliminal") stimuli: Dissociation of unconscious from conscious cognition. *Experimental Psychology: General, 124*(1), 22–42.

Greer, A. E., & Buss, D. M. (1994). Tactics for promoting sexual encounters. *Journal of Sex Research, 31*(3), 185–201.

Gregory, A. M., Light-Häusermann, J., Rijsdijk, F., & Eley, T. C. (2009). Behavioral genetic analyses of prosocial behavior in adolescents. *Developmental Science, 12*(1), 165–174.

Gregory, R. L. (2005). Seeing after blindness. *Nature Neuroscience, 6,* 909–910.

Gregory, S. W., & Webster, S. (1996). A nonverbal signal in voices of interview partners effectively predicts communication accommodation and social status perceptions. *Journal of Personality and Social Psychology, 70,* 1231–1240.

Gren-Landell, M., Tillfors, M., Furmark, T., Bohlin, G., Andersson, G., & Svedin, C. G. (2009). Social phobia in Swedish adolescents: Prevalence and gender differences. *Social Psychiatry and Psychiatric Epidemiology, 44,* 1–7.

Greven, C. U., Harlaar, N., Kovas, Y., Chamorro-Premuzic, T., & Plomin, R. (2009). More than just IQ: School achievement is predicted by self-perceived abilities—but for genetic rather than environmental reasons. *Psychological Science, 20,* 753–762.

Griesinger, C. B., Richards, C. D., & Ashmore, J. F. (2005). Fast vesicle replenishment allows indefatigable signalling at the first auditory synapse. *Nature, 435,* 212–215.

Griffeth, R. W., Hom, P. W., & Gaertner, S. (2000). A meta-analysis of antecedents and correlates of employee turnover: Update, moderator tests, and research implications for the next millennium. *Journal of Management, 26,* 463–488.

Griffin, M. A., & Neal, A. (2000). Perceptions of safety at work: A framework for linking safety climate to safety performance, knowledge, and motivation. *Journal of Occupational Health Psychology, 5,* 347–358.

Griffitt, W. B., & Guay, P. (1969) "Object" evaluation and conditioned affect. *Journal of Experimental Research in Personality, 4,* 1–8.

Grigorenko, E. L. (2002). In search of the genetic engram of personality. In D. Cervone & W. Mischel (Eds.), *Advances in personality science* (pp. 29–82). New York: The Guilford Press.

Grigorenko, E. L. (2002). In search of the genetic engram of personality. In D. Cervone & W. Mischel (Eds.), *Advances in personality science* (pp. 29–82). New York: The Guilford Press.

Grinspoon, S., Thomas, E., Pitts, S., Gross, E., Mickley, D., Killer, K., et al. (2000). Prevalence and predictive factors for regional osteopenia in women with anorexia nervosa. *Annals of Internal Medicine, 133,* 790–794.

Griskevicius, V., Tybur, J. M., Gangestad, S. W., Perea, E. F., Shapiro, J. R., & Kenrick, D. T. (2009). Aggress to impress: Hostility as an evolved context-dependent strategy. *Journal of Personality and Social Psychology, 96,* 980–994.

Grob, C., & Dobkin de Rios, M. (1992). Adolescent drug use in cross-cultural perspective. *Journal of Drug Issues, 22*(1), 121–138.

Grønnerød, C. (2003). Temporal stability in the Rorschach method. *Journal of Personality Assessment, 80,* 272–293.

Groopman, J. (2000, January 24). Second opinion. *The New Yorker,* pp. 40–49.

Groopman, J. (2002, July 29). Hormones for men. *The New Yorker,* pp. 34–38.

Groopman, J. (2007, January 29). What's the trouble? *The New Yorker,* 36–41.

Grosbras, M. H., Jansen, M., Leonard, G., McIntosh, A., Osswald, K., Poulsen, C., et al. (2007). Neural mechanisms of resistance to peer influence in early adolescence. *Journal of Neuroscience, 27*(30), 8040–8045.

Gross, J. J. (2001). Emotion regulation in adulthood: Timing is everything. *Current Directions in Psychological Science, 10,* 214–219.

Grossberg, S., & Seidman, D. (2006). Neural dynamics of autistic behaviors: Cognitive, emotional, and timing substrates. *Psychological Review, 113,* 483–525.

Grossman, M., & Ash, S. (2004). Primary progressive aphasia: A review. *Neurocase, 10*(1), 3–18.

Grote, N. K., & Clark, M. S. (2001). Perceiving unfairness in the family: Cause or consequence of marital distress? *Journal of Personality and Social Psychology, 80,* 281–293.

Groth-Marnat, G. (1997). *Handbook of psychological assessment* (3rd ed.). New York: Wiley.

Grubb, P. L., Roberts, R. K., Swanson, N. G., Burnfield, J. L., & Childress, J. H. (2005). Organizational factors and psychological aggression: Results from a nationally representative sample of US companies. In V. Bowie, B. S. Fisher, & C. L. Cooper (Eds.), *Workplace violence: Issues, trends, strategies* (pp. 37–59). Portland, OR: Willan Publishing.

Grucza, R. A., Bucholz, K. K., Rice, J. P., & Beirut, L. J. (2008). Secular trends in the lifetime prevalence of alcohol dependence in the United States: A re-evaluation. *Alcoholism: Clinical and Experimental Research, 32,* 763–770.

Grunberg, N. E. (1994). Overview: Biological processes relevant to drugs of dependence. *Addiction, 89*(11), 1443–1446.

Grusec, J. E., Davidov, M., & Lundell, L. (2002). Prosocial and helping behavior. In P. K. Smith & C. H. Hart (Eds.), *Blackwell handbook of childhood social development* (pp. 457–474). Malden, MA: Blackwell.

Grusec, J. E., & Goodnow, J. J. (1994). Impact of parental discipline methods on the child's internalization of values. *Developmental Psychology, 30,* 4–19.

Guadagno, R. E., Asher, T., Demaine, L. J., & Cialdini, R. B. (2001). When saying yes leads to saying no: Preference for consistency and the reverse foot-in-the-door effect. *Personality and Social Psychology Bulletin, 27,* 859–867.

Gualtieri, C. T., & Johnson, L. G. (2006). Antidepressant side effects in children and adolescents. *Journal of Child and Adolescent Psychopharmacology, 16,* 147–157.

Gueguen, N. (2008). The receptivity of women to courtship solicitation across the menstrual cycle: A field experiment. *Biological Psychology, 80*(3), 321–324.

Guilford, J. P. (1959). Traits of creativity. In H. H. Anderson (Ed.), *Creativity and its cultivation* (pp. 142–161). New York: Harper & Row.

Guilleminault, C., Palombini, L., Pelayo, R., & Chervin, R. D. (2003). Sleepwalking and sleep terrors in prepubertal children: What triggers them? *Pediatrics, 111,* 17–25.

Guimon, J. (2004). Evidence-based research studies on the results of group therapy: A critical review. *European Journal of Psychiatry, 18*(Suppl.), 49–60.

Gump, B. B., Reihman, J., Stewart, P., Lonky, E., & Darvill, T. (2005). Terrorism and cardiovascular responses to acute stress in children. *Health Psychology, 24,* 594–600.

Gupta, A. R., & State, M. W. (2007). Recent advances in the genetics of autism. *Biological Psychiatry, 61,* 429–437.

Gupta, V. K., & Reiter, E. R. (2004). Current treatment practices in obstructive sleep apnea and snoring. *American Journal of Otolaryngology, 25,* 18–25.

Gur, R. C., Skolnic, B. E., & Gur, R. E. (1994). Effects of emotional discrimination tasks on cerebral blood flow: Regional activation and its relation to performance. *Brain and Cognition, 25*(2), 271–286.

Gura, T. (1999). Leptin not impressive in clinical trial. *Science, 286,* 881–882.

Gurman, A. S. (Ed.). (2008). *Clinical handbook of couple therapy* (4th ed.). New York: Guilford.

Gushue, G. V. (2004). Race, color-blind racial attitudes, and judgments about mental health: A shifting standards perspective. *Journal of Counseling Psychology, 51,* 398–407.

Guthrie, R. M., & Bryant, R. A. (2005). Auditory startle response in firefighters before and after trauma exposure. *American Journal of Psychiatry, 162,* 283–290.

Guyton, A. C. (1991). *Textbook of medical physiology* (8th ed.). Philadelphia: Saunders.

Ha, H., Tan, E. C., Fukunaga, H., & Aochi, O. (1981). Naloxone reversal of acupuncture analgesia in the monkey. *Experimental Neurology, 73,* 298–303.

Haaga, D. A. (2000). Introduction to the special section on stepped care models in psychotherapy. *Journal of Consulting and Clinical Psychology, 68,* 547–548.

Haake, M., Müller, H.-H., Schade-Brittinger, C., Basler, H. D., Schäfer, H., Maier, C., Endres, H. G., Trampisch, H. J., & Molsberger, A. (2007). German acupuncture trials (GERAC) for chronic low back pain: Randomized, multicenter, blinded, parallel-group trial with 3 groups. *Archives of Internal Medicine, 167,* 1892–1898.

Haber, R. N. (1979). Twenty years of haunting eidetic imagery: Where's the ghost? *The Behavioral and Brain Sciences, 2,* 583–629.

Haberlandt, K. (1999). *Human memory: Exploration and application.* Boston: Allyn & Bacon.

Haberstroh, J. (1995). *Ice cube sex: The truth about subliminal advertising.* South Bend, IN: Cross Cultural Publications/Crossroads.

Hacking, I. (1995). *Rewriting the soul: Multiple personality and the sciences of memory.* Princeton, NJ: Princeton University Press.

Hackman, J. R. (1998). Why don't teams work? In R. S. Tindale, J. Edwards, & E. J. Posavac (Eds.), *Applications of theory and research on groups to social issues.* New York: Plenum.

Hackman, J. R., & Oldham, G. R. (1980). *Work redesign.* Reading, MA: Addison-Wesley.

Haddad, S. K., Reiss, D., Spotts, E. L., Ganiban, J., Lichtenstein, P., & Neiderhiser, J. M. (2008). Depression and internally directed aggression: Genetic and environmental contributions. *Journal of the American Psychoanalytic Association, 56*(2), 515–550.

Hadjikhani, N., & de Gelder, B. (2003). Seeing fearful body expressions activates the fusiform cortex and amygdale. *Current Biology, 13,* 2201–2205.

Hagen, E. P. (1980). *Identification of the gifted.* New York: Teachers College Press.

Hake, R. R. (1998). Interactive-engagement vs. traditional methods: A six-thousand-student survey of mechanics test data for introductory physics courses. *American Journal of Physics, 66,* 64–74.

Hakuta, K., Bialystok, E., & Wiley, E. (2003). Critical evidence: A test of the critical-period hypothesis for second language acquisition. *Psychological Science, 14,* 31–38.

Halford, G. S., Baker, R., McCredden, J. E., & Bain, J. D. (2005). How many variables can humans process? *Psychological Science, 16*(1), 70–76.

Hall, C., Smith, K., & Chia, R. (2008). Cognitive and personality factors in relation to timely completion of a college degree. *College Student Journal, 42,* 1087–1098.

Hall, C. S., Lindzey, G., & Campbell, J. P. (1998). *Theories of personality* (4th ed.). New York: Wiley.

Hall, L. K., & Bahrick, H. P. (1998). The validity of metacognitive predictions of widespread learning and long-term retention. In G. Mazzoni & T. Nelson (Eds.), *Metacognition and cognitive neuropsychology: Monitoring and control processes* (pp. 23–36). Mahwah, NJ: Erlbaum.

Hall, W., & Degenhardt, L. (2003). Medical marijuana initiatives: Are they justified? How successful are they likely to be? *CNS Drugs, 17,* 689–697.

Hallam, B. J., Brown, W. S., Ross, C., Buckwalter, J. G., Bigler, E. D., Tschanz, J. T., Norton, M. C., Welsh-Bohmer, K. A., & Breitner, J. C. S. (2008). Regional atrophy of the corpus callosum in dementia. *Journal of the International Neuropsychological Society, 14*(3), 414–423.

Halligan, P. W., & David, A. S. (Eds.). (1999). *Conversion hysteria: Towards a cognitive neuropsychological account.* Hove, UK: Psychology Press.

Halloran, M. J., & Kashima, E. S. (2004). Social identity and worldview validation: The effects of ingroup identity primes and mortality salience on value endorsement. *Personality and Social Psychology Bulletin, 30,* 915–925.

Halperin, J. M., & Schulz, K. P. (2006). Revisiting the role of the prefrontal cortex in the pathophysiology of attention-deficit/hyperactivity disorder. *Psychological Bulletin, 132,* 560–581.

Halpern, D. F. (1997). Sex differences in intelligence. *American Psychologist, 52,* 1091–1102.

Halpern, D. F. (2005). Psychology at the intersection of work and family: Recommendations for employers, working families, and policymakers. *American Psychologist, 60,* 397–409.

Halpern, D. F., & Hakel, M. D. (2003). *Applying the science of learning to university teaching and beyond: New directions for teaching and learning.* San Francisco: Jossey-Bass.

Hamad, G. G. (2004). The state of the art in bariatric surgery for weight loss in the morbidly obese patient. *Clinics in Plastic Surgery, 31,* 591–600.

Hamann, S., Herman, R. A., Nolan, C. L., & Wallen, K. (2004). Men and women differ in amygdala response to sexual stimuli. *Nature Neuroscience, 7,* 411–416.

Hamarat, E., Thompson, D., Steele, D., Matheny, K., & Simons, C. (2002). Age differences in coping resources and satisfaction with life among middle-aged, young-old, and oldest-old adults. *Journal of Genetic Psychology, 163*(3), 360–367.

Hamer, M., Molloy, G. J., & Stamatakis, E. (2008). Psychological distress as a risk factor for cardiovascular events. *Journal of the American College of Cardiology, 52,* 2156–2162.

Hamilton, C. E. (2000). Continuity and discontinuity of attachment from infancy through adolescence. *Child Development, 71,* 690–694.

Hamilton, N. A., Gallagher, M. W., Preacher, K. J., Stevens, N., Nelson, C. A., Karlson, C., & McCurdy, D. (2007). Insomnia and well-being. *Journal of Consulting and Clinical Psychology, 75,* 939–946.

Hamilton, W. D. (1964). The evolution of social behavior: Parts I and II. *Journal of Theoretical Biology 7,* 1–52.

Hammad, T. A., Laughren, T., & Racoosin, J. (2006). Suicidality in pediatric patients treated with antidepressant drugs. *Archives of General Psychiatry, 63,* 332–339.

Hammerness, P., Basch, E., & Ulbricht, C. (2003). St. John's wort: A systematic review of adverse effects and drug interactions for the consultation psychiatrist. *Journal of Consultation Liaison Psychiatry, 44*(4), 271–282.

Hampson, S. E. (2008). Mechanisms by which childhood personality traits influence adult well-being. *Current Directions in Psychological Science, 17,* 264–268.

Hampson, S. E., Goldberg, L. R., Vogt, T. M., & Dubanoski, J. P. (2006). Forty years on: Teachers' assessments of children's personality traits predict self-reported health behaviors and outcomes at midlife. *Health Psychology, 25,* 57–64.

Hampton, T. (2008). Researchers seek ways to stem STDs. *Journal of the American Medical Association, 299*(16), 1888–1889.

Hamrick, N., Cohen, S., & Rodriguez, M. S. (2002). Being popular can be healthy or unhealthy: Stress, social network diversity, and incidence of upper respiratory infection. *Health Psychology, 21,* 294–298.

Hane, A. A., Cheah, C., Rubin, K. H., & Fox, N. A. (2008). The role of maternal behavior in the relation between shyness and social reticence in early childhood and social withdrawal in middle childhood. *Social Development, 17,* 795–811.

Haney, M., Ward, A. S., Comer, S. D., Foltin, R. W., & Fischman, M. W. (1999). Abstinence symptoms following smoked marijuana in humans. *Psychopharmacology, 141,* 395–404.

Hankin, B. L., & Abramson, L. Y. (2001). Development of gender differences in depression: An elaborated cognitive vulnerability-transactional stress theory. *Psychological Bulletin, 127,* 773–796.

Hankin, B. L., Fraley, R. C., & Abela, J. R. Z. (2005). Daily depression and cognitions about stress: Evidence for a traitlike depressogenic cognitive style and the prediction of depressive symptoms in a prospective daily diary study. *Journal of Personality and Social Psychology, 88,* 673–685.

Hankin, B. L., Fraley, R. C., Lahey, B. B., & Waldman, I. D. (2005). Is depression best viewed as a continuum or discrete category? A taxometric analysis of childhood and adolescent depression in a population-based sample. *Journal of Abnormal Psychology, 114,* 96–110.

Hanson, G., & Venturelli, P. J. (1995). *Drugs and society* (4th ed.). Boston: Jones & Bartlett.

Hanson, S. J., & Burr, D. J. (1990). What connectionist models learn: Learning and representations in connectionist networks. *Behavioral and Brain Sciences, 13,* 471–518.

Hara, K., Kubota, N., Tobe, K., Terauchi, Y., Miki, H., Komeda, K., et al. (2000). The role of PPARg as a thrifty gene both in mice and humans *British Journal of Nutrition, 84*(Suppl. 2), S235–S239.

Hardell, L., Carlberg, M., Söderqvist, F., Mild, K. H., & Morgan, L. L. (2007). Long-term use of cellular phones and brain tumours: Increased risk associated with use for > or =10 years. *Occupational and Environmental Medicine, 64*(9), 626–632.

Hardesty, D. E., & Sackeim, H. A. (2007). Deep brain stimulation in movement and psychiatric disorders. *Biological Psychiatry, 61,* 831–835.

Harding, K. J., Skritskaya, N., Doherty, E., & Fallon, B. A. (2008). Advances in understanding illness anxiety. *Current Psychiatry Reports, 10*(4), 311–317.

Hare, R. D. (1993). *Without conscience: The disturbing world of the psychopaths among us.* New York: Pocket Books.

Hariri, A. R., Drabant, E. M., Munoz, K. E., Kolachana, B. S., Mattay, V. S., Egan, M. F., et al. (2005). A susceptibility gene for affective disorders and the response of the human amygdala. *Archives of General Psychiatry, 62,* 146–152.

Harlow, H. F. (1959, June). Love in infant monkeys. *Scientific American,* pp. 68–74.

Harman, W. S., Lee, T. W., Mitchell, T. R., Felps, W., & Ownes, B. P. (2007). The psychology of voluntary turnover. *Current Directions in Psychological Science, 16,* 51–54.

Harmon-Jones, E. (2004). On the relationship of frontal brain activity and anger: Examining the role of attitude toward anger. *Cognition and Emotion, 18,* 337–361.

Harmon-Jones, E., & Harmon-Jones, C. (2007). Cognitive dissonance theory after 50 years of development. *Zeitschrift für Sozialpsychologie, 38,* 7–16.

Harmon-Jones, E., & Sigelman, J. (2001). State anger and prefrontal brain activity: Evidence that insult-related relative left prefrontal activation is associated with experienced anger and aggression. *Journal of Personality and Social Psychology, 80,* 797–804.

Harré, N., Brandt, T., & Houkamau, C. (2004). An examination of the actor-observer effect in young drivers' attributions for their own and their friends' risky driving. *Journal of Applied Social Psychology, 34,* 806–824.

Harris, C. V., & Goetsch, V. L. (1990). Multi-component flooding treatment of adolescent phobia. In E. L. Feindler & G. R. Kalfus (Eds.), *Adolescent behavior therapy handbook* (Vol. 22). New York: Springer.

Harris, G. C., & Aston-Jones, G. (1995). Involvement of D2 dopamine receptors in the nucleus acumbens in opiate withdrawal syndrome. *Nature, 371,* 155–157.

Harris Interactive. (2007). Handwashing survey fact sheet. Retrieved January 22, 2009, from http://www.asm.org/ASM.

Harris, J. R. (1995). Where is the child's environment? A group socialization theory of development. *Psychological Review, 102,* 458–489.

Harris, J. R. (1998). *The nurture assumption.* New York: Free Press.

Harris, J. R. (2000). Context-specific learning, personality, and birth order. *Current Directions in Psychological Science, 9,* 174–177.

Harrison, B. J., Pujol, J., López-Solà, M., Hernández-Ribas, R., Deus, J., Ortiz, H., Soriano-Mas, C., Yücel, M., Pantelis, C., & Cardoner, N. (2008). Consistency and functional specialization in the default mode brain network. *Proceedings of the National Academy of Sciences, 105*(28), 9781–9786.

Harrison, D. A., Newman, D. A., & Roth, P. L. (2006). How important are job attitudes? Meta-analytic comparisons of integrative behavioral outcomes and time sequences. *Academy of Management Journal, 49,* 305–325.

Harrison, K. (2003). Fitness and excitation. In J. Bryant, & D. Roskos-Ewoldsen (Eds.), *Communication and emotion: Essays in honor of Dolf Zillmann* (pp. 473–489). Mahwah, NJ: Erlbaum.

Harrow, M., & Jobe, T. H. (2005). Longitudinal studies of outcome and recovery in schizophrenia and early interventions: Can they make a difference? *Canadian Journal of Psychiatry, 50,* 879–880.

Hart, A. J., Whalen, P. J., Shin, L. M., McInerney, S. C., Fischer, H., & Rauch, S. L. (2000). Differential response in the human amygdala to racial outgroup vs. ingroup face stimuli. *Neuroreport, 11,* 2351–2355.

Hart, C. L., Taylor, M. D., Smith, G. D., Whalley, L. J., Starr, J. M., Hole, D. J., et al. (2003). Childhood IQ, social class, deprivation, and their relationships with mortality and morbidity risk in later life: Prospective observational study linking the Scottish mental survey of 1932 and the midspan studies. *Psychosomatic Medicine, 65,* 877–883.

Harter, S. (2006). The self. In W. Damon & R. M. Lerner (Series Eds.) & N. Eisenberg (Vol. Ed.), *Handbook of child psychology: Vol. 3. Social, emotional, and personality development* (6th ed.). New York: Wiley.

Hartung, C. M., & Widiger, T. A. (1998). Gender differences in the diagnosis of mental disorders: Conclusions and controversies of *DSM-IV. Psychological Bulletin, 123,* 260–278.

Hartup, W. W., & Stevens, N. (1997). Friendships and adaptation in the life course. *Psychological Bulletin, 121,* 355–370.

Harvey, A. G. (2008). Insomnia, psychiatric disorders, and the transdiagnostic perspective. *Current Directions in Psychological Science, 17,* 299–303.

Harvey, S. B., Stanton, B. R., & David, A. S. (2006). Conversion disorder: Towards a neurobiological understanding. *Neuropsychiatric Disease and Treatment, 2,* 13–20.

Harwood, K., McLean, N., & Durkin, K. (2007). First-time mothers' expectations of parenthood: What happens when optimistic expectations are not matched by later experiences? *Developmental Psychology, 43,* 1–12.

Hase, M., Schallmayer, S., & Sack, M. (2008). EMDR reprocessing of the addiction memory: Pretreatment, posttreatment, and 1-month follow-up. *Journal of EMDR Practice and Research, 2*(3), 170–179.

Hashioka, S., McGeer, P. L., Monji, A., & Kanba, S. (2009). Anti-Inflammatory Effects of Antidepressants: Possibilities for Preventives Against Alzheimer's Disease. *Central Nervous System Agents in Medicinal Chemistry, 9*(1), 12–19.

Hasin, D. S., Goodwin, R. D., Stinson, F. S., & Grant, B. F. (2005). Epidemiology of major depressive disorder: Results from the national epidemiologic survey on alcoholism and related conditions. *Archives of General Psychiatry, 62,* 1097–1106.

Haskett, M. E., Nears, K., Sabourin Ward, C., & McPherson, A. V. (2006). Diversity in adjustment of maltreated children: Factors associated with resilient functioning. *Clinical Psychology Review, 26,* 796–812.

Hassabis, D., Kumaran, D., Vann, D. S., Maguire, E. A. (2007). Patients with hippocampal amnesia cannot imagine new experiences. *Proceedings of the National Academy of Sciences, 104,* 1726–1731.

Hatcher, D., Brown, T., & Gariglietti, K. P. (2001). Critical thinking and rational emotive behavior therapy. *Inquiry: Critical Thinking Across the Disciplines, 20,* 6–18.

Hatfield, E., & Rapson, R. L. (2006). Passionate love, sexual desire, and mate selection: Cross-cultural and historical perspectives. In P. Noller & J. Feeney (Eds.), *Close relationships: Functions, forms and processes* (pp. 227–243). Hove, England: Psychology Press/Taylor & Francis.

Hatfield, J., Job, R. F. S., Hede, A. J., Carter, N. L., Peploe, P., Taylor, R., & Morrell, S. (2002). Human response to environmental noise: The role of perceived control. *International Journal of Behavioral Medicine, 9,* 341–359.

Hathaway, W. (2002, December 22). Henry M: The day one man's memory died. *Hartford Courant.*

Hattori, M., Fujiyama A., Taylor, T. D., Watanabe, H., Yada, T., Park, H. S., et al. (2000). The DNA sequence of human chromosome 21. *Nature, 405,* 311–319.

Hauck, F. R., Moore, C. M., Herman, S. M., Donovan, M., Kalelkar, M., Christoffel, K. K., et al. (2002). The contributions of prone sleeping to the racial disparity in sudden infant death syndrome: The Chicago Infant Mortality Study. *Pediatrics, 110,* 772–780.

Hausknecht, J. P., Day, D. V., & Thomas, S. C. (2004). Applicant reactions to selection procedures: An updated model and meta-analysis. *Personnel Psychology, 57,* 639–683.

Haw, R. M., & Fisher, R. P. (2004). Effects of administrator-witness contact on eyewitness identification accuracy. *Journal of Applied Psychology, 89,* 1106–1112.

Hawkins, H. L., Kramer, A. R., & Capaldi, D. (1993). Aging, exercise, and attention. *Psychology and Aging, 7,* 643–653.

Hayden, E. P., & Nurnberger, J. I. (2006). Molecular genetics of bipolar disorder. *Genes, Brain & Behavior, 5,* 85–95.

Hayes, E., & Silberman, L. (2007). Incorporating video games into physical education. *JOPERD: The Journal of Physical Education, Recreation & Dance, 78*(3), 18–24.

Haynes, S. R., Cohen, M. A., & Ritter, F. E. (2009). Designs for explaining intelligent agents. *International Journal of Human-Computer Studies, 67*(1), 90–110.

Hays, K. F. (2006). Being fit: The ethics of practice diversification in performance psychology. *Professional Psychology: Research and Practice, 37,* 223–232.

Hays, P. A., & Iwamasa, G. Y. (Eds.). (2006). *Culturally responsive cognitive- behavioral therapy: Assessment, practice, and supervision.* Washington, DC: American Psychological Association.

Hays, W. L. (1981). *Statistics* (3rd ed). New York: Holt, Rinehart & Winston.

Hazeltine, E., & Ivry, R. B. (2002). Neuroscience: Can we teach the cerebellum new tricks? *Science, 296,* 1979–1980.

He, L. F. (1987). Involvement of endogenous opioid peptides in acupuncture analgesia. *Pain, 31,* 99–121.

Heatherton, T. F., Macrae, C. N., & Kelley, W. M. (2004). What the social brain sciences can tell us about the self. *Current Directions in Psychological Science, 13,* 190–193.

Hebb, D. O. (1955). Drives and the C. N. S. (conceptual nervous system). *Psychological Review, 62,* 243–254.

Hedden, T., Ketay, S., Aron, A., Markus, H. R., & Gabrieli, J. D. E. (2008). Cultural influences on neural substrates of attentional control. *Psychological Science 19,* 12–17.

Hedge, A., & Yousif, Y. H. (1992). Effects of urban size, urgency, and cost of helpfulness: A cross-cultural comparison between the United Kingdom and the Sudan. *Journal of Cross-Cultural Psychology, 23,* 107–115.

Hedge, J. W., Borman, W. C., & Lammlein, S. E. (2006). *The aging workforce: Realities, myths, and implications for organizations.* Washington, DC: American Psychological Association.

Hegerl, U., Plattner, A., & Moller, H. J. (2004). Should combined pharmaco- and psychotherapy be offered to depressed patients? A qualitative review of randomized clinical trials from the 1990s. *European Archives of Psychiatry and Clinical Neuroscience, 254,* 99–107.

Heiby, E. M., DeLeon, P. H., & Anderson, T. (2008). A debate on prescription privileges for psychologists. In D. N. Bersoff (Ed.), *Ethical conflicts in psychology* (4th ed., pp. 370–375). Washington, DC: American Psychological Association.

Heilman, K. M., Barrett, A. M., & Adair, J. C. (1998). Possible mechanisms of anosognosia: A defect in self-awareness. *Philosophical Transactions of the Royal Society of London: Series B. Biological Sciences, 353*(1377), 1903–1909.

Heilman, K. M., & Gonzalez-Rothi, L. (2003). Apraxia. In K. M. Heilman & E. Valenstein (Eds.), *Clinical neuropsychology* (4th ed.). New York: Oxford University Press.

Heilman, K. M., & Valenstein, E. (Eds.). (2003). *Clinical neuropsychology* (4th ed.). New York: Oxford University Press.

Heilman, K. M., Valenstein, E., & Watson, R. T. (2000). Neglect and related disorders. *Seminars in Neurology, 20*(4), 463–470.

Heilman, K. M., Watson, R. T., & Valenstein, E. (2003). Neglect and related disorders. In K. M. Heilman & E. Valenstein (Eds.), *Clinical neuropsychology* (4th ed.). New York: Oxford University Press.

Heilman, M. E., & Haynes, M. C. (2008). Subjectivity in the appraisal process: A facilitator of gender bias in work settings. In E. Borgida & S. T. Fiske (Eds.), *Beyond common sense: Psychological science in the courtroom* (pp. 127–155). Malden: Blackwell Publishing.

Heim, S., Eickhoff, S. B., & Amunts, K. (2008). Specialisation in Broca's region for semantic, phonological, and syntactic fluency? *NeuroImage, 40*(3), 1362–1368.

Heiman, J. R. (2002). Sexual dysfunction: Overview of prevalence, etiological factors, and treatments. *Journal of Sex Research, 39,* 73–78.

Heine, S. J. (2003). Self-enhancement in Japan? A reply to Brown & Kobayashi. *Asian Journal of Social Psychology, 6,* 75–84.

Heine, S. J., & Buchtel, E. A. (2009). Personality: The universal and the culturally specific. *Annual Review of Psychology, 60,* 369–394.

Heine, S. J., Harihara, M., & Niiya, Y. (2002). Terror management in Japan. *Asian Journal of Social Psychology, 5,* 187–196.

Heinrichs, R. W. (2005). The primacy of cognition in schizophrenia. *American Psychologist, 60,* 229–242.

Heinrichs, W. L., Youngblood, P., Harter, P. M., & Dev, P. (2008). Simulation for team training and assessment: Case studies of online training with virtual worlds. *World Journal of Surgery, 32*(2), 161–170.

Heiss, W. D., & Teasel, R. W. (2006). Brain recovery and rehabilitation. *Stroke, 37*(2), 314–316.

Hejmadi, A., Davidson, R. J., & Rozin, P. (2000). Exploring Hindu Indian emotion expressions: Evidence for accurate recognition by Americans and Indians. *Psychological Science, 11,* 183–187.

Hektner, J. M., Schmidt, J. A., & Csikszentmihalyi, M. (2007). *Experience sampling method: Measuring the quality of everyday life.* Thousand Oaks, CA: Sage Publications, Inc.

Heldt, E., Manfro, G. G., Kipper, L., Blaya, C., Isolan, L., & Otto, M. W. (2006). One-year follow-up of pharmacotherapy-resistant patients with panic disorder treated with cognitive-behavior therapy: Outcome and predictors of remission. *Behaviour Research and Therapy, 44,* 657–665.

Heller, S. (2008). *Design disasters: Great designers, fabulous failure, and lessons learned.* New York: St. Martin's Press.

Heller, W. (1993). Neuropsychological mechanisms of individual differences in emotion, personality, and arousal. *NeuroPsychology, 7*(4), 486–489.

Heller, W., Nitschke, J. B., & Miller, G. A. (1998). Lateralization in emotion and emotional disorders. *Current Directions in Psychological Science, 7,* 26–32.

Hellmuth, J. C., & McNulty, J. K. (2008). Neuroticism, marital violence, and the moderating role of stress and behavioral skills. *Journal of Personality and Social Psychology, 95,* 166–180.

Helms, J. E. (1992). Why is there no study of cultural equivalence in standardized cognitive ability testing? *American Psychologist, 47,* 1083–1101.

Helms, J. E. (1997). The triple quandary of race, culture, and social class in standardized cognitive ability testing. In D. P. Flanagan, J. L. Genshaft, & P. L. Harrison (Eds.), *Contemporary intellectual assessment: Theories, tests, and issues* (pp. 517–532). New York: Guilford Press.

Helson, R., & Moane, G. (1987). Personality change in women from college to midlife. *Journal of Personality and Social Psychology, 53,* 176–186.

Helzer, J. E., Canino, G. J., Yeh, E., Bland, R. C., Lee, C. K., Hwu, H., & Newman, S. (1990). Alcoholism—North America and Asia: A comparison of population surveys with the diagnostic interview schedule. *Archives of General Psychiatry, 47,* 313–319.

Helzer, J. E., & Hudziak, J. J. (Eds.). (2002). *Defining psychopathology in the 21st century: DSM-V and beyond.* Washington DC: American Psychiatric Publishing, Inc.

Henderson, J. M. (2008). Peripheral nerve stimulation for chronic pain. *Current Pain and Headache Reports, 12*(1), 28–31.

Hendrick, B. (2003, May 8). Exam day rituals help students feel lucky. *Naples Daily News.*

Hendrick, C., & Hendrick, S. S. (2003). Romantic love: Measuring cupid's arrow. In S. J. Lopez & C. R. Snyder (Eds.), *Positive psychological assessment: A handbook of models and measures* (pp. 235–249). Washington, DC: American Psychological Association.

Hendricks, P. S., & Thompson, J. K. (2005). An integration of cognitive-behavioral therapy and interpersonal psychotherapy for bulimia nervosa: A case study using the case formulation method. *International Journal of Eating Disorders, 37,* 171–174.

Henig, R. (2004, April 4). The quest to forget. *New York Times,* p. 32.

Henkel, L. A. (2004). Erroneous memories arising from repeated attempts to remember. *Journal of Memory and Language, 50,* 26–46.

Henkel, L. A., Franklin, N., & Johnson, M. K. (2000). Cross-modal source monitoring, confusion between perceived and imagined events. *Journal of Experimental Psychology: Learning, Memory and Cognition, 26,* 321–335.

Henker, F. O. (1979). Acute brain syndromes. *Journal of Clinical Psychiatry, 40*(3), 117–120.

Hennig, J., Reuter, M., Netter, P., Burk, C., & Landt, O. (2005). Two types of aggression are differentially related to serotonergic activity and the A779C TPH polymorphism. *Behavioral Neuroscience, 119,* 16–25.

Heppner, P. P., Heppner, M. J., Lee, D., Wang, Y.-W., Park, H., & Wang, L. (2006). Development and validation of a collectivist coping styles inventory. *Journal of Counseling Psychology, 53,* 107–125.

Hepworth, S. J., Schoemaker, M. J., Muir, K. R., Swerdlow, A. J., van Tongeren, M. J. A., & McKinney, P. A. (2006). Mobile phone use and risk of glioma in adults: Case control study. *British Medical Journal, 332,* 883–887.

Herbert, J. D., Lilienfeld, S. O., Lohr, J. M., Montgomery, R. W., O'Donohue, W. T., Rosen, G. M., & Tolin, D. F. (2000). Science and pseudoscience in the development of eye movement desensitization and reprocessing: Implications for clinical psychology. *Clinical Psychology Review, 20,* 945–971.

Heres, S., Davis, J., Maino, K., Jetzinger, E., Kissling, W., & Leucht, S. (2006). Why olanzapine beats risperidone, risperidone beats quetiapine, and quetiapine beats olanzapine: An exploratory analysis of head-to-head comparison studies of second-generation antipsychotics. *American Journal of Psychiatry, 163,* 185–194.

Hergenhahn, B. R., & Olson, M. (2007). *Introduction to theories of personality* (7th ed.). Upper Saddle River, NJ: Prentice Hall.

Herman, E. J., Ramsey, N. F., & van Honk, J. (2008). Exogenous testosterone enhances responsiveness to social threat in the neural circuitry of social aggression in humans. *Biological Psychiatry, 63,* 263–270.

Hermann, R. C., Dorwart, R. A., Hoover, C. W., & Brody, J. (1995). Variation in ECT use in the United States. *American Journal of Psychiatry, 152,* 869–875.

Heron, M. P. (2007). Deaths: Leading causes for 2004. *National Vital Statistics Reports, 56*(5), 1–96.

Herrmann, D. J., & Searleman, A. (1992). Memory improvement and memory theory in historical perspective. In D. Herrmann, H. Weingartner, A. Searlman, & C. McEvoy (Eds.), *Memory improvement: Implications for memory theory.* New York: Springer-Verlag.

Herrnstein, R. J., & Murray, C. (1994). *The bell curve: Intelligence and class structure in American life.* New York: Free Press.

Hershcovis, M. S., Turner, N., Barling, H., Arnold, K. A., Dupré, K. E., Innes, M., LeBlanc, M. M., & Sivanathan, N. (2007). Predicting workplace aggression: A meta-analysis. *Journal of Applied Psychology, 92,* 228–238.

Hertenstein, M. J., & Campos, J. J. (2004). The retention effects of an adult's emotional displays on infant behavior. *Child Development, 75,* 585–613.

Hertlein, K., & Ricci, R. J. (2004). A systematic research synthesis of EMDR studies: Implementation of the platinum standard. *Trauma, Violence, and Abuse, 5,* 285–300.

Herz, R. S., & Cahill, E. D. (1997). Differential use of sensory information in sexual behavior as a function of gender. *Human Nature, 8,* 275–286.

Herzog, D. B., Dorer, D. J., Keel, P. K., Selwyn, S. E., Ekeblad, E. R., Flores, A. T., et al. (1999). Recovery and relapse in anorexia and bulimia nervosa: A 7.5-year follow-up study. *Journal of the American Academy of Child and Adolescent Psychiatry, 38,* 829–837.

Herzog, D. B., Greenwood, D. N., Dorer, D. J., Flores, A. T., Ekeblad, E. R., Richards, A., et al. (2000). Mortality in eating disorders: A descriptive study. *International Journal of Eating Disorders, 28,* 20–26.

Herzog, T. A., & Blagg, C. O. (2007). Are most precontemplators contemplating smoking cessation? Assessing the validity of the stages of change. *Health Psychology, 26,* 222–231.

Hespos, S. J., & Baillargeon, R. (2001). Infants' knowledge about occlusion and containment events: A surprising discrepancy. *Psychological Science, 12,* 141–147.

Hetherington, E. M., & Clingempeel, W. G. (1992). Coping with marital transitions. *Monographs of the Society for Research in Child Development, 57*(2–3), 1–14.

Hettema, J. M., Annas, P., Neale, M. C., Kendler, K. S., & Fredrikson, M. (2003). A twin study of the genetics of fear conditioning. *Archives of General Psychiatry, 60,* 702–708.

Hettema, J. M., Prescott, C. A., Myers, J. M., Neale, M. C., & Kendler, K. S. (2005). The structure of genetic and environmental risk factors for anxiety disorders in men and women. *Archives of General Psychiatry, 62,* 182–189.

Heuer, H., Kleinsorge, T., Klein, W., & Kohlisch, O. (2004). Total sleep deprivation increases the costs of shifting between simple cognitive tasks. *Acta Psychologica (Amsterdam), 117,* 29–64.

Heward, W. L. (1997). Four validated instructional strategies. *Behavior and Social Issues, 7,* 43–51.

Heymsfield, S. B., Greenberg, A. S., Fujioa, K., Dixon, R. M., Kushner, R., Hunt, T., et al. (1999). Recombinant leptin for weight loss in obese and lean adults. *Journal of the American Medical Association, 282,* 1568–1575.

Hickey, C., Chisholm, T., Passmore, M. J., O'Brien, J. D., & Johnston, J. (2008). Differentiating the dementias. Revisiting synucleinopathies and tauopathies. *Current Alzheimer Research, 5*(1), 52–60.

Hicks, R. A., Fernandez, C., & Pelligrini, R. J. (2001). The changing pattern of sleep habits of university students: An update. *Perceptual and Motor Skills, 93,* 648.

Highley, J. R., Walker, M. A., Crow, T. J., Esiri, M. M., & Harrison, P. J. (2003). Low medial and lateral right pulvinar volumes in schizophrenia: A postmortem study. *American Journal of Psychiatry, 160,* 1177–1179.

Hightower, J. R. R. (2005). Women and depression. In A. Barnes (Ed.), *The handbook of women, psychology, and the law* (pp. 192–211). New York: Wiley.

Hildebrandt, M. G., Steyerberg, E. W., Stage, K. B., Passchier, J., Kragh-Soerensen, P., and the Danish University Antidepressant Group. (2003). Are gender differences important for the clinical effects of antidepressants? *American Journal of Psychiatry, 160,* 1643–1650.

Hilgard, E. R. (1965). *Hypnotic susceptibility.* New York: Harcourt, Brace & World.

Hilgard, E. R. (1977). *Divided consciousness: Multiple controls in human thought and action.* New York: Wiley.

Hilgard, E. R. (1979). *Personality and hypnosis: A study of imaginative involvement.* Chicago: University of Chicago Press.

Hilgard, E. R. (1982). Hypnotic susceptibility and implications for measurement. International *Journal of Clinical and Experimental Hypnosis, 30,* 394–403.

Hilgard, E. R. (1992). Divided consciousness and dissociation. *Consciousness and Cognition, 1,* 16–31.

Hilgard, E. R., Morgan, A. H., & MacDonald, H. (1975). Pain and dissociation in the cold pressor test: A study of "hidden reports" through automatic key- pressing and automatic talking. *Journal of Abnormal Psychology, 84,* 280–289.

Hill, C. (2005). Therapist techniques, client involvement, and the therapeutic relationship: Inextricably intertwined in the therapy process. *Psychotherapy: Theory, Research, Practice, Training, 42,* 431–442.

Hill, C. E., & Lent, R. W. (2006). A narrative and meta-analytic review of helping skills training: Time to revive a dormant area of inquiry. *Psychotherapy: Theory, Research, Practice, Training, 43,* 154–172.

Hill, C. T., & Peplau, L. A. (1998). Premarital predictors of relationship outcomes: A 15-year follow-up of the Boston Couples Study. In T. N. Bradbury (Ed.), *The developmental course of marital dysfunction* (pp. 237–278). New York: Cambridge University Press.

Hill, T., Lewicki, P., Czyzewska, M., & Boss, A. (1989). Self-perpetuating biases in person perception. *Journal of Personality and Social Psychology, 57,* 373–386.

Hilliard, R. B., Henry, W. P., & Strupp, H. H. (2000). An interpersonal model of psychotherapy: Linking patient and therapist developmental history, therapeutic process, and types of outcome. *Journal of Consulting and Clinical Psychology, 68,* 125–133.

Hillis, A. E., Gold, L., Kannan, V., Cloutman, L., Kleinman, J. T., Newhart, M., Heidler-Gary, J., Davis, C., Aldrich, E., Llinas, R., & Gottesman, R. F. (2008). Site of the ischemic penumbra as a predictor of potential for recovery of functions. *Neurology, 71*(3), 184–189.

Hilton, D. (2002). Thinking about causality: Pragmatic, social and scientific rationality. In P. E. Carruthers, S. Stich, & M. Siegal (Eds.), *The cognitive basis of science* (pp. 211–231). New York: Cambridge University Press.

Hilton, H. (1986). *The executive memory guide.* New York: Simon & Schuster.

Hines, A. R., & Paulson, S. E. (2007). Parents' and teachers' perceptions of adolescent storm and stress: Relations with parenting and teaching styles. *Family Therapy, 34*(2), 63–80.

Hines, M., Brook, C., & Conway, G. (2004). Androgen and psychosexual development: Core gender identity, sexual orientation, and recalled childhood gender role behavior in women and men with congenital adrenal hyperplasia (CAH). *Journal of Sex Research, 41*(1), 75–81.

Hinshaw, S. P., Zupan, B. A., Simmel, C., Nigg, J. T., & Melnick, S. (1997). Peer status in boys with and without attention-deficit hyperactivity disorder: Predictions from overt and covert antisocial behavior, social isolation, and authoritative parenting beliefs. *Child Development, 68,* 880–896.

Hinton, D., Um, K., & Ba, P. (2001). Kyol goeu ("wind overload") Part I: A cultural syndrome of orthostatic panic among Khmer refugees. *Transcultural Psychiatry, 38,* 403–432.

Hirota, K. (2006). Special cases: Ketamine, nitrous oxide and xenon. *Best Practice and Research: Clinical Anaesthesiology, 20*(1), 69–79.

Hiroto, D. S. (1974). Locus of control and learned helplessness. *Journal of Experimental Psychology, 102,* 187–193.

Hirschfeld, R. J., Jordan, M. H., Thomas, C. H., & Field, H. S. (2008). Observed leadership potential of personnel in a team setting: big five traits and proximal factors as predictors. *International Journal of Selection and Assessment, 16,* 385–402.

Hirschfeld, R. M. A., & Vornik, L. A. (2004). Newer antidepressants: Review of efficacy and safety of escitalopram and duloxetine. *Journal of Clinical Psychiatry, 65*(Suppl. 4), 46–52.

Hirsch-Pasek, K., Treiman, R., & Schneiderman, M. (1984). Brown and Hanlon revisited: Mothers' sensitivity to ungrammatical forms. *Journal of Child Language, 11,* 81–88.

Ho, B.-C., Andreasen, N. C., Nopoulos, P., Arndt, S., Magnotta, V., & Flaum M. (2003). Progressive structural brain abnormalities and their relationship to clinical outcome: A longitudinal magnetic resonance imaging study early in schizophrenia. *Archives of General Psychiatry, 60,* 585–594.

Ho, C., Bluestein, D. N., & Jenkins, J. M. (2008). Cultural differences in the relationship between parenting and children's behavior. *Developmental Psychology, 44,* 507–522.

Ho, D. Y., & Chiu, C. (1998). Component ideas of individual, collectivism, and social organization. In U. Kim, C. Kagitcibasi, & H. C. Triandis (Eds.), *Individualism and collectivism: Theory, method, and applications.* Thousand Oaks, CA: Sage.

Ho, Y.-C., Cheung, M., & Chan, A. S. (2003). Music training improves verbal but not visual memory: Cross-sectional and longitudinal explorations in children. *Neuropsychology, 17,* 439–450.

Hobson, J. (1997). Dreaming as delirium: A mental status analysis of our nightly madness. *Seminar in Neurology, 17,* 121–128.

Hobson, J. A. (2005). Sleep is of the brain, by the brain and for the brain. *Nature, 437,* 1254–1256.

Hobson, J. A., Pace-Schott, E. F., Stickgold, R., & Kahn, D. (1998). To dream or not to dream? Relevant data from new neuroimaging and electrophysical studies. *Current Opinions in Neurobiology, 8,* 239–244.

Hodgins, S. (2007). Persistent violent offending: What do we know? *British Journal of Psychiatry, 190 (supplement),* s12–s14.

Hoegl, M., & Parboteeah, K. P. (2006). Autonomy and teamwork in innovative projects. *Human Resource Management, 45,* 67–79.

Hoek, H. W. (2006). Incidence, prevalence and mortality of anorexia nervosa and other eating disorders. *Current Opinion in Psychiatry, 19*(4), 389–394.

Hoel, H., Faragher, B., & Cooper, C. L. (2004). Bullying is detrimental to health, but all bullying behaviors are not necessarily equally damaging. *British Journal of Guidance and Counseling, 32,* 367–387.

Hofer, S. B., Mrsic-Flogel, T. D., Bonhoeffer, T., & Hübener, M. (2009). Experience leaves a lasting structural trace in cortical circuits. *Nature, 457,* 313–317.

Hoffman, D. (1999, February 11). When the nuclear alarms went off, he guessed right. *International Herald Tribune,* p. 2.

Hoffmann, J. P., & Cerbone, F. G. (2002). Parental substance use disorder and the risk of adolescent drug abuse: An event history analysis. *Drug and Alcohol Dependence, 66,* 255–264.

Hofmann, S. G., Meuret, A. E., Smits, J. A., Simon, N. M., Pollack, M. H., Eisenmenger, K., et al. (2006). Augmentation of exposure therapy with D-cycloserine for social anxiety disorder. *Archives of General Psychiatry, 63,* 298–304.

Hogan, R. (2006). *Personality and the fate of organizations.* Mahwah, NJ: Lawrence Erlbaum Associates Publishers.

Hogarth, R. M., & Einhorn, H. J. (1992). Order effects in belief updating: The belief adjustment model. *Cognitive Psychology, 24,* 1–55.

Hoglinger, G. U., Widmer, H. R., Spenger, C., Meyer, M., Seiler, R. W., Oertel, W. H., & Sautter, J. (2001). Influence of time in culture and BDNF pretreatment on survival and function of grafted embryonic rat ventral mesencephalon in the 6-OHDA rat model of Parkinson's disease. *Experimental Neurology, 167,* 148–157.

Hohman, A. A., & Shear, M. K. (2002). Community-based intervention research: Coping with the "noise" of real life in study design. *American Journal of Psychiatry, 159,* 201–207.

Hoigaard, R., & Ingvaldsen, R. P. (2006). Social loafing in interactive groups: The effects of identifiability on effort and individual performance in floorball. *Athletic Insight: The Online Journal of Sport Psychology, 8.*Retrieved March 19, 2009, from http://www.athleticinsight.com/Vol8Iss2/Loafing.htm.

Hoigaard, R., Säfvenbom, R., & Tonnessen, F. E. (2006). The relationship between group cohesion, group norms, and perceived social loafing in soccer teams. *Small Group Research, 37,* 217–232.

Holbrook, A. L., Berent, M. K., Krosnick, J. A., Visser, P. S., & Boninger, D. S. (2006). Attitude importance and the accumulation of attitude-relevant knowledge in memory. *Journal of Personality and Social Psychology, 88,* 749–769.

Holden, C. (1996). Small refugees suffer the effects of early neglect. *Science, 274,* 1076–1077.

Holladay, C. L., & Quiñones, M. A. (2003). Practice variability and transfer of training: The role of self-efficacy generality. *Journal of Applied Psychology, 88,* 1094–1103.

Hollander, E., Braum, A., Simeon, D. (2008). Should OCD leave the anxiety disorders in DSM-V? The case for obsessive-compulsive-related disorders. *Depression and Anxiety, 25,* 317–329.

Hollander, E., & Simeon, D. (2009). Anxiety disorders. In R. E. Hales, S. C., Yudofsky, & G. O. Gabbard (Eds.), *Textbook of psychiatry* (pp. 505–567). Washington, DC: American Psychiatric Publishing.

Hollinger, R. C., Dabney, D. A., Lee, G., Hayes, R., Hunter, J., & Cummings, M. (1996). *1996 national retail security survey final report.* Gainesville: University of Florida.

Hollon, S. D., Jarrett, R. B., Nienberg, A. A., Thase, M. E., Trivendi, M., et al. (2005). Psychotherapy and medication in the treatment of adult and geriatric depression: Which monotherapy or combined therapy? *Journal of Clinical Psychiatry, 66,* 455–468.

Hollon, S. D., Stewart, M. O., & Strunk, D. (2006).Enduring effects for cognitive behavior therapy in the treatment of depression and anxiety. *Annual Review of Psychology, 57,* 285–315.

Hollon, S. D., Thase, M. E., & Markowitz, J. C. (2002). Treatment and prevention of depression. *Psychological Science in the Public Interest, 3,* 39–77.

Holman, B. R. (1994). Biological effects of central nervous system stimulants. *Addiction, 89*(11), 1435–1441.

Holman, E. A., Silver, R. C., Poulin, M., Andersen, J., Gil-Rivas, V., & McIntosh, D. N. (2008). Terrorism, acute stress, and cardiovascular health: A 3-year national study following the September 11th attacks. *Archives of General Psychiatry, 65,* 73–80.

Holmes, D. S. (1991). *Abnormal psychology.* New York: HarperCollins.

Holmes, T. H., & Rahe, R. H. (1967). The Social Readjustment Rating Scale. *Journal of Psychosomatic Research, 11,* 213–218.

Holtmaat, A., Wilbrecht, L., Knott, G. W., Welker, E., & Svoboda, K. (2006). Experience-dependent and cell-type-specific spine growth in the neocortex. *Nature, 441,* 979–983.

Holway, A. H., & Boring, E. G. (1941). Determinants of apparent visual size with distance variant. *American Journal of Psychology, 54,* 21–37.

Hommer, D. W., Momenan, R., Kaiser, E., & Rawlings, R. R. (2001). Evidence for a gender-related effect of alcoholism on brain volumes. *American Journal of Psychiatry, 158,* 198–204.

Hong, Y., Morris, M. W., Chiu, C., & Benet-Martinez, V. (2000). Multicultural minds: A dynamic constructivist approach to culture and cognition. *American Psychologist, 55,* 709–720.

Honts, C. R., & Quick, B. D. (1995). The polygraph in 1996: Progress in science and the law. *North Dakota Law Review, 71,* 997–1020.

Hoobler, J. M., & Brass, D. J. (2006). Abusive supervision and family undermining as displaced aggression. *Journal of Applied Psychology, 91,* 1125–1133.

Hood, B. M., Willen, J. D., & Driver, J. (1998). Adult's eyes trigger shifts of visual attention in human infants. *Psychological Science, 9,* 131–134.

Hood, M. Y., Moore, L. L., Sundarajan-Ramamurti, A., Singer, M., Cupples, L. A., & Ellison, R. C. (2000). Parental eating attitudes and the development of obesity in children: The Framingham children's study. *International Journal of Obesity, 24,* 1319–1325.

Hooker, E. (1993). Reflections of a 40-year exploration: A scientific view on homosexuality. *American Psychologist, 48,* 450–453.

Hooley, J. M. (2004). Do psychiatric patients do better clinically if they live with certain kinds of families? *Current Directions in Psychological Science, 13,* 202–205.

Hopf, H. C., Muller, F. W., & Hopf, N. J. (1992). Localization of emotional and volitional facial paresis. *Neurology, 42*(10), 1918–1923.

Hopper, K., & Wanderling, J. (2000). Revisiting the developed versus developing country distinction in course and outcome in schizophrenia: Results from ISoS, the WHO Collaborative Followup Project. *Schizophrenia Bulletin, 26,* 835–846.

Horne, J. A. (1988). *Why we sleep: The functions of sleep in humans.* Oxford: Oxford University Press.

Horner, P. J., & Gage, F. H. (2002). Regeneration in the adult and aging brain. *Archives of Neurology, 59,* 1717–1720.

Horney, K. (1937). *Neurotic personality of our times.* New York: Norton.

Horowitz, J. L., & Garber, J. (2006). The prevention of depressive symptoms in children and adolescents: A meta-analytic review. *Journal of Consulting and Clinical Psychology, 74,* 401–415.

Horowitz, L. M., Rosenberg, S. E., & Bartholomew, K. (1993). Interpersonal problems, attachment styles, and outcome in brief dynamic psychotherapy. *Journal of Consulting and Clinical Psychology, 61,* 549–560.

Horvath, A. O. (2005). The therapeutic relationship: Research and theory: An introduction to the special issue. *Psychotherapy Research, 15,* 3–7.

Horwitz, P., & Christie, M. A. (2000). Computer-based manipulatives for teaching scientific reasoning: An example. In M. J. Jacobson & R. B. Kozuma (Eds.), *Innovations in science and mathematics education: Advanced designs for technologies of learning* (pp. 163–191). Mahwah, NJ: Erlbaum.

Hoshino-Browne, E., Zanna, A. S., Spencer, S. J., Zanna, M. P., Kitayama, S., & Lackenbauer, S. (2005). On the cultural guises of cognitive dissonance: The case of Easterners and Westerners. *Journal of Personality and Social Psychology, 89,* 294–310.

Houghton, G. (2005). *Connectionist models in cognitive psychology.* New York: Psychology Press.

Houpt, T. R. (1994). Gastric pressure in pigs during eating and drinking. *Physiology and Behavior, 56*(2), 311–317.

House, J. S., Landis, K. R., & Umberson, D. (1988a). Social relationships and health. *Science, 241,* 540–545.

House, J. S., Landis, K. R., & Umberson, D. (1988b). Structures and processes of social support. *Annual Review of Sociology, 14,* 293–318.

House, R. J., Hanges, P. J., Ruiz-Quintanilla, S. A., Dorfman, P. W., Javidan, M., Dickson, M., et al. (1999). Cultural influences on leadership and organizations: Project GLOBE. In W. H. Mobley, M. J. Gessner, & V. Arnold (Eds.), *Advances in global leadership* (Vol. 1, pp. 171–233). Stamford, CT: JAI.

Hoven, C. W., Duarte, C. S., Lucas, C. P., Wu, P., Mandell, D. J., Goodwin, R. D., et al. (2005). Psychopathology among New York city public school children 6 months after September 11. *Archives of General Psychiatry, 62,* 545–552.

Howard, D. V. (1983). *Cognitive psychology.* New York: Macmillan.

Howe, M. J. A., Davidson, J. W., & Sloboda, J. A. (1998). Innate talent: Reality or myth? *Behavioral and Brain Sciences, 21,* 399–442.

Howe, M. L. (2003). Memories from the cradle. *Current Directions in Psychological Science, 12,* 62–65.

Hoyert, D. L., Kung, H.-C., & Smith, B. L. (2005). Deaths: Preliminary data for 2003. *National Vital Statistics Reports, 53,* 1–48.

Hoyle, R. H. (1993). Interpersonal attraction in the absence of explicit attitudinal information. *Social Cognition, 11,* 309–320.

Hoyle, R. H., Harris, M. J., & Judd, C. M. (2002). *Research methods in social relations.* Belmont, CA: Wadsworth.

Hser, Y. I., Hoffman, V., Grella, C. E., & Anglin, M. D. (2001). A 33-year follow-up of narcotics addicts. *Archives of General Psychiatry, 58,* 503–508.

Hu, P., Stylos-Allan, M., & Walker, M. P. (2006). Sleep facilitates consolidation of emotional declarative memory. *Psychological Science, 17,* 891–898.

Hu, S., Patatucci, A. M. L., Patterson, C., Li, L., Fulker, D. W., Cherny, S. S., et al. (1995). Linkage between sexual orientation and chromosome Xq28 in males but not females. *Nature Genetics, 11,* 248–256.

Hua, J. Y., & Smith, S. J. (2004). Neural activity and the dynamics of central nervous system development. *Nature Neuroscience, 7,* 327–332.

Huang, L., & Li, C. (2000). Leptin: A multifunctional hormone. *Cell Research, 10,* 81–92.

Hubel, D. H., & Wiesel, T. N. (1979). Brain mechanisms of vision. *Scientific American, 241,* 150–162.

Hudson, J. I., Hiripi, E., Pope, H. G., Jr, & Kessler, R. C. (2007). The prevalence and correlates of eating disorders in the National Comorbidity Survey replication. *Biological Psychiatry, 61,* 348–358.

Hudson, J. L., & Rapee, R. M. (2009). Familial and social environments in the eitology and maintenance of anxiety disorders. In M. M. Antony & M. B. Stein (Eds.) *Oxford handbook of anxiety and related disorders* (pp. 173–189). New York: Oxford University Press.

Hudson, W. (1960). Pictorial depth in perception in subcultural groups in Africa. *Journal of Social Psychology, 52,* 183–208.

Hudziak, J. J., Derks, E. M., Althoff, R. R., Rettew, D. C., & Boomsma, D. I. (2005). The genetic and environmental contributions to attention deficit hyperactivity disorder as measured by the Conners' Rating Scales—Revised. *American Journal of Psychiatry, 162,* 1614–1620.

Hudziak, J. J., van Beijsterveldt, C. E. M., Bartels, M., Rietveld, M. J. H., Rettew, D. C., Derks, E. M., et al. (2003). Individual differences in aggression: Genetic analyses by age, gender, and informant in 3-, 7-, and 10-year-old Dutch twins. *Behavior Genetics, 33,* 575–589.

Huesmann, L. R. (1995). *Screen violence and real violence: Understanding the link.* Auckland, NZ: Media Aware.

Huesmann, L. R. (1998). The role of social information processing and cognitive schema in the acquisition and maintenance of habitual aggressive behavior. In R. G. Geen & E. Donnerstein (Eds.), *Human aggression.* San Diego: Academic Press.

Huesmann, L. R., & Eron, L. D. (1986). *Television and the aggressive child: A cross-national comparison.* Hillsdale, NJ: Erlbaum.

Huesmann, L. R., Moise, J., Podolski, C., & Eron, L. (1997, April). *Longitudinal relations between early exposure to television violence and young adult aggression: 1977–1992.* Paper presented at the annual meeting of the Society for Research in Child Development, Washington, DC.

Huesmann, L. R., Moise-Titus, J., Podolski, C., & Eron, L. D. (2003). Longitudinal relations between children's exposure to TV violence and their aggressive and violent behavior in young adulthood: 1977–1992. *Developmental Psychology, 39,* 201–221.

Huffcutt, A. I., & Arthur, W. (1994). Hunter and Hunter (1984) revisited: Interview validity for entry-level jobs. *Journal of Applied Psychology, 79,* 184–190.

Huffcutt, A. I., Conway, J. M., Roth, P. L., & Stone, N. J. (2001). Identification and meta-analytic assessment of psychological constructs measured in employment interviews. *Journal of Applied Psychology, 86,* 897–913.

Hughes, B. M. (2006). Lies, damned lies, and pseudoscience: The selling of eye movement desensitization and reprocessing (EMDR). *PsycCritiques, 51,* 10.

Hughes, J. R., Higgins, S. T., & Bickel, W. K. (1994). Nicotine withdrawal versus other drug withdrawal syndromes: Similarities and dissimilarities. *Addiction, 89*(11), 1461–1470.

Hughes, R. N. (2007). Neotic preferences in laboratory rodents: Issues, assessment and substrates. *Neuroscience & Biobehavioral Reviews, 31*(3), 441–464.

Hui, C., Lam, S. S. K., & Law, K. K. S. (2000). Instrumental values of organizational citizenship behavior for promotion: A field quasi-experiment. *Journal of Applied Psychology, 85,* 822–828.

Huizink, A. C., Mulder, E. J. H., & Buitelaar, J. K. (2004). Prenatal stress and risk for psychopathology. *Psychological Bulletin, 130,* 115–142.

Hull, C. L. (1951). *Essentials of behavior.* New Haven, CT: Yale University Press.

Hull, S. A., Cornwell, J., Harvey, C., Eldridge, S., & Bare, P. O. (2001). Prescribing rates for psychotropic medication amongst east London general practices: Low rates where Asian populations are greatest. *Family Practice, 18,* 167–173.

Hulleman, J., & Humphreys, G. W. (2004). A new cue to figure-ground coding: Top-bottom polarity. *Vision Research, 44*(24), 2779–2791.

Hunsley, J. (2007). Addressing key challenges in evidence-based practice in psychology. *Professional Psychology: Research and Practice, 38,* 113–121.

Hunsley, J., Lee, C. M., & Wood, J. M. (2003). Controversial and questionable assessment techniques. In S. O. Lilienfeld & S. J. Lynn (Eds.), *Science and pseudoscience in clinical psychology* (pp. 39–76). New York: Guilford Press.

Hunsley, J., & Rumstein-McKean, O. (1999). Improving psychotherapeutic services via randomized trials, treatment manuals, and component analysis designs. *Journal of Clinical Psychology, 55,* 1507–1517.

Hunt, E. (1983). On the nature of intelligence. *Science, 219,* 141–146.

Hunt, M. (1982). *The universe within.* New York: Simon & Schuster.

Hunt, M., & Forand, R. (2005). Cognitive vulnerability to depression in never depressed subjects. *Cognition and Emotion, 19,* 763–770.

Hunt, R., & Rouse, W. B. (1981). Problem solving skills of maintenance trainees in diagnosing faults in simulated power plants. *Human Factors, 23,* 317–328.

Hunter, M. A., & Ames, E. W. (1988). A multifactor model of infants' preferences for novel and familiar stimuli. In C. Rovee-Collier & L. P. Lipsitt (Eds.), *Advances in infancy research* (Vol. 5, pp. 69–91). Norwood, NJ: Ablex.

Huprich, S. K. (2009). What should become of depressive personality in DSM-V? *Harvard Review of Psychiatry, 17,* 41–59.

Hurt, H., Brodsky, N. L., Betancourt, L., & Braitman, L. E. (1995). Cocaine-exposed children: Follow-up through 30 months. *Journal of Developmental and Behavioral Pediatrics, 16*(1), 29–35.

Huston, A. C., & Wright, J. C. (1989). The forms of television and the child viewer. In G. Comstock (Ed.), *Public communication and behavior* (Vol. 2, pp. 103–159). San Diego: Academic Press.

Huston, T. L., Caughlin, J. P., Houts, R. M., Smith, S. E., & George, L. J. (2001). The connubial crucible: Newlywed years as predictors of marital delight, distress, and divorce. *Journal of Personality and Social Psychology, 80,* 237–252.

Huttenlocher, P. R. (1990). Morphometric study of human cerebral cortex development. *Neuropsychologia, 28,* 517–527.

Hwang, W.-C. (2006). The psychotherapy adaptation and modification framework: Application to Asian Americans. *American Psychologist, 61,* 702–715.

Hybels, C. F., Pieper, C. F., Blazer, D. G., & Steffens, D. C. (2008). The course of depressive symptoms in older adults with comorbid major depression and dysthymia. *American Journal of Geriatric Psychiatry, 16,* 300–309.

Hyde, J. S. (1986). Gender differences in aggression. In J. S. Hyde & M. C. Linn (Eds.), *The psychology of gender: Advances through meta-analysis.* Baltimore: Johns Hopkins University Press.

Hyde, J. S. (2005). The gender similarities hypothesis. *American Psychologist, 60,* 581–592.

Hyde, J. S. (2007). New directions in the study of gender similarities and differences. *Current Directions in Psychological Science, 16,* 259–263.

Hyde, J. S., & Durik, A. M. (2000). Gender differences in erotic plasticity–Evolutionary or sociocultural forces? Comment on Baumeister (2000). *Psychological Bulletin, 126,* 375–379.

Hyde, K. L., Lerch, J., Norton, A., Forgeard, M., Winner, E., Evans, A. C., & Schlaug, G. (2009). Musical training shapes structural brain development. *The Journal of Neuroscience, 29,* 3019–3025.

Hyman, I. E., Jr. (2000). The memory wars. In U. Neisser & I. E. Hyman, Jr. (Eds.), *Memory observed* (2nd ed., pp. 374–379). New York: Worth.

Hyman, I. E., Jr., & Pentland, J. (1996). The role of mental imagery in the creation of false childhood memories. *Journal of Memory and Language, 35,* 101–117.

Hyman, R. (2002). Why and when are smart people stupid? In R. J. Sternberg (Ed.), *Why smart people can be so stupid* (pp. 1–23). New Haven, CT: Yale University Press.

Hyman, S. E., Malenka, R. C., & Nestler, E. J. (2006). Neural mechanisms of addiction: The role of reward-related learning and memory. *Annual Review of Neuroscience, 29,* 565–598.

Hypericum Depression Trial Study Group. (2002). Effect of *Hypericum perforatum* (St. John's wort) in major depressive disorder: A randomized, controlled trial. *Journal of the American Medical Association, 287,* 1

Iacono, W. G., & Patrick, C. J. (2006). Polygraph ("lie detector") testing: Current status and emerging trends. In I. B. Weiner & A. K. Hess (Eds.), *The handbook of forensic psychology* (3rd ed., pp. 552–588). Hoboken, NJ: Wiley.

Iancu, I., Poreh, A., Lehman, B., Shamir, E., & Kotler, M. (2005). The positive and negative symptoms questionnaire: A self-report in schizophrenia. *Comprehensive Psychiatry, 46,* 61–66.

Iani, C., Ricci, F., Ghem, E., & Rubichi, S. (2006). Hypnotic suggestion modulates cognitive conflict: The case of the flanker compatibility effect. *Psychological Science, 17,* 721–727.

Iervolino, A. C., Hines, M., Golombok, S. E., Rust, J., & Plomin, R. (2005). Genetic and environmental influences on sex-typed behavior during the preschool years. *Child Development, 76,* 826–840.

Igalens, J., & Roussel, P. (1999). A study of the relationships between compensation package, work motivation, and job satisfaction. *Journal of Organizational Behavior, 20,* 1003–1025.

Ilgen, D. R., & Pulakos, E. D. (Eds.). (1999). *The changing nature of performance: Implications for staffing, motivation, and development.* San Francisco, CA: Jossey-Bass.

Ilies, R., & Judge, T. A. (2003). On the heritability of job satisfaction: The mediating role of personality. *Journal of Applied Psychology, 88,* 750–759.

Ilies, R., Nahrgang, J. D., & Morgeson, F. P. (2007). Leader-member exchange and citizenship behaviors: A meta-analysis. *Journal of Applied Psychology, 92,* 269–277.

Ilies, R., Scott, B. A., & Judge, T. A. (2006). The interactive effects of personal traits and experienced states on intraindividual patterns of citizenship behavior. *Academy of Management Journal, 49,* 561–575.

Imtiaz, K. E., Nirodi, G., & Khaleeli, A. A. (2001). Alexia without agraphia: A century later. *International Journal of Clinical Practice, 55*(3), 225–226.

Inciardi, J. A., Surratt, H. L., & Saum, C. A. (1997). *Cocaine-exposed infants: Social, legal, and public health issues.* Thousand Oaks, CA: Sage.

Indovina, I., & Sanes, J. N. (2001). On somatotopic representation centers for finger movements in human primary motor cortex and supplementary motor area. *Neuroimage, 13,* 1027–1034.

Inness, M., Barling, J., & Turner, N. (2005). Understanding supervisor-targeted aggression: A within-person, between-jobs design. *Journal of Applied Psychology, 90,* 731–739.

Inoue, K., Tanii, H., Fukunaga, T., Abe, S., Kaiya, H., Nata, M., & Okazaki, Y. (2006). Letter to the editor: Significant correlation of yearly suicide rates with the rate of unemployment among men results in a rapid increase of suicide in Mie Prefecture, Japan. *Psychiatry and Clinical Neurosciences, 60*, 781–782.

Insel, T. R. (2008). Assessing the economic cost of serious mental illness. *American Journal of Psychiatry, 165*, 663–665.

Institute of Medicine. (2006, April 5). *Sleep disorders and sleep deprivation: An unmet public health problem* [Press release]. Retrieved September 26, 2006, from http://www.iom.edu/CMS/3740/23160/33668.aspx.

International Human Genome Sequencing Consortium. (2001). Initial sequencing and analysis of the human genome. *Nature, 409*, 860–921.

Inzitari, M., Pozzi, C., Ferrucci, L., Chiarantini, D., Rinaldi, L. A., Baccini, M., Pini, R., Masotti, G., Marchionni, N., & Di Bari, M. (2008). Subtle neurological abnormalities as risk factors for cognitive and functional decline, cerebrovascular events, and mortality in older community-dwelling adults. *Archives of Internal Medicine, 168*, 1270–1276.

Ironson, G., Freund, B., Strauss, J. L., & Williams J. (2002). Comparison of two treatments for traumatic stress: A community-based study of EMDR and prolonged exposure. *Journal of Clinical Psychology, 58*, 113–128.

Ironson, G., Wynings, C., Schneiderman, N., Baum, A., Rodriguez, M., Greenwood, D., et al. (1997). Posttraumatic stress symptoms, intrusive thoughts, loss, and immune function after Hurricane Andrew. *Psychosomatic Medicine, 59*, 128–141.

Ironson, G. H., Smith, P. C., Brannick, M. T., Gibson, W. M., & Paul, K. B. (1989). Constitution of a Job in General scale: A comparison of global, composite, and specific measures. *Journal of Applied Psychology, 74*, 193–200.

Irwin, M., Daniels, M., Smith, T., Bloom, E., & Weiner, H. (1987). Impaired natural killer cell activity during bereavement. *Brain, Behavior, and Immunity, 1*, 98–104.

Ishikawa, A., Kanayama, Y., Matsumura, H., Tsuchimochi, H., Ishida, Y., & Nakamura, S. (2006). Selective rapid eye movement sleep deprivation impairs the maintenance of long-term potentiation in the rat hippocampus. *European Journal of Neuroscience, 24*, 243–248.

Ivleva, E., Thaker, G., & Tamminga, C. (2008). Comparing genes and phenomenology in the major psychoses: Schizophrenia and bipolar 1 disorder. *Schizophrenia Bulletin, 34*(4), 734–742.

Iwahashi, K., Matsuo, Y., Suwaki, H., Nakamura, K., & Ichikawa, Y. (1995). CYP2E1 and ALDH2 genotypes and alcohol dependence in Japanese. *Alcoholism Clinical and Experimental Research, 19*(3), 564–566.

Iwamasa, G. Y., Sorocco, K. H., & Koonce, D. A. (2002). Ethnicity and clinical psychology: A content analysis of the literature. *Clinical Psychology Review, 22*, 932–944.

Izac, S. M., & Eeg, T. R. (2006). Basic anatomy and physiology of sleep. *American Journal of Electroneurodiagnostic Technology, 46*(1), 18–38.

Izard, C., Fine, S., Schultz, D. Mostow, A., Ackerman, B., & Youngstrom, E. (2001). Emotion knowledge as a predictor of social behavior and academic competence in children at risk. *Psychological Science, 12*, 18–23.

Izard, C. E. (1977). *Human emotions*. New York: Plenum.

Izard, C. E. (2007). Basic emotions, natural kinds, emotion schemas, and a new paradigm. *Perspectives on Psychological Science, 2*, 260–280.

Izumikawa, M., Minoda, R., Kawamoto, K., Abrashkin, K. A., Swiderski, D. L., Dolan, D. F., et al. (2005). Auditory hair cell replacement and hearing improvement by *Atoh1* gene therapy in deaf animals. *Nature, 11*, 271–276.

Jaccard, J., Blanton, H., & Dodge, T. (2005). Peer influences on risk behavior: An analysis of the effects of a close friend. *Developmental Psychology, 41*, 135–147.

Jack, F., & Hayne, H. (2007). Eliciting adults' earliest memories: Does it matter how we ask the question? *Memory, 15*(6), 647–663.

Jackson, B., Sellers, R. M., & Peterson, C. (2002). Pessimistic explanatory style moderates the effect of stress on physical illness. *Personality & Individual Differences, 32*, 567–573.

Jackson, C. J. (2003). Gray's Reinforcement Sensitivity Theory: A psychometric critique. *Personality and Individual Differences, 34*, 533–544.

Jackson, J. W. (2002). The relationship between group identity and intergroup prejudice is moderated by sociostructural variation. *Journal of Applied Social Psychology, 32*, 908–933.

Jackson, L. A., von Eye, A., Biocca, F. A., Barbatsis, G., Zhao, Y., & Fitzgerald, H. E. (2006). Does home internet use influence the academic performance of low-income children? *Developmental Psychology, 42*, 429–435.

Jacob, S., & McClintock, M. K. (2000). Psychological state and mood effects of steroidal chemosignals in women and men. *Hormones and Behavior, 37*, 57–78.

Jacob, S., Kinnunen, L. H., Metz, J., Cooper, M., & McClintock, M. K. (2001). Sustained human chemosignal unconsciously alters brain function. *Neuroreport, 12*, 2391–2394.

Jacob, T., Waterman, B., Heath, A., True, W., Bucholz, K. K., Haber, R., et al. (2003). Genetic and environmental effects on offspring alcoholism: New insights using an offspring-of-twins design. *Archives of General Psychiatry, 60*, 1265–1272.

Jacobi, C., Hayward, C., de Zwaan, M., Kraemer, H. C., & Agras, W. S. (2004). Coming to terms with risk factors for eating disorders: Application of risk terminology and suggestions for a general taxonomy. *Psychological Bulletin, 130*, 19–65.

Jacobs, B. L. (2004). Depression: The brain finally gets into the act. *Current Directions in Psychological Science, 13*, 103–106.

Jacobs, G. D., Pace-Schott, E. F., Stickgold, R., & Otto, M. W. (2004). Cognitive behavior therapy and pharmacotherapy for insomnia: A randomized controlled trial and direct comparison. *Archives of Internal Medicine, 164*, 1888–1896.

Jacobs, G. H. (2008). Primate color vision: A comparative perspective. *Vision Neuroscience, 25*(5–6), 619–631.

Jacobs, M., Snow, J., Geraci, M., Vythilingam, M., Blair, R. J. R., et al. (2009). Association between level of emotional intelligence and severity of anxiety in generalized social phobia. *Journal of Anxiety Disorders, 22*, 1487–1495.

Jacobs, N., Kenis, G., Peeters, F., Derom, C., Vlietinck, R., & van Os, J. (2006). Stress-related negative affectivity and genetically altered serotonin transporter function: Evidence of synergism in shaping risk of depression. *Archives of General Psychiatry, 63*, 989–996.

Jacobs, R., & Solomon, T. (1977). Strategies for enhancing the prediction of job performance from job satisfaction. *Journal of Applied Psychology, 62*, 417–421.

Jacobson, E. (1938). *Progressive relaxation*. Chicago: University of Chicago Press.

Jacobson, K. (2002). ADHD in cross-cultural perspective: Some empirical results. *American Anthropologist, 104*, 283–286.

Jacobson, N. S., Christensen, A., Prince, S. E., Cordova, J., & Eldridge, K. (2000). Integrative behavioral couples therapy: An acceptance-based, promising new treatment for couple discord. *Journal of Consulting and Clinical Psychology, 68*, 351–355.

Jaffari-Bimmel, N., Juffer, F., van IJzendoorn, M. H., Bakermans-Kranenburg, M. J., & Mooijaart, A. (2006). Social development from infancy to adolescence: Longitudinal and concurrent factors in an adoption sample. *Developmental Psychology, 42*(6), 1143–1153.

Jaffee, S., & Hyde, J. S. (2000). Gender differences in moral orientation: A meta-analysis. *Psychological Bulletin, 126*, 703–726.

Jaffee, S. R., Caspi, A., Moffitt, T. E., & Taylor, A. (2004). Physical maltreatment to antisocial child: Evidence of an environmentally mediated process. *Journal of Abnormal Psychology, 113*, 44–55.

Jago, R., Baranowski, T., Baranowski, J. C., Thompson, D., & Greaves, K. A. (2005). BMI from 3–6 y of age is predicted by TV viewing and physical activity, not diet. *International Journal of Obesity, 29*, 557–564.

Jahnke, J. C., & Nowaczyk, R. H. (1998). *Cognition*. Upper Saddle River, NJ: Prentice Hall.

Jain, A. (2005). Treating obesity in individuals and populations. *British Medical Journal, 331*, 1387–1390.

Jakobsen, K. D., Frederiksen, J. N., Hansen, T., Jansson, L., et al. (2005). Reliability of clinical ICD-10 schizophrenia diagnoses. *Nordic Journal of Psychiatry, 59*, 209–212.

James, J. E. (2004). Critical review of dietary caffeine and blood pressure: A relationship that should be taken more seriously. *Psychosomatic Medicine, 66*, 63–71.

James, L., Barnes, T. R. E., Lelliott, P., Taylor, D., & Paton, C. (2007). Informing patients of the teratogenic potential of mood stabilizing drugs: A case note review of the practice of psychiatrists. *Journal of Psychopharmacology, 21*(8), 815–819.

James, W. (1884). Some omissions of introspective psychology. *Mind, 9*, 1–26.

James, W. (1890). *Principles of psychology*. New York: Holt.

James, W. (1892). *Psychology: Briefer course*. New York: Holt.

Jameson, L. C., & Sloan, T. B. (2006). Using EEG to monitor anesthesia drug effects during surgery. *Journal of Clinical Monitoring and Computers, 20*, 445–472.

Jamieson, P., Jamieson, K. H., & Romer, D. (2003). The responsible reporting of suicide in print journalism. *American Behavioral Scientist, 46*, 1643–1660.

Jancke, L., & Kaufmann, N. (1994). Facial EMG responses to odors in solitude and with an audience. *Chemical Senses, 19*(2), 99–111.

Janis, I. L. (1989). *Crucial decisions: Leadership in policy making and crisis management*. New York: Free Press.

Janowiak, J. J., & Hackman, R. (1994). Meditation and college students' self- actualization and rated stress. *Psychological Reports, 75*(2), 1007–1010.

Janowitz, H. D. (1967). Role of gastrointestinal tract in the regulation of food intake. In C. F. Code (Ed.), *Handbook of physiology: Alimentary canal 1*. Washington, DC: American Physiological Society.

Jans, L. A. W., Riedel, W. J., Markus, C. R., & Blokland, A. (2007). Serotonergic vulnerability and depression: Assumptions, experimental evidence and implications. *Molecular Psychiatry, 12*, 522–543.

Jansen, P. G., & Vinkenburg, C. J. (2006). Predicting managerial career success from assessment center data: A longitudinal study. *Journal of Vocational Behavior, 68*, 253–266.

Jason, L. A., Witter, E., & Torres-Harding, S. (2003). Chronic fatigue syndrome, coping, optimism and social support. *Journal of Mental Health, 12*, 109–118.

Javitt, D. C., Kantowitz, J., & Lajtha, A. (Eds.) (2009). *Handbook of neurochemistry and molecular neurobiology: Schizophrenia* (3rd ed.). New York: Springer.

Jawahar, I. M., Meurs, J. A., Ferris, G. R., & Hochwarter, W. A. (2008). Self-efficacy and political skill as comparative predictors of task and contextual performance: A two-study constructive replication. *Human Performance, 21*(2), 138–157.

Jefferis, B. M. J. H., Power, C., & Hertzman, C. (2002). Birth weight, childhood socioeconomic environment, and cognitive development in the 1958 British birth cohort study [Electronic version]. *British Medical Journal, 325*, 305.

Jeffries, K. J., Fritz, J. B., & Braun, A. R. (2003). Words in melody: An H(2)15O PET study of brain activation during singing and speaking. *Neuroreport, 14*, 749–754.

Jemal, A., Ward, E., Hao, Y., & Thun, M. (2005). Trends in the leading causes of death in the United States, 1970–2002. *Journal of the American Medical Association, 294*, 1255–1259.

Jenkins, M. R., & Culbertson, J. L. (1996). Prenatal exposure to alcohol. In R. L. Adams, O. A. Parsons, J. L. Culbertson, & S. J. Nixon (Eds.), *Neuropsychology for clinical practice:*

Etiology, assessment, and treatment of common neurological disorders (pp. 409–452). Washington, DC: American Psychological Association.

Jenkins, R. O., & Sherbum, R. E. (2005). Growth and survival of bacteria implicated in sudden infant death syndrome on cot mattress materials. *Journal of Applied Microbiology, 99,* 573–579.

Jevtovic-Todorovic, V., Wozniak, D. F., Benshoff, N. D., & Olney, J. W. (2001). A comparative evaluation of the neurotoxic properties of ketamine and nitrous oxide. *Brain Research, 895,* 264–267.

Jex, S. M., Adams, G. A., Elacqua, T. C., & Bachrach, D. G. (2002). Type A as a moderator of stressors and job complexity: A comparison of achievement strivings and impatience-irritability. *Journal of Applied Social Psychology, 32,* 977–996.

Johansen, J. P., Fields, H. L., & Manning, B. H. (2001). The affective component of pain in rodents: Direct evidence for a contribution of the anterior cingulate cortex. *Proceedings of the National Academy of Sciences, 98,* 8077–8082.

John, O., Naumann, L., & Soto, C. (2008). Paradigm shift to the integrative big five trait taxonomy: History, measurement, and conceptual issues, In O. John, R. Robins, & L. Pervin (Eds.), *Handbook of personality: Theory and research* (3rd ed. pp., 114–158). New York: Guilford.

Johnson, B. T., Maio, G. R., & Smith-McLallen, A. (2005). Communication and attitude change: Causes, processes, and effects. In D. Albarracín, B. T. Johnson, & M. P. Zanna (Eds.), *Handbook of attitudes* (pp. 617–669). Mahwah, NJ: Erlbaum.

Johnson, D. R., Westermeyer, J., Kattar, K., & Thuras, P. (2002). Daily charting of posttraumatic stress symptoms: A pilot study. *Journal of Nervous & Mental Disease, 190,* 683–692.

Johnson, G. (2002). Comments on lithium toxicity. *Australian and New Zealand Journal of Psychiatry, 36,* 703.

Johnson, J., & Vickers, Z. (1993). Effects of flavor and macronutrient composition of food servings on liking, hunger and subsequent intake. *Appetite, 21*(1), 25–39.

Johnson, J. G., Cohen, P., Smailes, E. M., Kasen, S., & Brook, J. S. (2002). Television viewing and aggressive behavior during adolescence and adulthood. *Science, 295,* 2468–2471.

Johnson, J. M., & Endler, N. S. (2002). Coping with human immunodeficiency virus: Do optimists fare better? *Current Psychology: Developmental, Learning, Personality, Social, 21,* 3–16.

Johnson, J. S., & Newport, E. L. (1989). Critical period effects in second language learning. *Cognitive Psychology, 21,* 60–99.

Johnson, M. A., Dziurawiec, S., Ellis, H., & Morton, J. (1991). Newborns' preferential tracking of face-like stimuli and its subsequent decline. *Cognition, 4,* 1–19.

Johnson, M. K., & Raye, C. L. (1998). False memories and confabulation. *Trends in Cognitive Sciences, 2,* 137–145.

Johnson, S. L. (2003). *Therapist's guide to clinical intervention: The 1-2-3's of treatment planning.* San Diego, CA: Academic Press.

Johnson, S. L., & Birch, L. L. (1994).Parents' and children's adiposity and eating style. *Pediatrics, 94,* 653–656.

Johnson, S. P. (2005). Development of perceptual completion in infancy. *Psychological Science, 15,* 769–775.

Johnson, W., & Krueger, R. F. (2005). Higher perceived life control decreases genetic variation in physical health: Evidence from a national twin study. *Journal of Personality and Social Psychology, 88,* 165–173.

Johnson, W., Jung, R. E., Colom, R., & Haier, R. J. (2008). Cognitive abilities independent of IQ correlate with regional brain structure. *Intelligence, 36*(1), 18–28.

Johnson, W., McGue, M., & Krueger, R. F. (2005). Personality stability in late adulthood: A behavioral genetic analysis. *Journal of Personality, 73,* 523–551.

Johnson, W., McGue, M., Krueger, R. F., & Bouchard, T. J., Jr. (2004). Marriage and personality: A genetic analysis. *Journal of Personality and Social Psychology, 86,* 285–294.

Johnson, W. R., & Neal, D. (1998). Basic skills and the black-white earnings gap. In C. Jencks & M. Phillips (Eds.), *The black-white test score gap* (pp. 480–497). Washington, DC: Brookings Institute Press.

Johnson-Laird, P. N. (1983). *Mental models: Toward a cognitive science of language, inference, and consciousness.* Cambridge, MA: Harvard University Press.

Johnson-Laird, P. N., Mancini, F., & Gangemi, A. (2006). A hyper-emotion theory of psychological illnesses. *Psychological Review, 113,* 822–841.

Johnston, D. W., Tuomisto, M. T., & Patching, G. R. (2008). The relationship between cardiac reactivity in the laboratory and in real life. *Health Psychology, 27,* 34–42.

Johnston, K. (1988). Adolescents' solutions to dilemmas in fables: Two moral orientations. In C. Gilligan, J. V. Ward, J. M. Taylor, & B. Bardige (Eds.), *Mapping the moral domain: A contribution to psychological theory and education.* Cambridge: Harvard University Press.

Jolij, J., & Lamme, V. A. (2005). Repression of unconscious information by conscious processing: Evidence from affective blindsight induced by transcranial magnetic stimulation. *Proceedings of the National Academy of Sciences, 102,* 10747–10751.

Jonas, E., Schimel, J., Greenberg, J., & Pyszczynski, T. (2002). The Scrooge effect: Evidence that mortality salience increases prosocial attitudes and behavior. *Personality and Social Psychology Bulletin, 28,* 1342–1353.

Jones, E. E. (1982). Psychotherapists' impressions of treatment outcome as a function of race. *Journal of Clinical Psychology, 38,* 722–731.

Jones, G. V. (1990). Misremembering a common object: When left is not right. *Memory & Cognition, 18,* 174–182.

Jones, H. E. (2006). Drug addiction during pregnancy. *Current Directions in Psychological Science, 15,* 126–130.

Jones, J. R., & Schaubroeck, J. (2004). Mediators of the relationship between race and organizational citizenship behavior. *Journal of Managerial Issues, 16,* 505–527.

Jones, M. A., Botsko, M., & Gorman, B. S. (2003). Predictors of psychotherapeutic benefit of lesbian, gay, and bisexual clients: The effects of sexual orientation matching and other factors. *Psychotherapy: Theory, Research, Practice, Training, 40,* 289–301.

Jonides, J., Lacey, S. C., & Nee, D. E. (2005). Processes of working memory in mind and brain. *Current Directions in Psychological Science, 14,* 2–5.

Jordan, N., Grissom, G., Alonzo, G., Dietzen, L., & Sangsland, S. (2008). Economic benefit of chemical dependency treatment to employers. *Journal of Substance Abuse Treatment, 34,* 311–319.

Jordan, N. C., Huttenlocher, J., & Levine, S. C. (1992). Differential calculation abilities in young children from middle- and low-income families. *Developmental Psychology, 28,* 644–653.

Jorge, R. E., Moser, D. J., Acion, L., & Robinson, R. G. (2008). Treatment of vascular depression using repetitive transcranial magnetic stimulation. *Archives of General Psychiatry, 65,* 268–276.

Josephson, W. L. (1987). Television violence and children's aggression: Testing the priming, social script, and disinhibition predictions. *Journal of Personality and Social Psychology, 53,* 882–890.

Joska, J. A., & Stein, D. J. (2008). Mood disorders. In R. E. Hales, S. C. Yudofsky, & G. O. Gabbard (Eds.), *Textbook of psychiatry* (pp. 457–503). Washington, DC: American Psychiatric Publishing.

Jost, J. T., & Hamilton, D. L. (2005). *Stereotypes in our culture.* In J. F. Dovidio, P. Glick, & L. Rudman (Eds.), *On the nature of prejudice: Fifty years after Allport* (pp. 208–224). Malden, MA: Blackwell Publishing.

Joy, J. E., Watson, S. J., Jr., & Benson, J. A., Jr. (1999). *Marijuana and medicine: Assessing the science base.* Washington, DC: National Academy Press.

Judd, F. K., Jackson, H. J., Komiti, A., Murray, G., Hodgins, G., Fraser, C. (2002). High prevalence disorders in urban and rural communities. *Australian and New Zealand Journal of Psychiatry, 36,* 104–113.

Judge, T. A., Colbert, A. E., & Ilies, R. (2004). Intelligence and leadership: A quantitative review and test of theoretical propositions. *Journal of Applied Psychology, 89,* 542–552.

Judge, T. A., Piccolo, R. F., & Ilies, R. (2004). The forgotten ones? The validity of consideration and initiating structure in leadership research. *Journal of Applied Psychology, 89,* 36–51.

Judge, T. A., Thoresen, C. J., Bono, J. E., & Patton, G. K. (2001). The job satisfaction-job performance relationship: A qualitative and quantitative review. *Psychological Bulletin, 127,* 376–407.

Julien, R. M. (2005). *A primer of drug action* (10th ed.). New York: Worth.

Julien, R. M. (2008). *A primer of drug action* (11th ed.). New York: Worth.

Jung, C. G. (1916). *Analytical psychology.* New York: Moffat.

Jung, C. G. (1933). *Psychological types.* New York: Harcourt, Brace and World.

Jurcevic, S., Urlic, I., & Vlastelica, M. (2005). Denial and dissociation as coping strategies in mothers' postmortem identification of their sons. *American Imago, 62*(4), 395–418.

Jureidini, J. N., Doecke, C. J., Mansfield, P. R., Haby, M. M., Menkes, D. B., & Tonkin, A. L. (2004). Efficacy and safety of antidepressants for children and adolescents. *British Medical Journal, 328,* 879–883.

Jussim, L., & Eccles, J. S. (1992). Teacher expectations: II. Construction and reflection of student achievement. *Journal of Personality and Social Psychology, 63,* 947–961.

Just, M. A., Carpenter, P. A., Keller, T. A., Emery, L., Zajac, H., & Thulborn, K. R. (2001). Interdependence of nonoverlapping cortical systems in dual cognitive tasks. *Neuroimage, 14,* 417–426.

Just, N., & Alloy, L. B. (1997). The response styles theory of depression: Tests and an extension of the theory. *Journal of Abnormal Psychology, 106,* 221–229.

Kadotani, H., Kadotani, T., Young, T., Peppard, P. E., Finn, L., Colrain, I. M., et al. (2001). Association between apolipoprotein E epsilon4 and sleep-disordered breathing in adults. *Journal of the American Medical Association, 285,* 2888–2890.

Kagan, J. R., Snidman, N., Arcus, D., & Resnick, J. S. (1994). *Galen's prophecy: Temperament in human nature.* New York: Basic Books.

Kahn, E., & Rachman, A. W. (2000). Carl Rogers and Heinz Kohut: A historical perspective. *Psychoanalytic Psychology, 17,* 294–312.

Kahneman, D., & Tversky, A. (1973). On the psychology of prediction. *Psychological Review, 80,* 237–251.

Kahneman, D., & Tversky, A. (1984). Choices, values, and frames. *American Psychologist, 29,* 341–356.

Kahneman, D., Krueger, A. B., Schkade, D., Schwarz, N., & Stone, A. A. (2006). Would you be happier if you were richer? A focusing illusion. *Science, 312,* 1908–1910.

Kaiser, R. B., Hogan, R., & Craig, S. B. (2008). Leadership and the fate of organizations. *American Psychologist, 63,* 96–110.

Kaitaro, T. (2001). Biological and epistemological models of localization in the nineteenth century: From Gall to Charcot. *Journal of Historical Neuroscience, 10*(3), 262–276.

Kajantie, E. (2008). Physiological stress response, estrogen, and the male-female mortality gap. *Current Directions in Psychological Science, 17,* 348–352.

Kajantie, E. J., & Phillips, D. I. W. (2006). The effects of sex and hormonal status on the physiological response to acute psychosocial stress. *Psychoneuroendocrinology, 31,* 151–178.

Kajiya, K., Inaki, K., Tanaka, M., Haga, T., Kataoka, H., & Touhara, K. (2001). Molecular bases of odor discrimination: Reconstition of olfactory receptors that recognize overlapping sets of odorants. *Journal of Neuroscience, 21,* 6018–6025.

Kalb, L. M., & Loeber, R. (2003). Child disobedience and noncompliance: A review. *Pediatrics, 111,* 641–652.

Kalechstein, A. D., De La Garza, R., II, Mahoney, J. J., III, Fantegrossi, W. E., & Newton, T. F. (2007). MDMA use and neurocognition: A meta-analytic review. *Psychopharmacology* (Berlin), *189,* 531–537.

Kales, A., & Kales, J. (1973). Recent advances in the diagnosis and treatment of sleep disorders. In G. Usdin (Ed.), *Sleep research and clinical practice.* New York: Brunner/Mazel.

Kales, H. C., DiNardo, A. R., Blow, F. C., McCarthy, J. F., et al. (2006). International medical graduates and the diagnosis and treatment of late-life depression. *Academic Medicine, 81,* 171–175.

Kalivas, P. W., & Volkow, N. D. (2005). The neural basis of addiction: A pathology of motivation and choice. *American Journal of Psychiatry, 162,* 1403–1413.

Kalsbeek, A., Palm, I. F., La Fleur, S. E., Scheer, F. A., Perreau-Lenz, S., Ruiter, M., et al. (2006). SCN outputs and the hypothalamic balance of life. *Journal of Biological Rhythms, 21,* 458–469.

Kamin, L. J. (1969). Predictability, surprise, attention, and conditioning. In B. A. Campbell & R. M. Church (Eds.), *Punishment and aversive behavior* (pp. 279–296). New York: Appleton-Century-Crofts.

Kaminski, J. W., Valle, L. A., Filene, J. H., & Boyle, C. L. (2008). A meta-analytic review of components associated with parent training program effectiveness. *Journal of Abnormal Child Psychology, 36,* 567–589.

Kammers, M. P. M., de Vignemont, F., Verhagen, L., & Dijkerman, H. C. (2009). The rubber hand illusion in action. *Neuropsychologia, 47*(1), 204–211.

Kammeyer-Mueller, J. D., Wanberg, C. R., Glomb, T. M., & Ahlburg, D. (2005). The role of temporal shifts in turnover processes: It's about time. *Journal of Applied Psychology, 90,* 644–658.

Kammrath, L. K., Mendoza-Denton, R., & Mischel, W. (2005). Incorporating if . . . then . . . personality signatures in person perception: Beyond the person situation dichotomy. *Journal of Personality and Social Psychology, 88,* 605–618.

Kamphuis, J. H., & Emmelkamp, P. M. (2001). Traumatic distress among support-seeking female victims of stalking. *American Journal of Psychiatry, 158,* 795–798.

Kane, J. M., Eerdekens, M., Lindenmayer, J.-P., Keith, S. J., Lesem, M., & Karcher, K. (2003). Long-acting injectable risperidone: Efficacy and safety of the first long-acting atypical antipsychotic. *American Journal of Psychiatry, 160,* 1125–1132.

Kaner, A., & Prelinger, E. (2007). *The craft of psychodynamic psychotherapy* (2nd ed.). Lanham, MD: Jason Aronson Publishers.

Kanki, B. J., & Foushee, H. C. (1990). Crew factors in the aerospace workplace. In S. Oskamp & S. Spacepan (Eds.), *People's reactions to technology* (pp. 18–31). Newbury Park, CA: Sage.

Kanno, T., Mitsugi, M., Sukegawa, S., Hosoe, M., & Furuki, Y. (2008). Computer-simulated bi-directional alveolar distraction osteogenesis. *Clinical Oral Implants Research, 19*(12), 1211–1218.

Kapogiannis, D., Barbey, A. K., Su, M., Zamboni, G., Krueger, F., & Grafman, J. (2009). Cognitive and neural foundations of religious belief. *Proceedings of the National Academy of Sciences, 106,* 4876–4881.

Kaptchuk, T. J. (2001). Methodological issues in trials of acupuncture. *Journal of the American Medical Association, 285,* 1015–1016.

Kapur, S., Sridhar, N., & Remington, G. (2004). The newer antipsychotics: Underlying mechanisms and the new clinical realities. *Current Opinion in Psychiatry, 17*(2), 115–121.

Karasz, A. (2005). Cultural differences in conceptual models of depression. *Social Science and Medicine, 60,* 1625–1635.

Karni, A., Meyer, G., Adams, M., Turner, R., & Ungerleider, L. G. (1994). The acquisition and retention of a motor skill: A functional MRI study of long-term motor cortex plasticity. *Abstracts of the Society for Neuroscience, 20,* 1291.

Karon, B. P., & Widener, A. J. (1997). Repressed memories and World War II: Lest we forget. *Professional Psychology: Research and Practice, 28*(4), 338–340.

Karp, D. A. (1991). A decade of reminders: Changing age consciousness between fifty and sixty years old. In B. B. Hess & E. W. Markson (Eds.), *Growing old in America* (pp. 67–92). New Brunswick, NJ: Transaction.

Karver, M. S., Handelsman, J. B., Fields, S., & Bickman, L. (2006). Meta-analysis of therapeutic relationship variables in youth and family therapy: The evidence for different relationship variables in the child and adolescent treatment outcome literature. *Clinical Psychology Review, 26,* 50–65.

Kasagi, F., Akahoshi, M., & Shimaoki, K. (1995). Relation between cold pressor test and development of hypertension based on 28-year follow-up. *Hypertension, 25,* 71–76.

Kasen, S., Cohen, P., Chen, H., & Must, A. (2008). Obesity and psychopathology in women: A three decade prospective study. *International Journal of Obesity, 32,* 558–566.

Kasper, S., & Papadimitriou, G. N. (Eds.) (2009). *Schizophrenia* (2nd ed.). New York: Informa Health Care.

Kassin, S. M., Rigby, S., & Castillo, S. R. (1991). The accuracy-confidence correlation in eyewitness testimony: Limits and extensions of the retrospective self-awareness effect. *Journal of Personality and Social Psychology, 61,* 698–707.

Kassin, S., Fein, S., & Markus, H. (2008). *Social Psychology.* Boston, MA: Houghton-Mifflin.

Kastin, A. J., & Pan, W. (2005). Targeting neurite growth inhibitors to induce CNS regeneration. *Current Pharmaceutical Design, 11,* 1247–1253.

Katkin, E. S., Wiens, S., & Öhman, A. (2001). Nonconscious fear conditioning, visceral perception, and the development of gut feelings. *Psychological Science, 12,* 366–370.

Kato, S., Wakasa, Y., & Yamagita, T. (1987). Relationship between minimum reinforcing doses and injection speed in cocaine and pentobarbital self-administration in crab-eating monkeys. *Pharmacology, Biochemistry, and Behavior, 28,* 407–410.

Katsavelis, D., Siu, K.-S., Brown-Clerk, B., Lee, I. H., Oleynikov, D., & Stergiou, N. (2007). Learning robotic surgical skills with a virtual reality environment. *Journal of Sport & Exercise Psychology, 29,* S91–S92.

Katzell, R. A., & Thompson, D. E. (1990). Work motivation: Theory and practice. *American Psychologist, 45,* 144–153.

Kauffman, N. A., Herman, C. P., & Polivy, J. (1995). Hunger-induced finickiness in humans. *Appetite, 24,* 203–218.

Kaufman, J., & Charney, D. (2000). Comorbidity of mood and anxiety disorders. *Depression and Anxiety, 12*(Suppl. 1), 69–76.

Kaufman, J., Yang, B.-Z., Douglas-Palumberi, H., Crouse-Artus, M., Lipschitz, D., Krystal, J. H., & Gelernter, J. (2007). Genetic and environmental predictors of early alcohol use. *Biological Psychiatry, 61,* 1228–1234.

Kaufman, L., & Kaufman, J. H. (2000). Explaining the moon illusion. *Proceedings of the National Academy of Sciences, 97,* 500–505.

Kaulfuss, P., Mills, D. S. (2008). Neophilia in domestic dogs (*Canis familiaris*) and its implication for studies of dog cognition. *Animal Cognition, 11*(3), 553–556.

Kawakami, K., Dovidio, J. F., & van Kamp, S. (2005). Kicking the habit: Effects of nonstereotypic association training and correction processes on hiring decisions. *Journal of Experimental Social Psychology, 41,* 68–75.

Kawamura, N., Kim, Y., & Asukai, N. (2001). Suppression of cellular immunity in men with a past history of posttraumatic stress disorder. *American Journal of Psychiatry, 158,* 484–486.

Kawasaki, H., Adolphs, R., Kaufman, O., Damasio, H., Damasio, A. R., Granner, M., et al. (2001). Single-neuron responses to emotional visual stimuli recorded in human ventral prefrontal cortex. *Nature Neuroscience, 4,* 15–16.

Kaye, W. H., Klump, K. L., Frank, G. K., & Strober, M. (2000). Anorexia and bulimia nervosa. *Annual Review of Medicine, 51,* 299–313.

Kazantzis, N., Deane, F. P., Ronan, K., & L'Abate, L. (2005). *Using homework assignments in cognitive-behavioral therapy.* London: Taylor and Francis.

Kazantzis, N., Lampropoulos, G. K., & Deane, F. P. (2005). A national survey of practicing psychologists' use and attitudes toward homework in psychotherapy. *Journal of Consulting and Clinical Psychology, 73,* 742–748.

Kazarian, S. S., & Evans, D. R. (Eds.). (2001). *Handbook of cultural health psychology.* New York: Academic Press.

Kazdin, A. E. (1994). Methodology, design, and evaluation in psychotherapy research. In A. E. Bergin & S. L. Garfield (Eds.), *Handbook of psychotherapy and behavior change* (4th ed., pp. 19–71). New York: Wiley.

Kazdin, A. E. (2003). Clinical significance: Measuring whether interventions make a difference. In A. E. Kazdin (Ed.), *Methodological issues and strategies in clinical research* (3rd ed., pp. 691–710). Washington, DC: American Psychological Association.

Kazdin, A. E. (2008). *Behavior modification in applied settings* (6th ed.). Long Grove, IL: Waveland Press.

Kazdin, A. E., & Weisz, J. R. (1998). Identifying and developing empirically supported child and adolescent treatments. *Journal of Consulting and Clinical Psychology, 66,* 19–36.

Kazdin, A. E., & Weisz, J. R. (2003). *Evidence-based psychotherapies for children and adolescents.* New York: Guilford.

Kealy, E. M. (2005). Variations in the experience of schizophrenia: A cross-cultural review. *Journal of Social Work Research and Evaluation, 6,* 47–56.

Keating, D. P. (1990). Adolescent thinking. In S. S. Feldman & G. R. Elliott (Eds.), *At the threshold: The developing adolescent* (pp. 4–89). Cambridge, MA: Harvard University Press.

Keel, P. K., & Klump, K. L. (2003). Are eating disorders culture-bound syndromes? Implications for conceptualizing their etiology. *Psychological Bulletin, 129,* 749–769.

Keeling, L. J., & Hurink, J. F. (1996). Social facilitation acts more on the consummatory phase on feeding behaviour. *Animal Behaviour, 52,* 11–15.

Keenan, K., Hipwell, A., Feng, X., Babinski, D., Hinze, A., et al. (2008). Subthreshold symptoms of depression in preadolescent girls are stable and predictive of depressive disorders. *Journal of the American Academy of Child and Adolescent Psychiatry, 47,* 1433–1442.

Keenan, K., & Wakschlag, L. S. (2004). Are oppositional defiant and conduct disorder symptoms normative behaviors in preschoolers? A comparison of referred and nonreferred children. *American Journal of Psychiatry, 161,* 356–358.

Keenan, K., Wakschlag, L. S., Danis, B., Hill, C., Humphries, M., Daux, J., & Radiah, D. (2007). Further evidence of reliability and validity of DSM-IV ODD and CD in preschool children. *Journal of the American Academy of Child and Adolescent Psychiatry, 46,* 457–468.

Keenan, P. S. (2009). Smoking and weight change after new health diagnoses in older adults. *Archives of Internal Medicine, 169,* 237–242.

Keene, J. R., & Prokos, A. H. (2007). The sandwiched generation: Multiple caregiving responsibilities and the mismatch between actual and preferred work hours. *Sociological Spectrum, 27*(4), 365–387.

Keesey, R. E., & Powley, T. L. (1986). The regulation of body weight. *Annual Review of Psychology, 37,* 109–133.

Keller, M. B., McCullough, J. P., Klein, D. N., Arnow, B., Dunner, D. L., Gelenberg, A. J., et al. (2000). A comparison of nefazodone, the cognitive behavioral- analysis system of psychotherapy, and their combination for the treatment of chronic depression. *New England Journal of Medicine, 342,* 1462–1470.

Keller, R. T. (2006). Transformational leadership, initiating structure, and substitutes for leadership: A longitudinal study of research and development project team performance. *Journal of Applied Psychology, 91,* 202–210.

Keller-Cohen, D., Toler, A., Fiori, K., & Bybee, D. (2004, August). *Social contact and communication in people over 85.* Paper presented at the convention of the American Psychological Association, Honolulu, HI.

Kelley, A. E., & Berridge, K. C. (2002). The neuroscience of natural rewards: Relevance to addictive drugs. *Journal of Neuroscience, 22,* 3306–3311.

Kelley, K. W. (1985). Immunological consequences of changing environmental stimuli. In G. P. Moberg (Ed.), *Animal stress.* Bethesda, MD: American Physiological Society.

Kellman, P. J., & Arterberry, M. E. (2006). Infant visual perception. In W. Damon & R. M. Lerner (Series Eds.) & D. Kuhn & R. Siegler (Vol. Eds.), *Handbook of child psychology: Vol. 2. Cognition, perception, and language* (6th ed.). New York: Wiley.

Kellner, C. H., Fink, M., Knapp, R., Petrides, G., Husain, M., Rummans, T., et al. (2005). Relief of expressed suicidal intent by ECT: A consortium for research in ECT study. *American Journal of Psychiatry, 162,* 977–982.

Kellner, C. H., Knapp, R. G., Petrides, G., Rummans, T. A., Husain, M. M., Rasmussen, K., et al. (2006). Continuation electroconvulsive therapy vs pharmacotherapy for relapse prevention in major depression. *Archives of General Psychiatry, 63,* 1337–1344.

Kellum, K. K., Carr, J. E., & Dozier, C. L. (2001). Response-card instruction and student learning in a college classroom. *Teaching of Psychology, 28,* 101–104.

Kelly, D. J., Quinn, P. C., Slater, A. M., Lee, K., Ge, L., & Pascalis, O. (2007). The other-race effect develops during infancy: Evidence of perceptual narrowing. *Psychological Science 18,* 1084–1089.

Kelly, G. A. (1980). A psychology of the optimal man. In A. W. Landfield & L. M. Leitner (Eds.), *Personal construct psychology: Psychotherapy and personality.* New York: Wiley.

Kelly, J. F. (2003). Self-help for substance-use disorders: History, effectiveness, knowledge gaps and research opportunities. *Clinical Psychology Review, 23*(5), 639–663.

Kelly, T., Yang, W., Chen, C.-S., Reynolds, K., & He, J. (2008). Global burden of obesity in 2005 and projections to 2030. *International Journal of Obesity, 32,* 1431–1437.

Kelly, T. H., Foltin, R. W., Emurian, C. S., & Fischman, M. W. (1990). Multidimensional behavioral effects of marijuana. *Progress in Neuro-Psychopharmacology and Biological Psychiatry, 14,* 885–902.

Keltner, D., & Buswell, B. N. (1996). Evidence for the distinctiveness of embarrassment, shame, and guilt: A study of recalled antecedents and facial expressions of emotion. *Cognition and Emotion, 10,* 117–125.

Kemble, E. D., Filipi, T., & Gravlin, L. (1985). Some simple classroom experiments on cerebral lateralization. *Teaching of Psychology, 12,* 81–83.

Kemeny, M. E. (2003). The psychobiology of stress. *Current Directions in Psychological Science, 12,* 124–129.

Kendall, P. C., & Chambless, D. L. (Eds.). (1998). Special section: Empirically supported psychological therapies. *Journal of Consulting and Clinical Psychology, 66,* 3–167.

Kendall, P. C., & Choudhury, M. S. (2003). Children and adolescents in cognitive-behavioral therapy: Some past efforts and current advances, and the challenges in our future. *Cognitive Therapy and Research, 27,* 89–104.

Kendall, P. C., Hudson, J. L., Gosch, A., Flannery-Schroeder, E., & Suveg, C. (2008). Cognitive-behavioral therapy for anxiety disordered youth: A randomized clinical trial evaluating child and family modalities. *Journal of Consulting and Clinical Psychology, 76,* 282–297.

Kendell, R., & Jablensky, A. (2003). Distinguishing between the validity and utility of psychiatric diagnoses. *American Journal of Psychiatry, 160,* 4–12.

Kendler, K. S. (2005). "A gene for . . .": The nature of gene action in psychiatric disorders. *American Journal of Psychiatry, 162,* 1243–1252.

Kendler, K. S., Gardner, C. O., & Prescott, C. A. (2006). Toward a comprehensive developmental model for major depression in men. *American Journal of Psychiatry, 163,* 115–124.

Kendler, K. S., Gatz, M., Gardner, C. O., & Pedersen, N. L. (2006). A Swedish national twin study of lifetime major depression. *American Journal of Psychiatry, 163,* 109–114.

Kendler, K. S., Hettema, J. M., Butera, F., Gardner, C. O., & Prescott, C. A. (2003). Life event dimensions of loss, humiliation, entrapment, and danger in the prediction of onsets of major depression and generalized anxiety. *Archives of General Psychiatry, 60,* 789–796.

Kendler, K. S., Jacobson, K. C., Myers, J., & Prescott, C. A. (2002). Sex differences in genetic and environmental risk factors for irrational fears and phobias. *Psychological Medicine, 32,* 209–217.

Kendler, K. S., Jacobson, K. C., Prescott, C. A., & Neale, M. C. (2003). Specificity of genetic and environmental risk factors for use and abuse/dependence of cannabis, cocaine, hallucinogens, sedatives, stimulants, and opiates in male twins. *American Journal of Psychiatry, 160,* 687–695.

Kendler, K. S., Kuhn, J., & Prescott, C. A. (2004). The interrelationship of neuroticism, sex, and stressful life events in the prediction of episodes of major depression. *American Journal of Psychiatry, 161,* 631–636.

Kendler, K. S., Thornton, L. M., & Prescott, C. A. (2001). Gender differences in the rates of exposure to stressful life events and sensitivity to their depressogenic effects. *American Journal of Psychiatry, 158,* 587–593.

Kenrick, D. T., Groth, G., Trost, M., & Sadalla, E. K. (1993). Integrating evolutionary and social exchange perspectives on relationships: Effects of gender, self- appraisal, and involvement level on mate selection. *Journal of Personality and Social Psychology, 64,* 951–969.

Kenrick, D., Neuberg, S., & Cialdini, R. (2005). *Social psychology: Unraveling the mystery* (3rd ed.). Boston, MA: Pearson.

Kenrick, D., Neuberg, S., & Cialdini, R. (2007). *Social psychology: Goals in interaction* (4th ed.). Upper Saddle River, NJ: Pearson.

Kensinger, E. A., & Corkin, S. (2004). Two routes to emotional memory: Distinct neural processes for valence and arousal. *Proceedings of the National Academy of Sciences, 101,* 3310–3315.

Kent, S., Rodriguez, F., Kelley, K. W., & Dantzer, R. (1994). Reduction in food and water intake induced by microinjection of interleukin-1b in the ventromedial hypothalamus of the rat. *Physiology and Behavior, 56*(5), 1031–1036.

Kenworthy, J. B., Turner, R. N., Hewstone, M., & Voci, A. (2006). Intergroup contact: When does it work, and why. In J. Dovidio, P. Glick, & L. Rudman (Eds.), *On the nature of prejudice: Fifty years after Allport.* Boston, MA: Blackwell.

Keogh, E., Bond, F. W., & Flaxman, P. E. (2006). Improving academic performance and mental health through a stress management intervention: Outcomes and mediators of change. *Behaviour Research and Therapy, 44,* 339–357.

Keough, M. E., Timpano, K. R., & Schmidt, N. B. (2009). Ataques de nervios: Culturally-bound and distinct from panic attacks? *Depression and Anxiety, 26,* 16–21.

Kepner, J. (2001). Touch in Gestalt body process psychotherapy: Purpose, practice, and ethics. *Gestalt Review, 5,* 97–114.

Kermer, D. A., Driver-Linn, E., Wilson, T. D., & Gilbert, D. T. (2006). Loss aversion is an affective forecasting error. *Psychological Science, 17,* 649–653.

Kern, M. L., & Friedman, H. S. (2008). Do conscientious individuals live longer? A quantitative review. *Health Psychology, 27,* 505–512.

Kerr, M. P., & Payne, S. J. (1994). Learning to use a spreadsheet by doing and by watching. *Interacting with Computers, 6,* 3–22.

Kerr, N. L., & Tindale, R. S. (2004). Group performance and decision making. *Annual Review of Psychology, 55,* 623–655.

Kersting, K. (2004, September). Cross-cultural training: 30 years and going strong. *Monitor on Psychology,* 48–49.

Kertesz, A. (1993). Clinical forms of aphasia. *Acta Neurochirurgica. Supplementum (Wien), 56,* 52–58.

Keselman, H. J., Othman, A. R., Wilcox, R. R., & Fradette, K. (2004). The new and improved two-sample t test. *Psychological Science, 15,* 47–51.

Keshavan, M. S., Diwadkar, V. A., Montrose, D. M., Rajarethinam, R., & Sweeny, J. A. (2005). Premorbid indicatgors and risk for schizophrenia: A selective review and update. *Schizophrenia Research, 79,* 45–57.

Kessels, R. P. C., Kortrijk, H. E., Wester, A. J., & Nys, G. M. S. (2008). Confabulation behavior and false memories in Korsakoff's syndrome: Role of source memory and executive functioning. *Psychiatry and Clinical Neurosciences, 62*(2), 220–225.

Kessler, R. C., Adler, L., Barkley, R., Biederman, J., Conners, C. K., Demler, O., et al. (2006). The prevalence and correlates of adult ADHD in the United States: Results from the National Comorbidity Survey Replication. *American Journal of Psychiatry, 163,* 716–723.

Kessler, R. C., Berglund, P., Borges, G., Nock, M., & Wang, P. S. (2005). Trends in suicide ideation, plans, gestures, and attempts in the United States, 1990–1992 to 2001–2003. *Journal of the American Medical Association, 293,* 2487–2495.

Kessler, R. C., Berglund, P., Demier, O., Jin, R., & Walters, E. E. (2005). Lifetime prevalence of and age of onset distributions of DSM-IV disorders in the national comorbidity survey replication. *Archives of General Psychiatry, 62,* 593–602.

Kessler, R. C., Chiu, W. T., Demier, O., & Walters, E. E. (2005). Prevalence, severity, and comorbidity of 12-month DSM-IV disorders in the national comorbidity survey replication. *Archives of General Psychiatry, 62,* 617–627.

Kessler, R. C., Chiu, W. T., Jin, R., Ruscio, A. M., Shear, K., & Walters, E. E. (2006). The epidemiology of panic attacks, panic disorder, and agoraphobia in the National Comorbidity Survey Replication. *Archives of General Psychiatry, 63,* 415–424.

Kessler, R. C., Demler, O., Frank, R. G., Olfson, M., Pincus, H. A., et al. (2005). Prevalence and treatment of mental disorders, 1990 to 2003. *New England Journal of Medicine, 352,* 2515–2523.

Kessler, R. C., Galea, S., Gruber, M. J., Sampson, N. A., Ursano, R. J., & Wessely, S. (2008). Trends in mental illness and suicidality after Hurricane Katrina. *Molecular Psychiatry, 13,* 374–384.

Kessler, R. C., Heeringa, S., Lakoma, M. D., Petukhova, M., Rupp, A. E., Schoenbaum, M., Wang, P. S., & Zaslavsky, A. M. (2008). Individual and societal effects of mental disorders on earnings in the United States: Results from the national comorbidity survey replication. *American Journal of Psychiatry, 165*(6), 703–711.

Kessler, R. C., Ruscio, A., Shear, K., & Wittchen, H.-U. (2009). Epidemiology of anxiety disorders. In M. M. Antony & M. B. Stein (Eds.), *Oxford handbook of anxiety and related disorders* (pp. 19–33). New York: Oxford University Press.

Kest, B., Wilson, S. G., & Mogil, J. S. (1999). Sex differences in supraspinal morphine analgesia are dependent on genotype. *Journal of Pharmacology & Experimental Therapeutics, 289,* 1370–1375.

Kety, S. S., Wender, P. H., Jacobsen, B., Ingraham, L. J., Jansson, L., Faber, B., & Kinney, D. K. (1994). Mental illness in the biological and adoptive relatives of schizophrenic adoptees. *Archives of General Psychiatry, 51,* 442–455.

Keverne, E. B., & Curley, J. P. (2008). Epigenetics, brain evolution and behaviour. *Frontiers in Neuroendocrinology, 29*(3), 398–412.

Khan, A., Leventhal, R. M., Khan, S., & Brown, W. A. (2002). Suicide risk in patients with anxiety disorders: A meta-analysis of the FDA database. *Journal of Affective Disorders, 69,* 183–190.

Khan, J., Wei, J. S., Ringner, M., Saal, L. H., Ladanyi, M., Westermann, F., et al. (2001). Classification and diagnostic prediction of cancers using gene expression profiling and artificial neural networks. *Nature Medicine, 7,* 673–679.

Khanna, C., & Medsker, G. J. (2007). 2006 income and employments survey results for the Society of Industrial and Organizational Psychology. *The Industrial-Organizational Psychologist, 45,* 17–34.

Khashan, A. S., McNamee, R., Abel, K. M., Pedersen, M. G., Webb, R. T., Kenny, L. C., Mortensen, P. B., & Baker, P. N. (2008). Reduced infant birthweight consequent upon maternal exposure to severe life events. *Psychosomatic Medicine, 70,* 688–694.

Khot, U. N., Khot, M. B., Bajzer, C. T., Sapp, S. K., Ohman, E. M., Brener, S. J., et al. (2003). Prevalence of conventional risk factors in patients with coronary heart disease. *Journal of the American Medical Association, 290,* 898–904.

Kiecolt-Glaser, J. K., & Glaser, R. (2001). Stress and immunity: Age enhances the risks. *Current Directions in Psychological Science, 10,* 18–21.

Kiecolt-Glaser, J. K., Loving, T. J., Stowell, J. R., Malarkey, W. B., Lemeshow, S., Dickinson, S. L., et al. (2005). Hostile marital interactions, proinflammatory cytokine production, and wound healing. *Archives of General Psychiatry, 62,* 1377–1384.

Kiecolt-Glaser, J. K., McGuire, L., Robles, T. F., & Glaser, R. (2002). Psychoneuroimmunology: Psychological influences on immune function and health. *Journal of Consulting & Clinical Psychology, 70,* 537–547.

Kiecolt-Glaser, J. K., & Newton, T. L. (2001). Marriage and health: His and hers. *Psychological Bulletin, 127,* 472–503.

Kiecolt-Glaser, J. K., Page, G. G., Marucha, P. T., MacCallum, R. C., & Glaser, R. (1998). Psychological influences on surgical recovery: Perspectives from psychoneuroimmunology. *American Psychologist, 11,* 1209–1218.

Kiecolt-Glaser, J. K., Preacher, K. J., MacCallum, R. C., Atkinson, C., Malarkey, W. B., & Glaser, R. (2003). Chronic stress and age-related increases in the proinflammatory cytokine IL-6. *Proceedings of the National Academy of Sciences, 100,* 9090–9095.

Kieffer, K. M., Schinka, J. A., & Curtiss, G. (2004). Person-environment congruence and personality domains in the prediction of job performance and work quality. *Journal of Counseling Psychology, 51,* 168–177.

Kiehl, K. A., Bates, A. T., Laurens, K. R., Hare, R. D., & Liddle, P. F. (2006). Brain potentials implicate temporal lobe abnormalities in criminal psychopaths. *Journal of Abnormal Psychology, 115,* 443–453.

Kieseppä, T., Partonen, T., Haukka, J., Kaprio, J., & Lönnqvist, J. (2004). High concordance of bipolar I disorder in a nationwide sample of twins. *American Journal of Psychiatry, 161,* 1814–1821.

Kiesler, D. J. (1996). *Contemporary interpersonal theory and research.* New York: Wiley.

Kiewra, K. A. (1989). A review of note-taking: The encoding storage paradigm and beyond. *Educational Psychology Review, 1,* 147–172.

Kihlstrom, J. F. (1999). The psychological unconscious. In L. Pervin & O. John (Eds.), *Handbook of personality* (pp. 424–442). New York: Guilford.

Kihlstrom, J. F. (2005). Dissociative disorders. *Annual Review of Clinical Psychology, 1,* 227–253.

Kihlstrom, J. F. (2008). The psychological unconscious. In O. John, R. Robins, & L. Pervin (Eds.), *Handbook of personality: Theory and research* (3rd ed. pp., 583–602). New York: Guilford.

Kilbourne, A. M., Haas, G. L., Musant, B. H., Bauer, M. S., & Picnus, H. A. (2004). Concurrent psychiatric diagnosis by age and race among persons with bipolar disorder. *Psychiatric Services, 55,* 931–933.

Kim, E. Y., Mahmoud, G. S., & Grover, L. M. (2005). REM sleep deprivation inhibits LTP in vivo in area CA1 of rat hippocampus. *Neuroscience Letters, 388,* 163–167.

Kim, J., & Hatfield, E. (2004). Love types and subjective well-being: A cross- cultural study. *Social Behavior and Personality, 32,* 173–182.

Kim, K., & Rohner, R. P. (2002). Parental warmth, control, and involvement in schooling: Predicting academic achievement among Korean American adolescents. *Journal of Cross-Cultural Psychology, 33*(2), 127–140.

Kim, N. S., & Ahn, W.-K. (2002). Clinical psychologists' theory-based representations of mental disorders predict their diagnostic reasoning and memory. *Journal of Experimental Psychology: General, 131,* 451–476.

Kimchi, R. (2003). Relative dominance of holistic and component properties in the perceptual organization of visual objects. In M. A. Peterson & G. Rhodes (Eds.), *Perception of faces, objects, and scenes* (pp. 235–268). New York: Oxford University Press.

Kim-Cohen, J., Arseneault, L., Caspi, A., Tomás, M. P., Taylor, A., & Moffitt, T. E. (2005). Validity of DSM-IV conduct disorder in 41/2-5-year-old children: A longitudinal epidemiological study. *American Journal of Psychiatry, 162,* 1108–1117.

King, C. R., Knutson, K. L., Rathouz, P. J., Sidney, S., Liu, K., & Lauderdale, D. S. (2008). Short sleep duration and incident coronary artery calcification. *Journal of the American Medical Association, 300,* 2859–28566.

King, D. B., & DiCicco, T. L. (2007). The relationships between dream content and physical health, mood, and self-construal. *Dreaming, 17,* 127–139.

King, J. E., Weiss, A., & Farmer, K. H. (2005). A chimpanzee (*pan troglodytes*) analogue of cross-national generalization of personality structure: Zoological parks and an African sanctuary. *Journal of Personality, 73,* 389–410.

King, M., Nazareth, I., Levy, G., Walker, C., Morris, R., et al. (2008). Prevalence of common mental disorders in general practice attendees across Europe. *British Journal of Psychiatry, 192,* 362–367.

King, M., Smith, G., & Bartlett, A. (2004). Treatments of homosexuality in Britain since the 1950s—an oral history: The experience of professionals. *British Medical Journal, 328,* 429–432.

Kingdom, F. A. (2003). Color brings relief to human vision. *Nature Neuroscience, 6,* 641–644.

Kingsbury, K., & McLeod, K. (2008, June 30). Postcard: Gloucester. *Time,* 8.

Kingston, D. A., Fedoroff, P., Firestone, P., Curry, S., & Bradford, J. (2008). Pornography use and sexual aggression: The impact of frequency and type of pornography use on recidivism among sexual offenders. *Aggressive Behavior, 34,* 341–351.

Kinsbourne, M., & Cook, J. (1971). Generalized and lateralized effects of concurrent verbalization on a unimanual skill. *Quarterly Journal of Experimental Psychology, 23,* 341–345.

Kinsey, A. C., Pomeroy, W. B., & Martin, C. E. (1948). *Sexual behavior in the human male.* Philadelphia: Saunders.

Kinsey, A. C., Pomeroy, W. B., Martin, C. E., & Gebhard, P. H. (1953). *Sexual behavior in the human female.* Philadelphia: Saunders.

Kipps, C. M., Nestor, P. J., Acosta-Cabronero, J., Arnold, R., & Hodges, J. R. (2009). Understanding social dysfunction in the behavioural variant of frontotemporal dementia: The role of emotion and sarcasm processing. *Brain, 132,* 592–603.

Kircher, J. C., Horowitz, S. W., & Raskin, D. C. (1988). Meta-analysis of mock crime studies of the control question polygraph technique. *Law and Human Behavior, 12,* 79–90.

Kirkpatrick, B., Buchanan, R. W., Ross, D. E., & Carpenter, W. T., Jr. (2001). A separate disease within the syndrome of schizophrenia. *Archives of General Psychiatry, 58,* 165–171.

Kirsch, I. (1994a). Clinical hypnosis as a nondeceptive placebo: Empirically derived techniques. *American Journal of Clinical Hypnosis, 37*(2), 95–106.

Kirsch, I. (1994b). Defining hypnosis for the public. *Contemporary Hypnosis, 11*(3), 142–143.

Kirsch, I., & Braffman, W. (2001). Imaginative suggestibility and hypnotizability. *Psychological Science, 10,* 57–61.

Kirsch, I., Lynn, S. J., Vigorito, M., & Miller, R. R. (2004). The role of cognition in classical and operant conditioning. *Journal of Clinical Psychology, 60*(4), 369–392.

Kirsch, I., Moore, T. J., Scoboria, A., & Nicholls, S. S. (2002). The emperor's new drugs: An analysis of antidepressant medication data submitted to the U.S. Food and Drug Administration [Electronic version]. *Prevention and Treatment, 5,* np.

Kirsch, I., Scoboria, A., & Moore, T. J. (2002). Antidepressants and placebos: Secrets, revelations, and unanswered questions. *Prevention and Treatment, 5,* np.

Kirschenbaum, H., & Jourdan, A. (2005). The current status of Carl Rogers and the person-centered approach. *Psychotherapy: Theory, Research, Practice, Training, 42,* 37–51.

Kishi, T., & Elmquist, J. K. (2005). Body weight is regulated by the brain: A link between feeding and emotion. *Molecular Psychiatry, 10,* 132–146.

Kishioka, S., Miyamoto, Y., Fukunaga, Y., Nishida, S., & Yamamoto, H. (1994). Effects of a mixture of peptidase inhibitors (Amastatin, Captopril and Phosphoramidon) on met enkephalin, beta-endorphin, dynorphin (1–13) and electroacupuncture induced antinociception in rats. *Japanese Journal of Pharmacology, 66,* 337–345.

Kisilevsky, B. S., Hains, S. M. J., Lee, K., Xie, X., Huang, H., Ye, H. H., et al. (2003). Effects of experience on fetal voice recognition. *Psychological Science, 14,* 220–224.

Kitano, H., Chi, I., Rhee, S., Law, C., & Lubben, J. (1992). Norms and alcohol consumption: Japanese in Japan, Hawaii, and California. *Journal of Studies on Alcohol, 53,* 33–39.

Kitayama, N., Vaccarino, V., Kutner, M., Weiss, P., & Bremner, J. D. (2005). Magnetic resonance imaging (MRI) measurement of hippocampal volume in posttraumatic stress disorder: A meta-analysis. *Journal of Affective Disorders, 88,* 79–86.

Kitayama, S., & Markus, H. R. (1992, May). *Construal of self as cultural frame: Implications for internationalizing psychology.* Paper presented to the Symposium on Internationalization and Higher Education, Ann Arbor, Michigan.

Kitayama, S., Duffy, S., Kawamura, T., & Larsen, J. T. (2003). Perceiving an object and its context in different cultures: A cultural look at new look. *Psychological Science, 14,* 201–206.

Kitayama, S., Duffy, S., & Uchida, Y. (2007). Self as cultural mode of being. In S. Kitayama & D. Cohen (Eds.), *Handbook of cultural psychology.* New York: Guilford Press.

Kitayama, S., Snibbe, A. C., Markus, H. R., & Suzuki, T. (2004). Is there any "free" choice?: Self and dissonance in two cultures. *Psychological Science, 15,* 527–533.

Kiviniemi, V. (2008). Endogenous brain fluctuations and diagnostic imaging. *Human Brain Mapping, 29,* 810–817.

Kjaer, T. W., Bertelsen, C., Piccini, P., Brooks, D., Alving, J., & Lou, H. C. (2002). Increased dopamine tone during meditation-induced change of consciousness. *Cognitive Brain Research, 13,* 255–259.

Klahr, D., & Simon, H. (1999). Studies of scientific discovery: Complementary approaches and convergent findings. *Psychological Bulletin, 125,* 524–543.

Klaus, M. H., & Kennell, J. H. (1976). *Maternal infant bonding: The impact of early separation or loss on family development.* St. Louis: Mosby.

Klausner, H. A., & Lewandowski, C. (2002). Infrequent causes of stroke. *Emergency Medicine Clinics of North America, 20,* 657–670.

Kleemola, P., Jousilahti, P., Pietinen, P., Vartiainen, E., & Tuomilehto, J. (2000). Coffee consumption and the risk of coronary heart disease and death. *Archives of Internal Medicine, 160,* 3393–3400.

Klein, D., Lewinsohn, P. M., Seeley, J. R., & Rohde, P. (2001). A family study of major depressive disorder in a community sample of adolescents. *Archives of General Psychiatry, 58,* 13–20.

Klein, D. C., & Seligman, M. E. P. (1976). Reversal of performance deficits and perceptual deficits in learned helplessness and depression. *Journal of Abnormal Psychology, 85,* 11–26.

Klein, D. N., Santiago, N. J., Vivian, D., Blalock, J. A., Kocsis, J. H., Markowitz, J. C., et al. (2004). Cognitive-behavioral analysis system of psychotherapy as a maintenance treatment for chronic depression. *Journal of Consulting and Clinical Psychology, 72,* 681–688.

Klein, F. (1990). The need to view sexual orientation as a multivariable dynamic process: A theoretical perspective. In McWhirter, D. P., Sanders, S. A., & Reinisch, J. M. (Eds.), *Homosexuality/heterosexuality: Concepts of sexual orientation. The Kinsey Institute series* (Vol. 2, pp. 277–282). New York, NY: Oxford University Press.

Klein, H. J., Noe, R. A., & Wang, C. (2006). Motivation to learn and course outcomes: The impact of delivery mode, learning goal orientation, and perceived barriers and enablers. *Personnel Psychology, 59,* 665–702.

Klein, M. (1975). *The writings of Melanie Klein: Vol. 3.* London: Hogarth Press.

Klein, P. D. (1997). Multiplying the problems of intelligence by eight: A critique of Gardner's theory. *Canadian Journal of Education, 22,* 377–394.

Kleinknecht, R. A. (1991). *Mastering anxiety: The nature and treatment of anxious conditions.* New York: Plenum.

Kleinknecht, R. A. (1994). Acquisition of blood, injury, and needle fears and phobias. *Behaviour Research and Therapy, 32,* 817–823.

Kleinknecht, R. A. (2000). Social phobia. In M. Hersen & M. K. Biaggio (Eds.), *Effective brief therapies: A clinician's guide.* New York: Academic Press.

Kleinman, A. (1991, April). *Culture and DSM-IV: Recommendations for the introduction and for the overall structure.* Paper presented at the National Institute of Mental Health–sponsored Conference on Culture and Diagnosis, Pittsburgh, PA.

Kleinman, A. (2004). Culture and depression. *New England Journal of Medicine, 351,* 951–953.

Klepp, K.-I., Kelder, S. H., & Perry, C. L. (1995). Alcohol and marijuana use among adolescents: Long-term outcomes of the class of 1989 study. *Annals of Behavioral Medicine, 17,* 19–24.

Kline, S., & Groninger, L. D. (1991). The imagery bizarreness effect as a function of sentence complexity and presentation time. *Bulletin of the Psychonomic Society, 29,* 25–27.

Klinesmith, J., Kasser, T., & McAndrew, F. T. (2006). Guns, testosterone, and aggression: An experimental test of a mediational hypothesis. *Psychological Science, 17,* 568–571.

Kling, K. C., Hyde, J. S., Showers, C. J., & Buswell, B. N. (1999). Gender differences in self-esteem: A meta-analysis. *Psychological Bulletin, 125,* 470–500.

Klintsova, A. Y., & Greenough, W. T. (1999). Synaptic plasticity in cortical systems. *Current Opinion in Neurobiology, 9,* 203–208.

Klohnen, E., & Bera, S. (1998). Behavioral and experiential patterns of avoidantly and securely attached women across adulthood: A 31-year longitudinal perspective. *Journal of Personality and Social Psychology, 74,* 211–223.

Kluger, A. N., & DeNisi, A. (1998). Feedback interventions: Toward the understanding of a double-edged sword. *Current Directions in Psychological Science, 7,* 67–72.

Klump, K. L., & Culbert, K. M. (2007). Molecular genetic studies of eating disorders: Current status and future directions. *Current Directions in Psychological Science, 16,* 37–41.

Knack, W. A. (2009). Psychotherapy and Alcoholics Anonymous: An integrated approach. *Journal of Psychotherapy Integration, 19,* 86–109.

Knafo, A., Iervolino, A. C., & Plomin, R. (2005). Masculine girls and feminine boys: Genetic and environmental contributions to atypical gender development in early childhood. *Journal of Personality and Social Psychology, 88,* 400–412.

Knopman, D., & Selnes, O. (2003). Neuropsychology of dementia. In K. M. Heilman & E. Valenstein (Eds.), *Clinical neuropsychology* (4th ed.). New York: Oxford University Press.

Knopman, D. S. (2006). Dementia and cerebrovascular disease. *Mayo Clinic Proceedings, 81*(2), 223–230.

Kochanska, G., Aksan, N., & Joy, M. E. (2007). Children's fearfulness as a moderator of parenting in early socialization: Two longitudinal studies. *Developmental Psychology, 43,* 222–237.

Koechlin, E., & Hyafil, A. (2007). Anterior prefrontal function and the limits of human decision-making. *Science, 318,* 594–598.

Koger, S. M., Schettler, T., & Weiss, B. (2005). Environmental toxicants and developmental disabilities: A challenge for psychologists. *American Psychologist, 60,* 243–255.

Koh, P. O., Undie, A. S., Kabbani, N., Levenson, R., Goldman-Rakic, P. S., & Lidow, M. S. (2002). Up-regulation of neuronal calcium sensor-1 (NCS-1) in the prefrontal cortex of schizophrenic and bipolar patients. *Proceedings of the National Academies of Science, 100,* 313–317.

Kohlberg, L., & Gilligan, C. (1971). The adolescent as a philosopher: The discovery of the self in a postconventional world. *Daedalus, 100,* 1051–1086.

Köhler, W. (1924). *The mentality of apes.* New York: Harcourt Brace.

Köhler, W. (1976). *The mentality of apes* (E. Winter, Trans.). Oxford, UK: Liveright.

Kohnert, K. (2004). Cognitive and cognate-based treatments for bilingual aphasia: A case study. *Brain and Language, 91,* 294–302.

Kohut, H. (1984). Selected problems of self-psychological theory. In J. D. Lichtenberg & S. Kaplan (Eds.), *Reflections on self psychology* (pp. 387–416). Hillsdale, NJ: Erlbaum.

Kok, M. R., & Boon, M. E. (1996). Consequences of neural network technology for cervical screening: increase in diagnostic consistency and positive scores. *Cancer, 78,* 112–117.

Kolassa, I.-T., Kolassa, S., Bergmann, S., Lauche, R., Dilger, S., Miltner, W. H. R., & Musial, F. (2009). Interpretive bias in social phobia: An ERP study with morphed emotional schematic faces. *Cognition & Emotion, 23*(1), 69–95.

Kolata, G. (2002, August 19.). Male hormone therapy popular but untested. *New York Times.*

Kolata, G. (2003, April 22). Hormone studies: What went wrong? *New York Times.*

Kolata, G., & Markel, H. (2001, April 29). Baby not crawling? Reason seems to be less tummy time. *New York Times.*

Kolb, B., Gorny, G., Li, Y., Samaha, A.-N., & Robinson, T. E. (2003). Amphetamine or cocaine limits the ability of later experience to promote structural plasticity in the neocortex and nucleus accumbens. *Proceedings of the National Academy of Sciences, 100,* 10523–10528.

Kolonin, M. G., Saha, P. K., Chan, L., Pasqualini, R., & Arap, W. (2004). Reversal of obesity by targeted ablation of adipose tissue. *Nature Medicine, 10,* 625–632.

Komsi, N., Räikkönen, K., Heinonen, K., Pesonen, A.-K., Keskivaara, P., Järvenpää, A.-L., & Strandberg, T. E. (2008). Continuity of father-rated temperament from infancy to middle childhood. *Infant Behavior & Development, 31,* 239–254.

Kondoh, T., & Torii, K. (2008). Brain activation by unami substances via gustatory and visceral signaling pathways, and physiological significance. *Biological and Pharmaceutical Bulletin, 31*(10), 1827–1832.

Konecná, M., Lhota, S., Weiss, A., Urbánek, T., Adamová, T., & Pluhácek, J. (2008). Personality in free-ranging Hanuman langur (Semnopithecus entellus) males: Subjective ratings and recorded behavior. *Journal of Comparative Psychology, 122*(4), 379–389.

Kong, L. L., Allen, J. J. B., & Gilsky, E. L. (2008). Interidentity memory transfer in dissociative identity disorder. *Journal of Abnormal Psychology, 117,* 686–692.

Konijn, E. A., Bijvank, M. N., & Bushman, B. J. (2007). I wish I were a warrior: The role of wishful identification in the effects of violent video games on aggression in adolescent boys. *Developmental Psychology, 43,* 1038–1044.

Konrad, K., Neufang, S., Hanisch, C., Fink, G. R., & Herpertz-Dahlmann, B. (2006). Dysfunctional attentional networks in children with attention deficit/hyperactivity disorder: Evidence from an event-related functional magnetic imaging study. *Biological Psychiatry, 59,* 643–651.

Kontoghiorghes, C. (2004). Reconceptualizing the learning transfer conceptual framework: Empirical validation of a new systemic model. *International Journal of Training and Development, 8,* 210–221.

Konuk, E., Knipe, J., Eke, I., Yuksek, H., Yurtsever, A., & Ostep, S. (2006). The effects of eye movement desensitization and reprocessing (EMDR) therapy on posttraumatic stress disorder in survivors of the 1999 Marmara, Turkey, earthquake. *International Journal of Stress Management, 13*(3), 291–308.

Koob, G., & Kreek, M. J. (2007). Stress, dysregulation of drug reward pathways, and the transition to drug dependence. *American Journal of Psychiatry, 164,* 1149–1159.

Kop, W. J., Berman, D. S., Gransar, H., Wong, N. D., Miranda-Peats, R., White, M. D., et al. (2005). Social network and coronary artery calcification in asymptomatic individuals. *Psychosomatic Medicine, 67,* 343–352.

Koppenaal, L., & Glanzer, M. (1990). An examination of the continuous distractor task and the "long-term recency effect." *Memory & Cognition, 18,* 183–195.

Kordower, J. H., Emborg, M. E., Bloch, J., Ma, S. Y., Chu, Y., Leventhal, L., et al. (2000). Neurodegeneration prevented by lentiviral vector delivery of GDNF in primate models of Parkinson's disease. *Science, 290,* 767–773.

Korman, M., Doyon, J., Doljansky, J., Carrier, J., Dagan, Y., & Karni, A. (2007). Daytime sleep condenses the time course of motor memory consolidation. *Nature Neuroscience, 10,* 1206–1213.

Korner, J., & Leibel, R. L. (2003). To eat or not to eat—How the gut talks to the brain. *The New England Journal of Medicine, 349,* 926–928.

Korochkin, L. I. (2000). New approaches in developmental genetics and gene therapy: Xenotransplantation of Drosophila embryonic nerve cells into the brain of vertebrate animals. *Genetika, 36,* 1436–1442.

Kotani, N., Hashimoto, H., Sato, Y., Sessler, D. I., Yoshioka, H., Kitayama, M., et al. (2001). Preoperative intradermal acupuncture reduces postoperative pain, nausea and vomiting, analgesic requirement, and sympathoadrenal responses. *Anesthesiology, 95,* 349–356.

Kouider, S., & Dupoux, E. (2005). Subliminal speech priming. *Psychological Science, 16,* 617.

Kounios, J. Frymiare, J. L., Bowden, E. M., Fleck, J. L., Subramaniam, K., Parrish, T. B., & Jung-Beeman, M. (2006). The prepared mind: Neural activity prior to problem presentation predicts subsequent solution by sudden insight. *Psychological Science, 17,* 882–890.

Kouri, E. M., Pope, H. G., & Lukas, S. E. (1999). Changes in aggressive behavior during withdrawal from long-term marijuana use. *Psychopharmacology, 143,* 302–308.

Kouyoumdjian, H. (2004). Influence of unannounced quizzes and cumulative exams on attendance and study behavior. *Teaching of Psychology, 31,* 110–111.

Kozak, M. J., Liebowitz, M. R., & Foa, E. B. (2000). Cognitive behavior therapy and pharmacotherapy for obsessive-compulsive disorder: The NIMH-sponsored collaborative study. In W. K. Goodman, M. V. Rudorfer, & J. D. Maser (Eds.), *Obsessive-compulsive disorder: Contemporary issues in treatment* (pp. 501–530). Mahwah, NJ: Erlbaum.

Kozorovitskiy, Y., Gross, C. G., Kopil, C., Battaglia, L., McBreen, M., Stranahan, A. M., et al. (2005). Experience induces structural and biochemical changes in the adult primate brain. *Proceedings of the National Academy of Sciences, 102,* 17478–17482.

Krain, A. L., & Castellanos, F. X. (2006). Brain development and ADHD. *Clinical Psychology Review, 26,* 433–444.

Krakauer, J. (1997). *Into thin air.* New York: Villard.

Kramer, A. F., & Willis, S. (2002). Enhancing the cognitive vitality of older adults. *Current Directions in Psychological Science, 11,* 173–177.

Kramer, G. P., Bernstein, D. A., & Phares, V. (2009). *Introduction to clinical psychology* (7th ed.) Upper Saddle River, NJ: Prentice Hall.

Krantz, D., Contrada, R., Hill, D., & Friedler, E. (1988). Environmental stress and biobehavioral antecedents of coronary heart disease. *Journal of Consulting and Clinical Psychology, 56,* 333–341.

Krantz, D., & Durel, L. (1983). Psychobiological substrates of the Type A behavior pattern. *Health Psychology, 2,* 393–411.

Krantz, D. S., & McCeney, M. K. (2002). Effects of psychological and social factors on organic disease: A critical assessment of research on coronary heart disease. *Annual Review of Psychology, 53,* 341–369.

Kraus, W. E., Houmard, J. A., Duscha, B. D., Knetzger, K. J., Wharton, M. B., McCartney, J. S., et al. (2002). Effects of the amount and intensity of exercise on plasma lipoproteins. *The New England Journal of Medicine, 347,* 1483–1492.

Krause, M. S. (2005). How the psychotherapy research community must work toward measurement and why. *Journal of Clinical Psychology, 61,* 269–283.

Krause, M. S., & Lutz, W. (2006). How we really ought to be comparing treatments for clinical purposes. *Psychotherapy: Theory, Research, Practice, Training, 43,* 359–361.

Krause, N., & Shaw, B. A. (2000). Role-specific feelings of control and mortality. *Psychology and Aging, 15,* 617–626.

Kraut, R., Olson, J., Banaji, M., Bruckman, A., Cohen, J., & Couper, M. (2004). Psychological research online: Report of board of scientific affairs' advisory group on the conduct of research on the Internet. *American Psychologist, 59,* 105–117.

Krauzlis, R. J. (2002). Reaching for answers. *Neuron, 34,* 673–674.

Krauzlis, R. J., & Lisberger, S. G. (1991). Visual motion commands for pursuit eye movements in the cerebellum. *Science, 253,* 568–571.

Kray, L. J., & Galinsky, A. D. (2003). The debiasing effect of counterfactual mind-sets: Increasing the search for disconfirmatory information in group decisions. *Organizational Behavior and Human Decision Processes, 91,* 69–81.

Krebs, D. L., & Denton, K. (2005). Toward a more pragmatic approach to morality: A critical evaluation of Kohlberg's model. *Psychological Review, 112,* 629–649.

Kreek, M. J., Nielsen, D. A., Butelman, E. R., & LaForge, K. S. (2005). Genetic influences on impulsivity, risk taking, stress responsivity and vulnerability to drug abuse and addiction. *Nature Neuroscience, 8,* 1450–1457.

Kreppner, J. M., Rutter, M., Beckett, C., Castle, J., Colvert, E., Groothues, C., Hawkins, A., O'Connor, T. G., Stevens, S., & Sonuga-Barke, E. J. S. (2007). Normality and impairment following profound early institutional deprivation: A longitudinal follow-up into early adolescence. *Developmental Psychology, 43,* 931–946.

Kreuger, R. F., & Johnson, W. (2008). Behavioral genetics and personality: A new look at the integration of nature and nurture. In O. John, R. Robins, & L. Pervin (Eds.), *Handbook of personality: Theory and research* (3rd ed., pp. 287–310). New York: Guilford.

Kring, A. M., & Gordon, A. H. (1998). Sex differences in emotion: Expression, experience, and physiology. *Journal of Personality & Social Psychology, 74,* 686–703.

Kristof, N. D. (1997, August 17). Where children rule. *New York Times Magazine.*

Krohne, H. W., & Slangen, K. E. (2005). Influence of social support on adaptation to surgery. *Health Psychology, 24,* 101–105.

Krosnick, J. A., Betz, A. L., Jussim, L. J., & Lynn, A. R. (1992). Subliminal conditioning of attitude. *Personality and Social Psychology Bulletin, 18,* 152–162.

Krueger, F., McCabe, K., Moll, J., Kriegeskorte, N., Zahn, R., Strenziok, M., Heinecke, A., & Grafman, J. (2007). Neural correlates of trust. *Proceedings of the National Academies of Science, 104*(50), 20084–20089.

Krueger, R. F., & Markon, K. E. (2006). Understanding psychopathology: Melding behavior genetics, personality, and quantitative psychology to develop an empirically based model. *Current Directions in Psychological Science 15,* 113–117.

Krueger, R. F., South, S., Johnson, W., & Iacono, W. (2008). The heritability of personality is not always 50%: Gene-environment interactions and correlations between personality and parenting. *Journal of Personality, 76,* 1485–1522.

Krueger, R. F., Watson, D., & Barlow, D. H. (2005). Introduction to the special section: Toward a dimensionally based taxonomy of psychopathology. *Journal of Abnormal Psychology, 114,* 491–493.

Kruger, D. J. (2003). Evolution and altruism: Combining psychological mediators with naturally selected tendencies. *Evolution and Human Behavior, 24,* 118–125.

Kruger, J., Wirtz, D., & Miller, D. T. (2005). Counterfactual thinking and the first instinct fallacy. *Journal of Personality and Social Psychology, 88,* 725–735.

Kryger, M. H., Roth, T., & Dement, W. C. (2000). *Principles and practice of sleep medicine* (3rd ed.). Philadelphia: Saunders.

Krykouli, S. E., Stanley, B. G., Seirafi, R. D., & Leibowitz, S. F. (1990). Stimulation of feeding by galanin: Anatomical localization and behavioral specificity of this peptide's effects in the brain. *Peptides, 11*(5), 995–1001.

Kubzansky, L. D., Davidson, K. W., & Rozanski, A. (2005). The clinical impact of negative psychological states: Expanding the spectrum of risk for coronary artery disease. *Psychosomatic Medicine, 67*(S1), S10–S14.

Kubzansky, L. D., Koenen, K. C., Jones, C., & Eaton, W. W. (2009). A prospective study of posttraumatic stress disorder symptoms and coronary heart disease in women. *Health Psychology, 28,* 125–130.

Kuhn, D., & Franklin, S. (2006). The second decade: What develops (and how)? In W. Damon & R. M. Lerner (Series Eds.) & D. Kuhn & R. Siegler (Vol. Eds.), *Handbook of child psychology: Vol. 2. Cognition, perception, and language* (6th ed.). New York: Wiley.

Kuhnen, C. M., & Knutson, B. (2005). The neural basis of financial risk taking. *Neuron, 47,* 763–770.

Kukull, W. A., Higdon, R., Bowen, J. D., McCormick, W. C., Teri, L., Schellenberg, G. D., et al. (2002). Dementia and Alzheimer disease incidence: A prospective cohort study. *Archives of Neurology, 59,* 1737–1746.

Kumanyika, S. K. (2008). Environmental influences on childhood obesity: Ethnic and cultural influences in context. *Physiology & Behavior, 94*(1), 61–70.

Kuncel, N. R., Hezlett, S. A., & Ones, D. (2004). Academic performance, career potential, creativity, and job performance: Can one construct predict them all? *Journal of Personality and Social Psychology, 86,* 148–161.

Kunen, S., Niederhauser, R., Smith, P. O., Morris, J. A., & Marx, B. D. (2005). Race disparities in psychiatric rates in emergency departments. *Journal of Consulting and Clinical Psychology, 73,* 116–126.

Kunkel, D., Wilson, B. J., Linz, D., Potter, J., Donnerstein, E., Smith, S. L., et al. (1996). *The national television violence study.* Studio City, CA: Mediascope.

Kuo, L. E., Kitlinska, J. B., Tilan, J. U., Li, L., Baker, S. B., Johnson, M. D., Lee, E. W., Burnett, M. S., Fricke, S. T., Kvetnansky, R., Herzog, H., & Zukowska, Z. (2007). Neuropeptide Y acts directly in the periphery on fat tissue and mediates stress-induced obesity and metabolic syndrome. *Nature Medicine 13,* 803–811.

Kuo, Y.-L., Liao, H.-F., Chen, P.-C., Hsieh, W.-S., & Hwang, A.-W. (2008). The influence of wakeful prone positioning on motor development during the early life. *Journal of Developmental & Behavioral Pediatrics, 29*(5), 367–376.

Kurbat, M. A. (1997). Can the recognition of living things really be selectively impaired? *Neuropsychologia, 35*(6), 813–827.

Kurdek, L. A. (2005). What do we know about gay and lesbian couples? *Current Directions in Psychological Science, 14,* 251–254.

Kushner, M. G., Thuras, P., Kaminski, J., Anderson, N., Neumeyer, B., & Mackenzie, T. (2000). Expectancies for alcohol to affect tension and anxiety as a function of time. *Addictive Behaviors, 25,* 93–98.

Kutchins, H., & Kirk, S. A. (1997). *Making us crazy: The psychiatric bible and the creation of mental disorders.* New York: Free Press.

Kwan, M., Greenleaf, W. J., Mann, J., Crapo, L., & Davidson, J. M. (1983). The nature of androgen action on male sexuality: A combined laboratory-self- report study on hypogonadal men. *Journal of Clinical Endocrinology and Metabolism, 57,* 557–562.

Kwate, N. O. A. (2001). Intelligence or misorientation? *Journal of Black Psychology, 27,* 221–238.

Kymalainen, J. A., Weisman, A. G., Resales, G. A., & Armesto, J. C. (2006). Ethnicity, expressed emotion, and communication deviance in family members of patients with schizophrenia. *Journal of Nervous and Mental Disease, 194,* 391–396.

Kyrios, M., Sanavio, E., Bhar, S., & Liguori, L. (2001). Associations between obsessive-compulsive phenomena, affect, and beliefs: Cross-cultural comparisons of Australian and Italian data. *Behavioural and Cognitive Psychotherapy, 29,* 409–422.

Laan, E., Everaerd, W., Van Aanhold, M. T., & Rebel, M. (1993). Performance demand and sexual arousal in woman. *Behavior Research and Therapy, 31,* 25–36.

Labouvie-Vief, G. (1982). Discontinuities in development from childhood. In T. M. Field, A. Huston, H. C. Quay, L. Troll, & G. E. Finley (Eds.), *Review of human development.* New York: Wiley.

Labouvie-Vief, G. (1992). A new-Piagetian perspective on adult cognitive development. In R. J. Sternberg & C. A. Berg (Eds.), *Intellectual development.* New York: Cambridge University Press.

Lack, L. C., & Wright, H. R. (2007). Chronobiology of sleep in humans. *Cellular & Molecular Life Sciences, 64*(10), 1205–1215.

Lacor, P. N. (2007). Advances on the Understanding of the Origins of Synaptic Pathology in AD. *Current Genomics, 8*(8), 486–508.

Ladd, G. (2005). *Peer relationships and social competence of children and youth.* New Haven, CT: Yale University Press.

LaFrance, M., Hecht, M. A., & Paluck, E. L. (2003). The contingent smile: A meta-analysis of sex differences in smiling. *Psychological Bulletin, 129,* 305–334.

Lagerspetz, K. M. J., & Lagerspetz, K. Y. H. (1983). Genes and aggression. In E. C. Simmel, M. E. Hahn, & J. K. Walters (Eds.), *Aggressive behavior: Genetic and neural approaches.* Hillsdale, NJ: Erlbaum.

Lagopoulos, J., & Malhi, G. S. (2008). Transcranial magnetic stimulation. *Acta Neuropsychiatrica, 20*(6), 301–317.

LaGreca, A. M., Silverman, W. K., Vernberg, E. M., & Prinstein, M. J. (1996). Symptoms of posttraumatic stress in children after Hurricane Andrew: A prospective study. *Journal of Consulting and Clinical Psychology, 64,* 712–723.

Lahey, B. B., Loeber, R., Burke, J. D., & Applegate, B. (2005). Predicting future antisocial personality disorder in males from a clinical assessment in childhood. *Journal of Consulting and Clinical Psychology, 73,* 389–399.

Lahey, B. B., Loeber, R., Hart, E. L., Frick, P. J., & Applegate, B. (1995). Four-year longitudinal study of conduct disorder in boys: Patterns and predictors of persistence. *Journal of Abnormal Psychology, 104,* 83–93.

Lahey, B. B., Van Hulle, C. A., Keenan, K., Rathouz, P. J., D'Onofrio, B. M., Rodgers, J. L., & Waldman, I. D. (2008). Temperament and parenting during the first year of life predict future child conduct problems. *Journal of Abnormal Child Psychology, 36,* 1139–1158.

Lai, C. S. L., Fisher, S. E., Hurst, J. A., Vargha-Khadem, F., & Monaco, A. P. (2001). A forkhead-domain gene is mutated in severe speech and language disorder. *Nature, 413,* 519–523.

Laird, R. D., Jordan, K. Y., Dodge, K. A., Pettit, G. S., & Gates, J. E. (2001). Peer rejection in childhood, involvement with antisocial peers in early adolescence, and the development of externalizing behavior problems. *Development and Psychopathology, 13,* 337–354.

Lakin, J. L., & Chartrand, T. L. (2003). Using nonconscious behavioral mimicry to create affiliation and rapport. *Psychological Science, 14,* 334–339.

Lalumière, M. L., Blanchard, R., & Zucker, K. J. (2000). Sexual orientation and handedness in men and women: A meta-analysis. *Psychological Bulletin, 126,* 575–592.

Lam, B., Sam, K., Mok, W. Y., Cheung, M., Fong, D. Y., Lam, J. C., et al. (2006). A randomised study of three non-surgical treatments in mild to moderate obstructive sleep apnoea. *Thorax, 62,* 354–359.

Lam, D. H., Watkins, E. R., Hayward, P., Bright, J., Wright, K., Kerr, N., Parr-Davis, G., & Sham, P. (2003). A randomized controlled study of cognitive therapy for relapse prevention for bipolar affective disorder: outcome of the first year. *Archives of General Psychiatry, 60,* 145–152.

Lamar, J. (2000). Suicides in Japan reach a record high. *British Medical Journal, 321,* 528.

Lamb, M. E. (1998). Assessments of children's credibility in forensic contexts. *Current Directions in Psychological Science, 7,* 43–46.

Lamb, M. E. (Ed.). (1997). *The role of the father in child development* (3rd ed.). New York: Wiley.

Lamb, M. E., & Ahnert, L. (2006). Nonparental child care. In W. Damon & R. M. Lerner (Series Eds.) & K. A. Renninger & I. E. Sigel (Vol. Eds.), *Handbook of child psychology: Vol. 4. Child psychology in practice* (6th ed.). New York: Wiley.

Lamberg, L. (2004). Impact of long working hours explored. *Journal of the American Medical Association, 292,* 25–26.

Lambert, M. J., & Barley, D. E. (2001). Research summary on the therapeutic relationship and psychotherapy outcome. *Psychotherapy, 38,* 357–361.

Lambert, N. M. (1999). Developmental trajectories in psychology: Applications to education and training. *American Psychologist, 54,* 991–1002.

Lambert, T., & Norman, T. R. (2008). Ethnic differences in psychotropic drug response and pharmacokinetics. In C. H. Ng, K. Lin, B. S. Singh, & E. Chiu (Eds.), *Ethno-psychopharmacology: Advances in current practice* (pp. 38–61). New York: Cambridge University Press.

Lamm, E., & Jablonka, E. (2008). The nurture of nature: Hereditary plasticity in evolution. *Philosophical Psychology, 21*(3), 305–319.

Landrigan, C. P., Rothschild, J. M., Cronin, J. W., Kaushal, R., Burdick, E., Katz, J. T., et al. (2004). Effect of reducing interns' work hours on serious medical errors in intensive care units. *New England Journal of Medicine, 351,* 1838–1848.

Landrine, H. (1991). Revising the framework of abnormal psychology. In P. Bronstein & K. Quina (Eds.), *Teaching a psychology of people.* Washington, DC: American Psychological Association.

Landsdale, M., & Laming, D. (1995). Evaluating the fragmentation hypothesis: The analysis of errors in cued recall. *Acta Psychologica, 88,* 33–77.

Lang, A. R., Goeckner, D. J., Adesso, V. J., & Marlatt, G. A. (1975). Effects of alcohol on aggression in male social drinkers. *Journal of Abnormal Psychology, 84,* 508–518.

Lang, C., Barco, A., Zablow, L., Kandel, E. R., Siegelbaum, S. A., & Zakharenko, S. S. (2004). Transient expansion of synaptically connected dendritic spines upon induction of hippocampal long-term potentiation. *Proceedings of the National Academy of Sciences, 101,* 16665–16670.

Lang, P. J. (1995). The emotion probe: Studies of motivation and attention. *American Psychologist, 50*(5), 372–385.

Lang, P. J., & Melamed, B. G. (1969). Avoidance conditioning therapy of an infant with chronic ruminative vomiting. *Journal of Abnormal Psychology, 74,* 1–8.

Lange, C., & Byrd, M. (2002). Differences between students' estimated and attained grades in a first-year introductory psychology course as a function of identity development. *Adolescence, 37*(145), 93–108.

Langenberg, P., Ballesteros, M., Feldman, R., Damron, D., Anliker, J., Havas, S. (2000). Psychosocial factors and intervention-associated changes in those factors as correlates of change in fruit and vegetable consumption in the Maryland WIC 5 a day promotion program. *Annals of Behavioral Medicine, 22,* 307–315.

Langenbucher, J., & Nathan, P. E. (2006). Diagnosis and classification. In F. Andrasik (Ed.), *Comprehensive handbook of personality and psychopathology: Vol. 2. Adult psychopathology* (pp. 3–20). New York: Wiley.

Langens, T. A., & Schüler, J. (2007). Effects of written emotional expression: the role of positive expectancies. *Health Psychology, 26,* 174–182.

Langlois, J. H., Kalakanis, L., Rubenstein, A. J., Larson, A., Hallam, M., & Smoot, M. (2000). Maxims or myths of beauty: A meta-analytic and theoretical review. *Psychological Bulletin, 126,* 390–423.

Lansford, J. E., & Dodge, K. A. (2008). Cultural norms for adult corporal punishment of children and societal rates of endorsement and use of violence. *Parenting: Science & Practice, 8*(3), 257–270.

Lansky, D., & Wilson, G. T. (1981). Alcohol, expectations and sexual arousal in males: An information processing analysis. *Journal of Abnormal Psychology, 89,* 528–538.

Lanzenberger, R. R., Mitterhauser, M., Spindelegger, C., Wadsak, W., Klein, N., Mien, L. K., et al. (2007). Reduced serotonin-1a receptor binding in social anxiety disorder. *Biological Psychiatry, 61,* 1081–1089.

Lapierre, L. M., & Allen, T. D. (2006). Work-supportive family, family-supportive supervision, use of organizational benefits, and problem-focused coping: Implications for work-family conflict and employee well-being. *Journal of Occupational Health Psychology, 11,* 169–181.

Lapointe, L. (1990). *Aphasia and related neurogenic language disorders.* New York: Thieme Medical.

LaRoche, M. J., & Martin, J. (2005). The cultural context and the psychotherapeutic process: Toward a culturally sensitive psychotherapy. *Journal of Psychotherapy Integration, 15,* 169–185.

Larsen, J. T., McGraw, A. P., Mellers, B. A., & Cacioppo, J. T. (2004). The agony of victory and thrill of defeat: Mixed emotional reactions to disappointing wins and relieving losses. *Psychological Science, 15,* 325–330.

Larsen, R., & Buss, D. M. (2005). *Personality psychology: Domains of knowledge about human nature* (2nd ed.). New York: McGraw-Hill.

Larson, E. B., Wang, L., Bowen, J. D., McCormick, W. C., Teri, L., Crane, P., & Kukull, W. (2006). Exercise is associated with reduced risk of incident dementia among persons 65 years of age and older. *Annals of Internal Medicine, 144,* 73–81.

Larson, J. R., Jr., Christensen, C., Franz, T. M., & Abbott, A. S. (1998). Diagnosing groups: The pooling, management, and impact of shared and unshared case information in team-based medical decision making. *Journal of Personality and Social Psychology, 75,* 93–108.

Larson, R. W., & Verma, S. (1999). How children and adolescents spend time across the world: Work, play, and developmental opportunities. *Psychological Bulletin, 125,* 701–736.

Larsson, H., Andershed, H., & Lichtenstein, P. (2006). A genetic factor explains most of the variation in the psychopathic personality. *Journal of Abnormal Psychology, 115,* 221–230.

Latané, B. (1981). The psychology of social impact. *American Psychologist, 36,* 343–356.

Latané, B., & Rodin, J. (1969). A lady in distress: Inhibiting effects of friends and strangers on bystander intervention. *Journal of Experimental Social Psychology, 5,* 189–202.

Latham, G. P. (2004). Motivate employee performance through goal-setting. In E. A. Locke (Ed.), *Handbook of principles of organizational behavior* (pp. 107–119). Malden, MA: Blackwell.

Latham, G. P., Skarlicki, D., Irvine, D., & Siegel, J. P. (1993). The increasing importance of performance appraisals to employee effectiveness in organizational settings in North America. In C. L. Cooper & I. T. Robertson (Eds.), *International review of industrial and organizational psychology 1993* (pp. 87–132). Chichester, UK: Wiley.

Lau, M. A., Pihl, R. O., & Peterson, J. B. (1995). Provocation, acute alcohol intoxication, cognitive performance, and aggression. *Journal of Abnormal Psychology, 104,* 150–155.

Laughery, K. R. (1999). Modeling human performance during system design. In E. Salas (Ed.), *Human/technology interaction in complex systems* (Vol. 9, pp. 147–174). Stamford, CT: JAI Press.

Laughlin, P. L. (1999). Collective induction: Twelve postulates. *Organizational Behavior and Human Decision Processes, 80,* 50–69.

Laumann, E. O., Gagnon, J. H., Michael, R. T., & Michaels, S. (1994). *The social organization of sexuality: Sexual practices in the United States.* Chicago: University of Chicago Press.

Laumann, E. O., & Michael, R. T. (Eds.). (2000). *Sex, love, and health in America: Private choices and public policies.* Chicago: University of Chicago Press.

Laumann, E. O., Paik, A., & Rosen, R. C. (1999). Sexual dysfunction in the United States: Prevalence and predictors. *Journal of the American Medical Association, 281,* 537–544.

Laurenceau, J.-P., Hayes, A. M., & Feldman, G. C. (2007). Some methodological and statistical issues in the study of change processes in psychotherapy. *Clinical Psychology Review, 27,* 682–695.

Laurenceau, J.-P., Stanley, S. M., Olmos-Gallo, A., Baucom, B., & Markman, H. J. (2004). Community-based prevention of marital dysfunction: Multilevel modeling of a randomized effectiveness study. *Journal of Consulting and Clinical Psychology, 72,* 933–943.

Laureys, S. (2004). Functional neuroimaging in the vegetative state. *NeuroRehabilitation, 19*(4), 335–341.

Laursen, B., Bukowski, W. M., Aunola, K., & Nurmi, J.-E. (2007). Friendship moderates prospective associations between social isolation and adjustment problems in young children. *Child Development, 78,* 1395–1404.

Law, D. J., Pellegrino, J. W., & Hunt, E. B. (1993). Comparing the tortoise and the hare: Gender differences and experience in dynamic spatial reasoning tasks. *Psychological Science, 4,* 35–40.

Law, K. L., Stroud, L. R., LaGasse, L. L., Niaura, R., Liu, J., & Lester, B. M. (2003). Smoking during pregnancy and newborn neurobehavior. *Pediatrics, 111,* 1318–1323.

Law, M. H., Cotton, R. G. H., & Berger, G. E. (2006). The role of phospholipases A2 in schizophrenia. *Molecular Psychiatry, 11,* 547–556.

Lawford, B. R., Young, R. M., Rowell, J. A., Qualichefski, J., Fletcher, B. H., Syndulko, et al. (1995). Bromocriptine in the treatment of alcoholics with the D2 dopamine receptor A1 allele. *Nature Medicine, 1*(4), 337–341.

Lawless, H. T., & Engen, T. (1977). Associations to odors: Interference, memories and verbal learning. *Journal of Experimental Psychology, 3,* 52–59.

Lawson, C. A. (2004). Treating the borderline mother: Integrating EMDR with a family systems perspective. In M. M. MacFarlane (Ed.), *Family treatment of personality disorders: Advances in clinical practice* (pp. 305–334). Binghamton, NY: Haworth Clinical Practice Press.

Lazarus, A. A. (1971). *Behavior therapy and beyond.* New York: McGraw-Hill.

Lazarus, C. N., & Lazarus, A. A. (2002). EMDR: An elegantly concentrated multimodal procedure? In F. Shapiro (Ed.), *EMDR as an integrative psychotherapy approach: Experts of diverse orientations explore the paradigm prism* (pp. 209–223). Washington, DC: American Psychological Association.

Lazarus, R. S. (1966). *Psychological stress and the coping process.* New York: McGraw-Hill.

Lazarus, R. S. (1991). *Emotion and adaptation.* New York: Oxford University Press.

Lazarus, R. S. (1999). *Stress and emotion: A new synthesis.* New York: Springer.

Lazarus, R. S., & Folkman, S. (1984). *Stress, appraisal, and coping.* New York: Springer-Verlag.

Lazarus, R. S., Opton, E. M., Nomikos, M. S., & Rankin, M. O. (1965). The principle of short-circuiting of threat: Further evidence. *Journal of Personality, 33,* 622–635.

Leamon, M. H., Wright, T. M., & Myrick, H. (2008). Substance-related disorders. In R. E. Hales, S. C. Yudofsky, & G. O. Gabbard (Eds) *Textbook of psychiatry* (pp. 365–406). Washington, DC: American Psychiatric Publishing.

Leary, M. R. (2001).Shyness and the self: Attentional, motivational, and cognitive self-processes in social anxiety. In R. Crozier & L. Alden (Eds.), *International handbook of social anxiety: A handbook of concepts, research, and interventions relating to the self and shyness* (pp. 217–234). New York: John Wiley and Sons.

LeBlanc, M. M., & Barling, J. (2004). Workplace aggression. *Current Directions in Psychological Science, 13,* 9–12.

LeBlanc, M. M., Dupre, K. E., & Barling, J. (2006). Public-initiated violence. In K. E. Kelloway, J. Barling, & J. J. Hurrell (Eds.), *Handbook of workplace violence* (pp. 261–280). Thousand Oaks, CA: Sage.

LeDoux, J. E. (1995). Emotion: Clues from the brain. *Annual Review of Psychology, 46,* 209–235.

Lee, C. M., Ryan, J. J., & Kreiner, D. S. (2007). Personality in domestic cats. *Psychological Reports, 100*(1), 27–29.

Lee, C. W., Taylor, G., & Drummond, P. D. (2006). The active ingredient in EMDR: Is it traditional exposure or dual focus of attention? *Clinical Psychology & Psychotherapy, 13*(2), 97–107.

Lee, H. S., Nelms, J. L., Nguyen, M., Silver, R., & Lehman, M. N. (2003). The eye is necessary for a circadian rhythm in the suprachiasmatic nucleus. *Nature Neuroscience, 6,* 111–112.

Lee, J. (2006). Human factors and ergonomics in automation design. In G. Salvendy (Ed.), *Handbook of human factors and ergonomics* (3rd ed., 1570–1596). Hoboken, NJ: John Wiley & Sons Inc.

Lee, J. L. C., Everitt, B. J., & Thomas, K. L. (2004). Independent cellular processes for hippocampal memory consolidation and reconsolidation. *Science, 304,* 839–843.

Lee, K., Ogunfowora, B., & Ashton, M. C. (2005). Personality traits beyond the big five: Are they within the HEXACO space? *Journal of Personality, 73,* 1437–1463.

Lee, L., Loewenstein, G., Ariely, D., Hong, J., & Young, J. (2008). If I'm not hot, are you hot or not? Physical-attractiveness evaluations and dating preferences as a function of one's own attractiveness. *Psychological Science, 19,* 669–677.

Lee, R. M., & Yoo, H. C. (2004). Structure and measurement of ethnic identity for Asian American college students. *Journal of Counseling Psychology, 51,* 263–269.

Lee, S., Colditz, G., Berkman, L., & Kawachi, I. (2003). Caregiving to children and grandchildren and risk of coronary heart disease in women. *American Journal of Public Health, 93,* 1939–1944.

Lee, T. M. C., Aua, R. K. C., Liud, H.-L., Tingf, K. H., Huangg, C.-M., & Chan, C. C. H. (2009). Are errors differentiable from deceptive responses when feigning memory impairment? An fMRI study. *Brain and Cognition, 69,* 406–412.

Lee, Y. S., & Silva, A. J. (2009). The molecular and cellular biology of enhanced cognition. *National Review of Neuroscience, 10*(2), 126–140.

Leff, J. (2006). Whose life is it anyway? Quality of life for long-stay patients discharged from psychiatric hospitals. In H. Katschnig, H. Freeman, & N. Sartorius (Eds.), *Quality of life in mental disorders* (2nd ed., pp. 247–255). New York: Wiley.

Legare, C. H., & Gelman, S. A. (2008). Bewitchment, biology, or both: The co-existence of natural and supernatural explanatory frameworks across development. *Cognitive science, 32,* 607–642.

Legerstee, M., Anderson, D., & Schaffer, A. (1998). Five- and eight-month-old infants recognize their faces and voices as familiar and social stimuli. *Child Development, 69,* 37–50.

le Grange, D., Crosby, R. D., Rathouz, P. J., & Leventhal, B. L. (2007). A randomized controlled comparison of family-based treatment and supportive psychotherapy for adolescent bulimia nervosa. *Archives of General Psychiatry, 64,* 1049–1056.

Lehman, D. R., Chiu, C., & Schaller, M. (2004). Psychology and culture. *Annual Review of Psychology, 55,* 689–714.

Lehman, H. E. (1967). Schizophrenia: IV. Clinical features. In A. M. Freedman, H. I. Kaplan, & H. S. Kaplan (Eds.), *Comprehensive textbook of psychiatry.* Baltimore: Williams & Wilkins.

Leibel, R. L., Rosenbaum, M., & Hirsch, J. (1995). Changes in energy expenditure resulting from altered body weight. *New England Journal of Medicine, 332*(10), 621–628.

Leibowitz, H. W., Brislin, R., Perlmutter, L., & Hennessy, R. (1969). Ponzo perspective illusion as a manifestation of space perception. *Science, 166,* 1174–1176.

Leibowitz, S. F. (1992). Neurochemical-neuroendocrine systems in the brain controlling macronutrient intake and metabolism. *TINS, 15,* 491–497.

Leichsenring, F., Rabung, S., & Leibing, E. (2004). The efficacy of short-term psychodynamic psychotherapy in specific psychiatric disorders: A meta-analysis. *Archives of General Psychiatry, 61,* 1208–1216.

Leigh, B. C., & Stacy, A. W. (2004). Alcohol expectancies and drinking in different age groups. *Addiction, 99,* 215–227.

Leiner, H. C., Leiner, A. L., & Dow, R. S. (1993). Cognitive and language functions of the human cerebellum. *Trends in Neuroscience, 16,* 444–447.

Leippe, M. R., Manion, A. P., & Romanczyk, A. (1992). Eyewitness persuasion: How and how well do fact finders judge the accuracy of adults' and children's memory reports? *Journal of Personality and Social Psychology, 63,* 181–197.

Leiser, D., & Azar, O. H. (2008). Behavioral economics and decision making: Applying insights from psychology to understand how people make economic decisions. *Journal of Economic Psychology, 29*(5), 613–618.

Leiser, D., Azar, O. H., & Hadar, L. (2008). Psychological construal of economic behavior. *Journal of Economic Psychology, 29*(5), 762–776.

Lejuez, C. W., Hopko, D. R., Levine, S., Gholkar, R., & Collins, L. (2005). The therapeutic alliance in behavior therapy. *Psychotherapy: Theory, Research, Practice, and Training, 42,* 456–468.

Lemly, B. (2000, February). Isn't she lovely? *Discover,* 43–49.

Lemmer, B., Kern, R. I., Nold, G., & Lohrer, H. (2002). Jet lag in athletes after eastward and westward time-zone transition. *Chronobiology International, 19,* 743–764.

Lemoine, P., Kermadi, I., Garcia-Acosta, S., Garay, R. P., & Dib, M. (2006). Double-blind, comparative study of cyamemazine vs. bromazepam in the benzodiazepine withdrawal syndrome. *Progress in Neuro-Psychopharmacology & Biological Psychiatry, 30,* 131–137.

Lenneberg, E. H. (1967). *Biological foundations of language.* New York: Wiley.

Lenzenweger, M. F., McLachlan, G., & Rubin, D. B. (2007). Resolving the latent structure of schizophrenia endophenotypes using expectation-maximization-based finite mixture modeling. *Journal of Abnormal Psychology, 116,* 16–29.

Leonard, B. E. (1992). *Fundamentals of psychopharmacology.* New York: Wiley.

Leonhardt, D. (2000, May 24). Management: On Testing for Common Sense; A Business School Thinks It Makes Sense. Yes? No? *New York Times,* p. C1.

LePage, J. P., DelBen, K., Pollard, S., McGhee, S., Vanhorn, L., Murphy, J., et al. (2003). Reducing assaults on an acute psychiatric unit using a token economy: A 2-year follow-up. *Behavioral Interventions, 18,* 179–190.

Lepore, S. J. (1995). Cynicism, social support, and cardiovascular reactivity. *Health Psychology, 14,* 210–216.

Lerner, J. S., Gonzalez, R. M., Small, D. A., & Fischhoff, B. (2003). Effects of fear and anger on perceived risks of terrorism: A national field experiment. *Psychological Science, 14,* 144–150.

Lesko, A. C., & Corpus, J. H. (2006). Discounting the difficult: How high math-identified women respond to stereotype threat. *Sex Roles, 54*(1–2), 113–125.

Leung, H. T., & Westbrook, F. R. (2008). Spontaneous recovery of extinguished fear responses deepens their extinction: A role for error-correction mechanisms. *Journal of Experimental Psychology: Animal Behavior Processes, 31,* 277–288.

Levant, R. F. (2005). Evidence-based practice in psychology. *Monitor on Psychology, 36,* 5.

Levenson, H. (2003). Time-limited dynamic psychotherapy: An integrationist perspective. *Journal of Psychotherapy Integration, 13,* 300–333.

Levenson, R. W., Ekman, P., & Friesen, W. V. (1990). Voluntary facial action generates emotion-specific autonomic nervous system activity. *Psychophysiology, 27*(4), 363–384.

Levenson, R. W., Ekman, P., Heider, K., & Friesen, W. V. (1992). Emotion and autonomic nervous system activity in the Minangkabau of West Sumatra. *Journal of Personality and Social Psychology, 62*(6), 972–988.

Leventhal, T., & Brooks-Gunn, J. (2000). The neighborhoods they live in: The effects of neighborhood residence on child and adolescent outcomes. *Psychological Bulletin, 126,* 309–337.

Levine, D., McCright, J., Dobkin, L., Woodruff, A. J., & Klausner, J. D. (2008). SEXINFO: A sexual health text messaging service for San Francisco Youth. *American Journal of Public Health, 98*(3), 393–395.

Levine, M. W., & Shefner, J. M. (1981). *Fundamentals of sensation and perception.* Reading, MA: Addison-Wesley.

Levine, R., Sato, S., Hashimoto, T., & Verna, J. (1995). Love and marriage in eleven cultures. *Journal of Cross-Cultural Psychology, 26,* 554–571.

Levine, R. V., Martinez, T. M., Brase, G., & Sorenson, K. (1994). Helping in 36 U.S. cities. *Journal of Personality and Social Psychology, 67,* 69–82.

Levine, R. V., Reysen, S., & Ganz, E. (2008). The kindness of strangers revisited: A comparison of 24 US cities. *Social Indicators Research, 85,* 461–481.

Levine, S. (1999, February 1). In a loud and noisy world, baby boomers pay the consequences. *International Herald Tribune.*

Levinson, D. F. (2006). The genetics of depression: A review. *Biological Psychiatry, 60,* 84–92.

Levinson, D. F., Evgrafov, O. V., Knowles, J. A., Potash, J. B., Weissman, M. M., Scheftner, W. A., et al. (2007). Genetics of recurrent early-onset major depression (GenRED): Significant linkage on chromosome 15q25-q26 after fine mapping with single nucleotide polymorphism markers. *American Journal of Psychiatry, 164,* 259–264.

Levinson, D. J., Darrow, C. N., Klein, E. B., Levinson, M. H., & McKee, B. (1978). *The seasons of a man's life.* New York: Knopf.

Levinthal, C. F. (2001). *Drugs, behavior, and modern society* (3rd ed.). Boston: Allyn & Bacon.

Levitt, P., Ebert, P., Mirnics, K., Nimgaonkar, V. L., & Lewis, D. A. (2006). Making the case for a candidate vulnerability gene in schizophrenia: Convergent evidence for regulator of g-protein signaling 4 (RGS4). *Biological Psychiatry, 60,* 534–537.

Levy, B. R., Slade, M. D., Kunkel, S. R., & Kasl, S. V. (2002). Longevity increased by positive self-perceptions of aging. *Journal of Personality & Social Psychology, 83*(2), 261–270.

Levy, D. A., Bayley, P. J., & Squire L. R. (2004). The anatomy of semantic knowledge: Medial vs. lateral temporal lobe. *Proceedings of the National Academies of Science, 101,* 6710–6715.

Levy, R. L., Cain, K. C., Jarrett, M., & Heitkemper, M. M. (1997). The relationship between daily life stress and gastrointestinal symptoms in women with irritable bowel syndrome. *Journal of Behavioral Medicine, 20,* 177–194.

Levy, R., & Ablon, J. S. (Eds.) (2009). *Handbook of evidence-based psychodynamic psychotherapy: Bridging the gap between science and practice.* Totowa, NJ: Humana Press.

Levy-Shiff, R. (1994). Individual and contextual correlates of marital change across the transition to parenthood. *Developmental Psychology, 30,* 591–601.

Lewicki, P. (1992). Nonconscious acquisition of information. *American Psychologist, 47,* 796–801.

Lewin, T. (2003, October 29). A growing number of video viewers watch from crib. *New York Times,* p. 1.

Lewinsohn, P. M., Joiner, T. E., & Rohde, P. (2001). Evaluation of cognitive diathesis-stress models in precicting Major Depressive Disorder in adolescents. *Journal of Abnormal Psychology, 110,* 203–215.

Lewinsohn, P. M., & Rosenbaum, M. (1987). Recall of parental behavior by acute depressives, remitted depressives, and nondepressives. *Journal of Personality and Social Psychology, 52,* 611–619.

Lewis, J. E. (2008). Dream reports of animal rights activists. *Dreaming, 18,* 181–200.

Lewis, J. W., Brefczynski, J. A., Phinney, R. E., Janik, J. J., & DeYoe, E. A. (2005). Distinct cortical pathways for processing tool versus animal sounds. *Journal of Neuroscience, 25*(21), 5148–5158.

Lewis, T. (2006). Seeking health information on the Internet: Lifestyle choice or bad attack of cyberchondria? *Media, Culture & Society, 28*(4), 521–539.

Lewis, T. T., Everson-Rose, S. A., Powell, L. H., Matthews, K. A., Brown, C., Karavolos, K., et al. (2006). Chronic exposure to everyday discrimination and coronary artery calcification in African-American women: The SWAN heart study. *Psychosomatic Medicine, 68,* 362–368.

Lewith, G. T., White, P. J., & Pariente, J. (2005). Investigating acupuncture using brain imaging techniques: The current state of play. *Evidence Based Complementary and Alternative Medicine, 2,* 315–319.

Lewy, A. J., Lefler, B. J., Emens, J. S., & Bauer, V. K. (2006). The circadian basis of winter depression. *Proceedings of the National Academy of Sciences, 103,* 7414–7419.

Ley, J. M., Bennett, P. C., & Coleman, G. J. (2009). A refinement and validation of the Monash Canine Personality Questionnaire (MCPQ). *Applied Animal Behaviour Science, 116*(2–4), 220–227.

Lezak, M. D., Loring, D. W., & Howieson, D. B. (2004). *Neuropsychological assessment* (4th ed.). New York: Oxford University Press.

Li, D.-K., Willinger, M., Petitti, D. B., Odouli, R., Liu, L., & Hoffman, H. J. (2006). Use of a dummy (pacifier) during sleep and risk of sudden infant death syndrome (SIDS): Population based case-control study. *British Medical Journal, 332,* 18–22.

Li, F., Harmer, P., McAuley, E., Duncan, T., Duncan, S. C., Chaumeton, N., & Fisher, K. J. (2001). An evaluation of the effects of Tai Chi exercise on physical function among older persons: A randomized controlled trial. *Annals of Behavioral Medicine, 23,* 139–146.

Li, J. (2005). Mind or virtue: Western and Chinese beliefs about learning. *Current Directions in Psychological Science, 14,* 190–194.

Li, L. C., & Kim, B. S. K. (2004). Effects of counseling style and client adherence to Asian cultural values on counseling process with Asian American college students. *Journal of Counseling Psychology, 51,* 158–167.

Li, M. D. (2006). The genetics of nicotine dependence. *Current Psychiatry Reports, 8,* 158–164.

Li, N. P., & Kenrick, D. T. (2006). Sex similarities and differences in preferences for short-term mates: What, whether, and why. *Journal of Personality and Social Psychology, 90,* 468–489.

Li, S., Cullen, W., Anwyl, R., & Rowan, M. J. (2003). Dopamine-dependent facilitation of LTP induction in hippocampal CA1 by exposure to spatial novelty. *Nature Neuroscience, 6,* 526–531.

Li, S. C., Lindenberger, U., Hommel, B., Aschersleben, G., Prinz, W., & Baltes, P. B. (2004). Transformations in the couplings among intellectual abilities and constituent cognitive processes across the life span. *Psychological Science, 15,* 155–163.

Liao, H., & Rupp, D. E. (2005). The impact of justice climate and justice orientation on work outcomes: A cross-level multifoci framework. *Journal of Applied Psychology, 90,* 242–256.

Liben, L. (1978). Perspective-taking skills in young children: Seeing the world through rose-colored glasses. *Developmental Psychology, 14,* 87–92.

Liben-Nowell, D., Novak, J., Kumar, R., Raghaven, P., & Tomkins, A. (2005). Geographic routing in social networks. *Proceedings of the National Academy of Sciences, 102,* 11623–11628.

Liberman, R. P., Wallace, C. J., Blackwell, G., Kopelowicz, A., Vaccaro, J. V., & Mintz, J. (1998). Skills training versus psychosocial occupational therapy for persons with persistent schizophrenia. *American Journal of Psychiatry, 155,* 1087–1091.

Lickey, M., & Gordon, B. (1991). *Medicine and mental illness: The use of drugs in psychiatry.* San Francisco: Freeman.

Lickliter, R. (2008). The growth of developmental thought: Implications for a new evolutionary psychology. *New Ideas in Psychology, 26*(3), 353–369.

Liden, R. C., Wayne, S. J., Jaworski, R. A., & Bennett, N. (2004). Social loafing: A field investigation. *Journal of Management, 30,* 285–304.

Lieberman, J. A., Stroup, T. S., McEvoy, J. P., Swartz, M. S., Rosenheck, R. A., Perkins, D. O., et al. (2005). Effectiveness of antipsychotic drugs in patients with chronic schizophrenia. *New England Journal of Medicine, 353,* 1209–1223.

Lieberman, J. A., Tollefson, G., Tohen, M., Green, A. I., Gur, R. E., Kahn, R., et al. (2003). Comparative efficacy and safety of atypical and conventional antipsychotic drugs in first-episode psychosis: A randomized, double-blind trial of olanzapine versus haloperidol. *The American Journal of Psychiatry, 160,* 1396–1404.

Lieberman, M. A., & Tobin, S. (1983). *The experience of old age.* New York: Basic Books.

Liebert, R. M., & Spiegler, M. D. (1994). *Personality: Strategies and issues.* Pacific Grove, CA: Brooks/Cole.

Liechti, M. E., Gamma, A., & Vollenweider, F. X. (2001). Gender differences in the subjective effects of MDMA. *Psychopharmacology, 154,* 161–168.

Liepert, J., Bauder, H., Miltner, W. H. R., Taub, E., & Weiller, C. (2000). Treatment-induced cortical reorganization after stroke in humans. *Stroke, 31,* 1210.

Lievens, F., Harris, M. M., Van Keer, E., & Bisqueret, C. (2003). Predicting cross-cultural training performance: The validity of personality, cognitive ability, and dimensions measured by an assessment center and a behavior description interview. *Journal of Applied Psychology, 88,* 476–489.

Lievens, F., Peeters, H., & Schollaert, E. (2008). Situational judgment tests: A review of recent research. *Personnel Review, 37,* 426–441.

Light, K. C., Girdler, S. S., Sherwood, A., Bragdon, E. E., Brownley, K. A., West, S. G., & Hinderliter, A. L. (1999). High stress responsivity predicts later blood pressure only in combination with positive family history and high life stress. *Hypertension, 33,* 1458–1464.

Light, K. J. (2008, August). Virtual fitness gets real. *BioMechanics Magazine,* 22–29.

Light, L. K., Grewen, K. M., Amico, J. A., Brownley, K. A., West, S. G., Hinderliter, A. L., et al. (2005). Oxytocinergic activity is linked to lower blood pressure and vascular resistance during stress in postmenopausal women on estrogen replacement. *Hormones and Behavior, 47,* 540–548.

Lilienfeld, S. O. (2007). Psychological treatments that cause harm. *Perspectives on Psychological Science, 2,* 53–70.

Lilienfeld, S. O., & Arkowitz, H. (2007, December). EMDR: Taking a closer look. *Scientific American, 17*(4), 10–11.

Lilienfeld, S. O., & Lynn, S. J. (2003). Dissociative identity disorder: Multiple personalities, multiple controversies. In S. O. Lilienfeld & S. J. Lynn (Eds.), *Science and pseudoscience in clinical psychology* (pp. 109–142). New York: Guilford.

Lilienfeld, S. O., Lynn, S. J., Namy, L. L., & Wolff, N. J. (2009). *Psychology: From inquiry to understanding.* Boston, MA: Pearson.

Lim, B.-C., & Ployhart, R. E. (2004). Transformational leadership: Relations to the five-factor model and team performance in typical and maximum contexts. *Journal of Applied Psychology, 89,* 610–621.

Lim, R. F. (Ed.). (2006). *Clinical manual of cultural psychiatry.* Washington, DC: American Psychiatric Publishing, Inc.

Lim, S.-L., & Kim, J.-H. (2005). Cognitive processing of emotional information in depression, panic, and somatoform disorder. *Journal of Abnormal Psychology, 114,* 50–61.

Lim, V. K. G., Teo, T. S. H., & Loo, G. L. (2003). Sex, financial hardship and locus of control: An empirical study of attitudes towards money among Singaporean Chinese. *Personality and Individual Differences, 34,* 411–429.

Lin, J. G., & Chen, W. L. (2008). Acupuncture analgesia: A review of its mechanisms of actions. *American Journal of Chinese Medicine, 36*(4), 635–645.

Lin, L., Umahara, M., York, D. A., & Bray, G. A. (1998). Beta-casomorphins stimulate and enterostatin inhibits the intake of dietary fat in rats. *Peptides, 19,* 325–331.

Lin, S., Thomas, T. C., Storlien, L. H., & Huang, X. F. (2000). Development of high fat diet-induced obesity and leptin resistance in C57BI/6J mice. *International Journal of Obesity Related Metabolic Disorders, 24,* 639–646.

Lin, Y., & Raghubir, P. (2005). Gender differences in unrealistic optimism about marriage and divorce: Are men more optimistic and women more realistic? *Personality and Social Psychology Bulletin, 31,* 198–207.

Lin, Y., Wu, M., Yang, C., Chen, T., Hsu, C., Chang, Y., et al. (2008). Evaluation of assertiveness training for psychiatric patients. *Journal of Clinical Nursing, 17,* 2875–2883.

Lindau, S. T., Schumm, L. P., Laumann, E. O., Levinson, W., O'Muircheartaigh, C. A., & Waite, L. J. (2007). A study of sexuality and health among older adults in the United States. *The New England Journal of Medicine, 357,* 762–774.

Linde, K., Allais, G., Brinkhaus, B., Manheimer, E., Vickers, A., & White, A. R. (2009). Acupuncture for tension-type headache. *Cochrane Database Systematic Review,* 1, article no. CD007587. Retrieved March 25, 2009, from http://mrw.interscience.wiley.com/cochrane/clsysrev/articles/CD007587/frame.html.

Lindsay, D. S., Hagen, L., Read, J. D., Wade, K., & Gary, M. (2004). True photographs and false memories. *Psychological Science, 15,* 149–154.

Lindvall, O., & Hagell, P. (2001). Cell therapy and transplantation in Parkinson's disease. *Clinical Chemistry and Laboratory Medicine, 39,* 356–361.

Linnet, K. M., Dalsgaard, S., Obel, C., Wisborg, K., Henriksen, T. B., Rodriguez, A., et al. (2003). Maternal lifestyle factors in pregnancy risk of attention deficit hyperactivity disorder and associated behaviors: Review of the current evidence. *American Journal of Psychiatry, 160,* 1028–1040.

Linnet, K. M., Wisborg, K., Obel, C., Secher, N. J., Thomsen, P. H., Agerbo, E., & Henriksen, T. B. (2005). Smoking during pregnancy and the risk for hyperkinetic disorder in offspring. *Pediatrics, 116,* 462–467.

Linz, D., Donnerstein, E., & Penrod, S. (1987). The findings and recommendations of the Attorney General's Commission on Pornography: Do the psychological facts fit the political fury? *American Psychologist, 42,* 946–953.

Lippa, R. A. (2003). Are 2D:4D finger-length ratios related to sexual orientation? Yes for men, no for women. *Journal of Personality and Social Psychology, 85,* 179–188.

Lipscombe, D., & Raingo, J. (2006). Internalizing channels: A mechanism to control pain? *Nature Neuroscience, 9*(1), 8–10.

Lisanby, S. H. (Ed.). (2004). *Brain stimulation in psychiatric treatment.* Washington, DC: American Psychiatric Association.

Lisspers, J., Sundin, Ö., Öhman, A., Hofman-Bang, C., Rydén, L., & Nygren, Å. (2005). Long-term effects of lifestyle behavior change in coronary artery disease: Effects on recurrent coronary events after percutaneous coronary intervention. *Health Psychology, 24,* 41–48.

Liston, C., McEwen, B. S., & Casey, B. J. (2009). Psychosocial stress reversibly disrupts prefrontal processing and attentional control. *Proceedings of the National Academy of Sciences, 106,* 912–917.

Littlewood, R. (1992). Psychiatric diagnosis and racial bias: Empirical and interpretative approaches. *Social Science & Medicine, 34,* 141–149.

Liu, G., & Akira, H. (1994). Basic principle of TCM. In Liu, G., Akira, H. (Eds.), *Fundamentals of acupuncture and moxibustion.* Tianjin, China: Tianjin Science and Technology Translation and Publishing Corporation.

Lively, W. M. (2001). Syncope and neurologic deficits in a track athlete: A case report. *Medicine and Science in Sports and Exercise, 33,* 345–347.

Livianos-Aldana, L., Rojo-Moreno, L., & Sierra-Sanmiguel, P. (2007). F. J. Gall and the phrenological movement. *American Journal of Psychiatry, 164*(3), 414–414.

Locke, E. A. (2000). Motivation, cognition, and action: An analysis of studies of task goals and knowledge. *Applied Psychology: An International Review, 49,* 408–429.

Locke, E. A., & Latham G. P. (1990). *A theory of goal setting & task performance.* Englewood Cliffs, NJ: Prentice Hall.

Locke, E. A., & Latham, G. P. (2002). Building a practically useful theory of goal setting and task motivation: A 35-year odyssey. *American Psychologist, 57,* 705–717.

Lockhart, R. S., & Craik, F. I. M. (1990). Levels of processing: A retrospective commentary on a framework for memory research. *Canadian Journal of Psychology, 44,* 87–112.

Loehlin, J. C. (1989). Partitioning environmental and genetic contributions to behavioral development. *American Psychologist, 44,* 1285–1292.

Loehlin, J. C. (1992). *Genes and environment in personality development.* Newbury Park, CA: Sage.

Loehlin, J. C., McCrae, R. R., Costa, P. T., & John, O. P. (1998). Heritabilities of common and measure-specific components of the Big Five personality factors. *Journal of Research in Personality, 32*(4), 431–453.

Loehlin, J. C., Neiderhiser, J. M., & Reiss, D. (2003). The behavior genetics of personality and the NEAD study. *Journal of Research in Personality, 37,* 373–387.

Loewenstein, G. (1994). The psychology of curiosity: A review and reinterpretation. *Psychological Bulletin, 116*(1), 75–98.

Loftus, E. F. (1992). When a lie becomes memory's truth: Memory distortion after exposure to misinformation. *Psychological Science, 3,* 121–123.

Loftus, E. F. (1997a). Memory for a past that never was. *Current Directions in Psychological Science, 6,* 60–65.

Loftus, E. F. (1997b). Repressed memory accusations: Devastated families and devastated patients. *Applied Cognitive Psychology, 11,* 25–30.

Loftus, E. F. (1998). The price of bad memories. *Skeptical Inquirer, 22,* 23–24.

Loftus, E. F. (2003, January). *Illusions of memory.* Presentation at the 25th Annual National Institute on the Teaching of Psychology, St. Petersburg Beach, Florida.

Loftus, E. F. (2004). Memories of things unseen. *Current Directions in Psychological Science, 13,* 145–147.

Loftus, E. F., & Hoffman, H. G. (1989). Misinformation and memory: The creation of new memories. *Journal of Experimental Psychology: General, 118,* 100–104.

Loftus, E. F., & Ketcham, K. (1991). *Witness for the defense.* New York: St. Martin's Press.

Loftus, E. F., & Ketcham, K. (1994). *The myth of repressed memory: False memories and allegations of sexual abuse.* New York: St. Martin's Press.

Loftus, E. F., & Palmer, J. C. (1974). Reconstruction of automobile destruction: An example of the interaction between language and memory. *Journal of Verbal Learning and Verbal Behavior, 13,* 585–589.

Loftus, E. F., & Pickrell, J. E. (1995). The formation of false memories. *Psychiatric Annals, 25,* 720–725.

Loftus, E. F., Garry, M., & Hayne, H. (2008). Repressed and recovered memory. In E. Borgida, & S. Fiske, (Eds.) *Beyond common sense: Psychological science in the courtroom* (pp. 177–194). Malden, MA: Blackwell Publishing.

Loftus, E., & Guyer, M. (2002). Who abused Jane Doe? The hazards of the single case history (Part 1). *Skeptical Inquirer, 26,* 24–32.

Loftus, T. M., Jaworsky, D. E., Frehywot, G. L., Townsend, C. A., Ronnett, G. V., Lane, M. D., & Kuhajda, F. P. (2000). Reduced food intake and body weight in mice treated with fatty acid synthase inhibitors. *Science, 288,* 2379–2381.

Logue, A. W. (1985). Conditioned food aversion in humans. *Annals of the New York Academy of Sciences, 104,* 331–340.

Logue, J. N. (2008, January 1). Violent death in American schools in the 21st century: Reflections following the 2006 Amish school shootings. *Journal of School Health,* pp. 58–61.

Loher, B. T., Noe, R. A., Moeller, N. L., & Fitzgerald, M. P. (1985). A meta-analysis of the relation of job characteristics to job satisfaction. *Journal of Applied Psychology, 70,* 280–289.

Lohman, D. F. (2004). Aptitude for college: The importance of reasoning tests for minority admissions. In R. Zwick (Ed.), *Rethinking the SAT: The future of standardized testing in college admissions* (pp. 41–56). New York: RoutledgeFalmer.

Lohman, D. F. (2005). The role of non-verbal ability tests in identifying academically gifted students: An aptitude perspective. *Gifted Child Quarterly, 49,* 111–138.

Lohman, D. F., & Hagen, E. (2001). *Cognitive abilities test (Form 6): Interpretive guide for teachers and counselors.* Itasca, IL: Riverside.

Lohr, J. M., Hooke, W., Gist, R., & Tolin, D. F. (2003). Novel and controversial treatments for trauma-related stress disorders. In S. O. Lilienfeld, S. J. Lynn, & J. M. Lohr (Eds.), *Science and pseudoscience in clinical psychology* (pp. 243–272). New York: Guilford Press.

Lohrenz, T., McCabe, K., Camerer, C. F., & Montague, P. R. (2007). Neural signature of fictive learning signals in a sequential investment task. *Proceedings of the National Academy of Sciences, 104,* 9493–9498.

LoLordo, V. M. (2001). Learned helplessness and depression. In M. E. Carroll & J. B. Overmier (Eds.), *Animal research and human health: Advancing human welfare through behavioral science* (pp. 63–77). Washington, DC: American Psychological Association.

London Daily Telegraph. (1998, September 19). "'Cat' that turned out to be a clock." *London Daily Telegraph.*

Longo, N., Klempay, S., & Bitterman, M. E. (1964). Classical appetitive conditioning in the pigeon. *Psychonomic Science, 1,* 19–20.

Lonn, S., Ahlbom, A., Hall, P., & Feychting, M. (2004). Mobile phone use and the risk of acoustic neuroma. *Epidemiology, 15,* 653–659.

Loos, R. J. F., Rankinen, T., Chagnon, Y., Tremblay, A., Pérusse, L., & Bouchard, C. (2006). Polymorphisms in the leptin and leptin receptor genes in relation to resting metabolic rate and respiratory quotient in the Québec Family Study. *International Journal of Obesity, 30,* 183–190.

Lopes, P. N., Salovey, P., Côté, S., & Beers, M. (2005). Emotion regulation abilities and the quality of social interaction. *Emotion, 5,* 113–118.

Lopez, S. R. (1989). Patient variable biases in clinical judgment: Conceptual overview and methodological considerations. *Psychological Bulletin, 106,* 184–203.

Lopez-Garcia, E., van Dam, R. M., Li, T. Y., Rodriguez-Artalejo, F., & Hu, F. B. (2008). The relationship of coffee consumption with mortality. *Annals of Internal Medicine, 148,* 904–914.

López-Ibor, J. J., López-Ibor, M.-I., & Pastrana, J. I. (2008). Transcranial magnetic stimulation. *Current Opinion in Psychiatry, 21*(6), 640–644.

Lord, C. G. (1997). *Social psychology.* Fort Worth: Harcourt, Brace.

Lotze, M., Scheler, G., Tan, H.-R. M., Braun, C., & Birbaumer, N. (2003). The musician's brain: Functional imaging of amateurs and professionals during performance and imagery. *NeuroImage, 20*(3), 1817.

Louzá, M. R., & Bassitt, D. P. (2005). Maintenance treatment of severe tardive dyskinesia with Clozapine: 5 years' follow-up. *Journal of Clinical Psychopharmacology, 25,* 180–182.

Love, J. M., Kisker, E. E., Ross, C., Raikes, H., Constantine, J., Boller, K., et al. (2005). The effectiveness of early head start for 3-year-old children and their parents: Lessons for policy and programs. *Developmental Psychology, 41,* 885–901.

Loving, T. J., Heffner, K. L., & Keicolt-Glaser, J. K. (2006). Physiology and interpersonal relationships. In A. Vangelisti & D. Perlman (Eds.), *The Cambridge handbook of personal relationships* (pp. 385–405). New York: Cambridge University Press.

Low, C. A., Stanton, A. L., & Danoff-Burg, S. (2006). Expressive disclosure and benefit finding among breast cancer patients: Mechanisms for positive health effects. *Health Psychology, 25*, 181–189.

Löw, K., Crestani, F., Keist, R., Benke, D., Brunig, I., Benson, J. A., et al. (2000). Molecular and neuronal substrate for the selective attenuation of anxiety. *Science, 290*, 131–134.

Löwe, B., Mundt, C., Herzog, W., Brunner, R., Backenstass, M., Kronmueller, K., & Henningsen, P. (2008). Validity of current somatoform disorder diagnoses: Perspective for classification in DSM-V and ICD-11. *Psychopathology, 41*, 4–9.

Lu, J., Sherman, D., Devor, M., & Saper, C. B. (2006). A putative flip-flop switch for control of REM sleep. *Nature, 441*, 589–594.

Lubinski, D., Benbow, C. P., Webb, R. M., & Bleske-Rechek, A. (2006). Tracking exceptional human capital over two decades. *Psychological Science, 17*(3), 194–199.

Lubinski, D., Webb, R. M., Morelock, M. J., & Benbow, C. P. (2001). Top 1 in 10,000: A 10 year follow-up of the profoundly gifted. *Journal of Applied Psychology, 86*, 718–729.

Luborsky, L. (1972). Another reply to Eysenck. *Psychological Bulletin, 78*, 406–408.

Luborsky, L., Rosenthal, R., & Diguer, L. (2003). Are some psychotherapies much more effective than others? *Journal of Applied Psychoanalytic Studies, 5*(4), 455–460.

Luborsky, L., Rosenthal, R., Diguer, L., Andrusyna, T. P., Berman, J. S., Levitt, J. T., et al. (2002). The dodo bird verdict is alive and well—mostly. *Clinical Psychology: Science and Practice, 9*, 2–12.

Luborsky, L., Singer, B., & Luborsky, L. (1975). Comparative studies of psychotherapies: Is it true that everyone has won and all must have prizes? *Archives of General Psychiatry, 32*, 995–1008.

Lucas, J. A. (2005). Disorders of memory. *Psychiatric Clinics of North America, 28*(3), 581–597.

Lucas, R. E. (2007). Adaptation and the set-point model of subjective well-being: Does happiness change after major life events? *Current Directions in Psychological Science, 16*, 75–79.

Ludwig-Rosenthal, R., & Neufeld, R. W. (1988). Stress management during noxious medical procedures: An evaluative review of outcome studies. *Psychological Bulletin, 104*, 326–342.

Luhrmann, T. M. (2008). "The street will drive you crazy": Why homeless psychotic women in the institutional circuit in the United States often say no to offers of help. *American Journal of Psychiatry, 165*, 15–20.

Luna, D., Ringberg, T., & Peracchio, L. A. (2008). One individual, two identities: Frame switching among biculturals. *Journal of Consumer Research, 35*(2), 279–293.

Lund, T., Labriola, M., Christensen, K. B., Bultmann, U., & Villadsen, E. (2006). Physical work environment risk factors for long-term sickness absence: Prospective findings among a cohort of 5357 employees in Denmark. *British Medical Journal, 332*, 449–452.

Lundy, R. F., Jr. (2008). Gustatory hedonic value: Potential function for forebrain control of brainstem taste processing. *Neuroscience & Biobehavioral Reviews, 32*(8), 1601–1606.

Luntz, B. K., & Widom, C. S. (1994). Antisocial personality disorder in abused and neglected children grown up. *American Journal of Psychiatry, 151*, 670–674.

Luria, Z. (1992, February). *Gender differences in children's play patterns.* Paper presented at University of Southern California, Los Angeles.

Lussier, J. P., Heil, S. H., Mongeon, J. A., Badger, G. J., & Higgins, S. T. (2006). A meta-analysis of voucher-based reinforcement therapy for substance use disorders. *Addiction, 101*, 192–203.

Lustig, R. H., Sen, S., Soberman, J. E., & Velasquez-Mieyer, P. A. (2004). Obesity, leptin resistance, and the effects of insulin reduction. *International Journal of Obesity, 28*, 1344–1348.

Luthar, S. S., & Latendresse, S. J. (2005). Children of the affluent. *Current Directions in Psychological Science, 14*, 49–53.

Lutz, D. J., & Sternberg, R. J. (1999). Cognitive development. In M. H. Bornstein & M. E. Lamb (Eds.), *Developmental psychology: An advanced textbook* (4th ed.). Mahwah, NJ: Erlbaum.

Lykken, D. T. (1998a). The genetics of genius. In A. Steptoe (Ed.) *Genius and mind: Studies of creativity and temperament* (pp. 15–37). New York, NY: Oxford University Press.

Lykken, D. T. (1998b). *A tremor in the blood: Uses and abuses of the lie detector.* Cambridge, MA: Perseus Publishing.

Lykken, D. T. (1999). *Happiness: What studies on twins show us about nature, nurture, and the happiness set point.* New York: Golden Books.

Lynam, D. R. (1996). The early identification of chronic offenders: Who is the fledgling psychopath? *Psychological Bulletin, 120*, 209–234.

Lynam, D. R., & Widiger, T. A. (2001). Using the five-factor model to represent the *DSM-IV* personality disorders: An expert consensus approach. *Journal of Abnormal Psychology, 110*, 401–412.

Lynch, F. L., Hornbrook, M., Clarke, G. N., Perrin, N., Polen, M. R., O'Connor, E., et al. (2005). Cost-effectiveness of an intervention to prevent depression in at-risk teens. *Archives of General Psychiatry, 62*, 1241–1248.

Lynn, R. (2006). *Race differences in intelligence: An evolutionary analysis.* Augusta, GA: Washington Summit Publishers.

Lynn, R., & Mikk, J. (2007). National differences in intelligence and educational attainment. *Intelligence, 35*, 115–121.

Lynn, S. J., & Kirsch, I. (2006). *Essentials of clinical hypnosis: An evidence-based approach.* Washington, DC: American Psychological Association.

Lynn, S. J., Lilienfeld, S. O., & Lohr, J. M. (Eds.). (2003). *Science and pseudoscience in clinical psychology.* New York: Guilford Press.

Lynn, S. J., Myers, B., & Malinoski, P. (1997). Hypnosis, pseudomemories, and clinical guidelines: A sociocognitive perspective. In J. D. Read & D. S. Lindsay (Eds.), *Recollections of trauma: Scientific evidence and clinical practice. NATO ASI series: Series A: Life sciences* (Vol. 291, pp. 305–336). New York: Plenum Press.

Lynn, S. J., & Rhue, J. W. (1986). The fantasy-prone person: Hypnosis, imagination, and creativity. *Journal of Personality and Social Psychology, 51*, 404–408.

Lynn, S. J., Vanderhoff, H., Shindler, K., & Stafford, J. (2002). Defining hypnosis as a trance vs. cooperation: Hypnotic inductions, suggestibility, and performance standards. *American Journal of Clinical Hypnosis, 44*, 231–240.

Lynskey, M. T., Heath, A. C., Bucholz, K. K., Slutske, W. S., Madden, P. A. F., Nelson, E. C., et al. (2003). Escalation of drug use in early-onset cannabis users vs. co-twin controls. *Journal of the American Medical Association, 289*, 427–433.

Lyubomirsky, S. (2001). Why are some people happier than others? The role of cognitive and motivational processes in well-being. *American Psychologist, 56*, 239–249.

Lyubomirsky, S., King, L., & Diener, E. (2005). The benefits of frequent positive affect: Does happiness lead to success? *Psychological Bulletin, 131*, 803–855.

Lyubomirsky, S., & Nolen-Hoeksema, S. (1995). Effects of self-focused rumination on negative thinking and interpersonal problem solving. *Journal of Personality and Social Psychology, 69*, 176–190.

Ma, M. (2007). Encoding olfactory signals via multiple chemosensory systems. *Critical Reviews in Biochemistry and Molecular Biology, 42*(6), 463–480.

Maandag, N. J., Coman, D., Sanganahalli, B. G., Herman, P., Smith, A. J., Blumenfeld, H., et al. (2007). Energetics of neuronal signaling and fMRI activity. *Proceedings of the National Academies of Sciences, 104*(51), 20546–20551.

MacAndrew, C., & Edgerton, R. B. (1969). *Drunken comportment.* Chicago: Aldine.

Maccoby, E. E., & Martin, J. A. (1983). Socialization in the context of the family: Parent-child interaction. In E. M. Hetherington (Ed.) and P. H. Mussen (Series Ed.), *Handbook of child psychology: Vol. 4. Socialization, personality, and social development* (pp. 1–101). New York: Wiley.

MacDonald, M., & Bernstein, D. A. (1974). Treatment of a spider phobia with in vivo and imaginal desensitization. *Journal of Behavior Therapy and Experimental Psychiatry, 5*, 47–52.

MacEvoy, S. P., & Paradiso, M. A. (2001). Lightness constancy in primary visual cortex. *Proceedings of the National Academy of Sciences, 98*, 8827–8831.

Macey, P. M., Henderson, L. A., Macey, K. E., Alger, J. R., Frysinger, R. C., Woo, M. A., et al. (2002). Brain morphology associated with obstructive sleep apnea. *American Journal of Respiratory and Critical Care Medicine, 166*, 1382–1387.

Machado, R. F., Laskowski, D., Deffenderfer, O., Burch, T., Zheng, S., Mazzone, P. J., et al. (2005). Detection of lung cancer by sensor array analyses of exhaled breath. *American Journal of Respiratory and Critical Care Medicine, 171*, 1286–1289.

Mack, A. (2003). Inattentional blindness: Looking without seeing. *Current Directions in Psychological Science, 12*, 180–184.

Mack, A., & Rock, I. (1998). *Inattentional blindness.* Cambridge, MA: MIT Press.

Mackay, D. G. (2006, March 29). Aging, memory, and language in amnesic H. M. *Hippocampus.* Retrieved Septeptember 26, 2006, from http://www3.interscience.wiley.com/cgi-bin/jissue/112597200.

MacMillan, H. L., Fleming, J. E., Steiner, D. L., Lin, E., Boyle, M. H., Jamieson, E., et al. (2001). Childhood abuse and lifetime psychopathology in a community sample. *American Journal of Psychiatry, 158*, 1878–1883.

MacMillan, N. A., & Creelman, C. D. (2004). *Detection theory: A user's guide* (2nd ed.). Hillsdale, NJ: Erlbaum.

MacQueen, G. M., Hajek, T., & Alda, M. (2005). The phenotypes of bipolar disorder: Relevance for genetic investigations. *Molecular Psychiatry, 10*, 811–826.

Maddi, S. R., & Khoshaba, D. M. (2005). *Resilence at work.* New York: American Management Association.

Maddux, J. E., & Gosselin, J. T. (2003). Self-efficacy. In M. R. Leary & J. P. Tangney (Eds.), *Handbook of self and identity* (pp. 218–238). New York: Guilford Press.

Madon, S., Guyll, M., Spoth, R., & Willard, J. (2004). Self-fulfilling prophecies. *Psychological Science, 15*, 837–845.

Madon, S., Willard, J., Guyll, M., Trudeau, L., & Spoth, R. (2006). Self-fulfilling prophecy effects of mothers' beliefs on children's alcohol use: Accumulation, dissipation, and stability over time. *Journal of Personality and Social Psychology, 90*, 911–926.

Madsen, M. V., Gøtzsche, P. C., and Hróbjartsson, A. (2009). Acupuncture treatment for pain: Systematic review of randomized clinical trials with acupuncture, placebo acupuncture, and no acupuncture groups. *British Medical Journal, 338*, a3115.

Magee, W. L. (2007). Music as a diagnostic tool in low awareness states: Considering limbic responses. *Brain Injury, 21*(6), 593–599.

Magnavita, J. J. (2006). In search of unifying principles of psychotherapy: Conceptual, empirical, and clinical convergence. *American Psychologist, 61*, 882–892.

Mahler, S. V., Smith, K. S., & Berridge, K. C. (2007). Endocannabinoid hedonic hotspot for sensory pleasure: Anandamide in nucleus accumbens shell enhances 'liking' of a sweet reward. *Neuropsychopharmacology, 32*(11), 2267–2278.

Mahroo, O. A., & Lamb, T. D. (2004). Recovery of the human photopic electroretinogram after bleaching exposures: Estimation of pigment regeneration kinetics. *Journal of Physiology, 554,* 417–437.

Maier, S. F., & Watkins, L. R. (2000). The immune system as a sensory system: Implications for psychology. *Current Directions in Psychological Science, 9,* 98–102.

Mains, J. A., & Scogin, F. R. (2003). The effectiveness of self-administered treatments: A practice-friendly review of the research. *Journal of Clinical Psychology, 59,* 237–245.

Maio, G., Haddock, G., Manstead, A., & Spears, R. (In press.) Attitudes and intergroup relations. In J. F. Dovidio, M. Hewstone, P. Glick, & V. M. Esses (Eds.), *Handbook of prejudice, stereotyping, and discrimination.* London: Sage.

Maj, M., Gaebal, W., Lopez-Ibor, J. J., & Sartorius, N. (Eds.). (2002). *Psychiatric diagnosis and classification.* New York: Wiley.

Major, B., Sciacchtinano, A. M., & Crocker, J. (1993). In-group versus out-group comparisons and self-esteem. *Personality and Social Psychology Bulletin, 19,* 711–721.

Makeover, R. B. (2004). *Treatment planning for psychotherapists* (2nd ed.). Washington, DC: American Psychiatric Publishing.

Makin, T. R., Holmes, N. P., & Ehrsson, H. H. (2008). On the other hand: Dummy hands and peripersonal space. *Behavioural Brain Research, 191*(1), 1–10.

Malamuth, N. M. (1998). The confluence model as an organizing framework for research on sexually aggressive men: Risk moderators, imagined aggression, and pornography consumption. In R. G. Geen & E. Donnerstein (Eds.), *Human aggression* (pp. 230–247). San Diego: Academic Press.

Malamuth, N., & Addison, T. (2001). Helping and altruism. In G. Fletcher & M. Clark (Eds.), *Blackwell handbook of social psychology: Interpersonal processes* (pp. 162–195). Oxford, UK: Blackwell.

Malamuth, N. M., Addison, T., & Koss, M. (2000). Pornography and sexual aggression: Are there reliable effects and can we understand them? *Annual Review of Sex Research, 11,* 26–91.

Malamuth, N. M., & Check, J. V. P. (1983). Sexual arousal to rape depictions: Individual differences. *Journal of Abnormal Psychology, 92,* 55–67.

Malarkey, W. B., Kiecolt-Glaser, J. K., Pearl, D., & Glaser, R. (1994). Hostile behavior during marital conflict alters pituitary and adrenal hormones. *Psychosomatic Medicine, 56,* 41–51.

Malaspina, D., Goetz, R. R., Friedman, J. H., Kaufmann, C. A., Faraone, S. V., Tsuang, M., et al. (2001). Traumatic brain injury and schizophrenia in members of schizophrenia and bipolar disorder pedigrees. *American Journal of Psychiatry, 158,* 440–446.

Maldonado, J. R., & Spiegal, D. (2008). Dissociative disorders. In R. E. Hales, S. C. Yudofsky, & G. O. Gabbard (Eds.), *Textbook of psychiatry* (pp. 665–728). Washington, DC: American Psychiatric Publishing.

Maldonado, R., Valverde, O., & Berrendero, F. (2006). Involvement of the endocannabinoid system in drug addiction. *Trends in Neuroscience, 29,* 225–232.

Malenka, R. C. (1995). LTP and LTD: Dynamic and interactive processes of synaptic plasticity. *The Neuroscientist, 1,* 35–42.

Malenka, R. C., & Nicoll, R. A. (1999). Long-term potentiation—a decade of progress? *Science, 285,* 1870–1874.

Malgrange, B., Rigo, J. M., Van de Water, T. R., Staecker, H., Moonen, G., & Lefebvre, P. P. (1999). Growth factor therapy to the damaged inner ear: Clinical prospects. *International Journal of Pediatric Otorhinolaryngology, 49*(Suppl. 1), S19–S25.

Malhotra, S. (2008). Impact of the sexual revolution: Consequences of risky sexual behaviors. *Journal of American Physicians & Surgeons, 13*(3), 88–90.

Maljaars, P. W. J., Peters, H. P. F., Mela, D. J., & Masclee, A. A. M. (2008). Ileal brake: A sensible food target for appetite control. A review. *Physiology & Behavior, 95*(3), 271–281.

Malojcic, B., Mubrin, Z., Coric, B., Susnic, M., & Spilich, G. J. (2008). Consequences of mild traumatic brain injury on information processing assessed with attention and short-term memory tasks. *Journal of Neurotrauma, 25*(1), 30–37.

Malone, D. A., Jr., Dougherty, D. D., Rezai, A. R., Carpenter, L. L., Friehsf, G. M., Eskandar, E. N., Rauch, S. L., Rasmussen, S. A., Machado, A. G., Kubu, C. S., Tyrka, A. R., Price, L. H., Stypulkowski, P. H., Giftakis, J. E., Rise, M. T., Malloy, P. F., Salloway, S. P., & Greenberg, B. D. (2009). Deep brain stimulation of the ventral capsule/ventral striatum for treatment-resistant depression. *Biological Psychiatry, 65,* 267–275.

Malouff, J. M., Rooke, S. E., & Schutte, N. S. (2008). The heritability of human behavior: Results of aggregating meta-analyses. *Current Psychology, 27*(3), 153–161.

Maltby, N., Kirsch, I., & Mayers, M. (2002). Virtual reality exposure therapy for the treatment of fear of flying: A controlled investigation. *Journal of Consulting and Clinical Psychology, 70*(5), 1112–1118.

Mancinelli, R., Binetti, R., & Ceccanti, M. (2007). Woman, alcohol and environment: Emerging risks for health. *Neuroscience & Biobehavioral Reviews, 31*(2), 246–253.

Mandelid, L. J. (2003). Dodofugl-dommen og psykoterapeuters credo. [The Dodo-bird verdict and the beliefs of psychotherapists]. *Tidsskrift for Norsk Psykologforening, 40*(4), 307–312.

Maner, J. K., Luce, C. L., Neuberg, S. L., Cialdini, R. B., Brown, S., & Sagarin, B. J. (2002). The effects of perspective taking on motivations for helping: Still no evidence for altruism. *Personality and Social Psychology Bulletin, 28,* 1601–1610.

Manfield, P., & Shapiro, F. (2004). Application of eye movement desensitization and reprocessing (EMDR) to personality disorders. In J. J. Magnavita (Ed.), *Handbook of personality disorders: Theory and practice* (pp. 304–328). New York: Wiley.

Manheimer, E., White, A., Berman, B., Forys, K., & Ernst, E. (2005). Meta-analysis: Acupuncture for low back pain. *Annals of Internal Medicine, 142,* 651–663.

Manini, T. M., Everhart, J. E., Patel, K. V., Schoeller, D. A., Colbert, L. H., Visser, M., et al. (2006). Daily activity energy expenditure and mortality among older adults. *Journal of the American Medical Association, 296,* 171–179.

Mann, J. J., Apter, A., Bertolote, J., Beautrais, A., Currier, D., Haas, A., et al. (2005). Suicide prevention strategies: A systematic review. *Journal of the American Medical Association, 294,* 2064–2074.

Mann, K., Roschke, J., Nink, M., Aldenhoff, J., Beyer, J., Benkert, O., & Lehnert, H. (1992). Effects of corticotropin-releasing hormone administration in patients suffering from sleep apnea syndrome. *Society for Neuroscience Abstracts, 22,* 196.

Manning, C. (2004). Beyond memory: Neuropsychologic features in differential diagnosis of dementia. *Clinical Geriatric Medicine, 20*(1), 45–58.

Mansfield, P. K., Voda, A., & Koch, P. B. (1995). Predictors of sexual response changes in heterosexual midlife women. *Health Values, 19*(1), 10–20.

Manti, L., Braselmann, H., Calabrese, M. L., Massa, R., Pugliese, M., Scampoli, P., Sicignano, G., & Grossi, G. (2008). Effects of modulated microwave radiation at cellular telephone frequency (1.95 GHz) on X-ray-induced chromosome aberrations in human lymphocytes in vitro. *Radiation Research, 169*(5), 575–583.

Manto, M. (2008). The cerebellum, cerebellar disorders, and cerebellar research—Two centuries of discoveries. *Cerebellum, 7*(4), 505–516.

Maquet, P. (2001). The role of sleep in learning and memory. *Science, 294,* 1048–1052.

March, J., Silva, S., Petrycki, S., Curry, J., Wells, K., Fairbank, J., et al. (2004). Fluoxetine, cognitive-behavioral therapy, and their combination for adolescents with depression: Treatment for Adolescents with Depression Study (TADS) randomized controlled trial. *Journal of the American Medical Association, 292,* 807–820.

Marchman, T. (2008, October 24). You Call That Bling? *Wall Street Journal—Eastern Edition, 252*(98).

Marcus, G. F. (1996). Why do children say "breaked"? *Current Directions in Psychological Science, 5,* 81–85.

Marcus, S. V. (2008). Phase 1 of integrated EMDR: An abortive treatment for migraine headaches. *Journal of EMDR Practice and Research, 2*(1), 15–25.

Marenco, S., & Weinberger, D. R. (2000). The neurodevelopmental hypothesis of schizophrenia: Following a trail of evidence from cradle to grave. *Developmental Psychopathology, 12,* 501–527.

Margetic, S., Gazzola, C., Pegg, G. G., & Hill, R. A. (2002). Leptin: A review of its peripheral actions and interactions. *Obesity, 26,* 1407–1433.

Marin, S., Vinaixa, M., Brezmes, J., Llobet, E., Vilanova, X., Correig, X., Ramos, A. J., & Sanchez, V. (2007). Use of a MS-electronic nose for prediction of early fungal spoilage of bakery products. *International Journal of Food Microbiology, 114,* 10–16.

Markman, E. M. (1994). Constraints children place on word meanings. In P. Bloom (Ed.), *Language acquisition: Core readings* (pp. 154–173). Cambridge, MA: MIT Press.

Markoff, J. (2008, November 25). Microsoft examines causes of 'cyberchondria.' *New York Times.*

Markon, K. E., Krueger, R. F., & Watson, D. (2005). Delineating the structure of normal and abnormal personality: An integrative hierarchical approach. *Journal of Personality and Social Psychology, 88,* 139–157.

Markov, D., & Goldman, M. (2006). Normal sleep and circadian rhythms: Neurobiologic mechanisms underlying sleep and wakefulness. *Psychiatric Clinics of North America, 29,* 841–853.

Marks, I. M. (2002). Reduction of fear: Towards a unifying theory. *Psicoterapia Cognitiva e Comportamentale, 8*(1), 63–66.

Markus, H. R. (2008). Pride, prejudice, and ambivalence: Toward a unified theory of race and ethnicity. *American Psychologist, 63*(8), 651–670.

Markus, H. R., & Kitayama, S. (1991). Culture and the self: Implications for cognition, emotion, and motivation. *Psychological Review, 98,* 224–253.

Markus, H. R., Kitayama, S., & Heiman, R. J. (1996). Culture and "basic" psychological principles. In E. T. Higgins & A. W. Kruglanski (Eds.), *Social psychology: Handbook of basic principles* (pp. 857–913). New York: Guilford.

Marmarosh, C., Holtz, A., & Schottenbauer, M. (2005). Group cohesiveness, group-derived collective self-esteem, group-derived hope, and the well-being of group therapy members. *Group Dynamics: Theory, Research, and Practice, 9,* 32–44.

Maron, E., Nikopensius, T., Koks, S., Altmae, S., Heinaste, E., Vabrit, K., et al. (2005). Association study of 90 candidate gene polymorphisms in panic disorder. *Psychiatric Genetics, 15,* 17–24.

Marsh, A. A., Ambady, N., & Kleck, R. E. (2005). The effects of fear and anger facial expressions on approach- and avoidance-related behaviors. *Emotion, 5,* 119–124.

Marshall, S. J., Biddle, S. J., Gorely, T., Cameron, N., & Murdey, I. (2004). Relationships between media use, body fatness and physical activity in children and youth: A meta-analysis. *International Journal of Obesity, 28,* 1238–1246.

Marshall, W. L. (1989). Pornography and sex offenders. In D. Zillmann & J. Bryant (Eds.), *Pornography: Research advances and policy considerations.* Hillsdale, NJ: Erlbaum.

Marti, P. R., Singleton, C. K., & Hiller-Sturmhofel, S. (2003). The role of thiamine deficiency in alcoholic brain disease. *Alcohol Research Health, 27*(2), 134–142.

Martin, C. L., & Fabes, R. A. (2001). The stability and consequences of young children's same-sex peer interactions. *Developmental Psychology, 37,* 431–446.

Martin, D. J., Garske, J. P., & Davis, M. K. (2000). Relation of the therapeutic alliance with outcome and other variables: A meta-analytic review. *Journal of Consulting & Clinical Psychology, 68,* 438–450.

Martin, G., Guadano-Ferraz, A., Morte, B., Ahmed, S., Koob, G. F., De Lecea, L., & Siggins, G. R. (2004). Chronic morphine treatment alters N-methyl-D-aspartate receptors in freshly isolated neurons from nucleus accumbens. *Journal of Pharmacology and Experimental Therapeutics, 311,* 265–273.

Martin, G., & Pear, J. (2006). *Behavior modification* (8th ed.). New York: Prentice Hall.

Martin, J. A., Hamilton, B. E., Sutton, P. D., Ventura, S. J., et al. (2009). Births: Final data for 2006. *National Vital Statistics Reports, 57*(7), 1–102.

Martin, J. G. A., & Réale, D. (2008). Temperament, risk assessment and habituation to novelty in eastern chipmunks, Tamias striatus. *Animal Behaviour, 75*(1), 309–318.

Martin, R., & Hewstone, M. (2003). Majority versus minority influence: When, not whether, source status instigates heuristic or systematic processing. *European Journal of Social Psychology, 33,* 313–330.

Martin, R., Gardikiotis, A., & Hewstone, M. (2002). Levels of consensus and majority and minority influence. *European Journal of Social Psychology, 32,* 645–665.

Martin, R. A. (2001). Humor, laughter, and physical health: Methodological issues and research findings. *Psychological Bulletin, 127,* 504–519.

Martinez, C. R., & Forgatch, M. S. (2001). Preventing problems with boys' noncompliance: Effects of a parent training intervention for divorcing mothers. *Journal of Consulting and Clinical Psychology, 69,* 416–428.

Martinez, D., Gil, R., Slifstein, M., Hwang, D.-R., Huang, Y., Perez, A., et al. (2005). Alcohol dependence is associated with blunted dopamine transmission in the ventral striatum. *Biological Psychiatry, 58,* 779–786.

Martinez, M. (2000). *Education as the cultivation of intelligence.* Mahwah, NJ: Erlbaum.

Martinez-Taboas, A. (2005). The plural world of culturally sensitive psychotherapy: A response to Castro-Blanco's (2005) comments. *Psychotherapy: Theory, Research, Practice, Training, 42,* 17–19.

Martinot, M.-L. P., Bragulat, V., Artiges, E., Dolle, F., Hinnen, F., Jouvent, R., et al. (2001). Decreased presynaptic dopamine function in the left caudate of depressed patients with affective flattening and psychomotor retardation. *American Journal of Psychiatry, 158,* 314–316.

Masand, P., Popli, A. P., & Welburg, J. B. (1995). Sleepwalking. *American Family Physician, 51*(3), 649–653.

Maslach, C. (2003). Job burnout: New directions in research and intervention. *Current Directions in Psychological Science, 12,* 189–192.

Masland, R. H. (2001). Neuronal diversity in the retina. *Current Opinion in Neurobiology, 11,* 431–436.

Maslow, A. H. (1943). A theory of human motivation. *Psychological Review, 50, 370–396.*

Maslow, A. H. (1954). *Motivation and personality.* New York: Harper.

Maslow, A. H. (1970). *Motivation and personality* (2nd ed.). New York: Harper & Row.

Maslow, A. H. (1971a). *The farther reaches of human nature.* New York: McGraw-Hill.

Maslow, A. H. (1971b). *Toward a psychology of being.* Princeton, NJ: Van Nostrand.

Mass, R., Hölldorfer, M., Moll, B., Bauer, R., & Wolf, K. (2008). Why we haven't died out yet: Changes in women's mimic reactions to visual erotic stimuli during their menstrual cycles. *Hormones and Behavior, 55*(2), 267–271.

Massaro, D. W., & Cowan, N. (1993). Information processing models: Microscopes of the mind. *Annual Review of Psychology, 44,* 383–425.

Masson, M. E. J., & MacLeod, C. M. (1992). Reenacting the route to interpretation: Enhanced perceptual identification without prior perception. *Journal of Experimental Psychology: General, 121,* 145–176.

Masters, J. C., Burish, T. G., Hollon, S. D., & Rimm, D. C. (1987). *Behavior therapy: Techniques and empirical findings* (3rd ed.). San Diego: Harcourt Brace Jovanovich.

Masters, W. H., & Johnson, V. E. (1966). *Human sexual response.* Boston: Little, Brown & Co.

Masuda, T., Gonzalez, R., Kwan, L., & Nisbett, R. E. (2008). Culture and aesthetic preference: Comparing the attention to context of East Asians and Americans. *Personality and Social Psychology Bulletin, 34*(9), 1260–1275.

Mather, M., & Carstensen, L. L. (2005). Aging and motivated cognition: The positivity effect in attention and memory. *Trends in Cognitive Sciences, 9,* 496–502.

Mathew, S. J., Amiel, J. M., & Sackeim, H. A. (2005). Electroconvulsive therapy in treatment-resistant depression. *Primary Psychiatry, 12,* 52–56.

Matlin, M. W. (1998). *Cognition* (4th ed.). Fort Worth, TX: Harcourt Brace.

Maton, K., Kohout, J. L., Wicherski, M., Leary, G. E., & Vinokurov, A. (2006). Minority students of color in the psychology graduate pipeline: Disquieting and encouraging trends, 1989–2003. *American Psychologist, 61,* 117–131.

Matson, J., Sevin, J., Fridley, D., & Love, S. (1990). Increasing spontaneous language in autistic children. *Journal of Applied Behavior Analysis, 23,* 227–233.

Matson, J. L., & Boisjoli, J. A. (2009). The token economy for children with intellectual disability and/or autism: A review. *Research in Developmental Disabilities, 30,* 240–248.

Matsumoto, D. (2000). *Culture and psychology: People around the world.* Belmont, CA: Wadsworth.

Matsumoto, D., & Ekman, P. (1989). American-Japanese cultural differences in intensity ratings of facial expressions of emotion. *Motivation and Emotion, 13,* 143–157.

Matsumoto, D., & Willingham, B. (2006). The thrill of victory and the agony of defeat: Spontaneous expressions of medal winners of the 2004 Athens Olympic games. *Journal of Personality and Social Psychology, 91,* 568–581.

Matsumoto, D., Yoo, S. H., Hirayama, S., & Petrova, G. (2005). Development and validation of a measure of display rule knowledge: The display rule assessment inventory. *Emotion, 5,* 23–40.

Matsumoto, D., Yoo, S. H., & Nakagawa, S. (2008). Multinational study of cultural display rules. Culture, emotion regulation, and adjustment. *Journal of Personality and Social Psychology, 94,* 925–937.

Mattanah, J. F., Hancock, G. R., & Brand, B. L. (2004). Parental attachment, separation-individuation, and college student adjustment: A structural equation analysis of mediational effects. *Journal of Counseling Psychology, 51,* 213–225.

Mattar, A. A. G., & Gribble, P. L. (2005). Motor learning by observing. *Neuron, 46,* 153–160.

Matthews, C. A. (2009). Phenomenology of obsessive-compulsive disorder. In M. M. Antony & M. B. Stein (Eds.), *Oxford handbook of anxiety and related disorders* (pp. 56–64). New York: Oxford University Press.

Matthews, G. (2008). Reinforcement Sensitivity Theory: A critique from cognitive science. In P. J. Corr (Ed.) *The reinforcement sensitivity theory of personality* (pp. 482–507). Cambridge: Cambridge University Press.

Matthews, K. A., Katholi, C. R., McCreath, H., Whooley, M. A., Williams, D. R., Zhu, S., et al. (2004). Blood pressure reactivity to psychological stress predicts hypertension in the CARDIA study. *Circulation, 110,* 74–78.

Matthews, K. A., Salomon, K., Kenyon, K., & Zhou, F. (2005). Unfair treatment, discrimination, and ambulatory blood pressure in black and white adolescents. *Health Psychology, 24,* 258–265.

Matthies, E., Hoeger, R., & Guski, R. (2000). Living on polluted soil: Determinants of stress symptoms. *Environment and Behavior, 32,* 270–286.

Maupin, H. E., & Fisher, J. R. (1989). The effects of superior female performance and sex-role orientation in gender conformity. *Canadian Journal of Behavioral Science, 21,* 55–69.

Maviel, T., Durkin, T. P., Menzaghi, F., & Bontempi, B. (2004). Sites of neocortical reorganization critical for remote spatial memory. *Science, 305,* 96–99.

Maxwell, J. P. (2003). The imprint of childhood physical and emotional abuse: A case study on the use of EMDR to address anxiety and a lack of self-esteem. *Journal of Family Violence, 18,* 281–293.

May, E. R., & Zelikow, P. D. (Eds.). (1997). *The Kennedy tapes: Inside the White House during the Cuban Missile Crisis.* New York: Belknap Press.

May, G. L., & Kahnweiler, W. M. (2000). The effect of a mastery practice design on learning and transfer in behavior modeling training. *Personnel Psychology, 53, 353–373.*

Mayberry, R. I., & Lock, E. (2003). Age constraints on first versus second language acquisition. *Brain and Language, 87,* 369–384.

Mayberry, R. I., Lock, E., & Kazmi, H. (2002). Linguistic ability and early language exposure. *Nature, 417,* 38.

Mayer, D. J., & Price, D. D. (1982). A physiological and psychological analysis of pain: A potential model of motivation. In D. W. Pfaff (Ed.), *The physiological mechanisms of motivation.* New York: Springer-Verlag.

Mayer, F. S., & Sutton, K. (1996). *Personality: An integrative approach.* Upper Saddle River, NJ: Prentice Hall.

Mayer, J. D. (2005). A tale of two visions: Can a new view of personality help integrate psychology? *American Psychologist, 60,* 294–307.

Mayes, L., Cicchetti, D., Acharyya, S., & Zhang, H. (2003). Developmental trajectories of cocaine-and-other-drug-exposed and non-cocaine-exposed children. *Journal of Developmental Behavioral Pediatrics, 24,* 323–335.

Mayes, L. C., Molfese, D. L., Key, A. P. F., & Hunter, N. C. (2005). Event-related potentials in cocaine-exposed children during a Stroop task. *Neurotoxicology and Teratology, 27*(6), 797–813.

Mayeux, R. (2003). Epidemiology of neurodegeneration. *Annual Review of Neuroscience, 26,* 81–104.

Maynard, D. C., Joseph, T. A., & Maynard, A. M. (2006). Underemployment, job attitudes, and turnover intentions. *Journal of Organizational Behavior, 27, 509–536.*

Mayou, R., Kirmayer, L. J., Simon, G., Kroenke, K., & Sharpe, M. (2005). Somatoform disorders: Time for a new approach in DSM-V. *American Journal of Psychiatry, 162,* 847–855.

Mazoyer, B., Tzouri-Mazoyer, N., Mazard, A., Denis, M., & Mellet, E. (2002). Neural basis of image and language interactions. *International Journal of Psychology, 37,* 204–208.

Mazzoni, G., & Memon, A. (2003). Imagination can create false autobiographical memories. *Psychological Science, 14,* 186–188.

Mazzoni, G. A., & Loftus, E. F. (1996). When dreams become reality. *Consciousness and Cognition, 5,* 442–462.

McAdams, D. P., & Pals, J. L. (2006). A new big five: Fundamental principles for an integrative science of personality. *American Psychologist, 61,* 204–217.

McAllister-Williams, R. H. (2006). Relapse prevention in bipolar disorder: A critical review of current guidelines. *Journal of Psychopharmacology, 20*(Suppl. 2), 12–16.

McAuley, E. (1992). The role of efficacy cognitions in the prediction of exercise behavior in middle-aged adults. *Journal of Behavioral Medicine, 15,* 65–88.

McAuley, E., Kramer, A. F., & Colcombe, S. J. (2004). Cardiovascular fitness and neurocognitive function in older adults: A brief review. *Brain, Behavior, and Immunity, 18,* 214–220.

McCabe, D. P., & Castel, A. D. (2008). Seeing is believing: The effect of brain images on judgments of scientific reasoning. *Cognition, 107*(1), 343–352.

McCabe, K. M. (2002). Factors that predict premature termination among Mexican-American children in outpatient psychotherapy. *Journal of Child and Family Therapy, 11,* 347–359.

McCaffery, E. J., & Baron, J. (2006). Thinking about tax. *Psychology, Public Policy, and Law, 12,* 106–135.

McCaffrey, R., & Locson, R. (2006). The effect of music on pain and acute confusion in older adults undergoing hip and knee surgery. *Holistic Nursing Practice, 20*(5), 218–224.

McCarley, J. S., Kramer, A. F., Wickens, C. D., Vidoni, E. D., & Boot, W. R. (2004). Visual skills in airport-security screening. *Psychological Science, 15,* 302–306.

McCaul, K. D., Hockemeyer, J. R., Johnson, R. J., Zetocha, K., Quinlan, K., & Glasgow, R. E. (2006). Motivation to quit using cigarettes: A review. *Addictive Behaviors, 31,* 42–56.

McClain, M., & Foundas, A. (2004). Apraxia. *Current Neurology and Neuroscience Reports, 4*(6), 471–476.

McClelland, D. C. (1958). Risk-taking in children with high and low need for achievement. In J. W. Atkinson (Ed.), *Motives in fantasy, action, and society* (pp. 306–321). Princeton, NJ: Van Nostrand.

McClelland, D. C. (1985). *Human motivation.* Glenview, IL: Scott, Foresman.

McCloskey, M. (1983). Naïve theories of motion. In D. Gentner & K. Stevens (Eds.), *Mental models* (pp. 299–324). Northvale, NJ: Erlbaum.

McClure, E. B. (2000). A meta-analytic review of sex differences in facial expression processing and their development in infants, children, and adolescents. *Psychological Bulletin, 126,* 424–453.

McConaghy, N., Hadzi-Pavlovic, D., Stevens, C., Manicavasagar, V., Buhrich, N., & Vollmer-Conna, U. (2006). Fraternal birth order and ratio of heterosexual/homosexual feelings in women and men. *Journal of Homosexuality, 51*(4), 161–174.

McCormick, D. A., & Thompson, R. F. (1984). Cerebellum essential involvement in the classically conditioned eyelid response. *Science, 223,* 296–299.

McCormick, E. J., Jeanneret, P. R., & Mecham, R. C. (1972). A study of job characteristics and job dimensions as based on the position analysis questionnaire (PAQ). *Journal of Applied Psychology, 56,* 347–368.

McCrae, R. R. (2001). Trait psychology and culture: Exploring intercultural comparisons. *Journal of Personality, 69*(6), 819–846.

McCrae, R. R., & Costa, P. T., Jr. (2004). A contemplated revision of the NEO Five-Factor Inventory. *Personality and Individual Differences, 36,* 587–596.

McCrae, R. R., & Costa, P. T., Jr. (2006). Cross-cultural perspectives on adult personality trait development. In D. Mroczek, & T. Little (Eds.) *Handbook of personality development* (pp. 129–145). Mahwah, NJ: Lawrence Erlbaum Associates.

McCrae, R. R., & Costa, P. T., Jr. (2008). The Five-Factor theory of personality. In O. John, R. Robins, & L. Pervin (Eds.), *Handbook of personality: Theory and research* (3rd ed., pp. 159–181). New York: Guilford.

McCrae, R. R., Costa, P. T., Jr., Martin, T. A., Oryol, V. E., Rukavishnikov, A. A., et al. (2004). Consensual validation of personality traits across cultures. *Journal of Research in Personality, 38,* 179–201.

McCrae, R. R., & John, O. (1992). An introduction to the five-factor model and its applications. *Journal of Personality, 60,* 175–215.

McCrae, R., Terracciano, A., & Personality Profiles of Cultures Project (2005). Personality profiles of cultures: Aggregate personality traits. *Journal of Personality and Social Psychology, 89,* 407–425.

McCusker, R. R., Goldberger, B. A., & Cone, E. J. (2006). Caffeine content of decaffeinated coffee. *Journal of Analytical Toxicology, 30,* 611–613.

McDermott, K. B. (2002). Explicit and implicit memory. In V. S. Ramachandran (Ed.), *Encyclopedia of the human brain* (Vol. 2, pp. 773–781). New York: Academic Press.

McDermott, K. B., & Chan, J. C. K. (2006). Effects of repetition on memory for pragmatic inferences. *Memory and Cognition.*

McDermott, K. B., & Roediger, H. L. (1998). Attempting to avoid illusory memories: Robust false recognition of associates persists under conditions of explicit warnings and immediate testing. *Journal of Memory and Language, 39,* 508–520.

McDermott, K. B., Szpunar, K. K., & Christ, S. E. (in press). Laboratory-based and autobiographical retrieval tasks differ substantially in their neural substrates. *Neuropsychologia.*

McDiarmid, M. A., & Condon, M. (2005). Organizational safety culture/climate and worker compliance with hazardous drug guidelines: Lessons from the blood-borne pathogen experience. *Journal of Occupational and Environmental Medicine, 47,* 740–749.

McDonald, R., & Siegel, S. (2004). The potential role of drug onset cues in drug dependence and withdrawal: Reply to Bardo (2004), Bossert and Shaham (2004), Bouton (2004), and Stewart (2004). *Experimental and Clinical Psychopharmacology, 12,* 23–26.

McDougall, W. (1908). *An introduction to social psychology.* London: Methuen.

McElroy, S. L., Zarate, C. A., & Cookson, J. (2004). A 52-week, open-label continuation study of lamotrigine in the treatment of bipolar depression. *Journal of Clinical Psychiatry, 65*(2), 204–210.

McEvoy, G. M., & Beatty, R. W. (1989). Assessment centers and subordinate appraisals of managers: A seven-year examination of predictive validity. *Personnel Psychology, 42,* 37–52.

McEwen, B. S., & Seeman, T. (1999). Protective and damaging effects of mediators of stress: Elaborating and testing concepts of allostasis and allostatic load. *Annals of the New York Academy of Sciences, 896,* 30–47.

McGaugh, J. L. (2003). *Memory and emotion.* New York: Columbia University Press.

McGehee, D. S., Heath, M. J. S., Gelber, S., Devay, P., & Role, L. W. (1995). Nicotine enhancement of fast excitatory synaptic transmissions in CNS by presynaptic receptors. *Science, 269,* 1692–1696.

McGlashan, T. H., & Hoffman, R. E. (2000). Schizophrenia as a disorder of reduced synaptic connectivity. *Archives of General Psychiatry, 57,* 637–648.

McGlynn, F. D., Moore, P. M., Lawyer, S., & Karg, R. (1999). Relaxation training inhibits fear and arousal during in vivo exposure to phobia-cue stimuli. *Journal of Behavior Therapy and Experimental Psychiatry, 30,* 155–168.

McGlynn, S. M., & Schacter, D. L. (1989). Unawareness of deficits in neuropsychological syndromes. *Journal of Clinical and Experimental Neuropsychology, 11*(2), 143–205.

McGorry, P. D., Yung, A. R., Phillips, L. J., Yuen, H. P., Francey, S., Cosgrave, E. M., et al. (2002). Randomized controlled trial of interventions designed to reduce the risk of progression to first-episode psychosis in a clinical sample with subthreshold symptoms. *Archives of General Psychiatry, 59,* 921–928.

McGue, M., & Bouchard, T. J. (1998). Genetic and environmental influences on human behavioral differences. *Annual Review of Neuroscience, 21,* 1–24.

McHugh, 2009 (cited in memory chapter)

McHugh, P. R. (2005). Striving for coherence: Psychiatry's efforts over classification. *Journal of the American Medical Association, 293,* 2526–2528.

McHugh, P. R. (2009). *Try to remember: Psychiatry's clash over meaning, memory, and mind.* Chicago: Dana Press.

McLaughlin, N. C. R., & Westervelt, H. J. (2008). Odor identification deficits in frontotemporal dementia: A preliminary study. *Archives of Clinical Neuropsychology, 23*(1), 119–123.

McLeod, J. D., Kessler, R. C., & Landis, K. R. (1992). Speed of recovery from major depressive episodes in a community sample of married men and women. *Journal of Abnormal Psychology, 101,* 277–286.

McLoyd, V. C. (1998). Socioeconomic disadvantage and child development. *American Psychologist, 53,* 185–204.

McMahon, P. (2000, January 31). Oregon man leads life without frills, leaves $9 million to charities, children. *USA Today,* p. 4A.

McMurrich, S. L., & Johnson, S. L. (2008). Dispositional rumination in individuals with a depression history. *Cognitive Therapy and Research, 32,* 542–553.

McNally, R. J. (2003). Recovering memories of trauma: A view from the laboratory. *Current Directions in Psychological Science, 12,* 32–35.

McNally, R. J. (2007). Mechanisms of exposure therapy: How neuroscience can improve psychological treatments for anxiety disorders. *Clinical Psychology Review, 27,* 750–759.

McNally, R. J., Clancy, S. A., Barrett, H. M., & Parker, H. A. (2005). Reality monitoring in adults reporting repressed, recovered, or continuous memories of childhood sexual abuse. *Journal of Abnormal Psychology, 114,* 147–152.

McNally, R. J., Clancy, S. A., & Schacter, D. L. (2001). Directed forgetting of trauma cues in adults reporting repressed or recovered memories of childhood sexual abuse. *Journal of Abnormal Psychology, 110,* 151–156.

McNally, R. J., Clancy, S. A., Schacter, D. L., & Pittman, R. K. (2000a). Cognitive processing of trauma cues in adults reporting repressed, recovered, or continuous memories of childhood sexual abuse. *Journal of Abnormal Psychology, 109,* 355–359.

McNally, R. J., Clancy, S. A., Schacter, D. L., & Pittman, R. K. (2000b). Personality profiles, dissociation, and absorption in women reporting repressed, recovered, or continuous memories of childhood sexual abuse. *Journal of Consulting and Clinical Psychology, 68,* 1033–1037.

McNally, R. J., & Geraerts, E. (2009). A new solution to the recovered memory debate. *Perspectives on Psychological Science, 4,* 126–134.

McNay, E. C., McCarty, R. C., & Gold, P. E. (2001). Fluctuations in brain glucose concentration during behavioral testing: Dissociations between brain areas and between brain and blood. *Neurobiology of Learning and Memory, 75,* 325–337.

McNulty, J. K., & Karney, B. R. (2004). Positive expectations in the early years of marriage: Should couples expect the best or brace for the worst? *Journal of Personality and Social Psychology, 86,* 729–743.

McTigue, K. M., Harris, R., Hemphill, B., Lux, L., Sutton, S., Bunton, A. J., & Lohr, K. N. (2003). Screening and interventions for obesity in adults: Summary of the evidence for the U.S. Preventive Services Task Force. *Annals of Internal Medicine, 139,* 933–949.

Medin, D. L., & Bazerman, M. H. (1999). Broadening behavioral decision research: Multiple levels of cognitive processing. *Psychonomic Bulletin & Review, 6,* 533–546.

Medin, D. L., Ross, B. H., & Markman, A. B. (2001). *Cognitive psychology* (3rd ed.). Fort Worth, TX: Harcourt.

Mednick, S., Nakayama, K., & Stickgold, R. (2003). Sleep-dependent learning: A nap is as good as a night. *Nature Neuroscience, 6,* 697–698.

Mehl, M. R., & Pennebaker, J. W. (2003a). The social dynamics of a cultural upheaval: Social interactions surrounding September 11, 2001. *Psychological Science, 14,* 579–585.

Mehl, M. R., & Pennebaker, J. W. (2003b). The sounds of social life: A psychometric analysis of students' daily social environments and natural conversations. *Journal of Personality and Social Psychology, 84,* 857–870.

Mehle, T. (1982). Hypothesis generation in an automobile malfunction inference task. *Acta Psychologica, 52,* 87–116.

Meichenbaum, D. (1977). *Cognitive behavior modification: An integrative approach.* New York: Plenum.

Meichenbaum, D. (2003). *Treatment of individuals with anger-control problems and aggressive behaviors.* Bethel, CT: Crown House Publishing.

Meiser, T., & Hewstone, M. (2006). Illusory and spurious correlations: Distinct phenomena or joint outcomes of exemplar-based category learning? *European Journal of Social Psychology, 36,* 315–336.

Melamed, S., Fried, Y., & Froom, P. (2001). The interactive effect of chronic exposure to noise and job complexity on changes in blood pressure and job satisfaction: A longitudinal study of industrial employees. *Journal of Occupational Health Psychology, 6,* 182–195.

Melby, T. (2008). The myth of teen promiscuity. *Contemporary Sexuality, 42*(9), 1–5.

Melchior, C. L. (1990). Conditioned tolerance provides protection against ethanol lethality. *Pharmacology, Biochemistry and Behavior, 37,* 205–206.

Meltzer, H. Y. (1997). Treatment-resistant schizophrenia: The role of clozapine. *Current Medical Research Opinion, 14,* 1–20.

Melzack, R., & Wall, P. D. (1965). Pain mechanisms: A new theory. *Science, 150,* 971–979.

Memon, A., Vrij, A., & Bull, R. (2004). *Psychology and law: Truthfulness, accuracy and credibility* (2nd ed.). New York: Wiley.

Menaker, M., & Vogelbaum, M. A. (1993). Mutant circadian period as a marker of suprachiasmatic nucleus function. *Journal of Biological Rhythms, 8,* 93–98.

Mendez, I., Sanchez-Pernaute, R., Cooper, O., Vinuela, A., Ferrari, D., Bjorklund, L., et al. (2005). Cell type analysis of functional fetal dopamine cell suspension transplants in the striatum and substantia nigra of patients with Parkinson's disease. *Brain, 128,* 1498–1510.

Mendez, I., Viñuela, A., Astradsson, A., Mukhida, K., Hallett, P., Robertson, H., Tierney, T., Holness, R., Dagher, A., Trojanowski, J. Q., & Isacson, O. (2008). Dopamine neurons implanted into people with Parkinson's disease survive without pathology for 14 years. *Nature Medicine, 14,* 507–509.

Mendl, M. (1999). Performing under pressure: Stress and cognitive function. *Applied Animal Behaviour Science, 65,* 221–244.

Menini, A., Picco, C., & Firestein, S. (1995, February 2). Quantal-like current fluctuations induced by odorants in olfactory receptor cell. *Nature, 373,* 435–437.

Menon, G. J., Rahman, I., Menon, S. J., & Dutton, G. N. (2003). Complex visual hallucinations in the visually impaired: The Charles Bonnet syndrome. *Survey Ophthalmology, 48,* 58–72.

Mente, A., de Koning, L., Shannon, H. S., & Anand, S. S. (2009). A systematic review of the evidence supporting a causal link between dietary factors and coronary heart disease. *Archives of Internal Medicine, 169,* 659–669.

Merchant, J. A., & Lundell, J. A. (2001). *Workplace violence: A report to the nation.* Iowa City: University of Iowa.

Merckelbach, H., Devilly, G. J., & Rassin, E. (2002). Alters in dissociative identity disorder: Metaphors or genuine entities? *Clinical Psychology Review, 22,* 481–497.

Meredith, E., & Baker, M. (2007). Factors associated with choosing a career in clinical psychology–Undergraduate minority ethnic perspectives. *Clinical Psychology and Psychotherapy, 14,* 475–487.

Meriac, J. P., Hoffman, B. J., Woehr, D. J., & Fleisher, M. S. (2008). Further evidence for the validity of assessment center dimensions: A meta-analysis of the incremental criterion-related validity of dimension ratings. *Journal of Applied Psychology, 93,* 1042–1052.

Merritt, M. M., Bennett, G. G., Jr, Williams, R. B., Edwards, C. L., & Sollers, J. J., III. (2006). Perceived racism and cardiovascular reactivity and recovery to personally relevant stress. *Health Psychology, 25,* 364–369.

Merry, T., & Brodley, B. T. (2002). The nondirective attitude in client-centered therapy: A response to Kahn. *Journal of Humanistic Psychology, 42,* 66–77.

Mesman, J., & Koot, H. M. (2000). Common and specific correlates of preadolescent internalizing externalizing psychopathology. *Journal of Abnormal Psychology, 109,* 428–437.

Mesquita, B., & Frijda, N. H. (1992). Cultural variations in emotions: A review. *Psychological Bulletin, 112,* 179–204.

Messer, S. B. (2004). Evidence-based practice: Beyond empirically supported treatments. *Professional Psychology: Research and Practice, 35,* 580–588.

Messer, S. B., & Wampold, B. E. (2002). Let's face facts: Common factors are more potent than specific therapy ingredients. *Clinical Psychology: Science and Practice, 9,* 21–25.

Messick, S. (1989). Validity. In R. Linn (Ed.), *Educational measurement* (3rd ed., pp. 13–103). New York: American Council on Education/Macmillan.

Messinger, A., Squire, L. R., Zola, S. M., & Albright, T. D. (2001). Neuronal representations of stimulus associations develop in the temporal lobe during learning. *Proceedings of the National Academy of Sciences, 98,* 12239–12244.

Messinger, D. S., Bauer, C. R., Das, A., Seifer, R., Lester, B. M., Lagasse, L. L., et al. (2004). The maternal lifestyle study: Cognitive, motor, and behavioral outcomes of cocaine-exposed and opiate-exposed infants through three years of age. *Pediatrics, 113,* 1677–1685.

Meston, C. M., & Buss, D. M. (2007). Why humans have sex. *Archives of Sexual Behavior, 36,* 477–507.

Mesulam, M. M. (1990). Large-scale neurocognitive networks and distributed processing for attention, language, and memory. *Annals of Neurology, 28*(5), 597–613.

Mesulam, M. M. (2001). Primary progressive aphasia. *Annals of Neurolology, 49*(4), 425–423.

Metzinger, T. (Ed.). (2000). Neural correlates of consciousness: Empirical and conceptual questions. Cambridge: MIT Press.

Meyer, G. J., Finn, S. E., Eyde, L. D., Kay, G. G., Moreland, K. L., Dies, R. R., et al. (2001). Psychological testing and psychological assessment: A review of evidence and issues. *American Psychologist, 56,* 128–165.

Meyer, G. J., Mihura, J. L., & Smith, B. L. (2005). The interclinician reliability of Rorschach interpretation in four data sets. *Journal of Personality Assessment, 84,* 296–314.

Meyer, I. H. (2003). Prejudice, social stress, and mental health in lesbian, gay, and bisexual populations: Conceptual issues and research evidence. *Psychological Bulletin, 129,* 674–697.

Meyer, J. D., & Salovey, P. (1997). What is emotional intelligence? In P. Salovey & D. Sluyter (Eds.), *Emotional development and emotional intelligence* (pp. 3–31). New York: Basic Books.

Meyer, R. G. (1975). A behavioral treatment of sleepwalking associated with test anxiety. *Behavior Therapy and Experimental Psychiatry, 6,* 167–168.

Meyer, U., Feldon, J., Schedlowski, M., & Yee, B. K. (2005). Toward and immuno-precipitated neurodevelopmental animal model of schizophrenia. *Neuroscience & Biobehavioral Reviews, 29,* 913–947.

Meyer-Bahlburg, H. F. L., Dolezal, C., Baker, S., & New, M. (2008). Sexual orientation in women with classical or non-classical congenital adrenal hyperplasia as a function of degree of prenatal androgen excess. *Archives of Sexual Behavior, 37*(1), 85–99.

Meyers, C., & Jones, T. B. (1993). *Promoting active learning: Strategies for the college classroom.* San Francisco: Jossey-Bass.

Mezey, E., Key, S., Vogelsang, G., Szalayova, I., Lange, G. D., & Crain, B. (2003). Transplanted bone marrow generates new neurons in human brains. *Proceedings of the National Academy of Sciences, 100,* 1364–1369.

Mezulis, A. H., Abramson, L. Y., Hyde, J. S., & Hankin, B. L. (2004). Is there a universal positivity bias in attributions? A meta-analytic review of individual, developmental, and cultural differences in the self-serving attributional bias. *Psychological Bulletin, 130,* 711–747.

Mezzacappa, E. S., Katkin, E. S., & Palmer, S. N. (1999). Epinephrine, arousal and emotion: A new look at two-factor theory. *Cognition and Emotion, 13,* 181–199.

Miceli, G., Fouch, E., Capasso, R., Shelton, J. R., Tomaiuolo, F., & Caramazza, A. (2001). The dissociation of color from form and function knowledge. *Nature Neuroscience, 4,* 662–667.

Michael, R. T., Wadsworth, J., Feinleib, J., Johnson, A. M., Laumann, E. O., & Wellings, K. (1998). Private sexual behavior, public opinion, and public health policy related to sexually transmitted diseases: A US-British comparison. *American Journal of Public Health, 88,* 749–754.

Michel, C., Rossion, B., Han, J., Chung, C.-S., & Caldara, R. (2006). Holistic processing is finely tuned for faces of one's own race. *Psychological Science, 17,* 608–615.

Michelena, P., Sibbald, A. M., Erhard, H. W., & McLeod, J. E. (2009). Effects of group size and personality on social foraging: The distribution of sheep across patches. *Behavioral Ecology, 20*(1), 145–152.

Mick, E., Biederman, J., Prince, J., Fischer, M. J., & Faraone, S. V. (2002). Impact of low birth weight on attention-deficit hyperactivity disorder. *Journal of Developmental and Behavioral Pediatrics, 23,* 16–22.

Miklowitz, D. J. (2008). Adjunctive psychotherapy for bipolar disorder: State of the evidence. *American Journal of Psychiatry, 165,* 1408–1419.

Miklowitz, D. J., & Alloy, L. B. (1999). Psychosocial factors in the course and treatment of bipolar disorder: Introduction to the special section. *Journal of Abnormal Psychology, 108,* 555–557.

Miklowitz, D. J., Otto, M. W., Frank, E., Reilly Harrington, N. A., Wisniewski, S. R., Kogan, J. N., et al. (2007). Psychosocial treatments for bipolar depression. *Archives of General Psychiatry, 64,* 419–426.

Mikulincer, M., & Shaver, P. R. (2005). Mental representations of attachment security: Theoretical foundation for a positive social psychology. In M. W. Baldwin (Ed.), *Interpersonal cognition* (pp. 233–266). New York: Guilford Press.

Milak, M. S., Parsey, R. V., Keilp, J., Oquendo, M. A., Malone, K. M., & Mann, J. J. (2005). Neuroanatomic correlates of psychopathologic components of major depressive disorder. *Archives of General Psychiatry, 62,* 397–408.

Milan, G., Lamenza, F., Iavarone, A., Galeone, F., Lorè, E., De Falco, C., Correntino, P., & Postiglione, A. (2008). Frontal Behavioural Inventory in the differential diagnosis of dementia. *Acta Neurologica Scandinavica, 117*(4), 260–265.

Milev, P., Ho, B. C., Arndt, S., & Andreasen, N. C. (2005). Predictive values of neurocognition and negative symptoms on functional outcome in schizophrenia: A longitudinal first-episode study with 7-year follow-up. *American Journal of Psychiatry, 162,* 495–506.

Milgram, S. (1963). Behavioral study of obedience. *Journal of Abnormal and Social Psychology, 67,* 371–378.

Milgram, S. (1965). Some conditions of obedience and disobedience to authority. *Human Relations, 18,* 57–76.

Milgram, S. (1974). *Obedience to authority.* New York: Harper & Row.

Milgram, S. (1977, October). Subject reaction: The neglected factor in the ethics of experimentation. *Hastings Center Report* (pp. 19–23).

Milisen, K., Braes, T., Fick, D. M., & Foreman, M. D. (2006). Cognitive assessment and differentiating the 3 Ds (dementia, depression, delirium). *Nursing Clinics of North America, 41*(1), 1–22.

Millar, H. R., Wardell, F., Vyvyan, J. P., Naji, S. A., Prescott, G. J., & Eagles, J. M. (2005). Anorexia nervosa mortality in Northeast Scotland, 1965–1999. *American Journal of Psychiatry, 162,* 753–757.

Miller, B. L. (2007). Frontotemporal dementia and semantic dementia: Anatomic variations on the same disease or distinctive entities?. *Alzheimer Disease & Associated Disorders, 21*(4), S19-s22.

Miller, G. (1956). The magical number seven, plus or minus two: Some limits on our capacity to process information. *Psychological Review, 63,* 81–97.

Miller, G. (2003). Spying on the brain, one neuron at a time. *Science, 300,* 78.

Miller, G. (2005a). Neuroscience: The dark side of glia. *Science, 308,* 778–781.

Miller, G. (2005b). Neuroscience: Reflecting on another's mind. *Science, 308,* 945–947.

Miller, G., Tybur, J. M., & Jordan, B. D. (2007). Ovulatory cycle effects on tip earnings by lap dancers: Economic evidence for human estrus? *Evolution and Human Behavior, 28,* 375–381.

Miller, G. A. (1991). *The science of words.* New York: Scientific American Library.

Miller, G. A., Heise, G. A., & Lichten, W. (1951). The intelligibility of speech as a function of the context of the test materials. *Journal of Experimental Psychology, 41,* 329–335.

Miller, J. (2001). The cultural grounding of social psychological theory. In A. Tesser & N. Schwarz (Eds.), *Blackwell handbook of social psychology: Intraindividual processes* (pp. 22–43). Oxford, UK: Blackwell.

Miller, J. D., Lynam, D., Zimmerman, R. S., Logan, T. K., Leukefeld, C., & Clayton, R. (2004). The utility of the Five Factor Model in understanding risky sexual behavior. *Personality and Individual Differences, 36,* 1611–1626.

Miller, J. G. (2002). Bringing culture to basic psychological theory—Beyond individualism and collectivism: Comment on Oyserman et al. *Psychological Bulletin, 128,* 97–109.

Miller, J. G., & Bersoff, D. M. (1994). Cultural influences on the moral status of reciprocity and the discounting of endogenous motivation. *Personality and Social Psychology Bulletin, 20,* 592–607.

Miller, K. F., Smith, C. M., Zhu, J., & Zhang, H. (1995). Preschool origins of cross-national differences in mathematical competence: The role of number-naming systems. *Psychological Science, 6,* 56–60.

Miller, L. C., Putcha-Bhagavatula, A., & Pedersen, W. C. (2002). Men's and women's mating preferences: Distinct evolutionary mechanisms? *Current Directions in Psychological Science, 11,* 88–93.

Miller, L. T., & Vernon, P. A. (1997). Developmental changes in speed of information processing in young children. *Developmental Psychology, 33,* 549–554.

Miller, N. E. (1959). Liberalization of basic S-R concepts: Extensions to conflict behavior, motivation, and social learning. In S. Koch (Ed.), *Psychology: A study of science* (Vol. 2, pp. 196–292). New York: McGraw-Hill.

Miller, T. W., Nigg, J. T., & Miller, R. L. (2009). Attention deficit hyperactivity disorder in African American children: What can we conclude from the past ten years? *Clinical Psychology Review, 29,* 77–86.

Miller, W. R., & Rollnick, S. (2002). *Motivational interviewing: Preparing people for change* (2nd ed.). New York: Guilford.

Millon, T., & Davis, R. D. (1996). *Disorders of personality.* DSM-IV *and beyond* (2nd ed.). New York: Wiley.

Mills, P. E., Cole, K. N., Jenkins, J. R., & Dale, P. S. (1998). Effects of differing levels of inclusion on preschoolers with disabilities. *Exceptional Children, 65,* 79–90.

Milner, B. (1966). Amnesia following operation on temporal lobes. In C. W. M. Whitty & O. L. Zangwill (Eds.), *Amnesia.* London: Butterworth.

Milner, B. (2005). The medial temporal-lobe amnesic syndrome. *Psychiatric Clinics of North America, 28*(3), 599–611.

Milner, D. (1983). *Children and race.* Beverly Hills, CA: Sage.

Miltenberger, R. G. (2007). *Behavior modification: Principles and procedures* (4th ed.). New York: Cengage Learning.

Mineka, S., & Zinbarg, R. (2006). A contemporary learning theory perspective on the etiology of anxiety disorders: It's not what you thought it was. *American Psychologist, 61,* 10–26.

Miner, J. L., & Clarke-Stewart, K. A. (2008). Trajectories of externalizing behavior from age 2 to age 9: Relations with gender, temperament, ethnicity, parenting, and rater. *Developmental Psychology, 44,* 771–786.

Ming, E. E., Adler, G. K., Kessler, R. C., Fogg, L. F., Matthews, K. A., Herd, J. A., & Rose, R. M. (2004). Cardiovascular reactivity to work stress predicts subsequent onset of hypertension: The air traffic controller health change study. *Psychosomatic Medicine, 66,* 459–465.

Minshew, N. J., & Williams, D. L. (2007). The new neurobiology of autism: Cortex, connectivity, and neuronal organization. *Archives of Neurology, 64,* 945–950.

Minsky, S., Vega, W., Miskimen, T., Gara, M., & Escobar, J. (2003). Diagnostic patterns in Latino, African American, and European American psychiatric patients. *Archives of General Psychiatry, 60,* 637–644.

Minzenberg, M. J., Jong, H. Y., & Cameron, S. C. (2008). Schizophrenia. In R. E. Hales, S. C. Yudofsky, & G. O. Gabbard (Eds.), *Textbook of psychiatry* (pp. 407–456). Washington, DC: American Psychiatric Publishing.

Minzenberg, M. J., Watrous, A. J., Yoon, J. H., Ursu, S., & Carter, C. S. (2008). Modafinil shifts human locus coeruleus to low-tonic, high-phasic activity during functional MRI. *Science, 322*(5908), 1700–1702.

Miotto, K., Darakjian, J., Basch, J., Murray, S., Zogg, J., & Rawson, R. (2001). Gamma-hydroxybutyric acid: Patterns of use, effects and withdrawal. *American Journal on Addictions, 10,* 232–241.

Miranda, J., & Green, B. L. (1999). The need for mental health services research focusing on poor young women. *Journal of Mental Health Policy and Economics, 2,* 73–89.

Mischel, W. (2004a). *Introduction to personality: Toward an integration.* Hoboken, NJ: Wiley.

Mischel, W. (2004b). Toward an integrative science of the person. *Annual Review of Psychology, 55,* 1–22.

Mischel, W., & Shoda, Y. (1999). Integrating dispositions and processing dynamics. In L. Pervin & O. John (Eds.), *Handbook of personality: Theory and research* (2nd ed., pp. 197–218). New York: Guilford.

Mischel, W., & Shoda, Y. (2008). Toward a unified theory of personality: Integrating dispositions and processing dynamics within the cognitive-affective processing system. In O. John, R. Robins, & L. Pervin (Eds.), *Handbook of personality: Theory and research* (3rd ed., pp. 208–241). New York: Guilford.

Mischel, W., Shoda, Y., & Smith, R. (2004). *Introduction to personality: Toward an integration* (7th ed.). New York: Wiley.

Mitchell, D. B. (2006). Nonconscious priming after 17 years: Invulnerable implicit memory? *Psychological Science, 17,* 925–929.

Mitchell, J. P. (2008). Contributions of functional neuroimaging to the study of social cognition. *Current Directions in Psychological Science, 17,* 142–146.

Mitchell, K. J., & Zaragoza, M. S. (1996). Repeated exposure to suggestion and false memory: The role of contextual variability. *Journal of Memory and Learning, 35,* 246–260.

Mitte, K. (2005a). A meta-analysis of the efficacy of psycho- and pharmacotherapy in panic disorder with and without agoraphobia. *Journal of Affective Disorders, 88,* 27–45.

Mitte, K. (2005b). Meta-analysis of cognitive-behavioral treatments for generalized anxiety disorder: A comparison with pharmacotherapy. *Psychological Bulletin, 131,* 785–795.

Miyagawa, T., Kawashima, M. Nishida, N., Ohashi, J., Kimura, R., Fujimoto, A., Shimada, M., Morishita, S., Shigeta, T., Lin, L., Hong, S.-C., Faraco, J., Shin, Y.-K., Jeong, J.-H., Okazaki, Y. Tsuji, S., Honda, M., Honda, Y., Mignot, E., & Tokunaga, K. (2008). Variant between CPT1B and CHKB associated with susceptibility to narcolepsy. *Nature Genetics, 40,* 1324–1328.

Miyamoto, S., Duncan, G. E., Marx, C. E., & Lieberman, J. A. (2005). Treatments for schizophrenia: A critical review of pharmacology and mechanisms of action of antipsychotic drugs. *Molecular Psychiatry, 10,* 79–104.

Miyamoto, Y., & Kitayama, S. (2002). Cultural variation in correspondence bias: The critical role of attitude diagnosticity of socially constrained behavior. *Journal of Personality and Social Psychology, 83,* 1239–1248.

Miyamoto, Y., Nisbett, R. E., & Masuda, T. (2006). Culture and the physical environment: Holistic versus analytic perceptual affordances. *Psychological Science, 17,* 113–119.

Moffitt, T. E. (2002). Teen-aged mothers in contemporary Britain. *Journal of Child Psychology & Psychiatry & Allied Disciplines, 43,* 727–742.

Moffitt, T. E., Caspi, A., & Rutter, M. (2005). Strategy for investigating interactions between measured genes and measured environments. *Archives of General Psychiatry, 62,* 473–481.

Mogenson, G. J. (1976). Neural mechanisms of hunger: Current status and future prospects. In D. Novin, W. Wyrwicka, & G. Bray (Eds.), *Hunger: Basic mechanisms and clinical applications.* New York: Raven.

Moghaddam, F. M. (2005). The staircase to terrorism: A psychological exploration. *American Psychologist, 60,* 161–169.

Moghaddam, F. M. (2008). *Multiculturalism and intergroup relations: Psychological implications for democracy in global context.* Washington, DC: American Psychological Association.

Mohr, C., Binkofski, F., Erdmann, C., Buchel, C., & Helmchen, C. (2005). The anterior cingulate cortex contains distinct areas dissociating external from self-administered painful stimulation: A parametric fMRI study. *Pain, 114,* 347–357.

Mohr, C., Rohrenbach, C. M., Landis, T., & Regard, M. (2001). Associations to smell are more pleasant than to sound. *Journal of Clinical and Experimental Neuropsychology, 23,* 484–489.

Mokdad, A. H., Marks, J. S., Stroup, D. F., & Gerberding, J. L. (2004). Actual causes of death in the United States, 2000. *Journal of the American Medical Association, 291,* 1238–1245.

Molden, D. C., & Dweck, C. S. (2000). Meaning and motivation. In C. Sansone & J. M. Harackiewicz (Eds.), *Intrinsic and extrinsic motivation: The search for optimal motivation and performance.* San Diego: Academic Press.

Moller, A. C., Elliot, A. J., & Friedman, R. (2008). When competence and love are at stake: Achievement goals and perceived closeness to parents in an achievement context. *Journal of Research in Personality, 42,* 1386–1391.

Molsa, P. K., Marttila, R. J., & Rinne, U. K. (1995). Long-term survival and predictors of mortality in Alzheimer's disease and multi-infarct dementia. *Acta Neurologica Scandinavica, 91,* 159–164.

Monane, M., Leichter, D., & Lewis, O. (1984). Physical abuse in psychiatrically hospitalized children and adolescents. *Journal of the American Academy of Child and Adolescent Psychiatry, 23,* 653–658.

Moncrief, W. C., Babakus, E., Cravens, D. W., & Johnston, M. W. (2000). Examining gender differences in field sales organizations. *Journal of Business Research, 49,* 245–257.

Moncrieff, J., & Kirsch, I. (2005). Efficacy of antidepressants in adults. *British Medical Journal, 331,* 155–157.

Mongillo, G., Barak, O., & Tsodyks, M. (2008). Synaptic theory of working memory. *Science, 319,* 1543–1546.

Monroe, S., Thase, M., & Simons, A. (1992). Social factors and psychobiology of depression: Relations between life stress and rapid eye movement sleep latency. *Journal of Abnormal Psychology, 101,* 528–537.

Montague, P. R., Hyman, S. E., & Cohen, J. D. (2004). Computational roles for dopamine in behavioural control. *Nature, 431,* 760–767.

Montelone, P., & Maj, M. (2008). The circadian basis of mood disorders: Recent developments and treatment implications. *European Neuropsychopharmacology, 18*, 701–711.

Montgomery, S., Baldwin, D. S., Blier, P., Fineberg, N., Kasper, S., Lader, M., et al. (2007). Which antidepressants have demonstrated superior efficacy? A review of the evidence. *International Clinical Psychopharmacology, 22*, 323–329.

Moon, R., Calabrese, T., & Aird, L. (2008). Reducing the risk of sudden infant death syndrome in child care and changing provider practices: Lessons learned from a demonstration project. *Pediatrics, 122*, 788–798.

Moon, Y. (2003). Don't blame the computer: When self-disclosure moderates the self-serving bias. *Journal of Consumer Psychology, 13*, 125–137.

Moore, J. W., Tingstom, D. H., Doggett, R. A., & Carlyon, W. D. (2001). Restructuring an existing token economy in a psychiatric facility for children. *Child & Family Behavior Therapy, 23*, 53–60.

Moore, S. A., Zoellner, L. A., & Bittinger, J. N. (2004). Combining cognitive restructuring and exposure therapy: Toward an optimal integration. In S. Taylor (Ed.), *Advances in the treatment of posttraumatic stress disorder: Cognitive-behavioral perspectives* (pp. 129–149). New York: Springer.

Moore, T. H. M., Zammit, S., Lingford-Hughes, A. Barnes, T. R. E., Jones, P. B., Burke, M., & Lewis, G. (2007). Cannabis use and risk of psychotic or affective mental health outcomes: A systematic review. *The Lancet, 370*, 319–328.

Moorman, R. H., & Byrne, Z. S. (2005). How does organizational justice affect organizational citizenship behavior? In J. Greenberg & J. A. Colquitt (Eds.), *Handbook of organizational justice* (pp. 355–380). Mahwah, NJ: Erlbaum.

Moos, R., Schaefer, J., Andrassy, J., & Moos, B. (2001). Outpatient mental health care, self-help groups, and patients' one-year treatment outcomes. *Journal of Clinical Psychology, 57*, 273–287.

Moradi, B., Dirks, D., & Matteson, A. V. (2005). Roles of sexual objectification experiences and internalization of standards of beauty in eating disorder symptomatology: A test and extension of objectification theory. *Journal of Counseling Psychology, 52*, 420–428.

Moran, C. C. (2002). Humor as a moderator of compassion fatigue. In C. R. Figley (Ed.), *Treating compassion fatigue* (pp. 139–154). New York: Brunner-Routledge.

Moran, D. R. (2000, June). *Is active learning for me?* Poster presented at APS Preconvention Teaching Institute, Denver.

Moran, R. (2006). Learning in high-tech and multimedia environments. *Current Directions in Psychological Science, 15*, 63–67.

Morewedge, C. K., Gilbert, D. T., & Wilson, T. D. (2005). The least likely of times: How remembering the past biases forecasts of the future. *Psychological Science, 16*(8), 626–630.

Morgan, C. A., Doran, A., Steffian, G., Hazlett, G., & Southwick, S. M. (2006). Stress-induced deficits in working memory and visuo-constructive abilities in special operations soldiers. *Biological Psychiatry, 60*, 722–729.

Morgan, C. D., & Murray, H. A. (1935). A method for investigating fantasy: The Thematic Apperception Test. *Archives of Neurology and Psychiatry, 34*, 289–306.

Morgan, S. E., Stephenson, M. T., Harrison, T. R., Afifi, W. A., & Long, S. D. (2008). Facts versus "feelings": How rational is the decision to become an organ donor? *Journal of Health Psychology, 13*(5), 644–658.

Morin, C. M., Bélanger, L., LeBlanc, M., Ivers, H., Savard, J., Espie, C. A., Mérette, C., Baillargeon, L., & Grégoire, J.-P. (2009). The natural history of insomnia: A population-based 3-year longitudinal study. *Archives of Internal Medicine, 169*, 447–453.

Morino, M., Toppino, M., Forestieri, P., Angrisani, L., Allaix, M. E., Scopinaro, N. (2007). Mortality after bariatric surgery: Analysis of 13,871 morbidly obese patients from a national registry. *Annals of Surgery, 246*, 1002–1007.

Morisky, D. E., Stein, J. A., Chiao, C., Ksobiech, K., & Malow, R. (2006). Impact of a social influence intervention on condom use and sexually transmitted infections among establishment-based female sex workers in the Philippines: A multilevel analysis. *Health Psychology, 25*, 595–603.

Morling, B., & Kitayama, S. (2008). Culture and motivation. In J. Y. Shah, & W. L. Gardner (Eds.), *Handbook of motivation science* (pp. 417–433). New York: Guilford Press.

Morris, J. S., DeGelder, B., Weiskrantz, L., & Dolan, R. J. (2001). Differential extrageniculostriate and amygdala responses to presentation of emotional faces in a cortically blind field. *Brain, 124*, 1241–1252.

Morris, J. S., Friston, K. J., Buchel, C., Frith, C. D., Young, A. W., Calder, A. J., et al. (1998). A neuromodulatory role for the human amygdala in processing emotional facial expressions. *Brain, 121*, 47–57.

Morris, L. (2000, December 5). Hold the anaesthetic. I'll hypnotise myself instead. *Daily Mail*, p. 25.

Morris, M. C., Evans, D. A., Tangney, C. C., Bienias, J. L., & Wilson, R. S. (2006). Associations of vegetable and fruit consumption with age-related cognitive change. *Neurology, 67*, 1370–1376.

Mortimer, J. A., Snowdon, D. A., & Markesbery, W. R. (2003). Head circumference, education, and risk of dementia: Findings from the nun study. *Journal of Clinical and Experimental Neuropsychology, 25*, 671–679.

Mortimer, R. G., Goldsteen, K., Armstrong, R. W., & Macrina, D. (1988). *Effects of enforcement, incentives, and publicity on seat belt use in Illinois*. University of Illinois, Dept. of Health & Safety Studies, Final Report to Illinois Dept. of Transportation (Safety Research Report 88–11).

Morton, G. J., Cummings, D. E., Baskin, D. G., Barsh, G. S., & Schwartz, M. W. (2006). Central nervous system control of food intake and body weight. *Nature, 443*, 289–295.

Moscovici, S. (1985). Social influence and conformity. In G. Lindzey & E. Aronson (Eds.), *The handbook of social psychology* (Vol. 2, 3rd ed.). New York: Random House.

Moser, J. (2008). Nursing students killed in school shooting. *American Journal of Nursing, 108*(4), 19.

Moses, E. B., & Barlow, D. H. (2006). A new unified treatment approach for emotional disorders based on emotion science. *Current Directions in Psychological Science, 15*, 146–150.

Moskowitz, G. B. (2005). *Social cognition: Understanding self and others*. New York: Guilford Press.

Moskowitz, J. T., Hult, J. R., Bussolari, C., & Acree, M. (2009). What works in coping with HIV? A meta-analysis with implications for coping with serious illness. *Psychological Bulletin, 135*, 121–141.

Moss, E., Bureau, J.-F., Cyr, C., Mongeau, C., & St.-Laurent, D. (2004). Correlates of attachment at age 3: Construct validity of the preschool attachment classification system. *Developmental Psychology, 40*, 323–334.

Motowidlo, S. J., Brownlee, A. L., & Schmit, M. J. (2008). Effects of personality characteristics on knowledge, skill, and performance in servicing retail customers. *International Journal of Selection and Assessment, 16*, 272–280.

Moussavi, S., Chatterji, S., Verdes, E., Tandon, A., Patel, V., & Ustun, B. (2007). Depression, chronic diseases, and decrements in health: Results from the World Health Surveys. *Lancet, 370*, 851–858.

Mozzachiodi, R., Lorenzetti, F. D., Baxter, D. A., & Byrne, J. H. (2008). Changes in neuronal excitability serve as a mechanism of long-term memory for operant conditioning. *Nature Neuroscience, 11*, 1146–1148.

Mroczek, D. K., & Spiro, A., III. (2005). Changing life satisfaction during adulthood: Findings from the Veterans Affairs normative aging study. *Journal of Personality and Social Psychology, 88*, 189–202.

Mucchi-Faina, A., & Pagliaro, S. (2008). Minority influence: The role of ambivalence toward the source. *European Journal of Social Psychology, 38*, 612–623.

Muchinsky, P. M. (2003). *Psychology applied to work* (7th ed.). Belmont, CA: Thomson.

Mueser, K. T., & Jeste, D. V. (Eds.) (2009). *Clinical handbook of schizophrenia*. New York: Guilford Press.

Mufson, L., Dorta, K. P. Moreau, D., & Weissman, M. M. (2004). *Interpersonal psychotherapy for depressed adolescents* (2nd ed.). New York: Guilford Press.

Mühlberger, A., Wiedemann, G., Herrmann, M. J., & Pauli, P. (2006). Phylo- and ontogenetic fears and the expectation of danger: Differences between spider- and flight-phobic subjects in cognitive and physiological responses to disorder-specific stimuli. *Journal of Abnormal Psychology, 115*(3), 580–589.

Muir, J. L. (1997). Acetylcholine, aging, and Alzheimer's disease. *Pharmacological and Biochemical Behavior, 56*(4), 687–696.

Mullen, B. (1986). Atrocity as a function of lynch mob composition: A self- attention perspective. *Personality and Social Psychology Bulletin, 12*, 187–197.

Müller, T. D., Föcker, M., Holtkamp, K., Herpertz-Dahlamnn, B., & Hebebrand, J. (2009). Leptin-mediated neuroendocrine alterations in anorexia nervosa: Somatic and behavioral implications. *Child and Adolescent Psychiatric Clinics of North America, 18*(1), 117–129.

Mullin, R. E. (2000). *The new handbook of cognitive therapy techniques*. New York: Norton.

Mullis, I. V. S., Martin, M. O., Gonzales, E. J., & Chrostowski, S. J. (2004). *TIMSS 2003 international mathematics report: Findings from IEA's Trends in International Mathematics and Science Study at the fourth and eighth grades*. Chestnut Hill, MA: Boston College.

Mullis, I. V. S., Martin, M. O., Kennedy, A. M., & Foy, P. (2007). *PIRLS 2006 international report: IEA's Progress in International Reading Literacy Study in primary school in 40 countries*. Chestnut Hill, MA: Boston College.

Mumford, M. D., Connelly, M. S., Helton, W. B., Strange, J. M., & Osburn, H. K. (2001). On the construct validity of integrity tests: Individual and situational factors as predictors of test performance. *International Journal of Selection and Assessment, 9*, 240–257.

Mumme, D. L., & Fernald, A. (2003). The infant as onlooker: Learning from emotional reactions observed in a television scenario. *Child Development, 74*, 221–237.

Munakata, Y. (2006). Information processing approaches to development. In W. Damon & R. M. Lerner (Series Eds.) & D. Kuhn & R. Siegler (Vol. Eds.), *Handbook of child psychology: Vol. 2. Cognition, perception, and language* (6th ed.). New York: Wiley.

Munley, P. H. (2002). Comparability of MMPI-2 scales and profiles over time. *Journal of Personality Assessment, 78*, 145–160.

Munn, M. A., Alexopoulos, J., Nishino, T., Babb, C. M., Flake, L. A., Singer, T., Ratnanather, J., Huang, H., Todd, R. D., Miller, M. I., Botteron, K. N. (2007). Amygdala volume analysis in female twins with major depression. *Biological Psychiatry, 62*(5), 415–422.

Muñoz, R. F., & Mendelson, T. (2005). Toward evidence-based interventions for diverse populations: The San Francisco General Hospital prevention and treatment manuals. *Journal of Consulting and Clinical Psychology, 73*, 790–799.

Munte, T. F., Altenmuller, E., & Jancke, L. (2002). The musician's brain as a model of neuroplasticity. *Nature Reviews: Neuroscience, 3*, 473–478.

Murphy, M. C., Steele, C. M., & Gross, J. J. (2007). Signaling threat: How situational cues affect women in math, science, and engineering settings. *Psychological Science, 18*, 879–885.

Murray, B. (2000). Learning from real life. *APA Monitor, 31*, 72–73.

Murray, E. A., & Mishkin, M. (1985). Amygdalectomy impairs crossmodal association in monkeys. *Science, 228,* 604–606.

Murray, H. A. (1938). *Explorations in personality.* New York: Oxford University Press.

Murray, H. A. (1971). *Thematic Apperception Test.* Cambridge: Harvard University Press.

Murray, J. A., & Terry, D. (1999). Parental reactions to infant death: The effects of resources and coping strategies. *Journal of Social and Clinical Psychology, 18,* 341–369.

Murrell, W., Feron, F., Wetzig, A., Cameron, N., Splatt, K., Bellette, B., et al. (2005). Multipotent stem cells from adult olfactory mucosa. *Developmental Dynamics, 233,* 496–515.

Mussweiler, T. (2003). "Everything is relative": Comparison processes in social judgment: The 2002 Jaspars Lecture. *European Journal of Social Psychology, 33,* 719–733.

Mustanski, B. S., Chivers, M. L., & Bailey, J. M. (2002). A critical review of recent biological research on human sexual orientation. *Annual Review of Sex Research, 13,* 89–140.

Myers, B. J. (1987). Mother-infant bonding as a critical period. In M. H. Bornstein (Ed.), *Sensitive periods in development: Interdisciplinary perspectives.* Hillsdale, NJ: Erlbaum.

Myers, D. G. (2000). *The American paradox: Spiritual hunger in an age of plenty.* New Haven, CT: Yale University Press.

Myers, D. G. (2004). *Intuition: Its powers and perils.* New Haven, CT: Yale University Press.

Myers, K. M., & Davis, M. (2007). Mechanisms of fear extinction. *Molecular Psychiatry, 12,* 120–150.

Myers, M. G., Reeves, R. A., Oh, P. I., & Joyner, C. D. (1996). Overtreatment of hypertension in the community? *American Journal of Hypertension, 9,* 419–425.

Myers, S. L. (2001, March 12). Sub's crew may have hesitated to question a trusted captain. *New York Times.*

Nabeshima, T., & Yamada, K. (2000). Neurotrophic factor strategies for the treatment of Alzheimer disease. *Alzheimer Disease & Associated Disorders, 14*(Suppl. 1), S39–46.

Nadeau, S., & Crosson, B. (1995). A guide to the functional imaging of cognitive processes. *Neuropsychiatry, Neuropsychology, and Behavioral Neurology, 8,* 143–162.

Nader, K., Schafe, G. E., & Le Doux, J. E. (2000). Fear memories require protein synthesis in the amygdala for reconsolidation after retrieval. *Nature, 406,* 722–726.

Naëgelé, B., Thouvard, V., Pépin, J.-L., Lévy, P., Bonnet, C., Perret, J. E., et al. (1995). Deficits of cognitive functions in patients with sleep apnea syndrome. *Sleep, 18*(1), 43–52.

Nägerl, U. V., Willig, K. I., Hein, B., Hell, S. W., Bonhoeffer, T. (2008). Live-cell imaging of dendritic spines by STED microscopy. *Proceedings of the National Academy of Sciences, 105,* 18982–18987.

Nagy, T. F. (1999). *Ethics in plain English: An illustrative casebook for psychologists.* Washington, DC: American Psychological Association.

Nairne, J. S. (2003). Sensory and working memory. In A. F. P. Healy, R. W. Proctor, & I. B. Weiner (Eds.), *Handbook of psychology: Vol. 4. Experimental psychology* (pp. 423–444). New York: Wiley.

Naito, M., & Miura, H. (2001). Japanese children's numerical competencies: Age-and schooling-related influences on the development of number concepts and addition skills. *Developmental Psychology, 37,* 217–230.

Nakamura, J., & Csikszentmihalyi, M. (2001). Catalytic creativity. *American Psychologist, 56,* 337–341.

Nakano, K., & Kitamura, T. (2001). The relation of the anger subcomponent of Type A behavior to psychological symptoms in Japanese and foreign students. *Japanese Psychological Research, 43,* 50–54.

Narayan, V. M., Narr, K. L., Kumari, V., Woods, R. P., Thompson, P. M., Toga, A. W., & Sharma, T. (2007). Regional cortical thinning in subjects with violent antisocial personality disorder or schizophrenia. *American Journal of Psychiatry, 164,* 1418–1427.

Nardone, I. B., Ward, R., Fotopoulou, A., & Turnbull, O. H. (2007). Attention and emotion in anosognosia: Evidence of implicit awareness and repression? *Neurocase, 13*(5), 438–445.

Narrow, W. E., Rae, D. S., Robins, L. N., & Regier, D. A. (2002). Revised prevalence based estimates of mental disorders in the United States: Using a clinical significance criterion to reconcile two survey estimates. *Archives of General Psychiatry, 59,* 115–123.

Nash, A. J., & Fernandez, M. (1996). P300 and allocation of attention in dual-tasks. *International Journal of Psychophysiology, 23,* 171–180.

Nash, I. S., Mosca, L., Blumenthal, R. S., Davidson, M. H., Smith, S. C., Jr., & Pasternak, R. C. (2003). Contemporary awareness and understanding of cholesterol as a risk factor: Results of an American Heart Association national survey. *Archives of Internal Medicine, 163,* 1597–1600.

Nathan, P. E., & Gorman, J. M. (2007). *A guide to treatments that work* (3rd ed.). New York: Oxford University Press.

Nathan, P. E., Stuart, S. P., & Dolan, S. L. (2000). Research on psychotherapy efficacy and effectiveness: Between Scylla and Charybdis? *Psychological Bulletin, 126,* 964–981.

Nathanson, M., Bergman, P. S., & Gordon, G. G. (1952). Denial of illness: Its occurrence in one hundred consecutive cases of hemiplegia. *Archives of Neurology and Psychiatry, 68,* 380–397.

National Association of Anorexia Nervosa and Associated Disorders. (2002). *Facts about eating disorders.* Retrieved August 26, 2003, from http://www.altrue.net/site/anadweb/content.php?type=1&id=6982.

National Center for Chronic Disease Prevention and Health Promotion. (2002). Trends in Sexual Risk Behaviors Among High School Students—United States, 1991–2001. *Morbidity and Mortality Weekly Report, 51,* 856–859.

National Center for Complementary and Alternative Medicine (2008, March). St. Johns wort. *Herbs at a Glance.* NCCAM Publication No. D269. Retrieved April 21, 2009, at http://nccam.nih.gov/health/stjohnswort/ataglance.htm#science.

National Center for Education Statistics. (2000). *National assessment of education progress.* Washington, DC: NCES.

National Center for Education Statistics. (2002). *Digest of education statistics, 2001.* Washington, DC: Office of Educational Research & Improvement, U.S. Dept. of Education.

National Center for Health Statistics. (2000). *Trends in pregnancies and pregnancy rates by outcome: Estimates for the United States, 1976–1996.* Washington, DC: Centers for Disease Control and Prevention.

National Center for Health Statistics. (2001). *Births, marriages, divorces, and deaths: Provisional data for January–December 2000.* Hyattsville, MD: Public Health Service.

National Center for Health Statistics. (2003). Births: Final data for 2002. *National Vital Statistics Reports, 52*(10). Washington, DC: Centers for Disease Control and Prevention.

National Center for Health Statistics. (2004). *Health, United States, 2004: With chartbook on trends in the health of Americans.* Hyattsville, MD: U.S. Department of Health and Human Services.

National Center for Health Statistics. (2007). *Sexual behavior and selected health measures: Men and women 15–44 years of age, United States, 2002.* Hyattsville, MD: U.S. Department of Health and Human Services.

National Computer Systems. (1992). *Catalog of assessment instruments, reports, and services.* Minneapolis: National Computer Systems.

National Highway Traffic Safety Administration. (2008). 2007 traffic safety annual assessment—Alcohol-impaired driving fatalities. *Traffic Safety Facts.* Retrieved April 9, 2009, from http://www-nrd.nhtsa.dot.gov/Pubs/811016.PDF.

National Institute for Occupational Safety and Health. (1999). *Stress at work.* Washington, DC: NIOSH Publication No. 99–101.

National Institute of Mental Health (2008a). The numbers count: Mental disorders in America. Retrieved 25 February 2009 from http://www.nimh.nih.gov/health/publications/the-numbers-count-mental-disorders-in-america/index.shtml.

National Institute of Mental Health (2008b). Study probes environment-triggered genetic changes in schizophrenia. Retrieved March 6, 2009 from http://www.nimh.nih.gov/science-news/2008/study-probes-environment-triggered-genetic-changes-in-schizophrenia.shtml.

National Institute of Mental Health. (1995). *Medications.* Washington, DC: U.S. Department of Health and Human Services.

National Institute of Mental Health. (2004, April 23). *Statement on antidepressant medications for children: Information for parents and caregivers.* Retrieved April 24, 2004, from www.nimh.nih.gov/press/StmntAntidepmeds.cfm.

National Institute of Mental Health. (2006). *The numbers count: Mental disorders in America.* Retrieved August 8, 2006, from http://www.nimh.nih.gov.publicat/numbers.cfm.

National Institute on Alcohol Abuse and Alcoholism. (2000). *Tenth special report to the U.S. Congress on alcohol and health* (Publication No. 00–1583). Washington, DC: National Institutes of Health.

National Institute on Alcohol Abuse and Alcoholism. (2001). *Alcoholism: Getting the facts.* Bethesda, MD: National Institute on Alcohol Abuse and Alcoholism.

National Institute on Drug Abuse. (2000). Facts about MDMA (Ecstacy). *NIDA Notes, 14.* Retrieved December 13, 2004, from http://drugabuse.gov/NIDA_Notes/NNVol14N4/tearoff.html.

National Institutes of Health Consensus Conference. (1998). Acupuncture. *Journal of the American Medical Association, 280,* 1518–1524.

National Institutes of Health. (2001). *Eating disorders: Facts about eating disorders and the search for solutions.* NIH Publication No. 01–4901. Washington, DC: U.S. Department of Health and Human Services.

National Safety Council. (2004). *Reports on injuries in America, 2003.* Itasca, IL: Author.

National Science Foundation. (2004). *Doctoral scientists and engineers: 2001 profile tables.* Arlington, VA: Author.

Navarrete-Palacios, E., Hudson, R., Reyes-Guerrero, G., & Guevara-Guzman, R. (2003). Lower olfactory threshold during the ovulatory phase of the menstrual cycle. *Biological Psychology, 63,* 269–279.

Neary, D., & Snowden, J. (1996). Fronto-temporal dementia: Nosology, neuropsychology, and neuropathology. *Brain and Cognition, 31*(2), 176–187.

Neary, D., Snowden, J. S., & Mann, D. M. (1993). The clinical pathological correlates of lobar atrophy. *Dementia, 4*(3–4), 154–159.

Neff, L. A., & Karney, B. R. (2005). To know you is to love you: The implications of global adoration and specific accuracy for marital relationships. *Journal of Personality and Social Psychology, 88,* 480–497.

Neher, A. (1991). Maslow's theory of motivation: A critique. *Journal of Humanistic Psychology, 31,* 89–112.

Neighbors, H. W., Caldwell, C., Williams, D. R., Nesse, R., Taylor, R. J., Bullard, K. M., et al. (2007). Race, ethnicity, and the use of services for mental disorders. *Archives of General Psychiatry, 64,* 485–494.

Neighbors, H. W., Trierweiler, S. J., Fort, B. C., & Muroff, J. R. (2003). Racial differences in DSM diagnosis using a semi-structured instrument: The importance of clinical judgment in the diagnosis of African Americans. *Journal of Health and Social Behavior, 44,* 237–256.

Neil, A. L., & Christensen, H. (2009). Efficacy and effectiveness of school-based prevention and early intervention programs for anxiety. *Clinical Psychology Review, 29,* 208–215.

Neisser, U. (1998). *The rising curve: Long-term gains in I.Q. and related measures.* Washington, DC: American Psychological Association.

Neisser, U. (2000a). Memorists. In U. Neisser & I. E. Hyman, Jr. (Eds.), *Memory observed* (2nd ed., pp. 475–478). New York: Worth.

Neisser, U. (2000b). Snapshots or benchmarks? In U. Neisser & I. E. Hyman, Jr. (Eds.), *Memory observed* (2nd ed., pp. 68–74). New York: Worth.

Neisser, U., Boodoo, G., Bouchard, T. J., Boykin, A. W., Brody, N., Ceci, S. J., et al. (1996). Intelligence: Knowns and unknowns. *American Psychologist, 51,* 77–101.

Nelson, C. A. (1999). Neural plasticity and human development. *Current Directions in Psychological Science, 8,* 42–45.Neugarten, B. L. (1977). Personality and aging. In J. E. Birren & K. W. Schaie (Eds.), *Handbook of the psychology of aging.* New York: Van Nostrand Reinhold.

Nelson, C. A. (2007). A neurobiological perspective on early human deprivation. *Child Development Perspectives, 1,* 13–18.

Nelson, K., & Fivush, R. (2004). The emergence of autobiographical memory: A social cultural developmental theory. *Psychological Review, 111,* 486–511.

Nelson, T. D., & Steele, R. G. (2006). Beyond efficacy and effectiveness: A multifaceted approach to treatment evaluation. *Professional Psychology: Research and Practice, 37,* 389–397.

Nelson-LeGall, S., & Resnick, L. (1998). Help seeking, achievement motivation, and the social practice of intelligence in school. In S. A. Karabenick (Ed.), *Strategic help seeking* (pp. 39–60). Mahwah, NJ: Erlbaum.

Nemeroff, C. B., Heim, C. M., Thase, M. E., Klein, D. N., Rush, A. J., Schatzberg, A. F., et al. (2003). Differential responses to psychotherapy versus pharmacotherapy in patients with chronic forms of major depression and childhood trauma. *Proceedings of the National Academy of Sciences, 100,* 14293–14296.

Nemeth, C. J., Personnaz, B., Personnaz, M., & Goncalo, J. A. (2004). The liberating role of conflict in group creativity: A study in two countries. *European Journal of Social Psychology, 34,* 365–374.

Neovius, M., & Narbro, K. (2008). Cost-effectiveness of pharmacological anti-obesity treatments: a systematic review. *International Journal of Obesity, 32,* 1752–1763.

Nestadt, G., Hsu, F.-C., Samuels, J., Bienvenu, O. J., Reti, I. Costa, P. T., Jr., et al. (2005). Latent structure of the *Diagnostic and Statistical Manual of Mental Disorders, Fourth Edition,* personality disorder criteria. *Comprehensive Psychiatry, 47,* 54–62.

Nestler, E. J. (2001). Molecular basis of long-term plasticity underlying addiction. *National Review of Neuroscience, 2,* 119–128.

Nestler, E. J. (2005). Is there a common molecular pathway for addiction? *Nature Neuroscience, 8,* 1445–1449.

Nestoriuc, Y., Rief, W., & Martin, A. (2008). Meta-analysis of biofeedback for tension-type headache: Efficacy, specificity, and treatment moderators. *Journal of Consulting and Clinical Psychology, 76,* 379–396.

Netter, P. (2006). Dopamine challenge tests as an indicator of psychological traits. *Human Psychopharmacology: Clinical and Experimental, 21,* 91–99.

Neumann, C. S., Grimes, K., Walker, E. F., & Baum, K. (1995). Developmental pathways to schizophrenia: Behavioral subtypes. *Journal of Abnormal Psychology, 104,* 558–566.

Neumeister, A., Bain, E., Nugent, A. C., Carson, R. E., Bonne, O., Luckenbaugh, D. A., et al. (2004). Reduced serotonin type 1A receptor binding in panic disorder. *Journal of Neuroscience, 24,* 589–591.

Neuwelt, E. A. (2004). Mechanisms of disease: The blood-brain barrier. *Neurosurgery, 54,* 131–140.

Neves-Pereira, M., Cheung, J. K., Pasdar, A., Zhang, F., Breen, G., Yates, P., et al. (2005). BDNF gene is a risk factor for schizophrenia in a Scottish population. *Molecular Psychiatry, 10,* 208–212.

Newberg, A., Alavi, A., Baime, M., Pourdehnad, M., Santanna, J., & d'Aquili, E. (2001). The measurement of regional cerebral blood flow during the complex cognitive task of meditation: A preliminary SPECT study. *Psychiatry Research, 106,* 113–122.

Newcombe, N., & Fox, N. A. (1994). Infantile amnesia: Through a glass darkly. *Child Development, 65,* 31–40.

Newcombe, N. S., Drummey, A. B., Fox, N. A., Lie, E., & Ottinger-Alberts, W. (2000). Remembering early childhood: How much, how, and why (or why not). *Current Directions in Psychological Science, 9,* 55–58.

Newell, A., & Simon, H. A. (1972). *Human problem solving.* Englewood Cliffs, NJ: Prentice Hall.

Newhouse, P., Newhouse, C., & Astur, R. S. (2007). Sex differences in visual-spatial learning using a virtual water maze in pre-pubertal children. *Behavioural Brain Research, 183,* 1–7.

Newnam, S., Griffin, M. A., & Mason, C. (2008). Safety in work vehicles: A multilevel study linking safety values and individual predictors to work-related driving crashes. *Journal of Applied Psychology, 93,* 632–644.

Newpher, T. M., & Ehlers, M. D. (2008). Glutamate receptor dynamics in dendritic microdomains. *Neuron, 58*(4), 472–497.

Newsom, J. T., Mahan, T. L., Rook, K. S., & Krause, N. (2008). Stable negative social exchanges and health. *Health Psychology, 27,* 78–86.

Ng, C. H., Chong, S., Lambert, T., Fan, A., Hackett, L. P., Mahendran, R., et al. (2005). An inter-ethnic comparison study of clozapine dosage, clinical response, and plasma levels. *International Clinical Psychopharmacology, 20,* 163–168.

Ng, K.-Y., Ang, S., & Chan, K.-Yin. (2008). Personality and leader effectiveness: A moderated mediation model of leadership self-efficacy, job demands, and job autonomy. *Journal of Applied Psychology, 93,* 733–743.

Nguyen, B. H., Pérusse, D., Paquet, J., Petit, D., Boivin, M., Tremblay, R. E., & Montplaisir, J. (2008). Sleep terrors in children: A prospective study of twins. *Pediatrics, 122,* e1164–e1167.

Nicassio, P. M., Meyerowitz, B. E., & Kerns, R. D. (2004). The future of health psychology interventions. *Health Psychology, 23,* 132–137.

NICHD Early Child Care Research Network. (2001, April). *Further explorations of the detected effects of quantity of early child care on socioemotional adjustment.* Paper presented at the biennial meetings of the Society for Research in Child Development, Minneapolis.

NICHD Early Child Care Research Network. (2005). *Child care and child development: Results from the NICHD Study of Early Child Care and Youth Development.* New York: Guilford.

NICHD Early Child Care Research Network. (2006a). Infant-mother attachment classification: Risk and protection in relation to changing maternal caregiving quality. *Developmental Psychology, 42,* 38–58.

NICHD Early Child Care Research Network. (2006b). Child-care effect sizes for the NICHD study of early child care and youth development. *American Psychologist, 61,* 99–116.

Nichols, M. P. (2007). *Family therapy: Concepts and methods* (8th ed.). Boston, MA: Allyn & Bacon.

Nicholson, A., Fuhrer, R., & Marmot, M. (2005). Psychological distress as a predictor of CHD events in men: The effect of persistence and components of risk. *Psychosomatic Medicine, 67,* 522–530.

Nicholson, I. R., & Neufeld, R. W. J. (1993). Classification of the schizophrenias according to symptomatology: A two factor model. *Journal of Abnormal Psychology, 102,* 259–270.

Nickell, J. (1997, January/February). Sleuthing a psychic sleuth. *Skeptical Inquirer, 21,* 18–19.

Nickerson, R. A., & Adams, M. J. (1979). Long-term memory for a common object. *Cognitive Psychology, 11,* 287–307.

Niederhoffer, K. G., & Pennebaker, J. W. (2002). Sharing one's story: On the benefits of writing or talking about emotional experience. In C. R. Snyder & S. J. Lopez (Eds.), *Handbook of positive psychology* (pp. 573–583). London: Oxford University Press.

Niederman, R., & Richards, D. (2005). Evidence-based dentistry: Concepts and implementation. *Journal of the American College of Dentistry, 72,* 37–41.

Nienhuys, J. W. (2001). Spontaneous human combustion: Requiem for Phyllis. *Skeptical Inquirer, 25,* 28–34.

Nievar, M. A., & Becker, B. J. (2008). Sensitivity as a privileged predictor of attachment: A second perspective on De Wolff and Van IJzendoorn's meta-analysis. *Social Development, 17,* 102–114.

Nigg, J. T. (2001). Is ADHD a disinhibitory disorder? *Psychological Bulletin, 127,* 571–598.

Niiya, Y., Crocker, J., & Bartmess, E. N. (2004). From vulnerability to resilience: Learning orientations buffer contingent self-esteem from failure. *Psychological Science, 15,* 801–805.

Nijstad, B. A., Stroebe, W., & Lodewijkx, H. F. M. (2003). Production blocking and idea generation: Does blocking interfere with cognitive processes? *Journal of Experimental Social Psychology, 39,* 531–548.

Nilsson, G. (1996, November). Some forms of memory improve as people age. *APA Monitor,* 27.

Nisbett, R. E. (2003). *The geography of thought.* New York: The Free Press.

Nisbett, R. E., & Masuda, T. (2007). Culture and point of view. *Intellectica, 46*(2), 153–172.

Noble, H. B. (2000, January 25). Outgrowth of new field of tissue engineering. *New York Times.*

Noblett, K. L., & Coccaro, E. F. (2005). Molecular genetics of personality. *Current Psychiatry Reports, 7,* 73–80.

Nock, M. K., Kazdin, A. E., Hirpi, E., & Kessler, R. C. (2006). Prevalence, subtypes and correlates of DSM-IV conduct disorder in the National Comorbidity Survey Replication. *Psychological Medicine, 36,* 699–710.

Nock, M. K., & Kessler, R. C. (2006). Prevalence of and risk factors for suicide attempts versus suicide gestures: Analysis of the National Comorbidity Survey. *Journal of Abnormal Psychology, 115,* 616–623.

Noftle, E. E., & Robins, R. W. (2007). Personality predictors of academic outcomes: Big five correlates of GPA and SAT scores. *Journal of Personality and Social Psychology, 93,* 116–130.

Noftle, E. E., & Shaver, P. R. (2006). Attachment dimensions and the big five personality traits: Associations and comparative ability to predict relationship quality. *Journal of Research in Personality, 40,* 179–208.

Nolen-Hoeksema, S. (2001). Gender differences in depression. *Current Directions in Psychological Science, 10,* 173–176.

Nolen-Hoeksema, S. (2006). The etiology of gender differences in depression. In C. M. Mazure & G. P. Keita (Eds.), *Understanding depression in women: Applying empirical research to practice and policy* (pp. 9–43). Washington, DC: American Psychological Association.

Nolen-Hoeksema, S., Morrow, J., & Fredrickson, B. L. (1993). Response styles and the duration of episodes of depressed mood. *Journal of Abnormal Psychology, 102,* 20–28.

Noll, R. B. (1994). Hypnotherapy for warts in children and adolescents. *Journal of Developmental and Behavioral Pediatrics, 15*(3), 170–173.

Nomura, H., Inoue, S., Kamimura, N., Shimodera, S., Mino, Y., et al. (2005). A cross-cultural study on expressed emotion in careers of people with dementia and schizophrenia: Japan and England. *Social Psychiatry and Psychiatric Epidemiology, 40,* 564–570.

Norberg, M. M., Krystal, J. H., & Tolin, D. F. (2008). A meta-analysis of D-Cycloserine and the facilitation of fear extinction and exposure therapy. *Biological Psychiatry, 63,* 1118–1126.

Norcross, J. C. (2001). Purposes, processes and products of the task force on empirically supported therapy relationships. *Psychotherapy: Theory, Research, Practice, Training, 38*(4), 345–356.

Norcross, J. C. (2002). *Psychotherapy relationships that work.* New York: Oxford University Press.

Norcross, J. C., Beutler, L. E., & Levant, R. F. (2005). Prologue. In J. C. Norcross, L. E. Beutler, & R. F. Levant (Eds.), *Evidence-based practices in mental health: Debate and dialogue on the fundamental questions* (pp. 3–12). Washington, DC: American Psychological Association.

Norcross, J. C., & Goldfried, M. R. (2005). *Handbook of psychotherapy integration* (2nd ed.). New York: Oxford University Press.

Norcross, J. C., Hedges, M., & Castle, P. H. (2002). Psychologists conducting psychotherapy in 2001: A study of Division 29 membership. *Psychotherapy: Theory, Research, Practice, Training, 39,* 97–102.

Norcross, J. C., Santrock, J. W., Campbell, L. F., Smith, T. P., Sommer, R., & Zuckerman, E. L. (2000). *Authoritative guide to self-help resources in mental health.* New York: Guilford.

Nordberg, A. (2008). Amyloid plaque imaging in vivo: current achievement and future prospects. *European Journal of Nuclear Medicine & Molecular Imaging, 35,* 46–50.

Norman, T., & Olver, J. S. (2004). New formulations of existing antidepressants: Advantages in the management of depression. *CNS Drugs, 18,* 505–520.

North, M. M., North, S. M., & Burwick, C. B. (2008). Virtual reality therapy: A vision for a new paradigm. In L. L'Abate (Ed.), *Toward a science of clinical psychology: Laboratory evaluations and interventions* (pp. 307–320). Hauppauge, NY: Nova Science Publishers.

Nourkova, V. V., Bernstein, D. M., & Loftus, E. F. (2004). Biography becomes autobiography: Distorting the subjective past. *American Journal of Psychology, 117,* 65–80.

Nowak, M. A., Komarova, N. L., & Niyogi, P. (2001). Evolution of universal grammar. *Science, 291,* 114–118.

Noyes, R., & Hoehn-Saric, R. (2006). *The anxiety disorders.* London: Cambridge University Press.

Nurnberger, J. I., Jr., Foroud, T., Flury, L., Su, J., Meyer, E. T., Hu, K., et al. (2001). Evidence for a locus on chromosome 1 that influences vulnerability to alcoholism and affective disorder. *American Journal of Psychiatry, 158,* 718–724.

Nutt, D. J. (2005a). Death by tricyclic: The real antidepressant scandal? *Journal of Psychopharmacology, 19,* 123–124.

Nutt, D. J. (2005b). Overview of diagnosis and drug treatments of anxiety disorders. *CNS Spectrums, 10,* 49–56.

Nyberg, L., Petersson, K. M., Nilsson, L. G., Sandblom, J., Aberg, C., & Ingvar, M. (2001). Reactivation of motor brain areas during explicit memory for actions. *Neuroimage, 14,* 521–528.

Nye, C. D., Roberts, B. W., Saucier, G., & Zhou, X. (2008). Testing the measurement equivalence of personality adjective items across cultures. *Journal of Research in Personality, 42*(6), 1524–1536.

O'Brien, T. L. (1991, September 2). Computers help thwart "groupthink" that plagues meetings. *Chicago Sun Times.*

O'Donohue, W., Fisher, J. E., & Hayes, S. C. (Eds.). (2003). *Cognitive behavior therapy: Applying empirically supported techniques in your practice.* New York: Wiley.

O'Driscoll, M., Brough, P., & Kalliath, T. (2006). Work-family conflict and facilitation. In F. Jones, R. J. Burke, & M. Westman (Eds.), *Work-life balance: A psychological perspective* (pp. 117–142). New York: Psychology Press.

O'Leary, D. S., Block, R. I., Koeppel, J. A., Flaum, M., Schulz, S. K., Andreason, N. C., et al. (2002). Effects of smoking marijuana on brain perfusion and cognition. *Neuropsychopharmacology, 26,* 802–816.

O'Neill, H. (2000, September 24). After rape, jail—a friendship forms. *St. Petersburg Times,* pp. 1A, 14A.

O'Reardon, J. P., Solvason, H. B., Janicak, P. G., Sampson, S., Isenberg, K. E., Nahas, Z., McDonald, W. M., Avery, D., Fitzgerald, P. B., Loo, C., Demitrack, M. A., George, M. S., & Sackeim, H. A. (2007). Efficacy and safety of transcranial magnetic stimulation in the acute treatment of major depression: A multisite randomized controlled trial. *Biological Psychiatry, 62*(11), 1208–1216.

O'Reilly, R. C. (2006). Biologically based computational models of high-level cognition. *Science, 314,* 91–94.

Oatley, K. (1993). Those to whom evil is done. In R. S. Wyer & T. K. Srull (Eds.), *Toward a general theory of anger and emotional aggression: Advances in social cognition* (Vol. 6). Hillsdale, NJ: Erlbaum.

Oberman, L. M., & Ramachandran, V. S. (2007). The simulating social mind: The role of the mirror neuron system and simulation in the social and communicative deficits of autism spectrum disorders. *Psychological Bulletin, 133,* 310–327.

Ochsner, K. N. (2004). Current directions in social cognitive neuroscience. *Current Opinion in Neurobiology, 14,* 254–258.

Oden, M. H. (1968). The fulfillment of promise: 40-year follow-up of the Terman gifted group. *Genetic Psychology Monographs, 17,* 3–93.

Odgers, C. L., Caspi, A., Nagin, D. S., Piquero, A. R., Slutske, W. S., Milne, B. J., Dickson, N., Poulton, R., & Moffitt, T. E. (2008). Is it important to prevent early exposure to drugs and alcohol among adolescents? *Psychological Science, 19,* 1037–1044.

Ogden, C. L., Carroll, M. D., & Flegal, K. M. (2008). High body mass index for age among us children and adolescents, 2003–2006. *Journal of the American Medical Association, 299,* 2401–2405.

Ogden, C. L., Carroll, M. D., McDowell, M. A., & Flegal, K. M. (2007). *Obesity among adults in the United States—no change since 2003–2004.* NCHS data brief no 1. Hyattsville, MD: National Center for Health Statistics, 2007.

Ogrodniczuk, J. S., & Piper, W. E. (2003). The effect of group climate on outcome in two forms of short-term group therapy. *Group Dynamics: Theory, Research, and Practice, 7,* 64–76.

Ohayon, M. M., & Roth, T. (2003). Place of chronic insomnia in the course of depressive and anxiety disorders. *Journal of Psychiatric Research, 37,* 9–15.

Öhman, A., & Mineka, S. (2001). Fears, phobias, and preparedness: Toward an evolved module of fear and fear learning. *Psychological Review, 108,* 483–522.

Öhman, A., & Mineka, S. (2003). The malicious serpent: Snakes as a prototypical stimulus for an evolved module of fear. *Current Directions in Psychological Science, 12,* 5–9.

Öhman, A., & Soares, J. J. (1993). On the automatic nature of phobic fear: Conditioned electrodermal responses to masked fear-relevant stimuli. *Journal of Abnormal Psychology, 102*(1), 121–132.

Öhman, A., & Soares, J. J. (1994). "Unconscious anxiety": Phobic responses to masked stimuli. *Journal of Abnormal Psychology, 103*(2), 231–240.

Öhman, A., & Soares, J. J. F. (1998). Emotional conditioning to masked stimuli: Expectancies for aversive outcomes following nonrecognized fear-relevant stimuli. *Journal of Experimental Psychology: General, 127*(1), 69–82.

Öhman, A., Dimberg, U., & Öst, L. G. (1985). Animal and social phobias: A laboratory model. In S. Reiss & R. R. Bootzin (Eds.), *Theoretical issues in behavior therapy.* Orlando, FL: Academic Press.

Ohring, R., Graber, J. A., & Brooks-Gunn, J. (2002). Girls' recurrent and concurrent body dissatisfaction: Correlates and consequences over 8 years. *International Journal of Eating Disorders, 31*(4), 404–415.

Ohta, H., Yamazaki, S., & McMahon, D. G. (2005). Constant light desynchronizes mammalian clock neurons. *Nature Neuroscience, 8,* 267–269.

Oishi, S., Diener, E., Lucas, R. E., & Suh, E. M. (1999). Cross-cultural variations in predictors of life-satisfaction: Perspectives from needs and values. *Personality and Social Psychology Bulletin, 25,* 980–990.

Okonkwo, D. O. (2003). Basic science of closed head injuries and spinal cord injuries. *Clinics of Sports Medicine, 22*(3), 467–481.

Olatunji, B. O. (2006). Evaluative learning and emotional responding to fearful and disgusting stimuli in spider phobia. *Journal of Anxiety Disorders, 20,* 858–876.

Oldenberg, P.-A., Zheleznyak, A., Fang, Y.-F., Lagenaur, C. F., Gresham, H. D., & Lindberg, F. P. (2000). Role of CD47 as a marker of self on red blood cells. *Science, 288,* 2051–2054.

Olds, J. (1973). Commentary on positive reinforcement produced by electrical stimulation of septal areas and other regions of rat brain. In E. S. Valenstein (Ed.), *Brain stimulation and motivation: Research and commentary.* Glenview, IL: Scott, Foresman.

Olds, J., & Milner, P. (1954). Positive reinforcement produced by electrical stimulation of septal areas and other regions of the rat brain. *Journal of Comparative and Physiological Psychology, 47,* 419–427.

Olfson, M., Blanco, C., Liu, L., Moreno, C., & Laje, G. (2006). National trends in the outpatient treatment of children and adolescents with antipsychotic drugs. *Archives of General Psychiatry, 63,* 679–685.

Olfson, M., Marcus, S. C., & Shaffer, D. (2006). Antidepressant drug therapy and suicide in depressed children and adolescents: A case-control study. *Archives of General Psychiatry, 63,* 865–872.

Olfson, M., Mechanic, D., Hansell, S., Boyer, C. A., & Walkup, J. (1999). Prediction of homelessness within three months of discharge among inpatients with schizophrenia. *Psychiatric Services, 50,* 667–673.

Oliner, S. P., & Oliner, P. M. (1988). *The altruistic personality: Rescuers of Jews in Nazi Europe.* New York: Free Press.

Olio, K. A. (1994). Truth in memory. *American Psychologist, 49,* 442–443.

Ollendick, T. H., & Prinz, R. J. (2002). Editors' comment: International consensus statement on attention deficit hyperactivity disorder (ADHD). *Clinical Child and Family Psychology Review, 5,* 87.

Olshansky, S. J., Passaro, D. J., Hershow, R. C., Layden, J., Carnes, B. A., Brody, J., et al. (2005). A potential decline in life expectancy in the United States in the 21st century. *New England Journal of Medicine, 352,* 1138–1145.

Olson, I. R., Rao, H., Moore, K. S., Wang, J., Detre, J. A., & Aguirre, G. K. (2006). Using perfusion fMRI to measure continuous changes in neural activity with learning. *Brain and Cognition, 60,* 262–271.

Olson, J. M., & Stone, J. (2005). The influence of behavior on attitudes. In D. Albarracín, B. T. Johnson, & M. P. Zanna (Eds.), *Handbook of attitudes* (pp. 223–271). Mahwah, NJ: Erlbaum.

Olson, J. M., Vernon, P. A., Harris, J. A., & Jang, K. L. (2001). The heritability of attitudes: A study of twins. *Journal of Personality and Social Psychology, 80,* 845–860.

Olson, L. (1997). Regeneration in the adult central nervous system. *Nature Medicine, 3,* 1329–1335.

Olson, M. B., Krantz, D. S., Kelsey, S. F., Pepine, C. J., Sopko, G., Handberg, E., et al. (2005). Hostility scores are associated with increased risk of cardiovascular events in women undergoing coronary angiography: A report from the NHLBI-sponsored WISE study. *Psychosomatic Medicine, 67,* 546–552.

Olsson, C. J., Jonsson, B., Larsson, A., & Nyberg, L. (2008). Motor representations and practice affect brain systems underlying imagery: An FMRI study of internal imagery in novices and active high jumpers. *The Open Neuroimaging Journal, 2,* 5–13.

Oltmanns, T. F., & Turkheimer, E. (2009). Person perception and personality pathology. *Current Directions in Psychological Science, 18,* 32–36.

Ölveczky, B. P., Baccus, S. A., & Meister, M. (2003). Segregation of object and background motion in the retina. *Nature, 423,* 401–408.

Omaha, J. (2004). *Psychotherapeutic interventions for emotion regulation: EMDR and bilateral stimulation for affect management.* New York: Norton.

Oman, D., Hedberg, J., & Thoreson, C. E. (2006). Passage meditation reduces perceived stress in health professionals: A randomized controlled trial. *Journal of Consulting and Clinical Psychology, 74,* 714–719.

Ones, D., & Viswesvaran, C. (1996). Bandwidth-fidelity dilemma in personality measurement for personnel selection. *Journal of Organizational Behavior, 17,* 609–626.

Ones, D., & Viswesvaran, C. (2001). Personality at work: Criterion focused occupational personality scales used in personnel selection. In R. Hogan & B. Roberts (Eds.), *Personality psychology in the workplace* (pp. 63–92). Washington, DC: American Psychological Association.

Ones, D. S., Viswesvaran, C., & Schmidt, F. L. (2003). Personality and absenteeism: A meta-analysis of integrity tests. *European Journal of Personality, 17,* S19–S38.

Onishi, K. H., & Baillargeon, R. (2005). Do 15-month-old infants understand false beliefs? *Science, 308,* 255–258.

Ono, Y., Kawakami, N., Nakane, Y., Nakamura, Y., Tachimori, H., et al. (2008). Prevalence of and risk factors for suicide-related outcomes in the World Health Organization Mental Health Surveys Japan. *Psychiatry and Clinical Neurosciences, 62,* 442–449.

Operario, D., & Fiske, S. T. (2001). Stereotypes: Processes, structures, content, and context. In R. Brown & S. Gaertner (Eds.), *Blackwell handbook in social psychology: Intergroup processes* (pp. 22–44). Oxford, UK: Blackwell.

Oppel, S. (2000, March 5). Managing ABCs like a CEO. *St. Petersburg Times,* 1A, 12–13A.

Oquendo, M. A., Ellis, S. P., Greenwald, S., Malone, K. M., Weissman, M. M., & Mann, J. J. (2001). Ethnic and sex differences in suicide rates relative to major depression in the United States. *American Journal of Psychiatry, 158,* 1652–1658.

Oquendo, M. A., & Mann, J. J. (2000). The biology of impulsivity and suicidality. *Psychiatric Clinics of North America, 23,* 11–25.

Orban, P., Rauchs, G., Balteau, E., Degueldre, C., Luxen, A., Maquet, P., et al. (2006). Sleep after spatial learning promotes covert reorganization of brain activity. *Proceedings of the National Academy of Sciences, 103,* 7124–7129.

Organ, D. W., Podsakoff, P. M., & MacKenzie, S. B. (2006). *Organizational citizenship behavior: Its nature, antecedents, and consequences.* Thousand Oaks, CA: Sage.

Orne, M. T., & Evans, F. J. (1965). Social control in the psychological experiment: Antisocial behavior and hypnosis. *Journal of Personality and Social Psychology, 1,* 189–200.

Orne, M. T., Sheehan, P. W., & Evans, F. J. (1968). Occurrence of posthypnotic behavior outside the experimental setting. *Journal of Personality and Social Psychology, 9,* 189–196.

Oshima, N. (2008). Beneficial and adverse effects of pharmacotherapy with risperidone on behavioral and psychological symptoms of dementia (BPSD). *Psychogeriatrics, 8*(4), 175–177.

Oskamp, S., & Schultz, P. W. (1998). *Applied social psychology* (2nd ed.). Upper Saddle River, NJ: Prentice Hall.

Öst, L.-G. (1978). Behavioral treatment of thunder and lightning phobia. *Behavior Research and Therapy, 16,* 197–207.

Öst, L.-G., Hellström, K., & Kåver, A. (1992). One- versus five-session exposure in the treatment of needle phobia. *Behavior Therapy, 23,* 263–282.

Öst, L.-G., Svensson, L., Hellström, K., & Lindwall, R. (2001). One-session treatment of specific phobias in youths: A randomized clinical trial. *Journal of Consulting and Clinical Psychology, 69,* 814–824.

Ostrov, J. M. (2006). Deception and subtypes of aggression during early childhood. *Journal of Experimental Child Psychology, 93,* 322–336.

Otto, M. W., Bruce, S. E., & Deckersbach, T. (2005). Benzodiazepine use, cognitive impairment, and cognitive-behavioral therapy for anxiety disorders: Issues in the treatment of a patient in need. *Journal of Clinical Psychiatry, 66*(Suppl. 2), 34–38.

Otto, M. W., Pollack, M. H., Gould, R. A., Worthington, J. J., III, McArdle, E. T., Rosenbaum, J. F., & Heimberg, R. G. (2000). A comparison of the efficacy of clonazepam and cognitive-behavioral group therapy for the treatment of social phobia. *Journal of Anxiety Disorders, 14,* 345–358.

Oudiette, D., De Cock, V. C., Lavault, S., Leu, S., Vidailhet, M., & Arnulf, I. (2009). Nonviolent elaborate behaviors may also occur in REM sleep behavior disorder. *Neurology, 72,* 551–557.

Overbeek, G., Stattin, H., Vermulst, A., Ha, T., & Engels, R. C. M. E. (2007). Parent-child relationships, partner relationships, and emotional adjustment: A birth-to-maturity prospective study. *Developmental Psychology, 43,* 429–437.

Overmier, J. B. (2002). On learned helplessness. *Integrative Physiological & Behavioral Science, 37,* 4–8.

Overmier, J. B., & Seligman, M. E. P. (1967). Effects of inescapable shock upon subsequent escape and avoidance learning. *Journal of Comparative and Physiological Psychology, 63,* 23–33.

Overton, D. A. (1984). State dependent learning and drug discriminations. In L. L. Iverson, S. D. Iverson, & S. H. Snyder (Eds.), *Handbook of psychopharmacology* (Vol. 18). New York: Plenum.

Ovsiew, F. (2006). An overview of the psychiatric approach to conversion disorder. In M. Hallet et al. (Eds.), *Psychogenic movement disorders: Neurology and neuropsychiatry* (pp. 112–121). New York: Lippincott Williams & Wilkins.

Oyama, H., Koida, J., Sakashita, T., & Kudo, K. (2004). Community-based prevention for suicide in elderly by depression screening and follow-up. *Community Mental Health Journal, 40,* 249–263.

Pachankis, J. E., & Goldfried, M. R. (2004). Clinical issues in working with lesbian, gay, and bisexual clients. *Psychotherapy: Theory, Research, Practice, Training, 41,* 227–246.

Packer, D. J. (2008). Identifying systematic disobedience in Milgram's obedience experiments: A meta-analytic review. *Perspectives on Psychological Science, 3,* 301–304.

Paik, H., & Comstock, G. (1994). The effects of television violence on antisocial behavior: A meta-analysis. *Communication Research, 21,* 516–546.

Palincsar, A. S. (2003). Ann L. Brown: Advancing a theoretical model of learning and instruction. In B. J. Zimmerman and D. H. Schunk (Eds.), *Educational psychology: A century of contributions,* pp. 459–475. Mahwah, NJ: Erlbaum.

Palkovitz, R., Copes, M. A., & Woolfolk, T. N. (2001). It's like . . . you discover a new sense of being: Involved fathering as an evoker of adult development. *Men & Masculinities, 4*(1), 49–69.

Palmer, S. E., & Ghose, T. (2008). Extremal edges: A powerful cue to depth perception and figure-ground organization. *Psychological Science, 19*(1), 77–84.

Palmisano, M., & Herrmann, D. (1991). The facilitation of memory performance. *Bulletin of the Psychonomic Society, 29,* 557–559.

Pandharipande, P., Jackson, J., & Ely, E. W. (2005). Delirium: Acute cognitive dysfunction in the critically ill. *Current Opinion in Critical Care, 11*(4), 360–368.

Paoletti, M. G. (1995). Biodiversity, traditional landscapes and agroecosystem management. *Landscape and Urban Planning, 31*(1–3), 117–128.

Paradise, A. (2007). *State of the Industry: ASTD's annual review of trends in workplace learning and performance.* Alexandria, VA: ASTD.

Pardini, D. A., & Lochman, J. E. (2003). Treatment of oppositional defiant disorder. In M. A. Reinecke, F. M. Dattilio, & A. Freeman (Eds.), *Cognitive therapy with children and adolescents.* New York: Guilford Press.

Parents Television Council. (2006). *TV bloodbath: Violence on primetime broadcast TV: A PTC state of the television industry report, March.* Retrieved May 24, 2006, from http://www.parentstv.org/PTC/publications/reports/stateindustryviolence/main.asp#_ftn.

Pariente, J., White, P., Frackowiak, R. S., & Lewith, G. (2005). Expectancy and belief modulate the neuronal substrates of pain treated by acupuncture. *NeuroImage, 25,* 1161–1167.

Park, D., & Gutchess, A. (2006). The cognitive neuroscience of aging and culture. *Current Directions in Psychological Science, 15,* 105–108.

Park, D. C. (2001, August). *The aging mind.* Paper presented at the annual convention of the American Psychological Association, San Francisco.

Park, D. C., Lautenschlager, G., Hedden, T., Davidson, N. S., Smith, A. D., & Smith, P. (2002). Models of visuospatial and verbal memory across the adult life span. *Psychology & Aging, 17*(2), 299–320.

Park, G., Lubinski, D., & Benbow, C. P. (2008). Ability differences among people who have commensurate degrees matter for scientific creativity. *Psychological Science, 19,* 957–961.

Park, H. J., Li, R. X., Kim, J., Kim, S. W., Moon, D. H., Kwon, M. H., & Kim, W. J. (2009). Neural correlates of winning and losing while watching soccer matches. *International Journal of Neuroscience, 119*(1), 76–87.

Park, I.-H., Zhao, R., West, J. A., Yabuuchi, A., Huo, H., Ince, T. A., Lerou, P. H., Lensch, M. W., & Daley, G. Q. (2008). Reprogramming of human somatic cells to pluripotency with defined factors. *Nature, 451,* 141–146.

Park, N., Peterson, C., & Seligman, M. E. P. (2004). Strengths of character and well-being. *Journal of Social and Clinical Psychology, 23,* 603–619.

Park, W.-W. (2000). A comprehensive empirical investigation of the relationships among variables of the groupthink model. *Journal of Organizational Behavior, 21,* 873–887.

Parke, R. D. (2002). Fathers and families. In M. H. Bornstein (Ed.), *Handbook of parenting* (2nd ed., pp. 27–63). Mahwah, NJ: Erlbaum.

Parke, R. D., & Buriel, R. (2006). Child development and the family. In W. Damon & R. M. Lerner (Series Eds.) & N. Eisenberg (Vol. Ed.), *Handbook of child psychology: Vol. 3. Social, emotional, and personality development* (6th ed.). New York: Wiley.

Parker, E. S., Cahill, L., & McGaugh, J. L. (2006). A case of unusual autobiographical remembering. *Neurocase, 12,* 35–49.

Parker, G., Gladstone, G., & Chee, K. T. (2001). Depression in the planet's largest ethnic group: The Chinese. *American Journal of Psychiatry, 158,* 857–864.

Parker, J. G., Saxon, J. L., Asher, S. R., & Kovacs, D. M. (2001). Dimensions of children's friendship adjustment: Implications for understanding loneliness. In K. J. Rotenberg & S. Hymel (Eds.), *Loneliness in childhood and adolescence.* New York: Cambridge University Press.

Parolaro, D., Massi, P., Rubino, T., & Monti, E. (2002). Endocannabinoids in the immune system and cancer. *Prostaglandins Leukotrienes & Essential Fatty Acids, 66,* 319–332.

Parsons, T. J., Power, C., & Manor, O. (2005). Physical activity, television viewing and body mass index: A cross-sectional analysis from childhood to adulthood in the 1958 British cohort. *International Journal of Obesity, 29,* 1212–1221.

Pascual, A., & Guéguen, N. (2005). Foot-in-the-door and door-in-the-face: A comparative meta-analytic study. *Psychological Reports, 96,* 122–128.

Pascual-Leone, A. (2001). The brain that plays music and is changed by it. *Annals of the New York Academy of Science, 930,* 315–329.

Pascual-Leone, A., & Torres, F. (1993). Plasticity of the sensorimotor cortex representation of the reading finger in Braille readers. *Brain, 116,* 39–52.

Pashler, H., Rohrer, D., & Cepeda, N. J. (2006). Temporal spacing and learning. *APS Observer, 19,* 30, 38.

Patel, S. R., White, D. P., Malhotra, A., Stanchina, M. L., & Ayas, N. T. (2003). Continuous positive airway pressure therapy for treating sleepiness in a diverse population with obstructive sleep apnea: Results of a meta-analysis. *Archives of Internal Medicine, 163,* 565–571.

Pathela, P., Hajat, A., Schillinger, J., Blank, S., Sell, R., & Mostashari, F. (2006). Discordance between sexual behavior and self-reported sexual identity: A population-based survey of New York City men. *Annals of Internal Medicine, 145,* 416–425.

Patkowski, M. (1994). The critical age hypothesis and interlanguage phonology. In M. Yavas (Ed.), *First and second language phonology* (pp. 205–221). San Diego: Singular Publishing Group.

Patten, S. B., Williams, J. V. A., Wang, J., Adair, C. E., Brant, C. E., Casebeer, A., et al. (2005). Antidepressant pharmacoepidemiology in a general population sample. *Journal of Clinical Psychopharmacology, 25,* 285–287.

Patterson, C. H. (2000). *Understanding psychotherapy: Fifty years of client-centered theory and practice.* Ross-on-Wye, UK: PCCS Books.

Patterson, C. J. (2004). *Lesbian and gay parents and their children: Summary of research findings.* Washington, DC: American Psychological Association. Retrieved September 26, 2006, from http://www.apa.org/pi/parent.html.

Patterson, D. R. (2004). Treating pain with hypnosis. *Current Directions in Psychological Science, 13,* 252–255.

Patterson, D. R., Hoffman, H. G., Palacios, A. G., & Jenson, M. J. (2006). Analgesic effects of posthypnotic suggestions and virtual reality distraction on thermal pain. *Journal of Abnormal Psychology, 115,* 834–841.

Patterson, D. R., & Jensen, M. P. (2003). Hypnosis and clinical pain. *Psychological Bulletin, 129,* 495–521.

Patton, G. C., Coffey, C., Carlin, J. B., Degenhardt, L., Lynskey, M., & Hall, W. (2002). Cannabis use and mental health in young people: Cohort study. *British Medical Journal, 325,* 1195–1198.

Patton, G. C., McMorris, B. J., Toumbourou, J. W., Hemphill, S. A., Donath, S., & Catalano, R. F. (2004). Puberty and the onset of substance use and abuse [Electronic version]. *Pediatrics, 114*(3), e300–e306.

Pauk, W. (2005). *How to study in college* (8th ed.). Boston: Houghton Mifflin.

Pauk, W., & Fiore, J. P. (2000). *Succeed in college!* Boston: Houghton Mifflin.

Paul, G. L. (1969). Behavior modification research: Design and tactics. In C. M. Franks (Ed.), *Behavior therapy: Appraisal and status* (pp. 29–62). New York: McGraw-Hill.

Paul, G. L. (2000). Milieu therapy. In A. E. Kazdin (Ed.), *The encyclopedia of psychology.* Washington, DC: American Psychological Association.

Paul, G. L., Stuve, P., & Cross, J. V. (1997). Real-world inpatient programs: Shedding some light—A critique. *Applied and Preventive Psychology, 6,* 193–204.

Paulhus, D. L., Trapnell, P., & Chen, D. (1999). Birth order effects on personality and achievement within families. *Psychological Science, 10,* 482–488.

Pauli, E., Hildebrandt, M., Romstöck, J., Stefan, H., & Blümcke, I. (2006). Deficient memory acquisition in temporal lobe epilepsy is predicted by hippocampal granule cell loss. *Neurology, 67*(8), 1383–1389.

Paul-Labrador, M., Polk, D., Dwyer, J. H., Velasquez, I., Nidich, S., Rainforth, M., et al. (2006). Effects of a randomized controlled trial of transcendental meditation on components on the metabolic syndrome in subjects with coronary heart disease. *Archives of Internal Medicine, 166,* 1218–1224.

Paulussen-Hoogeboom, M. C., Stams, G. J. J. M., Hermanns, J. M. A., Peetsma, T. T. D., & van den Wittenboer, G. L. H. (2008). Parenting style as a mediator between children's negative emotionality and problematic behavior in early childhood. *Journal of Genetic Psychology, 169,* 209–226.

Paus, T., Keshavan, M., & Giedd, J. N. (2008). Why do many psychiatric disorders emerge during adolescence? *Nature Reviews Neuroscience, 9*(12), 947–957.

Paus, T., Zijdenbos, A., Worsley, K., Collins, D. L., Blumenthal, J., Giedd, J. N., et al. (1999). Structural maturation of neural pathways in children and adolescents: In vivo study. *Science, 283,* 1908–1911.

Payne, J. D., & Nadel, L. (2004). Sleep, dreams, and memory consolidation: The role of the stress hormone cortisol. *Learning and Memory, 11,* 671–678.

Pear, J., & Martin, G. L. (2002). *Behavior modification: What it is and how to do it* (7th ed.). Englewood Cliffs, NJ: Prentice Hall.

Pearson, M. M. (2008). Voices of hope. *Education & Urban Society, 41*(1), 80–103.

Pedersen, P. B., & Draguns, J. G. (2002). *Counseling across cultures.* Thousand Oaks, CA: Sage.

Peigneux, P., Laureys, S., Delbeuck, X., & Maquet, P. (2001). Sleeping brain, learning brain: The role of sleep for memory systems. *Neuroreport, 12,* A111–A124.

Pekrun, R., Elliot, A. J., & Maier, M. A. (2009). Achievement goals and achievement emotions: Testing a model of their joint relations with academic performance. *Journal of Educational Psychology, 101*(1), 115–135.

Peña, M., Maki, A., Kovaci, D., Dehaene-Lambertz, G., Koizumi, H., Bouquet, F., & Mehler, J. (2003). Sounds and silence: An optical topography study of language recognition at birth. *Proceedings of the National Academy of Sciences, 100,* 11702–11705.

Pendergrast, M. (1996). A retractor's story. *Victims of memory: Sex abuse accusations and shattered lives.* Hinesburg, VT: Upper Access Books.

Penedo, F. J., & Dahn, J. (2004). Psychoneuroimmunology and aging. In M. Irwin & K. Vedhara (Eds.), *Psychoneuroimmunology.* New York: Kluwer.

Pennebaker, J. W. (1995). *Emotion, disclosure, and health.* Washington, DC: American Psychological Association.

Pennebaker, J. W. (2000). The effects of traumatic disclosure on physical and mental health: The values of writing and talking about upsetting events. In J. M. Violanti, D. Paton, & C. Dunning (Eds.), *Posttraumatic stress intervention: Challenges, issues, and perspectives* (pp. 97–114). Chicago: Charles C. Thomas.

Pennebaker, J. W., & Chew, C. H. (1985). Deception, electrodermal activity, and inhibition of behavior. *Journal of Personality and Social Psychology, 49,* 1427–1433.

Pennebaker, J. W., & O'Heeron, R. C. (1984). Confiding in others and illness rate among spouses of suicide and accidental death victims. *Journal of Abnormal Psychology, 93,* 473–476.

Penner, L. A. (2002). Dispositional and organizational influences on sustained volunteerism: An interactionist perspective. *Journal of Social Issues, 58,* 447–467.

Penner, L. A., & Craiger, J. P. (1992). The weakest link: The performance of individual group members. In R. W. Swezey & E. Salas (Eds.), *Teams: Their training and performance* (pp. 57–74). Norwood, NJ: Ablex.

Penner, L. A., & Finkelstein, M. A. (1998). Dispositional and structural determinants of volunteerism. *Journal of Personality and Social Psychology, 74,* 525–537.

Penner, L. A., & Orom, H. (in press) Enduring Goodness: A Person by Situation Perspective on Prosocial Behavior. In M. Mikulincer & P. Shaver (Eds.) *Prosocial Motives, Emotions, and Behavior,* Washington, DC: American Psychological Association.

Penner, L. A., Dovidio, J., & Albrecht, T. L. (2001). Helping victims of loss and trauma: A social psychological perspective. In J. Harvey & E. Miller (Eds.), *Loss and trauma: General and close relationship perspectives* (pp. 62–85). Philadelphia: Brunner Routledge.

Penner, L. A., Dovidio, J. F., Piliavin, J. A., & Schroeder, D. A. (2005). Prosocial behavior: Multilevel perspectives. *Annual Review of Psychology, 56,* 365–392.

Penner, L. A., Fritzsche, B. A., Craiger, J. P., & Friefeld, T. R. (1995). Measuring the prosocial personality. In J. Butcher & C. D. Spielberger (Eds.), *Advances in personality assessment* (Vol. 10, pp. 147–163). Hillsdale, NJ: Erlbaum.

Penner, L., Brannick, M. T., Webb, S., & Connell, P. (2005). Effects on volunteering of the September 11, 2001 attacks: An archival analysis. *Journal of Applied Social Psychology, 35,* 1333–1360.

Penney, L. M., & Spector, P. E. (2005). Job stress, incivility, and counterproductive work behavior (CWB): The moderating role of negative affectivity. *Journal of Organizational Behavior, 26,* 777–796.

Penninx, B. W., Beekman, A. T., Honig, A., Deeg, D. J., Schoevers, R. A., van Eijk, J. T., van Tilburg, W. (2001). Depression and cardiac mortality: Results from a community-based longitudinal study. *Archives of General Psychiatry, 58,* 221–227.

Peplau, L. A. (2003). Human sexuality: How do men and women differ? *Current Directions in Psychological Science, 12,* 37–40.

Perkonigg, A., Pfister, H., Stein, M. B., Hofler, M., Lieb, R., Maercker, A., et al. (2005). Longitudinal course of posttraumatic stress disorder and posttraumatic stress disorder symptoms in a community sample of adolescents and young adults. *American Journal of Psychiatry, 162,* 1320–1327.

Perlis, M. L., Sharpe, M., Smith, M. T., Greenblatt, D., & Giles, D. (2001). Behavioral treatment of insomnia: Treatment outcomes and the relevance of medical and psychiatric morbidity. *Journal of Behavioral Medicine, 24,* 281–296.

Perls, F. S. (1969). *Ego, hunger and aggression: The beginning of Gestalt therapy.* New York: Random House.

Perls, F. S., Hefferline, R. F., & Goodman, P. (1951). *Gestalt therapy.* New York: Julian Press.

Perrin, M. A., DiGrande, L., Wheeler, K., Thorpe, L., Farfel, M., & Brackbill, R. (2007). Differences in PTSD prevalence and associated risk factors among World Trade Center disaster rescue and recovery workers. *American Journal of Psychiatry, 164,* 1385–1394.

Perry, E. K. (1980). The cholinergic system in old age and Alzheimer's disease. *Age and Ageing, 9*(1), 1–8.

Persons, J. B., Davidson, J., & Tompkins, M. A. (2001). *Essential components of cognitive-behavior therapy for depression.* Washington, DC: American Psychological Association.

Perthen, J. E., Lansing, A. E., Liau, J., Liu, T. T., & Buxton, R. B. (2008). Caffeine-induced uncoupling of cerebral blood flow and oxygen metabolism: A calibrated BOLD fMRI study. *NeuroImage, 40*(1), 237–247.

Pervin, L. A., Cervone, D., & John, O. P. (2005). *Personality: Theory and research.* New York: Wiley.

Pesonen, A.-K., Räikkönen, K., Heinonen, K., Komsi, N., Järvenpää, A.-L., & Strandberg, T. (2008). A transactional model of temperamental development: Evidence of a relationship between child temperament and maternal stress over five years. *Social Development, 17,* 326–340.

Pessiglione, M., Seymour, B., Flandin, G., Dolan, R. J., & Frith, C. D. (2006). Dopamine-dependent prediction errors underpin reward-seeking behaviour in humans. *Nature, 442,* 1042–1045.

Peters, E., Hess, T. M., Västfjäll, D., & Auman, C. (2007). Adult age differences in dual information processes: Implications for the role of affective and deliberative processes in older adults' decision making. *Perspectives on Psychological Science, 2,* 1–23.

Petersen, R. C., & Morris, J. C. (2005). Mild cognitive impairment as a clinical entity and treatment target. *Archives of Neurology, 62*(7), 1160–1163.

Petersen, R. C., Smith, G. E., Waring, S. C., Ivnik, R. J., Tangalos, E., & Kokmen, E. (1999). Mild cognitive impairment: Clinical characterization and outcome. *Archives of Neurology, 56,* 303–308.

Petersen, R. C., Thomas, R. G., Grundman, M., Bennett, D., Doody, R., Ferris, S., et al. (2005). Vitamin E and donepezil for the treatment of mild cognitive impairment. *New England Journal of Medicine, 352,* 2379–2388.

Peterson, A., Compas, B., Brooks-Gunn, J., Stemmler, M., Ey, S., & Brant, K. (1993). Depression in adolescence. *American Psychologist, 48,* 155–168.

Peterson, C. (2006a). *A primer in positive psychology.* New York: Oxford University Press.

Peterson, C. (2006b). The Values in Action (VIA) Classification of Strengths: The un-DSM and the real DSM. In M. Csikszentmihalyi & I. Csikszentmihalyi (Eds.), *A life worth living: Contributions to positive psychology* (pp. 29–48). New York: Oxford University Press.

Peterson, C., Maier, S. F., & Seligman, M. E. (1993). *Learned helplessness: A theory for the age of personal control.* New York: Oxford University Press.

Peterson, C., & Seligman, M. E. P. (1984). Causal explanations as a risk factor for depression: Theory and evidence. *Psychological Review, 91,* 347–374.

Peterson, C., & Seligman, M. E. P. (2004). *Character strengths and virtues: A handbook and classification.* New York: Oxford University Press/Washington, DC: American Psychological Association.

Peterson, C., Seligman, M. E. P., Yurko, K. H., Martin, L. R., & Friedman, H. S. (1998). Catastrophizing and untimely death. *Psychological Science, 9,* 127–130.

Peterson, L. R., & Peterson, M. J. (1959). Short-term retention of individual verbal items. *Journal of Experimental Psychology, 58,* 193–198.

Peterson, N. G., Mumford, M. D., Borman, W. C., Jeanneret, P. R., Fleishman, E. A., Levin, K. Y., et al. (2001). Understanding work using the Occupational Information Network (O*NET): Implications for practice and research. *Personnel Psychology, 54,* 451–492.

Peterson, R. S., Smith, D. B., Martorana, P. V., & Owens, P. D. (2003). The impact of chief executive officer personality on top management team dynamics: One mechanism by which leadership affects organizational performance. *Journal of Applied Psychology, 88,* 795–808.

Petrakis, I. L., Limoncelli, D., Gueorguieva, R., Jatlow, P., Boutros, N. N., Trevisan, L., et al. (2004). Altered NMDA glutamate receptor antagonist response in individuals with a family vulnerability to alcoholism. *American Journal of Psychiatry, 161,* 1776–1782.

Petrescu, N. (2008). Loud music listening. *McGill Journal of Medicine, 11*(2), 169–176.

Petrill, S. A., Plomin, R., Berg, S., Johansson, B., Pederson, N. L., Ahern, F., & McClearn, G. E. (1998). The genetic and environmental relationship between general and specific cognitive abilities in twins age 80 and older. *Psychological Science, 9,* 183–189.

Petrocelli, J. V. (2002). Effectiveness of group cognitive-behavioral therapy for general symptomatology: A meta-analysis. *Journal of Specialists in Group Work, 27,* 92–115.

Petroski, H. (2008a). Scientists as inventors. *American Scientist, 96*(5), 368–371.

Petroski, H. (2008b). *Success through failure: The paradox of design.* Princeton, NJ: Princeton University Press.

Petrovic, P., Dietrich, T., Fransson, P., Andersson, J., Carlsson, K., & Ingvar, M. (2005). Placebo in emotional processing: Induced expectations of anxiety relief activate a generalized modulatory network. *Neuron, 46,* 957–969.

Petry, N. M. (2001). Substance abuse, pathological gambling and impulsivity. *Drug and Alcohol Dependence, 63,* 29–38.

Pettigrew, T., & Tropp, L. R. (2006). Allport's intergroup contact hypothesis: Its history and influence: In J. Dovidio, P. Glick, & L. Rudman (Eds.), *On the nature of prejudice: Fifty years after Allport.* Boston, MA: Blackwell.

Pettigrew, T. F. (1979). The ultimate attribution error: Extending Allport's cognitive analysis of prejudice. *Personality and Social Psychology Bulletin, 5,* 461–476.

Pettit, D. L., Shao, Z., & Yakel, J. L. (2001). Beta-amyloid(1–42) peptide directly modulates nicotinic receptors in the rat hippocampal slice. *Journal of Neuroscience, 21,* RC120.

Petty, R. E., & Briñol, P. (2008). Persuasion: From single to multiple to metacognitive processes. *Perspectives on Psychological Science 3,* 137–147.

Pfefferbaum, A., Rosenbloom, M., Deshmukkh, A., & Sullivan, E. (2001). Sex differences in the effects of alcohol on brain structure. *American Journal of Psychiatry, 158,* 188–197.

Pfister, J. A., Stegelmeier, B. L., Gardner, D. R., & James, L. F. (2003). Grazing of spotted locoweed (*Astragalus lentiginosus*) by cattle and horses in Arizona. *Journal of Animal Science, 81,* 2285–2293.

Pham, L. B., Taylor, S. E., & Seeman, T. E. (2001). Effects of environmental predictability and personal mastery on self-regulatory and physiological processes. *Personality & Social Psychology Bulletin, 27,* 611–620.

Phares, E. J. (1976). *Locus of control in personality.* Morristown, NJ: General Learning Press.

Phares, V. (2008). *Understanding abnormal child psychology* (2nd ed.). New York: Wiley & Sons.

Phelan, J. C., Link, B. G., Stueve, A., & Pescosolido, B. A. (2000). Public conceptions of mental illness in 1950 and 1996: What is mental illness and is it to be feared? *Journal of Health and Social Behavior, 41,* 188–207.

Phelps, E. A., & LeDoux, J. E. (2005). Contributions of the amygdala to emotion processing: From animal models to human behavior. *Neuron, 48,* 175–187.

Phelps, E. A., O'Connor, K. J., Cunningham, W. A., Funayama, E. S., Gatenby, J. C., Gore, J. C., & Banaji, M. R. (2000). Performance on indirect measures of race evaluation predicts amygdala activation. *Journal of Cognitive Neuroscience, 12,* 729–738.

Philip, P., Vervialle, F., Le Breton, P., Taillard, J., & Horne, J. A. (2001). Fatigue, alcohol, and serious road crashes in France: Factorial study of national data. *British Medical Journal, 322,* 829–830.

Phillips, M. R., Li, X., & Zhang, Y. (2002). Suicide rates in China, 1995–99. *Lancet 359,* 835–840.

Phillips, N. A. (2000). Female sexual dysfunction: Evaluation and treatment. *American Family Physician, 62,* 127–136, 141–142.

Phillips, P. E., Stuber, G. D., Heien, M. L., Wightman, R. M., & Carelli, R. M. (2003). Subsecond dopamine release promotes cocaine seeking. *Nature, 422,* 614–618.

Phinney, J. S., Ferguson, D. L., & Tate, J. D. (1997). Intergroup attitudes among ethnic minority adolescents: A causal model. *Child Development, 68,* 955–969.

Phinney, J. S., Jacoby, B., Silva, C. (2007). Positive intergroup attitudes: The role of ethnic identity. *International Journal of Behavioral Development, 31,* 478–490.

Pia, L., & Conway, P. M. (2008). Anosognosia and Alzheimer's disease. *Brain Impairment, 9*(1), 22–27.

Piaget, J. (1952). *The origins of intelligence in children.* New York: International Universities Press.

Piasecki, T. M. (2006). Relapse to smoking. *Clinical Psychology Review, 26,* 196–215.

Pickering, A. D., & Gray, J. A. (1999). The neuroscience of personality. In L. Pervin & O. John (Eds.), *Handbook of personality: Theory and research* (2nd ed., pp. 277–299). New York: Guilford.

Pickler, N. (2002, November 19). *NTSB cites fatigue, sleep apnea in fatal train wreck.* Associated Press. Retrieved August 25, 2003, from http://newsobserver.com/24hour/nation/v-print/story/626769p-4807167c.html.

Pietro, P., Guazzeli, M., Basso, G., Jaffe, K., & Grafman, J. (2000). Neural correlates of imaginal aggressive behavior assessed by positron emission tomography in healthy subjects. *American Journal of Psychiatry, 157,* 1772–1781.

Pike, K. M., Walsh, B. T., Vitousek, K., Wilson, G. T., & Bauer, J. (2003). Cognitive behavior therapy in the posthospitalization treatment of anorexia nervosa. *American Journal of Psychiatry, 160,* 2046–2049.

Piko, B. F., Bak, J., Gibbons, F. X. (2007). Prototype perception and smoking: Are negative or positive social images more important in adolescents? *Addictive Behaviors, 32,* 1728–1732.

Piliavin, J. A., Dovidio, J. F., Gaertner, S. L., & Clark, R. D., III. (1981). *Emergency intervention.* New York: Academic Press.

Pillard, R. C., & Bailey, J. M. (1998). Human sexual orientation has a heritable component. *Human Biology, 70,* 347–365.

Pillemer, K., & Suitor, J. J. (2002). Explaining mothers' ambivalence towards their adult children. *Journal of Marriage and Family, 64,* 602–613.

Pilon, M., Montplaisir, J., & Zadra, A. (2008). Precipitating factors of somnambulism: Impact of sleep deprivation and forced arousals. *Neurology, 70,* 2284–2290.

Pinel, J. P., Lehman, D. R., & Assanand, S. (2002). Eating for optimal health: How much should we eat? Comment. *American Psychologist, 57,* 372–373.

Pinker, S. (1994). *The language instinct: How the mind creates language.* New York: Morrow.

Pipes, R. B., Holstein, J. E., & Aguirre, M. G. (2005). Examining the personal- professional distinction: Ethics codes and the difficulty of drawing a boundary. *American Psychologist, 60,* 325–334.

Pipitone, R. N., & Gallup, G. G., Jr. (2008). Women's voice attractiveness varies across the menstrual cycle. *Evolution and Human Behavior, 29,* 268–274.

Pittler, M. H., Verster, J. C., & Ernst, E. (2005). Interventions for preventing or treating alcohol hangover: Systematic review of randomised controlled trials. *British Medical Journal, 331,* 1515–1518.

Plant, E. A., & Peruche, B. M. (2005). The consequences of race for police officers' responses to criminal suspects. *Psychological Science, 16,* 180–183.

Plant, E. A., & Sachs-Ericsson, N. (2004). Racial and ethnic differences in depression: The roles of social support and meeting basic needs. *Journal of Consulting and Clinical Psychology, 72,* 41–52.

Plaud, J. J. (2003). Pavlov and the foundation of behavior therapy. *Spanish Journal of Psychology, 6*, 147–154.

Plomin, R. (1994). *Genetics and experience: The developmental interplay between nature and nurture.* Newbury Park, CA: Sage.

Plomin, R. (2004). *Two views about the nurture assumption.* Retrieved June 15, 2005, from PsycCRITIQUES database.

Plomin, R., Corley, R., Caspi, A., Fulker, D. W., & DeFries, J. C. (1998). Adoption results for self-reported personality: Not much nature or nurture? *Journal of Personality and Social Psychology, 75*, 211–218.

Plomin, R., & Crabbe, J. C. (2000). DNA. *Psychological Bulletin, 126*, 806–828.

Plomin, R., DeFries, J. C., Craig, I. W., & McGuffin, P. (2002). *Behavioral genetics in the postgenomic era.* Washington, DC: American Psychological Association.

Plomin, R., & McGuffin, P. (2003). Psychopathology in the postgenomic era. *Annual Review of Psychology, 54*, 205–228.

Plomin, R., & Spinath, F. M. (2004). Intelligence: Genetics, genes, and genomics. *Journal of Personality and Social Psychology, 86*, 112–129.

Ploner, M., Gross, J., Timmermann, L., & Schnitzler, A. (2002). Cortical representation of first and second pain sensation in humans. *Proceedings of the National Academy of Sciences, 99*, 12444–12448.

Plous, S. (1996). Attitudes toward the use of animals in psychological research and education: Results from a national survey of psychologists. *American Psychologist, 51*, 1167–1180.

Plous, S. L., & Zimbardo, P. G. (2004, September 10). How social science can reduce terrorism. *The Chronicle of Higher Education*, B9–B10.

Plum, F., & Posner, J. B. (2000). *Diagnosis of stupor and coma.* New York: Oxford University Press.

Plutchik, R., & Conte, H. R. (Eds.). (1997). *Circumplex models of personality and emotions.* Washington, DC: American Psychological Association.

Poczwardowski, A., & Conroy, D. E. (2002). Coping responses to failure and success among elite athletes and performing artists. *Journal of Applied Sport Psychology, 14*, 313–329.

Poland, J., & Caplan, P. J. (2004). The deep structure of bias in psychiatric diagnosis. In P. J. Caplan & L. Cosgrove (Eds.), *Bias in psychiatric diagnosis: A project of the association for women in psychology* (pp. 9–23). New York: Aronson.

Polivy, J., & Herman, C. P. (2002). If at first you don't succeed: False hopes of self-change. *American Psychologist, 57*, 677–689.

Pollack, I. (1953). The assimilation of sequentially coded information. *American Journal of Psychology, 66*, 421–435.

Pollack, V. (1992). Meta-analysis of subjective sensitivity to alcohol in sons of alcoholics. *American Journal of Psychiatry, 149*, 1534–1538.

Polusny, M. A., & Follette, V. M. (1995). Long-term correlates of child sexual abuse: Theory and review of the empirical literature. *Applied and Preventive Psychology, 4*, 143–166.

Pope, H. G., Jr., Hudson, J. I., Bodkin, J. A., & Oliva, P. (1998). Questionable validity of "dissociative amnesia" in trauma victims: Evidence from prospective studies. *British Journal of Psychiatry, 172*, 210–215.

Pope, H. G., Jr., Kouri, E. M., & Hudson, J. I. (2000). Effects of supraphysiologic doses of testosterone on mood and aggression in normal men: A randomized controlled trial. *Archives of General Psychiatry, 57*(2), 133–140.

Pope, H. G., Jr., & Yurgelun-Todd, D. (1996). The residual cognitive effects of heavy marijuana use in college students. *Journal of the American Medical Association, 275*, 521–527.

Pope, K. S. (1998). Pseudoscience, cross-examination, and scientific evidence in the recovered memory controversy. *Psychology, Public Policy, and Law, 4*, 1160–1181.

Porcerelli, J. H., Cogan, R., Kamoo, R., & Leitman, S. (2004). Defense mechanisms and self-reported violence toward partners and strangers. *Journal of Personality Assessment, 82*, 317–320.

Porges, S. W., Doussard, R. J. A., & Maita, A. K. (1995). Vagal tone and the physiological regulation of emotion. *Monographs of the Society for Research on Child Development, 59*(2–3), 167–186, 250–283.

Poropat, A. (2009). A meta-analysis of the five-factor model of personality and academic performance. *Psychological Bulletin, 135*, 322–338.

Port, C. L., Engdahl, B., & Frazier, P. (2001). A longitudinal and retrospective study of PTSD among older prisoners of war. *American Journal of Psychiatry, 158*, 1474–1479.

Porte, H. S., & Hobson, J. A. (1996). Physical motion in dreams: One measure of three theories. *Journal of Abnormal Psychology, 105*, 329–335.

Porter, J., Anand, T., Johnson, B., Khan, R. M., & Sobell, N. (2005). Brain mechanisms for extracting spatial information from smell. *Neuron, 47*, 581–592.

Porter, R. H. (1991). Human reproduction and the mother-infant relationship. In T. V. Getchell et al. (Eds.), *Taste and smell in health and disease.* New York: Raven Press.

Porter, R. H., Cernich, J. M., & McLaughlin, F. J. (1983). Maternal recognition of neonates through olfactory cues. *Physiology and Behavior, 30*, 151–154.

Porter, R. H., Makin, J. W., Davis, L. B., & Christensen, K. M. (1992). Breast-fed infants respond to olfactory cues from their own mother and unfamiliar lactating females. *Infant Behavior and Development, 15*, 85–93.

Porter, S., Birt, A. R., Yuille, J. C., & Lehman, D. R. (2000). Negotiating false memories: Interviewer and rememberer characteristics relate to memory distortion. *Psychological Science, 11*, 507–510.

Porter, S., & Peace, K. A. (2007). The scars of memory: A prospective, longitudinal investigation of the consistency of traumatic and positive emotional memories in adulthood. *Psychological Science 18*, 435–441.

Porter, S., Yuille, J. C., & Lehman, D. R. (1999). The nature of real, implanted, and fabricated memories for emotional childhood events: Implications for the recovered memory debate. *Law & Human Behavior, 23*, 517–537.

Posener, J. A., DeBattista, C., Williams, G. H., Kraemer, H. C., Kalehzan, B. M., & Schatzberg, A. F. (2000). 24-hour monitoring of cortisol and corticotropin secretion in psychotic and nonpsychotic major depression. *Archives of General Psychiatry, 57*, 755–760.

Posner, M. I., & Peterson, S. E. (1990). The attention system of the human brain. *Annual Review of Neurosciences, 13*, 24–42.

Posner, M. I., & Raichle, M. E. (1994). *Images of mind.* New York: Scientific American Books.

Posthuma, D., & deGeus, E. J. C. (2006). Progress in the molecular-genetic study of intelligence. *Current Directions in Psychological Science, 15*, 151–155.

Potkin, S. G., Saha, A. R., Kujawa, M. J., Carson, W. H., Ali, M., Stock, E., et al. (2003). Aripiprazole, an antipsychotic with a novel mechanism of action, and risperidone vs placebo in patients with schizophrenia and schizoaffective disorder. *Archives of General Psychiatry, 60*, 681–690.

Potter, P. T., & Zautra, A. J. (1997). Stressful life events' effects on rheumatoid arthritis disease activity. *Journal of Consulting and Clinical Psychology, 65*, 319–323.

Pottick, K. J., Bilder, S., VanderStoep, A., Warner, L. A., & Alvarez, M. F. (2008). US patterns of mental health service utilization for transition-age youth and young adults. *Journal of Behavioral Health Services and Research, 35*, 373–389.

Pottick, K. J., Kirk, S. A., Hsieh, D. K., & Tian, X. (2007). Judging mental disorder in youths: Effects of client, clinician, and contextual differences. *Journal of Consulting and Clinical Psychology, 75*, 1–8.

Povinelli, D. J., & Bering, J. M. (2002). The mentality of apes revisited. *Current Directions in Psychological Science, 11*, 115–119.

Powch, I. G., & Houston, B. K. (1996). Hostility, anger-in, and cardiovascular activity in White women. *Health Psychology, 15*, 200–208.

Powell, L. H., Shahabi, L., & Thoresen, C. E. (2003). Religion and spirituality: Linkages to physical health. *American Psychologist, 58*, 36–52.

Powell, R. A., & Boer, D. P. (1995). Did Freud misinterpret reported memories of sexual abuse as fantasies? *Psychological Reports, 77*, 563–570.

Powers, S. I., Pietromonaco, P. R., Gunlicks, M., & Sayer, A. (2006). Dating couples' attachment styles and patterns of cortisol reactivity and recovery in response to a relationship conflict. *Journal of Personality and Social Psychology, 90*, 613–628.

Powley, T. L., & Keesey, R. E. (1970). Relationship of body weight to the lateral hypothalamic feeding syndrome. *Journal of Comparative & Physiological Psychology, 70*, 25–36.

Poyares, D., Guilleminault, C., Ohayon, M. M., & Tufik, S. (2004). Chronic benzodiazepine usage and withdrawal in insomnia patients. *Journal of Psychiatric Research, 38*, 327–334.

Prabhudesai, S. G., Gould, S., Rekhraj, S., Tekkis, P. P., Glazer, G., & Ziprin, P. (2008). Artificial neural networks: Useful aid in diagnosing acute appendicitis. *World Journal of Surgery, 32*(2), 305–309.

Pratkanis, A., & Aronson, E. (2001). *The age of propaganda: The everyday use and abuse of propaganda.* New York: W. H. Freeman.

Pratkanis, A. R. (1992). The cargo-cult science of subliminal persuasion. *Skeptical Inquirer, 16*, 260–273.

Pratkanis, A. R., Eskenazi, J., & Greenwald, A. G. (1994). What you expect is what you believe (but not necessarily what you get): A test of the effectiveness of self-help audiotapes. *Basic and Applied Social Psychology, 15*, 251–276.

Prescott, J. W. (1996). The origins of human love and violence. *Pre- and Peri-Natal Psychology Journal, 10*, 143–188.

President's New Freedom Commission on Mental Health. (2003). *Achieving the promise: Transforming mental health care in America.* Rockville, Maryland: U.S. Department of Health and Human Services.

Press, C., Heyes, C., Haggard, P., & Eimer, M. (2008). Visuotactile learning and body representation: An ERP study with rubber hands and rubber objects. *Journal of Cognitive Neuroscience, 20*(2), 312–323.

Press, Y., Margulin, T., Grinshpun, Y., Kagan, E., Snir, Y., Berzak, A., & Clarfield, A. M. (2009). The diagnosis of delirium among elderly patients presenting to the emergency department of an acute hospital. *Archives of Gerontology & Geriatrics, 48*(2), 201–204.

Pressman, S. D., & Cohen, S. (2005). Does positive affect influence health? *Psychological Bulletin, 131*, 925–971.

Pressman, S. D., Cohen, S., Miller, G. E., Barkin, A., Rabin, B., & Treanor, J. J. (2005). Loneliness, social network size, and immune response to influenza vaccination in college freshman. *Health Psychology, 24*, 297–306.

Price, K. H., Harrison, D. A., & Gavin, J. H. (2006). Withholding inputs in team contexts: Member composition, interaction processes, evaluation structure, and social loafing. *Journal of Applied Psychology, 91*, 1375–1384.

Prikryl, R., Ceskova, E., Kasparek, T., & Kucerova, H. (2006). Neurological soft signs, clinical symptoms and treatment reactivity in patients suffering from first episode schizophrenia. *Journal of Psychiatric Research, 40*, 141–146.

Prinstein, M. J., & La Greca, A. M. (2002). Peer crowd affiliation and internalizing distress in childhood and adolescence: A longitudinal follow-back study. *Journal of Research on Adolescence, 12*, 35–351.

Prochaska, J. O. (1994). Strong and weak principles for progressing from precontemplation to action on the basis of twelve problem behaviors. *Health Psychology, 13*, 47–51.

Prochaska, J. O., DiClemente, C., & Norcross, J. (1992). In search of how people change: Application to addictive behaviors. *American Psychologist, 47,* 1102–1114.

Procopio, M., & Marriott, P. (2007). Intrauterine hormonal environment and risk of developing anorexia nervosa. *Archives of General Psychiatry, 64,* 1402–1407.

Program for International Student Assessment. (2004). *Learning for tomorrow's world: First results from PISA 2003.* Paris: OECD.

Program for International Student Assessment. (2005). *Learning for tomorrow's world: First results from PISA 2004.* Paris: OECD.

Pronin, E., Wegner, D. M., McCarthy, K., & Rodreguez, S. (2006). Everyday magical powers: The role of apparent causation in the overestimation of personal influence. *Journal of Personality and Social Psychology, 91,* 218–231.

Proske, E. (2006). Kinesthesia: The role of muscle receptors. *Muscle and Nerve, 34*(5), 545–558.

Pulakos, E. D., Schmitt, N., Dorsey, D. W., Arad, S., Hedge, J. W., & Borman, W. C. (2002). Predicting adaptive performance: Further tests of a model of adaptability. *Human Performance, 15,* 299–324.

Pulkki-Råback, L., Elovainio, M., Kivimäki, M., Raitakari, O. T., & Keltikangas-Järvinen, L. (2005). Temperament in childhood predicts body mass in adulthood: The cardiovascular risk in young Finns study. *Health Psychology, 24*(3), 307–315.

Purdon, C. (2009). Psychological approaches to understanding obsessive-compulsive disorder. In M. M. Antony & M. B. Stein (Eds.), *Oxford handbook of anxiety and related disorders* (pp. 238–249). New York: Oxford University Press.

Putnam, F. W. (2003). Ten-year research update review: Child sexual abuse. *Journal of the American Academy of Child & Adolescent Psychiatry, 42,* 269–278.

Pyszczynski, T., Greenberg, J., Solomon, S., Arndt, J., & Schimel, J. (2004). Why do people need self-esteem? A theoretical and empirical review. *Psychological Bulletin, 130,* 435–468.

Pyszczynski, T., Rothschild, Z., & Abdollahi, A. (2008). Terrorism, violence, and hope for peace: A terror management perspective. *Current Directions in Psychological Science, 17,* 318–322.

Quinn, G. E., Shin, C. H., Maguire, M. G., & Stone, R. A. (1999). Myopia and ambient lighting at night. *Nature, 399,* 113–114.

Quinn, P., & Liben, L. S. (2008). A sex difference in mental rotation in young infants. *Psychological Science, 19,* 1067–1070.

Quinn, P. C., & Bhatt, R. S. (2005). Learning perceptual organization in infancy. *Psychological Science, 16,* 511–515.

Quintana, S. M. (1998). Children's developmental understanding of ethnicity and race. *Applied and Preventive Psychology, 7,* 27–45.

Rabasca, L. (1999, July/August). Behavioral interventions can cut the use of restraints. *APA Monitor,* p. 27.

Rabinowitz, J., De Smedt, G., Harvey, P. D., & Davidson, M. (2002). Relationship between premorbid functioning and symptom severity as assessed at first episode of psychosis. *American Journal of Psychiatry, 159,* 2021–2026.

Rabinowitz, J., Lichtenberg, P., Kaplan, Z., Mark, M., Nahon, D., & Davidson, M. (2001). Rehospitalization rates of chronically ill schizophrenic patients discharged on a regimen of risperidone, olanzapine, or conventional antipsychotics. *American Journal of Psychiatry, 158,* 266–269.

Racenstein, J. M., Harrow, M., Reed, R., Martin, E., Herbener, E., & Penn, D. L. (2002). The relationship between positive symptoms and instrumental work functioning in schizophrenia: A 10-year follow-up study. *Schizophrenia Research, 56,* 95–103.

Rachlin, H. (2000). *The science of self-control.* Cambridge, MA: Harvard University Press.

Rachlin, H., & Jones, B. A. (2008). Altruism among relatives and non-relatives. *Behavioural Processes, 79,* 120–123.

Rada, J. B., & Rogers, R. W. (1973). *Obedience to authority: Presence of authority and command strength.* Paper presented at the annual convention of the Southeastern Psychological Association.

Radcliffe, N. M., & Klein, W. M. (2002). Dispositional, unrealistic and comparative optimism: Differential relations with the knowledge and processing of risk information and beliefs about personal risk. *Personality & Social Psychology Bulletin, 28,* 836–846.

Radford, B. (2005). Voice of reason: Exorcisms, fictional and fatal. *Skeptical Inquirer.* Retrieved August 1, 2005, from http://www.csicop.org/specialarticles/exorcist-rituals.html.

Radford, B. (2008a, September/October). Psychic's false sex abuse claim threatens family. *Skeptical Inquirer, 32*(5), 11.

Radford, B. (2008b, December 20). Skeptic Benjamin Radford's psychic predictions for 2008. Retrieved January 15, 2009, from http://www.centerforinquiry.net/blog/skeptic_benjamin_radfords_psychic_predictions_for_2008.

Radford, B. (2008c, December 30). 5 predictions for 2008 that (thankfully) failed. Retrieved January 15, 2009, from http://www.livescience.com/strangenews/081230-bad-failed-predictions.html.

Radvansky, G. A. (1999). Aging, memory, and comprehension. *Current Directions in Psychological Science, 8,* 49–53.

Raffaelli, M., & Crockett, L. J. (2003). Sexual risk taking in adolescence: The role of self-regulation and attraction to risk. *Developmental Psychology, 39,* 1036–1046.

Raggatt, P. T. (1991). Work stress among long-distance coach drivers: A survey and correlational study. *Journal of Organizational Behavior, 12,* 565–579.

Raij, T. T., Numminen, J., Narvanen, S., Hiltunen, J., & Hari, R. (2005). Brain correlates of subjective reality of physically and psychologically induced pain. *Proceedings of the National Academy of Sciences, 102,* 2147–2151.

Raikes, H., Pan, B. A., Luze, G., Tamis-LeMonda, C. S., Brooks-Gunn, J., Constantine, J., et al. (2006). Mother-child bookreading in low-income families: Correlates and outcomes during the first three years of life. *Child Development, 77,* 924–953.

Raine, A., Brennan, P., & Mednick, S. (1994). Birth complications combined with early maternal rejection at age 1 year predispose to violent crime at age 18 years. *Archives of General Psychiatry, 51,* 984–988.

Raine, A., Lencz, T., Bihrle, S., LaCasse, L., & Colletti, P. (2000). Reduced prefrontal gray matter volume and reduced autonomic activity in antisocial personality disorder. *Archives of General Psychiatry, 57,* 119–127.

Raine, A., Moffitt, T. E., Caspi, A., Loeber, R., Stouthamer-Loeber, M., & Lynam, D. (2005). Neurocognitive impairments in boys on the life-course persistent antisocial path. *Journal of Abnormal Psychology, 114,* 38–49.

Raineteau, O. (2008). Plastic responses to spinal cord injury. *Behavioural Brain Research, 192*(1), 114–123.

Rains, G. C., Utley, S. L., & Lewis, W. J. (2006). Behavioral monitoring of trained insects for chemical detection. *Biotechnology Progress, 22,* 2–8.

Rajaram, S., & Barber, S. J. (2008). Retrieval processes in memory. In H. L. Roediger, III (Ed.), *Cognitive psychology of memory.* Oxford: Elsevier.

Rakic, P. (2002). Neurogenesis in adult primate neocortex: An evaluation of the evidence. *Nature Reviews Neuroscience, 3,* 65–71.

Ramachandran, V. S. (1988, August). Perceiving shape from shading. *Scientific American,* 76–83.

Ramachandran, V. S. (2008). *The man with the phantom twin: Adventures in the neuroscience of the human brain.* New York: Dutton.

Ramey, C. T., Ramey, S. L., & Lanzi, R. G. (2006). Children's health and education. In W. Damon & R. M. Lerner (Series Eds.) & K. A. Renninger & I. E. Sigel (Vol. Eds.), *Handbook of child psychology: Vol. 4. Child psychology in practice* (6th ed.). New York: Wiley.

Ramirez-Bermudez, J., Lopez-Gómez, M., Ana, L. S., Aceves, S., Nader-Kawachi, J., & Nicolini, H. (2006). Frequency of delirium in a neurological emergency room. *Journal of Neuropsychiatry & Clinical Neurosciences, 18*(1), 108–112.

Rapaport, M. H., Clary, C., Fayyad, R., & Endicott, J. (2005). Quality-of-life impairment in depressive and anxiety disorders. *American Journal of Psychiatry, 162,* 1171–1178.

Rapee, R., Brown, T., Antony, M., & Barlow, D. (1992). Response to hyperventilation and inhalation of 5.5% carbon dioxide-enriched air across *DSM-III* anxiety disorders. *Journal of Abnormal Psychology, 101,* 538–552.

Rapee, R., Kennedy, S., Ingram, M., Edwards, S., & Sweeney, L. (2005). Prevention and early intervention of anxiety disorders in inhibited preschool children. *Journal of Consulting and Clinical Psychology, 73,* 488–497.

Rapoport, J. L., Addington, A. M., & Frangou, S. (2005). The neurodevelopmental model of schizophrenia: Update 2005. *Molecular Psychiatry, 10,* 434–449.

Rapp, S. R., Brenes, G., & Marsh, A. P. (2002). Memory enhancement training for older adults with mild cognitive impairment: A preliminary study. *Aging & Mental Health, 6*(1), 5–11.

Rasch, B., & Born, J. (2008). Reactivation and consolidation of memory during sleep. *Current Directions in Psychological Science, 17,* 188–192.

Rasch, V. (2003). Cigarette, alcohol, and caffeine consumption: Risk factors for spontaneous abortion. *Acta Obstetric Gynecology Scandivia, 82,* 182–188.

Rasinski, K. A., Kuby, A., Bzdusek, S. A., Silvestri, J. M., & Weese-Mayer, D. E. (2003). Effect of a sudden infant death syndrome risk reduction education program on risk factor compliance and information sources in primarily black urban communities. *Pediatrics, 111,* 347–354.

Raskin, D. C. (1986). The polygraph in 1986: Scientific, professional and legal issues surrounding applications and acceptance of polygraph evidence. *Utah Law Review, 1,* 29–74.

Raskin, N. J., & Rogers, C. R. (2001). Person-centered therapy. In R. J. Corsini & D. Wedding (Eds.), *Current psychotherapies* (6th ed.). Itasca, IL: Peacock.

Raskin, N. J., & Rogers, C. R. (2005). Person-centered therapy. In R. J. Corsini & D. Wedding (Eds.), *Current psychotherapies* (7th ed., pp. 130–165). Belmont, CA: Thomson Brooks/Cole.

Rasmussen, K. G. (2003). Clinical applications of recent research on electro convulsive therapy. *Bulletin of the Menninger Clinic, 67*(1), 18–31.

Ratcliff, R., & McKoon, G. (1989). Memory models, text processing, and cue- dependent retrieval. In H. L. Roediger & F. I. M. Craik (Eds.), *Varieties of memory and consciousness.* Hillsdale, NJ: Erlbaum.

Rathbone, D. B., & Huckabee, J. C. (1999). *Controlling road rage: A literature review and pilot study.* Washington, DC: American Automobile Association.

Rattenborg, N., Lima, S. L., & Amlaner, C. J. (1999). Half-awake to the risk of predation. *Nature, 397,* 397–398.

Raudenbush, B., & Meyer, B. (2002). Effect of nasal dilators on pleasantness, intensity and sampling behaviors of foods in the oral cavity. *Rhinology, 39,* 80–83.

Rauscher, F. H., Shaw, G. L., Levine, L. J., Wright, E. L., Dennis, W. R., & Newcomb, R. L. (1997). Music training causes long-term enhancement of preschool children's spatial-temporal reasoning. *Neurological Research, 19,* 2–8.

Rawson, P. (2003). *Short-term psychodynamic psychotherapy: An analysis of the key principles.* London: Karnac Books.

Rawson, P. (2006). *Handbook of short-term psychodynamic psychotherapy.* London: Karnac Books.

Ray, D. W., Wandersman, A., Ellisor, J., & Huntington, D. E. (1982). The effects of high density in a juvenile correctional institution. *Basic and Applied Social Psychology, 3,* 95–108.

Raynor, H. A., & Epstein, L. H. (2001). Dietary variety, energy regulation, and obesity. *Psychological Bulletin, 127,* 325–341.

Raz, A., Fan, J., & Posner, M. I. (2005). Hypnotic suggestion reduces conflict in the brain. *Proceedings of the National Academy of Sciences, 102,* 9978–9983.

Razali, S. M., Aminah, K., & Umeed, A. (2002). Religious-cultural psychotherapy in the management of anxiety patients. *Transcultural Psychiatry, 39,* 130–136.

Reber, A. S. (1992). The cognitive unconscious: An evolutionary perspective. *Consciousness and Cognition: An International Journal, 1*(2), 93–133.

Redd, W. H. (1984). Psychological intervention to control cancer chemotherapy side effects. *Postgraduate Medicine, 75,* 105–113.

Redmond, D. E., Jr., Bjugstad, K. B., Teng, Y. D., Ourednik, V., Ourednik, J., Wakeman, D. R., Parsons, X. H., Gonzalez, R., Blanchard, B. C., Kim, S. U., Gu, Z., Lipton, S. A., Markakis, E. A., Roth, R. H., Elsworth, J. D., Sladek, J. R., Jr., Sidman, R. L., & Snyder, E. Y. (2007). Behavioral improvement in a primate Parkinson's model is associated with multiple homeostatic effects of human neural stem cells. *Proceedings of the National Academy of Sciences, 104,* 12175–12180.

Reed, P. L., Anthony, J. C., & Breslau, N. (2007). Incidence of drug problems in young adults exposed to trauma and posttraumatic stress disorder: Do early life experiences and predispositions matter? *Archives of General Psychiatry, 64,* 1435–1442.

Reed, S. K. (2000). *Cognition* (5th ed.). Belmont, CA: Wadsworth.

Reedy, M. N. (1983). Personality and aging. In D. S. Woodruff & J. E. Birren (Eds.), *Aging: Scientific perspectives and social issues* (2nd ed.). Monterey, CA: Brooks/Cole.

Rees, J., McKenna, P., Bell, V., Skucek, E., Nichols, E., & Fisher, P. (2008). The Rookwood Driving Battery: Normative older adult performance. *British Journal of Clinical Psychology, 47*(2), 139–151.

Reeve, J. M. (1996). *Understanding motivation and emotion.* New York: Harcourt, Brace, Jovanovich.

Reeves, G. K., Pirie, K., Beral, V., Green, J., Spencer, E., & Bull, D. (2007). Cancer incidence and mortality in relation to body mass index in the Million Women Study: Cohort study. *British Medical Journal, 335,* 1134.

Reeves, M. J., & Rafferty, A. P. (2005). Healthy lifestyle characteristics among adults in the United States, 2000. *Archives of Internal Medicine, 165,* 854–857.

Rehm, L. P., & DeMers, S. T. (2006). Licensure. *Clinical Psychology: Science and Practice, 13,* 249–253.

Reich, D. A. (2004). What you expect is not always what you get: The roles of extremity, optimism, and pessimism in the behavioral confirmation process. *Journal of Experimental Social Psychology, 40,* 199–215.

Reid, M. J., Webster-Stratton, C., & Baydar, N. (2004). Halting the development of conduct problems in Head Start children: The effects of parent training. *Journal of Clinical Child and Adolescent Psychology, 33,* 279–291.

Reif, A., & Lesch, K. P. (2003). Toward a molecular architecture of personality. *Behavioural Brain Research, 139,* 1–20.

Reilly, T., Atkinson, G., Edwards, B., Waterhouse, J., Åkerstedt, T., Davenne, D., Lemmer, Björn, Wirz-Justice, A. (2007). Coping with jet-lag: A position statement for the European College of Sport Science. *European Journal of Sport Science, 7*(1), 1–7.

Reilly, T., Waterhouse, J., Burke, L. M., & Alonso, J. (2007). Nutrition for travel. *Journal of Sports Sciences, 25,* 125–134.

Reinisch, J. M., Ziemba-Davis, M., & Sanders, S. A. (1991). Hormonal contributions to sexually dimorphic behavioral development in humans. *Psychoneuroendocrinology, 16,* 213–278.

Reis, B. F., & Brown, L. G. (2006). Preventing therapy dropout in the real world: The clinical utility of videotape preparation and client estimate of treatment duration. *Professional Psychology: Research and Practice, 37,* 311–316.

Reis, H. T., & Aron, A. (2008). Love: What is it, why does it matter, and how does it operate? *Perspectives on Psychological Science 3,* 80–86.

Reisenzein, R. (1983). The Schachter theory of emotion: Two decades later. *Psychological Bulletin, 94,* 239–264.

Reiss, A. J., & Roth, J. A. (1993). *Understanding and preventing violence.* Washington, DC: National Academy Press.

Reiss, D., Neiderhiser, J. M., Hetherington, E. M., & Plomin, R. (2000). *The relationship code: Deciphering genetic and social influences on adolescent development.* Cambridge, MA: Harvard University Press.

Ren, T. (2002). Longitudinal pattern of basilar membrane vibration in the sensitive cochlea. *Proceedings of the National Academy of Sciences, 99,* 17101–17106.

Rendall, D., Cheney, D. L., & Seyfarth, R. M. (2000). Proximate factors mediating "contact" calls in adult female baboons (*Papio cynocephalus ursinus*) and their infants. *Journal of Comparative Psychology, 114,* 36–46.

Reneman, L., Lavalaye, J., Schmand, B., de Wolff, F. A., van den Brink, W., den Heeten, G. J., & Booij, J. (2001). Cortical serotonin transporter density and verbal memory in individuals who stopped using 3, 4-methylenedioxymethamphetamine (MDMA or "ecstasy"). *Archives of General Psychiatry, 58,* 901–906.

Rentz, D. M., Huh, T. J., Faust, R. R., Budson, A. E., Scinto, L. F. M., Sperling, R. A., & Daffner, K. R. (2004). Use of IQ-adjusted norms to predict progressive cognitive decline in highly intelligent older individuals. *Neuropsychology, 18,* 38–49.

Rescorla, L. A. (1981). Category development in early language. *Journal of Child Language, 8,* 225–238.

Rescorla, R. A. (1968). Probability of shock in the presence and absence of CS in fear conditioning. *Journal of Comparative and Physiological Psychology, 66,* 1–5.

Rescorla, R. A. (2004). Spontaneous recovery varies inversely with the training- extinction interval. *Learning and Behavior, 32,* 401–408.

Rescorla, R. A. (2005). Spontaneous recovery of excitation but not inhibition. *Journal of Experimental Psychology: Animal Behavior Processes, 31,* 277–288.

Rescorla, R. A., & Wagner, A. R. (1972). A theory of Pavlovian conditioning: Variations in the effectiveness of reinforcement and nonreinforcement. In A. H. Black & W. F. Prokasy (Eds.), *Classical conditioning II.* New York: Appleton Century Crofts.

Reuter, J., Raedler, T., Rose, M., Hand, I., Glascher, J., & Buchel, C. (2005). Pathological gambling is linked to reduced activation of the mesolimbic reward system. *Nature Neuroscience, 8,* 147–148.

Reuter, M., Schmitz, A., Corr, P., & Hennig, J. (2006). Molecular genetics support Gray's personality theory: The interaction of COMT and DRD2 polymorphisms predicts the behavioural approach system. *International Journal of Neuropsychopharmacology, 9,* 155–166.

Revell, V. L., & Eastman, C. I. (2005). How to trick mother nature into letting you fly around or stay up all night. *Journal of Biological Rhythms, 20,* 353–365.

Revelle, W. (2008). The contribution of Reinforcement Sensitivity Theory to personality theory. In P. J. Corr (Ed.), *The reinforcement sensitivity theory of personality* (pp. 508–527). Cambridge, UK: Cambridge Press.

Reyna, V. F., & Farley, F. (2006). Risk and rationality in adolescent decision making: Implications for theory, practice, and public policy. *Psychological Science in the Public Interest, 7,* 1–44.

Reynolds, C. A., Finkel, D., McArdle, J. J., Gatz, M., Berg, S., & Pederson, N. L. (2005). Quantitative genetic analysis of latent growth curve models of cognitive abilities in adulthood. *Developmental Psychology, 41,* 3–16.

Reynolds, J. S., & Perrin, N. A. (2004). Mismatches in social support and psychosocial adjustment to breast cancer. *Health Psychology, 23,* 425–430.

Rhee, S. H., Hewitt, J. K., Young, S. E., Corley, R. P., Crowley, T. J., & Stallings, M. C. (2003). Genetic and environmental influences on substance initiation, use, and problem use in adolescents. *Archives of General Psychiatry, 60,* 1256–1264.

Ribases, M., Gratacos, M., Badia, A., Jimenez, L., Solano, R., Vallejo, J., et al. (2005). Contribution of NTRK2 to the genetic susceptibility to anorexia nervosa, harm avoidance and minimum body mass index. *Molecular Psychiatry, 10,* 851–860.

Riccio, D. C., Millin, P. M., & Gisquet-Verrier, P. (2003). Retrograde amnesia: Forgetting back. *Current Directions in Psychological Science, 12,* 41–44.

Rice, F., Harold, G. T., Shelton, K. H., & Thaper, A. (2006). Family conflict interacts with genetic liability in predicting childhood and adolescent depression. *Journal of the American Academy of Child and Adolescent Psychiatry, 45,* 841–848.

Rice, M. E. (1997). Violent offender research and implications for the criminal justice system. *American Psychologist, 52,* 414–423.

Richards, J. M., & Gross, J. J. (2000). Emotion regulation and memory: The cognitive costs of keeping one's cool. *Journal of Personality and Social Psychology, 79,* 410–424.

Richards, K. C., Anderson, W. M., Chesson, A. L., Jr., & Nagel, C. L. (2002). Sleep-related breathing disorders in patients who are critically ill. *Journal of Cardiovascular Nursing, 17,* 42–55.

Richards, P. S., & Bergin, A. E. (Eds.). (2000). *Handbook of psychotherapy and religious diversity* (pp. 105–129). Washington, DC: American Psychological Association Press.

Richardson, G. A., Goldschmidt, L., & Larkby, C. (2007). Effects of prenatal cocaine exposure on growth: A longitudinal analysis. *Pediatrics, 120,* e1017–e1027.

Richardson, R., & Hayne, R. (2007). You can't take it with you: The translation of memory across development. *Current Directions in Psychological Science, 16,* 223–227.

Richardson-Klavehn, A., & Bjork, R. A. (1988). Measures of memory. *Annual Review of Psychology, 39,* 475–543.

Richmond, J., & Nelson, C. A. (2007). Accounting for change in declarative memory: A cognitive neuroscience perspective. *Developmental Review, 27*(3), 349–373.

Rickels, K., & Rynn, M. (2002). Pharmocotherapy of generalized anxiety disorder. *Journal of Clinical Psychiatry, 63*(Suppl. 14), 9–16.

Rickels, K., Schweizer, E., Weiss, S., & Zavodnick, S. (1993). Maintenance drug treatment of panic disorder: II. Short- and long-term outcome after drug taper. *Archives of General Psychiatry, 50,* 61–68.

Rickels, K., Zaninelli, R., McCafferty, J., Bellew, K., Iyengar, M., & Sheehan, D. (2003). Paroxetine treatment of generalized anxiety disorder: A double-blind, placebo-controlled study. *American Journal of Psychiatry, 160,* 749–756.

Riddoch, M. J., Humphreys, G. W., Akhtar, N. A., Allen, H., Bracewell, R. M., & Schofield, A. J. (2008). A tale of two agnosias: Distinctions between form and integrative agnosia. *Cognitive Neuropsychology, 25*(1), 56–92.

Ridley, M. (2000). *Genome: The autobiography of a species in 23 chapters*. New York: HarperCollins.

Riggio, R. E. (1989). *Introduction to industrial/organizational psychology*. Glenview, IL: Scott, Foresman.

Riggs, K. J., McTaggart, J., Simpson, A., & Freeman, R. P. J. (2006). Changes in the capacity of visual working memory in 5- to 10-year-olds. *Journal of Experimental Child Psychology, 95*(1), 18–26.

Rihmer, Z. (2001). Can better recognition and treatment of depression reduce suicide rates? A brief review. *European Psychiatry, 16*, 406–409.

Riis, J., Loewenstein, G., Baron, J., Jepson, C., Fagerlin, A., & Ubel, P. A. (2005). Ignorance of hedonic adaptation to hemodialysis: A study using ecological momentary assessment. *Journal of Experimental Psychology: General, 134*, 3–9.

Rimes, K. A., & Watkins, E. (2005). The effects of self-focused rumination on global negative self-judgments in depression. *Behaviour Research and Therapy, 43*, 1673–1681.

Rind, B., Tromovitch, P., & Bauserman, R. (1998). A meta-analytic examination of assumed properties of child sexual abuse using college samples. *Psychological Bulletin, 124*, 22–53.

Rinn, W. E. (1984). The neuropsychology of facial expressions: A review of the neurological and psychological mechanisms for producing facial expressions. *Psychological Bulletin, 95*, 52–77.

Rioult-Pedotti, M.-S., Friedman, D., & Donoghue, J. P. (2000). Learning-induced LTP in neocortex. *Science, 290*, 533–536.

Ripple, C. H., Gilliam, W. S., Chanana, N., & Zigler, E. (1999). Will fifty cooks spoil the broth? The debate over entrusting Head Start to the states. *American Psychologist, 54*, 327–343.

Rips, L. J. (1994). *The psychology of proof: Deductive reasoning in human thinking*. Cambridge, MA: MIT Press.

Risen, J. (1998, July 7). CIA seeks "curmudgeon" to signal its mistakes. *New York Times*.

Ritchie, K., Carrière, I., de Mendona, A., Portet, F., Dartigues, J. F., Rouaud, O., Barberger-Gateau, P., & Ancelin, M. L. (2007). The neuroprotective effects of caffeine: A prospective population study (the Three City Study). *Neurology, 69*, 536–545.

Rittenhouse, C. D., Stickgold, R., & Hobson, J. A. (1994). Constraint on the transformation of characters, objects, and settings in dream reports. *Consciousness and Cognition, 3*(1), 100–113.

Rizzolatti, G., & Arbib, M. A. (1998). Language within our grasp. *Trends in Neuroscience, 21*, 188–194.

Rizzolatti, G., Fadiga, L., Gallese, V., & Fogassi, L. (1996). Premotor cortex and the recognition of motor actions. *Brain Research: Cognitive Brain Research, 3*, 131–141.

Robakis, T. K., & Hirsch, L. J. (2006). Literature review, case report, and expert discussion of prolonged refractory status epilepticus. *Neurocritical Care, 4*(1), 35–46.

Robbins, T. W., & Everitt, B. J. (1999). Interaction of the dopaminergic system with mechanisms of associative learning and cognition: Implications for drug abuse. *Psychological Science, 10*, 199–202.

Roberts, B. W., & Bogg, T. (2004). A longitudinal study of the relationships between conscientiousness and the social-environmental factors and substance-use behaviors that influence health. *Journal of Personality, 72*, 325–353.

Roberts, B. W., Caspi, A., & Moffitt, T. E. (2001). The kids are alright: Growth and stability in personality development from adolescence to adulthood. *Journal of Personality & Social Psychology, 81*(4), 670–683.

Roberts, B. W., & DelVecchio, W. F. (2000). The rank-order consistency of traits from childhood to old-age: A quantitative review of longitudinal studies. *Psychological Bulletin, 126*, 3–25.

Roberts, B. W., Helson, R., & Klohnen, E. C. (2002). Personality development and growth in women across 30 years: Three perspectives. *Journal of Personality, 70*, 79–102.

Roberts, B. W., Kuncel, N., Shiner, R. N., Caspi, A., & Goldberg, L. R. (2007). The power of personality: The comparative validity of personality traits, socio-economic status, and cognitive ability for predicting important life outcomes. *Perspectives in Psychological Science, 2*, 313–345.

Roberts, B. W., & Mroczek, D. (2008). Personality trait change in adulthood. *Current Directions in Psychological Science, 17*, 31–35.

Roberts, B. W., Smith, J., Jackson, J. J., & Edmonds, G. (2009). Compensatory conscientiousness and health in older couples. *Psychological Science, 20*, 553–559.

Roberts, B. W., Walton, K. E., & Viechtbauer, W. (2006). Patterns of mean-level change in personality traits across the life course: A meta-analysis of longitudinal studies. *Psychological Bulletin, 132*, 1–25.

Roberts, M. C. (2002). The process and product of the Felix decree review of empirically supported treatments: Prospects for change. *Clinical Psychology: Science and Practice, 9*, 217–219.

Robertson, I. H., & Murre, J. M. J. (1999). Rehabilitation of brain damage: Brain plasticity and principles of guided recovery. *Psychological Bulletin, 125*, 544–575.

Robertson, J., & Robertson, J. (1971). Young children in brief separation: A fresh look. *Psychoanalytic Study of the Child, 26*, 264–315.

Robiner, W. N. (2006). The mental health professions: Workforce supply and demand, issues, and challenges. *Clinical Psychology Review, 26*, 600–625.

Robins, L. N., & Regier, D. A. (Eds.). (1991). *Psychiatric disorders in America: The Epidemiologic Catchment Area study*. New York: Free Press.

Robinson, G. E., Fernald, R. D., & Clayton, D. F. (2008). Genes and social behavior. *Science, 322*, 896–900.

Robinson, J. H., & Pritchard, W. S. (1995). "The scientific case that nicotine is addictive": Reply. *Psychopharmacology, 117*(1), 16–17.

Robinson, N. M., Zigler, E., & Gallagher, J. J. (2000). Two tails of the normal curve: Similarities and differences in the study of mental retardation and giftedness. *American Psychologist, 55*, 1413–1424.

Robinson, S., Sandstrom, S. M., Denenberg, V. H., & Palmiter, R. D. (2005). Distinguishing whether dopamine regulates liking, wanting, and/or learning about rewards. *Behavioral Neuroscience, 119*, 5–15.

Robinson, T. N., Borzekowski, D. L. G., Matheson, D. M., Kraemer, H. C. (2009). Effects of fast food branding on young children's taste preferences. *Archives of Pediatric and Adolescent Medicine, 161*(8), 792–797.

Robinson, T. N., Wilde, M. L., Navracruz, L. C., Haydel, K. F., & Varady, A. (2001). Effects of reducing children's television and video game use on aggressive behavior: A randomized controlled trial. *Archives of Pediatrics and Adolescent Medicine, 155*, 17–23.

Robles, T. F., Glaser, R., & Kiecolt-Glaser, J. K. (2005). Out of balance: A new look at chronic stress, depression, and immunity. *Current Directions in Psychological Science, 14*, 111–115.

Robles, T. F., & Kiecolt-Glaser, J. K. (2003). The physiology of marriage: Pathways to health. *Physiology and Behavior, 79*, 409–416.

Rochon, P. A., Stukel, T. A., Sykora, K., Gill, S., Garfinkel, S., Anderson, G. M., et al. (2005). Atypical antipsychotics and Parkinsonism. *Archives of Internal Medicine, 165*, 1882–1888.

Rock, I. (1978). *An introduction to perception*. New York: Macmillan.

Rock, I. (1983). *The logic of perception*. Cambridge, MA: MIT Press.

Rodgers, J. (2000). Cognitive performance amongst recreational users of "ecstasy". *Psychopharmacology, 151*, 19–24.

Rodriguez de Fonseca, F., Carrera, M. R. A., Navarro, M., Koob, G. F., & Weiss, F. (1997). Activation of corticotropin-releasing factor in the limbic system during cannabinoid withdrawal. *Science, 276*, 2050–2054.

Roe, K. V. (2001). Relationship between male infants' vocal responses to mother and stranger at three months and self-reported academic attainment and adjustment measures in adulthood. *Psychological Reports, 89*(2), 255–258.

Roediger, H. L., & Gallo, D. A. (2001). Levels of processing: Some unanswered questions. In M. Naveh-Benjamin, M. Moscovitch, & H. L. Roediger (Eds.), *Perspectives on human memory and cognitive aging: Essays in hounour of Fergus Craik* (pp. 28–47). New York: Psychology Press.

Roediger, H. L., & McDermott, K. B. (2000). Tricks of memory. *Current Directions in Psychological Science, 9*, 123–127.

Roediger, H. L., Meade, M. L., & Bergman, E. T. (2001). Social contagion of memory. *Psychonomic Bulletin and Review, 8*, 365–371.

Roediger, H. L., III, Gallo, D. A., & Geraci, L. (2002). Processing approaches to cognition: The impetus from the levels-of-processing framework. *Memory, 10*, 319–332.

Roediger, H. L., III, Guynn, M. J., & Jones, T. C. (1995). Implicit memory: A tutorial review. In G. d'Ydewalle, P. Eelen, & P. Bertelson (Eds.), *International perspectives on psychological science: Vol. 2. The state of the art* (pp. 67–94). Hove, UK: Erlbaum.

Roediger, H. L., III, Jacoby, D., & McDermott, K. B. (1996). Misinformation effects in recall: Creating false memories through repeated retrieval. *Journal of Memory and Learning, 35*, 300–318.

Roediger, H. L., III, McDaniel, M., & McDermott, K. (2006). Test enhanced learning. *APS Observer, 19*, 28.

Roediger, H. L., III, & McDermott, K. B. (1995). Creating false memories: Remembering words not presented in lists. *Journal of Experimental Psychology: Learning, Memory, and Cognition, 21*, 803–814.

Roehrich, L., & Goldman, M. S. (1995). Implicit priming of alcohol expectancy memory processes and subsequent drinking behavior. *Experimental and Clincial Psychopharmocology, 3*, 402–410.

Roffman, J. L., & Gerber, A. J. (2008). Neural models of psychodynamic concepts and treatments: Implications for psychodynamic psychotherapy. In R. A. Levy & J. S. Ablon (Eds.), *Handbook of evidence-based psychodynamic psychotherapy* (pp. 305–339). Totowa, NJ: Humana Press.

Roffwarg, H. P., Muzio, J. N., & Dement, W. C. (1966). Ontogenetic development of the human sleep-dream cycle. *Science, 152*, 604–619.

Rog, D. J., Nurmikko, T. J., Friede, T., & Young, C. A. (2005). Randomized, controlled trial of cannabis-based medicine in central pain in multiple sclerosis. *Neurology, 65*, 812–819.

Rogalski, Y., & Edmonds, L. A. (2008). Attentive reading and constrained summarisation (ARCS) treatment in primary progressive aphasia: A case study. *Aphasiology, 22*(7–8), 763–775.

Rogers, A. A., Aldrich, M. S., & Lin, A. (2001). A comparison of three different sleep schedules for reducing daytime sleepiness in narcolepsy. *Journal of Sleep and Sleep Disorders Research, 24*, 385–391.

Rogers, C. R. (1961). *On becoming a person*. Boston: Houghton Mifflin.

Rogers, C. R. (1970). *Carl Rogers on encounter groups*. New York: Harper & Row.

Rogers, C. R. (1980). *A way of being*. Boston: Houghton Mifflin.

Rogers, J., Madamba, S. G., Staunton, D. A., & Siggins, G. R. (1986). Ethanol increases single unit activity in the inferior olivary nucleus. *Brain Research, 385*, 253–262.

Rogers, M. R., & Molina, L. E. (2006). Exemplary efforts in psychology to recruit and retain graduate students of color. *American Psychologist, 61*, 143–156.

Rogers, R. (1995). *Diagnostic and structured interviewing: A handbook for psychologists.* Odessa, FL: Psychological Assessment Resources.

Rogers, R. (2003). Standardizing DSM-IV diagnoses: The clinical application of structured interviews. *Journal of Personality Assessment, 81,* 220–225.

Rogoff, B., & Waddell, K. J. (1982). Memory for information organized in a scene by children from two cultures. *Child Development, 53,* 1224–1228.

Rohan, M. J., & Zanna, M. P. (1996). Value transmission in families. In C. Seligman, J. M. Olson, & M. P. Zanna (Eds.), *The psychology of values: The Ontario symposium* (Vol. 8, pp. 253–276). Mahwah, NJ: Erlbaum.

Rohrer, D., & Pashier, H. (2007). Increasing retention without increasing study time. *Current Directions in Psychological Science, 16,* 183–186.

Roid, G. H. (2003). *Stanford-Binet Intelligence Scale* (5th ed.). Itasca, IL: Riverside.

Roisman, G. I. (2007). The psychophysiology of adult attachment relationships: Autonomic reactivity in marital and premarital interactions. *Developmental Psychology, 43,* 39–53.

Roisman, G. I., Masten, A. S., Coatsworth, J. D., & Tellegen, A. (2004). Salient and emerging developmental tasks in the transition to adulthood. *Child Development, 75,* 123–133.

Rokach, A. (2008). How do the homeless cope with loneliness? *Psychology Journal, 5*(4), 215–227.

Rolls, E. T. (1997). Taste and olfactory processing in the brain and its relation to the control of eating. *Critical Review of Neurobiology, 11,* 263–287.

Romeo, R. D., Richardson, H. N., & Sisk, C. L. (2002). Puberty and the maturation of the male brain and sexual behavior: Recasting a behavioral potential. *Neuroscience and Biobehavioral Review, 26,* 381–391.

Romer, D., Jamieson, K. H., & deCoteau, N. J. (1998). The treatment of persons of color in local television news: Ethnic blame discourse or realistic group conflict? *Communication Research, 25,* 286–305.

Romer, D., Jamieson, P. E., & Jamieson, K. H. (2006). Are news reports of suicide contagious? A stringent test in six U.S. cities. *Journal of Communication, 56,* 253–270.

Ronnestad, M. H., & Ladany, N. (2006). The impact of psychotherapy training: Introduction to the special section. *Psychotherapy Research, 16,* 261–267.

Roorda, A., & Williams, D. R. (1999). The arrangement of the three cone classes in the living human eye. *Nature, 397,* 520–522.

Root, J. C., Wong, P. S., & Kinsbourne, M. (2006). Left hemisphere specialization for response to positive emotional expressions: A divided output methodology. *Emotion, 6,* 473–483.

Rooy, D. L. V., Dilchert, S., Viswesvaran, C., & Ones, D. (2006). Multiplying intelligences: Are general, emotional, and practical intelligences equal? In K. R. Murphy (Ed.), *A critique of emotional intelligence: What are the problems and how can they be fixed?* (pp. 235–262). Mahwah, NJ: Erlbaum.

Rosch, E., Mervis, C. B., Gray, W. D., Johnson, D. M., & Boyes-Braem, P. (1976). Basic objects in natural categories. *Cognitive Psychology, 8,* 382–439.

Rose, A. J., & Rudolph, K. D. (2006). A review of sex differences in peer relationship processes: Potential trade-offs for the emotional and behavioral development of girls and boys. *Psychological Bulletin, 132,* 98–131.

Rose, S. A., & Feldman, J. F. (1995). Prediction of IQ and specific cognitive abilities at 11 years from infancy measures. *Developmental Psychology, 31,* 685–696.

Roseborough, D. J. (2006). Psychodynamic psychotherapy: An effectiveness study. *Research on Social Work Practice, 16,* 166–175.

Rosen, B. C., & D'Andrade, R. (1959). The psychosocial origins of achievement motivation. *Sociometry, 22,* 188–218.

Rosen, D., Stukenberg, K. W., & Saeks, S. (2001). The group-as-a-whole-object relations model of group psychotherapy. *Bulletin of the Menninger Clinic, 65,* 471–488.

Rosen, G. M. (1999). Treatment fidelity and research on eye movement desensitization and reprocessing (EMDR). *Journal of Anxiety Disorders, 13,* 173–184.

Rosen, M. L., & López, H. H. (2009). Menstrual cycle shifts in attentional bias for courtship language. *Evolution and Human Behavior, 30*(2), 131–140.

Rosen, R. (1991). *The healthy company.* Los Angeles: Tarcher.

Rosenbaum, M., & Bennett, B. (1986). Homicide and depression. *American Journal of Psychiatry, 143,* 367–370.

Rosenbaum, R. S., Moscovitch, M., Foster, J. K., Schnyer, D. M., Gao, F., Kovacevic, N., Verfaellie, M., Black, S. E., & Levine, B. (2008). Patterns of autobiographical memory loss in medial-temporal lobe amnesic patients. *Journal of Cognitive Neuroscience, 20*(8), 1490–1506.

Rosenbaum, R. S., Priselac, S. K., Black, S. E., Gao, F., Nadel, L., & Moscovitch, M. (2000). Remote spatial memory in an amnesiac person with extensive bilateral hippocampal lesions. *Nature Neuroscience, 3,* 1044–1048.

Rosenberg, R. N. (2009). Consciousness, coma, and brain death--2009. *Journal of the American Medical Association, 301*(11), 1172–1174.

Rosenfarb, I. S., Bellack, A. S., & Aziz, N. (2006). A sociocultural stress, appraisal, and coping model of subjective burden and family attitudes toward patients with schizophrenia. *Journal of Abnormal Psychology, 115,* 157–165.

Rosenfarb, I. S., Goldstein, M. J., Mintz, J., & Nuechterlein, K. H. (1995). Expressed emotion and subclinical psychopathology observable within the transactions between schizophrenic patients and their family members. *Journal of Abnormal Psychology, 104,* 259–267.

Rosenfarb, I. S., Nuechterlein, K. H., Goldstein, M. J., & Subotnik, K. L. (2000). Neurocognitive vulnerability, interpersonal criticism, and the emergence of unusual thinking by schizophrenic patients during family transactions. *Archives of General Psychiatry, 57,* 1174–1179.

Rosenfeld, J. P. (1995). Alternative views of Bashore and Rapp's (1993) alternatives to traditional polygraphy: A critique. *Psychological Bulletin, 117*(1), 159–166.

Rosenstock, I. M. (1974). Historical origins of the health belief model. *Health Education Monographs, 2,* 328–335.

Rosenthal, R. R. (1966). *Experimenter effects in behavioral research.* New York: Appleton-Century-Crofts.

Ross, C. A. (1997). *Dissociative identity disorder: Diagnosis, clinical features, and treatment of multiple personality.* New York: Wiley.

Ross, E. D. (1981). The aprosodias: Functional-anatomic organization of the affective components of language in the right hemisphere. *Archives of Neurology, 38*(9), 561–569.

Ross, E. D. (2006). The Aprosodias. In M. J. Farah & T. E. Feinberg (Eds.), *Patient-based approaches to cognitive neuroscience* (2nd ed.) (pp. 259–269). Cambridge, MA: The MIT Press.

Ross, E. D., & Monnot, M. (2008). Neurology of affective prosody and its functional–anatomic organization in right hemisphere. *Brain & Language, 104*(1), 51–74.

Ross, M. W. (2002). Sexuality and health challenges: Responding to a public health imperative. *Journal of Sex Research, 39,* 7–9.

Ross, S. M., & Ross, L. E. (1971). Comparison of trace and delay classical eyelid conditioning as a function of interstimulus interval. *Journal of Experimental Psychology, 91,* 165–167.

Roth, A., & Fonagy, P. (2005). *What works for whom: A critical review of psychotherapy research* (2nd ed.). New York: Guilford.

Roth, H. L., Lora, A. N., & Heilman, K. M. (2002). Effects of monocular viewing and eye dominance on spatial attention. *Brain, 125,* 2023–2035.

Roth, P. L., Huffcutt, A. I., & Bobko, P. (2003). Ethnic group differences in measures of job performance: A new meta-analysis. *Journal of Applied Psychology, 88,* 694–706.

Rothbart, M. K. (2007). Temperament, development, and personality. *Current Directions in Psychological Science, 16,* 207–212.

Rothbart, M. K., & Derryberry, D. (2002). Temperament in children. In C. von Hofsten & L. Baeckman (Eds.), *Psychology at the turn of the millennium: Vol. 2. Social, developmental, and clinical perspectives* (pp. 17–35). Florence, KY: Taylor & Frances/Routledge.

Rothbaum, B. O. (2006). Virtual reality in the treatment of psychiatric disorders. *CNS Spectrums, 11,* 34.

Rothbaum, B. O., Hodges, L., Anderson, P. L., Price, L., & Smith, S. (2002). Twelve-month follow-up of virtual reality and standard exposure therapies for fear of flying. *Journal of Consulting and Clinical Psychology, 70,* 428–432.

Rothbaum, B. O., Hodges, L., Smith, S., Lee, J. H., & Price, L. (2000). A controlled study of virtual reality exposure therapy for the fear of flying. *Journal of Consulting and Clinical Psychology, 68,* 1020–1026.

Rothbaum, B. O., Hodges, L. F., Alarcon, R., Ready, D., Shahar, F., Graap, K., et al. (1999). Virtual reality exposure therapy for PTSD Vietnam veterans: A case study. *Journal of Traumatic Stress, 12,* 263–271.

Rothbaum, B. O., Hodges, L. F., Kooper, R., & Opdyke, D. (1995). Effectiveness of computer-generated virtual reality graded exposure in the treatment of acrophobia. *American Journal of Psychiatry, 152,* 626–628.

Rothbaum, F., Pott, M., Azuma, H., Miyake, K., & Weisz, J. (2000). The development of close relationships in Japan and the United States: Paths of symbiotic harmony and generative tension. *Child Development, 71,* 1121–1142.

Rothwell, P. M. (2003). Incidence, risk factors and prognosis of stroke and TIA: The need for high-quality, large-scale epidemiological studies and meta- analyses. *Cerebrovascular Disease, 16*(Suppl. 3), 2–10.

Rottenstreich, Y., & Tversky, A. (1997). Unpacking, repacking, and anchoring: Advances in support theory. *Psychological Review, 104,* 406–415.

Rotter, J. B. (1954). *Social learning and clinical psychology.* New York: Prentice Hall.

Rotter, J. B. (1982). The development and application of social learning theory. New York: Praeger.

Rotton, J., & Kelly, I. W. (1985). Much ado about the full moon: A meta-analysis of lunar-lunacy research. *Psychological Bulletin, 97,* 286–306.

Rouach, N., Koulakoff, A., Abudara, V., Willecke, K., & Giaume, C. (2008). Astroglial metabolic networks sustain hippocampal synaptic transmission. *Science, 322*(5907), 1551–1555.

Rouch, I., Wild, P., Ansiau, D., & Marquie, J.-C. (2005). Shiftwork experience, age, and cognitive performance. *Ergonomics, 48,* 1282–1293.

Rouéché, B. (1986, December 8). Cinnabar. *New Yorker.*

Rounsaville, B. J., & Carroll, K. M. (2002). Commentary on dodo bird revisited: Why aren't we dodos yet? *Clinical Psychology: Science & Practice, 9*(1), 17–20.

Rouse, S. V. (2007). Using reliability generalization methods to explore measurement error: An illustration using the MMPI2 PSY-5 Scales. *Journal of Personality Assessment, 88,* 264–275.

Rovee-Collier, C. (1999). The development of infant memory. *Current Directions in Psychological Science, 8,* 80–85.

Rowe, D. C. (1997). Genetics, temperament, and personality. In R. Hogan, J. Johnson, & S. Briggs (Eds.), *Handbook of personality psychology* (pp. 367–386). San Diego: Academic Press.

Rowe, D. C. (2005). Under the skin: On the impartial treatment of genetic and environmental hypotheses of racial differences. *American Psychologist, 60*, 60–70.

Rowe, D. C., Jacobson, K. C., & Van den Oord, E. J. C. G. (1999). Genetic and environmental influences on vocabulary IQ: Parental education level as moderator. *Child Development, 70*, 1151–1162.

Rowe, M. L., & Goldin-Meadow, S. (2009). Differences in early gesture explain SES disparities in child vocabulary size at school entry. *Science, 323*, 951–953.

Roy, D. K., & Pentland, A. P. (2002). Learning words from sights and sounds: A computational model. *Cognitive Science, 26*, 113–146.

Roy-Byrne, P., Stang, P., Wittchen, H.-U., Ustun, B., Walters, E. E., & Kessler, R. (2000). Lifetime panic-depression comorbidity in the National Comorbidity Survey. *British Journal of Psychiatry, 176*, 229–235.

Roy-Byrne, P. P., Craske, M. G., Stein, M. B., Sullivan, G., Bystritsky, A., Katon, W., et al. (2005). A randomized effectiveness trial of cognitive-behavioral therapy and medication for primary care panic disorder. *Archives of General Psychiatry, 62*, 290–298.

Rozin, P. (1982). "Taste-smell confusions" and the duality of the olfactory sense. *Perception and Psychophysics, 31*, 397–401.

Rozin, P. (2007). Food and eating. In S. Kitayama & D. Cohen (Eds.), *Handbook of cultural psychology* (pp. 391–416). New York, NY: Guilford Press.

Rubens, A. B., & Benson, D. F. (1971). Associative visual agnosia. *Archives of Neurology, 24*, 304–316.

Rubin, E. (1915). *Synsoplevede figure*. Copenhagen: Gyldendalske.

Rubin, K. H., Bukowski, W., & Parker, J. G. (2006). Peer interactions, relationships, and groups. In W. Damon & R. M. Lerner (Series Eds.) & N. Eisenberg (Vol. Ed.), *Handbook of child psychology: Vol. 3. Social, emotional, and personality development* (6th ed.). New York: Wiley.

Rubinstein, S., & Caballero, B. (2000). Is Miss America an undernourished role model? *Journal of the American Medical Association, 283*, 1569.

Ruble, D. N., Martin, C. L., & Berenbaum, S. A. (2006). Gender development. In W. Damon & R. M. Lerner (Series Eds.) & N. Eisenberg (Vol. Ed.), *Handbook of child psychology: Vol. 3. Social, emotional, and personality development* (6th ed., pp. 858–932). New York: Wiley.

Rudolph, K. D., Lambert, S. F., Clark, A. G., & Kurlakowsky, K. D. (2001). Negotiating the transition to middle school: The role of self-regulatory processes. *Child Development, 72*, 929–946.

Rueckert, L., Baboorian, D., Stavropoulos, K., & Yasutake, C. (1999). Individual differences in callosal efficiency: Correlation with attention. *Brain and Cognition, 41*, 390–410.

Ruiz, J. M., Matthews, K. A., Scheier, M. F., & Schulz, R. (2006). Does who you marry matter for your health? Influence of patient's and spouses' personality on their partners' psychological well-being following coronary artery bypass surgery. *Journal of Personality and Social Psychology, 91*, 255–267.

Ruiz-Padial, E., & Vila, J. (2007). Fearful and sexual pictures not consciously seen modulate the startle reflex in human beings. *Biological Psychiatry, 61*, 996–1001.

Rumelhart, D. E., & McClelland, J. L. (1986). *Parallel distributed processing: Explorations in the microstructure of cognition: Vol. 1. Foundations*. Cambridge, MA: Bradford.

Rusbult, C. E., & Van Lange, P. A. M. (1996). Interdependence processes. In E. T. Higgins & A. W. Kruglanski (Eds.), *Social psychology: Handbook of basic principles* (pp. 564–596). New York: Guilford.

Rusbult, C. E., Arriaga, X. B., & Agnew, C. R. (2001). Interdependence in close relationships. In G. Fletcher & M. Clark (Eds.), *Blackwell handbook of social psychology: Interpersonal processes* (pp. 359–387). Oxford, England: Blackwell.

Rusbult, C. E., & Van Lange, P. A. M. (2003). Interdependence, interaction and relationships. *Annual Review of Psychology, 54*, 351–375.

Ruscio, J. (2005). Exploring controversies in the art and science of polygraph testing. *Skeptical Inquirer, 29*, 34–39.

Rushton, J. P., & Bons, T. A. (2005). Mate choice and friendship in twins. *Psychological Science 16*, 555–559.

Rushton, J. P., & Jensen, A. R. (2005). Thirty years of research on race differences in cognitive ability. *Psychology, Public Policy, and Law, 11*, 235–294.

Ruskin, P. E., Silver-Aylaian, M., Kling, M. A., Reed, S. A., Bradham, D. D., Hebel, J. R., et al. (2004). Treatment outcomes in depression: Comparison of remote treatment through telepsychiatry to in-person treatment. *American Journal of Psychiatry, 161*, 1471–1476.

Russ, S. (2006). Psychodynamic treatments. In R. T. Ammerman (Ed.), *Comprehensive handbook of personality and psychopathology* (Vol. 3, pp. 425–437). New York: Wiley.

Russell, J. A. (1991). Culture and the categorization of emotions. *Psychological Bulletin, 110*, 426–450.

Russell, J. A. (1994). Is there universal recognition of emotion from facial expression? A review of the cross-cultural studies. *Psychological Bulletin, 155*(2), 102–141.

Russell, J. A. (1995). Facial expressions of emotion: What lies beyond minimal universality? *Psychological Bulletin, 118*, 379–391.

Russell, M. C. (2006). Treating combat-related stress disorders: A multiple case study utilizing eye movement desensitization and reprocessing (EMDR) with battlefield casualties from the Iraqi War. *Military Psychology, 18*, 1–18.

Russell, M. C., Silver, S. M., Rogers, S., & Darnell, J. N. (2007). Responding to an identified need: A joint Department of Defense/Department of Veterans Affairs training program in eye movement desensitization and reprocessing (EMDR) for clinicians providing trauma services. *International Journal of Stress Management, 14*(1), 61–71.

Rutkowski, G. K., Gruder, C. L., & Romer, D. (1983). Group cohesiveness, social norms, and bystander intervention. *Journal of Personality and Social Psychology, 44*, 545–552.

Rutledge, T., Reis, S. E., Olson, M., Owens, J., Kelsey, S. F., Pepine, C. J., et al. (2004). Social networks are associated with lower mortality rates among women with suspected coronary disease: The National Heart, Lung, and Blood Institute-Sponsored Women's Ischemia Syndrome Evaluation study. *Psychosomatic Medicine, 66*, 882–888.

Rutter, M. (2007). Proceeding from observed correlation to causal inference: The use of natural experiments. *Perspectives on Psychological Science, 2*(4), 377–395.

Rutter, M., O'Connor, T. G., & ERA Study Team. (2004). Are there biological programming effects for psychological development? Findings from a study of Romanian adoptees. *Developmental Psychology, 40*, 81–94.

Rutter, M., & Schopler, E. (1992). Classification of pervasive developmental disorders: Some concepts and practical considerations. *Journal of Autism and Developmental Disorders, 22*, 459–482.

Ryan, R. H., & Geiselman, R. E. (1991). Effects of biased information on the relationship between eyewitness confidence and accuracy. *Bulletin of the Psychonomic Society, 29*, 7–9.

Ryder, A. G., Yang, J., Zhu, X., Yao, S., Yi, J., Heine, S. J., & Bagby, R. M. (2008). The cultural shaping of depression: Somatic symptoms in China, psychological symptoms in North America? *Journal of Abnormal Psychology, 117*, 300–313.

Rymer, R. (1993). *Genie: A scientific tragedy*. New York: HarperCollins.

Rynders, J., & Horrobin, J. (1980). Educational provisions for young children with Down's syndrome. In J. Gottlieb (Ed.), *Educating mentally retarded persons in the mainstream* (pp. 109–147). Baltimore: University Park Press.

Rynes, S. L., Gerhart, B., & Parks, L. (2005). Performance evaluation and pay for performance. *Annual Review of Psychology, 56*, 571–600.

Saarni, C. (2006). Emotion regulation and personality development in childhood. In D. K. Mroczek & T. D. Little (Eds.), *Handbook of personality development* (pp. 245–262). Mahwah, NJ: Erlbaum.

Sabbagh, M. A., Xu, F., Carlson, S. M., Moses, L. J., & Lee, K. (2006). The development of executive functioning and theory of mind: A comparison of Chinese and U.S. preschoolers. *Psychological Science, 17*, 74–81.

Sachs, J. (1967). Recognition memory for syntactic and semantic aspects of connected discourse. *Perception and Psychophysics, 2*, 437–442.

Sackeim, H. A., Haskett, R. F., Mulsant, B. H., Thase, M. E., Mann, J. J., Pettinati, H. M., et al. (2001). Continuation pharmacotherapy in the prevention of relapse following electroconvulsive therapy: A randomized controlled trial. *Journal of the American Medical Association, 285*, 1299–1307.

Sackeim, H. A., Prudic, J., Devanand, D. P., Nobler, M. S., Lisanby, S. H., Peyser, S., et al. (2000). A prospective, randomized, double-blind comparison of bilateral and right unilateral electroconvulsive therapy at different stimulus intensities. *Archives of General Psychiatry, 57*, 425–434.

Sackett, P. R., Borneman, M. J., & Connelly, B. S. (2008). High stakes testing in higher education and employment: Appraising the evidence for validity and fairness. *American Psychologist, 63*, 215–227.

Sackett, P. R., Hardison, C. M., & Cullen, M. J. (2004). On interpreting stereotype threat as accounting for African American-White differences on cognitive tests. *American Psychologist, 59*, 7–13.

Sackett, P. R., Kuncel, N. R., Arneson, J. J., Cooper, S. R., & Waters, S. D. (2009). Does socioeconomic status explain the relationship between admissions tests and post-secondary academic performance? *Psychological Bulletin, 135*, 1–22.

Sackett, P. R., & Lievens, F. (2008). Personnel selection. *Annual Review of Psychology, 59*, 419–450.

Sackett, P. R., Schmitt, N., Ellington, J. E., & Kabin, M. B. (2001). High-stakes testing in employment, credentialing, and higher education: Prospects in a post-affirmative action world. *American Psychologist, 56*, 302–318.

Sacks, O. (1985). *The man who mistook his wife for a hat*. New York: Summit Books.

Sacks, O. (1992, July 27). The landscape of his dreams. *New Yorker*.

Sacks, O. (2002, October 7). The case of Anna H. *New Yorker*, pp. 62–73.

Sadetzki, S., Chetrit, A., Jarus-Hakak, A., Cardis, E., Deutch, Y., Duvdevani, S., Zultan, A., Novikov, I., Freedman, L., & Wolf, M. (2008). Cellular Phone use and risk of benign and malignant parotid gland tumors—A nationwide case-control study. *American Journal of Epidemiology, 167*, 457–467.

Sadler, L. S., Swartz, M. K., Ryan-Krause, P., Seitz, V., Meadows-Oliver, M., Grey, M., & Clemmens, D. A. (2007). Promising outcomes in teen mothers enrolled in a school-based parent support program and child care center. *Journal of School Health, 77*(3), 121–130.

Saffran, J. R., Senghas, A., & Trueswell, J. C. (2001). The acquisition of language by children. *Proceedings of the National Academy of Sciences, 98*, 12874–12875.

Safren, S. A., Gershuny, B. S., Marzol, P., Otto, M. W., Pollack, M. H. (2002). History of childhood abuse in panic disorder, social phobia, and generalized anxiety disorder. *Journal of Nervous and Mental Disease, 190*, 453–456.

Sagan, C. (1996). *The demon-haunted world*. New York: Ballantine.

Sahraie, A., Trevethan, C. T., MacLeod, J., Murray, A. D., Olson, J. A., & Weiskrantz, L. (2006). Increased sensitivity after repeated stimulation of residual spatial channels in blindsight. *Proceedings of the National Academy of Sciences, 103*, 14971–14976.

Saiz, P. A., Garcia-Portilla, M. P., Arango, C., Morales, B., Bascaran, M., et al. (2008). Association study between obsessive-compulsive disorder and serotonegic candidate genes. *Progress in Neuro-Psychopharmacology and Biological Psychiatry 32*, 765–770.

Sakairi, Y. (1992). Studies on meditation using questionnaires. *Japanese Psychological Review, 35*(1), 94–112.

Sakuma, M., Endo, T., & Muto, T. (2000). The development of self-understanding in preschoolers and elementary school children: Analysis of self-descriptions and self-evaluations. *Japanese Journal of Developmental Psychology, 11*, 176–187.

Salgado, J. F., Anderson, N., Moscoso, S., Bertua, C., de Fruyt, F., & Rolland, J. P. (2003). A meta-analytic study of general mental ability validity for different occupations in the European community. *Journal of Applied Psychology, 88*, 1068–1081.

Salin-Pascual, R., Gerashchenko, D., Greco, M., Blanco-Centurion, C., & Shiromani, P. J. (2001). Hypothalamic regulation of sleep. *Neuropsychopharmacology, 25*(Suppl. 5), S21.

Salokangas, R. K. R. (2004). Gender and the use of neuroleptics in schizophrenia. *Schizophrenia Research, 66*, 41–49.

Salovey, P., & Grewal, D. (2005). The science of emotional intelligence. *Current Directions in Psychological Science, 14*, 281–285.

Salovey, P., Mayer, J. D., & Rosenhan, D. L. (1991). Mood and helping: Mood as a motivator of helping and helping as a regulator of mood. In M. S. Clark (Ed.), *Review of personality and social psychology: Vol. 12. Prosocial behavior* (pp. 215–237). Newbury Park, CA: Sage.

Salzer, M. S., Rappaport, J., & Segre, L. (1999). Professional appraisal of professionally led and self-help groups. *American Journal of Ortho-Psychiatry, 69*, 536–540.

Sambunaris, A., & Hyde, T. M. (1994). Stroke-related aphasias mistaken for psychotic speech: Two case reports. *Journal of Geriatric Psychiatry and Neurology, 7*(3), 144–147.

Sanai, N., Tramontin, A. D., Quinones-Hinojosa, A., Barbaro, N. M., Gupta, N., Kunwar, S., et al. (2004). Unique astrocyte ribbon in adult human brain contains neural stem cells but lacks chain migration. *Nature, 427*, 740–744.

Sanders, M. R., Markie-Dadds, C., Tully, L. A., & Bor, W. (2000). The triple p-positive parenting program: A comparison of enhanced, standard, and self-directed behavioral family intervention for parents of children with early onset conduct problems. *Journal of Consulting and Clinical Psychology, 68*, 624–640.

Sanderson, W. C. (2003). Why empirically supported psychological treatments are important. *Behavior Modification, 27*, 290–299.

Sanderson, W. C., Rapee, R. M., & Barlow, D. H. (1989). The influence of an illusion of control on panic attacks induced via inhalation of 5.5% carbon dioxide- enriched air. *Archives of General Psychiatry, 46*, 157–162.

Sanders Thompson, V. L., Bazile, A., & Akbar, M. (2004). African Americans' perceptions of psychotherapy and psychotherapists. *Professional Psychology: Research and Practice, 35*, 19–26.

Santry, H. P., Gillen, D. L., & Lauderdale, D. S. (2005). Trends in bariatric surgical procedures. *Journal of the American Medical Association, 294*, 1909–1917.

Saper, C. B., Chou, T. C., & Scammell, T. E. (2001). The sleep switch: Hypothalamic control of sleep and wakefulness. *Trends in Neurosciences, 24*, 726–731.

Saper, C. B., Scammell, T. E., & Lu, J. (2005). Hypothalamic regulation of sleep and circadian rhythms. *Nature, 437*, 1257–1263.

Sarafino, E. P., & Goehring, P. (2000). Age comparisons in acquiring biofeedback control and success in reducing headache pain. *Annals of Behavioral Medicine, 22*, 1–9.

Sarason, B. R., Sarason, I. G., & Gurung, R. A. R. (1997). Close personal relationships and health outcomes: A key to the role of social support. In S. Duck (Ed.), *Handbook of personal relationships* (pp. 547–573). New York: Wiley.

Sarason, I. G., Johnson, J., & Siegel, J. (1978). Assessing impact of life changes: Development of the life experiences survey. *Journal of Clinical and Consulting Psychology, 46*, 932–946.

Sarin, S., Abela, J. R. Z., & Auerbach, R. P. (2005). The response styles theory of depression: A test of specificity and causal mediation. *Cognition and Emotion, 19*, 751–761.

Sasaki, Y., Jadjikhani, N., Fischl, B., Liu, A. K., Marret, S., Dale, A. M., & Tootell, R. B. H. (2001). Local and global attention are mapped retinotopically in human occipital cortex. *Proceedings of the National Academy of Sciences, 98*, 2077.

Sass, D. A., Twohig, M. P., & Davies, W. H. (2004). Defining the independent variables and ensuring treatment integrity: A comparison across journals of different theoretical orientations. *Behavior Therapist, 27*, 172–174.

Sattler, D. N., Kaiser, C. F., & Hittner, J. B. (2000). Disaster preparedness: Relationships among prior experience, personal characteristics, and distress. *Journal of Applied Social Psychology, 30*, 1396–1420.

Saucier, G., Georgiades, S., Tsaousis, I., & Goldberg, L. R. (2005). The factor structure of Greek personality adjectives. *Journal of Personality and Social Psychology, 88*, 856–875.

Saudino, K. J., Ronald, A., & Plomin, R. (2005). The etiology of behavior problems in 7-year-old twins: Substantial genetic influence and negligible shared environmental influence for parent ratings and ratings by same and different teachers. *Journal of Abnormal Child Psychology, 33*, 113–130.

Sauter, S., Murphy, L., Colligan, M., Swanson, N., Hurrell, J., Jr., Scharf, F., Jr., et al. (1999). *Stress at work* (DHHS [NIOSH] Publication No. 99–101). Washington, DC: National Institute on Occupational Health and Safety.

Saveliev, S. V., Lebedev, V. V., Evgeniev, M. B., & Korochkin, L. I. (1997). Chimeric brain: Theoretical and clinical aspects. *International Journal of Developmental Biology, 41*, 801–808.

Savelkoul, M., Post, M. W. M., de Witte, L. P., & van den Borne, H. B. (2000). Social support, coping, and subjective well-being in patients with rheumatic diseases. *Patient Education and Counseling, 39*, 205–218.

Savic, I., Berglund, H., Gulyas, B., & Roland, P. (2001). Smelling of odorous sex hormone-like compounds causes sex-differentiated hypothalamic activations in humans. *Neuron, 31*, 661–668.

Saville, B. K., Zinn, T. E., Neef, N. A., Van Norman, R., & Ferreri, S. J. (2006). A comparison of interteaching and lecture in the college classroom. *Journal of Applied Behavior Analysis, 39*, 49–61.

Savin-Williams, R. C. (2006). Who's gay? Does it matter? *Current Directions in Psychological Science, 15*, 40–44.

Savin-Williams, R. C., & Demo, D. H. (1984). Developmental change and stability in adolescent self-concept. *Developmental Psychology, 20*, 1100–1110.

Saxe, L., & Ben-Shakhar, G. (1999). Admissibility of polygraph tests: The application of scientific standards post-Daubert. *Psychology, Public Policy, and Law, 5*, 203–223.

Saxe, R., Tzelnic, R., & Carey, S. (2007). Knowing who dunnit: Infants identify causal agent in an unseen causal interaction. *Developmental Psychology, 43*, 149–158.

Sayal, K., Heron, J., Golding, J., Alati, R., Smith, G. D., Gray, R., & Emond, A. (2009). Binge pattern of alcohol consumption during pregnancy and childhood mental health outcomes: Longitudinal population-based study. *Pediatrics, 123*, e289–e296.

Sayers, J. (1991). *Mother of psychoanalysis*. New York: Norton.

Scandura, T. A., & Lankau, M. J. (1997). Relationships of gender, family responsibility and flexible work hours to organizational commitment and job satisfaction. *Journal of Organizational Behavior, 18*, 377–391.

Scandura, T. A., & Schriesheim, C. A. (1994). Leader-member exchange and supervisor career mentoring as complementary constructs in leadership research. *Academy of Management Journal, 37*, 1588–1602.

Scarr, S. (1998). How do families affect intelligence? Social environmental and behavior genetic prediction. In J. J. McArdle & R. W. Woodcock (Eds.), *Human cognitive abilities in theory and practice* (pp. 113–136). Mahwah, NJ: Erlbaum.

Scarr, S., & Carter-Saltzman, L. (1982). Genetics and intelligence. In R. Sternberg (Ed.), *Handbook of human intelligence* (pp. 792–896). Cambridge, UK: Cambridge University Press.

Schabracq, M. J. (2003). Organizational culture, stress, and change. In M. J. Schabracq, J. A. M. Winnubst, & C. L. Cooper (Eds.), *Handbook of work and health psychology* (pp.37–62). West Sussex, UK: Wiley.

Schacter, D. L. (2001). *The seven sins of memory*. Boston: Houghton Mifflin.

Schacter, D. L., Chiu, C.-Y. P., & Ochsner, K. N. (1993). Implicit memory: A selective review. *Annual Review of Neuroscience, 16*, 159–182.

Schacter, D. L., Cooper, L. A., Delaney, S. M., Peterson, M. A., & Tharan, M. (1991). Implicit memory for possible and impossible objects: Constraints on the construction of structural descriptions. *Journal of Experimental Psychology: Learning, Memory, and Cognition, 17*, 3–19.

Schacter, D. L., Norman, K. A., & Koutstaal, W. (1998). The cognitive neuroscience of constructive memory. *Annual Review of Psychology, 49*, 289–318.

Schachter, S., & Singer, J. (1962). Cognitive, social and physiological determinants of emotional state. *Psychological Review, 69*, 379–399.

Schaefer, J., Sykes, R., Rowley, R., & Baek, S. (1988, November). *Slow country music and drinking*. Paper presented at the 87th annual meeting of the American Anthropological Association, Phoenix, AZ.

Schaefer, M., Heinze, H. J., & Rotte, M. (2008). My third arm: Shifts in topography of the somatosensory homunculus predict feeling of an artificial supernumerary arm. *Human Brain Mapping, 6*, 6.

Schafer, J., & Brown, S. A. (1991). Marijuana and cocaine effect expectancies and drug use patterns. *Journal of Consulting and Clinical Psychology, 59*, 558–565.

Schatzberg, A. F., Rush, A. J., Arnow, B. A., Banks, P. L., Blalock, J. A., Borian, F. E., et al. (2005). Chronic depression: Medication (nefazodone) or psychotherapy (CBASP) is effective when the other is not. *Archives of General Psychiatry, 62*, 513–520.

Schaubroeck, J., Jones, J. R., & Xie, J. J. (2001). Individual differences in utilizing control to cope with job demands: Effects on susceptibility to infectious disease. *Journal of Applied Psychology, 86*, 265–278.

Schaufeli, W. B., & Buunk, B. P. (2003). Burnout: An overview of 25 years of research and theorizing. In M. J. Schabracq, J. A. M. Winnubst, & C. L. Cooper (Eds.), *Handbook of work and health psychology* (pp.383–428). West Sussex, UK: Wiley.

Schaztberg, A. F., Cole, J. O., & DeBattista, C. (2007). *Manual of clinical psychopharmacology* (6th ed.). Arlington, VA: American Psychiatric Publishing.

Scheerer, M., Rothmann, R., & Goldstein, K. (1945). A case of "idiot savant": An experimental study of personality organization. *Psychology Monograph, 58*(4), 1–63.

Scheidinger, S. (2004). Group psychotherapy and related helping groups today: An overview. *American Journal of Psychotherapy, 58*, 265–280.

Scheier, M. F., Matthews, K. A., Owens, J. F., Magovern, G. J., Lefebvre, R. C., Abbott, R. A., et al. (1989). Dispositional optimism and recovery from coronary artery bypass surgery: The beneficial effects on physical and psychological well-being. *Journal of Personality and Social Psychology, 57*, 1024–1040.

Scheier, M. F., Matthews, K. A., Owens, J. F., Schulz, R., Bridges, M. W., Magovern, G. J., et al. (1999). Optimism and rehospitalization after coronary artery bypass graft surgery. *Archives of Internal Medicine, 159*, 829–835.

Schell, T. L., Martino, S. C., Ellickson, P. L., Collins, R. L., & McCaffrey, D. (2005). Measuring developmental changes in alcohol expectancies. *Psychology of Addictive Behaviors, 19,* 217–220.

Schellenberg, E. G. (2004). Music lessons enhance IQ. *Psychological Science, 15,* 511–514.

Schenck, C. H., & Mahowald, M. W. (1992). Motor dyscontrol in narcolepsy: Rapid eye movement (REM) sleep without atonia and REM sleep behavior disorder. *Annals of Neurology, 32*(1), 3–10.

Scheufele, P. M. (2000). Effects of progressive relaxation and classical music on measurements of attention, relaxation, and stress responses. *Journal of Behavioral Medicine, 23,* 207–228.

Schiff, N. D., Rodriguez-Moreno, D., Kamal, A., Kim, K. H., Giacino, J. T., Plum, F., et al. (2005). fMRI reveals large-scale network activation in minimally conscious patients. *Neurology, 64*(3), 514–523.

Schiffman, S. S., Graham, B. G., Sattely-Miller, E. A., & Warwick, Z. (1999). Orosensory perception of dietary fat. *Current Directions in Psychological Science, 7,* 137–143.

Schleicher, D. J., Watt, J. D., & Greguras, G. J. (2004). Reexamining the job satisfaction–performance relationship: The complexity of attitudes. *Journal of Applied Psychology, 89,* 165–177.

Schloss, P., & Williams, D. C. (1998). The serotonin transporter: A primary target for antidepressant drugs. *Journal of Psychopharmacology, 12,* 115–121.

Schmader, T., Johns, M., & Forbes, C. (2008). An integrated process model of stereotype threat effects on performance. *Psychological Review, 115,* 336–356.

Schmidt, F. L., & Hunter, J. E. (2004). General mental ability in the world of work: Occupational attainment and job performance. *Journal of Personality and Social Psychology, 86,* 162–173.

Schmidt, J. R., Crump, M. J. C., Cheesman, J., & Besner, D. (2007). Contingency learning without awareness: Evidence for implicit control. *Consciousness and Cognition, 16,* 421–435.

Schmidtke, A., & Hafner, H. (1988). The Werther effect after television films: New evidence for an old hypothesis. *Psychological Medicine, 18,* 665–676.

Schmitt, D. P. (2003). Universal sex differences in the desire for sexual variety: Tests from 52 nations, 6 continents, and 13 islands. *Journal of Personality and Social Psychology, 85,* 85–104.

Schmolck, H., Buffalo, E. A., & Squire, L. R. (2000). Memory distortions over time: Recollections of the O. J. Simpson trial verdict after 15 and 32 months. *Psychological Science, 11,* 39–47.

Schnall, S., & Laird, J. D. (2003). Keep smiling: Enduring effects of facial expressions and postures on emotional experience and memory. *Cognition & Emotion, 17,* 787–797.

Schnee, M. E., Lawton, D. M., Furness, D. N., Benke, T. A., & Ricci, A. J. (2005). Auditory hair cell-afferent fiber synapses are specialized to operate at their best frequencies. *Neuron, 47,* 243–254.

Schneider, B. (1985). Organizational behavior. *Annual Review of Psychology, 36,* 573–611.

Schneider, B. H., Atkinson, L., & Tardif, C. (2001). Child-parent attachment and children's peer relations: A quantitative review. *Developmental Psychology, 37,* 86–100.

Schneider, K. T., Hitlan, R. T., & Radhakrishnan, P. (2000). The nature and correlates of ethnic harassment experiences in multiple contexts. *Journal of Applied Psychology, 85,* 3–12.

Schneider, R. H., Alexander, C. N., Staggers, F., Rainforth, M., Salerno, J. W., Hartz, A., et al. (2005). Long-term effects of stress reduction on mortality in persons [GTE] 55 years of age with systemic hypertension. *American Journal of Cardiology, 95,* 1060–1064.

Schneider, T. R., Ring, C., & Katkin, E. S. (1998). A test of the validity of the method of constant stimuli as an index of heartbeat detection. *Psychophysiology, 35,* 86–89.

Schneider, W., & Bjorklund, D. F. (1998). Memory. In W. Damon, D. Kuhn, & R. Siegler (Eds.), *Handbook of child psychology: Vol. 2. Cognition, language and perception* (5th ed., pp. 467–521). New York: Wiley.

Schneiderman, N. (2004). Psychosocial, behavioral, and biological aspects of chronic diseases. *Current Directions in Psychological Science, 13,* 247–251.

Schneiderman, N., Antoni, M. H., Saab, P. G., & Ironson, G. (2001). Health psychology: Psychosocial and biobehavioral aspects of chronic disease management. *Annual Review of Psychology, 52,* 555–580.

Schnur, T. T., Schwartz, M. F., Kimberg, D. Y., Hirshorn, E., Coslett, H. B., & Thompson-Schill, S. L. (2009). Localizing interference during naming: Convergent neuroimaging and neuropsychological evidence for the function of Broca's area. *Proceedings of the National Academy of Sciences, 106*(1), 322–327.

Schnurr, P. P., Friedman, M. J., Engel, C. C., Foa, E. B., Shea, T., Chow, B. K., et al. (2007). Cognitive behavior therapy for posttraumatic stress disorder in women: A randomized controlled trial. *Journal of the American Medical Association, 297,* 820–830.

Schoemaker, M. J., Swerdlow, A. J., Ahlbom, A., Auvinen, A., Blaasaas, K. G., Cardis, E., et al. (2005). Mobile phone use and risk of acoustic neuroma: Results of the Interphone case-control study in five North European countries. *British Journal of Cancer, 93,* 842–848.

Schoenbaum, M., Sherbourne, C., & Wells, K. (2005). Gender patterns in cost effectiveness of quality improvement for depression: Results of a randomized controlled trial. *Journal of Affective Disorders, 87,* 319.

Schofield, H.-L., Bierman, K. L., Heinrichs, B., & Nix, R. L. (2008). Predicting early sexual activity with behavior problems exhibited at school entry and in early adolescence. *Journal of Abnormal Child Psychology, 36*(8), 1175–1188.

Scholz, H., Franz, M., & Heberlein, U. (2005). The *hangover* gene defines a stress pathway required for ethanol tolerance development. *Nature, 436,* 845–847.

Schooler, C. (2007). Use it--and keep it, longer, probably: A reply to Salthouse (2006). *Perspectives on Psychological Science, 2,* 24–29.

Schott, B. H., Henson, R. N., Richardson-Klavehn, A., Becker, C., Thoma, V., Heinze, H. J., & Duzel, E. (2005). Redefining implicit and explicit memory: The functional neuroanatomy of priming, remembering, and control of retrieval. *Proceedings of the National Academy of Sciences, 102,* 1257–1262.

Schreiber, G. B., Robins, M., Striegel-Moore, R., Obarzanek, E., Morrison, J. A., & Wright, D. J. (1996). Weight modification efforts reported by black and white preadolescent girls: National Heart, Lung, and Blood Institute Growth and Health Study. *Pediatrics, 98,* 63–70.

Schroeder, D. A. (1995). An introduction to social dilemmas. In D. Schroeder (Ed.), *Social dilemmas: Perspectives on individuals and groups* (pp. 1–13). Westport, CT: Praeger.

Schroeder, D. A., Penner, L. A., Dovidio, J. F., & Piliavin, J. A. (1995). *The psychology of helping and altruism: Problems and puzzles.* New York: McGraw-Hill.

Schuckit, M. A. (1998). Biological, psychological, and environmental predictors of alcoholism risk: A longitudinal study. *Journal of Studies in Alcoholism, 59,* 485–494.

Schulden, J., Chen, J., Kresnow, M., Arias, I., Crosby, A., Mercy, J., et al. (2006). Psychological responses to the sniper attacks: Washington DC area, October, 2002. *American Journal of Preventive Medicine, 31,* 324–327.

Schultheiss, O. (2008). Implicit motives. In O. John, R. Robins, & L. Pervin (Eds.), *Handbook of personality: Theory and research* (3rd ed., 603–633). New York: Guilford.

Schultheiss, O. C., & Rohde, W. (2002). Implicit power motivation predicts men's testosterone changes and implicit learning in a contest situation. *Hormones and Behavior, 41,* 195–202.

Schultz, D., & Schultz, S. (2009). *Theories of personality* (9th ed.). Florence, KY: Cengage Learning.

Schultz, D., & Schultz, S. E. (2002). *Psychology and work today: An introduction to industrial and organizational psychology* (8th ed.). Upper Saddle River, NJ: Prentice Hall.

Schultz, D. P., & Schultz, S. E. (2000). *A history of modern psychology* (7th ed.). Fort Worth, TX: Harcourt Brace.

Schultz, D. P., & Schultz, S. E. (2002). *A history of modern psychology* (8th ed.). Fort Worth, TX: Harcourt Brace.

Schultz, D. P., & Schultz, S. E. (2005). *Theories of personality* (8th ed.) Belmont, CA: Wadsworth.

Schultz, P. W., Nolan, J. M., Cialdini, R. B., Goldstein, N. J., & Griskevicius, V. (2007). The constructive, destructive, and reconstructive power of social norms. *Psychological Science, 18,* 429–434.

Schulz, R. (1978). *The psychology of death, dying, and bereavement.* Reading, MA: Addison-Wesley.

Schulz, R., Beach, S. R., Lind, B., Martire, L. M., Zdaniuk, B., Hirsch, C., et al. (2001). Involvement in caregiving and adjustment to death of a spouse: Findings from the caregiver health effects study. *Journal of the American Medical Association, 285,* 3123–3129.

Schulz-Hardt, S., Frey, D., Luthgens, C., & Moscovici, S. (2000). Biased information search in group decision making. *Journal of Personality and Social Psychology, 78,* 665–669.

Schumann, A., Meyer, C., Rumpf, H. J., Hannover, W., Hapke, U., & John, U. (2005). Stage of change transitions and processes of change, decisional balance, and self-efficacy in smokers: A transtheoretical model validation using longitudinal data. *Psychology of Addictive Behaviors, 19,* 3–9.

Schwartz, C. E., Wright, C. I., Shin, L. M., Kagan, J., & Rauch, S. L. (2003). Inhibited and uninhibited infants "grown up": Adult amygdala response to novelty. *Science, 300,* 1952–1953.

Schwartz, J. (2004, September 5). Always on the job, employees pay with health. *The New York Times,* p. 1.

Schwartz, J. R. (2005). Modafinil: New indications for wake promotion. *Expert Opinion in Pharmacotherapy, 6,* 115–129.

Schwartz, M. W., Woods, S. C., Porte, Jr., D., Seeley, R. J., & Baskin, D. G. (2000). Central nervous system control of food intake. *Nature, 404,* 661–671.

Schwarz, N., & Bohner, G. (2001). The construction of attitudes. In A. Tesser & N. Schwarz (Eds.), *Blackwell handbook of social psychology: Intraindividual processes* (pp. 436–457). Oxford, UK: Blackwell.

Schwarz, N., & Scheuring, B. (1992). Frequency reports of psychosomatic symptoms: What respondents learn from response alternatives. *Zeutschrift fur Klinische Psychologie, 22,* 197–208.

Schwarzbold, M., Diaz, A., Martins, E. T., Rufino, A., Amante, L. N., Thais, M. E., Quevedo, J., Hohl, A., Linhares, M. N., & Walz, R. (2008). Psychiatric disorders and traumatic brain injury. *Neuropsychiatric Disease and Treatment, 4*(4), 797–816.

Schwarzer, R. (2001). Social-cognitive factors in changing health-related behaviors. *Current Directions in Psychological Science, 10,* 47–51.

Schwender, D., Klasing, D., Daunderer, M., Maddler, C., Poppel, E., & Peter, K. (1995). Awareness during general anesthetic: Definition, incidence, clinical relevance, causes, avoidance, and medicolegal aspects. *Anaesthetist, 44,* 743–754.

Schyns, B. (2006). Are group consensus in leader-member exchange (LMX) and shared work values related to organizational outcomes? *Small Group Research, 37,* 20–35.

Scott, K. M., Bruffaerts, R., Simon, G. E., Alonso, J., Angermeyer, M., de Girolamo, G., Demyttenaere, K., Gasquet, I., Haro, J. M., Karam, E., Kessler, R. C., Levinson, D., Mora, M. E. M., Browne, M. A. O., Ormel, J., Villa, J. P., Uda, H., & Von Korff, M. (2008). Obesity and mental disorders in the general population: results from the world mental health surveys. *International Journal of Obesity, 32,* 192–200.

Scott, T. F. (2006). The neurological examination. In P. J. Snyder & P. D. Nussbaum (Eds.), *Clinical neuropsychology: A pocket handbook for assessment,* 2nd ed. (pp. 17–33). Washington, DC: American Psychological Association.

Scourfield, J., Van den Bree, M., Martin, N., & McGuffin, P. (2004). Conduct problems in children and adolescents: A twin study. *Archives of General Psychiatry, 61,* 489–496.

Scoville, W. B., & Milner, B. (1957). Loss of recent memory after bilateral hippocampal lesions. *Journal of Neurology, Neurosurgery, and Psychiatry, 20,* 11–21.

Sears, R. (1977). Sources of satisfaction of the Terman gifted men. *American Psychologist, 32,* 119–128.

Sederberg, P. B., Schulze-Bonhage, A., Madsen, J. R., Bromfield, E. B., Litt, B., Brandt, A., & Kahana, M. J. (2007). Gamma oscillations distinguish true from false memories. *Psychological Science, 18,* 927–932.

Seegert, C. R. (2003). Token economies and incentive programs: Behavioral improvement in mental health inmates housed in state prisons. *Behavior Therapist, 26*(1), 208, 210–211.

Seeley, K. (2006). *Cultural psychotherapy: Working with culture in the clinical encounter.* Northvale, NJ: Aronson.

Seeman, M. V. (2004). Gender differences in the prescribing of antipsychotic drugs. *American Journal of Psychiatry, 161,* 1324–1333.

Seeman, P., Weinshenker, D., Quirion, R., Srivastava, L. K., Bhardwaj, S. K., Grandy, D. K. (2005). Dopamine supersensitivity correlates with D2High states, implying many paths to psychosis. *Proceedings of the National Academy of Sciences, 102,* 3513–3518.

Seeman, T., & Chen, X. (2002). Risk and protective factors for physical functioning in older adults with and without chronic conditions: MacArthur studies of successful aging. *Journals of Gerontology: Series B. Psychological Sciences & Social Sciences, 57*(3), S135–S144.

Segal, Z. V., Gemar, M., & Williams, S. (2000). Differential cognitive response to a mood challenge following successful cognitive therapy or pharmacotherapy for unipolar depression. *Journal of Abnormal Psychology, 108,* 3–10.

Segall, M. H., Dasen, P. R., Berry, J. W., & Poortinga, Y. H. (1990). *Human behavior in global perspective: An introduction to cross-cultural psychology.* Elmwood, NY: Pergamon Press.

Segerstrom, S. C., Taylor, S. E., Kemeny, M. E., & Fahey, J. L. (1998). Optimism is associated with mood, coping, and immune change in response to stress. *Journal of Personality and Social Psychology, 74,* 1646–1655.

Segurado, R., Conroy, J., Meally, E., Fitzgerald, M., Gill, M., & Gallagher, L. (2005). Confirmation of association between autism and the mitochondrial aspartate/glutamate carrier *SLC25A12* gene on chromosome 2q31. *American Journal of Psychiatry, 162,* 2182–2184.

Seiger, A., Nordberg, A., Vonholst, H., Backman, L., Ebendal, T., Alafuzoff, I., et al. (1993). Intracranial infusion of purified nerve growth factor to an Alzheimer patient: The 1st attempt of a possible future treatment strategy. *Behavioral Brain Research, 57,* 255–261.

Sejnowski, T. J., Chattarji, S., & Stanton, P. K. (1990). Homosynaptic long-term depression in hippocampus and neocortex. *Seminars in the Neurosciences, 2,* 355–363.

Sejnowski, T. J., & Destexhe, A. (2000). Why do we sleep? *Brain Research, 886,* 208–223.

Selemon, L. D., Mrzljak, J., Kleinman, J. E., Herman, M. M., & Goldman-Rakic, P. S. (2003). Regional specificity in the neuropathologic substrates of schizophrenia: A morphometric analysis of Broca's area 44 and area 9. *Archives of General Psychiatry, 60,* 69–77.

Seligman, M. (2002). Positive psychology, positive prevention, and positive therapy. In C. Snyder & S. Lopez (Eds.), *Handbook of positive psychology.* NewYork: Oxford University Press.

Seligman, M. E. P. (1975). *Helplessness: On depression, development, and death.* San Francisco: Freeman.

Seligman, M. E. P. (1991). *Learned optimism.* New York: Knopf.

Seligman, M. E. P. (1995). The effectiveness of psychotherapy: The *Consumer Reports* study. *American Psychologist, 50,* 965–974.

Seligman, M. E. P. (1996). Good news for psychotherapy: The *Consumer Reports* study. *Independent Practitioner, 16,* 17–20.

Seligman, M. E. P., Castellon, C., Cacciola, J., Shulman, P., Luborsky, L., Ollove, M., & Downing, R. (1988). Explanatory style change during cognitive therapy for unipolar depression. *Journal of Abnormal Psychology, 97,* 13–18.

Seligman, M. E. P., & Schulman, P. (1986). Explanatory style as a predictor of productivity and quitting among life insurance agents. *Journal of Personality and Social Psychology, 50,* 832–838.

Seligman, M. E. P., Steen, T. A., Park, N., & Peterson, C. (2005). Positive psychology progress: Empirical validation of interventions. *American Psychologist, 60,* 410–421.

Sell, R. L., Wells, J. A., & Wypij, D. (1995). The prevalence of homosexual behavior and attraction in the United States, the United Kingdom, and France: Results of national population-based samples. *Archives of Sexual Behavior, 24*(3), 235–248.

Selye, H. (1956). *The stress of life.* New York: McGraw-Hill.

Selye, H. (1975). *Stress without distress.* New York: Signet.

Selye, H. (1976). *The stress of life* (2nd ed.). New York: McGraw-Hill.

Semmler, C., Brewer, N., & Wells, G. L. (2004). Effects of postidentification feedback on eyewitness identification and nonidentification confidence. *Journal of Applied Psychology, 89,* 334–346.

Senghas, A., & Coppola, M. (2001). Children creating language: How Nicaraguan sign language acquired a spatial grammar. *Psychological Science, 12,* 323–328.

Sergeant, J. A., Geurts, H., & Oosterlaan, J. (2002). How specific is a deficit of executive functioning for attention deficit/hyperactivity disorder? *Behavioural Brain Research, 130,* 3–28.

Serpell, R. (1994). The cultural construction of intelligence. In W. J. Lonner & R. S. Malpass (Eds.), *Psychology and culture* (pp. 157–164). Boston: Allyn & Bacon.

Serretti, A., Chiesa, A., Calati, R., Perma, G., Bellodi, L., & De Ronchi, D. (2009). Common genetic, clinical, demographic and psychosocial predictors of response to pharmacotherapy in mood and anxiety disorders. *International Clinical Psychopharmacology, 24,* 1–18.

Servan-Schreiber, E., & Anderson, J. R. (1990). Learning artificial grammars with competitive chunking. *Journal of Experimental Psychology: Learning, Memory, and Cognition, 16,* 592–608.

Seta, J. J., Seta, C. E., & McElroy, T. (2006). Better than better-than-average (or not): Elevated and depressed self-evaluations following unfavorable social comparisons. *Self and Identity, 5,* 51–72.

Seth, A. K., Izhikevich, E., Reeke, G. N., & Edelman, G. M. (2006). Theories and measures of consciousness: An extended framework. *Proceedings of the National Academy of Sciences, 103,* 10799–10804.

Seto, M. C., Maric, A., & Barbaree, H. E. (2001). The role of pornography in the etiology of sexual aggression. *Aggression and Violent Behavior, 6,* 35–53.

Sewell, M. C., Goggin, K. J., Rabkin, J. G., Ferrando, S. J., McElhiney, M. C., & Evans, S. (2000). Anxiety syndromes and symptoms among men with AIDS: A longitudinal controlled study. *Psychosomatics, 41,* 294–300.

Seymour, N. E. (2008). VR to OR: A review of the evidence that virtual reality simulation improves operating room performance. *World Journal of Surgery, 32*(2), 182–188.

Shadish, W. R., & Baldwin, S. A. (2005). Effects of behavioral marital therapy: A meta-analysis of randomized controlled trials. *Journal of Counseling and Clinical Psychology, 73,* 6–14.

Shadish, W. R., Cook, T. D., & Campbell, D. T. (2002). *Experimental and quasi- experimental designs for generalized causal inference.* Boston: Houghton Mifflin.

Shadish, W. R., Matt, G. E., Navarro, A. M., & Phillips, G. (2000). The effects of psychological therapies under clinically representative conditions: A meta-analysis. *Psychological Bulletin, 126,* 512–529.

Shaffer, D. R. (1973). *Social and personality development* (Box 4–2). Pacific Grove, CA: Brooks/Cole.

Shaffer, D. R. (1999). *Developmental psychology: Childhood and adolescence.* Pacific Grove, CA: Brooks/Cole.

Shah, J. (2003). Automatic for the people: How representations of significant others implicitly affect goal pursuit. *Journal of Personality and Social Psychology, 84,* 661–681.

Shahin, A. J., Roberts, L. E., Chau, W., Trainor, L. J., & Miller, L. M. (2008). Music training leads to the development of timbre-specific gamma band activity. *NeuroImage, 41*(1), 113–122.

Shalev, A. Y., & Freedman, S. (2005). PTSD following terrorist attacks: A prospective evaluation. *American Journal of Psychiatry, 162,* 1188–1191.

Shalev, A. Y., Tuval, R., Frenkiel-Fishman, S., Hadar, H., & Eth, S. (2006). Psychological responses to continuous terror: A study of two communities in Israel. *American Journal of Psychiatry, 163,* 667–673.

Shamay-Tsoory, S. G., & Tomer, R. (2005). The neuroanatomical basis of understanding sarcasm and its relationship to social cognition. *Neuropsychology, 19,* 288–300.

Shand, M. A. (1982). Sign-based short-term memory coding of American Sign Language and printed English words by congenitally deaf signers. *Cognitive Psychology, 14,* 1–12.

Shankman, S. A., Klein, D. N., Tenke, C. E., & Bruder, G. E. (2007). Reward sensitivity in depression: A biobehavioral study. *Journal of Abnormal Psychology, 116,* 95–104.

Shanks, D. R. (1995). *The psychology of associative learning.* New York: Cambridge University Press.

Shapiro, A. F., Gottman, J. M., & Carrere, S. (2000). The baby and the marriage: Identifying factors that buffer against decline in marital satisfaction after the first baby arrives. *Journal of Family Psychology, 14,* 59–70.

Shapiro, D. H., & Walsh, R. N. (Eds.). (1984). *Meditation: Classical and contemporary perspectives.* New York: Aldine.

Shapiro, F. (1989a). Efficacy of the eye movement desensitization procedure in the treatment of traumatic memories. *Journal of Traumatic Stress, 2,* 199–223.

Shapiro, F. (1989b). Eye movement desensitization: A new treatment for post- traumatic stress disorder. *Journal of Behavior Therapy and Experimental Psychiatry, 20,* 211–217.

Shapiro, F. (1991). Eye movement desensitization and reprocessing procedure: From EMD to EMD/R—A new treatment model for anxiety and related traumata. *Behavior Therapist, 15,* 133–135.

Shapiro, F., & Forrest, M. S. (2004). *EMDR: The breakthrough therapy for overcoming anxiety, stress, and trauma.* New York: Basic Books.

Shapiro, J. P. (2008). Integrating outcome research and clinical reasoning in psychotherapy planning. *Professional Psychology: Research and Practice, 40,* 46–53.

Shapiro, K. A., Moo, L. R., & Caramazza, A. (2006). Cortical signatures of noun and verb production. *Proceedings of the National Academy of Sciences, 103,* 1644–1649.

Shaver, P. R., & Mikulincer, M. (2005). Attachment theory and research: Resurrection of the psychodynamic approach to personality. *Journal of Research in Personality, 39,* 22–45.

Shaw, D. S., Dishion, T. J., Supplee, L., Gardner, F., & Arnds, K. (2006). Randomized trial of a family-centered approach to the prevention of early conduct problems: 2-year effects of the family check-up in early childhood. *Journal of Consulting and Clinical Psychology, 74,* 1–9.

Shaw, D. S., Owens, E. B., Giovannelli, J., Winslow, E. B. (2001). Infant and toddler pathways leading to early externalizing disorders. *Journal of the American Academy of Child and Adolescent Psychiatry, 40,* 36–43.

Shaw, J. S., III. (1996). Increases in eyewitness confidence resulting from persistent questioning. *Journal of Experimental Psychology: Applied, 2,* 126–146.

Shayer, M. (2008). Intelligence for education: As described by Piaget and measured by psychometrics. *British Journal of Educational Psychology, 78*(1), 1–29.

Shaywitz, B. A., Shaywitz, S. E., Pugh, K. R., Constable, R. T., Skudlarski, P., Fulbright, R. K., et al. (1995). Sex differences in the functional organization of the brain for language. *Nature, 373,* 607–609.

Shea, M. T., Stout, R., Gunderson, J., Morey, L. C., Grilo, C. M., McGlashan, T., et al. (2002). Short-term diagnostic stability of schizotypal, borderline, avoidant, and obsessive-compulsive personality disorders. *American Journal of Psychiatry, 159,* 2036–2041.

Shechtman, Z. (1992). A group assessment procedure as a predictor of on-the-job performance of teachers. *Journal of Applied Psychology, 77,* 383–387.

Shedler, J., & Westen, D. (2004). Refining personality disorder diagnoses: Integrating science and practice. *American Journal of Psychiatry, 161,* 1350–1365.

Sheehy, R., & Horan, J. J. (2004). Effects of stress inoculation training for 1st-year law students. *International Journal of Stress Management, 11*(1), 41–55.

Sheldon, K. M., & Kasser, T. (2001). Getting older, getting better? Personal striving and psychological maturity across the life span. *Developmental Psychology, 37,* 491–501.

Sheldon, K. M., & King, L. (2001). Why positive psychology is necessary. *American Psychologist, 56,* 216–217.

Shen, J., & Dicker, B. (2008). The impacts of shiftwork on employees. *International Journal of Human Resource Management, 19,* 392–405.

Shenker, J. I. (2005, April). *When you only see trees, is there still a forest?* Paper presented at the American Academy of Neurology Annual Meeting, Miami Beach, FL.

Shenker, J. I., Wylie, S. A., Fuchs, K., Manning, C. A., & Heilman, K. M. (2004). On-line anosognosia: Unawareness for chorea in real time but not on videotape delay. *Neurology, 63*(1), 159–160.

Shepard, R. N., & Metzler, J. (1971). Mental rotation of three-dimensional objects. *Science, 171,* 701–703.

Shepherd, C., Kohut, J. J., & Sweet, R. (1989). *News of the weird.* New York: New American Library.

Shepherd, R. K., Coco, A., Epp, S. B., & Crook, J. M. (2005). Chronic depolarization enhances the trophic effects of brain-derived neurotrophic factor in rescuing auditory neurons following a sensorineural hearing loss. *Journal of Comparative Neurology, 486,* 145–158.

Shepherd, R. K., & McCreery, D. B. (2006). Basis of electrical stimulation of the cochlea and the cochlear nucleus. *Advances in Otorhinolaryngology, 64,* 186–205.

Sher, K. J., Walitzer, K., Wood, P., & Brent, E. (1991). Characteristics of children of alcoholics: Putative risk factors, substance use and abuse, and psychopathology. *Journal of Abnormal Psychology, 100,* 427–448.

Sher, K. J., Wood, M. D., Wood, P. K., & Raskin, G. (1996). Alcohol outcome expectancies and alcohol use: A latent variable cross-lagged panel study. *Journal of Abnormal Psychology, 105,* 561–574.

Shera, C. A., Guinan, J. J., & Oxenham, A. J. (2002). Revised estimates of human cochlear tuning from otoacoustic and behavioral measurements. *Proceedings of the National Academy of Sciences, 99*(5), 3318–3323.

Sherer, M. R., & Schreibman, L. (2005). Individual behavioral profiles and predictors of treatment effectiveness for children with autism. *Journal of Consulting and Clinical Psychology, 73,* 525–538.

Shergill, S. S., Brammer, M. J., Williams, S. C., Murray, R. M., & McGuire, P. K. (2000). Mapping auditory hallucinations in schizophrenia using functional magnetic resonance imaging. *Archives of General Psychiatry, 57,* 1033–1038.

Sherif, M. (1937). An experimental approach to the study of attitudes. *Sociometry, 1,* 90–98.

Sherman, J. W., & Bessenoff, G. R. (1999). Stereotypes as source-monitoring cues: On the interaction between episodic and semantic memory. *Psychological Science, 10,* 106–110.

Sherman, R. T., & Thompson, R. A. (2004). The female athlete triad. *Journal of School Nursing, 20,* 197–202.

Sherman, S. J. (1980). On the self-erasing nature of errors of prediction. *Journal of Personality and Social Psychology, 39,* 211–221.

Sherman, S. M. (2007). The thalamus is more than just a relay. *Current Opinion in Neurobiology, 17*(4), 417–422.

Sherwin, B. B., & Gelfand, M. M. (1987). The role of androgen in the maintenance of sexual functioning in oophorectomized women. *Psychosomatic Medicine, 49,* 397–409.

Sherwin, B. B., Gelfand, M. M., & Brender, W. (1985). Androgen enhances sexual motivation in females: A prospective crossover study of sex steroid administration in the surgical menopause. *Psychosomatic Medicine, 47,* 339–351.

Shields, L. B. E., Hunsaker, D. M., Muldoon, S., Corey, T. S., & Spivack, B. S. (2005). Risk factors associated with sudden unexplained infant death: A prospective study of infant care practices in Kentucky. *Pediatrics, 116,* e13–e20.

Shifman, S., Bhomra, A., Smiley, S., Wray, N. R., James, M. R., Martin, N. G., Hettema, J. M., An, S. S., Neale, M. C., van den Oord, E. J. C. G., Kendler, K. S., Chen, X., Boomsma, D. I., Middeldorp, C. M., Hottenga, J. J., Slagboom, P. E., & Flint, J. (2008). A whole genome association study of neuroticism using DNA pooling. *Molecular Psychiatry, 13,* 302–312.

Shiller, R. J. (2001). *Irrational exuberance.* Princeton, NJ: Princeton University Press.

Shimamura, A. P., Berry, J. M., Mangels, J. A., Rusting, C. L., & Jurica, P. J. (1995). Memory and cognitive abilities in university professors: Evidence for successful aging. *Psychological Science, 6,* 271–277.

Shimazu, T., Kuriyama1, S., Ohmori-Matsuda, K., Kikuchi, N., Nakaya, N., & Tsuji, I. (2009). Increase in body mass index category since age 20 years and all-cause mortality: A prospective cohort study (the Ohsaki Study). *International Journal of Obesity, 33,* 490–496.

Shin, L. M., Rauch, S. L., & Pitman, R. K. (2006). Amygdala, medial prefrontal cortex, and hippocampal function in PTSD. *Annals of the New York Academy of Sciences, 1071,* 67–79.

Shin, S.-M., Chow, C., Camacho-Gonzalves, T., Levy, R. J., Allen, I. E., & Leff, H. S. (2005). A meta-analytic review of racial-ethnic matching for African American and Caucasian American clients and clinicians. *Journal of Counseling Psychology, 52,* 45–56.

Shinskey, J. L., & Munakata, Y. (2005). Familiarity breeds searching. *Psychological Science, 16,* 596–600.

Shiraev, E., & Levy, D. (2004). *Cross-cultural psychology: Critical thinking and contemporary applications* (2nd ed.). Boston: Allyn & Bacon.

Shiwach, R. S., Reid, W. H., & Carmody, T. J. (2001). An analysis of reported deaths following electroconvulsive therapy in Texas, 1993–1998. *Psychiatric Services, 52,* 1095–1097.

Shneidman, E. S. (1987). A psychological approach to suicide. In G. VandenBos & B. K. Bryant (Eds.), *Cataclysms, crises, and catastrophes: Psychology in action. The master lectures* (Vol. 6, pp. 147–183). Washington, DC: American Psychological Association.

Shoda, Y., & LeeTiernan, S. (2002). What remains invariant? Finding order within a person's thoughts, feelings, and behavior across situations. In D. Cervone & W. Mischel (Eds.), *Advances in personality science* (pp. 241–270). New York: Guilford Press.

Shoda, Y., & Mischel, W. (2006). Applying meta-theory to achieve generalisability and precision in personality science: Comment. *Applied Psychology: An International Review, 55,* 439–452.

Shook, N. J., & Fazio, R. H. (2008). Interracial roommate relationships: An experimental field test of the contact hypothesis. *Psychological Science, 19,* 717–723.

Shorter, E., & Healy, D. (2007). *Shock therapy: A history of electroconvulsive treatment in mental illness.* Piscataway, NJ: Rutgers University Press.

Shreeve, J. (1993, June). Touching the phantom. *Discover,* 35–42.

Shu, S. Y., Wu, Y. M., Bao, X. M., Wen, Z. B., Huang, F. H., Li, S. X., et al. (2002). A new area in the human brain associated with learning and memory: Immunohistochemical and functional MRI analysis. *Molecular Psychiatry, 7,* 1018–1022.

Shweder, R. A., Much, N. C., Mahapatra, M., & Park, L. (1994). The "big three" of morality (autonomy, community, and divinity), and the "big three" explanations of suffering, as well. In A. Brandt & P. Rozin (Eds.), *Morality and health.* Stanford, CA: Stanford University Press.

Siber, L. (2005, December). Precious metal. *Skiing, 58*(4), 16E.

Sibley, C. G., Wilson, M. S., & Duckitt, J. (2007). Effects of dangerous and competitive worldviews on right-wing authoritarianism and social dominance orientation over a five-month period. *Political Psychology, 28,* 357–371.

Siebert, S. E., & Kraimer, M. L. (2001). The five-factor model of personality and career success. *Journal of Vocational Behavior, 58,* 1–21.

Siegel, J. M. (2005). Clues to the functions of mammalian sleep. *Nature, 437,* 1264–1271.

Siegal, M. (1997). *Knowing children: Experiments in conversation and cognition* (2nd ed.). Hove, UK: Psychology Press/Erlbaum/Taylor & Francis.

Siegel, S. (2005). Drug tolerance, drug addiction, and drug anticipation. *Current Directions in Psychological Science, 14,* 296–300.

Siegel, S., Hirson, R. E., Krank, M. D., & McCully, J. (1982). Heroin "overdose" death: The contribution of drug associated environmental cues. *Science, 216,* 430–437.

Siegler, R. S. (1994). Cognitive variability: A key to understanding cognitive development. *Current Directions in Psychological Science, 3,* 1–4.

Siegler, R. S. (2003). Thinking and intelligence. In M. H. Bornstein, L. Davidson, C. L. M. Keyes, & K. A. Moore (Eds.), *Well-being: Positive development across the life course. Crosscurrents in Contemporary Psychology* (pp. 311–320). Mahwah, NJ: Lawrence Erlbaum Associates Publishers.

Siegler, R. S. (2006). Microgenetic analysis of learning. In W. Damon & R. M. Lerner (Series Eds.) & D. Kuhn & R. Siegler (Vol. Eds.), *Handbook of child psychology: Vol. 2. Cognition, perception, and language* (6th ed.). New York: Wiley.

Siep, N., Roefs, A., Roebroeck, A., Havermans, R., Bonte, M. L., & Jansen, A. (2009). Hunger is the best spice: An fMRI study of the effects of attention, hunger and calorie content on food reward processing in the amygdala and orbitofrontal cortex. *Behavioural Brain Research, 198*(1), 149–158.

Siever, L. J. (2008). Neurobiology of aggression and violence. *American Journal of Psychiatry, 165,* 429–442.

Sigalovsky, N. (2003). Awareness under general anesthesia. *American Association of Nurse Anesthetists Journal, 71,* 373–379.

Silber, M. H. (2001). Sleep disorders. *Neurology Clinics, 19,* 173–186.

Silbert, M. H., & Pines, A. M. (1984). Pornography and sexual abuse of women. *Sex Roles, 10,* 857–868.

Silver, E. (1995). Punishment or treatment? Comparing the lengths of confinement of successful and unsuccessful insanity defendants. *Law and Human Behavior, 19,* 375–388.

Silver, E., Cirincione, C., & Steadman, H. J. (1994). Demythologizing inaccurate perceptions of the insanity defense. *Law and Human Behavior, 18,* 63–70.

Silver, S. M., Rogers, S., Knipe, J., & Colelli, G. (2005). EMDR therapy following the 9/11 terrorist attacks: A community-based intervention project in New York City. *International Journal of Stress Management, 12,* 29–42.

Silverman, K., Evans, A. M., Strain, E. C., & Griffiths, R. R. (1992). Withdrawal syndrome after the double-blind cessation of caffeine consumption. *New England Journal of Medicine, 327,* 1109–1114.

Silverthorne, C. (2001). Leadership effectiveness and personality: A cross cultural evaluation. *Personality & Individual Differences, 30,* 303–309.

Simcock, G., & Hayne, H. (2002). Breaking the barrier? Children fail to translate their preverbal memories into language. *Psychological Science, 13,* 225–231.

Simeon, D., Greenberg, J., Knutelska, M., Schmeidler, J., & Hollander, E. (2003). Peritraumatic reactions associated with the World Trade Center disaster. *The American Journal of Psychiatry, 160,* 1702–1705.

Simion, F., Cassia, V. M., Turati, C., & Valenza, E. (2003). Non-specific perceptual biases at the origins of face processing. In O. Pascalis & A. Slater (Eds.), *The development of face processing in infancy and early childhood* (pp. 13–25). Hauppauge, NY: Nova Science.

Simon, G. E., Savarino, J., Operskalski, B., & Wang, P. S. (2006). Suicide risk during antidepressant treatment. *American Journal of Psychiatry, 163,* 41–47.

Simon, G. E., & von Korff, M. (2006). Medical co-morbidity and validity of DSM-IV depression criteria. *Psychological Medicine, 36,* 27–36.

Simons, D. J., & Ambinder, M. S. (2005). Change blindness: Theory and consequences. *Current Directions in Psychological Science, 14,* 44–48.

Simons, R., & Valk, P. J. L. (2009). Melatonin for commercial aircrew? *Biological Rhythm Research, 40*(1), 7–16.

Simons, T., & Roberson, Q. (2003). Why managers should care about fairness: The effects of aggregate justice perceptions on organizational outcomes. *Journal of Applied Psychology, 88,* 432–443.

Simonton, D. K. (1984). *Genius, creativity and leadership.* Cambridge, MA: Harvard University Press.

Simonton, D. K. (1999). Creativity and genius. In L. Pervin & O. John (Eds.), *Handbook of personality research* (2nd ed., pp. 629–652). New York: Guilford.

Simonton, D. K. (2002). In C. R. Snyder & J. Shane (Eds.), *Handbook of positive psychology* (pp. 189–201). London: Oxford University Press.

Simonton, D. K. (2004). *Creativity in science: Chance, logic, genius, and zeitgeist.* Cambridge, UK: Cambridge University Press.

Simonton, D. K., & Song, A. V. (2009). Eminence, IQ, physical and mental health, and achievement domain: Cox's 282 geniuses revisited. *Psychological Science, 20,* 429–434.

Simpson, J. A., & Kenrick, D. T. (1997). *Evolutionary social psychology.* Mahwah, NJ: Erlbaum.

Simpson, J. A., Winterheld, H. A., Rholes, W. S., & Oriña, M. M. (2007). Working models of attachment and reactions to different forms of caregiving from romantic partners. *Journal of Personality and Social Psychology, 93,* 466–477.

Simpson, S., Hurtley, S. M., & Marx, J. (2000). Immune cell networks. *Science, 290,* 79.

Simpson, S. G., McMahon, F. J., McInnis, M. G., MacKinnon, D. F., Edwin, D., Folstein, S. E., et al. (2002). Diagnostic reliability of bipolar II disorder. *Archives of General Psychiatry, 59,* 736–740.

Simpson, S. H., Eurich, D. T., Majumdar, S. R., Padwal, R. S., Tsuyuki, R. T., et al. (2006). A meta-analysis of the association between adherence to drug therapy and mortality. *British Medical Journal, 333.*

Sinclair, R. C., Hoffman, C., Mark, M. M., Martin, L. L., & Pickering, T. L. (1994). Construct accessibility and the misattribution of arousal. *Psychological Science, 5*(1), 15–19.

Singer, L. T., Arendt, R., Minnes, S., Farkas, K., Salvator, A., Kirchner, L., & Kliegman, R. (2002). Cognitive and motor outcomes of cocaine-exposed infants. *Journal of the American Medical Association, 287*(15), 1952–1960.

Singer, L. T., Arendt, R., Minnes, S., Salvator, A., Siegel, C., & Lewis, B. A. (2001). Developing language skills of cocaine-exposed infants. *Pediatrics, 107,* 1057–1064.

Singer, L. T., Minnes, S., Short, E., Arendt, R., Farkas, K., Lewis, B., et al. (2004). Cognitive outcomes of preschool children with prenatal cocaine exposure. *Journal of the American Medical Association, 291,* 2448–2456.

Singh, H., & O'Boyle, M. W. (2004). Interhemispheric interaction during global-local processing in mathematically gifted adolescents, average-ability youth, and college students. *Neuropsychology, 18,* 371–377.

Singh, S. M., & O'Reilly, R. (2009). (Epi)genomics and neurodevelopment in schizophrenia: Monozygotic twins discordant for schizophrenia augment the search for disease-related (epi)genomic alterations. *Genome, 52*(1), 8–19.

Sinha, R., & Parsons, O. A. (1996). Multivariate response patterning of fear and anger. *Cognition and Emotion, 10,* 173–198.

Sirvio, J. (1999). Strategies that support declining cholinergic neurotransmission in Alzheimer's disease patients. *Gerontology, 45,* 3–14.

Sitzmann, T., Brown, K. G., Casper, W. D., Ely, K., & Zimmerman, R. D. (2008). A review and meta-analysis of the nomological network of trainee reactions. *Journal of Applied Psychology, 93,* 280–295.

Skaar, D. A., Shao, Y., Haines, J. L., Stenger, J. E., Jaworski, J., Martin, E. R., et al. (2005). Analysis of the RELN gene as a genetic risk factor for autism. *Molecular Psychiatry, 10,* 563–571.

Skinner, B. F. (1961). *Cumulative record* (3rd ed.). Englewood Cliffs, NJ: Prentice Hall.

Skitka, L. J., Bauman, C. W., & Sargis, E. G. (2005). Moral conviction: Another contributor to attitude strength or something more? *Journal of Personality and Social Psychology, 88,* 895–917.

Skre, I., Onstad, S., Toregersen, S., Lyngren, S., & Kringlin, E. (2000). The heritability of common phobic fear: A twin study of a clinical sample. *Journal of Anxiety Disorders, 14,* 549–562.

Slade, E. P., & Wissow, L. S. (2004). Spanking in early childhood and later behavior problems: A prospective study of infants and young toddlers. *Pediatrics, 113,* 1321–1330.

Slamecka, N. J., & McElree, B. (1983). Normal forgetting of verbal lists as a function of their degree of learning. *Journal of Experimental Psychology: Learning, Memory, and Cognition, 9,* 384–397.

Slater, A., Mattock, A., Brown, E., & Bremmer, J. G. (1991). Form perception at birth. *Journal of Experimental Child Psychology, 51,* 395–406.

Slavin, K. V. (2008). Peripheral nerve stimulation for neuropathic pain. *Neurotherapeutics, 5*(1), 100–106.

Slentz, C. A., Duscha, B. D., Johnson, J. L., Ketchum, K., Aiken, L. B., Samsa, G. P., et al. (2004). Effects of the amount of exercise on body weight, body composition, and measures of central obesity: STRRIDE—A randomized controlled study. *Archives of Internal Medicine, 164,* 31–39.

Sloan, D. M., Marx, B. P., & Epstein, E. M. (2005). Further examination of the exposure model underlying the efficacy of written emotional disclosure. *Journal of Consulting and Clinical Psychology, 73,* 549–554.

Sloan, D. M., Strauss, M. E., & Wisner, K. L. (2001). Diminished response to pleasant stimuli by depressed women. *Journal of Abnormal Psychology, 110,* 488–493.

Slocombe, K. E., & Zuberbühler, K. (2005). Functionally referential communication in a chimpanzee. *Current Biology, 15,* 1779–1784.

Slomkowski, C., & Dunn, J. (1996). Young children's understanding of other people's beliefs and feelings and their connected communication with friends. *Developmental Psychology, 32,* 442–447.

Slotnick, S. D., & Schacter, D. L. (2004). A sensory signature that distinguishes true from fales memories. *Nature Neuroscience, 7,* 664–672.

Slutske, W., Eisen, S., Xian, H., True, W., Lyons, M. J., Goldberg, J., et al. (2001). A twin study of the association between pathological gambling and antisocial personality disorder. *Journal of Abnormal Psychology, 110,* 297–308.

Small, B. J., & Bäckman, L. (1999). Time to death and cognitive performance. *Current Directions in Psychological Science, 8,* 168–172.

Small, D. M., Gregory, M. D., Mak, Y. E., Mesulam, M. M., & Parrish, T. (2003). Dissociation of neural representation of intensity and valuation in human gustation. *Neuron, 39,* 701–711.

Small, G., & Dubois, B. (2007). A review of compliance to treatment in Alzheimer's disease: potential benefits of a transdermal patch. *Current Medical Research & Opinion, 23*(11), 2705–2713.

Smillie, L. D., Pickering, A. D., & Jackson, C. J. (2006). The new Reinforcement Sensitivity Theory: Implications for personality measurement. *Personality and Social Psychology Review, 10,* 320–335.

Smith, A. M., Malo, S. A., Laskowski, E. R., Sabick, M., Cooney, W. P., III, Finnie, S. B., et al. (2000). A multidisciplinary study of the 'yips' phenomenon in golf: An exploratory analysis. *Sports Medicine, 30,* 423–437.

Smith, A. P., & Maben, A. (1993). Effects of sleep deprivation, lunch, and personality on performance, mood, and cardiovascular function. *Physiology and Behavior, 54*(5), 967–972.

Smith, E., & Mackie, D. (2007). *Social psychology.* Philadelphia, PA: Psychology Press.

Smith, E., & Quellar, S. (2001). Mental representations. In A. Tesser & N. Schwarz (Eds.), *Blackwell handbook of social psychology: Intraindividual processes* (pp. 499–517). Oxford, UK: Blackwell.

Smith, E. E., Geva, A., Jonides, J., Miller, A., Reuter-Lorenz, P., & Koeppe, R. A. (2001). The neural basis of task-switching in working memory: Effects of performance and aging. *Proceedings of the National Academy of Sciences, 98,* 2095–2100.

Smith, G. C. S., & White, I. R. (2006). Predicting the risk for sudden infant death syndrome from obstetric characteristics: A retrospective cohort study of 505,011 live births. *Pediatrics, 117,* 60–66.

Smith, G. T., Simmons, J. R., Flory, K., Annus, A. M., & Hill, K. K. (2007). Thinness and eating expectancies predict subsequent binge-eating and purging behavior among adolescent girls. *Journal of Abnormal Psychology, 116,* 188–197.

Smith, K. M., Larive, L. L., & Romananelli, F. (2002). Club drugs: Methylenedioxymethamphetamine, flunitrazepam, ketamine hydrochloride, and gamma-hydroxybutyrate. *American Journal of Health Systems Pharmacology, 59,* 1067–1076.

Smith, L. B., & Sera, M. D. (1992). A developmental analysis of the polar structure of dimensions. *Cognitive Psychology, 24,* 99–142.

Smith, M. L., Glass, G. V., & Miller, T. I. (1980). *The benefits of psychotherapy.* Baltimore: Johns Hopkins University Press.

Smith, N. T. (2002). A review of the published literature into cannabis withdrawal symptoms in human users. *Addiction, 97,* 621–632.

Smith, P. B., & Bond, M. H. (1999). *Social psychology across cultures: Analysis and perspectives* (2nd ed.). Boston: Allyn & Bacon.

Smith, P. C., & Kendall, L. M. (1963). Retranslation of expectations: An approach to the construction of unambiguous anchors for rating scales. *Journal of Applied Psychology, 47,* 149–155.

Smith, P., Frank, J., Bondy, S., & Mustard, C. (2008). Do changes in job control predict differences in health status? Results from a longitudinal national survey of Canadians. *Psychosomatic Medicine, 70,* 85–91.

Smith, P. K., & Drew, L. M. (2002). Grandparenthood. In M. H. Bornstein (Ed.), *Handbook of parenting* (2nd ed.). Mahwah, NJ: Erlbaum.

Smith, R. M., Tivarus, M., Campbell, H. L., Hillier, A., & Beversdorf, D. Q. (2006). Apparent transient effects of recent "ecstasy" use on cognitive performance and extrapyramidal signs in human subjects. *Cognitive & Behavioral Neurology, 19*(3), 157–164.

Smith, R. W., Uchino, B. N., Berg, C. A., Florsheim, P., Pearce, G., Hawkins, M., Henry, N. J. M., Beveridge, R. M., Skinner, M. A., Hopkins, P. N., & Yoon, H.-C. (2008). Associations of self-reports with spouse ratings of negative affectivity, dominance, and affiliation with coronary artery disease: Where should we look and who should we ask when studying personality and health? *Health Psychology, 27,* 676–684.

Smith, S., & Freedman, D. G. (1983, April). *Mother-toddler interaction and maternal perception of child temperament in two ethnic groups: Chinese-American and European-American.* Paper presented at the meeting of the Society for Research in Child Development, Detroit, MI.

Smith, S. L., & Donnerstein, E. (1998). Harmful effects of exposure to media violence: Learning of aggression, emotional desensitization, and fear. In R. G. Geen & E. Donnerstein (Eds.), *Human aggression* (pp. 230–247). San Diego: Academic Press.

Smith, S. M., Glenberg, A. M., & Bjork, R. A. (1978). Environmental context and human memory. *Memory & Cognition, 6,* 342–355.

Smith, S. M., Vela, E., & Williamson, J. E. (1988). Shallow input processing does not induce environmental context-dependent recognition. *Bulletin of the Psychonomic Society, 26,* 537–540.

Smith, S. S., O'Hara, B. F., Persico, A. M., Gorelick, D. A., Newlin, D. B., Vlahov, D., et al. (1992). Genetic vulnerability to drug abuse: The D2 dopamine receptor Taq i B1 restriction fragment length polymorphism appears more frequently in polysubstance abusers. *Archives of General Psychiatry, 49,* 723–727.

Smith, T. B., Constantine, M. G., Dunn, T. W., Dinehart, J. M., & Montoya, J. A. (2006). Multicultural education in the mental health professions: A meta-analytic review. *Journal of Counseling Psychology, 53,* 132–145.

Smith, T. W., Orleans, C. T., & Jenkins, C. D. (2004). Prevention and health promotion: Decades of progress, new challenges, and an emerging agenda. *Health Psychology, 23,* 126–131.

Smith, T. W., Uchino, B. N., Berg, C. A., Florsheim, P., Pearce, G., Hawkins, M., Hopkins, P. N., & Yoon, H.-C. (2007). Hostile personality traits and coronary artery calcification in middle-aged and older married couples: Different effects for self-reports versus spouse ratings. *Psychosomatic Medicine 69,* 441–448.

Smith, V. L. (1991). Prototypes in the courtroom: Lay representations of legal concepts. *Journal of Personality and Social Psychology, 44,* 787–797.

Smith-Crowe, K., Burke, M. J., & Landis, R. S. (2003). Organizational climate as a moderator of safety knowledge–safety performance relationships. *Journal of Organizational Behavior, 24,* 861–876.

Smither, J. W., London, M., & Reilly, R. R. (2005). Does performance improve following multisource feedback? A theoretical model, meta-analysis, and review of empirical findings. *Personnel Psychology, 58,* 33–66.

Smits, J. A. J., O'Cleirigh, C. M., & Otto, M. W. (2006). Combining cognitive-behavioral therapy and pharmacotherapy for the treatment of panic disorder. *Journal of Cognitive Psychotherapy, 20,* 75–84.

Smoller, J. W. (2008). Genetics of mood and anxiety disorder. In J. W. Smoller, B. R. Sheidley, & M. T. Tsaung (Eds.), *Psychiatric genetics: Applications in clinical practice* (pp. 131–176). Arlington: American Psychiatric Publishing.

Snarey, J. (1987). A question of morality. *Psychological Bulletin, 97,* 202–232.

Snellingen, T., Evans, J. R., Ravilla, T., & Foster, A. (2002). Surgical interventions for age-related cataract. *Cochrane Database System Review, 2,* CD001323.

Snowden, L. R., & Cheung, F. (1990). Use of inpatient mental health services by members of ethnic minority groups. *American Psychologist, 45,* 347–355.

Snyder, C. R., & Lopez, S. J. (2006). *Handbook of positive psychology.* New York: Oxford University Press.

Snyder, C. R., & Lopez, S. J. (2007). *Positive psychology: The scientific and practical explorations of human strengths.* New York: Sage.

Snyder, T. D., Dillow, S. A., & Hoffman, C. M. (2008). *Digest of Education Statistics: 2007* (Report No. NCES 2008-022). Washington, D. C.: National Center for Education Statistics, Institute of Education Sciences, U. S. Department of Education. Retrieved June 9, 2009, from http://nces.ed.gov/programs/digest/d07.

Snyderman, M., & Rothman, S. (1987). Survey of expert opinion on intelligence and aptitude testing. *American Psychologist, 42,* 137–144.

Sobel, D. M., & Kirkham, N. Z. (2006). Blickets and babies: The development of causal reasoning in toddlers and infants. *Developmental Psychology, 42,* 1103–1115.

Sohlberg, S., & Jansson, B. (2002). Unconscious responses to "mommy and I are one": Does gender matter? In R. F. Bornstein & J. M. Masling (Eds.), *The psychodynamics of gender and gender role.Vol. 10: Empirical studies in psychoanalytic theories* (pp. 165–201). Washington, DC: American Psychological Association.

Sohler, N., & Bromet, E. J. (2003). Does racial bias influence psychiatric diagnoses assigned at first hospitalization? *Social Psychiatry and Psychiatric Epidemiology, 38,* 463–472.

Soken, N. H., & Pick, A. D. (1992). Intermodal perception of happy and angry expressive behaviors by seven-month-old infants. *Child Development, 63,* 787–795.

Sokolowska, M., Siegel, S., & Kim, J. A. (2002). Intraadministration associations: Conditional hyperalgesia elicited by morphine onset cues. *Journal of Experimental Psychology: Animal Behavior Processes, 28,* 309–320.

Solomon, R. L. (1980). The opponent-process theory of acquired motivation: The costs of pleasure and the benefits of pain. *American Psychologist, 35,* 691–712.

Solomon, R. L., Kamin, L. J., & Wynne, L. C. (1953). Traumatic avoidance learning: The outcomes of several extinction procedures with dogs. *Journal of Abnormal and Social Psychology, 48,* 291–302.

Solomonson, A. L., & Lance, C. E. (1997). Examination of the relationship between true halo and halo error in performance ratings. *Journal of Applied Psychology, 82,* 665–674.

Solowij, N., Stephens, R. S., Roffman, R. A., Babor, T., Kadden, R., Miller, M., et al. (2002). Cognitive functioning of long-term heavy cannabis users seeking treatment. *Journal of American Medical Association, 287,* 1123–1131.

Sombrero, S. (2008, December 29). Failed apocalyptic psychic predictions for 2008. Retrieved January 15, 2009, from http://www.panicwatch.org/article.pl?title=Failed%20Apocalyptic%20Psychic%20Predictions%20for%202008.

Song, H., & Baillargeon, R. (2008). Infants' reasoning about others' false perceptions. *Developmental Psychology, 44,* 1789–1795.

Song, H., Onishi, K. H., Baillargeon, R., & Fisher, C. (2008). Can an actor's false belief be corrected by an appropriate communication? Psychological reasoning in 18.5-month-old infants. *Cognition, 109,* 295–315.

Sorce, J., Emde, R., Campos, J., & Klinnert, M. (1981, April). *Maternal emotional signaling: Its effect on the visual cliff behavior of one-year-olds.* Paper presented at the meeting of the Society for Research in Child Development, Boston, MA.

Sørensen, H. J., Mortensen, E. L., Reinisch, J. M., & Mednick, S. A. (2003). Do hypertension and diuretic treatment in pregnancy increase the risk of schizophrenia in offspring? *American Journal of Psychiatry, 160,* 464–468.

Sorrentino, R. M., & Roney, C. J. R. (2000). *The uncertain mind: Individual differences in facing the unknown.* Philadelphia: Psychology Press.

Soto, D., Funes, M. J., Guzmán-García, A., Warbrick, T., Rotshtein, P., & Humphreys, G. W. (2009). Pleasant music overcomes the loss of awareness in patients with visual neglect. *Proceedings of the National Academy of Sciences, 106*(14), 6011–6016.

South, S. C., & Krueger, R. F. (2008). An interactionist perspective on genetic and environmental contributions to personality. *Social and Personality Psychology Compass, 2*(2), 929–948.

Sowdon, J. (2001). Is depression more prevalent in old age? *Australian & New Zealand Journal of Psychiatry, 35,* 782–787.

Sowell, E. R., Delis, D., Stiles, J., & Jernigan, T. L. (2001). Improved memory functioning and frontal lobe maturation between childhood and adolescence: A structural MRI study. *Journal of the International Neuropsychological Society, 7,* 312–322.

Sowell, E. R., Peterson, B. S., Thompson, P. M., Welcome, S. E., Henkenius, A. L., & Toga, A. W. (2003). Mapping cortical change across the human life span. *Nature Neuroscience, 6,* 309–315.

Sowell, T. (2005). *Black rednecks and white liberals.* San Francisco: Encounter Books.

Spalletta, G., Serra, L., Fadda, L., Ripa, A., Bria, P., & Caltagirone, C. (2007). Unawareness of motor impairment and emotions in right hemispheric stroke: a preliminary investigation. *International Journal of Geriatric Psychiatry, 22*(12), 1241–1246.

Spanagel, R., & Weiss, F. (1999). The dopamine hypothesis of reward: Past and current status. *Trends in Neuroscience, 22,* 521–527.

Spangler, G., Fremmer-Bombik, E., & Grossman, K. (1996). Social and individual determinants of infant attachment security and disorganization. *Infant Mental Health Journal, 17,* 127–139.

Spano, M. S., Ellgren, M., Wang, X., & Hurd, Y. L. (2007). Prenatal cannabis exposure increases heroin seeking with allostatic changes in limbic enkephalin systems in adulthood. *Biological Psychiatry, 61,* 554–563.

Spanos, N. P. (1994). Multiple identity enactments and multiple personality disorder: A sociocognitive perspective. *Psychological Bulletin, 116,* 143–165.

Spanos, N. P., Burnley, M. C. E., & Cross, P. A. (1993). Response expectancies and interpretations as determinants of hypnotic responding. *Journal of Personality and Social Psychology, 65*(6), 1237–1242.

Sparing, R., Dafotakis, M., Meister, I. G., Thirugnanasambandam, N., & Fink, G. R. (2008). Enhancing language performance with non-invasive brain stimulation—A transcranial direct current stimulation study in healthy humans. *Neuropsychologia, 46*(1), 261–268.

Sparks, K., Cooper, C., Fried, Y., & Shirom, A. (1997). The effects of hours of work on health: A meta-analytic review. *Journal of Occupational and Organizational Psychology, 70,* 391–408.

Sparks, K., Faragher, B., & Cooper, C. L. (2001). Well-being and occupational health in the 21st century workplace. *Journal of Occupational and Organizational Psychology, 74,* 489–509.

Spears, R., Postmes, T., Lea, M., & Watt, S. E. (2001). A SIDE view of social influence. In J. P. Forgas & K. D. Williams (Eds.), *Social influence: Direct and indirect processes. The Sydney symposium of social psychology* (pp. 331–350). Philadelphia, PA: Psychology Press.

Speckhard, A. (2002). Voices from the inside: Psychological responses to toxic disasters. In J. M. Havenaar & J. G. Cwikel (Eds.), *Toxic turmoil: Psychological and societal consequences of ecological disasters* (pp. 217–236). New York: Plenum.

Specter, M. (2004, February 2). Miracle in a bottle. *New Yorker,* 64–75.

Specter, M. (2005, May 23). Higher risk. *New Yorker,* 38–45.

Spector, P. E. (1985). Measurement of human service staff satisfaction: Development of the Job Satisfaction Survey. *American Journal of Community Psychology, 13,* 693–713.

Spector, P. E. (2002). Employee control and occupational stress. *Current Directions in Psychological Science, 11,* 133–136.

Spector, P. E. (2003). *Industrial & organizational psychology: Research and practice* (3rd ed.). New York: Wiley.

Spector, P. E., Fox, S., & Domalgaski, T. (2006). Emotions, violence, and counterproductive work behavior. In E. K. Kelloway, J. Barling, & J. J. Hurrell (Eds.), *Handbook of workplace violence* (pp. 29–46). Thousand Oaks, CA: Sage.

Spelke, E. S., Breinlinger, K., Macomber, J., & Jacobson, K. (1992). Origins of knowledge. *Psychological Review, 99,* 605–632.

Spence, S. H., Sheffield, J. K., & Donovan, C. L. (2005). Long-term outcome of a school-based, universal approach to prevention of depression in adolescents. *Journal of Consulting and Clinical Psychology, 73,* 160–167.

Spencer, T. J. (2002). Attention-deficit/hyperactivity disorder. *Archives of Neurology, 59,* 314–316.

Sperry, R. W. (1968). Hemisphere deconnection and unity in conscious awareness. *American Psychologist, 23,* 723–733.

Spiegel, D. (Ed.). (1994). *Dissociation: Culture, mind, and body.* Washington, DC: American Psychiatric Press.

Spiegel, D. A., & Bruce, T. J. (1997). Benzodiazepines and exposure-based cognitive behavior therapies for panic disorder: Conclusions from combined treatment trials. *American Journal of Psychiatry, 151,* 876–881.

Spiegler, M. E., & Guevremont, D. C. (2009). *Contemporary behavior therapy* (5th ed.). New York: Cengage Learning.

Spinath, F. M., Harlaar, N., Ronald, A., & Plomin, R. (2004). Substantial genetic influence on mild mental impairment in early childhood. *American Journal of Mental Retardation, 109,* 34–43.

Spinhoven, P., Kuile, M., Kole-Snijders, A. M., Mansfeld, H. M., Ouden, D. L., & Vlaeyen, J. W. (2005). Catastrophizing and internal pain control as mediators of outcome in the multi-disciplinary treatment of chronic low back pain. *European Journal of Pain, 8,* 211–219.

Spitzer, R. L., Gibbon, M., Skodol, A. E., & Williams, J. B. W., & First, M. B. (Eds.). (1994). *DSM-IV casebook: A learning companion to the Diagnostic and Statistical Manual of Mental Disorders* (4th ed.). Washington, DC: American Psychiatric Association.

Springer, K., & Belk, A. (1994). The role of physical contact and association in early contamination sensitivity. *Developmental Psychology, 30*(6), 864–868.

Spychalski, A. C., Quinones, M. A., Gaugler, B. B., & Pohley, K. (1997). A survey of assessment center practices in organizations in the U.S. *Personnel Psychology, 50,* 71–90.

Squire, L. R. (1986). Mechanisms of memory. *Science, 232,* 1612–1619.

Squire, L. R. (1992). Memory and the hippocampus: A synthesis from findings with rats, monkeys, and humans. *Psychological Review, 99,* 195–231.

Squire, L. R. (2009). The legacy of patient H. M. for neuroscience. *Neuron, 61*(1), 6–9.

Srivastava, A., Locke, E. A., & Bartol, K. M. (2001). Money and subjective well- being: It's not the money, it's the motives. *Journal of Personality and Social Psychology, 80,* 959–971.

Srivastava, S., John, O. P., Gosling, S. D., & Potter, J. (2003). Development of personality in early and middle adulthood: Set like plaster or persistent change? *Journal of Personality and Social Psychology, 84,* 1041–1053.

Srivastava, S., Tamir, M., McGonigal, K. M., John, O. P., & Gross, J. J. (2009). The social costs of emotional suppression: A prospective study of the transition to college. *Journal of Personality and Social Psychology, 96,* 883–897.

Sroka, J. J., & Braida, L. D. (2005). Human and machine consonant recognition. *Speech Communication, 45,* 401–423.

St. John, W. (2003, September 28). In U.S. funeral industry, triple-wide isn't a trailer. *The New York Times,* p. 1.

Stacey, J., & Biblarz, T. J. (2001). (How) Does the sexual orientation of parents matter? *American Sociological Review, 66,* 159–183.

Staddon, J. E. R., & Ettinger, R. H. (1989). *Learning: An introduction to the principles of adaptive behavior.* San Diego: Harcourt Brace Jovanovich.

Stahl, S. M. (2002). Selective actions on sleep or anxiety by exploiting GABA-A/benzodiazepine receptor subtypes. *Journal of Clinical Psychiatry, 63,* 179–180.

Staley, J. K., Sanacora, G., Tamagnan, G., Maciejewski, P. K., Malison, R. T., Berman, R. M., et al. (2006). Sex differences in diencephalon serotonin transporter availability in major depression. *Biological Psychiatry, 59,* 40–47.

Stanley, B. G., Willett, V. L., Donias, H. W., & Ha-Lyen, H. (1993). The lateral hypothalamus: A primary site mediating excitatory aminoacid-elicited eating. *Brain Research, 63*(1–2), 41–49.

Stansfeld, S. A., & Marmot, M. G. (Eds.). (2002). *Stress and the heart: Psychosocial pathways to coronary heart disease.* London: BMJ Books.

Stapleton, S. (2001, February 19). Miles to go before I sleep: America is becoming a culture of sleeplessness. *Amednews.* Retrieved December 7, 2004, from http://www.ama-assn.org/sci-pubs/amnews/pick_01/hlsa0219.htm.

Starkman, N., & Rajani, N. (2002). The case for comprehensive sex education. *AIDS Patient Care & STDs, 16,* 313–318.

Starkstein, S. E., Fedoroff, J. P., Price, T. R., Leigguarda, R., & Robinson, R. G. (1992). Anosognosia in patients with cerebrovascular lesions: A study of causative factors. *Stroke, 23,* 1446–1453.

Stasser, G., Stewart, D., & Wittenbaum, G. M. (1995). Expert roles and information exchange during discussion: The importance of knowing who knows what. *Journal of Experimental Social Psychology, 31,* 244–265.

Staudt, M., Grodd, W., Niemann, G., Wildgruber, D., Erb, M., & Krageloh-Mann, I. (2001). Early left periventricular brain lesions induce right hemispheric organization of speech. *Neurology 2001, 57,* 122–125.

Stauffer, J. M., & Buckley, M. R. (2005). The existence and nature of racial bias in supervisory ratings. *Journal of Applied Psychology, 90,* 586–591.

Staw, B. M., Bell, N. E., & Clausen, J. A. (1986). The dispositional approach to job attitudes: A lifetime longitudinal test. *Administrative Science Quarterly, 31,* 56–77.

Staw, B. M., & Cohen-Charash, Y. (2005). The dispositional approach to job satisfaction: More than a mirage, but not yet an oasis. *Journal of Organizational Behavior, 26,* 59–78.

Steadman, H. J. (1993). *Reforming the insanity defense: An evaluation of pre- and post- Hinckley reforms.* New York: Guilford.

Steele, C. M. (1997). A threat in the air: How stereotypes shape intellectual identity and performance. *American Psychologist, 52,* 613–629.

Steele, C. M., & Aronson, J. (2000). Stereotype threat and the intellectual test performance of African Americans. In C. Stangor (Ed.), *Stereotypes and prejudice: Essential readings* (pp. 369–389). Philadelphia: Psychology Press/Taylor & Francis.

Stefanacci, L., Buffalo, E. A., Schmolck, H., & Squire, L. R. (2000). Profound amnesia after damage to the medial temporal lobe: A neuroanatomical and neuropsychological profile of patient E. P. *Journal of Neuroscience, 20*(18), 7024–7036.

Steiger, H., Young, S. N., Ng Ying Kin, N. M. K., Koerner, N., Israel, M., Lageix, P., & Paris, J. (2001). Implications of impulsive and affective symptoms for serotonin function in bulimia nervosa. *Psychological Medicine, 31,* 85–95.

Stein, D. J. (2006). Specific phobia: A disorder of fear conditioning and extinction. *CNS Spectrums, 11,* 248–251.

Stein, D. J., Seedat, S., Herman, A., Moomal, H., Heeringa, S. G., Kessler, R. C., et al. (2008). Lifetime prevalence of psychiatric disorders in South Africa. *British Journal of Psyciatry, 192,* 112–117.

Stein, E. (1999). *The mismeasure of desire: The science, theory and ethics of sexual orientation.* New York: Oxford University Press.

Stein, K. D., Goldman, M. S., & Del Boca, F. K. (2000). The influence of alcohol expectancy priming and mood manipulation on subsequent alcohol consumption. *Journal of Abnormal Psychology, 109,* 106–115.

Stein, M. A. (1993, November 30). Spacewalking repair team to work on Hubble flaws; shower head inspires a device to improve focusing ability. *Los Angeles Times,* A1, A5.

Steinberg, L. (2007). Risk taking in adolescence: New perspectives from brain and behavioral science. *Current Directions in Psychological Science, 16*(2), 55–59.

Steinberg, L. (2008). A social neuroscience perspective on adolescent risk-taking. *Developmental Review, 28*(1), 78–106.

Steinberg, L., Dornbusch, S. M., & Brown, B. B. (1992). Ethnic differences in adolescent achievement: An ecological perspective. *American Psychologist, 47,* 723–729.

Steinberg, L., Lamborn, S. D., Darling, N., Mounts, N. S., & Dornbusch, S. M. (1994). Over-time changes in adjustment and competence among adolescents from authoritative, authoritarian, indulgent, and neglectful families. *Child Development, 65,* 754–770.

Steindler, D. A., & Pincus, D. W. (2002). Stem cells and neuropoiesis in the adult human brain. *Lancet, 359,* 1047–1054.

Steiner, J. E., Glaser, D., Hawilo, M. E., & Berridge, K. C. (2001). Comparative expression of hedonic impact: Affective reactions to taste by human infants and other primates. *Neuroscience and Biobehavioral Reviews, 25,* 53–74.

Steiner, J. M., & Fahrenberg, J. (2000). Authoritarianism and social status of former members of the Waffen-SS and SS and of the Wehrmacht: An extension and reanalysis of the study published in 1970. *Koelner Zeitschrift fuer Soziologie und Sozialpsychologie, 52,* 329–348.

Stepanski, E. J., & Perlis, M. L. (2000). Behavioral sleep medicine. An emerging subspecialty in health psychology and sleep medicine. *Journal of Psychosomatic Research, 49,* 343–347.

Stephan, B. C. M., & Caine, D. (2009). Aberrant pattern of scanning in prosopagnosia reflects impaired face processing. *Brain and Cognition, 69,* 262–268.

Stephan, K. E., Marshall, J. C., Friston, K. J., Rowe, J. B., Ritzl, A., Zilles, K., & Fink, G. R. (2003). Lateralized cognitive processes and lateralized task control in the human brain. *Science, 301,* 384–386.

Stephens, R. S., Roffman, R. A., & Simpson, E. E. (1994). Treating adult marijuana dependence: A test of the relapse prevention model. *Journal of Consulting and Clinical Psychology, 62*(1), 92–99.

Stephenson, J. (2007, June 20). Jet lag relief? *Journal of the American Medical Association, 297*(23), 2578–2578.

Steptoe, A., Peacey, V., & Wardle, J. (2006). Sleep duration and health in young adults. *Archives of Internal Medicine, 166*, 1689–1692.

Steptoe, A., Wardle, J., & Marmot, M. (2005). Positive affect and health-related neuroendocrine, cardiovascular, and inflammatory processes. *Proceedings of the National Academy of Sciences, 102*, 6508–6512.

Steriade, M., & McCarley, R. W. (1990). *Brainstem control of wakefulness and sleep*. New York: Plenum.

Stern, K., & McClintock, M. K. (1998). Regulation of ovulation by human pheromones. *Nature, 392*, 177–179.

Sternberg, R. (2009). A duplex theory of love. In R. Sternberg & K. Weis (Eds.), *The new psychology of love* (pp. 184–199). New Haven, CT: Yale University Press.

Sternberg, R. J. (1985). *Beyond IQ: A triarchic theory of human intelligence*. Cambridge, England: Cambridge University Press.

Sternberg, R. J. (1988a). Triangulating love. In R. J. Sternberg & M. L. Barnes (Eds.), *The psychology of love* (pp. 500–520). New Haven: Yale University Press.

Sternberg, R. J. (1988b). *The triarchic mind*. New York: Cambridge Press.

Sternberg, R. J. (1996). *Successful intelligence*. New York: Simon & Schuster.

Sternberg, R. J. (1999). Ability and expertise: It's time to replace the current model of intelligence. *American Educator Spring 1999*, pp. 10–51.

Sternberg, R. J. (2001). What is the common thread of creativity? Its dialectical relation to intelligence and wisdom. *American Psychologist, 56*, 360–362.

Sternberg, R. J. (2004). Culture and intelligence. *American Psychologist, 59*, 325–338.

Sternberg, R. J., & Dess, N. K. (2001). Creativity for the new millennium. *American Psychologist, 56*, 332.

Sternberg, R. J., & Grigorenko, E. L. (Eds.). (2004a). *Creativity: From potential to realization*. Washington, DC: APA Books.

Sternberg, R. J., & Grigorenko, E. L. (Eds.). (2004b). *Culture and competence: Contexts of life success*. Washington, DC: APA Books.

Sternberg, R. J., & Kaufman, J. C. (1998). Human abilities. *Annual Review of Psychology, 49*, 479–502.

Sternberg, R. J., Lautrey, J., & Lubart, T. I. (2003). Where are we in the field of intelligence, how did we get here, and where are we going? In R. J. Sternberg, J. Lautrey, et al. (Eds.), *Models of intelligence: International perspectives* (pp. 3–25). Washington, DC: American Psychological Association.

Sternberg, R. J., & Lubart, T. I. (1992). Buy low and sell high: An investment approach to creativity. *Current Directions in Psychological Science, 1*(1), 1–5.

Sternberg, R. J., & O'Hara, L. A. (1999). Creativity and intelligence. In R. J. Sternberg, et al. (Eds.), *Handbook of creativity* (pp. 251–272). New York: Cambridge University Press.

Sternberg, R. J., & The Rainbow Project Coordinators. (2006). The Rainbow Project: Enhancing the SAT through assessments of analytical, practical, and creative skills. *Intelligence, 34*, 321–350.

Sternberg, R. J., Wagner, R. K., Williams, W. M., & Horvath, J. A. (1995). Testing common sense. *American Psychologist, 50*, 912–927.

Sternberg, R. J., & Williams, W. M. (1997). Does the graduate record examination predict meaningful success of graduate training of psychologists? A case study. *American Psychologist, 52*, 630–641.

Stettler, D. D., Yamahachi, H., Li, W., Denk, W., & Gilbert, C. D. (2006). Axons and synaptic boutons are highly dynamic in adult visual cortex. *Neuron, 49*, 877–887.

Steunenberg, B., Beekman, A. T. F., Deeg, D. J. H., & Kerkhof, A. J. F. M. (2006). Personality and the onset of depression in late life. *Journal of Affective Disorders, 92*, 243–251.

Stevens, A. (1996). *Private myths: Dreams and dreaming*. Cambridge, MA: Harvard University Press.

Stevens, A. A., & Weaver, K. E. (2009). Functional characteristics of auditory cortex in the blind. *Behavioural Brain Research, 196*, 134–138.

Stevens, R. D., & Bhardwaj, A. (2006). Approach to the comatose patient. *Critical Care Medicine, 34*(1), 31–41.

Stevenson, H. (1992). *A long way from being number one: What we can learn from East Asia*. Washington, DC: Federation of Behavior, Psychological and Cognitive Sciences.

Stevenson, R. J., & Boakes, R. A. (2003). A mnemonic theory of odor perception. *Psychological Review, 110*, 340–364.

Stewart, G. L. (2006). A meta-analytic review of relationships between team design features and team performance. *Journal of Management, 32*, 29–55.

Stewart, J. H. (2005). Hypnosis in contemporary medicine. *Mayo Clinic Proceedings, 80*, 511–524.

Stewart, S. E., Platko, J., Fagerness, J., Birns, J., Jenike, E., Smoller, J. W., et al. (2007). A genetic family-based association study of OLIG2 in obsessive-compulsive disorder. *Archives of General Psychiatry, 64*, 209–214.

Stewart, W. F., Ricci, J. A., Chee, E., Hahn, S. R., & Morganstein, D. (2003). Cost of lost productive work time among US workers with depression. *Journal of the American Medical Association, 289*, 3135–3144.

Stewart-Williams, S. (2004). The placebo puzzle: Putting together the pieces. *Health Psychology, 23*, 198–206.

Stice, E. (2001). A prospective test of the dual-pathway model of bulimic pathology: Mediating effects of dieting and negative affect. *Journal of Abnormal Psychology, 110*, 124–135.

Stice, E., & Fairburn, C. G. (2003). Dietary and dietary-depressive subtypes of bulimia nervosa show differential symptom presentation, social impairment, comorbidity, and course of illness. *Journal of Consulting and Clinical Psychology, 71*, 1090–1094.

Stice, E., & Shaw, H. (2004). Eating disorder prevention programs: A meta-analytic review. *Psychological Bulletin, 130*, 206–227.

Stice, E., Ragan, J., & Randall, P. (2004). Prospective relations between social support and depression: Differential direction of effects for parent and peer support? *Journal of Abnormal Psychology, 113*, 155–159.

Stice, E., Shaw, H., & Nathan, C. (2006). A meta-analytic review of obesity prevention programs for children and adolescents: The skinny on interventions that work. *Psychological Bulletin, 132*, 667–691.

Stickgold, R., James, L., & Hobson, J. A. (2000). Visual discrimination learning requires sleep after training. *Nature Neuroscience, 3*, 1237–1238.

Stickgold, R., Malia, A., Maguire, D., Roddenberry, D., & O'Connor, M. (2000). Replaying the game: Hypnagogic images in normals and amnesics. *Science, 290*, 350–353.

Stickgold, R., Rittenhouse, C. D., & Hobson, J. A. (1994). Dream splicing: A new technique for assessing thematic coherence in subjective reports of mental activity. *Consciousness and Cognition, 3*(1), 114–128.

Stiles, W. B., Barkham, M., Twigg, E., Mellor-Clark, J., & Cooper, M. (2006). Effectiveness of cognitive-behavioural, person-centered and psychodynamic therapies as practised in UK national health service settings. *Psychological Medicine, 36*, 555–566.

Stillman, J. A. (2002). Gustation: Intersensory experience par excellence. *Perception, 31*, 1491–1500.

Stillwell, M. E. (2002). Drug-facilitated sexual assault involving gamma- hydroxybutyric acid. *Journal of Forensic Science, 47*, 1133–1134.

Stipek, D. J., & Ryan, R. H. (1997). Economically disadvantaged preschoolers: Ready to learn but further to go. *Developmental Psychology, 33*, 711–723.

Stoff, D. M., Breiling, J., & Maser, J. D. (Eds.). (1997). *Handbook of antisocial behavior*. New York: Wiley.

Stone, J. (2003). Self-consistency for low self-esteem in dissonance processes: The role of self-standards. *Personality and Social Psychology Bulletin, 29*, 846–858.

Stone, J., & Cooper, J. (2001). A self-standards model of cognitive dissonance. *Journal of Experimental Social Psychology, 37*, 228–243.

Stone, J., & Fernandez, N. C. (2008). To practice what we preach: The use of hypocrisy and cognitive dissonance to motivate behavior change. *Social and Personality Psychology Compass, 2*, 1024–1051.

Stone, S. P., Halligan, P. W., & Greenwood, R. J. (1993). The incidence of neglect phenomena and related disorders in patients with acute left or right hemisphere stroke. *Age and Ageing, 22*, 46–52.

Stoney, C. M., & Finney, M. L. (2000). Social support and stress: Influences on lipid reactivity. *International Journal of Behavioral Medicine, 7*, 111–126.

Stoney, C. M., & Hughes, J. W. (1999). Lipid reactivity among men with a parental history of myocardial infarction. *Psychophysiology, 36*, 484–490.

Stoney, C. M., & Matthews, K. A. (1988). Parental history of hypertension and myocardial infarction predicts cardiovascular responses to behavioral stressors in middle-aged men and women. *Psychophysiology, 25*, 269–277.

Stoney, C. M., Bausserman, L., Niaura, R., Marcus, B., & Flynn, M. (1999). Lipid reactivity to stress: II. Biological and behavioral influences. *Health Psychology, 18*, 251–261.

Stoney, C. M., Niaura, R., Bausserman, L., & Matacin, M. (1999). Lipid reactivity to stress: I. Comparison of chronic and acute stress responses in middle-aged airline pilots. *Health Psychology, 18*, 241–250.

Strain, E. C., Mumford, G. K., Silverman, K., & Griffiths, R. R. (1994). Caffeine dependence syndrome: Evidence from case histories and experimental evaluations. *Journal of the American Medical Association, 272*(13), 1043–1048.

Strakowski, S. M., DelBello, M. P., & Adler, C. M. (2005). The functional neuroanatomy of bipolar disorder: A review of neuroimaging findings. *Molecular Psychiatry, 10*, 105–116.

Strauss, E., & Wada, J. (1983). Lateral preferences and cerebral speech dominance. *Cortex, 19*(2), 165–177.

Strauss, R. S., & Pollack, H. A. (2001). Epidemic increases in childhood overweight: 1986–1998. *Journal of the American Medical Association, 286*, 2845–2848.

Strayer, D. L., & Drews, F. A. (2007). Cell-phone-induced driver distraction. *Current Directions in Psychological Science, 16*(3), 128–131.

Stricker, G. (2006). Assimilative psychodynamic psychotherapy integration. In G. Stricker & J. Gold (Eds.), *A casebook of psychotherapy integration* (pp. 55–63). Washington, DC: American Psychological Association.

Stricker, L. J., & Ward, W. C. (2004). Stereotype threat, inquiring about test takers' ethnicity and gender, and standardized test performance. *Journal of Applied Social Psychology, 34*, 665–693.

Stright, A. D., Gallagher, K. C., & Kelley, K. (2008). Infant temperament moderates relations between maternal parenting in early childhood and children's adjustment in first grade. *Child Development, 79*, 186–200.

Stroebe, W., Papies, E. K., & Aarts, H. (2008). From homeostatic to hedonic theories of eating: Self-regulatory failure in food-rich environments. *Applied Psychology: An International Review, 57*(Suppl. 1), 172–193.

Strohmetz, D. B., Rind, B., Fisher, R., & Lynn, M. (2002). Sweetening the till: The use of candy to increase restaurant tipping. *Journal of Applied Social Psychology, 32,* 300–309. Stromberg, C. D., Haggarty, D. J., Leibenluft, R. F., McMillian, M. H., Mishkin, B., et al. (1988). *The psychologist's legal handbook.* Washington, DC: Council for the National Register of Health Service Providers in Psychology.

Stroop, J. R. (1935). Studies of interference in serial verbal reactions. *Journal of Experimental Psychology, 18,* 643–662.

Strote, J., Lee, J. E., & Wechsler, H. (2002). Increasing MDMA use among college students: Results of a national survey. *Journal of Adolescent Health, 30,* 64–72.

Strümpfer, D. J. W. (2005). Standing on the shoulders of giants: Notes on early positive psychology (psychofortology). *South African Journal of Psychology, 35,* 21–45.

Strunk, D. R., Lopez, H., & DeRubeis, R. J. (2006). Depressive symptoms are associated with unrealistic negative predictions of future life events. *Behaviour Research and Therapy, 44,* 875–896.

Stuart, R. B. (2004). Twelve practical suggestions for achieving multicultural competence. *Professional Psychology: Theory and Practice, 35,* 3–9.

Stuart, S., & Robertson, M. (2003). *Interpersonal psychotherapy: A clinician's guide.* London: Arnold Publishers.

Stürmer, T., Hasselbach, P., & Amelang, M. (2006). Personality, lifestyle, and risk of cardiovascular disease and cancer: Follow-up of population based cohort. *British Medical Journal, 332,* 1359.

Su, J. C., Tran, A. G. T. T., Wirtz, J. G., Langteau, R. A., & Rothman, A. J. (2008). Driving under the influence (of stress): Evidence of a regional increase in impaired driving and traffic fatalities after the September 11 terrorist attacks. *Psychological Science, 20,* 59–65.

Su, Z., Korstanje, R., Tsaih, S.-W., & Paigen, B. (2008). Candidate genes for obesity revealed from a C57BL/6J 129S1/SvImJ intercross. *International Journal of Obesity, 32,* 1180–1189.

Sue, D. W., Capodilupo, C. M., Torino, G. C., Bucceri, J. M., Holder, A. M. B., Nadal, K. L., & Esquilin, M. (2007). Racial microaggressions in everyday life: Implications for clinical practice. *American Psychologist, 62,* 271–286.

Sue, S., & Okazaki, S. (1990). Asian-American educational achievements: A phenomenon in search of an explanation. *American Psychologist, 45,* 913–920.

Sue, S., Zane, N., Hall, G. C. N., & Berger, L. K. (2009). The case for cultural competency in psychotherapeutic interventions. *Annual Review of Psychology, 60,* 525–548.

Suh, E., Diener, E., & Fujita, F. (1996). Events and subjective well-being: Only recent events matter. *Journal of Personality and Social Psychology, 70,* 1091–1102.

Suinn, R. M. (2001). The terrible twos: Anger and anxiety. *American Psychologist, 56,* 27–36.

Sullivan, H. S. (1954). *The psychiatric interview.* New York: Norton.

Sullivan, J. W., & Horowitz, F. D. (1983). The effects of intonation on infant attention: The role of the rising intonation contour. *Journal of Child Language, 10,* 521–534.

Sullivan, P. F., Kendler, K. S., & Neale, M. C. (2003). Schizophrenia as a complex trait: Evidence from a meta-analysis of twin studies. *Archives of General Psychiatry, 60,* 1187–1192.

Suls, J., & Bunde, J. (2005). Anger, anxiety, and depression as risk factors for cardiovascular disease: The problems and implications of overlapping affective dispositions. *Psychological Bulletin, 131,* 260–300.

Suls, J., & Rothman, A. (2004). Evolution of the biopsychosocial model: Prospects and challenges for health psychology. *Health Psychology, 23,* 119–125.

Suls, J., & Wan, C. K. (1993). The relationship between trait hostility and cardiovascular reactivity: A quantitative review and analysis. *Psychophysiology, 30,* 1–12.

Suomi, S. (1999). Attachment in rhesus monkeys. In J. Cassidy & P. Shaver (Eds.), *Handbook of attachment* (pp. 181–197). New York: Guilford.

Suomi, S. (2004). Aggression, serotonin, and gene-environment interactions in rhesus monkeys. In J. T. Cacioppo & G. G. Berntson (Eds.), *Essays in social neuroscience* (pp. 15–27). Cambridge, MA: MIT Press.

Suslow, T., Ohrmann, P., Bauer, J., Rauch, A. V., Schwindt, W., Arolt, V., et al. (2006). Amygdala activation during masked presentation of emotional faces predicts conscious detection of threat-related faces. *Brain and Cognition, 61,* 243–248.

Suzdak, P. D., Glowa, J. R., Crawley, J. N., Schwartz, R. D., Skolnick, P., & Paul, S. M. (1986). A selective imidazobenzodiazepine antagonist of ethanol in the rat. *Science, 234,* 1243–1247.

Svartberg, M., Stiles, T. C., & Seltzer, M. H. (2004). Randomized, controlled trial of the effectiveness of short-term dynamic psychotherapy and cognitive therapy for cluster C personality disorders. *American Journal of Psychiatry, 161,* 810–817.

Swaab, D. E., & Hofman, M. A. (1995). Sexual differentiation of the human hypothalamus in relation to gender and sexual orientation. *Trends in Neuroscience, 18*(6), 264–270.

Swan, G. E. (1996, December). Some elders thrive on working into late life. *APA Monitor,* 35.

Swan, G. E., & Carmelli, D. (1996). Curiosity and mortality in aging adults: A 5-year follow-up of the Western Collaborative Group Study. *Psychology and Aging, 11,* 449–453.

Swann, W. B., Jr., De la Ronde, C., & Hixon, J. G. (1994). Authenticity and positivity strivings in marriage and courtship. *Journal of Personality and Social Psychology, 66,* 857–869.

Swarte, N. B., van der Lee, M. L., van der Bom, J. G., van den Bout, J., & Heintz, A. P. M. (2003). Effects of euthanasia on the bereaved family and friends: A cross sectional study. *British Medical Journal, 327,* 189.

Swartz, H. A., Zuckoff, A., Grote, N. K., Spielvogle, H. N., Bledsoe, S. E., Shear, M. K., & Frank, E. (2007). Engaging depressed patients in psychotherapy: Integrating techniques from motivational interviewing and ethnographic interviewing to improve treatment. participation. *Professional Psychology: Research and Practice, 38,* 430–439.

Swartz, M. S., Perkins, D. O., Stroup, T. S., Davis, S. M., Capuano, G., Rosenheck, R. A., et al. (2007). Effects of antipsychotic medications on psychosocial functioning in patients with chronic schizophrenia: Findings from the NIMH CATIE study. *American Journal of Psychiatry, 164,* 428–436.

Swets, J. A. (1992). The science of choosing the right decision threshold in high-stakes diagnostics. *American Psychologist, 47,* 522–532.

Swets, J. A. (1996). *Signal detection theory and ROC analysis in psychology and diagnostics.* New Jersey: Erlbaum.

Swets, J. A., Dawes, R. M., & Monahan, J. (2000). Psychological science can improve diagnostic decisions. *Psychological Science in the Public Interest, 1,* 1–26.

Swinburn, B. (2009). Obesity prevention in children and adolescents. Child *and Adolescent Psychiatric Clinics of North America, 18*(1), 209–223.

Swindle, R., Jr., Heller, K., Pescosolido, B., & Kikuzawa, S. (2000). Responses to nervous breakdowns in America over a 40-year period: Mental health policy implications. *American Psychologist, 55,* 740–749.

Swithers, S. E., Davidson, T. L. (2008). A role for sweet taste: Calorie predictive relations in energy regulation by rats. *Behavioral Neuroscience, 122*(1), 161–173.

Swithers, S. E., & Hall, W. G. (1994). Does oral experience terminate ingestion? *Appetite, 23*(2), 113–138.

Symons, D. (1979). *The evolution of human sexuality.* Oxford, UK: Oxford University Press.

Szasz, T. (1972). *The myth of mental illness.* New York: Paladin.

Szasz, T. (2003). The psychiatric protection order for the "battered mental patient." *British Medical Journal, 327,* 1449–1451.

Szasz, T. (2009). *Coercion as cure.* Edison, NJ: Transaction Publishers.

Szegedi, A., Kohnen, R., Dienel, A., & Kieser, M. (2005). Acute treatment of moderate to severe depression with hypericum extract WS 5570 (St John's wort): Randomised controlled double blind non-inferiority trial versus paroxetine. *British Medical Journal, 330,* 503.

Szpunar, K. K., Chan, J. C., & McDermott, K. B. (in press). Contextual processing in episodic future thought. *Cerebral Cortex.*

Szpunar, K. K., Watson, J. M., & McDermott, K. B. (2007). Neural substrates of envisioning the future. *Proceedings of the National Academy of Sciences, 104,* 642–647.

Szymanski, K., Garczynski, J., & Harkins, S. (2000). The contribution of the potential for evaluation to coaction effects. *Group Processes and Intergroup Relations, 3,* 269–283.

Tabert, M. H., Manly, J. J., Liu, X., Pelton, G. H., Rosenbaum, S., Jacobs, M., et al. (2006). Neuropsychological prediction of conversion to Alzheimer disease in patients with mild cognitive impairment. *Archives of General Psychiatry, 63,* 916–924.

Taggar, S., Hackett, R., & Saha, S. (1999). Leadership emergence in autonomous work teams: Antecedents and outcomes. *Personnel Psychology, 52,* 899–926.

Takahashi, K., & Yamanaka, S. (2006). Induction of pluripotent stem cells from mouse embryonic and adult fibroblast cultures by defined factors. *Cell, 126*(4), 663–676.

Takashima, A., Petersson, K. M., Rutters, F., Tendolkar, I., Jensen, O., Zwarts, M. J., et al. (2006). Declarative memory consolidation in humans: A prospective functional magnetic resonance imaging study. *Proceedings of the National Academy of Sciences, 103,* 756–761.

Takeuchi, N., Uchimura, N., Hashizume, Y., Mukai, M., Etoh, Y., Yamamoto, K., et al. (2001). Melatonin therapy for REM behavior disorder. *Psychiatry and Clinical Neurosciences, 55,* 267–269.

Takkouche, B., Etminan, M., & Montes-Martinez, A. (2005). Personal use of hair dyes and risk of cancer. *Journal of the American Medical Association, 293,* 2516–2525.

Talarico, J. F., & Rubin, D. C. (2003). Confidence, not consistency, characterizes flashbulb memories. *Psychological Science, 14,* 455–461.

Talbott, J. A. (2004). Deinstitutionalization: Avoiding the disasters of the past. *Psychiatric Services, 55,* 1112–1115.

Tallman, B. A., Altmaier, E., & Garcia, C. (2007). Finding benefit from cancer. *Journal of Counseling Psychology, 54,* 481–487.

Talmi, D., Grady, C. L., Goshen-Gottstein, Y., & Moscovitch, M. (2005). Neuroimaging the serial position curve: A test of single-store versus dual-store models. *Psychological Science, 16,* 716–723.

Tam, K. P., Chiu, C. Y., Lau, I. Y. M. (2007). Terror managements among Chinese: Worldview defence and intergroup bias in resource allocation. *Asian Journal of Social Psychology 10,* 93–102.

Tamashiro, K. L. K., & Bello, N. T. (Eds.) (2008). Special issue on leptin. *Physiology & Behavior, 94*(5).

Tamir, M. (2009). What do people want to feel and why? Pleasure and utility in emotion regulation. *Current Directions in Psychological Science, 18,* 101–105.

Tamminga, C. A., & Holcomb, H. H. (2005). Phenotype of schizophrenia: A review and formulation. *Molecular Psychiatry, 10,* 27–39.

Tan, G., Hammond, D. C., & Joseph, G. (2005). Hypnosis and irritable bowel syndrome: A review of efficacy and mechanism of action. *American Journal of Clinical Hypnosis, 47,* 161–178.

Tanaka, H., Taira, K., Arakawa, M., Toguti, H., Urasaki, C., Yamamoto, Y., et al. (2001). Effects of short nap and exercise on elderly people having difficulty sleeping. *Psychiatry and Clinical Neurosciences, 55,* 173–174.

Tanaka, S. C., Balleine, B. W., & O'Doherty, J. P. (2008). Calculating consequences: brain systems that encode the causal effects of actions. *The Journal of Neuroscience, 28,* 6750–6755.

Tanda, G., Pontieri, F. E., & Di Chiara, G. (1997). Cannabinoid and heroin activation of me-solimbic dopamine transmission by a common mu1 opioid receptor mechanism. *Science, 276*, 2048–2050.

Tandon, R., Keshavan, M. S., & Nasrallah, H. A. (2008). Schizophrenia, "Just the facts" What we know in 2008: 2. Epidemiology and etiology. *Schizophrenia Research, 102*(1–3), 1–18.

Tang, Y. Y., Ma, Y., Wang, J., Fan, Y., Feng, S., Lu, Q., Yu, Q., Sui, D., Rothbart, M. K., Fan, M., & Posner, M. I. (2007). Short-term meditation training improves attention and self-regulation. *Proceedings of the National Academies of Science, 104*, 17152–17156.

Tan-Laxa, M. A., Sison-Switala, C., Rintelman, W., & Ostrea, E. M. (2004). Abnormal audi-tory brainstem response among infants with prenatal cocaine exposure. *Pediatrics, 113*, 357–360.

Tannen, D. (2001). *You just don't understand: Women and men in conversation*. New York: HarperCollins.

Tanner, J. M. (1978). *Foetus into man: Physical growth from conception to maturity*. London: Open Books.

Tarabar, A. F., & Nelson, L. S. (2004). The gamma-hydroxybutyrate withdrawal syndrome. *Toxicological Reviews, 23*, 45–49.

Targino, R. A., Imamura, M., Kaziyama, H. H., Souza, L. P., Hsing, W. T., Furland, A. D., Imamura, S. T., & Azevedo Neto, R. S. (2008). A randomized controlled trial of acupunc-ture added to usual treatment for fibromyalgia. *Journal of Rehabilitation Medicine, 40*(7), 582–588.

Task Force on Promotion and Dissemination of Psychological Procedures. (1995). Training in and dissemination of empirically validated psychological treatments: Report and recom-mendations. *Clinical Psychologist, 48*, 3–23.

Tasker, F., & Golombok, S. (1995). Adults raised as children in lesbian families. *American Jour-nal of Orthopsychiatry, 65*(2), 203–215.

Tassi, P., & Muzet, A. (2001). Defining states of consciousness. *Neuroscience and Biobehavioral Reviews, 25*, 175–191.

Taub, A. (1998). Thumbs down on acupuncture. *Science, 279*, 159.

Tavris, C. (2003). Mind games: Psychological warfare between therapists and scientists. *The Chronicle of Higher Education, 49*, B7–B9.

Taylor, H. A., & Tversky, B. (1992). Spatial mental models derived from survey and route descriptions. *Journal of Memory and Language, 31*, 261–292.

Taylor, J. G. (2002). Paying attention to consciousness. *Trends in Cognitive Science, 6*, 206–210.

Taylor, R. L., & Richards, S. B. (1991). Patterns of intellectual differences of Black, Hispanic, and White children. *Psychology in the Schools, 28*, 5–8.

Taylor, S. (2004). Efficacy and outcome predictors for three PTSD treatments: Exposure therapy, EMDR, and relaxation training. In S. Taylor (Ed.), *Advances in the treatment of posttraumatic stress disorder: Cognitive-behavioral perspectives* (pp. 13–37). New York: Springer.

Taylor, S., & Asmundson, G. J. G. (2008). Hypochondriasis. In J. S. Abramowitz, D. McKay, & S. Taylor. *Clinical handbook of obsessive-compulsive disorder and related problems* (pp. 304–315). Baltimore, MD: Johns Hopkins University Press.

Taylor, S., Peplau, A., & Sears, D. (2006). *Social psychology* (12th ed.). Upper Saddle River, NJ: Pearson/Prentice Hall.

Taylor, S., Thordarson, D. S., Maxfield, L., Fedoroff, I. C., Lovell, K., & Ogrodniczuk, J. (2003). Comparative efficacy, speed, and adverse effects of three PTSD treatments: Exposure therapy, EMDR, and relaxation training. *Journal of Consulting and Clinical Psychology, 71*, 330–338.

Taylor, S. E. (1995). *Health psychology* (3rd ed.). New York: McGraw-Hill.

Taylor, S. E. (1999). *Health psychology* (4th ed.). New York: McGraw-Hill.

Taylor, S. E. (2002). *Health psychology* (5th ed.). New York: McGraw-Hill.

Taylor, S. E., & Aspinwall, L. G. (1996). Mediating processes in psychosocial stress: Appraisal, coping, resistance, and vulnerability. In H. B. Kaplan (Ed.), *Psychosocial stress: Perspectives on structure, theory, life course, and methods* (pp. 71–110). New York: Academic Press.

Taylor, S. E., Dickerson, S. S., & Klein, L. C. (2002). Toward a biology of social support. In C. R. Snyder & S. L. Lopez (Eds.), *Handbook of positive psychology* (pp. 556–569). London: Oxford University Press.

Taylor, S. E., & Lobel, M. (1989). Social comparison activity under threat: Downward evalua-tion and upward contacts. *Psychological Review, 96*, 569–575.

Taylor, S. E., Gonzaga, G. C., Klein, L. C., Hu, P., Greendale, G. A., & Seeman, T. E. (2006). Relation of oxytocin to psychological stress responses and hypothalamic-pituitary-adrenocortical axis activity in older women. *Psychosomatic Medicine, 68*, 238–245.

Taylor, S. E., Kemeny, M. E., Aspinwall, L. G., Schneider, S. G., Rodriguez, R., & Herbert, M. (1992). Optimism, coping, psychological distress, and high-risk sexual behavior among men at risk for acquired immunodeficiency syndrome (AIDS). *Journal of Personality and Social Psychology, 63*, 460–473.

Taylor, S. E., Kemeny, M. E., Reed, G. M., Bower, J. E., & Gruenewald, T. L. (2000). Psycho-logical resources, positive illusions, and health. *American Psychologist, 55*, 99–109.

Taylor, S. E., Klein, L. C., Lewis, B. P., Gruenewald, T. L., Gurung, R. A. R., & Updegraff, J. A. (2000). Biobehavioral responses to stress in females: Tend-and-befriend, not fight-or-flight. *Psychological Review, 107*, 411–429.

Taylor, S. E., Lerner, J. S., Sherman, K. D., Sage, R. M., & McDowell, N. K. (2003). Are self-enhancing cognitions associated with health or unhealthy biological profiles? *Journal of Personality and Social Psychology, 85*, 605–615.

Taylor, S. E., Lewis, B. P., Gruenewald, T. L., Gurung, R. A. R., Updegraff, J. A., & Klein, L. C. (2002). Sex differences in biobehavioral responses to threat: Reply to Geary and Flinn (2002). *Psychological Review, 109*, 751–753.

Teachman, J. D. (2008). The living arrangements of children and their educational well-being. *Journal of Family Issues, 29*, 734–761.

Teigen, K. H. (1994). Yerkes-Dodson: A law for all seasons. *Theory and Psychology, 4*(4), 525–547.

Telegraph Correspondent. (2005, April 18). Scratching your cars was art, says vandal. *Daily Telegraph*, p. 5.

Tellegen, A., Lykken, D. T., Bouchard, T. J., Wilcox, K. J., Segal, N. L., & Rich, S. (1988). Per-sonality similarity in twins reared apart and together. *Journal of Personality and Social Psychology, 54*, 1031–1039.

Tellegen, A., Lykken, D. T., Bouchard, T. J., Wilcox, K. J., Segal, N. L., & Rich, S. (1988). Per-sonality similarity in twins reared apart and together. *Journal of Personality and Social Psychology, 54*, 1031–1039.

Tenenbaum, H. R., & Leaper, C. (2003). Parent-child conversations about science: The social-izations of gender inequities? *Developmental Psychology, 39*, 34–47.

Teng, Y. D., Lavik, E. B., Qu, X., Park, K. I., Ourednik, J., Zurakowski, D., et al. (2002). Func-tional recovery following traumatic spinal cord injury mediated by a unique polymer scaffold seeded with neural stem cells. *Proceedings of the National Academy of Sciences, 99*, 3024–3029.

Teplin, L. A., McClelland, G. M., Abram, K. M., & Weiner, D. A. (2005). Crime victimization in adults with severe mental illness. *Archives of General Psychiatry, 62*, 911–921.

Terman, J. S., Terman, M., Lo, E. S., & Cooper, T. B. (2001). Circadian time of morning light administration and therapeutic response in winter depression. *Archives of General Psy-chiatry, 58*, 69–75.

Terman, L. M. (1906). Genius and stupidity: A study of the intellectual process of seven "bright" and seven "stupid" boys. *Pedagogical Seminary, 13*, 307–373.

Terman, L. M. (1916). *The measurement of intelligence*. Boston: Houghton Mifflin.

Terman, L. M., & Oden, M. H. (1947). *The gifted child grows up: Vol. 4. Genetic studies of genius*. Stanford, CA: Stanford University Press.

Terman, L. M., & Oden, M. H. (1947). *The gifted child grows up: Vol. 4. Genetic studies of genius*. Stanford, CA: Stanford University Press.

Terman, L. M., & Oden, M. H. (1959). *The gifted group at midlife*. Stanford, CA: Stanford University Press.

Terman, M., & Terman, J. S. (2005). Light therapy for seasonal and nonseasonal depression: Efficacy, protocol, safety, and side effects. *CNS Spectrums, 10*, 647–663.

Terracciano, A., Löckenhoff, C. E., Zonderman, A. B., Ferrucci, L., & Costa, P. T. (2008). Personality predictors of longevity: Activity, emotional stability, and conscientiousness. *Psychosomatic Medicine, 70*, 621–627.

Tesser, A. (2001). Self-esteem: The frequency of temporal-self and social comparisons in peo-ple's personal appraisals. In A. Tesser & N. Schwarz (Eds.), *Blackwell handbook of social psychology: Intraindividual processes* (pp. 479–498). Oxford, UK: Blackwell.

Thakkar, R. R., Garrison, M. M., & Christakis, D. A. (2006). A systematic review for the effects of television viewing by infants and preschoolers. *Pediatrics, 118*, 2025–2031.

Thaler, E. R., Kennedy, D. W., & Hanson, C. W. (2001). Medical applications of elec-tronic nose technology: Review of current status. *American Journal of Rhinology, 15*, 291–295.

Thanos, P. K., Volkow, N. D., Freimuth, P., Umegaki, H., Ikari, H., Roth, G., et al. (2001). Overexpression of dopamine D2 receptors reduces alcohol self-administration. *Journal of Neurochemistry, 78*, 1094–1103.

Thase, M. E. (2002). Antidepressant effects: The suit may be small, but the fabric is real. *Prevention & Treatment, 5*, Article 32. Retrieved December 13, 2004, from http://www.journals.apa.org/prevention/volume5/pre0050032c.html.

Thase, M. E., Friedman, E. S., Biggs, M. M., Wisniewski, S. R., Trivedi, M. H., Luther, J. F., et al. (2007). Cognitive therapy versus medication in augmentation and switch strate-gies as second-step treatments: A STAR*D report. *American Journal of Psychiatry, 164*, 739–752.

Thelen, E. (1995). Motor development: A new synthesis. *American Psychologist, 50*, 79–95.

Theofilopoulos, S., Goggi, J., Riaz, S. S., Jauniaux, E., Stern, G. M., & Bradford, H. F. (2001). Parallel induction of the formation of dopamine and its metabolites with induction of tyrosine hydroxylase expression in foetal rat and human cerebral cortical cells by brain-derived neurotrophic factor and glial-cell derived neurotrophic factor. *Brain Research: Developmental Brain Research, 127*, 111–122.

Thiessen, E. D., Hill, E. A., & Saffran, J. R. (2005). Infant-directed speech facilitates word seg-mentation. *Infancy, 7*, 53–71.

Thom, A., Sartory, G., & Jöhren, P. (2000). Comparison between one-session psychologi-cal treatment and benzodiazepine in dental phobia. *Journal of Consulting and Clinical Psychology, 68*, 378–387.

Thomas, A., & Chess, S. (1977). *Temperament and development*. New York: Brunner/Mazel.

Thomas, E. L., & Robinson, H. A. (1972). *Improving reading in every class: A sourcebook for teachers*. Boston: Allyn & Bacon.

Thomas, J. A., & Walton, D. (2007). Measuring perceived risk: Self-reported and actual hand positions of SUV and car drivers. *Traffic Psychology and Behavior, 10*, 201–207.

Thomas, R., & Forde, E. (2006). The role of local and global processing in the recognition of living and nonliving things. *Neuropsychologia, 44*(6), 982–986.

Thompson, C., Koon, E., Woodwell, W., Jr., & Beauvais, J. (2002). *Training for the next economy: An ASTD state of the industry report on trend in employer- provided training in the United States.* Washington, DC: American Society for Training and Development.

Thompson, D. S., & Pollack, B. G. (2001, August 26). Psychotropic metabolism: Gender-related issues. *Psychiatric Times, 14.* Available: http://www.mhsource. com/pt/p010147.html.

Thompson, E. M., & Morgan, E. M. (2008). "Mostly straight" young women: Variations in sexual behavior and identity development. *Developmental Psychology, 44,* 15–21.

Thompson, J. K. (1996). Introduction: Assessment and treatment of binge eating disorder. In J. K. Thompson (Ed.), *Body image, eating disorders, and obesity* (pp. 1–22). Washington, DC: American Psychological Association.

Thompson, P. M., Giedd, J. N., Woods, R. P., Macdonald, D., Evans, A. C., & Toga, A. W. (2000). Growth patterns in the developing brain detected by using continuum mechanical tensor maps. *Nature, 404,* 190–193.

Thompson, P. M., Hayashi, K. M., Simon, S. L., Geaga, J. A., Hong, M. S., Sui, Y., et al. (2004). Structural abnormalities in the brains of human subjects who use methamphetamine. *Journal of Neuroscience, 24,* 6028–6036.

Thompson, R. A. (2006). The development of the person: Social understanding, relationships, self, conscience. In W. Damon & R. M. Lerner (Series Eds.) & N. Eisenberg (Vol. Ed.), *Handbook of child psychology: Vol. 3. Social, emotional, and personality development* (6th ed.). New York: Wiley.

Thompson, R. R., George, K., Walton, J. C., Orr, S. P., & Benson, J. (2006). Sex- specific influences of vasopressin on human social communication. *Proceedings of the National Academy of Sciences, 103,* 7889–7894.

Thompson-Brenner, H., Glass, S., & Westen, D. (2003). A multidimensional meta-analysis of psychotherapy for bulimia nervosa. *Clinical Psychology: Science and Practice, 10,* 269–287.

Thomsen, L., Green, E. G. T., & Sidanius, J. (2008).We will hunt them down: How social dominance orientation and right-wing authoritarianism fuel ethnic persecution of immigrants in fundamentally different ways. *Journal of Experimental Social Psychology, 44,* 1455–1464.

Thomson, C. P. (1982). Memory for unique personal events: The roommate study. *Memory & Cognition, 10,* 324–332.

Thomson Healthcare (2007). *PDR drug guide for mental health professionals* (3rd ed.). Washington, DC: Physician's Desk Reference.

Thorens, B. (2008). Glucose sensing and the pathogenesis of obesity and type 2 diabetes. *International Journal of Obesity, 32,* S62–S71.

Thoresen, C. J., Kaplan, S. A., Barsky, A. P., Warren, C. R., & deChermont, K. (2003). The affective underpinnings of job perceptions and attitudes: A meta-analytic review and integration. *Psychological Bulletin, 129,* 914–945.

Thorndike, E. L. (1898). Animal intelligence: An experienced study of the associative process in animals. *Psychological Monographs, 2*(Whole No. 8).

Thorndike, E. L. (1905). *The elements of psychology.* New York: Seiler.

Thorndike, R. L., & Hagen, E. P. (1996). *Form 5 CogAT interpretive guide of school administrators: All levels.* Chicago: Riverside.

Thorngren, J. M., & Kleist, D. M. (2002). Multiple family group therapy: An interpersonal/postmodern approach. *Family Journal–Counseling and Therapy for Couples and Families, 10,* 167–176.

Thurston, I. B., & Phares, V. (2008). Mental health service utilization in African American and Caucasian mothers and fathers. *Journal of Consulting and Clinical Psychology, 76,* 1058–1067.

Tienari, P., Wynne, L. C., Läksy, K., Moring, J., Nieminen, P., et al. (2003). Genetic boundaries of the schizophrenia spectrum: Evidence from the Finnish Adoptive Family Study of Schizophrenia. *American Journal of Psychiatry, 160,* 1587–1594.

Tierney, J. (2009, March 10). What do dreams mean? Whatever your bias says. *New York Times,* D2.

Tiihonen, J., Kuikka, J., Bergstrom, K., Hakola, P., Karhu, J., Ryynänen, O.-P., & Föhr, J. (1995). Altered striatal dopamine re-uptake site densities in habitually violent and non-violent alcoholics. *Nature Medicine, 1*(7), 654–657.

Timms, P. (2005). Is there still a problem with homelessness and schizophrenia? *International Journal of Mental Health, 34,* 57–75.

Tinbergen, N. (1989). *The study of instinct.* Oxford, UK: Clarendon.

Tindale, R. S., & Kameda, T. (2000). "Social sharedness" as a unifying theme for information processing in groups. *Group Processes and Intergroup Relations, 3,* 123–140.

Tippmann-Piekert, M., Park, J. G., Boeve, B. F., Shepard, J. W., & Silber, M. H. (2007). Pathologic gambling in patients with restless legs syndrome treated with dopaminergic agonists. *Neurology, 68,* 301–303.

Tobler, P. N., Fiorillo, C. D., & Schultz, W. (2005). Adaptive coding of reward value by dopamine neurons. *Science, 307,* 1642–1645.

Todd, P. M., & Gigerenzer, G. (2007). Environments that make us smart: Ecological rationality. *Current Directions in Psychological Science, 16,* 167–171.

Tohen, M., Zarate, C. A., Jr., Hennen, J., Khalsa, H.-M. K., Strakowski, S. M., Gebre-Medhin, P., et al. (2003). The McLean-Harvard first-episode mania study: Prediction of recovery and first recurrence. *American Journal of Psychiatry, 160,* 2099–2107.

Tolman, E. C., & Honzik, C. H. (1930). Introduction and removal of reward and maze performance in rats. *University of California Publication in Psychology, 4,* 257–265.

Tomasello, M. (2000). Culture and cognitive development. *Current Directions in Psychological Science, 9,* 37–40.

Tomasello, M. (2006). Why don't apes point? In J. Enfield & S. C. Levinson (Eds.), *Roots of human sociality: Culture, cognition, and interaction* (pp. 506–524). New York: Berg.

Tomberlin, J. K., Rains, G. C., & Sanford, M. R. (2008). Development of Microplitis croceipes as a biological sensor. *Entomologia Experimentalis et Applicata, 128*(2), 249–257.

Tomes, H. (1999, April). The need for cultural competence. *APA Monitor,* p. 31.

Toni, N., Buchs, P. A., Nikonenko, I., Bron, C. R., & Muller, D. (1999). LTP promotes formation of multiple spine synapses between a single axon terminal and a dendrite. *Nature, 402,* 421–425.

Topakian, R., & Aichner, F. T. (2008). Vascular dementia: A practical update. *Current Medical Literature: Neurology, 24*(1), 1–8.

Torpy, J. A. (2008). Delirium. *Journal of the American Medical Association, 300*(24), 2936–2936.

Tougas, F., Rinfret, N., Beaton, A. M., & de la Sablonnière, R. (2005). Policewomen acting in self-defense: Can psychological disengagement protect self-esteem from the negative outcomes of relative deprivation? *Journal of Personality and Social Psychology, 88,* 790–800.

Touzani, K., Puthanveettil, S. V., & Kandel, E. R. (2007). Consolidation of learning strategies during spatial working memory taks requires protein synthesis in the prefrontal cortex. *Proceedings of the National Academy of Sciences, 104,* 5632–5637.

Trabasso, T. R., & Bower, G. H. (1968). *Attention in learning.* New York: Wiley.

Tramer, M. R., Carroll, D., Campbell, F. A., Reynolds, D. J., Moore, R. A., & McQuay, H. J. (2001). Cannabinoids for control of chemotherapy induced nausea and vomiting: quantitative systematic review. *British Medical Journal, 323,* 16–21.

Tranter, L. J., & Koutstaal, W. (2008). Age and flexible thinking: An experimental demonstration of the beneficial effects of increased cognitively stimulating activity on fluid intelligence in healthy older adults. *Aging, Neuropsychology, and Cognition, 15*(2), 184–207.

Treboux, D., Crowell, J. A., & Waters, E. (2004). When "new" meets "old": Configurations of adult attachment representations and their implications for marital functioning. *Developmental Psychology, 40,* 295–314.

Treiber, F. A., Musante, L., Kapuku, G., Davis, C., Litaker, M., & Davis, H. (2001). Cardiovascular (CV) responsivity and recovery to acute stress and future CV functioning in youth with family histories of CV disease: A 4-year longitudinal study. *International Journal of Psychophysiology, 41,* 65–74.

Treisman, A. (1999). Feature binding, attention, and object perception. In G. W. Humphreys, J. Duncan., & A. Treisman (Eds.), *Attention, space, and action* (pp. 91–111). New York: Oxford University Press.

Tremblay, R. E., Pagani-Kurtz, L., Mâsse, L., Vitaro, F., & Pihl, R. O. (1995). A bimodal preventive intervention for disruptive kindergarten boys: Its impact through mid-adolescence. *Journal of Consulting and Clinical Psychology, 63,* 560–568.

Tremblay, R. E., Pihl, R. O., Vitaro, F., & Dobkin, P. (1994). Predicting early onset of male antisocial behavior from preschool behavior. *Archives of General Psychiatry, 51,* 732–739.

Trevor, C. O. (2001). Interactions among actual ease-of-movement determinants and job satisfaction in the prediction of voluntary turnover. *Academy of Management Journal, 44,* 621–638.

Triandis, H. C., & Trafimow, D. (2001). Cross-national prevalence of collectivism. In C. Sedikides & M. B. Brewer (Eds.), *Individual self, relational self, collective self* (pp. 259–276). New York: Psychology Press.

Trierweiler, S. J., Muroff, J. R., Jackson, M. S., Neighbors, H. W., & Munday, C. (2005). Clinician race, situational attributions, and diagnoses of mood versus schizophrenia disorders. *Cultural Diversity & Ethnic Minority Psychology, 11,* 351–364.

Trierweiler, S. J., Neighbors, H. W., Munday, C., Thompson, E. E., Binion, V. J., & Gomez, J. P. (2000). Clinician attributions associated with the diagnosis of schizophrenia in African American and non-African American patients. *Journal of Consulting and Clinical Psychology, 68,* 171–175.

Trifiletti, L. B., Shields, W., McDonald, E., Reynaud, F., & Gielen, A. (2006). Tipping the scales: Obese children and child safety seats. *Pediatrics, 117,* 1197–1202.

Trillin, A. S. (2001, January 29). Betting your life. *New Yorker,* pp. 38–41.

Tronick, E. Z., Messinger, D. S., Weinberg, M. K., Lester, B. M., LaGasse, L., Seifer, R., et al. (2005). Cocaine exposure is associated with subtle compromises of infants' and mothers' social-emotional behavior and dyadic features of their interaction in the face-to-face still-face paradigm. *Developmental Psychology, 41,* 711–722.

Trope, Y., Cohen, O., & Alfieri, T. (1991). Behavior identification as a mediator of dispositional inference. *Journal of Personality and Social Psychology, 61,* 873–883.

Tropp, L. R., & Pettigrew, T. F. (2005). Relationships between intergroup contact and prejudice among minority and majority status groups. *Psychological Science, 16,* 951–957.

Tropp, L. R., & Wright, S. (2001). In group identification as the inclusion of ingroup in the self. *Personality and Social Psychology Bulletin, 27,* 585–600.

Trotter, M. I., & Morgan, D. W. (2008). Patients' use of the Internet for health related matters: A study of Internet usage in 2000 and 2006. *Health Informatics Journal, 14*(3), 175–181.

Trout, J., & Christie, B. (2007). Interactive Video Games in Physical Education. *JOPERD: The Journal of Physical Education, Recreation & Dance, 78*(5), 29–45.

Truelsen, T., & Bonita, R. (2003). Advances in ischemic stroke epidemiology. *Advances in Neurology, 92,* 1–12.

Trull, T. J., & Sher, K. J. (1994). Relationship between the five-factor model of personality and Axis I disorders in a nonclinical sample. *Journal of Personality and Social Psychology, 103,* 350–360.

Trunzo, J. J., & Pinto, B. M. (2003). Social support as a mediator of optimisim and distress in breast cancer survivors. *Journal of Consulting and Clinical Psychology, 71*, 805–811.

Tryon, W. W. (2005). Possible mechanisms for why desensitization and exposure therapy work. *Clinical Psychology Review, 25*, 67–95.

Tsai, J. L., Knutson, B., & Fung, H. H. (2006). Cultural variation in affect evaluation. *Journal of Personality and Social Psychology, 90*, 288–307.

Tsai, J. L., Levenson, R. W., & McCoy, K. (2006). Cultural and temperamental variation in emotional response. *Emotion, 6*, 484–497.

Tsang, J. S., Naughton, P. A., Leong, S., Hill, A. D. K., Kelly, C. J., & Leahy, A. L. (2008). Virtual reality simulation in endovascular surgical training. *Surgeon, 6*(4), 214–220.

Tsuang, M. T., Stone, W. S., & Faraone, S. V. (2000). Toward reformulating the diagnosis of schizophrenia. *American Journal of Psychiatry, 157*, 1041–1950.

Tuch, S. A., & Martin, J. K. (1991). Race in the workplace: Black/white differences in the sources of job satisfaction. *The Sociological Quarterly, 32*, 103–116.

Tucker, C. M., & Herman, K. C. (2002). Using culturally sensitive theories and research to meet the academic needs of low-income African American children. *American Psychologist, 57*, 762–773.

Tuller, D. (2004, January 27). Britain poised to approve medicine derived from marijuana. *New York Times*, p. F5.

Tulving, E. (1983). *Elements of episodic memory*. New York: Oxford University Press.

Tulving, E. (2000). Introduction to memory. In M. S. Gazzaniga (Ed.), *The new cognitive neurosciences* (pp. 727–732). Cambridge, MA: MIT Press.

Tulving, E. (2005). Episodic memory and autonoesis: Uniquely human? In H. S. Terrace and J. Metcalfe (Eds.), *The missing link in cognition: Origins of self-reflective consciousness* (pp. 3–56). New York: Oxford University Press.

Tulving, E., & Psotka, J. (1971). Retroactive inhibition in free recall: Inaccessibility of information available in the memory store. *Journal of Experimental Psychology, 87*, 1–8.

Tuomilehto, J., Lindstrom, J., Eriksson, J. G., Valle, T. T., Hamalainen, H., Ilanne-Parikka, P., et al. (2001). Prevention of type 2 diabetes mellitus by changes in lifestyle among subjects with impaired glucose tolerance. *New England Journal of Medicine, 344*, 1343–1350.

Turati, C. (2004). Why faces are not special to newborns: An alternative account of the face preference. *Current Directions in Psychological Science, 13*, 5–8.

Turiel, E. (2006). The development of morality. In W. Damon & R. M. Lerner (Series Eds.) & N. Eisenberg (Vol. Ed.), *Handbook of child psychology: Vol. 3. Social, emotional, and personality development* (6th ed.). New York: Wiley.

Turkheimer, E., Haley, A., Waldron, M., D'Onofrio, B., & Gottesman, I. I. (2003). Socioeconomic status modifies heritability of IQ in young children. *Psychological Science, 14*, 623–628.

Turkheimer, E., & Waldron M. (2000). Nonshared environment: A theoretical, methodological, and quantitative review. *Psychological Bulletin, 126*, 78–108.

Turkington, C. (1987). Special talents. *Psychology Today*, pp. 42–46.

Turkington, D., Kingdon, D., & Weiden, P. J. (2006). Cognitive therapy for schizophrenia. *American Journal of Psychiatry, 163*, 365–373.

Turnbull, C. (1961). Some observations regarding the experiences and behavior of the Bambuti Pygmies. *American Journal of Psychology, 74*, 304–308.

Turner, E. H., Matthews, A. M., Linardatos, E., Tell, R. A., & Rosenthal, R. (2008). Selective publication of antidepressant trials and its influence on apparent efficacy. *New England Journal of Medicine, 358*, 252–260.

Turner, J. C. (1991). *Social influence*. Pacific Grove, CA: Brooks/Cole.

Turner, M., Mitchell, T., R., Limon, M. S., & Zuckerman-Hyman, C. (2007). The moderators and mediators of door-in-the-face requests: Is it a negotiation or a helping experience? *Communication Monographs, 74*, 333–356.

Turner, M. S., Cipolotti, L., Yousry, T. A., & Shallice, T. (2008). Confabulation: Damage to a specific inferior medial prefrontal system. *Cortex, 44*(6), 637–648.

Turner, R. J., & Lloyd, D. A. (2004). Stress burden and the lifetime incidence of psychiatric disorder in young adults: Racial and ethnic contrasts. *Archives of General Psychiatry, 61*, 481–488.

Turner, S. M., DeMers, S. T., Fox, H. R., & Reed, G. M. (2001). APA's guidelines for test user qualifications: An executive summary. *American Psychologist, 56*, 1099–1113.

Turner, T. H., Drummond, S. P. A., Salamat, J. S., & Brown, G. G. (2007). Effects of 42 hr of total sleep deprivation on component processes of verbal working memory. *Neuropsychology, 21*, 787–795.

Tuszynski, M. H., Grill, R., Jones, L. L., McKay, H. M., & Blesch, A. (2002). Spontaneous and augmented growth of axons in the primate spinal cord: Effects of local injury and nerve growth factor-secreting cell grafts. *Journal of Comparative Neurology, 449*, 88–101.

Tuszynski, M. H., Thal, L., Pay, M., Salmon, D. P., U, H. S., Bakay, R., et al. (2005). A phase 1 clinical trial of nerve growth factor gene therapy for Alzheimer disease. *Nature Medicine, 11*, 551–555.

Tversky, A., & Kahneman, D. (1974). Judgment under uncertainty: Heuristics and biases. *Science, 185*, 1124–1131.

Tversky, A., & Kahneman, D. (1981). The framing of decisions and the psychology of choice. *Science, 211*, 453–458.

Tversky, A., & Kahneman, D. (1991). Loss aversion in riskless choice: A reference dependent model. *Quarterly Journal of Economics, 106*, 1039–1061.

Tversky, A., & Kahneman, D. (1993). Probabilistic reasoning. In A. Goldman (Ed.), *Readings in philosophy and cognitive science* (pp. 43–68). Cambridge: MIT Press.

Tversky, B., & Tuchin, M. (1989). A reconciliation of the evidence on eyewitness testimony: Comments on McCloskey and Zaragoza. *Journal of Experimental Psychology: General, 118*, 86–91.

Tyler, K. L., & Malessa, R. (2000). The Goltz-Ferrier debates and the triumph of cerebral localizationalist theory. *Neurology, 55*(7), 1015–1024.

Tziner, A., Murphy, K. R., & Cleveland, J. N. (2005). Contextual and rater factors affecting rating behavior. *Group and Organization Management, 30*, 89–98.

U.K. Statistical Bulletin. (1999). *Electro convulsive therapy: Survey covering the period from January 1999 to March 1999, England*. London: Department of Health.

U.S. Bureau of Labor Statistics. (2006). *Occupational projections and training data 2006–2007*. Bulletin 2602. Washington, DC: U.S. Bureau of Labor Statistics.

U.S. Bureau of Labor Statistics. (2007). *Injuries, illnesses, and fatalities, 2005*. Washington, DC: U.S. Department of Labor. Retrieved May 9, 2007, from http://www.bls.gov/iif/home.htm#tables.

U.S. Bureau of Labor Statistics. (2008a). *Occupational outlook handbook, 2008–09*. Washington, DC: U.S. Bureau of Labor Statistics. Retrieved July 16, 2009, from http://www.bls.gov/oco.

U.S. Bureau of Labor Statistics. (2008b). *Occupational projections and training data 2008–2009*. Bulletin 2702. Washington, DC: U.S. Bureau of Labor Statistics.

U.S. Census Bureau. (2008). *Current population reports: Income, poverty, and health insurance coverage in the United States: 2007*. Washington, DC: U.S. Government Printing Office.

U.S. Department of Health and Human Services Office of Applied Studies. (2003). *Results from the 2002 National Survey on Drug Use and Health: Summary of national finding* (DHHS Publication No. SMA 03-3836, NHSDA Series H-22). Rockville, MD: Substance Abuse and Mental Health Services Administration.

U.S. Department of Health and Human Services. (2001a). *Alzheimer's disease fact sheet*. Washington, DC: U.S. Public Health Service (NIH Publication No. 01–3431).

U.S. Department of Health and Human Services. (2001b). *Mental health: Culture, race, and ethnicity. A supplement to mental health: A report of the Surgeon General*. Washington, DC: United States Public Health Service.

U.S. Department of Health and Human Services. (2001c). *Women and smoking: A report of the Surgeon General*. Atlanta: Centers for Disease Control and Prevention.

U.S. Department of Justice. (1999). *Eyewitness evidence: A guide for law enforcement*. Washington, DC: National Institute of Justice.

U.S. Department of Justice. (2002). *Recidivism of prisoners released in 1994*. Washington, DC: U.S. Department of Justice, Bureau of Justice Statistics.

U.S. Department of Justice. (2007). *Crime characteristics*. Retrieved January 31, 2007, from http://www.ojp.usdoj.gov/bjs/cvict_c.htm#relate.

U.S. Drug Enforcement Administration. (2002). Drug intelligence brief: OxyContin. Retrieved September 12, 2004, from http://www.usdoj.gov/dea/pubs/intel/02017/02017.html.

U.S. Surgeon General. (1999). *Mental health: A report of the surgeon general*. Rockville, MD: U.S. Department of Health and Human Services.

U.S. Surgeon General. (2009). Other Disorders in Children and Adolescents. In *Mental Health: A Report of the Surgeon General*. Rockville, Md.: Dept. of Health and Human Services, U.S. Public Health Service. Retrieved February 26, 2009, from http://www.surgeongeneral.gov/library/mentalhealth/chapter3/sec6.html.

Uchida, Y., Kitayama, S., Mesquita, B., & Reyes, J. A. (2001, June). *Interpersonal sources of happiness: The relative significance in Japan, the Philippines, and the United States*. Paper presented at Annual Convention of American Psychological Society, Toronto, Canada.

Uchino, B. N., Cacioppo, J. T., & Kiecolt-Glaser, J. K. (1996). The relationship between social support and physiological process: A review with emphasis on underlying mechanisms and implications for health. *Psychological Bulletin, 119*, 488–531.

Udry, J. R., & Chantala, K. (2003). Masculinity-femininity guides sexual union formation in adolescents. *Personality and Social Psychology Bulletin, 30*, 44–55.

Ugajin, T., Hozawa, A., Ohkubo, T., Asayama, K., Kikuya, M., Obara, T., et al. (2005). White-coat hypertension as a risk factor for the development of home hypertension: The Ohasama study. *Archives of Internal Medicine, 165*, 1541–1546.

Uhl, G. R., Sora, I., & Wang, Z. (1999). The mu opiate receptor as a candidate gene for pain: polymorphisms, variations in expression, nociception, and opiate responses. *Proceedings of the National Academy of Sciences, 96*, 7752–7755.

Uhl-Bien, M., Marion, R., & McKelvey, B. (2007). Complexity leadership theory: Shifting leadership from the Industrial Age to the Knowledge Era. *Leadership Quarterly, 18*, 298–318.

Uleman, J. S., Blader, S. L., & Todorov, A. (2005). Implicit impressions In R. Hassin, J. Uleman, & J. Bargh (Eds.), *The new unconscious* (pp. 362–392). New York: Oxford University Press.

Ulett, G. A. (2003). Acupuncture, magic, and make-believe. *The Skeptical Inquirer, 27*(2), 47–50.

Ullmann, L. P., & Krasner, L. (1965). *Case studies in behavior modification*. New York: Holt, Rinehart & Winston.

Ulrich, W. L., Richards, P. S., & Bergin, A. E. (2000). Psychotherapy with Latter-Day Saints. In P. S. Richards & A. E. Bergin (Eds.), *Handbook of psychotherapy and religious diversity* (pp. 185–209). Washington DC: American Psychological Association.

Umbreit, J., Ferro, J., Liaupsin, C. J., & Lane, K. L. (2006). *Functional behavioral assessment and function-based intervention: An effective, practical approach.* Upper Saddle River, NJ: Prentice Hall.

Ungemach, C., Chater, N., & Stewart, N. (2009). Are probabilities overweighted or underweighted when rare outcomes are experienced (rarely)? *Psychological Science, 20,* 473–479.

Ungerleider, L. G., & Mishkin, M. (1982). Two cortical visual systems. In D. J. Ingle, M. A. Goodale, & R. J. W. Mansfield (Eds.), *Analysis of visual behavior.* Cambridge, MA: MIT Press.

Ungless, M. A., Whistler, J. L., Malenka, R. C., & Bonci, A. (2001). Single cocaine exposure in vivo induces long-term potentiation in dopamine neurons. *Nature, 411,* 583–587.

United Nations Office on Drugs and Crime. (2007). Intentional homicide, rate per 100,000 population. Retrieved March 19, 2009, from http://www.unodc.org/documents/data-and-analysis/IHS-rates-05012009.pdf.

Urbach, T. P., Windmann, S. S., Payne, D. G., & Kutas, M. (2005). Mismaking memories. *Psychological Science, 16,* 19–24.

Urry, H. L., Nitschke, J. B., Dolski, I., Jackson, D. C., Dalton, K. M., Mueller, C. J., et al. (2004). Making a life worth living: Neural correlates of well-being. *Psychological Science, 15,* 367–372.

Uttal, W. R. (2003). *The new phrenology: The limits of localizing cognitive processes in the brain.* Cambridge, MA: MIT Press.

Uvnas-Moberg, K., Arn, I., & Magnusson, D. (2005). The psychobiology of emotion: The role of the oxytocinergic system. *International Journal of Behavioral Medicine, 12,* 59–65.

Uwe, H. (2005). Therapeutic alliance: The best synthesizer of social influences on the therapeutic situation? On links to other constructs, determinants of its effectiveness, and its role for research in psychotherapy in general. *Psychotherapy Research, 15,* 9–23.

Vahia, I. V., & Cohen, C. I. (2009). Psychosocial factors. In K. T. Mueser & D. V. Jeste (Eds.), *Clinical handbook of schizophrenia.* (pp. 74–81). New York: Guilford Press.

Vaish, A., Grossmann, T., & Woodward, A. (2008). Not all emotions are created equal: The negativity bias in social-emotional development. *Psychological Bulletin, 134,* 383–403.

Vaitl, D., Birbaumer, N., Gruzelier, J., Jamieson, G. A., Kotchoubey, B., Kubler, A., et al. (2005). Psychobiology of altered states of consciousness. *Psychological Bulletin, 131,* 98–127.

Valent, F., Brusaferro, S., & Barbone, F. (2001). A case-crossover study of sleep and childhood injury. *Pediatrics, 107,* e23.

Valenza, E., Simion, F., Assia, V. M., & Umilta, C. (1996). Face preference at birth. *Journal of Experimental Psychology: Human Perception and Performance, 22,* 892–903.

Valkenburg, P. M., & Peter, J. (2007a). Preadolescents' and adolescents' online communication and their closeness to friends. *Developmental Psychology, 43*(2), 267–277.

Valkenburg, P. M., & Peter, J. (2007b). Online communication and adolescent well-being: Testing the stimulation versus the displacement hypothesis. *Journal of Computer-Mediated Communication, 12*(4), 1169–1182.

Valkenburg, P. M., & Peter, J. (2009). Social consequences of the Internet for adolescents: A decade of research. *Current Directions in Psychological Science, 18,* 1–5.

Valli, K., Revonsuo, A., Pälkäs, O., & Punamäki, R.-L. (2006). The effect of trauma on dream content—A field study of Palestinian children. *Dreaming, 16,* 63–87.

Vallotton, C. D. (2008). Signs of emotion: What can preverbal children "say" about internal states? *Infant Mental Health Journal, 29,* 234–258.

Valuck, R. J., Libby, A. M., Benton, T. D., & Evans, D. L. (2007). A descriptive analysis of 10,000 suicide attempters in the Unites States managed care plans, 1998–2005. *Primary Psychiatry, 14,* 52–60.

Van Bezooijen, R., Otto, S. A., & Heenan, T. A. (1983). Recognition of vocal expression of emotion: A three-nation study to identify universal characteristics. *Journal of Cross-Cultural Psychology, 14,* 387–406.

van Bokhoven, I., van Goozen, S. H. M., van Engeland, H., Schaal, B., Arseneault, L., Séguin, J. R., et al. (2006). Salivary testosterone and aggression, delinquency, and social dominance in a population-based longitudinal study of adolescent males. *Hormones and Behavior, 50,* 118–125.

van Dam, R. M., Li, T., Spiegelman, D., Franco, O. H., & Hu, F. B. (2008). Combined impact of lifestyle factors on mortality: prospective cohort study in US women. *British Medical Journal, 337,* a1440.

Vandello, J. A., & Cohen, D. (1999). Patterns of individualism and collectivism across the United States. *Journal of Personality and Social Psychology, 77,* 279–292.

Van de Vijver, F. J. R., & Leung, K. (2001). Personality in cultural context: Methodological issues. *Journal of Personality, 69*(6), 1007–1031.

Vandewater, E. A., Rideout, V. J., Wartella, E. A., Huang, X., Lee, J. H., & Shim, M. S. (2007). Digital childhood: Electronic media and technology use among infants, toddlers, and preschoolers. *Pediatrics, 119,* 1006–1015.

Van den Bergh, B. R., & Marcoen, A. (2004). High antenatal maternal anxiety is related to ADHD symptoms, externalizing problems, and anxiety in 8- and 9-year-olds. *Child Development, 75,* 1085–1097.

van der Does, W. (2006). Has everyone won, and must all have prizes? *Psycholoog, 41*(12), 650–657.

van der Hart, O., Bolt, H., & van der Kolk, B. A. (2005). Memory fragmentation in dissociative identity disorder. *Journal of Trauma & Dissociation, 6*(1), 55–70.

van der Kolk, B. A.,Spinazzola, J., Blaustein, M. E., Hopper, J. W., Korn, D. L., & Simpson, W. B. (2007). A randomized clinical trial of eye movement desensitization and reprocessing (EMDR), fluoxetine, and pill placebo in the treatment of posttraumatic stress disorder: treatment effects and long-term maintenance. *Journal of Clinical Psychiatry, 68*(1), 37–46.

Van der Molen, J. H. W. (2004). Violence and suffering in television news: Toward a broader conception of harmful television content for children. *Pediatrics, 113,* 1771–1775.

Van Deusen, K. M. (2004). Bilateral stimulation in EMDR: A replicated single-subject component analysis. *Behavior Therapist, 27,* 79–86.

Van Eerde, W., & Thierry, H. (1996). Vrooms's expectancy models and work- related criteria: A meta-analysis. *Journal of Applied Psychology, 81,* 575–586.

van Griensven, F., Chakkradband, S., Thienkrua, W., Pengjuntr, W., Cardozo, B. L., Tantipiwatanaskul, P., et al. (2006). Mental health problems among adults in tsunami-affected areas in southern Thailand. *Journal of the American Medical Association, 296,* 537–548.

Van Hiel, A., & Mervielde, I. (2004). Openness to experience and boundaries in the mind: Relationships with cultural and economic conservative beliefs. *Journal of Personality, 72,* 659–686.

Van Hoesen, G. W., Hyman, B. T., & Damasio, A. R. (1991). Entorhinal cortex pathology in Alzheimer's disease. *Hippocampus, 1*(1), 1–8.

van IJzendoom, M. H., & Juffer, F. (2005). Adoption as a successful natural intervention enhancing adopted children's IQ and school performance. *Current Directions in Psychological Science, 14,* 326–330.

van IJzendoorn, M. H. (1995). Adult attachment representations, parental responsiveness, and infant attachment: A meta-analysis on the predictive validity of the Adult Attachment Interview. *Psychological Bulletin, 117,* 387–403.

Vanman, E. J., Saltz, J. L., Nathan, L. R., & Warren, J. A. (2004). Racial discrimination by low-prejudiced whites. *Psychological Science, 15,* 711–714.

van Os, J., Rutten, B. P. F., Poulton, R. (2008). Gene-environmental interactions in schizophrenia: Review of epidemiological findings and future directions. *Schizophrenia Bulletin, 34,* 1066–1082.

Van Sickel, A. D. (1992). Clinical hypnosis in the practice of anesthesia. *Nurse Anesthesiologist, 3,* 67–74.

van Wel, F., ter Bogt, T., & Raaijmakers, Q. (2002). Changes in the parental bond and the well-being of adolescents and young adults. *Adolescence, 37*(146), 317–333.

Varnum, M. E. W., Grossmann, I., Katunar, D., Nisbett, R. E., & Kitayama, S. (2008). Holism in a European cultural context: Differences in cognitive style between Central and East Europeans and westerners. *Journal of Cognition & Culture, 8*(3–4), 321–333.

Vasey, P. L., & VanderLaan, D. P. (2007). Birth order and male androphilia in Samoan fa'afafine. *Proceedings of the Royal Society: Biological Sciences, 274*(1616), 1437–1442.

Vasilakopoulou, A., & le Roux, C. W. (2007). Could a virus contribute to weight gain? *International Journal of Obesity, 31,* 1350–1356.

Vasquez, M. J. T. (2007). Cultural difference and the therapeutic alliance: An evidence-based analysis. *American Psychologist, 62,* 878–885.

Vattano, F. (2000). *The mind: Video teaching modules* (2nd ed.). Fort Collins, CO: Colorado State University and Annenberg/CPB.

Vazza, G., Bertolin, C., Scudellaro, E., Vettori, A., Boaretto, F., Rampinelli, S., et al. (2007). Genome-wide scan supports the existence of a susceptibility locus for schizophrenia and bipolar disorder on chromosome 15q26. *Molecular Psychiatry, 12,* 87–93.

Veale, D. (2009). Body dysmorphic disorder. In M. M. Antony & M. B. Stein, (Eds.). *Oxford handbook of anxiety and related disorders* (pp. 541–550). New York: Oxford University Press USA.

Vecera, S. P., Vogel, E. K., & Woodman, G. F. (2002). Lower region: A new cue for figure-ground assignment. *Journal of Experimental Psychology: General, 131,* 194–205.

Velakoulis, D., Wood, S. J., Wong, M. T., McGorry, P. D., Yung, A., Phillips, L., et al. (2006). Hippocampal and amygdala volumes according to psychosis stage and diagnosis: A magnetic resonance imaging study of chronic schizophrenia, first-episode psychosis, and ultra-high-risk individuals. *Archives of General Psychiatry, 63,* 139–149.

Velicer, C. M., Heckbert, S. R., Lampe, J. W., Potter, J. D., Robertson, C. A., & Taplin, S. H. (2004). Antibiotic use in relation to the risk of breast cancer. *Journal of the American Medical Association, 291,* 827–835.

Velligan, D. I., Bow-Thomas, C. C., Huntzinger, C., Ritch, J., Ledbetter, N., Prihoda, T. J., & Miller, A. L. (2000). Randomized controlled trial of the use of compensatory strategies to enhance adaptive functioning in outpatients with schizophrenia. *American Journal of Psychiatry, 157,* 1317–1328.

Vemuganti, R., Kalluri, H., Yi, J., Bowen, K. K., & Hazell, A. S. (2006). Gene expression changes in thalamus and inferior colliculus associated with inflammation, cellular stress, metabolism and structural damage in thiamine deficiency. *European Journal of Neuroscience, 23*(5), 1172–1188.

Vennemann, M. M., Bajanowski, T., Brinkmann, B., Jorch, G., Sauerland, C., & Mitchell, E. A. (2009a). Sleep environment risk factors for sudden infant death syndrome: The German sudden infant death syndrome study. *Pediatrics, 123,* 1162–1170.

Vennemann, M. M., Bajanowski, T., Brinkmann, B., Jorch, G., Yücesan, K., Sauerland, C., & Mitchell, E. A. (2009b). Does breastfeeding reduce the risk of sudden infant death syndrome? *Pediatrics, 123,* e406–e410.

Venter, J. C., et al. (2001). The sequence of the human genome. *Science, 291,* 1304–1351.

Verghese, J., LeValley, A., Derby, C., Kuslansky, G., Katz, M., Buschke, H., et al. (2006). Leisure activities and the risk of amnestic mild cognitive impairment in the elderly. *Neurology, 66,* 821–827.

Verghese, J., Lipton, R. B., Katz, M. J., Hall, C. B., Derby, C. A., Kuslansky, G., et al. (2003). Leisure activities and the risk of dementia in the elderly. *New England Journal of Medicine, 348,* 2508–2516.

Vernacchio, L., Corwin, M. J., Lesko, S. M., Vezina, R. M., Hunt, C. E., Hoffman, H. J., et al. (2003). Sleep position of low birth weight infants. *Pediatrics, 111,* 633–640.

Vernet, M. E., Robin, O., & Dittmar, A. (1995). The ohmic perturbation duration, an original temporal index to quantify electrodermal responses. *Behavioural Brain Research, 67*(1), 103–107.

Vernon, P. A., Martin, R. A., Schermer, J. A., & Mackie, A. (2008). A behavioral genetic investigation of humor styles and their correlations with the big-5 personality dimensions. *Personality and Individual Differences, 44*(5), 1116–1125.

Vernon, P. A., Villani, V. C., Vickers, L. C., & Harris, J. A. (2008). A behavioral genetic investigation of the Dark Triad and the Big 5. *Personality and Individual Differences, 44*(2), 445–452.

Verona, E., Patrick, C. J., Curtin, J. J., Bradley, M. M., & Lang, P. J. (2004). Psychopathy and physiological response to emotionally evocative sounds. *Journal of Abnormal Psychology, 113,* 99–108.

Verster, J. C., & Volkerts, E. R. (2004). Clinical pharmacology, clinical efficacy, and behavioral toxicity of alprazolam: A review of the literature. *CNS Drug Reviews, 10,* 45–76.

Verweij, K., Shekar, S. N., Zietsch, B. P., Eaves, L. J., Bailey, J. M., Boomsma, D. I., & Martin, N. G. (2008). Genetic and environmental influences on individual differences in attitudes toward homosexuality: An Australian twin study. *Behavior Genetics 38,* 257–265.

Vetter, M. L., Cardillo, S., Rickels, M. R., & Iqbal, N. (2009). Narrative review: effect of bariatric surgery on type 2 diabetes mellitus. *Annals of Internal Medicine, 150*(2), 94–103.

Vierikko, E., Pulkkinen, L., Kaprio, J., & Rose, R. J. (2006). Genetic and environmental sources of continuity and change in teacher–rated aggression during early adolescence. *Aggressive Behavior, 32,* 308–320.

Vieta, E., & Phillips, M. L. (2007). Deconstructing bipolar disorder: A critical review of its diagnostic validity and a proposal for DSM-V and ICD-11. *Schizophrenia Bulletin, 33,* 886–892.

Vignoles, V. L., Regalia, C., Manzi, C., Golledge, J., & Scabini, E. (2006). Beyond self-esteem: Influence of multiple motives on identity construction. *Journal of Personality and Social Psychology, 90,* 308–333.

Vijayalaxmi, V. T. J. (2008). Genetic damage in mammalian somatic cells exposed to radiofrequency radiation: a meta-analysis of data from 63 publications (1990–2005). *Radiation Research, 169*(5), 561–574.

Villalta-Gil, V., Vilaplana, M., Ochoa, S., Dolz, M., Usall, J., Haro, J. M., et al. (2006). Four symptom dimensions in outpatients with schizophrenia. *Comprehensive Psychiatry, 47,* 384–388.

Vincent, C. A., & Richardson, P. H. (1986). The evaluation of therapeutic acupuncture: Concepts and methods. *Pain, 24,* 1–13.

Vingerhoets, G., Berckmoes, C., & Stroobant, N. (2003). Cerebral hemodynamics during discrimination of prosodic and semantic emotion in speech studied by transcranial Doppler ultrasonography. *Neuropsychology, 17,* 93–99.

Vink, T., Hinney, A., van Elburg, A. A., van Goozen, S. H. M., Sandkuijl, L. A., Sinke, R. J., et al. (2001). Association between an agouti-related protein gene polymorphism and anorexia nervosa. *Molecular Psychiatry, 6,* 325–328.

Vinod, K. Y., Yalamanchili, R., Xie, S., Cooper, T. B., & Hungund, B. L. (2006). Effect of chronic ethanol exposure and its withdrawal on the endocannabinoid system. *Neurochemistry International, 49,* 619–625.

Visser, P. J., Krabbendam, L., Verhey, F. R., Hofman, P. A., Verhoeven, W. M., Tuinier, S., et al. (1999). Brain correlates of memory dysfunction in alcoholic Korsakoff's syndrome. *Journal of Neurology, Neurosurgery, and Psychiatry, 67*(6), 774–778.

Visser, P. S., Krosnick, J. A., & Lavrakas, P. J. (2000). Survey research. In H. T. Reis & C. Judd (Eds.), *Handbook of research methods in social and personality psychology* (pp. 223–252). Cambridge, UK: Cambridge University Press.

Viswesvaran, C., & Ones, D. S. (2000). Measurement error in "Big Five factors" personality assessment: Reliability generalization across studies and measures. *Educational and Psychological Measurement, 60,* 224–235.

Vitaliano, P. P., Zhang, J. M., & Scanlan, J. M. (2003). Is caregiving hazardous to one's physical health? A meta-analysis. *Psychological Bulletin, 129,* 946–972.

Vitiello, B., & Swedo, S. (2004). Antidepressant medications in children. *New England Journal of Medicine, 350,* 1489–1491.

Vocisano, C., Klein, D. N., Arnow, B., Rivera, C., Blalock, J. A., Rothbaum, B., et al. (2004). Therapist variables that predict symptom change in psychotherapy with chronically depressed outpatients. *Psychotherapy: Theory, Research, Training, Practice, 41,* 255–265.

Vogel, I., Brug, J., van der Ploeg, C. P. B., & Raat, H. (2009). Strategies for the prevention of mp3-induced hearing loss among adolescents: Expert opinions from a delphi study. *Pediatrics, 123,* 1257–1262.

Vokey, J. R. (2002). Subliminal messages. In J. R. Vokey & S. W. Allen (Eds.), *Psychological sketches* (6th ed., pp. 223–246). Lethbridge, Alberta, Canada: Psyence Ink.

Vokey, J. R., & Read, J. D. (1985). Subliminal messages: Between the devil and the media. *American Psychologist, 40,* 1231–1239.

Volk, H. E., Scherrer, J. F., Bucholz, K. K., Todorov, A., Heath, A. C., Jacob, T., & True, W. R. (2007). Evidence for specificity of transmission of alcohol and nicotine dependence in an offspring of twins design. *Alcohol Dependence, 87,* 225–232.

Volkow, N. D., Chang, L., Wang, G. J., Fowler, J. S., Franceschi, D., Sedler, M. J., et al. (2001). Higher cortical and lower subcortical metabolism in detoxified methamphetamine abusers. *American Journal of Psychiatry, 158,* 383–389.

Vollset, S. E., Tverdal, A., & Gjessing, H. K. (2006). Smoking and deaths between 40 and 70 years of age in women and men. *Annals of Internal Medicine, 144,* 381–389.

Volz, J. (2000). Successful aging. The second 50. *APA Monitor, 31,* 24–28.

Von Wright, J. M., Anderson, K., & Stenman, U. (1975). Generalization of conditioned GSRs in dichotic listening. In P. M. A. Rabbitt & S. Dornic (Eds.), *Attention and performance V.* New York: Academic Press.

Voracek, M., & Fisher, M. L. (2002). Shapely centrefolds? Temporal change in body measures: trend analysis. *British Medical Journal, 325,* 1447–1448.

Vorstman, J. A. S., Staal, W. G., van Daalen, E., van Engeland, H., Hochstenbach, P. F. R., & Franke, L. (2006). Identification of novel autism candidate regions through analysis of reported cytogenetic abnormalities associated with autism. *Molecular Psychiatry, 11,* 18–28.

Vroom, V. (1964). *Work and motivation.* New York: Wiley.

Vygotsky, L. S. (1991). Genesis of the higher mental functions. In P. Light, S. Sheldon, & M. Woodhead (Eds.), *Learning to think: Child development in social context* (Vol. 2, pp. 32–41). London: Routledge.

Vyse, S. A. (2000). *Believing in magic: The psychology of superstition* (Rep. ed.). New York: Oxford University Press.

Waagenaar, W. (1986). My memory: A study of autobiographical memory over six years. *Cognitive Psychology, 18,* 225–252.

Wacker, J., Chavanon, M.-L., & Stemmler, G. (2006). Investigating the dopaminergic basis of extraversion in humans: A multilevel approach. *Journal of Personality and Social Psychology, 91,* 171–187.

Wadden, T. A., Berkowitz, R. I., Sarwer, D. B., Prus-Wisniewski, R., & Steinberg, C. (2001). Benefits of lifestyle modification in the pharmacologic treatment of obesity: A randomized trial. *Archives of Internal Medicine, 161,* 218–227.

Wadden, T. A., Berkowitz, R. I., Womble, L. G., Sarwer, D. B., Phelan, S., Cato, R. K., et al. (2005). Randomized trial of lifestyle modification and pharmacotherapy for obesity. *New England Journal of Medicine, 353,* 2111–2120.

Wade, C. (1988, April). *Thinking critically about critical thinking in psychology.* Paper presented at the annual meeting of the Western Psychological Association, San Francisco, CA.

Wade, J. B. (2004). Neuropsychologists diagnose traumatic brain injury. *Brain Injury, 18*(7), 629–643.

Wade, W. A., Treat, T. A., & Stuart, G. L. (1998). Transporting an empirically supported treatment for panic disorder to a service clinic setting: A benchmarking strategy. *Journal of Consulting and Clinical Psychology, 66,* 231–239.

Waelti, P., Dickinson, A., & Schultz, W. (2001). Dopamine responses comply with basic assumptions of formal learning theory. *Nature, 412,* 43–48.

Wager, T. D. (2005). The neural bases of placebo effects in pain. *Current Directions in Psychological Science, 14,* 175–179.

Wager, T. D., Rilling, J. K., Smith, E. E., Sokolik, A., Casey, K. L., Davidson, R. J., et al. (2004). Placebo-induced changes in fMRI in the anticipation and experience of pain. *Science, 303,* 1162–1167.

Wagg, J. (2008, October 21). Yamaha Yakidding? Retrieved January 15, 2009, from http://www.randi.org/site/index.php/swift-blog/242-yamaha-yakidding.html.

Wagner, K. D., Ambrosini, P., Rynn, M., Wohlberg, C., Yang, R., Greenbaum, M. S., et al. (2003). Efficacy of sertraline in the treatment of children and adolescents with major depressive disorder: Two randomized controlled trials. *Journal of the American Medical Association, 290,* 1033–1041.

Wagner, U., Gais, S., & Born, J. (2001). Emotional memory formation is enhanced across sleep intervals with high amounts of rapid eye movement sleep. *Learning and Memory, 8,* 112–119.

Wagner, U., Hallschmid, M., Rasch, B., & Born, J. (2006). Brief sleep after learning keeps emotional memories alive for years. *Biological Psychiatry, 60,* 788–790.

Wai, J., Lubinski, D., & Benbow, C. P. (2005). Creativity and occupational accomplishments among intellectually precocious youth: An age 13 to age 33 longitudinal study. *Journal of Educational Psychology, 97,* 484–492.

Wakefield, J. C. (1992). The concept of mental disorder: On the boundary between biological facts and social values. *American Psychologist, 47,* 373–388.

Wakimoto, R. (2006). Mortality salience effects on modesty and relative self-effacement. *Asian Journal of Social Psychology, 9,* 176–183.

Wakschlag, L. S., Briggs-Gowan, M. J., Hill, C., Danis, B., Leventhal, B. L., Keenan, K., Egger, H. L., Cicchetti, D., Burns, C., & Carter, A. S. (2008). Observational assessment of preschool disruptive behavior, Part II: Validity of the Disruptive Behavior Diagnostic

Observation Schedule (DB-DOS). *Journal of the American Academy of Child & Adolescent Psychiatry, 47*(6), 632–641.

Wakschlag, L. S., Leventhal, B. L., Pine, D. S., Pickett, K. E., & Carter, A. S. (2006). Elucidating early mechanisms of developmental psychopathology: The case of prenatal smoking and disruptive behavior. *Child Development, 77,* 893–906.

Waldman, I. D., & Gizer, I. R. (2006). The genetics of attention deficit hyperactivity disorder. *Clinical Psychology Review, 26,* 396–432.

Walker, E. F., & Diforio, D. (1998). Schizophrenia: A neural diathesis-stress model. *Psychological Review, 104,* 667–685.

Walker, L. (1991). The feminization of psychology. *Psychology of Women Newsletter of Division, 35,* 1, 4.

Walker, M. P., Brakefield, T., Hobson, J. A., & Stickgold, R. (2003). Dissociable stages of human memory consolidation and reconsolidation. *Nature, 425,* 616–620.

Walker, M. P., & Stickgold, R. (2006). Sleep, memory, and plasticity. *Annual Review of Psychology, 57,* 139–166.

Walkup, J. T., Albano, A. M., Piacentini, J., Birmaher, B., Compton, S. N., Sherrill, J. T., Ginsburg, G. S., Rynn, M. A., McCracken, J., Waslick, B., Iyengar, S., March, J. S., & Kendall, P. C. (2008). Cognitive behavioral therapy, sertraline, or a combination in childhood anxiety. *The New England Journal of Medicine, 359,* 2753–2766.

Wall, T. L., Shea, S. H., Chan, K. K., & Carr, L. G. (2001). A genetic association with the development of alcohol and other substance use behavior in Asian Americans. *Journal of Abnormal Psychology, 110,* 173–178.

Wall, T. L., Shea, S. H., Luczak, S. E., Cook, T. A., & Carr, L. G. (2005). Genetic associations of alcohol dehydrogenase with alcohol use disorders and endophenotypes in white college students. *Journal of Abnormal Psychology, 114,* 456–465.

Wallace, J. C., Popp, E., & Mondore, S. (2006). Safety climate as a mediator between foundation climates and occupational accidents: A group-level investigation. *Journal of Applied Psychology, 91,* 681–688.

Wallace, R. K., & Benson, H. (1972). The physiology of meditation. *Scientific American, 226,* 84–90.

Wallen, K., & Lovejoy, J. (1993). Sexual behavior: Endocrine function and therapy. In J. Shulkin (Ed.), *Hormonal pathways to mind and brain.* New York: Academic Press.

Wallerstein, R. S. (2002). The growth and transformation of American ego psychology. *Journal of the American Psychoanalytic Association, 50,* 135–169.

Walsh, R., & Shapiro, S. L. (2006). The meeting of meditative disciplines and Western psychology: A mutually enriching dialogue. *American Psychologist, 61,* 227–239.

Walther, E., & Langer, T. (2008). Attitude formation and change though association: An evaluative conditioning account. In R. Prislin & W. B. Crano (Eds.), *Attitudes and Persuasion* (pp. 87–110). New York: Psychology Press.

Walton, G. E., Bower, N. J. A., & Bower, T. G. R. (1992). Recognition of familiar faces by newborns. *Infant Behavior and Development, 15,* 265–269.

Wampold, B. E. (2005). Estimating variability in outcomes attributable to therapists: A naturalistic study of outcomes in managed care. *Journal of Consulting and Clinical Psychology, 73,* 914–923.

Wampold, B. E. (2007). Psychotherapy: The humanistic (and effective) treatment. *American Psychologist, 62,* 857–873.

Wampold, B. E., Ahn, H., & Coleman, H. L. K. (2001). Medical model as metaphor: Old habits die hard. *Journal of Counseling Psychology, 48,* 263–273.

Wampold, B. E., Minami, T., Tierney, S. C., Baskin, T. W., & Bhati, K. S. (2005). The placebo is powerful: Estimating placebo effects in medicine and psychotherapy from randomized clinical trials. *Journal of Clinical Psychology, 61,* 835–854.

Wanders, F., Serra, M., & de Jongh, A. (2008). EMDR versus CBT for children with self-esteem and behavioral problems: A randomized controlled trial. *Journal of EMDR Practice and Research, 2*(3), 180–189.

Wanek, J. E., Sackett, P. R., & Ones, D. S. (2003). Towards an understanding of integrity test similarities and differences: An item-level analysis of seven tests. *Personnel Psychology, 56,* 873–894.

Wang, C., Collet, J. P., & Lau, J. (2004). The effect of Tai Chi on health outcomes in patients with chronic conditions: A systematic review. *Archives of Internal Medicine, 164,* 493–501.

Wang, O. (2006). Earliest recollections of self and others in European American and Taiwanese young adults. *Psychological Science, 17,* 708–714.

Wang, P. S., Aguilar-Gaxiola, S., Alonso, J., Angermeyer, M. C., Borges, G., Bromet, E. J., et al. (2007). Use of mental health services for anxiety, mood, and substance disorders in 17 countries in the WHO world mental health surveys. *Lancet, 370,* 841–850.

Wang, P. S., Demler, O., Olfson, M., Pincus, H. A., Wells, K. B., & Kessler, R. C. (2006). Changing profiles of service sectors used in mental health care in the United States. *American Journal of Psychiatry, 163,* 1187–1198.

Wang, P. S., Lane, M., Olfson, M., Pincus, H. A., Wells, K. B., & Kessler, R. C. (2005). Twelve-month use of mental health services in the United States: Results from the National Comorbidity Survey Replication. *Archives of General Psychiatry, 62,* 629–640.

Wang, Q. (2008). Emotion knowledge and autobiographical memory across the preschool years: A cross-cultural longitudinal investigation. *Cognition, 108,* 117–135.

Wang, S., M., Kain, Z. N., & White, P. (2008). Acupuncture analgesia: I. The scientific basis. *Anesthesia and Analgesia, 106*(2), 602–610.

Wang, X., Merzenich, M. M., Sameshima, K., & Jenkins, W. M. (1995). Remodelling of hand representation in adult cortex determined by timing of tactile stimulation. *Nature, 378,* 71–75.

Wang, Y. (2007). Cognitive informatics: Exploring the theoretical foundations for natural intelligence, neural informatics, autonomic computing, and agent systems. *International Journal of Cognitive Informatics and Natural Intelligence, 1*(1), i–x.

Warburton, D. M. (1995). Effects of caffeine on cognition and mood without caffeine abstinence. *Psychopharmacology, 119,* 66–70.

Ward, C. (1994). Culture and altered states of consciousness. In W. J. Lonner & R. S. Malpass (Eds.), *Psychology and culture.* Boston: Allyn & Bacon.

Warneken, F., & Tomasello, M. (2006). Altruistic helping in human infants and young chimpanzees. *Science, 311,* 1301–1303.

Warner, L., Kessler, R., Hughes, M., Anthony, J., & Nelson, C. (1995). Prevalence and correlates of drug use and dependence in the United States. *Archives of General Psychiatry, 52,* 219–229.

Watanabe, S., Sakamoto, J., & Wakita, M. (1995). Pigeons' discrimination of paintings by Monet and Picasso. *Journal of Experimental Analysis of Behavior, 63,* 165–174.

Watanabe, T., Náñez, J. E., & Sasaki, Y. (2001). Perceptual learning without perception. *Nature, 413,* 844–848.

Waterhouse, L. (2006a). Inadequate evidence for multiple intelligences, Mozart Effect, and emotional intelligence theories. *Educational Psychologist, 41*(4), 247–255.

Waterhouse, L. (2006b). Multiple Intelligences, the Mozart Effect, and emotional intelligence: A critical review. *Educational Psychologist, 41*(4), 207–225.

Waterman, A. S. (1982). Identity development from adolescence to adulthood: An extension of theory and a review of research. *Developmental Psychology, 18,* 341–358.

Waters, E., Merrick, S., Treboux, D., Crowell, J., & Albersheim, L. (2000). Attachment security in infancy and early adulthood: A twenty-year longitudinal study. *Child Development, 71,* 684–689.

Watkins, K. E., Smith, S. M., Davis, S., & Howell, P. (2008). Structural and functional abnormalities of the motor system in developmental stuttering. *Brain, 131,* 50–59.

Watson, J. B. (1913). Psychology as the behaviorist views it. *Psychological Review, 20,* 158–177.

Watson, J. B. (1919). *Psychology from the standpoint of a behaviorist.* Philadelphia: Lippincott.

Watson, J. B. (1925). *Behaviorism.* London: Kegan Paul, Trench, Trubner.

Watson, R. T., & Heilman, K. M. (1979). Thalamic neglect. *Neurology, 29*(5), 690–694.

Waugh, C. E., Wager, T. D., Fredrickson, B. L., Noll, D. C., & Taylor, S. F. (in press). The neural correlates of trait resilience when anticipating and recovering from threat. *Social Cognitive and Affective Neuroscience.*

Wearden, A. J., Tarrier, N., Barrowclough, C., Zastowny, T. R., & Rahill, A. A. (2000). A review of expressed emotion research in health care. *Clinical Psychology Review, 20,* 633–666.

Weaver, F. M., Follett, K., Stern, M., Hur, K., Harris, C., Marks, W. J., Jr., et al. (2009). Bilateral deep brain stimulation vs best medical therapy for patients with advanced Parkinson disease: A randomized controlled trial. *Journal of the American Medical Association, 301*(1), 63–73.

Webb, T. L., & Sheeran, P. (2006). Does changing behavioral intentions engender behavior change? A meta-analysis of the experimental evidence. *Psychological Bulletin, 132,* 249–268.

Weber, J. M., Kopelman, S., & Messick, D. M. (2004). A conceptual review of decision making in social dilemmas: Applying a logic of appropriateness. *Personality and Social Psychology Review, 8,* 281–307.

Weber, M. A., Klein, N. J., Hartley, J. C., Lock, P. E., Malone, M., & Sebire, N. J. (2008). Infection and sudden unexpected death in infancy: A systematic retrospective case review. *The Lancet, 371,* 1848–1853.

Weber, R. J. (1992). *Forks, phonographs, and hot air balloons: A field guide to inventive thinking.* New York: Oxford University Press.

Wechsler, D. (1939). *The measurement of adult intelligence.* Baltimore: Williams & Wilkins.

Wechsler, D. (1949). *The Wechsler Intelligence Scale for Children.* New York: Psychological Corporation.

Wechsler, D. (2003). *Wechsler Intelligence Scale for Children* (4th ed.). San Antonio, TX: Psychological Corporation.

Wecker, N. S., Kramer, J. H., Hallam, B. J., & Delis, D. C. (2005). Mental flexibility: Age effects on switching. *Neuropsychology, 19,* 345–352.

Weekes, J. R., Lynn, S. J., Green, J. P., & Brentar, J. T. (1992). Pseudomemory in hypnotized and task-motivated subjects. *Journal of Abnormal Psychology, 101,* 356–360.

Wegge, J., & Haslam, S. A. (2005). Improving work motivation and performance in brainstorming groups: The effects of three group goal-setting strategies. *European Journal of Work and Organizational Psychology, 14,* 400–430.

Wegner, D. M., Wenzlaff, R. M., & Kozak, M. (2004). Dream rebound: The return of suppressed thoughts in dreams. *Psychological Science, 15,* 232–236.

Weihs, K. L., Enright, T. M., & Simmens, S. J. (2008). Close relationships and emotional processing predict decreased mortality in women with breast cancer: Preliminary evidence. *Psychosomatic Medicine, 70,* 117–124.

Weiler, B. L., & Widom, C. S. (1996). Psychopathy and violent behavior in abused and neglected young adults. *Criminal Behaviour and Mental Health, 6,* 253–271.

Weinberg, R. A., Scarr, S., & Waldman, I. D. (1992). The Minnesota transracial adoption study: A follow-up of IQ test performance at adolescence. *Intelligence, 16,* 117–135.

Weiner, B. (1980). *Human motivation.* New York: Holt, Rinehart & Winston.

Weinfield, N. S., Sroufe, L. A., & Egeland, B. (2000). Attachment from infancy to early adulthood in a high-risk sample: continuity, discontinuity, and their correlates. *Child Development, 71,* 695–702.

Weinraub, M., Horvath, D. L., & Gringlas, M. B. (2002). Single parenthood. In M. H. Bornstein (Ed.), *Handbook of parenting: Vol. 3. Being and becoming a parent* (2nd ed., pp. 109–140). Mahwah, NJ: Erlbaum.

Weinstein, E. A., & Kahn, R. L. (1955). *Denial of illness: Symbolic and physiological aspects.* Springfield, IL: Thomas.

Weisman, A. (2005). Integrating culturally based approaches with existing interventions for Hispanic/Latino families coping with schizophrenia. *Psychotherapy: Theory, Research, Practice, Training, 42,* 178–197.

Weiss, A., Bates, T. C., & Luciano, M. (2008). Happiness is a personal(ity) thing: The genetics of personality and well-being in a representative sample. *Psychological Science 19,* 205–210.

Weiss, A., King, J. E., & Perkins, L. (2006). Personality and subjective well-being in orangutans (*pongo pygmaeus and pongo abelii*). *Journal of Personality and Social Psychology, 90,* 501–511.

Weiss, S., & Moore, M. (1990). Cultural differences in the perception of magazine alcohol advertisements by Israeli Jewish, Moslem, Druze, and Christian high school students. *Drug and Alcohol Dependence, 26,* 209–215.

Weiss, S. J., St. Jonn-Seed, M., & Harris-Muchell, C. (2007). The contribution of fetal drug exposure to temperament: Potential teratogenic effects on neuropsychiatric risk. *Journal of Child Psychology and Psychiatry, 48*(8), 773–784.

Weiss, V. (2007). Percentages of children living in poverty determine IQ averages of nations. *European Journal of Personality.* Special Issue: *European personality reviews, 21,* 761–763.

Weissberg, R. P., Kumpfer, K. L., & Seligman, M. E. P. (2003). Prevention that works for children and youth. *American Psychologist, 58,* 425–432.

Weissman, M. M., Markowitz, J. C., & Kierman, G. L. (2007). *Clinician's quick guide to interpersonal psychotherapy.* New York: Oxford University Press.

Weissman, M. M., Wickramaratne, P., Nomura, Y., Warner, V., Verdeli, H., Pilowsky, D. J., et al. (2005). Families at high and low risk for depression: A 3-generation study. *Archives of General Psychiatry, 62,* 29–36.

Weisz, J. R., Doss, A. J., & Hawley, K. M. (2005). Youth psychotherapy outcome researcy: A review and critique of the evidence base. *Annual Review of Psychology, 56,* 337–363.

Weisz, J. R., McCarty, C. A., & Valeri, S. M. (2006). Effects of psychotherapy for depression in children and adolescents: A meta-analysis. *Psychological Bulletin, 132,* 132–149.

Weisz, J. R., Weersing, V. R., & Henggeler, S. W. (2005). Jousting at straw men: Comment on Westen, Novotry, and Thompson-Brenner (2004). *Psychological Bulletin, 131,* 418–426.

Wells, A., & Matthews, G. (2006). Cognitive vulnerability to anxiety disorders: An integration. In L. B. Alloy & J. H. Ruskind (Eds.), *Cognitive vulnerability to emotional disorders* (pp. 303–325). New York: Erlbaum.

Wells, G. L., & Bradfield, A. L. (1999). Distortions in eyewitness' recollections: Can the postidentification-feedback effect be moderated? *Psychological Science, 10,* 138–144.

Wells, G. L., & Olson, E. A. (2003). Eyewitness testimony. *Annual Review of Psychology, 54,* 277–295.

Wells, G. L., & Quinlivan, D. S. (2009). Suggestive eyewitness identification procedures and the Supreme Court's reliability test in light of eyewitness science: 30 years later. *Law and Human Behavior, 33*(1), 1–24.

Wells, G. L., Malpass, R. S., Lindsay, R. C. L., Fisher, R. P., Turtle, J. W., & Fulero, S. M. (2000). From the lab to the police station: A successful application of eyewitness research. *American Psychologist, 55,* 581–598.

Wells, G. L., Memon, A., & Penrod, S. D. (2006). Eyewitness evidence: Improving its probative value. *Psychological Science in the Public Interest, 7,* 45–75.

Wells, G. L., Olson, E. A., & Charman, S. D. (2002). The confidence of eyewitnesses in their identifications from lineups. *Current Directions in Psychological Science, 11,* 151–154.

Wells, G. L., Olson, E. A., & Charman, S. D. (2003). Distorted retrospective eyewitness reports as functions of feedback and delay. *Journal of Experimental Psychology: Applied, 9,* 42–52.

Wells, S., Graham, K., & West, P. (2000). Alcohol-related aggression in the general population. *Journal of Studies on Alcohol, 61,* 626–632.

Welsh, T. N., Ray, M. C., Weeks, D. J., Dewey, D., & Elliot, D. (2009). Does Joe influence Fred's action? Not if Fred has autism spectrum disorder. *Brain Research, 1248,* 141–148.

Weltzin, T. E., Bulik, C. M., McConaha, C. W., & Kaye, W. H. (1995). Laxative withdrawal and anxiety in bulimia nervosa. *International Journal of Eating Disorders, 17*(2), 141–146.

Weng, X., Odouli, R., & Li, D.-K. (2008). Maternal caffeine consumption during pregnancy and the risk of miscarriage: A prospective cohort study. *American Journal of Obstetrics and Gynecology, 198,* 279.e1–279.e8.

Wengenack, T. M., Jack, C. R., Garwood, M., & Poduslo, J. F. (2008). MR Microimaging of amyloid plaques in Alzheimer's disease transgenic mice. *European Journal of Nuclear Medicine & Molecular Imaging, 35,* 82–88.

Wenzel, A., Sharp, I. R., Brown, G. K., Greenberg, R. L., & Beck, A. T. (2006). Dysfunctional beliefs in panic disorder: The Panic Belief Inventory. *Behaviour Research and Therapy, 44,* 819–833.

Werner, E. (2003, January 28). Police: Sons kill mom, dismember her after seeing it done on "The Sopranos." *Naples Daily News.*

Wernig, M., Zhao, J. P., Pruszak, J., Hedlund, E., Fu, D., Soldner, F., et al. (2008). Neurons derived from reprogrammed fibroblasts functionally integrate into the fetal brain and improve symptoms of rats with Parkinson's disease. *Proceedings of the National Academy of Sciences, 105*(15), 5856–5861.

West, M. A., Borrill, C. S., & Unsworth, K. L. (1998). Team effectiveness in organizations. In C. L. Cooper & I. T. Robertson (Eds.), *International review of industrial and organizational psychology 1998* (pp. 1–48). Chichester, UK: Wiley.

West, S. L., D'Aloisio, A. A., Agans, R. P., Kalsbeek, W. D., Borisov, N. N., & Thorp, J. M. (2008). Prevalence of low sexual desire and hypoactive sexual desire disorder in a nationally representative sample of US women. *Archives of Internal Medicine, 168,* 1441–1449.

Westen, D. (2005). Implications of research in cognitive neuroscience for psychodynamic psychotherapy. In G. Gabbard, J. Beck, & J. Holmes (Eds.), *Oxford textbook of psychotherapy* (pp. 447–454). Oxford: Oxford University Press.

Westen, D., & Bradley, R. (2005). Empirically supported complexity. *Current Directions in Psychological Science, 14,* 266–271.

Westen, D., Glen, O., Gabbard, G. O., & Ortigo, K. M. (2008). Psychoanalytic approaches to personality. In O. John, R. Robins, & L. Pervin (Eds.), *Handbook of personality: Theory and research* (3rd ed., pp. 61–113). New York: Guilford.

Westen, D., Novotny, C. M., & Thompson-Brenner, H. (2004). The empirical status of empirically supported psychotherapies: Assumptions, findings, and reporting in controlled clinical trials. *Psychological Bulletin, 130,* 631–663.

Westen, D., Shedler, J., & Bradley, R. (2006). A prototype approach to personality disorder diagnosis. *American Journal of Psychiatry, 163,* 846–856.

Weuve, J., Kang, J. H., Manson, J. E., Breteler, M. M. B., Ware, J. H., & Grodstein, F. (2004). Physical activity, including walking, and cognitive function in older women. *Journal of the American Medical Association, 292,* 1454–1461.

Wexler, M. (2005). Anticipating the three-dimensional consequences of eye movements. *Proceedings of the National Academy of Sciences, 102,* 1246–1251.

Whalen, P. J. (1998). Fear, vigilance, and ambiguity: Initial neuroimaging studies of the human amygdala. *Current Directions in Psychological Science, 7,* 177–188.

Whalen, P. J., Kagan, J., Cook, R. G., Davis, F. C., Kim, H., Polis, S., et al. (2004). Human amygdala responsivity to masked fearful eye whites. *Science, 306,* 2061.

Whaley, A. L. (2001). Cultural mistrust: An important psychological construct for diagnosis and treatment of African-Americans. *Professional Psychology: Research and Practice, 32,* 555–562.

Whalley, L. J., & Deary, I. J. (2001). Longitudinal cohort study of childhood IQ up to age 76. *British Medical Journal, 322,* 819.

Wharton, C. M., Grafman, J., Flitman, S. S., Hansen, E. K., Brauner, J., Marks, A., & Honda, M. (2000). Toward neuroanatomical models of analogy: A positron emission tomography study of analogical mapping. *Cognitive Psychology, 40,* 173–197.

Wheaton, L. A., & Hallett, M. (2007). Ideomotor apraxia: A review. *Journal of the Neurological Sciences, 260*(1–2), 1–10.

Wheeler, B. W., Gunnell, D., Metcalfe, C., Stephens, P., & Martin, R. M. (2008). The population impact on incidence of suicide and non-fatal self harm of regulatory action against the use of selective serotonin reuptake inhibitors in under 18s in the United Kingdom: Ecological study. *British Medical Journal, 336,* 542–545.

Wheeler, M. E., & Fiske, S. T. (2005). Controlling racial prejudice. *Psychological Science, 16,* 56–63.

Whiffin, V. E. (2006). *A secret sadness: The hidden relationship patterns that make women depressed.* Oakland, CA: New Harbinger Publications.

Whimbey, A. (1976). *Intelligence can be taught.* New York: Bantam.

Whitaker, D. J., Morrison, S., Lindquist, C., Hawkins, S. R., O'Neil, J. A., Nesius, A. M., et al. (2006). A critical review of interventions for the primary prevention of perpetration of partner violence. *Aggression and Violent Behavior, 11,* 151–166.

Whitam, F. L., Diamond, M., & Martin, J. (1993). Homosexual orientation in twins: A report on 61 pairs and three triplet sets. *Archives of Sexual Behavior, 22*(3), 187–206.

White, A. T., & Spector, P. E. (1987). An investigation of age-related factors in the age-job satisfaction relationship. *Psychology and Aging, 2,* 261–265.

White, F. J. (1998). Nicotine addiction and the lure of reward. *Nature Medicine, 4,* 659–660.

White, K. S., Brown, T. A., Somers, T. J., & Barlow, D. H. (2006). Avoidance behavior in panic disorder: The moderating influences of perceived control. *Behaviour Research and Therapy, 44,* 147–157.

Whitlock, J. R., Heynen, A. J., Shuler, M. G., & Bear, M. F. (2006). Learning induces long-term potentiation in the hippocampus. *Science, 313,* 1093–1097.

Whitney, P. (2001). Schemas, frames, and scripts in cognitive psychology. In N. J. Smelser & P. B. Baltes (Eds.), *International encyclopedia of the social and behavioral sciences* (pp. 13522–13526). New York: Elsevier.

Whittington, C. J., Kendall, T., & Pilling, S. (2005). Are SSRIs and atypical antidepressants safe and effective for children and adolescents? *Current Opinion in Psychiatry, 18,* 21–25.

Wichers, M. C., Myin-Germeys, I., Jacobs, N., Kenis, G., Dermon, C., Vlietinck, R., et al. (2008). Susceptibility to depression expressed as alterations in cortisol day curve: A cross-twin, cross-trait study. *Biological Psychology, 79,* 80–90.

Wicherski, M., & Kohout, J. (2007). *2005 doctorate employment survey.* Washington, D. C.: American Psychological Association, APA Center for Psychology Workforce Analysis and Research.

Wickens, C. D. (1989). Attention and skilled performance. In D. Holding (Ed.), *Human skills* (pp. 71–105). New York: Wiley.

Wickens, C. D. (1992). *Engineering psychology and human performance* (2nd ed.). New York: HarperCollins.

Wickens, C. D. (2002). Situation awareness and workload in aviation. *Current Directions in Psychological Science, 11,* 128–133.

Wickens, C. D., & Carswell, C. M. (2006). Information processing. In G. Salvendy (Ed.), *Handbook of human factors and ergonomics* (3rd ed.). Hoboken, NJ: Wiley Interscience.

Wickens, C. D., Stokes, A., Barnett, B., & Hyman, F. (1992). The effects of stress on pilot judgment in a MIDIS simulator. In O. Svenson & J. Maule (Eds.), *Time pressure and stress in human judgment and decision making* (pp. 271–292). New York: Plenum.

Wicker, B., Keysers, C., Plailly, J., Royet, J. P., Gallese, V., & Rizzolatti, G. (2003). Both of us disgusted in My insula: The common neural basis of seeing and feeling disgust. *Neuron, 40,* 655–664.

Wickham, D. (2001, September 3). Castration often fails to halt offenders. *USA Today.*

Widiger, T. A. (2008). Personality disorders. In J. Hunsley, E. J. Mash (Eds.), *A guide to assessments that work* (pp. 413–435). New York: Oxford University Press.

Widiger, T. A., & Clark, L. A. (2000). Toward *DSM-V* and the classification of psychopathology. *Psychological Bulletin, 126,* 946–963.

Widiger, T. A., & Lowe, J. R. (2008). A dimensional model of personality disorder: Proposal for DSM-V. *Psychiatric Clinics of North America, 31,* 363–378.

Widiger, T. A., & Samuel, D. B. (2005). Diagnostic categories or dimensions? A question for the *Diagnostic and Statistical Manual of Mental Disorders—Fifth Edition. Journal of Abnormal Psychology, 114,* 494–504.

Widiger, T. A., Simonsen, E., Sirovatka, P., & Reiger, D. A. (2006). *Dimensional models of personality disorders: Refining the research agenda for DSM-V.* Washington, DC: American Psychiatric Publishing.

Widom, C. S. (1989). The cycle of violence. *Science, 244,* 160–166.

Widom, C. S. (2000). Childhood victimization: Early adversity, later psychopathology. *National Institute of Justice Journal, 19,* 2–9.

Widom, C. S., Czaja, S. J., & Dutton, M. A. (2008). Childhood victimization and lifetime revictimization. *Child Abuse and Neglect, 32,* 785–796.

Widom, C. S., Kahn, E. E., Kaplow, J. B., Sepulveda-Kozakowski, S., & Wilson, H. W. (2007). Child abuse and neglect: Potential derailment from normal developmental pathways. *NYS Psychologist, 19*(5), 2–6.

Wiech, K., Ploner, M., & Tracey, I. (2008). Neurocognitive aspects of pain perception. *Trends in Cognitive Sciences, 12*(8), 306–313.

Wiederhold, B. K., & Wiederhold, M. D. (2005). *Virtual reality therapy for anxiety disorders: Advances in evaluation and treatment.* Washington, DC: American Psychological Association.

Wiens, S., Mezzacappa, E. S., & Katkin, E. S. (2000). Heartbeat detection and the experience of emotions. *Cognition & Emotion, 14,* 417–427.

Wiesner, W. H., & Cronshaw, S. F. (1988). A meta-analytic investigation of the impact of interview format and degree of structure on the validity of the employment interview. *Journal of Occupational Psychology, 61,* 275–290.

Wigfield, A., & Eccles, J. S. (2000). Expectancy-value theory of achievement motivation. *Contemporary Educational Psychology, 25,* 68–81.

Wilcox, H. C., Grados, M., Samuels, J., Riddle, M. A., Beinvenu, O. J., III, Pinto, A., et al. (2008). The association between parental bonding and obsessive-compulsive disorder in offspring at high familial risk. *Journal of Affective Disorders, 111,* 31–39.

Wilhelm, K., Mitchell, P. B., Niven, H., Finch, A., Wedgwood, L., et al. (2006). Life events, first depression onset, and the serotonin transporter gene. *British Journal of Psychiatry, 188,* 210–215.

Wilhelm, K., Siegel, J. E., Finch, A. W., Hadzi-Pavlovic, D., Mitchell, P. B., Parker, G., & Schofield, P. R. (2007). The long and the short of it: Associations between 5-HTT genotypes and coping with stress. *Psychosomatic Medicine 69,* 614–620.

Wilkowski, B. M., & Robinson, M. D. (2008). The cognitive basis of trait anger and reactive aggression: An integrative analysis. *Personality & Social Psychology Review, 12*(1), 3–21.

Willams, R. B. (2001). Hostility and heart disease: Williams et al. (1980). *Advances in Mind-Body Medicine, 17,* 52–55.

Willford, J. A., Leech, S. L., & Day, N. L. (2006). Moderate prenatal alcohol exposure and cognitive status of children at age 10. *Alcoholism: Clinical and Experimental Research, 30,* 1051–1059.

Williams, C. L., & Pleil, K. E. (2008). Toy story: Why do monkey and human males prefer trucks? *Hormones and Behavior, 54,* 355–358.

Williams, E., Thomas, K., Sidebotham, H., & Emond, A. (2008). Prevalence and characteristics of autistic spectrum disorders in the ALSPAC cohort. *Developmental Medicine and Child Neurology, 50,* 672–677.

Williams, J. (2008). Working toward a neurobiological account of ADHD: Commentary on Gail Tripp and Jeff Wickens' dopamine transfer deficit. *Journal of Child Psychology and Psychiatry, 49,* 705–711.

Williams, J. E., & Best, D. L. (1990). *Measuring stereotypes: A multination study* (Rev. ed.). Newbury Park, CA: Sage.

Williams, J. H. G., Waiter, G. D., Gilchrist, A., Perrett, D. I., Murray, A. D., et al. (2006). Neural mechanisms of imitation and 'mirror neuron' functioning in autistic spectrum disorder. *Neuropsychologica, 44,* 610–621.

Williams, K. D., & Sommer, K. L. (1997). Social ostracism by coworkers: Does rejection lead to loafing or compensation? *Personality and Social Psychology Bulletin, 23,* 693–706.

Williams, L. M. (1994). What does it mean to forget child sexual abuse? A reply to Loftus, Garry, and Feldman (1994). *Journal of Consulting and Clinical Psychology, 62,* 1182–1186.

Williams, N. L., Reardon, J. M., Murray, K. T., & Cole, T. M. (2005). Anxiety disorders: A developmental vulnerability-stress perspective. In B. L. Hankin & J. R. Z. Abela (Eds.), *Development of psychopathology: A vulnerability-stress perspective* (pp. 289–327). Newberry Park, CA: Sage.

Williams, R. A. (2005). A short course in family therapy: Translating research into practice. *Family Journal: Counseling and Therapy for Couples and Families 13,* 188–194.

Williams, R. J., & Connolly, D. (2006). Does learning about the mathematics of gambling change gambling behavior? *Psychology of Addictive Behavior, 20,* 62–68.

Williams, T. J., Pepitone, M. E., Christensen, S. E., Cooke, B. M., Huberman, A. D., Breedlove, N. J., et al. (2000). Finger-length ratios and sexual orientation. *Nature, 404,* 455–456.

Williams-Piehota, P., Pizarro, J., Schneider, T. R., Mowad, L., & Salovey, P. (2005). Matching health messages to monitor-blunter coping styles to motivate screening mammography. *Health Psychology, 24,* 58–67.

Willis, J., & Todorov, A. (2006). First impressions: Making up your mind after a 100-ms exposure to a face. *Psychological Science, 17,* 592–598.

Willis, S. L., & Schaie, K. W. (1999). Intellectual functioning in midlife. In S. L. Willis & J. D. Reid (Eds.), *Life in the middle: Psychological and social development in middle age* (pp. 233–247). San Diego: Academic Press.

Wilson, B. S., & Dorman, M. F. (2008). Cochlear implants: A remarkable past and a brilliant future. *Hearing Research, 242*(1–2), 3–21.

Wilson, E. J., MacLeod, C., Matthews, A., & Rutherford, E. M. (2006). The causal role of interpretive bias in anxiety reactivity. *Journal of Abnormal Psychology, 115,* 103–111.

Wilson, G. T. (1985). Limitations of meta-analysis in the evaluation of the effects of psychological therapy. *Clinical Psychology Review, 5,* 35–47.

Wilson, G. T. (1995). Behavior therapy. In R. J. Corsini & D. Wedding (Eds.), *Current psychotherapies* (5th ed., pp. 197–228). Itasca, IL: Peacock.

Wilson, G. T. (1997). Dissemination of cognitive behavioral treatments: Commentary. *Behavior Therapy, 28,* 473–475.

Wilson, G. T., Loeb, K. L., Walsh, B. T., Labouvie, E., Petkova, E., Liu, X., & Waternaux, C. (1999). Psychological versus pharmacological treatments of bulimia nervosa: Predictors and processes of change. *Journal of Consulting and Clinical Psychology, 67,* 451–459.

Wilson, G. T., Nathan, P. E., O'Leary, K. D., & Clark, L. A. (1996). *Abnormal psychology.* Boston: Allyn & Bacon.

Wilson, J. M., Straus, S. G., & McEvily, B. (2006). All in due time: The development of trust in computer-mediated and face-to-face teams. *Organizational Behavior and Human Decision Processes, 99,* 16–33.

Wilson, K., & French, C. C. (2006). The relationship between susceptibility to false memories, dissociativity, and paranormal belief and experience. *Personality and Individual Differences, 41,* 1493–1502.

Wilson, R. S., Beck, T. L., Bienias, J. L., & Bennett, D. A. (2007a). Terminal cognitive decline: Accelerated loss of cognition in the last years of life. *Psychosomatic Medicine, 69,* 131–137.

Wilson, R. S., Beckett, L. A., Barnes, L. L., Schneider, J. A., et al. (2002). Individual differences in rates of change in cognitive abilities of older persons. *Psychology & Aging, 17*(2), 179–193.

Wilson, R. S., Scherr, P. A., Schneider, J. A., Tang, Y., & Bennett, D. A. (2007b). Relation of cognitive activity to risk of developing Alzheimer disease. *Neurology, 69,* 1911–1920.

Winer, G. A., Cottrell, J. E., Gregg, V., Fournier, J. S., & Bica, L. A. (2002). Fundamentally misunderstanding visual perception: Adults' belief in visual emissions. *American Psychologist, 57,* 417–424.

Winerman, L. (2005, July/August). A virtual cure. *Monitor on Psychology,* 87–89.

Winkelmayer, W. C., Stampfer, M. J., Willett, W. C., & Curhan, G. C. (2005). Habitual caffeine intake and the risk of hypertension in women. *Journal of the American Medical Association, 294,* 2330–2335.

Winkielman, P., Bernston, G. G., & Cacioppo, J. T. (2001). The psychophysiological perspective on the social mind. In A. Tesser & N. Schwarz (Eds.), *Blackwell handbook of social psychology: Intraindividual processes* (pp. 89–109). Oxford, UK: Blackwell.

Winkielman, P., & Berridge, K. C. (2004). Unconscious emotion. *Current Directions in Psychological Science, 13,* 120–123.

Winn, P. (1995). The lateral hypothalamus and motivated behavior: An old syndrome reassessed and a new perspective gained. *Current Directions in Psychological Science, 4,* 182–187.

Winner, E. (2000). Giftedness: Current theory and research. *Current Directions in Psychological Science, 9,* 153–156.

Winson, J. (1990, November). The meaning of dreams. *Scientific American,* pp. 86–96.

Winston, A., Been, H., & Serby, M. (2005). Psychotherapy and psychopharmacology: Different universes or an integrated future? *Journal of Psychotherapy Integration, 15,* 213–223.

Winter, D. G. (1996). *Personality: Analysis and interpretation of lives.* New York: McGraw-Hill.

Winterer, G. (2006). Cortical microcircuits in schizophrenia—The dopamine hypothesis revisited. *Pharmacopsychiatry, 39,* S68–S71.

Wisborg, K., Kesmodel, U., Bech, B. H., Hedegaard, M., & Henriksen, T. B. (2003). Maternal consumption of coffee during pregnancy and stillbirth and infant death in first year of life: Prospective study. *British Medical Journal, 326*, 420.

Wiseman, R., West, D., & Stemman, R. (1996, January/February). Psychic crime detectives: A new test for measuring their successes and failures. *Skeptical Inquirer, 21*, 38–58.

Wismer Fries, A. B., Ziegler, T. E., Kurian, J. R., Jacoris, S., & Pollak, S. D. (2005). Early experience in humans is associated with changes in neuropeptides critical for regulating social behavior. *Proceedings of the National Academy of Sciences, 102*, 17237–17240.

Witt, C., Brinkhaus, B., Jena, S., Linde, K., Streng, A., Wagenpfeil, S., et al. (2005). Acupuncture in patients with osteoarthritis of the knee: A randomised trial. *Lancet, 366*, 136–143.

Wittchen, H. U., & Hoyer, J. (2001). Generalized anxiety disorder: Nature and course. *Journal of Clinical Psychiatry, 62*, 15–19.

Wixted, J. T. (2004). The psychology and neuroscience of forgetting. *Annual Review of Psychology, 55*, 235–269.

Wixted, J. T. (2005). A theory about why we forget what we once knew. *Current Directions in Psychological Science, 14*, 6–9.

Wohl, J. (1995). Traditional individual psychotherapy and ethnic minorities. In J. F. Aponte, R. Y. Rivers, & J. Wohl (Eds.), *Psychological interventions and cultural diversity* (pp. 74–91). Boston: Allyn & Bacon.

Wohlfarth, T., Storosum, J. G., Elferink, A. J. A., van Zweiten, B. J., Fouwels, A., & van den Brink, W. (2004). Response to tricyclic antidepressants: Independent of gender? *American Journal of Psychiatry, 161*, 370–372.

Woldt, A. L., & Toman, S. M. (Eds.). (2005). *Gestalt therapy: History, theory, and practice.* Newbury Park, CA: Sage.

Wolf, H., Angleitner, A., Spinath, F., Reimann, R., & Strelau, J. (2004). Genetic and environmental influences on the EPQ-RS scales: A twin study using self- and peer reports *Personality and Individual Differences. 37*, 579–590.

Wolf, P. A. (2003). Fifty years at Framingham: Contributions to stroke epidemiology. *Advances in Neurology, 92*, 165–172.

Wolfe, J. M., Horowitz, T. S., Van Wert, M. J., Kenner, N. M., Place, S. S., & Kibbi, N. (2007). Low target prevalence is a stubborn source of errors in visual search tasks. *Journal of Experimental Psychology, 136*(4), 623–638.

Wollert, R. (2007). Poor diagnostic reliability, the Null-Bayes Logic Model, and their implications for sexually violent predator evaluations. *Psychology, Public Policy, and Law, 13*, 167–213.

Wolpaw, J. R., & Chen, X. Y. (2006). The cerebellum in maintenance of a motor skill: A hierarchy of brain and spinal cord plasticity underlies H-reflex conditioning. *Learning & Memory, 13*, 208–215.

Wolpe, J. (1958). *Psychotherapy by reciprocal inhibition.* Stanford, CA: Stanford University Press.

Wolpert, I. (1924). Die Simultanagnosie: Störung der Gesamtauffassung. *Archiv für Psychiatrie und Nervenkrankheiten, vereinigt mit Zeitschrift für die gesamte Neurologie und Psychiatrie, 93*, 397–413.

Wolraich, M. L., Wibbelsman, C. J., Brown, T. E., Evans, S. W., Gotlieb, E. M., Knight, J. R., et al. (2005). Attention-deficit/hyperactivity disorder among adolescents: A review of the diagnosis, treatment, and clinical implications. *Pediatrics, 115*, 1734–1746.

Wong, C. G., Gibson, K. M., & Snead, O. C. (2004). From the street to the brain: Neurobiology of the recreational drug gamma-hydroxybutyric acid. *Trends in Pharmacological Science, 25*, 29–34.

Wong, K. F. E., & Kwong, J. Y. Y. (2005). Between-individual comparisons in performance evaluation: A perspective from prospect theory. *Journal of Applied Psychology, 90*, 284–294.

Wood, J. (2006). Effect of anxiety reduction on children's school performance and social adjustment. *Developmental Psychology, 42*, 345–349.

Wood, J. M., Nezworski, M. T., Lilienfeld, S. O., & Garb, H. N. (2003). *What's wrong with the Rorschach? Science confronts the controversial inkblot test.* San Francisco, CA: Jossey-Bass.

Wood, N. D., Crane, D. R., Shaalje, G. B., & Law, D. D. (2005). What works for whom: A meta-analytic review of marital and couples therapy in reference to marital distress. *American Journal of Family Therapy, 33*, 273–287.

Wood, W. (2000). Attitude change: Persuasion and social influence. *Annual Review of Psychology, 51*, 539–570.

Wood, W., & Eagly, A. H. (2002). A cross-cultural analysis of the behavior of women and men: Implications for the origins of sex differences. *Psychological Bulletin, 128*, 699–727.

Wood, W., Wong, F. Y., & Chachere, G. (1991). Effects of media violence on viewers' aggression in unconstrained social interaction. *Psychological Bulletin, 109*, 371–383.

Woods, B. T., Schoene, W., & Kneisley, L. (1982). Are hippocampal lesions sufficient to cause lasting amnesia? *Journal of Neurology, Neurosurgery, and Psychiatry, 45*(3), 243–247.

Woods, S. C., Schwartz, M. W., Baskin, D. G., & Seeley, R. J. (2000). Food intake and the regulation of body weight. *Annual Review of Psychology, 51*, 255–277.

Woodward, A. L. (2009). Infants' grasp of others' intentions. *Current Directions in Psychological Science, 18*, 53–57.

Woodward, T. S., Moritz, S., Cuttler, C., & Whitman, J. C. (2006). The contribution of a cognitive bias against disconfirmatory evidence (BADE) to delusions in schizophrenia. *Journal of Clinical and Experimental Neuropsychology, 28*, 605–617.

Woodworth, R. S., & Schlosberg, H. (1954). *Experimental psychology.* New York: Holt.

Woolfolk-Hoy, A. (1999). Psychology applied to education. In A. Stec & D. Bernstein (Eds.), *Psychology: Fields of application* (pp. 61–81). Boston: Houghton Mifflin.

Woolley, J. D. (1997). Thinking about fantasy: Are children fundamentally different thinkers and believers from adults? *Child Development, 68*, 991–1011.

Workman, M. (2004). Expert decision support system use, disuse, and misuse: A study using the theory of planned behavior. *Computers in Human Behavior, 21*, 211–231.

World Health Organization. (2003). *AIDS epidemic update.* Geneva, Switzerland: WHO.

World Health Organization. (2008). *World health report 2008: Primary health care now more than ever.* Geneva, Switzerland: World Health Organization. Retrieved June 11, 2009, from http://www.who.int/whr/2008/whr08_en.pdf.

World Health Organization. (2009). *World health organization mental health surveys.* Cambridge, MA: Cambridge University Press.

World Health Organization Mental Health Survey Consortium. (2004). Prevalence, severity, and unmet need for treatment of mental disorders in the World Health Organization World Mental Health Surveys. *Journal of the American Medical Association, 291*, 2581–2590.

Worthington, R. L., Navarro, R. L., Savoy, H. B., & Hampton, D. (2008). Development, reliability, and validity of the Measure of Sexual Identity Exploration and Commitment (MOSIEC). *Developmental Psychology, 44*, 22–33.

Wren, C. S. (1999, February 24). U.N. drug board urges research on marijuana as medicine. *New York Times.* Retrieved December 13, 2004, from http://nytimes.com.

Wright, E. F., Voyer, D., Wright, R. D., & Roney, C. (1995). Supporting audiences and performance under pressure: The home-ice disadvantage in hockey championships. *Journal of Sport Behavior, 18*, 21–28.

Wujcik, D. M. (2008, November). Are you part of the sandwich generation? *ONS Connect, 23*(11), 7.

Wupperman, P., & Neumann, C. S. (2006). Depressive symptoms as a function of sex-role, rumination, and neuroticism. *Personality and Individual Differences, 40*, 189–201.

Wurtman, R. J. (2006). Narcolepsy and the hypocretins. *Metabolism, 55*(10 Suppl. 2), S36–S39.

Wynne, C. L. (2004). *Do animals think?* Princeton, NJ: Princeton University Press.

Xiao, Y., Seagull, F. J., Mackenzie, C. F., Klein, K. J., & Ziegert, J. (2008). Adaptation of team communication patterns. Exploring the effects of leadership at a distance (pp. 71–96). In S. Weisband (Ed.), *Leadership at a distance: Research in technologically-supported work.* New York: Erlbaum.

Xue, Y., Leventhal, T., Brooks-Gunn, J., & Earls, F. J. (2005). Neighborhood residence and mental health problems of 5- to 11-year-olds. *Archives of General Psychiatry, 62*, 554–563.

Yaffe, K., Barnes, D., Nevitt, M., Lui, L.-Y., & Covinsky, K. (2001). A prospective study of physical activity and cognitive decline in elderly women. *Archives of Internal Medicine, 161*, 1703–1708.

Yakimovich, D., & Saltz, E. (1971). Helping behavior: The cry for help. *Psychonomic Science, 23*, 427–428.

Yalom, E. D. (2005). *The theory and practice of group psychotherapy* (5th ed.). New York: Basic Books.

Yamagata, S., Suzuki, A., Ando, J., Ono, Y., Kijima, N., Yoshimura, K., Ostendorf, F., Angleitner, A., Riemann, R., Spinath, F. M., Livesley, W. J., Jang, K. L. (2006). Is the genetic structure of human personality universal? A cross-cultural twin study from North America, Europe, and Asia. *Journal of Personality and Social Psychology, 90*(6), 987–998.

Yamamoto, R., Iseki, E., Higashi, S., Murayama, N., Minegishi, M., Sato, K., Hino, H., Fujisawa, K., Kosaka, K., Togo, T., Katsuse, O., Uchikado, H., Furukawa, Y., Yoshida, M., Hashizume, Y., & Arai, H. (2009). Neuropathological investigation of regions responsible for semantic aphasia in frontotemporal lobar degeneration. *Dementia & Geriatric Cognitive Disorders, 27*(3), 214–223.

Yan, B., Li, K., Xu, J., Wang, W., Li, K., Liu, H., et al. (2005). Acupoint-specific fMRI patterns in human brain. *Neuroscience Letters, 383*, 236–240.

Yan, Z., Chi, Y., Wang, P., Cheng, J., Wang, Y., Shu, Q., & Huang, G. (1992). Studies on the luminescence of channels in rats and its law of changes with "syndromes" and treatment of acupuncture and moxibustion. *Journal of Traditional Chinese Medicine, 12*(4), 283–287.

Yang, C.-M., & Spielman, A. J. (2001). The effect of delayed weekend sleep pattern on sleep and morning functioning. *Psychology and Health, 16*, 715–725.

Yang, C.-M., Spielman, A. J., & Glovinsky, P. (2006). Nonpharmacologic strategies in the management of insomnia. *Psychiatric Clinics of North America, 29*, 895–919.

Yang, T., & Kubovy, M. (1999). Weakening the robustness of perspective: Evidence for a modified theory of compensation in picture perception. *Perception and Psychophysics, 61*, 456–467.

Yantis, S. (1993). Stimulus-driven attentional capture. *Current Directions in Psychological Science, 2*, 156–161.

Yarlagadda, A., Helvink, B., Chou, C., Gladieux, K., Keller, A., & Clayton, A. (2008). Glutamic acid decarboxylase (GAD) antibodies in tardive dyskinesia (TD) as compared to patients with schizophrenia without TD and normal controls. *Schizophrenia Research, 105*, 287–288.

Yates, W. R. (2000). Testosterone in psychiatry. *Archives of General Psychiatry, 57*, 155–156.

Yearta, S. K., Maitlis, S., & Briner, R. B. (1995). An exploratory study of goal setting in theory and practice: A motivational technique that works? *Journal of Occupational and Organizational Psychology, 68,* 237–252.

Yela, C., & Sangrador, J. L. (2001). Perception of physical attractiveness throughout loving relationships. *Current Research in Social Psychology, 6,* 57–75.

Yerkes, R. M. (Ed.). (1921). Psychological examining in the U.S. Army. *Memoirs of the National Academy of Sciences,* No. 15.

Yeung, L. M., Linver, M. R., & Brooks-Gunn, J. (2002). How money matters for young children's development: Parental investment and family processes. *Child Development, 73,* 1861–1879.

Yip, T., Gee, G. C., & Takeuchi, D. T. (2008). Racial discrimination and psychological distress: The impact of ethnic identity and age among immigrant and United States-born Asian adults. *Developmental Psychology, 44,* 787–800.

Yonas, A., Arterberry, M. E., & Granrud, C. D. (1987). Space perception in infancy. In R. Vasta (Ed.), *Annals of child development* (Vol. 4, pp. 1–34). Greenwich, CT: JAI Press.

Yonke, A., & Barnett, M. (2001). Persistence of early psychoanalytic thought about women. *Gender & Psychoanalysis, 6*(1), 53–73.

Yoo, S.-S., Hu, P. T., Gujar, N., Jolesz, F. A., & Walker, M. P. (2007). A deficit in the ability to form new human memories without sleep. *Nature Neuroscience, 10,* 385–392.

Yoshimasu, K., Washio, M., Tokunaga, S., Tanaka, K., Liu, Y., Kodama, H., et al. (2002). Relation between Type A behavior pattern and the extent of coronary atherosclerosis in Japanese women. *International Journal of Behavioral Medicine, 9,* 77–93.

Youm, Y., & Laumann, E. O. (2002). Social network effects on the transmission of sexually transmitted diseases. *Sexually Transmitted Diseases, 29,* 689–697.

Young, M. E. (1995). On the origin of causal theories. *Psychonomic Bulletin & Review, 2,* 83–104.

Young, M. S., Turner, J., Denny, G., & Young, M. (2004). Examining external and internal poverty as antecedents of teen pregnancy. *American Journal of Health Behavior, 28,* 361–373.

Yousif, Y., & Korte, C. (1995). Urbanization, culture, and helpfulness: Cross- cultural studies in England and the Sudan. *Journal of Cross-Cultural Psychology, 26,* 474–489.

Yovel, I., & Mineka, S. (2005). Emotion-congruent attentional biases: The perspective of hierarchical models of emotional disorders. *Personality and Individual Differences, 38,* 785–795.

Yu, J., Vodyanik, M. A., Smuga-Otto, K., Antosiewicz-Bourget, J., Frane, J. L., Tian, S., Nie, J., Jonsdottir, G. A., Ruotti, V., Stewart, R., Slukvin, I. I., & Thomson, J. A. (2007). Induced pluripotent stem cell lines derived from human somatic cells. *Science, 318*(5858), 1917–1920.

Yuan, J., Kerr, D., Park, J., Liu, X. H., & McDonough, S. (2008). Treatment regimens of acupuncture for low back pain—A systematic review. *Complementary Therapies in Medicine, 16*(5), 295–304.

Yücel, M., Solowij, N., Respondek, C., Whittle, S., Fornito, A., Pantelis, C., & Lubman, D. I. (2008). Regional brain abnormalities associated with long-term heavy cannabis use. *Archives of General Psychiatry, 65,* 694–701.

Yukl, G., & Van Fleet, D. D. (1992). Theory and research on leadership in organizations. In M. D. Dunnette & L. M. Hough (Eds.), *Handbook of industrial and organizational psychology* (Vol. 3, 2nd ed., pp. 147–198). Palo Alto, CA: Consulting Psychologists Press.

Yun, S., Faraj, S., & Sims, H. P. (2005). Contingent leadership and effectiveness of trauma resuscitation teams. *Journal of Applied Psychology, 90,* 1288–1296.

Zaccarco, S. J. (2007). Trait-based perspectives of leadership. *American Psychologist, 62,* 6–16.

Zadnik, K. (2001). Association between night lights and myopia: True blue or a red herring? *Archives of Ophthalmology, 119,* 146.

Zadra, A., Desjardins, S., & Marcotte, E. (2006). Evolutionary function of dreams: A test of the threat simulation theory in recurrent dreams. *Consciousness and Cognition, 15,* 450–463.

Zadra, A., & Donderi, D. C. (2000). Nightmares and bad dreams: Their prevalence and relationship to well-being. *Journal of Abnormal Psychology, 109,* 273–281.

Zahn-Waxler, C., Radke-Yarrow, M., Wagner, E., & Chapman, M. (1992). Development of concern for others. *Developmental Psychology, 28,* 1038–1047.

Zahrani, S. S., & Kaplowitz, S. A. (1993). Attributional biases in individualistic and collectivist cultures: A comparison of Americans with Saudis. *Social Psychology Quarterly, 56*(3), 223–233.

Zajonc, R. B. (1965). Social facilitation. *Science, 149,* 269–274.

Zajonc, R. B. (1998). Emotions. In D. Gilbert, S. T. Fiske, & G. Lindzey (Eds.), *Handbook of social psychology* (Vol. 1, 4th ed., pp. 591–634). Boston: McGraw-Hill.

Zakriski, A. L., Wright, J. C., & Underwood, M. K. (2005). Gender similarities and differences in children's social behavior: Finding personality in contextualized patterns of adaptation. *Journal of Personality and Social Psychology, 88,* 844–855.

Zakzanis, K. K., & Young, D. A. (2001). Memory impairment in abstinent MDMA ("Ecstasy") users: A longitudinal investigation. *Neurology, 56,* 966–969.

Zald, D. H., & Pardo, J. V. (1997). Emotion, olfaction, and the human amygdala: Amygdala activation during aversive olfactory stimulation. *Proceedings of the National Academy of Sciences, 94*(8), 4119–4124.

Zalta, A. K., & Keel, P. K. (2006). Peer influence on bulimic symptoms in college students. *Journal of Abnormal Psychology, 115,* 185–189.

Zambelis, T., Paparrigopoulos, T., & Soldatos, C. R. (2002). REM sleep behaviour disorder associated with a neurinoma of the left pontocerebral angle. *Journal of Neurology, Neurosurgery, and Psychiatry, 72,* 821–822.

Zammit, S., Allebeck, P., Andreasson, S., Lundberg, I., & Lewis, G. (2002). Self reported cannabis use as a risk factor for schizophrenia in Swedish conscripts of 1969: Historical cohort study. *British Medical Journal, 325,* 1199.

Zang, Y. (2008). Undergraduate students' mental models of the web as an information retrieval system. *Journal of the American Society for Information Science and Technology, 59,* 2087–2098.

Zaragoza, M. S., Payment, K. E., Ackil, J. K., Drivdahl, S. B., & Beck, M. (2001). Interviewing witnesses: Forced confabulation and confirmatory feedback increase false memories. *Psychological Science, 12,* 473–477.

Zatorre, R. J. (2003). Music and the brain. *Annals of the New York Academy of Sciences, 999,* 4–14.

Zebrowitz, L., White, B., & Wieneke, K. (2008). Mere exposure and racial prejudice: Exposure to other-race faces increases liking for strangers of that race. *Social Cognition, 26,* 259–275.

Zeldow, P. B. (2009). In defense of clinical judgment, credentialed clinicians, and reflective practice. *Psychotherapy: Theory, Research, Practice, Training, 46,* 1–10.

Zeman, A. (2001). Consciousness. *Brain, 124,* 1263–1289.

Zeman, A., Britton, T., Douglas, N., Hansen, A., Hicks, J., Howard, R., et al. (2004). Narcolepsy and excessive daytime sleepiness. *British Medical Journal, 329,* 724–728.

Zhang, Y., Hoon, M. A., Chandrashekar, J., Mueller, K. L., Cook, B., Wu, D., et al. (2003). Coding of sweet, bitter, and umami tastes: Different receptor cells sharing similar signaling pathways. *Cell, 112,* 293–301.

Zhang, Y., Proenca, R., Maffei, M., Barone, M., Leopold, L., & Friedman, J. M. (1994). Positional cloning of the mouse obese gene and its human homologue. *Nature, 372,* 425–432.

Zhang, Y., Qin, W., Liu, P., Tian, J., Liang, J., von Deneen, K. M., & Liu, Y. (2009). An fMRI study of acupuncture using independent component analysis. *Neuroscience Letter, 449*(1), 6–9.

Zhao, G., Ford, E. S., Dhingra, S., Li, C., Strine, T. W., & Mokdad, A. H. (2009). Depression and anxiety among US adults: Associations with body mass index. *International Journal of Obesity, 33,* 257–266.

Zhao, H., & Seibert, S. E. (2006). The big five personality dimensions and entrepreneurial status: A meta-analytical review. *Journal of Applied Psychology, 91,* 259–271.

Zhao, M., Momma, S., Delfani, K., Carlen, M., Cassidy, R. M., Johansson, C. B., et al. (2003). Evidence for neurogenesis in the adult mammalian substantia nigra. *Proceedings of the National Academy of Sciences, 100,* 7925–7930.

Zhou, J.-N., Hofman, M. A., Gooren, L. J. G., & Swaab, D. F. (1995). A sex difference in the human brain and its relation to transsexuality. *Nature, 378,* 68–70.

Zhou, Q., Eisenberg, N., Wang, Y., & Reiser, M. (2004). Chinese children's effortful control and dispositional anger/frustration relations to parenting styles and children's social functioning. *Developmental Psychology, 40,* 352–366.

Ziegler-Graham, K., Brookmeyer, R., Johnson, E., & Arrighi, H. M. (2008). Worldwide variation in the doubling time of Alzheimer's disease incidence rates. *Alzheimer's & Dementia: The Journal of the Alzheimer's Association, 4*(5), 316–323.

Zigler, E., & Seitz, V. (1982). Social policy and intelligence. In R. J. Sternberg (Ed.), *Handbook of human intelligence* (pp. 586–641). Cambridge, UK: Cambridge University Press.

Zigurs, I. (2003). Leadership in virtual teams: Oxymoron or opportunity? *Organizational Dynamics, 31,* 339–351.

Zillmann, D. (1984). *Connections between sexuality and aggression.* Hillsdale, NJ: Erlbaum.

Zillmann, D. (1988). Cognition-excitation interdependencies in aggressive behavior. *Aggressive Behavior, 14,* 51–64.

Zillmann, D. (2003). Theory of affective dynamics: Emotions and moods. In J. Bryant & D. Roskos-Ewoldsen (Eds.), *Communication and emotion: Essays in honor of Dolf Zillmann* (pp. 533–567). Mahwah, NJ: Erlbaum.

Zillmann, D., Katcher, A. H., & Milavsky, B. (1972). Excitation transfer from physical exercise to subsequent aggressive behavior. *Journal of Experimental Social Psychology, 8,* 247–259.

Zimbardo, P. G. (1973). The psychological power and pathology of imprisonment. In E. Aronson & R. Helmreich (Eds.), *Social psychology.* New York: Van Nostrand.

Zimmerman, B. J., & Schunk, D. H. (2003). Albert Bandura: The scholar and his contributions to educational psychology. In B. J. Zimmerman (Ed.), *Educational psychology: A century of contributions* (pp. 431–457). Mahwah, NJ: Erlbaum.

Zimmerman, F. J., & Christakis, D. A. (2007). Associations between content types of early media exposure and subsequent attentional problems. *Pediatrics, 120*(5), 986–992.

Zimmerman, F. J., Christakis, D. A., & Meltzoff, A. N. (2007). Associations between media viewing and language development in children under age 2 years. *The Journal of Pediatrics, 151*(4), 364–368.

Zimmerman, M., McDermut, W., & Mattia, J. I. (2000). Frequency of anxiety disorders in psychiatric outpatients with major depressive disorder. *American Journal of Psychiatry, 157,* 1337–1340.

Zimmerman, M., Posternak, M. A., Attiullah, N., Freidman, M., Michael, R. J., et al. (2005). Why isn't bupropion the most frequently prescribed antidepressant? *Journal of Clinical Psychiatry, 66,* 603–610.

Zimmerman, M. E., Pan, J. W., Hetherington, H. P., Katz, M. J., Verghese, J., Buschke, H., et al. (2008). Hippocampal neurochemistry, neuromorphometry, and verbal memory in nondemented older adults. *Neurology, 70*(18), 1594–1600.

Zinbarg, R. E., & Griffith, J. W. (2008). Behavior therapy. In J. L. Lebow (Ed.), *Twenty-first century psychotherapies: Contemporary approaches to theory and practice* (pp. 8–42). Hoboken, NJ: Wiley.

Zinbarg, R. E., & Mineka, S. (1991). Animal models of psychopathology: II. Simple phobia. *The Behavior Therapist, 14,* 61–65.

Zittoun, T., Gillespie, A., Cornish, F., & Psaltis, C. (2007). The metaphor of the triangle in theories of human development. *Human Development, 50*(4), 208–229.

Zoellner, L. A., Foa, E. B., Brigidi, B. D., & Przeworski, A. (2000). Are trauma victims susceptible to "false memories"? *Journal of Abnormal Psychology, 109,* 517–524.

Zoellner, T., & Maercker, A. (2006). Posttraumatic growth in clinical psychology: A critical review and introduction of a two component model. *Clinical Psychology Review, 26,* 626–653.

Zola-Morgan, S. (1995). Localization of brain function: The legacy of Franz Joseph Gall (1758–1828). *Annual Review of Neuroscience, 18,* 359–383.

Zou, Z., & Buck, L. B. (2006). Combinatorial effects of odorant mixes in olfactory cortex. *Science, 311,* 1477–1481.

Zou, Z., Li, F., & Buck, L. B. (2005). Odor maps in the olfactory cortex. *Proceedings of the National Academy of Sciences, 102,* 7724–7729.

Zuberbühler, K. (2005). The phylogenetic roots of language. *Current Directions in Psychological Science, 14,* 126–130.

Zubieta, J.-K., Bueller, J. A., Jackson, L. R., Scott, D. J., Xu, Y., Koeppe, R. A., et al. (2005). Placebo effects mediated by endogenous opioid activity on [MU]-opioid receptors. *Journal of Neuroscience, 25,* 7754–7762.

Zubin, J., & Spring, B. (1977). Vulnerability—A new view of schizophrenia. *Journal of Abnormal Psychology, 86,* 103–126.

Zucker, A. N., Ostrove, J. M., & Stewart, A. J. (2002). College-educated women's personality development in adulthood: Perceptions and age differences. *Psychology & Aging, 17*(2), 236–244.

Zuckerman, E. (2003). Finding, evaluating, and incorporating Internet self-help resources into psychotherapy practice. *Journal of Clinical Psychology: In Session, 59,* 217–227.

Zuckerman, M. (1984). Sensation seeking: A comparative approach to a human approach. *Behavioral and Brain Sciences, 7,* 413–471.

Zuckerman, M. (1990). Some dubious premises in research and theory on racial differences. *American Psychologist, 45,* 1297–1303.

Zuckerman, M. (1993). Out of sensory deprivation and into sensation seeking: A personal and scientific journey. In G. G. Brannigan & M. R. Merrens (Eds.), *The undaunted psychologist: Adventures in research* (pp. 45–57). Philadelphia: Temple University Press.

Zuckerman, M. (1996). "Conceptual clarification" or confusion in "The study of sensation seeking" by J. S. H. Jackson and M. Maraun. *Personality and Individual Differences, 21,* 111–114.

Zuckerman, M. (2004). The shaping of personality: Genes, environments, and chance encounters. *Journal of Personality Assessment, 82,* 11–22.

Zufall, F., & Leinders-Zufall, T. (2007). Mammalian pheromone sensing. *Current Opinion in Neurobiology, 17*(4), 483–489.

Zuroff, D. C., & Blatt, S. J. (2006). The therapeutic relationship in the brief treatment of depression: Contributions to clinical improvement and enhanced adaptive capacities. *Journal of Consulting and Clinical Psychology, 74,* 130–140.

Zuvekas, S. H., Vitiello, B., & Nordquist, G. S. (2006). Recent trends in stimulant medication use among U.S. children. *American Journal of Psychiatry, 163,* 579–585.

GLOSSARY

Key terms, which appear in boldface, are followed by their definitions. Entries that appear in blue refer to the optional Industrial and Organizational Psychology or Neuropsychology chapters.

absolute threshold The minimum amount of stimulus energy that can be detected 50 percent of the time.

accessory structures Structures, such as the outer part of the ear, that modify a stimulus.

accommodation The process of modifying schemas as an infant tries out familiar schemas on objects that do not fit them.

achievement motivation (need for achievement or n-Ach) The degree to which a person establishes specific goals, cares about meeting them, and experiences satisfaction by doing so.

acoustic memory Mental representations of stimuli as sounds.

acoustic nerve The bundle of axons that carries messages from the hair cells of the cochlea to the brain.

action potential The electrochemical impulse or message that is sent down an axon and stimulates release of a neurotransmitter.

actor-observer effect The tendency to attribute other people's behavior to internal causes while attributing one's own behavior to external causes.

actualizing tendency An innate inclination toward growth and fulfilment that motivates all human behavior.

addiction Development of a physical need for a psychoactive drug.

affective disorder (mood disorder) A condition in which a person experiences extremes of moods for long periods, shifts from one extreme mood to another, and experiences moods that are inconsistent with events.

aggression (aggressive behavior) An act that is intended to harm another person.

agonists Drugs that bind to a receptor and mimic the effects of the neurotransmitter that normally fits that receptor.

agoraphobia A strong fear of being alone or away from the safety of home.

algorithms Systematic procedures that cannot fail to produce a correct solution to a problem.

altered state of consciousness A condition that exists when changes in mental processes are extensive enough to produce noticeable differences in psychological and behavioral functioning.

altruism An unselfish concern with another's welfare.

Alzheimer's disease Dementia resulting from a neurogenerative disease, characterized by the loss of cognitive functions.

amnestic disorders Neuropsychological disorders (such as anterograde amnesia) that involve memory loss.

amplitude The distance between the peak and the baseline of a wave.

amygdala A forebrain structure that links information from various systems and plays a role in emotions.

anal stage The second of Freud's psychosexual stages, in which the focus of pleasure shifts from the mouth to the anus; occurs during the second year of life.

analgesia Reduction in the sensation of pain in the presence of a normally painful stimulus.

anchoring bias (anchoring heuristic) A shortcut in the thought process that involves adding new information to existing information to reach a judgment.

androgens Masculine hormones that circulate in the bloodstream.

anorexia nervosa An eating disorder characterized by self-starvation and dramatic weight loss.

antagonists Drugs that bind to a receptor and prevent the normal neurotransmitter from binding.

anterograde amnesia A loss of memory for events that occur after a brain injury.

antidepressant drugs Drugs that reduce depression.

antisocial personality disorder A long-term, persistent pattern of impulsive, selfish, unscrupulous, even criminal behavior.

anxiety disorder A condition in which intense feelings of fear and dread are long-standing or disruptive.

anxiolytics (see tranquilizing drugs)

aphasias (see language disorders)

apraxias (see movement disorders)

arousal: cost-reward theory A theory which describes the decision to provide assistance as motivated by efforts to reduce the unpleasant arousal people feel when confronted with a suffering victim while also considering the costs involved.

arousal theory A theory that people are motivated to maintain what is an optimal level of arousal for them.

artificial intelligence (AI) The field that studies how to program computers to imitate the products of human perception, understanding, and thought.

assertiveness training A set of methods for helping clients learn to express their feelings and stand up for their rights in social situations.

assessment center An extensive set of exercises designed to determine an individual's suitability for a particular job.

assimilation The process of taking in new information about objects by using existing schemas on objects that fit those schemas.

assistance (helping behavior) Any act that is intended to benefit another person.

association cortex The parts of the cerebral cortex that integrate sensory and motor information and perform complex cognitive tasks.

attachment A deep, affectionate, close, and enduring relationship with a person with whom a baby has shared many experiences.

attachment behavior Actions such as crying, smiling, vocalizing, and gesturing that help bring an infant into closer proximity to its caretaker.

attachment theory The idea that children form a close attachment to their earliest caretakers and that this attachment pattern can affect aspects of the children's later life.

attention The process of directing and focusing certain psychological resources to enhance perception.

attitude A tendency toward a particular cognitive, emotional, or behavioral reaction to objects in one's environment.

attribution The process of explaining the cause of some event; the process of explaining the causes of people's behavior, including our own.

authoritarian parents Parents who are firm, punitive, and unsympathetic.

authoritative parents Parents who reason with their children and are firm but understanding.

autonomic nervous system The subsystem of the peripheral nervous system that carries messages between the central nervous system and the heart, lungs, and other organs and glands in the body.

autonomous work groups (AWGs) Self-managed employee groups that do not report to anyone for routine daily supervision.

availability heuristic A mental shortcut through which judgments are based on information that is most easily brought to mind.

aversion conditioning A method for reducing unwanted behaviors by using classical conditioning principles to create a negative response to some stimulus.

avoidance conditioning The process of learning particular responses that avoid an aversive stimulus.

axon A fiber that carries signals away from the cell body.

babblings Repetitions of syllables; the first sounds infants make that resemble speech.

basilar membrane The floor of the fluid-filled duct that runs through the cochlea.

behavioral approach A view based on the assumption that human behavior is determined mainly by what a person has learned in life, especially by rewards and punishments.

behavioral genetics The study of the effect of genes on behavior.

behavior modification Treatments that use operant conditioning methods to change behavior.

behavior therapy Treatments that use classical conditioning principles to change behavior.

biased sample A group of research participants selected from a population each of whose members did not have an equal chance of being chosen.

biological approach The view that behavior is the result of physical processes, especially those relating to the brain, to hormones, and to other chemicals.

biological psychologists Psychologists who analyze the biological factors influencing behavior and mental processes.

biological psychology The study of physical and chemical changes involved in behavior and mental processes.

biopsychosocial approach An explanation for mental disorders that sees them as the result of a combination of biological, psychological, and sociocultural factors.

bipolar disorder A condition in which a person alternates between the two emotional extremes of depression and mania.

bisexuality Sexual desire or behavior that is focused on members of both sexes.

blind spot The point at which the optic nerve exits the eyeball.

blood-brain barrier A characteristic of blood vessels in the brain that prevents some substances from entering brain tissue.

body dysmorphic disorder A somatoform disorder characterized by intense distress over imagined abnormalities of the skin, hair, face, or other areas of the body.

bottom-up processing Aspects of recognition that depend first on information about stimuli that come up to the brain from the sensory systems.

brightness The overall intensity of the wavelengths making up light.

Broca's aphasia A language disorder in which there is a loss of fluent speech.

Brown-Peterson distractor technique A method for determining how long unrehearsed information remains in short-term memory.

bulimia An eating disorder that involves eating massive quantities of food, then eliminating it by self-induced vomiting or laxatives.

burnout A pattern of physical and psychological dysfunctions in response to continuous stressors.

bystander effect A phenomenon in which the chances that someone will help in an emergency decrease as the number of people present increases.

case studies Research involving the intensive examination of some phenomenon in a particular individual, group, or situation.

central nervous system (CNS) The brain and spinal cord.

cerebellum The part of the hindbrain that controls finely coordinated movements.

cerebral cortex The outer surface of the forebrain.

cerebrospinal fluid A clear liquid that surrounds and buffers the brain against vibration.

cerebrovascular accident (stroke) A loss of blood supply to some part of the brain, resulting in disruption of some aspect of behavior or mental processes.

chromosomes Structures in every biological cell that contain genetic information in the form of genes.

chunking Organizing individual stimuli so that they will be perceived as larger units of meaningful information.

circadian rhythm (human biological rhythm) A cycle, such as waking and sleeping, that repeats about once a day.

classical conditioning A procedure in which a neutral stimulus is paired with a stimulus that triggers a reflexive response until the neutral stimulus alone comes to trigger a similar response.

client-centered therapy (person-centered therapy) A type of therapy in which the client decides what to talk about and when without direction, judgment, or interpretation from the therapist.

clinical, counseling, and community psychologists Psychologists who seek to assess, understand, modify, and prevent behavior disorders.

CNS depressant drugs Psychoactive drugs that inhibit the functioning of the central nervous system.

CNS stimulating drugs Psychoactive drugs that increase behavioral and mental activity.

cochlea A fluid-filled spiral structure in the inner ear in which auditory transduction occurs.

cognitive approach A view that emphasizes research on how the brain takes in information, creates perceptions, forms and retrieves memories, processes information, and generates integrated patterns of action.

cognitive behavior therapy Behavioral treatment methods that help clients change the way they think as well as the way they behave.

cognitive dissonance theory A theory that attitude change is driven by efforts to reduce tension caused by inconsistencies between attitudes and behaviors.

cognitive map A mental model that represents familiar parts of the environment; a mental representation of the environment.

cognitive psychologists Psychologists whose research focus is analysis of the mental processes underlying judgment, decision making, problem solving, imagining, and other aspects of human thought or cognition.

cognitive therapy An organized problem-solving approach in which the therapist actively collaborates with clients to help them notice how certain negative thoughts precede anxiety and depression.

color saturation The purity of a color.

community psychology A mental health approach whose goal is to minimize or prevent psychological disorders by promoting social change and making treatment methods more accessible to those who normally have little or no access to psychological services.

competition Any type of behavior in which individuals try to attain a goal while denying others access to that goal.

compliance Adjusting one's behavior because of a direct request.

compulsions Repetitive behaviors that interfere with daily functioning but are performed in an effort to prevent dangers or events associated with obsessions.

concepts Categories of objects, events, or ideas that have common properties.

concrete operations According to Piaget, the third stage of cognitive development, during which children can learn to count, measure, add, and subtract.

conditioned response (CR) The response triggered by a conditioned stimulus.

conditioned stimulus (CS) An originally neutral stimulus that now triggers a conditioned response.

conditions of worth According to Rogers, circumstances in which an individual experiences positive regard from others only when displaying certain behaviors or attitudes.

cones Photoreceptors in the retina that are less light sensitive than rods but that can distinguish colors.

confabulation A characteristic of some neuropsychochogical disorders in which patients report false memories.

confirmation bias The tendency to pay more attention to evidence in support of one's hypothesis about a problem than to evidence that refutes that hypothesis.

conflict What occurs when a person or group believes that another person or group interferes with the attainment of a goal.

conformity Changing one's behavior or beliefs to match those of others, generally as a result of real or imagined (though unspoken) group pressure.

confounding variable Any factor that affects the dependent variable along with, or instead of, the independent variable.

congruence In client-centered therapy, a consistency between the way therapists feel and the way they act toward clients.

consciousness The awareness of external stimuli and our own mental activity.

consciousness disturbances Neuropsychological disorders in which there are impairments in the ability to be conscious, or accurately aware, of the world.

consciousness state The characteristics of consciousness at any particular moment.

conservation The ability to recognize that the important properties of substances or objects, such as quantity, volume, or weight, remain constant despite changes in shape, length, or position.

contact hypothesis The idea that stereotypes and prejudice toward a group will diminish as contact with the group increases.

context-specific learning (see **context-specific memory**)

context-specific memory Memories that are helped or hindered by similarities or differences between the contexts in which they are learned and recalled.

control group The group that receives no treatment or provides some other baseline against which to compare the performance or response of the experimental group.

conventional reasoning Moral reasoning that reflects a concern about other people as well as the belief that morality consists of following rules and conventions.

convergent thinking The ability to apply the rules of logic and what one knows about the world to narrow down the possible solutions to a problem.

conversion disorder A somatoform disorder in which a person appears to be (but actually is not) blind, deaf, paralyzed, or insensitive to pain.

cooperation Any type of behavior in which people work together to attain a goal.

cornea The curved, transparent, protective layer through which light rays enter the eye.

corpus callosum A bundle of fibers that connects the left and right cerebral hemispheres.

correlation The degree to which one variable is related to another.

correlational studies Research methods that examine relationships between variables in order to analyze trends, test predictions, evaluate theories, and suggest new hypotheses.

couples therapy A form of therapy that focuses on improving communication between partners.

creativity The capacity to produce original solutions or novel compositions.

critical period An interval during which certain kinds of growth must occur if development is to proceed normally.

critical thinking The process of assessing claims and making judgments on the basis of well-supported evidence.

cultural-familial mental retardation Cases of mild retardation for which no environmental or genetic cause can be found.

culture The accumulation of values, rules of behavior, forms of expression, religious beliefs, and occupational choices for a group of people who share a common language and environment.

cutaneous senses Senses including touch, temperature, pain, and kinesthetic perception that are spread throughout the body rather than located in a specific organ. Also called somatosensory systems.

cyclothymic personality (cyclothymic disorder) An affective disorder characterized by an alternating pattern of mood swings that is less extreme than that of bipolar disorder.

dark adaptation The increasing ability to see in the dark as time passes.

data Numbers that represent research findings and provide the basis for conclusions.

decay theory The view that sees forgetting as the gradual disappearance of information from memory.

defense mechanisms Unconscious tactics that either prevent threatening material from surfacing or disguise it when it does.

deindividuation A psychological state occurring in group members that results in loss of individuality and a tendency to do things not normally done when alone.

delirium Periods of abnormally impaired and/or abnormally elevated levels of consciousness.

delusions False beliefs, such as those experienced by people suffering from schizophrenia or severe depression.

dementia Neuropsychological disorders in which there are significant and disruptive impairments in memory as well as in perceptual ability, language, or learned motor skills.

dendrites Fibers that receive signals from the axons of other neurons.

deoxyribonucleic acid (DNA) The molecular structure of a gene that provides the genetic code.

dependent variable In an experiment, the factor affected by the independent variable.

depth perception Perception of distance, allowing us to experience the world in three dimensions.

developmental psychologists Psychologists who seek to understand, describe, and explore how behavior and mental processes change over the course of a lifetime.

developmental psychology The psychological specialty that documents the course of people's social, emotional, moral, and intellectual development over the life-span.

diathesis-stress model An approach that recognizes the roles of predispositions and situational factors in the appearance of psychological disorders.

discriminative conditioned stimuli Stimuli that signal whether reinforcement is available if a certain response is made.

diseases of adaptation Illnesses caused or worsened by stressors.

dissociative amnesia A psychological disorder marked by a sudden loss of memory for one's own name, occupation, or other identifying information.

dissociative disorders Conditions involving sudden and usually temporary disruptions in a person's memory, consciousness, or identity.

dissociative identity disorder (DID) A dissociative disorder in which a person appears to have more than one identity, each of which behaves in a different way.

dissociative fugue (see **fugue reaction**)

distributed practice Learning new information in many study sessions that are spaced across time.

divergent thinking The ability to generate many different solutions to a problem.

double-blind design A research design in which neither the experimenter nor the participants know who is in the experimental group and who is in the control group.

dreaming The production during sleep of story-like sequences of images, sensations, and perceptions that last from several seconds to many minutes; it occurs mainly during REM sleep.

drive A physiological state that arises from an imbalance in homeostasis and prompts action to fulfill a need.

drive reduction theory A theory that motivation arises from imbalances in homeostasis.

drug abuse (substance abuse) The use of psychoactive drugs in ways that deviate from cultural norms and cause serious problems for the user.

drug tolerance A condition in which increasingly larger drug doses are needed to produce a given effect.

drug withdrawal A set of symptoms associated with ending the use of an addictive substance.

dysthymic disorder A pattern of depression in which the person shows the sad mood, lack of interest, and loss of pleasure associated with major depression but to a lesser degree and for a longer period.

eardrum (see **tympanic membrane**)

educational psychologists Psychologists who study methods by which instructors teach and students learn and who apply their results to improving such methods.

ego According to Freud, the part of the personality that makes compromises and mediates conflicts between and among the demands of the id, the superego, and the real world.

elaboration likelihood model A model of attitude change suggesting that people can change their attitudes through a central route (by considering an argument's content) or through a peripheral route (by relying on irrelevant persuasion cues).

elaborative rehearsal A memorization method that relates new information to information already stored in memory.

Electra complex The notion that young girls develop an attachment to the father and compete with the mother for the father's attention.

electroconvulsive shock therapy (ECT) A brief electric shock administered to the brain, usually to reduce severe depression that does not respond to drug treatments.

embryo The developing individual from two weeks to two months after fertilization.

emotions Temporary positive or negative experiences that are felt as happening to the self, that are generated partly by interpretation of situations, and that are accompanied by learned and innate physical responses.

empathy In client-centered therapy, the therapist's attempt to appreciate how the world looks from the client's point of view.

empathy-altruism helping theory A theory suggesting that people assist others because they feel empathy toward them.

empirically supported therapies (ESTs) Treatments for psychological disorders whose effectiveness has been validated by controlled experimental research.

empiricism The view that knowledge comes from experience and observation.

encoding The process of putting information into a form that the memory system can accept and use; translation of the physical properties of a stimulus into a specific pattern of neural activity.

encoding specificity principle A principle that states that the ability of a cue to aid retrieval depends on how well it taps into information that was originally encoded.

endocrine system Cells that form organs called glands and that communicate with one another by secreting hormones.

engineering psychologists Psychologists who study and try to improve the relationships between human beings and the computers and other machines they use.

environmental psychologists Psychologists who study the relationship between people's physical environment and their behavior.

environmental psychology The study of the effects of the physical environment on people's behavior and mental processes.

epigenetics The study of potentially inheritable changes in gene expression that are caused by environmental factors that do not alter a cell's DNA.

episodic memory Memory for events in one's own past.

escape conditioning The process of learning responses that stop an aversive stimulus.

estrogens Feminine hormones that circulate in the bloodstream.

ethnic identity The part of a person's identity that reflects the racial, religious, or cultural group to which that person belongs.

evidence-based practice The selection of treatment methods based mainly on empirical evidence of their effectiveness.

evolutionary approach A view that emphasizes the inherited, adaptive aspects of behavior and mental processes.

excitation-transfer theory The theory that physiological arousal that stems from one situation is carried over to and enhances emotional experience in an independent situation.

existence, relatedness, growth (ERG) theory A theory of motivation that focuses on employees' needs at the levels of existence, relatedness, and growth.

expectancy theory A theory of workplace motivation that states that employees act in accordance with expected results and with how much they value those results.

expected value The total benefit to be expected of a decision if it were repeated on several occasions.

experiment A situation in which the researcher manipulates one variable and observes the effect of that manipulation on another variable, while holding all other variables constant.

experimental group The group that receives the experimental treatment.

experimenter bias A confounding variable that occurs when an experimenter unintentionally encourages participants to respond in a way that supports the hypothesis.

explicit memory Information retrieved through a conscious effort to remember something.

extinction The gradual disappearance of a conditioned response.

eye convergence A depth cue that results when the eyes rotate to project the image of an object on each retina.

family therapy A type of treatment involving two or more clients from the same family.

feature detectors Cells in the cortex that respond to a specific feature of an object.

fetal alcohol syndrome A pattern of defects found in babies born to women who drink heavily during pregnancy.

fetus The developing individual from the third month after conception until birth.

fiber tracts Bundles of axons that travel together.

fight-or-flight response Physical reactions triggered by the sympathetic nervous system that prepare the body to fight or to run from a threatening situation.

figure ground discrimination The ability to organize a visual scene so that it contains meaningful figures set against a less relevant ground.

figure The part of the visual field that has meaning.

Five Factor Personality Model (also called the **Big Five Personality Model**) A view based on studies using factor analysis that suggests the existence of five basic components of human personality: openness, conscientiousness, extraversion, agreeableness, and neuroticism.

flooding An exposure technique for reducing anxiety that keeps a client in a feared but harmless situation.

forebrain The part of the brain responsible for the most complex aspects of behavior and mental life.

forensic psychologists Psychologists who are involved in many aspects of psychology and law.

formal operational period According to Piaget, the fourth stage of cognitive development, characterized by the ability to engage in hypothetical thinking.

formal reasoning A set of rigorous procedures for reaching valid conclusions.

fovea A region in the center of the retina.

frequency The number of complete waves, or cycles, that pass a given point per unit of time.

frustration-aggression hypothesis A proposition stating that frustration always leads to some form of aggressive behavior.

fugue reaction (dissociative fugue) A psychological disorder involving sudden loss of memory and the assumption of a new identity in a new locale.

functional fixedness The tendency to think about familiar objects in familiar ways.

fundamental attribution error A bias toward attributing the behavior of others to internal factors.

gate control theory of pain A theory suggesting the presence of a "gate" in the spinal cord that either permits or blocks the passage of pain impulses to the brain.

generalized anxiety disorder A condition that involves long-lasting anxiety that is not focused on any particular object or situation.

gender roles Patterns of work, appearance, and behavior that society associates with being male or female.

general adaptation syndrome (GAS) A three-stage pattern of responses triggered by the effort to adapt to stressors.

generativity The concern of adults in their forties with generating something enduring.

genes Hereditary units, located on chromosomes, that contain biological instructions inherited from both parents, providing the blueprint for physical development.

genital stage The fifth and last of Freud's psychosexual stages, when sexual impulses begin to appear at the conscious level; begins during adolescence.

Gestalt therapy A form of treatment that seeks to create conditions in which clients can become more unified, more self-aware, and more self-accepting.

glands Organs that secrete hormones into the bloodstream.

glial cells Nervous system cells that hold neurons together and help them communicate with each other.

goal-setting theory A theory of workplace motivation focused on the idea that employees' behavior is shaped by their intention to achieve specific goals.

grammar A set of rules for combining the symbols, such as words, used in a given language.

ground The contourless part of the visual field; the background.

group psychotherapy Psychotherapy involving six to twelve unrelated individuals.

groupthink A pattern of thinking that renders group members unable to evaluate realistically the wisdom of various options and decisions.

habituation Reduced responsiveness to a repeated stimulus.

hallucinations False or distorted perceptions of objects or events.

hallucinogenic drugs Psychoactive drugs that alter consciousness by producing a temporary loss of contact with reality and changes in emotion, perception, and thought.

health care psychology (health psychology) A field focused on understanding how psychological factors affect health and illness and which interventions help maintain health and combat illness.

health promotion The process of altering or eliminating behaviors that pose risks to health and, at the same time, fostering healthier behavior patterns.

health psychologists Psychologists who study the effects of behavior on health and the impact of illness on behavior and emotion.

heterosexuality Sexual desire or behavior that is focused on members of the opposite sex.

heuristics Mental shortcuts or rules of thumb.

higher order conditioning A process through which a conditioned stimulus comes to signal another conditioned stimulus that is already associated with an unconditioned stimulus.

hindbrain The portion of the brain that lies just inside the skull and is a continuation of the spinal cord.

hippocampus A forebrain structure associated with the formation of new memories.

homeostasis The tendency for physiological systems to remain stable by constantly adjusting themselves in response to change.

homosexuality Sexual desire or behavior that is focused on members of one's own sex.

hormones Chemicals secreted by glands into the bloodstream, allowing stimulation of cells that are not directly connected.

hue The essential color determined by the dominant wavelength of a light.

humanistic approach A view of behavior as controlled by the decisions that people make about their lives based on their perceptions of the world.

humanistic psychology The school of psychology in which human behavior is viewed as being controlled by the decisions that people make about their lives based on their perceptions of the world.

hunger The general state of wanting to eat.

hypnosis A phenomenon that is brought on by special techniques and is characterized by varying degrees of responsiveness to suggestions for changes in a person's behavior and experiences.

hypnotic susceptibility The degree to which a person responds to hypnotic suggestion.

hypochondriasis A strong, unjustified fear of physical illness.

hypothalamus A forebrain structure that regulates hunger, thirst, and sex drives and has many connections to and from the autonomic nervous system and other parts of the brain.

hypothesis In scientific research, a specific, testable proposition about a phenomenon.

iconic memory The sensory register for visual information.

id According to Freud, a personality component containing basic instincts, desires, and impulses with which all people are born.

identity crisis The phase during which an adolescent attempts to develop an integrated self-image as a unique person by pulling together self-knowledge acquired during childhood.

images Mental representations of visual information.

immediate memory span The maximum number of items a person can recall perfectly after one presentation of the items.

immune system The body's first line of defense against invading substances and microorganisms.

implicit memory The unintentional recollection and influence of prior experiences.

implosive therapy An exposure technique in which clients are helped to imagine being kept in a feared but harmless situation.

incentive theory A theory that people are pulled toward behaviors that offer positive incentives and pushed away from behaviors associated with negative incentives.

independent variable In an experiment, the variable manipulated by the researcher.

industrial and organizational (I/O) psychology The science of behavior and mental processes in the workplace.

infant vocalizations Early sounds, such as **babblings**, made by babies.

informal reasoning The process of evaluating a conclusion based on the evidence available to support it.

information processing The process of taking in, remembering or forgetting, and using information.

information-processing model of memory A model that suggests that information must pass through sensory memory, short-term memory, and long-term memory in order to become firmly embedded in memory.

information-processing system Mechanisms for receiving information, representing it with symbols, and manipulating it.

insight A sudden understanding of what is required to solve a problem.

insomnia A sleep disorder in which a person has trouble falling asleep or staying asleep at night.

instinct doctrine A view that behavior is motivated by automatic, involuntary, and unlearned responses.

instinctive behaviors Innate, automatic dispositions to respond in particular ways to specific stimuli.

intelligence The possession of knowledge, the ability to efficiently use that knowledge to reason about the world, and the ability to use that reasoning adaptively in different environments.

intelligence quotient (IQ) A number that reflects the degree to which a person's score on an intelligence test differs from the average score of others in his or her age group.

interference The process through which storage or retrieval of information is impaired by the presence of other information.

iris The part of the eye that gives it its color and adjusts the amount of light entering it.

jet lag Fatigue, irritability, inattention, and sleeping problems caused by air travel across several time zones.

job analysis The process of collecting information about jobs and job requirements that is used to guide hiring and training decisions.

job performance A measure of how well employees are doing in various aspects of their work, usually recorded in an annual appraisal.

job satisfaction The degree to which people like or dislike their jobs.

just-noticeable difference (JND) The smallest detectable difference in stimulus energy. Also called difference threshold.

kinesthetic perception The proprioceptive sense that tells us where the parts of the body are with respect to one another.

Korsakoff's syndrome An amnestic condition in people whose thiamine (vitamin B1) level is depleted by inadequate nutrition or alcoholism.

language Symbols (and a set of rules for combining them) that are used as a means of communicating.

language disorders (aphasias) Neuropsychological disorders in which there are disruptions in the ability to speak, read, write, and understand language.

latency period The fourth of Freud's psychosexual stages, in which sexual impulses become dormant and the child focuses on education and other matters; usually begins during the fifth year of life.

latent learning Learning that is not demonstrated at the time it occurs.

law of effect A law stating that if a response made in the presence of a particular stimulus is rewarded, the same response is more likely to occur when that stimulus is encountered again.

leader-member exchange (LMX) theory A theory suggesting that leaders tend to supervise in-group and out-group employees in different ways.

learned helplessness A process in which a person or animal stops trying to exert control after experience suggests that no control is possible.

learning The modification of preexisting behavior and understanding.

lens The part of the eye directly behind the pupil.

lesion An damaged area in the brain.

levels-of-processing model of memory A model that suggests that memory depends on the degree or depth to which we mentally process information.

light intensity A physical dimension of light waves that refers to how much energy the light contains and that determines our experience of its brightness.

light wavelength A physical dimension of light waves that refers to their length and that produces sensations of different colors.

locus coeruleus A small nucleus in the reticular formation that is involved in directing attention.

logic A system of formulas for drawing valid conclusions.

long-term memory (LTM) The stage of memory that researchers believe has an unlimited capacity to store new information.

looming A motion cue whereby rapid expansion in the size of an image fills the available space on the retina.

loudness A psychological dimension of sound determined by the amplitude of a sound wave.

lucid dreaming Being aware that a dream is a dream while it is occurring.

maintenance rehearsal A memorization method that involves repeating information over and over to keep it in memory.

major depression (major depressive disorder) A condition in which a person feels sad and hopeless for weeks or months, often losing interest in all activities and taking pleasure in nothing.

mania An elated, active emotional state.

massed practice Trying to learn complex new information in a single long study period.

matching hypothesis The notion that people are most likely to form committed relationships with others who are similar to themselves in physical attractiveness.

maturation Natural growth or change triggered by biological factors independent of the environment.

medulla The area of the hindbrain that controls vital autonomic functions such as heart rate, blood pressure, and breathing.

mental models Sets of propositions that represent people's understanding of how things look and work.

mental set The tendency for old patterns of problem solving to persist.

midbrain A small region between the hindbrain and the forebrain that, among other things, helps produce smooth movements.

middle ear The part of the ear that contains the hammer, anvil, and stirrup, which transmit sound from the tympanic membrane to the oval window.

mnemonic strategies Methods for organizing information in order to remember it.

modeling A behavioral therapy method in which desirable behaviors are demonstrated for clients.

moral development The growth of an individual's understanding of the concepts of right and wrong.

motivation The influences that account for the initiation, direction, intensity, and persistence of behavior.

motive A reason or purpose for behavior.

motor cortex The part of the cerebral cortex that controls voluntary movement.

motor neurons The neurons that influence muscles and other organs to respond to the environment in some way.

movement disorders (apraxias) Neuropsychological disorders in which there are impairments in the ability to perform or coordinate previously normal motor skills.

narcolepsy A daytime sleep disorder in which a person suddenly switches from an active waking state into REM sleep.

naturalistic observation The process of watching without interfering as a phenomenon occurs in the natural environment.

needs Biological requirements for well-being.

negative reinforcers The removal of unpleasant stimuli.

nervous system A network of billions of cells that detects what is going on inside or outside the body and guides appropriate responses.

neural networks Neurons that operate together to perform complex functions.

neural plasticity A property of the central nervous system that has the ability to strengthen neural connections at synapses as well as to establish new connections.

neural receptors Cells that are specialized to detect certain types of energy and convert it into neural activity.

neurodegenerative diseases Conditions in the brain that result in the gradual loss of nerve cells and of the cognitive or other functions in which those cells are normally involved.

neuroleptic drugs Drugs that relieve the symptoms of schizophrenia or other severe forms of psychological disorder. Also called antipsychotics.

neurons Specialized cells of the nervous system that send and receive messages.

neuropsychological assessment Testing a patient's intelligence, memory, reading, motor coordination, and other cognitive and sensory functions in an effort to locate problems in the brain responsible for neuropsychological symptoms.

neuropsychology The subfield of psychology whose goal is to explore and understand the relationship between brain processes, human behavior, and psychological functioning.

neurotransmitter A chemical that transfers messages across synapses.

nightmares Frightening dreams that take place during REM sleep.

noise The spontaneous random firing of nerve cells that occurs because the nervous system is always active.

nonprojective personality measures Tests that list clear, specific questions, statements, or concepts to which people are asked to respond.

norms Descriptions of the frequency of particular scores on a test.

NREM (nonrapid eye movement) sleep Sleep stages 1, 2, 3, and 4; they are accompanied by gradually slower and deeper breathing; a calm, regular heartbeat; reduced blood pressure; and slower brain waves. (Stages 3 and 4 are called slow-wave sleep.)

nuclei Clusters of nerve cell bodies in the central nervous system.

obedience Changing behavior in response to a demand from an authority figure.

obesity A condition in which a person is severely overweight.

object permanence The knowledge that an object exists even when it is not in view.

observational learning (social learning) Learning by watching the behavior of others.

observational methods Procedures for systematically watching behavior in order to summarize it for scientific analysis.

obsessions Persistent, upsetting, and unwanted thoughts that interfere with daily life and may lead to compulsions.

obsessive-compulsive disorder (OCD) An anxiety disorder in which a person becomes obsessed with certain thoughts or feels a compulsion to do certain things.

occupational health psychology A field concerned with psychological factors that affect the health, safety, and well-being of employees.

ocular accommodation The ability of the lens to change its shape and bend light rays so objects are in focus.

Oedipal complex The notion that young boys' impulses involve sexual feelings for the mother and the desire to eliminate the father.

olfactory bulb A brain structure that receives messages regarding smell.

olfactory perception (sense of smell) The sense that detects chemicals that are airborne. Also called olfaction.

one-word stage A stage of language development during which children tend to use only one word at a time.

operant A response that has some effect on the world.

operant conditioning A process in which responses are learned on the basis of their rewarding or punishing consequences.

operational definitions Statements that define phenomena or variables by describing the exact research operations or methods used in measuring or manipulating them.

opiates Psychoactive drugs that produce both sleep-inducing and pain-relieving effects.

opponent-process theory A theory of color vision stating that the visual elements that are sensitive to color are grouped into red-green, blue-yellow, and black-white pairs.

optic nerve A bundle of fibers that carries visual information to the brain.

oral stage The first of Freud's psychosexual stages, in which the mouth is the center of pleasure; occurs during the first year of life.

organizational citizenship behavior (OCB) A willingness to go beyond formal job requirements in order to help co-workers and/or the organization.

panic disorder Anxiety in the form of severe panic attacks that come without warning or obvious cause.

papillae Structures in the mouth on which taste buds are grouped.

parallel distributed processing (PDP) models of memory Memory models in which new experiences are seen as changing one's overall knowledge base.

parasympathetic nervous system The subsystem of the autonomic nervous system that typically influences activity related to the protection, nourishment, and growth of the body.

parenting style The varying patterns of behavior—ranging from permissive to authoritarian—that parents display as they interact with and discipline their children.

partial reinforcement effect A phenomenon in which behaviors learned under a partial reinforcement schedule are more difficult to extinguish than those learned on a continuous reinforcement schedule.

perception The process through which people take raw sensations from the environment and give them meaning, using knowledge, experience, and understanding of the world.

perceptual constancy The perception that objects retain the same size, shape, color, and other properties despite changes in their retinal image.

perceptual disturbances Neuropsychological disorders in which there are impairments in the ability to organize, recognize, interpret, and make sense of incoming sensory information.

peripheral nervous system The part of the nervous system that sends messages to and from the central nervous system.

permissive parents Parents who give their children complete freedom and lax discipline.

personality The pattern of psychological and behavioral characteristics by which each person can be compared and contrasted with others.

personality disorders Long-standing, inflexible ways of behaving that become styles of life that create problems, usually for others.

personality psychologists Psychologists who focus on people's unique characteristics.

personality traits A set of stable characteristics that people display over time and across situations.

phallic stage The third of Freud's psychosexual stages, in which the focus of pleasure shifts to the genital area; lasts from approximately age three to age five.

pheromones Chemicals that are released by one creature and detected by another, shaping the second creature's behavior or physiology.

phobia An anxiety disorder that involves strong, irrational fear of an object or situation that does not objectively justify such a reaction.

photoreceptors Specialized cells in the retina that convert light energy into neural activity.

physiological arousal A general level of activation reflected in several physiological systems.

pinna The crumpled part of the outer ear that collects sound waves.

pitch How high or low a tone sounds; pitch depends on the frequency of a sound wave.

place theory A theory of hearing that states that hair cells at a particular place on the basilar membrane respond most to a particular frequency of sound.

placebo A treatment that contains no active ingredient but produces an effect because the person receiving it believes it will.

pleasure principle The operating principle of the id, which guides people toward whatever feels good.

positive psychology A field of research that focuses on people's positive experiences and characteristics, such as happiness, optimism, and resilience.

positive reinforcement Presenting a positive reinforcer (reward) after a desired response.

positive reinforcers Stimuli that strengthen a response if they follow that response.

postconventional reasoning Moral reasoning that reflects moral judgments based on personal standards or universal principles of justice, equality, and respect for human life.

posttraumatic stress disorder (PTSD) A pattern of adverse reactions following a traumatic event, commonly involving reexperiencing the event through nightmares or vivid memories.

preconventional reasoning Moral reasoning that is not based on the conventions or rules that guide social interactions in a society.

prejudice A positive or negative attitude toward people in certain groups.

preoperational period According to Piaget, the second stage of cognitive development, during which children begin to understand, create, and use symbols that represent things that are not present.

primacy effect A characteristic of memory in which recall is particularly good for the first two or three items in a list.

primary drives Drives that arise from basic biological needs.

primary reinforcers Events or stimuli that satisfy physiological needs basic to survival.

proactive inhibition A cause of forgetting whereby previously learned information interferes with the ability to remember new information.

procedural knowledge A type of memory containing information about how to do things.

procedural memory (see procedural knowledge)

progestational hormones (progestins) Feminine hormones that circulate in the bloodstream.

projective personality measures Personality tests made up of relatively unstructured stimuli in which responses are seen as reflecting the individuals' unconscious needs, fantasies, conflicts, thought patterns, and other aspects of personality.

propositions Mental representations that express a relationship between concepts.

proprioception The sensory processes that tell us about the location of our body parts and what each is doing.

proprioceptors Neural receptors that provide information about movement and body position.

prototype A member of a natural concept that possesses all or most of its characteristic features.

psychiatrists Medical doctors who have completed special training in the treatment of mental disorders.

psychoactive drugs Chemical substances that act on the brain to create psychological effects.

psychoanalysis A method of psychotherapy that seeks to help clients gain insight into and work through unconscious thoughts and emotions presumed to cause psychological problems.

psychoanalytic theory Freud's view that human behavior and personality are determined largely by psychological factors, many of which are unconscious.

psychodynamic approach A view developed by Freud that emphasizes unconscious mental processes in explaining human thought, feelings, and behavior.

psychologists In the area of treatment, therapists with advanced training in clinical or counseling psychology.

psychology The science that seeks to understand behavior and mental processes and to apply that understanding in the service of human welfare.

psychosexual development In Freud's psychodynamic theory, personality development in which internal and external conflicts focus on particular issues during particular periods or stages.

psychoneuroimmunology The field that examines the interaction of psychological and physiological processes affecting the body's ability to defend itself against disease.

psychopathology Patterns of thinking and behaving that are maladaptive, disruptive, or uncomfortable for the affected person or for others.

psychopharmacology The study of psychoactive drugs and their effects.

psychotherapy The treatment of psychological disorders through psychological methods, such as analyzing problems, talking about possible solutions, and encouraging more adaptive ways of thinking and acting.

puberty The condition of being able, for the first time, to reproduce.

punishment The presentation of an aversive stimulus or the removal of a pleasant one following some behavior.

pupil An opening in the eye just behind the cornea through which light passes.

quantitative psychologists Psychologists who develop statistical methods for evaluating and analyzing data from psychological research.

random assignment A procedure through which random variables are evenly distributed in an experiment by placing participants in experimental and control groups on the basis of a coin flip or some other random process.

random sample A group of research participants selected from a population each of whose members had an equal chance of being chosen.

random variables Uncontrolled or uncontrollable factors that affect the dependent variable along with, or instead of, the independent variable.

rational-emotive behavior therapy (REBT) A treatment that involves identifying illogical, self-defeating thoughts that clients have learned, then helping clients replace these thoughts with more realistic and beneficial ones.

reality principle The operating principle of the ego, which takes into account the constraints of the social world.

reasoning The process by which people generate and evaluate arguments and reach conclusions about them.

recall Retrieving information stored in memory.

recency effect A characteristic of memory in which recall is particularly good for the last few items in a list.

recognition Awareness, based on retrieval cues, that particular information is in one's memory.

reconditioning The relearning of a conditioned response following extinction.

reference groups Categories of people with whom individuals compare themselves.

reflexes Simple, involuntary, unlearned behaviors directed by the spinal cord without instructions from the brain.

refractory period A short recovery time after cell firing, during which the cell cannot fire again.

reinforcement The process through which a particular response is made more likely to recur.

reinforcement schedules In operant conditioning, rules that determine how and when certain responses will be reinforced. They are usually based on the number of responses made (ratio schedules) or the amount of time since the last reinforced response (interval schedules).

reinforcer A stimulus event that increases the probability that the response immediately preceding it will occur again.

relationship-motivated leaders Leaders who provide loose supervision, ask for group members' ideas, and are generally concerned with subordinates' feelings.

relative deprivation The sense that one is not getting all that one deserves.

relearning method A method for measuring forgetting.

reliability The degree to which test results or other research evidence occurs repeatedly.

REM (rapid eye movement) sleep The stage of sleep during which muscle tone decreases dramatically but the EEG resembles that of someone who is awake.

representative sample A sample of research participants chosen from a larger population such that their age, gender, ethnicity, and other characteristics are typical of that larger population.

representativeness heuristic A mental shortcut that involves judging whether something belongs in a given class on the basis of its similarity to other members of that class.

repressed memory A painful memory that is said to be kept out of consciousness by psychological processes.

response bias (response criterion) The internal rule a person uses to decide whether or not to report a stimulus.

reticular formation A collection of cells and fibers in the hindbrain and midbrain that are involved in arousal and attention.

retina The surface at the back of the eye onto which the lens focuses light rays.

retinal disparity A depth cue based on the difference between the retinal images received by each eye.

retrieval The process of finding information stored in memory.

retrieval cues Stimuli that allow or help people to recall information.

retroactive inhibition A cause of forgetting whereby new information placed in memory interferes with the ability to recall information already in memory.

retrograde amnesia A loss of memory for events that occurred prior to a brain injury.

rods Photoreceptors in the retina that allow sight even in dim light but that cannot distinguish colors.

role theory A theory proposing that hypnotized people act in accordance with a social role that provides a reason to follow a hypnotist's suggestions.

sampling The process of selecting participants who are members of the population that the researcher wishes to study.

satiation The satisfaction of a need such as hunger.

satiety The condition of no longer wanting to eat.

schemas Mental representations of categories of objects, places, events, and people; mental representations of what we know and expect about the world; generalizations about categories of objects, places, events, and people; mental representations about people and social situations.

schizophrenia A pattern of severely disturbed thinking, emotion, perception, and behavior that constitutes one of the most serious and disabling of all mental disorders.

school psychologists Psychologists who test IQ, diagnose students' academic problems, and set up programs to improve students' achievement.

scripts Mental representations of familiar sequences of activity.

secondary drives Stimuli that take on the motivational properties of primary drives through learning.

secondary reinforcers Rewards that people or animals learn to like.

selective attention The process of focusing mental resources on only part of the stimulus field.

self-actualization The reaching of one's fullest potential; the complete realization of a person's talents, faculties, and abilities.

self-concept The way one thinks of oneself.

self-efficacy According to Bandura, the learned expectation of success in given situations.

self-esteem The evaluations people make about their worth as human beings.

self-fulfilling prophecy A process in which an initial impression causes us to bring out behavior in another that confirms the impression.

self-serving bias The tendency to attribute one's successes to internal characteristics while blaming one's failures on external causes.

semantic memory Memory for generalized knowledge about the world.

sensations Raw information from the senses.

sense A system that translates data from outside the nervous system into neural activity.

sense of equilibrium (vestibular sense) The proprioceptive sense that provides information about the position of the head and its movements.

sensitivity The ability to detect a stimulus.

sensorimotor period According to Piaget, the first stage of cognitive development, when the infant's mental activity is confined to sensory perception and motor skills.

sensory adaptation Decreasing responsiveness to an unchanging stimulus.

sensory cortex The part of the cerebral cortex located in the parietal, occipital, and temporal lobes that receives stimulus information from the skin, eyes, and ears, respectively.

sensory memory A type of memory that is very brief but lasts long enough to connect one impression to the next.

sensory neurons The neurons that provide the brain with information about the environment.

sensory registers Memory systems that briefly hold incoming information.

sex hormones Chemicals in the blood that organize and motivate sexual behavior.

sex roles (see **gender roles**)

sexual arousal Physiological arousal that arises from sexual contact or erotic thoughts.

sexual function disturbances Problems with sexual motivation, arousal, or orgasmic response.

sexual response cycle The pattern of arousal before, during, and after sexual activity.

shaping The reinforcement of responses that come successively closer to some desired response.

short-term memory (STM) A stage of memory in which information normally lasts less than twenty seconds; a component of working memory.

signal detection theory A mathematical model of what determines a person's report of a near-threshold stimulus.

sleep apnea A sleep disorder in which a person briefly but repeatedly stops breathing during the night.

sleep deprivation A condition in which people do not get enough sleep; it may result in reduced cognitive abilities, inattention, and increased risk of accidents.

sleep terror disorder (night terrors) The occurrence of horrific dream images during stage 4 sleep, followed by a rapid awakening and a state of intense fear.

sleepwalking A phenomenon that starts primarily in non-REM sleep, especially in stage 4, and involves walking while asleep.

social cognition Mental processes associated with people's perceptions of and reactions to other people.

social-cognitive approach An approach that views personality as a label that summarizes the unique patterns of thinking and behavior that a person learns.

social comparison Using other people as a basis of comparison for evaluating oneself.

social dilemmas Situations in which actions that produce rewards for one individual will produce negative consequences for all if they are adopted by everyone.

social discrimination Differential treatment of people in certain groups; the behavioral component of prejudice.

social facilitation A phenomenon in which the presence of others improves a person's performance.

social identity The beliefs we hold about the groups to which we belong.

social interference A reduction in performance due to the presence of other people.

socialization The process by which parents, teachers, and others teach children the skills and social norms necessary to be well-functioning members of society.

social loafing Exerting less effort when performing a group task than when performing the same task alone.

social neuroscience A specialty that focuses on the influence of social processes on biological processes and on the influence of biological processes on social psychological phenomena.

social norms Learned, socially based rules that prescribe what people should or should not do in various situations.

social perception The processes through which people interpret information about others, draw inferences about them, and develop mental representations of them.

social phobias Strong, irrational fears related to social situations.

social psychologists Psychologists who study how people influence one another's behavior and attitudes, especially in groups.

social psychology The subfield of psychology that explores the effects of the social world on the behavior and mental processes of individuals and groups.

social support The friends and social contacts on whom one can depend for help and support.

sociocultural factors Social identity and other background factors, such as gender, ethnicity, social class, and culture; characteristics or conditions that can influence the appearance and form of maladaptive behavior, such as gender, age, and marital status; physical, social, and economic situations; and cultural values, traditions, expectations, and opportunities.

sociocultural perspective An approach to explaining mental disorder that emphasizes the role of factors such as gender and age, physical situations, cultural values and expectations, and historical era.

somatic nervous system The subsystem of the peripheral nervous system that transmits information from the senses to the central nervous system and carries signals from the CNS to the muscles that move the skeleton.

somatization disorder A psychological problem in which a person has numerous physical complaints without verifiable physical illness.

somatoform disorders Psychological problems in which a person shows the symptoms of some physical (somatic) disorder for which there is no physical cause.

somatoform pain disorder A somatoform disorder marked by complaints of severe, often constant pain with no physical cause.

sound A repetitive fluctuation in the pressure of a medium such as air.

specific phobias Phobias that involve fear and avoidance of specific stimuli and situations such as heights, blood, and specific animals.

spinal cord The part of the central nervous system that receives information from the senses, passes these signals to the brain, and sends messages from the brain to the body.

spontaneous recovery The temporary reappearance of a conditioned response after extinction.

sport psychologists Psychologists whose research is aimed at maximizing athletic performance.

spreading activation In semantic network theories of memory, a principle that explains how information is retrieved.

Stanford-Binet Intelligence Scale A test for determining a person's intelligence quotient, or IQ.

state theory A theory proposing that hypnosis creates an altered state of consciousness.

state-dependent learning (see **state-dependent memory**)

state-dependent memory Memory that is helped or hindered by similarities or differences in a person's internal state during learning versus recall.

statistical reliability The degree to which test results or other research evidence occurs repeatedly.

statistical validity The degree to which test scores are interpreted appropriately and used properly.

statistically significant Referring to a correlation, or a difference between two groups, that is larger than would be expected by chance.

stereotypes False assumptions that all members of some group share the same characteristics.

stimulus discrimination A process through which people learn to differentiate among similar stimuli and respond appropriately to each one.

stimulus generalization A process in which a conditioned response is triggered by stimuli similar to the original conditioned stimulus.

storage The process of maintaining information in the memory system over time.

stress The process of adjusting to circumstances that disrupt or threaten to disrupt a person's daily functioning.

stressors Events or situations to which people must adjust.

stress reactions Physical and psychological responses to stressors.

stroboscopic illusion An illusion of motion that is created when we see slightly different images or slightly displaced lights flashed in rapid succession.

stroke (see **cerebrovascular accident**)

subconscious A term that describes the mental level at which influential but normally inaccessible mental processes take place.

substance-related disorders Problems involving the use of psychoactive drugs for months or years in ways that harm the user or others.

sudden infant death syndrome (SIDS) A disorder in which a sleeping baby stops breathing but does not awaken and dies.

superego According to Freud, the component of personality that tells people what they should and should not do.

surveys Research that involves giving people questionnaires or interviews designed to describe their attitudes, beliefs, opinions, and intentions.

sympathetic nervous system The subsystem of the autonomic nervous system that readies the body for vigorous activity.

synapse The tiny gap between the axon of one neuron and the dendrites of another.

syndrome A pattern of symptoms associated with a particular neuropsychological disorder.

systematic desensitization therapy A behavioral method for treating anxiety in which clients visualize a graduated series of anxiety-provoking stimuli while remaining relaxed.

task-motivated leaders Leaders who provide close supervision, lead by giving directions, and generally discourage group discussion.

taste perception The sense that detects chemicals in solution that come into contact with receptors inside the mouth. Also called gustatatory sense.

temperament An individual's basic, natural disposition that is evident from infancy.

teratogens Harmful substances, such as alcohol and other drugs, that can cause birth defects.

terminal drop A sharp decline in mental functioning that tends to occur in late adulthood, a few months or years before death.

test A systematic observation of behavior in a standard situation, described by a numerical scale or category.

thalamus A forebrain structure that relays messages from most sense organs to higher brain areas.

theory An integrated set of propositions used to explain certain phenomena, including behavior and mental processes.

thinking The manipulation of mental representations.

timbre The quality of a sound that identifies it.

token economy program A system for improving the behavior of clients in institutions by rewarding desirable behaviors with tokens that can be exchanged for various rewards.

top-down processing Aspects of recognition guided by higher-level cognitive processes and by psychological factors such as expectations.

trait approach A perspective on personality that views it as the combination of stable characteristics that people display over time and across situations.

tranquilizing drugs (anxiolytics) Drugs that reduce tension and symptoms of anxiety.

transduction The process of converting incoming physical energy into neural activity.

transfer-appropriate processing model of memory A model that suggests that memory depends on how the encoding process matches up with what is later retrieved.

traumatic brain injury (trauma) A impact on the brain caused by a blow or sudden violent movement of the head.

trichromatic theory A theory of color vision stating that information from three types of visual elements combines to produce the sensation of color.

tympanic membrane (eardrum) A tightly stretched membrane in the middle ear that generates vibrations that match the sound waves striking it.

unconditional positive regard In client-centered therapy, the therapist's attitude that expresses caring for and acceptance of the client as a valued person.

unconditioned response (UCR) The automatic, unlearned, reflexive reaction to a stimulus.

unconditioned stimulus (UCS) A stimulus that triggers a response without conditioning.

unconscious The term used to describe a level of mental activity said by Freud to contain unacceptable sexual, aggressive, and other impulses of which an individual is unaware.

uninvolved parents Parents who invest as little time, money, and effort in their children as possible.

utility In decision making, any subjective measure of value.

validation studies Research projects that determine how well a test, interview, or other assessment method predicts job performance.

validity The degree to which evidence from a test or other research method measures what it is supposed to measure.

variables Specific factors or characteristics that can take on different numerical values in research.

vascular dementia A form of dementia caused by multiple restrictions of the brain's blood supply.

visual memory Mental representations of stimuli as pictures.

volley theory A theory of hearing that states that the firing rate of an acoustic nerve matches a sound wave's frequency. Also called frequency-matching theory.

wavelength The distance between peaks in a wave of light or sound.

Weber's law A law stating that the smallest detectable difference in stimulus energy (just-noticeable difference) is a constant fraction of the intensity of the stimulus.

well-being (subjective well-being) A cognitive judgment of satisfaction with life, the frequent experiencing of positive moods and emotions, and the relatively infrequent experiencing of unpleasant moods and emotions.

Wernicke's aphasia A language disorder in which there is a loss of ability to understand written or spoken language and to produce sensible speech.

work group At least two people who interact with one another as they perform the same or different workplace tasks.

working memory Memory that allows us to mentally work with, or manipulate, information being held in short-term memory.

work team A work group in which the members' specialized activities are coordinated and interdependent as they work toward a common goal.

NAME INDEX

Italicized page numbers show the locations of figures. Entries that appear in blue refer to the optional *Industrial and Organizational Psychology or Neuropsychology chapters.*